KU-438-866

Nelson's
ENCYCLOPAEDIA

Nelson's
ENCYCLOPAEDIA

Compiled and edited by

H. L. GEE

THOMAS NELSON AND SONS LTD

LONDON EDINBURGH PARIS MELBOURNE

TORONTO AND NEW YORK

House of Commons Library

54056000174992

THOMAS NELSON AND SONS LTD
Parkside Works Edinburgh 9
3 Henrietta Street London WC2
312 Flinders Street Melbourne C1
5 Parker's Buildings Burg Street Cape Town

THOMAS NELSON AND SONS (CANADA) LTD
91–93 Wellington Street West   Toronto 1

THOMAS NELSON AND SONS
19 East 47th Street New York 17

SOCIÉTÉ FRANÇAISE D'EDITIONS NELSON
25 rue Henri Barbusse Paris Ve

———

First published 1951

PREFACE

LARGE encyclopaedias are often far more useful to specialists than they are to the general reader, and in any case they are necessarily expensive. Short encyclopaedias are relatively much cheaper to buy, but in dealing with subjects of major importance they are all too often sketchy and superficial. A short encyclopaedia which seeks to overcome this common defect by varying the breadth of treatment according to the nature and importance of each particular subject has long been urgently required. NELSON'S ENCYCLOPAEDIA has been specially designed to meet this need.

Although comparatively low in price, this one-volume work, expressly prepared for the general reader, contains well over 500,000 words and nearly 9,000 entries, excluding cross-references. In common with most works of reference of similar proportions it supplies a wealth of purely factual information, e.g. geographical and statistical data, brief biographies, hundreds of useful mathematical and chemical formulae, etc. It differs from most one-volume encyclopaedias in that strict compression and the adoption of a ' notebook style ' in all merely factual contexts has made it possible to include many articles of much greater length and much wider scope than are usually to be found in similar works.

Thus many topics of general interest and lasting importance—such as architecture, aviation, Bible, Church history, electricity, Fascism, internal-combustion engine, poetry, politics, radar, radioactivity, ships, World War II, to name only a few—are dealt with on a generous scale. These, and scores of other major articles, have been specially planned as *keys* to a fuller understanding of more detailed sub-articles elsewhere in this work. Key-articles and sub-articles are abundantly supplied with cross-references.

The treatment throughout is adapted to the reader's most probable requirements. In dealing with subjects likely to be of interest chiefly to specialists, the compiler's approach has been frankly introductory—though in general he has set himself the task of discussing *every* subject as fully as the space at his disposal would allow. Moreover, as the list of acknowledgments following this preface shows, he has had much expert assistance, and has spared no effort in an attempt to ensure the accuracy of all facts and figures given.

But no encyclopaedia can be *purely* factual. Every reader who wonders on occasion why some subjects have been dealt with at much greater length than others is instinctively aware of this; for in deciding what to include, and what to omit, the compiler of an encyclopaedia is not dealing with matters of fact but with questions concerning value. It is possible of course to make it a principle that questions about values should not be discussed in the text of such a book (in which case many questions that the reader will naturally ask must go unanswered) : but of necessity its whole governing plan—the scope of reference, the emphasis accorded to opposed points of view, and (most vital of all) the actual selection of the facts—is determined ultimately by judgments that, rightly seen, are value-judgments. This assessing of values is indeed one of the most difficult tasks the encyclopaedist has to grapple with ; and it is one the compiler of this work has not shirked. Sometimes he has implied or stated the commonly accepted judgment of the moment ; often he has, quite frankly, been guided only by his own sense of values.

NELSON'S ENCYCLOPAEDIA defines briefly and carefully. Where necessary it supplies English, and in many cases foreign, pronunciations. It gives Bible references precisely. It mentions, and also quotes, scores of the world's most important books, plays and poems, and refers the reader to hundreds of technical or authoritative works to which he may turn for further reading.

It is sincerely hoped that, by reason of the many special features already mentioned, NELSON'S ENCYCLOPAEDIA will also be eminently useful to the younger generation, particularly those who have reached the higher classes in school, or are engaged in academic studies at home or at college or university.

For this reason illustrations have been provided on an exceptionally lavish scale. Most of the line-drawings in the text, including many sketch-maps and explanatory diagrams, have been specially prepared for this book. They illustrate natural history, the sciences, technology, world politics, and many personalities of outstanding historical and present-day importance.

The black-and-white half-tone illustrations (80 pages in all) comprise two distinct but complementary themes : (a) 64 pages representing modern civilisation seen in its main economic aspects, e.g. agriculture, industry, transport, intercommunication ; (b) 16 pages illustrating what might be called the ' permanent record,' i.e. the development of western architecture from its earliest beginnings to our own time. Each of these half-tones illustrates information mentioned in the text—and in the text the reference is duly noted ; but the arrangement of the half-tones in a grouped and ordered series enables the youthful reader to gain a many-sided and coherent panorama of the modern world not only in relation to its contemporary aspects but also (taking architecture as a case in point) in relation to the past.

A somewhat similar plan has been followed in assembling the 16 pages in full colour, which illustrate the theme : *Colour in nature, life and art.*

The compilation and production of a work of this kind is not easy, particularly in times like these, but the compiler owes much to the publishers, who throughout have been consistently helpful and encouraging. He wishes to acknowledge his very great indebtedness to all who have supplied information, e.g. various embassies and legations, British Overseas Airways Corporation, Cadbury Brothers Ltd., Central Electricity Board, Chance Brothers Ltd., the Colonial Office, Courtaulds Ltd., the Public Relations Department of the General Post Office, Imperial Chemical Industries, Lever Brothers Ltd., London Passenger Transport Board, the Society of the Men of the Trees, the National Book League, the Pilgrim Trust, the Royal National Lifeboat Institution, Singer Sewing Machine Co., Ltd., and many others. He is indebted to the following artists, Mr H. Lutry, Miss B. D. Inglis, Mr R. C. Robertson, Miss Mary Shillabeer and Mr A. C. Wolffe, for their valued assistance. Among many who helped to assemble the half-tone plates, the compiler wishes especially to thank Mrs G. A. Langdon of the Courtauld Institute and Mrs H. M. Herrick of the Exclusive News Agency.

The compiler gratefully acknowledges the co-operation of Messrs J. H. Barker; E. E. Cook, B.A., B.Sc.; J. Dodson; Mrs Grace Eling; Sir Howard Florey; Messrs E. W. Fryer, F.L.A.; Edward Fryer, Secretary of the Automobile Association; H. M. Hill, Engineer-in-Charge, BBC, Edinburgh; Clifford Hindley, B.A.; Rev. H. R. Hindley; Messrs Maurice A. R. Horspool; F. Austin Hyde, M.A.; Mr and Mrs A. P. Masser; Miss Gertrude Miller of the BBC; Mr E. Morris; Principal Hugh B. Nisbet, Ph.D., D.Sc., F.R.I.C., F.R.S.E., of the Heriot-Watt College, Edinburgh; Messrs K. O'Brien, B.A.; R. Pearson, B.A.; Herbert Perkin, F.S.I.; the late G. T. Reeve, M.A.; Miss Doreen Ripley; Mr James S. Ross and Messrs George G. Harrap & Co., Ltd., for a diagram from *Groundwork of Educational Psychology*; Rev. Dr W. E. Sangster, M.A.; Messrs Jas. B. Sloan of Imperial Studios; John Snagge of the BBC; Miss M. Stoddart, B.Sc.; Messrs F. S. Thompson, B.Sc.; S. T. Thompson, A.L.A.; A. C. Warner, M.A.; Dr Leonard Watson, L.R.C.P.&S.(Edin.), L.R.F.P.&S.(Glasgow); Messrs G. V. Welbourne, M.A.; Mrs Whitaker, L.R.A.M.; Messrs Maurice T. Woodhouse, B.A., M.Ed.; F. Yates. Finally, the compiler wishes to express his thanks to the publisher's editorial staff, and to the readers and compositors who have so nobly responded to every demand that has been made upon them.

H. L. GEE

THE PLATES

Throughout the text, the colour illustrations are referred to as Plates I, II, III etc.; the black-and-white half-tone illustrations as Plates 1, 2, 3 etc.

ABBREVIATIONS

AC	alternating current	LNER	London and North-Eastern Railway
b	born	m	miles
BR	British Railways	mm	millimetres
c.	century	mgm	milligrammes
c.	circa	MP	Member of Parliament
cc	cubic centimetres	mps	miles per second
cap.	capital	MSS	manuscripts
cgs	centimetre gram seconds	Mt	Mount
co.tn	county town	mts.	mountains
cm	centimetres	N.	North
d	died	NT	New Testament
DC	direct current	NZ	New Zealand
E.	east	OE	Old English
emf, EMF	electromotive force	OT	Old Testament
Eng.	English	pop.	population
Fr.	French	Rom.	Roman
ft	feet	S.	South
Ger.	German	sec	seconds
Gk	Greek	sg, sp.gr	specific gravity
GWR	Great Western Railway	sq.m	square miles
hp	horsepower	sq.yd	square yards
HMS	His Majesty's Ship	UK	United Kingdom
I., Is.	Island(s)	USA	United States of America
in	inches	USSR	Union of Soviet Socialist Republics (Russia)
It.	Italian	W.	west
L.	Lake	wt	weight
Lat.	Latin	yd	yards
lat.	latitude		
LMS	London Midland and Scottish Railway		

GUIDE TO PRONUNCIATION

VOWELS

$\ddot{a}$	as in father	o	as in pot
$\bar{a}$	as in late	$\bar{o}$	as in bone
au, aw	as in daughter	$\breve{o}$	as in lord
e	as in sell	oo	as in room
$\bar{e}$	as in meet	ou, ow	as in doubt, cow
i, $\bar{i}$	as in fit	$\breve{u}$	as in burn
$\bar{i}$	as in fine	$\bar{u}$	as in mute

CONSONANTS

ch	as in chime	g	as in good	th	as in think
ch	as in loch	j	as in jug	th	as in thus
		on, etc.	as in Fr. bon, etc.		

viii

A

A, chemical symbol for Argon.

Aachen or **Aix-la-Chapelle,** *ä'chen ; eks-lä-shäpel,* Rhineland city of Germany ; *c.*45m W. of Cologne. Its cathedral was begun *c.*AD796 by Charlemagne, and contains his tomb. Charlemagne, who died here, made Aachen the capital of his dominions N. of the Alps. Long famous for its mineral springs and baths, Aachen has been noted for woollen yarn, cloth, machinery and chemicals ; the city was almost completely destroyed by bombing in World War II ; pop. 165,000.

aard-vark, African burrowing animal ; has a snout like that of a pig, huge ears, and a thick tail ; feeds at night on ants etc.

aard-wolf, animal, resembling a hyena, found in S. and E. Africa ; yellowish with black stripes ; has a long bushy tail ; feeds on decaying flesh.

Aaron, *är'on,* first high priest of Israel ; spokesman for his brother, Moses, before Pharaoh (Exodus 4, 7) ; made the golden calf (Exodus 32).

ab'acus, wooden frame with 10 wires, each with 10 coloured beads, an aid to counting still used much as in ancient Greek and Roman times. Also (in architecture) the upper portion of a column.

Ab'ana, Syrian river flowing through Damascus (2 Kings 5), now called Barada.

Abbotsford, Sir Walter Scott's country house (Roxburghshire) by the R. Tweed, *c.*2½m from Melrose. In ' baronial ' style, the house was begun 1811. Here Sir Walter wrote many of his books, and here he died. The library and the armoury (rich in examples of Scottish weapons) are shown to visitors Apr.–Oct.

Abélard, PIERRE, *ab'e-lärd* (1079–1142), French scholar and churchman ; chiefly remembered as the lover of the beautiful Héloïse ; each wrote the other fascinating letters, now famous. The two lovers are buried in one tomb in Paris.

Abercrom'by, SIR RALPH (1734–1801), *b* Menstrie, Scotland, general ; commander in the Netherlands against Napoleon ; mortally wounded at the battle of Aboukir Bay, Egypt. Notable with Sir John Moore for restoring discipline to the British army, and for his humane and honourable conduct when commanding troops in Ireland, 1798.

The story is told that while being carried to his ship after his last fight, Abercromby asked, ' What have you placed under my head ? '

' Only a soldier's blanket,' someone replied.

' Take it back to him at once,' Abercromby ordered.

Aberdare, town, Glamorganshire ; centre

of a coal-mining district ; manufactures cables ; pop.42,000.

Aberdeen, co.tn, Aberdeenshire ; between Rs. Dee and Don ; chief port of NE. Scotland ; called the ' granite city ' ; industries include fishing, fish-curing, engineering, granite-polishing, linen, woollen and cotton goods, paper, chemicals, tobacco ; the university was founded 1494 ; pop.182,000.

Aberdeenshire, county, NE. Scotland ; has a rocky coast ; is mountainous in the W. ; rivers include Dee, Don, Deveron, all noted for salmon and trout ; agriculture is important ; co.tn Aberdeen.

Abertillery, *ab-er-til-ä'ri,* town in a coal-mining district, Monmouthshire ; pop.32,000.

Aberystwyth, *-ŭst'with,* seaside and university town, Cardiganshire ; has the National Library of Wales.

Abiathar, *a-bi'athär,* Jewish high priest and friend of King David (1 Samuel 22).

Abigail, wife of David, King of Israel (1 Samuel 25) ; term used for a serving-maid.

Abishai, *a-bish'i,* OT hero, nephew of King David ; one of three men who risked their lives for a cup of water for the King (2 Samuel 23).

Abner, OT Hebrew general killed by Joab (1 Samuel 14 ; 2 Samuel 2, 3).

Abolition of Slavery, see SLAVERY

aborigines, *ab-or-ij'i-nēz,* first people to live in a country, e.g. the Blackfellows of Australia, who were there long before Europeans arrived.

Abou Ben Adhem, see HUNT, LEIGH

Abraham, *ä-brä-ham,* grand figure of the OT who lived *c.*2300BC. The Bible story tells how he moved his flocks from Ur of the Chaldees, *c.*50m SE. of Babylon, to Canaan, his nephew (Lot) going with him. There he settled with his wife, Sarah, mother of Isaac, from whom the Jewish (Hebrew) nation claims descent. Abraham worshipped one God, and is known as ' father of the faithful.'

Abraham was a typical ' patriarch,' i.e. head of a large family living and working together as one unit in an age when men, hitherto wandering shepherds (' pastoral nomads '), were just beginning to settle as farmers in fixed habitations.

The story of his long life is told in Genesis 11–25.

Abraham, PLAINS OF, high ground on the N. bank of the R. St Lawrence, and near the city of Quebec, Canada. Here Wolfe defeated Montcalm, 1759. The site is now known as the National Battlefield Park.

Ab'salom, handsome and ambitious, raised a rebellion against his father David,

1

King of Israel. Caught by his hair in the branches of an oak while flying for his life, he was overtaken and killed (2 Samuel 13–18). How David learnt of his son's terrible death is one of the most moving OT stories :

And the king said unto Cushi, ' Is the young man, Absalom, safe ? '

And Cushi answered, ' The enemies of my Lord, the King, and all that rise against thee to do thee hurt, be as that young man is.'

And the king was much moved, and went up to the chamber over the gate, and wept : and as he went thus he said : ' O my son Absalom, my son, my son Absalom ! Would God I had died for thee, O Absalom, my son, my son ! '

absolute units, see ELECTRICITY

absolute zero, see ZERO

Abydos, *a-bī'dos,* (1) old city, Asia Minor ; home of Leander, who swam the Hellespont to visit his sweetheart Hero ; scene of the bridge of boats built 480BC by Xerxes. (2) Former city of Egypt, its temple and tombs now in ruins.

Abyssinia, see ETHIOPIA

AC, see ELECTRICITY

acacia, *akā'sha,* spiny shrub or small tree found at the edge of deserts ; known as wattle in Australia.

Academy, see PLATO

Aca'dia, name for Nova Scotia prior to 1713.

acanthus, *a-kan'thŭs,* prickly plant of S. Europe. The deeply-cut leaves were probably the model from which Greek sculptors evolved the decoration of the capital of the Corinthian column.

accelera'tion (Lat. *accelerare,* to hasten) in physics, increasing (+) or decreasing (−) speed ; may be uniform or variable. Equations of motion for a body travelling with *uniform acceleration* are :

$$v = u + at$$
$$s = \frac{u + v}{2}t \quad \text{or} \quad ut + \tfrac{1}{2}at^2$$
$$v^2 = u^2 + 2as,$$

where *u* is initial velocity, *v* is final velocity, *a* is acceleration, *t* is time, and *s* is distance.

Acceleration due to gravity (*g*) is 32·17ft per sec. per sec. or 980·655cm per sec. per sec. in the latitude of the British Is. See MECHANICS

The distance covered by a body falling from rest in a vacuum is 16ft in the first second, (16 + 32) ft in the second, (16 + 48) ft in the third, etc., and in the *n*th second 16 + 32 (*n* − 1) ft. The total distance a body has fallen by the end of the *n*th second is found by multiplying the square of the time in seconds by 16. Owing to air resistance a bomb released from a plane a mile high takes 19 seconds to reach the earth.

accent has four meanings :

(1) taken together, the differences between one person's way of pronouncing a language and the pronunciations accepted as standard. Accent in this sense may be peculiar to one person, or shared by many, in which case it may indicate to what district or social group the speaker belongs.

(2) the musical pitch of a syllable, i.e. whether ' higher ' or ' lower ' than another.

(3) the stress or emphasis given to particular syllables.

(4) in some languages, as written, special marks called ' accents ' are used as a means of indicating stress or less often pitch accents. Greek and French are especially rich in various accents. In ancient Greek the accent showed pitch —in modern Greek it shows stress. In French the *acute accent* (´) indicates sharpening of a vowel sound ; the *grave accent* (`) a marked but diminishing stress ; the *circumflex* (^) indicates that a vowel is lengthened (to make up for an *s* that has fallen out, e.g. *être* for old Fr. *estre*) ; and the *cedilla* under a *c* (ç) indicates that it is pronounced like *s*. Other important accents are : the *diaeresis* (*dī-ēr'esis*) (¨) over the second of two vowels indicates that each vowel is to be sounded ; *umlaut* (*oom'lowt*), a German accent with the same form as diaeresis (¨), is used to shorten the long vowels, and may be replaced by an *e* following the vowel ; the *tilde* (~) in Spanish, which adds a *y* sound when over *n*, e.g. *cañon* is pronounced *canyon*.

accentor or **hedge sparrow,** British bird, *c.*5½in long ; plumage dusky brown ; its nest, of moss, wool, etc., is lined with hair ; lays 4–5 bluish-green eggs. Though often called the hedge sparrow it is no relation to the house sparrow.

accidence, see GRAMMAR

account'ancy, profession which has to do with the records and business figures of a person or firm. An accountant examines and certifies (' audits ') the correctness of accounts, and is usually a member of a chartered society such as the Incorporated Society of Accountants and Auditors, or the Institute of Chartered Accountants.

Accra', cap. and port, British Gold Coast colony ; exports cocoa, palm-oil, ivory, rubber, timber ; pop.75,000.

Ac'crington, industrial town, Lancashire ; industries include cotton-spinning, bleaching, dyeing, also textile machinery, bricks, chemicals ; pop.39,000.

accumulators and **batteries.** Electric cells ; may be (*a*) primary, i.e. *supplying* electricity (batteries), or (*b*) secondary, i.e. *storing* electricity (accumulators). (*a*) A zinc plate connected by a wire to a copper plate, and both plates immersed in dilute acid. A current flows but this is later reduced as bubbles of hydrogen accumulate on the copper plate (or pole), a phenomenon called polarisation. Depolarisation was successfully achieved in the BICHROMATE CELL, much used last century. It gave a steady electro-motive force (EMF) of *c.*2 volts.

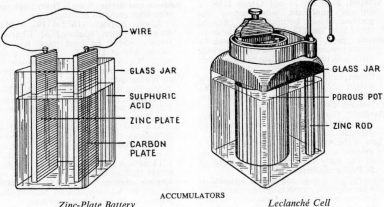

ACCUMULATORS

Zinc-Plate Battery   *Leclanché Cell*

In LECLANCHÉ CELLS often used for bells, sal-ammoniac (NH$_4$Cl) is employed, also zinc and carbon rods and a porous pot filled with carbon (to act as a conductor) and manganese dioxide (MnO$_2$), which 'depolarises' by oxidising the hydrogen to form water. In the 'wet' cell the MnO$_2$ is in fairly large grains, and its action is slow. Capable of delivering current for short periods only (after which it needs time to recover), it is used for electric bells. In the 'dry' cell the MnO$_2$ is finely divided. The cell delivers a moderate current continuously, hence its use in flash-lamps and electric torches. The 'dry' cell of this type has the depolariser embedded in a paste of sal-ammoniac and flour. The voltage is c.1·5.

(b) Storage batteries, or ACCUMULATORS, are much used in cars, radio-sets, etc. A typical accumulator has two lead plates (or lead and antimony) in dilute sulphuric acid. When charged, the positive plate (*anode*) is coated with lead peroxide. While the accumulator is discharging, oxygen is freed from the lead peroxide until pure lead remains. Edison's nickel-iron accumulator gives an EMF of 1·4 volts.

acetic acid, *a-sē'tik,* CH$_3$COOH, acid produced by many plants by fermentation ; present in vinegar from 3 to 6 per cent ; combines with many metals to form acetates, used commercially and in medicine.

acetone, *as'ē-tōn,* clear liquid, CH$_3$.CO. CH$_3$; dissolves fats.

acetylene, *a-set'i-lēn,* poisonous gas, C$_2$H$_2$, prepared by adding water to calcium carbide ; may be used for lighting. Burned with oxygen, it gives the oxy-acetylene flame, temperature 3,500°C, which is used for welding and cutting metals.

Achaeans, *a-kē'ans,* Homer's name for the Greeks in the Trojan war. Achaea was part of the Peloponnese.

Achill or **Eagle Isle,** *äch'il,* largest island off the W. coast of Eire.

Achilles, *ä-chil'ēz,* in old Greek tales, son of Peleus and Thetis. Most famous of the Greek heroes in the Trojan war, his deeds are described by Homer in the *Iliad.* Holding him by the heels, his mother dipped him, as an infant, in the R. Styx so that he could not be wounded by any weapon, except in the heel. Hence the phrase 'heel of Achilles,' meaning a weak spot.

acicular iron, see IRON AND STEEL

acid, substance readily giving hydrogen ions in solution ; always contains hydrogen, which may be replaced by a metal to form a salt ; may be defined as a proton-donor. Sour to the taste, an acid is the opposite of an alkali ; it turns blue litmus red ; if dilute it is less active. Among commonly used acids are sulphuric, H$_2$SO$_4$; nitric, HNO$_3$; hydrochloric, HCl, all inorganic ; and oxalic (COOH)$_2$, an organic acid.

Ackworth, *ak'wĕrth,* town 4m from Pontefract, Yorkshire ; has a noted Quaker school.

Aconcagua, *a-kŏn-käg'wä,* extinct volcano, Andes Range ; highest mt. (22,976 ft) in the New World.

aconite or **monk's hood,** *ak'on-īt,* poisonous plant common in England ; has spindle-shaped root, toothed leaves, and large blue hood-shaped flowers. See WINTER ACONITE

acoustics, see SOUND

Acre, *ä'kĕr,* port, Israel, between the Mediterranean and Mt Carmel ; scene of Richard Lion-heart's conquest 1191 ; taken from the Turks by the British 1918.

acropolis, *a-krop'o-lis,* highest part (citadel) of a Greek city ; notably the Acropolis at Athens, a rock 500ft high on which are the ruins of the Parthenon and other magnificent buildings of the time of Pericles (c.430BC) when Greek art was at its best. See ARCHITECTURE ; PLATE 67

Actaeon, *ak-tē'on,* in old Greek tales, a famous huntsman who, seeing the goddess Diana bathing, was changed into a stag, and killed by his own hounds.

actinic rays, invisible electromagnetic waves present in sunlight. They include ultra-violet rays, and affect photographic films.

actinium, radioactive element, Ac ; atomic weight 227·2 ; atomic number 89 ; discovered 1899. The element was isolated 1948. See RADIUM

Actium, Greek headland near which Octavian (later the Emperor Augustus) defeated Antony and Cleopatra 31BC.

Acts of the Apostles, 5th book of the NT ; written after AD60 ; gives an account of the early Christian Church, and of St Paul's missionary journeys.

actuary, *ak'tū-ar-i,* one whose business is with figures, especially averages for insurance. In England, actuaries belong to the Institute of Actuaries, London ; in Scotland, to the Faculty of Actuaries, Edinburgh.

AD, short for the Latin *Anno Domini,* in the year of our Lord, i.e. since the birth of Christ.

Adam, in Hebrew mythology, the first man created by God. His story, told in Genesis 2–5, symbolises the beginnings of human life on earth. Adam's wife was Eve ; his sons were Cain, Abel, and Seth.

Adam, ROBERT (1728–92), Scottish architect and designer of furniture. Robert was the most celebrated of four brothers who brought a new dignity to architecture, especially classical interior decoration.

adamant, *ad'ä-mant,* hard stone found in the Greek island of Naxos ; hence anything exceedingly hard.

Adam Bede, see ELIOT, GEORGE

Adams, JOHN (1735–1826), 2nd president of the USA (1797–1801) ; helped to prepare the *Declaration of Independence.*

Adams, JOHN COUCH (1819–92), brilliant astronomer, born near Launceston, Cornwall. His calculations led to the discovery of the planet Neptune. See LEVERRIER, U. J. J.

Adams, JOHN QUINCY (1767–1848), 6th president of the USA (1825–29) ; supported the abolition of slavery ; favoured high tariffs into the USA.

Adam's apple, see LARYNX

Adam's Bridge, series of rocks and sandbanks (*c.*17m) between India and Ceylon.

Adam's Peak, mt. of Ceylon (7,360ft), visited by pilgrims. An impression 5ft long is said by Arabs to be Adam's footprint ; by Hindus it is claimed as Buddha's.

Addis Ababa, cap., Ethiopia ; is on the equator, but at 8,000ft above sea-level enjoys spring-like weather all the year ; linked by air with Cairo etc., and by rail with Jibuti ; though still old-fashioned it is being rapidly modernised ; occupied by Italians 1936–41 ; pop. 180,000. See ETHIOPIA ; HAILE SELASSIE

Addison and Steele, friends from boyhood who later enriched our literature.

JOSEPH ADDISON (1672–1719), *b* Milston, Wiltshire, educated at Charterhouse, where he first met Richard Steele, and at Oxford. Addison, early wrote Latin verse, travelled much in Europe, became MP, and was buried in Westminster Abbey.

SIR RICHARD STEELE (1672–1729), *b* Dublin ; entered Parliament ; wrote plays and essays ; was a kindly, genial man, but almost always in debt.

The two friends founded their first periodical, the *Tatler,* 1709. The more famous *Spectator* (a word meaning looker-on) appeared daily 1 March 1711 until 6 Dec 1712. Today the 555 essays (published in book form) are an English classic. Of these, 274 were written by Addison, 236 by Steele ; the remainder by less notable writers.

It is in the pages of the *Spectator* that we read of Sir Roger de Coverley, an imaginary gentleman of Worcestershire, kindly but odd, a perfect portrait of the typical English squire of his day. Addison wrote about him, and so did Steele. Here is part of the former's account of Sir Roger's visit to Westminster Abbey :

Our conductor then pointed to that monument where there is a figure of one of our English kings without a head ; and upon giving us to know that the head, which was of beaten silver, had been stolen away several years since : ' Some Whig, I'll warrant,' says Sir Roger, ' you ought to lock up your kings better ; they will carry off the body too, if you do not take care.'

The glorious names of Henry V and Queen Elizabeth gave the knight great opportunities of shining, and of doing justice to Sir Richard Baker, ' who,' as our knight observed with some surprise, ' had a great many kings in him whose monuments he had not seen in the abbey.'

For my own part, I could not but be pleased to see the knight shew such an honest passion for the glory of his country, and such a respectful gratitude to the memory of its princes.

Adelaide, *ad'e-lād,* (1792–1849) queen of William IV, whom she married 1818. Her meddling with politics made her unpopular.

Adelaide, cap., S. Australia ; a great trading centre ; does much business in mining shares ; exports wool, wine, wheat, silver, copper ore, etc. ; named after Adelaide, queen of William IV. An exceedingly well-planned town, it is set amid parks and gardens, and abounds in tree-lined roads ; pop.370,000.

Aden, *ä'den,* British colony of great military importance on the Red Sea trade-route between Europe and the E. ; area 75sq.m ; pop. *c.*86,000. British since 1839, it became a Crown Colony in 1937 ; includes the islands of

Perim, Kamaran, etc. ; also a protectorate, area *c*.112,000sq.m ; estimated pop. *c*.600,000. The port of Aden, a coaling station, exports salt and coffee.

Adenauer, KONRAD (1876–), since 1949 Democratic Chancellor of the Western German Federal Republic.

adenoids, see TONSILS

Adige, *a'de-jä*, river of Italy ; flows *c*.240m to the Adriatic Sea.

Adirondack Mountains, *adi-ron'dak*, mountain and forest region of New York State, USA ; has many lakes and rivers.

adjutant bird, Indian stork 5ft high ; has a bald head, a large pouch, and a huge beak ; feeds on carrion.

' **Admiral Graf Spee,**' see PLATE, RIVER

Admiralty Arch, triumphal arch designed by Sir Aston Webb. Built *c*.1910, it leads from Trafalgar Square to St James's Park, London.

Admiralty, BOARD OF, see GOVERNMENT

Adonijah, *a-don-ī'jä*, 4th son of David, King of Israel (2 Samuel 3, 1 Kings 1–2).

Adonis, *ä-dō'nis* ; *ä-don'is*, in old Greek tales, a handsome young man loved by Aphrodite, goddess of love. There are different forms of the story, but in all of them Adonis has to die each year and spend some time in the Lower World (Hades). In the story, Adonis stands for the vegetation, or perhaps the corn, which dies in autumn, and Aphrodite represents the power of Nature to make it grow again.

Adour, *ä'door*, French river ; flows 208m from the Pyrenees to the Bay of Biscay.

Adrian IV, *ä'dri-an*, only Englishman to become pope (1154–59) ; *b* Langley, Hertfordshire ; actually named Nicholas Breakspear.

Adriatic Sea, *ä-dri-at'ik*, part of the Mediterranean between Italy and Yugoslavia ; length *c*.470m.

' **Advancement of Learning,**' see BACON, FRANCIS

Advent (Latin *adventus*, coming), period between the Sunday nearest St Andrew's Day (30 Nov.) and Christmas. See CALENDAR

advowson, in England, right of appointing a clergyman to a living, i.e. a rectory or vicarage. One who presents a living is a patron.

aedile, *ē'dīl*, Roman magistrate whose chief duty was the oversight of buildings, water supply, national games, police, etc. ; instituted 494BC.

Aegean Civilisation, *ē-jē'an*, flourished in islands of the Agean Sea (E. Mediterranean) and on the Greek mainland from *c*.3000BC. Enriched by trade with Egypt and Asia Minor, and centred in Crete, Aegean owed much to Egyptian culture. The Cretan capital was Cnossos, where modern archaeologists, notably Sir Arthur Evans, have dug up remains of one of the most luxurious civilisations of the ancient world.

The sanitation of the king's palace was surprisingly modern in design. The palace itself contains a bewildering number of rooms, doubtless the origin of Gk stories about the Cretan Labyrinth (the word itself is pre-Greek and probably Aegean), or maze, in which King Minos kept the Minotaur, a monster half bull, half man, which was killed by the Athenian hero Theseus. Aegean art is notable for its freshness, and shows delight in simple things, e.g. flowers. Wall-paintings, vases and other objects of great beauty have been found, also clay tablets with writing on them not yet deciphered.

Cnossos was destroyed *c*.1400BC, probably by sea-raiders, and in Crete the Aegean civilisation was obliterated, although it flourished for some time afterwards in Mycenae, legendary home of the Greek hero Agamemnon. Mycenae was destroyed *c*.468BC. At Mycenae many carvings, ruined buildings and treasures of gold and silver have been unearthed.

Aegean Sea, *ē-jē'an*, part of the Mediterranean between Greece and Asia Minor ; noted for its many islands.

Aegina, *ē-jī'nä*, Greek island 20m SW. of Athens ; noted for sponges ; has remains of ancient Greek civilisation.

Aegir, *ä'gir*, in old Norse tales, giant of the seashore.

aegir, tidal wave or bore, especially in the English R. Trent.

aegis, *ē'jis*, in old Greek tales, name of the shield of Zeus ; hence the word now means *protection*.

Aelred, *al'red*, (*d* 1166), English monk and saint ; *b* Hexham ; wrote a life of Edward the Confessor.

' **Aeneid,**' see VIRGIL

aeolian harp, *ē-ō'liän*, box with wires or strings that give a musical note when a breeze passes over them.

Aeolus, *ē-ō'lŭs*, god of the winds in old Greek tales.

aerodynamics, see AVIATION

aeromodelling, see HOBBY

aeronautics, see AVIATION

aeroplane, see AVIATION

Aeschines, *ēs'ki-nēz*, (389–314BC), Greek orator and statesman, a rival of Demosthenes.

Aeschylus, *es'ki-lus*, (525–456BC), ' the father of Greek Tragedy ' ; *b* Eleusis, Attica ; fought against the Persians at Marathon and Salamis ; *d* Gela, Sicily.

The *Agamemnon* is Aeschylus's noblest play and one of the greatest ever written. With the *Choephoroe* and the *Eumenides* (Furies) it makes up a trilogy (group of three plays) called the *Oresteia*. King Agamemnon has sacrificed his daughter Iphigenia in order to obtain a favourable wind for the Greek army and fleet, and is bringing home with him from Troy Cassandra, a Trojan slave-woman. Agamemnon's wife Clytaemnestra murders Agamemnon and Cassandra. Agamemnon's son Orestes now has to avenge his father by slaying Clytaemnestra, his own mother. Afterwards he is pursued by the Furies, who have him tried for murder at Athens. The judges' votes are evenly divided ; but Athena, goddess of Athens, who is presiding, gives her casting vote for Orestes, and he is absolved. This myth was used for plays also by Sophocles and Euripides, and also by the modern American dramatist Eugene O'Neill.

Aeschylus wrote 70 plays, but only the *Oresteia* and four others (*Suppliants, Persians, Seven against Thebes* and *Prometheus Bound*) survive today. Aeschylus is called the father of Greek tragedy because it was he who developed it from religious pageants full of ritual and solemn music into what we understand the word, i.e. plays about human beings involved in some great conflict with one another. His plays are the first which try to show the characters of human beings in any detail ; but in them the human beings are less important than the gods and goddesses.

With their profoundly religious spirit Aeschylus's plays are among the noblest in the world. Although written 2,500 years ago, they are still often performed, usually in English translations (of which those by Gilbert Murray are best known), but sometimes in the original Greek. Well-known quotations from Aeschylus's works, which express some of his ideas, are as follows : Τὸ τῆς ἀνάγκης ἔστ' ἀδήριτον σθένος (the force of fate is irresistible) ; οὐ γὰρ δοκεῖν ἄριστος ἀλλ' εἶναι, θέλει (he does not wish to be thought best, but to be best) ; ποντίων τε κυμάτων ἀνήριθμον γέλασμα (the innumerable laughter of the sea-waves) ; πάθει μάθος (we learn by suffering).

The story that he was killed by an eagle (which dropped a tortoise on his bald head, mistaking it for a big white stone) is probably not true.

Aesculapius, *ĕskŭ-lā'pĭ-ŭs,* Greek god of medicine ; his symbol, a staff with a twisted snake, is now the badge of the Royal Army Medical Corps.

Aesop, *ē'sop,* (*d* 560BC), said to have been ugly and deformed, was perhaps a Greek slave. It is told that Croesus, King of Lydia, sent him on an errand to Delphi, where the witty little man vexed the people so much that they threw him over a precipice.

Whether Aesop wrote all the tales attributed to him is doubtful, but what are known as *Aesop's Fables* (stories usually about birds, animals, etc.) illustrate moral truths, e.g.

THE THIRSTY CROW

A crow, almost dying of thirst, saw a pitcher. Joyously he flew towards it, only to find, to his great disappointment, that he could not reach the water at the bottom. He tried to roll the pitcher over, but it was too heavy. Then he tried to break it, but could not. At last, however, he thought of a plan. Seeing some pebbles near by, he dropped them into the pitcher one by one till the level of the water rose, and he was able to quench his thirst.

The lesson or moral of the fable is : *Where there's a will there's a way.*

Two other notable tellers of fables are Jean de La Fontaine (1621–95), a Frenchman, and Lessing. See LESSING, GOTTHOLD EPHRAIM.

aestivation, see HIBERNATION

AFC, see DECORATIONS

afforestation, see FORESTS

Afghanistan, country on the NW. frontier of Pakistan ; area 250,000sq.m ; largely mountainous (Hindu Kush) and with a general elevation of 4,000ft. The climate is dry and extreme. Inhabited by a mixed but generally industrious people, it usually produces two harvests a year, e.g. wheat, barley, lentils, also rice, millet, etc. The exports include timber, carpets, fruit, and Persian lamb skins. Motor transport is gradually replacing beasts of burden. The capital is Kabul, though Dar-ul-Aman may eventually be the capital.

The British were at war with Afghanistan (owing to Russian influence), 1838–42, when a massacre occurred in the Khyber Pass, a narrow defile in places only 10ft wide. There was also war, 1879, and there has since been much unrest ; pop. *c.*10,000,000.

Africa, continent linked to Asia by the isthmus of Suez ; is almost equally N. and S. of the equator ; area *c.*11,699,000 sq.m.

Africa is largely a vast plain with the highest mt. ranges in the E., the loftiest peaks being Kilimanjaro (19,321ft), Kenya (17,040ft), and Ruwenzori (16,794ft) ; other mt. ranges include the Abyssinian Highlands, Drakensberg and Atlas. The chief rivers are the Nile, Congo and Zambesi. Among lakes are Victoria (26,200sq.m), Tanganyika, Nyasa, Chad, etc. The deserts include, in the N., Sahara, Libyan, Nubian, and in the S., the Kalahari. The Sahara and Kalahari are almost rainless, but Central Africa has tropical rainfall ; the Mediterranean coasts have winter rains. The estimated pop. is 158,000,000, the natives being (*a*) yellow-skinned Bushmen and Hottentots in the S., or Pygmies in the equatorial forests ; (*b*) Negro races either (i) Bantu, including Kaffirs, Zulus, etc., or (ii) Sudan Negroes ; (*c*) Hamitic races, e.g. Berber, Somali, Fulbe, etc., mostly in the N. and NE., often mingled with Arabs.

Long known as the Dark Continent, the early history of Africa was chiefly that of Egypt and Carthage. Portuguese settlements began *c.*1450 ; Diaz discovered the Cape of Good Hope, 1487, rounded by Vasco da Gama 10 years later. The British African Company was founded 1588. The Dutch colonised S. Africa *c.*1650. Livingstone explored the interior 1840–73 ; Speke and Grant discovered one of the sources of the Nile 1862 ; Sir Samuel Baker first saw L. Albert Nyanza 1864 ; Stanley explored the Congo 1879–80. See ALL-AFRICA HIGHWAY

Since World War II Africa has swiftly grown in importance in the defence of the British Empire. Aviation, atomic warfare, and the withdrawal of troops from Palestine, India, etc., and other considerations compel Britain to regard the continent as the keystone of Imperial security. hence plans for far-reaching development, notably in Kenya, which is likely to become a great army base. An All-Africa Conference was held in 1948.

The Katanga copper belt of the Belgian Congo is now supremely important as one of the world's two most productive sources of uranium. Since supplies of uranium are required for atomic warfare, it is imperative that control of the African sources should belong to the democratic powers.

Afridi, *ä-frē'dē,* warlike tribe on the NW. frontier of India.

Afrikaans, *afri-käns',* formerly called Taal, language (originally Dutch) spoken by descendants of Dutch settlers in S. Africa, where it enjoys equality of status with English.

Ag, chemical symbol for silver ; Latin *argentum.*

Agamemnon, Greek leader in the Trojan War. Probably there was actually a king of Mycenae called Agamemnon, but he is known to us only in legends. See AEGEAN CIVILISATION ; AESCHYLUS

agar-agar, jelly made from seaweed ; used for cultivating bacteria.

Agassiz, JEAN LOUIS RODOLPHE, *ag'äs-ē* (1807–73), Swiss naturalist ; a pioneer of careful inquiry ; studied much in USA.

agate, *ag'it,* form of silica ; coloured varieties are used as ornaments.

Agate, JAMES, *ag'āt* (1877–1947), dramatic critic, *b* Manchester. His books include *Here's Richness,* and *Ego,* an autobiography in many volumes.

agave, see SISAL

' age-hardening,' see ALUMINIUM

agenda, *ä-jen'dä,* list of topics to be discussed at a meeting. It is usually prepared by the secretary for the guidance of the chairman, and is circulated beforehand to those who will be present.

Agesilaus, *ä-jēs-i-lā'ŭs* (*d* 360BC), limping King of Sparta ; fought against the Persians ; hated Thebes.

Agincourt, *ä-zhan'koor,* village *c.*25m from Boulogne, France ; scene 25 Oct 1415 (St Crispin's Day) of a brilliant English victory.

Having marched from Harfleur with *c.*6,000 sick, tired, and disheartened men, Henry V of England gave battle to 30,000 Frenchmen, who were ' confident and over-lusty.' The attack began when Sir Thomas Erpingham gave the word, ' Now strike ! ' The English advanced with the cry, ' God for Harry, England,

and St George,' and later halted behind pointed stakes while the French, heavily armoured, came up slowly over wet soil, thus offering an excellent target for the bowmen.

Though the English are said to have lost only 200, the French lost *c.*8,000, including the Constable of France and the Duke of Brabant. The victory resulted in Henry becoming the hero of his people, but the immediate gain was small. Celebrated in song, Agincourt is immortalised by Shakespeare in *King Henry the Fifth.*

agora, *ag'o-rä,* public meeting-place in a Greek city.

agouti, *ä-goo'ti,* animal rather like a rabbit ; found in S. America and the W. Indies ; *c.*18in long ; is destructive in sugar-plantations.

Agra, *ä'grä,* city of India ; on the R. Jumna *c.*140m SE. of Delhi ; capital of the Mogul Empire in the 16th c. ; has a fortress built by Akbar, and is noted for the palace of Sha Jehan, also other palaces and mosques. Near is the Taj Mahal. Agra is an important rail and trading centre ; pop.284,000. See AGRAPHA

Agra and Oudh, *owd,* united provinces known as the NW. Provinces and Oudh prior to 1902. A portion of the Ganges plain W. of Bengal, it produces rice, wheat, barley, pulse, millet, cotton, sugar, etc.

Agrapha, *ag'rä-fä,* words and sayings attributed to Jesus but not recorded in the NT. Dr Bernard Grenfell and Dr Arthur Hunt found (1903) in the sands of Egypt many scraps of papyrus (bills, letters, exercises done in school, etc.) among which were sayings of Jesus previously unknown, e.g. *Wherever there is one alone, I say, I am with him. Raise the stone, and there thou shalt find Me ; cleave the wood, and there am I.*

Another saying of Jesus not found in the NT is written above the gateway of a Mohammedan mosque near Agra, India : *Jesus, on whom be peace, has said : The world is merely a bridge ; ye are to pass over it and not to build your dwellings on it.*

Agricola, JULIUS, *ä-grik'ō-lä* (AD37–93), Roman general ; governor of Britain AD78–87 ; defeated the Caledonians led by Calgacus at Mons Graupius ; his life-story, written by his son-in-law, Tacitus, gives a vivid picture of Britain in the 1st c. AD.

agriculture, farming or husbandry, i.e. cultivation of the soil, also the rearing of animals for food, etc., hence, growing crops (as wheat, oats, barley, turnips, beet, peas, beans), and raising stock, e.g. sheep, cattle, horses, pigs ; is one of the oldest of all occupations ; has become much more scientific in the last 20 years. See PLATES 1–12, 15–20

Crops were long sown ' broadcast ' (as the parable of the sower, Matthew 13, reminds us), but in the 18th c. Jethro

Tull introduced sowing in straight drills or furrows to allow room for hoeing. By using suitable manures the nitrogenous content of the soil may be increased, thus ensuring better crops ; and by rotation of crops the farmer arranges to put back into the soil some of the elements taken out, so preventing soil exhaustion. One example of a 4-year rotation is a succession of wheat, roots, barley, clover ; but this may be widely varied to suit local needs, e.g. oats may replace barley, or peas and beans may replace clover. Manures include (a) a mixture of straw and dung from the fold yard and cow-house, (b) such inorganic fertilisers as basic slag, superphosphate, ammonium sulphate and sodium nitrate.

Farm implements include (a) *plough*, which may have 1 to 5 shares or blades, or (as in USA) as many as 25 shares. Deep ploughing serves to bring to the surface fresh and unexhausted soil, (b) *drills*, by means of which the seed is automatically dropped into the soil and then covered to the correct depth, and often supplied with a suitable amount of fertiliser, (c) *harrow*, for turning over the soil by means of teeth or discs, (d) machinery for harvesting crops, as the *self-binder*, which cuts, binds and throws out grain crops (wheat, oats, barley, etc.) in sheaves, where they are left in stooks or shocks to dry ; also the more recent *combined harvesters*, much used in America, and now being increasingly used on British farms. These not only cut the corn, but at the same time thresh and bag the grain. Since 1936 many large farms have employed machinery that transforms green grass into hay and dried grassmeal. At one time all farm implements were drawn by horses or oxen, but powerful tractors, running on cheap fuel, have now largely replaced such methods.

Livestock rearing requires suitable grazing pastures, and a knowledge of (a) correct feeding and housing, (b) milking cows by hand and with mechanical milking machinery, (c) sheep-shearing, (d) animal breeding, and the control of diseases, e.g. foot-and-mouth disease, one of the most serious infectious maladies among cattle, sheep and pigs. When an outbreak is discovered, all movement of these animals in the affected area is prohibited by the Ministry of Agriculture. Other diseases are liver fluke in sheep, swine fever in pigs.

In summer, stock is fed by grazing ; for winter feeding farmers store hay, straw, oats, mixed pulses, etc., and cattle cake (i.e. the material left over after oil has been extracted from such vegetable products as linseed, cotton-seed and soya beans). In recent years agriculturists have made great use of silage, i.e. green fodder mixed with molasses. See SILAGE

Researchers have gone a long way this century in improving crops and stocks, and farmers today owe much to experiments carried out at the Rothamsted Experimental Station, Harpenden, Hertfordshire (founded 1843), and to various agricultural schools, e.g. Harper Adams Agricultural College, Newport, Shropshire ; the National Institute of Agricultural Botany, Cambridge, and the Newton Rigg Farm School, Penrith, Cumberland ; also to the Diploma Courses in Agriculture at many universities, e.g. Oxford, Cambridge, Edinburgh, Aberdeen, London, Leeds, etc, some giving Degree Courses.

It is supremely important that we should view agriculture from the world standpoint since possibly the most vital problem before mankind is the production of sufficient food. There is no doubt that most of our political and economic difficulties today can be traced back finally to lack of food—one of several reasons for the swift rise of Communism all over the world. Experts have declared that 2·5 acres of land need to be farmed per head of the population, but in Europe only 0·88 of an acre is available, and in the UK only 0·3 of an acre. Nor is the future bright with hope since, in spite of two world wars this century, the world's population has increased enormously. Moreover much farming is done badly, leading to soil erosion or to over-grassing. Instead, therefore, of destroying each other by war, nations need to realise the urgent necessity for co-operation in the production of food, the conservation of farm land, and the widespread application of scientific methods of production in order to ensure a supply of food for all. See WORLD WAR II (POLITICAL BACKGROUND)

Read *Holdfast*, A. G. Street

agrimony, plant of dry places ; has a spire of small yellow five-petalled flowers ; the green calyx is bell-like with five points ; the leaflets, dark and hairy, have saw edges.

Agrippa I, *ä-grip'ä* (d AD44), ruler of Judaea ; grandson of Herod the Great ; condemned St James to death ; imprisoned St Peter ; mentioned in Acts 12. His son Agrippa II (d c.AD100) listened to St Paul's defence, and said, ' Almost thou persuadest me to be a Christian ' (Acts 25–26).

Ahab, *ä'hab*, King of Israel, 875–863BC (1 Kings 16–22).

Ahasuerus, *ähaz-ū-ē'rŭs* (d c.465BC), Persian king (Ezra 4, Daniel 9, and Esther).

Ahaz, *ä'haz*, (d c.715BC), King of Judah (2 Kings 16, 2 Chronicles 28).

Ahmedabad, *ä-mŭd-ä-bäd'*, city, c.300m N. of Bombay, India ; founded in the 15th c., and of great importance in the Mogul Empire ; manufactures cotton ; pop.591,000.

Ai or **Hai**, ancient town, Canaan (Genesis 13, Joshua 7–8).

CULTIVATION   *plate 1*

Top : Rice-cultivation in Burmese paddy-fields. The ploughs are drawn by bullocks. (*Topical Press*). *Bottom :* Horse-ploughing on an English farm. (*Picture Post Library*)

plate 2 FARMING

Top : Croft-farming in Stenness and Harray, Orkney. Each crofting family works a relatively small amount of land. Inshore fishing makes a valuable addition to the family budget. (*W. S. Thomson Esq.*). *Bottom :* Contour-ploughing for wheat, Montana, U.S.A. The soil is ploughed along the contour lines so as to minimise erosion of top-soil by rain-water. (*U.S. Information Service*)

CANADIAN WHEAT HARVEST   *plate 3*

Top : Stooked wheat on a prairie-land farm near Rosebud, Alberta, Canada. *Bottom :*
Combine harvesters at work near Rouleau, Saskatchewan.
(Both *Canadian National Film Board*)

plate 4   THRESHING AND STORING

Top : Wheat-threshing, Oregon, U.S.A. The grain goes into the sacks : the chaff is a useful by-product. (*U.S. Information Service*). *Bottom :* Grain is stored in silos until it is time to load it on to ships. (*Canadian National Film Board*)

Aidan, *ā'dan* (*d* 651), monk of Iona and a Christian missionary; converted Oswald of Northumbria; lived on the island of Lindisfarne (Holy I.), being its first bishop.

Ainsworth, WILLIAM HARRISON (1805–82), *b* Manchester; author of many historical novels, e.g. *The Tower of London, Old St Paul's.*

Aintree, suburb of Liverpool; scene (March or April) since 1839 of the Grand National, the most famous of English steeplechases. The course of 4½m has 30 jumps.

Ainu, old race of *c.*20,000 partly civilised people in N. Japan. They have long, black, wavy hair.

air, see ATMOSPHERE

air-conditioning, see VENTILATION

aircraft, see AVIATION

Airdrie, mining and cotton town, Lanarkshire; pop.26,000.

Aire, Yorkshire river flowing through Airedale and Leeds to the Ouse.

Airgraph, trade name for a form of correspondence adopted 1940 by the British Post Office, and first operated 1941 as a service to troops in the Middle East during World War II. Correspondents obtained a form at a Post Office, wrote their letter on this, and posted it. The forms were then collected, photographed, and reduced by a special process, dispatched by air, and later enlarged. 1,700 messages, when reduced, weighed only 5½oz. As many as 250,000 letters were handled in one day. By 1945 no less than 350,000,000 Airgraphs had been mailed.

Air Lift, see BERLIN

air, LIQUID, see LIQUID AIR

air mail, see POST OFFICE

Air Ministry, see GOVERNMENT

air raids, attacks on enemy civil population by aircraft; those by Germany on Britain resulted in 1,316 deaths in World War I, and in 60,584 in World War II.

air records, see AVIATION

air routes, see AVIATION

airship, see AVIATION

airstrip, name of a specially laid runway for planes. More specifically, a floating metal 'carpet' laid on water to form a flexible airfield. The idea of linking together a large number of 6-sided cans was the invention of R. M. Hamilton of London. Experimented with as a floating base for planes or as a harbour for seaplanes, the airstrip has been known as Lily since 1940.

Air Training Corps, see YOUTH ORGANISATIONS

Aisne, *ān*, French river flowing 175m to join the Oise near Compiègne. See WORLD WAR I

Aix-la-Chapelle, *eks-lä-shä-pel'*, TREATY OF, 1748; ended the War of the Austrian Succession, Prussia retaining Silesia. See AACHEN

Aix-les-Bains, *eks'lā-ba*n, health resort, Savoie, France; has warm springs and Roman remains; pop.130,000.

Ajaccio, *ä-yät'chō*, cap., Corsica; a port with a large harbour; Napoleon's birthplace; pop.40,000.

Ajanta, narrow valley, Hyderabad, India; famous for Buddhist cave-temples, *c.*1,300–2,100 years old.

Ajax, *ā'jaks*, in old Greek tales, Greek hero of the Trojan war; son of Telamon; fought in single combat with Hector of Troy.

Ajmer, *ŭj-mēr'*, capital of the province of Ajmer-Merwara, Rajputana, India; pop.120,000.

Akbar the Great (1542–1605), most famous of Mogul emperors; conqueror of much of India; abolished slavery within his domains; introduced beneficial reforms.

à Kempis, THOMAS, (1379–1471), German monk and writer, chiefly remembered for his devotional book, *The Imitation of Christ,* 1418.

Akhenaton, *ä-ke-nä'tun*, Egyptian king who attempted, without much success, to reform Egyptian religion by introducing the idea that there is only one God, whereas the Egyptians believed there were many. He died *c.*1360BC, and was succeeded by Tutankhamen, who undid his reforms.

Al, chemical symbol for aluminium.

Alabama, *al-ä-bä'mä*, river, USA; also a state of USA; has cultivated lowlands, great timber forests, and (in the S.) a cotton belt; cap. Montgomery.

Al'aric I (376–410), King of the Visigoths (or W. Goths); captured and sacked Rome, AD410. This event marked the end of 'classical antiquity' and the beginning of the Dark Ages.

Alaska, *ä-las'kä*, NW. territory (586,000 sq.m) of USA; bought from Russia 1867; extremely mountainous, Mt McKinley, 20,300ft, being the highest peak. The rivers include the Yukon. Alaska is largely inhabited by Indians and Eskimos, but has had a white population since the Klondyke Gold Rush, 1896. The products include salmon and furs. The capital is Juneau.

The ALASKAN HIGHWAY continues the Inter-American Highway (16,800m) from Alaska to the Argentine, the N. American section being opened 1942.

Alban, *ŏl'ban*, 3rd c. British saint and martyr; believed to have been born Verulamium (now St Albans).

Albania, *al-bā'niä*, mountainous republic E. of the Adriatic Sea; area *c.*11,000 sq.m; pop.1,000,000. Agriculture is somewhat primitive. The industries include the mining of copper, iron, etc. Oil is a valuable export. The only harbour is Durazzo.

Albania was invaded by the Italians (under Mussolini) 1939. During World War II the people bravely resisted Axis troops, and patriot forces entered the capital (Tirana) 1944.

Albany, cap., New York State, USA; on the Hudson R.; terminal point of the Erie Canal; pop.131,000.

2

albatross, *al'bä-tros,* largest of all seabirds ; wing span 12ft ; plumage] white with black on the wings ; the feet are webbed. The bird is common in the S. Pacific. Sailors once believed that ill-luck followed the killing of an albatross, hence Coleridge's *Rime of the Ancient Mariner.*

Albert (1819–61), husband of Queen Victoria, whom he married 1840 ; known as the Prince Consort from 1857 ; the Great Exhibition in Hyde Park 1851 was his inspiration. See VICTORIA

Albert, KING OF THE BELGIANS (1875–1934), *b* Brussels ; became king 1909 ; ruled wisely and kindly. Germany invaded his country 1914, and the king and government took refuge at Le Havre, the king later commanding a successful Allied army. He was killed while mountain-climbing.

Alberta, *al-bŭrt'ä,* province of Canada between Saskatchewan and British Columbia ; area 255,285sq.m ; pop. *c.*800,000 ; noted for wheat, oats, barley, etc. ; cap. Edmonton. Alberta gave the Social Credit theory a practical but unsuccessful test. See SOCIAL CREDIT

Albert Hall, S. Kensington, London, completed 1871 in memory of Prince Albert ; seats 8,000 ; noted for prom-enade concerts and for great public meetings.

Albert Memorial, Kensington Gardens, London, a tribute to Prince Albert ; completed 1872 ; has a spire 150ft high, and carvings of sculptors, artists, musicians, etc.

albino, *al-bē'nō,* person or animal with white hair and pink eyes.

Albion, *al'bi-on,* ancient name for Britain ; possibly of Celtic origin, Albainn being still the Gaelic and Irish name for Scotland ; associated by the Romans with Latin *albus,* white, from the white cliffs of Dover.

Albuera, *äl-bwä'rä,* village 13m from Badajoz, Spain ; scene 1811 of a British victory over the French in the Peninsular War.

albumen or **albumin,** *al-bū'men, -min,* one group among many of the protein compounds ; an important part of all animal matter, e.g. eggs, and also of most vegetable matter.

' Alchemist, The,' see DRAMA

alchemy, *al'kemi,* unscientific chemistry of the Middle Ages. The chemist today knows much about the materials he deals with, whereas the alchemist eked out his small store of knowledge with a belief in magic.

The first alchemists were Egyptians, Greeks, Arabs, etc. ; later, alchemy was practised in Britain and Germany, search being made for the so-called PHILOSOPHER'S STONE which, it was thought, would transmute base metals (e.g. lead or iron) into gold ; and also for the ELIXIR OF LIFE, a liquid supposed to give eternal youth. Alchemists be-

lieved that the planets influenced metals. Roger Bacon ; Albertus Magnus, a 13th c. German scholar ; Thomas Aquinas ; Paracelsus (*d* 1541) ; Sir George Ripley and Dr Dee were all noted alchemists. It should be remem-bered that the alchemists stumbled on many useful discoveries during their experiments, and were pioneers of modern chemistry.

Alcibiades, *äl-si-bī'adēz* (*d* 404BC), hot-headed Athenian statesman, general and orator ; kinsman of Pericles ; friend of Socrates.

Alclad, see METALS

Alcock, SIR JOHN WILLIAM, *öl'kok* (1892–1919), Manchester airman who, in company with Sir Arthur Whitten Brown, made the first official Atlantic flight (Newfoundland to Ireland) 14 June 1919.

al'cohol, name of a group of hydrocarbon compounds with a hydrogen atom re-placed by one or more hydroxyl (HO) groups. What is commonly called alcohol is actually ethyl alcohol, C_2H_5OH, the usual source of which is the fermentation of sugar. This occurs in beer, wine and spirits. Among the alcohols of commerce is methyl alcohol, CH_3OH, usually obtained by the syn-thetic process of passing a mixture of one part of carbon monoxide and two parts of hydrogen over zinc and chromium oxides heated to 350–400°C, when

$$CO + 2H_2 = CH_3OH.$$

Other alcohols include propyl and butyl alcohol, both used as solvents.

Alcohol burns with a non-luminous flame ; dissolves fats, oils ; is used in the manufacture of polishes and as a sub-stitute for petrol.

Alcott, LOUISA MAY, *öl'kot* (1832–88), American author of several charming books, including *Little Women.*

Alcuin, *al'kwin* (735–804), English scholar, historian and poet, *b* York ; became a teacher in the palace of the Emperor Charlemagne at Aix-la-Chapelle.

aldehyde, *al'dē-hīd,* a group of compounds produced from primary alcohols ; they contain the -CHO group. See FORMAL-DEHYDE

alder, *öl'dĕr,* British tree usually found near rivers ; 20–40ft high ; has oval leaves with toothed edges ; the catkins mature in March.

alderman (OE *elder* man), senior member of a town or council in England and Wales. He is elected by the councillors. The Scottish equivalent is a bailie. See LOCAL GOVERNMENT

Alderney, *öl'dĕr-ni,* one of the Channel Islands, *c.*4m long ; noted for a fine breed of (Alderney) cows.

Aldershot, town, Hampshire ; has had a military camp since 1855 ; noted for its summer tattoo ; pop.34,000.

Aldington, RICHARD, *öld'ing-tŭn* (1892–), British author and poet, notable for his war-book *Death of a Hero* ; also *All Men are Enemies* ; *Artifex* ; *Rejected Guest.*

Aldred, *al'dred* (*d* 1069), English monk ; Archbishop of York 1061 ; crowned William I (1066), but later rebuked him for his evil deeds.

Aleppo, *ä-lep'ō*, city of N. Syria. It is a great trading centre, and a terminus of the Iraq pipe-line ; pop.298,000.

Aleutian Islands, *ā-loo'shan*, *c*.150 islands curving W. from Alaska ; mostly bare rocks, some with active volcanoes. The inhabitants are of Eskimo stock. The islands were the scene of fighting between USA and the Japanese in World War II, and are of strategic importance.

Alexander, name of several kings of Scotland : ALEXANDER I, *d* 1124 ; ALEXANDER II (1198–1249), who helped the English barons to compel King John to agree to *Magna Carta* ; ALEXANDER III (1241–86), king when only eight ; a strong ruler, unfortunately killed by riding over a cliff.

Alexander, name of eight popes, among them Alexander III (*d* 1181) who made Henry II of England do penance for the murder of Becket.

Alexander, name of several tsars of Russia, including Alexander I (1777–1825), who compelled Napoleon's army to retreat from Moscow 1812.

Alexander, FIELD-MARSHAL VISCOUNT (1891–), soldier and statesman, *b* Ulster ; in command of troops in the first days of World War II ; last to leave the beaches of Dunkirk in the evacuation 1940 ; as supreme Allied Commander in Italy displayed superb skill against the Germans 1943–45 after aiding the Eighth Army to win a resounding victory in N. Africa ; appointed Governor-General of Canada from Sept 1945.

ALEXANDER THE GREAT 356–323 B.C.

Alexander the Great (356–323BC), King of Macedonia ; distinguished himself in battle at 16 ; defeated immensely powerful enemies before he was 25 ; planned and achieved some of the most ambitious conquests ever dreamed of ; died at 32.

Son of Philip II, Alexander, *b* Pella, strikingly handsome, was taught by Aristotle. Only 20 when his father was murdered, he gathered an army of

THE EMPIRE OF ALEXANDER THE GREAT IN 323 B.C.

Starting from Macedon in 333, Alexander overran Asia Minor, Syria and Egypt, then turned against the Persian Empire. After his death his own empire broke up into separate kingdoms.

Macedonians and Greeks, and marched against Darius, the 'great king' of Persia, who ruled all W. Asia ; defeated one of the armies of Darius at the R. Granicus 334BC ; conquered Asia Minor ; met Darius and his huge mass of troops on the banks of the R. Issus, and there (333BC) won a complete victory.

Success followed success. Egypt submitted without a fight, the young Macedonian building his own city of Alexandria near the mouth of the Nile. He marched along the valley of the Tigris to Babylon (331BC), shattering the 3rd army Darius had gathered at Gaugamela, and ransacked the great city of Persepolis. When Darius was murdered, Alexander, at 26, found himself lord of all the world the Greeks knew E. of the Adriatic Sea. He then conquered part of India, crossing the R. Indus, 326BC ; but three years later, while preparing an advance into Arabia, he died of fever.

Alexander's vast empire crumbled after his death, but his work had an immense effect on the development of the E. Mediterranean world for the next three centuries, and helped to form the background prevailing in the lifetime of Jesus Christ. He was not only a matchless general but also a statesman with a genius for exploiting the weaknesses of conquered races.

Alexandra Palace, place of entertainment N. London ; now a BBC television station.

Alexandra, QUEEN (1844–1925), Danish princess called by Tennyson ' sea-king's daughter ' ; married the Prince of Wales (later Edward VII), 1863 ; greatly beloved in England.

Alexandra Rose Day (26 June), anniversary of the day Princess Alexandra arrived in England ; is in aid of hospitals.

Alexandria, city and chief seaport of Egypt ; founded by Alexander the Great 332BC ; linked at one time by viaduct with the island of Pharos ; became a great trading centre and home of learning with royal palaces, a famous library, temples, etc. ; declined under Turkish rule, but revived in the 19th c.; captured by Napoleon 1798 ; under British rule after Nelson's victory at Aboukir (Battle of the Nile) from 1801 ; now Egypt's most important commercial city and a great cotton market ; pop.682,000.

Alexandrine, see METRE

alfalfa or **lucerne**, *al-fal'fä*, cloverlike plant for feeding cattle etc. ; will produce a crop every 40 days. Possibly the oldest forage plant known, it grows wild in Britain, has a smooth upright stem, leaves in groups of 3, and clusters of purple flowers. It enriches the soil with nitrates, and hence is widely cultivated.

Alfonso XIII (1886–1941), King of Spain from his birth ; was compelled in 1931 to abdicate.

Alfred the Great (849–901), one of the noblest kings of England, found his kingdom weak, left it strong ; came to a divided nation and gave his people a sense of national unity.

At first King of Wessex, later of half England, Alfred, *b* Wantage, Berkshire, was the son of Ethelwulf and Osburga, the latter teaching him to read at twelve. When the Danes invaded Wessex 871 they were defeated at Ashdown, chiefly through Alfred's skill.

Alfred became king 872, and for a time hid from the Danes in the island of Athelney, Somerset, the story of his burning the cakes (if true) belonging to this period. Gathering an army, he defeated the Danes at Ethandune, compelling their leader Guthrum to become a Christian, and to divide England into 2 parts, Alfred ruling in London and W. of the old Roman road (Watling Street), Guthrum in the E., a region called Danelagh. Alfred also drew up the *Treaty of Wedmore* (in Somerset) 878, a turningpoint in English history.

Becoming overlord of all England, Alfred was the first to build our ' wooden walls,' i.e. a navy. He taught his people how to fight ; gathered together and improved the laws of the land, and may, therefore, be regarded as the founder of our English legal code ; loved learning, and brought scholars from other countries ; built schools ; declared that all churchmen should know Latin ; translated books, including those of Bede ; sent sailors to explore distant seas ; is believed to have ordered the writing of the *Anglo-Saxon Chronicle*, i.e. a national diary of events from the earliest times, which went on after his death until 1154. Alfred, who never wasted a minute, was a man of prayer as well as of action, and loved only to serve his people.

Alfreton, *öl'frē-tun*, industrial town 14m from Derby ; pop.21,000.

algebra, generalised form of arithmetic ; said to have been used by the Egyptians over 3,000 years ago. The quantities dealt with are not definite numbers as in arithmetic but are represented by letters. Algebra is used to solve problems in arithmetic and to discover the fundamental laws that apply to all quantities. It introduces most important principles that are far beyond the scope of arithmetic.

algebraic factors, see FACTORS

Algeria, overseas region of France in NW. Africa ; area estimated at 222,120sq.m ; pop. *c*.7,240,000 ; exports include wines, cereals, sheep, cattle, fruits, olive oil, cork, esparto grass, zinc and iron ores, etc. ; cap. Algiers.

Algiers, cap., Algeria ; Mediterranean coaling station and harbour ; has ruins of Roman, Moorish and Christian buildings ; pop.252,000.

Alicante, *ali-kan'tē*, Mediterranean seaport, Spain ; pop.113,000.

alimentary canal, see DIGESTION

aliquot parts, i.e. parts which divide a whole

without a remainder, e.g. 10s = £½.

alkali, *al'kä-lī,* any substance, soluble in water, that neutralises acids, forming salts, and turns red litmus blue ; more exactly, a soluble hydroxide of ammonia and certain metals, particularly sodium and potassium. Originally the name alkali was given to the ashes of vegetable substances which had a soapy feel when dissolved in water.

All-Africa Highway, road system from the Cape to Algiers now in course of construction ; includes, with its feeder roads, over 48,000m of highways. In conjunction with the Cape to Cairo Railway and with the increasing air services (*a*) a flying-boat service from Durban to Cairo via Mozambique, Dares-Salaam, Khartoum and Luxor, and (*b*) a landplane service from the Union of S. Africa to Cairo, including Khartoum, Nairobi and Johannesburg, this highway should open up the continent for trade, transport, tourist travel, etc.

Allah, *al'ä,* Mohammedan name for God. See MOHAMMED

Allahabad, city, cap. of the United Provinces, India ; has government offices and an ancient fort ; pop.261,000.

Allegheny, *al'ē-gäni,* tributary of the R. Ohio, USA.

Allegheny Mountains, low range of the Appalachians between the Atlantic and the R. Mississippi, USA.

allegory, *al'ē-gor-i,* picture, story, play, poem, etc., with a hidden meaning, e.g. Bunyan's *Pilgrim's Progress,* not merely the story of Christian's journey to the Celestial City, but intended also as a sermon on right living. A short allegory in which animals, birds, etc., speak, is a FABLE, e.g. *Aesop's Fables* ; and akin to these are PARABLES, i.e. stories teaching great truths, e.g. Christ's parable of the Good Samaritan, which is not only an account of a kind action, but also an illustration of a fundamental principle of Christianity.

Allen, BOG OF, see BOG

Allenby, VISCOUNT (1861–1936), British general ; fought in the S. African War ; knighted 1915 ; went to Egypt 1917, eventually capturing Jerusalem, and winning the battle of Megiddo, thus driving the Turks out of Palestine ; created Viscount Allenby of Megiddo and Felixstowe.

alligator, see CROCODILE

All-India Council, see INDIA

alliteration, see FIGURES OF SPEECH

allotment, piece of ground (usually *c.*300 sq.yd) cultivated to produce vegetables etc. for the occupier and his family The Allotments Act dates from 1922.

allotropy, *al'o-tro-pi,* property of some (and possibly all) chemical elements of taking more than one form, e.g. sulphur, which may appear as an amorphous solid or in crystalline form ; also carbon, which exists as graphite, charcoal, or diamond, all burning in oxygen to give carbon dioxide.

Alloway, *al'ō-wä,* Ayrshire village ; birthplace of Robert Burns, whose cottage may still be seen.

alloy, *al'oi,* mixture of two or more elements or compounds, at least one being a metal, e.g. steel, chiefly an alloy of iron and carbon. Other immensely important alloys include brass (copper and zinc) ; bronze (copper and tin) ; solder (tin and lead) ; duralumin, nickel-chromium, etc. See METALS

All-Purpose Authorities, see LOCAL GOVERNMENT

Almeria, *äl-mä-rē'ä,* port, Spain, on the Gulf of Almeria ; exports grapes ; pop.80,000.

almond, *ä'mond,* nut of the cultivated tree of the same name ; grows from 20 to 30ft high ; has pink flowers which bloom before the oval leaves ; the nuts have valuable medicinal properties.

Alnwick, *an'ik,* co.tn, Northumberland ; has the castle of the Duke of Northumberland, now partly a college.

alpaca, see SALT, SIR T.

alphabet, see WRITING

Alpha Centauri, see ASTRONOMY

alpha particles, see RADIUM

Alps, highest mountains in Europe. The snow-capped ranges and groups extend 600m from the Gulf of Genoa almost to Vienna, and are *c.*130m broad in Tirol. They form a great barrier between Italy and N. Europe, named variously Swiss Alps, Maritime Alps, Bernese Oberland. The loftiest peak is Mont Blanc (15,732ft). The most important pass (Italy–Germany) is the Brenner, along which the first railway over the Alps was built 1867 ; tunnels include Mont Cenis and St Gothard. Alpine climbing became popular *c.*1850. See SWITZERLAND

Alsace-Lorraine, *al'sas lo-rän',* province between the Rhine and the Vosges Mts ; ceded to Germany 1871, restored to France 1919 ; area 5,600sq.m ; chiefly agricultural, but noted for coal, cotton and potash.

Altai Mountains, *al-tī',* ranges (up to 14,800 ft) in the S. of Asiatic Russia ; rich in minerals.

alternating current, see RECTIFIER

Althing, see ICELAND

altitude records, see AVIATION

alto, see SINGING

Altrincham, *öl'tring-am,* town, Cheshire ; supplies Manchester with fruit and vegetables ; pop.40,000.

alum, *al'ŭm,* name of a series of compounds, including the double sulphate of aluminium and potassium ; found in Italy, England (Yorkshire), Scotland, etc. ; used in dyeing.

aluminium, white metal and element, A1 ; atomic weight 26·97 ; atomic number 13 ; very light, easily hammered or drawn into very fine wire ; good conductor of electricity ; produced commercially by electrolysis from bauxite ; much used in various alloys, e.g. aluminium bronze, aluminium brass. Being light and resisting corrosion, the metal and its alloys are largely used in aircraft. The statue of Eros, Piccadilly Circus, London, is of aluminium. Aluminium is given still further anti-corrosion qualities by anodising, i.e. adding a film of oxide by an electrolytic process. It is much used also for cooking utensils and (in thin sheets) for wrapping foodstuffs.

An alloy of aluminium, copper, manganese and magnesium was discovered 1906, and named duralumin, this reaching its highest strength and hardness a few days after manufacture. See PLATE 36

Alva, DUKE OF (1508–83), cruel Spanish soldier sent by Philip II of Spain to govern the Netherlands 1567–73, his tyranny prompting the Dutch to rebel, and eventually win independence.

Alwar, *ŭl'wŭr*, native state, Rajputana, India, and now one of the Mateya groups of states ; cap. Alwar, a walled city ; pop.54,000.

Amalekites, *ä-mal'e-kīts*, fierce wandering tribe frequently at war in OT times with the Israelites in Canaan.

amalgam, alloy of mercury and another metal, e.g. mercury + tin, once much used for silvering mirrors. See MERCURY

amaranth, *am'ä-ranth* (Gk *amarantos*, unfading), plant of warm countries ; has flowers that retain their colour long after being cut.

Amazon, *am'ä-zon*, S. American river, *c.*4,000m long. The third longest river in the world, it drains an area (2,700,000 sq.m) greater than that of the Mississippi and Nile combined ; rises in the Andes ; flows into the Atlantic near Pará ; navigable for ocean-going vessels to Iquitos, 2,500m. Its tributaries, winding amid vast and little-explored tropical forests, include Napo, Marañon, Putumayo, Rio Negro, Juruá, Purus, Madeira, Tapajos, Xingu, etc.

The Amazon Basin has been less changed by man than almost any other region of the earth, apart from Polar wastes and deserts. Various areas once yielded large supplies of wild rubber, but (1881) seeds from Brazilian rubber trees were taken to Kew, and from the young plants reared there have come almost all the cultivated rubber plantations of Malaya and the E. Indies, wild rubber being now in little demand.

UNESCO, which has recently renamed the Amazon Basin Hylea, is preparing huge development schemes for this vast region. See RUBBER ; WALLACE, A. R.

Amazons, in old Greek tales, female warriors who went to battle on horseback.

amber, fossilised resin ; usually yellow or brown ; actually a solidified gum, probably from larch or pine. ' Electricity ' is derived from *electron*, the Greek name for amber, because it is electrified by rubbing. See RESIN

ambergris, *-grēs*, grey fatty substance found in the intestines of whales ; used in making perfumes.

Ambleside, attractive town near L. Windermere, Westmorland ; beloved by Wordsworth.

ambrosia, *am-brō'ziä*, in old Greek tales, the supposed food of the gods.

ameer or **emir,** *ä-mēr* ; *e-mēr*, commander, ruler, or high official among Mohammedans.

America, continent comprising 2 triangular masses of land linked by the narrow Isthmus of Panama ; total area *c.* 16,000,000sq.m ; estimated pop. *c.* 275,000,000. Murchison Peninsula in the N. is 9,000m from Cape Horn in the S. N. America (area 8,300,000 sq.m) includes Alaska, Canada, Newfoundland, USA, Mexico, etc. ; Central America includes Honduras, Nicaragua, Panama, etc. ; S. America (area over 7,300,000sq.m) includes Brazil, Argentine, Peru, Chile, Venezuela, Bolivia, etc. The largest mountain ranges are near the Pacific coast, e.g. Rocky Mts (N.), Andes (S.).

America is possibly named after Amerigo Vespucci, an Italian. Known as the New World, S. America was discovered by Columbus 1492 ; N. America, probably known to the Norsemen in the 10th c., was rediscovered by Cabot 1497.

America, Cup, prize offered 1851 by the Royal Yacht Squadron of England for an international yacht race ; won by *The America*, and never regained.

American Civil War, struggle between the N. states (chiefly industrial) and the S. states (e.g. Virginia, Tennessee, Mississippi, Georgia, etc.) peopled by farmers and great landowners employing Negro slaves ; essentially a contest between the Federals of the N., who wished to keep the USA as one nation (Federation), and the S. (Confederates), who wished to cut adrift from the N. and form an independent country with its own capital at Richmond, Virginia, its own flag, and its own president. The Federals, led by Abraham Lincoln, had declared that slavery must be abolished. The Confederates objected to this, as their prosperity was founded on the existence of slavery, and went to war on this issue.

The Federal generals included Ulysses S. Grant, who later was twice president of the USA ; the Confederate generals included Robert E. Lee and Thomas Jonathan Jackson, whose courage and stern discipline earned him the nickname Stonewall Jackson.

The war began 1861 with the bombardment of Fort Sumter by the Confederates ; in July was fought the battle of Bull Run, after which, during 4 years of strife, over 2,200 battles, skirmishes, and sieges were fought, 600 of them in Virginia. Much fighting occurred in the neighbourhood of the R. Potomac. The turning-point of the war was the victory of the Federals at Gettysburg 1863, General Lee finally surrendering to

General Grant 9 April 1865 at Appomattox Court House. The triumph of the Federals meant that the Confederate states were to remain united with the Federals, and also the abolition of slavery throughout the USA. Note that the US central government is of the kind called ' federal,' i.e. the governments of all the states of the federation have limited independence, but are ultimately subject to the central government, of which the President is head.

Read *Gone With the Wind*, Margaret Mitchell's best-seller. There is also a brilliant discussion of the Civil War in Bertrand Russell's *Freedom and Organization*, 1815–1914.

American Independence, WAR OF, 8 years' struggle (1775–83) between Britain and the American colonists.

The causes go back to the Seven Years' War, as a result of which Britain was heavily taxed. It seemed only fair that our American colonies should contribute something towards the cost of an army in their own country, hence George III and his ministers favoured the Stamp Act (1765), intended to impose a small direct tax ; but the colonists refused to pay the tax unless they were represented in the British Parliament, and the Stamp Act was repealed. Parliament later (1767) ordered the colonists to pay certain import duties ; that on tea led to the so-called Boston Tea Party (1773), a riot in which colonists, disguised as Indians, threw 340 chests of tea into Boston harbour. The colonists withstood all British demands ; and though Edmund Burke pleaded for conciliation, fighting began 1775 with the battle of Lexington.

The British General Gage found himself opposed by a group of American states led by George Washington. Thirteen of these states sent representatives to Philadelphia, where (4 July 1776) the *Declaration of American Independence* was signed. Washington gave his countrymen a national flag (the Stars and Stripes or ' Old Glory ') 1777. His armies suffered many defeats, and further resistance often seemed futile. A British army led by General William Howe defeated Washington's ill-equipped army at Brandywine ; but General Burgoyne was compelled to surrender at Saratoga (1777), and later, with aid from France, the Americans were winning successes. Lord Cornwallis defeated General Gates at Camden (1780), but the war went steadily against the British, and Cornwallis surrendered at Yorktown 19 Oct 1781, thus bringing the struggle to an end.

By the *Treaty of Paris* (Versailles) 1783, the British left New York, their last stronghold, and Britain recognized the thirteen states as the United States of America.

American Indians, original inhabitants of N. and S. America ; called Indians because Columbus (1492) mistook the New World for India. Among best-known tribes of N. American Indians (or Redskins) were Crees, Ojibwas, Blackfeet, Pawnees, Iroquois, Cherokees, Mohawks, Chickasaws, Sioux, Dakotas, etc. The Eskimos of the Far N., and the Tehuelche of Patagonia are of the same stock as the Red Indians. Notable Red Indian chiefs were Pontiac, Tammany, Red Cloud, Almighty Voice (the last Redskin to oppose white men, or Pale Faces), and Hiawatha.

Longfellow's epic *Hiawatha* (1855) tells us much of the American Indians, especially those living near L. Superior (Big-Sea-Water). Indians of the prairies, they hunted beaver and bison ; lived in wigwams ; paddled birch-bark canoes ; covered themselves with tattooing, had bright feather headdresses, and a wampum, i.e. a string of beads or shells used as money. They wore shoes called moccasins ; used a tomahawk (a light hatchet) to scalp enemies ; and smoked the calumet, or peace-pipe, with friendly tribes. A Redskin who reached manhood and proved himself worthy was called a brave.

SEQUOIA (*d* 1843) a Cherokee half-breed, invented an Indian alphabet.

The Red Indians are almost extinct now, but some still live in ' reserves ' in the USA and Canada.

American literature, see UNITED STATES OF AMERICA

American Loan, loan of *c*.£1,400,000,000 to Britain from USA, negotiated 1945 by Lord Keynes ; an effort to enable British trade to recover after World War II. See ECONOMICS

Amiens, *äm'ya*n, town, France, on the R. Somme ; noted for its beautiful 13th c. cathedral ; suffered much in World War I ; pop.90.000.

ami′no-acids, derivatives of the fatty acids in which one or more hydrogen atoms have been replaced by an amino group, i.e. the univalent NH_2. They form an essential constituent of proteins, which compose a large part of living matter, build up body-tissue, and depend for their usefulness on the particular amino-acid from which they are derived. They include albumen (e.g. white of egg), keratin (from which hair and nails are formed), haemoglobin (the red pigment of blood), casein (found in cheese). The hydrolysis of proteins gives amino-acids.

amino-plastics, see PLASTICS

ammeter, see ELECTRICITY

ammo′nia, gas, NH_3 ; has a pungent smell; is soluble in water ; found in small quantities in the atmosphere ; is a product of all animal and plant decay (see NITROGEN) ; prepared as a by-product of coal-gas or, more commonly, by the Haber process in which nitrogen and hydrogen at high pressure are passed over finely divided iron and other substances as activators at a temperature of 500°C, whereby $N_2 + 3H_2 = 2NH_3$, one process for the fixation of nitrogen.

Ammonium compounds are derived from ammonium, NH_4, a univalent radical which has not been isolated ; and among them are AMMONIUM CHLORIDE, NH_4Cl (sal ammoniac) used in various batteries and cells ; AMMONIUM HYDROXIDE, NH_4OH, i.e. ammonia dissolved in water and strongly alkaline ; AMMONIUM NITRATE, NH_4NO_3, used in various explosives ; AMMONIUM SULPHATE $(NH_4)_2SO_4$, a valuable fertiliser obtained from ammonia, and also as a by-product of coal-gas. NITROUS OXIDE, N_2O, or laughing gas, is derived from ammonium nitrate by gently heating.

Ammonites, *am'on-īts*, tribes often mentioned in the OT as the enemies of the Israelites.

ammonites, fossil sea-snails abundant in Triassic, Jurassic and Cretaceous rocks.

amoeba, *ă-mē'bä*, humble form of animal life found in the mud of ponds etc. ; looks like a speck of jelly ; reproduces itself by division.

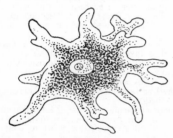

THE AMOEBA

Amos, *ā'mos*, earliest of the Hebrew prophets ; lived *c*.750BC ; urged the need for social justice and righteousness.

Amoy, treaty port, China ; E. of Canton. The E. India Company traded here 1670 ; exports, tea, sugar, paper, etc. ; pop.240,000.

ampere, *am'pār*, from Ampère, a French scientist ; often written amp. It is the unit of electric current. One ampere = the current produced by 1 volt acting through a resistance of 1 ohm, hence

$$amperes = \frac{volts}{ohms} \, .$$

The international ampere is defined as the electric current which, when passed through a solution of silver nitrate, deposits silver at the rate of 0·001118gm per sec.

The practical unit of quantity of electricity is the *ampere-hour*, i.e. the quantity represented by the flow of 1 ampere for a period of 1 hour. One ampere-hour = 3,600 coulombs. See ELECTRICITY

Ampère, ANDRÉ MARIE, *än'-pār* (1775-1836), French scientist ; gave his name to the ampere, unit of electric current.

amphibian, *am-fib'ian*, creature at home in water and on land. Amphibians are vertebrate animals often able to go for months without food. They include (*a*) FROG, beginning as an egg in a mass of jelly or spawn, hatches as a tadpole which breathes (as fish do) through gills ; grows limbs, gradually loses the tail, and finally breathes with lungs. Frogs feed on insects etc., catching them with a long sticky tongue. In France the thighs of some frogs are eaten as a delicacy. (*b*) TOAD, similar to the frog but with a broader head, shorter limbs, and a dry pimply skin ; the eggs are laid in double chains of jelly. In *As You Like It* Shakespeare is mistaken in saying the toad ' ugly and venomous, wears yet a precious jewel in his head.' There is no jewel, and the toad is not venomous. (*c*) NEWT or EFT, tailed creature ; the three British species include the common newt, *c*.3in long, brown and black above, spotted on the yellowish under-

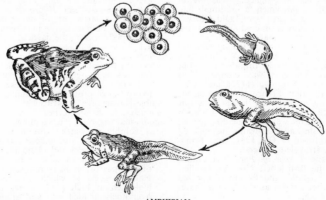

AMPHIBIAN
Life Cycle of the Frog

side, the male having a frill from head to tail. Newts spend much time on land, e.g. under stones ; they are found in water during spring ; the eggs are laid singly on water plants. (*d*) SALA-MANDER, not found in Britain, resembles the newt ; common in many parts of Europe and Asia Minor. There was a belief long ago that it could live in fire.

amphitheatre, *am'fi-*, round or slightly oval open-air theatre, usually of stone, especially one built by the Romans, e.g. the Colosseum at Rome, completed for the emperors Vespasian and Titus *c.*AD80. This had room for 50,000 spectators. Roman amphitheatres were for public games, gladiator and wild beast fights, chariot races, etc.

amphora, *am'fora*, ancient Greek or Roman earthenware vessel with two handles and usually a pointed base. Partly buried in the ground, it was used for storing wine etc.

Amritsar, *ŭm-rit'sar*, holy city of the Sikhs ; in the Punjab, India ; commercially important ; manufactures cashmere shawls ; pop.391,000 .

Amsterdam, port built on 96 islands of the N. Netherlands ; has a spacious harbour and 300 bridges ; is a great trade and banking centre ; noted especially for diamond-polishing, also for shipbuilding, sugar-refining, printing, dyeing ; has a famous university ; scene 1948 of a great meeting of the World Council of Churches ; pop. 794,000.

amulet, *am'ū-let*, charm ignorantly believed to protect the wearer from evil.

Amundsen, ROALD, *ä'mŭn-sen* (1872–1928), Norwegian explorer ; reached the S. Pole Dec 1911, thus beating Captain Scott by a few days ; with Lincoln Ellsworth flew by airship (*Norge*) over the N. Pole 1926 ; lost his life while attempting to rescue another Arctic explorer, the Italian, General Nobile. See POLAR REGIONS

Anabasis, *a-nab'a-sis*, account by Xenophon of the march of the 10,000 Greeks from Cunaxa to Trebizond. Actually, though the work is generally called *Anabasis*, the return journey is known to scholars as the *Catabasis* (*ka-tab'ä-sis*). A summary of the march of the 10,000 is given under XENOPHON. Anabasis is Greek for ' march up country.'

anachronism, *anak'ron-izm*, mistake in time made by a writer, e.g. Shakespeare's reference to striking clocks in *Julius Caesar*.

anaconda, S. American python or boa ; often 25ft long ; is brown with black spots ; found in forest rivers.

Anacreon, *a-nak'rē-on* (*c.*563–478BC), Greek lyric poet.

anaesthetic, *an-ēs-thet'ik*, means of producing temporary unconsciousness so that an operation may be performed painlessly. Sir Humphry Davy suggested the use of ' laughing gas ' (nitrous oxide) 1800 ; but the actual pioneer of

anaesthetics was the Scottish doctor, Sir James Young Simpson, who, 1847, thus used chloroform, $CHCl_3$. Chloroform, ether, etc., are known as general anaesthetics ; cocaine, eucaine, Novocaine, etc. causing numbness in one part of the body only, are local anaesthetics. Since 1947 trilene has been used as an emergency treatment. It deadens pain but does not cause unconsciousness. See SIMPSON, SIR JAMES YOUNG

' Analects,' see CONFUCIUS

Anatolia, *an-a-tō'liä*, ' Land of the Rising Sun ' or the Orient, i.e. Asia Minor or Turkey in Asia.

anatomy, *an-at'o-mi*, literally ' cutting up,' scientific study of bodies (especially human and animal) in which their structure is revealed by cutting up (dissecting) dead bodies.

Anatomy provides knowledge about the structure of various systems of the body, i.e. *locomotive* (bones and the muscles that move them), *alimentary* (digestive), *lymphatic* (that which transfers absorbed matter from food to the blood and removes waste matter), *respiratory* (breathing), *circulatory* (heart, arteries and veins), *nervous* (brain, nerves and organs of sense). Anatomy does not include the study of how the living body works, which is called physiology.

In former times it was difficult for anatomy schools to obtain adequate supplies of dead bodies for dissection and *c.*1800 the ' resurrectionists ' (people who dug up recently buried corpses and sold them to teachers of anatomy) were very active. Burke and Hare were two criminals tried in Edinburgh 1827 for murdering people whose bodies they sold in this way. R. L. Stevenson wrote a gruesome story about this called *The Anatomists.*

anchorite, see HERMIT

ancient lights, windows, at least 20 years old, which may not, therefore, be darkened by newer buildings.

Ancona, *än-kō'nä*, Adriatic port, Italy ; has a fine harbour ; pop.90,000.

Andalusia, *an-dä-loo'shiä*, old division of S. Spain, now including various provinces, e.g. Granada, Almeria, etc.

Andamans and Nicobars, *an'da-man ; nikō-bär*, chain of 200 islands in the Bay of Bengal ; noted for timber ; the 21 Nicobars (S.) have been British since 1869 ; exports include coconuts.

Andean Highway, see ROADS

Andersen, HANS CHRISTIAN (1805–75), Danish story-teller, *b* Odense ; son of a poor cobbler. A rather ugly child, awkward and shy, he listened entranced to tales of witches and fairies told by his grandmother ; delighted in his toy theatre, and wrote plays for cardboard actors. As a young man he travelled abroad, and won fame with his novels and poems. Later he became still more famous for his charming fairy-tales. Of these he used to say, ' They tap at my forehead and cry, *Here we are* ! ' He visited England 1847, staying with Charles Dickens. Hans Andersen *d* Copenhagen. His story *The Ugly Duckling* may be read as a fanciful account of his own life.

Anderson, SHERWOOD (1876–1941), American novelist and poet ; author of *Dark Laughter* etc.; frequently deals with the mentality of the Negro.

Andes, *an'dēz*, vast mt. range of S. America, 4,000m. N.–S. and parallel to the Pacific coast ; comprises various chains known as *cordilleras* ; noted for magnificent scenery and series of snow-clad peaks, many of them active volcanoes, e.g. Chimborazo, Cotopaxi (19,612ft), the loftiest volcano in the world. Aconcagua (22,976ft) is the highest mt. in N. or S. America. L. Titicaca (Peru) is over 12,000ft above sea-level. The Andes are rich in minerals, e.g. gold, tin, copper, silver, lead, etc.

Andorra, *an-dor'ä*, republic in the Pyrenees; area 175sq.m ; noted for cattle-raising ; has been independent since AD790 ; pop.5.500 ; cap. Andorra.

Andrew, patron saint of Scotland ; a fisherman, brother of Simon Peter ; disciple of Jesus (John 1) ; believed to have been martyred AD70 on a cross like a letter X, hence the Saltire (white X on blue) or Scottish national flag. His day is 30 November.

Andromeda, *an-drom'ē-dä*, in old Gk tales, a maiden offered as a sacrifice to a dragon, but rescued by Perseus ; also a conspicuous group of stars named after her. The Andromeda nebula is possibly a vast universe far beyond the Milky Way.

anemone or **windflower,** *a-nem'ony*, plant (family *Ranunculaceae*) found in Britain, e.g. the wood anemone, with white flowers ; also garden varieties of many hues.

aneroid, see BAROMETER

Angelico, FRÀ, *än-jel'ē-kō* (1387–1455), Italian artist who painted religious pictures ; *d* Rome.

Angers, *än-zhā'* ; *an-jerz'*, city on the R. Maine, France ; was the ancient cap. of Anjou ; pop. *c*.85,000.

angle (Latin *angulus*, corner), in mathematics and geometry, the amount of turning or rotation required to make two intersecting straight lines coincide.

If the amount of turning is a complete circle, four right angles are described : a right angle is $\frac{1}{4}$ of a complete revolution, and is the standard unit of angular measure. A smaller angle is *acute* ; a larger *obtuse* if less than two right angles. A *reflex angle* is greater than two right angles but less than four. A degree (°) in angular measure is 1/90th right angle, and this is divided into 60 minutes ('), each minute into 60 seconds (").

Angles, Teutonic tribe that gave its name to England ; came from N. Germany in the 5th c., and settled chiefly in what is now E. Anglia.

Anglesey, island and county, N. Wales ; separated from the mainland by the Menai Strait. Noted for its bird-life ; co.tn Beaumaris, but Holyhead is the chief port.

Anglicans, see CHURCH

Anglo-Egyptian Sudan, see SUDAN

Anglo-Saxon Chronicle, see ALFRED THE GREAT

Anglo-Saxons, descendants of various Teutonic tribes that settled in England after the withdrawal of the Roman legions *c*.AD410. First came the Saxons, joined in the 5th c. by Angles and Jutes, later (*c*.520) settling in villages on the ' open-field ' system, and eventually founding the kingdoms of Kent, Sussex, E. Anglia, Bernicia and Deira, Middlesex, Wessex and Mercia, the conquest being completed *c*.613, by which time Roman-British civilisation was destroyed. Local affairs were discussed at moots, i.e. meetings ; wrongdoers paid fines ; trial by fire was a common practice ; chiefs were buried under mounds ; gold and bronze ornaments and weapons were employed, nobles and thanes using 2-edged swords.

A remarkable ship-burial unearthed at Sutton Hoo (Suffolk) 1939 proved to be the last resting-place of an Anglo-Saxon king or prince who died *c*.600. He had been in the cabin of his ship, and among a host of treasures was a huge silver dish made in Constantinople.

Old English literature (Anglo-Saxon) includes books and poems written from the 7th–11th c., e.g. *Beowulf*, the story of how Beowulf killed the monster Grendel. The first English song or poem may be regarded as the *Creation* composed by Caedmon, a herdsman of Whitby Abbey, Yorkshire, traditionally inspired by a vision he had when asleep in a stable. Caedmon died *c*.675. For the *Anglo-Saxon Chronicle* see ALFRED THE GREAT

Angora, see ANKARA

Angora goat, sheep-like animal of Asia Minor, from which comes angora wool.

Angström unit, *ang'strŭm*, unit for wavelengths of light, ultra-violet radiations, X-rays, etc. ; equals 10^{-8} cm ; often written briefly as AU ; named after the Swedish scientist A. V. Angström (1814–74).

Angular or **Circular Measure,** see WEIGHTS AND MEASURES

Angus, formerly Forfarshire, Scottish county N. of the R. Tay ; co.tn Forfar but Dundee is much more important.

Anhalt, former German state (once a duchy) ; has great forests ; noted for its chemical industries ; cap. Dessau.

anhy'dride, compound obtained by removing water from another compound, e.g. sulphur trioxide, SO_3, is obtained when water is removed from sulphuric acid H_2SO_4.

anhy'drite, white crystalline mineral, calcium sulphate, $CaSO_4$.

aniline, *an'i-līn*, one of the chief deriva-

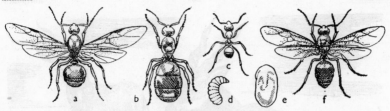

THE WOOD ANT

(a) *the young winged queen*　(b) *after shedding her wings the queen becomes a life prisoner in the nest*　(c) *the worker*　(d) *the larva*　(e) *the cocoon*　(f) *the male*

tives of coal-tar ; colourless oily liquid ($C_6H_5NH_2$) used in making aniline dyes, which are of great commercial importance.

animals, see ZOOLOGY

Anjou, *än-zhoo',* once a province of N. France, hence Henry II, *Count of Anjou.*

Ankara or **Angora,** *äng'kä-rä,* city, cap. Turkey since 1923 ; terminus of the Anatolian railway (to Baghdad) ; largely modernised. Angora goats are bred hereabouts, the fleeces being exported as mohair ; airport on the Cairo–Istanbul route ; pop.230,000.

'Anna Karenina,' see TOLSTOY, COUNT LEO

Annam, *a-nam',* French protectorate along the China Sea ; cap. Hué ; exports rice, cotton, silk, etc. ; area 57,000sq.m ; pop.6,220,000 ; in 1946 the region was united with Tonkin to form Viet-Namh.

Anne (1665–1714), Queen of Great Britain and Ireland ; *b* London ; daughter of James II ; began to rule 1702 ; married Prince George of Denmark ; of her 17 children only one lived to be 10. Anne was long overruled by the strong-minded Sarah Jennings (later the Duchess of Marlborough) or by her other favourite, Mrs Masham. Her reign was famous for Marlborough's victories, and its many literary giants, e.g. Swift, Addison, Steele, etc.

Anne of Cleves (1515–57), 4th queen of Henry VIII of England. A German, she was married to Henry 1540, but the king disliked her, and she lived in retirement.

Anno Domini, see AD

annuals, see PERENNIAL

anode, see CATHODE

Anschluss, *än'shlooss,* enforced union of Austria with Germany, 1938. It violated existing international treaties, and was accomplished by a combination of treachery with force. Austria was thus the first independent state overwhelmed by Hitler, and her destruction was one of the main steps in Germany's preparation for war. See SCHUSCHNIGG

Anselm (*c.*1033–1109), saint and Archbishop of Canterbury, *b* Aosta, Italy. He had frequent disputes with William II and Henry I about Church matters. Anselm believed that his only superior was the pope, but ultimately agreed that although the archbishop had spiritual authority in England, he should do homage to the king for the lands belonging to the cathedral. Brave, learned and kindly, Anselm (who was especially fond of animals) was the author of many books on religion and philosophy, and is chiefly remembered as the author of what philosophers call the ' ontological ' proof that a God exists who is the embodiment of all perfections.

Anson, LORD (1697–1762), admiral, born in Staffordshire ; sailed in the *Centurion* for the Pacific 1740, rounded Cape Horn, and returned 1744 via the Cape of Good Hope, having thus sailed round the world and returned with treasure worth £500,000. He defeated the French off Cape Finisterre 1747, and greatly improved administration in the navy.

ant, among the most intelligent of insects. Ants form highly organised communities, and appear to have some means of communication. Some varieties of ants keep ' slaves,' making them work as drudges ; some may be said to keep ' cows,' i.e. plant-lice supplying a sweet juice, honeydew.

Closely related to bees and wasps, ants are of three classes : queens (fertile females), which sometimes live 15 years, winged males, and wingless workers (barren females). An ants' nest is riddled with narrow tunnels, and here the queen lays eggs that hatch in about 16 days, the young larvæ (grubs) being fed by the workers until they become pupæ, often wrapping themselves in silken cocoons, the so-called ants' eggs. British ants sleep most of the winter. See TERMITES

Antarctic, see POLAR REGIONS

Antarctica, see POLAR REGIONS

Antarctic Ocean, S. portion of the Atlantic, Pacific and Indian oceans, the limit being regarded as lat. 60°S ; includes Weddell Sea, Biscoe Sea, Ross Sea, etc.

ant-eater, toothless S. American animal related to the sloths and armadillos ; has a long tube-like muzzle and a sticky tongue ; feeds on ants. The GREAT ANT-EATER (*c.*4ft long) walks on its knuckles ; the TAMANDUA, which is smaller, lives in trees.

antelope, name of a group of *c.*150 sorts of animals related to cattle, sheep and goats ; almost all are graceful, swift and shy, and many have horns ; they belong chiefly to Africa. Typical

ANTELOPES
(1) *Eland*   (2) *Addax*   (3) *Hartebeest*

antelopes include addax, eland, gazelle, hartebeest.

anthem, strictly, a sacred song for a church choir, sung with or without accompaniment.

The term national anthem implies a stirring song or hymn expressing patriotism. National anthems include *La Brabançonne* of Belgium, and *La Marseillaise* of France, composed 1792 by Rouget de Lisle, and so named because it was sung by rebels from Marseilles during the French Revolution. It begins

Allons enfants de la patrie,
Le jour de gloire est arrivé.

In the USA the patriotic songs *Star Spangled Banner* and *Hail Columbia* are more or less national anthems.

The author of the British national anthem (*God Save the King*) is unknown. Possibly the tune was composed by John Bull (1562–1628), and the words may have been written by Henry Carey (*d* 1743). In recent years William Blake's *Jerusalem* has come to be regarded as a second national anthem. The Scottish national anthem is *Scots Wha Hae*, by Robert Burns.

anthracite, see COAL

anthropology (Gk *anthropos,* human being), that branch of natural history which studies mankind. Man is studied (*a*) in time, i.e. his beginnings and development, including his tools and weapons, customs, folk-lore, etc., and (*b*) in space, i.e. the variety of races and their distribution over the face of the earth, also how man's surroundings (environment) have affected him and how he has changed his surroundings. Anthropology includes the classification and relationship of the races of mankind (ethnology), and is closely associated with evolution, geography, archaeology, pre-history and religion.

Anticosti, Canadian island in the Gulf of St Lawrence ; area 2,500sq.m.

' **Antigone,**' see SOPHOCLES

Antigua, *an-tē'gwä,* island, British W. Indies ; cap. St John, governing the Leeward Is. ; the chief exports are sugar and molasses ; pop.41,000.

Antilles, *an-til'ēz,* islands of the W. Indies, comprising (*a*) GREATER ANTILLES (Cuba, Haiti, etc., Jamaica, Puerto Rico) ; and (*b*) the LESSER ANTILLES, shared among Britain, France, Netherlands, USA, etc. ; pop.10,500,000.

an'timony, white metal and element, Sb ; atomic weight 121·76 ; atomic number 51 ; has the peculiar property of expanding when cooling ; prepared from stibnite, Sb_2S_3, it is used for alloys, especially type metal ; also lead-tin alloys used as solders.

antinode, see SOUND

Antioch, *an'ti-ok,* town, now in Turkey, 60m W. of Aleppo. The followers of Christ were first called Christians here ; pop.30,000.

antipodes, *an-tip'ō-dēs,* regions at opposite sides of the world, i.e. places that would be joined by a straight line through the centre of the earth ; thus Wellington,

NZ, is almost at the antipodes of Madrid, Spain.

antirrhinum, see SNAPDRAGON

antisep′tics, chemicals etc., that kill or arrest the development of bacteria ; first used in surgery by Lord Lister, who insisted on cleanliness in operating theatres and sick-rooms, and introduced the cleansing of instruments and wounds with a solution of phenol (carbolic acid). Other antiseptics include iodine, nascent oxygen, potassium permanganate (Condy's Fluid), various aniline dyes, Lysol, Dettol.

The theory that bacteria cause festering, etc., was derived from Pasteur's discoveries (*a*) that diseases (e.g. diphtheria, cholera, hydrophobia) are due to the presence of bacteria, and that these may be destroyed by the use of suitable vaccines or sera, (*b*) that mould on cheese, fermentation of wine, and the sourness of milk are the result of bacteria *from the air*. Pasteur found that if milk is kept for 30 mins at 140°–145°F, and is stirred all the time, bacteria are killed, including the tuberculosis bacilli. This process is known as pasteurisation. He also found that food canned at a high temperature will keep for long periods if air-tight. Pasteur, Professor of Chemistry at the Sorbonne, struggled long to convince the medical profession of the value of his discoveries, but finally won the highest honours.

antithesis, see FIGURES OF SPEECH

antlers, horn-like branches on the heads of deer ; they are shed yearly.

Antofagasta, busy port, Chile ; exports silver ore, nitrate of soda, lead, copper, etc. ; pop.51,000.

Antoinette, MARIE, see LOUIS XVI

Antonine Wall, Roman wall (mainly of turf) between Rs. Forth and Clyde, Scotland ; built when Antoninus Pius was emperor (AD138–161) ; traces may still be seen.

Antrim, county, N. Ireland ; noted for the Giant's Causeway ; produces potatoes, oats, flax ; co.tn Belfast.

Antwerp, Belgian city and chief port ; on the R. Schelde, and 55m from the sea ; noted for its cathedral of Notre Dame, the Guild House, and the Hôtel de Ville ; birthplace of Franz Hals and Vandyck (artists) ; has immense docks and a great trade ; manufactures sugar, textiles, etc. ; is also an airport ; pop.257,000.

Anubis, *ä-nū′bis,* ancient Egyptian god, guardian of the dead.

Anuradhapura, sacred city, Ceylon, *c.*70m from Kandy ; noted for Buddhist ruins, and the Sacred Bo Tree, said to have grown from a branch of the tree under which Buddha first saw the 'light.'

Anzac, word possibly made from the initial letters of the *Australian* (and) *New Zealand Army Corps* of 1914–18 ; it now means Australian and NZ troops.

Anzio, *än′tsē-ō,* port, Italy, 30m S. of Rome ; scene of bitter fighting 1944 when Allied forces established a beach-

head there behind the enemy lines.

AP, see ARITHMETICAL PROGRESSION

Apache, *ä-pach′ē,* various tribes of N. American Indians once found in New Mexico, Arizona and Texas.

Apelles, *a-pel′ēz,* 4th c. BC Greek artist ; painted a famous portrait of Alexander the Great. When a cobbler dared to criticise his drawing of a shoe, the artist made no reply, but when the cobbler found other faults, Apelles retorted, ' Let the cobbler stick to his last.'

Apennines, *ap′e-nīnz,* mountain range forming the ' backbone ' of Italy, and extending into Sicily.

apes and **monkeys,** animals termed *Primates,* an order including man. Apes, the most man-like of all animals, have no tails, or only very short ones ; the thumb is almost human ; there are 32 teeth (as in man), but monkeys, usually smaller than apes, have tails used in climbing ; also pouches in the cheeks.

Among apes the smallest are GIBBONS, found in Malay, Sumatra and Iraq ; they walk easily on their hind legs ; the ORANG (or orangutan), found only in Borneo and Sumatra, swings from branch to branch, is often over 4ft high, and has very long arms ; the CHIMPANZEE (like a little old man) is shy and clever. The GORILLA, largest and fiercest of apes, lives in African forests, the male being over 6ft, with black hair.

Monkeys include the BABOON, a savage dog-headed animal of Africa and Arabia ; the DIANA monkey, black and white, and a native of W. Africa ; the DOUROUCOULI, a little monkey of S. America ; the COLOBUS of Africa ; and the CAPUCHIN of Brazil.

aphis, *ā′fis ; af′is,* small (usually wingless) insect popularly known as green-fly ; sucks juice from plants ; sometimes domesticated by ants. (Plural, APHIDES)

aphorism, *af′or-izm,* short saying expressing a deep truth ; e.g. *Life is short, art is long.*

Aphrodite, *afrō-dī′tē,* Gk goddess of love, corresponding to the Roman Venus. She was the mother of Eros (Gk) or Cupid (Rom.), who is usually represented as a beautiful youth or as a small, winged boy with bow and arrows. A famous statue of Aphrodite, the Venus de Milo, carved *c.*400BC, was discovered at Melos 1820.

Apia, *ä′pē-ä,* chief town, Upolu, Samoa.

apiary, see BEE

Apocalypse, *a-pok′alips* (Gk for revelation, discovery), name given by the Jews and early Christians to sacred writings about the future, especially the *Revelation of St John.*

Apocrypha, *a-pok′rifa,* literally, hidden or secret writings, especially (*a*) the 14 sacred books like those of the OT, but not included in it, e.g. *Esdras, Maccabees, Judith,* etc., and (*b*) similar books not included in the NT. Lessons from the *Apocrypha* are still sometimes read in church, for example :

APES AND MONKEYS

(1) *Diana Monkey* (2) *Capuchin* (3) *Guereza Colobus* (4) *Douroucouli* (5) *Orang family*
(6) *Gorilla* (7) *Gibbon* (8) *Hamadryas Baboon* (9) *Chimpanzee and Young*

22

Let us now praise famous men. . . .
Their seed shall remain for ever, and
their glory shall not be blotted out.
Their bodies are buried in peace, but
their name liveth for evermore
(Ecclesiasticus 44).

Apollo, *a-pol'ō,* Greek god and the supreme
type of manly beauty ; son of Zeus ;
born in Delos ; mentioned by Homer ;
was the god of healing, prophecy,
colonisation, etc., and was worshipped
by athletes. His most famous temple
was at Delphi.

apostle, *a-pos'l,* one who is sent forth. The
Twelve Apostles, friends of Jesus, were
Simon (also called Peter), Andrew,
James, John, Philip, Bartholomew,
Thomas, Matthew, James the son of
Alphaeus, Thaddaeus, Simon the Zealot,
and Judas Iscariot. Jesus also appointed
70 more apostles to go forth preaching
two and two. Paul and Barnabas were
apostles. See CHRIST

Apostles' Creed, see CREED

apostrophe, *a-pos'trofē,* (') , raised comma
used in English (*a*) to show possession :
the girl's frock, i.e. the frock of the girl ;
the girls' frocks, i.e. the frocks of two or
more girls. Note especially : *Mr Jones's
children,* not *Mr Jones' children* ; *Jesu's,*
not *Jesus's* ; *St James's,* not *St James'* ;
also note that the apostrophe is *not* used
if there is a separate word for the genitive case, i.e. *hers, its, ours, yours* (not
her's, etc.) . (*b*) To show that a letter
has been omitted, e.g. *I'm* for *I am,*
where the apostrophe indicates that the
letter *a* has been dropped ; similarly
you're for *you are, don't* for *do not,*
we've for *we have, it's* for *it is.* Note
Ma'am for *madam* ; *'twas* for *it was* ;
o'er for *over.*

Appalachians, *ap-a-lā'chian,* mt. system of
USA extending from the Gulf of St
Lawrence to Alabama.

appeasement, British policy of compromis-
ing with Nazi and Fascist dictators before
World War II ; supported by Neville
Chamberlain, condemned by Winston
Churchill.

appendicitis, *a-pen'di-sī-tis,* inflammation of
the appendix, a small tube leading from
the large intestine. The appendix, now
useless, is a relic of some earlier stage
in man's development. Food, or some
foreign body, lodged in it may cause
bacterial infection (appendicitis) usually
remedied by removing the appendix.

Appian Way, *ap'ian,* ancient Roman road
from Rome to Brundusium (Brindisi) ;
begun by the censor Appius Claudius
312BC. St Paul journeyed along it as
a prisoner.

apple, fruit of the tree known as crab
or crab-apple when wild. The apple
is widely cultivated, e.g. in Britain,
California, Canada, Australia, NZ, etc.
Varieties of apple include Bramley's
Seedlings, Cox's Orange Pippins, Newton Wonder, etc. Cider is made from
apples, especially in Devon and Somerset. See PLATE 7 (*bottom*)

Appleby, town, Westmorland ; on the
R. Eden.

Appleton, SIR EDWARD (1892–   ),
scientist, born in Yorkshire ; associated
with the development of the atom bomb
1945 ; appointed Principal of Edinburgh
University 1948. He discovered the
Appleton layer, an ionised region of the
stratosphere sometimes called the F-
layer, *c.*300km high at night, 200km by
day. Radio waves reaching the Appleton layer are reflected towards the earth
and so are not lost in space. See
ATMOSPHERE

Appomattox, *ap-ōmăt'oks,* river, Virginia,
USA.

apprentice, one learning a trade or profession. The Guilds of the Middle Ages
saw to it that a term of 7 years was
strictly kept, and the custom remained
till 1814. One result of apprenticeship
was that almost every youth who had
served his term was master of his trade.
Specialised or technical training has now
largely (but not altogether) replaced the
old system.

Approved Schools, formerly known as re-
formatories or industrial schools, are
controlled by the Home Office (not
Ministry of Education), and are designed
for the education of certain young
persons who have appeared before a
Juvenile Court, either because they are
offenders against the law, or, in a few
cases, because they need care and protection.

The schools give a general education
which keeps in view some definite occupation in life ; e.g. for boys, there are
nautical schools and farming schools ;
in some carpentry, gardening and
engineering are taught. The methods
of discipline employed are intended to
form good habits. See BORSTAL

apricot, fruit tree grown in Britain since
*c.*1524.

April Fool's Day, see CALENDAR

Apsley House, stately mansion, Piccadilly,
London, presented (1820) to the first
Duke of Wellington. Part of it is now
a museum. Popularly known as
' Number One, London.'

apteryx, see KIWI

aqua fortis, see NITROGEN

aquarium, pond or, more usually, a glass
tank, in which fish are kept ; should be
stocked first with water plants, then
snails. Diving-beetles and water-bugs
should never be introduced. Suitable
fish include goldfish, carp, tench (bought
at a pet stores), all fed on crushed
vermicelli and so-called ants' eggs. A
marine (sea water) aquarium is difficult
to look after. For the London aquarium,
see LONDON (ZOO)

aqueduct, *ak'wē-dukt,* bridge or channel
along which water flows. The Romans
were famous for their great stone
aqueducts ; the oldest (built 310BC,
and 19,000yd long) conveyed water to
Rome. The Roman aqueduct of Segóvia,
Spain, one of the most remarkable, is

still standing. Modern aqueducts are usually *pipes*, e.g. the one carrying water 95m from Thirlmere to Manchester, or the aqueduct linking Catskill and New York, 120m apart.

Aquila, ak'wil-ä, with his wife Priscilla, was a friend of St Paul (Acts 18 ; Romans 16).

Aquinas, THOMAS, ä-kwī'nas (1227–74), Italian saint, scholar, hymn-writer, born near Naples ; author of the *Summa contra gentiles* and the *Summa Theologica*, two treatises representing the culmination of medieval philosophy. Aquinas combined Christian Doctrine with Aristotelian philosophy, and his work is the basis of most later Catholic philosophy.

Aquitaine, ak-wi-tān', name for an old division of S. France.

Arabia, group of Arab states forming a kingdom between the Red Sea and the Persian Gulf ; area 1,200,000sq.m, mostly desert ; now includes (*a*) kingdom of Saudi Arabia, founded 1932, and comprising Nejd and Hejaz, etc., (*b*) the shaikhdom of Kuwait, (*c*) the kingdom of Yemen in the SW., (*d*) Bahrain Is. in the Persian Gulf, long famous for pearls, now also noted for oil-refineries, (*e*) the sultanate of Muscat and Oman. The total pop. is *c*.10,000,000, including wandering Bedouins and settled Arabs, also many Jews.

Arabia is noted for sheep, camels, skins, dates, pearls, coffee (exported via Aden), carpets and rugs, and (since 1938) oil. The towns include MECCA (pop.60,000), birthplace of Mohammed (Mahomet) *c*.AD570, visited annually by 50,000 pilgrims who worship in El Haram (a mosque) with its famous Ka'aba, a building in which is the sacred Black Stone (oval, and *c*.7in long), said to have been given by Gabriel to Abraham, and kissed by all pilgrims ; MEDINA (mä-dē'nä), 820m by rail from Damascus, with the Mosque of the prophet, and the grave of Mohammed who died here 632 ; pop. *c*.30,000 ; also Jedda and Muscat.

The great days of Arabia were in the reigns of the three caliphs, Mansur (754–755), Haroun al Raschid (786–809), and Mamun (809–833). Excellent prose and verse in Arabic were written prior to the 13th c., though the *Arabian Nights* seems to have come from Persia ; science and mathematics (especially algebra) once flourished ; the Arabian horse-shoe arch has become the distinctive feature of Oriental architecture.

Arabian Sea, part of the Indian Ocean between Arabia and India.

Arab League, organisation of the Arab States (Egypt, Syria, Jordan, Iraq, etc.), supporting Egypt in its claim to the Sudan (1947) and demanding control of Palestine.

Aragon, ar'a-gon, kingdom of NE. Spain prior to 1497.

Aral, SEA OF, salt lake, USSR; 26,000sq.m.

Aram, EUGENE, ä'ram (1704–59), Yorkshire scholar ; murdered a shoemaker at Knaresborough 1745 ; arrested 13 years later in Dorset ; executed at York. Thomas Hood wrote *The Dream of Eugene Aram.*

Aran Islands, ar'an, 3 islands in Galway Bay, Eire.

Ararat, ar'ä-rat, mountainous region, Armenia, where Noah's ark is traditionally said to have rested (Genesis 8). Highest point is 17,325ft.

arbalest, see Bow

Arbela, ancient town, Assyria, where Alexander the Great defeated Darius 331BC ; one of the oldest continuously inhabited towns in existence ; now Erbil, Iraq ; pop.181,000.

arbitration, settlement of disputes or differences between persons, groups, or nations by appointing someone (an *arbitrator*) to decide on a just agreement. Both disputants agree beforehand to accept the arbitrator's decision.

Arbor Day, school holiday in the USA (and some other countries) for the planting of trees ; Latin *arbor*, tree.

arboretum, är-bo-rē'tum, collection of growing trees, as the one at Kew, London.

Arcadia, är-kä'diä, hilly country of ancient Greece. See SIDNEY, SIR P.

arch, see ARCHITECTURE ; TRIUMPHAL ARCH

archaeology, ark-ē-ol'ŏji, scientific study of the way people lived long ago. Archaeologists dig up and study traces of ancient civilisations, bringing to light houses, temples, fortresses, weapons, utensils, ornaments, etc. of the period.

We owe much of our knowledge of ancient Egypt, Greece, Syria, Crete, Troy and Herculaneum to the patient work of archaeologists. Sir Austen Layard revealed the splendours of Nineveh and Babylon ; Sir Flinders Petrie made astonishing discoveries in Egypt ; and in the Valley of the Kings (Egypt) Lord Carnarvon and Howard Carter found, 1922, the tomb of Tutankhamen, one of the most thrilling of all archaeological discoveries. Tutankhamen, King of Egypt *c*.1350BC, was buried at Thebes ; round him were golden beds, richly carved chariots, caskets, candlesticks, and his throne, sparkling with jewels ; the flowers, fresh at his funeral, were found unharmed after more than 3,000 years.

Recent excavations by Sir Leonard Woolley show that at Ur in Mesopotamia there was a high degree of civilisation 3500BC.

The British Museum and various universities in Britain and USA send archaeological expeditions abroad. Archaeologists have brought to light remains of the Stone Age and of Celtic, Roman and Saxon Britain.

The use of air reconnaissance as an instrument of archaeological discovery is now generally recognised. Sites of lost settlements of the Stone Age and later periods, may be revealed by suitable aerial photography.

Read *Ur of the Chaldees* and *Digging up the Past*, Sir Leonard Woolley ; *The Ancient World*, T. R. Glover, *What Happened in History* and *Man Makes Himself*, Gordon Childe.

archaeopteryx, see GEOLOGY

Archangel, *ärk'ān-jel*, Soviet port near the Arctic Circle and on the R. Dvina ; has a spacious harbour free from ice June–Sept. There are large fisheries. Archangel was the port for hazardous convoys to Russia in World War II ; pop. 280.000.

Archbishop of Canterbury, see CANTERBURY

archery, see BOW

Archimedes, *ärki-mē'dēz* (*d* 212BC), Greek scholar, *b* Syracuse, Sicily. Archimedes was the first to discover the theory of levers, and used to say that if only he could find somewhere in space to rest a lever, he would move the earth. He is credited with inventing the Archimedean screw, a mechanical means of raising water.

Archimedes also discovered a principle known by his name concerning the apparent loss of weight of a body when immersed in a fluid. The story is told that Hiero of Syracuse invited him to find whether or not his crown was of pure gold, and that when stepping into his bath, Archimedes observed that some of the water overflowed, whereupon he cried, ' *Eureka !* ' i.e. ' I have found it,' namely, the principle that a solid body immersed in a fluid appears to lose as much of its weight as the weight of the fluid displaced by the body. From this he was able to solve the problem of the crown.

Archimedes was also a pioneer in geometry, especially of the circle, sphere, spiral and cylinder. He was killed (no doubt in error) by a Roman soldier. See SPECIFIC GRAVITY

archipelago, *är-ki-pel'agō*, group of islands, e.g. the Malay Archipelago.

architect, one who designs buildings, and sees that the work is properly done. The registration of architects has been compulsory since 1940.

architecture, art of building beautifully and well. Buildings are needed in the first place to provide shelter. Two things which affect the development of architecture in any country are the climate and the nature of the materials available. A third consideration is that buildings are needed for many different purposes. In its long history architecture has had to provide palaces, tombs, temples, fortresses, houses, railway stations, shops, offices, etc., and new types of buildings are always emerging in response to changing needs.

Thus the ancient Greeks did business in the open air, so that they did not need office buildings. Again, their religious ceremonies were unlike our Christian worship. It is partly for this reason that the Greek temple and the Christian cathedral are so different in general design, although both were meant to serve a religious purpose.

In our age, with its rapidly changing needs, architecture has moved far in the direction of *functionalism*, the doctrine that what makes a building beautiful is perfect adaptation to a particular purpose or function. It is certainly true that functional adaptation can be very pleasing to the eye, but it is not the only

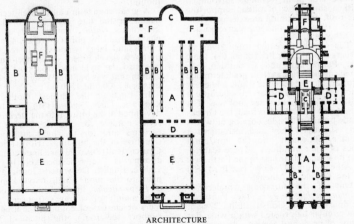

ARCHITECTURE

(*Left*) San Clemente, Rome : A—*Nave* B—*Aisles* C—*Apse* D—*Narthex* E—*Atrium* F—*Choir* (*Middle*) Old St Peter's, Rome (AD326), *destroyed to make room for the present cathedral* : A—*Nave* B—*Aisles* C—*Apse* D—*Narthex* E—*Atrium* F—*Transverse Aisle* (*Right*) Winchester Cathedral : A—*Nave* B—*Aisles* C—*Choir* D—*Transepts* E—*Presbytery* F—*Lady Chapel*

feature of a building that makes for beauty. Even the largest building is not impressive unless the design is harmonious and well-proportioned, both in its general effect and in every detail ; while grace and elegance can only be achieved by architects who have good taste and subtle sense of style.

Among the oldest examples of architecture in existence are the temples and pyramids of *ancient Egypt*. The pyramids were built over 5,000 years ago as tombs of the Pharaohs. The Great Pyramid of Ghizeh (near Cairo) stands 481ft high on a base 775ft square, and contains 88 million cu.ft of solid masonry. Other notable pyramids are : Khafra's, 454ft high ; Menkaura's 219ft high ; and the pyramids at Abusir and Saqqara.

Egyptian temples consist of lofty halls, roofed over (since timber was scarce) with stone slabs supported by pillars. (This is known as post-and-lintel construction.) The pillars were bulbous in shape and richly carved ; and because the roofing slabs were not strong enough to span a wide gap, the pillars were set very close together, as in the hypostyle of the Great Temple at Karnak (PLATE 65). Light was excluded by the windowless exterior wall, and the whole effect was highly imposing and mysterious.

Ancient Greek Architecture (6th–3rd c. BC) displays a grace and elegance never attained by the Egyptians. The Greeks too used the post-and-lintel principle— they had no knowledge of the arch—but timber was available for roof construction. Consequently the inner hall of the Greek temple is an empty space, whereas the interior of an Egyptian temple is filled with pillars. In plan the normal Greek temple is a plain rectangle surrounded with a single row of pillars supporting the roof, and forming an exterior colonnade with a shady and impressive portico at either end.

The Greeks invented three styles or Orders : Doric (see PLATES 66, 67), Ionic (see PLATE 67), and Corinthian. In Greek architecture certain predetermined proportions between the whole and every part are carefully observed. Because a pillar with straight sides looks as if it might give way under its load, the Greeks made pillars with sides curving outwards very slightly. They also introduced a similar refinement into the horizontal lines of their buildings. These features can be seen at their best in the Parthenon at Athens, built 447–438BC (see PLATE 67) as the Temple of Athene.

One of the surviving wonders of *Roman architecture* is the Pantheon (temple of all the Gods). Built *c.*27BC, it is a circular hall roofed with a wide, flat dome of brick and cement. It was converted into a Christian church AD609. Rome's most important legacy in architecture was the semi-circular or Roman arch, which is much used in such buildings as the Colosseum (amphitheatre at

Rome used for public games and gladiatorial contests) and in great aqueducts like the Pont du Gard at Nîmes. The Roman arch is much used also in *Romanesque architecture*, a style which developed in Italy in the Dark Ages (e.g. San Vitale, Ravenna, see PLATE 68), and was later adopted by the Normans in France and England (e.g. Durham Cathedral, see PLATE 71).

When Christianity became the official religion of the Roman Empire (4th c. AD), the Christians began to build Christian churches. In some cases they simply took over the Roman Basilica or law courts, normally in the form of a long hall flanked with pillars and side aisles, and ending in a recess where the judges used to sit (see PLATE 68). This plan was well adapted to early Christian ritual, and when ritual became more complicated a transept was added. This is the origin of the cross-shaped or cruciform church.

Norman architecture is dignified and heavy, with thick walls and massive pillars. The round arches are usually carved with grotesque heads, foliage, or zigzag patterns, but apart from this decoration is reduced to a minimum. Besides cathedrals—e.g. Durham, Ely, Winchester, Hereford, etc.—the Normans in England built many castles— e.g. Dover, Castle Hedingham (PLATE 70), Rochester and the Tower of London. A typical Norman castle has massive outer walls, sometimes protected by a moat (a ditch filled with water), its gateway or barbican reached by a drawbridge, and two courtyards, in one of which stood the keep, a round or squarish building, often set upon a mound.

A great change in church architecture began in the late 12th c. Popularly known as *Gothic*, the new style was characterised by pointed arches, slender pillars and large windows. It reached its finest development in France, but it was also the style used in almost every church that was built in Western Europe between 1200 and 1500.

In England the earliest Gothic is known as *Early English* (13th c.), which developed in the 14th c. into the *Decorated* style, notable for the richness of its carvings and for the light and open structure of the building. Holy Trinity Church, Hull (PLATE 73), is a fine example: another is Exeter Cathedral. In the 15th c. English Decorated Gothic gave place to the purely English style known as *Perpendicular*, in which the wall consists mainly of windows (between the piers or clusters of columns required to support the roof), the pitch of the pointed arches is flattened, and the roof is covered with an elaborate fan-tracery in stone. In the 16th c. Perpendicular gave rise to *Tudor*, in which Gothic is adapted to non-religious needs. In mansion houses, such as Mapledurham

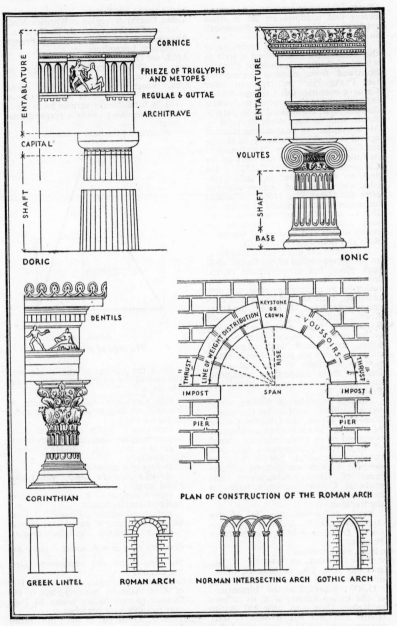

ARCHITECTURE

Showing the Grecian Orders—Doric, Ionic, Corinthian—and the evolution of Roman into Gothic architecture.   See also Plates 66 (bottom), 67, 68, 72, 73.

27

(PLATE 74) brick is used instead of stone, except that windows are set in stone mullions ; timber is used as a framework in town houses.

Meanwhile in Italy the architects of the Renaissance had evolved a style in which much use was made of elements borrowed from classical architecture (see PLATE 75). In Italy and other Catholic countries this *Classical Revival* led in the end to the gorgeous and ornate *Baroque* style, exemplified in St Peter's, Rome, with its huge dome designed by Michelangelo. In England the classical revival inspired such buildings as Hampton Court Palace (PLATE 75) and reached its fullest expression in the work of Sir Christopher Wren (1632–1723), the architect who designed St Paul's Cathedral and many other London churches after the Great Fire (1666). Classical influences were dominant through the 18th c., and were combined with large-scale town-planning to produce the stately streets and circuses of Georgian Bath and Edinburgh (PLATE 80).

In England and elsewhere in the 19th c. an attempted revival of the Gothic style took place, but in conditions of the Industrial Revolution the need was rather for an entirely new style, and new materials, such as steel, glass and concrete were at hand. In Britain, the USA, Russia, Holland, Germany, France and Scandinavia many schools of *modern architecture* have arisen. Houses, factories, government and commercial office buildings are planned with attention to simplicity of line and mass, freedom from unnecessary ornament, and specialisation of function (see PLATES 78, 79).

Notable examples of modern architecture in Britain are London University, Shell-Mex House, the Glasgow College of Art, etc. Much modern architecture is marred by its crude vulgarity. Some of it is starkly impressive and even genuinely beautiful, but it may be doubted whether the greatest achievement of Greek, Romanesque and medieval Gothic architects have yet been surpassed by their successors in the tradition.

Read *An Introduction to Modern Architecture*, J. M. Richards ; *An Outline of European Architecture*, Nikolaus Pevsner.

arc-lamp, see LIGHTING
Arc of the Covenant, see TEMPLE
Arcot, city 65m SW. of Madras, India ; once the capital of the Carnatic ; pop. *c.*15,000 ; regarded as the 'birthplace' of the Indian Empire after its defence by Robert Clive who, with 200 British troops and 300 native Sepoys, took possession of the fort, and defended it 23 Sept–14 Nov 1751 against the French who were 10,000 strong. After the French failure to take the city British power in India rapidly increased.
Arctic, see POLAR REGIONS

Arctic towns, see SIBERIA
Arden, FOREST OF, region in Warwickshire ; scene of Shakespeare's *As You Like It*.
Ardennes, *är-den'*, range of hills in France, Belgium, Luxemburg.
Ardil, see GROUND-NUT
are, *är*, 100sq.metres, i.e. 119·6sq.yd or 0·0988 rood.
area, measure of surface. For *square measure*, see WEIGHTS AND MEASURES. Useful formulae for various areas are :
   parallelogram : base × perpendicular height
   triangle : (i) ½ base × height

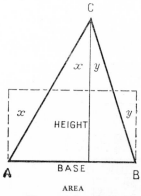

AREA

The area of a triangle

   (ii) ½ the product of any 2 sides and the sine of the angle between them, i.e. ½*bc* sin A
   (iii) $\sqrt{s(s-a)(s-b)(s-c)}$, where *a*, *b* and *c* are lengths of the sides, and *s* is ½(*a*+*b*+*c*)
   trapezium : ½(sum of parallel sides) × perpendicular distance between them
   circle : πr^2, i.e. 3·1416 × radius² (approx.)
   surface of a sphere : $4\pi r^2$
   curved surface of cylinder : with radius *r* and length *l* is $2\pi rl$
   curved surface of a cone : π × base-radius × slanting height
   surface of regular pyramid : ½ slant height × perimeter of base + area of base
   ellipse : longest diameter × shortest diameter × $\frac{\pi}{4}$; or πab, where *a* and *b* are the semi-major and semi-minor axes. See ELLIPSE
Areopagus, *ar-ē-op'agus*, court on the Hill of Ares, Athens ; meeting-place of the famous council before whom St Paul may possibly have preached.
Ares, *är'ēz*, Greek god of war ; the Roman Mars ; had a temple on the Hill of Ares, Athens.
Argand, AIMÉ, *är'gand ; är-gän'* (1755–1803), Swiss chemist who invented the Argand gas-burner.
Argentine, *är-jen-tīn*, republic, S. America,

from Bolivia to Cape Horn, c.2,300m ; area c.1,113,000sq.m ; rises to the Andes in the W., but is largely a country of great plains, with woods N. forming El Gran Chaco, and the treeless grasslands (the Pampas) further S. (La Plata). The extreme S. is known as Patagonia. The chief rivers are La Plata, Paraná, Rio Negro.

The Argentine is notable for agriculture, especially cattle-raising (see PLATE 15, *bottom*), though copper, manganese and wolfram are produced, also oil ; exports include wheat, maize, sugar, wool, hides, frozen beef and mutton.

Colonised by Spain 1535, the Argentine won independence 1816, and has had a settled government since 1853, being a republic with a president (who chooses his own Cabinet) and a National Congress with a Senate and House of Deputies. The cap. is Buenos Aires ; other towns are Rosario, Tucuman, Santa Fé, Cordoba, La Plata. Boundary disputes with Chile led to a settlement 1902, and to the erection in the Andes of a bronze statue, 26ft high, of Christ the Redeemer (made from old cannon) to commemorate friendly relations ; pop. (which has more than doubled in the last 34 years) is c.16,000,000.

argentite, the sulphide of silver, Ag_2S, an ore from which silver is obtained. See SILVER

Argo, see JASON AND THE GOLDEN FLEECE

argon, inert gas and element, A ; atomic weight 39·944 ; atomic number 18 ; its presence in the air was discovered in 1894 by Rayleigh and Ramsay.

Argonauts, see JASON AND THE GOLDEN FLEECE

Argos, town, Greece, with ruins of an ancient city once famous for its sculptors and musicians.

Argyll, *är-gīl'*, county of W. Scotland ; it includes the Inner Hebrides, Mull, Iona, Staffa, Lismore, etc. ; is mountainous with many deer forests ; co.tn Lochgilphead.

Argyll, *är-gīl'*, title of a famous old Scottish family of Campbells, e.g. Archibald Campbell, the ' good Marquis ' of Argyll (1607–61), known as Lord Lorne ; supported the Covenanters, also Cromwell, but crowned Charles II at Scone 1651 ; beheaded at Edinburgh. Also the 9th earl, who fought for Charles II at Dunbar ; joined Monmouth's rebellion ; executed at Edinburgh 1685. Also John Douglas Campbell (1845–1914), Governor-General of Canada 1878–83.

Ariadne, see THESEUS

Ariosto, LUDOVICO (1474–1533), Italian poet, *b* Reggio ; famous for his epic poem, *Orlando Furioso.*

Aristides, *aris-tī'dēz* (550–467BC), Athenian general and democratic statesman ; fought at Marathon and Platæa ; greatly improved the status of the poorer classes ; died in extreme poverty. He is said to have been ostracised (banished). Requested by a fellow-citizen, who did not recognise him, to give his vote for the banishment of Aristides he said, ' Why do you wish him to be banished ? ' ' Because,' replied the other, ' I'm tired of hearing him called The Just.'

Aristophanes, *aris-tof'änēz* (d 385BC), Greek playwright. Though little is known of him, eleven of his fifty-four brilliantly witty comedies are extant, e.g. *The Knights, The Wasps, The Birds*, the latter particularly notable for its exquisite lyrics. Full of broad humour the plays of Aristophanes might be termed the ' revues ' of antiquity.

Typical quotations from Aristophanes include :

Ἀπ' ἐχθρών πολλὰ μανθάνουσιν οἱ σοφοί (the wise learn many things from their foes).

Οὔποτε ποιήσεις τὸν καρκίνον ὀρθὰ βαδίζειν (you cannot make a crab walk straight).

Aristotle, *är'is-tot-l* (384–322BC), Greek thinker, possibly the greatest the world has seen ; *b* Stagira, Macedonia ; for twenty years studied at Athens under Plato ; became tutor to Alexander the Great ; returned to Athens 332BC and founded his own school, the Peripatos ; died at Chalcis.

Dante called him father of them that know. No other philosopher has left writings of such importance about so many subjects. Even his early teaching challenged some of Plato's most important doctrines, but the two remained friends. After Plato's death, Aristotle intensified his studies of natural history and pure science, thus moving further than ever from Plato's thought.

His greatest originality appears in his masterly books on logic, physics, psychology and biology. He was the first thinker who put these subjects on a scientific basis. Scarcely less important are his writings about metaphysics (treated by him as the study of existence, and therefore the science that governs all others), ethics (the study of goodness and badness in man), politics and literary criticism, of which again he was the real founder. These books, translated into Arabic, then into Latin, influenced deeply most philosophers of the Middle Ages. His views on all these subjects are still widely studied, which attests the astonishing range and power of his mind.

Arithmetic, see MATHEMATICS

arithmetical progression, series of numbers increasing or decreasing by a common difference, e.g. 1, 3, 5, 7, 9 etc., or 100, 95, 90, 85 etc. If *a* is the first term, *d* the difference, *n* the number of terms, L the last term, and S the sum of *n* terms, then

(i) $S = \dfrac{n}{2} [2a + (n-1)d]$ or $\dfrac{n}{2}(a + L)$

(ii) $L = a + (n-1)d$

Note that the Arithmetic Mean of any arithmetic series

$$= \frac{a + L}{2}$$

Arizona, mountainous state in the S. of USA ; noted for the grandeur of its scenery, especially in the region of the Colorado R., its canyons including the Grand Canyon, a national park. The capital is Phoenix, pop.474,000. Read *Spin of a Silver Coin*, Alberta Hannum. See SHOOTING STARS

Arkansas, state, USA ; produces wheat, cotton, etc. ; the industries include coal, manganese, lead and lumbering ; cap. Little Rock.

Ark of the Covenant, chest of acacia wood made by the Israelites according to God's command to Moses. In the ark were the stones of the Ten Commandments. Emblem of the Jewish faith, the Ark had a place of honour in the Temple at Jerusalem (Exodus 25 ; 1 Kings 8).

Arkwright, SIR RICHARD, *ärk'rit* (1732–92), barber who gave Lancashire its great cotton industry ; *b* Preston ; had the idea of replacing the old hand method of spinning by a new and quicker method. With the help of John Kay and John Smalley, Arkwright built a mechanical water-driven spinning machine 1769 ; later he employed steam. In spite of rioters who destroyed his mills, he made a fortune.

Arles, *ärl* ; *ärlz*, town, S. France ; on the R. Rhone ; noted for Roman remains.

Arlington, name of the USA National Cemetery, near Washington, Virginia, last resting place of the American Unknown Warrior.

arma'da, Spanish word meaning fleet of warships, especially the Great Armada of 1588.

Philip II of Spain, rich and powerful, hoped that Elizabeth of England would marry him, thus uniting the two nations so that he might conquer France. Champion of the RC faith, and hated by the English, Philip decided on invasion after the execution of Mary Queen of Scots, the plan being to send a huge fleet up the English Channel, and take on board soldiers in the Netherlands commanded by the Duke of Parma.

His attempt was unlucky from the start : (*a*) Sir Francis Drake made a daring raid on shipping and stores in Cadiz harbour 1587, thus delaying preparations, ' singeing the King of Spain's beard,' as Drake expressed it ; (*b*) the Spanish admiral died and was replaced by Medina Sidonia, an inexperienced landsman ; (*c*) the clumsy galleons were at the mercy of the nimbler English ships ; and (*d*) a storm shattered the vessels not captured or sunk by the English.

Sailing 12 July 1588, the Armada comprised 130 ships, many rowed by galley slaves. The English ships were commanded by Lord Howard of Effingham, aided by Drake, Hawkins, Frobisher, etc. England's navy was small, but there were ships from nearly every port, possibly 197 all told, only 50 over 200 tons, the Spaniards having 60 ships over 300 tons, and twice as many men and guns.

The story is told that Drake was playing bowls on Plymouth Hoe when news came that the Armada had been sighted. Cool as ever, he replied, ' There is plenty of time to win this game and thrash the Spaniards too.' Warning beacons blazed on every headland ; ships were manned, soldiers mustered. Queen Elizabeth rode among her troops at Tilbury, saying, ' I have the body of a weak and feeble woman, but I have the heart of a king, *and of a king of England, too.*'

Boldly attacked by the little English ships, the Armada sailed in a half-moon to Calais, where the English sent down fire-ships which caused the Spaniards to put out to sea. The Spanish ships were driven by a strong wind into the N. Sea, many being wrecked.

From the defeat of the Armada the might of Spain steadily decreased. She ceased to menace the growing strength of England. English seamen travelled without fear. A medal struck by the English bore the inscription : *Dominus flavit et dissipati sunt,* i.e. God blew and they were scattered.

armadillo, toothless animal of Central and S. America. Protected by bony plates, the armadillo can roll up like a hedgehog. The giant armadillo is 3ft long, with a tail 20in long. The armadillo feeds chiefly on ants and beetles.

THE BANDED ARMADILLO

Armagh', *är-mä'*, county, N. Ireland. The co.tn Armagh, is the seat of RC and Protestant bishops.

armature, see ELECTRICITY

Armenia, *är-mē'nia,* republic of USSR since 1920 ; is between Asia Minor and the Caspian Sea. Largely agricultural, it is capable of much development, and has sulphur, naphtha, bitumen, nitre, copper, etc. Carpets are manufactured. The Armenians, mostly Christian, have been much persecuted by Turks, Kurds, etc., notably during the Armenian massacres 1915–17 ; area 11,580sq.m ; pop. 1,280,000 ; cap. Erevan.

Also, somewhat vaguely, a region (between the Black Sea and the Caucasus Mts) ruled by Turkey and Iran.

Armistice Day, originally Nov 11, anniversary of the end of World War I ; day on which the Two Minutes' Silence is kept ; now the Sunday before Nov 11, a national Day of Remembrance.

armour, protective equipment in warfare ; was at first of leather, the word cuirass (a breastplate and back-covering worn by ancient Greeks) coming from the Latin *coriaceus,* i.e. made of leather. Anciently, Greek soldiers wore a bronze cuirass, a helmet with a high crest, bronze greaves (rather like cricket-pads), and carried a round shield. Roman armour was usually of iron, the helmet being smaller. The legs were unprotected.

Norman armour (11th c.) was of leather with metal plates, the conical helmet having a nose-guard. Iron rings attached to leather or cloth made up a suit of 'mail.' Later, the rings were linked together to form chain armour. Plate armour reached perfection in the 15th and 16th c. A poor man then could afford little or no armour, but a knight was encased in hinged armour, often enriched with engraving. For jousting at tournaments, knights, clad in superb armour, carried lances, and rode horses also protected by armour. Intended to ward off blows from sword or spear, armour was gradually discontinued (*c.*1650) after the widespread use of firearms.

Armour is still used today in various ways, e.g. the steel helmet worn by soldiers and civil defence workers in World War II ; also armoured cars, tanks and battleships, the latter having plating 15in thick, or more. The difficulty about armour is that it always slows down the man, vehicle, or ship it protects. This loss of speed often outweighs the advantage of the extra protection.

Armstrong, THOMAS (1899–), novelist, *b* Yorkshire ; author of *Crowthers of Bankdam* ; *King Cotton,* etc.

army, national armed force for use on land. ' Army ' can mean the whole of a nation's land forces, or a group of *corps* fighting under one commander in a particular theatre of war, e.g. Montgomery's Eighth Army. A modern army consists of *field units* and *formations* (the fighting troops) ; *services* (to supply fighting troops with everything they need) ; and *staff* (to co-ordinate and direct operations). Of field formations the most important is the *division.* A division is commanded by a major-general, is self-contained and consists of two or three infantry or armoured brigades, with its own artillery, services, etc., totalling about 16,000 men.

The British army has developed in part from the Saxon *fyrd,* when all men between 16 and 60 (if free land-owners) were liable for military service. In medieval England the wealthy classes usually supplied the cavalry, the infantry consisting of the *militia,* i.e. a citizen army as distinct from professional fighters. Prior to the 15th c. the English bowmen were supreme on the Continent (e.g. the battle of Agincourt, 1415), but the introduction of fire-arms weakened the militia, who were supposed to supply their own weapons, and it was not till 1645, when Cromwell founded the New Model Army of professional fighting men, well disciplined and trained, that the army became truly effective.

Reconstituted 1663, the army was directed by a Secretary at War—hence the War Office. After that, the main outlines of the modern British army began to appear. At the battle of Waterloo (1815) the British army included cavalry and infantry of the line, artillery and ' ancillary ' (supporting) services. The artillery consisted of Horse Artillery (for supporting the cavalry) and Field Artillery (for supporting the Infantry). In addition to the Line Cavalry and Infantry, there were several regiments of Household Cavalry and Footguards whose first duty, at any rate in peace time, was to guard the person of the king. The fighting efficiency of Wellington's army and its high standard of training were due largely to Sir John Moore and Sir Ralph Abercromby.

In 1870, the British army was re-organised by Cardwell, then in charge of the War Office. The Line Infantry regiments were officially given the names so familiar to us, e.g. Buffs, Black Watch, King's Shropshire Light Infantry, Hampshire, Gordon Highlanders, etc., and every regiment consisted of a depot (usually stationed in the county town of the county in which it was recruited) and two regular battalions, of which one at a time served overseas.

In the Boer War (1899–1902) many weaknesses in training and organisation came to light, and in 1906 Haldane introduced many reforms, of which the most important were the creation of an Imperial General Staff and the institution of a Territorial Army, consisting of civilians trained in their spare time. In 1914–15 these Territorials bridged the gap between the small regular army, nearly overwhelmed at Mons, and the

New Army, consisting of volunteers recruited after the outbreak of war, who had to be trained for several months before they could be sent overseas.

In 1914, the British Army consisted entirely of volunteers, but in 1916 conscription was introduced, i.e. all men of a certain age were ' called up,' and compelled to serve as soldiers whether they liked it or not, unless they were physically unfit or required for other essential occupations, e.g. coal-mining, munition-making, etc. Conscription was abolished after 1918, but in 1939 it was reinstated. In World War II the Territorial and to some extent the regular army were used at the outset as a framework (cadre) on which to build the wartime army.

World War I saw an immense increase of mechanical transport, mainly behind the lines, and of ancillary services. Even more important was the invention of tanks : but for the time being tanks were only used to help the infantry to get through the first crust of the enemy resistance. Infantry still fought on foot, and the artillery relied solely on horse-transport to draw their guns and feed them with ammunition. Cavalry was not much used.

Between 1918 and 1938 mechanisation was carried much further. The infantry and artillery were lavishly re-equipped with motor transport, thus enormously increasing their effective range of action within a given time. Cavalry was converted into an armoured fighting force with its own artillery (RHA) and reorganised in Armoured Divisions independent of the ordinary Infantry Divisions. There was a further expansion of the ancillary services. After World War II, conscription was retained, but the army was reduced in size. Now its main components are Royal Armoured Corps ; Infantry, now highly specialised and armed with many different weapons ; Royal Artillery, consisting of RHA (for service with armoured formations), Field, Medium, Anti-Tank, Anti-Aircraft, etc. ; Royal Corps of Signals ; Royal Engineers ; services, including the Royal Army Medical Corps, Royal Army Service Corps, Royal Army Ordnance Corps, Royal Electrical and Mechanical Engineers, etc., etc.

During World War II the RAF co-operated with the army wherever it fought, and for certain purposes both were combined with the Royal Navy under unified command. In outline the old army pattern of brigades, divisions, corps, persisted : but its role was changing. Essentially, it had to defend land-areas affording air-bases, ports, or supplies of vital raw materials, or to attack similar areas held by the enemy. These were important in themselves, but subsidiary to the airborne assault in the enemy's homeland. This shift of emphasis has been confirmed by the invention of atom bombs, first used by US forces against Japan in 1945 ; but the army is still an essential component of a nation's armed forces and has not lost its importance.

Arne, THOMAS AUGUSTINE, *ärn* (1710–78), musician, *b* London ; composed the music for several of Shakespeare's songs, e.g. *Where the bee sucks* ; also the tune of *Rule, Britannia.*

Arnhem, port on the Rhine, Netherlands ; scene 1944 of bitter fighting when Allied ground forces failed to break through to support advance paratroops dropped behind the enemy lines ; pop.80,000.

Arnim, GENERAL VON, see WORLD WAR II

Arno, Italian river ; flows 150m to the Mediterranean near Pisa.

Arnold, MATTHEW (1822–88) ; English poet, critic and educationalist ; eldest son of Arnold of Rugby. Best-known among his poems are *Sohrab and Rustum, The Scholar Gipsy* and *Thyrsis.* At its best his poetry is very good, but has a characteristic weakness that spoils it. Like most Victorians who had the courage to think for themselves, Matthew Arnold suffered from ' doubts.' His doubts begin in intellectual honesty but end in self-pity. He does not share the Victorian belief in ' progress,' i.e. that everything is continuously improving and will soon be perfect ; but his Victorian world seems so unshakeable that although he does not really admire it, there is nothing else in which he can believe. Arnold never really faced this difficulty. So he doubted but did nothing, hence the wistfulness which pervades and weakens his poetry.

This explains the inner meaning of *The Scholar Gipsy,* a long and very moving poem about a 17th c. scholar who forsook Oxford because he found the world too busy and too full of mere cleverness, went off to learn wisdom from the mysterious gipsies of the countryside, and did not return. (If he had been more adventurous Matthew Arnold himself would have liked to escape from the world he lived in.) The following lines from *Thyrsis* are typical of Arnold at his best, but reveal the weakness mentioned above :

So, some tempestuous morn in early June
When the year's primal burst of bloom
    is o'er,
Before the roses and the longest
    day . . .
So have I heard the cuckoo's parting cry,
From the wet field, through the vext
    garden-trees,
Come with the volleying rain and
    tossing breeze :
' The bloom is gone, and with the bloom
    go I ! '

Arnold, THOMAS (1795–1842) ; at 33 headmaster of Rugby, which he made a model for other public schools in a quickly-changing England. Formerly the more famous public schools had been for the sons of the noblemen and landed gentry who until then ruled England. In Arnold's time a new class of wealthy industrialists was demanding its share of political power, hence, for example, the Reform Act (1832). Arnold made Rugby a school in which the sons of these industrialists mixed with the sons of the older ruling class and were brought up to undertake the same responsibilities. The story of this is told in *Tom Brown's Schooldays*.

Arnold stressed the need for character as well as cleverness, and allowed manly games to become an important part of a boy's education.

arquebus, *är'kwē-bus,* hand-gun resembling a musket ; first used in the 15th c.

Arran, rugged and beautiful island in the Firth of Clyde.

Arras, city, France, 38m NE. of Amiens ; famous for tapestries ; hence *arras,* a coloured woven fabric hung on the wall for decoration or to keep out draughts, first made at Arras in the 14th c. ; pop.26,000.

Arromanches, *ar-o-monsh,* village, Normandy (France), scene 6 June 1944 of the historic Allied D-Day landings in World War II.

Arrowrock Dam, dam, 350ft high, holding back the waters of the R. Boise, Idaho, USA, thus making fertile about 200,000 acres.

arrowroot, plant of tropical America and the W. Indies. From the root comes a rich starch food.

ar'senic, crystalline element, As ; atomic weight 74·91 ; atomic number 33 ; its many compounds are highly poisonous.

art, general name for any human activity that has the object of making beautiful things. See ARCHITECTURE ; MUSIC ; PAINTING ; SCULPTURE

Artemis, *är'tē-mis,* Greek goddess of the chase ; Latin name, Diana.

artery, see BLOOD

artesian well, see WELL

arthritis, see RHEUMATISM

arthropoda, *är-throp'ō-dä* (Gk *arthron,* joint ; *pous,* foot), large group of creatures without backbone, e.g. insects, spiders, centipedes, crabs, lobsters, etc. See SPIDERS

Arthur, largely mythical 5th or 6th c. British warrior-chief, possibly buried in the so-called I. of Avalon, said to have been Glastonbury, Somerset. Stories about him grew up much as did legends of Robin Hood, some being gathered *c.*1147 by Geoffrey of Monmouth ; but the chivalrous King Arthur of the Round Table was not a part of our national literature till Sir Thomas Malory wrote *Morte d'Arthur* (i.e. the Death of Arthur) *c.*1470. Regarded as the finest example of 15th c. English prose, this inspired Lord Tennyson's *Idylls of the King,* a group of epic poems in blank verse.

To King Arthur's court at Camelot (perhaps Caerleon-on-Usk, Monmouth-

shire) came the noblest knights of the day. They feasted at a huge round table said to have been made for Uther Pendragon by Merlin, the cunning magician described by Tennyson as having vast wit and a hundred winters. Among the 150 seats was one, the *Siege Perilous,* in which only the pure in heart could sit without being struck dead. Arthur's sword was the magic Excalibur, taken from the hand of the Lady of the Lake, who wore white samite i.e. silk. The knights of the Round Table included Geraint, who crowned a happy life with a fair death ; Lancelot, secretly in love with Guinevere, Arthur's queen ; Percival, whose wife was Elaine, and their son Galahad ; also Bors ; Kay ; Mordred, the traitor ; Gareth ; Gawain ; Tristram ; Bedivere, etc.

Many of the stories are about the quest of the Holy Grail, the Grail being the cup from which Christ drank at the Last Supper.

As an example of Sir Thomas Malory's style, take this passage about Sir Tristram who had been taunting two knights of the Round Table till they came at him ' as it had been thunder ' :

And Sir Dodinas' spear brast (broke) in sunder, but Sir Tristram smote him with a more might, that he smote him clean over the horse-croup, that nigh he had broken his neck. When Sir Sagramore saw his fellow fall he marvelled what knight he might be, and he dressed his spear with all his might, and Sir Tristram against him, and they came together as the thunder, and there Sir Tristram smote Sir Sagramore a strong buffet, that he bare his horse and him to the earth, and in the falling he brake his thigh. When this was done Sir Tristram asked them : ' Fair knights, will ye any more ? Be there no bigger knights in the court of King Arthur ? '

Arthur (1486–1502), eldest son of Henry VII of England ; married Catherine of Aragon (a Spanish princess) 1501.

Arthur, CHESTER ALAN (1830–86), President of USA 1881–85.

Arthur, DUKE OF BRITTANY (1187–1203), grandson of Henry II of England ; had a better claim to the throne than his uncle, King John. Captured by the king, he was murdered at Rouen, France. In Shakespeare's play *King John,* Hubert de Burgh is ordered to put out Prince Arthur's eyes ; he refuses, but the boy-prince takes his own life by jumping from the walls of Northampton Castle.

Arthur's Seat, hill, 822ft high ; almost like a lion crouching over Edinburgh.

artificial rain, rain produced when required. The first successful experiment was made over 20sq.m of Australia (1947) as a result of scattering ice crystals or dry-ice, i.e. powdered solid carbon dioxide. Dropped from a high-flying aircraft on clouds, they cause rain to fall soon after. Artificial rain has been induced over Britain.

artificial respiration, see LUNGS
artificial silk, see RAYON ; SILK
arts, in universities today usually means the study of classics, philosophy, modern languages and literature. Mathematics is sometimes included. See DEGREES
Arundel, *är'ŭn-del,* Sussex town 10m from Chichester ; noted for its castle, home of the Duke of Norfolk.
Arundel, EARL OF, title of the Duke of Norfolk, oldest of its kind. Henry, 6th Duke, bequeathed to Oxford University (1667) a collection of statues, including the famous Arundel Marbles from ancient Greece.
Aryan, race of people from whom have come the present inhabitants of India and Europe ; also the name of the group of languages spoken by these people, e.g. Greek, Latin, Celtic, German, Persian, Hindu. Hitler's use of Aryan as opposed to Jewish was incorrect. See LANGUAGE
asbes'tos, fibrous mineral found in various forms, of which the chief is calcium magnesium silicate, occurring chiefly in Canada and USSR ; its fire-resisting properties give it a wide range of uses from fireproof mill-boards to brakelinings.
Ascalon or **Ashkelon,** Philistine city of Bible times ; gave its name to eschalot (or shallot), i.e. onion.
Ascension, *ä-sen'shon,* Christ's ascent to heaven 40 days after his resurrection ; Mark 16 ; Luke 24 ; Acts 1. Ascension Day or Holy Thursday is the 40th day after Easter Sunday.
Ascension, volcanic island in the S. Atlantic ; is 760m NW. of St Helena ; discovered Ascension Day 1501 by the Portuguese ; British since 1815 ; noted for turtles ; pop. *c.*200.
Ascham, ROGER, *as'kam* (1515–68), English scholar, *b* Yorkshire. He was tutor to Princess (afterwards Queen) Elizabeth ; and author of *The Schoolmaster* and a book on archery.
Ascot, town, Berkshire, noted for its race-meeting in June, always attended by people of fashion.
asepsis, see LISTER, LORD
Asgard, home of the gods in old Norse stories.
ash, handsome British tree, often 80ft high ; has feathery leaves in 3–5 pairs with a terminal leaf. The fruits hang in clusters of ' keys ' or ' spinners ' that fly on the wind. Straight-grained and strong, the wood is used for making wooden wheel-spokes, spade handles, etc.
Ashanti, see GOLD COAST
Ashburton Treaty, agreement 1842 between USA and Canada, settling various matters, including the boundary between the two countries ; named after Lord Ashburton (1774–1848), British statesman.
Ashby-de-la-Zouch, *ash'bi de lä zoosh,* town, Leicestershire ; mentioned by Sir Walter Scott in *Ivanhoe.*

THE ASH

Ashdown, spot, Berkshire, where Ethelred and Alfred defeated the Danes 871. Wayland the Smith (hero of Old English tales) is supposed to have lived hereabouts.
Ashdown Forest, area of 14,000 acres, Sussex. Called by Londoners the ' poor man's Scotland.'
Ashes, THE, see CRICKET
Ashford, DAISY, author, when only 9, of a remarkably successful book, *The Young Visiters,* published 1919 with an introduction by J. M. Barrie.
Ashingdon, village, Essex (formerly Assandun), scene 1016 of Canute's defeat of Edmund Ironside.
Ashkelon, see ASCALON
Ashley-Cooper, ANTHONY, see SHAFTESBURY, LORD
Ashmole, ELIAS (1617–92), English scholar ; gave Oxford University a collection of antiques, some of which are now in the Ashmolean (*ash-mō'lēan*) Museum, built 1893–94.
Ashmolean Museum, see ASHMOLE, E.
Ashton-under-Lyne, Lancashire town noted for cotton-spinning, dyeing, bleaching, and hat-making ; pop. 52,000.
Ash Wednesday, see CALENDAR
Asia, continent ; area 17,206,000sq.m ; is over 5,300m N.–S. and 6,000m E.–W. ; has vast mt. ranges, e.g. Himalayas, Hindu Kush, Tien Shan, etc., and the immense Tibetan plateau over 12,000ft above sea-level. The deserts include the Arabian and Gobi (or Shamo). Great rivers include Yangtse and Hwangho (China) ; Ob, Yenisei and Lena flowing into the Arctic Ocean ; Ganges, Indus, Brahmaputra (India) ; Irrawaddy (Burma) ; also Mekong and Salween. The boundary between Asia and Europe comprises the Ural and Caucasus (moun-

tain ranges), also, the Caspian, Black and Mediterranean seas.

The chief countries include Afghanistan, Arabia, Burma, Ceylon, China, India, Iran, Iraq, Japan, Malaya, Pakistan, Palestine, Siam, Syria, Turkey, and part of USSR. The population of *c*.1,155,000,000 is largely Mongolian, though in India and Siberia it is mostly Aryan.

Asia Minor, name sometimes given to the W. of Asia occupied by Turkey in Asia or Anatolia.

asp, poisonous snake, usually a viper, found in S. Europe and N. Africa.

aspar′agus, plant used as a vegetable ; first grown in Britain in the 16th c. ; requires 5 years to mature.

Aspdin, JOSEPH, see CLAY

aspen, tree, usually 50–80ft high ; has grey bark and drooping oval leaves stirred by the slightest breeze.

asphalt, see BITUMEN ; PITCH ; TRINIDAD

asphodel, *as′fō-del,* garden plant with showy white or yellow flowers on an upright stem. Homer mentions an asphodel meadow in the underworld.

aspic, jelly often made from calves' feet.

Asquith, H. H., see OXFORD AND ASQUITH

ass, animal related to the horse and zebra ; has long ears and upright mane ; found wild in Asia and Africa. The domestic ass (or donkey) has been used in England as a beast of burden since the 16th c., and is widely used in Oriental countries. It is intelligent when treated kindly. Read G. K. Chesterton's poem, *The Donkey.*

assagai or **assegai,** spear used by some African tribes.

Assam, province of India, largely W. of Burma ; area 55,000sq.m ; pop. *c.* 10,200,000 ; has exceedingly heavy rainfall (over 425in a year). The chief river is the Brahmaputra. Assam produces silk and cotton, but is most famous for tea and rice. The people are mainly Hindu and Mohammedan ; cap. Shillong.

assassinate, to murder a notable person, usually for political reasons ; Lord Darnley (husband of Mary Queen of Scots), Henry IV of France, George Villiers (1st Duke of Buckingham) and Abraham Lincoln were assassinated. The assassination of the Archduke Francis Ferdinand at Serajevo was the immediate cause of World War I. Dr Dollfuss was assassinated 1934 ; Mahatma Gandhi 1948.

assaying, method of finding how pure a metal is, or how much metal is in the ore.

assets, term for (*a*) the possessions of a person or firm, (*b*) the property left by someone who has died after all debts have been paid; or (*c*) whatever possessions remain when someone is bankrupt.

Assisi, *äs-sē′zē,* town, Italy ; birthplace of St Francis (1182–1226).

Assistance Board, Government department which since 1940 has replaced the 1934 Unemployment Assistance Board. It pays unemployment allowances, and deals with Old Age Pensions and Widows' Pensions, etc.

assizes, visits of a High Court judge 2, 3, or 4 times yearly to a town or city (outside London) in England or Wales. Persons accused of minor offences may be tried by local magistrates ; more serious cases are taken to the assizes, legal institutions dating from the time of Edward I.

Association football, see FOOTBALL

assonance, see FIGURES OF SPEECH

Assur, see ASSYRIA

Assyria, ancient empire of Asia, now partly comprising Iraq ; began before 3000BC as a city-state (Assur). A highland region with rocks (from which stone was quarried in contrast to the mud bricks used in Babylonia) it had valleys where wheat and barley were grown. Here a warlike and powerful people became a nation, and built up an empire from the Persian Gulf to the Nile. Among its great rulers were Sargon II (722–705BC) and his son Sennacherib (705–681BC), great military leaders of armies with chariots, bowmen, battering-rams and iron weapons, the first used by large armies.

The cities included NINEVEH (N. of Assur) with walls 2½m along the R. Tigris, a great palace, and a remarkable system of government, also postal services, and libraries of clay tablets ; destroyed by the Chaldeans *c*.606BC

Assyût, *äs-yoot′,* town, Upper Egypt, *c.* 250m S. of Cairo ; noted for pottery ; is an important trade centre ; near it is a Nile barrage ; pop.60,000.

asterisk (Gk *asteriskos,* small star), sign used by printers thus * ; usually calls attention to a footnote.

Asteroids, see ASTRONOMY

astigmatism, see EYE

Astley, JACOB (1579–1652), Royalist who fought for Charles I at Edgehill. Before the battle he offered the famous prayer : *Lord, Thou knowest how busy I must be this day. If I forget Thee, do not forget me ;* then, more loudly : *March on, boys !*

Astor, WILLIAM WALDORF, 1st Viscount Astor (1848–1919), financier, came from New York to England ; made his home at Hever Castle, Kent. His son, WILLIAM WALDORF ASTOR, 2ND VISCOUNT ASTOR (1879–   ) was elected MP for Plymouth 1910. The 2nd Viscount's wife, VISCOUNTESS ASTOR (Nancy Witcher Astor), *b* Virginia, USA, was the first woman to sit in the British Parliament. She was elected MP for Plymouth 1919.

Astrakhan, *as-tra-kan′,* town on an island in the R. Volga, USSR, *c*.30m from the Caspian Sea ; noted for fisheries, and especially for caviare, i.e. the roe of sturgeon ; pop.260,000.

astrakhan, skin of the Persian lamb ; the short wool is usually dyed.

astrology, old-time belief that the stars

shaped human life, an idea still accepted by ignorant people and cranks, though even Shakespeare declared : *The fault, dear Brutus, is not in our stars, but in ourselves.* Astrologers divided the sky into 12 imaginary ' houses ' (the Zodiac) in order to foretell the future, a child's fortunes, it was thought, depending on the position of the sun, moon, planets, etc., at its birth. Such a diagram is termed a HOROSCOPE.

astronomy, science of the stars, planets, etc. ; shows that our Earth is only one of a family of worlds circling round the Sun, and that this Solar System (so big that the outermost planet is *c.*4,000,000,000m from the Sun) is nevertheless rather like a lonely swarm of gnats in a corner of a room as big as the Earth, since the universe of which we are a part comprises millions of stars at immense distances from one another. Yet all this is but one of a great number of universes. We consider here (*a*) the Stellar System (stars, nebulæ, etc.). (*b*) The Solar System.

(*a*) STELLAR SYSTEM : Our particular universe is apparently somewhat lens-shaped, with the Solar System some distance from the centre. When we look at the night sky we see the rim of this universe, crowded with stars, the so-called Milky Way or Galaxy, like a faint veil of light floating across the sky. This Galactic System is roughly 600,000,000,000,000,000m in diameter, and possibly 96,000,000,000,000,000m thick at the centre ; the total mass being probably *c.*160,000,000,000 times that of the Sun. Observed through a telescope, it resolves into myriads of stars and star-clusters, photographic examination suggesting a total of 50,000,000,000 ; but all this vastness is only one ' island universe ' in space. Other ' island universes,' e.g. the Andromeda nebula, *c.*5,400,000,000,000,000,000m distant, is thought to be as large as our Galactic System.

Owing to the rotation of the Earth, the stars, planets, Sun, Moon, etc., appear to travel E. to W., but the planets, because of their motion round the Sun, rise in a slightly different position each evening, and seem, therefore, to ' wander ' across the sky (Gk *planetes*, wandering). The so-called ' fixed stars ' keep relatively the same groupings ; hence, for example, the constellation of the Plough appears never to change its shape, though its stars are actually travelling at high speeds. They appear ' fixed ' only because they are so far from us.

Stellar distances being so great, astronomers are compelled to replace the mile as a unit of length by the ' light-year.' Light travels 186,300mps, i.e. 11,178,000m per minute, or 670,680,000 m per hour, or 6,000,000,000,000m per year (approx.). Astronomers speak of the distance of *Alpha Centauri* (our nearest neighbour in space, apart from the Solar System) as over 4 light-years; Sirius as 9 ; Vega 26, Capella 47, Betelgeuse 190, Rigel (18,000 times brighter than the Sun) over 540. Astronomers at Mt Wilson Observatory, California, noted, 1937, a new star (or star-cluster), *Nova Persei,* the light from which began its journey to the Earth 7,000,000 years ago.

Though the average size of a star seems to be about that of the Sun, millions are giants by comparison, e.g. Canopus has a diameter 180 times greater ; Betelgeuse is 24,000,000 times larger, having a diameter of 216,000,000m. *Alpha Herculis* is still greater, having a diameter of 346,000,000m, almost twice the size of the orbit described by the Earth in its annual journey round the Sun.

BINARIES, or double stars, have motions showing that they are linked by gravitational attraction, e.g. *Alpha Centauri, Epsilon Bootis* (Mira), also a bright star near Capella, proved by the spectroscope to be almost as large as our Solar System.

NEBULÆ are actually island universes, such as our Galactic Systems ; some are a vast mass of incandescent gas, and others have cooled sufficiently to break into separate worlds or star-clusters. Most nebulæ have apparently a spiral form, and the powerful telescopes at Mt Wilson Observatory can show about two million of them, all beyond the Milky Way, so distant that we measure them in units even greater than the light-year, namely megaparsecs. The parsec is 3¼ light-years, and the megaparsec a million parsecs.

See COMET ; EVOLUTION ; RELATIVITY ; SPECTROSCOPE

(*b*) SOLAR SYSTEM : the Sun and the group of planets travelling round it in almost circular paths. The system as a whole is travelling at 170mps towards Vega. The Sun, 1,300,000 times as large as the Earth, has a diameter of 886,000m ; surface area 2,280,000,000,000sq.m ; volume 339,300,000,000,000,000cu.m ; mass 1,998,000,000,000,000,000,000,000,000 tons. The average surface temperature may be *c.*6,000°C, a whirling furnace so fiercely hot that incandescent gas and molten matter send up flames 280,000m high, and every sq.ft radiates energy at the rate of 9,000hp. Dark spots on the surface—SUN-SPOTS—may be seen from time to time. These are actually immense funnels up which swirling gases, cooling as they approach the surface, are rushing from the interior. Some of the sun-spots are 40,000m across and there seems good reason to associate them with electrical storms and displays of Northern Lights on our planet, possibly due to the emission of electrically charged particles reaching the Earth's atmosphere. Of the Sun's total radiation, the Earth receives only one part in 2,200,000,000, but this amounts to almost 5,000,000hp for every sq.m of the Earth's surface. It has been estimated that the age of the Sun is probably 5,000,000,000,000 years.

Lord Kelvin supposed that the heat of the Sun was due to shrinkage, but modern scientists discount this theory as insufficient to explain its vast and prolonged radiation of energy. The answer is possibly that disruption of radioactive substances is continuously going on in the immense heat of the Sun's interior.

Round the Sun go the planets in their orbits (*a*) major planets, Mercury, Venus, Earth, Mars, Jupiter, Saturn, Uranus, Neptune, Pluto, (*b*) minor planets (or asteroids) and comets. The planets are :

(i) MERCURY, nearest the Sun ; has a mean orbital radius of 36,000,000m ; makes one complete revolution in 87 days ; diameter 3,100m. It is thought to be waterless and without air.

(ii) VENUS, mean distance from the Sun 67,000,000m ; completes its orbit in 224 days ; is about the size of the Earth, and similar in many ways. At its brightest it is the brightest planet in the sky. It has some atmosphere and much cloud.

(iii) EARTH, *c*.93,000,000m from the Sun ; travels 19mps as it speeds round the Sun (once in 365¼ days) ; area *c*.197,000,000sq.m. Prior to about 1930 the origin of the Earth and of the other planets could not be satisfactorily explained. The view generally held was that given by Sir James Jeans, namely, that long ago (possibly 5,000 million years ago) a star approached so close to the Sun that a vast tidal wave of incandescent matter was torn from it, and that out of this came lesser portions which, cooling and condensing, took the form of planets revolving round the parent. The most recent view is that the Solar System was not flung out of the Sun, but that at one time the Sun was one of two stars revolving round each other (that is, each was a binary), and that one of the stars exploded, its scattered fragments eventually becoming planets revolving round the star which remained—our Sun. This theory has none of the defects of the earlier one, and has already won general approval among modern astronomers.

(iv) MOON, our satellite, has a diameter of 2,163m as compared with the Earth's 7,926m. It takes one month to travel round the earth, and during its course changes from the crescent of the new moon to the complete circle of the full moon and then diminishes again. Its change of appearance is known as the phases of the moon. Its force of gravity is ⅙ that of the Earth, hence a boy who could jump 5ft here would easily leap 30ft on the Moon. It has been generally supposed that the Moon is without water and atmosphere, both having escaped into space long ago, though it has been suggested that there are possibly traces of vegetation, and this would imply the presence of both water and air. The surface of the Moon is a wilderness of mountains and plains, and appears to be crowded with ' craters.' We see only *one* side of the Moon, and this by reflected sunlight.

The Moon has much to do with our tides, its gravitational attraction piling up water on the Earth's surface. Since the Moon's average distance from the Earth is only *c*.250,000m, we may wonder (as Jules Verne and H. G. Wells did) if one day we shall find a means of reaching it in some kind of space-machine. Jet-propulsion brings this possibility much nearer, it would appear.

(v) MARS, mean distance from the Sun 142,000,000m ; has a year of 686 of our days ; diameter 4,230m ; appears red, hence the Romans named it after Mars, their god of war. There are two moons, Deimos and Phobos, both very small.

Mars brings to mind the fascinating question : Is there life beyond our Earth ? We do not know. Of the millions of stars, most seem either too hot or too cold to support life as we know it here, though a form of life might possibly exist on Venus or Mars. The Italian astronomer Schiaparelli thought, 1877, that he had discovered ' canals ' on Mars, and the theory was put forward that Mars, largely desert, had a race of intelligent beings who had built gigantic canals to bring water from the melting snow of the poles. The theory is intriguing, but careful examination of Mars gives no confirmation.

It should be noted, however, that very recently this question of life on other worlds has received new attention not only by astronomers but by biologists. The existence of life on Mars or any other of the planets in our Solar System is remotely possible though unlikely, but the new theory accounting for the creation of the Solar System makes it seem highly probable that there are many millions of millions of worlds revolving round their respective central suns, and since some of these may be presumed to have an adequate supply of heat and light, and also to be composed of elements including oxygen, hydrogen, carbon, nitrogen and phosphorus (the elements necessary for life) it seems reasonable to suppose, as do Fred Hoyle and C. D. Darlington, that living things of some kind may exist on a vast number of worlds beyond our own.

(vi) ASTEROIDS, *c*.44,000 very small worlds (the largest, Ceres, being 480m in diameter) moving in an orbit beyond that of Mars. Some of the asteroids are only 5m across, waifs of the Solar System.

(vii) JUPITER, the largest planet, mean distance from the Sun 483,000,000m, requires almost 12 Earth years to

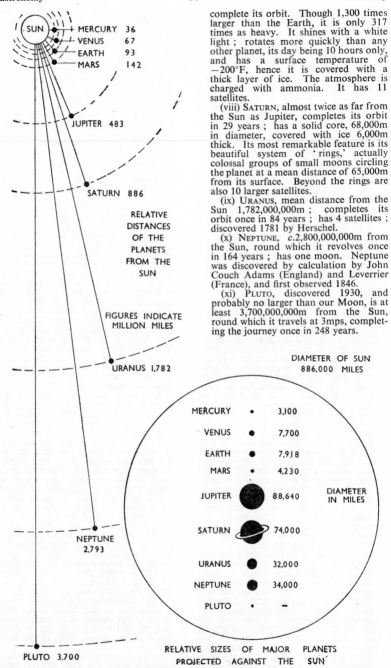

SUN

MERCURY 36
VENUS 67
EARTH 93
MARS 142

JUPITER 483

SATURN 886

RELATIVE
DISTANCES
OF THE
PLANETS
FROM THE
SUN

FIGURES INDICATE
MILLION MILES

URANUS 1,782

NEPTUNE
2,793

PLUTO 3,700

DIAMETER OF SUN
886,000 MILES

		DIAMETER IN MILES
MERCURY	•	3,100
VENUS	●	7,700
EARTH	●	7,918
MARS	•	4,230
JUPITER	●	88,640
SATURN	♄	74,000
URANUS	●	32,000
NEPTUNE	●	34,000
PLUTO	•	—

RELATIVE SIZES OF MAJOR PLANETS
PROJECTED AGAINST THE SUN

complete its orbit. Though 1,300 times larger than the Earth, it is only 317 times as heavy. It shines with a white light ; rotates more quickly than any other planet, its day being 10 hours only, and has a surface temperature of −200°F, hence it is covered with a thick layer of ice. The atmosphere is charged with ammonia. It has 11 satellites.

(viii) SATURN, almost twice as far from the Sun as Jupiter, completes its orbit in 29 years ; has a solid core, 68,000m in diameter, covered with ice 6,000m thick. Its most remarkable feature is its beautiful system of ' rings,' actually colossal groups of small moons circling the planet at a mean distance of 65,000m from its surface. Beyond the rings are also 10 larger satellites.

(ix) URANUS, mean distance from the Sun 1,782,000,000m ; completes its orbit once in 84 years ; has 4 satellites ; discovered 1781 by Herschel.

(x) NEPTUNE, c.2,800,000,000m from the Sun, round which it revolves once in 164 years ; has one moon. Neptune was discovered by calculation by John Couch Adams (England) and Leverrier (France), and first observed 1846.

(xi) PLUTO, discovered 1930, and probably no larger than our Moon, is at least 3,700,000,000m from the Sun, round which it travels at 3mps, completing the journey once in 248 years.

Astronomy (or, rather, astrology) was studied thousands of years ago, notably in Egypt, Assyria, India and China. It did not become a science till Nicolaus Copernicus (a Pole *b* 1473) showed that the Sun and stars did *not* (as was commonly supposed) revolve round the Earth. Johann Kepler, a German astronomer *b* 1571, first gave us the laws governing the motions of the planets. Galileo, *b* Pisa 1564, invented the astronomical telescope. The young Lancashire curate Jeremiah Horrocks, using a home-made instrument, 1639, was the first to observe the transit of Venus, i.e. the passing of that planet across the Sun. John Flamsteed (born near Derby 1646) was our first Astronomer Royal at Greenwich Observatory.

Since the days of Sir Frederick William Herschel (1738–1822) great progress has been made. More powerful telescopes are now used ; the spectroscope and camera have brought about tremendous advances in the hands of astronomers, such as Sir William Huggins, Sir Arthur Eddington, Sir James Jeans, Dr Shapley of America, and Sir H. Spencer Jones, whose *Worlds Without End* makes fascinating reading.

ASTROPHYSICS (i.e. the study of the composition of stars) has made great advances recently. Surprising though it may be, our rapidly increasing knowledge of nuclear physics has enabled scientists to solve many astronomical problems. The latest theories (e.g. those of Dr Fred Hoyle, Lecturer in Mathematics at Cambridge) provide us with explanations of the atomic nature of stars, nebulæ and interstellar space, and of the mechanics of the universe, grander and more reasoned in conception than any previously put forward. It seems that the hydrogen atom is the basis of all matter ; and Hoyle's most startling theory is that of 'continuous creation'—the perpetual appearance in space of atoms emerging from nothing.

Read *The Nature of the Universe*, Hoyle.

Asuncion, *ä-soon'si-on,* cap. and port of Paraguay ; pop.120,000.

Aswan, frontier town, at the first cataract on the Nile, Upper Egypt. Near by are famous ruins ; also the Great Nile Barrage (dam), 3m S.

Atahualpa, *ata-wal'pa* (1495–1533), last of the Inca rulers of Peru.

Atalanta, in old Greek tales, a maiden who declared she would marry only the man who could outrun her. Many young men tried, but she outstripped all until Milanion rolled 3 golden apples along the course. Atalanta delayed to pick them up, and thus lost the race.

Ataturk, KEMAL, see KEMAL ATATURK

ATC, see YOUTH ORGANISATIONS

atebrin, see MOSQUITO

Athelney, ISLE OF, area between the Rs. Tone and Parret (Somerset), where King Alfred hid from the Danes 878.

Athelstan (*d* 940), called the first King of the English ; grandson of Alfred the Great ; crowned at Kingston, Surrey ; defeated his rivals at Brunanburh 937.

Athena, *ä-thē'na,* one of the chief goddesses of old Greek tales ; known to the Romans as Minerva ; sometimes called Pallas or Pallas Athene ; associated with war, but was above all the goddess of wisdom.

Athens, cap. of Greece, with a harbour at Piraeus 4m away ; a great railway and business centre, with fine modern buildings, also famous ruins of ancient temples, etc., notably on the Acropolis (see ACROPOLIS) ; associated with Aristides, Pericles, Themistocles ; destroyed by Xerxes 480BC ; submitted to Alexander the Great 335BC ; a home of learning for over 2,500 years ; pop.481,000.

Said to be named after the goddess Athena, Athens began as a small state, later becoming a democracy. The Athenians took a leading part in the defeat of the Persians 490 and 480BC, and the triumphs inspired them to build anew and better, hence the so-called age of Pericles (say from 440BC), when the grandeur of the thriving city was the wonder of the world, and the fair perfection of the Acropolis buildings was untouched by the hand of time. War between Athens and Sparta continued from 431 to 371BC, the Athenians being defeated. Further humbled by the Macedonians (322BC), Athens came under Roman sway *c.*146BC.

Great Athenians were Solon, Themistocles, Aeschylus, Sophocles, Euripides, Thucydides, Plato, Socrates and Demosthenes.

athletics, physical exercises, vigorous games and racing. The ancient Greeks organised festivals at Olympia every four years from *c.*800BC, and the idea was revived 1896. Since 1901 the Amateur Athletic Association has arranged athletic meetings in Britain in co-operation with universities and schools.

Atlanta, cap., Georgia, USA; pop.302,000 ; is a great railway centre.

Atlantic Charter, joint declaration (Aug 1941) by Britain and USA of principles of their national policies on which they based their hopes of a better future. Drawn up by President Roosevelt and Winston Churchill, Prime Minister of Britain, the Charter declared that their countries sought no territorial gains ; wished to see no territorial changes against the wishes of the peoples concerned ; respected the right of all peoples to choose the form of government they thought best, and to see the right of self-government restored to those countries which had been deprived of it ; would endeavour to enable all nations, great and small, victor or vanquished, to enjoy equal opportunities for trade etc. ; desired to bring all nations into an era of improved labour conditions, economic advancement, and social security ; to establish (after destroying Nazi tyranny) a peace enabling all nations to dwell in safety and to enjoy freedom from fear and want ; to keep the high seas safe for all ; and lastly to strive to abolish armaments.

From this historic Charter sprang not only new hopes for war-stricken nations, but all the energies detailed under UNO. See UNO

Atlantic City, holiday resort, New Jersey, USA ; pop.64,000.

Atlantic Ocean, area c.31,530,000sq.m ; greatest depth yet found Porto Rico Deep, 30,143ft. No doubt crossed by the Norsemen, the first recorded crossing was that of Columbus 1492 ; the first crossing under steam power was made by the *Sirius* and *Great Western* 1838 ; the first successful Atlantic cable was laid 1866 ; the first Atlantic flights were made 1919 ; first crossed by pilotless plane 1947.

Atlantic Pact, see NORTH ATLANTIC PACT

Atlantis, island said by Plato to have been in the Atlantic Ocean (perhaps not far from Gibraltar) till it vanished in a day and a night.

Bacon's *New Atlantis* describes a perfect commonwealth.

Atlas, in old Greek tales, a giant who rebelled against Zeus. As punishment he was made to support the earth on his shoulders.

Atlas Mountains, range extending 1,500m in NW. Africa.

atmosphere, ' ocean ' of air, possibly 500m deep, above the surface of the earth. Dry air is composed by weight of 75·5% nitrogen, 23·2% oxygen ; 1·8% argon ; *circa* 0·05% carbon dioxide ; 0·028% krypton ; 0·005% xenon ; 0·00086% neon ; 0·000056% helium ; variable amount of water vapour, say 0·5%. The probable total weight of the atmosphere is c.4,000,000,000,000,000 tons ; the normal pressure (at sea level) is approx. 14·8lb per sq.in ; i.e. the weight of the air is enough to support a column of mercury 30in or 76cm high, or a column of water 34ft high. See BAROMETER

Air in motion becomes WIND. The 2 general principles at work are (a) warm air expands, becomes lighter, and rises, being pushed up by the colder air ; (b) the E. rotation of the earth causes deflection, i.e. winds *from* the equator are deflected towards the E., winds *to* the equator towards the W. There is a belt of high pressure in the neighbourhood of lat. 30°N and 30°S, giving us 4 chief world systems of air currents (see diagram). From latitudes 30°N and 30°S approx., cool air blows towards the equator. This air flows from regions where the rotating earth is moving c.900mph, and travels at ground level towards a region where the speed is c.1,000mph. Air from, say, the N., lags behind the quicker-moving

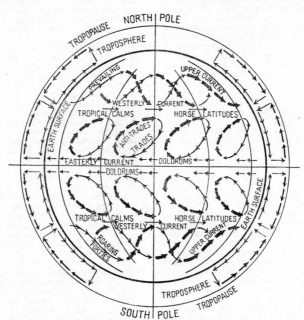

Diagram of theoretical atmosphere circulation in the absence of continents and mountain ranges. The upper winds are indicated by thicker arrows.

FRUIT FARMING   *plate 5*

A 2½ h.p. tractor at work on an English market garden.   (*The Farmer and Stockbreeder*)

plate 6   FRUIT GROWING

Top : A grape-harvest scene near Kimberley. *Bottom :* Citrus-groves in the Northern
Transvaal.   (Both *South African Railways and Harbours*)

BANANAS AND APPLES

plate 7

Top : The ripening fruit in a banana plantation, Puerto Rico, West Indies. (*Lotte Jay-Pix*).
Bottom : Fruit must be graded before sale. These Canadian girls are grading apples.
(*Fox Photos Ltd*)

plate 8 PINEAPPLES

Top : Removing the crowns and butts from ripe pineapples on a Hawaii plantation. (*E.N.A.*).
Bottom : Much canned pineapple comes from Malaya. Here a Chinese worker is slicing out the eyes of the fruit. (*C.O.I.*)

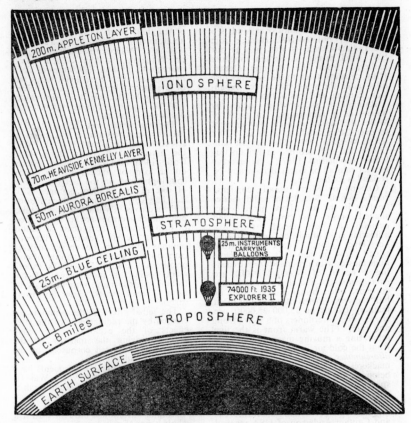

Diagram of the atmospheric layers above the earth's surface

earth, and, relative to the earth's surface, travels to the W., thus becoming a NE. wind ; a similar wind from the S. becomes a SE. wind. These are the persistent trades, i.e. steady breezes once of great value to sailing ships.

Farther from the equator (lat. 30°N or S) are warm winds travelling towards the poles. These travel to a region rotating less quickly, and thus gain upon the earth, and are deflected relative to the earth's surface so as to become a SW. wind N. of the equator, a NW. wind S. of the equator. These are the *prevailing westerlies* that blow so frequently across Britain.

Many factors cause variations in these great general air currents, notably the size and relief of land masses. Land becomes warm more quickly than water, therefore during the day the air above the land rises, and a cool wind blows *from* the sea *to* the land, giving us sea-breezes by day ; at night, as water does not cool as quickly as land, cool winds blow *from* the land *to* the sea.

On a larger scale this principle is responsible for the MONSOONS that are of vital importance in India. From Oct. to Apr. Central Asia is intensely cold, hence cold air flows S., is deflected W. by the rotation of the earth, and becomes a steady NE. wind ; from Apr. to Oct. Central Asia is intensely hot, giving rise to a SW. wind blowing towards that region from the Indian Ocean ; it is this wind (the SW. monsoon) which carries 60–90 % of India's rainfall.

The cause of RAIN is evaporation. Water evaporates into the air as invisible water vapour ; and as air is almost always in motion, this vapour is carried long distances. Air at, say, 45°F cannot hold more than 1 % water vapour by weight ; air at 62·5°F may hold 2 %. If, then, air at 62·5°F rises and in consequence expands and becomes cooler, it cannot hold all its moisture

3

hence some falls as rain after appearing first as cloud. The NE. monsoon travelling almost wholly over land is a dry wind ; but the SW., coming from the Indian Ocean, is wet, just as our SW. wind brings to Britain moisture gathered from the Atlantic Ocean. Hilly districts tend to be wet because hills make the wind rise, hence expansion, cooling, and loss of moisture.

Rainfall is measured in inches by means of a rain-gauge. In parts of Wales the annual rainfall may amount to over 246in, while as little as 9·29in fell at Margate 1921. The greatest rainfall in one day recorded in Britain was 9·56in (Somerset) 1917 ; the average annual rainfall of Great Britain and N. Ireland is c.42in.

CLOUDS or MISTS usually condense round minute particles of solid matter floating in the air. Low, great dome-shaped masses of cloud are called *cumulus*, i.e. ' heap ' clouds ; those like a floating layer of mist or fog are *stratus*, i.e. ' layer ' clouds ; dark clouds from which snow or rain falls are *nimbus* ; huge masses with a rounded form (reaching a height of 10,000–25,000ft) are *cumulo-nimbus*, and have strong up-currents, often bringing heavy rain or hail showers. Wisps of white and often feathery clouds at 25,000–35,000ft are *cirrus*, often forerunners of a warm front and rain. (The warm front is the line separating a moving mass of warm air from the cold air it is displacing.) The *alto-cumulus* is commonly called a mackerel sky. Both winds and clouds belong to the lower regions of the atmosphere (troposphere) ; but c.8m up is the *stratosphere*, where the temperature is c.–50°F. Professor Piccard pioneered into this region 1931, and Captain Stevens and Captain Anderson of USA reached 72,395ft in *Explorer II*, 1935. Balloons carrying instruments only have reached 25m, where ultra-violet rays from the sun change most of the oxygen in the atmosphere to ozone, thus making a kind of blue ceiling. Above 50m the aurora borealis may form like the glow of an X-ray tube. Higher still is the Heaviside-Kennelly layer of ionised air-molecules ; this reflects radio waves, and thus prevents them going off into space and being lost (see RADIO), though the Appleton layer, still higher (c.150m by day, but lower at night), also affects radio waves, and accounts for better transmission after dark.

The intense cold and the low density of the upper atmosphere are prime factors in aviation, requiring high-flying planes to be equipped with ' pressurised ' and heated cabins. See CLIMATE

Read *Weather Study*, David Brunt, and *The Weather*, George Kimble and Raymond Bush.

atoll, see CORAL

atom, see ELEMENT ; H-BOMB ; MATTER ; RADIOACTIVITY ; VALENCY

atom bomb, wholly new type of high explosive, first used in warfare on 6 Aug 1945 when a US plane dropped an atom bomb on Hiroshima, a Japanese war base. A second bomb was dropped on Nagasaki, 9 Aug. Each bomb, more powerful than 20,000 tons of TNT, had a blast effect over 2,000 times that of the largest bomb ever used before. The two bombs, small in size, killed c.70,000 Japanese, injured 120,000, and destroyed both cities.

The new bomb was the result of intensive research by British and American scientists during World War II. With the assistance of Niels Bohr, Mme Curie-Joliot, etc., various teams worked out a form of nuclear fission (atom-splitting) based on the fact that fission of one of the uranium isotopes U235 may be secured by bombarding its atoms with neutrons. When this fission takes place more neutrons are set free ; these in turn continue the process of fission, and this ' chain reaction ' liberates millions of times the energy derived from burning the same quantity of coal or oil. At a cost of £500,000,000 experiments resulted in finding a way of controlling this enormous output, partly by using ' heavy water,' later by using carbon.

The lethal effect of the bomb is increased by the radioactivity of the after effects of the explosion, radioactive rays destroying the marrow of the bones where the red corpuscles of the blood are made.

Various atom bomb experiments have been carried out since World War II, e.g. the explosion, 1946, of atom-bomb 5, which succeeded in wrecking large naval vessels in the Pacific. See BIKINI

Atomic warfare has brought with it a whole series of world problems. Armed with such weapons (against which no defence has been devised) a nation might now destroy an enemy in a matter of hours, and the annihilation of civilisation, or a major part of it, is not merely probable but indeed certain unless (a) some adequate defence is found, or (b) the outlawing of atomic warfare can be guaranteed. The atom bomb brings mankind face to face with the fact that science has outstripped moral progress, and that if civilisation is to continue it must be based on the principle of mutual understanding among nations. Governments and committees are now striving to establish world security, but security can never be attained in a world where such gigantic forces of destruction can be let loose unless fear, suspicion and aggression are replaced by a universal and sincere application of Christian principles to individual and national life. See WORLD WAR II and Plates 46, 47

Read John Hersey's book *Hiroshima*.

atomic numbers, see ELEMENT

atomic pile, apparatus for producing a variety of radioactive isotopes. One type comprises a mass of some hundreds of tons of graphite into which bars of uranium metal are inserted. Cold air is blown through the pile, and the whole is surrounded by more graphite and by layers of steel and concrete to absorb escaping neutrons, all injurious to life. Such a pile is at the Clinton Laboratories, Tennessee, USA, where isotopes are produced, and a still more powerful pile (heavy water) is at Chalk River, Ontario, Canada. There is a pile at Hanford (USA), and another, which is named ZOË, at Fort Chantillon, near Paris.

Britain's first atomic energy plant was at Harwell. This has been operating since August 1948, and one of its nuclear piles produces over 10^{17} neutrons per second. The first pile built at Harwell was nicknamed GLEEP, i.e. graphite low energy experimental pile, its uranium providing neutrons from the fission of U235. The second pile (BEPO) was designed to develop a higher intensity of radiation, and is air-cooled. See also ATOM BOMB ; HARWELL ; SELLAFIELD

Atomic Theory, see MATTER
atomic warfare, see ATOM BOMB
atomic weight, see ELEMENT
Atropos, see FATES
ATS, see WOMEN'S ROYAL ARMY CORPS
attainder, in feudal and later times disinheritance. A person found guilty of treason was attainted, i.e. his heirs could not inherit his property.
At'tica, state of ancient Greece, having Boeotia to the N. and the Aegean Sea on the E. The capital of the territory was Athens. Modern Attica is a department of Greece.
At'tila (d AD453), King of the Huns ; conquered much of Europe, reaching the gates of Rome.
Attlee, CLEMENT RICHARD (1883–   ), British statesman ; Labour MP 1922 ; Leader of the Opposition 1935–40 ; Prime Minister from 1945, carrying out a programme devised by his party, and showing energetic statesmanship in solving the Indian dilemma. He continued as Prime Minister after the General Election of 1950, though with a perilously small majority. In Dec. 1950 he flew to America for talks with President Truman ; and (1951) secured the nationalisation of Iron and Steel.
attorney, a-těr'ni, in English law, one who acts for others, his work being similar to that of a solicitor. The Attorney-General, the chief lawyer, is a member of the government.
Power of Attorney is the authority given by A to B to do business on A's behalf, usually during his absence or inability for health reasons to do it for himself. In America legal practitioners are still called attorneys. See SOLICITOR
Au, chemical symbol for gold, from the Latin, *aurum.*
AU, see ANGSTRÖM UNIT
Auckland, largest city, NZ ; capital of the

province of Auckland (N. Island) ; has a fine harbour and much shipping ; manufactures glass etc. ; has shipyards and sugar refineries ; pop.264,000.
auctioneer, one licensed to sell goods or property to the highest bidder.
Auden, WYSTAN HUGH, *aw'den* (1907–   ), English poet now an American citizen ; has written satiric and lyric poems, many of them obscure, and has evolved a technique which has influenced modern drama. See CHAUCER
audit, see ACCOUNTANCY
audition, trial or rehearsal to discover if a person speaks or sings sufficiently well to be allowed to broadcast or take part in some play, film, or similar production.
auditor, in Britain, one who examines accounts to see if they are correct. For information regarding auditing as a career write : British Association of Accountants and Auditors, 7 Union Court, Old Broad Street, London, E.C.2
Augsburg, *owks'bur*ch, city, Bavaria (Germany) ; pop.186,000.
Augustine, *au-gust'in* (AD354–430), saint ; born near Tunis, N. Africa. His mother, Monica, a devout Christian, influenced his life for good. He was a professor at Carthage, Rome and Milan, but at 32 was converted to Christianity, and after studying the Bible became Bishop of Hippo (N. Africa) 395. He taught men to trust God and to do good ; preached powerful sermons ; wrote many books, among them one explaining the *Psalms* ; but his most famous books are his *Confessions* and *The City of God.* He had subsequently a great influence on Luther and Calvin, and thus on the Reformation.
Augustine (d c.604), saint, known as the Apostle of the English. He was prior of a monastery in Rome till 597, when Pope Gregory I sent him (with 40 monks) as a missionary to convert the Angles to Christianity. Received by Ethelbert, King of Kent, whose wife, Bertha, was a Christian, Augustine became the first Archbishop of Canterbury 601.
Augustinians, see MONKS AND NUNS
Augustus (63BC–AD14), known as Gaius Octavius, later as Gaius Julius Caesar Octavianus or Octavian, 1st emperor of Rome, was the adopted son and heir of Julius Caesar ; became supreme in the Roman world when only 33, having defeated Mark Antony, his rival, in the naval battle of Actium, 31BC ; ruled wisely for over 40 years ; had immense power but took care not to abuse it ; was styled *Imperator,* that is, emperor, though he avoided using the title.

Though actually a dictator, Augustus lived only to make the Roman empire prosperous and united, and it was due to him that the Roman world enjoyed the *Pax Romana,* i.e. the Roman peace, of which it was in need after long years of warfare. He gave his name to the month *Sextilis,* now our month of August ; reorganised the senate ; saw

AUGUSTUS CAESAR 63 B.C.–14 A.D.

that the provinces of the empire were governed by well-chosen administrators; improved the city of Rome, so that of him it was said, *He found it of brick and left it of marble.* Great writers flourished in his day (the Augustan Age), among them Virgil, Horace, Ovid and Livy.

auk, name of two seabirds (*a*) little auk, which visits the coast of Scotland in winter, (*b*) great auk, once found from the Bay of Biscay to Greenland, now extinct, the last being killed 1844. The great auk was as large as a goose, but unable to fly.

'Auld Lang Syne,' *lang sīn,* song written by Robert Burns 1789 ; the words mean *the days of long ago.*

Auld Reekie, name for Edinburgh, ' reek ' being the smoke from chimneys in the old part of the city.

Aurelian, *au-rē'li-an* (murdered AD275), peasant's son who became emperor of Rome AD270 ; known as *Restitutor Orbis* because of his attempts to prevent the empire crumbling ; persecuted Christians.

aureole, *au'rē-ōl,* light or radiance about figures of Christ and saints as shown in paintings ; a circle or ring round or above the head only is a nimbus or halo.

auricle, see BLOOD

Auriol, VINCENT (1886–   ), first Socialist to become President of the French Republic (1947).

aurochs, *au'roks,* huge European wild ox ; had large horns ; extinct since the 17th c. ; some breeds of domestic cattle are descendants, e.g. Chillingham.

Aurora, *au-rō'rä,* Latin name for Eos, Greek goddess of the dawn.

auro'ra borealis or **northern lights,** *-bō-rē-āl'is,* patches of light, quivering beams, or immense ' curtains ' with swaying folds appearing in the night sky ; may be white, red, yellow, green, violet. Usually from 70 to 100m above the earth, the aurora is often seen in Scotland, but more frequently in Arctic regions or (as *aurora Australis*) in the Antarctic. The apparent cause is ionisation of the stratosphere by electromagnetic waves. The lights are in some way associated with sun-spots. The same effect is produced artificially in neon tubes when a rarefied gas is subjected to high voltage. See PLATE IV (*top*)

Austen, JANE (1775–1817), author, born in the rectory, Steventon, Hampshire. Of her novels *Pride and Prejudice* (1797) is perhaps the best and most widely read ; others are *Sense and Sensibility, Northanger Abbey, Mansfield Park* and *Emma.* In all the author reveals a sly sense of humour. Exciting incidents are rare, but the characters are intensely alive.

Austerlitz, town in Czechoslovakia, the scene of Napoleon's victory 1805 over the Austrians and Russians, after he had given up his plan of invading Britain.

Australasia, collective name for Australia, NZ, and islands near by ; sometimes also includes the Malay archipelago, Philippines, etc.

Australia, continent (sometimes regarded as the world's largest island) and British commonwealth, 2,500m E.–W., about 2,000m N.–S. ; area 2,974,581sq.m ; coastline over 12,000m.

Australia is mostly a plateau (parts of which are below sea-level) rising towards the coast, though the highest mt. peak (Mount Kosciusko, New South Wales) is only 7,328ft. There are few large rivers, the Murray, with its tributaries, Darling and Murrumbidgee, being the chief. Much of the interior is desert, notably in the W., with sand, stones, scrub (i.e. spinifex, a wiry grass, and mulga) ; salt lakes ; rainfall (except in the SW., extreme N., E., and SE.) is scanty, and attempts to make provision for periods of drought have led to the sinking of artesian wells, and to huge irrigation undertakings, e.g. the reservoirs in New S. Wales.

Long ago separated from Asia, the country is particularly interesting for its animals and plants, many of which are peculiar to Australia, e.g. kangaroo, dingo, platypus, cassowary, kiwi among animals and birds, eucalyptus and acacia among plants. Of pests menacing farming the chief are the rabbit and dingo. The rapid growth of prickly pear threatened to eliminate farming till the caterpillar of a moth which blights it (cactoblastis) was introduced c.1925.

Australia has more sheep than any other country, also great herds of cattle ; its agricultural exports include butter, meat, wool, fruits, wheat, wines, tallow, hides, honey, cane sugar, etc. ; its mineral resources include gold, silver, copper, zinc, iron, coal, and also antimony, tin, magnesite, etc. Synthetic ammonia is now manufactured on a large scale, two plants being in New S. Wales. Uranium deposits in the neighbourhood of the Flinders Range are being prospected. A new goldfield was discovered 1948 in Northern Territory.

The climate is healthy. The seasons are opposite to those of Britain. The native pop. (now *c*.50,000) live much as in the Stone Age, have no permanent dwellings, and are without any knowledge of cultivation of the land, but are remarkable for their keen eyesight and their powers of ' tracking.'

The continent is now divided into 6 states, exclusive of 2 territories (Northern and Capital), namely New S. Wales, Victoria, Queensland, S. Australia, W. Australia and Tasmania, an island S. of Bass Strait. The chief towns are Canberra (federal cap.), Sydney, Melbourne, Adelaide, Brisbane and Perth. The pop. of Australia is *c*.7,500,000.

De Torres, a Portuguese, was the first European to sight Australia 1605 ; the Dutch navigator Tasman discovered Tasmania 1642, and the English navigator William Dampier landed in Australia 1688 ; but it was not till Captain Cook landed at Botany Bay 1770 that Australia was actually placed on the map. Colonisation began with a convict settlement at Sydney. The ' Gold Rush ' 1851 took many thousands to the Melbourne area. Federation of the 6 states dates from 1901, when the first Parliament met. Today the Commonwealth is governed by a Governor-General, Prime Minister, and a Federal Parliament with a Senate of 36 members (6 from each state), and a House of Representatives.

Australia rendered magnificent service in World War II, mustering over 578,000 men and women, suffering 95,746 casualties. The discovery of paludrine (an anti-malarial drug) was made by the Australian Army Medical Service.

In December 1949 Australia's Labour Government was defeated at the General Election, Robert Gordon Menzies, a former Prime Minister and leader of the Liberal Party, forming a Government which dealt severely with Communists.

Read *Australia*, D. S. Anderson (Nelson) ; *Cobbers*, T. Wood ; *Waltzing Matilda*, A. L. Haskell.

Australia Day or **Wattle Day**, 26 Jan., i.e. the anniversary of the founding of Sydney.

Austria, central European country straddling the R. Danube between Germany and Hungary ; capital Vienna ; pop. *c*.7,000,000. Austria produces cereals, potatoes, sugar-beet, etc. Mountainous districts produce cattle and timber. Other products include coal, salt, and electricity from water-power.

Before 1918 Austria was a great empire, containing speakers of German (the modern Austrians), Czech, Slovak, Serbe-Croat, Magyar, and other languages. Starting as a *mark* or border district on the Danube, it became a duchy in 1156, and later included the territories of modern Hungary, Czechoslovakia, Yugoslavia and Albania ; also Transyl-vania, Galicia and Bukovina (now parts of Rumania, Poland and Russia). During the 16th and 17th c., most of Hungary and parts of Yugoslavia were occupied, ruled and devastated by the Turks. During the 18th c., the whole territory was ruled by the Austrian Hapsburgs as Holy Roman Emperors ; after 1804 as Emperors of Austria. In 1867 Hungary, which had retained its own parliament, became more independent, and until 1918 the Empire was known as the Dual Monarchy of Austria and Hungary, or Austria-Hungary for short.

In 1914 Austria fought beside Germany against Russia and Italy. In 1918 the Empire collapsed. Czechoslovakia, Hungary, Yugoslavia, etc., declared themselves independent. The peoples of these states were Magyars (Hungarians), Czechs, Slovaks, Croats, Slovenes, Serbs; other areas, populated mainly by Germans, continued after 1918 as Austria, and became a democratic republic. The new Austria was far from wealthy and encountered many difficulties. In 1934, Dollfuss became dictator in Austria after overthrowing the democratic constitution, but was murdered soon afterwards by German and Austrian Nazis. Schuschnigg, the next dictator, bravely but unsuccessfully resisted Hitler, who in 1938 invaded Austria and made it part of Germany. Without Austria Hitler could not have mastered Czechoslovakia nearly so easily as he did. After World War II, Austria became in name once more an independent republic, but for a time was occupied jointly by Russia, the USA, Britain and France. This hampered its recovery.

Famous Austrians include Andreas Hofer, Haydn, Mozart, Mendel, Freud.

Austrian Succession, WAR OF, began when the Emperor Charles VI of Austria *d* 1740, leaving his possessions to his daughter Maria Theresa. Charles Albert of Bavaria proclaimed himself Emperor, and Frederick (afterwards Frederick the Great) of Prussia took Silesia, a part of Austria. France and Spain supported Charles Albert and Frederick, but Britain stood by Maria Theresa.

Thus we found ourselves at war with France and Spain. The British (1743) fought the French at Dettingen, Bavaria, being led to victory by George II, the last time a king of Britain actually fought in battle, but they were defeated by the French at Fontenoy, 1745, though at sea they secured two victories off Cape Finisterre, one by Admiral Anson 1747, the other by Hawke, 1748. The war ended with the peace of Aix-la-Chapelle 1748, by which Prussia retained Silesia ; but the agreement proved unsatisfactory, and the Seven Years' War began in 1756.

Authorised Version, see BIBLE

autobahnen, see GERMANY

autobiography, story of your life written by yourself. Sometimes the writer weaves fancy into the facts, as Charles Dickens did in his partly autobiographical novel or story *David Copperfield.*

auto-da-fé, *ä-oo'tō dä-fä,* service attended by heretics condemned to death by the Spanish Inquisition ; also the public burning of heretics. The first auto-da-fé took place in Spain 1481 ; the last 1813.

autogyro, see AVIATION ; HELICOPTER

autumn, see SEASONS

Auvergne, *ōver'ny',* former province of S. France.

AV, see BIBLE

avalanche, *av'a-lanch,* fall of loose snow, ice and rock from a mountain into a valley, especially among the Alps. Such a fall has often destroyed a village.

Avebury, *āv'bĕri ; ā'bĕr-i,* prehistoric stone circle, Wiltshire ; may be compared with Stonehenge.

Avebury, LORD, *ā'bĕr-i* (1834–1913), known earlier as Sir John Lubbock, *b* London ; banker, scientist and MP ; persuaded Parliament to pass the Bank Holidays Act 1871, ensuring a number of holidays a year for working people ; also the Shop Hours Act 1881 regulating the working hours of shop assistants ; wrote *Ants, Bees, and Wasps* ; *The Pleasures of Life,* etc.

Ave Maria, *ä've mä-rē'ä,* Latin for Hail, Mary ! See BEADS

av'ens, name of two British plants (*a*) common avens or herb bennet, with flowers similar to those of the buttercup, (*b*) water avens, with purple and orange flowers.

'Avesta,' see ZEND-AVESTA

aviation (Lat. *avis,* bird), human flight by means of various types of aircraft. These types may be grouped :

the possibilities of flight ; and the famous Italian artist Leonardo da Vinci (*d* 1519) not only knew something of the air-screw, but came very near to designing a helicopter.

Aviation may be said to have begun when balloons were used as a means of transport. The Chinese are thought to have had balloons as early as the 14th c., but European experiments date from *c.*1783, when the brothers Stephen and Joseph Montgolfier, Frenchmen, released a balloon which reached 500ft, travelled 5 miles, and had two passengers. At first the Montgolfier brothers imagined that balloons rose because they were filled with smoke, only later discovering that the actual cause was due to the presence of hot air. The fundamental hydrostatic principle is that if the weight of the envelope etc., and the gas inside (either hot air, hydrogen or helium) be less than the weight of an equal volume of the normal surrounding air, the balloon will rise till it reaches a point where its total weight equals the weight of air (at that height) which it displaces.

From *c.*1850 ballooning became the subject of much experiment in Europe and USA, and as early as 1852 Henry Giffard added to the undercarriage a 4hp steam engine so that while the balloon lifted him above the earth the engine propelled him in a given direction. By 1884 Captain Charles Renard had improved on the more-or-less spherical envelope by building a streamlined airship which was electrically driven. The rubber envelope of the first balloons and airships was replaced by an aluminum outer cover (1897), hence the rigid type of airship ; and a series of successful

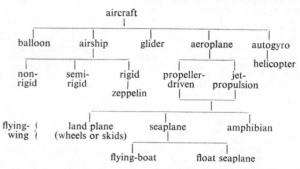

aircraft

| balloon | airship | glider | aeroplane | autogyro |

helicopter

| non-rigid | semi-rigid | rigid | propeller-driven | jet-propulsion |

zeppelin

| flying-wing | land plane (wheels or skids) | seaplane | amphibian |

flying-boat float seaplane

(1) *balloons and airships* : The story of man's conquest of the air, one of the most thrilling in history, may be said to have sprung from his envy of the birds. Thus, the Psalmist long ago sighed : *O that I had wings like a dove, for then would I fly* ; and in *The Arabian Nights* we read of the giant roc which carried Sinbad over sea and land. In the 13th c. Roger Bacon had some knowledge of

experiments by Count Zeppelin (1838–1917), whose workshops were near L. Constance, led to Germany building huge airships filled with hydrogen. During World War I these immense aircraft were much used for night bombing.

The British airship R34, which made a trans-Atlantic flight 1919, was 643ft long, 90ft from keel to top, and weighed 59 tons when loaded. The world's largest airship, R38, built at Cardington, Bedfordshire, contained 2,700,000cu.ft of gas, was 695ft long, and was driven by 6 Sunbeam Cossack 350hp engines. She crashed over the Humber 1921, only 5 of her crew of 49 being saved. Roald Amundsen flew over the N. Pole (1926) in the airship *Norge*, and (1929) the German *Graf Zeppelin* flew round the world in 21 days. The British R101 fell in flames in France (1930) while on her way to India.

Though the building and navigation of huge airships had been brought to a high degree of perfection by 1930, it became increasingly obvious that such craft were difficult to handle, expensive to moor, comparatively slow, and (unless filled with helium) liable to catch fire. Development ceased *c.*1933, aircraft builders concentrating on the development of heavier-than-air machines.

Note, however, that ballooning is not altogether discounted even now. Small balloons fitted with automatic self-recording apparatus are sent up for weather study and for investigation of the stratosphere ; and scientists have made notable ascents in recent years, especially in connection with the study of cosmic rays, e.g. Professor Piccard, who reached an altitude of over 54,000ft, 1931, and Captains Stevens and Anderson of the USA Air Corps, who (1935) reached a height of 72,395ft (over 13½m) in *Explorer II*.

(II) *aeroplanes* : It should be noted that progress in mechanical flight was long delayed because (*a*) the principles were not understood, (*b*) even when much theoretical knowledge had been gained there were no means of propelling a heavier-than-air machine at sufficiently high speed. Steam and electricity were tried, but the size and weight of such power-units were wholly out of proportion to the speed attained. Sir George Caley, a Yorkshire squire, was far ahead of his times (the early 19th c.) in his knowledge of streamlining, steering and surface pressures, and Lilienthal in Germany, Sir Hiram Maxim in USA, and others, made useful experiments, thus greatly advancing the science of aeronautics. But it was the brothers Wilbur and Orville Wright of Dayton, Ohio, who, realising that the petrol engine was the ideal source of power, built the first heavier-than-air machine to make a sustained flight with a passenger. That historic achievement, the true beginning of modern aircraft, was made by Wilbur Wright 17 Dec 1903. His plane, a contraption of wood and wire, travelled 852ft in 59 seconds. Ballooning and the construction of airships went on, but the Wrights' petrol-driven aircraft was destined to lead to the vast network of airlines that now bring the world's capitals within a few minutes' or (at most) a few hours' distance of each other.

From 1903 the progress of the aeroplane was phenomenal. The first flight in Europe (by A. Santos-Dumont) was made in France 1906, the year in which Orville Wright flew 20½m. The English Channel was first flown (by plane) 1909, Louis Blériot, a Frenchman, being the pilot. The first seaplane (hydroplane) was built and flown 1911, a year before Harry Hawker remained in the air 8 hr 23 min. Sir John Alcock and Sir A. Whitten Brown made the first Atlantic crossing (Newfoundland–Ireland) by plane 1919, and (1924) Imperial Airways (now the British Overseas Airways Corporation, known as BOAC) was founded.

The startling advances made in construction, speed, range and size from 1919 to 1939 were due, in no small degree, to the technical experience gained during World War I. Single-engined aircraft were followed by twin-engined, and the tendency was towards greater hp for relatively less weight. The biplane (2 pairs of wings) gave place gradually to the monoplane, and engineers were discovering new principles concerning stresses and pressures. Air resistance was minimised by the introduction of the retractable undercarriage and streamlining generally. By 1931 there was a regular air mail from London to Australia. A flight over Mt Everest was made 1933 ; in 1934 an Italian seaplane reached 440mph. From 1934 to the beginning of World War II air races became the most exciting events in the news, e.g. records set up by Miss Jean Batten and Miss Amy Johnson, by Tommy Rose and Squadron-Leader Gillian who (1938) flew from Edinburgh to London at 409mph.

Meanwhile immense technical progress was being made (*a*) in engines, (*b*) in design, a pioneer of new grace and strength in construction, and hence of greatly improved performance and speed, being the English inventor Reginald Mitchell, to whom we owe the fighting *Spitfire*, supplies of which were only just enough to enable our pilots to win the Battle of Britain, 1940.

(III) *World War II* : It has been said that the science of aeronautics made a century's progress during the 6 years of World War II. The Germans and Italians were producing far more fighting planes at the beginning of the war than Britain and (later) America, but gradually the United Nations gained superiority in numbers, and in range and capability. The *Hurricane* remained a front-line machine till the end of the war, one type carrying 12 machine-guns, another 8 rocket projectiles. *Spitfires* travelled 450mph at 45,000ft, sometimes more. Other fighters were the twin-engined *Bristol Beaufighter*, heavily armoured and powered by 2 Bristol Hercules engines of 1,650hp, and the *Mosquito*, employed for day and night fighting and also for bombing. A *Mosquito* flew the

Atlantic (1945) at 445 mph. *Hawker Tempests, Gladiators, Wellington* bombers, *Whitleys, Stirlings, Halifaxes* and *Lancasters*, these were a few of the British planes employed against the Axis in World War II.

Among USA fighting aircraft were the famous bombers : *Flying Fortress, Liberator* and *Super Fortress*, the first two having a crew of 6 or 10, a bombload of 5,000lb and a range of 2,500m. The *Super Fortress*, the biggest bomber used during the war, was driven by 4 2,200hp engines, each with 18 cylinders and a 4-bladed screw. The plane weighed 53tons, had air-pressurised cabins in the fuselage, and was defended by 10 machine-guns in electrically controlled turrets. *Super Fortresses* were used against Japan ; and it was a *Super Fortress* which dropped the atom bombs on Hiroshima and Nagasaki. Other American military aircraft were the *Mustang, Thunderbolt, Airacobra, Mohawk,* etc.

The success of British and US aircraft in World War II was due to many factors, including the skill and daring of pilots and crews. But this would have availed little had not superiority in numbers, design and performance been wrested from the Germans and Italians. By the end of the war aircraft construction incorporated a host of refinements, not least of which were new alloys for vital parts of engines ; new materials for fuselage, wings, etc., including a variety of plastics ; and new instruments of remarkable precision. Gyroscopic compasses made more reliable navigation possible ; radio facilitated instant intercommunication between a squadron leader and the pilots under his direction, and also with the base. Radar was developed at an amazing speed, so that by the end of the war aircraft were flying blind along narrow ' roads,' thus avoiding collision, and being enabled to land through fog and without guiding lights. Moreover, new devices made it possible for the ground to be ' seen ' through fog on the screen of the cathode-ray tube, hence night bombing and bombing through cloud (see RADAR). Not only was bullet-proof armour used in many planes, but the air-conditioning and control of air-pressure in cabin or cockpit enabled planes to fly at much higher altitudes than formerly. Undercarriages were retractable (i.e. they could be drawn up so as not to offer resistance to wind pressure) ; and great advances in meteorology supplied pilots with weather forecasts of the utmost importance. Chemists improved the fuels used, providing aero-spirit of high octane number. Engineers devised floating landing stages (operation Lily) ; shipbuilders improved the aircraft-carrier so that the British Fleet Air Arm had at its disposal such vessels as *Illustrious,* one of the latest achievements in this class being *Indomitable*, with 23,000 tons dis-placement, and a complement of 1,600 ; another, HMS *Eagle,* Britain's largest aircraft-carrier, was launched 1946.

(IV) *jet propulsion* : It was during World War II that the greatest revolution in aircraft was made. At the moment when aero-engines seemed to have reached perfection, combining tremendous hp with an amazing conservation of weight, a wholly new idea was introduced. Experiments had been going on for some years before the war, and Italian and German experts had designed types of jet-propulsion planes, but it was the English inventor Sir Frank Whittle who made jet-propulsion a practical proposition. For many years his ideas were disregarded, and it was not till 1941 that the first British jet-propelled plane made a successful flight. Within two years British and US firms were producing jet-propelled fighting aircraft on a large scale. By 1944 the *Gloster Meteor* (using Rolls Royce Derwent engines) was employed against the German flying-bombs, also the De Havilland *Vampire,* which had a speed of 500mph.

There are two types of jet-propulsion. In one, air is pumped into the engine from the atmosphere, burned with vapourised kerosene or some other oil, and the resulting gases shot backwards to give a forward impulse to the plane. The Lockheed P-80 *Shooting Star* is of this type, and the power unit requires no cooling and no elaborate ignition system.

The other type of jet-propulsion has a supply of oxygen either in the form of a compressed gas in cylinders, or derived from solids chemically rich in oxygen. The other components of the combustible mixture may be alcohol or some solid fuel. Strictly speaking, the name jet-propulsion is confined to the 1st type, the 2nd being rocket propulsion. In this the gases are electrically exploded, and in this class was the German V_2 rocket-bomb used against England with devastating results during the last months of World War II. It was claimed that the V_2 attained a speed of 2,500mph, and reached a height of 60m.

Jet-propulsion does not, as is sometimes imagined, depend on a blast of hot gases pushing against a cushion of air. It is simply that, having one outlet only, the expanding gases push the plane forward in a direction opposite to that in which they escape. In the rocket type, jet-propulsion functions independently of atmospheric pressure, the plane flying at high altitudes as easily as at lower levels where the air is denser. Hence, also, in theory the rocket could travel in outer space where there is no atmosphere, and it seems possible that we shall ultimately be able to reach the Moon by means of some variation of the rocket-plane. At present it is difficult to achieve interplanetary travel because of the tremendous power required to

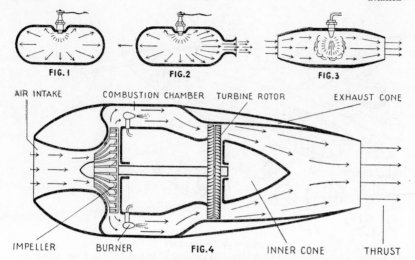

FIG.1   FIG.2   FIG.3

AIR INTAKE   COMBUSTION CHAMBER   TURBINE ROTOR   EXHAUST CONE

IMPELLER   BURNER   FIG.4   INNER CONE   THRUST

THE PRINCIPLE OF JET PROPULSION

(1) *Combustion in a closed vessel results in the uniform distribution of internal pressure, but no tendency for the vessel to move.* (2) *Combustion in a rocket. The unbalanced internal pressure tends to propel the vessel in the direction opposite to the issuing jet.* (3) *A Thermal Duct (with a divergent entry nozzle and a convergent discharge nozzle) into which fuel is injected and burnt so that the heat is released directly into the air stream, causing a forward thrust.* (4) *A sketch diagram of the principle of Whittle's jet engine for aircraft*

overcome the earth's gravitational pull, but inventors are now working on this problem, and there seems no reason to suppose that the difficulty will not be solved.

The jet became a practical proposition when combined with a gas-turbine as its pumping engine, and the success of the gas-turbine depended largely on finding alloys (especially for the blades) that would not melt when subjected to high temperatures. Gas-turbines are now employed in propeller units, and planes are provided with jet-propulsion for high speeds, the propeller for take-off.

At the moment it looks as if the *flying-wing* is the culmination of aircraft design. This was developed in USA by Jack Northrop, head of Northrop Aircraft Incorporated, California. The *flying-wing* has no fuselage and no tail. It is all wing, hence there is no fuselage surface to create merely 'drag' without 'lift,' and the whole of the upper and lower surfaces contribute to 'lift.' Northorp's experimental *flying-wing*, XB-35, has 4 engines at the rear developing, in all, 12,000hp. The plane weighs 90,000lb, and when loaded will take-off with a total weight of over 200,000 lb. Flying at 30,000ft, it cruises at 400mph. New types of this aircraft are now being planned. They are twice as big as XB-35, and are equipped with turbo-jets. The XF89 all-weather fighter, built 1948 by Northrop Aircraft, is a high-speed plane equipped with so-

called 'X-ray eyes' capable of penetrating night darkness and fog. Supersonic speeds (i.e. speeds greater than the speed of sound in air) are now becoming the order of the day, various types of aircraft exceeding 760mph.

One of the features of our time is the rapidly increasing network of 'skyways' across the world, especially in Europe, Canada, Australia, etc. In S. America many republics are finding that air transport of passengers and goods is of exceptional value where road and rail services are few. Among the most notable of air routes is that controlled by Pan-American Airways, famous for its giant luxury passenger planes, e.g. the Stratocruiser *Flying Cloud*, linking New York and London in 11½hr, though the smaller British jet-driven De Havilland *Comet* carries 36 passengers in only 7½hr.

British aircraft today (see PLATES 58, 59) may be grouped as (a) *military*, e.g. planes of the Royal Air Force (see RAF), the Fleet Air Arm, etc., and (b) *civil*. Civil aviation, nationalised in 1946, includes British Overseas Airways Corporation, now incorporating British European and British South American Airways. Among the corporation's aircraft are some of the finest ever built, their heated and pressurised accommodation enabling them to travel at high altitudes, and hence at great speed. One of Britain's most notable planes is *Brabazon I*, a giant 1948 air-liner built

3 a

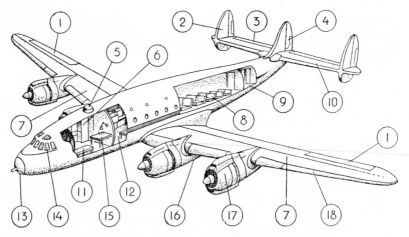

PARTS OF AN AIRCRAFT

(1) *Aileron*   (2) *Vertical Stabilising Fin*   (3) *Elevator*   (4) *Rudder*   (5) *Astro Dome for celestial navigation*   (6) *Galley*   (7) *Wing*   (8) *Pressurised Passenger Cabin*   (9) *Toilets*   (10) *Tailplane*   (11) *Crew Sleeping Berth*   (12) *Freight Hold and Crew's Rest Cabin*   (13) *Headlight*   (14) *Control Cabin*   (15) *Navigator's Position*   (16) *Twin Wheels of main Undercarriage housed in the rear of the Motor*   (17) *one of the four Motors*   (18) *Leading Edge fitted with Rubber De-Icing Strip*

by the Bristol Aeroplane Company. The plane weighs *c*.130tons, has a wing-span of 230ft, a fuselage 177ft long, and 8 engines developing in all 20,000hp. The body is of duralumin, and 100 passengers are carried. British *Viscounts* are the first air-liners to be propelled by air-screw turbines.

Flying records of recent years include a flight of 2,400m (1946) by two 'drones,' i.e. unmanned planes, namely, US *Flying Fortresses* ; a record London–Australia flight by a *Lancaster Aries* in 45hr 35min ; the crossing of the Atlantic by a pilotless aircraft (a 4-engined US *Skymaster*) in Sept 1947, and an altitude record (1948) attained by a De Havilland *Ghost Vampire*, a jet-fighter which reached 59,492ft (i.e. over 11m) in 47min. In May 1949 a jet plane (P1052) flew from London to Paris in 21min, i.e. 618mph. Russian scientists are said to have launched at Peenemunde, on the shores of the Baltic, rockets attaining speeds approaching 7,000mph, and American experts are believed to be perfecting rockets capable of carrying atom bombs half-way round the world. The development of guided missiles has been rapidly advanced since 1945, notably by the Americans.

In Nov 1949 the Pan-American Clipper, *Mayflower*, flew from Gander to London Airport in 6hr 2min ; in April 1950 a Gloster *Meteor VIII* made the return journey Northolt–Copenhagen at an average speed of over 478mph, though a similar aircraft reached 580mph in May. Flying a converted Mustang

fighter aircraft powered by a Packard-built Rolls-Royce Merlin engine, Captain Blair, a Pan-American Airways pilot, flew (1951) from New York to London in 7hr 48min.

We may note that great advances have recently been made in the development of the autogyro, and that now, as the helicopter, this seems likely to become the popular taxi of the air. Gliding is becoming increasingly popular also. The British Gliding Association has its HQ in Park Lane, London. The gliding altitude record is at present 15,300ft, the greatest distance flown is 216m.

For flying as a career see BRITISH OVERSEAS AIRWAYS CORPORATION ; also Air Ministry pamphlets, e.g. *Commissioned Service in the Royal Air Force* ; *The Aircraft Apprentice* ; *Careers in the RAF*, the latter including a list of RAF recruiting offices.

Magazines for those interested in aircraft include *Aero Modeller* ; *Aeronautics* ; *Aeroplane* ; *Air Transport* ; *Aircraft Engineering* ; *Aircraft Production* ; *Flight* ; and books to read include *British Aircraft*, R. A. Saville-Sneath ; *Aircraft of the USA* ; *Flight and Engines*, G. V. Welbourne ; *Air Navigation* E. R. Hamilton ; *Aerodynamics of the Aeroplane*, W. L. Cowley ; *Chemistry and the Aeroplane*, Vernon J. Clancey ; *The Men Who Fly*, Hector Hawton ; *Modern Air Transport*, F. S. Stuart and H. C. Biard ; *Gliding and Advanced Soaring*, A. C. Douglas ; Jane's *All the World's Aircraft*.

See BRITISH OVERSEAS AIRWAYS COR-

PORATION ; HELICOPTER ; LILY ; PAN-AMERICAN AIRWAYS ; RAF, etc.

Avignon, *ä-vē-nyön,* ancient city of S. France, on the R. Rhône. The popes resided here 1307–77, during which period they lost much of their power. Manufactures silk ; pop.57,000. See POPE

Avogadro, COUNT AMADEO (1776–1856), Italian scientist ; discovered what is known as Avogadro's hypothesis : *Under the same conditions of pressure and temperature, equal volumes of all gases contain an equal number of molecules.*

Avon, *ā'von,* name of several rivers in Britain, e.g. Bristol Avon, 75m, and Warwickshire Avon, 95m, both flowing to the R. Severn.

Awe, loch (lake) in Argyllshire ; noted for salmon.

Axholme, ISLE OF, *aks'hōm,* district in N. Lincolnshire ; area *c.*50,000 acres ; drained in the 17th century.

axiom, statement, e.g. in geometry, which cannot be proved but is necessary for the proof of subsequent propositions (in geometry, theorems). Axioms may be regarded either as self-evident truths or as preliminary statements of principle accepted without proof so as to afford a starting point. An example in geometry is the familiar axiom ' A point is that which has position but no magnitude.'

axis, used politically since a speech at Milan 1936 by Mussolini for an alliance between two or more major countries with similar political and foreign policies, these having control of a sphere about a common ' axis,' especially the Rome-Berlin axis of the Fascist régime.

Axminster, town, Devon, once famous for carpets.

aye-aye, *ī'ī,* night-hunting animal peculiar to Madagascar. The size of a hare, it has a large bushy tail.

Aylesbury, industrial co.tn, Buckingham-shire ; pop.20,000.

Aylesford, town on the R. Medway, Kent.

Aylesham, Kent garden-village built for miners *c.*1922.

Ayrshire, Scottish SW. coastal county, noted for dairy-farming, especially the Ayrshire breed of cows. The co.tn, Ayr (pop.43,000), is a port and holiday town associated with Robert Burns.

Aytoun, SIR ROBERT (1570–1638), one of the first Scottish poets to write English ; *b* Kinaldie, Fife.

Aytoun, WILLIAM EDMONDSTOUNE (1813–1865), Scottish poet, *b* Edinburgh ; re-membered for his *Bon Gaultier Ballads,* and *Lays of the Scottish Cavaliers.*

azalea, *ä-zā'lē-a,* slow-growing shrub with fragrant bell-shaped flowers.

Azerbaijan, *az-er-bī-jan',* see USSR

Azores, *ä-zōrz',* 9 Portuguese islands in the N. Atlantic. The climate is mild ; in-dustries include basket-making, woollen goods, hats, etc. Oranges are grown. Flores is one of the islands.

Azov, SEA OF, *ä'zôf,* gulf of the Black Sea NE. of the Crimea. Azov is also a town on the R. Don, USSR.

Aztecs, Indian tribe of the Mexican table-land, their descendants (known as Mexicano) numbering *c.*500,000 today. Founded about the 12th c., the Aztec civilisation existed alongside that of the Mayas. Warlike, skilled in com-merce, ruled by priests, the Aztecs were overthrown when Montezuma II, their last emperor, was captured by Cortés 1520. See MEXICO

B

B, chemical symbol for boron.

Ba, chemical symbol for barium.

Babel, TOWER OF, see BABYLONIA

Babington, ANTHONY (1561–86), con-spirator, *b* Dethick, Derbyshire ; headed RC plot to murder Queen Elizabeth and set Mary Queen of Scots free ; hanged.

babirusa, wild pig of the East Indies. The male has very long teeth piercing the skin of the snout and curving backwards.

baboon, see APES AND MONKEYS

Babylonia, ancient empire in what is now Mesopotamia (Iraq), N. of the Persian Gulf. Watered by ' the Two Rivers,' i.e. Euphrates and Tigris, Babylonia was first inhabited by Sumerians, who settled in southern Mesopotamia before 3000BC. They built houses of mud bricks ; were largely farmers but traded to the north ; used copper, and were

perhaps the first people to employ wheeled vehicles. The Sumerians wrote on clay tablets in cuneiform (see WRIT-ING) ; were skilled in pottery-making ; built temples on cube-like towers of baked brick, e.g. those at Nippur, Babylon. (These towers are called ziggurats ; the Tower of Babel was probably a ziggurat.) They were con-quered by Sargon 2750BC, a Semitic chief from the north. Another leader was Hammurabi, 2100BC, King of Babylon, famous for his code of laws, his love of justice, and also for his letters. The empire revived under Nebuchad-nezzar I *c.*1140BC, but was later con-quered by the Assyrians, and raised to its greatest glory 604–562BC by Nebuchad-nezzar II, after which its history merged into that of Persia.

At the height of its splendour, BABYLON was one of the richest cities of the East, famous for many-coloured palaces, gateways (ruins of the Ishtar Gateway may still be seen), and the so-called Hanging Gardens of Nebuchadrezzar's palace, i.e. terraces amid palms and ferns.

It was to this city that the Hebrews were taken as captives.

Bacchus, *băk'ŭs,* in old Roman tales, god of wine ; known as Dionysus to the Greeks. Characterised by drunkenness, the *Bacchanalia* (festival of Bacchus) were introduced into Rome from Etruria. Men were excluded at first ; later they were admitted. The Bacchanalia were banned in Rome from 186BC.

Bach, JOHANN SEBASTIAN, *bä*ch (1685–1750), one of the world's greatest musicians, *b* Eisenach, Germany. The son of a violinist, an orphan at ten, young Sebastian lived with his elder brother, a clever musician, who forbade him to play some of the difficult organ music he possessed ; the boy, however, secretly copied it at night, and permanently injured his eyes by doing so. In later life he became blind.

At eighteen Bach was organist at Arnstadt ; later at Weimar, Cöthen and Leipzig, where he died. He was twice married, and had in all twenty children.

A brilliant organist, Bach won immortal fame as a composer, inspiring Mozart, Haydn and Beethoven, who all owed much to his masterly compositions, e.g. masses, passions, 223 cantatas, a vast amount of orchestral music, etc. ' The Forty Eight ' (preludes and fugues) are unequalled. His *High Mass in B Minor* is also of exceptional merit, yet his genius was not generally recognised for nearly a century after his death.

He perfected the polyphonic style of music, and his great number of organ compositions are of timeless worth.

Bach's third son, KARL PHILIPP EMANUEL BACH (1714–88) was also a notable musician.

bacillus, *bä-sil'ŭs,* (plural, *bacilli*), rod-like bacterium. See BACTERIA

backgammon, dice game for two players ; known in the 14th c. as tables.

' Back to Methuselah,' see SHAW, BERNARD

bacon, flesh from the back or sides of the pig ; cured by being salted or smoked ; exported by Scotland, Ireland, Denmark, Canada, USA and other countries.

Bacon, FRANCIS (1561–1626), statesman and thinker, *b* London ; became a noted barrister ; displeased Queen Elizabeth but was knighted by James I ; Lord Chancellor 1618, when he was created Lord Verulam, taking his title from Verulamium, the Roman name for St Albans, his home in later years. He was created Viscount St Albans 1621 ; he died from a chill caught when experimenting with snow and ice in an attempt to preserve food by refrigeration.

One of the strangest of all famous Englishmen, Bacon was imprisoned for accepting bribes from people who desired a favourable legal decision, but there was no cleverer man in England. A pioneer of the new way of studying science, he taught men to observe first and then examine cause and effect. He was ever on the lookout for new wonders.

His *Essays,* models of their kind, are full of moral philosophy ; his *Advancement of Learning* (1605), almost an encyclopedia of the knowledge of his day, deals with memory, reason and imagination ; his *Novum Organum* (The New Learning) was published 1620 ; his *New Atlantis* is a fable about an island or Utopia where life is perfect.

Bacon has been described as ' the wisest, brightest, and meanest of mankind.' Attempts have been made to prove that he wrote the plays attributed to SHAKESPEARE, but this theory is not generally accepted.

Bacon, ROGER (1214–94), learned friar, *b* Ilchester, Somerset ; known as *doctor mirabilis* (i.e. the ' wonderful teacher ') ; studied at Oxford and in Paris. His advanced ideas and experiments angered ignorant people who believed that he dealt in black magic. He was imprisoned in France 1277–92.

Bacon wrote about steamships, microscopes, cameras, air-pumps and telescopes before others even dreamed of such inventions. He experimented with charcoal, sulphur and saltpetre, mixing these to make gunpowder ; his *Opus Majus* is a kind of encyclopedia ; he declared that there are two ways of gaining knowledge, one by argument, the other by experiment ; he may be counted among the early pioneers of experimental research.

bacteria, *bak-tēr'iä* (Greek *bakterion,* small rod), minute forms of life studied by the bacteriologist with the aid of a powerful microscope, of aniline dyes with which to stain specimens, and of a serum or jelly (e.g. agar-agar) in which bacteria are cultivated at suitable temperatures. A bacterium may be (*a*) rod-like (*bacillus*) or (*b*) round (*coccus*) or (*c*) curved (*spirilla*) ; most are 0·005–0·0005cm long, i.e. 25,000 in a line would not measure 1in. A colony as big as a mustard seed would contain at least 1,000,000,000 bacteria.

These micro-organisms multiply by splitting in two every 20–30min, hence, in favourable conditions, one bacterium would produce 75,000,000,000,000 bacteria in 24hrs.

Bacteria that are friends of man include those that break down farmyard manure into a valuable fertiliser ; turn nitrogen in the air into nitrogen compounds ; enrich the soil with nitrates by unceasing activity ; form the mould from which penicillin is derived ; change milk-sugar into lactic acid ; cause useful fermentation (e.g. yeast) ; transform cellulose into methane and sugar into glycerine. As foes of man bacteria cause countless diseases, e.g. diphtheria, typhoid, the common cold, consumption; also various poisons, e.g. that caused by *Bacillus botulinus*, one of the astonishing anaerobic bacteria that live without oxygen, the only known creatures to do so.

Notable pioneers of bacteriology include Anton van Leeuwenhoek (1632–1723), a Dutch naturalist ; Robert Koch (1843–1910), the German scientist who proved that *Bacillus anthracis* is the cause of anthrax in cattle ; Louis Pasteur, Lord Lister, Sir Alexander Fleming, Sir Patrick Manson, Sir David Bruce and Sir Ronald Ross.

A knowledge of bacteria has led to remarkable conquests of disease and methods of preventing it, e.g. various drugs to destroy or lessen the activities of bacteria ; the canning of food (especially in USA) at high temperature, thus preserving it for years if air-tight ; sterilising surgical instruments, dressings and wounds ; the use of disinfectants, among which, it should be noted, is sunlight, ultra-violet rays being deadly to bacteria ; also many forms of vaccination and immunisation.

Smaller even than the smallest bacteria are Viruses, so minute that the pathologist cannot see them with an ordinary microscope or ' catch ' them by filtration. The virus of cow-pox is thought to be 0·00002cm in diameter ; that of foot-and-mouth disease only 0·0000008 cm. Little is known about these micro-organisms, possibly the smallest and simplest of all living creatures.

Read *Man, Microbe and Malady*, Dr John Drew.

bactris, slender S. American palm.

Bacup, *bä'kup*, industrial Lancashire town noted for spinning and weaving cotton ; pop.20,000.

Badajoz, *bä-thä-hōth'*, Spanish city on the R. Guadiana ; 315m SW. of Madrid ; has an old cathedral and ruins of a Moorish castle ; scene 1812 of Wellington's victory over the French ; pop. 57,000.

Baden, *bä'den*, German state ; includes the Black Forest area. Rich in minerals and timber, it is noted for its hot springs, especially at the town of Baden-Baden, which has medicinal baths dating back to Roman times.

Baden, health-resort, Switzerland ; noted for its hot mineral springs since Roman times ; pop.8,300

Baden-Powell, Lord Robert Stephenson, *bä'den pō'el* (1857–1941), British general, founder of the Boy Scout Movement. Though a soldier, he worked for peace, and lived up to his motto, *Be Prepared*.

Nicknamed B.P., he was the son of an Oxford professor. He became a cavalry officer ; served in Afghanistan ; won fame by his defence of Mafeking (1899–

1900) during the Boer War, and came home to find himself the hero of the hour. While in Africa he learned the art of scouting ; the Zulus called him *The Man who lies down to Shoot*, the Matabele renamed him *The Wolf that Never Sleeps*.

Founding the Boy Scout Association 1908, he made it a training for citizenship, friendship and international understanding. Knighted 1909, he became Lord Baden-Powell 1929. He died in Kenya. His favourite quotation was : *We were born not for ourselves but to help others*.

His sister Agnes, who was Girl Guide Number One, *d* 1945.

Read Baden-Powell's *Rovering to Success*. See Boy Scouts

badger, British night-hunting animal *c*.3ft long ; grey with a black and white head ; lives in woods and among hills ; defends itself bravely when attacked.

THE BADGER

Badoglio, Pietro, *bä-dō'lyo* (1871–   ), Italian soldier and statesman ; was Prime Minister 1943–44.

Baffin, William (1584–1622), explorer, *b* London ; searched for the NW. Passage ; gave his name to a bay he discovered in N. America 1615.

Baffin Bay, sea between Canada and Greenland, and within the Arctic Circle ; discovered by William Baffin 1615. It abounds in whales and seals.

Baffin Land, island W. of Baffin Bay ; area 240,000sq.m ; inhabited by Eskimos.

Baghdad, capital city of Iraq. Silk and leather goods are manufactured ; the exports include skins, carpets and wool. From AD750 until its capture by the Mongols (1258), Baghdad was the capital of the Caliphs (including Haroun-al-Rashid, 763–89), rulers of the Eastern Mohammedans. The modern part of the city (eastern section) contains the governor's palace, chief European consulates and chief bazaars ; the western section is made up of mud buildings and low brick walls. The whole city, which is built on both banks of the river Tigris and crossed by a bridge of boats, is encircled with groves and date palms ; pop.400,000. Near Baghdad stand the ruins of Babylon.

bagpipe, wood-wind musical instrument, played throughout Europe and elsewhere for 2,000 years. Best known is the (Scottish) Highland bagpipe, of great musical interest because it divides the octave somewhat differently from the familiar diatonic scale. Pibroch (Gaelic *piobaireachd*), the name given in Scotland to a piece of classical bagpipe music, is a highly developed art-form, and includes salutes, marches, laments, etc. A pibroch usually consists of ground and variations.

Baha'i, religion founded by the Persian, Baha'u'llah (1817–92) ; stresses world brotherhood and the need for spiritual life.

Bahamas, *ba-hä'maz*, large group of coral islands in the British West Indies. Mostly very small, they are mainly inhabited by descendants of liberated African slaves. The islands have a pleasant climate and are much visited in winter by Americans. Exports include sponges, tomatoes, timber. Discovered by Columbus 1492, the Bahamas have been British since 1783 ; cap. Nassau. The USA has leased a naval base there since 1940.

Bahia, *ba-ē'a*, Atlantic state of Brazil occupying middle and north Sâo Francisco valley ; produces diamonds, sugar, cotton, coffee, cocoa, tobacco ; 165,000sq.m ; pop.3,859,000.

Bahia or **Sao Salvador,** capital of Bahia ; important port ; pop.382,000.

Bahrain Islands, *bä-rän'*, Arabian islands in the Persian Gulf ; noted for dates, white donkeys, pearls, etc. ; oil was discovered 1932 ; pop.100,000.

Baikal, *bĭ-käl'*, lake S. of Siberia, almost 400m long ; area 13,500sq.m.

bail, legal term. If A is in custody he may be allowed to go free, pending his trial, on condition that B undertakes to make sure he will appear in court when required, and that if A fails to appear B will pay a stated sum. This is called admitting bail.

bailey, see ARCHITECTURE

bailie, see MAGISTRATE

Baillie, LADY GRIZEL (1665–1746), daughter of Sir Patrick Hume of Redbraes, Berwickshire. When Grizel was twelve, one of Sir Patrick's friends (Robert Baillie of Jerviswood) was in prison on a charge of having taken part in the Rye House plot. Grizel smuggled a letter into his cell, where she met and fell in love with Robert Baillie's son, George, whom in happier times she married. Lady Baillie wrote much charming verse.

Baillie, JOANNA (1762–1851), dramatist and poet, *b* Bothwell, Lanarkshire.

Baird, SIR DAVID (1757–1829), Scottish soldier ; won distinction in India at the

storming of Seringapatam 1799, and also by his dramatic desert march (1801) to the Nile.

Baird, JOHN L. (1888–1946), Scottish inventor ; won distinction 1925 by his successful demonstration of television (in outline) ; demonstrated (1926) radio transmission of the human face in light and shade ; achieved television in colour 1928, when he televised across the Atlantic. The Baird system was adopted by the German Post Office and was employed by the BBC 1929, but Baird's mechanical scanning is now done much more rapidly by an electric beam in a cathode-ray tube. Baird demonstrated television in both colour and relief 1941. He also invented the TELEFILM, by which an audience may watch what is happening elsewhere at the moment of the occurrence.

' Bakelite,' see PLASTICS

Baker, SIR BENJAMIN (1840–1907), engineer, *b* Somerset ; associated with the building of the Forth Bridge ; brought Cleopatra's Needle to London.

Baker, SIR SAMUEL WHITE (1821–93), explorer, *b* London. He and his Hungarian wife shared many adventures, e.g. a journey from Cairo to explore Central Africa. While searching for the sources of the Nile, Baker discovered L. Albert Nyanza 1864. He also did much to suppress the slave trade in the Upper Nile region.

Bakewell, Derbyshire health resort ; ancient town ; has chalybeate springs.

Bakewell, ROBERT, see CATTLE

baking powder, mixture of tartaric acid, bicarbonate of soda, and ground rice or flour. When moist it forms carbon dioxide, thus making dough ' rise.'

Baku, *bä-koo*, town, USSR ; on the Caspian Sea ; capital of Azerbaijan ; centre of petroleum industry ; rail communications with Batum, Tiflis and Moscow ; pop.809,000.

Bala, *bä'lä*, largest lake in Wales ; 4m long ; also a town, Merionethshire.

Balaam, *bä'lam*, OT magician ; Numbers 22–24.

balaclava, woollen helmet first worn in the Crimean War, *c.*1854.

Balaclava, village and harbour in the Crimea, S. Russia ; scene 1854 of the ' Thin Red Line ' formed by the Argyll and Sutherland Highlanders ; also of the famous charge of the Light Brigade.

Lord Raglan sent an order by Captain Nolan : *Lord Raglan wishes the cavalry to advance rapidly to the front, and try to prevent the enemy carrying away the guns.* The order referred to some British guns near at hand ; but Lord Lucan, who received the order, imagined that Raglan intended to prevent the Russians from removing some of their own guns, which were posted at the end of a valley. Lucan therefore ordered Lord Cardigan to lead the Light Brigade (673 men) into what Tennyson describes as the valley of death, where—

Cannon to right of them,
Cannon to left of them,
Cannon in front of them
Volley'd and thunder'd.

In spite of the fierce crossfire the brigade cut down the Russian gunners, losing 110 killed, with 134 wounded.

balance sheet, statement of accounts showing profit and loss, liabilities and assets, of a person or company.

Balboa, VASCO NUÑEZ DE, *bal-bo'ä* (1475–1517), courageous Spanish sailor and explorer ; led an expedition to Darien, the old name for what is now Panama. There (1513) he climbed a mt., looked beyond tropical forests, and was the first European to see the ocean which he christened the Pacific.

Keats in his sonnet *On First Looking into Chapman's Homer*, speaks of

stout Cortés when with eagle eyes
He stared at the Pacific,

but this is an error. It was Balboa, not Cortés, conqueror of Mexico, who ' stood silent upon a peak in Darien.'

Balder the Beautiful, *böl'dĕr*, in old Norse tales, the sun god, husband of Nanna, the moon goddess. His house, Broad-Shining, was at Asgard ; he was killed by a mistletoe dart thrown by Hoder, and was buried at sea.

Read Matthew Arnold's poem, *Balder Dead.*

Baldwin, STANLEY, *böld'win* (1867–1947), English statesman ; cousin of Rudyard Kipling ; entered his father's engineering works at Stourport, Worcestershire ; was Unionist MP for Bewdley 1908 ; Prime Minister 1923, also 1924–29 and also 1935–37 ; created Earl Baldwin of Bewdley ; instrumental in securing the abdication of Edward VIII. Baldwin excused his failure to warn Britain that Germany was re-arming by the plea that in a democracy it takes time to persuade the people to face unpleasant facts.

Balearic Isles, *bal-ē-ar'ik*, 11 islands off the E. coast of Spain. They include Minorca, noted for lemons, figs, almonds ; and Majorca (largest), noted for its caves, also pottery (majolica) ; cap. Palma (in Majorca).

Balfour, ARTHUR JAMES, *bal'fur* (1848–1930), statesman, *b* Whittingehame, E. Lothian ; Conservative MP for Hertford 1874, and for E. Manchester for 21 years after 1885. In 1887 he began five years of stern rule in Ireland as Chief Secretary. Prime Minister 1902–05, he was responsible for the Education Act (1902) and the Licensing Act. Sent by Lloyd George on a mission to USA in World War I, he made the famous *Balfour Declaration* (1917) that the British favoured a national home for the Jews in Palestine. He was created Earl Balfour after his return from the Washington Conference 1922, and had much to do with Allied war debts.

Balfour never married. A lover of

sport, he had intellectual interests and great charm of manner.

Bali with **Lombok**, *bä'lē*, islands of the Netherlands East Indies, producing rice, coffee, sugar, etc. ; the peak of Lombok is volcanic.

Baliol, JOHN, *bä'l-yol* (1249–1315), son of John de Baliol, founder (1265) of Balliol College, Oxford. As a descendant of David I of Scotland, he claimed the throne after the death of the Maid of Norway 1290, was supported by Edward I of England, and became king of Scots 1292. Disliked in Scotland because he had acknowledged Edward as his overlord, he was forced by his subjects to ally himself with France. Edward invaded Scotland and deposed Baliol 1296.

Balkan Mountains, *böl'kan*, mt. range, Bulgaria ; highest point 7,780ft.

Balkans or **Balkan Peninsula**, region between the Adriatic and Aegean Sea. The Balkan States are Greece, Albania, Yugoslavia, Rumania, Bulgaria.

Ball, JOHN (*d* 1381), English priest and rebel. For 20 years he declared that all men are equal in the sight of God ; and asked

When Adam delved and Eve span,
Who was then the gentleman ?

(To *delve* is to dig ; *span* is the past tense of spin.) Dissatisfied peasants in Kent and Essex who had joined Wat Tyler's rebellion (Peasants' Revolt) 1381 released John Ball, then in prison at Maidstone. The rebels were met by Richard II at Mile End, and later at Smithfield (London), where Tyler was killed by the Lord Mayor, Sir William Walworth. The rebellion was soon quelled, Ball being hanged, drawn and quartered at St Albans. See BLACK DEATH

ballad, poem telling a story in a simple, musical and dramatic way, usually in stanzas of two or four lines. Generally anonymous, having grown generation after generation, the ballad is midway between a lyric and an epic, the name coming, it is said, from the Latin *ballare*, to dance, ballads being at one time chanted to the accompaniment of dancing. The theme, often crude, is frequently a love story or some heroic deed, and the ending is often unhappy. Among our best-known ballads are those of Robin Hood, the *Ballad of Sir Patrick Spens*, and *Chevy Chase*. Few English or Scottish ballads are earlier than the 14th century.

Ballantrae', small holiday town, Ayrshire.

Ballantyne, ROBERT MICHAEL (1825–94), Scottish writer of over 80 adventure stories for boys, e.g. *The Lighthouse*, *Coral Island*, etc.

Ballarat, *bal'a-rat*, city, Victoria, Australia ; centre of a gold-mining region. The industries include textiles, iron smelting and brewing ; pop.39,000.

ballet, see DANCING

Balliol College, *bäl'yol*, one of the oldest

and largest Oxford colleges, founded
*c.*1265 by John de Baliol the elder
(*d* 1269) and further endowed by his
widow Dervorguilla ; famous as a school
of statesmen, constitutional lawyers and
classical scholars. Among noted
' Balliol men ' are Wycliffe, Benjamin
Jowett, Asquith and Milner.

ballista, *bal-is'tä,* Roman and medieval
war machine for throwing heavy stones.

balloon, see AVIATION

ballot, see ELECTION

balm of Gilead, *gil'ē-ad,* yellowish gum
from trees in Arabia and Ethiopia ;
that mentioned in the Bible may have
been resin from the lentisk plant.

Balmoral, castle (rebuilt *c.*1853) in Aberdeenshire ; overlooks the R. Dee ; was
Queen Victoria's favourite residence.
The estate of 25,000 acres includes deer
forests.

Balquhidder, *bal-hwid'er,* village, Perthshire, where Rob Roy (immortalised by
Sir Walter Scott) was buried 1734.

balsa, *böl'sä,* tree of Central and S. America.
Its wood is exceedingly light, and much
used for making model aeroplanes.

Baltic Sea, *böl'tik,* tideless sea ; area
160,000sq.m ; linked with the N. Sea
by the Skagerrack, Kattegat, and other
channels ; also by the Kiel Canal. The
Baltic is usually frozen Dec.–Apr.

Baltimore, *böl'ti-mör,* city, Maryland,
USA ; noted for its large harbour, and
as a great railway centre ; industries
include textiles, flour and iron. The
exports include grain ; pop.859,000.

Baluchistan, *bä-loo'-chi-stän,* upland region
of Pakistan ; area *c.*55,000sq.m, part
of it a cold desert, though the fertile
areas produce rice, cotton, indigo. Oil
is found. The capital is Quetta.

Balzac, HONORÉ DE, *bäl'zäk* (1799–1850),
French novelist, *b* Tours. His schooldays
were unhappy, and as a young man he
lived for a time in an attic in Paris. He
won fame with his story *The Wild Ass's
Skin,* published 1831. Though kindly,
he was critical and impulsive, hard-
working but temperamental and highly
imaginative, so much so that he sometimes confused characters in his books
with actual people. He had a great
interest in money, and loved power.
Among his novels are *Eugénie Grandet,
Father Goriot, César Birotteau,* and *Lost
Illusions* ; the group as a whole is called
The Human Comedy (La Comédie
Humaine), and gives a vivid picture of
early 19th c. France.
Read *Balzac,* Stefan Zweig.

bamboo, giant grass with a rigid tubular
stem ; may be 50ft high and even 100ft ;
belongs especially to India, China, Japan,
Malaya ; has been known to grow 18in
a day.

Bamburgh, village, Northumberland ; the
castle stands magnificently on a rock
above the sea ; in the churchyard, close
by, is the grave of Grace Darling.

banana, though usually spoken of as a tree,
is actually a large tropical plant. The

stem, or trunk, is not woody, but green
and pulpy, being the lower part of the
huge leaves, generally 8–10ft long, and
over 1ft wide. Cultivated bananas produce clusters of fruit weighing up to 70lb.
Britain normally imports large quantities of bananas from the W. Indies,
Canary Is., Columbia, E. Indies, etc.
See PLATE 7 (*top*)

bandicoot, Australian animal like a small
kangaroo ; feeds mostly on insects.

Band of Hope, organisation to induce
children to become life-abstainers from
alcohol ; founded 1847 by Mrs Carlile
of Dublin, the first festival being held
at Leeds (1847).

Banff, *bamf,* co.tn, Banffshire, a county of
NE. Scotland ; also a holiday resort,
Alberta, Canada, noted for sulphur
springs and magnificent scenery.

Bangalore, city and cap., Mysore, S. India ;
manufactures carpets, silks, woollen
goods ; pop.248,000.

Bangkok, see SIAM

Bangor, cathedral city, Caernarvonshire ;
a noted tourist centre.

banjo, musical instrument with 5, 6, or 7
strings plucked or struck with the finger
nails ; popular among Negroes of USA ;
said to be of African origin.

bank, place of security for the deposit of
money. A bank receives money on
deposit accounts upon which interest is
allowed, but its chief business is the
keeping of *current* accounts for customers, and the paying of cheques drawn
thereon. See CHEQUE
A customer's current account at a
bank is one to which he pays in money
daily, or at intervals, and upon which
he draws cheques as required for business or other purposes. A banker will
not open a current account with a
person unknown to him without first
obtaining satisfactory references as to
the proposed customer's integrity and
responsibility. A bank always takes a
specimen of each customer's signature
for comparison in case of need.
A bank lends money in two ways :
(*a*) by allowing a customer to overdraw
his current account ; (*b*) by granting a
loan on a separate loan account. Of
these (*a*) is the method more frequently
adopted, i.e. by overdraft. The bank
records the balance of an overdraft in
red ink, and charges interest for the use
of the money. Borrowers must state the
purpose for which an overdraft or loan
is required, and suitable security is
usually called for by the bank. Un-
secured lending is not uncommon,
however, the character and earning
capacity of the borrower sometimes
being the only security on which the
bank relies for repayment.
The business of a bank embraces
nearly every transaction connected with
the borrowing, lending and exchanging
of money, e.g. collecting cheques, bills,
etc. for customers ; buying and selling
Stock Exchange securities ; acting as

trustee or executor under a Will ;
making periodical payments, on the due
dates, of subscriptions, insurance premiums, etc. ; taking care of valuables
and securities entrusted to the bank for
safe custody. The unique function of a
bank is the provision of a convenient
mechanism by which people can make
payments to each other without having
to go round to each other's houses or
places of business with bags of coin.

The profits of a bank are derived
largely from the difference between the
rate of interest it pays on the money deposited with it and the rate of interest it
earns on the money it lends and invests.

A *Savings Bank* is for the deposit of
money, the depositor receiving interest
thereon. The money and interest may
be drawn out by the depositor as and
when required. Depositors cannot issue
cheques. The funds of the savings banks
are invested with the Government, and
repayment of the money is guaranteed
by Act of Parliament.

Bank notes are promissory notes issued
by a bank and payable to bearer on demand. In England and Wales only the
Bank of England is now allowed to issue
notes, but eight banks in Scotland and
nine in Ireland issue notes.

The banking system depends on the
confidence of the public in the ability of
the banks to meet their liabilities on
demand ; it is confidence which determines the amount entrusted to the banks.

The BANK OF ENGLAND, sometimes
referred to as ' the Old Lady of Thread-
needle Street' was founded 1694 by a
Scotsman, William Paterson (1658–1719).
It was nationalised 1946. The Bank
conducts the business of a ' central
bank ' ; its chief customer is the Govern-
ment, and it is the Bankers' bank. The
' Big Five ' English banks—Barclays,
Lloyds, Midland, National Provincial,
Westminster—have accounts with the
Bank of England. Scotland has its own
banks, the Royal Bank of Scotland, the
Bank of Scotland, etc.

bank rate, advertised minimum rate at
which the Bank of England will discount approved bills of exchange or
grant short loans ; but in practice the
Bank discounts bills for customers at
market rate, which is usually a little
lower. Bank Rate influences all rates.

bankrupt, in law, a person unable to pay
his debts. Bankruptcy is failure to carry
on business, but a man is not properly
bankrupt till he has been declared so in
a court of law. Bankruptcy in Scotland
differs slightly from that in England.

When bankrupt, all a man's assets are
realised and shared out proportionately
among his creditors, i.e. those to whom
he owes money.

Banks, SIR JOSEPH (1743–1820), naturalist,
b London ; accompanied Captain Cook
on a voyage round the world 1768.

Bannockburn, town, 3m SE. of Stirling ;
manufactures carpets, tartans, etc. ;
scene 1314 of Robert the Bruce's victory
over the English, led by Edward II,
whereby Scottish national independence
was secured.

bantam, small fowl, said to have come
originally from Bantam, Java. Now
almost any diminutive breed of poultry.

banteng, brown or black ox of Burma,
Malay, Borneo, Java, etc. ; fierce when
wild in the jungle, but is widely domesticated.

Banting, SIR FREDERICK GRANT (1891–
1941), Canadian scientist and discoverer
of Insulin for the treatment of diabetes.
See INSULIN

Bantock, SIR GRANVILLE (1868–1946),
musician ; *b* London ; knighted 1930 ;
his musical pieces include *The Fire
Worshippers, Atalanta in Calydon*, and
Omar Khayyam, etc.

Bantry, town overlooking Bantry Bay,
County Cork (Eire) ; manufactures
tweeds ; scene 1689 of a slight encounter
between the English and French fleets.

Bantu, group of 400 African languages
spoken by Bushmen, Hottentots, Pygmies,
Zulus and Kaffirs, possibly 50,000,000
in all, living chiefly south of lat. 5°N.

banyan, *ban'yan,* Indian fig sacred to
Hindus. Stems from the branches of the
tree take root in the ground, and thus
the tree-colony extends until an immense
area is covered, one tree having given
shelter to 7,000 people.

baobab, *bā'ō-bab,* African tree with a
massive trunk often 30ft round, though
rarely over 70ft high ; has dark green
leaves, white flowers, and a fruit known
as sour gourd or monkey-bread.

BAOBAB
The flower, the leaves and the fruit

Baptists, Protestants who, among other beliefs, hold that one must be completely covered by water when baptised, and that grown men and women (not children) should receive baptism when prepared to repent of their sins and declare their faith in God and in His Son, Jesus Christ. The sect was founded in the 16th c., and today in the UK numbers c.368,000. World membership is c.13,000,000, over 8,000,000 being in USA.

A great Baptist preacher was CHARLES HADDON SPURGEON (1834–92), who attracted 6,000 people every Sunday for 30 years to the Tabernacle, Southwark, London.

Barbados, *bär-bā´doz*, island of the British W. Indies ; colonised 1627 ; exports sugar, rum, cotton, molasses, etc. ; cap. Bridgetown ; pop. (chiefly Negro) 203,000.

barbar´ians, uncivilised peoples ; word used by the ancient Greeks for all who did not speak Greek ; by the Romans for those outside the Roman Empire.

Barbary, old name for some of the states of N. Africa (especially Morocco and Algeria) inhabited by Berbers, a white race related to the Egyptians. Barbary pirates (Berbers and Moors) infested the Mediterranean 15th–19th c., and had HQ at Tunis, Algiers and Sallee.

Barbary ape, only wild monkey in Europe ; found at Gibraltar, and also in N. Africa, e.g. Morocco, Algiers ; is yellowish-brown with flesh-coloured buttocks.

barber, one whose occupation is shaving and cutting hair. Formerly, barbers were also amateur doctors and dentists, their favourite remedy being letting blood by opening a vein in the arm, or applying leeches.

The barber's pole symbolises an arm red with blood and bound with a white bandage.

' **Barber of Seville, The,**' see BEAUMARCHAIS, P. ; ROSSINI, G. A.

barberry, spiny British shrub ; may be 5ft high ; has egg-shaped leaves and drooping yellow flowers in May ; the berries are orange-red.

barbican, see ARCHITECTURE

Barbirolli, JOHN (1899–), conductor, *b* London of Italian and French parents ; conducts the Hallé orchestra.

Barbour, JOHN (*d* 1395), Scottish poet ; wrote *The Bruce*, a patriotic epic of 14,000 lines ; was possibly the author of *Legends of the Saints*.

Barbuda, see LEEWARD ISLANDS

Barcelona, city and Mediterranean port, Spain, with a large harbour and much shipping ; manufactures include cotton ; pop.1,250,000.

bard, trained poet, especially a Celtic bard, who was frequently a historian, and sometimes led armies into battle. Bardic songs, usually sung to the harp, and generally warlike, could be very tender. Wales still has its bards, acclaimed annually at the Eisteddfodau. The word

is still used in Scottish Gaelic for anyone who makes songs and poems. See CELTIC LANGUAGE AND LITERATURE

Barents, WILLEM (*d* 1597), Dutch explorer ; made three attempts to find the NE. Passage ; discovered Spitzbergen. The hut where he and his companions perished in the far N. was found 1871. Barents Sea, part of the Arctic Ocean, is named after him.

Barfleur, port from which the *White Ship* sailed 1120 ; now a holiday resort (French coast) 15m from Cherbourg.

Barham, RICHARD HARRIS, *bär´am*, (1788–1845), humorous writer, *b* Canterbury ; author of the delightful and often ghostly *Ingoldsby Legends*, among which is *The Jackdaw of Rheims*.

baritone, man's singing voice between tenor and bass.

barium, *bār´i-ŭm*, (Gk *barys*, heavy), silvery metal and element, Ba ; atomic weight 137·36 ; atomic number 56 ; occurs naturally as barytes, $BaSO_4$.

bark, covering of trees and shrubs. Botanically the *periderm*, it usually consists of cork. Being a poor conductor of heat, the bark protects the trunk and branches from sudden changes in temperature ; it is also waterproof. The bark of many trees is valuable as a medicine, e.g. Peruvian bark, source of quinine.

Barker, SIR HERBERT (1869–1950), manipulative surgeon, *b* Southport, Lancashire ; skilled in bloodless operations on joints ; knighted 1922.

Barking, manufacturing town, Essex ; has jute factories, chemical works, a large electric power-station ; pop.78,000.

BARBERRY
A cluster of leaves and flowers

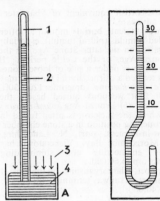
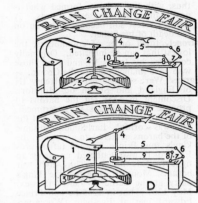

BAROMETER

A *illustrates the principle of a barometer :* (1) *a vacuum* (2) *a column of mercury balancing the pressure of air on mercury in the bowl* (3) *the air pressing down with a weight of 14·7 lb per square inch.* B *is an ordinary mercury barometer.* C *the aneroid barometer :* (1) *Spring* (2) *Rod* (3) *Metal Box with a vacuum inside* (4) *the hand on a pivot* (5, 6, 7, 8) *levers* (9) *the chain that turns the hand* (10) *the hair spring.* D : (1) *the spring pulled down by compressed lid of box at* (3) (4) *the hand pivot pulled round by the chain* (9) *the chain unwound by levers* (5) (6) (7) *and* (8)

barley, cereal ; may be (*a*) race I, having 6 rows of grain in the head, (*b*) race II, called bere or brigg, and having 4 rows of grain, and (*c*) race III, which is 2-rowed barley. The best crops are grown on chalky soil in a dry climate. Barley is used for brewing ale, and for distilling certain whiskies. It is also used for animal feeding. Pearl barley is the dehusked grain.

barleycorn, old British measure taken from the length of a grain of barley, three or four of which make up an inch.

Barnabas, saint ; friend of St Paul ; *b* Cyprus ; Acts 4, 9, 11 ; also 13–15.

barnacle, shell-protected sea-creature, e.g. the acorn barnacle, which attaches itself to rocks ; another attaches itself to floating timber or the sides of ships, thus making periodic scraping necessary.

Barnardo, THOMAS JOHN, *bär-när'dō* (1845–1905), philanthropist, *b* Dublin. When a child of two he was thought to be dead, but the undertaker noticed a spark of life, and the infant was nursed back to health.

Becoming a doctor in a London hospital, he founded Dr Barnardo's Homes 1866. The work has continued since his death, and altogether over 140,000 children have been cared for in the UK and Canada, *c.*8,000 being in residence at one time.

Barnes, residential district, Surrey ; on the R. Thames ; pop.41,000.

Barnes, WILLIAM (1801–86), English poet and clergyman, born in Dorset ; best known for his dialect poems, e.g. *Poems of Rural Life in Dorset.*

Barnet, town, Hertfordshire, still noted for its great horse fair in September.

Barnsley, manufacturing town, W. Yorkshire ; on the R. Dearne. Centre of a mining district, it is noted for textiles, wire, bleaching ; pop.72,000.

Barnstaple, *bärn'stab'l,* port, Devon, noted for lace, gloves, pottery and furniture ; on the estuary of the R. Taw.

Baroda, a princely state in NW. India.

barometer, instrument for measuring the pressure of the atmosphere, its pioneer being Evangelista Torricelli, a 17th c. Italian scientist.

In its simplest form a barometer is a glass tube over 30in long and closed at one end. It has a vacuum at the top, the open end being in a dish of mercury. Since there is no pressure above the mercury, its height in the tube depends solely on the pressure of the atmosphere on the mercury in the dish, and any increase in the atmospheric pressure will cause the mercury to rise in the tube, any decrease a corresponding fall. The normal atmospheric pressure at sea-level is sufficient to balance a column of mercury *c.*30in or 760mm high, or a column of water *c.*34ft high.

Since atmospheric pressure decreases with increase in height, an aneroid barometer may serve as an altimeter (height-finder), a special form being used in aircraft, though this is now being replaced by methods depending on the reflection of short radio waves from the ground.

baron, originally one who, after the Norman Conquest, held land directly from the king in return for military service. In Edward I's day barons were summoned to Parliament by special letter or writ. Later, heirs of such barons had the right to sit in Parliament, and thus, with the bishops, formed what is now called the House of Lords. A baron's eldest son becomes a baron on the death of his father.

baronet, titled order of commoners, the lowest that can be inherited. Originally conferred by James VI and I on those who gave financial aid to the Crown.

Barons' War, struggle between Henry III of England and Simon de Montfort. Discontent in 1258 led the barons to propose improvements in government, hence the *Provisions of Oxford* ; but the king was scornful. Earl Simon and some of the barons gathered an army, and the king's son, Prince Edward (afterwards Edward I) also gathered an army to fight for his father. Thus civil war began. Montfort defeated the king's party at the battle of Lewes (Sussex) May 1264 ; but in 1265 he and Prince Edward met at Evesham (Worcestershire), where the king's party won a notable victory. From the first, the Earl knew that defeat was sure, and exclaimed, ' God have mercy on our souls, for our bodies are theirs.' Montfort was killed, and the rebellion ended almost at once.

barque, *bärk,* sailing ship with 3, 4, or 5 masts, square sails on all except the aftermast.

Barrie, Sir JAMES MATTHEW (1860–1937), Scottish author and playwright, born in the village of Kirriemuir (Angus) of comparatively poor parents ; attended Edinburgh University ; became a journalist ; wrote many delightful books (e.g. *Auld Licht Idylls*) about his own village and its working people ; later called the village Thrums (the ends of threads used in weaving), and won still greater fame with *A Window in Thrums* and *The Little Minister,* books full of sympathy and humour. He wrote also *The Little White Bird* ; *Margaret Ogilvy* (a tribute to his mother).

Barrie's greatest successes were his plays, including *Quality Street* (1902) ; *The Admirable Crichton* ; *A Kiss for Cinderella* ; *Dear Brutus* ; *Boy David* ; but perhaps he is best remembered for his play *Peter Pan* (the tale of a boy who would not grow up), first produced at the Duke of York's theatre (London) 27 Dec 1904. In Kensington Gardens is a bronze statue (1912) of Peter Pan by Sir George Frampton.

Barrie, knighted 1913, was buried at Kirriemuir.

Barringer Meteor, see SHOOTING STARS

barrister, in England a lawyer who has been ' called to the bar ' by one of the Inns of Court, i.e. a member of the legal profession who has passed his examinations, attended at an Inn of Court for about three years, and proved himself worthy. The senior in knowledge and experience of a solicitor, he may be without the bar (outside or beyond it), or within the bar, when he is known as a King's Counsel (KC).

The Scottish equivalent of ' barrister ' is ' advocate.'

barrow, ancient burial mound ; often called tumulus (plural tumuli), especially if raised in the later Stone Age, or the Bronze Age, or the Celtic period. If the grave is under a pile of loose stones it is termed a cairn. Burial mounds may be (*a*) *long barrows,* sometimes 120 × 30ft, with flint weapons buried beside the skeleton, (*b*) Bronze Age *round barrows* in which the skeleton is often found in a crouching position in a stone chamber.

Barrow-in-Furness, port, N. Lancashire, on Morecambe Bay. Vickerstown has large engineering and shipbuilding works ; pop.66,000.

Barry, port, Glamorganshire, on the Bristol Channel ; a railway terminus with docks ; pop.40,000.

barter, see MONEY

Barth, KARL, *bärt* (1886–), Swiss religious thinker, *b* Basel ; opposed the anti-religious measures of the Nazis ; has called for a new belief in, and understanding of, the word of God.

Bartholomew, St, *bär-thol′o-mū,* one of Christ's apostles ; see Matthew 10, Mark 3, Luke 6.

St BARTHOLOMEW'S FAIR, London, was at one time England's chief cloth fair.

Bartholomew, MASSACRE OF St, name given to the massacre authorised by Catherine de Medici, Queen of France, on St Bartholomew's Day, 24 Aug 1572.

On account of Admiral Coligny's endeavour to draw Charles IX into a war with Spain, Catherine attempted his assassination, but this failed and she then resolved, with the support of the Catholic powers, to massacre all the Huguenot leaders.

The massacre spread throughout France, the number killed being estimated at 50,000.

Bartlett, VERNON (1894–), born in Wiltshire ; MP for Bridgwater 1938 ; well-known writer and broadcaster on foreign affairs.

Bartók, BÉLA, *bawr′-tōk* (1881–1946), Hungarian musician ; gathered 7,000 old Hungarian folk-tunes ; noted for *The Wooden Prince* (a pantomime ballet) ; choral music (e.g. *Cantata Profana*) ; and his magnificent concertos and series of string quartets. His *Concerto for Orchestra* is perhaps his most mature work.

Bartolommeo, Fra, *bärto-lōm-mā′ō* (1475–1517), Italian artist, friend of Raphael ; born near Florence.

' **Bart's,**' see St BARTHOLOMEW'S HOSPITAL

barytes, *bä-rī′tēz,* barium sulphate, $BaSO_4$, a mineral often found with lead ores. Lithopone, used as white paint, is a mixture of barium sulphate and zinc oxide. See BARIUM

basalt, *bä-sölt,* form of lava containing ferrous (i.e. iron) and magnesian silicates ; forms the sub-stratum of all the continents ; is usually grey or black. The Inner Hebrides, NE. Ireland, the

Faeroe Is., Iceland, Greenland, much of Colorado, and the Deccan (India) are examples of great outpourings of this kind of lava ; also the Giant's Causeway, which, with Fingal's Cave in the Scottish island of Staffa, is noted for basalt columns like thousands of upright pillars. Most of these have 5 or 6 sides ; the Causeway (Antrim, Ireland) has 40,000 columns. FINGAL'S CAVE (named after a legendary Irish hero) is *c.*230ft long, 60ft high, and is noted for the solemn music made by wind and wave.

base, in chemistry, substance which reacts with an acid to form a salt and water. In geometry, the base of a triangle is the side opposite the apex.

baseball, national game of USA, much like the game of rounders. The field is diamond-shaped (90ft square) ; the bat used is a long club ; the ball is *c.*9in round. The bowler is called the pitcher. The idea of the game is for the batsman to score runs and get round from his home plate to each of the 3 bases. There are 9 men to a side, and a side is out when 3 batsmen are dismissed. The National Baseball Association (of America) was founded 1858.

Basel, see BASLE

Bashan, *bā'shan,* region E. of the Sea of Galilee, Palestine, once noted for its fierce cattle.

Basic English, essentials of English evolved by C. K. Ogden ; comprises 850 words. Particulars may be obtained from the Orthological Institute.

Consult *The General Basic English Dictionary,* published by Evans Brothers. This gives in Basic English 40,000 senses of over 20,000 words.

The British Government bought the copyright of Basic English 1947.

basic slag, fertiliser rich in phosphates, also in lime, iron oxides and silica. A by-product in the manufacture of steel, it is excellent for clover crops. As clover gives the soil nitrogen, a good crop greatly enriches the soil.

Basle, *bäl, bä'zel,* Rhine city, Switzerland, manufactures silk, chemicals, etc. ; is a famous centre of learning ; pop.162,000.

Basques, *bäsks,* people living W. of the Pyrenees, or their descendants now living elsewhere, especially in the Argentine. A remarkable race, the Basques have many ancient traditions, old dances, and peculiar funeral ceremonies. They speak a language different from any other in Europe, and are unusually religious. The men are excellent soldiers, successful farmers, and daring sailors, many having been discoverers. Ignatius Loyola, the founder of the Jesuit order, was a Basque ; so was Francis Xavier, the 16th c. missionary.

By the BASQUE PROVINCES is meant part of NE. Spain now known as the provinces of Guipúzcoa, Vizcaya (that is, Biscay), and Álava.

Basra, *bŭs'rä,* town, Iraq, a port 60m from the Persian Gulf ; linked with Baghdad by rail, and on the England–India air route ; noted for dates ; pop.286,000.

Bass Rock, *bas,* basaltic rock, 350ft high, in the Firth of Forth ; inhabited by solan geese ; figures in R. L. Stevenson's *Catriona* in the tale of *Tod Lapraik.*

Bass Strait, channel, with isls and coral reefs, between Tasmania and Australia.

Bastille, *bas-tēl',* once a great prison in Paris ; begun *c.*1370 as a building with two towers ; later six more towers were added, and the lofty walls protected by a moat. So many prisoners were secretly or wrongly locked behind its heavy doors that the Bastille became a symbol of injustice, and its capture 14 July 1789 may be said to mark the beginning of the French Revolution. A mob attacked the fortress, and after some hours of furious fighting an entrance was gained, and the Governor killed ; the destruction of the building began next day. A bronze column with a figure of Liberty now stands on the site of the Bastille.

bastinado, *bas-ti-nä'dō,* Asiatic torture. The soles of the prisoner's feet are beaten till he is driven mad with pain.

Basutoland, *bä-soo-tō-,* Native Territory of S. Africa ; area 11,716sq.m ; pop. 560,000. Known as ' the Switzerland of S. Africa,' Basutoland has magnificent scenery among the Drakensberg Mts ; produces grain, cattle, horses (especially Basuto ponies), wool ; cap. Maseru. Basutoland is under British rule.

bat, animal rather like a mouse ; has fur and claws and large ears, but is most remarkable for its wings, which are in fact membrane stretched from the long fore limbs to the much shorter hind limbs.

In Britain bats wake with the dusk and hunt for insects, especially moths ; in winter they hibernate in church towers, caves, ruins, trees, etc., often clinging in large clusters, and always hanging headdownwards. British bats include the common bat or pipistrelle ; mousecoloured bat ; noctule bat, and the longeared bat.

Bats are found in America, Africa and India. The Australian fruit-eating bat (the kalong or flying-fox) is the largest ; S. and Central America have two kinds of blood-sucking bats known as vampires.

bat, see ELECTRONICS

Batavia, *bat-ā'via,* port and cap. of the Netherlands E. Indies ; on the NW. coast of Java ; an important air terminus ; pop.260,000.

Bates, HENRY WALTER (1825–92), naturalist ; *b* Leicester ; went to Brazil 1848 with Alfred Russel Wallace, another naturalist ; returned 1859 with a vast collection of insects and plants, of which *c.*8,000 had never been seen before ; published 1863 his fascinating book, *The Naturalist on the Amazons.*

Bates, HERBERT ERNEST (1905–   ), British novelist, dramatist and short-

BATS

(1) *Pipistrelle* (2) *Flying Fox* (3) *Noctule Bat* (4) *South American Vampire Bat*
(5) *Long-Eared Bat*

story writer, excelling as the latter ;
served in the RAF in World War II.
His novels include *The Two Sisters* ;
The Poacher, etc.

Bath, cathedral city and health resort on
the R. Avon, Somerset ; in great favour
with the Romans for its medicinal springs
and hot baths ; now noted for its
Roman remains, possibly the finest in
England. The city was heavily bombed
in World War II ; pop.77,000.

Bath, ORDER OF THE, see CHIVALRY

bathos, *bā'thos*, in speech or writing means
coming suddenly from the sublime to
the ridiculous ; e.g. Having gazed in
awe upon the mighty constellations,
Smith rode home on his bicycle.

baths, were popular among the Greeks in
the 5th c. BC, and in the 3rd c. BC almost
every Roman city had its public baths.
We may see ruins of magnificent Roman
baths not only in Italy, but also in
Britain, e.g. at Caerwent (Venta Silurum)
Monmouthshire, and at Bath.

A town noted for its springs is called
a spa (*spä*) after the health resort (or
watering-place) of Spa, Belgium. British
spas include Bath, Harrogate, Buxton
and Cheltenham. Droitwich, Nantwich
and Northwich have brine (i.e. salty)
bath waters ; famous spas abroad are
Aix-les-Bains, Vichy and Plombières,
France ; St Moritz and Baden, Switzerland ; and Abano, Italy.

A Turkish bath is a hot air or hot
vapour bath used to cleanse the skin
by inducing perspiration, or as treatment
for various ailments.

Bath-sheba, -*shē'bä*, wife of David, King
of Israel. She was the mother of Solomon (2 Samuel, 11, 12 ; 1 Kings, 1, 2).

Bathurst, town, New South Wales, Australia ; centre of an agricultural, fruit-
growing and mining region.

Bathurst, chief town and port, Gambia,
W. Africa ; near the mouth of the
Gambia R. ; exports ground-nuts.

Batley, woollen-manufacturing town, W.
Yorkshire ; pop.39,000.

Baton Rouge, *bat'ŭn roozh*, i.e. Fr. *red
stick*, port and cap., Louisiana, USA,
on the R. Mississippi ; has a spacious
harbour, much trade in sugar, cotton,
lumber, etc. ; pop.35,000.

Batten, JEAN (1909–   ), NZ aviator ;
flew alone from England to Australia
(Port Darwin) May 1934 ; set up many
records, including solo flight Australia–
England (5 days 21 hrs) Oct 1936. See
AVIATION

battering ram, old type of weapon for
knocking down walls or doors ; actually
a heavy beam swinging from supporting
scaffolding, and worked by as many as
100 men. Mentioned in the Bible, it
was used by the Romans, who named it
aries (a ram) because the end was
sometimes shaped like a ram's head.

Battersea, borough of London, S. of the
R. Thames ; noted for its electric
power-station ; pop.117,000.

battery, see ACCUMULATORS AND BATTERIES

battle-axe, weapon with a heavy, sharp
blade and long handle ; much used by
knights in the Middle Ages.

Battle of Britain, decisive air combat
(Aug–Sept 1940) of World War II.
The attack (largely planned by Field-
Marshal Hermann Goering) began
8 Aug 1940, and was chiefly aimed at
SE. England and London. It was intended to prepare the way for a sea-
borne invasion of SE. England, but the
German air-losses were so heavy that
they abandoned the attempt. Outnumbered, but exploiting to the full the
superiority of their Spitfires and Hurricanes, the RAF pilots fought a magnificent defensive battle. RAF losses were
375 pilots killed, 358 wounded. Speaking in Parliament 20 Aug. the Prime
Minister (Winston Churchill) made the
memorable declaration : *Never in the
field of human conflict was so much owed
by so many to so few.*

In commemoration of this battle the
road from London to Dover (A20) is
now known as Battle of Britain Avenue.

Battle of Britain Sunday is the Sunday
nearest to 15 Sept. The Battle of Britain
Chapel, Westminster Abbey, was opened
1947. See AVIATION

Batum, *bä-tūm'*, Black Sea port, Adjar,
USSR ; linked by rail and petroleum
pipe-line with Baku ; exports oil.

Baum, VICKI, *bowm* (1896–   ), German
woman novelist, *b* Vienna ; achieved
fame with *Grand Hotel.* Other books
include *Secret Sentence* ; *Falling Star* ;
The Weeping Wood, etc.

Baumé, ANTOINE, *bō-mā'* (1728–1804),
French chemist who invented the hydrometer ; studied the specific gravity of
liquids.

bauxite, *bawks'īt*, mineral, a hydrated
aluminium oxide, found in France,
Hungary, USA, etc. ; practically our
only source of aluminium. See PLATE 36

Bavaria, *bav-ār'iä*, German state ; area
29,486sq.m ; cap. Munich. Bavaria,
chiefly in the basin of the Danube, is
largely mountainous with dense forests ;
it produces salt, coal, iron, etc. The
capital of the Rhenish Palatinate (now
part of Bavaria, but separate from it) is
Speyer.

Bax, SIR ARNOLD (1883–   ), English
composer ; much of his music is based
on Celtic legend.

Baxter, RICHARD (1615–91). churchman,
b Rowton, Shropshire ; chiefly remembered for his book *The Saint's Everlasting
Rest.*

Bayard, PIERRE TERRAIL (1476–1524), brave
French soldier, known as ' the knight
without fear and without reproach ' ; is
said to have defended a bridge single-
handed against 200 Spanish soldiers
1503 ; was chiefly responsible for the
French victory at the Battle of Marig-
nano 1515 ; with 1,000 men defended
Mezières against 35,000. He was the
ideal soldier of his day.

Bayeux Tapestry, *bä-yě*, a most remarkable

example of old needlework to be seen at Bayeux, France ; is 200ft long and 19in wide ; of supreme interest for its 72 pictures illustrating in colour the history of England and Normandy from the day Harold II sailed for Normandy to his death at the battle of Hastings 1066. In all, there are 623 figures, 760 animals and birds, 41 ships, 37 buildings. The tapestry is said to have been worked by Matilda (wife of William the Conqueror).

bayonet, sword-like weapon said to be named from Bayonne, France, where bayonets were manufactured in the 17th century. It is attached to a rifle.

Bayreuth, *bī-roit'*, town, Bavaria, where the musician Wagner is buried, and where his memorial theatre stands ; pop.37,000.

bay tree, kind of laurel, an evergreen often 40ft high. The name is given to many evergreens and shrubs, but the true laurel is the bay tree. The ancient Greeks used its leaves to make crowns for brave soldiers, popular poets, and winners in the Olympic games ; hence *to crown somebody with laurels* is to confer an honour on him. Laureate comes from the word laurel ; see POET LAUREATE

BBC, short for British Broadcasting Corporation. See RADIO ; PLATES 61–63

BCG, see TUBERCULOSIS

BEA, short for British European Airways ; airlines link London with Copenhagen, Oslo, Prague, Stockholm, Madrid, etc.

Beachy Head, headland, Sussex, with chalk cliffs 533ft high ; an extension of the S. Downs.

beacon, *bē'kon* (OE *beacen*, a signal), fire kindled on a hill or headland to give warning, e.g. the beacons fired in England 1588 to spread news that the Spanish Armada was approaching.

Beaconsfield, *bek'-onz-fēld*, town, Buckinghamshire, where Edmund Burke is buried.

Beaconsfield, EARL OF, see DISRAELI, B.

beads, *bēds*, usually small ornaments of glass, amber, etc. The OE *bede* meant a prayer ; and Roman Catholics today wear a rosary, i.e. a crucifix hanging from a string of 50 beads. The small beads are fingered when saying an *Ave Maria*, the larger when saying a *Pater Noster*.

beagling, *bē'gling*, hunting hares with small dogs similar to foxhounds, known as beagles. The huntsmen follow on foot.

beam-radio, see RADIO

bean, plant probably brought to Britain by the Romans. It is highly nutritious. French or kidney-beans came from S. America 1597 ; runner beans are perhaps the easiest to grow ; SOY or SOYA BEANS are largely grown in Manchuria, and in recent years have taken up increased acreage in USA, S. Africa, etc. They are now employed in making soya flour, margarine, cattle-food, etc., and were experimented with in 1940 by Henry Ford with a view to using them in the manufacture of motor-car bodies. Fuel oil from soya beans is now being manufactured on an increasing scale.

bear, powerful animal with strong claws and thick fur ; was common in Britain till the 9th c. The European bear may weigh from 50–60st ; the grizzly bear of America is exceptionally fierce. Most bears climb trees, can stand upright,

BEARS
(1) *Grizzly Bear*   (2) *Malayan Honey Bear*

THE POLAR BEAR

sleep for months without food, and enjoy honey, especially the honey bear of Malaya. As a rule they live on vegetables, berries, etc. as well as flesh, but the polar bear (or white bear, *Thalarctos maritimus*) feeds on flesh only, and is notable for its exceedingly long neck. It is an excellent swimmer.

Bear-baiting was once a favourite but cruel sport in England, in which dogs were set against a chained bear, or one in a pit. A common pastime from the 12th to the 17th c., bear-baiting was forbidden 1835.

Beardmore Glacier, see POLAR REGIONS

beating the bounds, old English custom. Each district or parish had its boundary, often marked by stones, ditches, or hedges, and in May the parish priest, the churchwardens, beadle, and others used to go round the boundary, accompanied by boys who memorised the limits of the parish by beating the boundary stones, ditches, hedges, etc. with branches.

Beatitudes, *bē-at'i-tūds,* verses in the NT (Matthew 5) in which Jesus tells who are the blessed (or happy) people. The Beatitudes are almost a summary of what a Christian should be.

Beattie, JAMES, *bē'ti* (1735–1803), Scottish poet, *b* Laurencekirk, Kincardine ; remembered for his poem, *The Minstrel.*

Beatty, EARL, *bē'ti* (1871–1936), *b* Howbeck, Cheshire ; became an admiral (as Nelson did) when only 39 ; given command of the battle-cruiser squadron of the Home Fleet 1913. In World War I he fought the battle of Heligoland 1914 ; the battle of the Dogger Bank 1915 (when his flagship *Lion* was put out of action) ; and the memorable but unsatisfactory battle of Jutland (1916), after which the German fleet never again dared to put to sea. Admiral Sir David Beatty was created an earl 1919.

Beaumarchais, PIERRE AUGUSTIN CARON DE, *bō-mär-shā'* (1732–99), French dramatist, *b* Paris ; had a ready wit and a vivid imagination ; his greatest plays are *The Barber of Seville* and *The Marriage of Figaro.*

Beaumont and Fletcher, English dramatists of Shakespeare's day ; were among the friends he often met at the Mermaid Tavern, an inn in Cheapside, London.

FRANCIS BEAUMONT, *bō'mont* (1584–1616), born in Leicestershire, was a friend of Michael Drayton and Ben Jonson ; had a rare gift for poetry and humour ; noted for his poem *On the Tombs in Westminster Abbey.* While at the Mermaid Tavern he met JOHN FLETCHER (1579–1625), *b* Rye, Sussex. Fletcher died of plague, and was buried in Southwark Cathedral (London) ; his play *The Faithful Shepherdess* was written 1609.

The joint plays of Beaumont and Fletcher include *Cupid's Revenge, The Scornful Lady, The Knight of the Burning Pestle,* and *The Maid's Tragedy.* Beaumont was a master of plot, Fletcher of dialogue.

Beauvais, *bō-vā,* city, France, cap. of the Oise Department ; noted for its magnificent 13th c. cathedral, also for woven tapestries.

beaver, *bē'vĕr,* gnawing animal ; its body is often 30in long, not including a flat, hairless tail, another 12in in length ; has thick brown fur and webbed hind feet. European beavers (France, Poland and Norway) live in burrows ; the American beaver makes lodges of branches and mud in rivers and lakes, constructing dams across streams so as to keep the water deep enough to cover its home. It works at night. It feeds on river plants and the bark of trees.

There are no beavers in Britain now, though they were found in England till the 9th c., in Scotland till the 16th.

Beaverbrook, LORD (1879–   ), British statesman and newspaper proprietor, *b* New Brunswick (Canada) ; entered Parliament (Unionist) 1910 ; created Lord Beaverbrook 1917 ; Minister for Aircraft Production 1940–41 ; controls the *Daily Express* group of newspapers ; championed Empire Free Trade.

Bec, village, Normandy. In its 11th c. Benedictine monastery Anselm and Lanfranc were monks.

Bechuanaland, *bek-ū'änä-,* British protectorate of S. Africa, area 275,000sq.m, native pop.265,000. The products include Kaffir corn, mealies, beans ; great herds of cattle are reared. The region is administered from Mafeking.

Becket, THOMAS À, *bek'et* (*d* 1170) ; *b* London. As Chancellor of England he was on good terms with Henry II. Made Archbishop of Canterbury 1162, he was apparently pious and austere.

At that period there was a civil or lay court, often punishing offenders severely, and a Church court which frequently administered comparatively light punishment. Accused people, therefore, claimed the right to be tried in the

BEAVERS
at work on the construction of their house and dam

latter if they had the slightest connection with the Church. Henry II declared that all law-breakers should be tried in a civil court ; Becket denied this. In the *Constitutions of Clarendon* (16 laws drawn up by the king at Clarendon, Wiltshire, 1164) it was decreed that clerics might be tried in a Church court, and that if found guilty they should be punished in a civil court. To this Becket would not at first agree. He went to Rome to seek the Pope's advice.

Returning, he made his peace with Henry II, but was still troublesome, so much so that, in a fit of temper, the king gave a hint to four knights (Reginald FitzUrse, William de Tracey, Hugh de Morville and Richard Breto) that he would be glad to be rid of such an archbishop. The knights hurried to Canterbury, and there murdered Becket in his cathedral. His tomb was for many years visited by pilgrims, e.g. those described by Chaucer in *The Canterbury Tales*. The story has been used by T. S. Eliot in his play *Murder in the Cathedral*.

Becquerel, ANTOINE HENRI, *bek-rel'*, (1852–1908), French scientist ; studied uranium and discovered radioactivity ; shared the Nobel Prize (physics) with M. and Mme Curie 1903.

Beddgelert, see GELLERT

Bede, *bēd* (*d* 735), known as the Venerable Bede, monk of Jarrow, County Durham ; regarded as the most learned scholar of his day. One of our earliest historians, he wrote (in Latin) the *Historia Ecclesiastica*, an account of Saxon England ; also a translation of the Gospel of St John, which he finished a few hours before he died.

St Cuthbert, his pupil, tells us that towards evening a youth who was writing to Bede's dictation, said, ' There is yet one more sentence to write, dear master.'

' Write quickly,' answered Bede.

After a while the youth said, ' It is finished.'

' Thou hast spoken truly,' said Bede. ' It is finished.'

Then he bade the monks place him where he had always knelt to pray ; and, lying thus on the stone floor of his cell, he died singing, *Gloria Patri*. His tomb is in Durham Cathedral.

Bedford, co.tn, Bedfordshire ; on the R. Ouse ; manufactures agricultural machinery, lace, etc. ; has a noted grammar school. John Bunyan wrote *The Pilgrim's Progress* in prison there, and his birthplace (Elstow) is close by ; pop.52,000.

Near by is a Government aeronautical research station which will cost about £20,000,000, and is expected to employ 5,000 persons.

Bedfordshire, midland county of England ; mainly agricultural ; co.tn, Bedford.

Bedouins or **Beduins,** *bed'u-in*, wandering tribes of desert Arabs in Arabia and N. Africa ; have been keepers of flocks and herds for thousands of years ; dwell in tents.

bee, four-winged insect with a sting ; may be either solitary or social. Solitary bees include the carpenter-bee, which tunnels rotting wood and lays eggs there ; the mason-bee, which builds cells of grains of sand. The building genius of such bees has been vividly described by Jean Henri Fabre. Of bees living in a colony, examples are the humble-bee (a wild bee living in groups of 50–300) and the hive bee.

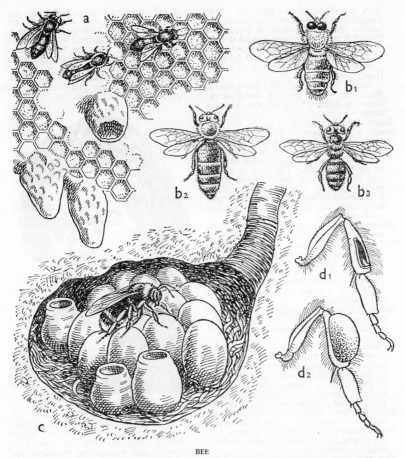

BEE

(a) *a portion of a honey-bee comb showing the queen cells—one is empty* (b) *honey bees :*
(1) *a drone* (2) *a queen* (3) *a worker* (c) *the underground nest of the humble bee, with the*
queen, the cocoons and the honey pots (d) *leg of the humble bee :* (1) *with the pollen basket*
(2) *with a load of pollen*

Social bees that have been domesticated form communities having (a) a
queen, usually larger than other bees,
often living 3 years, and able to lay
2–3,000 eggs a day, (b) drones, i.e. males,
non-workers, one of which mates with
the queen. The drones are driven from
the hives in autumn or killed by (c) the
workers, of which a hive may have
50,000–100,000. Workers, living only
6–8 weeks as perfect insects, have a
pollen-basket in each hind leg, and in
these pollen from flowers is carried,
later being made into ' bee-bread ' for
the grubs. Each worker has on its
underside eight pockets for secreting
the wax used in making the honey-comb.
Workers also gather nectar (i.e. the

sweet juices of flowers) by sucking it
through a tube in the lower lip. This,
when made into honey, is stored in the
honeycomb of the hive, the bee intending
it for winter use, though the bee-keeper
takes a share for himself. Bees have
been known to fly 60m in a day.
A new colony begins when the bees
swarm, leave the old hive to a new
queen and her following, and, being
taken, start life in a new hive. For 20
hours or more the newly-hived bees
may hang in a cluster while making
enough wax to begin building a new
comb, i.e. a series of six-sided cells
required for the first grubs. An egg
hatches in c.3 days, and out comes a
white grub, fed by the workers for 5

days on liquid food, then on ' bee-bread,' a mixture of honey, pollen and water. After c.20 days as pupa and nymph it becomes a fully-fledged bee.

As bees fertilise flowers they are friends of gardeners, fruit-growers and farmers.

A collection of bee-hives is an apiary (Latin *apis*, a bee).

Read *A Manual of Bee-Keeping*, Wedmore ; *The Joy of Bee-Keeping*, Kennedy-Bell ; *Life of the Bee*, Maeterlinck.

Beebe, DR, see DIVING

beech, tree, common in Britain ; may be 100ft high ; has a smooth and silvery green trunk ; finely toothed leaves that are light green in spring, brown, orange, or red in autumn. The fruit is a nut, and beech nuts (or beech mast) make good pig-food. The copper beech, a handsome tree with purplish leaves, was introduced into Britain from Germany c.100 years ago.

Beecham, SIR THOMAS (1879–   ), conductor and composer ; noted for his Promenade Concerts at the Albert Hall (London) ; chief founder of the Imperial League of Opera 1927 ; founded the London Philharmonic Orchestra 1932 ; long associated with the BBC ; a striking personality of the musical world.

Beecher, HENRY WARD (1813–87), American preacher, *b* Litchfield, Connecticut, USA ; supported the abolition of slavery.

beefeater, nickname for a Yeoman of the Guard, i.e. a British soldier who has a pension for bravery and is also a member of the Royal Household. The Warders of the Tower of London (closely related to the Yeomen of the Guard) still wear a quaint and picturesque Tudor costume.

beer, alcoholic drink made from malted barley, hops and yeast. See BREWING

Beersheba, town, Palestine; see Genesis 21; the phrase *from Dan to Beersheba* means from one end to the other.

beet, root crop, including the common beet and mangel-wurzel ; also *sugar-beet*, grown in Europe for many years before being raised in Britain on any considerable scale. One of the first sugar-beet factories in Britain was opened in 1912 at Cantley, Norfolk. Sugar-beet yields 15–20% sugar. Read *The New Farming*, D. H. Robinson (Nelson).

Beethoven, LUDWIG VAN, *bā'tō-ven* (1770–1827), one of the world's supreme musicians, *b* Bonn, Germany. At four he had written three sonatas ; at nine he knew all the music his drunken father could teach him. He early became notable as a pianist, and when only sixteen was given music lessons by Mozart. His mother died when he was seventeen, and he greatly missed her affection. Poor but ambitious, he had to shoulder the burden of supporting the family. At twenty-two, in Vienna, he had Haydn as his tutor.

A strange young man, he had high moral principles and a kindly disposition, but he was also proud, impatient and often suspicious. Before he was thirty he was afflicted with approaching deafness ; later he became stone deaf, one who lived, thought and felt in music and loved it with a burning passion, yet tortured in a silent prison, hence his ill-temper and rudeness, and also the pathos of his genius.

BEETHOVEN 1770–1827

It should be noted that to his brilliant inspirations this lonely and rugged master musician brought the most careful and painstaking revision after revision.

Among his superb legacy of immortal music may be mentioned his chamber music, including sixteen pieces for string quartets ; his sonatas for pianoforte and violin and the thirty-two for the pianoforte only ; his nine matchless symphonies ; his overtures ; and his opera *Fidelio* etc.

beetle, insect with wings completely covered by horny sheaths (*elytra*). Beetles appear to be dressed in shining ' armour,' actually a thick skin (cuticle) of *chitin*. The jaws are strong, and sight, hearing and smell are usually highly developed. Though few beetles fly, all are able to run quickly, and some are powerful swimmers. Of at least 150,000 species, 3,000 are found in Britain.

The world's largest beetle, found in S. America, is *Titanus giganteus*, sometimes almost 9in long.

Beeton, MRS, name by which Isabella Mary Mason (1836–65) is best known ; author of the famous book on household management.

BEF, short for British Expeditionary Force, i.e. any British army fighting overseas.

'**Beggar's Opera, The**,' see GAY, JOHN

begum, bē'gŭm, Mohammedan woman of high rank in India ; possibly the feminine of the Turkish word beg, a lord.

Beira, bā'rä, town, Portuguese East Africa ; airport on the Durban–Calcutta route.

Beirut, bā'root, Mediterranean port and cap. of the state of Lebanon ; exports silk, oils, coffee, cotton goods, etc. ; pop.234,000.

Beith, JOHN HAY, see HAY, IAN

Beke, CHARLES TILSTONE, bēk (1800–74), b Stepney (London); explored the sources of the Nile ; made discoveries near Mount Sinai when in Syria and Palestine.

Belem, see PARÁ

belemnite, bel'em-nīt, dart-shaped fossil of an extinct sea creature ; found in chalk.

Belfast, bel'fäst, cap., N. Ireland ; also the co.tn of County Antrim. A shipping port on Belfast Lough, Belfast has been a city since 1888, and is a centre of shipbuilding, linen, banking, commerce, etc.; severely bombed in World War II ; pop.438,000.

Belgae, bel'gē, ancient Celtic inhabitants of Gaul ; dwelt between the Marne and Seine ; conquered by Julius Caesar.

Belgian Congo, Belgian colony, Africa. The area (c.909,000sq.m) covers most of the R. Congo and its tributaries. The colony has a seaboard on the west coast, where the Congo enters the Atlantic at Banana ; the climate is tropical ; most of the country is fertile, producing palm-oil, palm-kernels, cotton, rubber and cocoa. Minerals include copper, tin, gold, manganese ; also radium. Railways and roads have been extensively built ; pop.11,000,000 ; cap. Leopoldville, an air-terminus.

Belgium, low-lying kingdom between France and Germany, formerly part of the Netherlands ; area c.12,000sq.m. The chief rivers are the Schelde and Meuse. Belgium has a short N. Sea coast. The Ardennes rise to over 2,000ft, but most of the country is flat, and that near the coast is divided into ' polders,' areas of low land reclaimed from the sea, and protected by dikes. The country has rich supplies of coal, iron, zinc, etc., and is largely industrial, its chief industries being mining, cotton, woollen and linen goods, lace and glassware. It has many important canals, e.g. the Albert Canal, 79m in length.

The inhabitants are chiefly (a) Flemish-speakers of German origin (b) Walloons, mostly speaking French ; almost all are RC. The towns include Antwerp, the chief port ; Ghent, Liége, Ostend, Bruges and Brussels, the capital.

An independent state since 1830, Belgium suffered much in World War I when Albert, King of the Belgians,

moved his capital to Havre, Germany having attacked his kingdom in spite of the Treaty of London 1839 (the so-called ' scrap of paper ') by which she had promised to respect Belgian neutrality. Belgium suffered again 1939–45, being under Nazi control 1940–44.

The population of Belgium is c.8,386,000, the density (710 per sq.m) being greater than that of any other European country.

Belgrade, bel-grād', city and cap., Yugoslavia. The name means ' white fortress.' The city stands where the Sava joins the Danube ; it has grown rapidly, and is now a centre of culture ; pop. 250,000.

Belisha beacon, see HORE-BELISHA, L.

bell, musical instrument, generally a metal cup ; may be rung by a clapper or tongue, or struck by hammers. A set of bells may be a chime or carillon. Bell metal is usually an alloy of copper and tin.

Church bells were known in Europe in the 6th century.

Notable bells include : Big Ben in the Clock Tower of the Houses of Parliament, which weighs 13 tons, and was named after Sir Benjamin Hall, Chief Commissioner of Works ; also the Tsar Kolokol (Moscow), 200 tons, 26ft high, cast 1735. Great Paul at St Paul's Cathedral, weighs 17 tons, and is the biggest in England. The largest bell of Liverpool Cathedral weighs 14½ tons. The most famous bell in USA is the Liberty Bell, Philadelphia, which rang out tidings of the signing of the Declaration of Independence 1776.

On ships at sea a bell rings every 30min, 8 bells being noon. The day is divided into 7 watches :

afternoon watch	noon to 4pm
first dog watch	4pm to 6pm
second dog watch	6pm to 8pm
first watch	8pm to midnight
middle watch	midnight to 4am
morning watch	4am to 8am
forenoon watch	8am to noon

In the Royal Navy the second dog watch is called the last dog watch.

For electric bell, see MAGNETISM

Bell, ALEXANDER GRAHAM (1847–1922), inventor of the telephone, b Edinburgh ; lived in USA ; patented his telephone 1876.

Bell, SIR CHARLES (1774–1842), Scottish surgeon, b Edinburgh ; made the discovery (1807) that there are two kinds of nerves, sensory and motor, one of the most important achievements in medical science.

Bell, GERTRUDE (1868–1926), English woman with a remarkable variety of talents ; was scholar, historian, nature-lover, poet and archaeologist, especially in Syria, Arabia, etc. ; served as a British intelligence agent in Iraq 1914–18 ; gathered treasures for Baghdad museum.

Bell, HENRY (1767–1830), Scottish inventor, *b* Linlithgow ; worked as a shipbuilder. While in Glasgow he began experimenting with a steamship ; his *Comet* began plying regularly from Glasgow to Greenock 1812, the first successful steamer on any river in Europe. She was 40ft long, and had paddles driven by a 3hp engine.

Belle Isle, *bel,* British island between Newfoundland and Labrador, and in Belle I. Strait, leading to the R. St Lawrence ; also an island off the W. coast of France.

Bellerophon, *bel-er′ō-fon,* in old Greek tales, a hero who caught and bridled a winged horse, the famous Pegasus.
Bellerophon was the British battleship on which Napoleon surrendered 1815.

belles-lettres, *bel-let′r,* French : fine literature, i.e. writing which shows good taste, especially poetry and essays.

Bellini, surname of three Italian artists : Jacopo (1400–70) and his sons (*a*) Gentile (1429–1507) and (*b*) Giovanni (1430–1516), whose masterpieces include *The Agony in the Garden* and *The Blood of the Redeemer,* formerly in the Northbrook collection. His portrait of the Doge of Venice (National Gallery) was painted about the year 1505.

bell-metal, alloy of copper and tin.

Belloc, HILAIRE, *bel′ok* (1870–), writer, born in France of a French father and an English mother ; became a British subject 1902 ; noted for his poetry, much of it humorous, his novels and essays, and a series of historical books, e.g. studies of Danton, Robespierre, Richelieu, Marlborough, Cromwell ; also *A History of England.* Others of his books include *The Old Road, Hills and the Sea, The Path to Rome,* etc.

Bell Rock, see INCHCAPE ROCK

Belorussia, see USSR

Belsen, German concentration camp (prison) near Hanover, scene of barbaric cruelties during World War II.

Belshazzar, *bel-shaz′ĕr* (*d* 538BC), Babylonian general, son (apparently) of Nabonidus the last king of Babylon. For the story of Belshazzar's feast and the writing on the wall which foretold the fall of Babylon, see Daniel 5, where Belshazzar is wrongly described as Nebuchadnezzar's son.

Bemersyde, *bēm′er-sīd,* house and park, Berwickshire ; near the R. Tweed ; for seven centuries the home of the Haigs ; presented 1921 to Earl Haig as a gift from the British Empire.

ben, in Scottish place-names, a mountain (gaelic *beinn,* a mountain, especially one with a sharp or pointed peak).

Benares, *be-nä′rez,* sacred city of the Hindus, India ; on the R. Ganges ; has 1,700 temples and a vast array of mosques and towers ; pilgrims crowd the steps to the river to bathe in its waters. Benares has a large trade in country produce, and is noted for jewellery, silks, shawls, toys, etc., and especially brass ware ; pop.263,000.

Benbow, JOHN (*d* 1702), gallant British admiral *b* Shrewsbury ; remembered for his fight against the French in the W. Indies 1702.

bench-mark, broad arrow carved or painted on buildings for use in an ordnance survey.

Benedict, *ben′e-dikt* (480–543), Italian saint ; founded an order of monks known as the Benedictine order. In Benedict's lifetime there were only 14 Benedictine monasteries, but in the 14th c. there were *c.*37,000, and at least 300 of the English monasteries closed by Henry VIII were Benedictine. Downside, Ampleforth and Buckfastleigh are English examples ; Cluny (France) was a famous Benedictine abbey. The Benedictine motto is, *Laborare est orare,* i.e. to work is to pray. See MONKS AND NUNS

Benedictines, see MONKS AND NUNS

Benelux, name given 1947 to a group of Western European countries—Belgium, Netherlands and Luxemburg—when they agreed to co-operate for mutual advantage. Full economic union began 1 July 1950.

Benes, DR EDUARD, *bā′nesh* (1884–1948), President of the Czechoslovak Government 1940, *b* Bohemia ; supporter of the League of Nations, voiced the rights of the smaller European countries.
Read *Dr Benes,* Compton Mackenzie.

benev′olences, loans to certain English kings. Though supposed to be made freely they were actually forced ; first demanded by Edward IV ; last employed by James I.

Bengal, *ben-göl,* region of which *c.*29,000 sq.m are in India, 54,000sq.m in Pakistan ; formerly a province of British India W. of Assam. Watered by the Ganges and Brahmaputra, and largely a productive plain, Bengal produces rice, jute, oil-seeds, sugar, silk, tea, etc. ; pop.60,000,000, both Mohammedans and Hindus.

Bengali, *ben-göl′i,* language spoken by *c.*40,000,000 people in Bengal (India) and Assam.

Benghazi, *ben-gä′zē,* province, Cyrenaica, N. Africa, inhabited chiefly by Arabs, Greeks, Maltese, etc. ; produces cereals and wool. The port, Benghazi (pop. *c.*63,000), was the scene of much fighting in World War II. See EL ALAMEIN

Benjamin, Jacob's youngest son. See Genesis 35.

Ben Macdhui, *mac-doo′e,* mountain, Aberdeenshire ; 4,296ft ; second highest in Britain.

Bennett, ARNOLD (1867–1931), novelist, born near Hanley, Staffordshire ; author of *The Grand Babylon Hotel*; *Buried Alive*; *Riceyman Steps,* etc., but his lasting fame rests on his stories of life in the Potteries, i.e. the drab district of Staffordshire which is the scene of *Anna of the Five Towns,* the towns being Tunstall, Burslem, Hanley, Stoke-on-Trent and Longton (called by Bennett, Turnhill, Bursley, Hanbridge, Knype and Longshaw). *Anna* was followed by *The Old Wives' Tale*, and the Clayhanger series : *Clayhanger* ; *Hilda Lessways* ; and *These Twain*. All are realistic pictures of provincial life.

Bennett was also a journalist and playwright. Parts of his remarkable diary were published after his death.

Ben Nevis, *nĕ'vis* ; *nev'is*, highest mt. in Britain ; in Inverness-shire ; rises 4,406ft ; pierced (1930) by a water-tunnel to Fort William.

Bentinck, LORD WILLIAM CAVENDISH (1774–1839), Governor-General of India (1833–1835) ; remembered as the Englishman who put an end to the Thugs, i.e. Indian murderers (at first Mohammedans, later Hindus) who strangled travellers, and robbed and buried them. He also prevented Indian widows from throwing themselves on the funeral pyres of their husbands, a practice known as *suttee*.

Bentley, PHYLLIS (1894–   ), *b* Halifax, Yorkshire ; critic, lecturer, author of a series of novels dealing with the industrial history of the W. Riding, including *Take Courage* ; *Inheritance* ; *Sleep in Peace*, etc.

benzene, *ben'zēn*, hydrocarbon compound ; often confused with benzol, the latter being the commercial name for benzene. Strictly, benzene, C_6H_6, is a highly inflammable by-product in the manufacture of coal-gas. Discovered by Michael Faraday 1825, it is much used in making drugs and aniline dyes. Nitrobenzene, $C_6H_5NO_2$, smells like almonds.

Beowulf, *bā'ō-wulf*, OE or Anglo-Saxon poem of over 3,000 lines ; possibly the oldest epic in any Teutonic language. It is thought to have been composed in the 7th or 8th c. See ANGLO-SAXONS

Béranger, PIERRE JEAN DE, *bārän-zhā'* (1780–1857), French poet whose clever and charming poems and songs are still greatly loved, among them *Le Roi d'Yvetot*.

Berchtesgaden, *bĕrch'tes-gä-den*, town among the Bavarian Alps (Germany). It is set amid magnificent scenery, and the people (*c*.4,000) are renowned for their skill as wood-carvers. Some 16m off Adolf Hitler had his private house, richly furnished and so strongly fortified that he believed no-one could force an entry.

berg, hot, dry, coastal wind in S. Africa.

Bergen, port and fortified town on the W. coast of Norway; has a fine harbour and important fisheries : is a noted tourist centre ; pop.107,000.

Bergson, PROFESSOR HENRI, *berg-sön* (1859–1941), French thinker and writer ; his books include *Laughter* (an essay on the meaning of ' comic '), and *Matter and Memory*. Bergson's theory of Creative Evolution had great influence on many writers of his generation in Britain as well as in France.

beri-beri, see RICE

Bering, VITUS (1680–1741), Danish navi-gator who sailed along the N. coast of Asia and discovered Alaska, N. America. Wrecked on the homeward voyage, he died on Bering I. in the Bering Sea, a part of the N. Pacific Ocean. Bering Strait separates Asia from America.

Berkeley, *bärk'li*, village, Gloucestershire. Here is the castle where Edward II was murdered 1327.

Berkeley, GEORGE (1685–1753), Bishop of Cloyne, Irish philosopher and church-man, *b* Kilkenny, Ireland. His great contribution to philosophical thought is his demonstration that the doctrine of matter, as held by scientists and philo-sophers of his day, was inconsistent and should therefore be abandoned. His theory of ' Immaterialism ' is expounded in *A New Theory of Vision* (1709) ; *The Principles of Human Knowledge* (1710) ; and *Three Dialogues between Hylas and Philonous* (1713), all written when he was quite young. His *Alciphron* (1732) is a comprehensive defence of Christian faith and order against the ' free-thinkers ' of the 18th c., and his last work, *Siris* (1744), is an odd com-bination of medical, philosophical and religious speculations. He realised early the immense importance which America would have in the future development of civilisation and formed a project for a Christian community and college in Bermuda ; but this failed through lack of support, and after spending three years (1728–31) in Rhode Island he returned to Ireland. He was made a Bishop in 1734.

Berkshire, *bärk'-*, small English county S. of the R. Thames ; has chalk downs ; co.tn Reading.

Berlin, *bur-lin'*, city and cap., Germany ; on the R. Spree. Prior to World War II, Berlin, also the capital of Prussia was a remarkably handsome city. Its many fine buildings included the royal and imperial palaces, the Reichstag, the library, university, etc., but immense damage was done by allied bombing before the city surrendered 2 May 1945. Its pop. 1939 was over 4,330,000. A great railway and canal centre, Berlin is also a centre of trade in cereals, wool, cattle, etc., and has long been noted for its manufacture of woollens and other textiles, bronze articles and beer. After World War II Berlin was governed by Britain, US, France and Russia, each responsible for a given sector. Russian blockade of other sectors gave rise to the Berlin Air Lift 1948, the Western zones being supplied with necessities by a continued air-shuttle maintained by British and American aircraft.

Berlin Conference, meeting 1884 at which representatives of many European countries and USA attempted to share out the African continent, especially the Congo region ; the Berlin Act was signed 1885 by all except representatives from USA.

Berlin, CONGRESS OF, brought about 1878

a re-arrangement of conditions between Turkey and Russia, and made further alterations in E. Europe. The congress was promoted by Lord Beaconsfield (Disraeli), who returned saying that he had secured peace with honour.

Berlin Decree, order made by Napoleon 1806 forbidding all trade between France and Britain.

Berlioz, HECTOR, *ber-lē-öz* (1803–69), French romantic musician remembered for his *Fantastic Symphony* ; his oratorio *The Childhood of Christ* ; and his operas *Benvenuto Cellini* and *Beatrice and Benedict*, etc.

Bermondsey, *bŭr'mund-zi*, London borough S. of the Thames.

Bermudas or **Somers Islands,** *bĕr-mū'däs*, group of British islands in the Atlantic, 580m from Cape Hatteras ; area 21sq.m. The climate is mild, and the islands are noted for junipers, onions, vegetables, flowers, etc. Discovered 1527 by Bermudez (a Spaniard), they were colonised by Admiral Somers (*sŭm'ĕrz*) 1609 ; cap. Hamilton. The USA leased a naval and air base in Bermuda 1940. Bermuda, a popular tourist centre, is a BOAC airport.

Bernadotte, COUNT FOLKE (1895–1948), Swede who was head of the Swedish Red Cross in World War II, later becoming mediator in Palestine for the United Nations. He was assassinated.

Bernadotte, JEAN BAPTISTE JULES, see CHARLES XIV

Bernard of Clairvaux, *-kler-vō'* (1090–1153), saint, born near Dijon, France ; was abbot of a monastery at Clairvaux in Champagne (France) where he won fame for his piety. Bernard urged Christians to join the Second Crusade 1146.

Berne, *bŭrn*, city and cap., Switzerland ; is 1,790ft above sea-level ; almost surrounded by the R. Aar ; has notable modern buildings ; is a famous centre of learning ; pop.130,000.

Bernese Oberland, *bŭr-nēz ō'bĕr-länt*, part of the Alps between lakes Geneva and Lucerne ; the peaks include the Jungfrau, 13,671ft, and Wetterhorn, 12,150ft.

Bernhardt, SARAH, *bern'härt* (1845–1923), known as ' the divine Sarah,' French actress with a stage presence that never failed to hold great audiences spellbound; *b* Paris ; played in Victor Hugo's *Hernani* etc.

Bernicia, see NORTHUMBRIA

Berwickshire, *ber'ik-*, county, SE. Scotland ; separated from England partly by the R. Tweed ; co.tn Duns.

Berwick-upon-Tweed, *ber'ik*, port, Northumberland ; was a neutral border town prior to 1885 ; scene of much border warfare.

beryllium, *beril'i-ŭm*, hard, white and very light metal and element, Be ; atomic weight 9·02 ; atomic number 4. Beryllium aluminium silicate is the gem, beryl, the emerald, being a green variety.

Berzelius, JONS JACOB, *bĕr-zē'li-ŭs* (1779–1848), Swedish chemist who checked

atomic and molecular weights of many chemical substances ; invented the system of symbols now used for the elements, e.g. Sn for tin, H for hydrogen, etc.

Besançon, *bĕ-zän-sŏn'*, town, France, on the R. Doubs ; noted for clocks and watches ; pop.60,000.

Bess'emer, SIR HENRY (1813–98), engineer and scientist, born near Hitchin, Hertfordshire ; discovered (*a*) that pig-iron contains an unknown quantity of carbon, (*b*) that by blowing air through the molten metal all the carbon can be burnt up, and (*c*) that when the carbon (with various impurities) is removed, a *known* amount of carbon may be added to produce fine steel of a required grade. This is called the Bessemer Process, important not only in the production of high-grade steels, but for the valuable waste (basic slag), rich in phosphorus, and used as a fertiliser.

Bess of Hardwick, see SHREWSBURY, EARL OF

beta (β), second letter of the Gk alphabet.

A β-particle is the name given to a fast-moving electron (actually a negatively charged particle) shot from certain radioactive substances as part of the product of their disruption. β-rays are streams of such particles. The betatron is an apparatus for greatly increasing the speed of an electron stream. See RADIOACTIVITY

Betelgeuse, see ASTRONOMY

Bethany, *beth'ä-ni*, village 2m from Jerusalem, Palestine ; mentioned in the NT as the home of Lazarus and his sisters, Martha and Mary.

Bethel, *beth'el* (i.e. house of God), town, now in ruins, *c*.12m from Jerusalem, Palestine. There Abraham pitched his tent, and Jacob dreamed of a ladder set up from earth to heaven (Genesis 28).

A small chapel is often called a bethel.

Bethesda, *bethes'-dä*, pool in Jerusalem. Formerly lame and blind people hoped to be healed by bathing in its waters ; read John 5.

Bethlehem, *beth'lē-hem*, town, Palestine, *c*.5m from Jerusalem ; now called Beit Lahm ; birthplace of King David, hence known as ' David's royal city ' (Luke 2). Near its gate was a spring (read 2 Sam. 23) ; the prophet Micah declared that the Messiah would be born in Bethlehem (Micah 5), and today, in what is believed to be the oldest church in the world, is the Grotto of the Nativity (a crypt) said to have been built for the wife of the Emperor Constantine on the spot where Jesus was born.

In recent years the bells of Bethlehem have frequently been broadcast at Christmas. Read H. V. Morton's *In the Steps of the Master*.

Bethsaida, *beth-sä'idä*, name of two villages in Galilee, Palestine, (*a*) W. of L. Galilee, home of Peter, Andrew and Philip, (*b*) NE. of the lake, and scene of the feeding of the Five Thousand.

betony, *bet'ōni*, woodland plant with heart-shaped leaves ; the purple flowers appear June–Aug.

betting, see GAMBLING ; TOTALISATOR

Beveridge, LORD (1879–), British economist, *b* Rangpur, India ; began his study of unemployment before 1914 ; chairman of Inter-Departmental Committee on Social Insurance etc. 1941 ; introduced the *Beveridge Plan for Social Security*, 1942. His Report outlined schemes whereby there should be in the UK a Ministry of Social Security with local Security Offices to help all insured persons. He planned a single weekly contribution by insured persons covering all benefits ; a minimum income for man and wife of £2 a week ; payment of unemployment benefit without a means test ; unlimited sick pay ; retirement pensions for men at 65, women at 60 ; revised workmen's compensation ; compulsory insurance for everyone ; increased allowances for children ; free medical treatment. Private industrial insurance was to become a public service. See SOCIAL SECURITY

Beverley, old town, E. Yorkshire ; noted for its superb 13th–15th c. minster.

Bevin, RT. HON. ERNEST (1881–1951), Socialist chairman, General Council of Trades Union Congress 1937 ; Minister of Labour and National Service, 1940 ; Secretary of State for Foreign Affairs, 1945. During the exceptionally difficult years following World War II, he proved a wise, patient and firm statesman in international affairs, doing much to retain good relations with USA and to build up a W. Europe Union in opposition to the menace of Russian Communism. His attitude towards Germany won widespread approval. See EUROPE ; NORTH ATLANTIC PACT

bey, *bā*, title of distinguished Turkish officials ; also of the ruler of Tunis.

bhang, see HEMP

Bharat, now the official name for the new republic of India, its first President being Dr Rajendra Prasad.

Bhopal, *bō-päl*, state, Central India.

Bhutan, *boo-tän*, country N. of Bengal, India ; area *c.*18,000sq.m ; cap. Punakha.

Bi, chemical symbol for bismuth.

Bialystok, *bē-lō-stŏk'*, town, Poland, noted for woollen, silk, linen goods, etc. ; pop.107,000.

Biarritz, *bēä-rēts'*, French pleasure resort overlooking the Bay of Biscay ; pop. 21,000.

Bible (Greek *ta biblia*, the books), collection of ancient sacred writings comprising the Old Testament (OT) and the New Testament (NT), and forming the body of belief on which Christianity is based. The OT is a progressive record which reveals how the Jewish nation advanced from crude beginnings to a lofty and noble idea of God, and how they came through many sufferings to have a deeper understanding of His purpose ; in the NT this process of revelation culminates in the life, teachings, self-sacrifice and triumph of Jesus Christ.

Modern scholars have shown that the OT was not completed in its present form until the 2nd c. BC. It contains many ancient Jewish documents woven together to form a single stream of narrative, and between the various accounts of Jewish history that have been combined in this way there are many obvious contradictions. It is now widely agreed that the *Hexateuch* (the first five books of the OT with *Joshua*) fuses together several strands of history and legend that reach back perhaps to the 10th c. *Kings* and *Judges* were probably put together similarly in the 5th c. They contain documents nearly contemporary with the events described, and also a later account of the same events, which reflects a more critical attitude than that which appears in the documents.

The prophetic books contained in the OT record the teaching of righteousness and repentance by men of outstanding spiritual insight. *Amos* and *Hosea* belong to the 8th c. BC. *Micah* is dated 8th–7th c. BC. *Jeremiah*, *Ezekiel* and part of *Isaiah* are early 6th c. BC (before or during the captivity, 586–538BC) : the rest of *Isaiah* contains prophecies (probably not Isaiah's own) uttered *c.*540BC. *Malachi* and *Joel* are 5th c. prophets ; *Jonah* belongs to the 4th c. BC.

The *Psalms* are a compilation made after the captivity, and contain in poetic form the inspired vision of seekers after God ; *Proverbs* was put together in its present form in the 4th c. BC but incorporates some material that is much older. Probably written in the 5th c., *Job*, based on a legend thought to be ancient, is a poetic drama of great beauty, which presents the problems of God's dealing with men. *Ecclesiastes* belongs entirely to the 4th c. It is thus one of the latest books in the OT.

The NT is likewise a compilation. The Gospels seem only to have been written when it became necessary to preserve in documentary form the existing traditions, which were *oral* up till then, of the life of Jesus ; but even at that early date, tradition had developed differently in different places, and the relations of the Gospels to the traditions and to one another are not easy to disentangle. It is clear however that both Luke and Matthew made use of Mark's Gospel, which is therefore the earliest gospel, for John's is later than either Mark's or Luke's. All four were probably written between AD65 and AD125. The *Acts of the Apostles* was probably written *c.*AD95 ; it is probable that most of *St Paul's Epistles* were actually written by St Paul, who died *c.*AD64.

Besides the books contained in the NT there were many other early Christian writings. What should be included in the NT was a question not finally decided

4

until the 4th c. AD. The whole of the Bible was translated into Latin (the *Vulgate*) by Jerome in the late 4th c. AD, and this was the only version available until the Middle Ages.

In the Dark and Middle Ages Bibles were scarce, and even if they had been more plentiful, most people were unable to read and did not in any case understand Latin, the only language in which the Bible was available. In the 16th c. printed versions of the Bible in English, French, German, etc. became available in larger numbers, and Bible-reading increased. It began to be widely realised that Church practices and traditions were in many points at variance with the Bible record. The shock of this discovery was one of the main causes of the Reformation. Our English Bible was born when John Wycliffe, often called ' the Morning Star of the Reformation,' translated St Jerome's *Vulgate* from Latin into English. Preacher and scholar, Wycliffe made his famous translation at Lutterworth in Leicestershire, where he died 1384. Copies of Wycliffe's Bible had been made by hand, but William Tyndale's translation of the NT was printed at Cologne 1525. He is said to have been put to death near Brussels in 1536 while at work, in hiding, on a translation of the OT. Other translations into English include that by Miles Coverdale (1488–1569), and the Authorised Version (AV), made by 54 scholars for James I. This was published in 1611, and no other English translation has such dignity, simplicity and melody. Since then Bible-reading has been one of the principal ways in which knowledge of Christ's teaching has been spread throughout the world. No book has been translated into so many languages or so widely read, and it is not too much to say that of all the books of ancient peoples that have come down to us the Bible is the most interesting, the most valuable and the most important. Since the AV other translations have been made. The Revised Version (RV), made 1881–84, though a more accurate translation, is much less popular than the AV. Modern editions of the Bible include R. F. Weymouth's *The New Testament in Modern Speech*, James Moffatt's translation, and (1946–49) Monsignor R. A. Knox's translation into the English of our common speech, which succeeds in relating the message of the Bible to our own times. Another important modern version is the American *Revised Standard Version* of the Bible, of which the New Testament was published in 1946.

In 1934 the British Government bought for £100,000 the *Codex Sinaiticus*, a handwritten copy of part of a Bible believed to be 1,600 years old. It was found in 1844 in a monastery on Mt Sinai, and is now in the British Museum. In 1948 several MSS of parts of the Bible were found in a cave near Jericho which were judged to be at least 2,000 years old, the oldest known versions of parts of the Bible.

Our modern knowledge of the Bible and how it came to be written is largely the work of modern Biblical scholars who set out to study the Bible in exactly the same way as classical scholars had studied ancient Greek and Latin literature. Before the 19th c. the Bible was generally regarded by Christians as something quite different from ordinary books in that it had been ' *verbally inspired*,' i.e. virtually dictated by God. It had always been recognised that some parts of the Bible contradict one another; and with the progress of scientific discovery, it became harder and harder to believe that everything in the Bible was literally and historically true. This difficulty came to a head in the 19th c. with Darwin's theory of evolution, which flatly contradicted the *Genesis* account of the creation, and yet was supported by masses of evidence.

By showing how the Bible was put together modern Bible-scholarship has undermined the doctrine of ' verbal inspiration ' ; and those who believed in that doctrine were afraid that religion would thereby suffer a setback. This has not been the case.

Much has been said above concerning the scholarly side of Bible-reading, but you have only to read the Bible for yourself in order to find out that to a greater extent than any other book of such importance in the world it is written in ordinary language and is meant for ordinary people.

biceps, *bī'seps,* muscle of the upper arm ; also a leg muscle that helps to bend the knee.

bichromate cells, see ACCUMULATORS AND BATTERIES

bicycle, two-wheeled vehicle developed from a machine pushed with the feet. The ' penny-farthing ' (*c.*1866) had one large and one small wheel. The addition of rubber tyres made for speed and comfort. Cycles with wheels of the same size were introduced *c.*1880. The freewheel was introduced later. The modern cycle is lighter, safer and handier than any of its predecessors, and the latest model is provided with a power unit for hill-climbing. The motor-cycle is a development of the bicycle ; also the popular recent development, the ' Corgi,' a cheap 2-stroke motor-cycle increasingly popular since 1946.

For practical information about cycles and cycling consult *Cycling Manual* (English University Press).

Bideford, *bid'ĕ-fĕrd,* port at the mouth of the R. Torridge, Devon ; birthplace of Sir Richard Grenville. Charles Kingsley wrote *Westward Ho !* here.

Biel or **Bienne,** *bēl ; byen,* town below the Jura, Switzerland ; noted for watch and clock manufacture ; pop.41,000.

Bielefeld, *bē'le-felt,* linen-manufacturing town, Germany ; pop.129,000.

Bienne, see BIEL

biennials, plants that live two seasons, flowering and dying in the second.

Big Ben, see BELL

big game, chiefly such wild animals as lions, tigers, elephants, etc. ; mostly hunted in S. Africa and India.

bight, *bīt,* large bay, e.g. the Great Australian Bight.

Bihar, *be-här',* Ganges province of India ; S. of Nepal ; products include rice, wheat, oil-seeds, sugar, etc., also mica. The city of Jamshedpur is famous for steel (see INDIA) ; the chief city is Patna.

Bikini, Pacific island with a lagoon where the third atom-bomb was dropped experimentally, July 1946 ; a fourth bomb was exploded some days later. At least 10,000,000 tons of water were thrown a mile into the air.

Bilbao, *bil-bä'ō,* cap. of the Basque province of Biscay, Spain ; long famous as a port, and for iron-ore ; celebrated for its swords in the 16th c. ; pop.216,000.

bilberry or **whortleberry,** low moorland shrub ; has oval leaves, reddish or green flowers, and a blue-black fruit ripe in Aug.

bile, yellowish or greenish liquid made in the liver ; aids the digestion of fats. Should it pass into the blood-stream the patient suffers from jaundice.

billabong, Australian word for a creek running into a river.

billiards (Fr. *bille,* a ball), game played with two white balls and one red ball. The table is usually 12ft by 6ft ; the players strike the balls with a cue. Walter Lindrum (*b* 1899), an Australian who won fame as a billiards player at twenty, is left-handed.

Snooker, a form of billiards played with 22 balls, is popular to-day, W. Smith and Joe Davis being among the champions.

Billingsgate, fish-market near London Bridge.

billion, in the UK and Germany a million million, i.e. 1,000,000,000,000 or 10^{12} ; in France and USA, a thousand million, i.e. 1,000,000,000, or 10^9.

Bill of Rights, statute (1689) based on a declaration made by Parliament after James II had left England (1688), and when William and Mary were to become king and queen. Founded on *Magna Carta* (1215), the statute stated again the principles of freedom and law, e.g. that the king must always rule legally ; that he cannot levy taxes without the consent of Parliament ; that a standing army in peacetime, without Parliament's consent, is illegal ; that all men have the right to speak freely, etc. The Bill was the inspiration of the constitution of USA.

Bilston, town, Staffordshire ; has ironfoundries, pottery-works ; pop.31,000.

binaries, see ASTRONOMY

bindweed, twining plant, a species of convolvulus ; has spearhead-shaped leaves, and white or pink funnel-shaped fragrant flowers.

Bingley, pleasant town, W. Yorkshire ; manufactures textiles ; pop.20,000.

binnacle, support of a ship's compass.

Binyon, LAURENCE (1869–1943), English poet, *b* Lancaster ; at twenty-four joined the staff of the British Museum where, later, he had charge of Oriental prints and drawings ; wrote on art ; most famous for his poem *For the Fallen* :

They shall grow not old, as we that are left grow old :
Age shall not weary them, nor the years condemn.
At the going down of the sun and in the morning
We will remember them.

biochemistry, *bī'ō-,* science of great and increasing importance. It deals with the chemistry of substances found in living plants and animals, and with the chemical changes in them, both in normal functions and in pathological conditions.

biography, see BOOKS

biology, science of life in plant and animal. The biologist tries to understand how living things *live,* in what ways they are alike, how they differ (and why), and into what groups to arrange them. *Botany,* the study of plants, and *zoology,* the study of animals, are branches of biological science. These studies include *morphology,* the outward appearance of plant or animal ; *anatomy,* its inner structure ; *histology,* the science of examining with a microscope the cells in the tissues ; *physiology,* i.e. how the various parts function (or work), and *embryology,* the study of birth and development.

The biologist must also be able to classify living things (*taxonomy*). He considers them in relation to their surroundings or environment, and endeavours to understand how they are distributed throughout the world.

Biology includes careful and scientific nature study out of doors ; the student must also experiment in the laboratory, e.g. study the growth of seeds, the opening of buds, also the structure of various plants or animals (the latter requires the examination of the skeleton and organs of fish, birds and mammals). The life-histories of such creatures as frogs and butterflies are part of his concern ; and in schools and colleges group activities are found extremely profitable.

Read *Direct Biology,* J. B. Palframan, B.Sc. (Nelson) ; *Fundamentals of Biology,* Stork and Renouf ; *Biology,* R. Berks (Nelson) ; *Everyday Biology,* E. P. Smith ; *A Child's Biology,* B. Vesey-Fitzgerald ; *Biology in Everyday Life,* J. R. Baker and J. B. S. Haldane ; and the excellent School Nature Study Union leaflets.

See BOTANY ; EVOLUTION ; GEOLOGY ; HEREDITY ; LIVING THINGS; ZOOLOGY, etc.

biometry, science in which higher mathematics is applied to biology.

birch, sometimes called the lady of the woods, slender and graceful tree, sometimes 60ft high, though the trunk, with its silvery bark, is rarely more than 12in across ; grows on bleak hillsides, has oval or wedge-shaped leaves with sharp points and saw-like edges ; winged seeds.

bird of paradise, bird found in Australia, E. Indies, etc. Though related to the crow, it is notable for its magnificent plumage, especially that of the male in the breeding season. Varieties include the long-tailed bird of paradise of New Guinea.

birds, feathered creatures that lay eggs ; have warm blood (usually from 108–112°F) ; a four-chambered heart, beating as frequently as 120 times a minute ; and air-filled tubular bones.

Descended from the *archaeopteryx,* the fossil remains of which show that it was a lizard-like animal with teeth, birds are now toothless and have bills or beaks adapted to their way of life. The breastbone (or sternum) is usually large, with a ridge (except in flightless birds as the emu, etc.) giving attachment for powerful wing muscles. Birds swallow their food whole, passing it to the crop, and then (in grain and fruit-eating birds) to the gizzard. They moult (i.e. lose their feathers) after the breeding season ; have acute hearing and keen eyesight.

British birds may be classed as (*a*) 120 resident species that remain all the year round, though not always in the same district, (*b*) migratory, of which *c.*40 species are summer visitors, 60 winter visitors. Of 11,000 species of birds nearly half are of the *passerine,* i.e. perching birds, including song-birds. The *Wild Birds Protection Act* forbids the shooting or snaring of certain birds during the breeding season. There are bird-sanctuaries in Hyde Park, London, and elsewhere. The Royal Society for the Protection of Birds has a Junior Bird Recorders' Club with a rapidly growing membership.

The scientific study of birds is called ornithology.

Read *Watching Birds,* James Fisher ; *Garden Birds,* Phyllis Barclay-Smith ; *The Charm of Birds,* Grey of Fallodon ; *Our Bird Book,* S. Rogerson and C. Tunnicliffe.

bird's-foot trefoil, *tre'foil,* meadow plant (family *Leguminosae*) ; blooms in late summer, and has bunches of pea-like flowers, the back petal often red on the outer side ; also known as lady's slipper.

Birkbeck, GEORGE (1776–1841), Yorkshire doctor, founder, 1823, of Mechanics' Institutes, i.e. meeting-places for working-men who wished to improve their education.

Birkenhead, port on the R. Mersey, Cheshire ; linked by the Mersey Tunnel with Liverpool ; noted for docks, shipbuilding yards, etc. ; pop.134,000.

' Birkenhead,' British troopship wrecked off Cape Agulhas, S. Africa, 1852. Of 500 soldiers, some women and children, and a crew of 134, only 200 were saved, as there were not enough boats for all, but the discipline of the troops remained perfect.

Birkett, SIR NORMAN (1883–), judge of the High Court ; for some time Liberal MP for E. Nottingham. He was one of the judges at the Nuremberg trials, 1946.

Birmingham, city, Warwickshire ; world famous for metal goods from cheap jewellery to locomotives, but especially for machine-tools, guns, brass goods, engines, steel pens, buttons, nails, cars, screws ; also plastics, glass, chemicals, electrical and radio apparatus ; claims that its Hospital Centre (Edgbaston) is the finest in Europe ; built an airport 1939. A relay television transmission station has recently been built ; pop. 1,076,000.

Birmingham, city, Alabama, USA ; noted for iron and steel ; pop.268,000.

Birrell, AUGUSTINE (1850–1933), born near Liverpool ; became a lawyer ; was Liberal MP for W. Fife ; President of the Board of Education 1905 ; remembered as a scholar, statesman and wit. Among his books are *Obiter Dicta* (passing remarks) 1884 ; essays ; and his study of Charlotte Brontë.

Biscay, BAY OF, bay of the Atlantic off W. France and N. Spain ; notably stormy when the wind is SW.

bishop, spiritual overseer (Gk *episkopos*) in the early Christian Church. Today there are bishops in the RC Church, Methodist Episcopal Church, etc. In the Anglican Church a bishop is a clergyman immediately below an archbishop. The district of which he has charge is his diocese, with HQ (the see, throne, or chair) in its cathedral. On ceremonial occasions he wears vestments, a ring, a mitre (a kind of crown), and carries a crosier. A suffragan bishop of the Church of England has care of a part only of a wide diocese.

Bisley, village, Surrey. Near by is Bisley Camp, famous for rifle ranges and its summer shooting competitions for the King's Prize, and others, including the Ashburton Shield, competed for by public schools. The shield was presented 1861 by the third Lord Ashburton. A silver medal is given to every member of the winning team.

Bis'marck, PRINCE, in full, Otto Eduard Leopold, Prince von Bismarck-Schönhausen (1815–98) ; German statesman. A Prussian, he was born near Stendal ; fought many duels at the university of Göttingen ; married a deeply religious woman ; became one of the greatest figures in Europe ; minister-president of the German Government 1862, and for 28 years strove to make Prussia the most powerful state in Germany. He ruled with a rod of iron ; engineered wars of aggression against Denmark and

macaw

bird-of-paradise

humming-bird

king vulture

penguin

sea eagle

toucan

peacock

ostrich

secretary-bird

kiwi

BIRDS

Birds-of-Paradise *inhabit some of the Pacific Islands : the males have beautiful plumage ; largest of the parrot family is the* Macaw *found in the New World, the home of* Humming-Birds, *which use their long tongues to suck honey ;* King Vultures, *found in tropical America, eat carrion ; Antarctic* King Penguins *use their wings as swimming paddles ;* Sea Eagles *eat grouse, rabbits and fish : they no longer breed in Britain ; a sub-tropical bird is the* Toucan, *characterised by its very large beak ; India is the home of* Peacocks *whose ' trains ' are not tail- but back-feathers ; in South Africa the* Secretary-Bird *kills and eats snakes ; there, too,* Ostriches *were formerly farmed for their wing and tail feathers ; a bird with flightless wings and hairlike feathers is the* Kiwi, *New Zealand.*

Austria ; directed the Franco-Prussian war 1870–71 ; and defeated the French at Sedan. His armies marched into Paris. He proclaimed Germany to be one nation, with William I as its kaiser (emperor) ; but William II had private ambitions, and at 75 the ' Iron Chancellor ' was compelled to make way for others. Bismarck spent his last days in retirement, brooding gloomily over changed conditions of which he disapproved.

Bismarck Archipelago, *c.*100 islands in the Territory of New Guinea, including New Britain ; noted for copra, coffee, cocoa, pearls, etc. ; mandated to Australia.

THE BLACKBIRD

bismuth, white metal and element, Bi ; atomic weight 209·00 ; atomic number 83 ; used in alloys with low melting-points ; has the peculiarity of expanding when cooling.

bison, *bī'son,* kind of ox, with the forepart of the body exceptionally massive, covered in winter with a thick mane. The bison is remarkable for a great hump above the shoulders, and a large head with low horns. Few bison are still found in Europe, but fossil remains show that they were once very numerous, and that huge herds roamed over Britain. The American bison was at one time found there in immense numbers, though only a few herds remain.

bittern, large European bird, once common in the fens of England ; somewhat like a heron, its yellowish plumage is streaked with black and brown ; has a long, thick neck ; lives on small fish and frogs ; noted for its deep booming call.

bitumen, *bi-tū'men,* dark brown or black substance like thick tar. A hydrocarbon, it is possibly a petroleum deposit. Petroleum and naphtha are forms of it ; another is asphalt, much used for making roads. Asphalt is dug out of the famous Pitch Lake on the I. of Trinidad. Mineral pitch may be found in the earth, or derived from coal-tar.

bivalve, see MOLLUSCA

Bizerta, town, port and naval base, Tunisia (N. Africa) ; pop.35,000.

Bizet, ALEXANDRE CÉSAR LÉOPOLD, *bē-ze'* (1838–75), better known as Georges Bizet, French musician ; composed the opera *Carmen.*

Björnson, BJÖRNSTJERNE, *byürn'sŭn* (1832–1910), Norwegian dramatist, poet, writer and statesman ; wrote the Norwegian national anthem. His ' problem plays ' rival those of Ibsen, e.g. the three Sigurd plays. He was the author of charming tales of old Norway.

Black, JOSEPH (1728–99), British chemist ; discovered carbon dioxide ; was the first scientist to outline the theory of latent heat.

blackberry, see BRAMBLE

blackbird, resident British singing bird ; has deep black plumage and a bright yellow or orange beak. The nest of fibres and grass is coated with mud and lined with grass, and is usually in a thick bush. The 4–5 eggs are light blue or green, freckled with reddish-brown.

Blackburn, town, Lancashire ; notable for cotton, also for engineering ; is on the Leeds–Liverpool Canal. The grammar school was established by Queen Elizabeth 1567 ; pop.109,000.

Black Country, industrial area, England (parts of Staffordshire, Warwickshire and Worcestershire). Coal, iron and clay are mined ; the chief towns are Birmingham and Wolverhampton.

Black Death, 14th c. plague, said to have killed one person in four ; was actually a bubonic infectious disease causing dark swellings under the skin ; possibly brought from China to Europe by traders ; was at its worst 1348–49, when at least 50,000 people are said to have died of it in London alone. Thousands more died at Yarmouth, Bristol, Oxford, Norwich, Leicester, York. The plague prevented the building of churches for many years.

The chief consequence of the plague was that fewer labourers remained. As they had more work to do they demanded increased wages, and Parliament passed a law (*Statute of Labourers* 1351), declaring that higher wages must *not* be paid. Angry peasants raised an insurrection known as the *Peasants' Revolt,* led 1381 by Wat Tyler and John Ball. Finally the life of the labourers improved, and higher wages were paid. See BALL, JOHN

Black Earth, region of exceedingly fertile soil in S. Russia, Hungary, etc.

Blackett, PROFESSOR PATRICK MAYNARD STUART (1897–   ), first to photograph the transmutation of the atom ; discoverer of the positron ; associated with the development of the atom-bomb of 1945. See POSITRON

Blackfeet, tribe of *c.*4,000 N. American Indians. They were once buffalo-hunters, and lived in tents (*tipi*).

Black Forest, mt. region of SW. Germany ; watered by the Rhine ; noted for its silver, copper, cobalt, lead, iron, etc. The inhabitants are skilled in wood-carving and clock-making. The district is a famous tourist centre abounding in pines.

Black Friars, group of preachers following the rule of St Dominic (*d* 1221) ; they wore a black cloak and hood. See MONKS AND NUNS

Blackheath, part of SE. London ; noted for its common of nearly 300 acres.

Black Hole of Calcutta, dungeon at Fort William, Calcutta, India. The British garrison of 146 was imprisoned in a space *c*.22ft square. The prisoners had been trying to hold the fort against Surajah Dowlah, and when they surrendered 20 June 1756, they were herded into this terrible place ; by morning only 23 were alive.

blackmail, threat to kill, injure, or expose a person unless he pays a sum of money. It is regarded as a serious crime, and is usually punished by imposing severe penalties.

Black Market, phrase much used in the later years of World War II, and afterwards. To buy in the Black Market means to obtain scarce or rationed goods in extra quantity by dealing secretly and paying higher prices than one would normally pay in a shop.

Blackmore, RICHARD DODDRIDGE (1825–1900), author, *b* Longworth, Berkshire ; attended Blundell's School, Tiverton ; became a lawyer ; lived chiefly at Teddington, Middlesex ; wrote *The Maid of Sker, Cripps the Carrier, Mary Anerley,* a tale of Yorkshire smugglers ; best known for *Lorna Doone,* a story of Exmoor in the reign of Charles II and James II. We read of John Ridd (' girt Jan Ridd ') a tall and strong young Exmoor farmer whose father is murdered by a clan of robbers, the Doones. There actually were Doones in the Badgworthy Valley, Exmoor, in the 17th century.

black-out, period from dusk to dawn during which no light was allowed to show from a window, and streets were either in total darkness or with only dimmed pilot lights, a precaution against air raids during World War II.

Blackpool, pleasure resort on the Lancashire coast ; noted for its Tower, 500ft high ; its illuminations, promenades, amusements, etc. ; also its sands and invigorating air ; pop.153,000.

Black Prince, see EDWARD THE BLACK PRINCE

Black Sea or Euxine, tideless sea between USSR and Turkey ; receives the waters of the Danube, Dneister, Dnieper, Bug, etc. ; its ports include Odessa.

Blackshirts, see MOSLEY, SIR O.

blackthorn, spiny shrub, sometimes called sloe ; its white flowers come before the oval leaves ; its fruit (the sloe), like a small purple damson, is very sour.

Blackwall, district of London noted for the E. India Docks and the Blackwall Tunnel, 6,200ft long, opened 1897 for pedestrians and vehicles.

Blake, ROBERT (1599–1657), English admiral, born at Bridgwater, Somerset ; in charge of the Commonwealth fleet, 1649, defeating Prince Rupert, who was then commanding the Royalist fleet ; commanded the English fleet in the Dutch war (1652–54), outwitting the Dutch admirals De Ruyter and Van Tromp. His most brilliant naval success was the total destruction, 1657, of a Spanish fleet off Teneriffe (Canary Is.) ; honoured as a great admiral and a chivalrous gentleman.

Blake, WILLIAM (1757–1827), artist and poet, *b* London. As a boy he dreamed dreams and saw visions. He was only four when he declared that God had looked in at the window ; at seven he saw a tree filled with angels ; at ten he was bidding for pictures at auction sales ; at twelve he wrote verse. Growing up to write strange and mystical poems and draw symbolical pictures, he married Catherine Boucher, a simple, loving girl, who made him a perfect wife. In spite of misfortunes Blake kept a brave heart, and though long poor won fame. He illustrated his own poems, e.g. *Songs of Innocence, Songs of Experience,* etc., and is especially remembered for his poem *Jerusalem,* beginning, *And did those feet in ancient time,* and ending with the famous lines :

I will not cease from mental fight,
    Nor shall my sword sleep in my hand,
Till we have built Jerusalem
    In England's green and pleasant land.

This, set to music by Sir Hubert Parry, *c*.1915, is now regarded as a second English national anthem.

blankets, see WITNEY

blank verse, verse that does not rhyme ; usually in pentameters, i.e. 5 feet in each line, the stress being on the 2nd, 4th, 6th, 8th, and last syllables, e.g. Shakespeare's *Friends, Romans, countrymen, lend me your ears.* Blank verse is sometimes in hexameters. See METRE

Blantyre, mining district, Lanarkshire ; birthplace of David Livingstone 1813.

Blarney, village, County Cork, Eire ; has a 15th c. castle with the ' Blarney Stone,' said to give persuasive speech to all who kiss it.

Blaydon, manufacturing town, Durham ; pop.32,000.

bleach, to remove colour with the use of chemicals, e.g. sulphur dioxide, chlorine, hydrogen peroxide and bleaching powder, $CaOCl_2$.

Blenheim, *blen'im,* Danube village in Bavaria ; scene 1704 of a battle during the War of the Spanish Succession, when the British (under the Duke of Marlborough) and the Austrians (under Prince Eugene) defeated the French and Bavarians.

Blenheim Palace, great house of the Duke of Marlborough, Oxfordshire, so called in memory of the victory at Blenheim, Bavaria, 1704.

Blenkinsop, JOHN (1783–1831), Yorkshire

inventor 1811 of a steam locomotive with cog-wheels.

Blériot, Louis, *blā-ryō'* (1872–1936), French airman ; first to fly the English Channel, 25 July 1909.   See Aviation

Bligh, William, see ' Bounty '

blimp, small non-rigid airship.   The term Colonel Blimp is applied to any officer with out-of-date ideas.

blindness, a misfortune less common now than formerly, conditions of living having greatly improved.   At one time little was done for the blind, but today many societies care for them, e.g. the National Institute for the Blind, 224 Great Portland Street, London, W ; St Dunstan's (Regent's Park, London), for blinded soldiers, sailors and airmen, founded 1915 by Sir Cyril Arthur Pearson (1866–1921), a famous newspaper owner who went blind.

Blind people need not forego the pleasures of reading, since books, magazines, etc. are now published in Braille, the invention of Louis Braille (1809–52), a Frenchman to whom we owe the system of raised dots for letters of the alphabet, etc.   There is now a Braille typewriter ;   also Braille shorthand. Braille publications include *The Braille Radio Times, The Braille Punch, The Braille Chess Magazine,* etc. ; there are also ' talking books.'   The invention (1950) of the electronic pencil (translating letters into sound) enables the blind to read ordinary books.

There are *c.*85,000 blind people in the UK.

Worcester College, a public school, educates blind boys and boys (known as ' Dims ') who have very weak sight.

blind spot, see Eye

blind-worm, harmless lizard without legs ; *c.*12in long ; usually feeds at night ; is *not* blind.

Bliss, Arthur (1891–   ), musician *b* London ; made a stir 1922 with his *Colour Symphony* ; noted for choralorchestral works, his ballet *Checkmate* (1937) and his incidental music for H. G. Wells' *Things to Come* ; especially notable for his ballet *Miracle in the Gorbals.*

blitz, short for blitzkrieg, German, *lightning war,* i.e. sudden and overwhelming attack by mechanised forces, or, more especially, by planes ; first successfully employed by Hitler in his attack on Poland 1939.

Bloemfontein, *bloom-'fon-tēn,* cap. Orange Free State, S. Africa ; on the Modder R.; has many handsome buildings.   The name means Fountain of Flowers, and the city is noted for its lawns and rose gardens ; a large telescope has recently been installed ; pop.64,000.

Blois, *blwä,* historic city of France on the R. Loire ; has a handsome château, once a royal residence ; pop.24,000.

Blondel, see Richard I

Blondin, Charles, *blŏn-dăn* (1824–97), stage name of Jean François Gravelet,

French tight-rope walker ; crossed Niagara Falls on a tight-rope 1,100ft long and 160ft above the water (1859).

blood, almost colourless fluid (*plasma*) in which float a vast number of exceedingly small disc-like corpuscles (or cells), some red, some white.   As many as 5,000,000 red corpuscles of human blood occupy a cubic millimetre.   Each has a speck of red matter (*haemoglobin*) which carries oxygen.   White corpuscles (roughly one for every 500 red) are our main and final defence against disease.

If bacteria enter the body these ' white knights ' rush to the attack, throw themselves on enemy bacteria, and die in destroying them.

The normal temperature of human blood is 98·4°F ; a full-grown man has about 15lb or 1½galls of blood.

The Circulation of the Blood was discovered 1628 by the English doctor, William Harvey, physician to James I and Charles I.   Blood warms the body, supplies the tissues with oxygen and nourishment, and removes unwanted carbon dioxide (CO_2) and other waste matter.   It is impelled by the Heart, a powerful muscular organ that beats 70–80 times a minute (say 3,000,000,000 times in 70 years), causing the blood to complete its tour of the body once every 23–30 seconds.

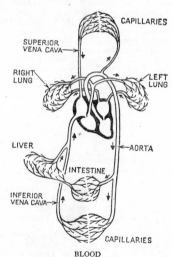

BLOOD

The arrows show the circulation of the blood as it is pumped through the body by the heart.

The heart weighs 8–12oz ; is the size of one's closed fist ; has four chambers : (*a*) *right auricle* and *left auricle* above, (*b*) *right* and *left ventricle* below.   Between the auricles and ventricles there is a wall of muscular tissue, but each auricle has a one-way valve to the ventricle

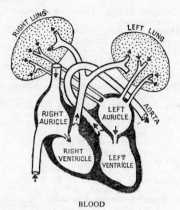

BLOOD

The four-chambered human heart : the arrows show the passage of the blood supply

below. Blood flows *from* the heart *through* arteries, and back *to* the heart through veins.

Beginning from the left ventricle, blood, bright red and newly charged with oxygen in the lungs, flows through the *aorta* to every part of the body. The farther it travels the smaller the arteries become, till they are no more than fine tubes, almost like hairs, called *capillaries.* The blood then begins to flow back towards the heart, becoming darker because it has lost its oxygen and taken up carbon dioxide and other waste. Lesser veins carry the blood to the two great veins of the body, i.e. the *superior vena cava* and the *inferior vena cava,* both opening into the right auricle. Thence the blood pours into the right ventricle, which pumps it out again on a circular tour of the *pulmonary system* (lungs), where it passes through a network of capillaries in the lungs, there receiving oxygen, and afterwards flowing on as a purified stream to the left auricle, to enter the left ventricle, and so begin its journey once more.

As the blood passes through the capillaries a little of its plasma leaks through the walls into the tissues. This fluid is *lymph* (Latin *lympha,* water) ; it is from lymphoid tissue and bone-marrow that our white corpuscles are made.

The beating of the heart is accompanied by the throbbing (expansion and contraction) of our arteries. We feel this if we place a finger, say, above the wrist on what is called the *pulse.*

Soon after flowing from a scratch, blood clots. This is due to its *fibrin,* nature's way of preventing excessive bleeding.

Hospitals now keep emergency supplies of blood so that *blood transfusions* may be made whenever a patient requires them. The blood is stored, as a liquid, in refrigerators, but not at freezing point; such reserves are called ' BLOOD BANKS. Often plasma only is stored. Blood is typed according to groups, e.g. AB, B, A, and O ; and those who give their blood (usually a pint at a time) are called blood-donors. A patient typed as AB must receive only blood so typed ; in emergencies group O is given. Since 1949 a substitute for blood plasma has been increasingly used. This is dextran plasma, the result of research by Professor M. Stacey of Birmingham University. The use of this substitute will not for some years, at least, diminish the urgent need for blood donors, especially overseas.

Blood, COLONEL (1618–80), bold adventurer who attempted (1671) to steal the English crown jewels from the Tower of London ; pardoned by Charles II.

blood transfusion, see BLOOD

Bloomfield, ROBERT (1766–1823), ploughman poet, *b* Honington, Suffolk ; always poor and ailing ; published 1800 a long outdoor poem *The Farmer's Boy.*

Bloomsbury, district of London, in which is the British Museum and the University of London.

Blore Heath, see ROSES, WARS OF THE

Blücher, GEBHARD LEBERECHT VON, *fon blü'cher* (1742–1819), Prussian general, *b* Rostock (Mecklenburg), Germany ; nicknamed Marshal Forwards because of his energy ; aided the Duke of Wellington in defeating Napoleon at Waterloo.

Blue, ' colour ' awarded at Oxford or Cambridge for representing one university against the other in one of the main athletic events of the year. For less important sports and games, a half-blue is awarded. A ' Blue ' is so called because he is allowed to wear a blue cap and blazer, etc. (dark blue at Oxford, light blue at Cambridge.) Blues are awarded for rowing, cricket, football (Rugby and Association), and athletics ; half Blues for tennis, swimming, boxing, shooting, chess, etc. Cambridge awards a full Blue for hockey.

bluebell or **wild hyacinth,** late spring flower ; grows from a bulb ; has tall leaves, and bell-like flowers, usually blue, but may be white or pink ; found chiefly in woods. In Scotland ' bluebell ' means the smaller flower known in England as the ' harebell.'

bluebird, N. American song bird, symbol of happiness ; hence Maurice Maeterlinck's charming play *The Blue Bird* (London 1910).

Blue Book, official British Government publication, usually with a blue cover, though periodical returns are bound in grey or white as well as blue covers. Occasional Government publications are known as White Papers.

' Blue Books ' of other governments are bound in a variety of colours, e.g. the ' Blue Book ' of the Supreme Soviet has red covers.

4 *a*

bluebottle or **blow-fly**, insect much like a house-fly, but larger ; lays eggs in meat.

Blue Coat School, name often given to Christ's Hospital (and certain other schools) because of the uniform worn by the boys, i.e. long blue woollen coat with narrow, red leather girdle, knee breeches, yellow stockings, and clergymen's neckbands. This uniform, which was the typical dress of a schoolboy in the 16th c., has been worn by the boys since the foundation of the school 1553.

The school, originally intended for foundlings and orphans, was in Newgate Street, London. The girls' school was moved to Hertford 1778, where a new school was built 1906. In 1902 the boys' school moved to W. Horsham, Sussex. Some places are still reserved for the children of persons distinguished in literature, science and art, and for the children of officers in H.M. Forces, but other places are awarded as the results of competitive examination to children from LCC primary schools and from certain city parishes. A royal nautical school was added to the original foundation by Charles II, and still forms part of the school.

Boys in the highest form of the school are known as Grecians, and many of these win Exhibitions to Oxford and Cambridge.

Among the distinguished men who were once Blue Coat boys were Charles Lamb, Samuel Taylor Coleridge, Leigh Hunt and Edmund Blunden.

Blue Mountains, range of mts., New South Wales (Australia), with rugged edges and immense forests. Here, also, are the famous limestone caves of Jenolan.

Blue Peter, flag flown by a ship about to sail ; it is blue with a white square.

blue print, plan or drawing of machinery, etc. It is first made on transparent tracing-cloth. This is laid over a sheet of photographic paper, and a print made by exposing to a bright light. When developed, the paper becomes blue, the lines and printing white. This method is now giving place to a process which produces black lines, the figures being inserted with the aid of a specially designed typewriter.

Blue Riband of the Atlantic, see SHIPS

blue tit, see TIT

Blum, LÉON (1872–1950), French Socialist politician ; advocated a Popular Front, including Communists, against Nazi and Fascist aggression ; Prime Minister 1936–37 ; 1938 ; also 1946.

Blundell's School, public school near Tiverton, Devon ; founded 1604 by Peter Blundell ; has scholarships to Oxford and Cambridge ; described in *Lorna Doone*.

Blunden, EDMUND (1896–), distinguished English poet, critic and writer, born in Kent ; lover of cricket ; author of *Undertones of War* ; *Cricket Country* ; *Shells by a Stream*, etc.

blunderbuss, 18th c. pistol with a trumpet-shaped muzzle. The name is Dutch for thunder-box.

Blunt, WILFRID SCAWEN (1840–1922), traveller and minor poet ; *b* Petworth House, Sussex ; travelled much in Asia and Africa ; his *Love Sonnets of Proteus* and his *Esther* are of great merit ; especially noted for *The Future of Islam*.

Blyth, port and holiday town, Northumberland ; pop.34,000.

boa, *bō'ä*, snake found in S. America and Madagascar ; may be 12ft long, or longer ; coils round its prey and crushes it to death ; lurks among the branches of trees ; is usually black with yellow markings.

BOAC, see AVIATION

Boadicea, *bō-ä-di-sē'ä*, British queen. Leader of the Iceni in E. Britain, she raised a rebellion against the Roman general Suetonius Paulinus, and set the Roman camps Londinium (London) and Camalodunum (Colchester) on fire. When defeated by Suetonius AD62 she took her own life rather than become a prisoner.

Read Cowper's poem, *Boadicea*.

boar, wild pig with strong tusks and coarse bristles ; found in Europe, Africa and Asia ; was hunted in Britain till the 17th century

Board of Trade, department of the British Government dealing chiefly with trade and navigation, mines, commercial treaties, trade-returns, Patent Office, etc ; is presided over by a member of the Cabinet.

Board of Trade Unit, usually written BTU, British unit of electrical energy, i.e. the kilowatt-hour. It is the work done when a rate of working of one kilowatt is maintained for one hour. See ELECTRICITY

Boar's Head, name of an old London tavern in Eastcheap ; vividly described by Shakespeare in *King Henry the Fourth* ; destroyed in the Great Fire 1666.

Boat Race, yearly rowing event since 1829 between the universities of Oxford and Cambridge. Each boat has a crew of eight and a coxswain ; the 4¼m race is held on the Thames between Putney and Mortlake. A new record (17min 50sec) was set up by Cambridge 1948. The race is usually held in March or April.

boatswain, *bō's'n*, ship's warrant officer in charge of sails, rigging, ropes, anchors, etc.

Boaz, see RUTH

Boccaccio, GIOVANNI, *bōk-kät'chō* (1313–1375), Italian poet ; lived in Florence ; was a friend of Petrarch and an admirer of Dante ; most famous for his collection of stories, *The Decameron*, from which Chaucer borrowed some of his *Canterbury Tales*.

Bochum, *bō'chum*, Ruhr town, Westphalia (Germany) ; noted for mining, also iron and steel ; pop.303,000.

Bodleian Library, *bod-lē'an*, library of Oxford University ; named after Sir

Thomas Bodley (1545–1613), who rebuilt it ; extended 1936–46 ; famous for the valuable MSS it contains.

Bodmin, *bod'min*, co.tn, Cornwall ; noted for its fairs.

Boeotia, *bē-ō'shi-ä*, part of ancient Greece north of Attica ; birthplace of Pindar ; its most important town was Thebes. By other Greeks, the Boeotians were thought to be dull-witted and stupid.

Boers, name given to Dutch settlers in South Africa and often applied to their descendants. ' Boer ' means ' farmer ' or ' peasant.' The first Boers to reach South Africa were those who were shipwrecked in Table Bay 1648. The descendants of settlers (mostly farmers) in the Cape of Good Hope spread rapidly to the Transvaal and Orange Free State. In 1899 a struggle which went on until 1902 took place between the British settlers and the Boers ; this is known as the *Boer War.*

The Transvaal Republic was a community of Boer farmers, very Biblical in outlook, but in 1886 gold was discovered on the Rand, and thousands of *Uitlanders* (foreigners, mainly British subjects) settled there. The Boers resented this invasion, and the Uitlanders began to demand political rights, in which they were supported by the British government. The Uitlanders were angered by promised reforms which failed to materialise ; the Boer police service, too, they thought was unnecessarily violent.

On 31 May 1899 Sir Alfred Milner (High Commissioner at the Cape) met Paul Kruger (President of the Transvaal) to try to solve the Uitlanders' problems, but the conference broke up, without result, on 5 June 1899.

Infuriated by what they regarded as unwarrantable British interference, the Boers eventually delivered an ultimatum, and war broke out on 12 Oct 1899, the Transvaal Republic being supported by the Orange Free State.

Boer forces invaded Natal and the Cape territory, and laid siege to Ladysmith, Kimberley and Mafeking. The Boers were expert marksmen and skirmishers. Early in the war the British met with serious reverses, but in January 1900 Lord Roberts and Kitchener took command, and the tide began to turn in favour of Britain. Under Botha, Beyers, Delarey, de Wet and others, the Boers gallantly held out and withstood British attacks until they were finally defeated months later. Peace was signed on 31 May 1902 at Vereeniging. Four years later the Transvaal Boers were granted responsible self-government and were incorporated in the Union of S. Africa 1910.

Read *My Early Life,* Winston Churchill.

bog, soft, spongy ground, useless for growing crops, but supplying peat, a mixture of decaying vegetation and moss, especially sphagnum, which is cut out in bricks, and used as fuel. Ireland is one-eighth bogland, the largest bog being the Bog of Allen, chiefly in County Offaly.

Bogotá, *bo-go-ta'*, cap., Colombia ; on a plateau over 8,500ft above sea-level ; pop.425,000.

Bohemia, see CZECHOSLOVAKIA

Bohr, NIELS, *bör* (1885–   ), Danish professor of physics at Copenhagen ; applied the quantum theory to the structure of the atom ; brought scientific secrets from Germany in World War II, and eventually escaped to USA, where he joined the scientists who produced the first atom-bomb, 1945. See MATTER

NIELS BOHR 1885–

boil, infection of a hair follicle by a germ. Pus is formed, and the region becomes inflamed.

boiler, vessel, usually cylindrical, for heating water. There are two main types (a) with the furnace inside the boiler, e.g. Cornish and Lancashire boilers, (b) with the water flowing in tubes inside the furnace, called tubular boilers, e.g. the Babcock and Wilcox, the Thornycroft, Yarrow, and Stirling.

boiling-point, temperature at which the vapour of a liquid is at the same pressure as that of the atmosphere. At this temperature vaporisation begins from within the liquid, and bubbles of vapour rise to the surface. At lower temperatures evaporation takes place from the *surface* only. For water the boiling-point is 100°C (212°F) when a column of mercury stands at 760mm. This is lowered 1°F for every 550ft above sea-level. Useful boiling-points are :

	°C		°C
air	−192·0	hydrogen	−252·7
alcohol (ethyl)	78·3	mercury	356·7
benzene	80·4	oxygen	−183·0
chloroform	61·0	water (pure)	100·0

Bois de Boulogne, *bwä dĕ boo-lön'y',* park on the outskirts of Paris ; area 2,155 acres ; bordered partly by the R. Seine ; has a lake of 27 acres, also a ruined abbey, a zoo, etc.

Bolan, *bō-lan',* pass between Baluchistan and Afghanistan.

bolas, *bo'läs,* weapon used by S. American natives in Patagonia. It is a strong cord with a stone at each end. Flung skilfully, it twines round an animal's legs.

Boleyn, ANNE, *bul'in* (1507–36), second queen of Henry VIII of England, and mother of Elizabeth ; was beheaded on Tower Green.

Bolingbroke, HENRY OF, see HENRY IV

Bolivar, SIMON, *bol'i-vĕr* (1783–1830), S. American patriot who enabled several countries there to overthrow Spanish rule ; *b* Caracas, Venezuela ; won independence for a larger republic (Colombia) 1821 ; became its first president ; helped Peru to win independence, and saw the S. provinces become a separate republic, called Bolivia, 1826 ; earned the title of ' the Liberator.'

Bolivar deserves to be better known. He was an amazing man of action ; directed nearly 500 battles in 15 years ; led a small army over the Andes, drove the Spaniards from an area as large as USA ; had great charm of manner ; hated dictatorship.

Read *Bolivar,* Emil Ludwig.

Bolivia, *bō-liv'iä,* republic SW. of Brazil, S. America ; area *c.*514,000sq.m ; pop. *c.*3,700,000. Largely mountainous (with lofty peaks of the Andes) and a great plateau 12,000ft above sea-level, Bolivia has vast mineral wealth, notably tin, gold, silver, copper, wolfram, oil, antimony. Exports include antimony, minerals, rubber, wool and hides. The country, largely undeveloped, is handicapped for trade purposes by having no coastline.

Ruled by the Incas prior to the 16th c., Bolivia became fully independent 1826, and was later named after Simon Bolivar (*d*1830), its liberator. The government is at La Paz, but the legal capital is Sucre.

Bologna, *bō-lō'nyä,* city, Italy, *c.*80m N. of Florence ; has many art treasures and an 11th c. university ; pop.279,000.

Bolshevism, see MARX, KARL

Bolton, cotton-spinning town, Lancashire ; noted also for iron, chemicals, bleaching, etc. ; pop.164,000.

bomb-aimer, instrument in bombing planes for aiming the bombs at the target.

A bomb leaves an aircraft with the horizontal velocity of the plane. In a vacuum it would retain this, while gravity would give it an increasing velocity, hence it would fall in a parabola, and strike immediately below the aircraft. Factors modifying this are (*a*) effect of air-drag on the horizontal component of the velocity, (*b*) effect of drag on vertical velocity, (*c*) effect of wind, etc. The factors (*a*)

and (*b*) vary with the weight and shape of the bomb. The bomb-sight must allow for (*c*), i.e. ' drift,' and for other factors. On the *automatic bomb-sight* all the factors are set, the bomb-aimer steers the aeroplane so as to keep the target in the ' finder,' and the bomb is released automatically at the right moment. Gyroscopes in the instrument counteract errors that would arise from curved or unsteady flight.

Bombay, *bom-bä',* western province of India, with a coastline on the Arabian Sea ; area *c.*77,000sq.m ; pop.21,000,000, chiefly Hindus and Mohammedans ; grows much cotton, and is also building cotton-mills ; chief city, Bombay.

Bombay, busy and progressive city and port in the province of Bombay. On an island, linked by causeway with the mainland, it has a magnificent harbour, and large docks, etc. The population (*c.*1,500,000) includes many nationalities. The trade in cotton and the manufacture of cotton goods is increasing. Near by are hills where the Parsees lay their dead on the ' Five Towers of Silence.' Bombay has developed from a trading station of the E. India Company.

bombazine, *bom-bä-zēn,* dress material, usually of silk and wool ; a black variety was once much used for mourning.

Bona, port, French Algeria ; has two harbours ; trades particularly with Marseilles ; pop.83,000.

Bonaparte, see NAPOLEON BONAPARTE

Bondfield, MARGARET (1873–   ), Trade Unionist and Labour leader, *b* Somerset ; writer and lecturer on Socialist and Labour movements ; first woman to sit in the British Cabinet (1929).

Bond Street, London street with fashionable shops ; joins Oxford Street and Piccadilly.

Bone, SIR MUIRHEAD (1876–   ), Scottish artist, *b* Glasgow ; famous for his black and white pictures of industry, architectural subjects, etc.

bones, see SKELETON

Boniface (680–755), English saint ; went as a missionary to Germany.

Bonn, *bon,* town, Germany ; on the R. Rhine ; has a noted university ; was the birthplace of Beethoven ; capital of the West German State founded 1949 ; pop.100,000.

Bonner, EDMUND (1500–69), Bishop of London ; went to Rome 1532 to secure permission for Henry VIII to divorce Catherine of Aragon ; deprived of his bishopric for refusing to order people to read Edward VI's new Prayer Book ; signed the death warrants of the Protestant martyrs Mary Tudor sent to the stake.

Bonnie Dundee, see DUNDEE, VISCOUNT

Bonnie Prince Charlie, see STUART, PRINCE CHARLES EDWARD

bonus, *bō'nŭs,* gift, or an addition to salary or wages. Some insurance companies pay not only profits on premiums but also bonuses, i.e. extra profits.

bonze, Buddhist monk in China, Japan, etc.

booby, seabird of the gannet kind, found only S. of the Equator ; the throat is bare.

booby trap, hidden bomb, mine, or other explosive, left behind by a retreating army.

bookplate, see BOOKS

books (OE *boc,* beech tree), bound volumes, i.e. a number of pages fastened together and protected by a cover.

A volume such as this was completely unknown hundreds of years ago when impressions of cuneiform writing were first recorded on baked clay tablets. A roll of *papyrus* (obtained from the plant of the same name, and from which our word ' paper ' is derived) was later used by the Egyptians instead of clay. The earliest paged books were made of sheets of *vellum* (the skins of kids and calves) or of *parchment* (goat or sheepskins) and these sheets were folded and thonged together to form pages.

In the 7th c. Celtic books, beautifully illuminated, were hand-written in script, and in later centuries monks used to enrich their manuscripts by ornamentation, particularly by drawing and colouring initial letters. Such books were, of course, extremely expensive to produce because they had always to be written and bound by hand. In Europe in the 15th c. books became cheap and plentiful when printing with moveable types was introduced. This invention transformed the civilisation of Western Europe (see PRINTING). Instead of a few people being able to buy expensive hand-made books, many people could afford to buy printed books, so that knowledge was spread throughout the land much more quickly than before.

Today there are hundreds of printing works employed in turning out books of all kinds, from text books for school use to novels for pleasure reading.

The *fly-leaf* of a book is the blank page at the beginning or end of a book ; the *frontispiece* is an illustration near, or facing, the *title-page* ; a *bookplate* is an engraved label pasted in by the owner and bearing his name ; a *preface* or *foreword* is a brief introductory section explaining the purpose of the book ; the *index* appears at the back of the book, and is an alphabetical list of the chief names or facts mentioned in the text, and is therefore a valuable aid to readers in search of information.

Formerly, authors were supported by wealthy men (' patrons ') interested in them or their work, and it was customary for the author to insert a *dedication* offering the book as a tribute or compliment to his patron. Nowadays authors are not to any large extent dependent on patronage and the dedication (if any) in a modern book is usually a personal tribute by the author to his wife, a relation, one of his friends, or somebody he particularly admires.

Books may be classified in many ways. Librarians as a rule make two main divisions : (*a*) *fiction,* i.e. books telling of imaginary adventures, e.g. R. L. Stevenson's *Treasure Island,* and (*b*) *non-fiction,* e.g. biography, autobiography (including diaries, journals and letters), essays, *belles-lettres,* criticism, history, philosophy, religion, poetry, drama, anthologies (collections of verse or prose), books on social matters, politics, science, travel, topography (about places), works of reference, etc. Some books are quickly forgotten, others are used or enjoyed for a long time. The latter are known as ' classics,' e.g. the works of ancient Greek or Roman writers, and English classics, which include books as old as (or older than) the *Pilgrim's Progress* by John Bunyan, and as recent as *David Copperfield,* by Charles Dickens, and *The Forsyte Saga,* by John Galsworthy.

We may use books in several ways : (*a*) for enjoyment, as when we read a thrilling detective yarn ; (*b*) to learn something, as when we do not merely read but also *study* a school text-book, say French or mathematics ; and (*c*) to find out. It is an excellent thing to know *where* to find the information we want, and to be well acquainted with some of the most reliable reference books, e.g. *The Dictionary of National Biography* (popularly known as the DNB), which gives the life-stories of British people who have been dead ten years or more ; *Who's Who,* giving information about *living* people ; *The Encyclopædia Britannica,* an immense storehouse of information on all subjects ; *Kelly's Directories,* giving up-to-date information about our cities, towns and villages ; *Oxford Dictionary of Quotations* ; Brewer's *Dictionary of Phrase and Fable* ; *The Oxford Companion to Music,* giving information about musical terms and musicians ; *Modern English Usage,* answering queries about spelling, grammar, punctuation, etc. ; *Whitaker's Almanack,* an annual giving innumerable facts about the Commonwealth, foreign countries, Government departments, sport, etc. ; *The Daily Mail Year Book.*

All the reference books mentioned above may be consulted in your nearest public library, and the librarian will always be willing to guide you to others. The wise student will make good use of libraries, but all who know how to value books aright will gradually build up a private library of the books he or she enjoys most and find most useful.

In recent years the practice of giving *book tokens* has become popular ; such tokens enable the recipient to choose his own book, provided his choice does not exceed the value of the token he has received. If this does happen it is permissible to pay the extra amount and still use the book token. Since 1949 junior book tokens, known as Book Tallies, have become increasingly popular. These are series of coloured cards, the detachable portion being worth sixpence.

boomerang, Australian hunting weapon, usually of hard wood. It is *c*.30in long, one side flat, the other rounded ; some boomerangs are only slightly curved, others form an obtuse angle. In flight the boomerang follows a wide curve, so that if it misses its target at some distance from the thrower, it tends to return to him.

Booth, ' GENERAL ' WILLIAM (1829–1912), founder of the Salvation Army ; *b* Nottingham ; first a Methodist minister; organised 1865 his own body of religious workers among London's poor. His Christian Mission in the East End of London grew into the Salvation Army (1880). In 1890 Booth published a remarkable book, *Darkest England and the Way Out*. His wife, Catherine (1829–1890), did much to help him in building up his ' Army.' Today over 80 countries have their Salvation Armies. The weekly newspaper, the *War Cry*, was founded 1879.

Bootis, see ASTRONOMY

Bootle, town, Lancashire, adjoining Liverpool ; noted for its Merseyside docks, engineering works, iron-smelting, etc. ; pop.67,000.

borage, *borij,* plant with sprays of blue flowers and hairy leaves that smell like cucumber.

borax, white crystalline salt, $Na_2B_4O_7$. $10H_2O$; boric or boracic acid, H_3BO_3, is used as an antiseptic. Of the world's supply of borax 94% comes from the USA.

Borchert, WOLFGANG (1921–47), German playwright, notable for *The Man Outside*.

Bordeaux, *bŏr-dō',* city and port, France, on the R. Garonne, *c*.60m from the sea ; has a spacious harbour and modern docks ; linked by canal with the Mediterranean ; centre of a wine-producing region ; noted for sugar-refining, pottery, glass, chemicals, fisheries ; pop.258,000.

Bordeaux, RICHARD OF, see RICHARD II

bore, see EAGRE

Boreas, *bor'-ēas,* in old Greek tales, god of the north wind.

Borgia, Italian family of Spanish origin which rose to power in Italy in the 15th c.
(*a*) CESAR BORGIA (1476–1507), created archbishop of Valencia in 1492 and became cardinal one year later. In 1497 Cesar was sent to Naples as papal legate, and in Aug 1498 was released from ecclesiastical obligations to carry out political schemes in which he was pitiless and unscrupulous in pursuit of ambition. (*b*) FRANCESCO (1510–72), Roman Catholic saint who helped to found the Society of Jesus, i.e. Jesuits. He married Eleanor de Castro, a Portuguese lady of high rank, and was created Marquis of Lombardy. In 1543 he succeeded his father in the dukedom.

He visited Rome in 1550, returning to Spain in 1551 when he was ordained a priest of the Jesuits and entered a life of penance and prayer. (*c*) LUCREZIA (1480–1519). At the time of her death she was reputed to be a patroness of culture, but later her name was linked, probably unjustly, with many crimes.

boring, method of sinking a narrow shaft into the earth (*a*) to discover the kind of rocks below, (*b*) for engineering purposes, (*c*) for tapping supplies of petroleum or water. Boring rods, 10–20ft long, are dropped and turned by steam power. Among the kinds of cutting tools used are the diamond boring-bit, studded with Brazilian black diamonds, and the Davis calyx drill, with hard steel teeth.

Boris III (1894–1943), King of Bulgaria, succeeded his father, Ferdinand, who abdicated 1918.

Borneo, *bŏr'nē-ō,* island of the Indian Archipelago, third largest in the world ; area 284,000sq.m ; crossed almost midway by the equator ; pop.1,850,000, chiefly Dyaks, also Chinese and Malays. Borneo has mts. rising to 13,000ft ; vast forests of teak, ebony, palms, etc. ; great rubber plantations ; large mineral wealth, including gold, copper, iron, tin, coal ; also petroleum. The island is politically divided into (*a*) NETHERLANDS BORNEO (about two-thirds), (*b*) the British colony of NORTH BORNEO, area 30,000sq.m ; pop. *c*.300,000 ; noted for rubber, timber, copra, manilla hemp, sago, with possibilities of producing sugar, pepper, tapioca ; cap. Sandakan, (*c*) SARAWAK (NW. coast), area 50,000sq.m, founded 1842 by Sir James Brooke (1803–68), English adventurer who became Rajah ; ceded to Britain 1946 ; produces sago, gutta-percha, rubber, gold, silver, petroleum ; chief town Kuching. See BRUNEI

Borodin, ALEXANDER (1834–87), Russian composer, noted for his opera *Prince Igor.*

boron, brown powder and element, B : atomic weight 10·82 ; atomic number 5; melting-point 2,300°C. See BORAX

borough, see LOCAL GOVERNMENT

Borrow, GEORGE, *bor'ō,* (1803–81), writer and traveller, born near E. Dereham, Norfolk ; loved outdoor life. As a young man he made friends with gipsies ; claimed that he had mastered over 30 languages ; began distributing Bibles for the British and Foreign Bible Society 1832 ; travelled in Russia, Spain and Portugal ; wrote *Lavengro* (the master of words), *The Romany Rye* (the gipsy gentleman), *The Bible in Spain* and *Wild Wales.* His love of ' the wind on the heath ' led others to find new enjoyment in the countryside and in outdoor activities.

Borstal, village near Rochester, Kent ; has given its name to a system for training young offenders. There are now 10 Borstal institutions, including one for girls, at Aylesbury. They are provided and managed by the Prison Commissioners for young offenders. At first Borstal was run on prison lines, but it is not a prison ; its aim is not to punish but to educate. The usual sentence is three years, but the period of training is often two years, or even less, and the young person is afterwards let out ' on licence.' Borstal training gives the young offenders a new outlook on life, sound character training, and help in preparing for an occupation. See APPROVED SCHOOLS

Boscawen, EDWARD, *bos-kō'en* (1711–61), noted admiral, born in Cornwall ; nicknamed Old Dreadnought ; shattered a French fleet off Gibraltar 1759.

Bos'cobel, parish, Shropshire, where Charles II hid after his defeat at Worcester 1651.

Bosphorus, *bos'pō-rŭs,* channel (½–2m wide and 16m long) between the Black Sea and the Sea of Marmora, thus separating Europe from Asia Minor.

Bosruck, tunnel through the Austrian Alps. It is 3m long, and was opened 1905.

Boston, port, Lincolnshire, on the R. Witham. The industries include fishing, engineering, brewing, and there is much agricultural trade. The church has a massive tower called Boston Stump ; pop.22,000.

Boston, cap., Massachusetts, USA. A great port with a spacious harbour, and huge export and import trade, it is an important railway centre, has varied industries, e.g. boots and shoes, and is a famous cultural and literary centre. Of great historical interest, and the scene of the ' Boston Tea Party ' 1773, the city possesses old churches, including one associated with Paul Revere. Boston, long noted for its educational institutions, was the home of Franklin, Emerson and Poe ; the Boston Symphony Orchestra has long been famous ; pop.771,000.

Boston Tea Party, see AMERICAN INDEPENDENCE, WAR OF

Boswell, JAMES, see JOHNSON, SAMUEL

Bosworth or **Market Bosworth,** village, Leicestershire, where Henry Tudor, Earl of Richmond, defeated Richard III, 1485. Richard was killed, and Henry became Henry VII, first of the Tudors.

botanic gardens, gardens planned for the study of plants and trees, e.g. those at Edinburgh, Oxford, Cambridge, Dublin, Paris (Jardin des Plantes), and especially Kew Gardens, Surrey, opened to the public 1841. The area of Kew Gardens is 300 acres ; the palm-house, begun 1844, is 362ft long and 70ft high. The herbarium contains over 3,000,000 plants ; the Kew orchids, cacti, etc. are world-famous.

botany (Greek *botane,* plant), scientific study of plant life.

Flowering plants may be grouped as *Gymnosperms,* i.e. those whose leaves bear uncovered seeds ; of *c.*500 species, most are conifers. *Angiosperms* are those

with enclosed seeds. Angiosperms are subdivided into *monocotyledons,* in which the young plant within the seed has only one leaf, and *dicotyledons,* which have two seed-leaves. A bean has two seed-leaves, but a grain of wheat (or an onion seed) has only one seed leaf.

The chief parts of a plant are the *root,* which holds the plant firmly in the soil, and absorbs water (containing mineral salts), the food-material of plants ; the *stem* or *axis,* which may be erect, trailing or climbing, and which bears leaves ; the *leaves,* which are actually living laboratories where the energy of sunlight is absorbed by the green cells and used to build up sugar (glucose), starch, from carbon dioxide of the air, and water which is absorbed through the root. This process (known as *photosynthesis*)

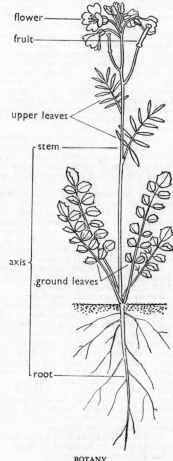

BOTANY
The parts of a plant

distinguishes plants from animals. All plants with *chlorophyll* (green colouring matter) are able to build up their own food from simple substances, whereas animals cannot do so, and must *feed* on plants (or on animals that have fed on plants). Plants *absorb* carbon dioxide through the *stomata* (pores) of their leaves (a leaf of, say, an apple-tree has as many as 100,000 stomata). Leaves differ greatly in shape, size and texture, most of them have leaf-stalks (*petiole*) and scale-leaves to form a protective covering for resting buds in winter.

Flowers are the reproductive part of flowering plants ; others, without flowers, reproduce themselves by means of tubers. A flower comprises a *calyx* (usually green) made up of leaves (*sepals*) round the stem ; the *corolla* (a group of petals) is sometimes brightly coloured, thus attracting the attention of insects ; *anthers* (part of the *stamen*) from which insects (especially bees) obtain pollen, and which are supported by a stalk or filament ; the *pistil*, made up of three parts, namely, the *stigma* which receives pollen carried by insects or the wind (a process known as *pollination*), and the *style*, a passage leading to the *ovary* where the *ovules* (eggs) are developed. Fertilisation takes place after pollination when a male cell inside the pollen grain unites with a female cell inside the ovule. See PLATE III

Once a flower is fertilised its ovules grow into seeds. These may be hidden in fleshy fruits, e.g. apples, pears, or may be in dry cases which eventually open to release the seeds, e.g. poppies, peas or nuts.

Plants find many ways of scattering seeds, e.g. by wind ('parachutes' of dandelions and the winged seeds of sycamores), by water, mechanical means, by birds or mammals e.g. cleavers (goosegrass), the seeds of which hook on the wool of sheep, and are thus carried some distance from the parent.

Much of our present system of plant classification we owe to Linnaeus (1707–78), the Swedish botanist.

Botany also includes *morphology*, i.e. the study of plant forms, including extinct species ; *phytopathology*, the study of diseases of plants, a science of increasing value, especially in agriculture, since it includes a study of the causes, also the removal or avoidance of various pests. Other branches of botany are *ecology*, the study of plant environment, and *genetics*, the breeding of plants, i.e. how they are affected by heredity, a branch of biology largely pioneered by Charles Darwin and such patient research students as Mendel, Luther Burbank and Bateson.

Student's Flora of the British Isles is the standard work for botanists in Britain.

See BIOLOGY ; EVOLUTION

Botany Bay, inlet on the E. coast of New South Wales, Australia ; discovered by

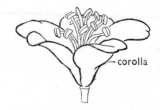

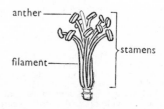

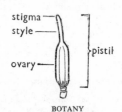

BOTANY
The parts of a flower

Captain Cook 1770 ; so named from its many flowering plants. A convict settlement was established 1787.

Botha, LOUIS, *bō'tä* (1862–1919), South African soldier and statesman ; son of a Boer farmer ; fought against the British in the Boer War, but later became a great supporter of the British ; first Prime Minister of the Union of S. Africa 1910.

Bothnia, GULF OF, extension of the Baltic Sea between Sweden and Finland.

Bothwell, 4TH EARL OF, see MARY, QUEEN OF SCOTS

bo-tree, kind of fig tree ; abundant in India and Ceylon, where it is sacred because of the belief that Buddha saw visions under a bo-tree.

Botticelli, SANDRO, *bot-tē-chel'lē* (1444–1510), Italian artist ; apprenticed to Fra

Filippo Lippi, under whose guidance he remained for 8 years. Fresh influences later led him to the style he adopts in two of his famous pictures, ' Primavera ' and ' The Birth of Venus.' Through all his paintings there runs the vein of poetical and mystical fantasy.

BOTU, see ELECTRICITY

Bouillon, COUNT OF, see GODFREY, COUNT OF BOUILLON

Boulder Dam, see DAM

boulevard, *bool'värd*, wide street shaded by trees ; originally an earthwork to protect a town. Paris is famous for its many boulevards.

Boulogne, *boo-lön'y'*, French Channel port ; has a fine harbour ; the Folkestone-Boulogne ferry is one of the most important cross-Channel services ; pop. 52,000.

Boult, SIR ADRIAN, *bōlt* (1889–), musician and conductor, born at Chester; studied music at Leipzig ; BBC musical director since 1930.

Boulton, MATTHEW (1728–1809), Birmingham engineer ; founded 1762 the great engineering works at Soho, where he and James Watt built steam engines.

' **Bounty**,' naval vessel ; sailed 1788 for the Society Is., with William Bligh (1754–1817), a Cornishman, as captain.

Led by Fletcher Christian, all but 18 of the crew mutinied 1789, made Bligh a prisoner, and cast him adrift in a small boat with a few sailors who had remained loyal. The *Bounty* then sailed for Tahiti, where nine of the mutineers, with native men and women, again embarked, and sailed for Pitcairn, an uninhabited island of the Pacific, where they founded, under John Adams, a colony still peopled by descendants of the mutineers.

A magnificent piece of seamanship enabled Bligh and his men to reach Timor I., whence they eventually reached England.

Read *Mutiny of the Bounty*, C. Nordhoff and J. N. Hall.

Bourbon, *boor'bu*n, old French family. The first of note was Adhemar, 10th c. ; the next was Louis, Duke of Bourbon, *d* 1341 ; from Louis were descended the Dukes of Bourbon, and also the Counts of La Marche, known later as the Counts and Dukes of Vendôme. Among the latter was Henry of Navarre, afterwards Henry IV of France ; his uncle, Louis, Prince of Condé, was the first of the great Condé family. Many French kings belonged to the Bourbon family, among them Louis XIII, XIV, XV, XVI, XVII, XVIII, and Charles X, who was the last Bourbon king (1824–30). One branch of the Bourbons included the Dukes of Orleans ; another, various kings of Spain and of Naples, 17th–19th c.

Bourges, *boorzh*, city, France, *c*.140m S. of Paris ; has a 12th c. cathedral ; pop.50,000.

Bournemouth, *börn'muth*, popular health resort, Hampshire, on Poole Bay ; noted for its ' Chines ' (ravines in the cliffs), pinewoods and gardens ; pop. 138,000.

Bourneville, see CADBURY

Bourse, *boorss*, Paris Stock Exchange.

Bouvines, *boo-vēn*, village near Lille, France ; scene of a French victory over King John of England and Otto IV of Germany, 1214.

bovate or **oxgang**, old English land measure, possibly 24 acres.

bow, *bō*, weapon for shooting arrows ; used by the ancient Greeks and Egyptians, etc. Poisoned arrows are still employed by backward tribes. William I is said to have introduced the arbalest (which fired arrows or bullets) into England. The cross-bow, a similar weapon, had a cord stretched by turning a handle and released by a trigger. The long bow (of yew) was in common use *c*.1300. The practice of shooting with bows and arrows is called archery.

Bow or **Stratford-le-Bow**, suburb of East London ; mentioned in Chaucer's *Canterbury Tales.*

Bowdler, THOMAS (1754–1825), *b* Bath, Somerset ; editor of *Family Shakespeare*, his best known work.

In 1818 he published his first edition of *Shakespeare*. In the Preface he wrote of Shakespeare's language :

' Many words and expressions occur which are of so indecent a nature as to render it highly desirable that they should be erased.'

Bowdler removed from Shakespeare's text all those expressions that seemed unsuitable for young readers, and by doing so has given us the word ' bowdlerise.'

bower bird, Australian bird of the starling family, which builds covered runs with twigs and grass, often adorning them with shells or pebbles.

bowie knife, *bow-*, large sheath knife named after James Bowie, American pioneer, *d* 1836.

Bow Street, London street near Covent Garden ; has a famous police court. ' Bow Street Runners ' acted as detectives before 1829.

box, slow-growing shrub with very hard wood ; often seen in gardens.

Boxer Rising, attempt by a Chinese secret society to kill, or drive out of the country, all foreigners. The word Boxer in Chinese means *righteous harmony fist.* The risings ended when Allied troops entered Peking 1900. Most European countries were doing their utmost in the 19th c. to exploit the Chinese, and the natural resentment felt by the Boxers was the beginning of modern Chinese Nationalism.

Box Hill, lovely spur of the North Downs near Dorking, Surrey ; has belonged to the National Trust since 1914.

boxing, art of attack and defence with the fists protected by padded gloves, as distinguished from prize fighting with *bare* fists (pugilism), now forbidden by law in Britain and USA. Boxing takes place in

a ring. Not more than 20 rounds of
3 minutes each are allowed ; each boxer
may have two assistants, called seconds. A
boxer who is knocked down must rise
to his feet again within 10 seconds or his
opponent is declared winner of the
match.

Standard championship weights include

fly weight	8st 0lb
bantam	8st 6lb
feather	9st 0lb
light	9st 9lb
welter	10st 7lb
middle	11st 6lb
light heavy	12st 7lb
heavy	over 12st 7lb

Boxing Day, see CALENDAR

boxwood, wood of the box tree, an evergreen ; has a very fine, close grain ;
will not float in water ; grows in Europe,
Asia and N. Africa. Boxes are *not*
made of boxwood.

boy bishop, any choir-boy who wore
6–29 Dec. the garments of a bishop, and
was allowed to preside over services in
church. The custom ceased in the
16th century.

Boyce, WILLIAM (1710–79), musician, *b*
London ; remembered as the composer
of *Heart of Oak*, 1759.

boycott, to refuse to have commercial or
social dealings with someone, as a kind
of punishment. It is named after Charles
Boycott (1832–97), thus dealt with by
his neighbours in Co. Mayo, Ireland,
because he refused to receive rents at
figures fixed by his tenants. *To send to
Coventry* is much the same.

Boyle, ROBERT (1627–91) Irish thinker and
scientist, *b* Lismore, Munster ; son of
the 1st Earl of Cork ; travelled in
France, Italy, etc., and later spent much
time experimenting at Oxford. He was
one of the founders of the Royal Society,
and was also deeply religious, doing
much to promote missions. He founded
the Boyle Lecture, an annual sermon
preached at St Mary-le-Bow, London.

Boyle is chiefly notable for his discovery of Boyle's Law, known abroad as
Mariotte's Law, after Edme Mariotte,
a French scientist who *d* 1684. Boyle's
Law states that *At a constant temperature,
the volume* (V) *of a given quantity of any
gas is inversely proportional to the
pressure* (P) *on the gas,* i.e.

$$V \propto \frac{1}{P}, \text{ or } PV = \text{constant}$$

Boyne, river in Eire ; flows 80m to the
Irish Sea near Drogheda. At the battle
of the Boyne, 1690, William III defeated
James II.

Boys' Brigade, youth organisation founded,
Glasgow, 1883 by Sir William Smith
(1854–1914) ; gives physical training,
culture, religious instruction, and is
usually associated with churches ; now
musters *c.*100,000 officers and boys, and
50,000 juniors.

Boy Scouts, members of the Boy Scout
Movement founded 1908 by Lord Robert

Baden-Powell. It is now a world-wide
organisation.

The Boy Scouts Association tries to
make good citizens by teaching boys to
be self-reliant, loyal, observant, and
able to work co-operatively with others.
The motto is : *Be Prepared.* The
youngest members (8–11) are Wolf Cubs;
11–17 are Scouts ; over 17 become
Rover, Sea or Air Scouts. A patrol
is usually 7 boys, one of them a leader ;
a troop is a group of not more than
36 boys under a scoutmaster.

Special badges are awarded to Scouts
who have proved themselves proficient
in various accomplishments, e.g. stalking, shooting, interpreting, signalling,
riding, pioneering, bee-keeping, etc. A
jamboree is an international rally of
Scouts. Total world membership is
*c.*5,000,000.

The official Scout magazine is *The
Scout,* founded 1908. Read *Scouting for
Boys,* Lord Baden-Powell ; *Rovering to
Success,* Lord Baden-Powell ; *Boy
Scouts' Companion,* M. Adams.

B.P., see BADEN-POWELL, LORD ROBERT

Br, chemical symbol for bromine

Brabant, *brä-bant'*, province (*a*) of central
Belgium, (*b*) N. of Holland.

brackets, in mathematics, show in what
order an operation must be performed.
If a bracket is preceded by a plus sign,
the signs in the bracket remain unchanged if the bracket is removed, e.g.
$x + (y - z) = x + y - z$; but if a
minus sign is before the bracket, the
signs inside the bracket must be changed
when the bracket is removed, e.g.
$x - (y - z)$ becomes $x - y + z$. A
bracket may be written $a - (b + c)$:

$$a - [b + c] \; ; \; a - \left\{ b + c \right\} \; ; \text{ or } a - \overline{b + c}.$$

In the latter, the line over $b + c$ is called
vinculum.

Bradfield College, public school 8m from
Reading, Berkshire ; founded 1850 ;
noted for its public performances of
Greek plays.

Bradford, city, W. Yorkshire ; noted for
spinning and weaving woollen goods,
but especially for marketing wool and
worsted ; other industries include coal,
iron, machinery ; pop.285,000.

Bradlaugh, CHARLES, *brad-law* (1833–91),
man of independent thought, *b* Hoxton
(London) ; called himself Iconoclast,
i.e. one who breaks down old beliefs ;
was 11 years MP for Northampton ; a
sincere reformer.

Bradman, SIR DONALD G. (1908–), better
known as Don Bradman, Australian
cricketer especially noted as a batsman ;
won great success in the Test Match
(Leeds) 1930 with 334 runs ; several
times captained the Australians, notably
1946–47, also 1948 ; knighted 1949.

Bradshaw, GEORGE (1801–53), *b* Salford
(Manchester) ; first publisher (1839) of
railway time-tables and guides.

Bradshaw, JOHN (1602–59), *b* Marple Hall,
Cheshire. As a judge he presided over

the ' Regicides ' who tried Charles I and condemned him to death. He was buried in Westminster Abbey, but at the Restoration his body was dug up and hanged at Tyburn.

Braemar, *brā-mär'*, tourist centre, Aberdeenshire ; scene of annual Highland games.

Bragg, SIR WILLIAM (1862–1942), scientist, *b* Wigton, Cumberland ; aided by his son, WILLIAM LAWRENCE BRAGG, made many discoveries concerning crystals, X-rays and radioactivity. He and his son received the Nobel Prize (physics) 1915.

Brahe, TYCHO, *brä* (1546–1601), Danish astronomer, though born in Sweden ; discovered a new star in Cassiopeia 1572. His remarkably accurate observations and calculations (despite the imperfection of his instruments) led the way to discoveries by Johann Kepler and Galileo.

Brahmanism, *brä'man-izm*, Hindu religion. Brahmans or Brahmins (*c.*15,000,000 in India) are priests of the highest order ; all other Hindu castes bow to them, but Brahmans bow to no-one except Brahma, chief god, creator of all things, essence of all good, believed by all Hindus to have been born from a golden egg or a lotus.

As early as 2000BC Hindus had sacred writings, e.g. the *Vedas*, collections in Sanskrit of prayers and hymns ; from these *c.*1000BC, came a religion made up almost entirely of ceremonials, leading to the belief that to perform faultless service was almost all that was required. The sacred writings include the *Rigveda*, *Samaveda*, *Yajurveda* and *Atharvaveda* ; also the *Arenyakas* and *Upanishads*, which describe what Brahma is like.

The Brahmans teach that we are born many times, and that happiness in the next rebirth depends on goodness in this life. Among their gods are Vishnu, the preserver of life, and Siva, usually shown with four hands and three eyes.

Brahmaputra, *brämä-poo'trä*, river of India ; rises in the Himalayas, and flows 1,680m to the Bay of Bengal. It has many tributaries in Assam.

Brahms, JOHANNES, *brämz* (1833–97), German musician, *b* Hamburg ; as a youth met Robert Schumann, who greatly encouraged him. He settled in Vienna 1862, and died there. His music is romantic and classical ; his greatest works include 4 symphonies, a violin concerto, 2 piano concertos, much fine chamber music, and many songs and choral pieces, among them his *German Requiem.*

In his *Hungarian Dances* a totally different style is evident ; perhaps the nearest approach to a blending of these two dissimilar styles is to be seen in his *Academic Festival Overture* (1880).

Braille, LOUIS, see BLINDNESS

brain, part of the nervous system. It may be regarded as the control-centre of the body to which the nerves convey messages, i.e. sensations of feeling, seeing, hearing, discomfort or pleasure ; ' commands ' are sent from the brain to the muscles, thus causing action, and it is the brain we use to do our thinking.

Protected by the skull, the human brain weighs *c.*49oz in men, 44oz in women. Intelligence does not depend greatly on the size of the brain, but rather its surface area, which is governed by the degree to which it is folded. Lower animals have almost smooth masses of nerve-cells at the end of the spinal cord, but the normal human brain is much wrinkled, and comprises several parts. (*a*) The *medulla oblongata*, or bulb ; its centre, is concerned with bodily processes, e.g. breathing, the beating of the heart, etc. (*b*) The *cerebellum*, a region at the back of and under the main part of the mass of grey matter filling the skull ; is responsible, among other functions, for our ability to balance. (*c*) The *mid-brain.* (*d*) The *cerebral hemispheres* (occupying by far the greater portion of the inside of the skull, growing backwards, and being folded like a walnut) : this part of the brain receives sensory impressions and controls voluntary movements, the cells (of which there are at least 3,000,000,000) of the right hemisphere controlling the muscles on the left side of the body, and vice versa.

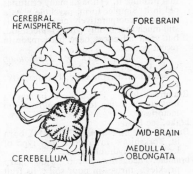

BRAIN
Diagram of the Human Brain

Various regions of the brain have been identified with certain functions : e.g. those interpreting smell and taste are below the speech area ; the auditory area is somewhat to the right ; the motor area (controlling muscles) is in front of the sensory area ; the visual area (curiously enough) is at the back of the brain. What is called the silent area, just behind the forehead, is believed to be closely associated with our sense of right and wrong, and is part of our ' thinking ' brain, while our emotions are centred, it seems, in the base of the brain, but are directly connected with the fore-brain so that in principle thinking and feeling are closely linked.

By ' brain ' we mean the nervous grey matter in the skull, i.e. tangible material ; but the *mind* is elusive. It is not the actual cells of the brain, but a mingling of thinking and feeling which goes on *in* them. The ancient Greeks called this *nous*, i.e. the part of us that knows, understands, is aware. We are conscious as long as the mind functions properly, but all our thinking is not conscious. Often we remember or understand as a result of the working of the *sub-conscious mind.* This is a region or state of mind frequently influenced by *repression*, i.e. thoughts or memories we want to forget, though they may come into our conscious thinking and cause anxieties or fears. Much of what we do is the result of *instinct*, i.e. a kind of race memory. Human instincts tend to be arranged in groups (called *complexes*), e.g. self-preservation; the inferiority complex, which is actually a feeling that we are not as good or as clever as another person, this causing lack of confidence, often disguised under a boastful or apparently careless pose.

Students of the mind, as distinct from the physical brain, are psychologists, and the business of psychology is to tell us about our behaviour, and to explain, as far as possible, the mental processes that produce it. Though many centuries old in its simpler form, psychology as a science is comparatively new. There is still much that is only partly understood, but great advances have been made in recent years.

Read *The A B C of Psychology,* C. K. Ogden.

See MIND; PSYCHIATRY; PSYCHOLOGY; PSYCHOTHERAPY

Braintree, town, Essex ; of increasing importance owing to Courtauld's rayon factories.

brake, see PUMP

Bramah, JOSEPH, *brä'mä* (1749–1814), born in Yorkshire ; invented a new type of lock, and a hydraulic press.

bramble, hedgerow shrub with sharp prickles ; thrives in poor soil ; its fruit (blackberry) ripens Sept.–Nov.

bran, see WHEAT

Brandenburg, (1) former electorate of Prussia ; its ruler was known as the Elector till he took the title of King of Prussia 1701. Brandenburg is now a German state ; cap. Potsdam. (2) A town 37m from Berlin.

branding, marking an animal or person with a hot iron. Cattle are branded for identification purposes. The Romans branded runaways with a capital F (*fugitivus*, fugitive). In England vagabonds were at one time branded with a V ; slaves in America were branded with their owner's initials.

brandy, alcoholic liquor distilled from wine ; acquires its golden tint from the oak casks in which it is stored ; contains *c.*53% alcohol. Cognac is brandy exported from Cognac, France.

Brandywine Creek, river of Pennsylvania, USA ; scene 1777 of a battle in the American War of Independnece.

Brangwyn, SIR FRANK, *brang'win* (1867–), British artist, *b* Bruges ; travelled much in the East ; early showed an amazing mastery of colour and form ; famous for superb designs representing historic themes, e.g. man's conquest of the world (Rockefeller Centre, New York), *Modern Commerce* (Royal Exchange, London).

Brasenose College, Oxford, founded 1509 ; several of the buildings are old. The college is thought to take its name from its first hall, which had a brass figure of a nose. A replica of this is to be seen above the modern gate.

brass, alloy of copper and zinc, though other metals are sometimes present.

A MONUMENTAL BRASS is an epitaph or portrait engraved on brass laid in the pavement or floor of a church over a tomb. England has over 3,000 portrait brasses ; the oldest is of Sir John d'Abernon (*d* 1277), Stoke d'Abernon, Surrey. A PALIMPSEST BRASS is one with a portrait on both sides. To make a rubbing of a brass, lay a sheet of paper smoothly over the engraving, and rub gently with a piece of heelball, i.e. cobbler's wax.

Bratislava, *brät'i-slävä*, port on the R. Danube, Czechoslovakia ; centre of wheat and vine growing district ; pop. 139,000. German name, Pressburg.

Brazil, *brä-zil'*, republic of S. America ; area *c.*3,300,000sq.m ; is 2,300m N.-S., and the same E.-W. ; and the Atlantic coast-line is over 3,500m. The N., mostly low, is covered with vast tropical forests (selvas) ; the E. and S. are hilly ; much of the centre (Matto Grosso) is 2,000ft above sea-level, and has a fine climate. Among the rivers is the immense basin of the Amazon, with tributaries flowing from the Andes and other uplands ; see AMAZON. Great areas are swamp and dense jungle, home of snakes, insects, brilliantly plumaged birds, etc. ; also of backward tribes.

The resources (only partly developed) include rubber, timber, maize, sugar (from cane, and now being cultivated in increasing quantities), cotton, cocoa, and especially coffee, Brazil producing about ¾ of the world's total. Cattle-raising is important, and hides are exported. The mineral wealth is known to be enormous, e.g. gold, manganese, iron, coal, monazite ; diamonds and topazes are also found. The population, *c.*44,000,000, includes many wandering tribes of Indians. The language is largely Portuguese, and the religion RC. The capital is Rio de Janeiro ; other towns are Sao Paulo, Sao Salvador (Bahia), Pernambuco and Pará. The Federal Republic is governed by a President. Discovered 1500 by a

Portuguese, the country became a republic 1889.

Brazil nut, seed of a tall S. American tree ; a single capsule contains *c*.20 nuts.

BRAZIL NUT
The capsule containing the nuts

breaching tower, old-time weapon like a wooden tower on wheels. The lower floor sometimes had battering rams, the upper a bridge from which the besiegers of a city or castle attempted to force an entry.

bread, food, usually made of flour, water, yeast and salt kneaded into dough, and baked as cakes or loaves. In hot countries the flour is of ground millet, maize, or rice ; in cold lands of rye, barley, or oats ; in temperate lands of milled wheat. Bread without yeast is called unleavened, e.g. the oatcakes of Scotland ; leavened (or aerated) bread is made light with yeast, or water containing carbon dioxide ; brown (or wholemeal) bread, the most wholesome, is made of wheat from which the husks have not been removed.

World food shortage obliged the British Government to impose bread rationing July 1946.

bread fruit, tree of many S. Pacific islands, but now grown in S. America and the W. Indies. The large green fruit becomes yellow when ripe, and may be eaten fresh or baked.

breathing, see LUNGS

Breconshire, county, S. Wales ; co.tn Brecon.

Breda, DECLARATION OF, *brā-dä'*, made by Charles II of England 1660 shortly before his restoration. The declaration promised free pardon and liberty of conscience. Breda is a Dutch town.

Breitenfeld, see GUSTAVUS II

Bremen, *brā'men*, state of NW. Germany ; includes Bremen (with Bremerhaven), a busy port on the R. Weser. A great trading and shipping centre, Bremen has many industries now being revived after Allied air-raids during World War II ; pre-war pop.342,000.

Brenner Pass, pass over the Alps ; links Italy, Germany, Austria ; rises *c*.4,500ft. Here, during World War II, Hitler and Mussolini met several times for consultations.

Brentford, co.tn, Middlesex ; includes Chiswick ; pop.63,000.

Brescia, *bresh'ya*, city of N. Italy ; is a notable railway junction ; industries include woollens, silks, wine ; pop.93,000.

Breslau, *bres'low*, town, Lower Silesia ; on the R. Oder ; pop. *c*.615,000 ; manufactures textiles on a large scale, e.g. silk, linen, cotton ; trades in cereals ; now in Poland, and known as Wroclaw (*vros'läv*).

Brest, naval port of NW. France ; has important shipbuilding yards, repair docks, etc. ; suffered heavily from British bombing while in German hands during World War II ; pop.80,000.

Bretton Woods, town in New Hampshire, USA ; scene 1944 of an International Monetary Conference.

BREAD FRUIT
The leaves and the fruit

breve, see NOTES

breviary, *brēv'i-ĕr-i*, book of hymns, psalms, portions of Scripture and stories of saints for daily use in the RC Church.

brewing, making of beer, an alcoholic drink prepared from barley which becomes malt when steeped and allowed to germinate. This is made into an infusion known as wort ; after boiling with hops it is cooled and then fermented with yeast.

Brewster, SIR DAVID (1781–1868), Scottish scientist, *b* Jedburgh ; invented the kaleidoscope, and greatly improved the lamps used in lighthouses.

Briand, ARISTIDE, *brē-än* (1862–1932), French statesman, *b* Nantes ; first Socialist Prime Minister of France, being re-elected 11 times. He was associated with every peace proposal, and

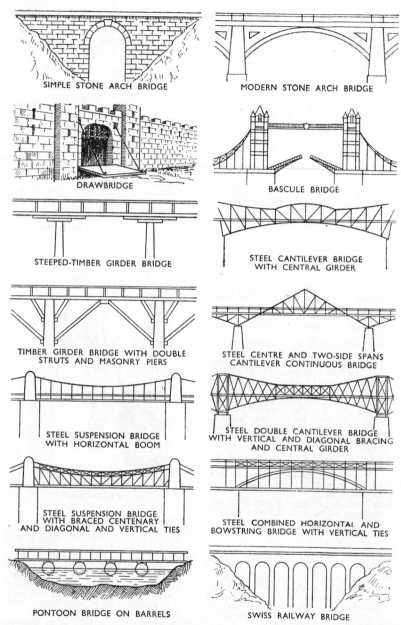

SIMPLE STONE ARCH BRIDGE

MODERN STONE ARCH BRIDGE

DRAWBRIDGE

BASCULE BRIDGE

STEEPED-TIMBER GIRDER BRIDGE

STEEL CANTILEVER BRIDGE
WITH CENTRAL GIRDER

TIMBER GIRDER BRIDGE WITH DOUBLE
STRUTS AND MASONRY PIERS

STEEL CENTRE AND TWO-SIDE SPANS
CANTILEVER CONTINUOUS BRIDGE

STEEL SUSPENSION BRIDGE
WITH HORIZONTAL BOOM

STEEL DOUBLE CANTILEVER BRIDGE
WITH VERTICAL AND DIAGONAL BRACING
AND CENTRAL GIRDER

STEEL SUSPENSION BRIDGE
WITH BRACED CENTENARY
AND DIAGONAL AND VERTICAL TIES

STEEL COMBINED HORIZONTAL AND
BOWSTRING BRIDGE WITH VERTICAL TIES

PONTOON BRIDGE ON BARRELS

SWISS RAILWAY BRIDGE

BRIDGES

Examples of various types of bridges from the simple stone or brick arch to those in which metal is employed either in the form of steel girders or wire (as in suspension bridges). In the cantilever bridge half the weight of one span is balanced by the half-span at the other side of the supporting pier

one of his dreams was to see the European nations drawn together as the United States of Europe.

bricks, anciently (and still in some hot countries), sun-baked clay or mud ; elsewhere, blocks of clay fired, and thus hardened, in a kiln.

Modern bricks are usually $c.9 \times 4\frac{1}{2} \times 3$in. Bonding means arranging bricks in one of various ways so as to overlap.

Bridgeport, port, Connecticut, USA ; pop.147,000.

bridges, means of spanning rivers. The ends of a bridge are *abutments* ; the arches rest on *piers* ; the width of the arch is the *span.*

Some of the earliest bridges were built by the Romans, e.g. Pons Fabricius in Rome 62BC. The old London Bridge, across the Thames, was built of stone *c.*1176. On it were houses and a chapel ; it was replaced 1831. The first iron bridges were built in the 18th c. Cantilever bridges comprise a network of girders leaning out from the piers, and balancing each other. Suspension bridges hang from wires passing over lofty towers. Pontoon bridges (much used in warfare) are floating roadways resting on boats or tanks. Swing bridges open sideways to allow ships to pass ; bascule bridges have sections rising for the same purpose, e.g. the Tower Bridge (London), 1894, each bascule, 100ft long, being raised by hydraulic power. Transporters have a platform or carriage travelling from end to end, e.g. that at Runcorn or Middlesbrough.

Notable bridges include (*a*) FORTH BRIDGE, 1890, 8,296ft long, with a clear headway of 152ft, the spans are 1,710ft ; cost *c.*£3,000,000 ; (*b*) (the second) TAY BRIDGE, *c.*2m long, built 1887 to replace the first Tay Bridge, which had collapsed in a storm 1879 ; (*c*) the new high-level bridge across the Tyne (at Newcastle) 1928, the span is 531ft ; (*d*) SYDNEY HARBOUR BRIDGE, Australia, completed 1932 ; has stone towers 285ft high ; between them is a single arch 1,650ft across, 440ft high, weighs over 42,000 tons. The total length of the bridge is 3,816ft, and the cost was *c.*£10,000,000 ; (*e*) GOLDEN GATE BRIDGE, San Francisco, the longest and highest single-span suspension bridge in the world ; has a main span of 4,200ft, total length 8,940ft, roadway 220ft above water-level, height of the two towers 746ft. The cables supporting the bridge contain 80,000m of wire ; total cost *c.*£16,000,000 ; completed 1936. In 1948 the world's first aluminium bascule bridge was opened at Sunderland.

Bridges, DR ROBERT (1844–1930), poet laureate from 1913, *b* Walmer, Kent ; was a London doctor for 20 years. Among his poetical works the greatest is *The Testament of Beauty,* 1929. These lines show his work at its best :
Spring goeth all in white,
Crowned with milk-white may.

Bridgetown, cap. and chief port, Barbados ; has a fine harbour.

Bridgwater, port, Somerset ; the only town in Britain to manufacture bathbrick ; pop.21,000.

Bridie, JAMES (1888–1951), pen-name of O. H. Mavor, *b* Glasgow, popular dramatist, e.g. *Dr Angelus,* etc.

Bridlington, seaside health resort, E. Yorkshire ; pop.23,000.

brief, *brēf* (Latin *brevis,* short), in legal practice, a summary of the relevant facts given by a solicitor to a barrister to help him in preparing a case.

Air pilots are ' briefed ' before taking off for a flight, i.e. they are given instructions, especially (in war) as to the target they may have to bomb etc.

Brienze, *brē-ent'sā* (1) lake, Switzerland ; (2) a tourist village on the shores of above, noted for wood-carving.

brigand, *brig'and,* robber, notably in the mountainous parts of Italy, Sicily and Spain.

Brigantes, *bri-gan'tēz,* in Roman Britain a Celtic people living between the Humber and the Forth.

Brighouse, industrial town, W. Yorkshire ; on the R. Calder ; manufactures woollen goods, soap, carpets, etc. ; pop.30,000.

Bright, JOHN (1811–89), statesman, *b* Rochdale, Lancashire. With Richard Cobden he did much to bring about the repeal of the Corn Laws. Bright was a Quaker who became MP for Birmingham 1857. His policy may be summed up in the phrase *Peace, retrenchment, and reform.* He was a gifted and powerful speaker, and is regarded as one of the great Liberals of the 19th century.

Brightlingsea, yachting port, Essex ; has oyster-fisheries.

Brighton, seaside holiday town, Sussex ; favourite with Londoners ; has a long promenade linking it with Hove ; pop.154,000.

brimstone, old name for sulphur. See SULPHUR.

Brindisi, *brēn'dē-zē,* city and Adriatic port of S. Italy ; has a large harbour with several islands ; was a point of embarkation for Greece in ancient times, and for Palestine in the Middle Ages. Since the opening of the Overland Route by rail it has grown in importance as a modern port, and is now an air station ; pop. 42,000.

Brindley, JAMES (1716–72), engineer who could scarcely write, but was able to work sums in his head. Associated with the Duke of Bridgewater in canal construction ; his greatest achievement was the Barton aqueduct over the Irwell.

Brisbane, *briz'bān,* port and cap., Queensland, Australia ; exports frozen meat, coal, tallow, wool, etc. The city is colourful with flowering trees and shrubs, e.g. poinsettia, hibiscus and jacaranda ; pop.384,000.

Bristol, *bris't'l,* city and west coast port, Gloucestershire ; on the R. Avon, 7m

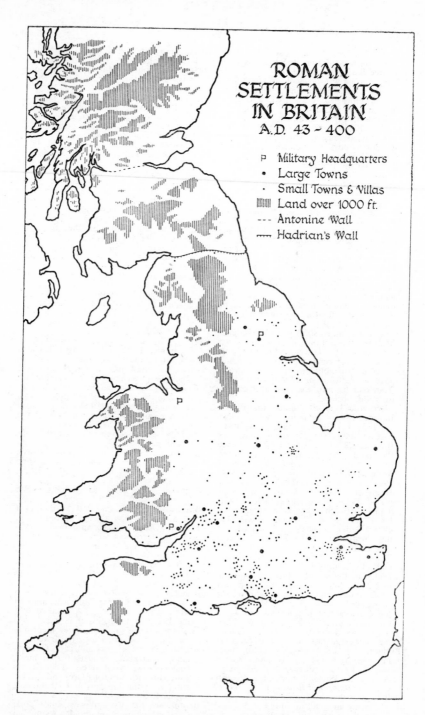

ROMAN
SETTLEMENTS
IN BRITAIN
A.D. 43 - 400

P   Military Headquarters
•   Large Towns
·   Small Towns & Villas
▥   Land over 1000 ft.
--- Antonine Wall
⁓   Hadrian's Wall

from the Bristol Channel ; has large docks, and trades with Ireland, the W. Indies, N. and S. America and India. The industries include tobacco on a great scale, boots and shoes, aircraft, milling, printing, chemicals and shipbuilding. Bristol has many historic buildings. It was the port from which Cabot sailed for N. America 1497. It was the scene of fighting in the Civil War, and suffered great damage from German air attack during World War II ; pop.436,000.

Bristol Channel, inlet on the west coast of England, between S. Wales and Devon and Somerset ; forms an estuary for the R. Severn.

Britain, ANCIENT, Roman province, i.e. parts of the British Isles conquered and occupied by the Romans between 55BC and AD410. After a brief reconnaissance 55BC, Julius Caesar invaded the Kentish peninsula 54BC but withdrew without attempting to establish permanent Roman rule. The Roman occupation began properly in AD43, when Aulus Plautius, a Roman general, invaded and conquered what is now SE. England. By AD75 the Romans had gained control of most of what are now the territories of England, Wales and southern Scotland. There was a good deal of resistance under such Celtic or British leaders as Caratacus (Welsh Marches) and Boadicea (Boudicca), queen of the Iceni (East Anglia). Galgacus, a Celtic leader in NE. Scotland, is said to have condemned Roman rule in the famous phrase ' they make a desert and call that peace.' Although Galgacus was defeated by Agricola (Roman governor) at Mons Graupius AD84, the Romans did not think it worth while to attempt to conquer and subdue the mountainous region north of the R. Forth. Hadrian's Wall (across the north of England, built c.AD120) became the frontier of Roman Britain proper. The Antonine Wall (across the waist of Scotland, between Forth and Clyde, built c.AD146) was not permanently garrisoned ; southern Scotland remained a frontier region under temporary occupation to protect the south from the north.

The Roman conquest destroyed in Britain a Celtic civilisation far more advanced, as modern archaeologists have shown, than it seemed to Julius Caesar and his successors. After the conquest Britain was thoroughly ' Romanised ' ; great highways were made, law and order were established, marshes were drained, agriculture was improved, mining was developed, market towns were built, trade flourished and wealth increased. Latin was spoken in the towns, Roman fashions and ways were adopted, and (among other religions) Christianity was introduced. Altogether, the Roman civilisation in Britain reached a high level, but it perished very quickly after the eventual withdrawal of

Roman legions (c.AD410). This is surprising and suggests that Romanisation although thorough had never taken root among the people.

Traces of the Roman occupation survive in modern Britain. There are the great Roman roads, e.g. Watling Street (Dover–London–Chester) Fosse Way (Cornwall–Lincoln), Ermine Street (London–York) : remains of many Roman villas (farm-houses) and of several towns, e.g. Wroxeter (Uriconium) have been dug up ; and many modern names (especially those beginning with Caer-, Strat- or Street-, or ending in -caster, -cester, -coln or -port) betray a Roman origin.

Read *Roman Britain*, by R. G. Collingwood. See CELTS ; CELTIC LANGUAGE AND LITERATURE

' **Britannia,**' see SHIPS

britannia metal, whitish alloy of tin, antimony and copper, and sometimes of bismuth and zinc.

British Association, British learned society ; has a yearly conference at which members discuss the latest discoveries in mathematics, science, geology, education, economics, agriculture, etc. ; founded by Sir David Brewster, and others, 1831.

British Broadcasting Corporation, see RADIO

British Columbia, province of Western Canada ; area c.366,000sq.m ; pop. 817,000 ; is between the Rocky Mts and the N. Pacific ; extremely mountainous ; the rivers include the Fraser and Columbia ; and the rocky coast (with many islands, e.g. Vancouver I.) has fine harbours. The products include vast quantities of timber and pulp. Agriculture and fisheries are important. The mines, as yet only partly developed, supply many ores, e.g. lead, copper, zinc and gold. Exports include fish, coal, gold, timber and wood-pulp. The cap. is Victoria ; Vancouver is the western terminus of the CPR.

British Commonwealth of Nations or **British Commonwealth and Empire,** voluntary partnership of peoples numbering in all c.540,000,000, and living in territories with a total area of 14,440,000 sq.m, i.e. one-quarter of the world's population, and one-quarter of the land area of the globe. Apart from the United Kingdom of Great Britain and Northern Ireland, the Commonwealth comprises Dominions, Colonies, Protectorates, Mandated Territories, etc.

Canada, the Commonwealth of Australia, New Zealand, the Union of South Africa, India, Pakistan and Ceylon are *Dominions*, officially defined in the Statute of Westminster (1931) as ' autonomous communities within the British Empire, equal in status and in no way subordinate to each other, though united by common allegiance to the Crown.'

Among the *Colonies* are some with an elected House of Assembly or House of Representatives and a nominated Legislative Council, e.g. Bahamas, Barbados, Bermuda and Jamaica ; some with a partly-elected Legislative Council, e.g. British Guiana, British Honduras, Gold Coast, Ashanti, Kenya, Leeward Islands, Mauritius, Northern Rhodesia, Singapore, Trinidad, the Windward Islands, Fiji, Sierra Leone ; some with a nominated Legislative Council, e.g. Aden, Cyprus, Falkland Islands, Gambia, Hong Kong, Nyasaland Protectorate, Seychelles, Uganda Protectorate and Zanzibar ; and some without a Legislative Council, e.g. British Solomon Islands Protectorate, Gibraltar, Somaliland, etc.

By a British *Mandated Territory* is meant an area in which responsibility for government was placed in the hands of Great Britain on the authority of a mandate (order) from the Supreme Council of the Allies after World War I. In 1946 Great Britain, Australia and New Zealand surrendered their mandates to the Assembly of the United Nations, the areas concerned including Tanganyika, parts of the Cameroons, Togoland, Palestine, Transjordan, New Guinea, etc. The Commonwealth also includes a number of Independent States, e.g. Malay States, Brunei, etc. It should be noted that Eire now regards herself as an independent republic associated with Britain.

A *Condominium* is an area jointly governed, e.g. Anglo-Egyptian Sudan.

Regions of the British Commonwealth in Europe total 125,000sq.m ; in Asia 2,346,000sq.m ; in Africa 4,652,000sq.m ; in North America 3,893,000sq.m ; in Central and South America 106,000sq.m ; in the West Indies *c*.12,000sq.m ; and in Oceania over 3,000,000sq.m. The white population of the Commonwealth is *c*.70,000,000. There are some 80,000,000 Christians, 13,000,000 of them being RC ; also 210,000,000 Hindus, 100,000,000 Moslems and *c*.750,000 Jews.

Built up over a period of 400 years by traders, soldiers, explorers, missionaries, pioneers and statesmen, the Commonwealth may be regarded today as comprising two associated groups : (*a*) equal and independent nations, namely the United Kingdom and the Dominions, and (*b*) the United Kingdom and various Dependencies, the latter forming what is sometimes called the Colonial Empire. In relation to (*a*) the United Kingdom is a member of a British *league of nations*, where a form of international co-operation exists ; in relation to (*b*) the United Kingdom must for many years remain the senior partner, ruling backward or primitive people while striving to raise the cultural standards and political status of mingled coloured races.

The growing empire began with the idea of a ' mother country ' (England) with ' children ' (colonies) overseas. The latter were thought of at home as *possessions*, and our statesmen tried to govern them from London, an experiment which led to rebellion and to the creation in George III's day of the USA, which broke away from all allegiance to the British crown. In the 19th c. it looked very much as if Canada also would secure similar independence, but Lord Durham (nicknamed Radical Jack) as Governor-General found (1839) the key to the problem of governing overseas regions peopled by the British. This was the British ' Cabinet System,' i.e. a Governor appointed by the king was to be guided, not by London, but by the majority in the colonial parliament, a system now known as *responsible self-government*. The Statute of Westminster (1931) clearly defined the relationship between Britain and the Dominions, the Act abolishing the right of the British Parliament to legislate for the Dominions or to disallow bills passed by the Dominions, and also empowering the Dominion parliaments to repeal or amend any act of the British Parliament applying to them. This statute is in itself proof that the Commonwealth is indeed a brotherhood of peoples bound together by mutual regard rather than by any form of coercion. Today wherever the British flag flies it is a symbol of a great heritage, of a common loyalty to one king, of mutual understanding and respect, and of a desire to work together and stand by each other.

Though Sir Walter Raleigh may be styled ' the father of British colonisation,' it was Sir Humphrey Gilbert who claimed Newfoundland for Queen Elizabeth in 1583, Raleigh's Virginia (N. America) being planted in 1607. New England was colonised by the Pilgrim Fathers 1620. Massachusetts was founded later ; Maryland was established by Lord Baltimore in 1634. Meanwhile, England secured also the Bermudas, the West Indies and Barbados, etc., and Jamaica was taken from the Spaniards 1655. William Penn founded his Quaker colony (Pennsylvania) 1682, and by Wolfe's victory over Montcalm at Quebec 1759 some 3,000,000sq.m were added to the British empire.

The loss through the American War of Independence of the American colonies was a severe blow to Britain, but the Empire was being built up elsewhere, notably in India, where the East India Company had begun as a number of trading ' stations.' There Robert Clive and Warren Hastings laid the foundations of the Indian Empire, but it was not till 1876 that Queen Victoria was proclaimed Empress of India. During this period settlements in Australia followed Captain Cook's exploration of that great continent *c*.1769 ; New Zealand was proclaimed British 1840. The

Cape of Good Hope had become part of the Empire in 1814, and other regions of Africa were added later, including (1882) the former British protectorate of Egypt and the Sudan.

Read *The British Commonwealth*, Sir Edward Grigg.

British Drama League, see DRAMA

British Guiana, see GUIANA

British Honduras, see CENTRAL AMERICA

British Isles, group of islands off the west coast of Europe. The largest is now called Great Britain (England, Wales and the mainland of Scotland). Next in size is Ireland (area 32,408sq.m). In all there are *c*.5,000, among them the Orkneys, Shetlands, Hebrides, I. of Man, I. of Wight, etc. (total area 121,000sq.m). See UNITED KINGDOM

British Legion, organisation founded 1921 by Earl Haig for the welfare of men who had served in World War I. It now includes ex-servicemen and women of World War II, and has over 3,500 branches besides those overseas and the British Legion Village at Maidstone, Kent. The funds are chiefly derived from local activities and from the sale of ' Flanders poppies ' on or before Armistice Day.

British Museum, THE, now the largest museum in the UK, was founded 1753. It is in Bloomsbury, London, though its natural history section is now housed in the Natural History Museum, South Kensington. The present building in Bloomsbury was designed by Sir Robert Smirke, and was completed 1847, the immense circular Reading Room ten years later. The library of the British Museum contains *c*.4,000,000 books, besides over 50,000 manuscripts. See LONDON

British Restaurants, see CANTEEN

British Ship Adoption Society, see SHIPS

British Thermal Unit (B.Th.U.), quantity of heat required to raise the temperature of 1lb of water 1°F, i.e. 252 calories (small) or 0·252 Calories, or 778 foot-pounds.

Brittain, VERA, writer and lecturer ; noted for her *Testament of Youth* and *Testament of Friendship* (life-story of Winifred Holtby).

Brittany, *brit'äni*, NW. peninsula of France, now divided into various departments, but formerly an independent duchy ; still keeps its individuality as the home of the Bretons, a deeply religious peasant people with customs, a Celtic language (not unlike Welsh), and folk-lore of their own. See CELTIC LANGUAGE AND LITERATURE

Britten, BENJAMIN (1913–   ), English musician, *b* Lowestoft ; won fame with his unaccompanied choral variations, *A Boy was Born*, 1934, and startled the musical world with his highly original operas *Peter Grimes* (1945), *The Rape of Lucretia* (1946) and *Albert Herring* (1947).

Brixham, coastal health resort, Devon ;

noted for its fisheries and safe harbour where William of Orange landed 1688.

Brno, *ber'nō* (formerly Brünn), industrial city, Czechoslovakia, where the first Bren gun was made ; pop.265,000.

broad arrow, mark placed on Government property, and on the clothes of convicts.

Broadcasting, see RADIO

Broads, flat district of Norfolk (and part of Suffolk), popular with tourists for its shallow fresh-water lakes ; famous for yachting, fishing and fowling.

broadsheet or **broadside,** single sheet with a song, the dying speech of a criminal, or a popular ballad, etc. printed on one side only ; popular in the 17th century.

Broadway, see NEW YORK

Brocken, highest point (3,730ft) of the Harz Mts, Germany. If one stands on the summit with the sun behind and a wall of mist in front, the shadow thrown on the mist sometimes seems gigantic. This has long been known as the Spectre of the Brocken.

Broken Hill, town, New S.Wales, Australia ; has what is claimed to be the largest silver mine in the world ; pop.26,000.

broker, in business, one who buys or sells on behalf of another, especially a stock-broker who deals in stocks and shares.

Bromborough, industrial town, Cheshire ; on the R. Mersey ; includes Bebington and Port Sunlight.

Bromfield, LOUIS (1896–   ), American author, dramatist, music critic, etc. ; noted for several important novels, e.g. *Early Autumn* and *The Green Bay Tree*, both in traditional style ; and of a more unusual type as *Twenty-four Hours, The Strange Case of Miss Annie Spragg*. Other brilliant books include *Wild is the River, Until the Day Break*.

bromine, *brō'mēn*, non-metallic element, Br ; atomic weight 79·916 ; atomic number 35 ; dark red liquid with a choking smell. Silver bromide (AgBr) is sensitive to light, hence bromide paper, plates, films used in photography, are coated with an emulsion containing silver bromide.

Bromley, market town, Kent ; part of Greater London ; pop.63,000 (with Bickley).

Brompton, residential district of Kensington, SW. London.

Brontë sisters, *bron'ti*, three famous English writers, *b* Thornton, Bradford, Yorkshire. Their father, Patrick Brontë (1777–1861) was an Irishman who had married a Cornish wife, Maria Branwell (1783–1821). Patrick became rector of Haworth, a small W. Riding town, 1820. His son, Patrick Branwell, *b* 1817, was clever and gifted, but a ne'er-do-well ; two daughters (Maria and Elizabeth) died in childhood.

The three remarkable sisters were Charlotte (1816–55) Emily (1818–48) ; Anne (1820–49). All were highly imaginative, living much in a world of fancy bounded by the walls of the dull parsonage at Haworth, beyond which were bleak moors. While at Roe Head School, Charlotte made a friend of Ellen Nussey. Emily and Anne eventually became governesses for a time ; later Charlotte and Emily went to Brussels (1842) to learn languages. After this, the ' dauntless three ' planned to open a school. This, however, was unsuccessful, so the girls published their collected verses, calling themselves Currer, Ellis and Acton Bell. Only two copies were sold.

In spite of disappointments and difficulties, and in spite of Branwell's follies, their father's strange behaviour, and their own frailty, the three sisters pressed on. Emily wrote her novel *Wuthering Heights*, published 1848, and the same year Anne's novel *Agnes Grey* appeared. Though Charlotte's story *The Professor* remained unpublished till after her death, her novel *Jane Eyre (ār)* (written in secret and by candle-light) was an instant and tremendous success 1847.

Unhappily there was little time for rejoicing in the Haworth parsonage. Branwell and Emily *d* 1848 ; Anne the following year, shortly after publishing *The Tenant of Wildfell Hall* ; and Charlotte had barely time to write *Shirley* and *Villette* (much of it about her experiences in Brussels) before she *d* 1855, shortly after marrying the Rev. A. B. Nicholls, her father's curate. Thus, old Patrick Brontë was left to mourn his losses, among them three daughters who had earned lasting fame.

Today the Haworth Parsonage is a Brontë museum.

Read *The Brontës*, Phyllis Bentley.

brontosaurus, see GEOLOGY

bronze, alloy of copper and tin, and sometimes zinc. We speak of *copper* coins, but they are actually bronze, the most recent containing much nickel.

Bronze Age, period between the Stone Age and Iron Age, when ornaments, weapons and tools were largely made of bronze. There seems reason to suppose that bronze was used in Egypt over 6,000 years ago ; in Britain the Bronze Age was roughly 1400–600BC.

Brooke, SIR JAMES (1803–68), *b* Benares (India). As a young man he bought a yacht and sailed to Borneo, where he became Rajah of Sarawak and showed himself an able ruler ; put down piracy ; controlled the head-hunting Dyaks ; and died in Devon, leaving the government of Sarawak in the hands of his nephew, SIR CHARLES JOHNSON BROOKE (1829–1917). The latter was succeeded by his son SIR CHARLES VYNER BROOKE (1874–   ), who, 1946, handed over Sarawak to the British Government.

Brooke, RUPERT (1887–1915), poet, *b* Rugby ; died in World War I at Scyros in the Aegean Sea. Handsome, a fine athlete, he showed great promise, and is noted for his poem *The Soldier*, a sonnet beginning :

If I should die, think only this of me :
That there's some corner of a foreign field
That is for ever England.

Brooklands, spot near Weybridge, Surrey ; formerly noted for its motor-racing track.

Brooklyn, see NEW YORK

broom, heath and moorland evergreen shrub with yellow pea-shaped flowers. The seeds are in small black pods.

Brophy, JOHN, *brō'fi* (1899–   ), novelist, *b* Liverpool ; author of *Gentleman of Stratford* ; *Immortal Sergeant*, etc.

Brougham, LORD, *broom* ; *brō'ŭm* (1778–1868), *b* Edinburgh ; a noted Whig and a great reformer ; Chancellor of the Exchequer 1830. He was an excellent speaker, but vain and rash ; designed the covered horse-drawn carriage known as a brougham.

Broughty Ferry, see DUNDEE

Brown, FORD MADOX (1821–93), artist, *b* Calais (France) of British parents ; friend of Dante G. Rossetti and William Morris ; designed stained glass windows. His pictures include *Christ Washing Peter's Feet* ; he is grouped with the Pre-Raphaelites.

Brown, JOHN (1810–82), Scottish doctor, *b* Biggar, Lanarkshire ; won fame with his book, *Rab and His Friends*, the story of a dog.

Brown, JOHN (1800–59), American farmer who, with his sons and a few followers, captured the Arsenal at Harper's Ferry, W. Virginia, USA, 1859, intending to raise a rebellion among the slaves in the neighbourhood, thus hoping to secure the abolition of slavery. His party was overwhelmed by Colonel E. Lee, and John Brown was tried by court-martial and hanged at Charlestown. His death gave America the anti-slavery song :

John Brown's body lies a-mouldering in the grave,
But his soul goes marching on !

Brown, THOMAS EDWARD (1830–97), Manx poet ; wrote *My Garden*, beginning : A garden is a lovesome thing.

Browne, HABLOT KNIGHT, *brown* (1815–82), artist, *b* Kennington, London ; illustrated books by Charles Dickens ; called himself Phiz, short for physiognomy, i.e. face.

Browne, SIR THOMAS (1605–82), doctor, a Royalist ; in *Religio Medici* (1643) he argues that it is possible for a doctor trained in science to remain a sincere Christian. Browne was a master of English prose.

Browning, ELIZABETH BARRETT, see BROWNING, ROBERT

Browning, ROBERT (1812–89), English poet, *b* Camberwell (London) ; being well-to-do he was able to devote himself to writing poetry, and to spend much of his life in Italy. A poet with a great love for humanity, a firm faith, a somewhat complex style full of dramatic power and rich imagery, he wrote plays; also *The Ring and the Book* ; his many long

poems, include the poetic drama
Pippa Passes ; also a host of shorter
poems, e.g. *Home Thoughts from Abroad* ;
Rabbi Ben Ezra ; *Prospice* ; *The Lost
Leader* ; and the ever-popular epic, *The
Pied Piper of Hamelin.*

Robert Browning met Elizabeth
Barrett, 1845. The most outstanding
woman poet England has known, Elizabeth (1806–61), was born at Coxhoe
Hall, near Durham. As a child she had
written plays in French and English ;
at 14 she had composed an epic on the
battle of Marathon. She early mastered
several languages, but falling from her
horse when a girl, she was long an invalid
at 50 Wimpole Street, London. Eventually she eloped with Robert (1846),
taking Wilson, her maid, and her dog
Flush, with her. The two poets lived in
Florence, Italy, and were ideally happy.

Elizabeth Barrett Browning's poetry
is full of fervour and melody, e.g.
Sonnets from the Portuguese ; *Aurora
Leigh* ; *The Cry of the Children* ;
Cowper's Grave.

Brownshirts, see STORM TROOPER

Brown Willy, hill rising 1,375ft in Cornwall.

Bruce, SIR DAVID (1855–1931), bacteriologist, *b* Australia ; specialist in tropical
diseases ; traced the cause of Malta
fever to goats' milk ; investigated sleeping sickness and made important discoveries.

Bruce, JAMES (1730–94), Scottish explorer,
b Kinnaird, Stirlingshire ; was the
second European to reach the source of
the Blue Nile.

Bruce, ROBERT, King of Scots (1274–1329).
Best-known of a family of Normans
owning estates in Scotland and elsewhere, Robert the Bruce led Scottish
national resistance against English
domination. He recaptured one Scottish
fortress after another from the English
occupation forces, was crowned King of
Scots in 1306, and in 1314, when only
Stirling remained in English hands,
defeated Edward II at Bannockburn.
Having thus secured Scottish independence, he ruled the kingdom of
Scotland wisely and well until his death
(of leprosy) in 1329. King Robert's
exploits inspired later generations, and
were celebrated by the poet Barbour in
his epic poem *The Bruce.*

Bruges, *broo'zh* (i.e. *bridges*), historic city
and port, Belgium ; has many canals
and *c*.50 bridges. It is noted for old and
pleasing buildings, e.g. the Hôtel de
Ville, the Halles (with its famous belfry)
and many churches. The industries
include textiles and chemicals, but
Bruges is not now the great trading centre
it was in the Middle Ages ; pop.60,000.
See ZEEBRUGGE

Brummell, GEORGE BRYAN, *brŭm'el* (1778–
1840), gentleman of fashion ; spent a
fortune of £30,000 ; died in an asylum ;
known as Beau Brummell—*beau* meaning dandy or fop.

Brunei, *bru'ni*, British state on the NW.

coast of Borneo ; area *c*.2,230sq.m ;
pop.40,000, chiefly Malays. The products include rubber and sago ; also
crude oil. Brunei has been under
British protection since 1888. The cap.,
Brunei, was recovered from the Japanese
invaders 1945. See BORNEO

Brunel, SIR MARC ISAMBARD, *brŭ-nel'*
(1769–1849), engineer ; *b* Normandy ;
came to England 1799 ; built the
Thames Tunnel, his inspiration being a
sea-worm that lines its tunnels with lime.

His son, ISAMBARD KINGDOM BRUNEL
(1806–59), *b* Portsmouth, was a railway
engineer who built bridges and docks.
He designed the *Great Britain*, the first
ocean vessel driven by a screw propeller,
and also the *Great Eastern.*

Brunhild, *brun-hilt*, warrior maiden, or
valkyrie, in Old Norse or Viking tales.
The Valkyries carried those who had
died most bravely in battle to Valhalla,
a vast hall with 540 doors. Odin (or
Woden) father of Brunhild, placed her
on a rock surrounded by fire, where she
slept till Sigurd or Siegfried rescued her ;
later she plotted his death, and threw
herself on his funeral pyre—or so runs
the 13th c. *Volsunga Saga*, a legend considerably altered in the *Song of the
Nibelungs* (the *Nibelungenlied*), where
the Nibelungs (dwarfs guarding a great
treasure buried in the Rhine) are associated with Siegfried, prince of the Netherlands, and Brunhild, a queen. Richard
Wagner's opera *Ring of the Nibelungs* is
based on the Norse story.

Brünn, see BRNO

Brunswick, *brunz'wik*, mountainous state
of N. Germany ; cap. Brunswick, a
commercial and industrial town with a
population of 201,000.

brush turkey, bird of the E. Indies and
Australia ; is like a small turkey ; lays
eggs in decaying vegetable matter.

Brussels, *brüss'elz*, cap., Belgium, on the
R. Senne ; notable for handsome
buildings, e.g. Palais de Justice overlooking the city, 15th c. town hall, and
the church of St Gudule. Brussels, with
its airport and many railways and
canals, is a great commercial centre, and
manufactures, lace, linen, ribbon, paper,
etc. The city was in Nazi hands 1940–
1944 ; pop.1,308,000.

Brut, see LAYAMON

Brutus, LUCIUS JUNIUS, *broo'tŭs* (*d* 509BC),
great figure of ancient Rome ; was one
of the first two consuls ; remembered
for his love of justice; condemning his
own sons to death when they were found
guilty of treachery.

Brutus, MARCUS JUNIUS (85–42BC), Roman;
fought against Julius Caesar, but was pardoned and shown favour, but was persuaded by Cassius to stab Caesar. It
was to him that Caesar's last words were
spoken, *Et tu, Brute?* i.e. *You, too,
Brutus?* Scholar, general and able administrator, Brutus was a man of high
ideals and great public spirit.

Bryant, WILLIAM CULLEN (1794–1878),

American poet and writer ; editor of the *New York Evening Post* for 50 years ; famous for his poem *Thanatopsis*, written when only 16.

Bryce, VISCOUNT (1838–1922), *b* Belfast ; became a lawyer. A Liberal, he was British ambassador to USA 1907–13, and wrote an important study of the American constitution ; author of *The Holy Roman Empire* and *Modern Democracies*.

Brythons, *brith'on,* Celtic-speaking peoples; came to Britain in the Iron Age, *c.*400BC ; forerunners of the people of Wales and Cornwall. See CELTS

B.Th.U., see BRITISH THERMAL UNIT

buccaneers and **pirates,** sea robbers. Strictly, buccaneers were British or French adventurers (with HQ in the W. Indies) who made war on Spanish ships in the 17th c. ; their captains included Sir Henry Morgan (*d* 1688), a Welshman who led many daring exploits against the Spaniards in Panama and Cuba. Later buccaneers became mere pirates, attacking ships of *any* nationality. Their flag was the Skull and Cross Bones.

Bucephalus, *bū-sef'ălŭs,* the name of Alexander the Great's favourite war-horse ; a city (Bucephala) was built over its grave.

Buchan, JOHN, see TWEEDSMUIR, LORD

Buchanan, GEORGE, *bū-kan'an* (1506–82), Scottish scholar and reformer ; had to fly from Scotland through writing against monastic orders ; became professor of Latin at Bordeaux and wrote many Latin plays. Scaliger declared that ' in Latin poetry Buchanan leaves all Europe behind.'

His democratic political treatise was condemned by Parliament and publicly burned by the University of Oxford.

Buchanan, JAMES (1791–1868), 15th president of USA, 1857–61.

Bucharest, *būkă-rest',* cap., Rumania ; on the R. Dimbovitza ; has immense trade with the Balkans, e.g. textiles, cereals, coal, cattle ; is an important airport ; liberated from Nazi rule 1944 ; pop. 985,000.

Buck, PEARL (1892–   ), American woman writer, *b* W. Virginia; lived much in China ; author of many novels, including *The Good Earth, The Promise* ; awarded the Nobel Prize (Literature), 1938.

Buckfastleigh, *-lē,* small town, Devon. Its ruined abbey, rebuilt by French Benedictine monks, was reconsecrated 1932.

Buckingham, GEORGE VILLIERS, 1ST DUKE OF (1592–1628), handsome courtier and ambitious statesman, born Brooksby, Leicestershire ; popular with James I and his son, Charles ; mismanaged foreign affairs. When about to lead a second expedition against La Rochelle he was stabbed to death at Portsmouth by John Felton.

Buckingham, GEORGE VILLIERS, 2ND DUKE

OF (1628–87), worthless courtier and politician, son of the 1st Duke ; brought up with the children of Charles I. A Royalist during the Civil War, he married the daughter of the Parliamentary general, Lord Fairfax.

Buckingham Palace, see LONDON

Buckinghamshire, county N. of the R. Thames ; has low hills, often with beeches and oaks ; is noted for dairy produce ; co.tn Aylesbury. Buckingham is a small town on the R. Ouse.

buckram, cotton or linen fabric often used for binding books.

buckwheat or **brank,** though included in grain crops is not a true cereal. A plant with heart-shaped leaves and pinkish flowers, it is grown in Britain as food for sheep, cattle and poultry. In America the flour, which is white but deficient in gluten, is used for cakes and porridge.

Budapest, *boo'dä-pesht,* cap., Hungary ; actually a twin city, i.e. Buda and Pest, separated by the R. Danube ; noted for wine ; pop.1,027,000.

Buddha, see BUDDHISM

Buddhism, *bud'izm,* religion of *c.*150,000,000 people, chiefly in India, Burma, Ceylon, China, Tibet and Japan. The founder was GAUTAMA BUDDHA, *b* India *c.*560BC ; at 30 he went in search of the perfect life, his quest ending 7 years later while meditating under a bo-tree. He became known as the Buddha, i.e. the wise or enlightened one.

Buddha taught men not to desire anything. Buddhist priests carry a bowl, for they must beg for their living ; they wear a yellow robe, and go bareheaded. Buddhists do not believe in killing any creature, and their faith is that the human soul passes from one living being to another till, finally, it reaches the blessed state of Nirvana or ' extinction ' ; this is known as the transmigration of souls.

budgerigar, see PARROT

Budget, *bŭj'et,* yearly statement of the country's income and expenditure, and of the way in which taxes are to be levied. The Budget speech is made in Parliament (sitting as the Committee of Ways and Means) by the Chancellor of the Exchequer, usually early in April. The word comes from the Fr. *bougette,* a leather bag, i.e. the case in which the Chancellor carries his Budget papers to Parliament.

Buenos Aires, *bwā'nōs ī'rās,* chief port and cap., Argentina ; largest American city S. of the equator ; is on the R. Plate, 150m from the Atlantic ; has a natural and also an artificial harbour with immense import and export trade, the latter including frozen meat; manufactures boots, shoes, cigars, cloth, etc. The population (3,000,000) includes many British.

Buffalo, city, New York State, USA ; on L. Erie ; packs meat, mills flour and manufactures iron and steel goods ; pop.576,000.

buffalo, large ox, wild in Africa, domesticated in India. The horns are low on the head. The N. American bison is sometimes called a buffalo.

Buffalo Bill, nickname given to William Frederick Cody (1845–1917), American horseman and guide, who founded a great Wild West show.

Buffon, GEORGES LOUIS LECLERC, COUNT OF, *boo-fön* (1707–88), French scientist and naturalist ; wrote a huge encyclopedia of natural history.

bugle, brass wind instrument usually without keys ; still used for signal-calls in the army.

building societies, organisations enabling people to buy property by instalments. Thus, Smith has not the money to buy a house outright, so he arranges for a building society to buy the house for him, paying the society an agreed sum per year for an agreed number of years, at the end of which period the house is his own. The first English building society was founded 1781, Birmingham ; now there are many reputable building societies, all regulated by the Building Societies Acts, 1874 and 1894.

Bulawayo, *boolä-wä'yō*, railway centre and busy town, S. Rhodesia ; associated with Lobengula, King of the Matabele ; gold is mined near by ; pop.40,000.

bulbs, modified leaf-buds of plants as snowdrop, hyacinth, tulip, daffodil. A solid bulb (e.g. crocus) is called a corm. Bulbs are exported from Holland, but E. Anglia is now famous for bulbgrowing.

Bulgaria, *bŭl-gār'iä*, republic of the Balkan states, W. of the Black Sea ; area 42,800sq.m, pop.8,640,000. A fertile region, it has mountains in the N., forests in the S., and being essentially agricultural it produces beet, rye, barley, tobacco, soya beans, cotton, and also exports hides, perfume, charcoal and copper-ore. There are many hot springs, and petroleum may eventually be produced.

Bulgaria, partly occupied by the Nazis 1941, attempted to remain neutral in World War II, but was forced by Russia to declare war on Germany Sept 1944. Tsar Simeon II (*b* 1937) succeeded his father, King Boris, 1943, and Bulgaria became a republic 1946. Its National Assembly is the Sobranyé. The cap., SOFIA (pop.400,000) near the R. Isker and on the railway to Istanbul, has been greatly modernised, and manufactures cloths, silks, leather, etc., and is noted for hot springs.

bull, solemn and important letter in Latin issued by the pope, and sealed with a *bulla*, i.e. a leaden seal.

bull-baiting, cruel old English sport (unlawful since 1835) in which dogs were set on a bull tied to a stake. What we now call bulldogs were once used in bull-baiting.

bulldozer, powerful vehicle, usually with caterpillar traction. It is used for levelling ground, and is capable of felling trees while doing so. It has a steel face with a forward-curving knife-edge forced forwards by a tractor in the rear.

Buller, SIR REDVERS HENRY (1839–1908), soldier, *b* Downes, Devonshire ; won the V.C. in the Zulu War ; in command of 70,000 men in the Boer War.

bull-fighting, national sport of Spain, Mexico and Spanish S. America. Spanish bull-rings are called the *plazas de toros* of which there are about 250 altogether, varying in size from that of Madrid, which holds 12,000 spectators, to those holding only 2,000 spectators.

Picadores (mounted pikemen) infuriate the bull by thrusting a short-pointed pike (a garrocha) into its back. Banderilleros divert the attention of the enraged bull from the picador, by means of their red cloaks. In the second division of the fight the banderillero steps towards the charging bull and plants two darts in the beast's neck. The espada, or matador, finally kills the bull by sword thrusts.

bullfinch, see FINCH

bullhead or **miller's thumb**, fish in British streams and ponds. It is *c*.4in long, the head broader than the body.

Bull Run, river, W. Virginia, USA ; scene 1861 and 1862 of Federal defeats in the American Civil War.

bulls and bears, see STOCK EXCHANGE

bulrush, water sedge, sometimes 8ft high ; has spikes of reddish-brown flowers, with tall spongy stems and lance-shaped leaves.

Bunhill Fields, garden and cemetery, Finsbury, London ; victims of the Great Plague were buried here 1665, also Bunyan, Defoe and Isaac Watts.

Bunker Hill, near Boston, USA, scene 1775 of the first important battle of the American War of Independence.

Bunsen, ROBERT WILHELM (1811–99), German chemist ; developed spectrum analysis ; invented the Bunsen burner which burns air and coal-gas ; also the Bunsen battery.

bunt, see WHEAT

bunting, bird rather like a finch ; 6–7in long ; dark brown above, mottled grey below, with yellow wing coverts. Its

THE YELLOW BUNTING

nest of grass, moss and hair is on or near the ground ; it lays five eggs, white with reddish marks. The REED BUNTING (head black, wings black and brown, and a white band under the neck) builds in reeds or small trees. The eggs are drab with purplish streaks. The YELLOW BUNTING (pure yellow underparts) builds under hedges a nest of grass and moss, lined with hair ; lays five eggs, whitish with reddish dots or streaks. The SNOW BUNTING is found in the Arctic.

Bunyan, JOHN (1628–88), preacher and writer, a tinker who won immortality ; b Elstow, near Bedford ; learned his father's trade ; fought in the Civil War ; married 1648 when so poor that he had neither dish nor spoon, though his wife brought him one or two books, and gave him a desire to be done with his careless living. He became deeply religious, and later won considerable distinction as a preacher.

At the Restoration (when Charles II came to the throne, 1660) no-one was allowed to preach unless he were a clergyman of the Church of England, but though a Nonconformist, Bunyan continued to preach in meeting-houses, chapels, farm-kitchens, etc., and for this suffered imprisonment at Bedford for 12 years. While he was in prison his wife died, leaving four small children. Bunyan married again, and his second wife cared for his children, among them his blind daughter, Mary.

Released 1672, Bunyan was again imprisoned 1675 ; and it was during this second term that, after a dream, he wrote *The Pilgrim's Progress,* one of 60 books from his inspired pen, the others including *Grace Abounding* and *The Holy War.*

The Pilgrim's Progress is an allegory, its story has a hidden meaning. One of our most famous English classics, it was published 1678–84, and tells how Christian journeys from the City of Destruction to the Celestial City. Christian's adventures are many, e.g. falling into the Slough of Despond, losing his burden (his sins) at the foot of the Cross, visiting Vanity Fair, being captured (along with his friend Hopeful) by Giant Despair, etc. The book has inspired millions of readers, and has been translated into over 100 languages. Characters include Obstinate, Pliable, Mr Charity, etc.

The simplicity and vividness of Bunyan's style is shown in the following quotation :

Then said Evangelist, pointing with his finger over a wide field, ' Do you see yonder wicket gate ? ' The man said, ' No.' Then said the other, ' Do you see yonder shining light ? ' He said, ' I think I do.' Then said Evangelist, ' Keep that light in your eye, and go up directly thereto.'

So I saw in my dream that the man began to run.

buoyancy, see MECHANICS

Burbank, LUTHER (1849–1926), American plant-expert, b Lancaster, Massachusetts. By experimenting he produced many new varieties of plants, e.g. a new kind of potato, a cactus without spines, a stoneless plum, etc.

Burckhardt, JOHN LEWIS, *burk'härt* (1784–1817), Swiss explorer who travelled much in north-east Africa and elsewhere ; was the first European to make a pilgrimage to the holy city of Mecca.

burdock, *bŭr'dok,* plant similar to the thistle ; its hooked seeds cling to the wool of sheep. The heart-shaped leaves are white below ; the flower is purple.

bureaucracy, *bū-rok'rä-si,* form of national government run by civil servants, and often hampered by ' red tape,' i.e. too much attention to correctness in mere details. (Government papers are usually tied with red tape, hence the nickname.) Bureaucracy, with its multiplication of officials and stereotyped forms promotes efficiency but tends to stifle initiative and to prevent adventurous and vigorous commercial enterprise.

burette, *bŭret',* graduated glass tube with a tap.

burgess, see LOCAL GOVERNMENT
burgh, see LOCAL GOVERNMENT
Burgh, HUBERT DE, *bŭrg* (d 1243), chief minister and justiciar in England 1215. Foremost English statesman in the early part of Henry III's reign, he resisted the power of the pope in England, and curbed the ambitions of the king's foreign favourites.

Burghley, LORD, *bŭr'li* (1520–98), Queen Elizabeth's most trusted minister of state, b Bourne, Lincolnshire ; was William Cecil till he became Lord Burghley 1571 ; strove to make England Protestant, and to decrease the power of Spain ; helped to improve trade while other countries on the Continent were at war ; built Burghley House, Northamptonshire ; was Lord High Treasurer from 1572. Burghley was the first of many Cecils to serve England.

burgomaster, mayor or chief magistrate of a Dutch, German or Belgian town.

Burgos, *boor'gōs,* city of N. Spain, famous for its cathedral ; pop.76,000.

Burgoyne, JOHN, *bŭr'goin* (1722–92), soldier, b Bedfordshire ; led an ill-equipped army in Canada, and was compelled to surrender to the Americans under General Gates at Saratoga 1777.

Burgundy, *bŭr'gŭndi,* name given at various periods to a region in E. France ; gave its name to a French wine, now produced in Australia and California as well.

Burke, EDMUND, *bŭrk* (1729–97), Irish statesman and writer, b Dublin ; entered Parliament. A harsh but eloquent speaker, he had a great influence on the political thought of his day ; stood for freedom, liberty of conscience in religion, a love of tradition ; condemned George III's unfortunate attitude towards the Americans ; deeply interested in Indian affairs ; brought about the trial (impeachment) of Warren Hastings.

Burke was famous as a writer of noble English prose, e.g. his essay on the *Sublime and Beautiful ; Thoughts on the Causes of the Present Discontents* (1770) ; *Speech on Conciliation with America* ; and *Reflections on the Revolution in France.* He was the bitterest English opponent of the French Revolution.

Burke, ROBERT O'HARA (1820–61), *b* Ireland ; emigrated to Australia ; met WILLIAM JOHN WILLS (1834–61), *b* Totnes, Devonshire, a surveyor. Burke and Wills, with a few others, set out 1860 to cross Australia S. to N. ; travelled from Melbourne to Cooper's Creek, then on to the Gulf of Carpentaria, being the first white men ever to do so. They returned to Cooper's Creek April 1861, where (June) they died of starvation.

Burke and Hare, see ANATOMY

Burma, country, separated from India 1937, which obtained complete self-government as an independent republic 1947. It is E. of Assam ; area *c*.261,000sq.m ; pop.18,000,000.

Largely drained by the Irrawaddy and Salween, N. Burma is a hilly country; S. Burma is flat delta land. The climate is moist and hot. There are vast teak forests ; other products are rice (grown in immense quantities), maize, cotton and beans. Minerals include rubies, wolfram, jade, and increasing quantities of petroleum.

Buddhism is the religion of 85 % of the population. The chief city of Lower Burma is RANGOON, pop.400,500, a great port on the Irrawaddy delta, and noted for its 6th c. Shwe Dagon pagoda, and its docks where rice, ivory, oil and teak are shipped. MANDALAY, cap. of Upper Burma (pop.150,000), is on the Irrawaddy, 360m N. of Rangoon. It is noted for silk-weaving, silver and ivory.

In World War II Burma was the scene of bitter fighting between the Japanese and Allied forces, pioneer work being done by General Wingate's airborne troops. China was isolated 1942 when the Japanese cut the BURMA ROAD (770m from Lashio, Burma, to Chungking, China ; built 1937–39). British and Indian forces captured Mandalay 1945 after superb organisation by Lord Louis Mountbatten, General Stilwell, etc.

The SHAN STATES, on the Burmese frontiers, are independent of, but closely related to, the administration of Burma. The Shans are a Mongol people numbering *c*.1,500,000.

Burma Road, see BURMA

Burne-Jones, SIR EDWARD, *bŭrn-* (1833–98), artist, *b* Birmingham ; friend of William Morris and student of Dante Gabriel Rossetti. His pictures are notable for exquisite design and rich colour. Burne-Jones was also a fine book illustrator and a designer of stained-glass windows.

Burnett, FRANCES ELIZA HODGSON, *bŭr-net'* (1849–1924), novelist, *b* Manchester, but lived mostly in USA ; author of *Little Lord Fauntleroy.*

Burney, FRANCES, *bŭr'ni* (1752–1840), better known as Fanny Burney, *b* King's Lynn, Norfolk. When only 26 her novel *Evelina* (in the form of letters) made a stir; other books were *Cecilia* and *Camilla.* She married General d'Arblay, a Frenchman. Fanny Burney was a friend of Dr Samuel Johnson, and her diary gives lively pictures of the England of her day.

Burnley, town, Lancashire ; on the Leeds–Liverpool Canal ; noted for cotton spinning and weaving ; has foundries and breweries ; pop.84,000.

Burns, ROBERT (1759–96), Scotland's national poet, *b* Alloway, Ayrshire. His father (*d* 1784) was poor but gave his sons a good education. With his brother Gilbert, Robert (' Rab ' or ' Robin ' for short) toiled hard to get his living on poor farms at Lochlea and Mossgiel. In 1786 he was about to give up the struggle and had booked a passage to Jamaica, when the unexpected success of a first volume of poems (published Kilmarnock) made him change his mind. The book caused a stir in Edinburgh, which he visited soon after. Although for a time made much of there by the fashionable, he returned to Ayrshire unspoilt by success but richer by £500. He settled with his wife (Jean Armour) at Ellisland, another poor farm (1788), lost all his money, became an excise officer at Dumfries, and died there, still young, worn out by continual poverty and unceasing misfortunes (many his own fault).

His life was wild and drunken. He had several disastrous and unhappy love affairs. Often in trouble with the Church, which had then much power and often interfered in private affairs, Burns in his satires (e.g. *Holy Willie's Prayer*) denounced the hypocrisy of the ' unco guid ' (' unnaturally good ') and the ' rigidly righteous,' and they hated him the more. Though savagely sarcastic, these satires are never mean- or small-minded. Burns had also an incomparable gift for song-writing. He refashioned old folk-songs, and wrote many new ones, often to old tunes. Many of these beautiful songs are still sung, especially on ' Burns Nicht ' (25 Jan.), which is kept as a national festival by Scotsmen throughout the world.

Burns sums up his views in the songs *Contented wi Little* and *A Man's a Man for a' That.* He wrote mostly what he himself called *Lallans,* i.e. Lowland Scots, the language of the common people, and was above all a people's poet.

His poetry is full of the glorious aliveness of the common man, and expresses a boisterous joy in living that triumphs

5

BUTTERCUPS
Meadow Crowfoot, the Bulbous and the Creeping Buttercups

over grinding poverty and all artificial restraints. Burns truly foretold his life in the words :
He'll hae misfortunes great and sma'
But aye a heart abune (above) them a'.
Burton, SIR RICHARD FRANCIS (1821–90), traveller and writer who, after being British Consul in Brazil, Damascus and Italy, won fame by his amazing travels, and by the writings in which he described them. His journeys include a daring pilgrimage to Mecca 1853 ; discovery of L. Tanganyika 1858 ; travels in the region of the Gold Coast ; and his wanderings among the Andes and in Brazil. He translated *The Arabian Nights.*
Burton-upon-Trent, town, Staffordshire ; noted for ale for 300 years ; pop.49,000.
Bury St Edmunds, *ber'i-*, city and agricultural centre, Suffolk.
Bushey Park, wooded area of 1,100 acres near Hampton Court, London ; famous for its horse-chestnuts.
Bushmen, nomad tribe ; probably the earliest inhabitants of many parts of Africa, from most of which they were driven out long ago. They now number *c.*26,000 ; are rarely over 5ft in height ; and resemble Negroes, but have a yellowish skin.
Bushrangers, robbers or escaped convicts in Australia, desperate men who lived in the wilds.

bustard, largest European land-bird (often 3ft high) seen occasionally in Britain. Its plumage is mottled grey, brown, and black.
butadiene, *būtä-dī'ēn*, chief ingredient of synthetic rubber. Its discovery was largely due to Professor Vladimir Ipatieff. See TRIPTANE
butane, *bū'tān*, paraffin hydrocarbon, C_4H_{10} ; is a gas at ordinary temperatures and is sold in compressed form in cylinders ; much used as a portable illuminant.
butcher-bird, see SHRIKE
Bute, fertile island with rugged coast off SW. Scotland ; chief town Rothesay. Bute is separated from the mainland by the Kyles of Bute (Gaelic *caol*, narrow).
Buteshire, Scottish county comprising the islands of Bute, Arran, Holy I., etc.
Butler, SAMUEL (1612–80), poet, *b* Strensham, Worcestershire ; noted for his satirical poem, *Hudibras* (1663), a witty and often bitter mockery of Puritans.
Butler, SAMUEL (1835–1902), artist, scholar, writer, *b* Langar, Nottinghamshire ; worked on a sheep farm, NZ, for 5 years ; author of *The Way of All Flesh* ; *Erewhon* ; and *Erewhon Revisited.* Like other Victorian writers (see ARNOLD, MATTHEW), Butler wondered whether the new industrial civilisation was progress

in the right direction and in *Erewhon* (*nowhere* backwards) he tells of a better country where the use of machinery is illegal, and it is a crime to be ill.

Butlin's camps, large, highly organised holiday camps with ample provision for recreation indoors and out. There are camps throughout the country. William Edmund Butlin (1900–   ), was born in S. Africa. His camps were taken over by the British Government 1939.

butter, see MILK

butterbur, plant with purple or flesh-coloured flowers ; the leaves (sometimes 3ft in diameter) are downy on the underside and appear in spring after the flowers.

buttercup, plant with bright yellow flowers ; species include (*a*) meadow buttercup, with roundish leaves in 3–7 lobes, (*b*) creeping, with oval leaves in 3 wedge-like segments, (*c*) bulbous, root like a bulb. All buttercups are avoided by cattle. All buttercups belong to the family *Ranunculaceae*.

butterflies and **moths,** insects belonging to the order *Lepidoptera*. Though much alike, butterflies and moths differ in many ways. Butterflies are active by day ; have *antennae* (or feelers) like hairs with knobs at the end ; place the wings back to back when at rest. Moths fly mostly at night ; the *antennae* are often feathery and never knobbed, and the wings are almost always closed when the insect is at rest, the upper pair over the lower.

Most butterflies are brightly coloured, the wings being covered with minute

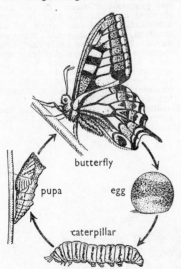

BUTTERFLY

The Life Cycle of the Swallow-Tail Butterfly

scales, and in tropical countries (e.g. Brazil) they may have a wing-span of 12in. Butterflies feed on flower juices, and their life-history is one of the most fascinating in Nature.

It begins as (*a*) an egg, often attached by a bead of glue to the leaves of bushes or plants ; becomes (*b*) the caterpillar, sometimes beautifully and vividly marked ; this from time to time sheds its old skin as it grows rapidly in size ; changes next (*c*) into a pupa or chrysalis (which sometimes is dormant for months). Eventually (*d*) the perfect insect emerges, but only after a hard struggle to escape its prison. Hence the ugly grub becomes one of the most beautiful and delicate creatures imaginable. Few butterflies survive the winter.

Many are coloured with spots or bands to resemble their environment. Among British butterflies are the cabbage whites, the red admiral, peacock, clouded yellow, etc.

Moths include the one that comes from the so-called silkworm. Others are the tiger moth, death's head, border white, lime hawk, etc.

Read *Butterflies and Moths* (Nelson) ; *Some British Moths*, Norman Ripley.

butterwort, -wŭrt, plant with a violet flower. The leaves, covered with a greasy fluid, trap insects.

buttress, bŭt′res, a projection of masonry from the face of the wall either to strengthen it or to resist the thrust of an arch or roof ; often richly ornamented, especially in church architecture. Modern buttresses are used only to strengthen walls and are usually of the simplest nature.

Buxton, health resort, Derbyshire ; noted for mineral springs.

buzzard, bird of prey closely related to eagles and hawks ; still found in Britain ; nests in trees or on mt. ledges ; feeds on rabbits and birds ; eggs bluish white, usually with brown spots.

Byblos, anciently a thriving Phoenician port on what is now the coastal plain between Palestine and Turkey. Called Gebal in the OT, it has been claimed as the oldest city in the world, rivalling Damascus. Recent excavations have brought to light relics of the Bronze Age, and of the Phoenician, Egyptian, Hittite, Assyrian, Persian, Macedonian, Roman, Saracen and Turkish civilisations.

by-election, see ELECTION

Byelorussia, see USSR

by-laws, see LAW

Byng, ADMIRAL JOHN, *bing* (1704–57), British sailor sent 1756 to relieve Minorca, which the French had attacked ; decided that it would be unwise to fight. As a result Fort St Philip surrendered and Byng was tried, deemed guilty of neglect of duty, and shot aboard the *Monarque* in Portsmouth Harbour—as Voltaire wittily said, ' *pour encourager les autres* ' (to encourage the rest).

by-product, substance formed during the preparation of another substance, e.g. tar, a by-product in the manufacture of coal-gas.

Byrd, RICHARD EVELYN, *bŭrd* (1888–   ), American explorer ; took part 1925 in an expedition to Greenland ; with Floyd Bennett flew over the N. Pole 1926, the first to do so ; flew over the S. Pole 1929. In 1946 he led an expedition to the Antarctic. Read *Skyward.*

Byrd, WILLIAM (1542–1623), English singer and composer ; organist at Lincoln Cathedral, later at the Chapel Royal ; composed anthems and madrigals ; declared :

Since singing is so good a thing,
I wish all men would learn to sing.

Byron, GEORGE GORDON NOEL, 6TH LORD (1788–1824), English romantic poet, *b* London. The Byrons were a violent family, Byron's grand-uncle being known as the ' wicked Lord ' ; Byron's father (*d* 1791) had spent his wife's fortune and then deserted her. Byron was therefore brought up by his mother, a Gordon from Aberdeenshire. She was selfish, self-contradictory and often cross, and she spoilt her son. As a boy Byron was ashamed of her, and of his own lame foot, which made him different from everybody else. For a time they lived in poverty at Aberdeen, but at ten years old Byron took possession of Newstead Abbey, a Byron property in Nottinghamshire.

At Harrow he read classical literature and often made mischief ; at Cambridge he kept a bear (he said it was going to become a fellow of the college) and gambled. Despite his deformity he played cricket and was good at swimming. In 1809, with his friend Hobhouse, Byron went abroad for two years. In 1815 he married, unhappily, and in 1816 his wife left him for ever. After this he went abroad and never returned. He spent some time in Italy, but the Near East exerted on him a still more powerful fascination, and in 1823 he went to Greece to take part in the Greek War of Independence against Turkey. He died of fever at Missolonghi on 19 Apr 1824.

LORD BYRON 1788–1824

Byron's *Hours of Idleness* (1807) attracted notice. *Childe Harold* (a fanciful account in verse of his early travels) created a sensation : later works, such as *Don Juan* and the *Vision of Judgment*, delighted or scandalised contemporaries. In England his poetry has never been widely regarded as of the highest quality ; on the Continent it was received with enthusiasm and has had enormous influence. Byron's outstanding characteristics as a poet are aristrocratic rebellism, hatred of all mankind, and a deep and desperate conviction of his own predestined (and therefore irremediable) wickedness ; and these characteristics agree with the spirit of 19th c. Continental romanticism to a far greater extent than with any important trend in English or Scottish literature during that period.

Byzantine Empire, see CONSTANTINE THE GREAT ; CRUSADES ; OTTOMAN EMPIRE

Byzantium, see ISTANBUL

C

C, chemical symbol for carbon.

Ca, chemical symbol for calcium.

cabal, *kä-bal'*, group of people pretending to be working for the public good, but actually in their own interest ; first used as a nickname for a group of politicians in Charles II's day, namely Clifford, Arlington, Buckingham, Ashley and Lauderdale (the initials of whose names form the word *cabal*). This group marked a step towards cabinet government, though it had no collective responsibility, and no leader corresponding to our modern prime minister.

caber, *kā'bĕr*, usually the lower trunk of a larch, *c.*20ft long. Tossing the caber is a favourite Highland sport.

cable, rope, chain, or wire hawser, especially for anchoring a ship. A cable-length is $\frac{1}{10}$th of a nautical mile, roughly 100 fathoms.

An electric cable, used for telephonic or telegraphic communication or for power, is usually a copper wire enclosed in gutta-percha or the plastic telothene. Deep-sea (submarine) cables are generally *c.*1in thick.

Cabinet, see PARLIAMENT

Cabinet system, see BRITISH COMMONWEALTH OF NATIONS

Cabot, JOHN, *kab'ō* (1450–98), navigator, *b* Genoa (Italy) ; came to England *c.*1484, and ten years later received from Henry VII permission to ' seek out, discover, and find ' unknown lands.

Accompanied by his son Sebastian and a crew of 18, he sailed from Bristol 1497 in the 100-ton ship *Matthew* and reached Cape Breton, N. America, two years before Columbus set foot on the mainland of S. America. Returning to England, he was rewarded by the king with a pension.

Sailing from Bristol 1498, Cabot reached Greenland, and continued still farther north till his crew mutinied.

His son Sebastian made maps for Henry VIII, planned several voyages to Russia, and is believed to have died *c.*1557.

cacao, see COCOA

cachalot, see WHALE

cactus, prickly plant found in hot, dry regions of America, though various species are now grown elsewhere. Mostly leafless, spiny plants with grotesquely-shaped stems and large, brightly-coloured flowers, cacti can live for months without water. Luther Burbank produced a spineless cactus.

Cadbury, RICHARD and GEORGE, built up a great Birmingham cocoa business on foundations laid by their father, John. Richard (1835–99) and George (1839–1922) founded for their employees the garden village of Bournville which served as a model for other social ventures of the kind. The Cadburys are well known as a Quaker family.

caddis fly, insect like a graceful moth ; the larvae live under water, surrounding themselves with a protective case or tube consisting of wood, small fragments of shells, or bits of stone, bound by juice from a ' spinning gland.'

Cade, JACK (*d* 1450), rebel, an Irishman by birth, who became leader of discontented peasants in Kent when they rose in rebellion against the practices of the King's soldiers.

After defeating Henry VI's forces at Sevenoaks, Cade and his men marched through London, where Cade robbed dwellings and ordered people to be put to death. A proclamation was issued against him, and a reward of 1,000 marks was offered to anyone who could bring him to the king dead or alive. Cade saw that he was in great danger so he disguised himself in order to evade his pursuers, but he failed, though not without a great struggle during which he received a fatal wound. He died while being conveyed to London.

Such a rising of hungry peasants against the wealthier people in the towns is known as a *jacquerie*, and has frequently occurred in European history.

Cader Idris, *kad'ĕr id'ris*, mt., Merionethshire, Wales, 2,915ft.

Cadiz, *ka'diz*, town and seaport on a peninsula, SW. Spain ; founded by the Phoenicians ; has an excellent natural harbour. Here Drake ' singed the King of Spain's beard ' 1587 ; pop.88,000.

cadmium, white metal and element, Cd ; atomic weight 112·41 ; atomic number 48 ; occurs in zinc ores ; the sulphide gives a bright yellow pigment used by artists.

Cadmus, *kad'mŭs*, in old Greek tales, founder of the city of Thebes.

Cadwaladr, *kad-wol'ädĕr*, name of two Welsh princes (*a*) ruler of the Britons in Wales, *d* 664, (*b*) patriot, who opposed Henry II ; *d* 1172.

Caedmon, *sĕd'mŭn* ; *kād'mŭn*, (*d c.*675), cowherd of Whitby Abbey, Yorkshire, of whom the story is told by Bede that as he could not sing, he crept out of the great hall whenever the other servants were making merry with the harp. Visited by an angel (i.e. inspired in a dream), he recited to St Hilda a poem, *The Creation*, regarded as the first notable example of Old English literature.

The opening words of Caedmon's *Creation* may be given in modern English as : ' Right it is that we praise the King of Heaven, the Lord of Hosts, and love him with all our hearts.'

Caen, *kän,* city, Normandy, France, on the R. Orne. Lace and cotton are the chief manufactures ; building stone is exported ; the university was begun by Henry VI, and the castle and church were founded by William the Conqueror, who is buried here ; pop.52,000.

Caerleon, *kär-lē'on,* historic town, Monmouthshire, on the R. Usk ; preserves many Roman remains—notably the fortress associated in legend with King Arthur.

Caernarvonshire, *kär-när'vŭn-,* mountainous county of N. Wales. The co.tn, Caernarvon, has Roman remains and an impressive 13th c. castle where Edward II, first Prince of Wales, was born.

Caesar, GAIUS JULIUS, *sē'zĕr,* (102–44BC) Roman soldier, statesman and dictator ; strove to build up a mighty Roman empire ; was poet, author, law-giver and brilliant orator ; before his death he was worshipped as a God.

When very young Caesar marched with the Roman legions and was captured by pirates. He became *pontifex maximus* (i.e. chief priest and law-maker) 63BC, *praetor* (a magistrate second only to a Roman consul) 62BC ; then governor of Spain. He marched into Gaul (largely what we now call France), twice crossed over to Britain (55BC and 54BC) ; made notes about the people he found (e.g. his *Gallic War,* containing the first written account of the Britons).

At that time the Roman Empire was governed by three men (the ' Triumvirate '), Pompey (in command of Spain), Crassus (Syria, Egypt and part of Greece), while Caesar commanded Gaul (including Britain, part of Germany, etc.). The triumvir Marcus Licinius Crassus was killed in Syria 53BC, and Pompey (*pom'pi*), once Caesar's friend, became his jealous enemy. Hearing of this, Caesar determined to make himself master of Italy, but if he and his armies crossed the small river, Rubicon, the boundary between Gaul and Italy, he would be a rebel against Rome. He took this vital step 49BC, and became dictator of Rome.

Caesar, made consul for five years, ruled sternly but wisely, and conquered N. Africa. In a famous dispatch 47BC after defeating an ally of Pompey he wrote : *veni, vidi, vici* (I came, I saw, I conquered). At the height of his glory the Romans wished to crown him, but he repeatedly refused this honour. Lesser men were envious of him, among them Cassius, who had been a friend of Pompey. Cassius persuaded Marcus Junius Brutus (whom Caesar greatly loved) to join in a conspiracy which ended in these, and others, stabbing Caesar to death, 15 March (Ides of March).

Many improvements in administration were due to Caesar, and he set in motion the reform of the calendar.

Caesar's *Commentaries* were compiled from his dispatches to the Senate in Rome, and resemble the dispatches of a modern commander-in-chief. They give a vivid picture of Gaul, and show that Caesar had a great care for his soldiers. See DE BELLO GALLICO

Caesarea, *sēzä-rē'ä,* port in Palestine named after Caesar, now called Qisarya.

Caesarea Philippi, *filip'-ī,* ancient town, Palestine, north of the sea of Galilee. Only a few remains are to be seen.

caesium, *sēz'i-ŭm,* white metal and element, Cs ; atomic weight 132·91 ; atomic number 55 ; resembles sodium and is extremely reactive ; first element to be discovered (1860) with the aid of the spectroscope.

caesura, *sē-zū'rä,* regular break or slight pause in the middle of a verse, e.g. :
Of man's first disobedience/and the fruit
Of that forbidden tree/whose mortal taste
Brought death into the world,/and all our woe . . .

caffeine, *kaf'ēn,* organic compound found in tea, coffee, etc. ; stimulates the heart and nerves.

Cagliari, *käl'yä-rē,* cap., Sardinia ; good harbour ; exports lead, zinc, salt ; pop.131,000.

Caillaux, JOSEPH, *kä-yō'* (1836–1944), French statesman ; prime minister 1911–12.

Cain, as told in *Genesis,* the first-born son of Adam and Eve ; killed his brother Abel, thus committing the first murder ; later founded Enoch, traditionally the first city.

cairn, pile of stones, often on a mountain top to serve as a landmark when the view is limited by mist. Cairns are common in the Scottish Highlands ; the word comes in fact from Gaelic *càrn,* stone.

Cairn Gorms, *kär'un gör'um,* a group of mountains in Banffshire, Scotland, forming a plateau cleft in two by a pass called the Lairig Gru, and having several peaks over 4,000ft. ' Cairn gorm ' is Gaelic for ' blue stones,' but the name is given to a quartzite like brown or yellow glass (used ornamentally in Scottish brooches, knife hilts, etc.) which is found mainly in the Cairn Gorms.

Cairo, *kī'rō,* cap., Egypt ; largest city in Africa ; on the east bank of the Nile immediately above its delta. The ancient portion has walls, gateways, mosques, Saladin's 12th c. citadel, bazaars, etc., all in contrast to the boulevards and hotels of the modern city. Cairo, noted for learning and trade, is a rail centre and airport of much importance ; location of British GHQ, Middle East, during World War II and scene (Nov 1943) of a war conference attended by Mr Churchill, President Roosevelt and General Chiang Kai-Shek ; pop. 1,307,000.

caisson, *kā'son*, metal or concrete box sunk to the bed of a river, lake, or sea, thus enabling men to work below water-level. As a rule the caisson is filled with masonry or concrete, and left as a foundation for the structure. Immense caissons were towed across the English Channel to build an invasion harbour, Mulberry, at Arromanches, 1944.

Caithness, county in the extreme NE. of Scotland ; has a rugged coast facing the North Sea ; co.tn Wick.

calabash, *kal'ä-bash*, name of a tree found in tropical America etc., the fruit of which is so hard that bowls or cooking vessels can be made from the rind.

Calais, *kal'ā*, fortified Channel port, France ; on the Straits of Dover ; has a fine harbour, many canals, large export trade. Termed the gateway to France for travellers from Britain, it is noted for lace and cotton. Calais was in English hands from the time of Edward III (1347) to Queen Mary (1558) ; suffered from bombardment during World Wars I and II ; pop.50,000.

calamine, zinc carbonate, $ZnCo_3$.

Calchas, *kal'kas*, the most famous soothsayer (or prophet) among the Greeks during the Trojan war.

calcination, heating a substance till it is reduced to a powder ; especially to calcine bones ; also the oxidation of metals.

calcite, *kal'sīt*, mineral, actually calcium carbonate, $CaCO_3$.

calcium, *kal'si-ŭm* (Lat. *calx*, lime), white metal and element, Ca, atomic weight 40·08 ; atomic number 20 ; first isolated by Sir Humphry Davy 1808. The metal, not found in nature, has little use in industry, but its compounds are widespread and important : (*a*) CALCIUM CARBONATE, $CaCO_3$, found in chalk, limestone and marble ; formed from the shells of sea animals, e.g. foraminifera, the different forms being due to heat and compression ; may appear as hills, e.g. the Wolds and Downs, which are geological features of Britain ; (*b*) CALCIUM SULPHATE, which occurs as gypsum, $CaSO_4.2H_2O$, from which plaster of paris is made by gentle heat ; (*c*) CALCIUM PHOSPHATE $Ca_3(PO_4)_2$, the chief constituent of bones. From the carbonate, quick lime, i.e. calcium oxide, CaO, is made by strong heat. By adding water, slaked lime, CALCIUM HYDROXIDE, $Ca(OH)_2$, is obtained, the reaction giving much heat. These two substances are much used for making mortar, cement and concrete. A solution of calcium hydroxide (lime water) is used as a test for carbon dioxide, giving a white precipitate of chalk. Plants absorb most of the nitrogen from the soil in the form of calcium nitrate, $Ca(NO_3)_2$.

Hardness of water is always due to the presence of calcium bicarbonate or calcium sulphate. The former causes temporary hardness, which can be removed by boiling ; the latter causes permanent hardness, which can be removed by washing soda. Both forms can be removed by running the water over sodium aluminium silicate. Hardness causes difficulty in getting a lather, and the degree of hardness is measured by the amount of a standard soap solution required to give a lather.

Calcutta, *kal-kŭt'ä*, city, Bengal, India ; on the R. Hooghly, 85m from the sea. It is sometimes styled ' the city of palaces ' from the many handsome buildings in the British quarter, but a large part of the city is squalid. Calcutta, which has a vast trade, is a great road- and rail-junction, and is growing in importance as an airport. The industries include iron, jute, coal, tea and timber. Founded by the E. India Company 1690, it was the scene of the ' Black Hole ' 1756, and was the capital of the Indian Empire prior to 1912 ; pop.2,109,000.

Calderon de la Barca (1600–81), Spanish dramatist, *b* Madrid ; wrote over 100 plays.

Caleb, *kā'leb*, Bible hero who, with Joshua, spied out the Promised Land for Moses. (Numbers 13, 14 ; Deuteronomy 1 ; Joshua 14).

Caledonia, Roman name given to those parts of Britain north of the Forth and Clyde ; now more generally a poetic name for Scotland.

Caledonian Canal, Scottish canal linking the N. Sea with the Atlantic (Inverness to Fort William) ; *c*.60m long ; completed 1823.

calendar, division of the tropical year of 365 days 5 hours 48 minutes 46 seconds into months, weeks and days. (The Jewish and Mohammedan calendar, based on the moon, has 354 days.)

The Roman calendar had at first 10 months and 304 days, each month being divided into Kalends, Nones and Ides. The Julian calendar, introduced 45BC by Julius Caesar, added 66 days, with an extra day in February every 4th year, thus giving what we now call Leap Year. This calendar was revised by Pope Gregory XIII (1502–85), who declared that 5 Oct 1582 should be called 15 Oct., thus losing 10 days, and also that a century should not be a Leap Year unless exactly divisible by 400, hence 1900 was not a Leap Year but 2000 will be. This Gregorian calendar was adopted in Britain and America 1752, when 3 Sept. became 14 Sept., from which time the Julian calendar has been known as Old Style (OS), the Gregorian as New Style (NS).

The months are:

Jan.	31 days	July	31 days
Feb.	28 or 29 „	Aug.	31 „
Mar.	31 „	Sept.	30 „
Apr.	30 „	Oct.	31 „
May	31 „	Nov.	30 „
June	30 „	Dec.	31 „

These are called calendar months. The lunar month (Latin *luna*, moon) is the

time from one full moon to the next,
i.e. 29 days 12 hours 44 minutes.

There are 52 weeks in the year, each
with 7 days, namely Sunday ; Monday
(moon's day) ; Tuesday (OE *Tiw*, god
of war) ; Wednesday (*Woden's* day) ;
Thursday (from *Thor*, Norse god of
thunder) ; Friday (from *Freya*, Norse
goddess of love) ; Saturday (probably
from *Saturn*, the Roman god).

For some years there has been talk of
calendar reform. The ' Desborough
Plan ' is for a 12 month year always
beginning on Sunday, with Easter Day
always 8 April, and the 365th day
regarded as New Year's Eve or as
December W, i.e. World Holiday.

The idea of Summer Time or daylight
saving was advocated by William
Willett (1857–1915), and the Summer
Time Act 1916 made compulsory the
advancing of clocks one hour, the extra
hour of daylight thus secured being
enjoyed from May to Oct. that year.
Double Summer Time (clocks being
advanced 2 hours) was introduced 1941
(4 May–10 Aug.).

Notable days and periods are :
Advent (Latin *adventus*, coming), four
weeks before Christmas
April Fool's Day, 1 Apr.
Ascension Day (Holy Thursday), 40th
day after Easter
Ash Wednesday, first day of Lent
Boxing Day, 26 Dec.
Christmas Day, 25 Dec.
Easter Sunday (in memory of Christ's
resurrection), first Sunday after the full
moon on, or next after, 21 Mar., a
date fixed by the Council of Nice, AD325
Empire Day (anniversary of Queen
Victoria's birthday), 24 May
Epiphany, see Twelfth Day (below)
Good Friday, Friday before Easter
Sunday, kept in remembrance of Christ's
crucifixion
Gunpowder Plot, 5 Nov.
Holy Thursday, see Ascension Day
(above)
Holy Week, week before Easter ;
begins on Palm Sunday
Independence Day (USA), 4 July
King's birthday, 8 June
Lent, period of 40 week-days from Ash
Wednesday to Easter Eve
Michaelmas Day, 29 Sept.
Midsummer Day, usually regarded as
21 June, and associated with our oldest
non-religious song, *Sumer is icumen in*
New Year's Day, now 1 Jan. ; was
Christmas Day from the 7th–13th c.
and 25 Mar. in the 14th c. The Income
Tax year begins 6 Apr.
Palm Sunday, Sunday before Easter
Pancake Day, see Shrove Tuesday
(below)
Primrose Day, 19 Apr.
Royal Oak Day (recalling Charles II's
escape 3 Sept. 1651 by hiding in an oak),
29 May
St Andrew's Day, 30 Nov.
St David's Day, 1 Mar.

St George's Day, 23 Apr.
St Patrick's Day, 17 Mar.
St Swithin's Day, 15 July
St Valentine's Day, 14 Feb.
Shrove Tuesday (OE shrive or confess),
day before Ash Wednesday
Trafalgar Day, 21 Oct.
Twelfth Day, i.e. 12th day after
Christmas, hence 6 Jan.; also known as
the Feast of Epiphany ; celebrated (with
Christmas) as wassail festival by the
Anglo-Saxons, wassail meaning *May
you have good health*
Wattle Day (Australia), 26 Jan.
Whit Sunday (formerly White Sunday
because new church members wore
white robes), 7th Sunday after Easter ;
commemorates the coming of the Holy
Spirit (Acts 2). See SEASONS

Calgacus (more correctly Galgacus), see
BRITAIN, ROMAN

Calgary, *kal'gäri*, town, Alberta, Canada ;
a busy centre with much trade in grain
and minerals ; pop.89,000.

calico, plain white cotton cloth, named
from Calicut, India.

Calicut, *kal'i-kŭt*, port, Madras, India ;
gave its name to *calico* ; pop.99,000.

California, SW. state of USA ; has a
Pacific coastline of *c*.1,000m ; area
156,000sq.m ; noted for magnificent
scenery, e.g. Yosemite Valley, with the
superb gorge of the R. Merced. The
south has an ideal climate. The immense film industry of the USA is centred
in California at Los Angeles and Hollywood. The products include films,
fruits, wheat, livestock, timber, gold,
quicksilver, copper, lead, petroleum,
sulphur, etc. ; cap. Sacramento ; chief
port San Francisco.

Caligula, *kä-lig'ūlä* (AD12–41), Roman
emperor, probably insane ; ruled
AD37–41 ; led an army to the coast of
Gaul, and there ordered his soldiers to
pick up shells which he called the spoils
of the conquered ocean ; was cruel and
extravagant ; murdered by a tribune.

calipers, instrument for measuring the
inside or outside dimensions of cylinders,
shafts, etc. The more accurate types
have screw adjustments and micrometer
or vernier scales.

caliph, *kal'if*, spiritual and political head
of Islam (Mohammedanism), a successor
of Mohammed. One of the greatest
was Haroun al Raschid (763–809),
Caliph of Baghdad, of whom we read
in *The Arabian Nights*. In Turkey the
rule of the caliphs ended 1924.

Callao, *käl-yä'ō*, port, Peru ; exports
sugar, cotton, hides, wool, vanadium ;
pop.84,000.

Calliope, *kalī'ō-pē*, in old Greek tales, muse
of epic poetry.

calomel, *kal'ō-mel*, mercurous chloride,
Hg_2Cl_2.

calor gas, fuel gas, a mixture of butane
and other hydrocarbons ; liquified under
pressure for easy transport.

Calorie (large), *kal'ō-ri*, unit of heat, used
in measuring the energy value of foods.

It equals the heat required to raise the temperature of 1 kilo of water through 1°C ; equivalent to 1,000 (small) calories, or 3·9682 B.Th.U., or 3,080 foot-pounds.

calorie (small), scientific unit of heat ; i.e. the amount of heat required to raise the temperature of 1 gram of water through 1°C ; equivalent to 0·001 Calorie, or 3·083968 B.Th.U., or 3·08 foot-pounds.

calumet, see AMERICAN INDIANS

Calvary, MOUNT, *kal'vă-ri* (Latin *calvaria*, skull) the hill outside the walls of Jerusalem on which Christ was crucified ; known to the Jews as *Golgotha*.

Calvin, JOHN (1509–64), *b* Noyon (France); greatest of Protestant reformers. Calvin studied to become a priest in the Roman church, then studied law and classics. Obliged by the persecution of Protestantism to leave Paris, he settled at Basel 1535 (where he wrote his *Institutes of the Christian Religion*) and later at Geneva, where as a prominent member of the Council, he set his face against those whose creed or whose morality differed from his own. Calvin strenuously opposed ritualism in Christian worship and superstition in Christian teaching. Like St Augustine he held that human nature is corrupt and wicked unless redeemed in Christ, and that only those who have been called by God enjoy salvation : all others are damned inevitably because in them human nature has not been redeemed. This doctrine is known as Predestination. There are passages in the New Testament which can hardly be interpreted otherwise, but many people have felt that the doctrine of Predestination is inconsistent with the spirit of Christ's own teaching, and most Protestants no longer believe in it, although it has had immense influence in many countries, especially Scotland, Switzerland, Hungary and New England.

cam, mechanical device for turning a rotating motion into linear motion of various kinds, especially that used on the valve-operating gear of a 4-stroke internal combustion engine ; another example is the shuttle-winding mechanism of a sewing machine.

Cambodia, *kam'bō-diä*, a region of *c.* 70,000sq.m by the Lower Mekong, Indo-China, with a coastline on the Gulf of Siam ; French protectorate since 1863 ; the chief product is rice ; pop. *c.*3,000,000 ; the cap. is Pnom-Penh.

Cambrai, *kän-bre'*, city, France, 37m from Lille ; noted for muslin ; gave its name to *cambric* ; pop.26,000.

Cambria, *kam'briä*, old name for Wales, home of the Cymry, a Celtic stock now represented by the Welsh. See CELTI

cambric, fine linen fabric said to have been made originally at Cambrai, France.

Cambridge, *kăm'brij*, university town and co.tn, Cambridgeshire, on the R. Cam ; has beautiful buildings and bridges, the Leys School and Perse Grammar School,

etc. ; noted for aircraft building, radio equipment, jam-making, etc. ; pop. 80,000.

CAMBRIDGE UNIVERSITY, founded in the 13th c., has many colleges and chapels centuries old. The men's colleges are : Christ's, Clare, Corpus Christi, Downing, Emmanuel, Gonville and Caius (pronounced *kēs*), Jesus, King's, Magdalene, Pembroke, Peterhouse (oldest), Queen's, Selwyn, Sidney Sussex, St Catherine's, St John's, Trinity, Trinity Hall. Girton and Newnham are the women's colleges. The libraries include the University Library, a handsome 1934 building ; there are also noted museums and laboratories. The University emphasises mathematics and science. Students for the degrees BA, LL.B, MB and B.Ch must be in residence for three years. There are *c.*8,000 students.

Cambridge, city, Massachusetts, USA ; on Charles R. ; situation of Harvard University ; pop.111,000.

Cambridgeshire, flat inland county of England ; co.tn Cambridge.

Cambyses, *kam-bī'sēz*, King of Persia 529–522BC.

Camden, *kam'den*, town, New Jersey, USA ; on the Delaware R., linked by ferry with Philadelphia ; is the terminus for six railways ; pop.118,000.

Camden, CHARLES PRATT, 1ST EARL (1714–1794), Whig politician ; presided at the trial of John Wilkes 1763 ; Lord Chancellor 1766–70.

Camden, WILLIAM (1551–1623 English), scholar whose *Britannia* (originally in Latin but translated into English), a survey of Britain, is still of great value.

camel, *kam'el*, hoofed animal, one of the oldest domestic animals. Because of its size, shape, and ability to go for some days without drinking (it has a complex stomach for storing water) it is particularly valuable for carrying heavy loads across deserts. Without water, a camel can carry 500–1,000lb for 25 miles a day for three days. Its feet, which are cushioned, are ideal for walking on yielding sand. Its food consists mainly of leaves of trees and scrub. The *dromedary* has one hump. The *bactrian* (or *Asiatic*) *camel* has two humps, is smaller than a dromedary, and grows a thick winter coat which it sheds in spring. A camel is known as ' the ship of the desert.' See illustration on next page.

camelopard, see GIRAFFE

Camelot, see ARTHUR

camera, see PHOTOGRAPHY

Cameroons, area (W. Africa) between Nigeria and French Equatorial Africa, a mandated territory shared between Britain and France, but was German till 1918 ; area *c.*177,000sq.m, of which the British portion is 34,000sq.m. The products include cocoa, timber (mahogany), palm-oil, rubber and bananas ; cap. Buea. The French Cameroons has an area of 143,000sq.m.

CAMELS
(1) *the Dromedary* (2) *the Bactrian Camel*

Camoëns, LUIS VAZ DE, *kam'ō-ens* (1525–1580), Portugal's greatest poet ; *b* Lisbon ; fought against the Moors ; spent many years in India where he wrote his great epic *Os Lusiadas*, the story of Portuguese exploration. He died in poverty.

camouflage, method of disguise used in war to prevent the enemy from observing or recognising troops, guns, military vehicles, or defended positions which have to be in areas where natural cover (e.g. trees) is too sparse to afford effective concealment.

Camouflage was first practised on a large scale in World War I. Since then it has become an important branch of military skill. Individual soldiers and large bodies of troops alike are trained to conceal themselves and their activities from possible enemy observers.

Many birds, animals and insects have a ' protective colouring ' which makes it difficult to recognise them when viewed against the background of their usual surroundings. Camouflage adapts the device of ' protective colouring ' to the needs of soldiers in war ; e.g. the khaki, drab or field-grey uniforms worn by soldiers of different nations, which merge more readily into normal backgrounds than the scarlet tunic of former times.

Mere protective colouring is not enough. In ordinary daylight, objects better concealed are given away to observers at a distance, especially to observers in aeroplanes, mainly by their shadows. However skilfully painted, a gun out in the open throws a shadow-pattern which can be recognised at once ; and the same is true of a man lying in the open, khaki-clad, whereas even a man in a scarlet tunic will be invisible so long as he stands in the deep shadow thrown by a rock or building. Hence effective camouflage depends as often as not on covering up the tell-tale shadows cast by the objects that have to be concealed. Nets are commonly used for this purpose. Often it is enough to break up the shadow-pattern. If it cannot be recognised, the chances are it will not be noticed.

Large bodies of troops are given away to air observation not only by the shadows of individual men, guns and vehicles, but by the tracks they make in moving about within the area occupied. Tracks are sure to be made, and if made they will be seen. But even if the enemy sees them he may not interpret them (i.e. guess their meaning) correctly. A track leading from a gate straight across a field to a gun concealed in the middle of the hedge on the far side will attract attention : but if the track goes round the edge of the field, past the gun, and back to the gate again, it will look like a path round four sides of a field, and no-one will bother about it. This result will be achieved if every soldier in approaching the gun goes round one end of the field and leaves it the other way. Such arrangements make up the ' track plan ' in modern warfare, a very important branch of camouflage.

Ships at sea are camouflaged by dazzle painting, the purpose of which is usually to make it look as if they were moving in a direction divergent from their actual course. Air-fields are camouflaged by various methods, such as burning the grass in strips to appear like shadows cast by hedges in a regular and innocent-looking field pattern.

campanile, -ē'li, large bell-tower belonging to, but usually detached from, a church ; e.g. the leaning tower of Pisa, or the famous campanile (St Mark's) Venice, rebuilt 1911. The word is Italian.

Campbell, THOMAS, kam'bel (1777–1844), poet ; b Glasgow. The success of The Pleasures of Hope which appeared in 1799 was immediate, but he is best remembered for his patriotic lyrics Ye Mariners of England and The Battle of the Baltic.

Campbell-Bannerman, SIR HENRY (1836–1908), statesman, b Glasgow. He was a staunch Liberal ; held various important offices in successive Liberal governments. His disapproval of the Boer War, however, caused a split in the Liberal Party. During his premiership (1906–1908) the Transvaal and the Orange River Colony were granted self-government.

Camperdown, Dutch coastal village c.25m north of Haarlem. In October 1797 Admiral Duncan, after a daring blockade led by himself in HMS Venerable and Vice-Admiral Onslow in the Monarch, defeated the Dutch under De Winter, for which he was raised to the peerage as Baron Duncan of Lundie and Viscount Duncan of Camperdown.

camphor, kam'fer, tree of Japan and China. The hydrocarbon camphor, a strongly-smelling, white, inflammable substance is distilled from the wood. It is used mainly for the manufacture of celluloid. It is also used medicinally as an antiseptic, and, in some degree, as a local anaesthetic. In the form of liniments, it is applied for the relief of lumbago, sciatica, etc.

campion, kam'pi-on, plant (family Caryophyllaceae) ; the several species include : (a) the common bladder campion, a summer flower of fields and lanes. Tall and slender, it has leaves in pairs with a swelling at the base ; white flowers with five petals growing from a calyx like a reddish bladder, (b) red campion, with pink flowers ; stem red and sticky.

campos, see GRASS

Cana, kā'nā, village of Galilee, about 4m from Nazareth ; scene of Christ's first miracle ; John 2.

Canaan, kā'nan, name given first to the coast of Palestine and land drained by R. Jordan. It was later applied to the whole of Palestine.

Canada, dominion of the British Commonwealth ; area 3,842,000sq.m ; comprises all American territory north of USA, except Alaska, which belongs to USA. The provinces (E.–W.) are Newfoundland, Nova Scotia, Prince Edward I., New Brunswick, Quebec, Ontario, Manitoba, Saskatchewan, Alberta, British Columbia with (N. of lat.60°N) Yukon and the North West Territories. The coastal region, Labrador, is part of the British Commonwealth, but not of the Dominion of Canada. The pop. is 13,203,000.

The chief climatic zones are (W.–E.) West Highlands, Prairies, Northern Region and Eastern Highlands. The Western Highlands are the region of the Rocky Mountains, with vast forests receiving abundant moisture on the Pacific slopes. The Prairies between the Rockies and the Great Lakes, now famous for wheat growing and stock rearing, were once grassland where bison roamed. This region is noted for the springtime westerly wind (chinook) which breaks the frost. The Northern Region is divided into plains and plateau. This area is valuable for its minerals and fur-bearing animals. Coniferous forests give place to tundra (treeless or swampy land), a region of intense winter cold. The Eastern Highlands are an area characterised by hot summers and cold winters. Fog occurs near the Atlantic coast, while the inland region enjoys sunshine and ' dry ' snow.

Rivers, lakes and mountains are features of Canada. The St Lawrence, with its tributaries, is the most important river ; others (all over 1,000m long) are the Mackenzie (flowing to the Arctic), Nelson, Churchill (entering Hudson Bay) and the Yukon. Lakes include the Great Lakes : Superior, Huron, Erie, Ontario, with Lake Winnipeg to the West ; others include the Great Bear and Great Slave lakes. Both rivers and lakes supply hydro-electric power, e.g. that of the Niagara and Shipshaw power-stations.

Communications include an Atlantic-Pacific highway completed in 1947, and the Alaska Highway completed 1942. Railways include the Canadian National and Canadian Pacific which run from Halifax to Vancouver. Civil aviation is expanding rapidly. The Trans-Canada Air Lines and the Canadian Pacific Air Lines are now in operation. There has been a great development of air transport in the north, and various services are operated on the Mackenzie R. route and by North-east Airways.

The Dominion ranks as a premier manufacturing country. The production of the important metal aluminium is rising rapidly, notably at Arvida (province of Quebec) ; and other mineral wealth includes nickel, asbestos, platinum, gold, silver, lead, cobalt, petroleum, copper, zinc and, in the far north-west, pitch-blende (which contains uranium) from which radium is extracted. Rich sources of haematite have been mined in Ontario since 1943. Over 87% of Canada's petroleum comes from the Turner Valley, Alberta. These supplies are now diminishing, but in NE. Alberta are vast supplies of oil-bearing sand, and at Vermilion Field (discovered 1944), and also near Edmonton, Canada has unlimited sources of petroleum. The forests exceed 1,220,000sq.m, among them the world's chief reserves of soft woods.

Forest products include maple, Douglas fir, red cedar, pine, oak, elm ; and among Canada's most important industries are lumbering, log-rolling, wood-pulping, paper-making, and the export of timber, notably from British Columbia, Ontario and Quebec. Canada has always exported valuable furs in great quantities. Trapping is carried out extensively in the north, and fox and mink farms have sprung up in various parts of the country. There are extensive fisheries of herring, cod, etc., also (in the west) salmon. Fish-canning is an important industry. Other products include cheese, honey, dried eggs, sugar-beet, tobacco and flax, and the central wheat area is considered one of the largest in the world. Nova Scotia, Ontario and British Columbia are among the great fruit-growing provinces. Imports include machinery, iron, steel, salt, clothing and coal.

A settlement was established about AD1000 by Norse explorers, but was overwhelmed by Indians who remained in possession until John Cabot reached the East coast 1497. Explored in the 16th c. by Jacques Cartier, who took possession in the name of France, and penetrated north by the Hudson Bay Company in the 17th c., Canada was early settled by the French and British, the contest for supremacy ending 1759 with General Wolfe's defeat of Montcalm on the Heights of Abraham. Canada was proclaimed a Dominion 1 July 1867, and has self-government under a Governor-general, the official representative of the King of Great Britain, and in his hands lies the executive power. He is appointed by the British Government but is advised by the Canadian Prime Minister and his colleagues. There is also a Cabinet, a Senate of 96 members and a House of Commons of 245. The federal capital is Ottawa. Education, which is compulsory, is free, and there are altogether 22 universities. Among the inhabitants are Scots, English, French and Indians ; the Scots and French form a large proportion of the population. Largest towns are Montreal, Quebec, Toronto and Vancouver. The principal denominations are Roman Catholic, Presbyterian and Anglican, but the Roman Catholic religion has the largest percentage of followers.

Canada has played a vital part in World Wars I and II, in the latter providing men, money and material, and having an important share in the production of the atom bomb. Field Marshal Viscount Alexander became Governor-general 1945.

Canadian Mounted Police, ROYAL, police in the Arctic, NW., and Yukon territories, and in Indian Reserves ; known as the ' Mounties ' ; first organised 1873 ; now have c.2,700 picked men who must be able to handle a canoe,

ride a horse, drive a dog-team and pilot an aircraft.

Canadian Pacific Railway (CPR), railway system opened 1886 from Montreal, via Ottawa, Great Lakes, Winnipeg, the Rocky Mts, British Columbia, to Vancouver, 2,903m ; including Quebec 3,078m ; total mileage with branches c.21,000m, spanning Canada from Halifax to Vancouver.

Canaletto, ANTONIO, kä-nä-let'tō (1697–1768), painter, b Venice ; famous for his pictures of Venice, which create a lasting impression of space, open air and light.

canals, open channels built for ships or barges. Many go up hill or down, usually by means of locks. A vessel enters a lock, the gates are then closed, water flows in till the level reaches that of the next section of the canal, the upper gates are opened, and the vessel moves forward. On some canals mechanical boat-lifts are employed, e.g. the Erie Canal (Canada). Britain has over 4,670m of canals.

Among notable artificial waterways are :

MANCHESTER SHIP CANAL, linking the Mersey (at Eastham) with Manchester, thus making a port of a city 35m from the sea ; opened by Queen Victoria 1895 ; cost c.£20,000,000 ; mostly 45ft deep and 120ft wide at the bottom ; used by vessels of 12,000 tons. The Trafford Park estate has great storage warehouses, docks and factories.

WELLAND CANAL, joining Lake Erie and Lake Ontario (Canada), 27m ; has 26 locks ; completed 1887, but reconstructed 1930.

France is famous for its canals, e.g. Marseilles-Rhône Canal, begun 1904.

Germany's most famous canal is the KIEL CANAL (kēl), opened 1895, reconstructed 1914 ; 61m ; is a short cut from the N. Sea to the Baltic.

The USSR has many huge canals, e.g. the Volga-Don, the Stalin Canal, and the Four Sea Ship Canal linking Moscow with the Baltic, White, Black, and Caspian Seas.

The CORINTH CANAL, Greece, 4m, saves ships 200 miles by sea. It was opened 1893.

The GÖTA CANAL, Sweden, 115m, was opened 1832.

The world's two most famous canals are the Suez and Panama. The Suez enables ships to reach India from Europe without going round S. Africa ; the Panama is a short cut from the Atlantic to the Pacific.

The SUEZ CANAL, linking the Mediterranean and the Red Sea, is 100m long, c.30ft deep and 197ft wide. Opened 1869, it cost c.£30,000,000. The builder was Ferdinand de Lesseps (1805–94), a Frenchman whose success in the Orient led him to the West, where (1879) he attempted to build the PANAMA CANAL. He died in disgrace because of his failure, due partly to increased cost, but largely because of a deadly enemy, malaria.

Sending men to Panama meant condemning them to death. This was so even in 1904 when the USA bought a strip of Panama, the Canal Zone (10m wide and 45m long) ; and no doubt the second attempt would have been a failure but for an American army surgeon, William Crawford Gorgas (1854–1920) who knew that malaria and yellow fever are due to germs carried by mosquitoes, and that mosquitoes begin as grubs under water. He caused oil to be poured on all ponds and ditches, and made Panama, once a death-trap, one of the healthiest regions in the world. Thus the canal was built from Colon to Panama ; and today vessels from the Atlantic are raised by huge locks to the level of the Gatun L., later descending by way of the Miraflores locks to the Pacific. The Gatun dam is 3¼m long. The canal, 50m long, 300ft wide, and 45ft deep, cost £75,000,000. It was first used 1914, but not officially opened till 1920.

canary, *kä-när'i*, bird of the finch kind, a native of the Canary Islands ; noted for its song. As a wild bird it is yellowish brown or green. As a cage-bird it needs ample room, feeds chiefly on millet, but requires canary-seed and green food, e.g. groundsel. The cage should never hang near a ceiling.

Canary Islands, 13 mountainous islands *c.*60m off the NW. coast of Africa ; area 2,800sq.m, pop.700,000, mainly Spanish, the Canaries forming two provinces of Spain. Of the inhabited islands, Grand Canary, Teneriffe and Palma are among the more important. Santa Cruz, the capital, is a busy port. The climate is pleasant. The islands are noted for wine, tomatoes and bananas. Ships may refuel at Las Palmas.

Canberra, *kan'berä*, capital of Australia ; *c.*200m from Sydney. Planning the city began 1911. The Parliament House was opened 1927 ; there are now government offices etc., also a university and cathedral. The city abounds in flowers and trees, and is beautiful in spring when the peach and cherry blossom are out ; pop.15,000.

cancer, *kan'ser*, growth composed of cells of the skin or the lining of internal organs. The reason for such multiplication is still unknown. Cancer is treated by operation, radium, X-rays, hormones or injections. The British Empire Cancer Campaign and the Imperial Cancer Research Fund are among many efforts now being made to deal with this serious menace to life.

Candia, *kan'diä*, ancient name for Crete ; also the old name (now Heraklion) for a port on the island.

candidate (Parliamentary), see ELECTION

Candlemas, Christian festival 2 Feb., named from the 11th c. church ceremony of blessing candles.

candle-power, measurement of the intensity of a source of light. One International c.p. is $\frac{1}{10}$th the illuminating power of the Harcourt pentane lamp burning pure pentane, C_5H_{12}. As the Harcourt pentane lamp is awkward to use, electric lamps operating from a carefully regulated voltage are usually employed as standards.

Canea, *kä-ne'ä*, chief port and cap., Crete ; pop.27,000.

Cannae, *kan'ē*, ancient village of SE. Italy, where (216BC) the Romans were crushingly defeated by the Carthaginians under Hannibal. The Roman state survived because Hannibal was unable to follow up his victory by marching on Rome itself.

Cannes, *kän*, Mediterranean health resort, France. Amid beautiful scenery, it has an excellent winter climate ; pop.50,000.

cannibals, tribes that eat human flesh, sometimes as food, more often as a ceremonial rite.

Canning, GEORGE (1770–1827), statesman, *b* London ; supported Catholic emancipation, but was for the most part an ardent Tory. Secretary for Foreign Affairs 1807, he was appointed Prime Minister 1827, but died four months later. Canning was a fine speaker, a man of strong will, and a great administrator. By first recognising the independence of the Spanish colonies in S. America, he (as he said) ' called a new world into existence to redress the balance of the old.'

canning industry, business of preserving and distributing meat, fruit, vegetables, etc. in hermetically sealed cans, a method invented *c.*1795.

Cannock, town, Staffordshire ; the moor, Cannock Chase, has coal and iron ; pop.41,000.

cannon, see GUN

Canopus, *kä-nō'püs*, ancient trading centre of Egypt.

Canopus, star in the constellation Argo ; may be 300 light-years distant. Its intensity is 22,000 times that of the sun. See ASTRONOMY

Canova, ANTONIO, *kä-nō'vä* (1757–1822), Italian sculptor. His most famous statues include *Perseus with the Head of Medusa* ; *Dancing Nymphs*, etc.

Cantab, short for *Cantabrigian*, a word made from the medieval Latin *Cantabrigienses*, i.e. Cambridge ; hence the name of a native of Cambridge or a student of Cambridge University.

cantaloupe, *kan'tä-loop*, kind of melon first grown in Europe at Cantalupo, Italy ; has a hard rough rind and delicious orange-coloured flesh.

canteen, *kan-tēn'*, establishment for rest and refreshments, especially a wartime institution enabling men and women in the Forces to buy and consume extra food and drink. Navy, Army and Air Force canteens (' Naffies ') were a feature of World War II, when also British Restaurants became popular for cheap meals for civilians. Many large commercial and industrial firms, etc. now have permanent canteens for employees ; as also many schools.

Canterbury, *kan'tĕr-ber-i,* religious cap. of England ; in E. Kent on the R. Stour ; trades largely in hops and grain ; pop. 25,000 ; has many old buildings and the remains of the city walls. It is noted for its schools, e.g. the Blue Coat School and King's School, traditionally founded in the 7th c., refounded 1541.

Canterbury's chief glory is the cathedral, much of it 12th, 14th and 15th c., though parts are Saxon. Founded 597 by St Augustine, it preserves the tomb of Becket (murdered here 1170), and is associated with Chaucer's *Canterbury Tales.*

The ARCHBISHOP OF CANTERBURY (primate of all England and the first peer of the realm) resides at the Old Palace here and at Lambeth. As primate of the Church of England he crowns our kings in Westminster Abbey.

Canterbury, province in South Island, NZ. Its plains are a rich grazing district for sheep. Canterbury lamb is exported.

canterbury bell, favourite old-fashioned garden plant *c.*3ft high. The flowers are like large blue, white, or lavender bells.

' **Canterbury Tales,**' see CHAUCER, GEOFFREY

Canton, *kan-ton',* port and chief commercial city of S. China ; 80m from the mouth of the Canton river ; has ancient walls ; is notable for its many houseboats, also numerous temples. The industries and exports include silk, porcelain, ivory, metalwork, etc. ; occupied by the Japanese 1938–45 ; pop.870,000.

canton, *kan'ton,* territorial division in Switzerland and France.

Canute I, *kä-nūt'* ; *k'noot* (994–1035), Danish king. After a bitter struggle against Edmund Ironside he became ruler of England 1017 ; restored law and order ; proved the folly of those flatterers who declared that he had command over the tide ; employed Englishmen as well as Danes to govern the country, and gave generous gifts to churches and monasteries. His permanent body of fighting men (the huscarls) was the earliest approach to a standing army in England.

Canvey Island, in the Thames estuary ; area *c.*7sq.m.

canyon, *kan'yon,* deep gorge, usually made by a river wearing down rocks, e.g. the Grand Canyon, Arizona, USA, the most remarkable of all. Shaped by the Colorado R., it is 1,000m long ; for 217m the gorge is 3,000–6,000ft deep.

capacity, see ELECTRICITY ; WEIGHTS AND MEASURES

Cape Breton Island, island of Nova Scotia, Canada ; area *c.*4,000sq.m ; pop. 150,000 ; has collieries and immense steel works. The chief town is Sydney.

Cape Cod, SE. point of Massachusetts Bay, USA.

Cape Griz Nez, *grē nā,* (Fr. ' grey nose '), headland, France. It is the nearest point to England.

Cape Hatteras, sandy headland of an island off N. Carolina (USA).

Cape Horn, S. America's farthest south ; a steep and rocky headland.

Capek, KAREL, *chä'pek* (1890–1938), Czechoslovak author and dramatist ; *b* Bohemia ; won fame with his play RUR (Rossum's Universal Robots) produced London 1923, in which mechanical giants devoid of emotion gain control of mankind. His drama *The Insect Play* foreshadows the Nazi régime.

Cape Matapan, *mät-ä-pän',* extreme southern headland of Greece, hence also Europe's farthest south ; scene of a British naval victory over the Italians 28 March 1941.

Cape of Good Hope, province of the Union of S. Africa ; area 277,169sq.m ; pop. 4,017,000. Much of the country is desert ; sheep and ostriches are reared ; there are diamond mines at Kimberley ; copper is exported ; cap. Cape Town.

Cape St Vincent, headland of SW. Portugal.

Capet, *kap'et* ; *kä-pe,* name of a French royal family which gave 118 rulers to Europe : 36 kings of France, 22 of Portugal, 11 of Naples and Sicily, 5 of Spain, 3 of Hungary, 3 of Navarre, 3 emperors of Constantinople, 17 dukes of Burgundy, 12 of Brittany, 2 of Lorraine, and 4 of Parma, all descendants of Robert the Strong, a Saxon count of Anjou in the 10th c.

Cape Town, legislative cap. and Mother City of the Union of S. Africa, also cap. of the Cape of Good Hope. Overlooking Table Bay, it has large docks, etc., and a spacious harbour. Behind the town is Table Mt, with a flat ridge 3,580ft high. Cape Town preserves relics of an early Dutch settlement. It has an airport at Wingfield. The SE. wind in midsummer is known as the Cape Doctor ; pop. 454,000.

Cape Trafalgar, *trä-fal'gĕr* ; *traf-al-gär',* headland on the SW. coast of Spain. See TRAFALGAR, BATTLE OF

Cape Verde Islands, *vŭrd,* 14 Portuguese islands, 350m W. of Cape Verde, Africa. They are largely mountainous ; cap. Praia.

Cape Wrath, *röth,* Scotland's farthest NW. point.

capillaries, see BLOOD

capillary action, *kä-pil'ĕr-i,* from *capillaris,* hair ; elevation or depression of a liquid in a narrow tube, due to the attraction of the molecules of the liquid for each other and for the sides of the tube.

capillary joining, see METALS

capital, top of a column or pilaster ; usually carved.

capital, in economics means more than it does in business. In economics the country's *capital* is the whole existing stock of goods owned by the country (including private persons, business or other associations, and the government) at any given time : *investment* is what is taken out of current *production* and added to *capital*, instead of being *consumed*. Thus *production* — *investment* = *consumption*. But some capital is always being used up in production, e.g. by wear and tear of machinery. This loss is known as *disinvestment*. Only if *investment* exceeds *disinvestment* does *capital* increase. If land is regarded as a form of capital, then it will be seen that goods are produced only in one way, i.e. by work applied to the capital existing at any given time. This is often a useful starting-point of economic investigation.

In politics the term capital is often used much more loosely for the class of capitalists, i.e. those who own among them a major share of a nation's capital (especially productive machinery and industrial raw materials). In some countries most of the nation's capital (in this sense) belongs to only a small number of people, and where this is the case there is often political strife between ' Capital ' and ' Labour,' the latter being those who work productive machinery which does not belong to them. When this is the case, ' Capitalism ' implies private enterprise as opposed to forms of ' Socialism ' or ' Communism ' in which the State is the owner of all means of production, distribution and exchange. In political discussions much confusion and prejudice is caused by people who use the names ' *Capital* ' and ' *Labour* ' too loosely.

capital punishment, death penalty. Prior to 1861 this was inflicted in England for many offences, e.g. forgery and petty theft ; later only for murder, piracy, treason and military crimes. In 1948 the House of Commons voted for the abolition of capital punishment for an experimental period of five years, but this was rejected by the House of Lords. Capital punishment is abolished in Italy, Portugal, Netherlands, etc., and is now hardly ever inflicted in Scotland. The method in the UK is usually by hanging ; sometimes by shooting ; in USA the electric chair is employed.

Capitol (*a*) one of the Seven Hills of Rome on which were a temple of Jupiter and other buildings, (*b*) the building where Congress assembles, Washington, USA, begun 1793, rebuilt 1815–27 ; noted for its lofty dome, Corinthian pillars and Statuary Hall.

Cappadocia, *kapä-dō'shi-ä*, ancient country of Asia Minor ; noted for sheep.

Capri, *kä'prē*, beautiful mountainous island in the Bay of Naples, Italy ; area 5sq.m ; famous for sea caves, e.g. the Blue Grotto.

Capua, *kap'u-ä*, formerly a prosperous town, Italy, 17m N. of Naples.

capybara, *kap-i-bä'rä*, animal, *c*.4ft long, with coarse reddish-brown hair ; found only in S. America ; feeds mainly on water-plants.

caracal, rare wild cat of Africa and S. Asia ; reddish-brown ; ears tufted ; has a long tail.

Caracalla (AD188–217), Roman emperor ; proclaimed at York as joint emperor with his brother Geta 211 ; slew Geta ; was extravagant and cruel, but bestowed rights of citizenship on all freemen in the empire.

Carácas, *kä-rä'käs*, cap., Venezuela ; is 3,000ft above sea-level ; has the tomb of Simon Bolivar who *d* 1830 ; pop. 400,000.

Carac'tacus (more correctly **Carata'cus**) or **Car'adoc**, British chief ; long resisted the Romans ; defeated AD51 ; taken in chains to Rome ; freed by the emperor Claudius ; died soon after. Caer Caradoc, a hill near Church Stretton, Shropshire, bears his name.

Caradoc, see CARACTACUS

carat, *kar'at*, jewellers' weight (3·16 gr. Troy). The metric carat of 200 milligrams is the legal standard weight for precious stones and pearls. Pure gold is 24 carat. Gold containing $\frac{2}{24}$th alloy is 22 carat, e.g. that normally used for wedding rings.

caravan, *kar-ä-van'*, in Asia Minor, Iran, Arabia, N. Africa, etc., a company of travellers, sometimes on pilgrimage (e.g. to Mecca), more often for trade. Camels, mules, asses, or horses may be used ; 20–25m per day is the average speed. Bus and plane services are now superseding the old caravans. In UK the word is used for any motor or horse-drawn ' house on wheels,' notably the gipsy caravan and the holiday touring type.

caraway, plant with hollow stem, fern-like leaves, white, umbrella-like flowers, and seeds used for flavouring.

carbide, compound of carbon and another element, e.g. boron, silicon, calcium, etc.; especially calcium carbide CaC_2 which gives acetylene gas when mixed with water.

carbohydrates, important group of organic chemical compounds of carbon, hydrogen and oxygen only, having the general formula $C_xH_{2y}O_y$. They include many heat and energy foods, e.g. starch and sugar ; also cellulose and gums ; all carbohydrates are produced by plant-forms with the aid of chlorophyll and sunlight.

carbolic acid, see PHENOL

carbon, *kär'bon*, non-metallic element, C ; atomic weight 12·01 ; atomic number 6 ; occurs in a variety of forms, e.g. animal charcoal, lamp-black, gas carbon, graphite and diamond ; has been called ' the life-giver ' because it is essential to all living plants and animals, and is therefore the basis of organic chemistry ; is present in a vast number of chemical compounds, e.g. metallic carbonates (limestone, chalk, etc.), and in mineral oils, coal, coal-tar products. As CARBON

DIOXIDE, CO_2 (a colourless gas with a faint, tingling smell), carbon is present in the atmosphere, the amount being increased when animals breathe out, and when coal or oil is burned, and decreased by being extracted by living plants which use carbon dioxide in the manufacture of starch, sugar, cellulose, etc.

Carbon dioxide may be produced in the laboratory by the action of dilute hydrochloric acid on chips of marble ; commercially it is obtained by heating limestone, or from fermentation, as in brewing ; the gas, heavier than air, is soluble in water, forming carbonic acid, H_2CO_3, the acid of various carbonates. CARBON MONOXIDE, CO, an odourless, invisible and poisonous gas, is formed during the incomplete combustion of coke, coal, etc., and is present in the exhaust fumes of motor cars ; a mixture of CO and hydrogen is known as water-gas ; CO and nitrogen form producer gas, a commercial fuel.

Recently, medical science has been aided by the experimental use of carbon 13, an isotope of carbon, by means of which the processes of digestion can be accurately traced, and also the progress of cellular disease.

Carbon 14 is now used in the treatment of cancer and diabetes.

carbon bisulphide or **disulphide**, CS_2, liquid formed when sulphur vapour is passed over heated charcoal. Colourless and inflammable, it is used for killing pests.

carbon dioxide, see CARBON

carbon tetrachloride, CCl_4, liquid resembling chloroform. Colourless, and with a boiling-point $c.77°C$, it has a pleasant odour, and is much used in fire-extinguishers (Pyrene), and as a solvent.

carborundum, see SILICON

carburettor, mechanism of the internal combustion engine for mixing air with petrol vapour in the correct proportions, and in a finely divided state in readiness for explosion by a timed electric spark.

Carcassonne, kär-kä-sön', walled city of S. France ; on the R. Aude ; pop. 35,000.

Carchemish, anciently a Hittite city by the R. Euphrates.

Cardiff, kär'dif, city and port, S. Wales ; co.tn, Glamorganshire, and commercial cap. of Wales ; noted for its fine civic centre, large docks and the export of coal. Its many industries include ship-repairing, steel, copper, patent fuels, chemicals, paper, ice, etc. ; pop.241,000.

Cardigan, co.tn and seaport, Cardiganshire, Wales ; site of the ruins of Cardigan Castle ; produces flannel, blanketcloth, etc. ; exports earthenware, bricks and tiles ; the R. Teifi is noted for salmon.

Cardigan Bay, bay on the west coast of Wales.

Cardiganshire, mountainous county, Wales; co.tn Cardigan.

cardinal, highest dignitary of the RC Church apart from the pope ; is chosen by the pope. A college of cardinals (usually 60–70) chooses a new pope. Cardinals wear a wide-brimmed red hat with tassels, or a scarlet biretta (a 3 or 4-cornered hat).

cardinal bird, singing bird of North and Central America ; also known as the Virginian nightingale ; has brilliant red plumage and a fine crest.

Carew, THOMAS, kä-roo' (d c.1639), English courtier and lyrical poet ; wrote *He that loves a rosy cheek.*

Carey, HENRY, kär'i (d 1743), English poet and musician ; best known for his poem *Sally in Our Alley.*

Carey, WILLIAM (1761–1834), Baptist missionary, b Northamptonshire ; was a shoemaker ; went to India 1793 , published parts of the Bible in 40 dialects

Caribbean Sea, kar-i-bē'an, part of the Atlantic between the Antilles and the coasts of Central and S. America.

caribou, kar'i-boo, wild reindeer of N. America (a) Barren Ground breed of the Arctic ; has slightly curved antlers, (b) Woodland breed, found in Canadian forests ; has shorter, much-branched antlers.

caricature, kar'i-kä-tŭr, drawing of a person, deliberately grotesque, or with some feature purposely exaggerated ; often used (e.g. in *Punch*) for ridiculing prominent politicians.

carillon, see BELL

Carisbrooke, kar'is-bruk, village, I. of Wight. Charles I was imprisoned in the castle there 1647–48.

Carlisle, kär-līl', cathedral city (also co.tn), Cumberland ; on the R. Eden ; is a notable railway centre ; has a castle with a Norman keep ; pop.66,000.

Carlos I (1863–1908), King of Portugal ; succeeded 1889 ; assassinated in Lisbon.

Carlow, kär'lō, county of Leinster, Eire ; also the co.tn.

Carl Rosa Opera Company, founded, London, 1875, by Carl August Nicholas Rosa (1842–89) ; tours the provinces and presents standard operas.

Carlyle, THOMAS, kär-līl' (1795–1881), Scottish author and historian, b Ecclefechan, Dumfriesshire ; studied German literature ; married Jane Welsh (1801–1866), an outspoken woman of genius and a noted letter-writer. At Craigenputtock, a moorland farm, Galloway, he wrote essays and *Sartor Resartus* (Latin for ' the tailor reclothed '). With great industry he completed the first volume of *The French Revolution* 1835. While the MS was being looked after by J. S. Mill, most of it was used by a servant for lighting fires, and Carlyle had to spend a year rewriting it. From 1834 Carlyle lived in Cheyne Row, Chelsea (London) ; won fame as a lecturer ; published also *Heroes and Hero Worship* ; *Oliver Cromwell's Letters and Speeches* ; *Past and Present* ; and *History of Frederick II of Prussia.*

Carlyle spoke plain broad Scots ; his contorted but often impressive English

LOCUST MENACE   *plate 9*

Locusts swarming near the Kenya-Uganda Border, East Africa. Last time locusts invaded
East Africa they caused damage costing £7,000,000. The grass was eaten up and thousands
of cattle died. (*Paul Popper*)

plate 10   WEST AFRICAN CROPS

Top : Threshing ground-nuts in the Gambia. Ground-nuts are a valuable source of vegetab!e oil. (*Government of Gambia*). *Bottom :* Inspecting cocoa pods at Bunsu, Gold Coast. Outbreaks of ' Swollen Shoot ' cocoa tree disease in 1947 necessitated the destruction of 46,000,000 trees in the Gold Coast alone. (*Pictorial Press*)

TEA AND COFFEE   *plate 11*

Top : Scene on a Kenya coffee plantation. (*C.O.I.*). *Bottom :* Tea-picking in a Ceylon
tea-garden. (*Empire Tea Bureau*)

plate 12   SUGAR AND VIRGIN LAND

Top : Caymanas Sugar Estate and Factory, Jamaica. *(C.O.I.). Bottom :* Virgin Territory :
Lamington National Park, a 48,000 acre reserve on a high table-land in Queensland, Australia.
(Australian News and Information Bureau)

style was probably an effort to overcome the difficulty of expressing himself in what was for him in many respects a foreign language. He worshipped force and virility for its own sake, probably because he was not fundamentally a strong man. Hence his admiration for such figures as Byron and Napoleon ; hence too the modern criticism that he was a fore-runner of Nazism in politics.

Carman, WILLIAM BLISS (1861–1929), Canadian poet, b Fredericton, New Brunswick ; lived mostly in USA ; his volumes of verse include *Songs from Vagabondia, Songs of the Sea Children, The Rough Riders,* etc.

Carmarthen, co.tn and port, Carmarthenshire, Wales ; has a ruined Norman castle.

Carmarthenshire, county of S. Wales ; mainly agricultural, but has iron and tin mines ; co.tn Carmarthen.

Carmel, MOUNT, hill near Acre, Palestine ; rises 1,887ft.

Carmelites, see MONKS AND NUNS

" **Carmen,**' see BIZET, A. C. L.

carmine, crimson pigment obtained from the cochineal insect.

carnation, herbaceous perennial with brightly-coloured flowers (June–Aug.) ; noted for its scent ; introduced into Britain by the Romans.

Carnegie, ANDREW, *kär-neg'i* (1835–1919), industrialist and philanthropist ; born of poor parents Dunfermline, Fife, he emigrated as a boy to USA. Starting as a telephone operator, he displayed exceptional ability in the iron and steel business, railways and oil, and became a multi-millionaire. Among other notable achievements, he built up the Pennsylvania Railroad Company, helped to develop the oil industry and founded (1901) the US Steel Corporation.

Carnegie gave away c.£100,000,000 in charities, mainly for founding various educational institutions, among which are many public libraries. He established the Carnegie Endowment for international peace, the Hero Fund and the Carnegie UK Trust.

Carnot, LAZARE NICOLAS MARGUERITE, *kär-nō* (1753–1823), French general who brilliantly reorganised and equipped the French army during the early days of the Revolution. In later life he devoted himself to scientific studies, especially to the investigation of heat. His work was carried still further by his son NICOLAS LÉONARD SADI CARNOT (1796–1832), who may be said to have laid the foundations of thermodynamics.

Caroline (1683–1737), queen of George II, known as Caroline the Good ; a supporter of Sir Robert Walpole and a patron of literature in the Church.

Caroline (1768–1821), wife of George IV, whom she married 1795. She and her husband separated soon after their marriage, and on his accession to the throne George had her name omitted from the liturgy. On this account she was the object of much popular sympathy.

carp, fresh-water fish, usually small, but may reach 25lb and be over 30in long ; has been known to live 200 years ; is olive green above, yellowish below ; found in ponds. Goldfish are a variety of carp.

Carpathians, *kär-pā'thi-an,* mt. range running from Czechoslovakia to Rumania in a curve c.900m long.

Carpentar'ia, GULF OF, opening c.350m long between Capes York and Arnhem, N. Australia.

carpets, woollen floor-coverings first used in the East ; made in France early in the 17th c. Today all except the most expensive carpets are woven on looms that work the pattern mechanically. The finest carpets come from Turkey, India and Iran. Pile carpets include Wilton, Brussels, Axminster ; those without pile (usually reversible) include Kidderminster.

Carrara, *ka-rä'ra,* town, Italy, 16m from Spezia ; noted for marble quarries.

Carroll, LEWIS (1832–98), pen-name of Charles Lutwidge Dodgson, b Daresbury, Cheshire ; lecturer in mathematics at Oxford 1855–81. He was very fond of little girls, and there were three in particular, Alice Liddell and her two sisters (daughters of the then Dean of Christ Church) whom he used to entertain by telling tales of the adventures of *Alice.* From these tales (at the suggestion of Alice Liddell herself) came the book *Alice's Adventures in Wonderland,* illustrated by Sir John Tenniel. This is the story of a little girl, who, in a dream, follows the White Rabbit into its burrow, and thence into a fantastic dreamworld where all sorts of things are liable to happen, and do. Other books include *Through the Looking-Glass*—further adventures of Alice, in which we meet Tweedledum and Tweedledee ; *The Hunting of the Snark* and *Sylvie and Bruno.*

Daresbury church has a memorial window showing, among others, Alice, the White Rabbit and the Mad Hatter.

Queen Victoria was so delighted by *Alice in Wonderland* that she gave instructions that every book Lewis Carroll had written should be sent to her. Great was her surprise when she received a large number of mathematical text-books and treatises. The original MS may now be seen in the British Museum.

carrot, root vegetable raised from seed usually sown in Feb. Seed should be sown in sandy soil in rows 9in apart. This vegetable has a yellow core while the outer rind is orange or red. It has a large sugar content ; is rich in vitamin A, and helps to overcome night blindness. Maturity is reached in the autumn, when the vegetable is stored, generally in sand, for use during the winter. The carrot-fly is a pest which attacks young carrots and once established can do much harm to the plants.

Carshalton, *kär-shŏl'tŭn,* town, Surrey, 11m south of London ; pop.57,000.

Carson, LORD (1854–1935), Irish lawyer and statesman ; championed the Ulster Unionists against Home Rule 1912–13, urging them to resist by force of arms, if necessary, though he rallied them to support the Government in World War I ; MP from 1892 to 1921.

Cartagena, *kär-tä-jē'nä,* city and Mediterranean port, Spain ; noted for its great naval harbour. The city was founded by the Carthaginians *c.*240BC ; pop. 117,000.

Cartagena, city and port, Colombia, S. America ; pop.90,000.

Carteret, JOHN, EARL GRANVILLE (1690–1763), British politician ; Lord-Lieutenant of Ireland 1724–30 ; an expert in foreign affairs ; highly regarded by George I and II. Usually in opposition to Walpole, he showed himself an able adviser in the War of the Austrian Succession. He joined the Pelham administration 1751.

Carthage, *kär'thij,* once a great and flourishing city of the Carthaginians near the present site of the town of Tunis, N. Africa ; founded *c.*850BC by Phoenician traders from Syria or Palestine. The Carthaginians long struggled against Rome (see PUNIC WARS). Destroyed by Publius Cornelius Scipio 146BC, Carthage rose to power again under the Caesars, but was burned AD698 by the Arabs. See HANNIBAL

Carthusians, see MONKS AND NUNS

Cartier, JACQUES, *kär'-tyā* (1494–1557), French explorer, *b* St Malo ; explored N. America 1534 ; discovered the St Lawrence River 1536.

cartilage, *kär'tilij,* body tissue or gristle without pores ; is firm but elastic ; found in the nose, etc., and on the joint surfaces of bones.

cartoon', rough sketch made before attempting the finished picture, or a humorous illustration in a periodical, often a summing-up of public feeling, or a CARICATURE of a well-known person.

Caruso, ENRICO, *kä-roo'zō* (1873–1921), world-famous Italian tenor opera singer ; *b* Naples.

Carver, DR G. W., see GROUND-NUT

carving, see SCULPTURE

Casabianca, see NILE, BATTLE OF

Casablanca, port, French Morocco ; pop. 257,000 ; scene, Jan 1943, of a World War II conference between Roosevelt and Churchill at which it was agreed that the Allies should demand unconditional surrender from Germany and Japan.

Casals, PABLO, *kä-säls'* (1876–   ), Spanish composer, conductor, and one of the world's greatest 'cellists.

Casals made his first public appearance in Barcelona 1889, and his first in England 1898. He has published chamber music and symphonic poems ; was exiled from Spain 1937 owing to his democratic views.

Casca, PUBLIUS SERVILIUS (*d* 42BC), Roman nobleman ; joined the conspiracy to murder Julius Caesar ; is said to have struck the first blow.

Casement, SIR ROGER (1864–1916), Irish patriot. Served in the British consular service 1895–1913, but during World War I he urged Irish prisoners in Germany to fight against England, and in 1916 was landed in Ireland by the Germans in order to lead an armed rising there. Casement was captured before he had achieved anything, taken to London, tried, found guilty of treason, and executed. In England he was regarded as a traitor, but it is now more widely recognised that he was moved by patriotic principles to do what he did. The Irish poet W. B. Yeats wrote of him :

> I say that Roger Casement
> Did what he had to do.

Cashmere, see KASHMIR

Caspian Sea, an almost tideless inland sea between Europe and Asia ; area 170,000sq.m ; is 85ft below the Mediterranean ; abounds in salmon and sturgeon.

Cassandra, *ka-san'dra,* in old Greek tales, daughter of Priam, King of Troy ; her gloomy predictions of the future were never believed by the people, and thus a ' cassandra ' has come to mean someone always foretelling disaster. See AESCHYLUS

Cassino, *käs-sē'nō,* town in Italy, 85m SE. of Rome ; noted for its Benedictine monastery founded AD529 and almost destroyed 1944 when defended by the Germans against Allied attack.

Cassius, CAIUS, *kas'i-ŭs* (*d* 42BC), Roman general and politician ; allied with Pompey ; pardoned by Julius Caesar, but conspired against him ; defeated by Antony at Philippi.

Casson, PETER, see HYPNOTISM

cassowary, *kas'ō-weri,* flightless bird similar to the ostrich and emu ; found only in Australia, New Guinea and islands near by ; is *c.*5ft high ; has a kind of bony helmet on its bare head ; black plumage.

caste, system of class-segregation among the Hindus in India. A caste is a group which keeps itself distinct, socially, from other groups. The Indian caste system is a development of Brahmanism.

Originally there were four main castes, namely, Brahmans (priests), Kshatriyas (military), Vaisyas (merchants) and Sūdras (the serving class). Out of these main classes have grown many sub-classes. The rule is that a man may not marry outside his group, and very often his occupation is determined by his caste. Thus the member of a warrior caste must not become, e.g. a cook or a sweeper. This system of grouping has proved to be a serious obstacle to social reform, but education, religion and economic needs have done much to break it down.

India has long had a group of people outside its caste system, namely the despised pariahs or Untouchables, a class whose welfare was championed by Gandhi.

Casterbridge, see DORCHESTER

Castile, *kas-tēl'*, once a kingdom of Spain; now a central province, comprising New and Old Castile.

castle, see ARCHITECTURE

Castleford, *käs'l'-fêrd*, W. Yorkshire town on the R. Aire ; noted for glass-making ; pop.42,000.

Castlereagh, ROBERT STEWART, VISCOUNT, *käs'l'-rā* (1769–1822), British statesman, *b* Dublin, son of the first Marquis of Londonderry. He suppressed the Irish Rebellion 1798 and persuaded the Irish parliament to pass the Act of Union 1800 ; held many high offices and played a leading part in forming the continental system of alliances by which Napoleon was ultimately defeated. He had Wellington made Commander-in-Chief in Portugal 1809, and planned the Walcheren expedition. He represented the UK at the Congress of Vienna, 1814, which arranged terms of peace after Napoleon's defeat. Finally, finding the strain of office too great, he committed suicide.

Castor and **Pollux,** in old Greek tales, twin sons of Zeus, Castor being famous as a tamer of horses, Pollux as a boxer ; traditionally said to have supported the Romans at the Battle of L. Regillus.

castor oil plant, small tree, probably a native of tropical Africa ; has 7-lobed leaves, green flowers, seeds yielding medicinal oil.

cat, name of a group of flesh-eating animals (e.g. lion, tiger, leopard, jaguar, ounce, puma, cheetah, etc.) and especially (*a*) the wild cat, still found in Scotland, (*b*) domestic cat, e.g. long-haired Persian, tailless Manx, etc. See next page.

'**Catabasis,**' see ' ANABASIS ' ; XENOPHON

catacombs, *kat'ä-koom* (Gk *kata,* down, *kymbe,* hollow), Roman underground burial-places where the early Christians excavated miles of galleries in which, prior to AD410, they buried *c*.7,000,000 of their dead. The most famous is that under the Appian Way, also used as a place of refuge by the early Christians who were persecuted. Similar burial-places are found in Egypt, Syria, Malta, etc.

Catalonia, formerly a north-east province of Spain ; now comprises Barcelona, Tarragona, Lerida and Gerona. The Catalonians are still an independent people with their own language and literature, of which there has been in recent generations a great revival.

catalyst, *kat'ä-list*, substance that alters the speed of a chemical reaction, but itself remains unchanged in the process ; thus, we may prepare oxygen by gently heating potassium chlorate, but if we add manganese dioxide, the potassium chlorate decomposes much more quickly at the same temperate, though the manganese dioxide is unchanged. The process, catalysis, is of great importance in industry.

Catania, *kä-tä'nyä* (1) province of Italy lying in the middle of the east side of Sicily, with Mt Etna in the north-east and fertile plains in the south. Exports include sulphur, grain, fruit, and silk ; (2) town and port, cap. of the above. An earthquake destroyed its Norman cathedral but it was rebuilt in 1693. Has Roman remains, university and former Benedictine monastery. Captured by British troops Aug 1943. Pop.290,000.

catch, see SINGING

catechism (Greek *katechein,* to teach orally), elementary form of teaching, especially of religious principles, by question and answer ; examples include the catechism of the *Book of Common Prayer,* used in the Anglican Church since the reign of Edward VI ; the Shorter Catechism (1647), which is used in the Church of Scotland, begins with the question ' What is the chief end of man ? ' the proper answering being ' To glorify God and enjoy Him for ever.'

Cathay, *ka'thä*, old (and now poetic) name for China.

cathedral, see CHURCH

Catherine de' Medici, *-dä med'ē-chē,* (1519–1589), daughter of Lorenzo de' Medici, Duke of Urbino (Italy), married Henry of France 1533 ; became queen regent after his death and that of their son Francis II ; sanctioned the massacre of St Batholomew. See BARTHOLOMEW, ST, MASSACRE OF

Catherine of Aragon (1485–1536), Spanish princess, daughter of Ferdinand and Isabella ; married, when only 16, Arthur Prince of Wales, who died 1502. Afterwards she married his brother, Henry VIII, being his first wife. Mother of Mary Tudor, she was divorced 1533, and died at Kimbolton Castle, Huntingdonshire.

Catherine of Braganza (1638–1705), daughter of John IV of Portugal. Married Charles II of England 1662. In her dowry was the ownership of Bombay.

Catherine of Valois, *-vä-lwä* (1401–37), *b* Paris ; youngest daughter of Charles VI of France ; in accordance with the Treaty of Troyes, she married Henry V of England 1420.

cathode, *kath'ōd*, negative electrode at which an electric current *leaves* an electrolyte or gas. It is the opposite of *anode,* the electrode through which a current *enters* an electrolytic cell or an electric discharge in a gas. The anode is at a positive potential to the cathode, hence it collects electrons or negative ions. In a thermionic or gas-discharge tube, the cathode is the source of electrons, the anode the collector of them.

Cathode rays are streams of negatively charged particles emitted from the

CATS

(1) *Wild Cat*   (2) *Puma*   (3) *Ounce*   (4) *Domestic Cats*   (5) *Siamese Cat*
(6) *Jaguar*   (7) *Leopards or Panthers*   (8) *Cheetah*   (9) *Tiger*   (10) *Lion and Lioness*

cathode during an electrical discharge in a rarefied gas ; and in television and radar apparatus the cathode-ray tube emits a narrow beam of electrons which passes through transverse electrostatic or magnetic fields and falls on a fluorescent viewing screen.

cathode-ray tube, see AVIATION

Ca'to, (1) MARCUS PORCIUS (234–149BC), Roman statesman. As censor (184BC) he legislated against luxury and extravagance ; urged the destruction of Carthage. He was a man of simplicity and integrity ; wrote on farming. (2) MARCUS PORCIUS (95–46BC), greatgrandson of the censor ; opposed Julius Caesar ; committed suicide.

Catskill Mountains, range in New York state, USA. With their precipices, waterfalls and streams, these well-timbered mountains are popular with tourists.

The adventures of Rip Van Winkle took place there.

Catterick, village and military camp in N. Yorkshire, 5m from Richmond. There was a Roman military station here.

cattle, domesticated members of the ox family, in the narrowest sense being pasture-fed animals, such as bulls and cows. In the broader sense, cattle include the European and American bison, buffaloes, yaks and other untamed members of the ox genus.

Oxen belong to the ruminants or animals that chew the cud, and have four stomachs, in the second of which the food is chewed at leisure.

Cattle provide us with meat and milk. See PLATES 15–18

Catull'us, GAIUS VALERIUS (c.87–54BC), Roman poet. Of his poems 116 (many very short) survive. Some are love poems addressed to the beautiful ' Lesbia ' (probably Clodia, sister of P. Clodius Pulcher). Those in which Catullus bitterly reproaches her heartless cruelty to him are unrivalled in literature as expressions of unrequited love.

Caucasia, kau-kā'zhyä, region between the Black and Caspian Seas, roughly 180,000 sq.m, with the Caucasus Mts rising to 18,465ft (Mt Elbruz). The region is now part of USSR.

caulking, see OAKUM

caustic, chemical (other than an acid) that burns or corrodes organic tissue, e.g. caustic potash, KOH, or caustic soda, NaOH.

caustic soda, see SODIUM

Cavalier, kav-ä-lēr' (Fr. chevalier ; Lat. caballus, a horse), originally a horseman or knight ; later applied to followers of Charles I in the Civil War, a Royalist as against a Parliamentarian.

Cavan, kav'an, inland county (Ulster) of Eire ; co.tn Cavan.

Cavell, EDITH, kav'el (1865–1915), nurse, b Swardleston, Norfolk. In 1907 she was appointed first Matron of the Birkendael Medical Institute in Brussels. During World War I Edith Cavell carried on her duties in Brussels, giving aid to wounded soldiers of all nationalities and helping Allied soldiers to get to the Dutch frontier. The German authorities were informed of the part she played in aiding men to escape, so they arrested her on 5 Aug 1915. After a brief trial she was sentenced to death in October, and despite the efforts of the US minister in Brussels to obtain a reprieve, she was shot on 12 October. Her last words were : ' I realise that patriotism is not enough. I must have no hatred towards anyone.' A statue to her memory stands in St Martin's Place, London.

Cav'endish, HENRY (1731–1810), English scientist, son of Lord Charles Cavendish, b Nice ; exceedingly wealthy, and very eccentric. He devoted his time to experiments concerning (a) the chemistry of gases, (b) hydrogen, (c) composition of air and water by volume, (d) the famous Cavendish experiment (' weighing the earth ') to discover the density of the earth by noting the attraction of two lead balls on a torsion balance ; result : mean density 5·52, (e) electricity and heat. Cavendish left over £1,170,000.

caves, hollows in rock, frequently the result of (a) waves beating on cliffs, (b) action of rain-water (containing carbon dioxide) slowly dissolving limestone formations, e.g. the caves in the Craven district of Yorkshire, those of Derbyshire, Kentucky, etc., (c) volcanic caves, which are actually air chambers or bubbles in lava once molten, e.g. those of Iceland and Mexico. Notable caves include Mammoth Cave, Kentucky ; Kent's Cavern ; the caves of Dordogne (France) where remains of Stone Age man have been found ; Fingal's Cave (see BASALT). Cave temples are to be seen at Abu-Simbel, Egypt and (mostly Buddhist) in India, e.g. at Karli (between Bombay and Poona) c.2,000 years old ; also at Nasik, Ajanta, etc.

caviare, kav-i-är', roe of the sturgeon after being beaten, strained and salted ; the finest comes from USSR ; eaten as a delicacy.

Cavour, COUNT, kä-voor' (1810–61), Italian statesman, advocate of a united Italy. He was closely associated with Garibaldi.

cavy, kā'vi, small gnawing animal of S. America ; grey or brown ; belongs to the rabbit family ; lives on roots, corn, etc ; in captivity must be protected from cold and damp.

Cawdor, village SW. of Nairn, Scotland ; said by Shakespeare to have been the scene of the murder (1040) of Duncan by Macbeth.

Cawnpore, kawn-poor', city on the R. Ganges, India ; an important railway centre ; industries include cotton, jute and tanning. Scene 1857 of a massacre of Europeans ; pop.487,000.

Caxton, WILLIAM, see PRINTING

Cayenne, kī-en', seaport and cap., French Guiana, S. America ; exports timber, gold, cotton, sugar, etc.

CATTLE

(1) *Highland Bull*   (2) *Welsh Black Bull*   (3) *Shorthorn Dairy Cow*   (4) *American Bison*
(5) *Cape Buffalo*   (6) *Yak*

CAVOUR 1810–61

cayman, see CROCODILE

Cayman Islands, *kī-män'*, three coral islands in the Caribbean Sea under the government of Jamaica ; discovered by Columbus ; chief town Georgetown.

Cecil, WILLIAM, see BURGHLEY, LORD

Cecil of Chelwood, 1ST VISCOUNT (1864–), Independent MP for Hitchin 1911–23 ; associated with foundation of the League of Nations ; joint author of *Principles of Commercial Law* ; author of *Our National* (i.e. English) *Church*, etc.

cedar, *sē'dĕr*, coniferous tree of Syria, Asia Minor, India, Australia, etc. ; has close-grained and fragrant timber. Of the famous cedars of Lebanon few remain in Palestine, but cedars of Lebanon grow in Scotland, and there is a fine avenue of them in Buckinghamshire. The so-called cedar wood of pencils, cigar boxes, etc., is usually a kind of juniper, e.g. the Bermuda cedar.

cedilla, see ACCENT

celandine, *sel'an-dīn*, plant of the poppy family ; has erect stem, deeply divided leaves, yellow flowers, pod-like fruit with valves to release the seeds. The LESSER CELANDINE, a distinct species (of the buttercup family) flowers in early spring, and is welcome for its golden stars and ivy-shaped leaves.

Celebes, *sel'ē-bēz*, island of Dutch Indonesia ; area 73,000sq.m ; has active volcanoes ; chief port Macassar.

cell, in biology, the material unit of all living things. Some creatures consist of one cell only, most animals or plants of many cells. A cell is a minute mass of jelly-like substance (*protoplasm*), a complex chemical mixture enclosed in a cell-wall of different material. Within the cell is (*a*) the *cytoplasm*, (*b*) *nucleoplasm*, containing densely packed granules especially rich in phosphorus.

A complex organism, e.g. a man, has groups of specialised cells, e.g. bone cells, locomotion cells, brain cells, etc.

In animal reproduction the cells concerned produce *chromosomes* responsible for handing on the characteristics of the species, reproduction occurring when the male cells (*spermatozoa*) unite with the female ova. In plants this occurs when male pollen grains and female ovules unite.

Cellini, BENVENUTO, *chel-lē'nē* (1500–71), Italian metal-worker and sculptor, *b* Florence ; hot-tempered and vain, but amazingly skilful ; famous for a gold salt-cellar made for Francis I of France, and his statues in bronze and marble. His memoirs are amusing to read.

'cello, see VIOLIN

cells, ELECTRIC, see ACCUMULATORS AND BATTERIES

celluloid, *sel'ū-loid*, mixture of nitrocellulose, camphor, etc. ; a thermoplastic that is elastic and durable.

cellulose, white, insoluble, odourless, and tasteless material of plant-tissues, e.g. cotton wool, purified wood-pulp. Chemically, cellulose ($C_6H_{10}O_5$)x, a carbohydrate closely related to starch, yields sugar (glucose) when treated with dilute acid. The molecule of natural cellulose may contain from several hundred to 20,000 or 40,000 molecules of glucose joined in a thread-like formation. Treatment with nitric acid gives various nitric acid esters (' nitrocelluloses ') including gun cotton. Purified cellulose from wood-pulp or cotton, treated with caustic soda and carbon disulphide, gives a viscous substance which is dissolved in dilute caustic soda, forming viscose. Forced through very fine holes into dilute acid, this forms fine threads of regenerated cellulose, now manufactured as viscose rayon (formerly called artificial silk) on a huge scale by Courtaulds. Of other forms of rayon, also from cellulose, the most important is cellulose acetate, manufactured by British Celanese and Courtaulds. See RAYON and PLATE 26

Celti, *seltē*, an ancient people who in Greek and Roman times occupied an area centred on the Alps and the Danube valley and spreading across south-west France and north Italy. The Celts were tall, fair-haired and reckless. They used a group of closely related languages and shared one civilisation. This Celtic civilisation reached a high level in the five centuries before Christ, the so-called La Tène period of Celtic culture. It is characterised by a great feeling for natural beauty, a subtle and delicate sense of form, and much skill in working metals, which was to give the Celts advantages over more backward peoples they came in contact with later on.

The development of La Tène culture was accompanied by an enormous expansion of the Celtic people. Celtic tribes overran Asia Minor and even

Russia as far east as the Sea of Azov. Those who swept southwards into Italy, and in 390BC sacked Rome, were eventually driven back by the Romans and confined within the Roman province of Gallia Cisalpina (i.e. Gaul This Side of the Alps). Westward the invading Celts passed through France (Gaul) into Spain and Britain.

The Celtic invasion of Britain probably began in the 5th c. BC. There were two main groups of invaders, (a) Brythons, (b) Goidels or Gaels. Brythonic tribes invaded Britain from the SE., where they fused together in Celtic kingdoms the previous inhabitants (' Iberians '). The Celtic kingdoms in southern Britain were with their culture in turn destroyed by the Roman invasion beginning AD43. Celtic influences survived in Roman Britain, and might have revived after the Roman withdrawal (c.AD410), if that had not been followed by the 5th c. Anglo-Saxon invasions, which drove the remaining Celtic culture back into Cornwall, Wales, and Strathclyde (SW. Scotland).

Strathclyde was later absorbed into the Kingdom of Scotland, and in Wales Celtic independence was destroyed by the Normans under Edward I of England c.1290 ; but the Welsh language, a form of Celtic, is still spoken, and the peoples of Wales and Cornwall are largely Celtic to this day.

The Goidels or Gaels invaded Ireland from France probably in the 4th c. BC. In Ireland they established a number of kingdoms loosely leagued together, and sharing a common Irish culture. During the 5th c. AD Ireland gave refuge to learned men driven out of continental Europe by invading barbarians (Huns, Goths and Vandals) and Christianity and classical learning (Latin and Greek) flourished side by side with Gaelic culture. Indeed it was largely by Gaelic Ireland that classical learning was kept alive for later European generations, and in the 9th c. the revival of European civilisation was partly due to the efforts of Irish missionaries, themselves refugees from the Vikings who were at that time harrying Ireland.

The Gaelic kingdoms in Ireland were overthrown by the Normans under Henry II of England (late 12th c.) : but Gaelic was still the language of the people, and Gaelic book-learning survived until the 16th c., when Ireland was finally subdued by England. There was a great revival of Gaelic learning in Ireland in the late 19th c., and in Eire Gaelic is now one of the official languages. Efforts to restore it to its former position have probably come too late, for although taught in schools it is now spoken by a minority in the south-west.

In AD470 the original Scots (Goidelic Celts from Ireland) crossed over to Scotland and founded there the kingdom of Argyll (i.e. ' eastern Gaels '). They eventually gained control of all the Highlands, and in the 9th c. the kingdom of Scotland was founded by the fusion of the Scots with the Picts, a nation of probably Brythonic Celts belonging to eastern and central Scotland. Later Scottish kings traced their descent from Kenneth MacAlpin, the first ' king of Picts and Scots.' Scottish Gaeldom was converted to Christianity by St Columba, who came over to Iona from Ireland in the 6th c. AD ; it developed no distinct culture of its own until cut off from the Gaels of Ireland by the 9th and 10th c. Viking raids.

Norman-English attempts to conquer Scotland failed at Bannockburn 1314, and a Scottish nation emerged which combined Brythonic, Goidelic, Anglic, Norse and Norman elements. Anglic (a dialect of west Teutonic) became the language of southern and eastern Scotland, and Gaelic was driven back into the Highlands. Gaelic culture in Scotland was shattered by the suppression of the last Jacobite rising (1745), and has now been almost completely exterminated. Gaelic is still spoken in the West Highlands and Islands, but as in Ireland it is the language of a dwindling minority.

After its age-long struggle with Normans and English, what is left of Celtic civilisation lingers on today in the outer fringes of the British Isles. The wonder is not that it is in decay, but that it has survived so long.

Read *The Aran Islands*, J. M. Synge ; *The Western Island*, Robin Flower.

Celtic language and literature. The Celtic languages are of great interest to scholars. Early Celtic closely resembled Greek and Latin. Dialects of Celtic fall into two groups : those which retain the Indo-European sound *qu*, and those which turn it into *p*, e.g. Lat. *quattuor*, four : Gaelic *ceithir* (modern pronunciation *kay'eer*) : Welsh *pedwar*. Celtic languages are for this reason classified as P-Celtic and Q-Celtic. Continental Celtic languages were mainly P-Celtic, and Goidelic was Q-Celtic. So modern Welsh, Cornish (now extinct) and Breton (spoken in Brittany) are P-Celtic, as also was Pictish, whereas Gaelic (both Irish and Scottish) and Manx (now extinct) are Q-Celtic.

The earliest Celtic literature of Ireland dates back to the 7th c. AD, but ' middle Irish ' literature (12th–16th c.) has collections of popular tales already ancient when first written down in books. This literature was the work of learned poets were honoured in all Celtic societies) and came to an end with the English conquest in the 16th c. A tradition of popular poetry sprang up c.1600 and still survives wherever Gaelic is spoken. (Learned poets were called *filid* : popular poets are *bards*.)

Early Welsh literature (including the

epic tales known as the *Mabinogion*)
were influenced by Irish and followed a
somewhat similar course. Learned
poetry perished with Welsh independence
but bardic poetry sprang up in its place
(13th c.). Greatest among the new
poets was David ap Gwilym (*b c.*1320).
There was a great 18th c. revival of
Welsh literature. Welsh lost ground in
the 19th c., both as spoken and as
written language. It is too early to say
whether the efforts of living Welsh writers
will succeed in saving it.

Scottish Gaelic literature developed
after the destruction of Gaelic learning
in Ireland mainly as a tradition of
popular songs. Its highest achievement
was in the 18th c., but some of its
greatest poetry has been written in the
present century.

It is possible that the great Latin poets
Virgil and Catullus, and the historian
Livy were of Celtic origin. Of books
in English, those of J. M. Synge are
mainly Celtic in idiom and feeling, and
the poetry and plays of W. B. Yeats owe
much to ancient Irish literature.

cement, see CLAY

Cenotaph, The, see LONDON

censor (Lat. *censere*, to assess), originally
a magistrate of ancient Rome, 443BC.
His chief duty was to take a census
(or count) of persons and property ;
also the administration of finance etc.
Today a censor is one who controls the
publication or broadcasting of news,
especially in wartime, or one who shares
in the censorship of films, plays, etc.,
more or less in the public interest.

census (Lat. *censere*, to assess), official
counting of the people in a country,
together with other information likely
to be useful to the government ; taken
in Rome from 443BC ; mentioned in
Luke. *Domesday Book* (1087) was a
form of census. A census has been
taken regularly (every 10 years) in
Britain since 1801, except 1941.

The census held in Great Britain on
8 Apr 1951 was more detailed than any
that had ever previously been taken.
See POPULATION

centaurs, in old Greek tales, monsters,
half man, half horse, mentioned by
Homer as dwelling in Thessaly. The
most famous was Chiron, supposed to
have taught many Greek heroes music,
medicine, etc.

Centigrade, see THERMOMETER

centipede, *sen'ti-pēd* (Lat. *centum,* 100, *pes,*
foot), creature of the order Myriopoda,
with many jointed legs (usually from
13 to 22 pairs) ; found under stones etc.

Central America, the isthmus joining N.
and S. America ; comprises BRITISH
HONDURAS, HONDURAS, COSTA RICA,
GUATEMALA, NICARAGUA, PANAMA,
SALVADOR. British Honduras is a
British Colony ; the rest are independent
republics.

BRITISH HONDURAS lies S. of Mexico ;
area 8,870sq.m ; pop.63,000. The
climate though hot and damp is not
unhealthy. The country has immense
forests varying from pine to mangrove,
and large areas of swamps. The products include mahogany and cedar ;
also cane sugar, pineapples, maize, rice,
coconuts, and *chicle* (used in making
chewing-gum) ; cap. Belize.

HONDURAS has an area of 44,370sq.m ;
is mountainous and only partly cultivated, but noted for bananas, also coffee,
coconuts, tobacco and horned cattle ;
cap. Tegucigalpa. The people are
mainly Spaniards, Indians and Negroes.

COSTA RICA lies across the isthmus ;
area 23,000sq.m ; pop. 772,000 ; has a
temperate climate on the inland plateau
(rising to 4,000ft), but is tropical in the
lowlands ; produces coffee, bananas,
rice, maize, cane sugar ; also gold,
silver, hides, timber ; cap. San José ;
chief ports Limon (Atlantic) and
Puntarenas (Pacific).

GUATEMALA (*gwä-tä-mä-lä*), area
45,452sq.m ; pop.3,300,000 ; is a land
of mts. and volcanoes ; is subject to
earthquakes ; has a hot climate and is
malarial near the coast ; exports coffee,
bananas, hides, timber and gold ; cap.
Guatemala.

NICARAGUA (*nik-ä-räg'wä*) has an area
of 51,660sq.m and coastlines on both
Atlantic and Pacific. Largest of the
Central American states, it is notable for
its forests of cedar, mahogany, etc.,
and for coffee, bananas, cane sugar.
Nicaragua is as yet largely undeveloped
but air transport is increasing ; cap.
Managua.

PANAMA has an area of 32,000sq.m ;
pop.632,000 ; produces bananas, coconuts, hides, etc. ; cap. Panama. The
country includes the Panama Canal
Zone (see CANALS).

SALVADOR is mountainous ; area
13,000sq.m ; pop.1,900,000. Though
healthy on the higher ground, it is unhealthy in the hot lowlands ; liable to
earthquakes, and has volcanoes, including Izalco, ' the lighthouse of the
Pacific ' ; exports include coffee, gold,
sugar, indigo, etc. ; cap. San Salvador,
linked by Pan-American Airways with
the USA.

Central Provinces and Berar, province N. of
Hyderabad, India ; cotton, rice, wheat,
etc. are grown, notably in Berar ; pop.
16,500,000 (mainly Hindu).

centre of gravity, fixed point of a solid body
through which the resultant force due to
the Earth's attraction passes. If a
vertical line from this point passes
outside its base, the body will fall. For
equilibrium the centre of gravity should
be as low as possible.

centrifugal force is the term applied to the
tendency which a rotating body has to
fly away from the centre round which
it is rotating. The simplest example is a
body revolving in a circle at the end of
a string. The term is not strictly scientific,
for the so-called centrifugal force is

properly the *reaction* to the force needed to make the body move in a curved path. In order to make the body move in a curve, force must be applied at right angles to the direction in which the body is moving ; the sharper the curvature of the path, the greater must be the force ; the faster the body travels, the greater must be the force of deflection to make the body move in a path of given curvature. The opposite of centrifugal force is *centripetal force*, i.e. the force required to keep a body moving in a circular path.

Centrifugal machines are used to separate molasses from sugar cane, water from clothes, and liquids of different weights. A cream separator depends upon the cream being lighter, bulk for bulk, than the milk. When a closed cylinder rotates at a given rate the cream will collect in the centre while the denser skim milk will be forced to the sides.

centripetal force, see CENTRIFUGAL FORCE

centurion, officer in the ancient Roman army ; originally in charge of 100 men.

ceorl, *che-örl*, OE for ' land-holder ' ; in the Anglo-Saxon period a person of some wealth and standing ; in feudal times a churl or peasant.

Cerberus, *sür'ber-ŭs*, in old Greek tales, the dog which guarded the entrance to Hades (the Underworld).

Cerdic, King of the West Saxons ; landed in Hampshire 495 ; *d* c.534.

cereals, cultivated grain products, e.g. wheat, barley, oats, rye, maize or Indian corn, rice, durra, millet ; named after Ceres, Roman goddess of agriculture, counterpart of the Greek goddess, Demeter.

Ceres, see DEMETER

cerium, *sē'ri-ŭm*, rare earth and element, Ce ; atomic weight 140·13 ; atomic number 58.

Cervantes, MIGUEL DE, *ther-vän'täs*, or *sĕr-van'tĕz* (1547–1616), Spanish writer, *b* Alcala de Henares ; had a life of adventure, bitterness and misery ; as a youth was page to a cardinal, but was condemned (it is said) to have a hand struck off for killing a sheriff in self-defence ; lived as an exile in Italy ; enlisted as a soldier ; was captured by Barbary pirates, and was for a time a galley-slave ; helped to supply stores for the Spanish Armada 1588 ; was several times imprisoned ; *d* Madrid on the same day as Shakespeare.

As a writer Cervantes produced plays and poetry of little worth, his fame resting on his novel *Don Quixote* (pronounced *don kwik'sōt* ; *kē-hō'tä*), published 1605–15, in which the hero, a mad nobleman, Don Quixote de la Mancha, and his faithful squire, Sancho Panza, have many amusing escapades. The book, full of humour and vivid description, is a satire on such tales of romance and chivalry as those of the knights of the Round Table. It ranks as one of

the world's greatest works of fiction.

Cetywayo, see ZULULAND

Ceuta, *thä-oo'tä*, fortified Spanish town and port on the coast of Morocco ; faces Gibraltar ; pop.60,000.

Cévennes, *sä-ven'*, low mt. range in Central France.

Ceylon, island of the British Commonwealth. It is in the Indian Ocean and to the SE. of India, from which it is separated by a narrow strait. The area is *c.*25,000sq.m, and the north of the island is mostly of coral formation with sand dunes and salt lagoons, but the south is mountainous, one of its two highest mountains being Adam's Peak, rising 7,360ft. The climate is tropical (except on the higher ground) and the vegetation rich and abundant.

Until very recently agriculture was almost the only occupation of the people, the two chief products being rice (on the flat coastal plains) and tea (on the hills). Now, however, rubber is being planted in increasing quantities, the area under cultivation exceeding that of the tea plantations (550,000 acres) by over 100,000 acres. Other products include grain, cacao, tobacco, copra, spices, areca nuts, etc. Though the island is not rich in minerals, graphite (plumbago) is worked, and it has long been famous for its precious stones, especially sapphires and rubies. Today a number of rare earths are mined.

Two very important changes of recent date are (*a*) the national industrial development, which is still being actively continued, increasing numbers of the people being engaged in the manufacture of leather goods, glass, plywood, a great variety of chemicals, rolled steel, textiles and drugs, including strychnine and pyrethrum extract ; and (*b*) the introduction of cottage industries, e.g. the making of mats, coir goods, rattanware, pottery, lacquerwork and brassware. The Dominion trades chiefly with the UK, Australia, India and the USA. There are over 900m of railways, and the island is well served by air lines. The capital is Colombo, and other important towns are Kandy and Jaffna.

Since 1945 education has been free ; and Ceylon became a self-governing Dominion of the British Commonwealth of Nations in 1948.

Of the island's population of 6,633,000 the most important are the Sinhalese, generally regarded as being descended from colonists who left the valley of the Ganges (India) to settle in the island about 540BC. The religion is mainly Buddhism, thousands of people making a yearly pilgrimage to Kandy (the old capital) to see what is believed to be a tooth of Buddha. After being under Portuguese and Dutch rule, Ceylon was ceded to Britain 1802. See INDIA

Cézanne, PAUL, *sä-zän'* (1839–1906), French painter, *b* Provence ; called the father of Impressionism ; noted for his landscapes and still life, especially flowers. See PLATE XIV

CGS, short for Centimetre-Gram-Second, a system of measurements in physics etc. See WEIGHTS AND MEASURES

CHA, see YOUTH ORGANISATIONS

Chaco, see EL CHACO

Chad, lake- in French Equatorial Africa ; area c.10,000 sq.m in the dry season.

chaffinch, common British bird 6–7in long ; has chestnut back, reddish throat and breast, yellowish bars on wings ; found mostly in hedges and gardens all the year round. The 5 eggs are greenish with purple blotches. The chaffinch feeds mostly on insects, and in this respect is most useful, but it also causes a great deal of destruction by feeding on seed crops.

THE CHAFFINCH

Chaillu, PAUL BELLONI DU (1835–1903), French author and traveller in Africa, where he travelled extensively and was among the first to see pygmies and gorillas.

chain, as a measure of length = 4 rods, poles, or perches ; 100 links ; 792in ; 22yd (length of a cricket pitch) ; 1/80th or 0·0125 mile ; 20·1168 metres, say 20·12.

chairman, one who presides at a meeting ; possibly so named from the time when chairs were scarce, and a seat had to be reserved for the president of a meeting. His duties are chiefly to maintain order, keep speakers to the business in hand, decide who shall speak, put resolutions to the vote, and announce the result. The chairman usually has a casting vote if ' for ' and ' against ' are equal. He or she is addressed as ' Mr Chairman ' or ' Madam Chairman.'

chalcedony, kal-sēd'ŏni, tinted precious stone of wax-like appearance, such as agate, jasper, onyx, etc. ; found at Chalcedon, an ancient town of Asia Minor.

Chaldea, kal-dē'ā, Bible name for North and South Babylonia.

Chalfont St Giles, village, Buckinghamshire, where Milton's cottage may still be seen, and where he wrote parts of *Paradise Lost.*

Chalgrove, village, Oxfordshire ; scene of a battle of the Civil War in 1643.

Chaliapin, FYODOR IVANOVICH shäl-yä'pen (1873–1938), Russian operatic bass singer, b Kazan. Made his first appearance in London 1913, and resided in Russia until 1921, thereafter in France.

Chalk, see CALCIUM

' Challenger,' see POLAR REGIONS

Chalmers, JAMES, chä'mĕrz (1841–1901), Scottish Congregational missionary, b Ardrishaig, Argyllshire ; worked with the London Missionary Society at Raratonga, S. Pacific and in New Guinea, where he met R. L. Stevenson ; killed by cannibals.

Chalmers, THOMAS (1780–1847), Scottish philanthropist, b Anstruther (Fife), became famous as a preacher in Glasgow, where he made important innovations in the system of administering relief to unemployed workmen ; appointed Professor of Moral Philosophy, St Andrews 1823, and of Divinity, Edinburgh 1828 ; leader of the movement for reforming the Church of Scotland which culminated 1843 in the Disruption and the foundation of the Free Kirk, of which he was the first Moderator.

Châlons-sur-Marne, shälawn' sür märn, French town 107m east of Paris ; has given its name to a battle AD451 in which the Roman general Aetius and the King of the Visigoths defeated Attila and his Huns.

Chalus, see RICHARD I

cham, see KHAN

Chamberlain, ARTHUR NEVILLE, chäm'bŭr-lin (1869–1940), British statesman, second son of Joseph Chamberlain, b Birmingham ; Lord Mayor of that city 1915 ; entered Parliament 1918, and held various cabinet offices in Conservative governments. From 1920 to 1931 he was chairman of the Conservative Party Organisation. Chancellor of the Exchequer, National Government 1931–37, he was responsible for the Tariff Act 1932, i.e. the abandonment of Free Trade in view of the world-wide trade depression of 1929–35.

In 1937 he became Prime Minister. Germany and Italy were rearming, and it was increasingly clear that their designs were a menace to world peace. The British people wanted above all to avoid war. Chamberlain tried to preserve world peace by what came to be known as Appeasement, i.e. by tolerating every fresh act of German aggression that did not directly affect British interests, in the hope that a time would come when Germany and Italy, realising that to go further would mean war, would rest content with what they had obtained by threats of force. In September 1938 Chamberlain flew to meet Hitler in Germany, first at Godesberg, then at Munich, where he signed a pact (the Munich Agreement) ceding the Sudetenland (frontier areas of Czechoslovakia with a large German population) to Hitler.

Returning to London, Chamberlain declared that like Disraeli in 1878 he had brought back ' Peace with Honour,' to which opponents retorted that it was the peace that passeth understanding and the honour that is common among thieves. Chamberlain seems actually to have believed that Hitler would at last keep his word, and ask no more ; but at the same time he took steps to hasten British rearmament. In March 1939, Germany, in defiance of the Munich agreement, invaded Czechoslovakia, and in September 1939 invaded Poland, as a result of which on 3 September 1939 Chamberlain announced that Britain was at war with Germany.

He remained in office for the time being : but when in April 1940 German forces invaded Norway, his own supporters turned against him in the House of Commons, and forced him to resign so that Churchill could become Prime Minister instead. There was general agreement that whatever his merits as a peacemaker, he was not able to lead the country in war. A broken man, he died in 1940. See WORLD WAR II

Chamberlain's appeasement policy did not succeed in preventing war, but it is defended on the grounds that it was at least a praiseworthy attempt to avert a catastrophe, and that by preventing war in 1938 it gave Britain a much needed opportunity to rearm. Against this it is urged that the breathing space was turned to better account by Germany, and that control of central and eastern Europe was an asset of immense value when war actually came. Behind Chamberlain's policy lay a difficult situation ; he could not rely on prompt US aid in any European war ; Britain and France had little military strength, and they could not in any case have defended Czechoslovakia and Poland against Germany without the assistance of Russia, which the French and British governments were not willing to accept on Russia's terms.

Chamberlain, JOSEPH (1836–1914), British statesman, *b* London ; partner in a manufacturing firm at Birmingham, where he made a fortune ; retired from business 1874. As mayor of Birmingham 1873–76 he erected improved municipal buildings and municipalised water and gas supplies. As well as abolishing much slum property he helped in the laying out of ground for recreation, and had a large share in founding Birmingham University, becoming its first chancellor 1900. From 1885 he was MP for W. Birmingham ; became a cabinet minister ; aided Gladstone to extend the franchise, but opposed Home Rule for Ireland. Resigning his seat in the cabinet, 1886, he became leader of the Liberal Unionists. In 1895 he was Colonial Secretary in Lord Salisbury's cabinet ; advocated old age pensions, Imperial tariffs, and worked for Imperial preference, his tariff reforms being defeated by Balfour. Chamberlain, a man of great ability and sincerity, wore an eyeglass. He was

seldom seen without an orchid in his buttonhole.

Chamberlain, SIR JOSEPH AUSTEN (1863–1937), English statesman, eldest son of Joseph Chamberlain ; Liberal-Unionist MP for East Worcestershire 1892–1914 ; for W. Birmingham 1914–37. Chancellor of the Exchequer 1903 and 1919 ; Secretary for India ; Leader of the House of Commons, and a supporter of Lloyd George ; Foreign Secretary 1924–1929 ; helped to shape the Treaty of Locarno 1925 ; made notable speeches on the Nazi movement in Germany 1933–34. He received the Garter for his services in the cause of peace and was awarded the Nobel Prize in 1925.

chamber music, music originally not for the theatre or church, but for a chamber or room, now has the meaning of large works in sonata form to be played by a small group of individual instruments, especially a quartet. Among the most prominent composers of chamber music are Haydn, Mozart and Beethoven.

chameleon, *ka-mē'le-un,* type of lizard found chiefly in Africa and Madagascar ; *c.*11in including the tail ; its tongue, which it flicks out to catch flies and moths, is *c.*6in long. It lives in trees and bushes, and has the curious ability to change its colour according to the colour of its surroundings.

THE CHAMELEON

chamois, *shä-mwä,* animal akin to the antelope ; *c.*24in at the shoulder ; has brown coat and small horns ; found in mountainous regions of S. Europe and W. Asia : noted for its agility. The skin (chamois pronounced *sham'y*) is valued as a fine leather, useful for polishing glass and other smooth and shiny surfaces.

Chamonix, *shä-mō-nē,* mountain valley and village in France ; starting-point for ascending Mont Blanc, Mer de Glace and six other glaciers ; tourist resort.

Champagne, *shän-pän'y,* formerly a province of NE. France ; noted for a sparkling white wine.

THE CHAMOIS

Champlain, *sham-plān'*, lake of NE. USA ; between New York State and Vermont ; contains about fifty islands ; can be navigated by the largest vessels. Champlain Lake and Hudson River communicate by Champlain Canal ; through traffic mainly coal and lumber ; area *c.*600sq.m.

Champlain, SAMUEL DE, *sham-plān'* (1567–1635), French explorer and 1st governor of Canada ; born near Rochefort ; sailed up the St Lawrence beyond Montreal 1603 ; discovered L. Champlain 1609 ; founded a settlement at Quebec, 1608, and established a fur trade ; was made prisoner by the British in 1629 when they captured Quebec, but in 1632 he resumed his former post as governor of Quebec, where he died three years later.

chancellor, formerly a clerk in a Roman law court. In England (since Edward I's time) a court official taking the place of the justiciar. The Lord High Chancellor is now keeper of the Great Seal and President of the House of Lords. He sits on the Woolsack, is head of our legal system, and advises the king on the appointment of judges.

The Chancellor of the Exchequer, a member of the Cabinet, is responsible for the country's finances.

Chancellor, RICHARD (*d* 1556), English navigator ; accompanied Sir Hugh Willoughby 1553 in his search for the NE. passage to India ; reached the White Sea, went on to Moscow, and laid the foundations of future British-Russian trade ; wrecked off the Scottish coast when returning from a second expedition.

Chanctonbury Ring, Stone Age hill-fortress on the Sussex Downs ; was also a Roman encampment.

Changing of the Guard, see LONDON

Channel Islands, British islands in the English Channel, near the Normandy coast ; Jersey, Guernsey, Alderney and Sark are the four largest ; noted for delightful scenery and a mild and sunny climate. Early flowers and vegetables are exported in large quantities to England, as is dairy produce. Famous for particular strains of cattle, and important lobster and oyster fisheries, these islands are popular as holiday resorts. The inhabitants are of Norman descent ; their official language is French, but English is taught in the schools and used in everyday life. Many ships have been wrecked in the vicinity of the islands because of the dangerous reefs which surround them. Each island has its own laws and is administered accordingly ; taxes are very low ; local copper coinage is used in Jersey and Guernsey, and each island has a local dialect. Occupied by the Germans in 1940, they were liberated in 1945. Island pop. 93,000.

Channel Tunnel, a proposal to build twin tunnels between England and France ; was much discussed 1876 and 1914. The tunnels were to link Dover and Calais, *c.*35m ; planned for electric transport. The scheme, estimated to cost £35,000,000, has not yet secured government support, though revived in 1948, and still being discussed.

chapbook, small book, often in the form of calendars, parts of the Bible put into rhyme, novels and riddles ; usually crudely illustrated ; sold 17th–18th c. by chapmen, i.e. pedlars.

Chaplin, CHARLES SPENCER (1889–), film star, *b* London ; went to USA 1910. A comedian with hard round hat, baggy trousers, small moustache, he won fame with *The Tramp, The Kid, The Gold Rush,* etc.

Chapman, GEORGE (1559–1634), English poet and dramatist, born near Hitchin, Hertfordshire ; worked with Marlowe, Ben Jonson, John Marston, and other Elizabethan dramatists ; most famous for his translation of *Homer,* praised by John Keats in the sonnet beginning, ' Much have I travelled in the realms of gold.'

charcoal, form of carbon frequently produced by charring wood or bones in an air-tight retort. Charcoal burning in the Middle Ages was the only method of smelting ores, e.g. iron in Kent and Sussex. Activated charcoal, usually prepared from coconuts, absorbs poison gases, hence its use in gas-masks.

Charing Cross, see LONDON

chariot, a two-wheeled vehicle largely employed in warfare, processions and horse-racing in ancient times, notably in Egypt, Persia, Greece and Rome. Chariots were usually made of wood or wicker, sometimes armour-plated, generally open at the back and drawn by two or three horses, the driver standing.

Chariots with scythed axles were used in Britain against Julius Caesar.

Charlemagne, *shär'le-mān,* i.e. Carolus

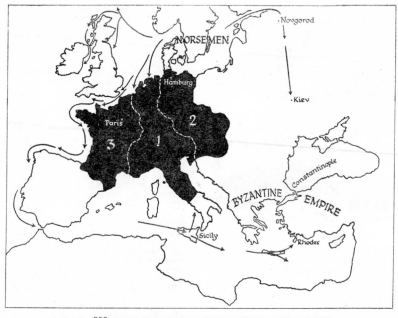

A.D. 800 : THE HOLY ROMAN EMPIRE UNDER CHARLEMAGNE

By the Treaty of Verdun (843) the Empire of Charlemagne was divided among his grandsons as shown above : (1) *The 'Empire,'* (2) *East Franks,* (3) *West Franks. The arrows show the paths of the 9th and 10th century Norse invasions.*

Magnus or Charles The Great (AD742–814) ; founder of the Holy Roman Empire. Charlemagne was a son of Pepin III, King of the Franks (French), and grandson of Charles Martel. As King of the Franks, he conquered the Lombards in N. Italy, declared himself their king (774), and occupied Rome.

The Lombards had been a menace to the power of the pope in Italy, but from 774 Popes Adrian I and Leo III did all in their power to help Charlemagne in his designs. Later he conquered most of Germany, where he forcibly converted the Saxons to Christianity, and in Spain 778 he acquired considerable territories. These conquests were achieved by able soldiers on whose assistance Charlemagne relied : he concerned himself mainly with the business of organising and consolidating the central government of his dominions.

On Christmas Day 800 Leo III crowned him emperor of the Holy Roman Empire It consisted of Charlemagne's possessions in France, Germany, Spain and Italy, and existed in name for over a thousand years. In reality it was effectively an Empire only when Pope and Emperor helped and supported one another, which was by no means often the case.

Charlemagne spent the rest of his life ruling his Empire, especially in codifying its laws. His court was the centre of a vigorous cultural revival, and learning flourished under Alcuin.

A famous figure in the history of Christianity, Charlemagne himself was not particularly notable for Christian virtues. His great achievement was that he gave men a new idea of strong and ordered government.

Charles, name of several kings of France, e.g. CHARLES III, the Simple (879–929) ; CHARLES V (1337–80) known as the Wise ; ruled a miserable France from 1364 ; CHARLES VI (1368–1422), ruled from 1380, lost the battle of Agincourt 1415 ; CHARLES VII, the Indolent—later Victorious (1403–61), crowned at Rheims as a result of aid given by Joan of Arc ; regained all France from the English except Calais ; CHARLES IX (1550–74), dominated by his mother Catherine de' Medici ; CHARLES X (1757–1836), before accession known as Comte d'Artois, leader of opposition to the Revolution, but lived mostly in England ; abdicated 1830.

Charles I (1600–49), King of Great Britain and Ireland from 1625 ; second son of James VI and I, *b* Dunfermline. As a young man he was much influenced by the Duke of Buckingham ; married Henrietta Maria, sister of Louis XIII of

France. Like his father, Charles Stuart believed in the divine right of kings ; quarrelled with Parliament over Puritanism and the king's right to raise money without Parliamentary authority. From 1629 to 1640 he ruled without Parliament, raising money (with the aid of ' Star Chamber ') as best he could, e.g. ship money, tunnage and poundage ; relied much on Thomas Wentworth (Lord Strafford) and Archbishop Laud ; failed to compel the Scots to accept the Church of England service and was driven to summoning the Short and then the Long Parliaments (1640). After his attempt to arrest five members of Parliament, Charles found himself (with Royalist supporters) at war 1642 with Parliament (Roundheads) ; see CIVIL WAR. He was tried for high treason, and beheaded Whitehall 30 Jan 1649, going to his death with great courage, so that although he was a failure as a king, he won admiration as a martyr. Of his execution Andrew Marvell, himself a Parliamentarian, wrote :

He nothing common did, or mean,
Upon that memorable scene,
But bowed his stately head
Down as upon a bed.

Charles II (1630–85), Stuart King of Great Britain and Ireland from the end of the Commonwealth 1660 ; son of Charles I ; *b* St James's Palace, London ; hurriedly sent out of the country in the Civil War ; received Scottish support for an invasion of England, but was defeated by Cromwell. He narrowly escaped to France and Holland, where for a time he was a penniless exile. By the *Declaration of Breda* 1660 he promised a free Parliament. He landed at Dover amid popular delight, determined (as he said) never to go on his travels again.

Charles had repeated disputes with Parliament ; concluded a secret treaty with France (*Treaty of Dover*) ; his reign saw the Dutch in the R. Medway, the Great Plague, Great Fire of London and the Popish Plot. He enjoyed increasing popularity in his last years ; died confessing himself a Catholic.

Charles II married Catherine of Braganza. Associated with Nell Gwyn, he was known as the Merry Monarch, but was an accomplished and shrewd master of diplomacy, a pioneer in science, and founder of the Royal Society. A lover of the sea, he improved the navy and extended trade. He was more tolerant in religious matters than his bickering Parliaments.

Charles V OF GERMANY AND THE HOLY ROMAN EMPIRE (1500–58), *b* Ghent ; son of Philip of Burgundy, from whom he inherited the Low Countries ; inherited Spain and Naples through his mother Joanna ; last German emperor actually crowned by the pope ; a rival of Francis I of France ; noted for his conflict with Martin Luther and Protestantism ; emperor from 1519 ; was also Charles I of Spain, taking an active part in Spanish conquests in S. America. Supreme in the Netherlands, he was for 40 years the most powerful ruler in Europe. After his abdication in favour of his son Philip 1556 he retired to a monastery in Estremadura.

Charles XII (1682–1718), King of Sweden from 1697. He had ambition, was brave but callous in his pursuit of military success. The Danes, Poles and Russians fought against him in 1699, and after defeating them he invaded Russia, and was beaten at Poltava by Peter the Great 1709. After taking refuge in Turkey he returned to Sweden but was killed during his invasion of Norway.

Charles XIV (1763–1844), King of Sweden and Norway ; a Frenchman, called Jean Baptiste Jules Bernadotte, who won fame as one of Napoleon's generals, and became King of Sweden and Norway 1818. He did much to improve the finances of his country.

Charles Edward, see STUART, CHARLES EDWARD

Charles Martel (*c.*688–741), Christian ruler of the Franks, son of Pepin II ; defeated the Saracens at Tours 732, which saved Christian civilisation in the West ; won the nickname Martel, i.e. *hammer* ; grandfather of Charlemagne.

Charles, PRINCE, see ELIZABETH, PRINCESS

Charles's law, see GAS

Charleston, city and busy port, S. Carolina, USA ; noted for cotton ; exports rice and timber ; pop.72,000.

charlock, plant found in cornfields in Britain, Europe, Asia and America ; sometimes called wild mustard ; often 2ft high ; has bristly stems and leaves ; four-petalled yellow flowers.

Charlotte, *shär′lot* (1744–1818), queen of George III from 1761 ; mother of 15 children.

Charlottetown, cap. of Prince Edward I., Canada. It is on Hillsborough Bay ; has a magnificent natural harbour.

Charon, *kā′ron,* in old Gk tales, a ferryman, son of Erebus and Nyx (night), who rowed the dead across the R. Styx to Hades, in payment for which he received an obolus which was placed in the mouth of the corpse. Regarded as probably a product of popular beliefs not mentioned in Hesiod or Homer.

chart, a map specially designed to enable navigators to reach port by steering in a straight line in a given direction. May be (*a*) *oceanic*, to a scale of 1·5in to a degree of longitude, or (*b*) *coastal*, 0·7–2·9in to a sea mile. This map shows, among other things, depths in fathoms, buoys, lighthouses and positions of sunken reefs ; sometimes gives much information about prevailing weather conditions. Gerardus Mercator, one of the earliest of chart makers (1512–94), had a method of arranging the lines of latitude and longitude at right angles which greatly helped navigation.

Charterhouse, a form of the French *Chartreuse*, i.e. a Carthusian monastery, now applied to a former Carthusian monastery in London, founded 1371 by Sir Walter de Mannay and later occupied by Queen Elizabeth (1558). Sir Thomas Sutton, a banker, purchased the site from the Earl of Suffolk and in 1611 it was turned into a home for 80 poor men and a school for 40 boys. Now a great public school. It was removed in 1872 to Godalming, Surrey.

Charter, THE GREAT, see MAGNA CARTA

Chartism, 19th c. working-class political movement in England. The movement began 1838 with demands by the London Working Men's Association, whose People's Charter demanded for every man the right to vote, the secret ballot, annual Parliaments, equal electoral districts, etc. In its day Chartism was regarded by the well-to-do as a dangerous revolutionary movement. The repeal of the Corn Laws 1846, which made bread cheaper for the town working-class, and other reforms, weakened the cause, but the general European upheavals of 1848 stirred up new agitation, and the Chartists carried a *Monster Petition* to the House of Commons. The movement collapsed after this, but it had helped to hasten the accomplishment of many overdue reforms.

Chartres, *shär'tr'*, town, N. France, 55m south-west of Paris ; famous for its 13th c. cathedral with magnificent carvings and old glass ; pop.21,000.

Charybdis, see SCYLLA AND CHARYBDIS

Chateaubriand, FRANÇOIS RENÉ, VICOMTE DE, *shä-tō-brē-än* (1768–1848), French thinker and novelist ; *b* St Malo. When revolution broke out in France he went to America to discover the NW. passage, but returned to France and joined the *émigrés* after Louis XVI had been arrested. At the siege of Thionville he was thought to be dead and was left behind, but he survived and escaped to London. It was there that he wrote the romance *Atala* and his prose poem *Les Natchez.* *René* appeared in 1802 ; he wrote in support of the Christian religion and was most famous for *Memoirs from Beyond the Grave.* A great master of prose, he was the founder of the romantic movement in 19th c. French literature. He held various diplomatic appointments under Napoleon, afterwards becoming ambassador in London, Rome and Berlin.

Chatham, town, port, and naval arsenal on the R. Medway, Kent ; pop.43,000.

Chatham, 1ST EARL OF, see PITT, WILLIAM

Chat Moss, bogland west of Manchester, now largely reclaimed.

Chatsworth, home of the Duke of Devonshire, 3m from Bakewell, Derbyshire.

Chattanooga, city, Tennessee, USA, on Tennessee River ; especially noted for iron, steel ; pop.128,000.

Chatterton, THOMAS (1752–70), English poet, *b* Bristol ; began writing verse at 10 ; read old parchments in St Mary Redcliffe church, and wrote poetry and prose which he submitted to Horace Walpole, declaring it to be the work of a 15th c. monk. Walpole treated the boy in a friendly manner until he heard that the MSS were forgeries, then he regarded Chatterton with silent contempt. In 1770 the poet left Bristol for London, and there committed suicide in a garret. He died aged 17 years 9 months, a genius with a disordered mind. Among the most interesting of his works are *Songe of Aella* and *The Balade of Charitie.*

Chaucer, GEOFFREY (*c*.1340–1400), poet who broke away from Anglo-Saxon traditions and wrote English poetry inspired by French and Italian models. Born and brought up in London, Chaucer was the son of a vintner. At 17 he became a member of the household of Edward III's daughter-in-law. Taken prisoner while soldiering in France 1359, he was ransomed by Edward III, whose personal attendant he then became. For some years after 1374 he was Controller of Customs in the Port of London, and was sent on diplomatic missions abroad, one to Italy. Falling from favour 1386, he became poorer ; but was again in office 1389–91 as Clerk of the Works, and received a pension from Henry IV which supported him until his death 1400. He was buried in Westminster Abbey.

Chaucer was familiar with the busy world of London, and with life at Court and in foreign countries, especially Italy and France. He was a man of broad sympathies and had a rich fellow-feeling for men and women he had met and mixed with in every walk of life ; but with keen good humour he observed and recorded all their little foibles and oddities.

His literary powers are most highly developed in the *Canterbury Tales,* which he was still working at when he died. In the *Romaunt of the Rose* he had merely translated the chivalric French *Roman de la Rose* ; and in *Troylus and Cryseyde* 1380–83 he had kept fairly close to his Italian original, Boccaccio's *Filostrato.* In the *Tales* however he gives a living picture of life in 14th c. England as he himself had lived it.

He begins by describing 29 people of all conditions who have met one another at a Southwark inn and are going to Canterbury as pilgrims to visit the tomb of Thomas Becket. There is a crusading knight, a reeve (sheriff), the wife of Bath (who has had five husbands and is looking for a sixth), a friar, a summoner (minor official who served summonses), a clerk, a business man, a franklin (well-to-do farmer), a prioress, a parson, Chaucer himself, and others.

The pilgrims agree that each of them

will tell a tale. Chaucer did not live to write all 29 of them, but the 23 he did write are astonishing in their rich variety. Many are taken from medieval romances, a form made fun of by Chaucer in his own story of Sir Thopas. Between the stories are Prologues in which Chaucer draws his picture of everyday life in England and gives his shrewd but always tolerant character-sketches of the people concerned.

The following quotation shows what Chaucer's poetry and language are like :

Her yelwë here was browded in a tresse
Byhynde her bak, a yerdë long, I gess.
And in the gardyn at the sonne upriste
She walketh up and doun, and as hir liste
Sche gadereth flourës, party whyte and reede,
To make a sotil gerland for hire heede,
And as an aungel hevenlyche sche song.

(*yelwë here,* yellow hair ; *browded,* braided ; *the sonne upriste,* the sun uprisen ; *as hir liste,* as it pleases her ; *gadereth,* gathers ; *party . . . reede,* some white, some red ; *sotil,* subtle ; *hire heede,* her head ; *hevenlyche,* heaven-like ; *song,* sang)

Chaucer's work is important, not only because it is good in itself, but because it gave English poetry an entirely new impetus by combining French with native English to make a new literary language in which he and his successors told stories and expressed ideas drawn partly from Continental sources. This Continental element has lasted in English literature until the present time, but much recent poetry (especially W. H. Auden's) is modelled on pre-Chaucerian Anglo-Saxon poetry. See AUDEN, W. H. ; LANGLAND

Cheadle, *chē'dl',* town, Cheshire, on the R. Mersey ; has bleaching and printing works ; pop.32,000 with Gatley.

Also market town, Staffordshire ; has silk mills and coal mines.

Cheddar, Mendip village, Somerset, which gives its name to a famous cheese made locally, and to a flower, the Cheddar pink, which will only grow in Britain on the limestone rocks of Cheddar. Nearby is the CHEDDAR GORGE, a famous beauty-spot with high cliffs and remarkable caves.

cheese, see MILK

cheetah, member of the cat family ; sometimes called the hunting leopard. A slender animal of Africa and southern Asia, it is tawny, long tailed, and thickly spotted with black ; is tamed in India and Persia to course antelopes and other game.

A cheetah can move almost as fast as an express train, but if it does not manage to overtake its prey in a few bounds, it gives up the pursuit and slinks away.

Chelmsford, co.tn, Essex ; industries include electrical engineering and the manufacture of motor cars ; has large corn and cattle markets ; pop.35,000.

Chelsea, borough of London, north of the Thames ; for long has been the home of artists and writers ; noted for CHELSEA ROYAL HOSPITAL, home for *c.*480 old soldiers (Chelsea Pensioners). The hospital was founded by Charles II 1681 and designed by Wren. Its inmates usually wear blue uniforms, but on Royal Oak Day (29 May) they dress in scarlet.

Cheltenham, fashionable inland health resort, Gloucestershire. Since 1716 noted for its mineral springs. Cheltenham Ladies' College was opened 1854 ; pop.62,000.

' Cheltenham Flyer,' see RAILWAYS

Chelyabinsk, city in the Urals, USSR ; manufactures tractors ; pop.274,000.

chemical symbols, see ELEMENT

chemist, see PHARMACY

chemistry, fundamentally the science of (*a*) the composition of substances (*b*) the ways in which elements may combine to form compounds, and (*c*) how these compounds react with each other and with elements.

The ancient Egyptians and Greeks had some practical knowledge of chemistry, but the Arabs were the first to make important advances, Geber being prominent *c.*AD900. While searching for the so-called philosopher's stone, the alchemists added to the sum of knowledge. They were followed by the medical chemists who tried to prepare the elixir of life, Paracelsus (*d* 1541) being a notable pioneer. Van Helmont (1577–1644) was the link between alchemy and modern chemistry, and Robert Boyle (1627–91) may be considered the first of the modern chemists because of his insistence on experimental method. He was also the first to distinguish clearly between elements and compounds.

The phlogiston theory of combustion led chemists astray for many years, but it had its value at the time. It was overthrown by Lavoisier (1743–94), helped by Joseph Priestley's discovery of oxygen 1774. Lavoisier gave us the modern theory of combustion, i.e. that combustion is due to the reaction of burning substances with the oxygen of the air.

Modern theories of combination are founded on John Dalton's Atomic Theory (*c.*1803), and it was he who gave to the old philosophical idea of atoms (going back at least to the ancient Greeks), a quantitative basis, so making it a sure foundation on which to build. Dalton's theory was probably deduced from (*a*) the Law of Conservation of Matter and (*b*) the Law of Constant Proportions. From his theory itself he probably deduced (*c*) the Law of Multiple Proportions.

These are the chief laws of chemical combination, and may be stated as follows : (*a*) *In a chemical reaction, matter is neither created nor destroyed.* (*b*) *A chemical compound always contains the same elements united in the same proportions by weight.* (c) *If two elements combine to form two or more compounds, the two or more weights of the one element that combine with a fixed weight of the other element, bear a simple ratio to one another.*

Other important laws are the Law of Reciprocal Proportions, i.e. *Elements combine in proportion to their equivalent weights* ; also Gay Lussac's Law of Volumes : *The volumes of gases entering into or formed by a chemical reaction bear a simple ratio to one another* ; also Dulong and Petit's Rule : *The atomic weight of an element × specific heat* = 6·4 (approx.). Note that this does not hold for elements of low atomic weights, e.g. carbon.

With the exception of Dulong and Petit's Rule, all the laws given above were for some time thought to be exact, but Einstein's theory of the equivalence of matter and energy makes the Law of Conservation of Matter inexact, though the error is too small to be measured by our balances. Note also that the discovery of isotopes has rendered the laws of Constant and of Multiple Proportions only *approximately* true, and Gay Lussac's Law is also inaccurate because gases do not obey Boyle's and Charles's laws precisely.

By the equivalent of an element is meant the number of grams of that element that will combine with or replace one gram of hydrogen or 8 grams of oxygen. The *atomic weight* of an element is the ratio between the weight of an atom of the element and $\frac{1}{16}$ of the weight of an atom of oxygen.

Dalton's theory made little progress until chemists distinguished clearly between atoms and molecules. The *molecular weight* of an element or compound is the ratio between the weight of a molecule of the substance and $\frac{1}{16}$ of the weight of an atom of oxygen.

Chemists represent each *element* by a symbol (e.g. O for oxygen, Au for gold, etc.), and a *compound* by a combination of symbols, e.g. water as H_2O, sulphuric acid H_2SO_4, etc. Chemical changes may be represented by equations, as $NaOH + HCl \longrightarrow NaCl + H_2O$, i.e. sodium hydroxide plus hydrochloric acid react to form sodium chloride and water. This is a *quantitative equation*, the number of atoms in each molecule being indicated. As the sides of the equation must balance each other, the quantities of each substance taking part in the chemical change and the quantities of the results can be calculated.

The *structure* of the molecules of a substance may be shown, not by a chemical formula, but by a *space diagram* ; see Diagram A : the *process* of the reaction by a *structural equation* ; see Diagram B. A process may also be shown by an *ionic equation* :

$$Ag^{\cdot} + NO'_3 + Na^{\cdot} + Cl'$$
$$\longrightarrow AgCl + Na^{\cdot} + NO'_3$$

where the sign · shows the valency of an electropositive ion or radical, and the sign ′ shows the valency of an electronegative ion or radical.

The chemist brings about chemical reactions in several ways, e.g. by mixing in the cold, by heating together, by electrolysis, etc. He distinguishes between (*a*) mixtures and (*b*) compounds,

A : SPACE DIAGRAMS

CH_4 (methane) C_6H_6 (benzene)

B : STRUCTURAL EQUATION

benzene   +   nitric acid $\longrightarrow$ nitrobenzene   +   water (H_2O)

(a) having components in *any* proportion, and capable of separation by physical means, the components retaining their respective properties.

The more important classes of reactions include (a) *decomposition*, i.e. breaking one substance into two or more ; (b) *combination*, i.e. uniting two or more substances to form one ; and (c) *mutual decomposition*, i.e. the reaction of two or more substances to form two or more fresh substances. Chemical changes are usually accompanied by changes of energy, generally in the form of the evolution of heat.

Elements are sometimes classified so as to bring similar elements together, e.g. lithium, sodium, potassium, etc., all soft, reactive metals with the same valency. When elements are arranged in order of their atomic numbers, the whole classification is known as the *Periodic Classification*, first put forward by a Russian chemist, Mendeléeff (d 1907). See ELEMENT

For convenience of study, chemistry is usually divided into three branches, (a) *inorganic*, which deals with the reactions and compounds of all elements, though only with very simple compounds of carbon, e.g. carbon monoxide, carbonates, etc., (b) *organic*, originally the chemistry of compounds needing, it was thought, a ' vital ' force for their preparation, but now the chemistry of the thousands of carbon compounds, (c) *physical*, which tries to explain how a reaction takes place, and, as far as it is ever possible, *why* it takes place.

Such is the importance of chemistry in the modern world that we might well call this the Chemical Age. To the chemist we owe high-grade and specialised steels, innumerable alloys, medicines, plastics, cellulose products, munitions (including the atom bomb), a host of synthetic substances, e.g. rayon, nylon, etc., the valuable and varied coal-tar products, penicillin, fertilisers, anaesthetics, dyes, unshrinkable wool, etc.

Those interested in chemistry have, broadly speaking, three possibilities before them, (a) industrial chemistry, (b) analytical chemistry, and (c) the teaching of chemistry. Details of these will be found in *Chemistry as a Profession*. See also booklets 19, 36, and 37 in *Careers for Men and Women*, published by the Ministry of Labour and National Service.

Read *The Chemical Age*, William Haynes ; *The Elements of Physical Chemistry*, Samuel Glasstone.

Chemnitz, chem'*nits*, manufacturing town, Saxony (Germany) ; noted for woollens, cottons and chemicals ; pop.335,000.

cheque, bill of exchange drawn on a banker payable on demand, i.e. an instruction by a customer of a bank, to his bank, to pay from his account a certain sum of money to, or to the order of, a specified person or to bearer. A cheque must bear the usual signature of the customer, and the amount must be stated in words and figures.

Cheques were known as early as the second half of the 17th c., but the great expansion of their use dates from the Bank Act of 1844, and similar enactments which limited the issue of notes by the Bank of England and other banks. This limitation was imposed at a time when the community was growing in size and wealth and had need of an ever increasing supply of money. The banks therefore turned to cheques as an alternative method of circulating and transferring money.

A cheque is usually acceptable in payment of a debt without prior reference to the bank upon which it is drawn to see if there are funds to meet it. The advantage of cheques is that they make it possible to pay a debt, however large, by means of a single piece of paper, thus doing away with the need for cash transactions which would involve carrying about, counting and recounting large sums of money. In Great Britain cheques are now by far the most frequently used method of transferring money.

The duty on a cheque is twopence, and the stamp may be impressed or adhesive. The banks provide cheque books for customers free of charge, the customer paying only for the impressed stamps, i.e. a book of twenty-four cheques costs four shillings. Every cheque bears the name of the bank and the branch of the bank from which it was issued. There follow the words, ' Pay . . . or Order ' and spaces for the amount of the cheque in words and figures and for the usual signature of the customer. Such cheques require endorsement (signing on the back) by the persons to whom they are made payable ; cheques bearing the words, ' Pay . . . or Bearer ' do not require endorsement Cheque books should be kept in a place of safety

Two transverse lines, which may be written, stamped, printed or perforated across the face of a cheque, constitute the crossing of a cheque. The object of crossing cheques is to ensure the safe transmission of the money from the sender to the receiver. An uncrossed cheque is called an ' open ' cheque.

The date on a cheque is important. A bank cannot pay a post-dated cheque, and a cheque dated on a Sunday will not be paid until the succeeding business day. A cheque is considered ' out of date ' six months after the date on the cheque, and it will be paid only after verification.

' Cashing a cheque ' means obtaining cash in exchange for the cheque. ' Open ' cheques may be cashed at that branch of the bank upon which they are drawn ;

' crossed ' cheques cannot be cashed, and must be paid into a banking account.

A bank may refuse to pay a cheque if the amount stated in words differs from the amount in figures, though it may sometimes agree to pay the lesser amount. Any alteration on a cheque must be initialled by the drawer. Payment may also be refused if the signature of the drawer differs from his usual signature.

If, when a cheque is presented for payment, the banker writes, ' Refer to Drawer ' in the top left-hand corner of the cheque, it implies that the drawer has insufficient money in his account to meet the cheque, or that the drawer has exceeded the arrangements he made with the bank to overdraw his account.

Chequers, *chek'ĕrz*, country seat in Buckinghamshire. Lord and Lady Lee of Fareham gifted it to the nation in 1917, as an official residence for the Prime Minister.

Cherbourg, *sher'boor*, Channel port and naval station, France ; pop.40,000 ; has a spacious roadstead for large vessels ; exports dairy produce and stone ; repairs ships. Among its chief industries are rope-making, fishing, sugar refining and shipbuilding.

Cherbourg was the first important French port secured by the Allied armies which invaded German-occupied France on and after D-Day 1944.

Cheribon, see INDONESIA

cherry, fruit of a tree of the same name. Both wild and cultivated trees grow in Britain. The fruit, which is small, round and sweet, has a stone in the centre ; generally is red, but some varieties are yellow, white, or black. Morello cherry trees thrive in any position, but others require S. or W. aspect. The flowering cherry (a feature of Japan, where it is a forest-tree notable for its timber) bears pink or white blossom.

' Cherry Ripe,' see HERRICK, ROBERT

Chesapeake Bay, *ches'ă-pēk*, largest opening on the Atlantic coast of USA, noted for oysters and wild fowl. Rivers James, Susquehanna and Potomac flow into the bay.

Cheshire, co. NW. England, noted for pastures, woods and meres (lakes). The fertile land is watered by the rivers Mersey and Dee. Dairying and market gardening are carried on extensively. Industries include shipbuilding, textile manufacturing, chemicals and fisheries. The co.tn is Chester. Other large towns are Crewe, Stockport, Birkenhead and Macclesfield. The district between the estuaries of the Mersey and Dee is the Wirral.

Chesil Bank, 16m shingle ridge on the Dorset coast linking the ' Isle ' of Portland with the mainland.

chess, game played by two opponents on a black and white chequered board having 64 squares. There are 16 ' pieces ' on each side (8 pawns, 2 rooks or castles, 2 knights, 2 bishops, a queen and a

king). The object is to force the opposing king into a position in which he cannot avoid being captured : this is known as ' check-mate.'

A game of chess between well-matched players usually passes through three phases : the *opening*, in which the object is to gain control of the centre of the board, and to secure minor advantages, which may make a great deal of difference later on ; the *middle game*, in which the object is to build up a powerful and flexible combination of pieces for attack or defence ; the *end game*, in which often only a few pieces remain on either side to fight it out to check-mate or a draw.

The rules governing the moves of the different pieces are complicated, and the game demands strenuous mental effort ; the beautiful subtlety of the various combinations by which the end is attained afford great pleasure to both players, and the game has its devotees in every continent. Chess probably began in India 1,400 years ago. Famous chess-players include Ruy Lopez 16th c., Morphy (1837–84), Alekhine (1892–1946), Capablanca (1888–1942).

Read *An Invitation to Chess*, Chernev and Harkness.

Chester, city and co.tn of Cheshire on the R. Dee ; still has its 14th c. walls, and 11th c. Gothic cathedral, many timbered houses and ' Rows ' (covered ways, boarded or flagged on the ground and having ceilings) ; public parks and a racecourse (Roodee) ; manufactures lead pipes, boots, shoes, chemicals, gloves and cheese ; was the Roman Deva ; pop.48,000.

Chesterfield, market town and municipal borough, Derbyshire ; its Gothic church has ancient monuments and a twisted spire 230ft high ; industries include the manufacture of silk, cotton hosiery, fishing tackle and machinery ; pop. 64,000.

Chesterfield, PHILIP DORMER STANHOPE, 4TH EARL OF (1694–1773), English statesman and author, *b* London ; was MP as a Whig 1715–23 ; appointed 1728 ambassador to the Hague, and 1744 lord-lieutenant of Ireland, where he proved to be a tolerant, though firm ruler ; in 1746 he became secretary of state in the Pelham administration, resigning two years later.

In 1747 Dr Johnson sent Chesterfield a prospectus of his *Dictionary* which was acknowledged by a subscription of £10. Chesterfield took little or no interest in the book until it was about to be published when he wrote its praises in a magazine. Johnson repudiated this belated recognition in a classic letter : ' . . . had it been early, it had been kind ; but it has been delayed . . . till I am known, and do not want it.' In 1751 Chesterfield distinguished himself in House of Lords debates on calendar reform and succeeded in having the

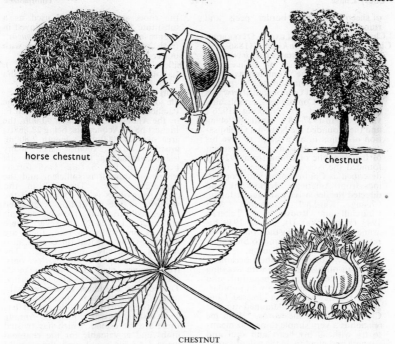

CHESTNUT

(left) the Horse Chestnut tree, its fruit (cut open to show seed) and its leaf; (right) the Chestnut tree, its leaf and fruit (with one of the four prickly bracts cut away to show three young nuts)

proposed New Style (see CALENDAR) adopted. He is famed for his *Letters to his Son*, which are witty and full of cynical wisdom, and *Letters to his Godson* (first published 1890).

Chester-le-Street, town, 6m north of Durham ; has collieries and iron works.

Chesterton, GILBERT KEITH (1874–1936), English author, *b* London. Educated at St Paul's School, where, at an early age, he won the ' Milton ' prize for English verse. When he left school in 1881 it was with the idea of studying art, but he was naturally inclined towards literature, so he became a free-lance journalist. Occasionally he did reviewing, and worked in the office of a publisher. He was an art and literary critic, paradoxical writer and satirist, and the author of the immensely popular detective stories of Father Brown. He was a Catholic convert who took part, not always with success, in many religious and theological controversies. Among his works are *What's wrong with the World ; Return of Don Quixote ; The Man who was Thursday ; New and Collected Poems.*

chestnut, the nut of the tree bearing the same name (thought to have been introduced to Britain 1550) of which there are three main kinds : the species known as the Spanish, French, European or Italian chestnut which grows in the forests of Europe and Asia ; the American chestnut generally found in North Carolina and central Mississippi, and in North America from Maine to Southern Michigan ; the Japanese chestnut found in China and Japan. The trees often grow 70ft in height, and in Britain they have yellow flowers in May. The wood of the trees is used for such purposes as the making of gateposts ; the fruit, which is called sweet chestnut, is very often candied or preserved (marrons glacés, crême de marrons), or roasted or boiled as a vegetable ; it can also be eaten raw.

HORSE CHESTNUTS (a distinct species) are trees often 60ft high ; have red or white spiky flowers. The fruit, which is green, is covered with spines and contains a red-brown nut popularly known as a ' conker.' This nut is used for feeding stock and manufacturing burner oil. The wood of the tree is soft and is used for fuel and for making charcoal.

Cheviots, *chĕv'i-ŭt ; chē'vi-ŭt,* range of hills forming eastern part of the border between England and Scotland, the highest point being 2,676ft ; these grassy hills extend for 35 miles from NE. to SW. ; famous for the Cheviot breed of sheep ; have many border 'peels' and ruins.

'Chevy Chase,' see BALLAD ; OTTERBURN

Chiang Kai-Shek, *chē'än kī-shek'* (1886–), Chinese general and statesman, *b* Ningpo; Kuomintang Dictator of China until driven out by the Communists 1949. Aided by the Communists, he gained military control of Canton, but afterwards broke with the Communists, establishing his government at Nanking 1926 ; visited Japan 1927–28 ; captured Peking and then founded the National Organisation of China in an attempt to give his country a sense of unity. As President of the Republic of China from 1928 he founded the New Life Movement (once described as Confucianism with borrowings from American Methodism), and directed the defensive war against Japan. Chiang Kai-Shek conferred with Churchill and Roosevelt at Teheran 1943 (World War II), but in 1949 his armies were defeated by the Communists, retreating first from Peking to Shanghai, then from Shanghai to Canton.

In 1927 Chiang Kai-Shek became a Christian on his marriage with Mayling Soong (1899–), a beautiful and accomplished woman who won popularity in USA, where she addressed Congress 1943. She has summed up her Christian faith in the words, ' With me religion is a very simple thing. It means to try with all my heart and soul and strength and mind to do the will of God.'

Chicago, *shi-kä'gō*, city, Illinois, USA ; on L. Michigan, second largest city in USA ; ' capital ' of the canned-meat industry, for which it is world-famous ; is also an immense railway centre ; has vast trade in grain, livestock and lumber. Noted for magnificent buildings and parks ; has grown with amazing rapidity, and now has a pop. of 3,400,000, including many Germans and Irish. Chicago has long been notorious for gangsters.

Chichester, *chich'istĕr*, city and municipal borough, Sussex ; has a port on the Channel ; noted for its 11th c. cathedral and old octagonal market cross ; was the Roman Regnum.

chicken-pox, contagious disease causing slight fever and crops of vesicles in the skin. The disease, which usually occurs in epidemics, generally affects children ; incubation period from ten to fifteen days ; one attack of this disease does not give immunity.

chickweed, feeble, straggling annual herb of the pink family. Sometimes called tongue-grass, winter weed or Satanflower ; has a green stem with smooth, oval leaves in pairs, small white-petalled flowers, each with five green sepals.

chicory, plant growing wild in Britain, most frequently by roadsides in chalky soil. The root is fleshy and long, leaves rather like those of a dandelion, and the bright blue flowers are almost 1–1½in in diameter. In France, Germany, Belgium and Holland it is cultivated ;

the roots are roasted and used as a substitute for coffee. Often enjoyed in France as the salad *Barbe de capucin* ; fresh roots are boiled and eaten with butter in Belgium.

Chifley, JOSEPH BENEDICT (1885–), Labour prime minister of Australia 1945–49.

Children's Crusade, see CRUSADES

Chile or **Chili,** *chil'ĕ*, republic on the Pacific coast of S. America ; bounded E. by the Andes, average height 9,000ft, the highest peak, Aconcagua, being 22,868ft; area over 285,000sq.m ; length 2,800m, breadth rarely 100m ; has many islands, including part of Tierra del Fuego. In the S. are vast forests where the rainfall is sufficient and the temperature low. The soil in the central provinces is very fertile and the majority of the population is engaged in agriculture and growing cereals and fruit ; in the N., however, where there is practically no rain, there are deserts. Chile is noted for copper, also nitrates, gold, silver and iodine. The products include wheat, barley, oats, fruits, wines, etc., and there is much sheep and cattle farming, also lumbering. The country is subject to severe earthquakes. Peumo, cacti, eucalyptus trees and cypress thrive in Chile, which has some distinct species of its own. Among these are the espino, which has twisted limbs and is valuable for the charcoal made from its wood, and the coquito palm which has been almost completely destroyed by collectors of the sweetened sap. The Chilean Pine, ' monkey-puzzle tree,' is valued for its nuts.

Many of the short, swift rivers generate electricity. Spanish is spoken. The government is republican ; the pop. *c.*5,100,000 ; capital Santiago. Other towns include Valparaiso and Concepcion (both ports), and Puntas Arenas, the most southerly town in the world. For the statue of Christ the Redeemer, see ARGENTINE

Chilean pine or **monkey-puzzle tree,** evergreen native of Chile, prized by natives who like the flavour of its small nuts ; may be 150ft high ; has horizontal branches ; pointed, leathery leaves ; cones 6–9in across.

Chiltern Hills, low range of chalk hills (noted for beech trees) extending from SW. to NE., mainly in Oxfordshire, Bedfordshire and Buckinghamshire, highest peak Wendover Hill. Formerly infested by robbers, the district was in charge of the Steward of the CHILTERN HUNDREDS. Today a member of Parliament may only resign by accepting this office.

Chiltern Hundreds, see CHILTERN HILLS

Chimborazo, *chim-bŏ-rä'zō*, (1) province, Ecuador, S. America. Area 2,989sq.m ; pop.125,000.

(2) Extinct volcano in the Andes, Ecuador ; craterless ; several glaciers ; first ascent made by Whymper (1879–80).

chimpanzee, see APES AND MONKEYS

China, in Chinese *Ta Chung-Hua Min Kuo,*
i.e. the Great Chinese Republic, is now
usually regarded as comprising (*a*) *China
Proper,* namely 18 provinces (the three
largest being Yunnan, Kansu and
Szechwan), with an area of *c.*1,405,860
sq.m, and a pop. of 400,000,000 ;
(*b*) *Manchuria,* namely ten provinces,
area 481,400sq.m, pop.41,088,000 ; (*c*)
Inner Mongolia, its three provinces
covering over 348,000sq.m, pop.
4,840,000 ; and (*d*) the *province of
Sinkiang,* the mountainous plateau of
Tibet Proper, and the island of *Taiwan*
or *Formosa.* The total area is estimated
at *c.*4,300,000sq.m, the pop. at nearly
458,000,000. In 1932 the Japanese conquered Manchuria (the northern territory
bounded by USSR), and ruled it as the
state of Manchukuo until 1945, when
the United Nations compelled Japan
to surrender unconditionally. Although
nominally reunited with China, Manchuria then fell into the hands of Russian
occupation forces.

China is generally mountainous,
especially in the West, but has many
extensive plains and broad river valleys,
its three great river systems being (*a*)
Hwang-ho or Yellow River, often called
' China's Sorrow ' because of disastrous
floods, though its fine yellow silt (*loess*)

is ideal for farming ; (*b*) Yangtse Kiang,
3,400m long, flowing through the densely
populated Red Basin area ; (*c*) Si-kiang
or West River.

Though the winters are severe in the
N., the climate is sub-tropical in the S.
and the Great Plain, with its yellow soil
requiring no manure, is well-named the
' flowery kingdom.' The long Pacific
coast, much indented, has the island of
Hainan in the extreme S. (lat.20°N).
There are many excellent harbours, and
canals are a feature of the country.
Between China Proper and Mongolia is
the Great Wall of China, over 1,500m
long, 20–30ft high, 15ft wide, and having
towers and forts at intervals. It was
built *c.*214BC as a defence against
barbarian invasions.

Primarily an agricultural country,
China has 360,000,000 people living on
farms, mostly very small, many of only
one acre or less ; their everyday routine
is vividly described in Pearl Buck's novel
The Good Earth. Crops include rice (the
staple food), also wheat, beans (including
soya), millet, barley, cotton (especially
in the lower Yangtse valley), tea, notably
in the S. and W. ; tobacco ; sugar-cane
and various seeds, including those producing vegetable oils. Raw silk, derived
from silkworms reared on millions of

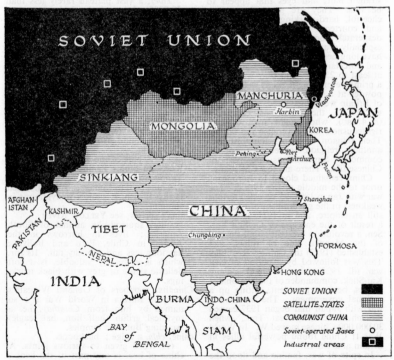

CHINA AND HER NEIGHBOURS

mulberry trees, is one of the chief exports. Pigs are found almost everywhere. Poverty and starvation are widespread.

There are vast reserves of coal (probably the richest in the world), also immense supplies of iron, copper (especially in Yunnan), gold, silver, lead, tungsten, etc., but as yet these have been little worked, though rapid progress is being made in mining, and already huge quantities of antimony are produced. The industries include iron, steel and textiles, but industrial advance awaits a great railway-building programme. There is now a N.–S. line with many branches, and through communication with Europe by the Manchurian railway. The line from Hunan to Kwangsi was opened to traffic 1939. Roads are lacking (China has only 0·03m of road for every sq.m, whereas the UK has 2m), but many great roads have been built recently, e.g. that from the border of Kweichow to Indo-China, completed 1940. (See BURMA ROAD.) Air services are being multiplied ; the ports include Shanghai, Canton, Amoy, Chefoo, Foochow, Hangchow and Wenchow.

Chinese civilisation is the oldest in the world. The people, belonging to the Mongolian type, have a yellow skin (though often only slightly so), black straight hair, and eyes that appear to be slits. They are generally patient, cheerful, hard-working, eager to learn and courteous ; most of them are desperately poor. They love poetry and especially drama, are highly artistic, and have long been famous for their pictures and porcelain. Their history goes back at least to 2300BC, and they were using a primitive printing-press as well as gunpowder at a time when the inhabitants of Britain were uncivilised. Their great teacher in the past was Confucius (d 478BC), who taught men to love righteousness and reverence the family. Their religion is mainly Buddhist, but another religion called Taoism is common. Superstitions are part of Chinese life. There are few Christians.

China remained closed to Europeans prior to the middle of the 19th c. The war with Japan 1894–95 revealed serious weakness in the government of what was still an empire, and in 1911, largely as a result of the energies of Dr Sun Yat-Sen, a revolution brought about the end of the Manchu line of rulers, and established (1912) the Chinese Republic. This was followed by a period of civil war till 1928, when General Chiang Kai-Shek, commander of the Nationalist armies, became president, setting up a national government. The devastating war with Japan that began 1937 caused the phenomenal 'Great Trek,' when 30,000,000 Chinese moved W. In World War II China found powerful allies in Britain and USA.

In spite of war, famine and flood the republic made progress under the leadership of Chiang Kai-Shek and the Kuo-Min-Tang, e.g. building over 160,000 schools ; establishing 70 or more universities ; improving health services and transport ; overhauling the whole legal system ; adopting Western ideas in industry and agriculture ; rebuilding cities ; reforming the army ; securing for the first time some sense of national unity, and carrying out Chiang Kai-Shek's 'New Life Movement,' a Chinese form of citizenship. A People's Political Council was formed 1938, and a new constitution was being planned to give China democratic representation when Communist elements brought about civil war, small farmers, young students and peasants joining the Communists, trained administrators, people with wealth, e.g. traders and industrialists joining the Kuo-Min-Tang. In 1949 the Communists advanced rapidly, occupying Peking and Shanghai and came within striking distance of Hong Kong. The Communists then proceeded to set up their own form of government throughout the area they had conquered.

Mongolia comprises Outer (i.e. NW.) and Inner Mongolia, total area *c*.1,360,000sq.m, where sheep and cattle are grazed, though the Gobi desert covers one-third of Inner Mongolia.

Tibet, a vast plateau rarely less than 10,000ft above sea-level, has an area of 463,000sq.m ; pop. *c*.3,000,000, many of whom are monks, over whom reigns the Dalai Lama, the present Lama being a boy when installed at Lhasa 1940.

Read *China*, one of Nelson's Practical Work Books ; *My Country and My People*, Lin Yutang.

China clay, white clay, the result of decomposition of felspar, a hydrated silicate of alumina ; is used for making porcelain. The largest British mines are in Cornwall (e.g. St Austell, Bodmin Moor) ; found also in France, Germany, China, etc.

China Sea, part of the Pacific Ocean from Korea to Malay Peninsula, includes the Yellow Sea S. of Korea ; extends (as the S. China Sea) to Malaya. The sea, which is rich in fish, is subject to typhoons in summer.

China's sorrow, see YELLOW RIVER

chinchilla, squirrel-like animal of South America ; lives in burrows in the Andes, in Chile, Peru and Bolivia ; has long legs and a bushy tail. Its fur, which is extremely valuable, is a soft delicate shade of grey with black markings.

Chindits, members of General Wingate's army in Burma in World War II ; so named by him from *Chinthay*, i.e. a mythical griffin (half lion, half eagle) guarding Burmese temples.

chine, *chīn,* a ridge ; backbone.

(1) Word given to various joints. A chine of beef is any part of the back ; that of a pig is the backbone and the

meat round it after the sides have been cut off to be cured ; two loins, generally called the saddle, is a chine of mutton.

(2) On the Hampshire coast this word is especially used for a ravine cut out of the rock by a stream which falls into the sea, e.g. Alum Chine near Bournemouth, and Shanklin Chine.

Chingford, town, Essex ; is at the edge of Epping Forest ; holiday resort ; pop.38,000.

Chino-Japanese War, (*a*) war fought 1894–1895 mainly in or near Korea, China resenting Japanese interference there ; won by the Japanese, largely owing to superior training of their army and navy ; (*b*) later struggle between China and the invading Japanese, who sought to secure a large portion of China, declaring war 1937, and being defeated, with aid from the United Nations, 1945.

chinook, (1) warm, dry wind from the Pacific that crosses the eastern slopes of the Rocky Mts, and in winter quickly melts the snow in USA and W. Canada ; sometimes called ' snow-eater.'

(2) Member of N. American tribe of Indians, now almost extinct. The Chinook language, which was the chief means of conversation between the servants of the Hudson Bay Company and the Indians, is still used occasionally. It is a mixture of English, Indian and Canadian French.

chintz, cotton cloth usually glazed with printed coloured designs. Originally meant pieces of imported Indian calico. A single piece was called a ' chint.'

Chios, *kī'os* or *kē'os*, (1) Greek island in the Ægean Sea ; has a fine climate ; the land is fertile and cultivated, though mountainous. Products include fruit and wine which are exported ; there are marble quarries and antimony mines ; subject to earthquakes ; pop.75,700.

(2) Chief town, Chios ; a traditional birthplace of Homer.

chipmunk, name of a ground squirrel common in Canada and the United States. It lives in thickets or rocky places but in the autumn it digs a burrow at the end of which it makes its nest, generally lined with grass. The chipmunk has lovely dark and buff stripes on its face and back, and a tail about the same length as its body—6in. Its food consists mainly of kernels of corn and small nuts.

Chippendale, THOMAS (*c.*1718–79), one of the most famous English cabinet-makers, son of John Chippendale, a Yorkshire joiner. It is not always easy to distinguish genuine from imitation Chippendale furniture. One well-attested example of Chippendale work is the Chinese bedroom in Claydon House, Buckingham ; and Robert Adam with Thomas Chippendale is known to have been employed in the furnishing of Harewood House, Yorkshire, 1765–71.

Sometimes a piece of his furniture is found to be a combination of three styles which he affected at different periods (Louis XV, Chinese and Gothic). His furniture, although strong, is not heavy, and construction was always his first consideration, especially in chairs, in which his work may be seen at its best. He introduced the cabriole leg from Holland ; the straight, early Georgian leg ; the fretwork leg ; the rococo leg with curled or hoofed foot ; the lattice-work Chinese leg ; the ancient Oriental claw and ball foot. Among his other successes were bookcases, cabinets, cases for long clocks, numerous tables, among which are those with fretwork galleries for displaying china.

Chiron, see CENTAURS

chiropody, *kīr-op'o-di* (Gk *cheir,* hand, *pous,* foot), professional care of the feet, especially the removal of corns, etc. Actually the word means the treatment of both hands and feet, but *chiropodist* is the word used for a person who treats ailments of the feet professionally, a *manicurist* being a person who treats and beautifies the hands and finger nails.

chitin, see INSECTS

Chitral, *chē-träl',* frontier state of Pakistan.

chivalry, *shiv'al-ri,* laws, customs and beliefs of medieval knights ; flourished especially in Edward III's day ; dealt also with personal honour and heraldry ; now suggests courtesy, adventure, courage and a great respect for women.

Among the orders of chivalry surviving as relics of the medieval world are the following British Orders : The Garter (English, founded 1349), motto : *Honi soit qui mal y pense,* ' cursed be he who thinks ill of it ' ; the Thistle (Scottish, founded 1687), motto : *Nemo me impune lacessit,* ' None provokes me (i.e. the Thistle) with impunity,' or more freely ' *Wha daur meddle wi' me ?* ' ; the St Patrick (Irish, founded 1783) motto : *Quis separabit ?* ' Who shall separate ? ' Britain has many other Orders of knighthood, of which the Order of the Bath dates from 1399.

chives, perennial plant, the leaves of which have a flavour similar to, but more delicate than, that of the onion ; are used as herbs for salads.

chlorates, *klō'rāt,* salts of chloric acid, $HClO_3$, e.g. potassium chlorate $KClO_3$.

chloric acid, oxyacid of chlorine, $HClO_3$.

chloride of lime, see CHLORINE

chlorine, *klō'rēn,* greenish-yellow choking gas and element, Cl ; atomic weight 35·457 ; atomic number 17 ; highly poisonous, hence its use (1915) as a war gas ; formed whenever hydrochloric acid reacts with an oxidising agent ; may be prepared in the laboratory by heating manganese dioxide with concentrated hydrochloric acid ; manufactured commercially by the electrolytic process ; valuable for bleaching : forms bleaching powder (chloride of lime) if passed over cold slaked lime ; is a powerful disinfectant.

6a

HYDROCHLORIC ACID (spirits of salts or muriatic acid) is a solution of hydrogen chloride (HC1) in water. It is colourless and corrosive. Chlorides are salts of hydrochloric acid.

chloromycetin, anti-bacterial drug derived from a mould or artificially produced ; used against typhoid and other fevers.

chlorophyll, see BOTANY

chloroquine, see MOSQUITO

chocolate, see COCOA

cholera, *kol'ĕr-ä*, infectious disease once known only in India, China, etc., but caused epidemics in Europe and America in 1826, 1832, 1854, 1866, 1891–96 ; generally conveyed by infected water, milk, etc.

Chopin, FRÉDÉRIC FRANÇOIS, *shō-pa*n (1810–49), Polish composer and pianist, born near Warsaw. He was a brilliant pianist at 9 ; gave pianoforte recitals in Berlin, Vienna, Paris, and in England and Scotland ; numbered Liszt, Balzac, Heine among his friends ; suffered from a chest complaint, and was nursed in Majorca by George Sand ; *d* Paris.

Chopin, who was a romantic, wrote exquisite scherzos, preludes, nocturnes, waltzes and polonaises for the piano, often based on Polish national dances. Most of these works are fairly short pieces of an emotional intensity difficult to sustain throughout longer compositions Chopin ranks as one of the greatest composers for the piano.

CHOPIN 1810–49

chopsticks, pair of slender rods of wood, bone, or ivory, used in China, Korea, Japan, for lifting food to the mouth. Both are held in the left hand.

Chorley, town, Lancashire ; noted for cotton, dyes, chemicals, railway wagons, etc. ; pop.31,000.

Chosen, *chō-sen*, republic of E. Asia, now usually called Korea. See KOREA

chough, *chŭf*, bird of the crow family. The one British species is found only in W. Britain ; has black plumage and bright red beak and legs ; rare bird, dying out quickly.

THE CHOUGH

Christ or **Jesus Christ,** founder of Christianity, regarded by Christians as the world's supreme religious example and teacher.

A Jew, he was probably born in the year we count as 6BC. His mother was Mary, whose husband was Joseph, a carpenter. Jesus (the Gk form of the Hebrew name Joshua) is said to have been born in a stable at Bethlehem, in Judea, Palestine, to which Mary and Joseph had gone for purposes of a census, though their home was at Nazareth, Galilee.

Of Christ's early life we know nothing apart from the scanty references given in the four Gospels (*Matthew, Mark, Luke, John*) in the NT ; but it seems that Jesus lived in Nazareth after about two years in Egypt, whither he had been taken because certain portents attending his birth had excited the enmity of Herod, the puppet Jewish king.

At Nazareth Jesus helped in the carpenter's shop ; but even at the age of 12 he had some intuition of his life's work, for when Mary and Joseph took him to Jerusalem, Jesus remained behind, talking with the scholars in the Temple, both asking and answering questions. He spoke even then of being ' about his Father's business.'

Not until he reached the age of 30 did he turn aside from earning a living, and thus supporting his mother and the family, by carpentry.

His cousin, John the Baptist, prepared his way by stirring the hearts of men and announcing the early coming of the Messiah, i.e. the leader whom the Jews hoped would enable them to overthrow their Roman masters.

John was still preaching when Jesus stepped into public life. The mission to which Christ gave himself was not the overthrow of the Romans, but the clearest teaching about God, and the plainest example of how men ought to live. He began by allowing John to baptise him in the waters of the R. Jordan ; and then spent 40 days and nights in the wilderness near by, a period in which he prepared for his great mission by listening to God in the silence and loneliness, and wrestling with the doubts in his own soul.

After that, for three years or so, Jesus moved about Palestine, teaching the truth of God as he had seen it, teaching, healing, and gathering about him 12 young men who gradually (but *only* gradually) came to understand a little of what his doctrine implied. The 12 disciples, or apostles, were Simon (also called Peter), Andrew, James, John, Philip, Bartholomew, Thomas, Matthew, James the son of Alphaeus, Thaddaeus, Simon the Zealot, and Judas Iscariot. Early in his ministry Jesus outlined his teaching in the memorable Sermon on the Mount, a summary of the highest moral teaching known to men. It is significant that the only serious criticism now offered of it is that it is almost too high for mortal men and women to achieve. Christ remains, therefore, beyond the onward march of mankind.

- It is only fair to admit that parts of the Sermon were anticipated in current Jewish teaching, though there the sublime morality was mixed with legal matters and details of ritual.

Christ's chief method of teaching, however, was not by sermons but by parables, i.e. stories summarising and illustrating the principles of his teaching, e.g. the parable of the Good Samaritan, the Prodigal Son, and he remains the world's supreme genius in this medium. In all he taught he laid stress on the fact of God, His loving character as a Father, from which it follows that men are God's children, and therefore brothers one of another. The irresistible inference Christ drew was that men ought to love and not to hate each other ; to forgive and help and serve.

But it was not only his teaching which impressed others (though he taught as one having authority), but his own nature and his daily life. He *lived* as well as preached his sermons, and was therefore in his day, as he has been ever since, the world's pattern of the perfect life. Nevertheless, Christ was opposed and, indeed, hated because his life and teaching showed others how imperfect they were, a truth of which they did not wish to be reminded ; and because, although he fulfilled the law of Moses in which the Jews (and especially their most religious sects, the priests, Scribes and Pharisees), believed, *he went far beyond it*, breaking through its petty outward observances, and showing men that it is the spirit, not the letter, of the law that counts. Inevitably there was increasing opposition to him ; and this came to a head at the Feast of the Passover, when Jesus, with matchless courage (and plainly foreseeing what the outcome would be) set his face towards Jerusalem, and challenged his opponents by assuming the role of the Messiah. Vested interests and religious bigotry combined against him. When he saw how things were going, he withdrew with his disciples for the Last Supper, and then went to the Garden of Gethsemane. There, being betrayed by one of his disciples, Judas Iscariot, he was captured by the Temple authorities, and tried before Pontius Pilate, the Roman governor, who declared that he could find no fault in him. Hoping, however, to avoid a revolt among the Jews, Pilate handed Jesus over for crucifixion.

Mocked, beaten with whips, he was compelled to carry his own cross to Calvary (or Golgotha, i.e. the place of the skull), a low hill outside Jerusalem, where he was nailed to the rough timber, and raised between two thieves. He died forgiving his enemies, and his death is commemorated throughout the Christian world on each Good Friday. He was buried in a cave (sepulchre), and on the 3rd day (commemorated as Easter Sunday) he rose from the dead, i.e. he appeared alive and active to the disciples and others in and near Jerusalem. He continued to appear for 40 days, when, as described in the NT, he ascended into heaven.

Such is a bare outline of the life and death of Jesus. His brief ministry in a corner of the world seemed at the time altogether unimportant, yet, over 1,900 years later, his is the most widely known name among men. His teaching has lived through changing times, and his faith has spread far and wide, so that today there are more than 450,000,000 Christians in Europe, 35,000,000 in Asia, and almost 180,000,000 in N. and S. America, a world total of nearly 700,000,000, roughly $\frac{1}{3}$ of the population of the globe. Yet Jesus never wrote a book. He was about 33 or 35 when he died. He had no money. He seemed of so little significance in his day, as far as world events were concerned, that there is no contemporary reference to him in Greek, Latin, or Hebrew authors.

Christ's teaching differs in many ways from that of all other great religious leaders, the most important difference, perhaps, being his claim to be, in a special sense, a revelation of God's will and of God's nature. He claimed that those who wished to be saved from sin, to live a victorious life, and to understand and love God, must follow *him*, walk in *his* way, and find in *him* not only the perfect example but the *power* to resist evil and to do and be good.

It is a mistake to think that the gentleness of Jesus included anything that was unmanly and weak. On the contrary, he is the world's most superb hero, one of indomitable will, of high moral and physical courage, a born leader of men. He had a hatred of all evil, and indeed of anything less than the best. In his lifetime he was in one place only at a time ; after his crucifixion it is the experience of millions that his spirit permeates all space and all time, so that those who ask him to come into their lives find that he does come in, and gives them just that strength and courage and patience and joy they need.

The story of Christianity begins with the Man of Galilee, and goes on to tell how the disciples, and others, being met in an upper room in Jerusalem at the feast of Pentecost were inspired and emboldened to go forth preaching salvation to all who would believe in Jesus. From the beginning, the early Church was persecuted, as Jesus had been. Stephen was the first Christian martyr, and it was at Antioch that the first little groups of the followers of Jesus were called Christians (Acts 2). The faith was vastly extended by the great missionary journeys of St Paul, a convert who had begun by persecuting Christians, but ended by going happily to a martyr's death because of his love for Christ. St Paul's life and labours, his carrying of the Gospel into Asia and Europe, and his letters and sermons established Christianity, though as a despised faith, throughout the known world, and led ultimately (4th c.) to the conversion of Constantine, the Roman emperor. Thereafter, with but brief intervals, Christianity became the state religion of the Roman empire.

Unhappily, many conflicting interpretations of Christ's teaching have been made, and much bitterness has been shown in past ages by one group of Christians to another. The major divisions of the Christian Church are between the Orthodox (Eastern) and the Roman (Western) Churches (8–11th c.) and between the Roman Church and Protestants (16th c.).

From Christ came Christianity ; and the Christian ideal of vision and service has had an immense influence for good on the lives of individuals and on the well-being of communities. Almost every great reform of the last 2,000 years has owed its conception to the teaching of Christ, e.g. the abolition of slavery, child-welfare movements, nursing, social advances towards equality or against injustice and oppression. Christ has inspired the building of churches and cathedrals, has moved artists to paint immortal pictures, musicians to compose immortal music (e.g. Handel's *Messiah*), writers to write immortal books (e.g. Thomas à Kempis who wrote *The Imitation of Christ*, Bunyan's *Pilgrim's Progress*) ; and though there is much wrong with the world, and though innumerable critics of Christ have scoffed at him, and still do so, the nobility and truth of his words remain. It is inescapable that if only men and nations *did* follow him more closely, and lived more as brothers, we should be rid of many of the ills that flesh is heir to, and should enter into a period of progress and happiness such as, so far, we have barely dared to dream.

Read *Ecce Homo*, J. R. Seeley ; *The Jesus of History*, T. R. Glover ; *The Days of His Flesh*, David Smith ; *The Man born to be King*, Dorothy Sayers ; *The History of the Christian Church*, F. J. Foakes-Jackson ; *The Robe*, Lloyd C. Douglas.

Christchurch, city, South Island, NZ, on the R. Avon ; centre of a rich agricultural district ; chills and exports mutton ; pop.135,000.

Christ Church, college of Oxford University ; founded by Cardinal Wolsey in 1525. The site included St Frideswide Priory, of which some old buildings still exist. Henry VIII remodelled the college which in 1546 was named Christ Church. Wolsey's buildings are of particular architectural interest ; the church of the Priory is used as cathedral and college chapel. Members are called students, not fellows. The college is known locally as ' The House.'

Christian, name of several kings of Denmark. Among the most notable are Christian IV (1577–1648), also king of Norway and founder of Christiania, the old name for Oslo, cap. of Norway ; Christian IX (1818–1906), father of Queen Alexandra ; Christian X (1870–1947), who became king 1912 and was succeeded by Frederick IX.

Christian Endeavour Union, see YOUTH ORGANISATIONS

Christianity, see CHRIST

Christian Science, religious faith founded by Mary Baker Eddy (1821–1910), *b* Bow, New Hampshire, USA ; author of *Science and Health* (1875). Her teaching, said to be based on the Bible, stressed the conquest of disease by faith. The Christian Science Church was first organised at Boston, Massachusetts, 1879. There are now *c.*2,000 other churches. The Boston Society publishes daily *The Christian Science Monitor.*

Christie's, popular name for a London firm of auctioneers, founded 1766 by James Christie (1730–1803) ; noted for the sale of valuable pictures, old china, and antiques. The famous salerooms were destroyed by German bombs, 1941.

Christmas, festival, 25 Dec., in honour of the birth of Christ ; associated with carol singing, parties and the giving and receiving of presents. RC and other churches often display a nativity scene (i.o. the Infant Christ in the stable), an idea we owe to St Francis of Assisi ; the decorating of Christmas trees, common in Germany in the 17th c., was introduced into Britain 1840 by

Prince Albert. *A Christmas Carol,* written 1843 by Charles Dickens, conveys all that is meant by 'the spirit of Christmas.' Recently the King's message to his people has become a feature of the BBC's Christmas Day programme.

Christ of the Andes, see ARGENTINE

Christ's College, college of Cambridge University ; founded 1442. Its most famous pupil was John Milton.

Christ's Hospital, see BLUE COAT SCHOOLS

chromatin, see HEREDITY

chromium, *krō'mi-ŭm,* metallic element, Cr; atomic weight 52·01 ; atomic number 24 ; melting-point 1,510°C ; found naturally as chromite or chrome iron stone ; since 1913 has been increasingly used in making stainless steels in which there is approx. 20% chromium and 10% nickel ; chromium plating resists corrosion. Lead chromate is used as a yellow pigment.

chromosome, see CELL

chromosphere, *krō'mō-sfēr,* layer of glowing gas which surrounds the sun. The chromosphere can be seen only during a total eclipse of the sun. The moon hides the whole of the disc of the sun, and the chromosphere appears as a brilliant ring of flame (due to burning hydrogen, helium, and calcium). Some flames shoot out fifty thousand miles or more from the sun's edge.

Chron'icles, 1ST AND 2ND BOOKS OF, OT books probably compiled in the 3rd c. BC. With *Ezra* and *Nehemiah* they review Jewish history to 538BC.

chronometer, see CLOCK

chrysalis, *kris'ä-lis,* pupal or resting-stage of insects, especially butterflies and moths, when the caterpillar forms a cocoon or a silk cradle, becomes dormant, and finally changes to the perfect insect. See BUTTERFLIES AND MOTHS

CHRYSALIS
A Peacock Moth chrysalis hanging from a nettle

chrysanthemum, *kris-an'thi-mŭm,* popular garden plant which flowers Oct.–Dec., often cultivated for exhibition ; said to have been introduced into Britain *c.*1764.

chub, fresh-water fish of most British rivers ; *c.*15in long, 2–5lb in weight ; dark green above, silvery or brassy below ; useless as food.

Chungking, town and commercial cap. (1937–46) of China ; a port on the R. Yangtse ; pop.623,000 ; has a great trade in both native and foreign goods.

church, as a building for Christian worship, see ARCHITECTURE

Church, as an institution, means *either,* in the widest sense, the spiritual fellowship of all believers in Christ, *or* a particular Christian community. The history of Christian churches as institutions from the earliest times to the present day is known as CHURCH HISTORY.

THE EARLY CHURCH

The first Christian community was that in Jerusalem. It started as a Jewish sect, but Paul's teaching that the Gospel was for all nations and not merely for the Jews prevailed, and before long Christian congregations were formed in Rome and many other cities in response to the missionary effort of the apostles. These scattered congregations kept closely in touch with one another, but to begin with they managed their affairs largely in independence of one another. It seems to have been the normal practice that in each congregation an *episcopus* (overseer) was appointed to administer the sacraments, to regulate the order of worship, to enforce Christian morality, and to supervise the congregational funds. In all this the *episcopus* was assisted by *presbyters* (elders) and *deacons,* and the normal method of appointment was election by the members of the congregation. This form of church government exists today among the Congregationalists, and also to a large extent among the Presbyterians.

In the 2nd c. disputes arose concerning doctrine, and several Church councils were held. The councils were attended largely by the *episcopi,* and in order to reinforce their decisions it was claimed that the *episcopi* had superior authority in deciding such questions, and further that this spiritual superiority had been conferred on them by the apostles. In this way a superior order of bishops (*episcopi*) came into existence before the end of the 2nd c. According to the theory of Apostolic Succession the appointment of a bishop was valid only if it was made by a bishop, and the bishops ceased thus to be elected by the people and came to be officials appointed to represent a priestly order claiming superior spiritual authority. It was also taught that saving grace, the legacy of the apostles, was mediated and transmitted to later generations only by the bishops. Thus arose the doctrine ' without bishops, no Church,' and with it the Catholic Church came into existence. This form of Church government (prelacy) is practised today by Anglicans, Roman Catholics and various Episcopalian Churches in many countries.

CONSTANTINE AND THEODOSIUS

The early Church was thus an ecclesiastical society within a pagan empire. The Christians refused to worship the emperors as gods, and for this reason were sometimes persecuted, especially by Nero and Domitian in the 1st c. and by Diocletian at the beginning of the 4th c. But Christianity was popular among the soldiers of Constantine, who became Emperor after Diocletian. Constantine proclaimed toleration of Christianity, and although he only became a Christian on his death-bed it was at his bidding that the first ecumenical or general council of the Church assembled at Nicaea (325). By Theodosius (379–396) Christianity was declared the official religion of the Empire, and the Church became in government almost an equal partner of the State.

After Constantine the Roman Empire was divided between East and West. Although not recognised officially until 1054, the corresponding separation of the Eastern Church (Greek Orthodox or Byzantine) from the Western Church (Roman Catholic) was complete already in the 7th c., and still exists.

THE ROMAN CHURCH

In the Western Church, the Bishop of Rome claimed supremacy over the whole of Christendom, and came to be recognised as Pope and Vicar-General of Christ on earth. In the Dark Ages (400–1000) the provinces of the Western Empire became separate kingdoms. The kings were for the most part Teutonic barbarians who had however accepted Christianity, and the Church of Rome was widely influential, so much so that when (800) he founded the Holy Roman Empire, Charlemagne the Great was crowned by the Pope. Charlemagne was instrumental in raising the status and the moral prestige of the clergy ; but later emperors came into conflict with the popes, whose claim to supreme power in spiritual matters overshadowed and undermined the temporal power of the emperors.

In the 11th c. Pope Gregory VII reformed the Roman Church by ridding it of many abuses, and thus enhanced enormously the moral influence of the Church. He worked for the subordination of civil authority to ecclesiastical authority, and if he had succeeded in this the Roman Church would have been both spiritually and politically supreme in Western Christendom. The result was a naked struggle between pope and emperor, the prize being absolute power. The popes enjoyed the great advantage of possessing the Power of

the Keys, i.e. it was generally believed that anybody excommunicated by the pope would assuredly go to hell ; and against such atheists as the Emperor Frederick II (*d* 1250) the popes did not hesitate to use this power.

THE REFORMATION AND AFTER

The acquisition of temporal power undid the good work done by Gregory VII. The Roman Church became corrupt, and the emergence of many national States in place of a single empire facilitated the great anti-Roman revolt known in history as the *Reformation*. In the 16th c. national Churches were formed in many countries. Those that did not acknowledge the supremacy of the pope are known as Protestant.

In some Protestant countries the national Church is in certain respects subordinated to the State, e.g. in England, where Anglican Bishops are nominated by the Prime Minister, and the King is head of the Church ; elsewhere, e.g. in Scotland, the national church is largely self-governing. The Church of England, like the Lutheran churches in Germany and Sweden, perpetuates the episcopal form of government, and also claims to have inherited the Apostolic Succession. It divides the country into the two archbishoprics or sees of Canterbury and York, which in their turn are divided into *dioceses* governed by bishops. Each diocese has a cathedral (Gk *cathedra*, seat) which is the seat of the bishop. In Scotland the form of government adopted at the Reformation was Presbyterian, and the Bible is looked to as the supreme authority in matters of doctrine. Each congregation is governed by a Kirk Session consisting of *elders* chosen from among the congregation ; elders and ministers form the governing body of the *presbytery* (which corresponds to the English diocese) ; presbyteries send delegates to regional *synods* and to the annual General Assembly of the Church.

Unlike the Roman Church, which with its rigid doctrine of authority has maintained its unity throughout the centuries, the Protestant Churches in many countries have become subdivided into a number of denominations, each differing from the others to a greater or less extent in its beliefs, its forms of worship and its method of government. Thus in England certain denominations trace their origin to the Puritans, who in the 17th c. sought to purify the life of the Church by doing away with some beliefs and practices of the Church of England which they regarded as sinful ; and in the 18th c. John Wesley founded the movement known as Methodism, which like the Anglican, Presbyterian and other Churches, has spread to many parts of the world. In England the members of these new churches came to be known as *Nonconformists*, i.e. those who were unable to conform to the Act of Uniformity (1662) which required the English clergy to declare their adherence to the Book of Common Prayer. In Scotland the number of religious denominations is no less great, but in 1929 the most important of them were re-united with the Church of Scotland.

The missionary movement of the 19th c. vastly increased the membership of the Protestant Churches. New Churches came into being in many countries where none had existed before ; old religious controversies ceased to have meaning both for these new Churches and for their parent Churches in Europe and America ; as a result the main problem of the 20th c. for the Protestant Churches has been that of re-uniting denominations, many of which are no longer divided by differences of belief but only by past history or geographical position. This movement towards reunion, known as the *Ecumenical Movement*, led to the establishment of the World Council of Churches in 1948.

The Roman Church does not recognise the Protestant Churches or the Eastern Orthodox Churches : for this reason it declined to send representatives to the meeting of the World Council of Churches (Amsterdam 1948). Since 1870 the pope has been regarded by Roman Catholics the world over as infallible, i.e. incapable of making mistakes in any formal pronouncement concerning faith or morals. In Dec 1948 the pope invoked the Power of the Keys by excommunicating those who took part in the arrest of Cardinal Mindszenty, Primate of Hungary ; in July 1949 he also excommunicated all those who belong to the Communist Party, or in any way support it in anti-Christian activities.

Church, RICHARD (1893–), English poet and author ; was 24 years in Whitehall ; is now Director of the English Festival of Spoken Poetry ; Examiner in Poetics for London University ; does much lecturing, broadcasting, reviewing. Read his collected poems ; also his *20th Century Psalter* ; *The Lamp*; *The Solitary Man*; also (prose) *The Porch* ; *The Stronghold* ; *The Room Within* (a trilogy) ; *Green Tide*, etc.

Churchill, JOHN, see MARLBOROUGH, DUKE OF

Churchill, LORD RANDOLPH (1849–95), son of the 7th Duke of Marlborough ; entered Parliament as a Conservative member 1874 ; critical of Gladstone, especially of his Home Rule Bill ; formed what was known as the Fourth Party ; twice Leader of the House of Commons ; Secretary of State for India 1885–86 ; father of Winston Churchill, who wrote his biography.

Churchill, WINSTON (1874–), statesman, descendant of the great Duke of Marlborough, son of Lord Randolph Churchill and Jennie Jerome of New York ; educated Harrow and Sandhurst ; joined the 4th Hussars ; found excitement and military experience in Cuba, on the Indian frontier, in Egypt, etc. often as a war correspondent ; captured by the Boers 1899, but made a daring escape ; entered Parliament 1900 as a Conservative.

Vigorous and independent, he joined the Liberals 1906, but rejoined the Conservatives 1924. As a Liberal, he was Under-Secretary for the Colonies in Sir H. Campbell-Bannerman's ministry ; went to the Admiralty 1911, and was First Lord when World War I began. He fought in France ; became Minister of Munitions, later Secretary for War ; Chancellor of the Exchequer 1924 ; and was highly critical of all governments for many years.

WINSTON CHURCHILL 1874–

As early as 1931 Churchill was pleading for a larger air force, and was in much disfavour for his criticism of our foreign policy and our failure to prepare for war. He remained in the background when Baldwin and Chamberlain in turn held office as Prime Minister ; made a name for himself as a writer and historian with his memoirs of the Great War (1914–18), *Life of Marlborough*, etc. ; and saw the menace of Hitlerism before most of his contemporaries. He became Prime Minister 1940 in the critical hour when Germany had overrun France and seemed about to invade Britain ; brought new hope and vigour ; infused all parties with a sense of responsibility and a need for united endeavour ; made stirring broadcasts to the nation and Empire ; promptly declared British support for Russia when the latter was invaded by Germany, June 1941 ; met President

Roosevelt at sea August 1941, and helped to draw up the Atlantic Charter ; flew to Moscow to confer with Stalin 1942 ; attended the Casablanca conference January 1943, went to Washington in May ; and (August) met Roosevelt and Chiang Kai-Shek in Canada. He had much to do with planning the D-Day attack on German-occupied France 1944 ; conferred with Stalin and Roosevelt at Yalta (Crimea) 1945. Defeated with his party at the general election 1945, he became leader of the Opposition. The first three volumes of *The Second World War* were published 1948–50. They will be regarded by future historians as one of the most important sources for World War II.

A man of foresight, genius, indomitable will, great administrative ability, a born soldier, a profound believer in democracy, orator, writer, statesman, adventurer, Churchill turned what seemed defeat to victory in the War of 1939–45, and with his massive figure, grim (although often smiling) face, and his cigar, has been (and still is) one of the world's greatest and most popular statesmen.

Church of England, see CHURCH

chyle, *chīl,* liquid (lymph) of the body containing digested food, including emulsified fats. It passes into the blood stream.

Ciano, COUNT, *chē-ä'no* (1903–44), Italian who married Edda Mussolini 1930, and was appointed Foreign Minister 1936. A Fascist, he organised the Italian invasion of Albania and the attack on France (1940), but later voted against Mussolini. His diaries are of considerable importance.

Cibber, COLLEY, *sib'ĕr* (1671–1757), actor and dramatist, *b* London ; poet laureate 1730.

cicada, *si-kā'dä,* large 4-winged insect like a grasshopper, found mostly in the tropics ; the male makes a curious chirping sound.

Cicero, MARCUS TULLIUS, *sis'erō* (106–43 BC), Roman orator, statesman, and writer, *b* Arpinum ; began his public career 77BC ; was aedile 69BC, consul 63, when he crushed the Catiline conspiracy (organised by Lucius Catiline) planned to overthrow the republic. Though a friend of Julius Caesar from boyhood, he joined Pompey ; henceforth he was sometimes an exile, sometimes in popular favour in Rome. He attacked Antony after Caesar's murder, and was slain by Antony's orders.

His fame rests on his writings, and it has been said of him that his unique and imperishable glory is that he used the Latin language to form a pure prose style which 20 centuries have not displaced ; 50 of his speeches remain, also his famous letters to his friend Atticus.

Note : *Justitia tanta vis est, ut ne illi quidem qui maleficio et scelere pascuntur, possint sine ulla particula justitiae vivere,* i.e. So great force is justice that not even those who live by ill-doing and crime can manage to exist without some small share of justice.

C.I.D., short for Criminal Investigation Department, a branch of Scotland Yard.

Cid Campeador, *sid* ; *thēth käm-pā-ä-thŏr,* (*d* 1099), Spanish hero who championed the Christians in their fight with the Moors ; many legends of his valour are preserved.

cider, *sī'der,* intoxicating drink made from fermented apple juice, particularly in France (Brittany, Normandy), also in England (Devon and Somerset).

Cincinnati, city, Ohio, USA ; important port on the R. Ohio ; a large industrial centre noted for the manufacture of clothing, tobacco, leather goods, etc. ; has a large market and is a great railway centre ; famous for musical festivals ; pop.455,000.

cinema, see FILMS

cinema organ, see ORGAN

cinnabar, *sin'ä-bär,* mercuric sulphide, HgS. An important ore of mercury, it is a red powder.

cinnamon, *sin'ä-mon,* spice of pale amber colour obtained from the inside bark of an evergreen tree grown in Ceylon. The spice is used for flavouring and as a medicine.

Cinque Ports, *singk* (Fr. five ports), the towns of Hastings, Romney, Hythe, Dover, Sandwich. (Winchelsea and Rye were added later.) These undertook the defence of the south coast from Saxon and Norman times, and enjoyed certain privileges granted by Henry VII.

cipher, any secret system of writing a message which uses letters, numerals, or other symbols having a special prearranged meaning known only to the sender and the receiver.

Ciphers were used by Caesar and Cicero, and one of the commonest methods of ancient times was that of the ' skytale ' i.e. a message that made sense only when wrapped round a cylindrical staff of such dimensions that the apparently jumbled letters arranged themselves to form a message. The zigzag cipher (once much used by gangsters in USA) is a series of slanting strokes, meaningless till one puts a pre-arranged alphabet over it and reads off the letter indicated by the points.

Many modern ciphers depend on a keyword, and as this can be changed from day to day, even from hour to hour, the enemy has hard work trying to decipher any messages intercepted.

Lord Wolsley's Square is a clever device. Any keyword may be chosen, say, DANGEROUS. This is written as shown in the diagram, and the remainder of the alphabet (except J). Suppose the clear is PLANE LOCATED. Our message begins with P, so we find P in square 10, and find the other square 10, which gives us U. We therefore write U for P. For L we write B, etc. Hence our cipher reads UBYXV BQKYRVZ. Had we occasion to use H we should use that letter without disguise.

1 D	2 A	3 N	4 G	5 E
8 R	9 O	10 U	11 S	6 B
7 C	12 F	H	12 I	7 K
6 L	11 M	10 P	9 Q	8 T
5 V	4 W	3 X	2 Y	1 Z

In modern British espionage coding and decoding, ciphering and deciphering are frequently done by accurate and complex instruments working at high speed, and the secrets of ROOM 40 in wartime are vital—i.e. the room where the Admiralty's cryptographic section is housed.

Circe, *sŭr'sē*, in old Greek tales, an enchantress on the island of Aeaea. Homer tells how Odysseus drank unharmed her magic potion which changed his companions into swine.

circle, in geometry a plane figure bounded by the *circumference* which is everywhere equidistant from a fixed point, the *centre* (O in the diagram) ; the *radius* (plural *radii*) is any straight line from the centre to the circumference ; a *chord* is a straight line joining any two points on the circumference ; a chord passing through the centre is the longest chord or a *diameter* (i.e. two radii in the same line) ; an *arc* is any portion of the circumference ; an area cut off by a chord is a *segment* ; a *secant* is a line of unlimited length cutting the circumference in two points ; a *tangent* is the

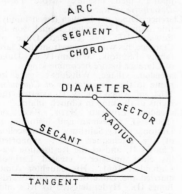

THE SECTIONS OF A CIRCLE

limiting position of a secant when the two points of intersection coincide ; an area cut off by two radii is a *sector* ; π, a Greek letter pronounced *pī*, is the circumference divided by the diameter, i.e. 3·1416 (approx.) or, more roughly, 3½. SQUARING THE CIRCLE (an impossibility) means finding the side of a square of the same area as a given circle. Note : circumference $= 2\pi r$; area $= \pi r^2$, or $d^2 \times 0.7854$, where d is diameter ; also diameter = circumference $\times 0.31831$.

circular measures, see WEIGHTS AND MEASURES

circumference, see CIRCLE

circumflex, see ACCENT

Cirencester, *si'ren-ses-tĕr* or *sis'itĕr*, market town, Gloucestershire ; contains the Royal Agricultural College ; the Roman Corinium.

Cistercians, see MONKS AND NUNS

citizenship, see LOCAL GOVERNMENT

citric acid, *sit'rik*, found in sour fruits as, say, lemons (6%) ; white crystalline acid $C_6H_8O_7$; hence citrus fruits, e.g. lemon, citron, orange, lime and grapefruit.

citron, *sit'rŭn*, fruit tree akin to the lemon ; originally found in India ; has purple and white flowers which give place to a yellow fruit.

civet, *siv'et*, flesh-eating animal, rather like the cat ; has slender body, tapering head, long tail, short legs. Its fur is coarse but finely mottled brownish-grey. The civet has peculiar scent glands near the tail. It is found in Asia and Africa.

civics, see LOCAL GOVERNMENT

civil engineer, one who designs or builds bridges, tunnels, dams, reservoirs, roads, docks, canals, etc. for peaceful (not military) purposes ; may also be responsible for irrigation. Courses may be taken at most universities.

Civil List, allowances paid to the king and other members of the royal family ; dates from the accession of William and Mary 1688. The *Civil List Pensions* of Britain include allowances made to people (or their dependents) who have rendered worthy service in literature, art, science, etc.

Civil Service, State administration other than in the navy, army or air-force ; includes all employment in government offices, e.g. Home Office, Treasury, Post Office, Customs, Inland Revenue, Ministry of Education, Ministry of Labour, Colonial Civil Service. Those who secure a post in the Civil Service are more or less assured of employment for the rest of their working life. The hours are never long, and there is usually opportunity for promotion.

Entrance into the Service is not easy, depending on *competitive* examinations held by the Civil Service Commissioners, to whom application for particulars should be made. See EXAMINATIONS

Civil War, THE ENGLISH : struggle between Crown and Parliament 1642–49

which resulted in complete supremacy (for the time being) of Parliament. This result was modified 1660 by the Restoration (of a king) but formed the basis of the Glorious Revolution 1688.

All through his reign Charles I (acceded 1625) was at loggerheads in England with the Commons, which opposed, as illegal, arbitrary taxation and arbitrary imprisonment by the king. The Commons were also in conflict with Laud (Archbishop of Canterbury) who maintained the Arminian doctrine that the king should have absolute supremacy. Another source of opposition was the Kirk of Scotland, which in 1637 had abolished the order of bishops and in the National Covenant had made it a condition for recognition of Royal authority that the king should protect religious liberty in Scotland instead of trying to extinguish it.

Matters came to a head in 1642 and all parties prepared for war.

Note that the king's followers, known as Royalists, usually wore their hair long, whereas the Parliamentarians (mostly Puritans) had their hair cut short, hence their nickname, Roundheads.

Charles raised his standard near Nottingham 22 Aug 1642, where the Earl of Lindsay had 15,000 men. Parliament had an army of 20,000, commanded by the Earl of Essex. In England, the king was supported by the gentry and nobility of the North and West, Parliament by the towns and independent farmers of the East and South. At the battle of Edgehill, Warwickshire, (1642) the king's troops under Prince Rupert and the Earl of Rochester, were barely saved from defeat ; but the Marquis of Newcastle secured several cities for the king, who made Oxford his headquarters ; and after a Royalist victory at Adwalton Moor (Yorkshire) Charles seemed almost sure of victory. But at the battle of Newbury (Berkshire), 1643, he suffered a reverse.

In spring 1644 the Scots invaded England and joined up with Cromwell's Ironsides, and on 2 July 1644 they won at Marston Moor, near York, a crushing victory ; this was followed by the battle of Naseby (Northamptonshire), 1645, a decisive victory for Cromwell's New Model Army of c.21,000 infantry and cavalry under Sir Thomas Fairfax, though trained and disciplined by Cromwell.

The Parliamentary forces then won success after success, securing Leicester, storming Bristol, defeating the Royalists at Rowton Heath, near Chester (Sept 1645), and compelling the king's army to surrender at Stow-on-the-Wold (Gloucestershire), March 1646. Charles took refuge with the Scots, who were willing to recognise his authority if he protected the Kirk of Scotland. When Charles rejected the settlement proposed

by the English Parliament, the Scots handed him over. He was a prisoner for two years. Meanwhile fighting broke out again. At the head of the New Model Army Cromwell crushed every insurrection ; and with the backing of the army, he gained control by purging the House of Commons of all but a Rump of 'Independents.' The Rump brought Charles to trial before a court whose jurisdiction he refused to acknowledge on the ground that it had been formed without the agreement of the House of Lords. Charles was condemned to death and executed 30 Jan 1649. The outcome of the Civil Wars was therefore a victory for Parliament, though for a time Parliament was dominated by Oliver Cromwell and the New Model Army.

Cl, chemical symbol for chlorine.

Clackmannanshire, smallest county in Scotland ; lies between Ochil Hills and the Forth ; rich in minerals, especially coal ; co. tn Clackmannan.

Clacton-on-Sea, seaside resort, Essex.

clad metals, see METALS

Clairvaux, *kler-võ*, village, France, 35m south-east of Troyes ; St Bernard founded an abbey here 1115.

clairvoyant, see PROPHET

Clapham, suburb of SW. London ; noted for its large common of 220 acres. Clapham Junction is one of the busiest in the world.

Clare (1194–1253), Italian saint, *b* Assisi, follower of St Francis of Assisi, and foundress of the religious order of nuns, the Poor Clares.

Clare, SW. county, Eire, bordering on the Atlantic ; important fisheries especially oysters ; agriculture neglected except oats and potatoes ; chief town Ennis.

Clare College, second oldest college of Cambridge University, founded 1326. The buildings (1638–1768) are exceedingly handsome. Hugh Latimer was a Fellow.

Clare, JOHN (1793–1864), poet, born near Peterborough ; a casual labourer, always poor ; died insane ; wrote *Poems Descriptive of Rural Life.*

Clarence, DUKE OF, English (royal family) title dating 1362, when Lionel, son of Edward III, was created Duke of Clarence, his wife coming from the Clare family of Suffolk. William IV was Duke of Clarence before becoming king.

Clarendon, village, Wiltshire ; gave its name to the *Constitutions of Clarendon* 1164, in which Henry II asserted the rights of the king in Church affairs.

Clarendon, EDWARD HYDE, EARL OF (1609–74), statesman and historian, *b* Dinton, near Salisbury ; Chancellor of the Exchequer 1643 ; supported Charles II, and at the Restoration was his chief minister ; created Earl of Clarendon 1661. His daughter Anne married the Duke of York (afterwards James II). Hyde, detested by RCs and Puritans alike, believed in constitutional government, and was a rigid churchman ; he left the country 1667, and died at Rouen, spending his last years writing a notable *History of the Great Rebellion*, the profits of which were used to build a printing house for the Oxford University Press. A statue of Clarendon was erected in 1721. Since the removal of the University Press in 1830, the original building has been known as the Clarendon Building.

claret (Latin *clarus*, clear), Bordeaux wine made chiefly at Gironde, France.

clarinet, wood-wind musical instrument consisting of a cylindrical tube with single reed ; there are many varieties. Mozart was the first composer to make a thorough use of it.

clarion, trumpet-like instrument, with a loud ringing note ; formerly used as a signal in war.

Clark, MAJOR-GENERAL MARK (1896–), American soldier ; led secret mission (by submarine) to N. Africa to prepare for an Allied invasion 1942 ; commanded the 5th Army in the invasion of Italy, capturing Rome 1944 ; in command of US forces in Austria 1945–47.

Classics, Classical Literature, terms used to denote the literature of Ancient Greece and Rome. Only a small proportion of this literature has been preserved ; during the ' Dark Ages ' after the fall of the Roman Empire all Greek and much Latin literature was lost to the Western world, and it was the rediscovery of many of the great works of the ancient authors which gave the decisive impetus to the Renaissance in Italy and the other countries of Western Europe. But it is certain that the quantity of what has been lost is greater than its quality. The surviving works of Latin and more especially of Greek authors are by common consent unequalled in certain respects ; hence the term ' classic ' is also extended to refer to any masterpiece of literature (or pre-eminent work of art) whether ancient or modern.

Greek literature has the freshness of a people making discoveries of a kind never made before : Aeschylus wrestling with the moral problems raised by human crimes and suffering ; Sophocles telling of the nightingale singing at Colonus ; Herodotus inquiring about the world in which he lived and setting down faithfully, if uncritically, all the information which he could obtain ; Thucydides observing human behaviour in such a way that he is both historian and social scientist, these are instances of the Greek power of apprehending human experience in a new way and making it live in literature. For this reason, even if there were no other, Greek literature deserves attention whether or not the subjects with which it deals have ceased to be of practical importance.

The habit of accurate observation, the avoidance of exaggeration, the emphasis on self-discipline and moderation and the desire to attain perfection of form are among the most important contributions of Greek literature to Western civilisation, and have led in modern times to the distinction between the *classical* and the *romantic* in all forms of art, including literature. This is a further sense in which the word ' classical ' is used : impossible to define in a few words, but taking its origin in the characteristic first mentioned.

Latin literature owes much to Greek both in its form and in its thought. But Lucretius, Horace and Virgil each developed the traditions of Greek poetry to an extent that made them much more than imitators of Greek tradition. Virgil's epic poem the *Aeneid* combines discipline of form and intensity of feeling in a way which can find no equal in Western literature, and Cicero's oratorical prose has been the foremost of its kind for writers of all the languages of Western Europe.

Claudius I (10BC–AD54), Roman emperor, nephew of Tiberius, *b* Lugdunum (Lyons), proclaimed emperor (AD41) after the murder of Caligula. The Roman conquest of Britain began during his moderately successful reign.

Read *I, Claudius* and *Claudius the God*, vivid fictional biographies by Robert Graves.

Claverhouse, see DUNDEE, VISCOUNT

clavichord, *klav'icord*, the first stringed instrument played by keys on a keyboard ; popular from the 14th to the 18th c. The strings are struck by metal ' tangents,' thus differing from the harpsichord, in which they are plucked by quills. Bach's *Well-tempered Clavier* was written for the clavichord.

clavicle, collar-bone ; joins the sternum (breast-bone) and shoulder-blade ; easily dislocated at its outer end.

clay, form of powdered rock, mainly aluminium silicate ; sticky if wet, becomes a hard, tough mass when dry or baked. Bricks are made of clay (see BRICKS) ; kaolin or China clay (used for crockery), a decayed form of granite, contains much silica ; it is mined in Cornwall. Clay coloured with ironoxide gives us the artist's colours sienna and umber. The fact that cement clays when heated with limestone become Portland cement was discovered by Joseph Aspdin, a Leeds bricklayer, *c.*1824, and Portland cement is now used in immense quantities. Reinforced cement (or concrete) has iron or steel rods or network inside. Portland cement is manufacutred near the mouth of the Thames ; also near Hull, Bridgwater, Cambridge, Cardiff, Newcastle and Rugby.

clay tablets, see CUNEIFORM

Clayton, REV PHILIP THOMAS BYARD (1885–), better known as Tubby Clayton, social worker and padre, *b*

Queensland ; one of the founders of Toc H, with HQ at All Hallows, Barking-by-the-Tower, London, since 1922. The Toc H movement began during World War I, when Talbot House, Poperinghe, near Ypres, was opened 1915 as a club and church in memory of Gilbert Talbot. The idea is to foster unselfishness and ideals of service. Toc H now has over 1,000 branches (marks) round the world ; and part of its ritual includes the beautiful ceremony of the lamp.

clearing house, institution for settling accounts between companies etc. in the same line of business, particularly banks. It facilitates business by doing away with the necessity of adjusting individual debit or credit amounts by totalling *all* transactions, and paying only the balance.

cleavers, wayside plant, 6–7ft long ; has whorls of hooked leaves. The small white flowers produce bristly purple fruits that cling to animals.

Clee Hills, range of hills in Shropshire.

Cleethorpes, seaside health resort, Lincolnshire ; noted for oysters ; pop.30,000.

clematis, *clem'atis,* climbing plant common in many English counties ; has white flowers ; known also as traveller's joy.

Clemenceau, GEORGES EUGENE, *klĕ-män-so'* (1841–1929), French statesman known as The Tiger ; *b* La Vendée ; implacable enemy of Germany ; Premier 1917 ; did much to ensure Allied victory in World War I ; established good relations between France and Britain ; presided over the Peace Conference, Versailles ; vigorous government critic ; author of several books.

Cleopatra (69–30BC), Queen of Egypt, daughter of Ptolemy XI, and therefore a Macedonian, not, as is often imagined, an Egyptian ; joint-ruler with her brother from 51BC, but removed after three years ; restored by Julius Caesar ; charmed Mark Antony, who fell in love with her, and was with him at the battle of Actium 31BC when both fled from the victorious Octavian (Augustus) ; is said to have taken her own life.

Cleopatra's Needle, see LONDON

Clerkenwell, *klär'-ken-wel,* western part of Finsbury, London ; watch-making and jewellery centre.

Clerk-Maxwell, JAMES, *klärk-* (1831–79), Scottish scientist and mathematician, *b* Edinburgh ; first professor of experimental physics at Cambridge University 1871 ; investigated Saturn's rings, the kinetic theory of gases, etc. ; but most famous for his work in electricity and magnetism. He advanced Faraday's theories, showed that the speed of electromagnetic waves is that of light ; and is rightly regarded as one of the pioneers of radio.

Cleveland, *klĕv-,* moorland district, N. Yorkshire ; noted for a fine breed of horses ; rich in iron ore. Its most important town is Middlesbrough.

Cleveland, city, Ohio, USA ; is on the south shore of L. Erie ; great railway centre ; chief centre in USA for iron ore ; iron manufacture in all branches ; pop.878,000.

climate, prevailing weather conditions which are the result of many factors, such as distance from the equator ; height of land ; distance from the sea. Temperature increases as the equator is approached, and tends to decrease as we ascend. Places near large areas of water tend to have less extremes of temperature, enjoying an *insular climate,* whereas those far inland have a *continental climate,* liable to great variations, e.g. Yakutsk (Siberia) may have a summer temperature 112° above its winter level, but in British Guiana the variation is not more than *c.*2°.

Prevailing winds considerably affect climate, and are partly responsible for changes in temperature, e.g. the chinook of N. America ; amount of cloud, and therefore the amount of sunshine ; rainfall, e.g. the south-west wind of Britain, usually bringing rain ; the Indian monsoon. Much is learned about climate from a study of ISOTHERMAL LINES, i.e. map-lines joining places with the same mean (or average) temperature.

WEATHER FORECASTING is now of great importance to shipping and farming,

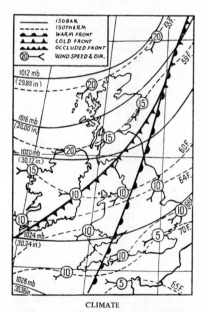

CLIMATE

An example of one kind of weather forecasting chart used to indicate the weather conditions that may be expected to prevail during a certain period of time over the whole or part of the country.

but most of all for aircraft in flight. It is based on the correlated readings, taken every 3 or 6 hours at many widely distributed meteorological stations, e.g. temperature, rainfall, wind-strength and direction, height of cloud, humidity and barometer pressure. From these a weather-map is constructed. Lines joining places having the same barometric pressure at sea-level are drawn, these being called *isobars*. Much information can be gleaned from the resulting pattern. Where the isobars are closest together the wind is strongest; a *warm front* is preceded by gradually thickening stratus cloud and finally by rain ; a *cold front* brings a shorter period of rain, often with squalls, and is accompanied by a drop in temperature.

From 1947 onwards thirteen countries, including Great Britain, Canada and USA, have maintained weather ships in the N. Atlantic, the vessels sending meteorological reports by radio, such reports being of special value to pilots of civil aviation services across the Atlantic.

The climate of the northern hemisphere is becoming gradually warmer. Since 1911 the period of pack-ice round the north coast of Iceland has shortened by almost two months. See ATMOSPHERE

Read *The Weather*, George Kimble and Raymond Bush.

clinic (Gk *kline*, bed), class where students learn from the surgeon or physician while he is examining patients. Nowadays the word is applied to an institution where people attend for medical treatment or medical advice, notably for schools and large factories.

Clive, ROBERT (1725–74), British administrator and soldier ; founder of the British Empire in India ; *b* Market Drayton, Shropshire. As a boy he was headstrong and adventurous. Clive sailed as a clerk in the E. India Company, and at 19 arrived in India penniless.

At that time (1744) no European country owned land in India, but British, French and Dutch companies had trading stations known as factories. Volunteering as a soldier, Clive fought against the French, earned a reputation as a skilled and daring leader, and 1751 with 200 Europeans and 300 Sepoys, seized the large city of Arcot, defended it against 10,000 men, and marched to Trichinopoli, thus outwitting the French governor, Dupleix, and establishing British interests in the region of the Carnatic. He was called by Pitt ' a heaven-born general.'

Clive returned to England, but 1756 he was again in India as Governor of St David's. He marched to Calcutta, and 1757 defeated the Nabob of Bengal (Suraj-ud-Dowlah), who had destroyed British trading stations, and suffocated 120 of his prisoners in the ' Black Hole.' By leading 1,000 Europeans and 2,000 Sepoys against the Nabob, Clive shattered

his force of 50,000 at Plassey (1757). Suraj-ud-Dowlah was captured and put to death, Mir Jaffer replacing him, the British being more or less in control of Bengal.

It seems that, as was then customary, Clive accepted large sums for himself. Though later he was received in England with great enthusiasm, and created Lord Clive of Plassey, his enemies attempted to bring about his impeachment in Parliament, the result, no doubt, of his reorganisation and administration (1765– 1767) which had compelled him to displace many employees, and put an end to much trickery in the E. India Company. Of a fiery disposition and liable to fits of depression, he is said to have taken his own life.

It cannot be questioned that British influence in India is due to Clive more than to any other person.

cloche, *klōsh*, glass covers for forcing early vegetables ; French market gardeners have long used this method.

clock, instrument for measuring time. Without clocks it is impossible to combine effectively in any but very simple plans the actions of large numbers of people, so that the efficiency of such civilisation as ours depends among other things on the reliability of its clocks ; and if there had been no reliable clocks, it could not possibly have come into existence.

In the ordered life of monks in monasteries during the Dark Ages (AD400–1000) it was necessary to have methods of measuring time, and the monasteries kept alive and in use a number of relatively simple, nonmechanical time-measuring devices (water clocks, sand glasses, graduated candles, etc.) invented in ancient times. The monastery bells were rung at regular intervals, thus giving the outside world a rough record of the lapse of time.

The increasing growth of trade and manufacture in medieval cities created a need for ever more accurate ways of measuring time, and the task of timekeeping passed from monasteries to the towns themselves. In the 13th c. there were already mechanical bell clocks, and the invention was rapidly developed in large cities such as Paris and trading centres like Nuremberg. In the 14th c. a dial and hands were incorporated in the bell-clock, and the division of hours into minutes and seconds was common *c.*1345. In the 16th c. Peter Henlein of Nuremberg was manufacturing watches, and by the end of the century small clocks were being taken into use in private dwelling houses in England and Holland.

With the development of clocks and watches a great change came over everyday life. Time in itself became valuable. Many kinds of work were paid for increasingly according to the time taken, and working life was regimented. The improvement of navigation was held up by want of clocks of extreme accuracy (needed for calculating longitude) until the 18th c. when John Harrison (1693–1776) invented the first modern chronometer ; he also invented the balance-wheel used in modern watches.

One of the difficulties that had to be solved by early clock-makers was that when a metal is heated it expands, and when a pendulum expands the clock loses time. Various devices have been invented for overcoming this defect, but even modern pendulum clocks may vary within two seconds a day. Nevertheless, clocks (as shown by the phrase ' as regular as clockwork ') have been among the most perfect mechanisms of their day. Some now in use, e.g. at Greenwich Observatory, are amazingly accurate. One is a type which is controlled by a small quartz crystal vibrating 100,000 times a second, and accurate within 1/1,000 second a day. This clock is responsible for our radio Time Signals. Still more accurate is the so-called atomic clock in Washington (USA), based on the vibration of atoms in an ammonia molecule.

Since 1936 the Post Office has made correct Greenwich Time available to telephone subscribers in large towns ; they ring the exchange and hear a recorded voice reading off the correct time on a series of discs with soundtracks scanned by light from a photoelectric cell. The device is popularly known as TIM. See also TIME

closed shop, name for the growing practice of requiring all employees in a factory, company, etc. to be members of a suitable trade union.

clothes, see COSTUME

clothing coupons, coupons issued in book form in the UK during World War II, and thereafter. Each civilian had a book of coupons, only so many of which could be used in a given period. Coupons were surrendered when purchasing articles of clothing, or material. Clothing coupons were discontinued 1949. See DOCKET ; RATIONING

Clotho, see FATES

clouds, see ATMOSPHERE ; CLIMATE

Clough, ARTHUR HUGH, *klŭf* (1819–61), English poet ; *b* Liverpool ; educated at Rugby and Oxford ; noted for his poem *Say Not the Struggle Naught Availeth,* and *The Bothie of Tober-na-Vuolich.* See ARNOLD, MATTHEW

clove, dried flower-bud of the clove tree ; used as spice. Cloves of the best quality are grown in the Moluccas on Amboyna I., but most of them come from East Africa ; although mostly used in this country to give additional flavour to apple tarts, cloves are used to flavour other food and mulled wine.

Clovelly, *klō-vel′i,* charming coastal holiday resort perched above Barnstaple Bay, N. Devon.

CLOVE

The flowers, the leaves, and (left) a flower bud (used for flavouring when dried)

clover, common field plant with three ovate leaves. The flower heads are bushy and have pointed petals curving upwards. Species include red clover (*Trifolium pratense*) and white clover (*Trifolium repens*), both flower in June–Aug. and have a very sweet scent. They form excellent pasture for farm stocks, enrich the soil with nitrogen, and provide nectar for bees, by which they are pollinated.

Clo′vis, (*c.*465–511) King of the Franks, and founder of the Frankish kingdom.

Cluniacs, see MONKS AND NUNS

Clwyd, *klŭd,* river, Denbighshire, N. Wales. The VALE OF CLWYD, 24m long, is a famous beauty-spot.

Clyde, *klīd,* river, Scotland ; flows 106m through Lanark and Hamilton to Glasgow, and enters the Firth of Clyde at Dumbarton. CLYDEBANK (near Glasgow) has huge shipbuilding and engineering yards (' cradle' of the *Queen Mary* and *Queen Elizabeth*). Clyde-built ships are recognised as being among the finest in the world. The Clyde valley is famous for Clydesdale horses, has fruit orchards, also coal and iron.

Clynes, JOHN ROBERT (1869–1949), politician, *b* Oldham ; Labour MP for NE. Manchester 1906–31 ; Home Secretary 1929–31.

Clytaemnestra, *klī-tem-nes′trä,* in old Greek tales, wife of Agamemnon, King of Argos. See AESCHYLUS

coal, mixture of carbon, volatile matter (hydrogen, oxygen, nitrogen, etc.), and ash. A black mineral, it is the decayed vegetable matter of the forests and swamps of over 300 million years ago, i.e. of the Carboniferous and sometimes Cretaceous periods (see GEOLOGY) ; hence coal is really fossilised cellulose, the result of chemical change, pressure (folding and weight of rocks above), and temperature.

Peat is probably an early stage in the

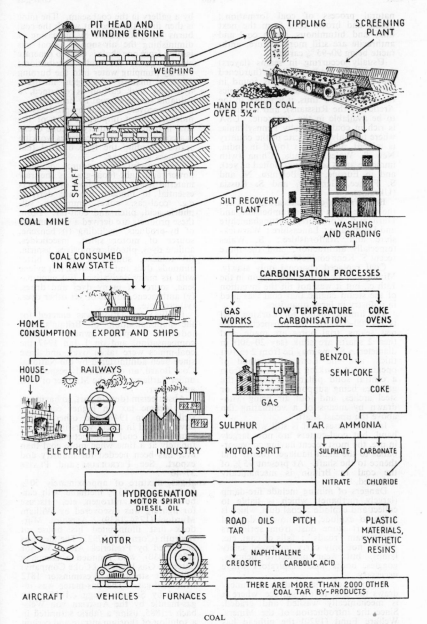

PIT HEAD AND WINDING ENGINE

WEIGHING

TIPPLING

SCREENING PLANT

SHAFT

COAL MINE

HAND PICKED COAL OVER 3½"

SILT RECOVERY PLANT

WASHING AND GRADING

COAL CONSUMED IN RAW STATE

CARBONISATION PROCESSES

HOME CONSUMPTION

EXPORT AND SHIPS

GAS WORKS

LOW TEMPERATURE CARBONISATION

COKE OVENS

BENZOL

SEMI-COKE

COKE

HOUSE-HOLD

RAILWAYS

GAS

ELECTRICITY

INDUSTRY

SULPHUR

TAR

AMMONIA

MOTOR SPIRIT

SULPHATE

CARBONATE

NITRATE

CHLORIDE

HYDROGENATION MOTOR SPIRIT DIESEL OIL

ROAD TAR

OILS

PITCH

PLASTIC MATERIALS, SYNTHETIC RESINS

MOTOR

NAPHTHALENE

AIRCRAFT

VEHICLES

FURNACES

CREOSOTE

CARBOLIC ACID

THERE ARE MORE THAN 2000 OTHER COAL TAR BY-PRODUCTS

COAL

The horizontal lines under the names of the three Carbonisation Processes show that many by-products of coal can be obtained from any one of them.

natural process of coal formation ; lignite and brown coal form the next link, and bituminous, steam coal and anthracite are still more mature, anthracite being 90–95% carbon.

Usually occurring in seams (layers) separated by beds of shale (hardened mud) and sandstone, coal is found in many areas, though less in the tropics than elsewhere ; thus, it is mined in the Arctic (by the Russians), and is known to be available in the Antarctic. USA is rich in coal (especially Pennsylvania, where the only anthracite in the country is mined), and coal is found in India, New S. Wales, Canada, China (with immense areas scarcely exploited as yet), and in Europe, e.g. Belgium, N. and S. France, Germany, and S. Russia (Ukraine).

Britain's chief coalfields are in W. Fife ; the Clyde basin ; Northumberland and Durham ; Yorkshire, Nottinghamshire and Derbyshire ; Lancashire ; Warwickshire and Staffordshire ; S. Wales (especially anthracite) ; and the more recent S. Kent coalfield.

Coal replaced charcoal only slowly. Mining may be said to have begun in the 13th c., but it was not till the invention of the steam engine that coal was used in industry in large quantities.

The limiting depth for working coal is c.4,000–5,000ft. In prospecting for new seams, trial bores are made, and then 2 shafts are sunk (say 20–30ft in diameter). Seams may be from 2 to 10ft thick, and the Longwall method of opening out working faces of coal from a central solid pillar is common, the galleries being supported by timber or steel arches, and foul air being withdrawn by means of a ventilating fan above the upcast shaft.

In some cases coal is still worked by hand, but coal-cutters are now largely in use, the most recent having conveyor-bands to the main haulage ' roads,' and thence to the shaft. At present 75% of the coal in Britain is mechanically extracted.

Dangers of mining include fire-damp (largely methane), which is liable to collect and explode ; coal dust, which is liable to explode, but now is damped with inert stone dust from sprinklers in the main ' roads ' ; falls of coal, etc. Miners not only carry improved safety lamps, but wear protective helmets, goggles, boots and respirators where necessary.

Steam or electric winding machinery draws the coal to the surface, where it is mechanically washed and graded. Since the introduction of the Miners' Welfare Fund (1920) the pithead has greatly improved, and many are provided with playing-fields, baths, rest-centres and educational facilities.

In USSR a remarkable development in mining has taken place since 1938 : Briefly, two shafts are sunk and joined by a gallery in the coal seam. The mine is then fired, the speed at which the coal burns being controlled by increasing or diminishing the air-supply. Coal gas issuing from one shaft is used to generate electric power for wide distribution ; and by pumping water into the burning mine, a mixture of oxygen, nitrogen, hydrogen and carbon is obtained, a valuable source of coal by-products.

The recovery of coal by-products is, indeed, a most important part of the coal industry. A battery of coke ovens is a common feature of colleries working seams affording the type of coal that produces good coke.

Coal, useful as a source of heat, power and light (coal-gas), is the raw material from which a host of products essential to modern life are derived, e.g. coal-gas, coke, ammonia, sulphuric acid, pitch and coal-tar. From these products are derived a vast number of by-products, including (i) benzene, source of motor spirit, insecticides, aniline dyes, phenol, explosives, aspirin, (ii) toluene, source of oil of bitter almonds, dyes and explosives, (iii) xylene with its many derivatives, (iv) naphthalene, source of many dyes and drugs, (v) anthracene, source of yet other dyes, (vi) creosote.

In 1945 legislation was enacted for the nationalisation of Britain's coal industry. Private owners received compensation, and on 1 Jan 1947 the coal-mines were taken over, and have since been administered by the National Coal Board, an official body responsible under Parliament to the Minister of Fuel and Power.

Absenteeism (due, in part, to having to pay income tax on higher earnings), strikes, as in 1947, and other factors have resulted in recent years in Britain's diminished coal production, unfortunately at a time when more coal than ever has been needed for industry and export. See PETROLEUM and PLATES 37–40

coal-gas, mixture of approximately 50% hydrogen and 33% methane with carbon monoxide, nitrogen, etc. Its use for lighting was discovered by William Murdock (1754–1839), b Ayrshire. Murdock first illuminated his house at Redruth (Cornwall) 1792. The idea was developed by Frederick Albert Winsor (1763–1830), who founded a company (later the Gas Light and Coke Company) which lit streets in Westminster 1812 with coal-gas. The gas-meter was invented by Samuel Clegg c.1815 ; the gas-mantle by the Austrian von Welsbach c.1885, using a fabric saturated in a solution of thorium nitrate and cerium nitrate.

In the manufacture of coal-gas, coal is heated in retorts operated by machinery, the gas (lighter than air) being cooled, separated from ammonia and tar, etc., and stored in gas-holders, either over water or in the more modern piston type ; it is then led to the mains. See diagram, p. 285

coalition, in politics, a temporary alliance of two or more parties for united effort, e.g. the Coalition Government of 1918–1922, and the Government which, in World War II, agreed to forget party differences. Coalitions are usually made only in time of national danger.

Coalport, village, Shropshire ; noted for pottery, especially richly decorated vases.

Coalville, -vil, mining town, Leicestershire ; pop.22,000.

coastguards, men recruited from the naval force for the purpose of maintaining signal and wireless stations round the coast. Originally known as preventative men, whose task it was to prevent smuggling and illicit trading ; assist shipwrecked vessels, and act as naval reserves.

Coatbridge, town, Lanarkshire ; centre of important iron and coal district ; pop.43,000.

Coates, ALBERT, kōts (1882–), English composer and conductor ; b Leningrad ; educated in England ; highly popular in the USA and Russia where he became conductor of the Imperial Orchestra. Conductor for Sir Thomas Beecham, 1919 ; produced his opera *Samuel Pepys* 1929 ; *Pickwick* 1936.

Coates, ERIC (1886–), composer, b Hucknall, Nottinghamshire ; held the post of principal viola player in the Queen's Hall Orchestra, but he later concentrated wholly on composition ; became a fellow of the Royal Academy of Music 1922. His works, which have a wide popular appeal, include *Country-side Suite, Summer Days Suite* and *Joyous Youth Suite* for orchestra. *Bird Songs at Eventide* is one of his best known and most popular songs.

cobalt, kō'bŏlt, white metal and element, Co ; atomic weight 58·94 ; atomic number 27 ; valuable metal resembling iron ; chiefly mined in the Belgian Congo, N. Rhodesia, French Morocco, Canada and Burma ; gives glass a rich blue tint ; largely used in making stellite for high-speed cutting tools, surgical instruments, etc. ; gives a brilliantly polished surface in electroplating.

Cobb, JOHN (1900–), British racing motorist ; first man to drive a car at over 400mph. He did this at Bonne-ville, Salt Lake Flats, Utah, in 1947, when he touched 403·135mph, his average top speed being 394·196mph.

Cobbett, WILLIAM, kob'et (1763–1835), writer and politician, b Farnham, Surrey ; won fame with his *History of the Pro-testant Reformation* and his *Rural Rides* (1830). From 1804 he was a fearless critic of the Government ; repeatedly prosecuted for libel ; imprisoned and fined for condemning flogging in the army. For over 30 years he edited *Cobbett's Weekly Political Register.* He

was a vigorous reformer and champion of the farm-labourer.

Cobden, RICHARD (1804–65), British states-man, born near Midhurst, Sussex ; became a calico-printer in Manchester 1830 ; visited USA and the Near East ; was convinced that prosperity depended on two things : free trade and non-intervention in foreign disputes. He was long associated with John Bright in a crusade for free trade ; was a founder of the Anti-Corn-Law League (see CORN LAWS) ; MP for Stockport 1841. He opposed Lord Palmerston's foreign policy and later lost his seat ; advocated peace ; negotiated a commercial treaty with France 1860 ; received £120,000 by public sub-scription.

Coblenz, kō'blents, city, c.60m from Cologne, Germany ; at the junction of the Rhine and Moselle ; manufactures wine and pianos ; pop.65,000.

cobra, see SNAKE

Cochin, kō'chin, native state of SW. India , it is in Madras province.

Cochin-China, republic, French Indo-China, SE. of Siam ; area 24,000sq.m ; pop. 5,000,000 ; noted for rice and sugar ; cap. and chief port Saigon.

cochineal, koch-i-nēl', bright scarlet dye used in cooking and for dyeing calico. It is made from the ground-up bodies of cochineal insects (c.70,000 to make 1lb). The insect feeds on cactus, and is found in Central America.

cockatoo, see PARROT

cockchafer, -chā-fĕr, brown beetle common in Europe and Britain ; the larva does much damage to crops.

Cockcroft, SIR JOHN DOUGLAS (1897–), scientist, b Yorkshire ; director of the Atomic Energy Establishment 1946.

cockfighting, sport common in Britain prior to 1849. The birds, specially reared, fought in round pits c.20ft across. The sport of pitting cocks to fight, and breeding and training them for the purpose has on account of its cruelty been prohibited by law in Great Britain since 1849.

Cockney, see ST MARY-LE-BOW

cocktail, short appetising drink, often iced and usually preceding a meal ; com-prises spirits (usually gin) mixed with bitters, sugar and a flavouring ingre-dient ; non-intoxicating varieties include fruit juice.

cocoa, kō'kō, the name of the fruit of the cocoa-tree, from which powdered cocoa is derived. Cocoa was used as a beverage by the Aztecs of Mexico, and Cortes saw the Emperor Montezuma drinking it from a golden goblet 1519. Cocoa clubs were common in London in the 17th century.

The cocoa-tree, c.20ft high, has pink or yellow flowers ; the fruit is a rough pod 5–11in long, growing on a short stalk from branch or trunk. Green, yellow, red, or purple, it encloses 30–40 beans. See PLATE 10

Cocoa is largely grown in the Gold Coast colony, which produces *c*.50% of the world's crop ; also in Ceylon, Java, Brazil, W. Indies and Ecuador (where trees have been attacked by disease greatly endangering future crops). It is manufactured in vast quantities in England, e.g. Messrs Cadbury Brothers Ltd at Bournville (Birmingham). The powder is used as cocoa (without its natural butter) or for chocolate, in which the butter is retained, sugar added, and also some flavouring. Moulded chocolate is sold in bars ; confectionery chocolate is used for making sweetmeats, such as nuts, crêmes and fruits. Cocoa and chocolate are easily digested, and have almost the highest energy-giving ratio of any food, hence their value to explorers.

coconut palm, *päm,* tall, graceful tree (family *Palmae*), native of the E. Indies, but found (especially near the coast) everywhere in the tropics. It is *c*.80ft high, with feathery leaves 20ft long. The nut is enclosed in an elliptical fibre case, and is the source of coir, used in ropemaking ; the kernel (copra) gives oil used in the manufacture of margarine, soap, oil-cake, etc.

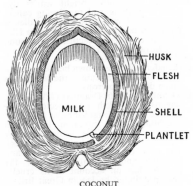

HUSK
FLESH
MILK
SHELL
PLANTLET

COCONUT
The longitudinal section

Cocos or **Keeling Islands,** *kō'kōs,* British possessions since 1857, lying 700m SW. of Batavia; part of Singapore politically; exports include coconuts, copra and oil.

cod, large ocean fish, usually 2–4ft long, spindle-shaped with conspicuous fins, the upper jaw projecting beyond the lower, a barbel on the chin ; back greenish, underparts grey ; weighs 30–50lb ; lays from 3 to 5 million eggs in spring ; shares with the herring the distinction of being our most important food fish. Cod are caught in vast quantities in the North Sea, off the Lofoten Islands, and on the Grand Banks off Newfoundland (April to October). Cod liver oil is especially rich in vitamin A. See PLATES 13 (*bottom*) and 14 (*top*)

C.O.D., i.e. 'Cash on Delivery.' See POST OFFICE

code (1) a statement of law by members in authority of a particular body, e.g military code, highway code ; rules of conduct (code of honour) ; (2) a table of rules used for ' encoding ' information or instructions. For example, you and I might arrange that I will ring you up at 10 a.m. tomorrow, and that if I say ' Bacon ' you will go out and buy me 500 shares in a certain company, but if I say ' Apple ' you will sell for me 250 shares in another company. In this case our arrangement is a *code* and ' Bacon ' and ' Apple ' are *code words.* A code may be secret, in which case its purpose is to enable me to give you instructions secretly : but where there is no need for secrecy, a code may still be useful because it saves time and avoids complications.

Codex Sinaiticus, see BIBLE

codicil, see WILL

coefficient of expansion, see EXPANSION

coelostat, see TELESCOPE

Coeur de Lion, see RICHARD I

coffee, drink made from coffee beans, which are seeds of the evergreen coffee-tree ; exported chiefly from Brazil ; roasted before being ground. Coffee-houses were first opened in London *c*.1652, some taking the place of social, political, or business clubs. See PLATE 11

cognac, see BRANDY

cohort, *kō'hört,* in the Roman army, body of troops forming the tenth part of a legion (i.e. *c*.600 men) ; roughly equivalent to a battalion of infantry.

coinage, see MONEY

coir, see COCONUT PALM

coke, more accurately, gas-coke, residue from the retorts used in manufacturing coal-gas ; is porous, brittle, and contains *c*.80% carbon.

Coke, SIR EDWARD (1552–1634), English lawyer and politician ; became Attorney-General 1594 ; brutally conducted the trials of the Earl of Essex (1600), Sir Walter Raleigh and the Gunpowder Plot conspirators ; opposed James I, and advocated the liberty of Parliament.

Colbert, JEAN BAPTISTE, *kawl-bār'* (1619–1683), French statesman who, in the reign of Louis XIV, vastly improved the country's financial affairs, created a fleet, developed the colonies, and advanced agriculture, though all his improvements were wrecked by an extravagant and foolish court.

Colchester, town, Essex, on R. Colne ; the Roman Camulodunum ; has Roman remains ; noted for its Norman castle. The industries include silk manufacturing and oyster fisheries ; pop.49,000.

Colenso, *kō-len'sō,* village, Natal, S. Africa; taken by the British 1900 during the S. African War ; has a great power-station.

Coleridge, SAMUEL TAYLOR (1772–1834), English poet and talker, *b* Ottery St Mary, Devon ; brought up after his father's death 1781 by an over-indulgent uncle ; educated at Christ's Hospital and Cambridge (1791–94). As a child Coleridge was idle, dreamy and self-centred. His life was marked by a deep emotional instability which showed itself in fickle and contradictory enthusiasms and an incapacity for sustained intellectual effort. It was as a gifted talker that he really shone : he was a man more easily appreciated by friends than as a husband, and his marriage (1795) was not happy.

His life-long friendship with Wordsworth began 1797, and in 1798 they published *Lyrical Ballads*, to which Coleridge contributed *The Ancient Mariner* and other poems. Soon afterwards, Coleridge's health broke down. He began taking opium to soothe the pain he suffered. Later efforts to overcome the habit succeeded, but only at the cost of so much mental and physical suffering that he relapsed. Opium ruined his bodily health and further damped his mental powers. In reading his poetry this should be borne in mind.

Most of Coleridge's poetry has very little logical meaning. It suggests more than it actually says. The effect is created by arranging in metrical patterns words used less for the sake of what they mean than for the feel they have acquired elsewhere ; e.g. (from *Youth and Age*) :

Verse, a breeze mid blossoms straying,
Where Hope clung feeding like a bee—
Both were mine !

His best known poems are *The Ancient Mariner*, *Christabel*, and *Kubla Khan*, which was composed in an opium-dream. Coleridge's poetry belongs to the dream-world. It ignores the realities encountered outside sleep.

Until 1819 Coleridge gave public lectures on philosophy, literary criticism and Shakespeare. They are full of grandiloquent language, and although of little value for their own sake, important in the history of criticism. After 1819, when his son Hartley was disgraced at Oxford, Coleridge gave up writing, but people still came to hear him talk According to Carlyle, Coleridge's talk was mostly ' the mistiest, wide, unintelligible deluge of things ' ; this is probably a shrewd judgment, but there can be no doubt that Coleridge made a tremendous impression on his contemporaries. Lamb described him as ' an Archangel—slightly damaged.'

Coligny, GASPARD DE, *kō-lē-nyē* (1519–72), French admiral, famous as a military reformer ; a devout Protestant, and leader of the Huguenots in the religious struggles of the period ; murdered in the Massacre of St Bartholomew's Eve.

collar-bone, see CLAVICLE

collectivism, see SOCIALISM

collimator, see SPECTRUM

Collingwood, CUTHBERT (1750–1810), British naval commander, *b* Newcastle-on-Tyne ; fought at the Glorious First of June 1794, and Cape St Vincent 1797 ; second in command at Trafalgar (1805) where he led a line of ships in *Royal Sovereign* ; succeeded Nelson ; created Baron Collingwood of Coldburne and Hethpoole in Northumberland. In his last years he planted acorns to ensure a supply of oaks for future warships.

Collingwood, R. G. (1889–1943), English philosopher and historian, Waynflete Professor of Metaphysics at Oxford 1935–41. Collingwood taught that metaphysics is really a historical study of the basic principles assumed in any age by scientists and thinkers. He was distinguished among his contemporaries by the clarity of his writing and by his insistence that philosophy is not a mere game of speculation but an activity of vital importance. His best known books are *Roman Britain* (1932), *Principles of Art* (1938), *Metaphysics* (1940), *New Leviathan* (1942 : morals and politics). His *Autobiography* (1939) is excellent reading.

Collins, WILLIAM WILKIE (1824–89), novelist, *b* London. Son of William Collins, RA, the landscape painter ; long associated with Charles Dickens. On his return from Italy, where he was taken as a boy of 12 by his parents, but later entered a firm of tea traders, but later abandoned his business career for law, being entered at Lincoln's Inn 1846 and called to the Bar three years later. He had no interest in his career, however, and after his father's death he wrote his first book—*The Life of William Collins* which was followed by many others. Best known are his *The Woman in White* ; *No Name* ; and *The Moonstone* (1868), one of the earliest detective stories.

colloid, substance that will not crystallise, e.g. starch, glue, and white of egg. The particles are larger than in true solutions of crystalloids, can be seen by the ultramicroscope as points of light. If a crystalloid and colloid are dissolved in water and poured on to parchment floating on water the crystalloid will go through the parchment but the colloid will remain.

Colmar, *kōl'mär*, French industrial town noted for cotton, silk, calico, wine, etc. ; pop.44,000.

Colne, *kōn*, town, Lancashire ; manufactures printed calicoes and fancy goods ; pop.24,000.

Cologne, *ko-lōn'*, historic city on the Rhine (Germany), *c*.20m S. of the Ruhr ; has many industries, e.g. tobacco, sugar and especially eau-de-Cologne ; centre of rail and river systems ; noted for its superb Gothic cathedral ; suffered immense damage from Allied bombing in World War II ; target for the first RAF 1,000 bomber raid (May 1942), and captured by the US 1st Army 1945 ; pre-war pop.768,000.

Colombia, *kō-lōm'bē-ä*, republic in the extreme NW. of S. America ; has both

Pacific and Atlantic coasts ; area *c.*
461,000sq.m ; pop.9,500,000. The mts.
include three great ranges of the Andes, the
W., Central and E. Cordilleras. There
are tropical forests, also lofty tablelands
with a healthy climate. The rivers
include Câuca, Patia, Magdalena ; the
forests yield dye-woods, medicinal plants,
cedar, mahogany, etc. Among agricultural products are coffee, cotton,
bananas and cereals, and among the
minerals are emeralds, for which
Colombia is world famous ; also gold,
silver, copper, platinum, lead, besides
rapidly increasing supplies of petroleum.
Air services are highly developed. The
language is Spanish , the official
religion RC. Colombia is governed by
a president elected for four years by
direct popular vote.

The name Colombia is derived from
Columbus, who landed 1502, Spanish
rule continuing till a republic was
established by Simon Bolivar 1819 ; cap.
Bogotá.

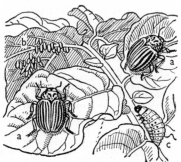

COLORADO BEETLE
(a) *the beetle*   (b) *the eggs*   (c) *the larva*

Colombo, *kō-lŏm'bō,* cap. and chief port,
Ceylon ; has a large artificial harbour
and many fine buildings, including the
hall of the legislative council (1930) ;
port of call for Eastern steamers ;
exports tea ; has been British since
1796 ; pop.356,000.
Colón, *kō-lŏn',* town and port, Panama;
is at the Atlantic terminus of the Panama
Canal ; pop.49,000.
Colonial Empire, BRITISH, see BRITISH
COMMONWEALTH OF NATIONS
Colonial Office, department (in Whitehall)
of the British Government ; is responsible for the colonies ; founded
1851 ; now under the Secretary of State
for the Colonies.
colonisation, see RALEIGH, SIR WALTER ;
RENAISSANCE
Colorado, *kol-ō-rä'dō,* (1) state of USA,
between Utah and Kansas ; area
103,000sq.m ; crossed by the Rocky
Mts, rising to 14,000ft ; has fruitful
valleys and treeless grazing plains, but
its wealth is in its minerals, e.g. gold,

silver, copper, lead, zinc, coal, petroleum.
Irrigation has made much otherwise
barren land richly productive ; cap.
Denver.

(2) River of USA and Mexico, flows
*c.*2,000m to the Gulf of California,
passing through the Grand Canyon ;
now controlled and made available for
irrigation by Boulder Dam (Arizona-
Nevada) 726ft high (highest in the world).
Colorado beetle, pest responsible for much
damage to potato crops ; it is *c.*½in long,
and is yellow with black marks.
colossus, *kō-los'ŭs,* ancient term for a huge
statue, especially that of the sun-god
Helios at Rhodes, a bronze, 100ft high,
probably completed 280BC.
colour, sensation of which we are aware
when the retina of the eye is stimulated
by light within a certain range of
frequencies ; see LIGHT, also EYE

The colours visible by means of the
human eye range from red, through
orange, yellow, green, blue and indigo
to violet ; in printing any of these
colours may be matched by suitably
adjusting the stimulations from the
three primary colours—red, green and
blue-violet ; but to artists and manufacturers of artists' colours the ' primary
colours ' are red, yellow and blue. In
mixing pigments (water-colour or oils) :

brown	= black + red
grey	= black + blue + white
pink	= red + white
chocolate	= black + Venetian red
purple	= blue + crimson
orange	= red + yellow

In photography the basic colours in
illumination (not pigments) are red,
green and blue, and colour photography is achieved either (*a*) by covering
the camera lens with suitable filters,
each cutting out various wave-lengths,
or (*b*) by combining in the emulsion on
the film various chemicals, each of
which is affected by one group of wave-
lengths only (those giving red or green
or blue). The latter is known as the
screen-plate process. A third method
(*c*) is the *Technicolour method* as used in
most coloured cinema films, a process
employing a three-colour analysis with
a beam-splitter camera, i.e. a camera
with a prism that breaks light into its
components or primary colours, each
component falling on a separate negative
film. Panchromatic emulsions are
sensitive to all colours, but have a
tendency to stress the red end of the
spectrum.

The British Colour Council has recently produced a colour ' dictionary '
intended to standardise some 400 colours
and thus to improve interior design.

COLOUR BLINDNESS takes several forms,
one being Daltonism, i.e. inability to
distinguish red from green. The use of
coloured traffic signals makes colour
blindness a serious defect in motorists.

colour blindness, see COLOUR
colour-printing, see PRINTING
colours (*a*) flags or standards of a regiment, at one time carried into battle, now often preserved in our churches ; (*b*) in sports, the cap and blazer worn by those who have excelled in, say, cricket, football, etc. ; known at Oxford and Cambridge as Blues. See BLUE
coltsfoot, plant of the family *Compositae* ; has a bright yellow flower in spring, scaly stalk, and (later) heart-shaped leaves.

COLTSFOOT

Columba, *kō-lum'bä* (521–97), Irish scholar, poet, and saint, *b* County Donegal ; founded a monastery on the island of Iona ; preached to the Picts and converted them to Christianity. See CELTS
Columbia or **Oregon,** *kō-lum'biä,* river of USA, flows 1,400m to the Pacific.
Columbia, district of USA ; centre of the government ; area *c.*69sq.m ; includes the US cap., Washington. The region is usually referred to as D.C., i.e. District of Columbia. It is on the Potomac R.
Columbus, *kō-lum'bŭs,* city and cap. of Ohio, USA ; noted as an industrial and a commercial centre ; pop.306,000.
Columbus, CHRISTOPHER (*c.*1446 or 1451–1506), Italian discoverer, *b* Genoa ; christened Cristoforo Colombo ; son of a weaver ; studied astronomy and geography ; delighted to talk with sailors. As a young man, fired by travellers' tales told by Marco Polo and others, he dreamed of a new route to the East, but for long was unable to find support for his daring schemes. Having married a Portuguese lady of high rank, he sought the help of King John of Portugal, and later laid his plans before the King of Spain, also before Henry VII of England, and Charles VIII of France. Finally, he again appealed to Ferdinand of Spain, enlisting the support of his queen, Isabella.
 Columbus sailed 3 Aug 1492 with three ships (*Santa Maria, Nina* and *Pinta*) from Palos. Many of his crew of 88 were convicts. His ships were unseaworthy. He left Teneriffe 6 Sept., and for five weeks sailed where no ship had ever sailed before. His crew mutinied, but he kept on ; and on the morning of 12 Oct. set foot on the island of San Salvador, now thought to have been Watling I. He went on to Cuba, lost his flagship, left a garrison on San Domingo, and returned to receive a great welcome.
 In Sept 1493 he again sailed west ; explored the W. Indies, and other islands. His third voyage (May 1498 to Dec 1500) was disastrous. He sighted Trinidad and the mainland of S. America, but failed to keep order among the colonists he had earlier left behind, and was taken back to Spain as a prisoner in chains. Pardoned by the king, he sailed for the last time, explored St Lucia and the coast of Honduras, beached his ship in Jamaica, escaped the fury of the natives by prophesying an eclipse, and returned to Spain, 1504, too ill to go to court again. He died at Valladolid in poverty though he had opened the way to the riches of two continents.
 It is strange that this pioneer and adventurer never knew that he had discovered the New World, believing to the end that he had found only a new way to Asia—hence his naming of the W. Indies.
 Read *The Life and Voyages of Columbus,* Washington Irving.
Colwyn Bay, *kol'win,* tourist centre and health resort, Denbighshire ; pop.24,000.
coma, *kō'mä,* state of unconsciousness ; may be due to head injuries or one of many diseases.
combined operations, see ARMY
combustion, burning ; essentially oxidation accompanied by heat and (as a rule) light. The commonest method is by the combination of carbon (in fuel, e.g. coal) and oxygen (in the air) ; *spontaneous combustion* occurs when the internal heat generated by the oxidation of, say, oily rags, damp hay or straw reaches ignition point.
comedy, see DRAMA
comet, *kom'et,* fragment of a shattered planet, or a collection of fragments. Comets travel in immense ellipses round the sun. The head is usually comparatively small, but the tail may extend for millions of miles, and is believed to comprise minute particles of matter blown out of the head by the pressure of radiation from the sun.
 One of the most famous comets is Halley's, discovered by Edmund Halley, *b* London 1656. Halley's Comet completes its orbit in 76 years, and its tail is *c.*20,000,000m in length. It was seen in AD70, and again March 1066, impressing Queen Matilda so much that she, or her helpers, embroidered a comet in the BAYEUX TAPESTRY. The comet's most recent appearance was 1910.
 Other famous comets include Encke's,

first seen 1786, and returning every 3 years ; also Brooke's Comet, which split in two in 1889. A new comet was seen at Cape Town in 1947.

' Comet,' see BELL, H ; SHIPS

comfrey, *kŭm'fri,* plant of moist places ; has hairy stem and hairy narrow pointed leaves with wavy edges. The bell-shaped flowers of the common comfrey (*Symphytum officinale*), in drooping clusters, are yellow or purple.

Comines, PHILIPPE DE, *ko-mēn'* (*d* 1511), French historian ; notable for his *Mémoires* giving word-pictures of France in the days of Louis XI and Charles VIII.

Cominform, name for the Communist Information Bureau, founded 1944 as an agency of Russian control of the Communist countries of E. Europe.

Comintern, short for 3rd Communist International, founded in Moscow 1919, and its successor 1936, a body designed to promote Communism outside Russia.

commando, in World War II, a small, permanent force of picked men, trained and equipped so as to be able to fight on its own in raids and other operations behind the enemy's lines. Commandos often took part in combined operations, as at Dieppe and St Nazaire 1942. Commandos were used against the British by the Boers in the Boer War.

commentator, one who writes notes to explain a book ; a radio commentator who broadcasts a running commentary, i.e. a description of some event such as a football match while it is actually taking place.

commercial traveller, *kom-ŭr'shäl,* representative of a wholesale firm who travels with samples which he displays to retailers ; he usually receives a salary plus a commission, i.e. percentage on everything he manages to sell.

Commodus, LUCIUS AELIUS AURELIUS, cruel Roman emperor AD180–92 ; son of Marcus Aurelius.

Commonwealth, BRITISH, see BRITISH COMMONWEALTH OF NATIONS

Communism, *kom'ū-nizm,* form of Socialism based on the common ownership of all property and production. The theory of Communism was inspired by the writings of Lenin, Engels, and above all Karl Marx.

Marx's political teaching is founded on the philosophical theory of dialectical materialism, which takes it for granted that mind and all its activities are merely the outcome or a reflection of physical processes which affect matter and are governed by natural laws. In Marx's opinion the ' social consciousness ' (i.e. established ways of thinking in any particular society) is caused by changes in the material environment (especially by changes in the methods of production), instead of helping to cause those changes, as most people who are not Marxists think.

This is what underlies Marx's political teaching. Marx held that every develop-

ment in politics can be explained as a stage in the ' class-struggle,' the political struggle between those who work the machines and those who own them. Marx also believed that it was possible to foretell the outcome of the ' class-struggle.'

According to him it would end in victory for the ' workers,' and after that there would be a new classless society.

The fundamental weakness of Marxian doctrine is that no effort is made to state clearly what is meant by ' mind ' and ' matter.' Marxism is important because (as revised by Lenin) it has become the official philosophy of the Soviet Union and of the Communist Party. In Russia the adoption of Marxism has not resulted in the emergence of a classless society in which there is government of the people by the people and for the people. Instead there is government of the people by the Communist Party, and that is a very different thing. See MARX, H. KARL ; SOCIALISM

commutator, see ELECTRICITY

Como, *kō'mō,* Alpine lake, N. Italy ; 31m long ; also a town on the lake, a famous beauty-spot ; pop.52,000.

compass, *kŭm-pās,* instrument for indicating the direction of the magnetic north; known in Europe since *c.*AD1300. The modern mariner's compass rests in a binnacle, the dial or card (attached to a number of light steel strips that have been magnetised) revolves in a bowl swung on gimbals so that it always remains level. The movement is immersed in liquid to prevent excessive swinging. The dial is divided into 4 cardinal points, N., S., E. and W., and each quarter is divided into 8 points. ' Boxing ' the compass means repeating all the points in correct order.

The practical invention of the gyro-compass or gyrostatic compass dates from *c.*1910. Of three types, the Sperry is the most popular, the invention of Elmer Ambrose Sperry (1860–1930), an American. Prior to the invention of radar (which seems likely to eliminate the need of compasses in ships, submarines and aircraft), the Sperry compass was very largely used at sea and in the air. It depends for success on the property of a rapidly revolving wheel to point steadily in one direction. In one type, the wheel, 12in in diameter, weighs 45lb and makes 8,600 revolutions per min. See GYROSCOPE

compost heap, see MANURES AND FERTILISERS

compound interest, see INTEREST

' **Comus,**' *kō'mŭs,* masque by John Milton ; first performed 1634. The name is taken from *kōmos,* Gk word meaning revelry. See MILTON, JOHN

concentration camps, see NUREMBERG ; PRISON

Concepcion, *kŏn-sep-syōn',* important town, S. Chile ; its port, Talcahuans, has a fine harbour ; pop. of both *c.*134,000.

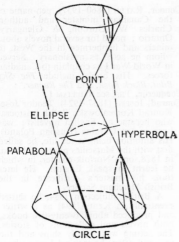

CONIC SECTIONS

concerto, *kön-cher'tō,* musical composition in sonata form designed for a solo instrument (usually piano or violin) with orchestral accompaniment. Masters of the concerto include Haydn, Mozart and Beethoven.

Concord, *kon'kĕrd,* city and cap. of New Hampshire, USA ; has granite quarries ; is a centre of printing and publishing ; pop.27,000 ; also town, Massachusetts, USA ; of great historical interest ; associated with the writers Emerson, Thoreau and Hawthorne.

concrete, see CLAY

concurrent lines, see TRIANGLE

Condé, title of a princely French family related to the Bourbons, and named by its founder (Louis de Bourbon, who *d* 1569) after Condé-sur-l'Escaut, near Valenciennes. The Great Condé was Louis de Bourbon (1621–86), a capable soldier and a friend of Molière.

condenser, may be (*a*) apparatus for cooling water-vapour or steam, usually in air- or water-cooled coils ; or (*b*) electrical condenser which, in its simplest form, is an arrangement of two metal plates separated by air or some other insulating material (the dielectric), the capacity of a parallel plate being $\dfrac{Ak}{4\pi d}$ where A = area of plate, *d* = thickness of dielectric, *k* = its specific inductive capacity.

condominium, see BRITISH COMMONWEALTH OF NATIONS

condor, large S. American bird, the vulture of the Andes ; body over 3ft exclusive of the tail feathers ; wing-span between 8 and 9ft ; plumage black with white round the neck. The condor feeds on carrion, but sometimes flies off with lambs ; it can fly at a tremendous height.

conduction, see HEAT

conductor (electrical), see ELECTRICITY

cone, solid figure, the base being a circle, the summit a point. If cut parallel to the base its section is a circle ; if in other ways an ellipse, parabola or hyperbola, these being known as *conic sections.* See AREA ; VOLUME

Coney Island, island at the SW. end of Long I., New York, USA ; a residential quarter famous for its pleasure beaches.

Confederates, see AMERICAN CIVIL WAR

Confucius, *kon-fū'shi-ŭs* (551–478BC), Latin form of the Chinese name K'ung Fu-tze, the great Chinese thinker. After holding important positions in the state, he devoted *c.*30 years of his life to teaching a band of disciples, and editing the ancient writings of his country. For a time he was governor of the state of Lu, but was so disgusted with the way the country was ruled that he resigned his position, and went travelling for 12 years.

CONFUCIUS *c.*551–478 B.C.

His teaching gave China its philosophy CONFUCIANISM. Strictly speaking this is not a religion but a way of thought. Confucius himself had no religious faith, though he taught that men should worship in the way their fathers had done ; his code of living is found in what are called the *Nine Classics,* and his golden rule is : *Do not do to others what you do not wish them to do to you.* He believed that knowledge is all-important; urged men to study poetry and music, to set a high regard on ceremonial and manners, to honour their ancestors, and to regard the state as supreme. His sayings were summarised by Mencius (372–289BC). Confucianism is now regarded as a traditional religion by some 350,000,000 people, mostly in Asia.

Among sayings of Confucius (from the *Analects*) are
To see what is right and not to do it is want of courage.
The cautious seldom err.
When you know a thing, to hold that you know it ; when you do not know a thing, to allow that you do not know it : this is knowledge.

Congo, *kong'gō,* river of Central Africa ; enters the Atlantic after *c.*3,000m ; drains the Congo Basin, an area over 1,300,000sq.m ; partly explored by Livingstone, Stanley, etc. ; navigable for 95m to Matadi. See BELGIAN CONGO

Congregationalists, members of a Nonconformist religious group in which each congregation is complete in itself, choosing its own minister and looking after its own affairs.

Congreve, WILLIAM, *kon'grēv* (1670–1729), English dramatist, *b* Bardsey, near Leeds, Yorkshire ; wrote *The Old Bachelor, Love for Love,* and *The Mourning Bride* ; but greater than these is *The Way of the World.*

congruent triangles, triangles equal in every respect.

conic sections, see CONE

conifer, see TREES

Coniston Water, lake, Lancashire ; *c.*5m long.

conjunctivitis, *-vī'tis,* inflammation of the *conjunctiva* or mucous membrane lining the inner surfaces of the eyelids, and continued over the white of the eye.

Connaught, *kon'awt,* province of western Eire ; area 6,800sq.m.

Connaught, DUKE OF (1850–1942), British prince, 3rd son of Queen Victoria, Commander-in-Chief in Bombay 1886–1890 ; afterwards in Ireland ; Governor General of Canada 1911–16 ; opened the first Parliament of the Union of S. Africa. His son, PRINCE ARTHUR OF CONNAUGHT (1883–1938), born at Windsor, married Alexandra, Duchess of Fife, their son being Alastair Arthur, Duke of Connaught (1914–43).

Connecticut, *ko-net'i-kŭt,* New England state of USA, with Massachusetts in the N., Rhode I. E., Long I. Sounds S., and New York W. ; temperate climate ; fertile river valleys. Cereals are largely produced, tobacco cultivated in great quantities. Connecticut is a great industrial state ; watch-making is carried on in Waterbury ; hats at Danbury and machinery at Bridgeport. Renowned as a centre of learning and culture.

Connelly, MARC, *kon'el-i* (1890–   ), American dramatist, his play *The Green Pastures* being generally regarded as one of the most original dramatic works produced in USA. It was banned in Britain and Russia, but it is a moving story in which God is portrayed as Negroes imagine Him. Marc Connelly was awarded the Pulitzer Prize 1930.

Connemara, *kon-ē-mä'rä,* W. division of County Galway, Eire ; has wild scenery in mt. areas ; noted for marble.

Connor, RALPH (1860–1937), pen-name of the Canadian minister and author, Charles W. Gordon, *b* Glengarry, Ontario ; noted for several novels about miners and lumbermen in the West, to whom he acted as missionary. Served in World War I as chaplain to Canadian forces. His books include *The Sky Pilot, Black Rock,* and *The Runner.*

Conqueror, THE, see WILLIAM I

Conrad, JOSEPH (1857–1924), Teodor Josef Konrad Korzeniowski, Polish aristocrat who became an English novelist ; was born in the Ukraine (Russian Poland). His ambition being a sea life, he sailed first with the Marseilles pilots, and then, in 1878, on a Norfolk coaster, in which he learnt to speak English. He later took his master's certificate in the British Merchant Service.

A British subject in 1884, he settled eventually in Kent (1894) as a writer, and produced about twenty-five books, both novels and collections of stories. The setting was usually ships and the sea, and often the tropical East ; there is an aroma of strange places about all his work. He was concerned with the qualities of restraint and self-sacrifice, loyalty and courage, particularly among ships' crews. He had the highest powers of description, atmosphere, character-creation and analysis, and a style at once intellectual and sensuous. Partly through a fondness for telling his stories in a roundabout way, out of the mouths of supposed witnesses, he is not an easy writer. Perhaps his masterpiece was *Lord Jim* (1900). Other permanent works are *The Nigger of the Narcissus* ; *Chance* ; *The Secret Agent* ; *Nostromo* ; *Youth* ; and *Typhoon.*

conscription, system under which ablebodied men are liable to be called up for military service ; introduced in World Wars I and II in Britain, and now applying to youths of 18, liable for a period of national service.

Conservation of Matter, see CHEMISTRY ; MATTER

Conservative, see PARLIAMENT

consols, *kon-solz',* short for Consolidated annuities, i.e. public stock formerly in several separate stocks but consolidated 1751 into one portion of the national debt, and bearing interest at 3 %, payable by the Bank of England.

Constable, JOHN (1776–1837), artist, *b* E. Bergholt, Suffolk ; delighted to paint Suffolk scenes ; won fame with his picture *Dedham Vale,* and particularly *Flatford Mill* ; *The Haywain* ; *Salisbury Cathedral* ; and *The Leaping Horse at Dedham Lock.* A pioneer of reality in nature pictures, he was a master in depicting the charm of rural England and the changing panorama of the sky. Though appreciated in France in his lifetime, he died before his own country recognised him as one of her greatest landscape painters. See PLATE XIV

Constance, *kon'stans,* lake between Ger-

FISHING VESSELS

plate 13

Top : Cod fishing off the Gaspe Peninsula, Canada. The annual catch is 35,000,000 codfish. Cod liver oil is rich in Vitamins A and D. (*Canadian National Film Board*). *Bottom :* The fishing-fleet off the Lofoten Is., Norway. (*Picture Post Library*)

plate 14   SEA HARVEST

Top : Fishermen on board their trawler drawing in their nets. (*Picture Post Library*).
Bottom : Crates of fish being dispatched from Halifax, Nova Scotia.
(*Canadian National Film Board*)

MEAT   plate 15

Top : These Canadian Herefords will eventually provide beef for export. (*Canadian National Film Board*). *Bottom :* Rounding-up on the Pampas, Argentine. (*Mrs. T. Muir*)

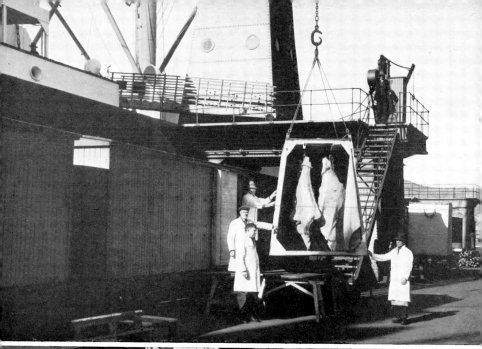

plate 16   FLESH AND HIDE

Top : Much of our meat comes from the Antipodes. New Zealand meat being loaded on to a refrigerator ship. (*N.Z. High Commissioner*). *Bottom :* Cattle-hide supplies the leather used in the manufacture of shoes. (*C.O.I.*)

NEW ZEALAND DAIRY AND SHEEP COUNTRY   *plate 17*

Top : Dairy Cattle grazing round the drinking pool : Otago, New Zealand. *Bottom :*
Behind, in the hills, sheep are pastured.   The Grasmere sheep-run, New Zealand.
(Both *N.Z. High Commissioner*)

plate 18   MILK

Top : Milking cows by modern hygienic methods, Fenton Barns, East Lothian. (*Ian Smith, Esq.*). *Bottom :* The bottling room in a large and modern British Dairy. (*E.N.A.*)

SHEEP *plate 19*

Early morning sheep-droving, North Island, New Zealand. (*N.Z. High Commissioner*)

plate 20 SHEEP IN SCOTLAND

Top : On the high tops of Breadalbane. In winter sheep and cattle are pastured in the glens. In summer they will find grazing higher up. *Bottom :* An Aberdeenshire shepherd driving his flock to market, on the motor-road, near Braemar. (*E.N.A.*)

many and Switzerland ; drained by the Rhine ; well-known beauty spot ; also a German health resort and tourist centre on L. Constance.

Constantine, DONATION OF, document in the form of a decree by Constantine the Great making the pope secular as well as spiritual ruler of Rome and its Western territories. The political power of medieval popes was founded on this document, which appeared to give legal authority to their political claims ; but in 1439 the scholar Lorenzo Valla, apostolic secretary of Pope Nicholas V, showed that the supposed Donation was a forgery. It is now generally admitted that it was made up in the 8th c. to justify church claims that the pope was rightful ruler in the West.

Constantine, KING OF GREECE, *kon'stan-tīn*, (1868–1923), *b* Athens ; ascended the throne 1913 ; deposed 1917 ; returned 1920 ; abdicated 1922.

Constantine the Great (Flavius Valerius Aurelius Constantinus) (AD?268–337), Roman emperor who made Christianity the official religion of the Roman Empire.

At York 306 the troops wanted to make him emperor, and his claim was recognised 307. He had to begin by eliminating possible competitors. In 311 only Maxentius and Licinius were left. Constantine allied himself with Licinius, and crossing the Alps 312 he defeated Maxentius at the battle of Pons Mulvius (Rome). He was now joint emperor with Licinius, and in the West supreme.

Licinius declared war on Constantine 324 but was soon defeated. Constantine was thus at last sole and undisputed emperor of the whole Roman Empire. He decided to move the seat of the government from Rome to Byzantium. The new capital was called Constantinople (Gk *Constantinou-polis*, Constantine's city), and the imperial government was established there 330.

Later in history it became the capital of the Eastern or Byzantine Empire. In order to understand why Constantine moved his government thither from Rome it is necessary to study the history of his dealings with the Christian church.

Constantine owed his success to his soldiers. In the army of the West Christianity was by this time a powerful influence, rather because Christians were well organised than because they were a majority. For this reason, perhaps also because he divined that Christianity could be used to strengthen his empire, Constantine favoured the Christian church and made Christianity the State religion, although he himself was only baptised on his deathbed.

At Milan 313 Constantine and Licinius proclaimed toleration of Christianity throughout the Empire, but Licinius resumed persecution in the Eastern Empire 321. Constantine himself summoned the COUNCIL OF NICAEA 325. His reason for moving the seat of government from Rome was that Rome was the stronghold of the pagan religions, hitherto enjoying privileges denied to Christianity : and Constantinople was founded as a Christian city so that the Christian church might become the dominant religion in fact as in name.

Constantine died 337 fighting against the Persians. His reign is one of the great turning points in history. His reforms perpetuated the division of the Roman Empire into two halves, Western and Eastern, begun by DIOCLETIAN. Later emperors sometimes managed to reunite the divided Empire, but the two halves grew increasingly apart. Both were Christian, each normally had its own ruler. In the Eastern or Byzantine half (roughly the area in which Greek was spoken) the emperor was supreme over the church : in the Western (Latin-speaking) the emperors were weaker and the pope (Bishop of Rome) became all-powerful. The split became final in 395 when the Eastern and Western churches separated as Greek Orthodox and Roman Catholic.

Constantinople, see ISTANBUL

Constantius I (*d* AD306), surnamed Chlorus (the Pale) ; Roman emperor 305–306, father of Constantine the Great ; *d* Eboracum (York).

Constant Proportions, see CHEMISTRY

constellation (Latin *con,* together, *stella,* star), a group of stars appearing close together in the sky, although in fact they are totally unrelated ; such groups have long been named, somewhat fancifully after heroes, goddesses, etc. In the 2nd c. Ptolemy listed 48 constellations : 52 are now recognised among stars visible in the northern hemisphere (e.g. Orion, Leo) ; 36 in the southern sky (e.g. the Southern Cross).

constitution, system of rules recognised by all concerned in politics as the proper way of doing things. For a discussion of some aspects of the British, American and Russian constitutions, see POLITICS.

Constitutions of Clarendon, see CLARENDON

consul, a chief magistrate (*praetor*) in Rome ; an office created 510BC when the two chief magistrates in the city were given high authority for the period of one year, during which time they had the power to inflict the death penalty, to control the spending of public money and, among other things, to summon the senate. After 31BC supreme authority was vested in the emperor, and the consul's office became correspondingly much less important. It ceased altogether AD536.

Each of the three chief magistrates during the French Republic of 1799–1804 was called a consul.

Today the term is applied to an official representative who attends to the business interests of his own country in another land, and generally deals with trading difficulties. He also protects

7

the interests of his own countrymen in the country in question. When there are many consuls of one nationality in a country, the chief is a consul-general.

consumption, see TUBERCULOSIS

continental shelf, see EUROPE

continents, see WORLD

continuum, see RELATIVITY

contour, *kon'toor,* geographical term for the relief of an area ; contour lines pass through points of equal elevation.

contraction, see EXPANSION

contralto, deepest type of woman's voice.

convection, see HEAT

conveyancing, act of legally conveying or transferring land or other property by deeds and documents. This generally entails payment of stamp duty, and is done by barristers or solicitors. Conveyancing is now usually used to describe all property transactions performed by solicitors.

convict, see PRISON

convulsion, involuntary muscular contraction ; a symptom of a variety of diseases, especially of fever in young children.

Conway, town and port, Caernarvonshire.

'Conway,' HMS, see MERCANTILE MARINE

Cook, CAPTAIN JAMES (1728–79), navigator and explorer, *b* Marton, N. Yorkshire, son of a poor farm labourer ; was apprenticed to a grocer, but ran away to sea, joining a ship at Whitby ; sailed to various Scandinavian ports and became mate before joining the Royal Navy 1755. Cook made an Admiralty chart of the R. St Lawrence ; surveyed the coast of Newfoundland, and wrote a book on sailing directions.

Given charge of a Royal Society geographical expedition in the S. Pacific, he sailed 1768 in the *Endeavour,* explored the Society Islands, visited Tahiti, made a chart of the New Zealand coast, and charted the east coast of Australia (then known as New Holland). Having proved that New Guinea was an island, he returned 1770.

His second and greatest voyage (in the *Resolution*) began 1772. He explored the Antarctic regions, Easter I., the Marquesas, Friendly Is. and the New Hebrides, and discovered New Caledonia before returning 1775. In an attempt to find the NW. Passage, he sailed again in the *Resolution* 1776, explored the Sandwich Is. and Hawaii, and was the first Englishman to reach the extreme west of America Returning to Hawaii, he was killed in an attempt to take the native king aboard.

Captain Cook was undoubtedly one of our greatest sailors. Whatever he did he did well. His charts are models of their kind ; his observations, as set out in his fascinating *Journals,* are remarkably accurate. He proved that sailors could remain long at sea without suffering from scurvy if they had plenty of fruit and vegetables. He preserved discipline. He was a modest man of fine character.

His boyhood home at Great Ayton was removed to Melbourne, Australia, 1934, as a memorial to the first Englishman to set foot in Victoria.

Cook Islands, group of coral atolls 1,640m from New Zealand ; the largest Rarotonga, is 26sq.m ; all belong to New Zealand.

Cook Strait, channel between the N. and S. Islands, New Zealand ; *c.*18m wide.

Coolidge, JOHN CALVIN (1872–1933), 30th President of USA ; a Republican ; he said little and was called ' Cautious Cal.'

coolie, unskilled Asiatic labourer, particularly Indian or Chinese ; generally imported to work in rubber plantations and the mines.

Cooper, SIR ALFRED DUFF (1890–), politician, Unionist MP for Oldham 1924–29 ; Financial Secretary to the War Office 1928–29 ; Secretary of State for War 1935–37 ; with Winston Churchill warned Britain of impending peril from Germany 1937 ; Minister of Information 1940–41 ; later British Ambassador to France ; author of several historical works.

Cooper, JAMES FENIMORE (1789–1851), American novelist, *b* Burlington, New Jersey, USA ; was some time in the navy. He was the first author to write sympathetically and vividly of the Red Indians. His books include *The Spy* ; *The Pilot* ; *The Two Admirals* ; and (most popular of all) *The Last of the Mohicans, The Pathfinder,* and *The Deerslayer.*

co-operation (acting together), name given to a movement begun in Rochdale (Lancashire) 1844 by disciples of Robert Owen, the idea being for a group of people to supply their own needs ; a large sum from profits is paid to the members as dividends. The Co-operative Society owns a large number of farms and hotels in the British Isles. Similar societies sprang up in industrial areas. The Co-operative Wholesale Society was formed 1864. There are now some 1,300 retail societies with a total annual turnover of at least £200,000,000. See OWEN, ROBERT

Co-operative Holiday Association, see YOUTH ORGANISATIONS

coot, water bird of the rail family ; frequents British ponds. The plumage is black, but the head of the male has a naked patch. Coots build large floating nests of reeds, etc. The eggs are buff with brown spots.

Coote, SIR EYRE, *koot,* (1726–83) British general, *b* Limerick ; distinguished himself in India 1760.

co-partnership, name for industrial and business experiments whereby workers share in the net profits, and in the control of an undertaking, e.g. Messrs Lever Bros. The principle goes far towards solving difficulties between Capital and Labour.

Copernicus, NICOLAUS (1473–1543), Polish astronomer who propounded the hypothesis, revolutionary in his day, that not the earth but the sun is the centre of our universe. Copernicus was a RC churchman who had travelled and taught in Italy. He early came to the conclusion that the earth has two motions : (1) a daily rotation about its own axis, (2) a yearly revolution in a circular path about the sun. His views were not published until the year of his death ; he rightly feared they would be condemned by the Church, which held that the earth was the centre of God's creation. The Copernican theory was denounced by Luther and Calvin, and the book *De Revolutionibus Orbium Coelestium* was banned in the time of Galileo (1564–1642) by the Roman Church.

In Copernicus' time telescopes did not exist, and it was not possible to make direct observations by which his theory might have been confirmed. The Copernican theory was not widely accepted until attention was drawn to it by Galileo and Kepler.

Cophetua, *kō-fē'tūä*, mythical African king who married a beggar maid, a tale referred to by Shakespeare, and illustrated by Sir Edward Burne-Jones.

Copley, JOHN SINGLETON, *kop'li* (1737–1815), Anglo-American artist, *b* Boston, USA ; settled in London 1775. Painted portraits and historical pictures ; most famous for *The Death of Chatham.*

copper, metal and element, Cu ; atomic weight 63·57 ; atomic number 29 ; the only red metal ; easily hammered and drawn into wire ; excellent conductor of electricity. Probably the first metal used by man, it was common in Europe 4000BC. Copper is mined in USA, Chile, Canada, N. Rhodesia, Belgian Congo, USSR, etc. ; used for electrical apparatus, and in many alloys, e.g. bronze, gun metal, and especially the brasses. With duralumin copper is much used in aircraft. British bronze coins at present contain *c.*95% copper and 5% zinc and tin ; copper sulphate or blue vitriol, $CuSO_4.5H_2O$, is used for making sprays for plants.

copra, see COCONUT PALM

Copts, influential Christian sect in Egypt ; their Church, with the patriarch of Alexandria as its head, preserves ancient ceremonies, but has no crucifix or sacrament. It was among the Copts (2nd and 3rd centuries AD) that the monasteries, or rather the monastic tradition, of the Christian Church first took shape.

copyright, legal right to prevent the copying of literary, artistic, or dramatic works. An original literary work is the copyright of the author for his lifetime, and of his heirs for 50 years after his death. The laws of copyright were revised in 1911 and 1933.

coracle, *kor'akl*, portable fishing boat made of wicker, covered with skins, and large enough to hold only one person ; commonly used by ancient Celtic races in Britain and France, and still employed in the West of Ireland and Wales. A boat of the same type but of bison skin was used in the Upper Missouri by Mandans. The word is of Celtic origin.

coral, *kor'al*, brittle, rock-like shapes, of different colours, forming reefs such as the Great Barrier Reef, which is over 1,200m long and is off the NE. coast of Australia. These are built by minute sea-water creatures (polyps) which take lime from the water. Red coral is valued more than any other and is used largely for making jewellery. As coral cannot grow at a depth of over 40 fathoms and must have a temperature of *c.*20°C, also very clear water, reefs are found only in or near tropical seas.

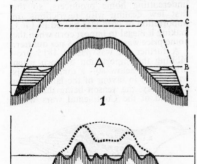

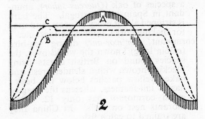

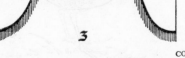

CORAL

(1) Darwin's subsidence theory : (A) *original island with fringing reef* (B) *the same after subsidence with barrier reef* (C) *the present atoll reef*
(2) Admiral Sir W. J. L. Wharton's suggestion : (A) *the formation of an atoll by the weathering down of an island* (B) *of volcanic ash to a platform* (C) *the building thereon of an atoll*
(3) *the formation of an atoll by erosion of land. The seaward edges are protected by the settlement of corals, nullipores, etc.*

Charles Darwin described how atolls —rings of coral—are formed : (1) a volcanic island, (2) polyps begin to build a reef in shallow water, (3) the island sinks and the reef grows higher, and (4) the island vanishes, leaving a reef enclosing a lagoon of calm water. See GREAT BARRIER REEF

Coral Sea, BATTLE OF, naval action fought 1942 in the vicinity of Port Moresby, the US and Australian forces defeating the Japanese, and thus preventing a Japanese invasion of Australia.

Corday d'Armont, MARIE ANNE CHARLOTTE better known as Charlotte Corday (1768–1793), French woman, born near Sées, Normandy. She was at first a supporter of the Revolution, but when Jean Paul Marat had demanded 200,000 executions, she found means of entering his house, and of stabbing him to death while in his bath. She was guillotined.

Cordoba, *kor'dōvä,* city, Spain ; on the R. Guadalquivir ; noted for a mosque used as a church since 1238 ; has skilled silversmiths and goldsmiths ; pop.172,000.

' Corgi,' see BICYCLE

Corinth, ancient Greek city on the isthmus joining the southern peninsula (the Peloponnese or Morea) with the northern mainland of Greece ; famous trading centre from early times ; destroyed by the Romans 146BC ; rebuilt by Julius Caesar ; home of one of the earliest colonies of Christians to whom Paul wrote his Letters to the Corinthians. A small new town now stands 3m from the ruins of the old ; exports currants.

Corinthian order, see ARCHITECTURE

Cork, county in SW. Eire, the largest in Ireland ; has much dairy farming and important fisheries ; the coast has many beautiful bays.

Cork, co.tn and port of County Cork ; on the R. Lee ; has a university college ; railway centre ; manufactures include milling, brewing, woollen goods. Eggs, butter, livestock, hides and provisions exported ; pop.75,000.

cork, outer bark of the evergreen cork-tree, a species of oak (*Quercus suber*), abundant in Spain and Portugal. The bark is stripped about every 10 years, and used for making corks, floor-coverings, etc.

cormorant, *kör'mor-ant,* diving sea-bird (*c.*36in long) known the world over, the species found on British coasts being blackish-brown with a slender crest, and naked yellow patches below the beak ; has 14 tail feathers, whereas the shag or green cormorant has only 12. Cormorants nest on cliffs. In China they are trained to catch fish.

corncrake or **landrail,** brown, insect-eating bird visiting Britain in summer from May to October ; roughly the same size as a partridge ; utters a harsh, creaking call.

cornea, see EYE

Corneille, PIERRE, *kor-nā'y'* (1606–84), French dramatist and poet, *b* Rouen ; abandoned law for play-writing. After being employed by Cardinal Richelieu he won success with his comedy, *Mélite* (1635). His play *Le Cid* 1636 was regarded as the first masterpiece of the French stage ; four superb tragedies followed : *Horace, Cinna, Polyeucte,* and *La Mort de Pompée* ; he also wrote *Le Menteur,* certainly the best French comedy before Molière.

Acknowledged as the creator of French classical tragedy, Corneille's construction owes much to Greece ; but his genius had romantic qualities, and he gives nobility to all his heroes.

cornflower, plant much like the thistle but without prickles. It has bright blue flowers (July and Aug.) crowning a cup of green scales ; the tall stem is often woolly ; leaves strap-shaped ; often cultivated in gardens.

Corn Law Rhymer, see CORN LAWS

Corn Laws, restrictions on the importation of grain to Britain.

In order to understand the need for Corn Laws in the 15th c. it is necessary to remember that before that time the agricultural class formed the largest part of the population, and were able to satisfy the needs of the country with ease.

After the 15th c., however, traders and craftsmen increased to such an extent and the agricultural class decreased so rapidly that it became impossible for the farmers to supply the whole population with grain.

At this point there arose the danger of importation of cheaper foreign corn at the expense of the British farmers. Something had to be done to prevent grain being imported at low prices and undercutting home producers, so the first law dealing with restrictions on importation of corn was passed in 1463, making it illegal to import corn when the home price was less than 6/8 per quarter.

A further act was passed 1815 prohibiting the importation of corn when prices were below 80/- a quarter. This was wholly in favour of the landowning aristocracy, the reason being that after the end of the Continental wars when

THE CORNCRAKE

large amounts of corn were imported from foreign countries, prices fell considerably, and this new act counteracted an otherwise worsening situation.

Later on the 1815 Act was modified by the introduction of a sliding scale by which the amount of duty decreased as prices increased. This sliding scale, however, encouraged much speculation and gambling. Opposition to the system grew up among the urban manufacturing populations, which gained power as the result of the Reform Act 1832, but resistance to the reform movement was maintained by the landowners and the Conservative party. It is extremely doubtful whether the Anti-Corn Law League (Manchester 1839) would have been successful had it not been for the energetic work of Cobden and Bright, the founders, assisted by Ebenezer Elliot (known as the Corn Law Rhymer) whose verses vividly revealed the sufferings of the poor during the Hungry Forties, when the price of bread reached an unprecedented level. All this encouraged a change of ideas in the minds of the people and Prime Minister, and in 1846 the Corn Laws were repealed. Thereafter the large and continued growth of the industrial working class and of the population generally provided a market for home grown grain until 1879, when, with the improvement of transportation, American competition began to make itself felt. This coincided with a series of bad harvests at home, and the combination of these two factors caused British agriculture to suffer a severe set-back, and virtually destroyed the remaining political power of the landowners. Free trade was introduced in 1903.

Cornwall, most south westerly county of England ; noted for deep inlets in its rugged coast ending in Land's End and Lizard Point ; includes the Scilly Isles. Tin and copper are mined, and China clay is worked. Dairy farming and fisheries (pilchard and mackerel) are important ; co.tn Bodmin.

The DUCHY OF CORNWALL, long owned by the Princes of Wales, comprises estates in Cornwall, Devon and London.

Cornwall, BARRY (1787–1874), pen-name of Bryan Waller Procter, poet and biographer ; b Leeds ; best known as a song-writer ; he also wrote memoirs of Charles Lamb and Edward Kean.

Cornwallis, CHARLES, 1st MARQUIS (1738–1805), English general. Though opposed to forcing the American colonists to pay taxes, was sent with reinforcements to N. America, finally surrendering at Yorktown 1781. As Governor-General in India he broke the power of Tippoo Sahib. He suppressed the Irish rebellion 1798, and supported Castlereagh in carrying out the Act of Union.

corona, gleaming irregular halo of rarefied incandescent gases seen round the sun during a total eclipse ; see CHROMOSPHERE

coronation (Lat. *corona*, crown), solemn public ceremony of crowning a monarch. It was adopted by Christian nations from the Jews, whose kings were anciently crowned by the high priest in the Temple. Alfred was the first Anglo-Saxon king to be anointed, i.e. to have oil poured on his head. All English sovereigns from Harold have been crowned in Westminster Abbey. During the coronation ceremony the monarch sits bareheaded in St Edward's chair, takes the oath, and is invested with the royal insignia, including the golden orb, the sceptres, the ring and the crown. Bishops, princes and peers then do homage, and after laying aside the crown the king takes the sacrament.

' **Coronation Scot,**' see RAILWAYS

coroner, law officer in England, usually a solicitor or medical doctor, whose duties include conducting an inquiry (called an *inquest*) concerning (*a*) any death from sudden, unnatural or unknown causes, and (*b*) treasure trove. In Scotland many of the duties of the English coroner are performed by the Procurator Fiscal.

Corot, JEAN BAPTISTE CAMILLE, *kō-rō'* (1796–1875), French artist, *b* Paris ; remembered chiefly as a poetic landscape painter. The Louvre, Glasgow Gallery and the Wallace Collection contain some examples of his work.

corpuscle, see BLOOD

Correggio, ANTONIO ALLEGRI (1494–1534), Italian artist ; a superb master in oils and fresco, and one of the greatest colourists of the Italian schools. He had great powers of invention and a remarkable ability to paint flesh tints ; his treatment of light and shade is excellent. All of his works are characterised by boldness and simplicity ; many of them may be seen in the National Gallery.

Correspondence Colleges, see EXAMINATIONS

corrosive sublimate, see MERCURY

Corsica, *kör'si-kä,* mountainous Mediterranean island near Sardinia ; belongs to France ; area 3,370sq.m ; central district mountainous, but a fertile plain extends to the E. coast ; produces grain, olives, fruit and chestnuts ; cap. Ajaccio, birthplace of Napoleon.

Cortés, HERNANDO, *kör-tez'* (1485–1547), Spanish soldier ; *b* Medellin, Estremadura ; assisted in conquering Cuba 1511 ; he sailed to Mexico, took prisoner the Aztec chief, Montezuma, and won a decisive victory 1520 over the Mexicans who worshipped him as a god ; captured Mexico City against tremendous odds ; founded Vera Cruz. Charles V of Spain rewarded him for his conquests. Cortés spent 10 years exploring the country, but his cruelties caused a rebellion, and he returned to Spain in disgrace. See BALBOA, B. N.

corundum, *kō-rŭn'dŭm,* aluminium oxide, Al_2O_3 ; almost as hard as a diamond, and used for polishing.

cosine, see TRIGONOMETRY

cosmic rays, either charged particles or high-frequency waves with a penetrating power vastly greater than those of X-rays. Probably produced in interstellar space, and thought to be shorter than any waves known in laboratories, they may be responsible, in some degree, for ionising the earth's atmosphere.

Cossacks, *kos'äk*, warlike tribes of the Russian steppes. They serve in the Red Army, as formerly in the armies of the Tsars, as skilled horsemen. They lived at one time in the valleys of the Don and Dnieper.

Costa Rica, see CENTRAL AMERICA

cost of living, economic term in use since July 1914 when the *cost of living index* of an average British working man with a wife and three children was assessed as 100, of which he was assumed to spend 60% on food, 16% on rent, 12% on clothing, 8% on lighting and heating, and 4% on luxuries, etc. By 1947 the cost of living had risen to 203, and in June a new index was introduced, including 24% not accounted for in the first index. By subsidising various essential foods the Government helps to keep down the cost of living. Money from taxation is paid to producers so that they receive more than the public pays in shops, but this method, useful in one way, is dangerous if protracted, since it gives the public a false sense of security.

cost price, see PROFIT

costume, clothing. The keynote of dress among the Greeks and Romans in ancient times was simplicity. Their garments were loosely cut and consisted of a tunic reaching to the knees, over which they wore a wrap.

The greatest change in British dress took place in the 16th c. when the long loose robes were discarded for less picturesque but neater apparel. Men wore closely fitting stockings, gartered below the knee, puffed out thighs, padded jerkins, short but ornate cloaks, ruffs, and high crowned hats. Women wore farthingales (wide spreading skirts on hoops), tight bodices and ruffs.

Very gradually the fashion changed until knee-breeches gave place to ankle length trousers for men, while women wore high-waisted dresses with low-cut necks and clinging skirts.

In later Victorian times dress for men included long trousers, frock coats and waistcoats, stiff upright collars and bowler hats ; umbrellas or walking-sticks were carried. Women wore crinoline dresses, a style popular for almost 15 years ; and what is now a very popular article of clothing was introduced—the blouse ; ' wasp ' waistlines were in fashion and small hats replaced earlier poke bonnets ; handbags came into favour.

In the 20th c. men sometimes wore pullovers ; ' Oxford bags '—wide flannels

—came into vogue as did tweed plus-fours. Women wore hobble skirts, flesh-coloured silk stockings and high heeled shoes. 1930 saw the appearance of knee-length dresses ; then came shorts for hiking and most outdoor sports ; in 1931 beach pyjamas were worn for holidays. Slacks for women became fashionable in 1936, but that fashion was adopted by comparatively few women, except of course later on in the women's services when, in some cases, it formed part of the uniform.

During World War II designers had to adjust their ideas to suit the smaller range of material and dyes available for clothes, and fashions became simple and clean-cut, often bordering on severity.

In post-war years, however, a more feminine touch was introduced in women's clothes, and longer skirts have now been accepted though with reluctance in some cases ; padded shoulders have been replaced by sloping ones ; waists are small ; skirts voluminous, and hemlines sometimes uneven.

Brighter clothes have been introduced for men ; ties are more colourful than formerly ; suede shoes and corduroy material enjoy popularity and are favoured by some who perfer them to more formal wear for every day use. In fact men's clothes generally have taken on a carefree informality never before adopted on such a wide scale in this country.

Cotman, JOHN SELL (1782–1842), artist, *b* Norwich ; famous for his water-colours, landscapes and architectural etchings.

Cotopaxi, world's highest active volcano (19,600ft) in the Andes, Ecuador, S. America. It is a perfect cone except for the rugged summit, and the gleaming whiteness of its snow is often aglow with blood-red reflections from the glare of its seething crater ; ascended first by Reiss (1872) ; first to reach the crater was Whymper (1880).

Cotswold Hills, *kots'wōld*, limestone hills, mostly in Gloucestershire ; once noted for their breed of sheep (now very scarce) ; highest peak 1,134ft (Cleeve Cloud).

cotton, the fleecy fibre attached to the seed of the cotton plant, used in the manufacture of cotton thread and other products.

Cotton seeds are sown annually, and the cotton is gathered about seventy days after the flowers appear.

Indian cotton (little used by British manufacturers) is exported to China and Japan. Cotton is grown in Kenya, Nyasaland, Tanganyika and Australia ; but especially in Egypt and in the southern states of the USA.

After the cotton has been gathered it is separated from the seeds by a mechanical process ; then, as cotton wool, it is packed to be sent to the mills, where it is spun, woven and made

(left) A typical example of picturesque Elizabethan dress (right) Early 18th-century fashions included farthingales for women.

(left) Clothes became simpler in the early 19th century (right) Ankle-length trousers for men and crinolines for women were worn in mid-Victorian times.

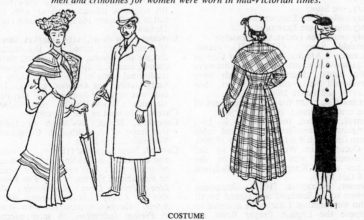

COSTUME

(left) In the early 20th century fashion dictated 'wasp' waistlines for women and bowler hats for men (right) 1949–50 clothes for women have button and pleat details on coats, jackets and skirts.

175

into cloth. Besides making thread and cloth, cotton can be used to provide a number of useful articles used in everyday life, such as cord and paper, although the increasing popularity of rayon is a serious competitor to cotton.

Lancashire became a great centre of cotton-spinning because (*a*) its enterprising people realised the importance of cotton before others did ; and (*b*) because it had abundant water-power when this was needed for driving machinery in the days before steam ; (*c*) the climate (west of the Pennines) is naturally moist, thus allowing the cotton threads to be drawn without snapping ; and (*d*) it is close to the sea, thus giving ready access to supplies from USA and Egypt, etc. See PLATES 23–25, 27 (*top*)

Prior to the end of the last century Lancashire had almost a monopoly of the cotton industry, exporting fabrics to nearly every part of the world, but many other countries now manufacture their own cotton goods, hence a decline that has caused much unemployment and suffering. Improved cotton fabrics and the mixing of cotton with artificial threads has recently brought about a revival.

Coulomb, CHARLES AUGUSTIN DE, *koo-lon'* (1736–1806), French scientist ; he investigated the laws of electricity and magnetism . his name now stands for the unit of quantity in electricity. See COULOMB ; ELECTRICITY

coulomb, *koo-lom'*, practical unit of quantity in electricity ; defined as the quantity of electricity which passes when one ampere flows for one second, or the quantity of electricity conveyed in one second by the current produced by an EMF of one volt acting in a circuit having a resistance of one ohm.

councillors, see ELECTION ; LOCAL GOVERNMENT

county, see SHIRE

county college, see EDUCATION

county council, see ELECTION

county court, see LOCAL GOVERNMENT

Courtauld, SAMUEL (1793–1881), manufacturer, *b* Albany, USA, son of George Courtauld, who introduced silk-throwing into Essex. Messrs Courtaulds later developed the invention of rayon. See RAYON and PLATE 26

court martial, court for trying members of the armed forces ; there is no jury.

Courtrai, *koor-trā*, town on the R. Lys, Belgium ; manufactures lace and table linen for which it is famous ; pop.38,000.

Occupied in World War I by the Germans, it was recaptured by the Allies under King Albert of Belgium (16 Oct 1918).

Covenant, NATIONAL (1638), document drawn up in Scotland and signed by all who were against Charles I's attempt to impose the English Prayer Book on Scotland ; it affirmed the willingness of the Church of Scotland to uphold Royal Authority, but on condition that the king should respect the independence of the Church of Scotland in matters of Church Government. In the great Civil War the Covenanters ultimately took sides against Charles I, because they considered that he had broken the Covenant. Charles I surrendered to the Covenanters in May 1646, whereupon he was handed over to the commissioners of the English Parliament, after he had refused to accept the *Solemn League and Covenant* (see COVENANTERS). After the Restoration of the monarchy (1660) the Presbyterian form of church government was by law abolished in Scotland, and those of the Covenanters who resisted these laws were subjected to savage persecution.

The SCOTTISH COVENANT of 1949 is a document affirming loyalty to the Crown of the United Kingdom, but pledging its adherents to do all in their power to obtain parliamentary Home Rule for Scotland. In the first 6 months of its existence the 1949 Covenant was signed by 1¼ million people, that is to say, over a third of the electorate in Scotland.

Covenanters, *kŭv-e-nan'tĕrs*, Scottish political party demanding religious liberty. Archbishop Laud ordered the Scots to worship in the English fashion 1637 ; this led to rioting, notably in St Giles's Cathedral, Edinburgh, when JENNY GEDDES, a vegetable seller, hurled a stool at the dean's head as he began Laud's new order of service. The Scots and the English Roundheads signed the *Solemn League and Covenant* 1643, revoked 1662, after which the more determined Scottish Presbyterians (known as Covenanters) held to their beliefs at the peril of their lives. They attended meetings (conventicles) on lonely moors, especially in Ayr and Lanarkshire ; were attacked by dragoons ; persecuted without mercy, but held to their faith till religious toleration came with the fall of the Stuarts 1688. See DRUMCLOG ; DUNBAR

Coventry, *kov'en-tri*, city, market town, Warwickshire ; noted for the manufacture of ribbons, cars, bicycles, aeroplanes, electrical apparatus and rayon ; traditional scene of the 11th c. story of Lady Godiva (see GODIVA, LADY). The city was severely damaged by German air-raids in World War II ; pop.243,000.

Coventry, to send to, see BOYCOTT

Coverdale, MILES, *kŭv'ĕr-dāl* (*d* 1569), translator of the Bible, *b* Coverham, Yorkshire. See BIBLE

Coward, NOEL, *kow'ĕrd* (1899–   ), actor and dramatist, *b* Teddington ; producer of many plays and reviews, for which he has written the music, e.g. *The Young Idea* ; *Private Lives* ; *Cavalcade* ; *Design for Living* ; *Bitter Sweet* ; *Blithe Spirit*. He has written his own story in *Present Indicative*. A later success was his play *Brief Encounter*.

Cowes, *kows*, seaside town and watering-place, I. of Wight ; noted for ship-

building, especially yachts ; HQ of the
Royal London Yacht Club. Edward VII
presented the former royal residence,
Osborne House, to the nation as an
officers' convalescent home ; Cowes
now builds aircraft.

Cowley, suburb of Oxford, noted for Lord
Nuffield's motor-works.

Cowper, WILLIAM, *koo'-* ; *kow'-* (1731–
1800), poet, *b* Great Berkhampstead,
Hertfordshire. Cowper's mother died
when he was six, and the shock affected
his whole life. Called to the Bar 1754,
he made little headway in his profession.
In 1763 he was disturbed by the prospect
of being interviewed for an appointment
as Clerk in the House of Commons.
He had a nervous breakdown and tried
to take his own life. Later he was befriended by a widow (Mrs Unwin) and
her daughter, who looked after him at
Olney. Here in collaboration with his
friend the Rev John Newton he wrote
and published the *Olney Hymns.* After
a further nervous breakdown 1773–76,
he obtained success 1782 with a second
volume of poems (including the ballad
John Gilpin), and in 1785 he followed
this with the *Task*, a more ambitious
work. In 1786 he was granted a pension of £300 a year, and began work on
his translation of Homer (published
1791). From 1794 until his death 1800
he was more or less insane.

Cowper's poetry has the form and,
despite his fits of madness, the clarity
of classical poetry, combined with a
tenderness of feeling foreshadowing the
romantics. His language is graceful and
pure, and his work is delightful to read.
Here is a sample of it (from the *Winter
Walk at Noon*) :

The night was winter in his roughest
    mood :
The morning sharp and clear. But
    now at noon
Upon the southern side of the slant
    hills,
And where the woods fence off the
    northern blast,
The season smiles, resigning all its
    rage.

cowslip, plant of the family *Primulaceae* ;
has wrinkled, spoon-shaped leaves springing directly from the root, and in spring
a mass of drooping, funnel-shaped yellow
flowers.

Cox, DAVID (1783–1859), artist, born near
Birmingham ; son of a blacksmith ;
noted for his water-colour landscapes,
many of them Welsh scenes.

coyote, *kī-ōt'*, prairie wolf of western
N. America ; has long fur and a bushy
tail ; usually lives in a burrow.

coypu, *koi'poo*, S. American aquatic
rodent with webbed hind-feet ; is rather
like a small beaver ; lives on roots,
water-plants, etc.

CP, short for Communist Party.

CPR, see CANADIAN PACIFIC RAILWAY

Cr, chemical symbol for chromium.

crab-apple, see APPLE

Crabbe, GEORGE (1754–1832), English poet,
b Aldeburgh, Suffolk ; composed poetry
in his leisure hours. Included among
his works are *The Village, The Borough,*
and *The Library.*

Cracow, city, Poland ; on the R. Vistula.
Near by is KOSCIUSKO HILL, a mound
built in honour of Kosciusko, the
famous soldier ; severely damaged by
enemy invasion during World War II ;
manufactures textiles, machinery, etc. ;
pop.259,000.

Craik, DINAH MARIA, *krāk* (1826–87),
English novelist, *b* Stoke-on-Trent ;
best remembered for her story *John
Halifax, Gentleman.*

cran (of herring), 37½ imperial gallons ;
roughly 750 fish.

Cranbourne, VISCOUNT, *kran'born* (1893–
), MP for Dorset 1929–40 ; created
a peer and became spokesman in the
Lords for the Foreign Office 1940 ;
Lord Privy Seal 1942 ; Dominions
Secretary 1943.

crane, mechanical device for lifting heavy
objects and putting them down where
required ; may be (*a*) jib, or (*b*) bridge
cranes.

The simplest example of (*a*) may often
be seen in a stonemason's yard, the jib
being simply a stout pole leaning forward
from the base, and having a rope passing
over a pulley at the top. The rope is
wound on a geared drum by means of a
handle. The reach of the jib is varied
by tilting. Larger jib cranes have jibs
of latticed girders, and power provided
by steam engines, electric motors, etc.,
some types, e.g. those at docksides,
lifting as much as 200 tons 175ft.

Of type (*b*) a common form is the
overhead gantry, the carriage or gantry
carrying the hoisting gear and engine
running on rails on the crossbar of an
H-shaped overhead steel framework,
and the crossbar itself being able to
travel along the sides of the H frame
from one end to the other of the machine
shop or yard. Another type of bridge-
crane is the hammerhead. The gantry
runs on a horizontal framework which
swivels on a vertical base. Such cranes
may lift over 250 tons. The snatch-
block or hook of a crane is sometimes
replaced by an electromagnet.

crane, wading bird with long legs, neck,
and bill ; has powerful wings ; noted
for its long migratory flights to Egypt
and India where it spends the winter ;
once common in the English fens, now
rare.

crane-fly, popularly known as daddy-longlegs, large two-winged insect. The
larvae, known as leather-jackets, are
destructive pests.

Cranford, see GASKELL, MRS ; KNUTSFORD

Cranmer, THOMAS (1489–1556), English
churchman, *b* Aslockton, Nottinghamshire ; proved useful to Henry VIII,
who made him Archbishop of Canterbury 1533. Cranmer declared Henry's
marriage with Catherine of Aragon to

7*a*

be invalid ; did much to abolish old Church ceremonies ; ordered the destruction of images, and greatly advanced the Reformation in England. In Edward VI's reign he introduced two prayer books, the second (1552) owing its beauty of language very largely to him. For his support of the cause of Lady Jane Grey he was imprisoned in Mary's reign.

All his life he had been weak-willed, and though he had long contended that the pope was not the supreme authority, he pretended in fear of death to believe this. At last he found new courage, and calmly denied that this was his true conviction. He was hurried to the stake at Oxford, thrusting first into the flames the hand with which he had earlier signed the recantation.

Cranwell, parish and village, Lincolnshire, 4m from Sleaford ; has an RAF College.

cravat, a tie for the neck made of muslin or linen edged with lace ; name given by the French to the scarf worn by Croatian soldiers enlisted in the royal Croatian regiment in the reign of Louis XIV.

crèche, *krāsh,* public day-nursery where the very young children of poor mothers are fed and cared for. The idea began in Paris 1844. Many day-nurseries are staffed by voluntary workers, but others are run by local authorities. The present day crèche is a nursery school where children are left in the hands of trained nursery workers while their mothers are away all day.

Crécy, BATTLE OF, *kres'i ; krā'-sē,* battle between the English (Edward III) and the French (Philip VI), 26 August 1346, when the English gained a great victory ; the longbow was used with much success by the English. Crécy is a village near Abbeville, N. France.

credit system, see MONEY

creed (Latin *credo,* I believe), short statement of fundamental points in Christian belief, acceptance or profession of a set creed being often made a condition for admission to membership of a particular church. The *Apostles' Creed* is thought to have been in existence before AD250. The ' Nicene ' Creed is in reality a later expansion of that adopted by the Council of Nicaea (325) : its insistence on the doctrine of the Trinity is a reaction against the Arian heresy, then at its height. The earliest creeds, those found in the New Testament, are much simpler, e.g. ' if thou shalt *confess with thy mouth* the " Lord Jesus " '—i.e. simply that Jesus is Lord—' and shalt *believe in thine heart* that God raised him from the dead, thou shalt be saved ' (Romans x.9).

The creed of the Church of England is set forth in the *Thirty-Nine Articles* ; that of the Church of Scotland in the *Westminster Confession* and the *Shorter Catechism.*

cremation, custom of burning the dead ; usually the ashes are collected and buried in jars or urns. The practice, common in the Bronze Age, was followed by the ancient Greeks and Romans, and is normal in India among the Hindus. In recent years the custom has been revived in USA and Britain. There are crematoria in most large towns in the British Isles. The practice of burying the dead unburnt is known as inhumation.

Cremona, *krē-mō'nä,* town, N. Italy ; on the R. Po ; noted for its 12th c. cathedral, numerous churches and palaces ; famous also as the home of Amati, Stradivarius and Guarneri, violin-makers; pop.63,000.

Creole, see HAITI

creosote, *krē'ō-sōt,* mixture obtained by distilling (*a*) coal-tar, giving the ' heavy oil ' used for preserving timber ; and (*b*) wood-tar (usually beech), with valuable medicinal properties.

cresols, constituents of coal-tar. The hydroxytoluene, $CH_3.C_6H_4.OH$, is much used as a liquid disinfectant.

Crete, *krēt,* large Mediterranean island (sometimes called Candia), in the S. Aegean Sea ; area 3,300sq.m ; mountainous but with fertile valleys ; warm climate ; under Greek rule since 1913 ; remains of ancient civilisation are at the palace of Knossos ; produces grain, wool, olive oil, flax, silk, fruits, fish, etc. ; cap. Canea ; the island was attacked by German airborne troops during World War II ; pop.336,000. See AEGEAN CIVILISATION

cretonne, *krē-ton',* strong cotton cloth printed on one or both sides, though sometimes with a woven pattern ; named from Creton, Normandy. This furnishing fabric has replaced the old-fashioned glazed chintz.

Creusot, see LE CREUSOT

crevasse, *kre-vǎs',* fissure or crack in a glacier.

Crewe, *kroo,* municipal borough, Cheshire ; noted for immense railway workshops ; also as a railway junction ; pop.55,000.

cricket, England's national summer game, possibly evolved from a game played on village greens in the 13th c.

Modern cricket may be said to have begun with the founding of the Hambledon Club *c.*1750, but cricket became a great national game only with the foundation of Lord's Cricket Ground, and the formation of the Marylebone Cricket Club (MCC), now the governing body of cricket the world over. Lord's, established first in Dorset Square, London (1787), has been at St John's Wood since 1814. The first Gentlemen *v.* Players match at Lord's took place 1806 ; the first Oxford *v.* Cambridge match 1827 ; the first recorded Eton *v.* Harrow match (in which Lord Byron played) 1805.

County cricket dates from *c.*1850. Though cricket is popular throughout the British Commonwealth, it is not played elsewhere. English teams visited Australia 1862–78, and the first Australian team to visit England came in 1878, and defeated the MCC by 9 wickets.

Test match cricket began 1880, when the first England v. Australia match was played, the first Australian victory being gained at the Oval 1882, with W. G. Grace batting for England. This was the occasion for the joke about 'the Ashes,' someone writing afterwards that the 'body' of English cricket would be cremated, and the ashes taken to Australia ; hence 'to win the Ashes' means to win the series.

Besides Lord's, famous cricket grounds include the Kennington Oval ; Old Trafford, Manchester ; Trent Bridge, Nottingham ; Bramall Lane, Sheffield ; Headingley, Leeds ; the Melbourne Ground, Sydney Oval (Australia), and the Wanderers' Ground at Johannesburg.

Famous cricketers include F. W. Lillywhite, C. G. Taylor, George Parr, Reginald Hankey, Alfred Mynn, V. E. Walker, W. G. Grace, who holds a unique place in the story of English cricket ; Ranjitsinhji, who became Jam Sahib of Nawanagar ; C. B. Fry, George Hirst, Albert Trott, T. Hayward, W. Rhodes. More recent exponents of the game include Sir Don Bradman, Leonard Hutton, W. R. Hammond, Hedley Verity, Maurice Turnbull, R. T. Simpson, H. Halliday, Herbert Sutcliffe, C. Washbrook, H. Larwood, Jack Hobbs, W. H. Ponsford, and the youthful Denis Compton.

For rules of the game consult *Wisden Cricketers' Almanack*.

cricket, insect closely related to the grasshopper ; the house cricket (*c.*1in long, pale yellow with brown) often infests bakehouses, kitchens, etc., and makes its chirping sounds by movement of the wing-covers. There is also the field cricket and mole cricket, the latter being confined to the south of England.

Crimea, *krī-mē'ä,* peninsula of the Black Sea ; linked to the mainland (USSR) by the Perekop isthmus ; area *c.*10,000sq.m ; has been Russian since 1783. It is fruitful in the S., where vines, olives, mulberries and cereals are cultivated ; scene of bitter fighting in World War II, and (1945) of the Yalta conference attended by Churchill, Roosevelt and Stalin.

Crimean War, attempt 1854–56 by England, France and Turkey to prevent Russia gaining too much power in E. Europe. Badly mismanaged from the first, the war chiefly centred in attacks on the fortress of Sebastopol, and was notable for the pioneer work of Florence Nightingale, though she and her nurses could do little to combat suffering due to lack of supplies, intensely cold weather, and disease (responsible for 15,700 of the 19,600 British lives lost). Another feature was the gallant charge of the Light Brigade (see BALACLAVA). The Russians were finally forced to abandon Sebastopol, and a peace was signed (1856) without actual advantage to either side.

crinoline, *krin'ō-lin,* was originally a fabric used for stiffening, made of linen, cotton, or horse hair, later applied to a skirt expanded over a frame worn *c.*1854.

Cripps, RT.HON. SIR STAFFORD (1889–), British statesman ; Labour MP for E. Bristol 1931, but expelled from the Labour Party 1939 ; Lord Privy Seal and Leader of the House of Commons 1942 ; Ambassador to USSR, he later attempted to solve the problem of government in India. He was President of the Board of Trade in the Labour Government 1945 ; appointed Minister of Economic Affairs 1947, his task being to lead a recovery drive at the moment when the gap between imports and exports was assuming alarming proportions. Later he became Chancellor of the Exchequer, and in 1949 devalued the pound sterling.

In Oct 1950 Sir Stafford resigned the Chancellorship owing to ill-health, being succeeded by Mr Hugh Gaitskell.

Crispin, ST (*d c.*287), patron saint of shoemakers. A legend relates how two brothers of noble Roman family, Crispin and Crispinian, made their way to Soissons, where they preached to the people and made their living by shoemaking. They were condemned to death by Emperor Maximianus. St Crispin's day is commemorated on 25 October, which is also the anniversary of the Battle of Agincourt 1415.

critical angle, see LIGHT

Croatia, see YUGOSLAVIA

Croce, BENEDETTO, *krō'chä* (1866–), Italian philosopher, *b* Pescasseroli (Aquila) ; famous as the learned author of many books on beauty, ethics, etc.

crocodile, large lizard-like reptile with horny skin. Crocodiles which are found in the rivers and lakes of Central America, Africa and India may be 20–24ft long. The gavial (an Indian crocodile) will attack land animals.

ALLIGATORS are common in S. American rivers ; the caiman or cayman, a S. American alligator, is *c.*14ft.

crocus, *krō'kŭs,* small plant (family *Iridaceae*) introduced into Britain from W. Asia and the Alps 1605. The flower is yellow, white, purple, or variegated.

Croesus, *krē'sus* (595–546BC), King of Lydia, country of Asia Minor ; was extremely wealthy ; decided to go to war against Persia, and was told by the Oracle at Delphi that if so he would ruin an empire—actually, as it proved, his own.

Crome, JOHN (1768–1821), artist, *b* Norwich ; often called 'Old Crome' to distinguish him from his son who was also an artist ; founder of Norwich School of Artists, 1805 ; excelled in landscapes.

Crompton, SAMUEL (1753–1827), English cotton spinner, *b* Firwood, near Bolton, Lancashire. Invented the mule (1779) a machine for spinning muslin yarn ; profited little from his invention, apart from a grant of £5,000 from Parliament, 1812.

Cromwell, OLIVER (1599–1658), soldier and statesman, *b* Huntingdon ; son of a well-to-do landowner ; inherited his father's estates while at Cambridge ; elected MP for Huntingdon before he was 30 ; became a fervent Puritan, and while eminently practical had a hint of the mystic. About 5ft 10in in height, he was broad and strong, with an impressive head and heavy features with several warts and pimples.

In the early days of the Civil War, Cromwell supported Parliament, raised forces in his own district, commanded a troop of horse at Edgehill (1642), and later trained soldiers who were so well disciplined that they became known as Ironsides. Parliament's new Model Army, organised by Cromwell, but commanded by Sir Thomas Fairax, won the battles of Marston Moor and Naseby. Parliament then attempted to bring the king to terms. Cromwell on behalf of the army forced Parliament to stiffen its attitude to the king. In December 1647 the king rejected Parliament's terms, and made an agreement with Scotland, whereby Scotland would fight for the Crown if the Crown allowed the Scots to be Presbyterians. In this way the second Civil War began (1648). Having crushed a Welsh rising and destroyed the Scots at Preston, Cromwell realised that only the death of Charles I could put an end to the struggle. Being appointed a member of the High Court of Justice which tried the king, he was fourth to sign the death warrant.

OLIVER CROMWELL 1599–1653

After the execution of Charles I the kingdom was declared a Commonwealth and was governed for the time being by a Council of State, of which Cromwell was a member. There was great unrest. Cromwell was sent to restore order in Ireland, where he crushed all resistance to the new Commonwealth by his terrible massacres at Drogheda (1649) and at Wexford. His harshness has made his name hated by Irishmen ever since ; it sprang from his determination that Catholic Ireland should not be, any more than Presbyterian Scotland, a menace to the supremacy of England. In 1650 he was marching against the Scots (Scotland had proclaimed Charles II king in return for his recognition of Presbyterianism) and routed them at Dunbar (3 Sept 1650), but did not finally quell them until the battle of Worcester (at which Charles himself was present) 3 Sept 1651. Leaving Monk to restore order in Scotland, Cromwell returned to London as Captain-general of the Army and was voted an income of £4,000 a year. In 1652 Parliament unwisely plunged the country into war with the Protestant Dutch, but Cromwell brought this to an end as soon as possible, and allied himself with France against Spain. Meanwhile he built up the finest fleet in the world, the foundation of our modern supremacy at sea.

At home Cromwell found Parliament incapable. With a file of musketeers (1653) he sent the so-called Rump scurrying home ; and though his Barebones Parliament drew up an *Instrument of Government* and appointed Cromwell Lord Protector of the Commonwealth, he dismissed it 1655. Provision was made for the government of Ireland and Scotland. A Parliament called 1656 offered him the crown, but he refused it, and by 1658 this Parliament, too, was dismissed. Thus, Cromwell ruled much as an autocrat—almost as a dictator—but he ruled wisely, was tolerant, evaded plots and revolutions, gave the people considerable liberty of conscience, kept order with a stern hand, raised English prestige abroad to unknown heights, and while Protector saw to it that England was the guardian of the Protestant faith.

Energetic, fervent, a lover of music, he was a great student of the Bible. He was good-humoured, kindly except when stern measures seemed necessary, and remarkably understanding. John Milton called him ' our chief of men.'

Cromwell wore himself out in his country's service, dying 3 Sept. His body was buried in Westminster Abbey, but at the Restoration it was dug up and hanged at Tyburn.

Of his four sons, Richard (1626–1712) who became Lord Protector of England was totally unfitted for such office, and lived in retirement from 1660.

Cromwell, RICHARD, see CROMWELL, OLIVER

Cromwell, THOMAS, EARL OF ESSEX (*c*.1485–1540), English statesman, *b* London. Henry VIII's minister, after the fall of Cardinal Wolsey, he was in royal favour, enriched with lands, given power over the Church, and is remembered for carrying out the suppression of the monasteries ; created an earl 1540. The reason for his execution was the failure of Henry's marriage with Anne of Cleves, which he helped to bring about.

Cronin, ARCHIBALD JOSEPH, *krō'nin* (1896–), Scottish doctor of medicine and author ; *b* Dumbartonshire. Well known books include *Hatter's Castle* (1931) ; *The Citadel* ; *The Stars Look Down,* and *The Keys of the Kingdom.* Also known as a playwright.

Crookes, SIR WILLIAM (1832–1919), English chemist and physicist, *b* London ; won fame with his discovery of thallium ; investigated radioactivity, and invented the Crookes tube. Received many public and scientific honours.

crooning, see SINGING

Cross Fell, one of the highest peaks (2,930ft) of the Pennines.

croup, *croop,* inflammation of the larynx ; occurs most frequently in children from 2 to 5.

crow, name of a family of birds (*Corvidae,* Latin *corvus,* raven) common in Britain, having black or black and white plumage, strong beaks, and laying greenish-blue eggs spotted or blotched with brown.

The crow, or carrion crow, is *c.*18in long. Usually solitary, or with one mate, it lays 4–6 eggs in a lofty nest.

Other members of the *Corvidae* include (*a*) *hooded crow,* more common in Scotland than in England, (*b*) *raven,* with purple reflections ; may be 25in long, (*c*) *rook,* similar to the crow, but distinguished by a whitish patch under the beak ; lives in colonies in tall trees, (*d*) *jackdaw,* smaller than the crow, has greyish neck and white eyes ; builds in towers ; is a notorious thief, (*e*) *jay,* handsome brown bird with a grey and

CROWS

(*below*) *the Rook*   (*above*) *the Jay*

black throat and vivid blue wings ; lays 3–7 eggs, (*f*) *magpie,* black with greenish-blue reflections and much white on the underside ; has a long tail ; lays 6–7 eggs in a domed nest of sticks and mud.

Crown Jewels, see LONDON

Croydon, town, Surrey ; now a suburb of London ; chiefly residential ; famous for its airport, opened for civil traffic 1920 ; pop.243,000.

crucifix, cross bearing a figure of Christ crucified.

Cruikshank, GEORGE, *kruk'shangk* (1792– 1878), English artist and book illustrator ; *b* London ; won fame with his illustrations (mostly etchings) for the works of Defoe, Scott, and especially Dickens.

Crusades, period of more or less continuous warfare 1096–1272 in which the armies of Western Christendom sought to acquire territories in Palestine and the Near East, where at that time a struggle for supremacy was in progress between the Greek or Byzantine Empire (Eastern Christendom) and the Seljuk Turks (Islam). The Crusades began when the Byzantine Empire appealed to the Pope for help.

Many of the Crusaders were genuinely inspired by the religious ideal of redeeming the Holy Land from non-Christian ownership, but the heavy cost of the Crusades was borne largely by Italian merchants who wanted to obtain trading-rights in the Near East, and even in blessing the First Crusade Urban II (the Pope) declared that in Palestine, by wresting the land from the ' wicked ' race of Moslems, the crusaders would find relief from the land-shortage, starvation and miseries of Europe, by reason of which ' you now murder and devour one another.' This shows that not only religious idealism but also European land-hunger was one of the driving forces of the Crusades.

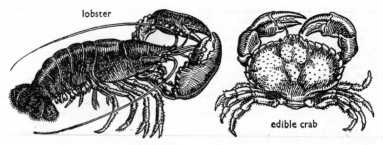

lobster

edible crab

CRUSTACEANS

The 1ST CRUSADE (1096–99) ended with the establishment of a Norman Kingdom in Jerusalem and of Norman principalities in Syria. Led by Louis VII (France) and Conrad III (Germany), the 2ND CRUSADE (1145–48) was a disastrously unsuccessful attempt to check Moslem inroads (under Nureddin), which culminated in the capture of Jerusalem (1187). In the 3RD CRUSADE Richard I (Cœur de Lion) and Philip Augustus (France) acted mainly on their own without much prompting from the Pope ; Acre was captured 1191 and a patched-up peace concluded with Saladdin. Meanwhile, Richard I had founded a Latin Kingdom in Cyprus. In other respects the 3rd Crusade was unsuccessful.

Byzantium and the Crusaders had long been at odds over the overlordship of reconquered territories in Syria and Palestine. The 4TH CRUSADE (1202–4) set out to attack Moslem Egypt but turned aside to invade Christian Byzantium. Constantinople fell 1204. The Byzantine Emperor was set aside and by his approval the Pope sanctified the dismemberment of the Eastern Empire, of which a large part was absorbed by the Venetian merchant-republic. (For later history of the Byzantine Empire see OTTOMAN EMPIRE.) The 5TH CRUSADE (1218–21) was directly instigated by the Pope (Innocent III). It was directed against Egypt. The Sultan offered terms including the restoration of the Kingdom of Jerusalem, but the Pope's representative insisted that he should also pay a large indemnity, and negotiations broke down. The Crusaders were driven out of Egypt and apart from the recovery of the pretended Holy Cross—it had been seized by Saladdin—the 5th Crusade was therefore a failure. For never taking part in a crusade, the Pope's redoubtable antagonist Frederick II (Holy Roman Emperor) was at length excommunicated. In his own good time he set sail for the Holy Land (which he intended to add to his own Kingdom of Sicily) ; obtained by friendly negotiation what ' Holy wars ' had failed to secure, crowned himself King of Jerusalem (no bishop would

crown him, because he had been excommunicated) ; returned home, and defeated the Pope's army, which had meanwhile invaded his Italian domains. This was the 6TH CRUSADE (1228–29) and by it Jerusalem was recovered for a period of 15 years ; but in 1244 it was recaptured for Islam by the Egyptian leader Bibars.

The leader of the 7TH CRUSADE (1249) was Louis IX (France), who defied the pope's intention of turning it into a private war against the Emperor (Frederick II). Louis invaded Egypt, but was taken prisoner and held to ransom. He returned home 1254 and died 1270 in the 8TH CRUSADE (1267–70) which was a successful attack on Tunis. From Tunis Edward of England went on to the Holy Land and occupied Acre 1271–72. After this there were no more Crusades, and in 1291 the Franks (Christian invaders) departed from the Holy Land for good.

The failure of the Crusades foreshadowed the enormous expansion of the Ottoman Empire, which was to overrun the whole of SE. Europe (see OTTOMAN EMPIRE). Launched in the name of Christianity, they caused untold misery, not least in Europe, where 10,000 Jews are said to have been massacred for the sake of their wealth by the starving and impoverished followers of Peter the Hermit, a religious fanatic who preached the 1st Crusade. (Another instance was the Children's Crusade 1212, in which 20,000 children were not merely allowed but encouraged to set out on a Crusade in which at last they were captured and sold to the Moors as slaves.) It may be said, however, that ultimately the Crusades contributed to European prosperity by increasing trade, and that they brought the West and East more closely into contact.

Crustaceans, *krŭs-tā'shanz,* name given to creatures whose outer coverings, as the name implies, are hard shells. Their muscles, which are exceptionally strong, are attached to the insides of these shells, and their bodies, in which there are no bones, are divided into sections (usually 22) to some of which is attached a pair of jointed limbs.

Well-known members of the class are crabs (various types), lobsters, crayfish, prawns, etc. Most Crustaceans dwell in the sea or on the shore, but there are fresh-water crabs, and land crabs, which, in the Bahamas and W. Indies, do a great deal of damage to sugar-cane.

cryptogram, see CIPHERS ; CODES

Crystal Palace, London pleasure resort with grounds of 200 acres noted for dirt-track and speed-boat racing, football finals, etc. ; once famous for its huge metal and glass hall designed by Sir Joseph Paxton ; destroyed by fire 1936. A new Crystal Palace is now being planned. Costing c.£15,000,000, it will have a great concert hall, theatre, opera house, etc., and a sports stadium for 100,000 spectators.

crystals, in chemistry, the geometrical forms many substances take when solidified, e.g. when a solution of copper sulphate is evaporated. The study of crystals is called crystallography. A crystal is bounded by surfaces (usually flat) arranged on a definite plan, thereby indicating the internal arrangement of the atoms. Sir William Bragg, and his son Laurence, made X-ray and other studies of crystals, discovering that they form a lattice. Generally, crystals may be divided into similar halves ; and it seems that there can be only 32 crystal systems, among which are cubic, hexagonal, monoclinic etc.

Cu, chemical symbol for copper (Latin *cuprum*, from Cyprus, anciently famous for its copper mines).

Cuba, $k\bar{u}'b\ddot{a}$, largest island of the W. Indies and most important of the Greater Antilles ; area c.44,170sq.m ; pop. 4,200,000. Largely mountainous, but has low-lying plains in the W. ; forests of mahogany and cedar ; sugar, tobacco, rum, fruit, iron, copper, manganese, also asphalt and oil are produced ; the climate is more temperate than that of other W. Indian islands ; cap. Havana. Cuba was discovered by Columbus 1492, and won independence 1902.

cube, regular hexahedron, *i.e.* a solid figure with 6 square faces ; volume = length × breadth × height, or any of these cubed, *e.g.* 1³. Note : 1³, *i.e. one cubed*, is $1 \times 1 \times 1 = 1$; $2^3 = 2 \times 2 \times 2$, i.e. 8, etc. The *cube root* ($\sqrt[3]{}$) of 27 is 3. Note

$1^3 =$	1	$11^3 =$	1,331
$2^3 =$	8	$12^3 =$	1,728
$3^3 =$	27	$13^3 =$	2,197
$4^3 =$	64	$14^3 =$	2,744
$5^3 =$	125	$15^3 =$	3,375
$6^3 =$	216	$16^3 =$	4,096
$7^3 =$	343	$17^3 =$	4,913
$8^3 =$	512	$18^3 =$	5,832
$9^3 =$	729	$19^3 =$	6,859
$10^3 =$	1,000	$20^3 =$	8,000

Also : the cube root of

2 =	1·2599210	7 =	1·9129312
3 =	1·4422496	8 =	2·0000000
4 =	1·5874011	9 =	2·0800837
5 =	1·7099759	10 =	2·1544347
6 =	1·8171206		

Cubism, see ART

cubit, old English measure of length ; 18in (approx.) ; the Egyptian cubit (in Bible times) was 18·24in.

cuckoo, hawk-like bird of the family *Cuculidae.* A summer visitant to Britain, it departs in August for S. Africa. What Wordsworth describes as its twofold note is heard mostly in May and June, hence the old rhyme :

In April the cuckoo shows his bill ;
In May he sings all day ;
In June he alters his tune ;
In July away he'll fly.

Grey, with black bars on the underside, the cuckoo lays eggs in nests of smaller birds, e.g. hedge-sparrow, meadow pipit, titlark, and others. The colour and marks of the eggs vary, and there seems ample evidence that the female often lays the egg on the ground and then carries it in her beak to some near-by nest. When the egg is hatched the young cuckoo is much larger than those with whom it shares the nest, and as it grows it needs more room, so it pushes the rightful occupants over the side of the nest until none remains. The parents appear to pay little attention to this behaviour and go on feeding the cuckoo until it is old enough to fend for itself.

cuckoo flower or **lady's smock,** meadow plant (family *Cruciferae*) ; lower leaves broader than those above. Its pale lilac flowers with 4 petals and 6 yellow stamens grow close together at the end of the stem.

THE CUCKOO FLOWER

cuckoo-pint, see POISONOUS PLANTS

cuckoo spit, froth seen on various plants, e.g. hawthorn, apple and chrysanthemum, produced by the plant-bug *Philaenus spumarius* (froghopper).

Cullinan diamond, see DIAMOND

Cumae, $k\bar{u}'m\bar{e}$, Gk settlement in S. Italy ; founded in the 8th c. BC. One of the caves in its acropolis was the home of the Cumaean Sibyl (prophetess). This can still be seen.

Cumberland, mountainous county, NW.

England ; has coal and iron mines ; noted for sheep and cattle ; there are several lakes ; co.tn Carlisle.

Cumbrian Mts, L. District mts of NW. England ; Scafell Pike (3,210ft) is the highest peak.

Cunard-White Star, see Ships

Cunaxa, *kū-nak'să*, site of a town (*c*.50m N. of Babylon), where Cyrus the Younger was killed in battle, 401BC.

cuneiform, *kū-nē-i-förm*, form of ancient writing with wedge-shaped strokes ; has been found on millions of clay tablets, and on inscriptions chiselled on stones and rocks. For 2,000 years no-one could read it, but the secret was discovered 1846 by Sir Henry Rawlinson.

A cliff 1,700ft high at Behistun, Iran, has inscriptions in Babylonian, Susian and Old Persian, all carved for King Darius 500BC. Here, on a ledge 12in wide, 500ft up, Rawlinson copied the inscriptions, and by comparing one with another discovered how to read cuneiform.

Beginning as picture-writing, cuneiform was a form of script by 3000BC, and was in common use in W. Asia by 2300BC. It was easily written on wet clay with a stylus making wedge-shaped impressions (Latin *cuneus*, wedge). The famous laws of Hammurabi (ruler of Babylon *c*.2100BC) were written in cuneiform. See Writing

Cunningham, Major-General Sir Alan Gordon (1887–ㅤ) ; led a victorious attack on Somaliland 1941. He became High Commissioner and Commander-in-Chief in Palestine 1945.

Cunningham, Allan (1784–1842), Scottish minor poet, *b* Keir, Dumfriesshire ; noted for his lyrics, ballads. Well known for his arrangement of *A Wet Sheet and a Flowing Sea*.

Cunningham, Admiral Sir Andrew (1883–ㅤ), served with distinction in World War I. In World War II he was Commander-in-Chief, Mediterranean Fleet, and led the naval attack on the Italians 1941 ; First Sea Lord 1943 ; created a viscount 1946.

Cupid, see Psyche

cupro-nickel, alloy proposed for British ' silver ' coins in 1946, i.e. 75 % copper, 25 % nickel.

Curaçao, *koorä-sä'ō*, isl (area 210sq.m) of the Netherlands W. Indies ; surrounded by coral reefs ; produces cotton, tobacco and sugar. Chief town Williamstadt ; pop.41,000.

curfew, see Bell

Curia Regis, see Henry I

Curie, Eve, see Curie, Pierre

Curie, Pierre, *kū-rē*, (1859–1906), scientist, *b* Paris ; a pioneer in the study of radioactive substances. He married, 1895, a Polish woman, Marie Skladowska (1867–1934) of Warsaw, who had been one of his pupils. The Curies laboured day and night, facing innumerable difficulties and disappointments, to obtain radium salts from pitchblende. They discovered

MADAME CURIE 1867–1934

polonium and radium 1898 ; and in 1903 they shared with Henri Becquerel the Nobel prize for physics. Pierre Curie and his brother also investigated the electrical properties of crystals, but Pierre's brilliant career was cut short by his death in a street accident in Paris. Mme Curie continued the work her husband had begun, succeeding him as Professor of Physics at the Sorbonne (Paris). She received the Nobel prize for chemistry 1911, and was appointed Professor of Radiology in Warsaw 1919. President Harding in 1921 presented her with a gramme of radium, on behalf of the women of USA in recognition of her work. Their daughter Irène married Joliot-Curie, *b* 1900, French Atomic Energy chief till removed (1950) because of his Communist sympathies.

Another daughter, Eve (1904–ㅤ), a lecturer and musician, has written a vivid biography of her mother. See Radium

curlew, *kŭrl'yū*, bird (*c*.17in long) of the plover family ; spring and summer visitor to moors, especially in Scotland ; has a long curved beak and somewhat rounded tail ; plumage greyish-brown ; nests on the ground ; known in Scotland as the whaup, after its wild cry. See Plate II

curling, Scottish winter sport. The ' roaring game ' is like bowls played on ice. The players send a round stone with an iron handle gliding over ice. Curling is now played also in England, USA, Switzerland, etc.

A curling match between members of one club is known as a spiel ; matches between different clubs are called bonspiels. Bonspiels for the whole of Scotland are held whenever the ice is bearing at Carsebreck and on Loch Leven.

A DOUBLE RAINBOW

Plate I

The source of colour is light, and in our lives the chief source of light is the sun. When an observer standing with his back to the sun sees sunlight falling on a sheet of raindrops, light of varying wave-lengths is scattered in different directions—this scattering is called 'refraction' —and a rainbow appears. In sunlight the component colours are, from shorter to longer wave-lengths, violet, blue, green, yellow, orange, red ; and beyond both ends of this scale there are wave-lengths—ultra-violet and infra-red—not visible to the human eye. Refraction also occurs when light passes through a prism, but in this case the resultant band of different colours is called a ' spectrum.' Spectrum-analysis of light emitted, e.g., by distant stars enables us to determine what they are made of, and the fact that different groups of wave-lengths can be separated from one another is used in colour-printing. (See *Plates X, XI*.)

(*J. F. Steljes, Esq.*)

Plate II   COLOUR FOR PROTECTION

Protective colouring, such as that of this nesting curlew, makes its possessor less
conspicuous against the background of its normal environment. But colouring is not
enough. In this case two features which draw attention are the bird's shadow and the shape
of its beak. (*David Stephen, Esq.*)

COLOUR FOR DISPLAY   *Plate III*

Bright colour draws attention, and when present in the flower of a plant, such as this
Parrot's Bill, which depends on insects for its pollination, helps to ensure the survival of
the species. (*R. Eudall, Esq.*)

Plate IV   AURORA BOREALIS

The Aurora or Polar Light, a phenomenon often seen in the more northerly parts of Britain, is associated with the occurrence of sunspots and other magnetic disturbances on the sun. When one of these magnetic ' storms ' occurs on the sun, there is an emission of particles (probably ionised atoms, etc.).   These move outwards in space at speeds of 1,000–1,500 m.p.h. On approaching the earth, any such stream of particles is caught in the earth's magnetic field and drawn towards the earth's magnetic poles.   There it forms a cloud of varying density— the shimmering, flickering, dancing Aurora illustrated above. (*J. R. Bell, Esq.*)

currant, a stoneless dried grape, small in size ; grown in Greece and used in this country in cakes and puddings, and sometimes bread. The name is also given to the fruit and bush of the genus *Ribes* which bears clusters of red, white, or black fruit ; named from Corinth, Greece, whence it was introduced.

curry, sauce for rice, composed of spices, e.g. turmeric, coriander seeds, cummin seeds, garlic, pepper ; eaten principally in India.

Curtin, JOHN (1885–1945), Prime Minister of Australia 1941 ; dealt boldly with the menace of Japanese invasion in World War II ; attended the prime ministers' conference in London in 1944.

Curwen, JOHN, see TONIC SOL-FA

Curzon, GEORGE NATHANIEL, MARQUIS OF KEDLESTON, *kur'zon* (1859–1925), British statesman ; *b* Kedleston, Derbyshire ; entered Parliament as Conservative MP for Southport 1886–98 ; when only 39 years of age was Viceroy of India until 1905, a position which he relinquished after his opposition to Kitchener over dual control of the Indian Army. Curzon was a deeply religious man who sincerely believed that God had called the English people to govern backward nations in India, Africa, etc., and although this made him somewhat narrow-minded he performed his great duties with strict and conscientious observance of religious principles. In 1907 he was Chancellor for Oxford University ; leader of the House of Lords 1916, became member of Lloyd George's war cabinet during the same year ; foreign secretary 1919–24 ; received many academic honours and wrote several books including *War Poems* (1915), *British Government in India* (1925).

Curzon line, see POLAND

customs, duties paid on imported goods. Importers, and also exporters, in the 11th c. paid *in goods* a toll to the king ; *c*.1200 this payment in kind was changed for payment in money, the amount depending, in the main, on what had become *customary*, hence the term customs.

Today duties are levied on practically all articles imported into the UK. The duties are collected by the Board of Customs and Excise.

By *excise* is meant taxes levied on goods produced within the country (e.g. beer and spirits). The department dealing with these was amalgamated with the Customs 1909.

Cutch, state of W. India bordering the Indian Ocean ; largely barren rocks.

Cuthbert, ST (*c*.635–687), probably *b* Northumbria ; became prior of Melrose Abbey, later converted Scots SE. lowlanders to Christianity ; bishop of Lindisfarne 685 ; lived as a hermit on Farne I. His tomb is in Durham Cathedral.

cutlass, heavy, straight-bladed sword formerly carried by sailors, especially when boarding enemy ships.

cutter (*a*) boat for the use of a ship's company, (*b*) single-masted sailing ship with foresail, mainsail, jib, topsail and flying jib.

cuttle-fish, see MOLLUSCA

' Cutty Sark,' see SHIPS

Cuvier, BARON, *kū'viä* (1769–1832), French anatomist ; professor in the Jardin des Plantes, Paris ; did much pioneer work in comparative anatomy, fossils, classification, and lectured with outstanding success. His work *Le Règne Animal* was once the standard for zoology.

Cuzco, *koos'kō*, city, Peru, 11,400ft above sea-level ; has Inca remains, and was once the Inca cap. ; pop.40,000.

Cyclades, *sik'lä-dēz*, group of *c*.200 mountainous Gk islands (volcanic origin) in the Aegean Sea ; mostly fertile ; principal islands include Syra, Naxos, Milos and Myconos.

cyclamen, *sik'lä-men*, plant of the family *Primulaceae*, much grown in greenhouses; has a tuberous rootstock ; flowers (waxy pink, white, or purple) with 5 petals curved backwards.

cycling, see BICYCLE ; YOUTH ORGANISATIONS

Cyclopes, *sī'klo-pes* (Gk *kyklos*, circle, *ops*, eye), in old Gk tales, giants with one eye ; described in Homer's *Odyssey* as cannibal shepherds who dwell in caves with their leader Polyphemus, who imprisoned Ulysses (Odysseus) and his men in a cave, and was blinded with a burning pole.

cyclotron, *sī'klō-tron*, apparatus for producing artificial radioactivity by imparting high speeds to a beam of electrons which are given a spiral movement. The electrons are produced by bombarding the nuclei of atoms, these travelling in a narrow path between the poles of a

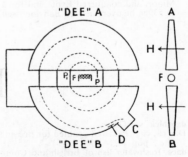

CYCLOTRON

Ions generated near the filament F *travel in a spiral path* P, P₁ *under the influence of the magnetic field at* H, *gaining an increment of energy at each crossing of the diametrical region between '* Dee *'* A *and '* Dee *'* B*. At the end of their path they are deflected by the deflecting electrode* D *into the target chamber at* C.

powerful magnet while being subjected to a changing electrostatic field.

cygnet, see SWAN

cylinder, solid figure traced out by a rectangle rotating round one side as axis, or, alternatively, a circular prism. See AREA ; VOLUME

cymbal, *sim'bal,* musical instrument composed of two brass plates ; used in orchestras and military bands to give a ringing sound which is produced by striking the plates together.

Cymric, form of Celtic speech used by the inhabitants of Wales and Brittany. The word survives in the name *Cumberland.*

Cynewulf, *kin'e-,* Northumbrian poet of the 8th c. ; author of religious poems, *Christ, The Fates of the Apostles, Juliana of Elene.*

Cyprus, *si'prŭs,* Mediterranean island, *c.*60m W. of Syria ; area 3,584sq.m ; pop. 350,000. Fertile though mountainous ; climate, good ; its products include potatoes, wine, almonds, raisins, oranges, cotton, cheese ; also pyrites, copper ore, asbestos, chromium ore, gypsum, etc. Administered by Great Britain since 1914, its constitution is now under review as there is a local demand for self-government ; cap. Nicosia.

Cyrenaica, *sir-ēn-ā'ikä,* province of Libya, N. Africa ; area 230,000sq.m ; conquered by Italy 1912, and developed as an Italian colony ; chief towns Cyrene, Benghazi, Derna and Tobruk, all scenes of bitter fighting (1940–43) in World War II. See LIBYA

Cyrus the Great, *si'rus, d* 529BC ; founder of the Persian Empire. In 612BC the Babylonians assisted by the Medes captured Nineveh, and thus completed the destruction of the Assyrian empire. Sixty years later, Cyrus of Anshan, a Persian, united the Medes and Persians, became king of Persia, overran Asia Minor, and conquered Lydia and Ionia. In 539BC he overwhelmed Babylon itself,

thus releasing the Jews who had been taken there as captives more than a generation before.

The work of Cyrus was carried on by Cambyses, who conquered Egypt, but further expansion in the Mediterranean was checked by Greek resistance in the Persian Wars (490–479BC).

Czechoslovakia, *chekō-slō-väk'iä,* Central European republic formed 1918 on the break-up of the Austrian Empire. It comprises Bohemia, Moravia and Slovakia : total area *c.*50,500sq.m, pop. (1948) 14,700,000 ; cap. Prague. Between the wars Czechoslovakia developed a vigorously democratic national life, but in 1938 Great Britain and France signed the Munich agreement (see CHAMBERLAIN) which allowed Germany to annex Czechoslovak frontier territories inhabited by Germans (Sudetens). In March 1939, Germany invaded Czechoslovakia, and it was not until 1945 that the country was finally liberated by Russian troops. Democratic government was restored ; but Czechoslovakia needs Russian military support in any European war, and this fact enabled the Czech Communist party to seize power 1948. This was followed by the suicide of the democrat Jan Masaryk, an event which greatly intensified anti-Russian feeling in the West.

The country is admirably developed agriculturally, producing rye, wheat, oats, sugar-beet, etc. ; also industrially e.g. coal, iron, steel, silver, copper, rock-salt, plywood, cellulose, rayon, Bohemian glass, chinaware, and especially textiles. Education is highly developed. Air services link the capital with all parts of Europe.

Czerny, KARL, *cher'nē* (1791–1857), Austrian composer and pianist, *b* Vienna; student of Beethoven ; teacher of Liszt ; well known for his educational music manuals.

D

dabchick, see GREBE

Dac'ca, city, Pakistan ; noted for rice and jute ; pop. *c.*214,000.

dace, freshwater fish of British and Continental rivers ; found in shoals ; weighs up to 6 ounces.

Dacia, *dä'shi-ä,* Roman province N. of the Danube, roughly the same as modern Rumania.

Dacoits, *dä-koits',* armed gangs of robbers in India and Burma, who used to raid villages, plunder, and often kill the inhabitants prior to the 18th c. Dacoity

(their robbing activities) was originally a religious and caste duty comparable with that of the Thugs.

daddy-longlegs, see CRANE-FLY

Daedalus, *dē'dä-lŭs,* in old Greek tales, an Athenian sculptor, architect and inventor ; excavated the labyrinth for King Minos of Crete. He and his son (Icarus) made wings which they affixed with wax. Daedalus reached Cumae, but when Icarus flew too near the sun, the wax melted, and he was drowned.

daffodil, popular name for a plant of the

family *Amaryllidaceae* ; has long spear-like leaves and usually a yellow, trumpet-like flower with six paler petals. See NARCISSUS

Dagenham, *dag'*- industrial town, Essex ; has extensive Ford motor works ; pop. 114,000.

Daghestan, *dä-ges-tän'*, republic of USSR, W. of the Caspian Sea ; rears sheep and cattle.

dagoba, *dä'gō-bä*, dome-shaped brick or stone shrine for relics of Buddha, or his followers, seen especially in Ceylon.

Dagon, *dä'gon*, national god of the Philistines ; Judges 16 ; 1 Samuel 5.

Daguerre, LOUIS, *dä-gär'* (1789–1851), French pioneer in photography ; *b* Cormeilles, Seine-et-Oise ; invented the daguerreotype, the forerunner of photography.

dahlia, *däl'yä*, plant (family *Compositae*), named after Andrew Dahl, Swedish botanist ; many varieties and colours of double and single flowers. The roots are used as food in Mexico.

Dahomey, *dä-hō'mä*, region of French W. Africa, area *c.*47,000sq.m ; once a notorious centre of the slave trade ; products include palm-oil ; pop. 1,400,000.

Dail Eireann, *däl är'in*, House of Representatives in the Parliament of Eire ; comprises 138 members. The other House (the Senate) is *Seanad Eireann*, with 60 members, 11 nominated by the *Taoiseach* (Prime Minister), the others elected partly according to employment. The two Houses form the National Parliament, *Oireachtas*, which came into operation on 29 Dec 1937 ; over all is the President (*Uachtaran na hEireann*), elected by direct vote for 5 years and not longer than 7 years.

Daimler, GOTTLIEB (1834–1900), German engineer ; *b* Württemberg ; made the first motor-cycle 1885, and the first petrol driven car 1887—one of the first Daimler cars.

Dai Nippon, see JAPAN

Dairen, *dī-ren'*, port, Kwantung peninsula, Manchuria ; pop.516,000.

daisy, small common plant (family *Compositae*) of Britain. The field daisy is *Bellis perennis*.

Dakar, *dä-kär'*, port (Senegal), and cap. of the Federation of French W. Africa ; pop.93,000.

Daladier, ÉDOUARD (1884–   ), French statesman ; Prime Minister of France at the time of the Munich Agreement (1938); for two years in a German prison camp during World War II.

Dalai Lama, *dä-lī' lä'mä* (' sea of wisdom '), or Grand Lama, ' pope ' of the Lamaist monks, Tibet, whose judgment is supreme ; he lives in seclusion and by Tibetans it is believed that a Dalai Lama does not die but puts aside his human form and is rejuvenated from time to time. New ' living Bhuddas ' are looked for and found in Tibet, when, generally, a boy of four or five years of age is

chosen because he is considered suitable for the training he has to undergo.

Dalcroze, ÉMIL JAQUES (1865–1950), Swiss composer ; *b* Vienna ; professor of harmony at Geneva Conservatoire ; won fame with his system of eurhythmics ; has written songs, symphonies and concertos.

Dalen, NILS GUSTAV, *dä-län'* (1869–1937), Swedish scientist, *b* Stenstorp ; though blinded 1913, he continued to invent and manufacture improved automatic lamps for lighthouses and light-ships ; he also made improvements in air compressors and milking machines ; Nobel Prize (physics) 1912.

Dalhousie, JAMES ANDREW, EARL OF, *dal-hoo'zi* (1812–60), administrator ; *b* Dalhousie Castle, near Edinburgh ; descended from a line of Scottish earls ; President of the Board of Trade 1845–46; Governor-General of India 1847–56, instituted many reforms, annexed the Punjab, Oudh and Pegu ; introduced reforms in India, including a system of railways, canals and post offices.

Dallas, city, Texas, USA ; centre of a cotton, petroleum and grain region ; fruit district ; pop.295,000.

Dalmatia, *dal-mä'shi-ä*, mountainous part of Yugoslavia ; is on the Adriatic coast ; produces wine, oil, honey, cereals, fruit.

Dalton, HUGH (1887–   ), Labour MP ; Minister of Economic Warfare 1940–42; President of the Board of Trade 1942–45 ; Chancellor of the Exchequer from 1945 until 1947, when he indiscreetly revealed the proposals in his budget to a journalist before making his budget speech in the House of Commons. The journalist published the details and Mr Dalton was obliged to resign. His place was taken by Sir Stafford Cripps. In 1948 Mr Dalton became Chancellor of the Duchy of Lancaster.

Dalton, JOHN, *döl'tŭn* (1766–1844), British chemist and physicist ; born near

THE OX-EYE DAISY

Cockermouth, Cumberland ; teacher of mathematics and natural philosophy at New College, Manchester, 1793 ; recorded over 200,000 weather observations : wrote the first scientific paper on colour-blindness ; but most famous for his pioneer work in atomic theory. It was Dalton who first made out a table of atomic weights c.1808.

Daltonism, see Colour

dam, structure of masonry or concrete built across a water course to store water or regulate its flow. Irrigation dams of vast size have been built in India and USA. Notable dams include those at Aswan (across the Nile) ; Hindiyah barrage across the Euphrates (Iraq) ; Hoover Dam, Colorado ; Boulder Dam across the Colorado, 726ft high (highest in the world) ; Grand Coulee Dam across the Columbia (Washington State), 550ft, largest concrete dam in the world. The Shasta Dam across the Sacramento R. is 602ft, and was completed 1944. See Plates 24 *(top)*, 41, 42

Damascus, *dä-mas'kŭs,* cap. Syria. One of the oldest cities in the world, it was the scene of the conversion of St Paul, and is believed by Mohammedans to have been the spot where Mohammed turned his back on the pleasures of life. Over 2,200ft above sea-level, it is set amid trees and flowers. For ages it has been a centre for the caravan trade ; taken from the Turks by the British 1918.

Damascus has long been famous for finely tempered swords, sharp as razors and often beautifully enriched with gold and silver ; and exquisite fabrics of coloured silks woven on primitive handlooms. For many centuries these have been known far and wide ; hence our word *damask.*

A great cemetery at Damascus, known as the City of the Dead, is a remarkable sight with its gravestones and flowers ; but for many tourists the street still called ' Straight ' is the most interesting feature. It is over a mile long, and remains, no doubt, much the same in appearance today as in the days of St Paul ; pop.286,000.

damask, *dam'ăsk,* fabric named from Damascus, famous for silks in the 12th c.; real damask is rich silk with raised pattern ; damask cloth contains only a proportion of silk.

Damien, Father, *dä-myan* (1840–89), Belgian RC missionary, *b* Tremeloo ; went to Hawaii 1864 ; became the only priest to 600 lepers on Molokai I., where he died of leprosy ; reburied Louvain 1936.

No praise is too great for this hero and martyr who lived and died for wretched sufferers, and was their greatest friend. Shortly before he died he was asked if he had any message to give to a distinguished churchman. Father Damien replied : *Only my thanks for sending me to Molokai.*

Damietta, *dam-i-et'tä,* town, Egypt ; on the Nile, 8m from the sea ; trades in grain, rice, cotton and hides; pop.40,000.

Damocles, *dam'ō-klēz,* flatterer of the tyrant Dionysius of Syracuse when he said the latter was the happiest man on earth, whereupon Dionysius invited him to take his (Dionysius's) place at a banquet. This he did and found a sword suspended over his head by a single hair, to show that a person in an exalted position is seldom free from the threat of danger, hence the expression ' the sword of Damocles.'

Damon and **Pythias,** 4th c. followers of Pythagoras, between whom there existed a great friendship. When Pythias was condemned to death by Dionysius the Tyrant of Syracuse, he was given leave to go home to attend to his affairs and Damon offered to take his friend's place until he returned. Pythias returned for execution, and both were released by the tyrant who begged their friendship.

Dampier, William, *dam'pēr* (1652–1715), English navigator and author, born near Yeovil ; commanded an expedition to the S. Seas, and wrote *A New Voyage Round the World.*

Dana, Richard Henry, *dä'nä* (1815–82), *b* Cambridge, Mass. ; American author of *Two Years Before the Mast.*

Danaë, *dan'ā-ē,* in old Gk tales, daughter of Acrisius King of Argos, who shut her up in a dungeon because an oracle announced that one day she would give birth to a son who would murder his grandfather. She was visited by Zeus in a shower of gold and became the mother of Perseus. Acrisius put both mother and child into a chest and cast it into the sea. They came to no harm, however, and drifted ashore on the island of Seriphos.

When Perseus and his mother returned to Argos, Acrisius fled but was slain accidentally by Perseus at Larissa.

Titian, Rembrandt and Correggio have all made paintings of the reunion of Danaë and Zeus.

dance, sequence or pattern in time of rhythmical bodily movements, usually to the accompaniment of music specially composed for the purpose. A dance may be for a single dancer. Many modern dances are for pairs of men and women dancing as separate couples ; others again, especially country dances, are for a set of dancers, i.e. a group of several couples. The impulse to express all sorts of emotion through dances is found in all ages and among all peoples. Thus there are many types of dances. These in turn have affected the development of musical forms.

The ancient Greeks brought dancing to a high level of perfection. The importance they attached to it is shown by the fact that one of their nine Muses, Terpsichore, was a Muse of dancing. Greek dances were performed as religious rites in honour especially of such deities as Demeter (corn goddess) and Aphrodite (goddess of love). It was thought that the performance of these dances made not only human beings but also the farm animals and the land more fertile. In ancient Greece, boys and girls danced together, men and women separately.

Oriental dances often have a religious meaning. (Our dances too had a religious origin but those who dance them are usually unaware of it.) Oriental dances often involve little movement of the feet but much swaying of the body : such are the Nautch dances of India, danced by trained dancers (usually girls) who use their arms and hands to express various ideas and emotions.

In Europe there have been two traditions of dancing, folk-dancing and court dancing. Both are now being superseded by forms of modern ballroom dancing imported from America.

In England folk-dancing nearly died out in the 19th c. That was because the social life of the countryside was transformed so completely by the Industrial Revolution. Traditional English folk-dances such as the Morris dance have survived only because folk-dancing societies were founded in the late 19th c. by educated people who thought it would be a pity if such dances were lost. There is something rather artificial about folk-dancing in modern England ; but in Scotland, Ireland, Wales and many other countries traditional folk-dances are still enjoyed as a natural self-expression, and are treasured as part of the national heritage. The neglect of the English folk-dance is part of the price England has had to pay for leading the world in the beginning of the industrial age.

Scottish folk-dances include the well-known Eightsome Reel, the Duke of Perth (Broun's Reel), Flouers o' Edinburgh, Reel of Tulloch (a foursome reel), and the strathspey, a slow and stately foursome for which many of the most beautiful Scottish airs were originally composed. The strathspey was danced at funeral wakes in the Scottish Highlands as late as the beginning of the 19th c. That suggests that this kind of dancing may have had a religious origin.

The court dance was often in origin a country dance that had been taken up by the court nobility and altered to make it suitable for dancing in polite society. Such was the Polish *mazurka* danced by the nobility of Tsarist Russia, and popular throughout Europe in the 19th c. Such too were the *pavan, galliard, chaconne, sarabande, gavotte, bourrée*, etc., of the 16th and 17th cs. These dances gave their names to corresponding musical forms much used by Bach and other well-known composers : but none of them has been so important in music as the 18th c. *minuet* (French), which rapidly ousted the older court dances and gave rise to a new musical form regularly used by Mozart and Haydn as the third movement of a symphony.

The *waltz* and the *polka* came in early in the 19th c. They differed from the earlier court dances in that they were danced by couples, whereas the older dances were for sets. Modern ballroom dancing is likewise mainly for couples, and owes much to the dances of the American Negroes. It is probable that the change-over from dancing in sets to dancing in couples is linked with the vast changes that have overtaken western society since the beginning of the industrial age. The communities in which set dances were danced as a matter of course were such that those who belonged to them had some idea of the community as a whole and of how everybody fitted into it ; modern societies are so vast that most people no longer have nearly so strong a feeling of community with others, and the relationship of one couple to the other dancers in a modern dance-hall is like the isolated position of the individual in the huge cities of modern industrial society.

The 20th c. has seen a frenzy of dancing reminiscent of the dance-madness that swept Europe in the 14th c. after the Black Death, and again, but less extensively after the Napoleonic Wars. This is probably because dancing is one of the few ways by which in times like these most ordinary people can express their thwarted desires for personal or social happiness.

Dancing has often developed into wild and abandoned forms, and for that reason has sometimes been denounced as immoral and wicked by religious authorities. In the late 19th c., for example, a famous American preacher asked parents whether they would willingly allow young men to embrace their daughters elsewhere as in the ballroom ; and in many parts of Britain even at the present time there are strong religious prejudices against ' promiscuous ' (i.e. mixed) dancing.

dandelion, plant, named from French *dent-de-lion*, lion's tooth, a fanciful description of the smooth arrow-head leaves springing from the rootstock ; the bright yellow flower is on a hollow stalk containing white juice ; the seeds have a downy tuft, often called a dandelion ' clock.'

danegeld, *dän'geld* ; *-gelt*, land-tax first levied in England 991 by Ethelred the Unready, with the consent of the Witan, and intended to buy off the raiding Danes ; abolished 1051 by Edward the Confessor, but revived for a different purpose by William I. The tax was originally 2s per hide (30–120 acres).

Danelagh, *dän'law* (OE), that part of England (E. Anglia, Northumbria, part of Mercia and Essex) where the law of the Danes prevailed after the Treaty of Wedmore 878.

Danes, the inhabitants of Denmark ;

descended from Scandinavian tribes that invaded Britain, from the 9th–10th c. Though defeated by Alfred, they returned in the reigns of Edward and Ethelred, their leader, Canute (*d* 1035), becoming king of England.

Daniel, Jew taken captive to Babylon by Nebuchadnezzar (605–562BC) ; won fame by his wisdom, uprightness, and ability to interpret dreams.

Dante, ALIGHIERI, *dan'tā* (1265–1321), greatest Italian poet, *b* Florence. As a boy of 9 he saw a beautiful girl of 8, Beatrice Portinari, who later became ' the glorious lady of his mind.' Falsely accused of dishonesty, Dante was condemned to death 1302. Escaping this fate, he became a poor wanderer in Northern Italy. He returned to Florence 1310, but was soon an exile again. His last years were spent at Ravenna, where he died.

DANTE 1265–1321

Dante's fame is due to his wonderful poem *La Divina Commedia*, i.e. *The Divine Comedy*, which is one of the greatest ever written. An epic in three parts, *Inferno, Purgatorio* and *Paradiso*, it describes (as in a vivid dream) how Dante was taken by Virgil through hell and purgatory, and then led through heaven by the spirit of his beloved Beatrice. Dante gives vivid descriptions of famous people, e.g. Noah, Moses, Cleopatra, Helen of Troy, Henry III of England, St Peter, etc.

As an example of Dante's style, take these lines describing certain hobgoblins writhing in boiling pitch :

As dolphins that, in sign
To mariners, heave high their arched backs,

That thence forwarn'd they may advise to save
Their threaten'd vessel : so, at intervals,
To ease the pain, his back some sinner show'd,
Then hid more nimbly than the lightning-glance.
E'en as the frogs, that of a watery moat
Stand at the brink, with the jaws only out,
Their feet and of the trunk all else conceal'd,
Thus on each part the sinners stood ; but soon
As Barbariccia was at hand, so they
Drew back under the wave. I saw, and yet
My heart doth stagger, one, that waited thus,
As it befalls that oft one frog remains,
While the next springs away : and Graffiacan,
Who of the fiends was nearest, grappling seized
His clotted locks, and dragg'd him sprawling up,
That he appear'd to me an otter.

Dan to Beersheba, see BEERSHEBA

Danton, GEORGES JACQUES, *dän-tön* (1759–1794), French Revolutionist ; *b* Arcis-sur-Aube ; a born orator, lawyer, and a statesman of no mean order ; Minister of Justice 1792, and for 19 months the leading figure in Paris ; allied himself with extremists, including Robespierre and Marat ; voted for the king's execution ; strove sincerely to establish civil order ; suspected by Robespierre, and guillotined. Danton gave France the rousing cry : *To dare, and again to dare, and always to dare !*

Danube, *dan'ūb*, river 1,750m long. A great waterway of SE. Europe, it rises in the Black Forest (Germany), flows by Ulm (where it becomes navigable), Ratisbon, Vienna, through Hungary, Yugoslavia and Rumania, to the Black Sea ; has over 60 navigable tributaries ; and in conjunction with the Rhine and various canals the system crosses Europe from the Black Sea to the N. Sea.

Danzig, *dän'tsi*ch, free state (754sq.m) guaranteed by the League of Nations 1919–39 ; claimed by Hitler for Germany 1939. The city of Danzig, on the R. Vistula, is a great Baltic port, dealing chiefly in timber and grain ; pop.415,000.

Dardanelles, *där-dä-nelz'*, (anciently the Hellespont), strait 1–4m broad between Europe and Asia. It links the Aegean with the Sea of Marmora, and was the scene of British landings (1915) which later suffered defeat. To gain control of the Straits has long been an objective of Russian policy.

Dare, VIRGINIA (1587–91 ?), said to have been the first child born to English parents in America, granddaughter of Governor White of Virginia. She lived with Raleigh's first colonists, but had vanished when a ship with further supplies reached Roanoke I. two years later. A stone found 1938 is believed by some to have an inscription proving that she died when only 4.

Dar-es-Salaam, *-sä-läm'*, ('harbour of peace '), cap. Tanganyika Territory, Africa ; pop.74,000 ; airport on the Durban–Calcutta route.

Darien, see BALBOA, VASCO NUNEZ DE

Darius I, *dä-rī'ŭs*, King of Persia 522–485 BC ; ruler of the whole of the Near East by 517BC ; defeated by the Greeks at Marathon 490BC. Notable as an able ruler who strove to make Persia a great naval power, Darius introduced coinage, improved communications, established a postal system, and greatly improved the efficiency of imperial administration.

Darius III, King of Persia 336–330BC ; killed at the battle of Arbela (Erbil) when trying to stem Alexander the Great's advance southward on Babylon.

Darjeeling, town and health resort in the Himalayas, over 7,100ft above sea-level. It is a popular retreat for white people in the hot season ; tea is grown in this district ; pop.26,000.

Dark Ages, see MIDDLE AGES

Darlan, JEAN FRANÇOIS (1881–1942), French admiral and politician ; was pro-German in World War II ; assassinated in N. Africa.

Darling, river 1,160m long, New S. Wales, Australia ; also hills in Queensland, noted for sheep.

Darling, GRACE HORSLEY (1815–42), English heroine ; *b* Bamburgh ; daughter of the lighthouse-keeper on Longstone Lighthouse (Farne Islands) ; with her father rescued nine survivors from the wreck of the *Forfarshire* 1838.

Darlington, town, Durham ; on the R. Tees ; important railway centre ; noted for iron and other works ; pop.84,000. See STOCKTON-ON-TEES

Darmstadt, *därm'shtät*, cap. Hesse Darmstadt (Germany) ; manufactures chemicals, iron goods, machinery, beer, etc. ; pop.116,000.

darnel, see TARE

Darnley, LORD, see MARY, QUEEN OF SCOTS

Dartford, *-fĕrd*, town, Kent, noted for chemical works and paper factories, a tunnel for road traffic is now being built under the Thames ; pop.35,000.

Dartmoor, uncultivated upland, Devon ; *c*.120,000 acres, noted for small sheep. At Princetown is a convict prison.

Dartmouth, port, Devon ; noted for yachting ; has a Royal Naval Cadet College.

Darwen, *dar'wen*, town, NE. Lancashire ; has blast furnaces ; also cotton mills and collieries ; pop.36,000.

Darwin, with Port Darwin, town and port, N. Territory, Australia. It is a growing airport ; bombed by the Japanese in World War II.

Darwin, CHARLES (1809–82), great Victorian naturalist who revolutionised accepted views of man's place in the universe. Born and schooled at Shrewsbury, Darwin was out of sympathy with the classical education he received. For two years he studied medicine at Edinburgh, and then went to Cambridge, intending to be a clergyman ; but in 1831 he was appointed naturalist to the survey expedition of HMS *Beagle* in Atlantic and Pacific waters. The voyage of the *Beagle*, which took five years, was Darwin's big chance. He married 1839, and settled at Downe in Kent, where he spent the rest of his life in scientific research.

A few thinkers, among them Lamarck and Charles Darwin's grandfather, Erasmus Darwin, had maintained the view that the different forms of life had developed gradually from a common ancestry, and that in certain conditions new features arose and were passed on to some members of the next generation, thus giving rise to the variety of species now in existence. This view is called the Theory of Evolution. Darwin brought forward, from his own researches, an enormous quantity of evidence in favour of the theory, and certainly deserves the credit of establishing it as almost unquestionably true. It is a mistake, however, to think that he invented it.

The theory of Evolution as stated by Darwin was bitterly opposed because it undermined accepted religious teaching about the place held by man in God's creation. The orthodox view had previously been that man had always been man since the creation of Adam and Eve, just as monkeys had always been monkeys : they could not change and had no relationship to one another. It was held that, unlike the animals, man was endowed from the beginning with a soul and moral qualities, i.e. the ability to tell good from bad, whereas animals were creatures without souls or moral qualities. If Darwin's theory were true, men were descended from animals, and therefore human nature could not be distinguished so sharply or fundamentally from the nature of animals : and if animals could not be held morally responsible for their actions because their nature was not moral, it was hard to see why the contrary should be true of human beings. (One answer to this difficulty is that man is certainly a moral being, but only in so far as he has *changed* in the course of evolution. But Darwin's teaching was so novel and so sharply in conflict with the accepted religious teachings of the time that there seemed to be no way of reconciling the two.)

Darwin's most original contribution to the Theory of Evolution was his explanation of how, according to his view (now considerably altered), evolution comes about. This explanation is summed up in Darwin's theory of Natural Selection. He assumed that certain alterations of physical make-up could occur in any member of a species ;

that once established these new characteristics could be passed on to the descendants of that particular animal or plant, thus bringing distinct new species into existence.

The next step was to show that such a development would have the effect of making the species in question fitter, or less fit, to cope with its *environment*, i.e. the surroundings in which it lived. Thus a flesh-eating species which happened to develop sharper and longer teeth would find it easier to kill its prey, and so get more food : and for this reason such an animal would stand a better chance of surviving to reproduce its kind than another member of the same species which had grown shorter and blunter teeth.

Darwin's theory of natural selection may therefore be summed up in the statement that among living creatures there is a struggle for existence (mainly because the food supply is limited) and that the outcome of the struggle is the ' survival of the fittest.' The fittest is not however necessarily the strongest : a species which became outstandingly good at killing its natural prey would tend to multiply rapidly, and the more efficient it was at killing its prey, the quicker the prey would be killed off. The prey might die out altogether and the efficient killer would then be deprived of its food supply. This aspect of Darwin's theory has been explored by modern ecologists, who have shown that interdependence is almost as important among animals and plants as fitness to compete at one another's expense. Darwin owed a great deal to the political and economic doctrines of his time ; it has often been pointed out that he simply applied Malthusian economics (see MALTHUS) to the study of nature. The idea that men are many individuals competing with one another for a limited food supply, and that the best type of human being is the one best fitted to compete with his fellows, runs through most Victorian thinking. This idea inspired Darwin : he strengthened it in turn. Modern criticism of Darwin's biological theories resembles modern criticism of the political views with which they were connected.

Darwin's great work, *The Origin of Species*, was published 1859.
See EVOLUTION

Darwin, SIR CHARLES G. (1887–   ), director of the National Physical Laboratory 1938 ; associated with the atom-bomb of 1945.

date, fruit of the date palm, a tree of N. Africa and India ; often 100ft high ; has feather-like leaves 12ft long. The soft sweet red-brown fruit surrounds a single seed. Once grown almost exclusively in the East, dates are now scientifically cultivated in USA, e.g. California, Arizona, Texas and Nevada.

Date Line, see TIME

Daudet, ALPHONSE, *dō-dā* (1840–97), French novelist ; *b* Nimes ; styled the Charles Dickens of France, his work being graceful, vivid, and full of humour and pathos ; became famous for his creation of the delightful yet boastful Tartarin, hero of *Les Aventures prodigieuses de Tartarin de Tarascon,* etc. Among his many works are *Le Nabab* ; *Lettres de mon Moulin* ; *Contes du Lundi,* and *Froment Jeune et Risler Aîné.*

Dauphin, *dō'fin,* title borne by the eldest son of the king of France 1349–1830.

Davenant, SIR WILLIAM, *dav'en-ant* (1606–1668), English poet laureate and dramatist ; *b* Oxford ; remembered for his poem *The lark now leaves her wat'ry nest,* and as the first playwright to introduce scene-shifting, operatic music and actresses on the English stage.

Daventry, town, Northamptonshire ; manufactures boots and shoes ; had a broadcasting station of the BBC, but this was dismantled 1947.

David, *dā'vid* (Hebrew ' beloved ') (c.1030–990BC), 2nd king of Israel, youngest son of Jesse of the tribe of Judah. As a shepherd-boy he became a skilled harpist, and fought the giant Goliath and slew him (1 Samuel 17 and 18). Friend of Jonathan, he was outlawed by the king (Saul). As king he waged war against the Philistines etc., and was succeeded by his son Solomon.

Though many of the *Psalms* of the OT were no doubt written by David, it seems impossible now to be sure for how many he was directly responsible, but the 23rd Psalm, at least, was in all probability his. See ABSALOM

David or **Dewi,** patron saint of Wales, died possibly AD601 ; his festival is 1 March.

David I (1084–1153), King of Scotland ; son of Malcolm Canmore and Margaret ; defeated at the battle of the Standard 1138 ; established several monasteries, which earned him the title ' Ane Sair Sanct for the crown.'

David II (1324–71), King of Scotland ; *b* Dunfermline ; son of Robert Bruce ; 11 years a prisoner in England after his defeat at Neville's Cross 1346.

David Pilgrim, see SAUNDERS, H. A. ; ST GEORGE

Davies, SIR HENRY WALFORD (1869–1941), British musician of Welsh parentage ;– *b* Oswestry ; 25 years organist and choirmaster of the Temple Church, London, and later at St George's Chapel, Windsor ; composed songs and orchestral pieces ; gave delightful broadcast talks on music. His most important work was *Everyman,* a setting of the medieval morality play. Master of the King's Music 1934–41. Published *The Pursuit of Music* 1935.

Davies, WILLIAM HENRY (1871–1940), ' tramp-poet,' *b* Newport, Monmouthshire ; wandered in America and Britain, voyaging in cattle ships ; told his own story in *Autobiography of a*

Super-Tramp, and wrote exquisite verse and prose, showing a great love of nature ; his works include *Collected Poems* ; and *My Birds* ; famous for
What is this life if, full of care,
We have no time to stand and stare ?

Davis, JOHN (*c.*1550–1605), navigator and explorer ; born near Dartmouth, Devon ; tried unsuccessfully to find the NW. Passage, but passed through and gave his name to Davis Strait.

Davis Cup, see LAWN TENNIS

Davis Strait, channel between Greenland and Baffin I. named after John Davis, English navigator and explorer.

Davy, SIR HUMPHRY (1778–1829), English scientist, *b* Penzance, Cornwall. As a young man he prepared nitrous-oxide (laughing gas). Davy had charge of the chemical laboratory of the Royal Institution, London ; became its first professor of chemistry. Famous as a lecturer, he proved that the diamond is a form of carbon ; discovered potassium and sodium ; experimented with chlorine ; wrote on agricultural chemistry ; and 1815 invented the miner's safety lamp.

    Coal mines (and also other mines) may become full of ' fire-damp,' (marsh-gas or methane), which causes explosions. Though George Stephenson invented an oil safety lamp, the most popular type was Davy's, based on the principle that a flame will not pass through wire gauze. The modern type is bolted to the base in such a way that it cannot be opened unless placed on a magnet which releases the bolt inside.

Dawes, CHARLES GATES (1865–   ), American statesman, *b* Ohio ; author of the Dawes Plan designed to secure payment of heavy war debts from Germany after World War I.

daylight saving, see CALENDAR

Day Nurseries, centres where young children are cared for while mothers are at work ; began in World War I, a pioneer being Margaret MacMillan.

days of the week, see CALENDAR

Dayton, *dā′tŭn*, town, Ohio, USA ; on the Miami R.; noted for iron and steel, electrical and aeroplane equipment ; pop.211,000.

Daytona Beach, *dā-tō′nä*, town, Florida, USA ; famous for motor speed-trials on its firm sands ; winter resort.

DC, see ELECTRICITY

D.C., see UNITED STATES OF AMERICA

DCM, see DECORATIONS AND MEDALS

D-Day, name in military plans for the day on which an operation is to begin. The day before D-Day is called D−1 (D minus one), and the day before that D−2, and so on ; the days after D-Day, D+1 (D plus one), D+2, etc. This makes it possible to work out a plan before deciding when the operation is to begin, and easier to keep the plan secret. Best known among D-Days of World War II was 6 June 1944 when the Allied Nations landed on the Normandy beaches, a dramatic beginning for their advance through France to Germany. By D+20 the Allies had become firmly established at Arromanches, between the Cotentin peninsula and the mouth of the R. Seine.

    A fascinating diorama of D-Day may be seen in the Imperial Services Museum, Whitehall, London.

DDT, short for dichlor diphenyl trichlorethane, a valuable insecticide ; first prepared 1874 by Zeidler, a German chemist but not widely used till 1942. A white waxy substance, it is a deadly poison to most insects. It was much used in World War II, and is now employed in many ways, e.g. against the Canadian budworm which infests spruce, and as an insecticide in the home.

deadly nightshade, see POISONOUS PLANTS

Dead Sea, a salt-water lake (Israel), 1,292ft below normal sea-level ; area 405sq.m. Fed by the R. Jordan, the water is intensely salt owing to evaporation. It is enclosed by mountains rising 6,000ft. Over 100,000 tons of potash are annually obtained by evaporation.

Deakin, ALFRED (1856–1919), prime minister of Australia three times between 1903 and 1910.

Deal, *dēl*, town, Kent ; supposed site of Julius Caesar's landing.

deal, common name for wood of the pine or fir.

Dean, FOREST OF, region of 22,000 acres, W. Gloucestershire ; has coal mines.

death duties, sums payable on the value of property, real or personal, at death. The duty payable (1948) on an estate valued at £2,000, and not exceeding £3,000, is 1%, over £3,000, 2%, rising to 75% on estates valued at £2,000,000 or more.

    Death duties have the effect of preventing the accumulation of unearned but inherited wealth in one family from one generation to another, and are one of the means by which the distribution of national income in Great Britain has been made more even since the beginning of the century.

death's head moth, largest British hawk moth. It is 4–5in across the wings ; mottled brown, yellow and black, with a mark on the thorax rather like a skull. The yellowish-green caterpillar (with purple streaks) may be 5in.

DEATH'S HEAD MOTH

Death Valley, valley in S. California, USA. A dry region 145m long, it was formerly the bed of a salt lake, and is *c.*480ft below sea-level. It winds among mts from 5,000–10,000ft high ; temperatures of 134°F have been registered, hence it is possibly the hottest place in the world.

Deauville, *dō-vēl,* fashionable seaside holiday town, Normandy, France.

De Bello Gallico, short Latin title for Julius Caesar's *Commentaries on the War in Gaul.* These war dispatches are models of military writing, and cover Caesar's nine years' long campaigns in Gaul. During this period he twice invaded Britain (55 and 54BC). Caesar's style is bald and uninspiring.

debenture, *dē-ben'tūr,* shares offered for sale to the public by a firm which wants to raise money for business purposes. Holders of shares known as *debenture stock* are entitled to receive interest before any others.

Debussy, Claude Achille, *de-bu'see* (1862-1918), French composer, *b* St Germain-en-Laye, *d* Paris. At twelve Debussy became a student at the Paris Conservatoire, and at 22 won a prize which enabled him to study music in Rome for three years. Later he spent a short time in Russia. In 1894 his tone-poem *Prelude to the Afternoon of a Faun* provoked much discussion, as did also his opera *Pelleas and Melisande* (1902). During his lifetime Debussy published a great deal of music for piano, including such nature impressions as *Gardens in Rain, Goldfish,* etc. His music is highly original and has been called impressionist because Debussy is interested in tone for its own sake just as the impressionist painters are interested in light. He often uses a ' whole-tone ' scale in which there are no semitones. His music is full of tender feeling but shaped throughout by a pleasing sense of form.

Deccan, fertile upland (2,000–3,000ft) o S. India.

deciduous, see Trees

decimals or **decimal fractions,** from Latin *decem,* 10 ; in mathematics they are distinguished from vulgar fractions by always having a denominator of 10 or a power of 10, e.g. 17·5, where ·5 is actually $\frac{5}{10}$; or ·03, which means $\frac{3}{100}$. The idea, though apparently due to Stevinus, a Dutchman, *b* 1584, was not commonly used prior to the 18th c.

' ·05 ' is read *point nought five,* and ' ·30 ' is read *point three,* not *point thirty.* Only those figures to the right of the decimal point are decimals.

When *multiplying decimals* we need in the product as many decimal figures as in the multiplier and multiplicand ; but 1,380 × ·005 is 6·900, i.e. 6·9 ; and 1·345 × ·04368 = 0·05874960, i.e. 0·0587496.

To divide a decimal by 10, move the decimal point one place to the *left,* e.g. ·037 ÷ 10 becomes ·0037 ; *to multiply* by 10 move the point to the *right,* e.g. 5·08 × 10 = 50·8. *To divide one decimal by another,* move the point (if necessary) in the divisor to the right till the divisor is a whole number, and move the point in the dividend the same number of places, e.g. ·02352 ÷ ·0048 = 235·2 ÷ 48, and ·13 ÷ ·007 = 130·0 ÷ 7.

To change a decimal into a vulgar fraction, write the figures to the right of the decimal point as the numerator, and for denominator write 1, followed by as many 0s as there are figures to the right of the point, e.g. 3·317 = $3\frac{317}{1000}$; ·005 = $\frac{5}{1000}$; *to express a vulgar fraction as a decimal,* divide the numerator by the denominator, e.g. $\frac{3}{8}$ = ·375, or $\frac{3}{80}$ = ·0375.

If, when dividing the numerator by the denominator, we get a figure, or a series of figures, continually repeating, the decimal is *recurring,* e.g. $\frac{1}{3}$, which gives 3)1·0000...

·3333 . . . to infinity: written (for short) $\cdot\dot{3}$; similarly, $\frac{11}{14}$ as a decimal gives ·7857142857142857142..., hence we write it as a recurring decimal $\cdot\dot{7}85714\dot{2}$. *To change a recurring decimal to a vulgar fraction,* write the period of the decimal as the numerator, and for denominator write as many 9s as there are figures in the period, e.g. $\cdot\dot{4}0\dot{7} = \frac{407}{999}$, and $\cdot\dot{6} = \frac{6}{9}$; but note that $\cdot\dot{0}2\dot{7} = \frac{27}{999}$, *not* $\frac{27}{99}$.

For a decimal with some repeaters and some non-repeating figures, the numerator is obtained by subtracting the non-repeating figures from *all* the figures, and the denominator by writing a 9 for each repeater and 0 for each non-repeater, e.g.

$\cdot 23\dot{4}\dot{5} = \frac{2345-23}{9900} = \frac{2322}{9900}$, i.e. $\frac{129}{550}$.

Decimalisation of money is simplified by noting that (*a*) 1s = £·05, and (*b*) $\frac{1}{4}$d is £·001 (approx.), actually an understatement, the exact figure being £·001$\frac{1}{24}$; hence (*a*) multiply the shillings by ·05, and (*b*) the pence, *when reduced to farthings,* by ·001.

The following table is an aid to changing decimals of £1 to shillings, pence, and farthings, *but only approximately* :

Conversion Table

Decimals of £1 to shillings and pence

£	s	£	s	d	£	d
·1 =	2	·01 =		2½	·001 =	0¼
·2 =	4	·02 =		4¾	·002 =	0½
·3 =	6	·03 =		7¼	·003 =	0¾
·4 =	8	·04 =		9½	·004 =	1
·5 =	10	·05 =	1	0	·005 =	1¼
·6 =	12	·06 =	1	2½	·006 =	1½
·7 =	14	·07 =	1	4¾	·007 =	1¾
·8 =	16	·08 =	1	7¼	·008 =	2
·9 =	18	·09 =	1	9½	·009 =	2¼

The following table may be found useful in converting shillings, pence, and farthings into *decimals of* £1 :

CONVERSION TABLE

Shillings and pence to decimals of £1

s	d	£		s	d	£
0	¼ =	·0010		5	0 =	·2500
0	½ =	·0021		6	0 =	·3000
0	¾ =	·0031		6	3 =	·3125
1	=	·0042		7	0 =	·3500
2	=	·0083		7	6 =	·3750
2½	=	·0104		8	0 =	·4000
3	=	·0125		8	9 =	·4375
4	=	·0167		9	0 =	·4500
5	=	·0208		10	0 =	·5000
6	=	·0250		11	0 =	·5500
7	=	·0292		12	0 =	·6000
8	=	·0333		13	0 =	·6500
9	=	·0375		13	9 =	·6875
10	=	·0417		14	0 =	·7000
11	=	·0458		15	0 =	·7500
1	0 =	·0500		16	0 =	·8000
1	3 =	·0625		16	3 =	·8125
1	6 =	·0750		17	0 =	·8500
2	0 =	·1000		17	6 =	·8750
2	6 =	·1250		18	0 =	·9000
3	0 =	·1500		19	0 =	·9500
3	9 =	·1875		20	0 =	1·0000
4	0 =	·2000				

Decius, dē-ci'ŭs (201–251), Roman emperor who persecuted Christians ; died in battle against Goths whose advance he tried to retard.

Declaration of Independence, 1776, statement setting forth the fundamental principles on which the Constitution of the USA was later founded. The War of American Independence began 1775, but it was not until 2 July 1776 that it was resolved in Congress that the American colonies should declare themselves independent. Meanwhile a draft Declaration of Independence had been drawn up, mainly by Jefferson, and on 4 July 1776 it was adopted by a majority of the delegates.

The Declaration begins by saying that when it becomes necessary for one people to break away from another to which it has been connected, it is only right that they should explain their reasons for doing so. Then follow these famous words :

We hold these truths to be self-evident, that all men are created equal ; that they are endowed by their Creator with certain inalienable rights, that among these are life, liberty, and the pursuit of happiness. That to secure these rights, governments are instituted among men, deriving their just powers from the consent of the governed. That whenever any form of government becomes destructive of these ends, it is the right of the people to alter or abolish it, and to institute new government. . . .

The Declaration then goes on to state the ways in which it was thought the British Government had violated these fundamental principles. In history the list of grievances has been less important than the statement of principles. Demo-

cracy came to Europe in the 19th c. from the USA, and the Declaration of Independence was the first coherent statement in a practical form of its fundamental beliefs and faith, and also of the doctrine of national self-determination (i.e. the doctrine that nations have a natural right to govern themselves) which was to be of such great importance later on.

Jefferson's political principles were derived from those put forward after the Glorious Revolution of 1688 by the English philosopher John Locke. It is important to realise that he lived before the industrial age, and that wide acceptance of his emphasis on the inalienable rights of individual men and nations has not made it any easier to solve the far more complicated political problems existing in modern societies. The doctrine that all men are created equal has not been fully accepted even in the USA, where coloured folk are not treated the same as white men ; and while it is rightly repugnant to modern minds that e.g. Czechs should be governed by Austrians or Russians, the doctrine that nations have certain inalienable sovereign rights is in the extreme form stated by Jefferson himself one cause of the inability of the nations at present to work out ways of peaceful co-operation and find solutions of major problems without recourse to mutually destructive wars.

decorations are honours given to people for outstanding service to their country. Among many decorations are :

VC (Victoria Cross) supreme award for gallantry. Instituted 1856, this is worn before all other decorations. It may be awarded to any member of the Naval, Military or Air Forces of the British Commonwealth.

DSO (Distinguished Service Order) instituted 1886, bestowed upon commissioned officers in the Navy, Army, Air Force and Mercantile Marine for special services in action.

GC (George Cross) instituted 1940, primarily intended for Civilians and the Fighting Services when military honours are not generally granted.

DSC (Distinguished Service Cross) instituted 1914, substituted for the Conspicuous Cross (1901) for officers below the rank of Captain and for Warrant Officers in the Royal Navy.

MC (Military Cross) 1915, awarded to Captains, Lieutenants, and Warrant Officers in the Army, Indian and Colonial Forces.

AFC (Air Force Cross) 1918, for acts of courage or devotion to duty when flying, although not necessarily in action against the enemy.

DCM (Distinguished Conduct Medal), for Warrant Officers, non-commissioned officers and men of the Army and Air Force.

DSM (Distinguished Service Medal)

DEER

(1) *Roe Deer*   (2) *Reindeer*
(3) *Red Deer*   (4) *Fallow Deer*

1914, awarded for outstanding services to Chief Petty Officers and all ranks down to boys in all branches of the Royal Navy and Mercantile Marine ; to non-commissioned officers and men of the Royal Marines and all those holding corresponding positions in HM services afloat.

de Coverley, SIR ROGER, see ADDISON AND STEELE

Dee, river in Wales and Cheshire, 80m long; its estuary has sandbanks ; also a river 87m long, entering the N. Sea at Aberdeen, Scotland ; noted for salmon.

deed, signed promise in writing. A deed between 2 parties (say a vendor and a purchaser) was formerly called an indenture from the old custom of cutting a wavy (*indented*) line across the parchment so that one part of the document fitted the other.

Deeping, GEORGE WARWICK (1877–1950), popular English novelist, *b* Southend-on-Sea ; practised as a doctor ; served in World War I ; made a name with romantic historical novels, later as the writer of novels dealing with modern conditions. His books include *Sorrell and Son* ; *Old Pybus* ; *Exiles* ; *The Dark House* ; *Corn in Egypt* ; and *Laughing House* ; several of his novels have been filmed.

deer, animal (family *Cervidae*), the male having solid, branching antlers that are shed every spring. Britain has (*a*) RED DEER, the largest ; roams chiefly in the Scottish highlands and on Exmoor ;

(*b*) ROE DEER, antlers only *c.*8in long ; (*c*) FALLOW DEER, *c.*3ft high, usually fawn, often dappled with white. All are wild game. The REINDEER (Siberia, Canada, USA), peculiar in having an antlered female, is the only domesticated species.

Defoe, DANIEL, *dē-fō′* (1661–1731), author, *b* London ; had a varied and unhappy career ; was in the brick-making trade, then became a dealer in cloth, a soldier, also a spy. Defoe was always busy writing, often getting himself into trouble by attacking the government, for which he was twice imprisoned ; stood in the pillory three times. A Non-conformist when Nonconformists were being severely persecuted, his health was never good, and he was almost always in debt.

Defoe was a noted pamphleteer, e.g. his plea for more kindly treatment of insane people, or on William III's plan for keeping an army always in readiness. He wrote *Journal of the Plague Year* and *Tour Through Great Britain.*

He was one of the founders of modern journalism, but is most famous for the skill with which he tells a story, and for his book *The Life and Strange Adventures of Robinson Crusoe of York, Mariner,* published 1719 ; based on the adventures of Alexander Selkirk (1676–1721), a Scotsman who sailed with William Dampier in the S. Seas, and for over 4 years was alone on the island of Juan Fernandez in the Pacific Ocean. *Robin-*

son *Crusoe* is now regarded as the starting-point of the modern English novel.

degrees (scholastic), see EXAMINATIONS ; UNIVERSITIES

dehydrated food has been in use for many years in the form of dried fruit, but it was not until World War II that the value of this food process was fully realised. Dehydrated eggs and milk were used extensively by forces and public alike during World War II, while dehydrated potatoes came into general use in the post-war period.

The advantages of dehydrated food are many—it does not deteriorate so quickly as food in its natural form ; it is easier to pack, uses less space, and is lighter to carry, being devoid of its water content which is easily replaced by mixing (in the case of eggs, milk, and potatoes) or soaking (in the case of fruit) in water. There is, after all, no reason for food + water-content being carried from place to place when the water may be removed without in any way detracting from the quality of the food.

dehydration, in chemistry, the removal of water (H_2O) from a compound by the action of heat or a chemical agent.

de-icing, see FROST

Deira, see NORTHUMBRIA

Dekker, THOMAS (*c.*1570–1641), dramatist and pamphleteer, *b* London ; portrayed life with humour ; was a lyric genius (e.g. *Art thou poor, yet hast thou golden slumbers?*). His best plays include *The Shoemaker's Holiday* ; *Old Fortunatus* ; *The Honest Whore* ; *The Witch of Edmonton*, etc.

Delafield, E. M., *del'ä-*, pen-name of Elizabeth M. Dashwood (*d* 1943), noted for *The Diary of a Provincial Lady*, and many other books portraying modern English life.

Delagoa Bay, *del-ä-gō'ä*, inlet on the SE. coast of Africa.

Delane, JOHN THADDEUS (1817–79), 36 years editor of *The Times*, which he raised to the foremost place in British journalism.

Delaware, *del'ä-wär*, river of USA ; rises in New York State and flows into Delaware Bay.

Delaware, small state of USA ; on the Atlantic coast ; named after Lord De la Warr, and founded 1610 ; grows fruit and grain ; cap. Dover.

Delft, town, S. Netherlands ; has many canals ; pop.60,000.

Delhi, *del'i*, ancient walled city and capital of India 1912–31 ; on the R. Jumna ; has remains of great buildings destroyed long ago, also the palace of Shah Jehan, built 1638–48, and now called ' The Fort ' ; also the Jamna Mesjid, one of the finest mosques in India. Some 10m off is the Kutb Minar, a fluted sandstone column 238ft high, one of the marvels of India. The manufactures include cotton, and also jewellery (often hand-made), wood-carvings, gold and silver trinkets, and woollen fabrics.

Long a centre of Mohammedan power, Delhi came under British control 1803, and was the scene of George V's coronation durbar 1911.

NEW DELHI, *c.*5m SW., planned by Sir Edward Lutyens, is famous for its handsome state buildings, among them two blocks of secretariats ; also the vast and imposing Indian Parliament House—a handsome building within a circular colonnade. There is the Durbar Hall, also Government House, which has a copper dome 177ft high. The pop. of Delhi is *c.*521,000, though at one time it was over 2,000,000. New Delhi has been the Indian capital since 1931.

deliquescence, in chemistry, taking up water from the air, as does calcium chloride.

Delius, FREDERICK (1862–1934), composer, *b* Bradford, of a German-Dutch father and German mother. Intended for a business career, he spent some time in Germany, Norway and Sweden, and went out to Florida as an orange-grower. He set up as a piano teacher in Danville, Virginia, and later studied music at Leipzig. He spent much of his life in France, where he died, and his music was for long more popular in Germany than in England, where it was popularised after World War I largely by the efforts of Sir Thomas Beecham. In later life he became blind and crippled. His music is romantic in feeling, and like Debussy he was an impressionist. His work includes operas, rhapsodies, and a Requiem based on words by the German romantic philosopher Nietzsche.

Delphi, *del'fi*, formerly a town before Mt Parnassus, Greece. The site of its temple of Apollo (famous for its oracle) has been excavated. See APOLLO

delta, area of alluvial deposit (river mud, usually fertile) at the mouth of a river, e.g. that of the Nile, Ganges, Mississippi and Danube. A river delta resembles in shape the Greek letter Delta (Δ).

Demerara, *dem-ĕ-rär'ä*, region of British Guiana, with a river of the same name entering the Atlantic at Georgetown ; noted for brown (demerara) sugar.

demesne, see VILLEIN

Demeter, *dē-mē'tĕr*, in old Greek tales, goddess of agriculture, known to the Romans as Ceres (see CEREAL) ; mother of Persephone, who was carried to the underworld by Pluto while gathering flowers in Sicily, whereupon the trees and flowers mourned for her (autumn). Demeter searched for her daughter, and eventually Persephone was allowed to return (springtime) for 6 months each year. The story is a nature allegory.

democracy, *dē-mok'rä-si* (Gk *demokratia*, government by the people), rule of the people by the people, at first contrasted with aristocracy, i.e. the rule of the wealthy, noble, or any privileged class, and later contrasted with Fascism or

Nazism, i.e. government of the people by dictators ; and with Communism, i.e. government of the people by a dictatorship of the Communist Party.

In the city-states of ancient Greece, citizens were called together to share in making laws and deciding public affairs. Later, the rise of large nations in Europe made this method impracticable, and the people chose representatives to act for them, the British parliamentary system being the model for many other countries, including (to some extent) that of USA.

In actual practice democracy does not work simply either in local or central governments, but the principle does allow the voice of the people to be heard, and with all its defects is no doubt the best for ensuring individual liberty. The ideal democracy is summed up in Lincoln's famous definition : *Government of the people, by the people, for the people.* See PARLIAMENT ; POLITICS

Democrat, *dem'ō-krat,* in USA, one who belongs to the Democratic Party, believing in decentralisation and self-government of the various states ; opposed to the Republican Party, founded 1854–56, long associated with policies of a strong central government, protective tariffs, and (later) with opposition to association with the League of Nations.

Democritus, *dē-mok'ri-tus* (460–370BC), Greek philosopher who with Leucippus invented the atomic theory, i.e. that everything is composed of atoms, which are supposed to be minute, indivisible particles differing from one another not in substance but only in their shapes and sizes, to which ultimately the differences between physical substances as known to us can be traced. Democritus worked out the theory in considerable detail, and it was taken up by later Greek philosophers, notably Epicurus.

The theory of atoms put forward by these philosophers was not based on systematic observation of nature, but was rather the outcome of mere speculation and intelligent guesswork. The modern atomic theory owes little if anything to Democritus and Leucippus. Their work was nevertheless a remarkable achievement. It was known to Aristotle, but probably not to Plato.

Democritus was known as 'the laughing philosopher.'

De Morgan, AUGUSTUS (1806–71), English mathematician, *b* Madura, India ; had a great deal to do with developing formal logic and introducing the metric system; professor of mathematics London University 1828–31 and 1836–66.

De Morgan, WILLIAM FREND (1839–1917), English artist, potter and author, *b* London ; noted for his novels *Joseph Vance* ; *Alice-for-Short* ; and *A Likely Story* ; invented new lustre-ware processes.

Demosthenes, *dē-mos'the-nēz* (c.383–322BC),

Athenian statesman and greatest of all Greek orators ; said to have cured himself of stammering by speaking with pebbles in his mouth. Fired by unbounded patriotism, his life was a struggle against Philip of Macedonia and, later, Alexander the Great. Some of his noblest speeches (e.g. the *Olynthiacs, Philippics*) call for united action against Macedonia. Though he turned coward at the battle of Chaeronea 338BC, it was proposed to award him a golden crown for his public services, hence his masterpiece of oratory *De Corona.* He took his own life to escape falling into the hands of the Macedonians.

One of his sayings was :

ὃ βούλεται, τοῦθ' ἕκαστος καὶ οἴεται

What each man wishes, that also he thinks.

Denbighshire, *den'bi-,* county of N. Wales ; has fine mt. scenery ; ponies and sheep are raised ; coal and lead are mined ; co.tn Denbigh.

Denis, ST (3rd c.), short for Dionysius, patron saint of France ; first bishop of Paris ; beheaded *c.*AD275 ; festival 9 Oct.

Denmark, Scandinavian kingdom in NW. Europe ; includes the peninsula of Jutland ; area *c.*16,580sq.m. The land is generally low and not exceptionally fertile, but the Danes have made the most of it, dividing it into small-holdings. Denmark, famous for dairy farming, exports butter, cheese, eggs, and bacon ; pop.4,000,000; cap. Copenhagen. The Germans invaded Denmark 1940, the capital being liberated by the Allies 1945. King Christian X *d* 1947, and was succeeded by Frederick IX.

The Danes are a highly educated and thrifty people, in many respects closely akin to the British. It was the Danes who, from the 5th c. AD, invaded E. England and SE. Scotland, and it was they who, in the 9th c., were the so-called Northmen or Norsemen who settled here in considerable numbers. Their language is interwoven with our own, hence such words as *stag, cur, egg, harbour, reindeer, sky, take, thrive, ugly, sleek, sly,* and such personal names as *Anderson, Davidson,* and *Thomson.*

denominator, see FRACTIONS

density, in physics, mass per unit volume, i.e. density $= \dfrac{\text{mass}}{\text{volume}}$.

See SPECIFIC GRAVITY

dentine, see TEETH

dentistry, see CAREERS

Denver, cap., Colorado, USA ; an important railway and industrial centre ; noted for its cattle market ; pop.322,000.

department, one of the 87 divisions of France (90 with the 3 in Algeria), each comparable to a county in the UK.

Deptford, *det'fĕrd,* London borough S. of the Thames, where Drake's *Golden Hind* docked ; suffered severely from air raids in World War II ; pop.57,000

de Quincey, THOMAS, *dē kwin'si* (1785–1859), English essayist, *b* Manchester, shy and imaginative as a child, delighted to wander out-of-doors ; lived in Wordsworth's old home, Grasmere, for 20 years ; suffered from an internal complaint that compelled him to take opium ; in 1828 he moved to Edinburgh. De Quincey, a master of Greek, Latin, German and philosophy, was an able critic, an imaginative, humorous writer, and a great stylist. His fame rests chiefly on his essays, among which are included *The English Mail Coach* ; *Confessions of an English Opium-Eater* ; and *On Murder Considered as a Fine Art.*

As an example of de Quincey's imaginative style consider :

Hitherto the human face had mixed often in my dreams, but not despotically, nor with any special power of tormenting. But now that which I have called the tyranny of the human face began to unfold itself. Perhaps some part of my London life might be answerable for this. Be that as it may, now it was that upon the rocking waters of the ocean the human face began to appear ; the sea appeared paved with innumerable faces, upturned to the heavens ; faces imploring, wrathful, despairing, surged upwards by thousands, by myriads, by generations, by centuries—my agitation was infinite—my mind tossed and surged with the ocean.

Derby, *där'bi* ; *dür'-*, co.tn, Derbyshire ; on the R. Derwent ; noted for the manufacture of silk, lace, net, hosiery ; also for engineering, and as a railway centre ; famous for Crown Derby china ; pop.142,000.

Derby, 14TH EARL OF (1799–1869), statesman, *b* Knowsley, Lancashire ; first a Whig, later a Tory ; Prime Minister 1852 ; again 1858–59 ; also 1866–68, during which period the 1867 Reform Bill was passed. A scholar, he is remembered for his famous speeches, and was called ' the Rupert of debate.'

Derby, THE, chief horse race in the UK since 1780 ; begun by the 12th Earl of Derby ; held annually May or early June at Epsom (Surrey) on a flat course of 1½m.

Derbyshire, midland county of England. Though largely a coalfield, it is noted for fine mountain scenery, notably in the Peak District ; and for beautiful winding valleys ; co.tn Derby.

dermatitis, see SKIN

Derry, see LONDONDERRY

De Ruyter, MICHAEL, *dē roi'tĕr* (1607–76), brilliant Dutch sailor, *b* Flushing ; served in first Dutch war with England 1653 ; with Danes against Swedes 1659 ; second Dutch war 1665, defeating Monk, chasing the English to the mouth of the Thames, and burning Chatham dockyard ; fought third Dutch war when he went into action against French and English fleets at Sole Bay, 1672.

dervish, *dür'vish*, Persian, Turkish or Arab religious man akin to the fakir ; some Dervishes dance till they fall in a fit ; others lead a wandering life ; others mutilate the body ; most are Mohammedan.

Derwentwater, lake, Cumberland. To the S. are the Falls of Lodore

Descartes, RENÉ, *dā'kart* (1596–1650), French philosopher, *b* La Haye (Touraine) ; saw military service in France and Germany ; *d* Stockholm. He founded analytical and algebraic geometry, and was the father of modern philosophy. He made it a rule in philosophy never to believe what he could possibly doubt, but found that it was impossible to doubt his own existence. This he summed up in the famous phrase ' *cogito, ergo sum* ' (I am thinking, therefore [it must be that] I exist), which he made the starting point of his philosophy.

desert, desolate uninhabited region where little or no vegetation exists. The world's chief deserts are the Sahara and Kalahari (Africa), Atacama (S. America), and Gobi (Asia). A desert is not necessarily a wilderness of sand.

In addition to natural deserts there are man-made wildernesses, e.g. those of N. America, the result of foolishly destroying forests, thus causing the soil to become dry dust, vast areas now being barren in Wyoming, Kansas, Colorado, etc. The building of dams and the sowing of soil-binding grasses is doing much to reclaim areas that have become nonproductive.

Desert Rats, name given to the Eighth Army in World War II. The 7th Armoured Division had a jerboa (desert rat) as its Divisional sign, hence the nickname for the troops which drove the Germans out of N. Africa.

Desmoulins, CAMILLE, *dā-moo-la*n' (1760–1794), French journalist, *b* Guise (France) ; urged abolition of monarchy and incited a Paris crowd to begin the Revolution by his call, ' To arms ! ' 12 July 1789 ; follower of Danton.

Detroit, *dē-troit'*, city, Michigan, USA, on the Detroit R. An important railway centre, it has a vast lake and river traffic ; noted for the Ford motor works ; pop.1,623,000.

Dettingen, *det'ing-en*, village, Bavaria (Germany), where British and Hanoverians, led by George II, defeated the French 1743.

deuterium, see HEAVY WATER

deuteron, see RADIOACTIVITY

Deuteronomy, *dū-ter-on'ō-mi*, 5th book of the OT. It deals with Jewish law.

de Valera, EAMON, *dā vä-lā'rä* (1882–   ), Irish statesman, *b* New York ; after being a teacher of French, mathematics and Latin, he became commandant in Irish National Rebellion, 1916 ; captured and sentenced to death ; released 1917 ; imprisoned 1918, but escaped. In America he raised funds 1919–20 for

Irish Republican government ; president of Sinn Fein Party 1917–26 ; leader of the party since then. Became president of Irish Free State 1932, and resigned 1948.

devaluation, see DOLLAR AREA

Devon, county of SW. England ; includes the bleak uplands of Dartmoor, but noted for seaside resorts and charming river valleys; co.tn Exeter. Tin, copper, iron, China clay and granite are mined. The county is famous for cider and clotted cream. ' Glorious Devon ' was the birthplace of such gallant adventurers as Drake, Raleigh and Gilbert, and its literary sons include Charles Kingsley.

Devonport, see PLYMOUTH

Devonshire, 1ST DUKE OF (1640–1707), English statesman ; raised the standard of rebellion at Derby for William of Orange ; rebuilt Chatsworth House.

Devonshire, 8TH DUKE OF (1833–1908), British statesman, *b* Holker Hall, N. Lancs ; Secretary for India 1880–82 ; became leader of Liberal Party when Gladstone retired ; invited to form government in 1880 (after the fall of the Beaconsfield government), but he declined in favour of Gladstone, later splitting with him over Home Rule (1886). Disagreed with and opposed Chamberlain on his Tariff Reform proposals.

dew, water deposit produced by condensation of water vapour in the air when the temperature falls (e.g. on clear nights) sufficiently for the vapour to reach saturation point.

DEW-PONDS (particularly common on the chalk of S. England) are hollows lined with straw, over which puddled clay is beaten, though concrete ponds are now being made.

The theory of dew-ponds may be stated simply as follows : (*a*) clay prevents drainage, (*b*) straw prevents inflow of heat from the ground, (*c*) the exposed hill-top position induces low night temperatures, hence condensation.

Dewar, SIR JAMES, *du'ĕr* (1842–1923), Scottish chemist and physicist, *b* Kincardine-on-Forth ; shared with Sir Frederick Abel the discovery of cordite ; investigated the liquefaction of gases and the physics of extreme cold, and invented the Dewar flask, forerunner of the modern vacuum flask.

de Wet, CHRISTIAN RUDOLF, *dĕ vet* (1854–1922), Boer soldier ; skilled leader of guerilla warfare ; joined the 1914 rebellion.

Dewsbury, town, W. Yorkshire ; manufactures blankets, shoddy, woollen cloth and carpets ; pop.46,000.

dextran plasma, see BLOOD

dextrin, see STARCH

dextrose, see GLUCOSE

dhow, *dow*, long, fast-sailing native ship of the Arabian Sea or Indian Ocean ; has one mast and a triangular sail ; this type of vessel was used for hundreds

of years in carrying on slave trade, gun-running, and normal trade.

diabetes, *dī-ä-bē'tēz*, disease caused by the presence of grape-sugar in the blood ; now very successfully treated with Insulin.

diaeresis, see ACCENT

diagnosis, see MEDICINE

dialect, see LANGUAGE

dialysis, in chemistry, separation of a colloid from a substance in true solution by allowing the latter to diffuse through a parchment.

diameter, see CIRCLE

diamond, *dī'ä-mŭnd*, precious stone of pure crystalline carbon ; hardest known substance ; the finest gems are crystal clear, but some are pink, yellow, or green ; cutting increases brilliance by adding reflecting facets ; inferior diamonds are used as pivots in watches, and as cutting tools, e.g. glass-cutting, boring, etching.

Notable diamonds include *Koh-i-noor* (Mountain of Light), now in the British crown, once in the eye of the peacock throne, Delhi, originally 186 carats, reduced to 106 ; *Cullinan* discovered 1905 in the Transvaal, now in the British sceptre, originally 3,025 carats (1¾ lb). Prior to 1729 most diamonds came from India ; later Brazilian diamonds were in great demand. Diamonds are now found in Borneo, Australia, British Guiana, USA and the Congo, but chiefly in S. Africa, where the centre is Kimberley. Black or green diamonds (worthless as gems) are used for rock-drills, wire-drawing, lathe tools, etc.

A remarkable diamond was discovered in Tanganyika Territory 1945.

Diamond Sculls, see SCULLING

Diana, see ARTEMIS

diary, book in which events of interest to the writer are recorded day by day. Many diaries kept for purely personal reasons have been of immense interest to later generations. Such are the diaries of Samuel Pepys, John Evelyn, Fanny Burney, Greville and Crocker. Diaries need not be about the private life of the writer : Gilbert White, 18th c. rector of Selborne, kept a nature diary which is delightful to read even though it is in note-form.

diasone, see TUBERCULOSIS

diastase, *dī'äs-tās*, enzyme that changes starch into maltose, a sugar employed in malting.

diatom, *dī'ä-tom*, minute single-celled plant-form akin to seaweeds. The cell-wall is rich in silica, and the creature may swim singly or in string-like colonies in fresh- or sea-water. *Diatomaceae* provide food for lower marine animals ; fossil forms are found in Britain, USA, and especially near Hanover (Germany).

Diaz, BARTOLOMEU (*d c.*1500), Portuguese explorer who rounded the Cape of Good Hope 1488.

Diaz, PORFIRIO, *dē'äs* (1830–1915), Mexican politician and soldier, *b* Oaxaca ; repeatedly president of Mexico, giving

WOOL *plate 21*

Top : Flinging an Australian fleece before passing it to the classer for grading. (*Australian News and Information Bureau*). *Bottom :* Making tweed. A loom in a Scottish woollen mill. (*Travel Press and Publicity Co.*)

plate 22   **WOOLLENS**

Stages in finishing lengths of woollen cloth (*top*), and (*bottom*) in the manufacture of woollen garments.   (*Travel Press and Publicity Co.*)

COTTON

plate 23

Much of the world's cotton comes from the U.S. Southern States, but post-war conditions necessitated development of cotton-growing inside the sterling area. A basketful of newly-picked cotton, Northern Provinces, Nigeria. (*C.O.I.*)

plate 24   COTTON CULTIVATION

Top : Irrigation is an important factor in cotton growing. The two-mile-long Sennar Dam on the Blue Nile, which feeds the irrigation system of the Gezira. *Bottom :* Cotton picking, Northern Provinces, Nigeria. (Both *C.O.I.*)

COTTON IN THE BOLL   *plate 25*

Close-up of a stem of cotton ready for picking.   (*C.O.I.*)

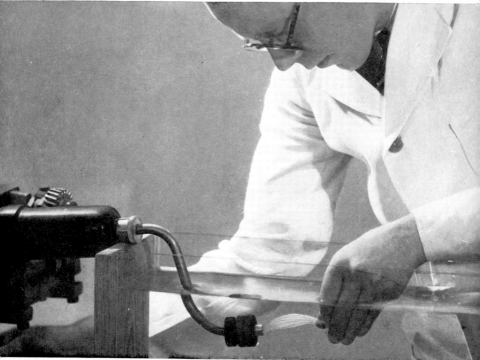

plate 26   **RAYON**

Top : Section-warping in Courtauld's textile mills. The warp comprises the lengthwise threads of a fabric. *Bottom :* Laboratory experiment demonstrating the extrusion of viscose from the 'spinning jet' into a bath of coagulating liquid so as to form a filament of rayon.
(Both *Courtaulds Ltd*)

TEXTILE PRODUCTION—NATURE AND SCIENCE   *plate 27*

Top : Inside a cotton-dyeing laboratory. (*I.C.I.*). *Bottom :* Silk moths with their eggs. (*E.N.A.*)

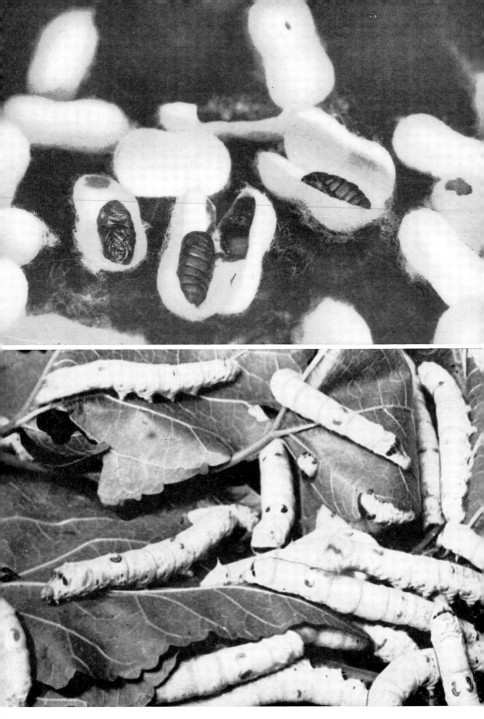

plate 28   **SILK**

Top : Silk-moth cocoons, some of them cut open to show the Pupa. Silk thread is obtained by unwinding the cocoon. *Bottom :* Silk worms feeding on Mulberry leaves. Soon they will turn into cocoons. (Both *E.N.A.*)

the country order and prosperity, but ruling as a dictator ; was overthrown in a revolution 1911.

dibasic acids, acids which contain two hydrogen atoms in each molecule replaceable by a metal, e.g. sulphuric acid, H_2SO_4.

Dibdin, CHARLES (1745–1814), English song-writer and popular entertainer, *b* Southampton. His songs, numbering 600, include *Tom Bowling* and *Poor Jack.*

Dickens, CHARLES (1812–70), novelist, *b* Portsea, a district of Portsmouth ; moved to Chatham 1816. Later (in London) the family were for a time so poor that Charles often pawned garments, and was sent to work in a blacking factory at 6s a week. While his family were in the Marshalsea prison for debt he was looked after by an old lady in Camden Town. After a brief schooling he became clerk in a solicitor's office, studied shorthand, and was reporting Parliamentary speeches 1832.

About this time Dickens began writing sketches of London life for the *Evening Chronicle* under the pen-name ' Boz ' ; and, 1836, he became famous as the author of the serial story *The Pickwick Papers.* This took England by storm, and was the first of many books which appeared first as serials. His marriage with Catherine Hogarth was not happy, and they separated 20 years later, though he found great joy in his 10 children, one of whom died in infancy. He visited America 1842, and was at the peak of his fame 1857 when he bought Gad's Hill (near Rochester, Kent), a house he is said to have longed for as a child. A nervous shock (the result of a railway accident 1865) clouded his last years, but he continued to give exceedingly popular readings from his own books. He died at Gad's Hill.

Dickens was peculiarly English. He understood and sympathised with the poor and oppressed. He portrayed English character more vividly and more fantastically than any other writer. His humour never fails ; his genius for plot is extraordinary ; his characters are as much alive now as when he created them, e.g. Mr Micawber, Sam Weller, Captain Cuttle, etc. He is over-sentimental at times, and his female characters are often weak and unreal, but his stories have an abiding place in our literature. Film and broadcast versions of his novels are extremely popular.

Among his novels are : *The Pickwick Papers* ; *Oliver Twist* ; *Nicholas Nickleby* ; *The Old Curiosity Shop* ; *Barnaby Rudge* ; *Martin Chuzzlewit* ; *A Christmas Carol* ; *David Copperfield* (partly the story of his own life) ; *Bleak House* ; *Little Dorrit* ; *A Tale of Two Cities* ; *Great Expectations* ; and the unfinished *Edwin Drood.*

Dickens championed the cause of the unfortunate, e.g. his novel *Nicholas Nickleby* led to the abolition of a type of corrupt school common in England prior to 1840.

Dickens, MONICA (1915–   ), a great-granddaughter of Charles Dickens, and a popular author, e.g. *One Pair of Hands.*

dicotyledon, see BOTANY

dictator, *dik-tā'tĕr*, in the ancient Roman republic, a magistrate who in some emergency was given extraordinary powers for six months ; e.g. those of life and death without appeal to the Senate, all other magistrates being compelled to obey him. Julius Caesar was several times dictator, and Fabius Maximus Cunctator and Sulla were others.

In modern times a dictator is the ruler of a totalitarian state, e.g. Hitler, Mussolini, etc. As there is no parliamentary opposition, he is almost inevitably compelled to resort to force rather than justice.

Diderot, DENIS, *dēd-rō'* (1713–84), French scholar, whose writings greatly advanced the scientific thought of his day.

Dido, *dī'dō*, in old Latin tales, founder and Queen of Carthage. One story of her (told by Virgil) is that she fell in love with Aeneas and killed herself because he deserted her in order to fulfil his destiny by founding Rome.

Didymus, see THOMAS

Dieppe, *dē-ep'*, Channel holiday town and port, France ; has a regular packet service with Newhaven. The industries include cotton-spinning and shipbuilding ; pop.26,000 ; scene (Aug 1942) of a large-scale British and Canadian raid, the town being then in German hands.

Diesel, RUDOLF, *dē'zel* (1858–1913), German engineer, *b* Paris ; inventor of the Diesel engine in which no electric spark is needed, the compression of the gases in the cylinder on the return-stroke of the piston causing a temperature sufficiently high to ignite a spray of fuel oil. Invented 1895, this type of engine, burning heavy oil, has recently made great advances, and is now used in London buses, as a marine engine, and has been tried with some success in aircraft engines.

diet, *dī'et*, a conference, congress or council. Among the most famous were the diets of Worms 1521 ; of Augsburg 1530 and 1547.

Dieu et Mon Droit, *dyü et mon drwä* (French for ' God and my right '), watchword given to his army by Richard I at the battle of Gisors 1198 ; adopted by Henry VI, and an English royal motto ever since.

diffraction, pattern of light and dark or coloured bands when a beam of light passes (*a*) through a small hole, or (*b*) beyond the edge of an opaque obstacle.

digestion, *dī-jes'chŭn*, process of assimilating food, i.e. changing the food we eat into flesh, bone, blood, heat, energy, etc. Food is digested as it passes along the

alimentary canal, i.e. the long tube
beginning at the mouth and ending with
the *anus*, where waste products are
expelled. Hence the digestive system
includes mouth, *oesophagus*, stomach,
and also the small and large intestine,
forming the bowel.

Food is broken up in the mouth by the
teeth and mixed with saliva which
partly changes starch into maltose
(i.e. malt sugar). When a mouthful of
food is swallowed it passes over the
epiglottis, is eased down the gullet
(*oesophagus*) by the frequent contraction
of the muscles behind the ball of food,
and the expansion of those in front. In
the *stomach*, a kind of muscular bag,
food is further acted on by mucus and
gastric juices, both produced in the cell-
lining. These juices (*pepsin* and *rennin*)
are accompanied by about ½ % hydrochloric acid. Pepsin is an *enzyme* which
breaks down proteins into nitrogen-
containing substances—*proteoses* and
peptones. Rennin acts on *casein* (the
protein of milk) and forms an emulsion
which is later absorbed into the blood-
stream.

Food then passes to the small intestine (about 20–24ft long, but only 1in
wide) where an alkaline liquid from the
pancreas acts on it ; also a greenish
yellow bile from the liver (the largest
organ in the body, weighing 50–60oz,
and having 5 lobes). The liver secretes
bile, and pours this into the earlier part
of the small intestine, the *duodenum*
(*du-ō-dē'nŭm*). The pancreatic juice in
the duodenum contains 3 enzymes (*a*)
trypsin, (*b*) *lipase*, (*c*) *amylase* ; (*a*) acts
still further on proteins and produces
proteoses, peptones, and amino-acids ;
(*b*) on fats, forming glycerol and fatty
acids with the help of the bile ; while
(*c*) changes starch into maltose. Finally,
food enters the large intestine (much
wider than the small intestine), where
the absorption of water from matter
that remains is accomplished.

Our food comprises water, carbohydrates, fats, proteins, vitamins, etc.,
and the digestive system is designed to
break these down chemically so that
they can be absorbed through the walls
of the alimentary canal and so reach the
blood-stream, as glucose, fatty acids,
glycerol and amino-acids, etc. This
chemical process is carried on by means
of water and various enzymes, to which
reference has already been made.

The precise nature of ENZYMES remains
a mystery. We know that they are found
only in living protoplasm, that each
affects a change only in its own appropriate substance ; that the change may
work either way, as, say, in the diastases,
which change sugar into starch or starch
into sugar ; that a very small amount of
an enzyme will act on a very large
amount of its appropriate substance ;
and that while changing another substance, the enzyme remains unchanged.

The liver-produced *glucose* is stored,
as *glycogen*, for emergency use. To do
this the pancreas supplies *insulin*, which
controls the percentage of sugar in the
blood, too much sugar causing diabetes.

Dijon, *dē-zhõn*, one of the most handsome
towns of France, formerly capital of
Burgundy ; a great railway centre ;
famous for wines. It is noted for its
many churches and educational facilities ;
pop.90,000.

dingo, wild dog of Australia which in size
is smaller than a wolf, but larger than a
jackal ; it has a long bushy tail, and the
colour varies from sandy-red in some,
to black in others. It preys on sheep
and poultry.

Diocletian, *dī-ō-klē'shan* (AD245–313),
Roman emperor (Gaius Aurelius
Valerius Diocletianus in full) ; son of
slave parents ; ruled AD284–305. He
was an able administrator who initiated
the division of the Roman Empire into
two halves, Eastern and Western, and
prepared the way for Constantine ; but
he was a cruel persecutor of Christians.

Diogenes, *di-oj'e-nēz* (*c*.412–323BC), Greek
philosopher, founder of the Cynic
school of thinkers. His father had been
sent to prison for defacing the coinage,
and Diogenes gave out that he wished
too to ' deface the coinage ' by showing
up all titles, honours and wordly
conventions as shams and falsehoods.
In furtherance of this aim he lived like
a dog, and is said to have dwelt in a
tub or large earthenware vessel. For
this reason he was first called a Cynic,
which in Greek means doglike. He was
not, however, cynical in our sense of the
word, the sense in which a cynic is ' a
man who knows the price of everything
and the value of nothing ' ; he believed
ardently in ' virtue,' and his eccentric
philosophy was an attempt to free true
' virtue ' from the insidious corruptions
of worldliness.

When Alexander the Great paid him
a visit and asked him whether he could
do anything for him, Diogenes replied,
' Just stand out of my light.'

On another occasion he was seen going
through the street in broad daylight
with a lighted lamp, and when asked
why he was doing that, he answered
that he was looking for a good man.

Dionysius the Elder, *dī-ō-niz'iŭs* (430–
367BC), soldier who became ruler of
Syracuse and other cities in Sicily ;
made war on the Carthaginians ; fostered
art, literature and architecture ; later
became suspicious and cruel.

Dionysus, in old Greek tales, a god
associated with the vine, and also
regarded as the patron of drama.
Festivals in his honour were a feature
of ancient Attica. Dionysus was known
to the Romans as Bacchus.

diphtheria, *dif-thēr'i-ä*, acute infectious
disease usually affecting the surface
tissues of the nose, throat and mouth ;
now largely prevented by immunisation

i.e. inoculating with a toxin-antitoxin vaccine.

diploma, *di-plō'mä,* certificate of efficiency in some branch of study. It is awarded by a university where a lower standard than a degree is achieved, or in some subject in which a degree is not conferred ; is also awarded to students who take an extra-mural course (i.e. outside the university). Specialised educational bodies not entitled to award degrees generally present diplomas. See EXAMINATIONS

dipper (or water ouzel), bird akin to the wren. It is *c.*7in long, with dark brown and white underparts, and a very short tail. It walks under water, and stands on stones bobbing up and down, hence its name.

DIPPER

direct current, see RECTIFIER

Directory, THE (Fr. Le Directoire), committee of 5 that governed France 1795–1799.

Disciples, see CHRIST

' Discobolus,' see SCULPTURE

discord, see SOUND

discount, reduction in the selling price of an article, sometimes made for an immediate cash payment, or when a retailer sells off some of his stock (especially millinery and drapery) during a ' sale.'

Discount is usually reckoned as a percentage, but may be expressed as, say, 1s in the £1.

' Discovery,' ship in which Captain Scott sailed on his Antarctic expedition 1901–4 ; presented 1931 by Australia to the Boy Scouts' organisation, and moored off the Thames Embankment, London.

disintegration, see MATTER

Disney, WALT(ER) (1901–   ), pioneer in technicolour film cartoons ; *b* Chicago ; became a commercial artist, and went to Hollywood 1923 ; produced the famous *Mickey Mouse, Silly Symphonies* (sound cartoons), and made his first full-length colour-cartoon *Snow White and the Seven Dwarfs* 1938 ; noted for *Pinocchio ; Fantasia ; Bambi ; Song of the South* (in which human beings and cartoon figures appear together) ; *Fun and Fancy Free,* and many others.

Displaced Persons, people rendered homeless in World War II, e.g. those expelled from Poland etc. ; later cared for by UNRRA, also by IRO (International Refugee Organisation) founded 1947, and responsible for settling many families in USA and Australia.

displacement, see SHIPS

Disraeli, BENJAMIN, *diz-rā'li* (1804–81), statesman, of Jewish descent, *b* London ; travelled in Egypt, Turkey and Spain ; elected Tory MP for Maidstone, Kent, 1837 ; married a rich widow—Mrs Wyndham Lewis—who called him her ' dear Dizzy ' ; became leader of the political party afterwards known as Conservative ; founded what he called ' Young England ' ; was Chancellor of the Exchequer, 1852, but only for a short time.

Prime Minister when Lord Derby retired, 1868, Disraeli was again Prime Minister 1874 ; claimed for Queen Victoria the title of Empress of India ; secretly secured for Britain complete control of the Suez Canal Company by buying shares to the value of £4,000,000 ; created Earl of Beaconsfield 1876. His last speech in the House of Lords was made 1881 ; and he died at his beautiful home, Hughenden Manor, Buckinghamshire, 19 April.

DISRAELI 1804–81

An imperialist, Disraeli was hated by many but loved and admired by those who knew him best. Queen Victoria trusted him as she trusted very few of her statesmen. His political novels, *Coningsby, Sybil,* and *Lothair,* were once widely read. He won fame by courage and brilliance ; his favourite flower was the primrose, and in 1883 the Conservatives founded the Primrose League among working people. On Primrose

Day (19 April) members of the League wear primroses, and place bunches of them on the London statue of Disraeli.

Dissenters, Nonconformists. See CHURCH

distillation, purification of a liquid by vaporising and then collecting the condensed vapour. This is a process in the manufacture of whisky and other liquors. By DESTRUCTIVE DISTILLATION we mean a process resulting in the decomposition of a solid, e.g. coke into tar, ammonia, gas. By FRACTIONAL DISTILLATION we mean the separation of various components of a liquid mixture in a fractionating column.

distributor, *dis-trib'ū-tĕr,* mechanical device for directing electric current along various circuits, particularly that used in a car engine, where electrical impulses are directed in correct sequence and correct timing to the sparking-plugs by means of a rotating arm which completes the respective circuits in the required order.

A somewhat similar mechanism is employed in the multiplex telegraph for sending a number of messages along a wire at the same time.

Divide, term used in USA and Australia for a range of mts between two valleys, e.g. Great Divide, Wyoming ; Great Dividing Range, Queensland, etc.

dividend (Lat. *dividendum,* something to be divided), usually money distributed from profits to shareholders in joint stock companies.

divination, see PROPHET

Divine Right, idea (which grew up, almost without notice, in Tudor times) that the monarch exercises authority by God's special grace, and that this is inherited, a notion which James I and Charles I exploited for their own ends. Challenged by the Parliamentarians, it was one of the chief causes of the Civil War, and was dismissed in Britain when the Hanoverians ascended the throne 1714, though it persisted in Germany where, as late as this century, William II believed in it.

diving for pearls, sponges, etc. is still undertaken without a diving-dress by divers who remain below the surface 2–3 min.

Where a diving-dress is used, skilled divers may work at a depth of 200–300ft for an hour or so. The dress is usually of rubber with a metal helmet, but for deep diving it is necessary to use a heavy metal water-tight armour, because the pressure increases as the diver descends, and at great depths is too much for the body of a rubber-clad diver to support. Air is supplied from a pump, and a valve allows used air to escape. The diver may communicate with those above by a telephone arrangement. He ascends by inflating the dress, taking care no‚ to surface too suddenly, as the difference in atmospheric pressure may be disastrous.

During World War II ' frog-men ' (powerful swimmers in rubber suits) performed many useful underwater services.

For building or engineering under water frequent use is made of the DIVING-BELL, usually rectangular, provided with an air-lock to enable workmen to enter or leave without raising the bell, and supplied with electric light, and telephone.

Using a steel sphere *c.*5ft in diameter, Dr Beebe has descended 2,200ft, observing strange sea creatures through a small window.

Employing a ' benthoscope,' Otis Barton, an American, in 1949 went down 4,500ft off the coast of California.

diving-bell, see DIVING

division, mathematical process of finding how often one number is contained in another. In such a sum as, $\dfrac{6)27}{4 \quad \text{r. } 3}$

27 is the *dividend,* 6 the *divisor,* 4 the *quotient,* 3 the *remainder* ; this may also be written $\dfrac{27}{6}$. When *dividing by factors,* note that to find the remainder we multiply each partial remainder by all the factors which precede it, except the factor that produced it, and add the products, thus : $17153 \div 216$ may be worked :

$$216 \begin{cases} 2 \\ 9 \\ 12 \end{cases} \begin{array}{|l} 17153 \\ \hline 8576 \text{ r. } 1 \qquad = 1 \\ \hline 952 \text{ r. } 8 \times 2 \quad = 16 \\ \hline 79 \text{ r. } 4 \times 9 \times 2 = \underline{72} \\ \qquad\qquad\qquad\qquad\quad 89 \end{array}$$

Ans. 79 r. 89

Or, briefly, $a \div b$ gives quotient c, and remainder r, $a = bc + r$.

Dixon, WILLIAM MACNEILE (1866–1946), *b* India ; Professor of English at Birmingham 1894–1904 and at Glasgow University 1904–35 ; author of *English Poetry from Blake to Browning* ; *The Human Situation* ; *An Apology for the Arts,* and many others.

DNB, see BOOKS

Dnieper, *nē'pĕr,* river of Ukraine etc., USSR ; rises in the Valdai plateau, and flows 1,340m to the Black Sea.

The dam (destroyed by the Red Army 1941) is now producing electricity again, each generator weighing 1,000 tons.

Dniepropetrovsk, *d-nēp-rŏ-pe-trofsk',* city, Ukraine, USSR ; noted for iron and coal ; pop.501,000.

Dniester, *nēs'tĕr,* river of Poland, Ukraine, etc. ; flows 650m to the Black Sea.

dock, enclosure of part of a harbour or river for the reception of vessels ; if gateless it is technically a tidal basin. A dock is *wet,* if used for loading or unloading a vessel ; *dry,* if the water can be drained away to enable a ship to be cleaned or repaired. The *floating dry dock* amounts to a movable repair-shop.

Dockland, see LONDON

doctor, see MEDICINE

Dodecanese, *dō-dek-ä-nēs'* (Greek *dodeca*

WILD DOGS

(1) *Wolf*   (2) *Fox*   (3) *Dingo*
(4) *Pariah*   (5) *Arctic Fox* (6) *Black-backed Jackal*

12), group of islands of the Aegean Sea.

Dodgson, CHARLES, see CARROLL, LEWIS

dodo, *dō'dō*, extinct bird of the pigeon variety that formerly inhabited Mauritius Isls. It was as large as a swan, grey in colour, and had a very strong beak. The colonists of the islands found the birds both good to eat and easy to catch (their wings and legs were so short that they could not move quickly), so that the birds were soon exterminated.

dog, family (*Canidae*) of flesh-eating mammals, including wolf, fox and jackal. Dogs walk on the toes (4 on the hind feet, 5 on the fore), and have usually long muzzles and 42 teeth. In the wild state they generally hunt in packs, mainly by scent, live in burrows, and clefts in rocks; examples include the dingo of Australia, the pariah dog of India, etc.

The domestic dog is almost certainly descended from the wolf, though the pupil of the wolf's eye is oblique, the dog's round. Domesticated in the New Stone Age (or earlier), the dog has a high degree of intelligence, and is regarded as man's best animal friend. It is favoured as a pet, and used for retrieving game, rounding up sheep, leading the blind, tracking down law-breakers, performing tricks, and as watch-dogs, also for racing, e.g. the over-specialised whippet.

Famous dogs include the fabled Argos of Ulysses ; King Arthur's hound, Cavall ; Lord Byron's Boatswain ;

Charles Lamb's Dash ; Elizabeth Browning's Flush ; ' Punch's ' dog, Toby ; Rin-tin-tin and Lassie, of film fame.

The owner of a dog (except a blind person) must pay a licence of 7s 6d a year.

doge, *dō'jā*, chief magistrate and official (in Venice and Genoa) elected by a committee. A doge held office from the day of his election until his death.

Dogger Bank, sand-bank in the N. Sea, midway between England and Denmark. It is *c.*150m long, and the water above it is *c.*60–120ft deep. The Dogger is noted for cod-fishing.

dog-rose, trailing shrub (family *Rosaceae*) of wayside hedges ; the stems have many hooked prickles (often red). The 5-petalled flower, usually pink, is above a seed-vessel which ripens into a bright red hip used for preparing rose-hip syrup, which is rich in vitamin C.

Dog Star, see SIRIUS

dog watch, see BELL

Doldrums, sailors' name for the equatorial region of calm, low pressure, and heavy rainfall where the NE. and SE. trade-winds meet. Its limits vary with the apparent seasonal movement of the sun.

dollar, coin (or bank note) used in Mexico and also in USA. The USA dollar, first issued 1794, has since 1837 weighed 26·730 grams of silver. It is equivalent to 100 cents. Since 1900 the London rate of exchange has varied from 4·486 to 2·80 to £1 (approx.). See USA

dollar area, region of the USA and other

DOMESTIC DOGS

(1) *Scottish Collie*   (2) *Bulldog*   (3) *Whippet*
(4) *Pointer*   (5) *Alsatian*

countries of America where payment for goods has to be made in dollars. One of the main problems of the world since the end of World War II has been that the countries outside the dollar area, especially those in the sterling area, have wanted to import from the dollar area a greater volume of goods than the dollar countries have been willing to take from them in exchange. The result of this has been that the non-dollar countries have found it exceedingly difficult to obtain dollars in exchange for sterling and other ' soft ' currencies, and have therefore been unable to pay for the goods imported by them from the dollar area. Recurrent crises, such as the UK currency crisis of August 1947, have been tided over by huge US loans of dollars enabling the soft currency countries to go on buying desperately needed supplies in the dollar area : but until the soft currency areas succeed in equating their dollar exports with their dollar imports the fundamental problem remains unsolved.

In a desperate attempt to ease her situation (Sept 1949), Britain devalued her currency against the dollar : £1 stg became equivalent to $2·80 instead of $4·30, the previous rate. In the short run, this had the effect of reducing British prices in terms of dollars, and this did, in fact, to some extent encourage American importers to increase their purchases of British goods, thus raising

British exports. But if the prices of British goods for export fell, the prices of American goods needed by Britain rose in the same proportion, and in the long run sterling devaluation can only be regarded as a partial remedy.

Read the annual *Economic Survey*, published by the Government as a White Paper and obtainable from HM Stationery Office. See ECONOMICS

Dollfuss, ENGELBERT (1892–1934), Austrian politician who became Chancellor of Austria 1932 as head of the Christian-Social party, set up a semi-Fascist government, and was eventually murdered by Nazis. The Christian-Social party was supported by big business, the Roman Catholic Church, and the peasants of Austria ; it had a rival of almost equal strength in the Social Democratic (Socialist) party, which was the party of the factory workers in Vienna. In their struggle for power both parties had illegal private armies which the police failed to disarm.

In 1933 there were strikes. Declaring that the Social Democrats intended to start a civil war, Dollfuss suspended the democratic constitution and without consulting Parliament made it illegal to belong to the Social Democratic party. In Feb 1934 there was further trouble. It developed into an armed rising by the Vienna workers, who barricaded themselves in their houses, and were there shot down. After quelling the Socialist rebellion which his own method of government had provoked, Dollfuss proceeded in May 1934 to set up a new non-democratic Constitution modelled on that of Fascist Italy. He had for long resisted the efforts of German and Austrian Nazis who wanted to make Austria part of Germany, and thus was forced to rely more and more on Italian help. Hitler did not like to see the growing dependence of Austria on Mussolini's Italy, and in June 1934 he had Dollfuss murdered by Nazis. He had meant then to invade and annex Austria on the excuse that it was necessary for Germany to maintain order in a neighbouring country, but Mussolini made it clear that he would fight Germany over Austria if this was attempted.

Hitler's Germany was not so strong as Italy in those days, so Hitler countermanded the invasion of Austria for the time being, and SCHUSCHNIGG became Fascist dictator of Austria in succession to Dollfuss.

Because he was murdered brutally and coldheartedly, Dollfuss came to be regarded throughout the civilised world as a martyr to Nazi tyranny, and so he was, but he was also the man who destroyed the democratic freedom of Austria between the two wars. See SCHUSCHNIGG

dolmen, Celtic word for a prehistoric grave covered by a flat unhewn stone resting on two or more upright stones. These were usually covered with earth at first, though many have long been exposed. Rare in England and Scotland, they are common in Wales, Ireland, France and the Mediterranean region.

dolomite, *dol′ō-mīt,* natural crystalline carbonate of calcium and magnesium, $MgCO_3.CaCO_3$; forms a source of carbon dioxide ; occurs in vast formations, e.g. the Dolomite Alps, often assuming fantastic shapes.

Dolomites, division of the E. Alps ; magnificent scenery and fantastically weathered rock pinnacles.

dolphin, see WHALE

Domesday Book, *doomz′dä,* survey of England (with the exception of the 4 northern counties, London, and Winchester) made 1086 for William I. The original may be seen in the Public Record Office, London.

The compilation was made so that the king might have a record of his rights, and of the income to which he was entitled from land-tax, rents and other dues ; and usually the entries give particulars of the king's own lands, those held by abbeys, bishops, etc., tenants-in-chief, villeins, cottars, etc. Comparisons were made between the value of the land in Edward the Confessor's time (1066) and the time of the survey. Other information included the number of plough-lands, oxen, churches, mills, etc. A typical example (for Westminster, then a rural area) reads :

In the villa where is situated the church of St Peter, the abbot of the same place holds 13½ hides. There is land for 11 plough teams. To the demesne belong 9 hides and 1 virgate, and there are 4 plough teams. The villeins have 6 plough teams, and one more might be made. There are 9 villeins with a virgate each, one villein with a hide, 9 villeins with a half virgate each, one cottar with 5 acres, and 41 cottars rendering a shilling each yearly for their gardens. There are 25 houses of the abbot's soldiers and of other men who render one shilling a year, or £10 in all ; when he received them the same : in the time of King Edward £12.

Here *villa* means village ; the *hide* was a means of assessing the tax, though based on the OE measure of land sufficient to support a single household ; its extent varied, but it was possibly *c.*120 acres ; *virgate* was the 4th part of a hide ; *villeins* were agricultural labourers ; *cottars* held a small plot of land and had a cottage.

domestic science, principles of effectively, economically and happily running a home. Much more an art than a science, it is an accomplishment to be desired in every girl and woman.

In its widest sense domestic science includes every aspect of home management, i.e. cleaning (scrubbing, polishing, dusting, the use of mechanical aids, and a knowledge of useful household hints) ; the correct way to wash up, e.g. washing glassware, silver and cutlery before greasy plates and cooking utensils ; clothes washing, including the correct way to wash delicate fabrics (a knowledge of such important details as e.g. that woollens are washed in warm soapy water, never boiled or washed in hot water, and that the soap must be thoroughly rinsed out before drying) ; the ability to carry out simple repairs in the home, such as renewing a washer on a tap, oiling a lock, and replacing a burnt-out fuse. It is advisable, too, to have some practical knowledge of electricity so that the unpleasantness of mild shocks and the dangers of severe ones may be avoided. Dressmaking is an added accomplishment, and the usefulness of being able to patch, darn and turn clothes correctly cannot be too highly emphasised. It is advisable, too, to have a working knowledge of cutting out clothes to a specified pattern, and making a garment ; the clever needlewoman should also be able to knit jumpers and baby clothes and to make soft toys.

All those who have to attend to the needs of a family should have some medical knowledge, especially elementary first-aid, and simple principles of hygiene, sick and child nursing. One of the most important duties that falls to the lot of a person who runs a home is cooking and baking. She should be able to cook food in a variety of ways ; bake, and follow a recipe (improving on it if necessary to suit the taste of those for whom she caters). Meals served attractively tend to make even plain fare interesting, and this art should be mastered by all students of domestic science.

Shopping is more important than is often realised. It includes the ability to shop advantageously and economically ; a knowledge of the various cuts of meat, etc., and when game is in season ; how to choose sound fruit, vegetables and fish ; the suitability of fabrics for various uses ; realisation that it is always cheaper in the long run to spend a little more on something that is obviously of better material and workmanship than to buy a cheap article, only to find that it is of inferior quality and may only last a short time. But a cheap article is not necessarily inferior ; that is where sound judgment and appreciation of quality are of inestimable value. It is also important for those who run a home to understand the need for setting aside money for repairs, insurance, rates and holidays ; the wisdom of saving, or investing one's savings, and the folly of living above one's means.

Mothercraft is a branch of science which cannot be neglected, and the ability to take complete charge of children is a valuable asset.

Importance must also be attached to etiquette—knowing the correct things to do and say in a variety of circumstances, also the correct dress for weddings and all social functions (even though there is not so much importance attached to this aspect of etiquette nowadays, and on most social occasions dress is optional) ; how to issue and accept invitations.

Domestic science courses may be taken at colleges in most large British towns where diplomas and certificates are awarded in most branches of training. After gaining these awards students may obtain managerial or administrative posts in institutions of all kinds. In 1946 was established the National Institute of Houseworkers, designed to improve conditions for all in domestic service.

Dominica, *dom-in'i-kä,* largest of the Windward Islands, British W. Indies ; volcanic and mountainous ; noted for lime-trees ; pop.54,000 ; cap. Roseau.

Dominican Republic, see SANTO DOMINGO

Dominicans, see MONKS AND NUNS

Dominions, BRITISH, see BRITISH COMMONWEALTH OF NATIONS

Domitian, *dō-mish'i-an,* (AD51–96), Roman emperor (Titus Flavius Domitianus Augustus) ; *b* Rome ; son of Vespasian; became emperor AD81. A wise administrator at first, though always a persecutor of Christians, he later lived in extravagant pomp, and was assassinated by his officers.

Don, name of various rivers, e.g. in Aberdeenshire ; also W. Yorkshire (a

tributary of the Ouse) ; also in USSR, flowing 1,325m to the Sea of Azov.

Donatello (1386–1466), Italian sculptor, *b* Florence ; did much work in Rome, Florence and Padua ; famous for his bronze *David,* one of many superb masterpieces.

Doncaster, market town, W. Riding Yorkshire ; on the R. Don ; manufactures iron and steel goods, machinery, rayon ; is the centre of a mining region, and noted for railway locomotive and carriage works ; large agricultural trade. The St Leger race meeting is run here annually (dating from 1776) in Sept. ; pop.80,000.

Donegal or **Tirconaill,** *don'e-göl,* Atlantic county of Eire ; has a rugged coastline ; co.tn Lifford.

Donetz, *dō-ni-ets',* region of the Ukraine (USSR), named after the Donetz, a tributary of the R. Don. The area is one of the most extensive coalfields known.

donkey, see Ass

Donne, JOHN, *dunn* (1571–1631), English divine and poet ; *b* London of a Catholic family but was converted to Anglicanism and was Dean of St Paul's 1621–31. Donne's poetry is strange and difficult, and was much neglected until quite recently, when interest in it revived. Since then it has influenced modern English poetry in many ways.

The following lines, addressed to a lady with whom he was in love, give some idea of his verse :

O my America ! my new-found-land,
My kingdome, safeliest when with one
man man'd,
My Myne of precious stones, My
Emperie,
How blest am I in thus discovering
thee !

Donne also wrote much religious verse full of deep feeling.

Donnybrook, suburb of Dublin, Eire ; notorious prior to 1855 for its disorderly fairs.

Don Quixote, see CERVANTES, MIGUEL DE

Doones, see BLACKMORE, R. D.

Doorn, *dorn,* castle 12m from Utrecht, Netherlands ; home of the exiled William II (the Kaiser) after World War I.

Doppler, CHRISTIAN JOHANN, *dōp'lĕr* (1803–1853), Austrian scientist, *b* Salzburg ; first explained the reason for sound being raised in pitch if the source is moving towards the listener, or lowered if source and listener are moving away from each other. The Doppler effect is also observable with light. Thus, the Fraunhofer lines in the sun's spectrum are shifted slightly to the red and blue ends, showing the sun's rotation ; and a similar shift in star spectra enables astronomers to calculate their velocity relative to the earth, though recent discoveries suggest that other factors are partly responsible.

DORA, popular short form for the Defence of the Realm Act, 1914.

Dorchester, co.tn, Dorset ; on R. Frome ;

associated with Thomas Hardy, who in his novels calls it Casterbridge ; agricultural district.

Dordogne, *dör-döny'*, river flowing 300m in the S. of France from Puy-de-Saucy into the estuary of the R. Garonne. At L'Aigle is a dam, also a hydraulic power station completed 1946 and developing 400,000,000 kilowatt-hours annually.

Dordrecht or **Dort**, *dör'drecht*, town, Netherlands ; artists' resort ; industries include shipbuilding, sugar refining and sawmills ; pop.62,000.

Doric order, see ARCHITECTURE

dormouse, British rodent, *c.*3in long exclusive of the tail (which is almost as long as its body) ; tawny above, yellowish with a white patch below. The British species, *Muscardinus avellanarius*, sleeps by day in a nest (continuously Oct.–Apr.) ; feeds at night on vegetable matter, sitting upright and lifting its food to its mouth with its fore-paws.

dorp, see UNION OF SOUTH AFRICA

Dorset, county, England, on the English Channel ; has chalk Downs noted for a breed of horned sheep ; co.tn Dorchester.

Dort, see DORDRECHT

Dortmund, *dört'moont*, industrial, mining and railway town, Germany, 47m NE. of Cologne ; linked by canal with Ems ; large coalfields ; iron and steel works ; pop. (1939) 537,000.

Dost Mahomed Khan, (1793–1863), ruler of Afghanistan who, in spite of earlier rebellion (1838) against the British later became a loyal ally.

Dostoievski, FYODOR, *do-sto-yev'ski* (1818–81), Russian novelist, *b* Moscow. In 1841 he obtained a commission as an officer in the Russian Army, but gave up soldiering three years later in order to write. His first novel *Poor Folk* (1845) was successful ; but *The Double* (1846) betrays a characteristic interest in madness and was laughed at, especially by the great novelist Turgeniev. Dostoievski was much hurt by this ridicule.

From 1849 to 1853 he was a convict at Omsk. *The House of Death* (1861), based on his impressions of prison life, was followed 1862 by *The Insulted and Injured*. In 1864 he had an unhappy love-affair and was heavily in debt. He began writing harder than ever in order to pay off his debts. He married a second time (1876), and by then his debts were so heavy that he had to live abroad, chiefly at Baden-Baden, where he gambled wildly.

Returning to Russia, he was more successful and became recognised as one of Russia's greatest writers. His finest work, done in later life, includes *Letters from the Underworld* (1864), *Crime and Punishment* (1866), *The Idiot* (1868), *The Possessed* (1871) and, greatest and oddest of all, *The Brothers Karamazov* (1880). *Karamazov* is the story of a family through which there runs a strain of madness and violence, but as a novel it is full of deep religious feeling.

Dostoievski has with his interest in madness and his emotional instability a profound sense of the tragedy of human existence, and a mystical sympathy for the poor. His religion was a very personal and striking interpretation of Christian teaching.

Douai, *doo'ā*, town, France, 18m S. of Lille ; noted for its English RC college (1568–1903) for the education of priests ; pop.42,000.

doublet, *dŭb'let*, close-fitting outer garment extending from the neck to just below the waist ; worn (France and England) 14th–17th c. by men and women ; originally it was doubled and wadded (for men) as a protection.

doubloon, *dŭb-loon'*, old gold coin of Spain and Spanish America, originally worth thirty-three to thirty-six shillings.

Doughty, CHARLES MONTAGU, *dow'ti* (1843–1926), English traveller, his *Travels in Arabia Deserta* being a fascinating description in magnificent style.

Douglas, *dŭg'las*, cap., I. of Man ; linked by ferry with Liverpool, Fleetwood, Glasgow, Belfast, etc. ; pop.20,000.

Douglas pine, tall evergreen tree (order *Coniferae*), common in N. America ; may be 300ft high ; has needle-like leaves arranged spirally ; also pendulous cones.

Douro, *doo'rō*, river of Spain and Portugal ; flows 450m to the Atlantic near Oporto.

dove, name for various kinds of pigeons, though no clear distinction is made ; species include the ring-dove (*Columba palumbis*) and the turtle-dove.

THE TURTLE DOVE

Dove Cottage, see GRASMERE

Dover, historic port, Kent ; faces Calais across the Straits (*c.*21m wide) ; has famous white cliffs, and remains of a Saxon fortress ; also a castle with a Norman keep. The port has regular sailings to Calais and Ostend. Dover suffered severely from German guns and planes 1939–45 ; pop. *c.*33,000.

Down, county of N. Ireland ; co.tn Downpatrick.

Downing College, college of Cambridge University, founded by Sir George Downing, who died 1749.

Downing Street, narrow street off White-hall, London, named after that Sir George Downing whose grandson founded Downing College. Number 10 is the official London home of the Prime Minister. Number 11 is the official home of the Chancellor of the Exchequer.

Downpatrick, co.tn, Down, N. Ireland, 27m SE. of Belfast ; reputed burial-place of St Patrick.

THE DRAGON-FLY

Downs, low chalk hills in SE. England : N. Downs, ending in Dover cliffs (Kent); S. Downs, ending in Beachy Head (Sussex) ; noted for sheep. The Downs is also an anchorage off the Kent coast.

Downside Abbey, Benedictine monastery and RC school near Bath, established 1814 by monks who arrived in England 1795, having fled from France ; the buildings were begun 1823.

Doyle, Sir Arthur Conan, *doil* (1859–1930), novelist, *b* Edinburgh ; studied medicine at Edinburgh under Dr Joseph Bell, Doyle's ' model ' for Sherlock Holmes. He is chiefly remembered for his stories of Sherlock Holmes ; was a pioneer of detective fiction. Published *The Adventures of Sherlock Holmes* (1891), followed by many more. His *Great Boer War* became a standard work; he was a firm believer in spiritualism.

Drachenfels, *drä′chen-fels* (German, dragon's rock), mountains near Bonn, Germany. The mountains are crowned with old castles, and the region abounds in legends.

' **drag,**' see Aviation

dragon-fly, British insect ; has a large head, conspicuous eyes, and a remarkably long brightly coloured body. The transparent wings are often brilliantly coloured ; the larva lives about a year in water.

Drake, Admiral Sir Francis (*c.*1545–1596), Elizabethan sea-dog, born near Tavistock, Devon ; cousin of Sir John Hawkins. Drake sailed 1572 to Panama, from a lofty point in which he was the first Englishman to sight the Pacific, praying ' Almighty God, grant me life and leave to sail an English ship upon that sea.' He captured much treasure, and was in high favour with Queen Elizabeth on his return.

With five ships he sailed 1577 on what proved to be his memorable circum-navigation of the globe. His flagship was the *Pelican,* later renamed the *Golden Hind.* Forcing a way round Tierra del Fuego, he sailed up the Pacific coast of S. and N. America, attacking Spanish ports, and carrying off merchandise ; captured the treasure-ship *Cacafuego* with her gold, silver and jewels, worth £200,000 ; landed in California, crossed the N. Pacific, rounded the Cape of Good Hope, and dropped anchor in Plymouth Sound 1580, the first Englishman to sail round the world. Philip of Spain demanded his punishment as a pirate, but the proud Elizabeth knighted him on board the *Golden Hind.*

When war with Spain became imminent, Drake took a small fleet and attacked Spanish ports (Vigo, San Domingo, etc.) 1585 ; and (1587) daringly ventured under the guns of Cadiz harbour, where the Armada was preparing to sail, and destroyed 10,000 tons of shipping, calling the gallant episode ' singeing the king of Spain's beard.' Second in command (under Lord Howard) in the fight against the Spanish Armada 1588, he urged attack in the open sea, but was overruled. To the end he went on attacking the Spaniards in port or at sea. He died of dysentery off Porto Bello, and was buried at sea.

A pirate, Drake was England's master mariner, cool, fearless, and a pioneer in the art of attack, thus laying the founda-tions of British naval supremacy at sea. He regarded the Spaniards as the enemies of England. In private life he was kindly, courteous and humorous, e.g. his remark while playing bowls on Plymouth Hoe : *There is plenty of time to win this game and to thrash the Spaniards, too.*

Ben Jonson wrote of Drake :

The stars above would make thee known
If men here silent were ;
The sun himself cannot forget
His fellow traveller.

Drakensberg, *drä′kenz-,* range of mountains in Natal, Orange Free State and Basutoland, S. Africa.

' Drake's Drum,' see NEWBOLT, SIR HENRY

drama, *drä′mä* (Greek *drän*, act or do), story acted instead of being told.

A play may last a few minutes (as Thornton Wilder's *The Angel that Troubled the Waters*) or five nights (Bernard Shaw's *Back to Methuselah*). The one-act play has some popularity, but usually a play is divided into several acts, which may be subdivided into scenes. It was customary for many years after Shakespeare's day for a play to be divided into five acts, each possibly having two or more scenes ; but the three-act play is common today.

Normally a play must obey the dramatic law first formulated by Aristotle (4th c. BC), who declared :

The play, since it is an imitation of action, should be the imitation of one action, and of the whole of it, and the parts of the action should be so arranged that, any one of them being transposed or taken away, the whole would become different.

That is, the action of a play must be a unity, even though many events take place.

Drama may be divided into (*a*) *tragedy*, a presentation of worthy, serious action, purifying the emotions by raising and discharging pity and terror ; (*b*) *comedy*, action and situation appealing to the sense of the ridiculous, but neither destructive nor painful. Note that these are extremes, and that between them are many varieties, e.g. tragi-comedy, comedy-drama, satirical comedy, farce, melodrama (deliberately and extravagantly ' tragic ' and therefore unreal). Closely related is mime, i.e. acting without words ; but drama, as such, implies the use of the spoken word, either in prose (John Galsworthy's *The Silver Box*) or in verse, e.g. most of Shakespeare's plays, in which blank verse is largely employed, or, more recently, T. S. Eliot's *Murder in the Cathedral*. A play may also be a mixture of prose and verse. Such are most of Shakespeare's plays.

Opera is drama having music as an explicit element in the presentation. See OPERA

In writing a play the dramatist requires (*a*) a theme, i.e. a basic idea, e.g. a principle of life, a theory about human nature, or a political view. To express this he invents (*b*) a plot, i.e. the ' story.' His success depends on his skill in making his characters live, in presenting a sequence of events so as to hold our interest by dramatic situations or by the brilliance of the dialogue, etc. True drama, it has been said, holds the mirror up to nature, and even if the image is distorted (as in J. M. Barrie's *Dear Brutus*, where the events are fantastic), the dramatist, if he is skilful enough, may bring truth home to us.

Note that the use of costume, scenic effects, sound effects. etc. is secondary ; *the essence of drama is theme, plot, characterisation, action and dialogue.*

European drama may be said to have begun in Greece *c.*535BC with Thespis of Attica, who added a recital (by one person) to the customary choruses and dances given in honour of Dionysus. Aeschylus (525–456BC) and Sophocles (495–406BC) added a second and a third player. Euripides (480–407BC) was the third of the greatest Greek tragic writers, and Aristophanes (*c.*445–388BC) was supreme in comedy.

Roman drama at first followed Greek models, but later a native drama sprang up, notably a type of farce acted at Atella in the 3rd c. BC. Of the few great Roman dramatists Plautus and Terence are notable for comedy, Seneca for tragedy. All three exerted a strong influence on European drama 1,500 years later.

Not till the Middle Ages was there again in Europe drama worthy of the name, though wandering minstrels, jongleurs and troubadours kept dramatic practice alive. From about the 10th c. Christian drama came into being, and in the following 400 years the Church encouraged it as a method of teaching religious truths by means of (*a*) MYSTERY PLAYS, performed by trade guilds, e.g. at York ; and (*b*) MIRACLE PLAYS, dealing with the legendary lives of the saints. Originally in Latin and acted by the clergy only, these plays at length were composed in common speech, and were acted almost solely by the guilds, especially on the Thursday after Trinity Sunday. Almost every guild in a town produced its play, e.g. the Plasterers in York presented *God Creating the Earth*, while the Shipwrights presented *God Warning Noah to Make an Ark*.

A later form of medieval religious drama was the MORALITY or allegorical play dealing with abstractions like truth, justice, etc. which were personified. These plays became popular when they began to deal with questions of the day, e.g. the early Scottish *Satire of the Thrie Estatis* by Sir David Lyndsay of the Mount (1539), though the most famous morality was *Everyman*, popular in the early 16th century.

Meanwhile, the Renaissance brought about a development of secular (i.e. non-religious) drama in Europe, and this was based on the plays of Plautus, Terence and Seneca. Spain and England produced genuinely national drama, but France naturalised classical drama, and in Germany so-called literary drama (to be read) did not blossom into acted drama before the middle of the 18th c., when Lessing introduced Shakespeare to the German stage.

English comedy, in some degree carrying on the tradition of the miracle plays, had possibly its first secular success in *Ralph Roister Doister* by Nicholas Udall (*c*.1534), but the earliest of all truly English comedies was *Gammer Gurton's Needle*, *c*.1575. The first English tragedy was *Gorboduc* (1562) by Thomas Norton and Thomas Sackville, historically important because written in blank verse. Christopher Marlowe followed with *Doctor Faustus*, later prompting Goethe to write one of the greatest of all German tragedies, *Faust*. Ben Jonson wrote the bitter comedies of ' humours,' e.g. *Every Man in his Humour, Volpone* and *The Alchemist*. It has been said that he found English blank verse a harpsichord and left it an orchestra, and it was Shakespeare (1564–1616) who brought that orchestra to perfection. See SHAKESPEARE, WILLIAM Elsewhere in Europe, 16th and 17th c. dramatists include Lope de Vega, the Spanish genius who wrote 1,500 plays ; and also Pedro Calderon. Supreme in French classical tragedy were Jean Racine and Pierre Corneille. Molière was France's master of comedy.

In England, Puritan opposition to the theatre, begun in Elizabeth's reign, was instrumental in closing all the theatres (1642), and it was not till the Restoration (1660) that drama was revived. We may note, in passing, John Dryden, William Wycherley, William Congreve and Sir John Vanbrugh ; but in the 18th and 19th c. came Oliver Goldsmith (*She Stoops to Conquer*), and Richard Brindsley Sheridan, whose witty plays, *The School for Scandal* and *The Rivals*, are still popular.

It was not, however, till the later years of the 19th c. that greatness again appeared on the English stage, e.g. after Sir A. W. Pinero's *The Second Mrs Tanqueray* (1893). A new generation of playwrights arose, e.g. Oscar Wilde, Bernard Shaw, Sir J. M. Barrie, John Galsworthy, Sir Harley Granville-Barker, John Drinkwater. Ireland produced W. B. Yeats, J. M. Synge and Sean O'Casey ; Norway, Henrik Ibsen, whose plays, based on social conditions, had been the inspiration of Shaw, Galsworthy, etc. In our own day Emlyn Williams, J. B. Priestley, Esther McCracken, Terence Rattigan, Noel Coward are popular dramatists. Two great American dramatists are Eugene O'Neill and Thornton Wilder ; and Marc Connelly's *The Green Pastures*, a Negro miracle play on modern lines, has great originality.

Play-going is excellent, but to act in a play is also both a delight and an education. So is producing a play.

All who are interested in drama for amateurs should consider becoming members of the British Drama League, particulars of which may be obtained from the Director. The league is helpful to youth clubs and rural groups.

Drave, *drä've*, tributary (450m) of the Danube ; rises in Tyrol, Austria.

Drayton, MICHAEL (1563–1631), English poet, *b* Hartshill, Warwickshire ; friend of Shakespeare ; best remembered for his sonnets, e.g. *Since there's no help, come, let us kiss and part*, and his *Ballad of Agincourt*, though his *Polyolbion*, a patriotic poem of 30,000 lines about England, is of great interest. His fancy and humour appear in *Nymphidia*. He is buried in Westminster Abbey.

Dreiser, THEODORE, *drī'sĕr* (1871–1945), American author, *b* Indiana ; editor-in-chief of Butterick publications ; a sympathetic and thoughtful observer of life ; a realist with a contempt for sentimentalism ; noted for *An American Tragedy* ; *Dawn* ; *The Financier* ; *The Genius* ; *Jennie Gerhardt* ; and *A Book about Myself*.

Dresden, *drez'den*, cap. Saxony (Germany); on the R. Elbe. Noted for its art treasures ; it manufactures machinery, hardware and chemicals ; pop.625,000. After 1710 the so-called Dresden china was actually made at Meissen, *c*.14m away. Dresden suffered severely from Allied bombing in World War II.

dress, see COSTUME

Dreyfus, ALFRED (1859–1935), French artillery officer of Jewish descent who was unjustly convicted of treachery 1894 and sent to Devil's Island. After years of public agitation he was at length retried (1899 and again 1906) and completely cleared. Dreyfus was the innocent victim in the first place of anti-Jewish prejudices and subsequently of the unwillingness of the military authorities to admit that they had been in the wrong. In order to prevent a retrial of Dreyfus, senior officers of the French War Office told lies and forged documents. At the time such crimes were almost incredible, but since then there have been many far more striking examples of the needless and horrible cruelties inspired by an unreasoning dislike of Jews.

Drinkwater, JOHN (1882–1937), English poet, playwright and critic ; noted for his historical plays, *Mary Stuart* ; *Oliver Cromwell* ; *Robert E. Lee* ; but most of all for *Abraham Lincoln* (1919). His chief prose work is *Pilgrim of Eternity* ; published *Collected Poems*.

Dritte Reich, see GERMANY ; REICH

Drogheda, *drŏ'chĕ-dä*, port, Co. Louth, Eire, on the R. Boyne. The garrison was massacred by Cromwell 1649.

Droitwich Spa, town, Worcestershire ; noted for rock-salt mines ; famous health-resort.

dromedary, see CAMEL

' drone,' see AVIATION

Druids, Celtic priests, more or less exterminated by the Romans. Their ceremonies are described in Caesar's *Gallic War*. Leaders of the people, they held the oak to be sacred, organised human sacrifices, and pretended to prophesy.

Drumclog, *drŭm-klog'*, village and moorland tract, Lanarkshire ; scene 1679 of a victory by the Covenanters over the king's troops.

Drummond, WILLIAM (1585–1649), Scottish poet, *b* Hawthornden, near Edinburgh ; noted for his sonnets, and for inventing the metre adopted by John Milton in his *Hymn to the Nativity* ; visited by Ben Jonson 1618–19. Drummond was the first great Scottish poet who wrote English. The HAWTHORNDEN PRIZE (£100) was founded 1919, and is awarded for literary work.

Druses, Syrian people with *c*.100 towns and villages scattered among other races of the Middle E. ; may number 200,000. Their language is largely Arabic, their religion a curious mixture of Mohammedanism, Judaism, and Christianity.

dryad, *drī'ad,* in old Greek tales, a nymph who lived as long as the tree in which she was supposed to dwell.

Dryburgh Abbey, *drī'bŭ-rŭ,* ruined abbey by the Tweed, Berwickshire. The abbey, founded 1150, was destroyed 1545. Here are buried Sir Walter Scott and Earl Haig.

Dryden, JOHN, *drī'den* (1631–1700), poet laureate 1670–89 ; *b* Aldwinkle, Northamptonshire ; inherited £60 a year from his father, adding to this by writing plays, few of which are of interest today, though *Marriage à la Mode, All for Love,* and *Don Sebastian* are notable exceptions.

In his day Dryden's dramas in rhymed couplets were highly popular. As a poet he is remembered for stanzas on the death of Oliver Cromwell, his *Annus Mirabilis* (dealing in quatrains with events of 1665–66, e.g. the Dutch war, and the Fire of London), and his great satirical poems, e.g. *Absalom and Achitophel,* in which he combines humour, wit and antithesis. He defended the Church of Rome in *The Hind and the Panther,* and made excellent translations of Juvenal and Virgil. His *Fables, Ancient and Modern* are delightful narrative poems.

Dryden remains a giant of English literature—critic, satirist, and a genius whose personality dominated the later 17th c.

DSC, see DECORATIONS
DSM, see DECORATIONS
DSO, see DECORATIONS
Dublin, county of E. Eire ; co.tn Dublin.
Dublin, port and cap. Eire ; on the R. Liffey ; has extensive docks and quays ; manufactures whisky, poplin ; home of the Irish Parliament (*Dail Eireann*) ; pop.503,000.

A new graving-dock is now being built ; the airport is at Collinstown.

ducat, *dŭk'at,* medieval coin (usually gold) circulating widely on the Continent ; value 9s 4d.

duce, *doo'chā,* Italian leader (Lat.*dux,* duke), and hence the *Il Duce,* the Leader, title assumed by Mussolini as Dictator of Fascist Italy. See MUSSOLINI, BENITO

duchy, see SHIRE

duck, bird (order *Anseres*) with short legs, webbed feet, depressed beak ; is an excellent swimmer, and usually powerful in flight. Most wild ducks migrate N. for the nesting season. Domestic varieties include the popular Aylesbury duck, white and boat-shaped, weighing often 8–10lb.

SCOTER
A large sea duck

duckbill, see PLATYPUS
ducking-stool, seat at the end of a long beam for ducking bad-tempered women (and sometimes men) in a pond or river ; last used in England at Leominster 1809.
Duddon Valley, beautiful river valley dividing Cumberland from N. Lancashire ; beloved by William Wordsworth.
Dudley, town, Worcestershire ; produces iron and steel goods and hardware ; pop.60,000.
Dudley, ROBERT, see LEICESTER, EARL OF
duel (Lat. *duo,* 2), old form of settling private disputes by fighting. Strict rules were observed, e.g. to govern the choice of weapons, usually swords or pistols. Duelling, a mania in France in the 16th and 17th c., was common in England in the 17th c. and especially in the reign of George III.
dugong, *doo'gong,* water mammal known as the sea-cow ; found in the Red Sea and near the E. Indies and Australia, etc. ; may be 8–12ft long.
Duisberg, *dü'iss-bur*ch, town and Rhine port, Germany ; on the Ruhr coalfield ; noted for iron, chemicals and textiles ; pop.431,000.
duke (Lat. *dux,* leader), highest title among British nobility. The first duke was Edward the Black Prince, created Duke of Cornwall 1337.
Duke of York's Camp, seaside holiday founded by King George VI when Duke of York. Every year *c*.300 boys spend a holiday together, half of them from Public Schools, others from factories and industrial centres, the idea

being to foster understanding and comradeship.

Duke of York's School, school for the sons of British soldiers ; founded Chelsea 1801, transferred to Dover 1909.

Dukeries, THE, beautiful district of NW. Nottinghamshire ; so named from the ducal homes of Clumber Park, Thoresby Park and Welbeck Abbey, etc.

Dulong and Petit's Law, see CHEMISTRY

Dulwich, *dŭl'ij* ; *-ich*, residential London suburb in the borough of Camberwell, noted for its College founded 1619.

Dumas, ALEXANDRE, *dü-mä* (1802–70), the elder (called Dumas *père*), son of a French marquis and a Negress, startled France with his play *Henri III et sa cour*, a brilliant historical romance, followed by many other dramatic successes, e.g. *Christine* ; *Charles VII* ; and *Antony* ; won still greater fame with his historical novels (covering a large part of French history from 1559 to 1848), among them those dealing with Henry of Navarre, e.g. *La Reine Margot* ; the Musketeer series, e.g. *Les Trois Mousquetaires* (The Three Musketeers), and *Le Vicomte de Bragelonne* ; and the Revolution series, e.g. *Mémoires d'un Médicin*.

Dumas was famous also for *La Tulipe Noire* (The Black Tulip) and his inimitable *Le Comte de Monte Cristo* (The Count of Monte Cristo). He is said to have written 1,200 works, many with help from other writers. He made a huge fortune, but lived extravagantly, dying in poverty, though in the care of his son, Dumas *fils*.

Dumas, ALEXANDRE (1824–95), son of Dumas *père*, and called Dumas *fils*, novelist and dramatist almost as famous as his father. His works are full of moralising, but he had his father's genius for characterisation. His novels include *La Dame aux camélias* ; *La Roman d'une femme* ; *Diane de Lys*. His plays include *Le Demi-monde* ; *Le Fils naturel*; *L'Ami des femmes* ; and *L'Etrangère*.

du Maurier, GEORGE, *dü maw'riä* (1834–96), British artist and author, *b* Paris ; now chiefly remembered for his novel *Trilby* His son, SIR GERALD DU MAURIER (1873–1934), was a noted actor. Sir Gerald's daughter, DAPHNE, is a popular writer, her books including *Jamaica Inn* and *Frenchman's Creek*.

Dumbarton, port and co.tn, Dumbartonshire ; noted for its castle ; has large shipbuilding yards, engineering works and brass foundries ; pop.22,000.

Dumbarton Oaks, meeting-place (1944), Washington, DC (USA), of chiefs of the United Nations, who prepared an outline of the *Charter of the United Nations*, published at San Francisco 1945. See UNO

Dumbartonshire, mountainous county, W. Scotland ; produces coal, iron, slate ; co.tn Dumbarton.

Dumfries, *dum-freess'*, co.tn, Dumfriesshire on R. Nith ; manufactures tweeds,

hosiery and hats ; has ironworks and tanneries ; burial-place of Robert Burns ; pop.27,000.

Dumfriesshire, border county, Scotland ; has a coastline along the Solway Firth ; co.tn Dumfries.

Dunbar, *dŭn-bär'*, Scottish town at the mouth of the R. Forth, 29m from Edinburgh ; famed for ' red soil ' potatoes ; holiday resort. Here 1650 Cromwell defeated the Scots under David Leslie.

Duncan, *dŭn'kan* (*d* 1040), King of Scots, succeeded Malcolm II 1034, slain by Macbeth of Cawdor. Shakespeare's play *Macbeth* is based on an old story about the murder.

Duncan, ADAM, 1ST VISCOUNT (1731–1804), Scottish admiral, *b* Lundie, Angus ; won a decisive victory over the Dutch fleet off Camperdown 1797 ; created Viscount Camperdown.

Dundee, *dŭn-dē'*, city and port, Angus ; on the R. Tay, which is crossed by the Tay (railway) Bridge 3,593yd long ; includes the town of BROUGHTY FERRY ; has a fine harbour ; noted for shipbuilding, confectionery and preserves, also jute and linen ; pop.182,000.

Dundee, VISCOUNT (*d* 1689), Scottish soldier (John Graham of Claverhouse), said to have saved the life of William of Orange; ruthlessly hunted down the Covenanters; a great supporter of the Stuart (Jacobite) cause ; killed at the battle of Killicrankie. Handsome, he was known as ' Bonnie Dundee.'

Dunedin, *dŭn-ē'din*, city of S. Island, New Zealand ; founded and named after Edinburgh by Scottish settlers (1848) ; exports wool, frozen meat and dairy produce ; became prosperous with the discovery of gold nearby, 1861 ; pop. 90,000.

Dunfermline, *dŭn-ferm'lin*, city, Fife, on the Firth of Forth ; once a favourite residence of the kings of Scotland, some of whom are buried in the Benedictine abbey ; birthplace of Andrew Carnegie who gave £500,000 to the town ; damask linen trade ; pop.45,000.

Dungeness, *dŭnj-nes*, low headland of Kent coast.

Dunkery Beacon, highest point on Exmoor, 1,707ft.

Dunkirk, *dŭn-kŭrk*, port of France on the Straits of Dover ; pop.32,000. From its beaches in 1940 British and French forces made a remarkable escape from the Germans, 337,130 troops being successfully evacuated with the aid of over 1,000 rescue ships.

Dunlop, JOHN BOYD (1840–1921), Scottish inventor, *b* Dreghorn, Ayrshire ; veterinary surgeon, Belfast, 1867 ; devised the first pneumatic tyre.

Dunmow Flitch, *dŭn'mō*, flitch or gammon of bacon awarded, after a more or less humorous trial, to a married couple who have had no quarrel for a year and a day ; chiefly associated with Little Dunmow, Essex.

Dunsinane, *dŭn-sin'nān*, peak of the Sidlaw Hills, Scotland, *c*.8m from Perth ; remains of a fort here are called Macbeth's Castle.

Dunstable, *dŭn'stä-bl'*, market town, Bedfordshire ; noted for straw-plaiting, printing and engineering.

Dunstan (924–988), English churchman ; born near Glastonbury ; abbot of Glastonbury 945 ; Archbishop of Canterbury 961, was the wisest and most powerful statesman in the England of his day.

duodenum, see DIGESTION

Dupleix, JOSEPH FRANÇOIS, *dü-plä* (1697–1763), French administrator ; *b* Landrecies ; Governor of Pondicherry 1741 ; planned to build up a French empire in India, but was beaten by Clive. See CLIVE, ROBERT

duralumin, see ALUMINIUM

Durban, *dŭr'ban*, port and health resort, Natal, S. Africa ; an important railway centre. There is much coal-mining near by. Durban is a centre for the sugar industry ; also an air terminus ; rickshaws drawn by Zulus are still in great favour ; pop.370,000.

durbar, *dŭr'bär*, word used in India for a court, council, or great state ceremony, e.g. the magnificent durbar at Delhi when Queen Victoria was proclaimed Empress of India 1877.

Dürer, ALBRECHT (1471–1528), German artist and engraver, *b* Nuremberg ; a scholar and superb craftsman greatly beloved by those who knew him ; supreme as an etcher and in woodcuts. The first artist in Germany to teach perspective, he had a great influence on German art. His works include *Feast of the Rosary* ; *Madonna and Child* ; his copperplates include *St Jerome in his Study* and *Death's Coat of Arms.*

Durham, county NE. England ; has 33m of coast ; noted for coal and iron ; co.tn Durham.

Durham, co.tn of County Durham ; almost surrounded by R. Wear ; famous for its cathedral (begun in the 11th c.) and the remains of a monastery. The castle is now the HQ of the University, founded 1832.

durra, kind of millet (often 15ft high) much grown by Negro farmers in W. Sudan.

Düsseldorf, *düs'el-dörf*, town, Rhineland, Germany ; busy port on the R. Rhine ; manufactures iron and steel, also textiles, dyes and paper ; pop.540,000.

dust, solid matter in a fine state ; exists in the atmosphere to a great height. From 100 to 14,000 particles per cu.cm have been found over Ben Nevis at over 4,000ft. Air over cities may contain 100,000 particles, and a puff of cigarette smoke 4,000 million. Much fine dust may come from disintegrated meteors. Dust particles often become laden with germs, and the presence of dust is therefore a menace to health.

dust-bowl, region where dust storms are common, in the Great Plains, USA., where over 110,000,000 acres of fertile land have been ruined.

Read *The Grapes of Wrath*, John Steinbeck.

Dutch metal, alloy of copper and zinc ; highly ductile.

Dutton, R. J. G., see SHORTHAND

Dvina, *dvē'nä*, river in USSR ; enters the White Sea at Archangel ; also a river flowing to the Gulf of Riga.

Dyaks, *dī'äk*, natives of Borneo, chiefly of the interior. Yellow-complexioned, they are farmers, and are considerably civilised in Sarawak, their former practice of head-hunting being now almost forgotten. Their chief weapon is the blow-pipe ; industries include cloth-weaving, metalwork and weapon making.

dyes, substances used to give colour to fabrics etc. Ideally they should be able to impart colour to the fabric ; attach themselves ; and be soluble or easily capable of transference. Once mainly obtained from vegetable or animal tissue (e.g. indigo and logwood), they are now chiefly synthesised by organic chemical processes. Artificial dyes can be classified into 12 groups, as, say : nitro-dye-stuffs, azo-dyes, xanthene dyes, sulphide dyes and vat dye-stuffs, including indigo.

Colour may be imparted by the dye itself or by a chemical reaction ; the power of attachment may be given by a mordant, usually a metallic salt. If the dye is not soluble it may be precipitated by a chemical process on the cloth, or used in the form of a colloidal solution called a ' lake.' Synthetic dyes were first made from coal-tar, and these are still widely used. The indigo dyes cover a wide range of colour, including the famous Tyrian purple.

Dye-stuffs are derived from benzene, toluene, phenol, naphthalene, anthracene, etc. Prior to 1914 90% of the artificial dyes came from Germany, but the UK, USA and France now produce their own.

The rapid and extensive development of dye-making in Germany before World War I is important in the history of modern industry. It was the first case of knowledge gained by independent scientific research being harnessed on a large scale to the needs of a developing industry. Previously the inventors of new industrial processes (e.g. Bessemer) had been manufacturers who made their discoveries by trial and error. In the new dye industry theoretical chemists were called upon to show the way.

dynamics, see MECHANICS

dynamite, explosive invented *c*.1867 by Alfred Nobel, the Swedish chemist. Dynamite is mainly nitroglycerine (glyceryl trinitrate, $C_3H_5(NO_3)_3$, a pale yellow oily liquid) usually mixed with kieselguhr, i.e. a mass of hydrated silica, SiO_2, but sometimes with other substances, such as wood-meal. Many varieties exist, all with the advantage of being plastic, hence relatively safe and easy to handle and transport.

dynamo, see ELECTRICITY ; FARADAY, MICHAEL

dyne, see MECHANICS

dysentery, *dis'en-tri,* affection of the bowel caused by an amoeba, i.e. a minute organism that enters the body from infected water, notably in the tropics ; and that caused by bacilli, an infectious disease common almost all over the world, but especially in hot climates, and until recently a menace to troops in warm countries. The latter is cured by treatment with M and B.

dysprosium, *dis-prō'shi-ŭm,* rare earth element, Dy ; atomic weight 162·46 ; atomic number 66.

dysticus, *dis'tik-ŭs,* fierce water-beetle in British ponds ; comes to the surface for air, a supply of which it carries under the wing-cases ; preys on tadpoles.

E

e, base of natural logarithms, equivalent to 2·7183.

eagle, largest member of the hawk family of birds of prey ; notable for strong, curved beak, wings when folded reaching to the tip of the tail; feathered toes ; soars to great heights ; popularly regarded as the king of birds. The chief British species is *Aquila chrysaëtus,* the GOLDEN EAGLE, 6ft across the expanded wings ; plumage brown, but head and neck golden-red ; now rare but increasing in Scottish highlands, where it nests in an ' eyrie ' on a rocky ledge. The ERNE (or sea-eagle), greyish-brown, is another British species.

Eagle Isle, see ACHILL ISLE

eagre, *ē'gĕr,* tidal wave, sometimes called a bore ; e.g. the bore of the R. Severn ; the eagre of the R. Trent.

ear, organ of hearing and balance.

As a sound-detector the ear gathers impression waves beyond the outer ear (*pinna*) and deflects them along a tube to the ear-drum (*tympanic membrane*), the vibrations of which are passed on by three small bones (hammer, anvil and stirrup) in the middle ear, which is air-filled from the Eustachian tube. The bones communicate the impulses to the small ear-drum, the intensified vibrations of which affect liquid in the inner ear, where there is a coiled spiral (*cochlea*), filled with liquid in which 5,000–6,000 nerve-ends from the brain ' pick up ' the various rates of vibration from 16 per sec. to 30,000 per sec. ; also the inner ear which contains the *labyrinth.* Movement of its liquid acting on nerve-ends enables us to keep our balance, and ' feel ' our position, whether upright, etc. See SOUND

Earhart, AMELIA (*d* 1937), American pilot ; first woman to fly the Atlantic alone (1932).

Earl's Court, see LONDON

Earth, a planet of the sun, is almost a sphere, the diameter at the equator being 7,926·7m ; at the poles 7,900m. The equatorial circumference is 24,902m ; surface area *c.*196,800,000sq.m ; volume *c.*26^{10}cu.m ; mass or weight *c.*6^{21} tons.

The Earth revolves round the sun in an orbit of *c.*580,000,000m in a year of 365 days 6 hours 9 minutes (approx.). The distance from the sun is between 91,000,000 and 94,000,000m ; average speed round the sun 66,000mph ; weight of atmosphere *c.*11·6^{17}lb. The Earth's equator is tilted at an angle of 23·5° to the ecliptic, hence the seasons ; it rotates on its own axis once in 23 hours 56 minutes (the sidereal day).

Of its surface *c.*141,000,000sq.m are water, 55,700,000sq.m land, comprising six great masses (continents) with a total pop. estimated at 2,200,000,000 :

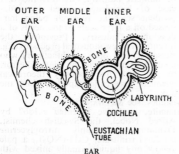

OUTER MIDDLE INNER
EAR EAR EAR

LABYRINTH

COCHLEA

EUSTACHIAN TUBE

EAR

Diagram of the Human Ear

	sq.m	pop.
Eurasia		
(*a*) Europe	2,085,000	403,000,000
(*b*) Asia	18,685,000	1,327,000,000
Africa	11,700,000	158,000,000
N. America	8,350,000	163,000,000
S. America and Central	7,355,000	112,000,000
Oceania	3,200,000	11,000,000
Antarctica	5,500,000	——

Chinese is spoken by *c.*400,000,000

people, English by 200,000,000, Russian by 130,000,000. Of the races of mankind there are approximately 680,000,000 Mongolians, 725,000,000 Caucasians, 210,000,000 Negroes and 234,000,000 comprising Semitic and Malayan, etc. The largest cities include London, New York, Tokyo, Berlin, Moscow, Shanghai, Chicago, Osaka, all with over 3,000,000 people. See also ISLAND ; MOUNTAIN ; OCEAN ; RIVER

earth-nut, see GROUND-NUT

earthquake, vibration of the solid crust of the earth due either to volcanic eruptions with only local effects, or to ' tectonic' causes, i.e. those due to continual internal strain, hence the movement of strata under pressure (the age-old faulting which raises mountains). Earthquake belts include the regions of the Pacific, Mediterranean and S. Asia. The range of vibrations (recorded by a seismograph) is usually c.1mm (though 76mm have been recorded) ; secondary *visible* waves in soft ground may be 12in high and 100ft long.
Notable earthquakes include Lisbon 1755 (death - roll c.50,000), Calabria 1783, San Francisco 1906, Tokyo 1923 (death-roll 150,000), India 1934 and 1935. London's worst earth-tremor was 7 June 1931.

earthworm, segmented worm (*Annelid*) ; swallows soil, digesting the vegetable matter and throwing up finely powdered soil as worm-castings. Darwin calculated that 53,000 worms inhabiting an acre bring to the surface 10 tons of earth per year, which helps to turn over the soil and is exceedingly beneficial.

earwig, straight-winged insect with pincerlike attachment at the rear ; regarded as useful to the farmer. It does *not* enter the ear.

East Anglia, kingdom of England from the 6th–9th c. ; founded by Angles. The name now means vaguely the region between the Wash and the Thames.

Eastbourne, town and health resort on the Sussex coast ; pop.57,000.

Easter, see CALENDAR

Easter Island, volcanic isl. of the S. Pacific; 2,300m W. of Chile, to which it belongs , area c.50sq.m ; has curious old carved lava figures, some 70ft high.

East Ham, town, Essex ; noted for the manufacture of chemicals and soap ; also for engineering ; pop.95,000.

East India Company, trading corporation to which a charter was granted by Queen Elizabeth 1600. It was owned by merchants in London, and had ' factories' (i.e. trading stations) at Surat (west coast of India), Fort St George (afterwards Madras), and at Hooghli, on the delta of the Ganges (later moved to Calcutta). Bombay (given to Charles II by the Portuguese 1661) later took the place of Surat. A rival company of William III's reign was incorporated 1701.
Attempts by Dupleix to secure pos-

session for the French were frustrated by Clive, and by 1765 the original trading company had become responsible for widespread administration. The E. India Company ceased to exist after the Indian Mutiny 1857. See INDIA ; LAMB, CHARLES

East Indiaman, see SHIPS

East Indies, name given vaguely to Indo-China, Malay Peninsula, islands of the Malay Archipelago, Sumatra, Java, Borneo, etc. The Netherlands E. Indies include Sumatra, Java, part of Borneo, and New Guinea. The total area of the Netherlands E. Indies is c.730,000sq.m ; pop.53,000,000 ; the islands are a great source of rubber. See INDONESIA

East London, wool-exporting port, Cape Province, S. Africa ; has a fine harbour ; pop.79,000. A new graving dock was opened by Princess Elizabeth 1947.

Eastman, GEORGE (1854–1932) American inventor, b Waterville, New York ; invented the photographic roll-film 1884, and the Kodak camera 1888 ; made a fortune, and left generous sums to charity, also for educational advancement.

eating, see DIGESTION ; FOOD

Ebbw Vale, *eb'oo,* district Monmouthshire ; noted for coal, iron mines and steelworks ; pop.28,000.

ebonite or **vulcanite,** *eb'ŭn-īt,* hard substance made by mixing 40% sulphur with pure rubber at 150°C. Easily moulded, it is an excellent insulating material.

ebony, *eb'oni,* tree found in Mauritius, India and Ceylon. The best timber is the heart-wood of the Ceylon variety, giving logs 2ft across and 10–15ft long ; may be black, red, or green ; takes a high polish.

Eboracum or **Eburacum,** *ē-bor-ä'kŭm,* Roman name for the legionary fortress (52 acres) on the site of which York now stands ; erected by the 9th Legion c.AD75.

Ebro, *ē'brō,* river flowing 460m in Spain to the Mediterranean.

ecce homo, *ek'sē,* Latin, ' behold the man,' i.e. Christ. See SEELEY, SIR J. R.

eccentric, *ek-sen'trik,* in engineering, metal disc with a shaft *not* in the centre, thus giving a reciprocating movement similar to the cam. It is used to operate the valves of a steam engine of the reciprocating type.

Eccles, industrial suburb of Manchester, noted for textiles ; gave its name to Eccles cakes ; pop.50,000.

Ecclesiastes, *e-klē-zē-as'tēz,* book of the OT ; treats of the vanity of earthly things ; once attributed to Solomon, but probably written long after his day.

Ecclesiastical and Church Estates Commissioners, commission dealing with the management of Church of England estates to the value of over £3,000,000 per annum.

echidna, *ē-kid'nä,* egg-laying ant-eater, about the size of a porcupine ; found in Australia and New Guinea ; has short

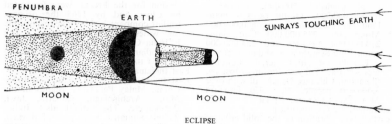

ECLIPSE
(left) of the moon   *(right)* of the sun

spines ; head with slender beak ; feeds at night on insects caught by its long, sticky tongue.

Echo, *ek'ō,* in old Greek tales, a mountain nymph who could speak only when spoken to. She pined away for love of Narcissus.

echo, in physics, reflection of a sound wave ; thus, shouting at a wall causes impulses in the molecules of air ; these spring back from the wall, and cause similar impulses in the *opposite* direction. In public buildings such echoes confuse the listener. To avoid them an architect covers the walls with ' acoustic plaster,' i.e. a mixture which absorbs rather than reflects sound waves, and designs the shape so that echoes do not reach the audience.

Sounding at sea at one time required the lowering of a plumb-line, a slow and clumsy method. This is now largely replaced by echo-sounding, in which an instrument records on sensitised paper the time (usually fractions of a second) taken by an inaudible sound wave from the hull to travel to the bed of the ocean, *and back* ; this, divided by 2 and multiplied by 1,440 metres (speed of sound in sea-water) gives the depth in metres, e.g. If the time interval $= \frac{1}{12}$ sec, the depth $= \frac{1}{12} \times \frac{1440}{2}$ metres, i.e. 60 metres, say, $32\frac{1}{2}$ fathoms. See also RADAR

ECITO, see UNO

eclipse, *ē-klips'* (Gk *ekleipsis,* failing), in astronomy, passing of one heavenly body between another and an observer, particularly the partial or total eclipse of the sun or moon due to the earth, the moon, and the sun being in a straight line, or nearly so. An eclipse of the moon occurs whenever the moon passes into the shadow of the earth, i.e. when the earth is between the sun and moon. A total lunar eclipse lasts *c.*105 minutes. An eclipse of the sun occurs when the moon apparently crosses the sun's face, its shadow (perhaps 150m across) sweeping over the earth from W. to E., any one place being in twilight for *c.*7 minutes. Total eclipses of the sun occur rarely in any one region.

ECO, see UNO

economics (Gk *ta oikonomika,* matters connected with problems of household management), a systematic study of the principles governing the production, exchange, distribution and consumption of *wealth.* By the term *wealth* economists mean anything that can normally be bought and sold. As far back as the 4th c. BC, Plato discussed some of the fundamental questions of economics in Book II of his *Republic,* but modern economics may be said to have begun with the publication (1776) of *The Wealth of Nations* by the great Scottish economist, Adam Smith.

The economics of our own day are so complex that even the men and women who devote all their thought and energy to the solution of its many problems are often baffled. Since many of the difficulties with which governments have to deal are fundamentally economic, it is desirable that all concerned with politics (see POLITICS) should also have some knowledge of economics. Unemployment and world trade are political problems, but their solution depends very largely, if not wholly, on economic principles. Thus, several important industries (e.g. coal, electricity, transport, etc.) were nationalised in Britain between 1945 and 1950, i.e. they were taken over by the State, acting in the name of the people as a whole. Economics supplies many weighty and powerful arguments both *for* and *against* nationalisation, but it may be doubted whether a majority of those who in 1945 voted either for or against the policy of nationalisation had enough knowledge of economics to form a sound opinion on the merits of the purely economic argument. (The term *economic argument* is here used for an argument which tends to prove that people will be better off—*wealthier*—if the step proposed is taken.)

From a political point of view Parliament is obliged to carry out the economic policies approved of by a majority of the voters, but economic measures inspired too much by political motives (such as, say, the desire of a party to obtain votes) are apt to have awkward economic consequences. Nationalisation was politically inevitable in 1945 when a Labour government was returned by the electorate. Whether, however, nationalisation is a sound economic policy is a question which time alone can answer.

Before 1936—when world-wide rearmament began—millions of workers in Britain, Germany, the USA and many other countries were out of work, and unemployment was the central problem of pre-war economics. Since 1945 Britain has aimed at *full employment*, a policy inspired by the general theory of employment put forward by Lord Keynes (1883–1946) and other economists. The Keynesian economists point out that those who have (say) £1,000 a year are likely to save a higher proportion of their income than those who have only (say) £300 a year. If, then, the *national income* (i.e. total wages + salaries + profits, or briefly, total production) increases, a higher proportion of it will be *saved* (i.e. not spent on current consumption) than would otherwise be the case.

We may say that what is *supposed* to happen is that the money saved is lent to enterprising business men who *invest* it, i.e. they spend it on buildings, new machinery, etc. (capital equipment), and by doing so help to increase production and thus still further to increase national income. But according to Keynesian economics what *actually* happens is that though the national income increases, and though the amount spent on current consumption increases, a higher proportion of the total is saved, and *what is spent on consumption does not go on increasing as rapidly as total production.* In other words the supply increases quicker than the demand, with the result that when manufacturers feel that the market for their goods is diminishing, they cancel their orders for new capital goods instead of maintaining and increasing orders, as they would have to do in order to absorb the increasing amount of money being saved. This has disastrous consequences. Thus, as orders fall off, the constructional and heavy industries (e.g. shipbuilding, engineering, etc.) dismiss workpeople. Therefore thousands of families must now spend less. Demands fall off still more steeply—hence we have still more unemployed people, hence still less is spent. Thus the process is repeated till finally mass unemployment prevails. This alternation of *boom* and *slump* (expanding and declining prosperity) is known as the *Trade Cycle*, a feature of the present century, and often catastrophic in its results.

The chief weapon of the full-employment policy in its attempt to fight against a slump is planned *redistribution of national income*, and such redistribution inevitably favours the lower income groups. Large personal incomes are taxed much more heavily. Under a full-employment policy the sums deducted in taxation of incomes are redistributed

by means of various benefits, e.g. food subsidies, intended to keep down the cost of living. The net result is that as the national income rises, a greater share in it is assigned to lower income groups, and therefore a greater proportion of every increase in national income is spent on current consumption. Obviously this counteracts the tendency (already mentioned) towards an excessive rise in savings (with consequent lessening of demand) as national income increases, and any rise in savings that does occur can then be met by governmental action to maintain capital investment at the necessary level.

The full-employment policy has been severely criticised on the ground that it does not provide *incentives*. That is to say, that especially among the lower income groups there tends to be little to persuade people to work hard, since various State benefits ensure them against extreme poverty and provide free medical attention, etc. Thus it comes about that one of the most important economic questions of our day is whether in view of Britain's financial and economic dependence on the USA we can successfully pursue a policy of full employment.

We see how closely economics and politics are intermingled if we consider this last question. Before 1939 (i.e. before the beginning of World War II) Britain derived a large income from the interest paid on loans for capital investment in many parts of the world, especially in the USA. This provided Britain with the dollars she needed to pay for her imports, the total value of which greatly exceeded the value of her exports to the USA. To pay for World War II Britain sold her right to the interest on her foreign investments, thus losing a large dollar income. But to maintain her high standard of living Britain must import a great deal from the USA, and to pay for these imports she must in future sell in the USA a much greater total of exports than she did before 1939. Immediately after the war Britain hoped to be able to achieve this aim by 1952, and in 1947 the USA lent her millions of dollars to enable her to buy the USA imports she needed. Great progress was made, but in 1949 British exports to the USA began to fall again. If a country cannot export as much as it imports, it must in the end cut down imports. It happens, however, that many British industries use raw materials which cannot be obtained in Britain but only in the USA ; with the result that if imports from the USA have to be cut down, some of those employed in such industries will be thrown out of work, and our ability to export more endangered.

It would seem that the root of the present economic difficulties is that if other countries are to balance their accounts, the USA, as universal creditor, must import more than she exports—as Britain did prior to 1939. While the USA continues to export far more than she imports, it follows that even a small American slump must cause an immediate and most devastating decline in the standard of living of other countries, this inevitably bringing about a host of political consequences.

We may say that the only remedy is that, wealthy as she is, America should plan for a further rise in her own standard of living in the hope that she would thus soon be importing more than she exports. For example, she might perhaps carry out policies designed to give various depressed classes a greater share in the US national income. Indeed, the Truman administration of 1948 had a mandate for such a policy, but was prevented from carrying it out by political considerations. The USA has certainly been very generous in extending loans and making Marshall Aid possible ; nevertheless until her own internal political obstacles can be overcome the present world economic crisis must continue.

Read *An Outline of Money*, Geoffrey Crowther ; *The Social Framework*, J. R. Hicks.

Ecuador, *ek'wä-dör*, republic of S. America so high that although on the equator (hence the name) the average temperature of Quito (the cap.) is only *c.*56°F. Its boundaries are still imperfectly defined, but its area is *c.*226,000sq.m ; pop. 3,250,000, mostly Indians and Spaniards.

Crossed by rugged and volcanic ranges of the Andes, Ecuador has vast forests yielding cinchona (for quinine) and dyewoods ; produces rice, vegetable ivory, bananas, cotton, coffee, rubber, sugar and tobacco ; cocoa crops have been much depleted by disease. Mineral wealth, not yet largely exploited, includes gold, petroleum, lead, iron, copper, precious stones and sulphur.

Now governed by a president, Ecuador was conquered in the 15th c. by the Incas of Peru, then by Pizarro of Spain, and became independent 1822. Now the President governs much as a dictator.

Eddington, SIR ARTHUR (1882–1944), astronomer, *b* Kendal ; was professor of astronomy, Cambridge University ; explained and advanced the theory of relativity ; noted for his books, e.g. *The Nature of the Physical World* and *The Expanding Universe.*

Eddy, MARY BAKER, see CHRISTIAN SCIENCE

eddy-currents, see ELECTRICITY

Eddystone Rock, reef, 14m SW. of Plymouth. Its first lighthouse, of wood, was built by Henry Winstanley, who perished with it 1703 ; the 2nd was burned down 1755 ; the 3rd dismantled. The 4th, completed 1882, is 168ft high.

Ede, JAMES CHUTER (1882–   ), Socialist politician, MP for S. Shields from 1929 ; Home Secretary 1945.

edelweiss, *ä'del-vīs*, plant (family *Compositae*), native of the Alps and the Himalayas. The foliage is white and woolly ; the yellowish flowers are *c.*6in from the ground.

Eden, ANTHONY, *ē'den* (1897–   ), English statesman ; Conservative MP for Warwick and Leamington 1923. A linguist and student of foreign affairs, he was greatly interested in the League of Nations ; Foreign Secretary 1935–38, and again 1940–45 ; leader of the House of Commons 1942–45 ; did much to establish good relations between Britain and allied countries.

Edgar (944–975), King of the English, succeeded his brother Edwy as king of all England 959. Known as ' the Peaceful,' his power was symbolised 973 (the year of his coronation) when 8 vassal kings rowed him across the R. Dee.

Edgbaston, see BIRMINGHAM

Edgehill, BATTLE OF, see CIVIL WAR

Edinburgh, *ed'in-bŭrŭ*, city, cap. of Scotland ; royal and municipal burgh on the S. bank of the Firth of Forth ; many hills stand in or on the outskirts of the city, including Arthur's Seat, Calton Hill, and the Pentland Hills ; has LEITH (*lēth*) as its port, with extensive docks, a large harbour, much trade, and important fisheries.

Built mostly of grey sandstone, Edinburgh is one of the most handsome cities in the world, and by its cultural achievements since 1750 has earned the title of the ' Athens of the North ' ; famous for its many imposing and historic buildings, e.g. the Castle, notable for its memorial to Scotland's heroes of World War I ; the Palace of Holyroodhouse (built for James IV *c.*1500, associated with Mary Queen of Scots, the scene of Rizzio's murder) ; the Parliament House, containing the Parliament Hall, Scottish National Library and the Law Courts ; John Knox's House ; the Royal Observatory ; and handsome museums and art galleries. The churches include St Giles' Cathedral, partly 14th c., scene of the riot caused 1637 by Jenny Geddes ; the 17th c. Canongate Church, and 16th c. Magdalen Chapel.

Long noted for learning, the city has the University, founded 1582, which is especially famous for medicine ; there are also many well-known schools, including Fettes College and Edinburgh Academy. At Corstorphine is the very fine Royal Zoological Park, one of the finest of its kind in the world ; in the New Town can be seen Sir Walter Scott's birthplace, as well as Robert Louis Stevenson's Memorial House and Museum, and his childhood home, 17 Heriot Row. Old Edinburgh, known as ' Auld Reekie,' is still quaint, having many steps and cobble stones in the old streets, high-storied buildings and quaint old-fashioned low-raftered houses. In direct contrast is Princes Street, one of the noblest and most beautiful thoroughfares in Europe. It has handsome buildings and shops on one side of the street which face the gardens and Castle on the other side. A feature of the gardens is the ' floral ' clock. Among the many memorial monuments in Princes Street gardens is one in memory of Sir Walter Scott which stands near the eastern end. Parks and gardens are numerous.

In recent years Edinburgh has attracted thousands of visitors to its annual International Festival of Music and Drama.

Among industries are brewing, distilling, biscuit-making, the manufacture of drugs, chemicals, rubber goods ; also engineering, and especially printing and publishing.

Called Edinburgh, i.e. Edwin's burgh or town, after Edwin, a 7th c. king of Northumbria, the city has been the cap. of Scotland since the 15th c. It is presided over by the Lord Provost, and sends 6 members to Parliament ; pop. 490,000.

Edinburgh, DUKE OF, see ELIZABETH, PRINCESS

Edinburgh University, founded 1582. The present buildings, on the site once known as Kirk of Field, scene of Darnley's death, were erected 1789. New science laboratories were begun 1920. The faculties include arts, science, divinity, law, music and medicine, the latter being of exceptional importance ; the number of students is usually over 4,000.

Edirne, *e-dir'ne,* city, Turkey, also known as Adrianople ; on the main road between Istanbul and Belgrade ; manufactures silks, perfumes, etc. ; pop. 45,000.

Edison, THOMAS ALVA, *ed'i-sŭn* (1847–1931), American inventor, *b* Milan, Ohio, USA, of Dutch and Scottish parents ; attended school for 3 months, and was always lowest in class ; was later educated by his mother ; began earning his living as a newsboy ; printed a small news-sheet on a train ; became an expert telegraphist, and while in Boston (*c.*1866) read Michael Faraday's book on electricity, the turning-point of his career.

Working in a small laboratory, Edison invented a vote-recording machine ; then (in New York) began a series of inventions for improving the electric telegraph, taking out a host of patents, e.g. the automatic repeater, the quadruplex and printing telegraph. He had works at Newark, New Jersey.

Edison vastly improved the telephone ; discovered the carbon filament 1879, and devoted much time to the first practical electric lamp ; perfected the dynamo, and made cheap distribution of electricity possible ; invented the phonograph, forerunner of the gramophone ; the kinetoscope, forerunner of the cinematograph ; a magnetic ore-separator ; and the Edison nickel-iron cell. In the realm of chemistry he established plants for the production of benzol etc.

In all, Edison took out over 1,000 patents. Shy and modest, he had a giant's capacity for patient work. He advanced practical science by leaps and bounds, brought new industries into existence, and more than any other man made electricity the servant of humanity. His favourite saying was : *Genius is one per cent inspiration and ninety-nine per cent perspiration.*

Edmonton, *ed'mŭn-tŭn,* city and cap., Alberta, Canada ; noted for flour mills, timber, meat-packing, mining. It is a great agricultural centre and a fur-trade depot ; pop.79,000.

Edmonton, industrial town, Middlesex ; home of Keats, and burial-place of Charles and Mary Lamb ; pop.106,000.

Edmund (841–70), saint and king of E. Anglia ; captured by the Danes and beheaded Hoxne, Suffolk ; buried Bury St Edmunds ; festival 20 Nov.

Edmund (*d* 946), King of the English, son of Edward the Elder ; ruled from 941 ; fought the Danes ; subdued Cumbria ; reformed Church and State.

Edmund (*d* 1240), saint ; born near Oxford ; Archbishop of Canterbury from 1233 ; vainly tried to persuade Henry III to rid himself of foreign favourites ; died Soissy, France.

Edmund Ironside (*c.*981–1016), King of the English. A fine soldier, he fought Canute the Dane ; won the mastery of Wessex, but he was defeated at Assandun and his kingdom broken up.

education (Lat. *educare,* to nourish, bring up), organised teaching of the younger generation by the older in a specially planned environment (e.g. a school or college) in order to help children as they grow up to acquire knowledge and skills, to develop talents and interests, to think clearly, honestly, logically and imaginatively, and to live rightly. Education is concerned also with physical development ; and the term applies, further, to instruction for youth and adults in evening classes by lectures and through correspondence courses.

Education in Britain owes much to the ancient Greeks and Romans, and to the work of European pioneers, e.g. Comenius, Rousseau, Pestalozzi and Froebel. In England from the 16th c. onwards children of the upper classes were educated in grammar and private schools, or by home tutors, but prior to 1800, poorer children had few opportunities. DAME SCHOOLS for children below 7 and COMMON DAY SCHOOLS were sometimes run for profit by private individuals charging 1d or 2d per week, while some CHARITY SCHOOLS, such as those of the SPCK and the SUNDAY SCHOOLS, gave a limited but free education to a small number of children of the ' lower orders.'

In Scotland after the Reformation a very different system prevailed. A sound schooling was made available for a great majority of the people, and a university education was open to all who were likely to benefit by it. Thus a Scottish 'lad o' pairts' who was the son of poor parents had a distinct advantage over his English counterpart, at any rate until with the reforms of 1870 English education for ordinary people began to catch up with Scottish standards.

Early in the 19th c. MONITORIAL SCHOOLS, founded by Joseph Lancaster and Andrew Bell, made possible a wider development of education, and two great societies (National Society and British and Foreign School Society) established schools in many parts of the country. In England and Wales the government showed its first practical interest in education 1833 by making a grant for building schools, but did not take an active part till 1870, when School Boards were established to provide accommodation for all children in all areas. Hence two kinds of elementary schools grew up : VOLUNTARY (provided by the religious denominations), and BOARD (later known as Council and now as County) SCHOOLS. In 1876 education was made compulsory up to the age of 10, and that age was gradually raised till it reached 15 in 1947.

The Education Act of 1902 laid down that elementary schools should receive financial aid from local rates as well as from government grants. Better buildings, more textbooks and equipment, and a wider curriculum resulted. By 1900 the State had made provision for handicapped children, e.g. the blind, deaf, epileptic, and mentally deficient, and by 1907 provision was made for school meals, milk, and a medical service.

The *Hadow Report*, published in 1926, led to a reorganisation of schools, especially for pupils over 11, but the task was only partially completed by 1939. By this time, however, all elementary schools (which catered for 90% of the school population) were free, and more opportunities for brighter pupils to proceed to SECONDARY SCHOOLS, JUNIOR TECHNICAL SCHOOLS and TECHNICAL COLLEGES were available, though they did not meet all needs. Private schools, good and bad, existed as well as so-called Public Schools for children whose parents could afford and wished to pay fees.

A new Education Act, which came into operation in 1945, marks a great step forward. It provides free secondary education for *all*. The term ' elementary education ' has gone : the stage from 2 to 11 is now called PRIMARY EDUCATION and embraces the NURSERY SCHOOL (2 to 5), INFANT SCHOOL (5 to 7) and JUNIOR SCHOOL (7 to 11). The SECOND-

ARY stage of education begins at 11, when the pupil proceeds according to his ability to either a GRAMMAR SCHOOL for academic training, which in many cases will lead to college or university ; a TECHNICAL SCHOOL for training for skilled occupations and, later, for posts of responsibility in industry and commerce ; or a MODERN SCHOOL for broader training on practical lines. A MULTILATERAL SCHOOL may cater for all three types of secondary education, under one head teacher. When accommodation is available and teachers are trained, the school leaving age will be raised to 16, and all young people not attending school full-time will attend part-time at a COUNTY COLLEGE until they are 18.

Some schools remain outside the national system, and fees can still be charged in some grammar schools as well as public and private schools, though a close supervision of these independent schools is exercised.

Education today is designed to cater for all-round development of the individual, and the curriculum is now considerably extended. Methods have changed. Smaller classes allow for more individual and group work. Activity is the keynote : pupils work together on real-life projects. Much work is done outside school buildings, in museums, art galleries, factories, and on farms. Schools are better equipped to allow freedom of movement, e.g. laboratories provide for experimental work ; practical rooms for arts and crafts, cookery, and dramatics. Radio, cinematograph projectors, and other mechanical aids, place children in contact with experiences which would otherwise be denied them. Social activities through school assemblies, hobbies clubs, school societies, and systems of self-government play an important part, and parents are encouraged to take an interest in school life. Health is of prime importance, and this is secured by medical inspection and treatment, school milk and meals, and the provision of gymnasia, playing fields, and swimming baths. Child Guidance Clinics are also provided to help children who are unhappy, or are not making progress in the ordinary school group. Finally, character-training, the backbone of education, is catered for through the school social life, religious instruction and school worship.

See EXAMINATIONS ; PUBLIC SCHOOLS ; TECHNICAL EDUCATION ; UNIVERSITIES

For recent alterations in School Certificate etc., see EXAMINATIONS

Edward I (1239–1307), King of England from 1272 ; *b* Westminster, supported his father, Henry III, in the struggle against the barons ; captured at Lewes 1264, but directed the royalist victory when Simon de Montfort was killed 1265 at Evesham. Edward conquered Wales and strove to conquer the Scots in an attempt to bring the whole of

Britain under the English Crown. He *d* Burgh-on-Sands (Cumberland) while marching against the Scots.

One of the greatest of our kings, Edward I was a strong ruler who gathered together English laws, and shaped the English Parliament by summoning the Model Parliament 1295, which included clergy, barons, knights and citizens. His motto was *Pactum serva* (Keep faith) ; and his tomb (Westminster Abbey) has the words *Malleus Scotorum*, ' Hammer of the Scots.'

Edward II (1284–1327), King of England, son of Edward I, *b* Caernarvon ; was the first Prince of Wales ; ruled from 1307 ; controlled by favourites, e.g. Piers Gaveston and the Despensers ; defeated by the Scots at Bannockburn 1314 ; deposed by followers of his wife, Isabella ; murdered at Berkeley Castle. Edward II was probably one of the most incompetent English kings.

Edward III (1312–77), King of England ; came to the throne 1327 when his father (Edward II) was deposed by Isabella and Roger Mortimer ; actual ruler from 1330. From war with Scotland he turned to France, beginning the Hundred Years' War 1338 ; won the naval victory of Sluys 1340 ; victorious at Crécy (1346) where English archers were supreme ; captured Calais 1347, and with the victory at Poitiers 1356 became ruler of Aquitaine. Edward increased commerce, especially with Flanders. His reign is notable for the Black Death, the teaching of John Wycliffe, and the feuds that led to the Wars of the Roses.

Edward IV (1442–83), King of England, *b* Rouen ; son of Richard, Duke of York. As leader of the Yorkists in the Wars of the Roses, he won the crown (1461) with the aid of Warwick the Kingmaker. Driven from the country when Warwick restored Henry VI, 1470, he finally regained the throne 1471, and reigned in peace. Edward only rarely summoned Parliament.

Edward V (1470–83), King of England ; son of Edward IV and Elizabeth Woodville ; succeeded 9 April 1483 ; imprisoned (with his brother) in the Tower of London by his guardian, Gloucester, who had himself crowned as Richard III, 6 July, and is believed to have had the two princes murdered.

Edward VI (1537–53), King of England, He was the son of Henry VIII and Jane Seymour ; succeeded 1547. His uncle, the Duke of Somerset, was Protector at first, followed by the Earl of Warwick (later Duke of Northumberland) who planned that his daughter-in-law, Lady Jane Grey, should become queen at Edward's death. From childhood Edward, always weak and ailing, was intensely religious. His reign is notable for the spread of Protestantism.

Edward VII (1841–1910), King and Emperor, eldest son of Queen Victoria ; *b* Buckingham Palace ; Prince of Wales till his accession 1901 in his 60th year. Married 1863 Princess Alexandra, daughter of Christian IX of Denmark. He was a great traveller (e.g. Canada and USA 1860 ; India 1875 ; Russia 1874 and 1908, and Germany 1909), also a lover of sport, especially racing ; had a genius for friendship, and was justly styled ' the Peacemaker.'

Edward VIII, see WINDSOR, DUKE OF

Edward the Black Prince (1330–76), son of Edward III ; ' won his spurs ' (i.e. proved himself a fine soldier) when 16 at the battle of Crécy 1346 ; led many successful raids against the French ; victorious at Poitiers 1356, capturing King John II of France ; ruled Gascony and Aquitaine ; married his cousin Joan (' the fair Maid of Kent ') ; and was buried in a handsome tomb in Canterbury Cathedral.

Remembered as ' the mirror of knightly chivalry,' he was a master of tactical warfare. Note : He was not called the Black Prince till long after his death, probably with reference to the black armour he is said to have worn.

Edward the Confessor (*c.*1005–66), King of the English, son of Ethelred the Unready ; half-brother of Hardicanute ; ruled from 1042. He was supported by Earl Godwin, whose daughter (Edith) he married. His reign was peaceful in spite of two struggles against the Normans. Deeply religious, Edward founded Westminster Abbey, which was consecrated 1065. He was made a saint 1161.

Edward the Elder (*d* 924), King of the English from 901 ; son of Alfred the Great ; conquered the Danes 918 ; overlord as far N. as the Humber.

Edward the Martyr (*d* 978), King of the English, son of Edgar ; slain by order of his stepmother, Elfrida, mother of Ethelred the Unready.

eel, food fish with long, snake-like body and no visible scales ; found in fresh water and at sea. The life-history was unknown prior to its examination by the Italian zoologist, Battista Grassi, *b* 1855. It now appears that mature eels migrate from ponds and rivers, to the sea in autumn, and spawn in deep water.

Besides the common eel there is the CONGER, sometimes over 6ft long. The ELECTRIC EEL, found in rivers of Brazil and Guiana, is also 6ft. How it generates a powerful shock remains a mystery.

eft, see AMPHIBIAN

Egbert (reigned 802–839), King of Wessex ; exiled at the court of Charlemagne ; returned as King of .the W. Saxons 802 ; subdued W. Wales or Cornwall, also Mercia and Kent, and became overlord of all the English kings 829 ; defeated Danish pirates at Hingston Down (Hengestdune) in Cornwall, 837.

eglantine, name given by poets to the sweet briar ; by it Milton may have meant the honeysuckle.

Egmont, mt. in N. Island, NZ ; height 8,270ft.

Egypt, kingdom of NE. Africa comprising *Egypt proper,* i.e. the delta and valley of the R. Nile, the Libyan desert, and the Arabian (or eastern) desert ; the *Peninsula of Sinai,* a part of Asia ; and *various islands* in the Gulf of Suez and the Red Sea. To the south Egypt marches with the Anglo-Egyptian Sudan; the western boundary lies chiefly along the 25th meridian ; area 386,000sq.m, of which only *c.*13,000sq.m are cultivated ; pop.19,000,000.

The outstanding feature of Egypt is the R. Nile, on which all cultivation depends. Its flood waters from Ethiopia are held back by the Aswan ' barrage,' and regulated also by the ' barrages ' at Asyut and Esna, the waters being led off right and left by a host of irrigation canals, thus providing a narrow green strip between deserts. The Nile floods (highest in Sept.), deposit mud for the growing of wheat, maize, cane sugar, rice, beans, tobacco, and especially cotton ; cattle, buffaloes, sheep and camels are reared, mostly in the Nile valley, which is rarely more than 20m wide, and often bounded by limestone or sandstone cliffs 1,000ft high. In the desert regions are depressions, often with oases, also *wadis* (seasonal riverbeds) with springs or wells, usually of brackish water.

Communications include 3,000m of railways, the Suez canal (linking Europe with the Far East and of great strategical importance), and the various civilian air stations. The few minerals worked include petroleum, manganese and phosphate rock ; among industries are cotton and woollen fabrics, silks, embroideries, much brass and copper ware, rugs, pottery and perfumes.

The native peasant population are called Fellahin ; in the deserts there are Bedouins (nomad Arab tribes), and Nubians.

The religion of a large part of the people is Mohammedan, but there are Coptic and Greek Christians. The country is a kingdom with a parliament (*Barlaman*) comprising a Senate and a Chamber of Deputies. Trade is largely with the UK, India, Turkey, France and the USA ; exports include raw cotton, cotton seed, minerals and onions ; the chief imports are textiles, metals, coal, chemicals, machinery, foodstuffs, timber and wood pulp.

The chief towns include Cairo, the capital, on the Nile delta ; Alexandria, port and centre of the cotton trade ; Port Said ; Mansura ; Asyut ; Faiyum; Zagazig ; Rosetta and Ismailia.

British influence in Egypt has been immense, and has led to great advances. Part of the Turkish empire from 1517, Egypt had a British army of occupation 1882–1936, and the country was a British Protectorate 1914–22. Sultan

Ahmed Fuad was proclaimed king, and Egypt became a sovereign-state by the Anglo-Egyptian Treaty 1936. In World War II Egypt narrowly missed falling into German hands 1942. After the War, successive Egyptian governments were influenced by an intensive popular agitation for the expulsion of British troops.

One of the earliest cradles of civilisation, ancient Egypt was famous for her religions, scholarship, literature, art and sculpture, social organisations, and especially her architecture, which flourished 6,000 years ago. Much was known of practical chemistry and medicine ; her astronomers divided the year into 365 days and into 12 months ; a decimal arithmetic was in use ; engineers and architects built huge temples, e.g. those at Karnak and Thebes ; the pyramids, including the Great Pyramid of Gizeh, the Sphinx, and the many royal tombs, e.g. those in the Valley of the Kings. Much of the glory of ancient Egypt has been brought to light comparatively recently, especially by Howard Carter and Sir Flinders Petrie. The art treasures of Luxor were revealed 1922 ; the temple of Pharaoh Akhenaton was discovered 1926. From Egypt (where they made bricks without straw) the Israelites journeyed to Palestine. In Egypt the earliest alphabet was used, the first paper (*papyrus*) invented, possibly the first metal weapon shaped, and the first medical book written. See SUDAN

Read *The Pyramids of Egypt,* I. E. S. Edwards

eider duck, *ī'der,* wild duck of the Farne Isls., Greenland, Iceland and Norway ; roughly twice as big as the common duck ; is reddish, spotted with black. The female lines the nest with fine down from her breast.

Eiffel Tower, *ī'fel,* building of 7,300 tons of iron erected in Paris 1889 by Alexandre Gustave Eiffel (1832–1923), a French engineer. The tower 985ft high is now used for broadcasting and for sightseeing.

Eighth Army, in World War II, the first British army to oppose German and Italian forces on a large scale ; eventually drove Axis forces out of N. Africa. Latterly, it was commanded by General (later Viscount) Montgomery, and afterwards invaded Sicily and Italy. Its 7th Armoured Division was known as the Desert Rats.

Einstein, ALBERT, *īn'stīn* (1879–), German scientist, author of the Theory of Relativity and of the later Unified Field Theory ; but see RELATIVITY

Eire, see IRELAND ; SINN FEIN

Eisenhower, GENERAL DWIGHT, *ī'zenow'r* (1890–), supreme commander in the European theatre of World War II ; *b* Texas, USA ; planned and carried through the brilliant invasion of Europe leading to the defeat of Germany 1945.

Read *Three Years with Eisenhower,* Captain H. C. Butcher's fine portrait of a great man, and *General Eisenhower*, Alden Hatch.

eisteddfod, *es-teth'vod*, Welsh assembly, said to have met in pre-Roman times, and for long centuries notable for the crowning of the chief bard (poet). Eisteddfods are still of great interest for their musical and poetical contests.

El Agheila, village in Cyrenaica, scene of fighting between the German Afrika Korps and the Eighth Army in World War II.

El Alamein, *-al'a-mān*, town on the coast of Egypt ; scene Nov 1942 of the British defeat of the German forces in World War II, and the beginning of an amazing British advance (1,350m in 82 days) across Cyrenaica, via El Agheila and Benghazi, and through Tripolitania, to meet Allied troops landed in Fr. N. Africa, and hence the expulsion of Axis forces. See EIGHTH ARMY

Elam, *ē'lam*, Bible name for a region of SW. Persia (Iran).

eland, *ē'land*, largest of the antelopes. Fawn or grey with twisted horns 2ft long, it is found in herds in E. Africa.

Elba, small rocky It. island in the Mediterranean. Trades in fish, fruit, iron ore, etc. ; home of the exiled Napoleon 1814–15.

Elbe, river, N. Germany ; 725m ; enters the N. Sea near Cuxhaven.

Elberfeld, *-felt*, industrial town 16m E. of Dusseldorf, Germany ; pop.150,000.

Elbing, Baltic port, Germany ; has one of the largest shipbuilding yards in the country ; pop.71,000.

Elbruz, *el'broos*, highest peak (18,526ft) of the Caucasus Mts, USSR.

Elburz, mt. range of N. Iran (Persia).

El Chaco, *el chä'kō*, region largely in Argentina. Part of El Gran Chaco, it has lakes and swamps ; much of the area (52,000sq.m) is unexplored, and the boundaries have frequently been in dispute.

elder, shrub-like tree, usually *c*.10ft high ; has clusters of cream flowers. The berries and flowers are used for making wine.

El Dorado, *el dō-rä'dō*, Spanish name for an imaginary region in S. America rich in gold and precious stones. Search for El Dorado has often been made by adventurers.

El Dorado is often used for an unattainable ideal ; hence R. L. Stevenson writes :

O unwearied feet, travelling ye know not whither ! Soon, soon, it seems to you, you must come forth on some conspicuous hilltop, and but a little way farther, against the setting sun, descry the spires of El Dorado. Little do ye know your own blessedness, for to travel hopefully is a better thing than to arrive, and the true success is to labour.

Eleanor, *el'ä-nĕr*, name of three queens of England : (1) ELEANOR (*d* 1204), wife of Henry II, and a daughter of William,

Duke of Aquitaine ; (2) ELEANOR (*d* 1291), wife of Henry III, *b* Provence ; very unpopular as queen ; (3) ELEANOR (*d* 1290), wife of Edward I ; daughter of Ferdinand III of Castile ; said to have saved Edward's life by sucking poison from a wound when he was at Acre. She *d* Harby, Nottinghamshire, Edward erecting 13 crosses on the route to Westminster Abbey, where she was buried. Of these only those at Northampton, Geddington and Waltham remain.

election, *ē-lek'shon*, choosing one out of many, e.g. shareholders elect others to speak for them at a company meeting, trusting those so elected to carry out the electors' wishes.

In politics and civics election by ballot has been the method in Britain since 1872. In early times a reeve and 4 men were chosen by villagers in a rough and ready way, and election was much the same for many representatives till the 19th c., a show of hands or shouting and cheering being enough to elect a knight of the shire or a burgess for a borough. Only slowly did election by ballot come into use. Ballot originally meant voting with balls—red for the person you wish to represent you, black for the other.

Today Parliamentary election is decided by *secret ballot*. As it is impossible for millions of men and women in the UK to come to London to decide important matters about the government of the kingdom, they choose *representatives*, known as Members of Parliament. Often 2 or 3 candidates hope to represent one division or constituency, though the people (the electorate) may have to choose only one MP. Before the election (polling day) candidates hold meetings, each trying to persuade the electors to choose him. When the electors go to the poll (*pōl*), i.e. to vote, at a polling booth (some convenient room) they receive a printed card with the name of each candidate ; and it is the elector's duty to put a cross opposite the name of the candidate he wishes to see elected. After the polling the votes for each candidate are counted, and the candidate with the biggest number (a majority) is ' returned ' to Parliament as MP for that constituency.

Parliamentary elections are of two kinds : (1) *general*, when the House of Commons is dissolved and a new one is required, which means that all over the country members must be elected or re-elected ; (2) *by-election*, i.e. election of a member in one constituency only, owing to the death or retirement of the previous member.

By *franchise* we mean all who are privileged to vote for an MP. An Act of Parliament 1430 decreed that only people whose land was worth 40s, or more, could vote, and the franchise remained unjust and unrepresentative till the famous Reform Act of 1832, first of several which reshaped Parliament, and gave more people the right to vote. Prior to 1832, Old Sarum, a parish in Wiltshire, returned two members of Parliament, though practically a ruin, while Birmingham and Manchester, growing towns with thousands of people, had not the right to elect even one member. By the Reform Act, 56 boroughs (often called rotten boroughs) were defranchised, i.e. lost the power to vote, and 42 were given the franchise for the first time. Later Acts brought about other alterations, greatly increasing the electorate ; thus W. E. Gladstone's Third Reform Act 1884 added 2,500,000 voters to the electorate ; and the Act of 1918 added 8,000,000 votes by giving the franchise to women, chiefly as a result of the work of the Suffragettes, led by Mrs Emmeline Pankhurst (1858–1928), and her daughters Christabel and Sylvia. Suffrage (Latin *suffragari*, to vote for) means the right to vote, and the Suffragettes were women who demanded votes for women. In the UK men over 21 have had a vote since 1918, women over 21 since 1928.

What is known as *indirect voting* is best illustrated by the way in which the President of USA is chosen, i.e. the people of America elect their representatives to Congress (Parliament), and these representatives, *not* the electors as a whole, choose the President.

Town and city councils (borough councils) in England are made up of representatives of the ratepayers. As one-third give up their position as councillors each year, it follows that every year (generally in May) the ratepayers have to chose a number of new councillors. This is a municipal election. County councillors (members of a committee dealing with the welfare of a county, or part of a county) are elected (or re-elected) every three years.

See LOCAL GOVERNMENT ; PARLIAMENT

elector, see HOLY ROMAN EMPIRE

Electra, *ē-lek´trä*, in old Gk tales, daughter of Agamemnon and Clytaemnestra ; goaded her brother Orestes to murder his mother. See SOPHOCLES

electrical capacity, charge that must be given to a body to raise its potential one volt. A body with a capacity of 1 farad requires a charge of 1 coulomb to raise its potential 1 volt, the farad being 9×10^{11} electrostatic units ; the practical unit is the microfarad, i.e. 1/1,000,000 farad.

electricity, phenomenon about which much has yet to be discovered, though electricity is daily employed in the service of man. A form of energy, its effects have long been known ; its name (from the Gk *elektron*, amber) reminds us that as early as *c.*640BC Thales, a Gk scientist, produced electricity by rubbing amber.

Among many who have added to our knowledge, and hence to the uses, of electricity are Sir Isaac Newton ; Cunaeus, inventor of the Leyden jar, for storing electricity ; Benjamin Franklin, who showed that lightning was caused by the discharge of electricity ; Volta, who constructed the first electric battery ; Sir Humphry Davy, discoverer of practical electrolysis, by which compounds could be split up into their elements by electric action ; Michael Faraday, to whom we owe the dynamo ; Ohm, who provided us with the basic idea of electrical resistance ; Hertz, discoverer of electromagnetic waves, which led in turn to radio, partly as a result of the pioneer work of Clerk-Maxwell and Marconi. Both Lord Kelvin and Edison did much to bring electricity into everyday use. Other notable names are those of Sir J. J. Thomson, Lord Rutherford, R. A. Millikan (first to measure accurately the charge on the electron), Chadwick, Einstein, A. K. Solomon, Niels Bohr, etc.

Electricity may be considered as *static*, and *current*, i.e. electricity in motion.

(I) *static electricity*, of more interest in the laboratory than outside it (except, perhaps, in the realm of atmospheric electricity) may be produced, e.g. by the friction of dry flannel on ebonite ; the former becomes charged with what is termed positive (+), the latter with negative (−) electricity.

Many experiments have been conducted to show that negative electrons *repel* one another ; so do positive ones ; whereas positive (+) and negative (−) *attract* one another. In such experiments, use is made of the electroscope, i.e. two thin gold leaves suspended from a metal rod.

If charged by touching (*conduction*), the charge on the leaves is similar to that of the charging body ; if charged by the *approach* of an electric field (*induction*), the charges are opposite.

Substances that offer comparatively little resistance to the passage of electricity are called *conductors*, e.g. most metals, especially silver and copper ; those offering great resistance are *insulators*, e.g. sulphur, wax, glass, porcelain, plastics, all of which (in ordinary circumstances) are non - conductors. See PLATE 45. Many experiments in static electricity employ the *electrophorus*, comprising (*a*) an ebonite sheet or a metal disc containing a mixture of paraffin wax and flowers of sulphur, (*b*) a circular sheet of metal with an insulating handle. The cake of wax and sulphur is charged by rubbing with flannel, when any number of charges may be taken off by lifting the metal disc after earthing it, an example of the conversion of mechanical energy into electricity.

The *Leyden jar* is a glass vessel coated inside and out (for about two-thirds of

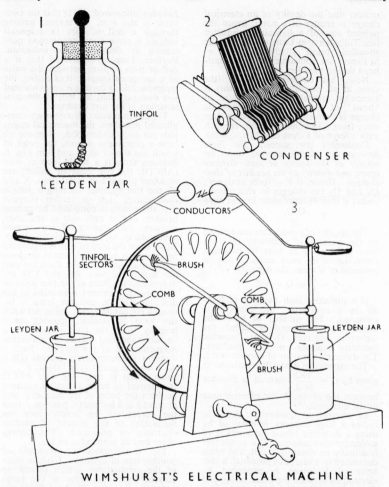

TINFOIL

LEYDEN JAR

CONDENSER

CONDUCTORS

TINFOIL SECTORS BRUSH

COMB COMB

LEYDEN JAR LEYDEN JAR

BRUSH

WIMSHURST'S ELECTRICAL MACHINE

its depth) with tin-foil. A metal rod and chain pass through an insulating stopper and touch the bottom of the jar. If the knob at the top of the rod is repeatedly charged from, say, the electrophorus, a high electrical potential (see Fig. 1) may be built up, and a bright spark produced when the jar is suitably discharged.

In effect, the Leyden jar is a form of *condenser*, the glass being the insulator (or *dielectric*), the tin-foil the conductor. In some types of condensers the dielectric is mica, paraffin wax, or paper ; in *variable condensers* (e.g. those used in radio apparatus) air is the dielectric. The *capacity* of a condenser depends on several factors (see CONDENSER and Fig. 2).

For laboratory work a useful piece of apparatus is the *wimshurst machine*

(Fig. 3), originally designed by James Wimshurst towards the end of the 19th c. An ' influence ' machine supplying frictional electricity, this comprises, in its simplest form, one or more pairs of circular glass or ebonite plates coated with shellac, over which, near the circumference, are thin sectors of foil (tin, brass, or copper). There are neutralising brushes and collecting combs. By rotating the discs in opposite directions, opposite charges are collected on two brass knobs. High potentials may be mounted and a long spark secured. The curious odour noticeable when the machine is working is due to the presence of ozone (O_3), a more active form of oxygen.

The fact that all the parts of a wimshurst machine are rounded is a reminder that the density of an electrical charge is greater at a point, hence the pointed tips of a lightning conductor (see THUNDER AND LIGHTNING), and the so-called ' brush ' discharge known as St Elmo's fire, sometimes seen at a mast-head during thundery weather.

Note that electrical potential (the same at all points of a conductor) is somewhat similar to the pressure of ' head ' of water. Unit electrostatic charge is that charge which, when 1cm away from a like charge, in air, repels it with a force of 1 dyne (see MECHANICS).

Coulomb's law states : *The force between two electric charges varies inversely as the square of their distance apart, and directly as the product of their charges.* Hence, if F = force in dynes ; Q_1 and Q_2 the charges in electrostatic units ; d their distance apart in cm : then

$$F = \frac{Q_1 Q_2}{d^2}$$

The *capacity* of a conductor is measured by the quantity of electricity that has been given to it to raise its potential unity, i.e. if Q units cause a rise in potential of V units, the capacity

$$C = \frac{Q}{V} \text{ or } Q = VC$$

If a dielectric such as mica replaces air in a condenser, the capacity is increased. The number of times the capacity is multiplied is called the dielectric constant (K) or ' specific inductive capacity ' of that insulator. The dielectric constant of ebonite is c.7.

The capacity of a parallel condenser is given by $C = \frac{AK}{4\pi d}$ where d is distance between the plates, A the effective area of the dielectric.

In electrolytic condensers (used in radio) a large capacity is obtained by using a dielectric whose thickness is of molecular dimensions. The condenser is actually an electrolytic cell, and when connected to a source of potential, a thin layer of hydrogen is produced by electrolysis between the outer casing and the liquid or jelly which is the electrolyte. This gas is the dielectric. With such condensers there is always a leakage current across the condenser.

(II) *current electricity*, fundamentally identical with static electricity, differs in its effects. Whereas static electricity passes instantly when a charged body is discharged (often giving a spark), current electricity *flows continuously*, hence its immense importance in modern life, since it provides heat, power and light. Of electric generators the *dynamo* is the most important. Here electricity and magnetism are both involved ; see MAGNETISM. As early as c.1820 it had been observed that an electric current flowing along a wire sets up circular magnetic fields in a clockwise direction to an observer facing the way of the current, and at right angles to the flow.

Faraday discovered (1831) that the converse is also true. A magnet passing through a coil of wire (a solenoid) induces a current, a phenomenon now known as electromagnetic induction. Further, Faraday discovered that if a coil of wire revolves between the poles of a horseshoe magnet, thus cutting the magnetic field, a current is again induced —a discovery led him to the construction of the first dynamo.

Though in practice dynamos are complicated machines, the theoretical essentials are easily understood, Suppose we have a permanent magnet, the poles of which are shown as N and S in Fig. 4. Between them is a single loop of wire (ABCD), the two ends of which are attached to two half metal rings, X and Y, the two together forming a simple *commutator*. Let us further suppose that the circuit is completed by carbon brushes, one at each side of the commutator, thus leading off any current generated to, say, a small electric lamp. Now, when the loop of wire is stationary no current is generated, but as the loop turns in an anticlockwise direction and the lengths of wire AB and CD are drawn past the faces of the two poles of the magnet, a current is induced in the direction DCBA, and the lamp is lit, though not continuously, going out when the loop is vertical, glowing most brightly when the loop is horizontal, i.e. when the loop crosses the maximum magnetic field of the magnet. Such a dynamo generates direct current (DC). At *a* on the graph (Fig. 5)—*a, b* . . . being points in time—the wire ABCD is supposed to be in a vertical position between the poles of the magnet ; and at point *b* in a horizontal position : then the curves on the graph show the fluctuation of the current of positive electricity so generated. The current effect may be graphed as in Fig. 5.

Fig. 6 illustrates the principle of another type of dynamo. Here, in place of the commutator (which picked up current from *both* sides of the loop) are two slip-rings (X, Y). Since the brush on the side X always takes current from the same half of the loop, it receives current in one direction (AB) when AB passes *down* the face of the pole N, and in the other direction (BA) when this half of the loop passes *up* the face of the pole S. So that the current reaching the lamp is reversed twice for every revolution of the loop, hence this current is *alternating* (AC). Fig. 7 shows a graph of this cycle.

This is the theory of the dynamo. In practice, the magnet is an electromagnet, which is much more powerful than any permanent magnet, or group of them ; the moving part (known as an *armature*) is not a single coil but a large number of coils of wire (sometimes miles in length) wound on a soft iron core, and thus greatly concentrating the magnetic field.

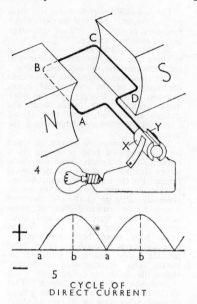

4

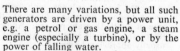

5

CYCLE OF
DIRECT CURRENT

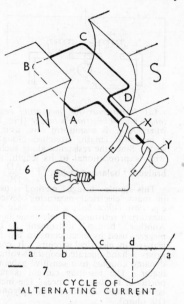

6

7

CYCLE OF
ALTERNATING CURRENT

There are many variations, but all such generators are driven by a power unit, e.g. a petrol or gas engine, a steam engine (especially a turbine), or by the power of falling water.

Note, however, that the principle of electromagnetic induction, on which the dynamo depends, is not a case of something for nothing. The induced current produces a magnetic field that always opposes the moving magnetic field causing it (Lenz's law). The magnetic field is, therefore, being moved against an opposing force, and mechanical work is being done. It takes effort (though too small an amount to be noticed) even to push a magnet into a coil, and power is required to turn a dynamo. The more the electricity load, the more power needed, i.e. more coal is consumed to generate steam to work the turbines that turn the generators.

The *electric motor* is an example of the opposite principle, i.e. the turning of electrical to mechanical energy. Such a motor often delivers 95% of the electrical energy supplied. See GRID ; INDUCTION COIL ; TRANSFORMER

One of the great assets in the use of electric power is the simplicity with which it can be transmitted, sometimes over long distances. Whereas it would be impossible to convey, say, water-power many miles, electricity flows along wires or cables with only comparatively small loss of potential (due to the resistance of the conducting material), hence, say, Battersea power house lights lamps in several counties, and the generating plant at Niagara drives machinery far from the source of power. But wherever current flows along a wire there is always some loss due to *resistance*, no matter how short the circuit ; hence the correct wiring of a house, a school, factory, etc. for electric light or power requires a thorough working knowledge on the part of the electrician.

The electrical energy lost when current flows along a conductor reappears as heat, and this loss, and the resultant rate of generation of heat, are proportional to the square of the current and to the resistance of the conductor, i.e. to C^2R. Thus, in any closed electrical circuit the greatest heat is generated where resistance is greatest, hence an electric lamp or fire glows (giving light and heat) because its resistance is great enough to make the wire red-hot or white-hot.

Whereas we require the resistance wire of a lamp or fire to be high, the electrician is careful to keep the resistance of the wiring of a building as low as possible. If, however, any wire becomes defective, but not broken, its resistance at that point may rise, and sufficient heat may be generated to cause a fire. To obviate this, a fuse-box is inserted somewhere in the circuit. The essentials of the fuse-box are described under FUSE.

Note that, especially in laboratory work, wiring may be (*a*) *in series*, when the same current flows through *all* the points where it is required, or (*b*) *in parallel*, where current is *divided* among the points.

The *measurement of electricity* has necessitated a wide range of instruments, among which may be noted :

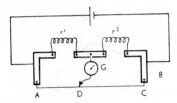

(a) *Instruments for measuring resistance*, e.g. *Wheatstone's bridge* (Fig. 8), where ADC is a uniform wire, usually 1 metre in length, stretched along a scale. Since the resistance along such a wire is proportional to its length, the bridge is ' balanced ' when $\frac{r_1}{r_2} = \frac{AD}{DC}$.

This simple ' bridge ' method is used in many electrical measuring devices, e.g. *Post Office box*, a device used for measuring resistance in telephone lines. Another ' bridge ' instrument is the *megger*, used by electricians to test for leakage in electrical circuits. It comprises a hand-operated constant-voltage dynamo coupled to a sensitive galvanometer. The resulting current is proportional to the resistance. The meter is sometimes calibrated in megohms (10^6 ohms).

(b) *Instruments for measuring current*, e.g. the *galvanometer*, types of which include the *tangent galvanometer* in which a magnetic needle is suspended at the centre of a circular coil through which a current (C) may be made to flow, thus creating a magnetic field, the earth's field exercising a restoring force. Current is proportional to the tangent of the angle of deflection.

The *ammeter*, another instrument for measuring current, may be (i) of the *moving-iron type*, i.e. depending on the attraction or repulsion of iron magnetised by a current. This type is suitable for measuring AC, and the more recent types, now using u-metal, are reasonably accurate and reliable ; (ii) *moving-coil ammeter*, now the most popular type, suitable for DC only. It comprises a suspended coil through which current passes. The coil turns in a magnetic field of a powerful permanent magnet ; (iii) *hot-wire ammeter*, in which the electric current causes a wire to become warm, and so expand, the increase in length being mechanically magnified. This type is suitable for high-frequency currents. There is also the *micro-ammeter* for detecting exceedingly small currents.

(c) *Instruments for measuring voltage or potential difference* (PD), e.g. the *voltmeter*. This is usually of the moving-coil or moving-iron (AC) type. Voltmeters differ from ammeters only in using high resistance coils instead of low resistance coils, those measuring very high voltages being known as electrostatic voltmeters.

The *household electric meter* is a form of wattmeter, an instrument which measures power, i.e. rate of consumption of electrical energy.

See POTENTIOMETER

There are two systems of *electrical units*, electrostatic and electromagnetic.

The *electrostatic system* is built round the notion of the mechanical forces between electric charges, and the work done against these forces when the charges are moved, hence they are all based on the mechanical force unit, the dyne.

The *electromagnetic system* is based on the magnetic field produced by a current, and magnetic fields are themselves defined in terms of mechanical forces. But electromagnetic units defined in this way soon proved to be inconveniently large or small, and therefore multiples or sub-multiples of these *absolute units* were taken and given names as *derived units*. These derived units have since been redefined in practical terms in various ways so as to provide ready means of ensuring accurate and international standards. Hence the following definitions :

Ampere, unit of *electric current* : That unvarying current which, when passed through a solution of nitrate of silver in water, in accordance with certain specifications, deposits silver at the rate of 0·001118 gram per sec. Ampere (from the French scientist, Ampère) is usually abbreviated amp.

Ohm, unit of *electrical resistance*, defined as equal to the resistance of a column of mercury 106·3cm long and of 1sq.mm cross-section at 0°C, its mass being 14·4521gm.

Volt, unit of *electrical potential difference* (PD), defined as that potenial difference which will maintain a current of 1 ampere through a conductor of 1 ohm resistance ; or the resistance offered to an unvarying electric current by a column of mercury (at the temperature of melting ice) 14·4521 gram in mass, 106·3cm in length. Note that $C = \frac{E}{R}$, where C is current, E is potential difference in volts, R is resistance in ohms ; also that $R = \frac{E}{C}$ and $E = CR$.

Coulomb, unit of *electrical quantity*, defined as the amount of electricity passing in a circuit when 1 ampere flows for 1 second.

Farad, unit of *electrical capacity* ; defined as the capacity of a condenser which holds 1 coulomb of electricity when the PD between the plates is 1 volt. Note that 1 microfarad = 10^{-6} farad, and that this is usually regarded as the unit.

Henry, unit of *self-inductance* or natural inductance. If a rate of change of electric current of 1 ampere per second in one coil produces an EMF (electromotive force) of 1 volt between the ends of another coil, the mutual inductance is said to be 1 henry. If it produces a back EMF in itself of 1 volt, it is said to have a self-inductance of 1 henry. Note that 10^{-6} henry = the microhenry, a unit commonly used in practice.

Joule, unit of *electrical work done* when 1 coulomb flows across a PD of 1 volt, i.e. the work done in 1 second by a current of 1 ampere flowing through a resistance of 1 ohm. Note that 1 joule = 10^7 ergs.

Hence we have : (i) if the EMF of a circuit be measured in volts, R = external resistance, r = internal resistance in ohms, then the current (C) in amperes is

$$C = \frac{EMF}{R+r}$$

and (ii) the total resistance (R) of r_1, r_2, r_3 *in series* is $R = r_1 + r_2 + r_3$; and *in parallel*

$$\frac{1}{R} = \frac{1}{r_1} + \frac{1}{r_2} + \frac{1}{r_3}$$

Watt, unit of *electrical power,* i.e. *rate* of consumption of electricity. Note that 1 watt is the consumption of 1 joule per second, and is equivalent to a rate of working of 10^7 ergs in the CGS (centimetre-gram-second) system. One horsepower is taken as 746 watts, and the value of the Board of Trade unit (BOTU) is 1,000 watt-hours, or 3,600,000 joules, or 1·3 hp-hours. Hence the important unit, the *Kilowatt,* i.e. 1,000 watts or 1,000 joules per sec.

Note that the dials of electric meters are calibrated in Kilowatt-hours (KWH), and that if a 100-watt lamp burns for, say, 12 hours at 6d per unit, we have 100 W = 0·1KW, therefore the energy consumed in 12 hours is 0·1 × 12, i.e. 1·2 KWH, or 1·2 × 6d, which is 7·2d.

The effects of current electricity may be (*a*) *magnetic,* hence electromagnetism, the magnetic crane, electric motor, etc. ; also the telegraph and telephone, electric relays, and the ordinary household electric bell ; (*b*) *chemical,* e.g. electrolysis, electroplating, chemical methods of manufacture, including the separation of aluminium from its ores, the purification of copper, etc. ; and in medicine, noticeably the treatment of asthma ; and (*c*) production of heat and light. In (*c*) use is made of the fact that increased resistance causes increased heat. The flex conveying electricity from a plug to an electric fire may be only slightly warmed by the current, but the special resistance wire in the fire offers a high resistance ; hence it glows red. In, say, the electric laundering-iron, heat is developed by a resistance element of ni-chrome wire wound on mica and clamped between heavy metal cheeks above and below. Electric resistance furnaces use the same principle, but a new type—the electric induction furnace —surrounds the metal to be treated with a coil carrying a high-frequency AC current. Eddy-currents induced in the metal cause heating, and the method is extremely satisfactory for small quantities of alloy.

A still more modern way of heating by electricity has quite recently been adapted for cooking. What is actually a high-frequency radio transmitter emits radio waves so short that they are practically heat waves near the infra-red end of the electro-magnetic spectrum. Absorption of these penetrating waves by the Sunday joint cooks it inside as well as outside.

If the resistance offered to a wire is sufficiently great, the wire will become white-hot, hence many types of *electric light bulbs.* Early electric lamps had carbon filaments, but today most have filaments of tungsten, which is extracted from the ore, wolfram. This has the highest melting-point of any metal (*c.*3,370°C). A coil of tungsten, or one of its alloys, in a bulb in which air has been replaced by one of the inert gases, as, say, argon, at low pressure, gives a high light-value for the current flowing through it.

Gas discharge tubes (neon tubes) are used extensively for display and advertisement. The high voltage (derived from a transformer) causes the gas, which is at low pressure, to glow. Different gases give different colours The current may be small, and as little heat is developed the lamps are very efficient. *Fluorescent lighting* depends on a high voltage across a tube containing mercury vapour. The discharge emission excites the coating on the tube's inner surface.

Electricity derived from various cells, etc. is dealt with under accumulators and batteries.

Many cross references have already been given in this entry, but the student may find the following alphabetical list of entries useful :

ACCUMULATORS AND BATTERIES ; CHEMISTRY ; CONDENSER ; COPPER ; COULOMB ; DYNE ; EDISON, T. A. ; ELECTRICAL CAPACITY ; ELECTRIC METER ; ELECTROLYSIS ; ELEMENT ; FARAD ; FARADAY, M. ; HEAT ; INDUCTION COIL ; JOULE ; KELVIN, LORD ; LIGHT ; MAGNETISM ; MATTER ; MECHANICS ; OHM ; POTENTIOMETER ; QUANTUM THEORY ; RADIO ; RADIOACTIVITY ; TELEGRAPH AND TELEPHONE ; THUNDER AND LIGHTNING ; VOLT ; WAVE MOTION ; X-RAYS.

Read *Sub-Atomic Physics,* Professor H. Dingle (Nelson) ; *Basic Radio,* G. L. Boltz (Nelson) ; *The World of Science,* Sherwood Taylor ; *General Physics,* Nightingale and Pearson ; *Electricity and Magnetism,* Reynolds, Chapter 14 ; *Science for the Citizen,* Lancelot Hogben; consult also *Chambers's Technical Dic-*

tionary ; *A Dictionary of Science*, E. B. Uvarov.

electrical units, see ELECTRICITY

electric spark, sudden discharge through a normally insulating medium (as air or gas) between two highly charged conductors of electricity, as that of influence machines or a flash of lightning. Passed through moist air the electric spark forms nitric acid, a principle used in the fixation of nitrogen from the air by the Birkeland Eyde method. The minimum sparking potential for air is *c*.300 volts ; 10,000 volts gives a spark 1⅜in long, the length depending partly on the number of ions present.

The electric spark is used in internal combustion engines for igniting an explosive charge by means of a sparking plug, usually a porcelain-lined tube, having within a metal conducting rod, the end of which is separated from the wall of a metal plug by *c*.1/50th in. The distributor is so timed that when the piston has fully compressed the charge by reaching the top of its stroke, an electric spark leaps the gap and ignites the gas, which, by suddenly expanding, forces the piston outward.

electro-chemical equivalent, see ELECTROLYSIS

electrolysis, *ē-lek-trol'i-sis*, process of chemical decomposition by means of an electric current flowing from one electrode to another through a solution called an electrolyte, usually an acid, base, or salt.

What happens is explained by the ionic theory, which supposes that, in solution, the molecules of the substance dissolved are partly broken up into ions which are not electrically neutral, e.g. copper sulphate is supposed to form, in part, copper ions (i.e. copper atoms carrying a positive charge) and sulphate ions (i.e. SO_4 atom-groups carrying negative charges), hence

$$CuSO_4 \longrightarrow Cu^+ + Cu^+ + SO_4^{--}$$

When two electrodes connected to a battery are dipped into the solution, migration of the copper ions to the negative electrode (*cathode*) takes place, and copper is deposited. The SO_4 ions move to the positive electrode (*anode*). If the positive electrode is copper they attack it to form copper sulphate. Thus the number of SO_4 ions is unaffected, but the result is gradually to transfer copper from the positive to the negative electrode.

This is the basis of the final purification of copper used for electrical purposes. If the anode is of platinum the SO_4 radical attacks the water instead, forming sulphuric acid and liberating oxygen

$$2SO_4^{++} + 2H_2O = 2H_2SO_4 + O_2$$

The amount of copper in solution decreases, and finally sulphuric acid only is left in solution. When this stage is reached the hydrogen ions, due to dissociation of the SO_4, travel to the cathode and are liberated, and as they carry electricity, a current flows round the circuit.

The quantitative treatment of electrolysis is summarised in Faraday's first law of electrolysis, which may be given as $Q = ect$, where $Q =$ quantity of substance deposited in grams, $c =$ current in amperes, $t =$ time in sec, and $e =$ the fraction of a gram of the substance deposited by 1 ampere flowing for 1 second. The latter is called the electro-chemical equivalent.

electromagnet, see MAGNETISM

electromagnetic waves, see RADIO ; WAVEMOTION

electromagnetism, see ELECTRICITY

electron, see MATTER ; VALENCY

electronic organ, see ORGAN

electronics, science of electrons. The development of electronics in recent years has been astonishing, and has led (among a host of applications) to radar ; weather forecasting by an adaptation of radar ; the radar beacon (' racon ') ; the bat, i.e. a radio-controlled glider bomb ; also to LORAN and SHORAN, i.e. long and short range radar systems used in aircraft navigation ; to television, electric heating, etc. See MATTER ; RADIO

electron microscope, see MICROSCOPE

electrophorus, see ELECTRICITY

electroscope, see ELECTRICITY

electrovalency, chemical bond in which an electron is transferred from one atom to another, resulting in the formation of positive and negative particles (ions).

electrum, native alloy of gold and silver.

elegy, see GRAY, THOMAS

element, *el'e-ment*, may be defined as a substance that cannot be broken down (decomposed) by chemical means into simpler substances, though this definition is not altogether adequate when we consider the ultimate foundations of matter, or for radioactive substances, or substances in which disintegration is caused by artificial nuclear bombardment.

For all practical purposes, however, we may consider, say, a molecule of water (H_2O) as capable of being decomposed into two atoms of hydrogen and one atom of oxygen, hydrogen and oxygen being elements that cannot be decomposed by any chemical means.

Another definition of an element is : *a substance consisting entirely of atoms of the same atomic number.* While recent investigation of atomic energy has led to new conceptions of matter and new means of splitting atoms by ' nuclear fission,' we may say that normally there are over 94 elements, each one with a different number of outer electrons, the lowest (hydrogen) having one outer electron revolving round a

TIMBER *plate 29*

Top : Logging operations in progress, Powell River, Canada. (*Canadian National Film Board*).
Bottom : Using a power-driven circular saw to convert tree-trunks into planks.
(*David Innes, Esq.*)

plate 30 TIMBER DISTRIBUTION

Top : Sawn timber ready for dispatch. Timber has to be well seasoned before it can be used. (*David Innes, Esq.*). *Bottom :* Timber awaiting shipment, Vancouver B.C. Canada ranks third among the producers of the world's timber-supply. (*Canadian National Film Board*)

USES OF TIMBER

plate 31

S.V. *Viking* in the West India Dock, London. Among the wooden objects shown in this
picture are the masts and spars of the ship. (*Stanley, Camera Artist*)

plate 32   PLASTICS

In this machine the plastic is thoroughly mixed with the plasticiser. The compound is then made into thin flexible sheeting used for such things as rainwear, curtains, aprons, table-covers, cable-sheathing, electrical conduits, dress belts and car harnesses for the motor industry. (*I.C.I.*)

nucleus comprising one proton and one neutron ; while one of the most complex (plutonium) has 94 outer electrons. Every atom, except those of the inert gases, has from 1–7 outer electrons, some of which can be detached, hence the many ways in which elements form compounds by sharing or rearranging electrons.

Below are two tables of elements : an alphabetical list ; and what is known as the periodic table, the columns giving

substances akin in the number of their outer electrons, the rows indicating elements grouped according to the number of outer electrons capable of chemically detaching themselves, and thus forming compounds. It will be noted that group O (i.e. elements having no detachable electrons) comprise the inert gases. The numbers above each element are atomic numbers, i.e. the number of outer electrons for each element.

(a) TABLE OF CHEMICAL ELEMENTS

name	symbol	atomic number	atomic weight	valency
actinium	Ac	89	227·2	3
aluminium	Al	13	26·97	3
antimony	Sb	51	121·76	3 or 5
argon	A	18	39·944	0
arsenic	As	33	74·91	3 or 5
astatine [1]	Ab	85		
barium	Ba	56	137·36	2
beryllium	Be	4	9·02	2
bismuth	Bi	83	209·00	3 or 5
boron	B	5	10·82	3
bromine	Br	35	79·916	1 or 7
cadmium	Cd	48	112·41	1 or 2
caesium	Cs	55	132·91	1
calcium	Ca	20	40·08	2
carbon	C	6	12·01	4
cerium	Ce	58	140·13	3 or 4
chlorine	Cl	17	35·457	1, 3, 5, 7
chromium	Cr	24	52·01	2, 3 or 6
cobalt	Co	27	58·94	2 or 3
copper	Cu	29	63·57	1 or 2
curium		95		
dysprosium	Dy	66	162·46	3
erbium	Er	68	167·2	3
europium	Eu	63	152·0	3
fluorine	F	9	19·00	1
gadolinium	Gd	64	156·9	3
gallium	Ga	31	69·72	3
germanium	Ge	32	72·60	4
gold	Au	79	197·2	1 or 3
hafnium	Hf	72	178·6	4
helium	He	2	4·003	0
holmium	Ho	67	163·5	3
hydrogen	H	1	1·0080	1
illinium	Il	61	146·0 (?)	
indium	In	49	114·76	3
iodine	I	53	126·92	1, 3, 5, 7
iridium	Ir	77	193·1	2 or 4
iron	Fe	26	55·85	2 or 3
krypton	Kr	36	83·7	0
lanthanum	La	57	138·92	3

[1] Name suggested for the undiscovered element with atomic number 85.

name	symbol	atomic number	atomic weight	valency
lead	Pb	82	207·21	2 or 4
lithium	Li	3	6·940	1
lutecium	Lu	71	174·99	3
magnesium	Mg	12	24·32	2
manganese	Mn	25	54·93	2, 3, 4, 6, 7
masurium [2]	Ma	43		
mercury	Hg	80	200·61	1 or 2
molybdenum	Mo	42	95·95	2 or 6
neodymium	Nd	60	144·27	3 or 4
neon	Ne	10	20·183	0
neptunium	Np	93	239·0 (?)	
nickel	Ni	28	58·69	2 or 3
niobium	Nb	41	92·91	5
nitrogen	N	7	14·008	3 or 5
osmium	Os	76	190·2	2 or 8
oxygen	O	8	16·0000	2 or 4
palladium	Pd	46	106·7	2 or 4
phosphorus	P	15	30·98	3 or 5
platinum	Pt	78	195·23	2 or 4
plutonium	Pu	94	239·0 (?)	
polonium	Po	84	210·0	2, 3 or 4
potassium	K	19	39·096	1
praseodymium	Pr	59	140·92	3 or 4
protoactinium	Pa	91	231·0	5
radium	Ra	88	226·05	2
radon	Rn	86	222·0	0
rhenium	Re	75	186·31	2, 3, 4, 6, 7
rhodium	Rh	45	102·91	2 or 3
rubidium	Rb	37	85·48	1
ruthenium	Ru	44	101·7	3, 4 or 8
samarium	Sm	62	150·43	3
scandium	Sc	21	45·10	3
selenium	Se	34	78·96	2, 4, or 6
silicon	Si	14	28·06	4
silver	Ag	47	107·880	1
sodium	Na	11	22·997	1
strontium	Sr	38	87·63	2
sulphur	S	16	32·06	2, 4 or 6
tantalum	Ta	73	180·88	5
tellurium	Te	52	127·61	2, 4 or 6
terbium	Tb	65	159·2	3
thallium	Tl	81	204·39	1 or 3
thorium	Th	90	232·12	4
thulium	Tm	69	169·4	3
tin	Sn	50	118·70	2 or 4
titanium	Ti	22	47·90	3 or 4
tungsten	W	74	183·92	4 or 6
uranium	U	92	238·07	2 or 6
vanadium	V	23	50·95	5
xenon	Xe	54	131·3	0
ytterbium	Yb	70	173·04	3
yttrium	Y	39	88·92	3
zinc	Zn	30	65·38	2
zirconium	Zr	40	91·22	4

[2] Now technetium.

(b) SIMPLIFIED PERIODIC TABLE OF ELEMENTS

GROUPS   ATOMIC NUMBERS

	1–2	3–10	11–18	19–36	37–54	55–86	87–94
IA	1 hydrogen	3 lithium	11 sodium	19 potassium	37 rubidium	55 caesium	87 [3]
IIA		4 beryllium	12 magnesium	20 calcium	38 strontium	56 barium	88 radium
IIIA				21 scandium	39 yttrium	57 [1] lanthanum, etc.	89 actinium
IVA				22 titanium	40 zirconium	72 hafnium	90 thorium
VA				23 vanadium	41 niobium	73 tantalum	91 protoactinium
VIA				24 chromium	42 molybdenum	74 tungsten	92 uranium
VIIA				25 manganese	43 [4] masurium	75 rhenium	93 neptunium
VIII				26 iron	44 ruthenium	76 osmium	94 plutonium
				27 cobalt	45 rhodium	77 iridium	95
				28 nickel	46 palladium	78 platinum	96
IB				29 copper	47 silver	79 gold	
IIB				30 zinc	48 cadmium	80 mercury	
IIIB		5 boron	13 aluminium	31 gallium	49 indium	81 thallium	
IVB		6 carbon	14 silicon	32 germanium	50 tin	82 lead	
VB		7 nitrogen	15 phosphorus	33 arsenic	51 antimony	83 bismuth	
VIB		8 oxygen	16 sulphur	34 selenium	52 tellurium	84 polonium	
VIIB		9 fluorine	17 chlorine	35 bromine	53 iodine	85 [2]	
O	2 helium	10 neon	18 argon	36 krypton	54 xenon	86 radon	

[1] and 14 rare earths, i.e. elements 57–71.   [2] Astatine is suggested as the name for this as yet undiscovered element.   [3] Similarly (group IA) an element with atomic number 87 has yet to be found, though francium has been suggested.   [4] Masurium is now called technetium.

ELEPHANTS

(1) *The Indian Elephant*　　　(2) *The African Elephant*

elephant, largest living animal except the whale. The two species are (1) the Asiatic elephant (*Elephas indicus*), much used for drawing or carrying heavy loads ; it has a large head but small ears, and four nails on the hind feet ; is dark grey, but sometimes blotched with white ; rarely more than 9ft high at the shoulders, and may live 100 years or more ; (2) the African elephant (*Elephas africanus*), usually fiercer ; has smaller head, large, fan-like ears, and three nails on the hind feet ; it is valuable for the ivory of its tusks. In both the nose is developed into a trunk used for conveying food and water to the mouth. Elephants are vegetarians.

Elephant Isle, see SHACKLETON, SIR E.

Eleusis, *ē-lū'sis,* ancient city of Attica, Greece ; famous for its Eleusinian mysteries, i.e. festivals in honour of Demeter.

Elgar, SIR EDWARD, *el'gĕr* (1857–1934), British composer, born near Worcester ; won fame with his *Enigma Variations* 1899 ; perhaps best remembered for his many choral works, e.g. *The Dream of Gerontius,* one of the finest by any Englishman, and his instrumental and orchestral works, e.g. his *First Symphony; Violin Concerto ; Second Symphony.* His rendering of the *National Anthem,* his *Pomp and Circumstance,* and his *Land of Hope and Glory* are well known.

Elgin, *el'gin,* co.tn and royal burgh, Morayshire ; noted for woollens.

Elgin, Scottish county, see MORAY

Elgin Marbles, collection of priceless Greek sculptures from the Parthenon, brought to England by the 7th Earl of Elgin 1806 ; bought for the nation for £35,000, and now in the British Museum.

El Greco, see GRECO, EL

Elia, see LAMB, CHARLES

Elias, see ELIJAH

Elijah, *ē-lī'jä,* OT prophet ; seems to have been a hermit of the 9th c. BC. He predicted a famine in Israel ; was fed by ravens when alone in the wilderness, and later cared for by a widow whose jar (or cruse) of oil never failed. Elijah dared to speak boldly to King Ahab, who had turned from the worship of the true god to that of Baal. The contest between 400 prophets of Baal and Elijah on Mount Carmel (1 Kings 18) is one of the most dramatic scenes in the Bible. We read that Elijah was carried up to heaven in a chariot of fire.

In the NT he is spoken of as Elias.

Eliot, GEORGE (1819–80), pen-name of Mary Ann (or Marian) Evans, English novelist, born near Nuneaton, and at 16 responsible for running her father's home. A student of languages and music, she mixed with intellectual people when the family removed to Coventry. On the death of her father (a carpenter with narrow religious views) she came to London, 1849, and was engaged in literary work. She married George Henry Lewes, who discovered her abilities as a novelist. Her many books include *Scenes of Clerical Life ; Adam Bede* (in which she portrays her father) ; *The Mill on the Floss ; Silas Marner ; Middlemarch* (a problem novel), and her historical novel *Romola,* the story of a girl in 15th c. Florence, the age of Savonarola.

With a genius for depicting rural scenes, George Eliot struggled in vain with intellectual problems, but has given us immortal characters.

Eliot, THOMAS STEARNS (1888–　　　), Anglo-American poet, dramatist, critic and

Christian philosopher ; *b* St Louis, Missouri, USA ; studied at Harvard, the Sorbonne and Oxford ; taught at Harvard 1913–14, and at Highgate School, near London 1915 ; edited various literary magazines 1917 onwards ; later a publisher ; naturalised a British subject 1927.

Eliot's poetry has gone through several phases of development. In *Prufrock* (1917) Eliot created a new poetic language, conversational in its expressions, but remarkably accurate. He also displayed notable virtuosity in adapting conventional metres to contemporary speech rhythm. The *Love Song of J. Alfred Prufrock* is a study in diffidence, the portrait in poetry of a literary man confronted by personal problems which, if possible, he wishes to evade :

I should have been a pair of ragged claws
Scuttling across the floors of silent seas.

In *Poems 1920* ' Prufrock ' is ousted by ' Apeneck Sweeney,' a somewhat crude personality typifying the Natural Man ; but the presence of unsolved personal problems continues to be felt.

The *Waste Land* (1922) is a single poem in five parts. The metre is blank verse, freely resolved in order to express a brooding sense of chaos. Through the eyes of Tiresias (in ancient mythology a blind Theban prophet who had been a woman as well as a man), Eliot contemplates the desolation of a world that has lost its faith :

Unreal City . . .
A crowd flowed over London Bridge, so many,
I had not thought death had undone so many.

The same desolation is contemplated again in *The Hollow Men* (1925) ; but in *Ash Wednesday* (1930) a new note is heard ; Eliot had become a convinced Anglo-Catholic. *Ash Wednesday* is a meditation on humility, grace, redemption and kindred themes ; it is dominated by the figure of a gracious lady (perhaps a symbol of the Church) who will pray ' for those who are terrified and cannot surrender.'

The Four Quartets (1935–43) are cast in a form rather like those which are used in chamber music, starting from four places which have special associations for T. S. Eliot. These remarkable poems are meditations on such themes as time and eternity, memory, and the mystery of the Incarnation. They contain some of Eliot's best poetry.

Murder in the Cathedral (1935), a poetic drama about the martyrdom of Thomas à Becket, created a deep impression ; but *Family Reunion* (1939) and *The Cocktail Party* (1949) have met with a somewhat mixed reception ; and the best critics are generally agreed that

Eliot's work in this field has not been so successful, technically or otherwise, as the rest of his poetry. Eliot's critical writing can be studied in such books as *The Sacred Wood* (4th edition 1928) and the *Use of Poetry* (1933). It contains a masterly restatement in modern terms of the classical point of view, and forms at the same time an illuminating commentary on certain aspects of Eliot's own poetry.

Elisha, *ē-lī′shä*, Hebrew prophet, disciple and successor of Elijah ; lived in the latter half of the 9th c. BC.

elixir of life, see ALCHEMY

Elizabeth (1533–1603), Queen of England and Ireland ; daughter of Henry VIII and Anne Boleyn, *b* London ; enjoyed comparative security in Mary Tudor's day ; imprisoned in the Tower of London for two months, but was cautious, living mostly in seclusion at Hatfield till her accession 1558.

QUEEN ELIZABETH 1533–1603

Among the features of her reign of 45 years were the exploits of her seamen (e.g. Hawkins, Frobisher, Drake, etc.), all more or less pirates who waged unofficial war against Spain ; the religious changes from fierce persecution of Protestants to a re-establishment of the ' English ' Church ; the *Act of Uniformity* 1559 ; a modified *Prayer Book* ; the queen's support of John Knox in Scotland ; her policy of playing off Spain against France, thus weakening both countries while English trade vastly increased, so that England, of little worth and in peril when her reign began, was rich and greatly to be feared when it ended ; the long-delayed execution of Mary Queen of Scots ; destruction of the Spanish Armada 1588, Elizabeth's skill in allowing many suitors to believe she would one day marry, e.g. Philip II of Spain, Don John of Austria, the Austrian Archduke, Charles, Henry III of France, besides her own subjects, the Earls of Leicester and

Essex ; the many Catholic plots against her ; the Poor Law of 1601 ; and the growing opposition of Parliament to her wishes.

Elizabeth loved dancing and riding, and had a violent temper ; was something of a scholar ; possessed (it is said) 1,000 dresses ; had a genius for gathering brilliant men about her (e.g. her great ministers Sir Francis Walsingham and Lord Cecil) ; inspired her people to high endeavour in discovery and commerce; drama and literature (hers was the golden age of Sir Philip Sidney, Sir Walter Raleigh, Shakespeare, Ben Jonson, etc.). She declared, ' I have the body of a weak and feeble woman, but I have the heart of a king, and a king of England, too.'

Elizabeth, PRINCESS (1926–   ), elder daughter of King George VI and sister of Princess Margaret Rose. Born at 12 Bruton Street, London, the Princess spent much of her childhood at Glamis Castle (Scotland), the home of her grandparents, Lord and Lady Strathmore. She lived also at Walden Bury (Herefordshire) and at Windsor Castle. She never attended school but studied at home.

When her father became King (1936) Princess Elizabeth became heiress-presumptive to the throne, after which she lived mostly at Buckingham Palace.

In World War II she was an honorary 2nd subaltern in the ATS, and took her NCO's course in mechanics at Aldershot. She was appointed Colonel of the Grenadier Guards 1943 ; made her first foreign tour when she accompanied the King and Queen to S. Africa (1947), where she was extremely popular. While at Cape Town she made a 21st birthday broadcast in which she dedicated her life to the service of the Empire.

Princess Elizabeth was married in Westminster Abbey (20 Nov 1947) to Philip Mountbatten (b 10 June 1921, created Duke of Edinburgh 1947, his father being Prince Andrew of Greece who died 1944). The Duke of Edinburgh's family came to England when Philip was one year old, and he spent his childhood at Viscount Mountbatten's home in Romsey (Hampshire). Later he attended a school at Cheam (Surrey) from which he went to Gordonstoun School, near Elgin. He entered the Navy 1936, and was mentioned in dispatches. He became a British citizen Feb 1947.

Princess Elizabeth and her husband, popular as the Duke and Duchess of Edinburgh, had hoped to set up housekeeping at Sunninghill Park immediately after their marriage, but a fire at the mansion caused an alteration of their plans, and led them later to purchase Windlesham Moor, Surrey. Their son, Prince Charles, was born 1948. His full name is Charles Philip Arthur George.

A daughter, the Princess Anne, was born in Aug 1950.

elk, largest of the deer family ; known in America as the *moose* ; occurs locally in N. Europe ; often over 6ft high at the withers ; has long legs, short neck, many-branched antlers ; inhabits forests, where it feeds on willow and birch.

Ellesmere Port, *elz'mēr*, town and canal-port, Cheshire.

Elliott, EBENEZER, see CORN LAWS

ellipse, *e-lips'*, one of the sections of a cone, or the path (locus) of a point, the sum of whose distances from two fixed points (foci) is constant. See AREA ; VOLUME

Ellis Island, island in New York harbour. Since 1892 immigrants have been examined here before being permitted to land in USA.

Ellora, *e-lōr'ä*, village of Hyderabad, India ; famous for its Buddhist and Hindu rock temples mostly 5th–10th c.

Ellsworth, LINCOLN (1880–   ), American explorer, *b* Chicago ; flew to the N. Pole with Amundsen 1926 ; was the first man to fly across Antarctica ; author of *Beyond the Horizon*.

Ellwood, THOMAS (1639–1713), Quaker author, *b* Crowell, Oxfordshire ; read to the blind John Milton, and suggested *Paradise Regained*.

elm, name of two British trees : (*a*) small-leaved elm (*Ulmus campestris*) ; has a rugged trunk with brushwood ; the somewhat pear-shaped leaves have a pointed tip and rough edges ; the tree may reach 80ft, but is liable to internal decay ; (*b*) wych elm (*Ulmus glabra*) or broad-leaved elm ; this has no brushwood and the leaves are larger.

THE ELM

El Paso, city and port, Texas, USA ; has a large trade in wool, hides and minerals ; pop.97,000.

Elsinore, port, Denmark ; has a fine harbour. It is possibly the scene of Shakespeare's *Hamlet*.

Elstow, *el'stō*, village, Bedfordshire ; close by is the birthplace of John Bunyan.

Elstree, town, Hertfordshire ; noted for film studios.

Ely, *ē'li,* cathedral city, Cambridgeshire ; on the R. Ouse ; scene of Hereward the Wake's last fight against William I c.1071.

Ely, ISLE OF, not now an island, but a fertile part of N. Cambridgeshire.

Elysée, *ā-lē-zā',* palace in Paris, separated by a garden from the Champs Elysées ; built 1718 ; now the official home of the president.

Elysium, *ē-lizh'ium,* or the Elysian Fields ; in Greek and Roman tales, the abode of the souls of the good ; a place of perpetual sunshine and flowers.

Emancipation Act, see SLAVERY

embalming, *em-bäm',* custom of preserving dead bodies ; still practised today, notably in USA, but chiefly associated with the ancient Egyptians, who removed the brains and intestines, rinsed the abdomen with palm wine, filled it with perfumes (myrrh, cassia, etc.), steeped the body in sodium carbonate for 70–90 days, and wrapped it in gummed linen cloths. A body so embalmed is called a mummy. The idea sprang from a belief in the resurrection of the body.

Embankment, THE, see LONDON

emblems, symbols for some person, idea, or country, somewhat similar to badges.

Much as a metal badge with a crown, horn, and the letters DLI represents the Durham Light Infantry, so a rose is the emblem of England. In the same way artists, sculptors, wood-carvers, makers of coloured windows in churches, etc., have used emblems for saints, e.g. a cross like the letter X for St Andrew, a spiked wheel for St Catherine, two keys for St. Peter, a lamb for St John the Baptist.

An old emblem for Christ was a fish, because the letters of the Greek word *ichthys,* fish, include those standing for *Jesus Christ, Son of God, the Saviour.* The cross (✝) is the usual emblem of Christ and Christianity, as the crescent is the emblem of the Moslem faith. A dove is the emblem of the Holy Ghost ; a hand coming out of a cloud the emblem of God the Father ; a phoenix symbolises the Resurrection because of the old belief that this imaginary bird lived 500 years, was then burned to death, and later rose again from its own ashes.

Many countries have what is known as a *national emblem,* e.g. the thistle for Scotland ; shamrock for Ireland, because St Patrick is said to have declared that its 3 leaves remind us that God is 3 persons, i.e. Father, Son, and Holy Ghost. The emblem of Wales, long regarded as the leek, has since 1911 been the daffodil. The emblem of France is the lily, i.e. the *fleur-de-lys (flŭr dĕ lē)* ; other national emblems include: Canada, maple leaf ; Japan, cherry blossom or chrysanthemum ; Netherlands, tulip ; Greece, laurel ; Switzerland, edelweiss ; Australia, wattle.

embroidery, art of decoration with needle and thread ; mentioned in the OT ; well known in ancient Greece ; associated with the Christian Church from the earliest times, e.g. the richly decorated gowns, copes, etc. of church officials, the vestments of 13th and 14th c. English bishops being exceptionally fine. An outstanding example of this art is the Bayeux Tapestry ; and in the Middle Ages ladies delighted to embroider scenes from the hunt, the Bible, and from history and legend. In Hanoverian times dresses were richly embroidered. Since 1944 many expert needlewomen have been at work on a tapestry (13ft by 7ft) illustrating the part played by women in World War II, an idea suggested by the West Sussex Women's Institute. In 1950 Martha Smith, a Yorkshire woman now living near New York, startled American needlewomen with her remarkable historical tapestries, among them one depicting the story of World War II, another telling the story of her own family.

embryology, *em-bri-ol'ōji,* science and study of the way in which living things (plants or animals) reproduce themselves and develop. All life, it seems, begins as a tiny speck of living matter which develops in the parent's body, and becomes a seed or an egg. How this happens is still partly a mystery ; and we are still puzzled by the question : *How did life begin on the earth?*

Embryology is a branch of biology. Comparative embryology was founded by Karl Ernst von Baer (1792–1876), Russo-German investigator, and one of the first to note that the growth of the individual creature often recapitulates much of its race history. See EVOLUTION

Emden, port, Germany, at the mouth of the R. Ems ; exports coal from the Ruhr ; imports iron and timber, etc. from Scandinavia ; pop.34,000.

emerald, precious stone, a green variety of beryl. It is a silicate of beryllium and aluminium. The finest emeralds come from Colombia.

Emerald Isle, THE, see IRELAND

Emerson, RALPH WALDO (1803–82), American poet, essayist and thinker, *b* Boston, Massachusetts ; travelled much in Europe, especially England and Scotland, where he met the famous men of his day, and began a long friendship with Thomas Carlyle. He won fame with his book on *Nature,* and later as a lecturer, and as the author of essays which stimulated thought. His teaching, above sect or party, is marked by lofty idealism. His lectures on *Representative Men* and his *English Traits* are excellent reading.

EMF, short for electromotive force. See ELECTRICITY

emigration, systematic movement of the

surplus population of one country to another, e.g. the Pilgrim Fathers (1620) and similar religious migrations. The Irish in the famines of the 19th c. emigrated to N. America, as also the Scots in great numbers. There have been Dutch emigrations to S. Africa, and British to Australia and NZ. There were amazing outpourings from Europe (especially from Russia, Italy, Ireland, etc.) to USA early in the 20th c. The opposite of emigration is *immigration*, i.e. the coming of settlers *into* a country.

Emin Pasha, *ā-mēn' pä'shä* (1840–92), Ger. administrator and traveller ; rescued in the Sudan 1888 by Stanley ; explored Central Africa.

Emir or **ameer,** Arabic word for a chief among Mohammedans, especially in Africa.

Emmanuel College, college of Cambridge University, founded 1584. The buildings include a chapel designed by Sir Christopher Wren. The college was long known for its Puritan members, e.g. John Harvard, founder of Harvard University, USA.

Empedocles, *em-ped'ō-klēz* (*d* 435BC), Gk thinker of Agrigentum, Sicily ; taught that all matter comprises fire, air, earth and water in some form. He is *said* to have flung himself into the crater of Etna.

emperors of Rome, see ROME

Empire, BRITISH, see BRITISH COMMONWEALTH OF NATIONS

Empire Day, see CALENDAR

Empire Free Trade, see FREE TRADE

Employment Exchange, local centre at which unemployed workers are guided in their search for work. Known at first as a Labour Exchange, the centre is organised by the Ministry of Labour and National Service. There are some 1,200 in Britain. They make unemployment payment ; deal chiefly with persons in such industries as building, textiles, machinery, agriculture and transport ; have departments for men, women and juveniles.

Ems, R. of Germany ; flows 200m to the N. Sea ; also German health resort, noted for its mineral springs.

emu, *ē'mū,* Australian bird very similar to the ostrich, but slightly smaller ; runs swiftly but cannot fly. The plumage is brown mottled with grey. The emu feeds in small flocks on fruits.

Encke, JOHANN FRANZ, *eng'ke* (1791–1865), German astronomer, *b* Hamburg ; associated with observations of Encke's comet, which has a normal period of 1,208 days, but the peculiarity of appearing unexpectedly.

enclosure, name for (*a*) enclosing land for sheep runs, the result of growing woollen trade in England from the 15th to 16th c., lords of the manor taking arable land as well as waste. As sheepfarming required fewer labourers than crop-raising, large numbers of farm labourers became workless ; (*b*) enclosing land for sport ; and (*c*) the abolition of the old open-field system of farming, a movement, encouraged late in the 18th c., leading to greatly improved methods, though yeomen farmers practically disappeared.

endowment policy, see INSURANCE

Endymion, *en-dim'i-on,* in old Gk tales, a beautiful young shepherd with whom Selene, the moon goddess, fell in love. The tale inspired John Keats to write his poem *Endymion.*

energy, in mechanics (*a*) *potential,* = mgh (where m = mass, g = acceleration due to gravity, h = height) ; and (*b*) *kinetic,* = $\frac{1}{2}mv^2$ (where m = mass, v = velocity). See MATTER ; MECHANICS ; QUANTUM THEORY ; RADIOACTIVITY ; RELATIVITY

Enfield, town, Middlesex ; noted for the manufacture of rifles ; pop.110,000.

engineering, profession of many branches such as military engineering ; civil engineering, i.e. the construction of docks, railways, harbours and bridges ; mechanical ; electrical ; motor ; telegraph ; radio ; and mining. In all, a general technical education is the foundation, with specialisation (generally university training in the case of civil engineers) later. Particulars may be obtained from the Institute of Civil Engineers.

England, *ing'gland,* originally Angleland, i.e. land of the Angles, is the larger southern part of Great Britain, area 50,337sq.m ; pop. *c.*37,000,000 ; extreme length (Lizard to Berwick-on-Tweed) 430m ; extreme width (Land's End to Lowestoft) 370m ; lies between latitudes 55° 46′ and 49° 57′ N, and between longitudes 1° 46′ E and 5° 43′ W.

In shape it is an irregular triangle with 1,800m of coast, no place inland being more than 70m from the sea. On the whole, England is more mountainous in the NW. and SW. than elsewhere, the hill districts including the Cheviots (on the Scottish border) reaching 2,676ft ; Pennine Chain ('backbone' of England), with Cross Fell (2,930ft) ; Cumbrian Mts, e.g. Scafell Pike (3,210ft), the highest point in England ; Yorkshire Moors, Peak District of Derbyshire, Dartmoor, Malvern Hills (1,395ft) in Worcestershire, and the Cotswolds of Gloucestershire.

Well watered by rivers, England has the Humber estuary draining the east side of the Pennines and also the area watered by the Trent ; the rivers emptying into the Wash ; the Thames (210m), its largest river, flowing to the N. Sea via London ; the small rivers of the south ; the Severn basin, with many tributaries draining over 8,500sq.m ; the Dee, Mersey, Ribble, Eden, etc. in the NW., and the Tyne and Tees, etc. in the NE.

Islands include Lundy (off the Devon coast) ; I. of Wight (separated from

Hampshire by the Solent) ; I. of Man ; and the Scilly Isls, 25m from Land's End.

The mean annual temperature is *c*. 50°F. The west tends to be mild and wet in winter, cool and less wet in summer, while the east is cool and dry in winter and spring but hot and rather wet in summer and autumn. The region of heaviest rainfall is the Lake District (Cumberland) ; the driest is E. Anglia ; average for the whole country *c*.30in. Climate is considerably influenced by the Gulf Stream, the surface waters of which are carried to our coasts by the prevailing westerly winds.

Since it is mostly more hilly and has a higher average rainfall than the east, the west of England, with its milder climate, favours pasture for sheep on the hills and for cattle in the valleys, while in the south and east (with more summer sunshine and wide plains) good crops are grown, especially wheat, barley and, in recent years, sugar-beet. Oats are grown almost everywhere.

Regionally there are the *chalk lands of the SE.*, e.g. the London Basin, with the Downs and the Weald ; the Hampshire Basin, with Salisbury Plain ; E. Anglia, with rich clay soil and sandy belts with pine plantations ; the *Inner Vale*, mainly clay, including the plains of the upper Thames and Great Ouse, and the Fens with their slow streams ; *Devon-Cornwall peninsula*, of Old Red Sandstone and granite rocks ; *Middle Plain* of clay, marl, and reddish sandstone, a region split by the south end of the Pennines. This is largely a grazing area, but has coalfields in the Black Country, where Birmingham and Wolverhampton use the iron readily to hand ; *Pennines and the NW.*, with mixed farming and vast industrial regions east and west of the Pennines, including cotton manufacture in Lancashire, woollen industries in Yorkshire, coal and iron being abundant.

England is divided into 40 counties, of which the largest are Yorkshire, Lincolnshire and Devon, and the smallest Rutland. The principal cities include London, Birmingham, Liverpool, Manchester, Sheffield, Leeds, Bristol, Hull, Bradford, Newcastle-upon-Tyne, Nottingham, Stoke-on-Trent, Portsmouth, Leicester, Plymouth, Sunderland, Bolton, Southampton and Coventry.

The history of Roman times is summarised under BRITAIN (ANCIENT). With the departure of the Roman legions *c*.410, the country became a prey to the Picts and Scots in the north ; to Irish invaders from the west ; and, in the east, to the Jutes from Denmark, who settled in Kent. Later, the Angles and Saxons gradually moved westwards. Christianity, brought to Kent by St Augustine *c*.597, spread northwards. There followed a long struggle against the Danes, Alfred the Great securing

overlordship (late 9th c.) though Canute, the Dane, regained power in the 11th c. Scarcely had the Danes been finally overcome when, after the more or less peaceful reign of Edward the Confessor, William, Duke of Normandy, shattered Harold's forces at Hastings 1066, and Saxon England became Norman.

Slowly the defeated English and their Norman conquerors commingled, hence changes in language, customs, form of government, etc., but with a growing sense of unity unknown in the days of warring kingdoms. For generations the Norman system of feudalism continued, the great barons holding land direct from the king in return for service, a principle applied to the relations of tenants-in-chief to the barons, etc. down to the labourer, who was in great measure ' bound to the soil.'

After the chaos of Stephen's reign, Henry II did much to organise government, establishing courts of justice, and wisely obtaining the approval of the Great Council before making important changes. In John's reign the great Council was strong enough to compel him to set his seal to *Magna Carta* (1215), the first charter of English liberties. Though for most of his long reign Henry III ruled with little attention to the wishes of the barons, the Great Council, under Simon de Montfort, made it plain that no king of England could continue to rule unconstitutionally.

In Edward I's reign the English nation became unified, law became more or less fixed, and the power of the king and the privileges of the people were clearly defined. The old quarrel between Church and State ended in the establishment of the civil law as supreme. Edward I subdued Wales and tried to subdue Scotland. (Ireland was not finally conquered until the 16th c.)

The 14th c saw the gradual breaking down of feudalism. Labourers were then working for wages ; foreign trade was increasing, and wool and hides were exported on a large scale. As the Hundred Years' War, begun by Edward III, was enormously costly the king found himself compelled to ask Parliament to find the money needed, hence the beginnings of Parliament's control of taxation, and, to a limited extent, of national policy. With one in three of the rural population carried off by the Black Death (*c*.1348), the surviving peasants demanded higher wages. This movement culminated in the Peasants' Revolt 1381.

Henry IV owed his crown to Parliament, and Parliament never allowed him to forget it ; moreover, the king had to deal with something very much like a pioneer Communist movement preached by the Lollards, and inspired by John Wycliffe, translator of the Bible and Morning Star of the Reformation.

Henry V's preposterous claim to the

9*a*

French throne led to more fighting against France in the Hundred Years' War, and to a brilliant victory at Agincourt 1415 ; but later, inspired by Joan of Arc, Frenchmen began to push back the English till (1453) England possessed only Calais overseas—no doubt a disaster at the time, but, freed from the impossible task of controlling France, England was able to build up a strong and vigorous nation.

But this could not be done immediately because of the Civil War (Wars of the Roses) between Yorkists and Lancastrians. The spark was kindled by Jack Cade's rebellion 1450, an attempt to dislodge the incapable Henry VI. This wretched and unprofitable period of English history ended with the establishment of the Tudors when (1485) Henry VII defeated Richard III at Bosworth. Henry put an end to private feuds, restored peaceful and orderly government, built up the navy, fostered commercial prosperity, and by consulting Parliament ruled constitutionally.

About this time came the first fruits of the Renaissance—new ideas stirring in men's minds, new movements in social life. Printing made knowledge easier to secure, and a new sense of nationalism took hold of the people because so many books were in English. The spirit of adventure was astir ; Cabot (with a charter from Henry VII) reached N. America 1497.

By Henry VIII's day a new idea of international relations was taking root, Wolsey fostering the policy known as the ' balance of power ' whereby great European nations (e.g. France, Spain, the Netherlands) were prevented from becoming too dangerous to England. Moreover, the Reformation had given Europe new ideas about religion. The king's dissolution of the monasteries, his defiance of the pope, and his subordination of the Church to the State, strengthened Protestantism and weakened the Roman Church, a process furthered by Edward VI's *Prayer Book*, and also by Mary Tudor's persecution of Protestants, for by burning alive some 300 heretics, she strengthened hostility to the cause of the Roman Church.

With the accession 1558 of Elizabeth the fortunes of England revived still more, and in the Elizabethan Age England became largely Protestant, trade increased, and the destruction of the Spanish Armada 1588 left her supreme at sea. Prosperity brought new wealth ; literature and drama flourished as never before ; commerce increased ; the Poor Law of 1601 was the first step towards subsequent social amenities ; the growing system of apprenticeship ensured good craftsmanship ; the multiplication of chartered mercantile companies encouraged trade.

The passing of the Tudors and the coming of the Stuarts (James VI and I, 1603) brought new struggles between king and Parliament, culminating, in Charles I's reign, in the Civil War, which led to the dominance of Parliament in the Commonwealth. As Lord Protector, Cromwell raised the status of England abroad to heights previously unknown. Meanwhile, earlier persecution of the Puritans had fostered colonisation, typified by the sailing of the Pilgrim Fathers in the *Mayflower* 1620. Steady migration to America continued.

At home, the party system of government was coming into being under Charles II, and in Queen Anne's day the age-old enmity between England and Scotland was, to some extent, cancelled by the *Act of Union* 1707, when the history of England became one with that of the UK. See UNITED KINGDOM

' **England expects,**' see TRAFALGAR, BATTLE OF

English Channel, channel linking the N. Sea with the Atlantic Ocean, and separating England from France ; narrowest at the Strait of Dover (21m) ; first swum by Captain Webb 1875 ; also swum 1949 by Philip Mickman of Ossett (Yorkshire) when only 18. See CHANNEL TUNNEL

English history, see ENGLAND

English language, see LANGUAGE

English literature, as distinct from that of Anglo-Saxon times, may be said to date from the romances of the 14th c., the most important examples being *Gawin and the Green Knight*, the mystical poem *Piers Plowman* (probably by William Langland), and the lyric *Sumer is i-comen in*, though the greatest name of this early period is that of Geoffrey Chaucer (*d* 1400), who gave us an immortal word-picture of the England of his day in *The Canterbury Tales*.

For nearly two centuries English literature had no equal to Chaucer, but the 15th c. was rich in Church drama—mysteries, miracle plays and moralities—and there was a vogue for ballads. Prose is represented by Sir Thomas Malory's *Morte d'Arthur* ; and later came a revival of learning in Italy which inspired English poets to experiment with the sonnet, e.g. Sir Thomas Wyatt, Sir Philip Sidney, Michael Drayton, etc., and (most successful of all) Shakespeare.

Meanwhile, our literature had been enriched by the publication (1579) of Edmund Spenser's *Shepherds' Calendar*, and his more famous allegorical romance *The Faerie Queene* (1596). Elizabethan poetry was crowned with George Chapman's superb translation of Homer.

Nothing in the 15th c. had equalled the serious drama, *Everyman*, followed by the 16th c. *Ralph Roister Doister* by Nicholas Udall. Based on Latin tragedies, this led on to the dramas of Christopher Marlowe (e.g. *Tamburlaine*), the first English plays (in blank verse) to have splendour of form and intense dramatic interest. Ben Jonson, Beaumont and Fletcher, Marston, Chapman, Middleton, Webster, Massinger, Ford, Shirley, all were dramatists of note ; and soaring above all was Shakespeare, whose comedies, tragedies and histories surpass anything produced by his fellows in grandeur of conception and plot, richness and power of expression, and deep understanding of the eternal truths of life.

Of late Elizabethan poets the outstanding names are John Donne and Ben Jonson, both of whom influenced Thomas Carew, Richard Lovelace, and John Suckling. There followed the incomparable Robert Herrick. Vaster than any other 17th c. poets was John Milton, who wedded fancy and great learning to sonorous lines in his shorter poems (e.g. *L'Allegro*, *Il Penseroso*), and his great religious epic *Paradise Lost*.

Unpopular now, John Dryden must be regarded as our first modern poet, writing (1659 to 1700) in the language we use today, a genius who was master of the lyric, the drama and satire. Akin to him was Alexander Pope, expert in epigrams.

Between 1597 and 1644 were published Bacon's *Essays*, Robert Burton's *Anatomy of Melancholy* (full of quiet and quaint humour in spite of its title), *Religio Medici* by Thomas Browne, and Milton's impassioned *Areopagitica* (a plea for freedom of the Press). What is still more important is that men were thinking and speaking in the language of the Authorised Version of the Bible (1611), its music sinking into their very souls so that almost all great English literature from that time echoed its melody. This is strikingly illustrated in all John Bunyan's writings, notably *The Pilgrim's Progress*, in Izaak Walton's gentle and conversational prose, and in the essays of Addison and Steele, whose periodicals *The Tatler* and *The Spectator*, challenged later writers to express themselves in pure English.

While essay-writing was becoming a fine art a new kind of literary expression was gaining ground. Jonathan Swift cast his satires into story-form, hence *The Tale of a Tub* and his immortal *Gulliver's Travels*. The influence of Cervantes, whose *Don Quixote* had set all Europe laughing in 1615, may be traced in Daniel Defoe's *Robinson Crusoe* ; and after Samuel Richardson had shown in his *Pamela* and *Clarissa Harlow* that realistic narrative portraying contemporary life and manners may hold the reader's attention, there came Henry Fielding, most truly the father of the English novel. His *Jonathan Wild* and *Tom Jones* were perhaps the greatest legacy to the 18th c. bequeathed to our literature. Other early novelists include Tobias Smollett, Laurence Sterne, author of *Tristram Shandy*, and Oliver Gold-

smith, author of the imperfect but gentle story *The Vicar of Wakefield*.

That prose in the 18th c. was acquiring flexibility, power and polish, we realise when we read Edward Gibbon's *Decline and Fall of the Roman Empire*, or Edmund Burke's masterly orations. There was also an exquisite finish on the best work of such poets as James Thomson, Thomas Gray (*Elegy Written in a Country Churchyard*), Goldsmith (*Deserted Village*), and the mystical William Blake. A new note in poetry was struck when William Wordsworth (1770–1850) turned to nature and wrote simple, outdoor verse without cumbersome reference to classic lore, and when Samuel Taylor Coleridge brought a vivid imagination to *The Rime of the Ancient Mariner*, *Kubla Khan*, etc. ; but before this poetry impressed the public Thomas More's songs were immensely popular, and Sir Walter Scott with his *Marmion* and *The Lay of the Last Minstrel*, was rivalling Lord Byron, whose *Childe Harold*, *Don Juan*, etc. were creating a stir by their superb mixture of lyric and epic, unhampered by moralising. There were also the impassioned Percy Bysshe Shelley, and matchless John Keats.

The romantic spirit of poetry breathes in 19th c. prose. Sir Walter Scott is now more famous for his *Waverley* novels, linking drama with description, and giving romance to the past, but like Burns' poems, these belong rather to Scottish than to English literature. Less spectacular but no less sure was Jane Austen who, paying attention only to the manners of her own day, drew exquisite portraits in her novels, e.g. *Pride and Prejudice*. Other early and mid-19th c. prose writers of outstanding merit were the essayists Charles Lamb (*Essays of Elia*), William Hazlitt, Thomas de Quincey, Leigh Hunt, and outspoken William Cobbett. There were the historians Lord Macaulay and James Anthony Froude ; and there was Thomas Carlyle, rugged and rebellious ; John Ruskin, pioneer of practical beauty, and George Borrow, happiest when out of doors.

Two novelists of exceptional genius were Charles Dickens, vivid, sentimental, humorous ; and the satirical William Makepeace Thackeray. Other Victorian novelists include George Eliot (*Adam Bede*, etc.), Charles Kingsley (*Westward Ho!*), Mrs. Gaskell, Charlotte Brontë (*Jane Eyre*), Anthony Trollope, Charles Reade (*The Cloister and the Hearth*), and Lord Lytton. Poetry had many phases, from the placid *Idylls of the King* and the pensive *In Memoriam* of Lord Tennyson, to the involved Robert Browning, and the amazing Elizabeth Barrett Browning. Never were there so many sweet singers—Matthew Arnold, Dante Gabriel Rossetti, William Morris, Algernon Charles Swinburne, Christina Rossetti, Edward Fitzgerald (translator of *Omar Khayyam*), John Keble, Lord Macaulay (*Lays of Ancient Rome*, etc.). Later still (out of the 19th into the 20th c.) we find poetry and prose flowing from the pen of Thomas Hardy (*The Dynasts* and the ' Wessex ' novels) ; and from that of Robert Louis Stevenson who wrote English as well as Scottish novels, and gave children simple poems, and boys their first thrilling adventure books (e.g. *Treasure Island*). Another writer of poetry and prose, alike vital, was Rudyard Kipling, master, too, of the short story. William Watson and Robert Bridges were also giving us verse of classical elegance. Yet other poets include William Butler Yeats (Irish), Francis Thompson (*The Hound of Heaven*), William E. Henley, William H. Davies (' The Super-Tramp '), Ralph Hodgson, Rupert Brooke (the poet who wrote *If I should die*) ; and along with these are dramatists, e.g. Bernard Shaw, stabbing us broad awake by his penetrating wit ; J. M. Barrie with his fancies and fairies ; John Drinkwater, St John Irvine, etc.

In recent years English literature has by no means lacked writers of merit. Poets include Walter de la Mare, John Masefield (*The Everlasting Mercy*, etc.), Edith, Osbert, and Sacheverell Sitwell, C. Day Lewis, etc. ; novelists number John Galsworthy (*The Forsyte Saga*), Hugh Walpole, Joseph Conrad, Somerset Maugham (novelist and dramatist), Aldous Huxley, J. B. Priestley (*The Good Companions*), Margaret Kennedy, Rose Macaulay, Rebecca West, Virginia Woolf, L. A. G. Strong, Edmund Blunden, etc. We have had provocative books from H. G. Wells, G. K. Chesterton and Hilaire Belloc ; history from Professor Trevelyan and Winston Churchill ; masterly descriptive writing and narrative in *The Seven Pillars of Wisdom* by Lawrence of Arabia ; social satire from Evelyn Waugh ; brilliant essays from Robert Lynd, popular philosophy from Professor Joad. The war of 1939–45 gave us tense and dramatic chronicles of a high order, e.g. *The Wooden Horse* by Eric Williams ; *Rommel*, Desmond Young's stirring biography ; *London Belongs to Me* by Norman Collins. Winston Churchill's *The Second World War* is written with admirable directness and has a distinctive style.

Read *A Short History of English Literature*, B. Ifor Evans. See BOOKS ; DRAMA ; NOVEL ; POETRY

English-Speaking Union, see YOUTH ORGANISATIONS

Ennis, co.tn of County Clare, Eire.

Ennius, QUINTUS (239–169BC), earliest of the great Latin poets ; noted for 20 tragedies, and the *Annales*, an epic of Roman history written in hexameters after the Greek model.

Enoch, see CAIN

ENSA, short for Entertainments National Service Association, an organisation which, in World War II, entertained troops, etc., giving 2,500,000 performances to over 500,000,000 spectators.

ensign, *en'sīn*, flag flown astern of a ship to show her nationality. British ships of the Royal Navy and Royal Yacht Squadron fly the white ensign. The Royal Navy Reserve flies the blue ensign ; the Merchant Service the red ensign.

ensilage, see SILAGE

Entebbe, see UGANDA

' Entente Cordiale,' friendly understanding established 1904 between Britain and France.

enzyme, see DIGESTION

eohippus, see EVOLUTION ; HORSE

Eos, see AURORA

Epaminondas, *ē-pami-non'das* (*c.*418–362 BC), Theban general, bitter enemy of the Spartans. He made Thebes the leading power in Greece.

Épernay, *āper-ne'*, town, France ; on the R. Marne ; noted for champagne ; pop.21,000.

epha, *ē'fä*, Bible measure of corn, equivalent to 6·477 gallons.

Ephesus, *ef'ē-zŭs*, ancient city of Asia Minor, now a ruin but once a great trading and administrative centre ; notable for the worship of Diana, whose temple was among the wonders of the world ; visited by St Paul.

ephod, *ef'od*, brightly coloured garment worn by Jewish high priests in the Temple. It covered the chest and back, and had a breastplate.

epic, see METRE ; POETRY

Epictetus, *ep-ik-tē'tŭs*, Greek thinker born *c.*AD60 ; he was lame, and as a child became a slave in Rome. He taught that patience, self-control and the simple life are of supreme importance ; his influence was far-reaching. One of his sayings was Οὐδεὶς διχὰ ἀπωλείας καὶ ζημίας κακός ἐστι (No one is wicked without loss and punishment).

epicure, see EPICURUS

Epicurus, *ep-i-kūr'ŭs* (341–270BC), Greek philosopher, *b* Samos ; taught at Athens; divided thought into logic (theory of knowledge), physics and ethics ; founded the school of thought known as Epicureanism, and taught that pleasure was the absence of pain, and that the soul perishes at death. Few of his many writings remain.

By *epicure* we now mean one who has discriminating taste in refined pleasure, especially food and wine. Epicurus himself lived simply and was content with very ordinary fare. One of his sayings was Ὧι ὀλίγον οὐχ ἱκανὸν, ἀλλὰ τούτῳ γε οὐδὲν ἱκανόν (Him whom a little will not content, nothing will content).

epidermis, see SKIN

epidiascope, *epi-dī'-*, instrument similar to the optical lantern. While capable of projecting enlargements of slides on a screen, it is specially designed to project

naturally coloured images of opaque bodies, e.g. coins, insects, leaves and diagrams.

epiglottis, thin, leaf-shaped cartilage behind the root of the tongue and forming a movable lid to the larynx. It prevents food going down the windpipe.

epigram, see FIGURES OF SPEECH

epilogue, see PROLOGUE

Épinal, *āpē-näl',* beautiful old town, France; on the R. Moselle ; noted for cotton, paper and brewing ; pop.30,000.

Epiphany, see CALENDAR

epiphyte, *ep'i-fīt,* plant that grows on other plants (usually trees), but does not feed on its host, e.g. some tropical orchids ; also ferns and mosses.

Epirus, *e-pī'rŭs,* NW. part of ancient Greece. Today the area is *c.*3,700sq.m.

epitaph (Greek *epi,* upon, *taphos,* tomb), inscription on a gravestone or monument, or a commendation of some dead person. Notable or curious epitaphs include :

Underneath this sable hearse
Lies the subject of all verse :
Sidney's sister, Pembroke's mother,
Death, ere thou hast slain another
Fair, and learn'd, and good as she,
Time shall throw a dart at thee.
    WILLIAM BROWNE (*or possibly* BEN
    JONSON) *on the Countess Dowager*
    of Pembroke

Fuller's earth.
            THOMAS FULLER (1608–61)

Warm summer sun shine kindly here ;
Warm southern wind blow softly here ;
Green sod above lie light, lie light—
Good night, dear heart, good night,
    good night.
    MARK TWAIN'S *epitaph for his*
    daughter Susy

Here lies Anne Mann ; she lived an
Old maid and died an old Mann.
Epitaph on ANNE MANN, *Bath Abbey*

O rare Ben Jonson.
        Epitaph in Westminster Abbey

        On a robin
Stand still awhile
And shed a tear,
Jane's little bird
Is buried here.

Ὦ ἄνθρωπε, ὅστις εἶ καὶ ὅθεν ἥκεις, ὅτι μὲν γὰρ ἥξεις, οἶδα, ἐγὼ Κῦρος εἰμὶ ὁ Πέρσαις κτησάμενος τὴν ἀρχήν. μὴ οὖν τῆς ὀλίγης μοι ταύτης γῆς φθονήσῃς ἢ τοὐμὸν σῶμα περικαλύπτει. (O man ! whosoever thou art, and whencesoever thou comest, for come I know thou wilt, I am Cyrus, founder of the Persian empire. Envy me not the little earth that covers my body.)
        On Cyrus (Plutarch's *Lives*)

Ὦ ξεῖν', ἄγγειλον Λακεδαιμονίοις ὅτι τῇδε κείμεθα, τοῖς κείνων ῥήμασι πειθόμενοι.
(Tell them in Sparta, passer-by,
We did our duty : here we lie.)
        SIMONIDES *on the Spartans who*
        fell at Thermopylae

Epping, town, Essex. EPPING FOREST, *c.*5,500 acres, is in SE. Essex.

Epsom, town, Surrey ; pop.61,000 ; scene of the Derby, a horse race held in June, and named after its originator, the Earl of Derby.

Epsom salts, magnesium sulphate ($MgSO_4$. $7H_2O$), in small rhombic prisms ; named from Epsom, Surrey.

Epstein, JACOB, *ep'stīn,* (1880–   ), sculptor, *b* New York of Russo-Polish parents; settled in London 1905 ; aroused storms of protest against his remarkable statues (e.g. Night, Rima, Genesis), but is undoubtedly a genius, excelling particularly in magnificent and vital bronze heads.

EPT, short for Excess Profits Tax.

Epworth, small market-town, Lincolnshire ; birthplace (1703) of John Wesley.

equation (Latin *aequare,* to make equal). In MATHEMATICS an equation is a statement of equality consisting of two expressions connected by the sign $=$. By *solving an equation* is meant finding the value of the unknown quantity or quantities which makes the statement true. The answer is called the *solution.* The Euclidean axioms concerning equations are : *Equals added to or subtracted from equals give equals ; equals multiplied or divided by equals give equals.*

Hence, solve, say, $x - 4 = 5$.
Add 4 to both sides, then $x = 5 + 4$
                        $\therefore x = 9$

Similarly, solve $7x = 21$.
Divide both sides by the coefficient of x, i.e. 7

            $x = \frac{21}{7}$
        $\therefore x = 3$

In each case the solution is seen to be correct by *substitution* of the answer in the given question. Note that with reference to addition and subtraction a term may cross the equals sign without disturbing the balance of the equation *if the sign be changed.*

SIMPLE EQUATIONS are those with only one unknown quantity of the first degree, e.g. the examples already given. Steps in finding the solution are (*a*) get rid of any fractions by multiplying *both sides* by the LCM of all the denominators ; (*b*) multiply out all brackets ; (*c*) collect ' like ' terms, those containing the unknown quantity to one side (usually the left), the rest to the other side ; (*d*) add up each side to a single term ; and (*e*) divide each side by the coefficient of the unknown quantity.

SIMULTANEOUS EQUATIONS : Consider, say, an equation of the first degree with two unknown quantities, e.g. $2x + 3y = 16$. If $x = 5$, it reads $10 + 3y = 16$, whence $3y = 6$, $\therefore y = 2$. Hence, when $x = 5$ and $y = 2$ the equation is true. Similarly, whatever value either x or y is assumed to have, the value of the other letter can be found, i.e. there is an infinite number of values for x and y which make $2x + 3y = 16$. There is likewise an infinite number of values for x and y in, say, $5x + 2y = 7$, but there is only *one*

equation 246 **Erie**

set of values for x and y which makes $2x + 3y = 16$ and $5x + 2y = 7$ true *at the same time*, i.e. simultaneously.

The method of solving a simultaneous equation is by *elimination* and *substitution*, e.g.

$$2x + 3y = 16 \ . \ . \ . \ . \ . \text{(i)}$$
$$5x + 2y = 7 \ . \ . \ . \ . \ . \text{(ii)}$$

Decide which letter to eliminate. Let it be y, whose coefficients are 3 in line (i), and 2 in line (ii). Multiply line (i) by 2 and line (ii) by 3, then

$$4x + 6y = 32$$
$$15x + 6y = 21$$

Subtract these two lines (or add if the y terms have opposite signs), whence

$$- 11x = 11$$
$$\therefore \ x = - 1$$

Substitute this in line (i) or (ii), say line (i) :

$$- 2 + 3y = 16$$
$$\therefore \ 3y = 18$$
$$\therefore \ y = 6$$

The answer, then, is $x = -1$ and $y = 6$, which is the only pair of values for x and y which makes *both* given equations true.

QUADRATIC EQUATIONS : If in an equation there is a term involving the square of the unknown quantity, but no higher power, the equation is a quadratic. If the unknown, say x, occurs only as x^2, and there is no term in x, the equation is a *pure quadratic*, e.g. $3x^2 - 27 = 0$. Generally there will be three terms (in x^2, x and one free from x, the latter being known as the constant term), e.g. $x^2 - 6x = 7$. Among a variety of ways of solving the equation, the first to be tried is always the Factor Method, this depending on the fact that if the product of two quantities is zero, one or other of the quantities must be 0. Thus the above equation can be solved as follows :

$$x^2 - 6x = 7$$
$$x^2 - 6x - 7 = 0$$
$$(x - 7) (x + 1) = 0$$

If $x = 7$ the first factor becomes 0, and if $x = -1$ the second becomes 0. These are the two solutions to the equation.

Another method is known as *Completing the Square*, and the same equation can be solved thus :

$$x^2 - 6x = 7$$

To make $x^2 - 6x$ a complete square a constant has to be added. This constant is *the square of half the coefficient* of x, i.e. $(-3)^2$ or $+9$

The left-hand side of this equation is now a complete square

$$x^2 - 6x + 9$$

As $+9$ has been added to the one side it must be added to the other also. This gives us

$$x^2 - 6x + 9 = 7 + 9 \ or \ (x - 3)^2 = 16$$

Taking the square root

$$x - 3 = \pm 4$$
$$\therefore \ x = + 7 \ or \ -1$$

LITERAL EQUATIONS may be of any of the foregoing types but with general coefficients, e.g. a, b, c, d, instead of

numbers. 'Solve $ax - b = cx - d$,' means : 'Find x in terms of the coefficients a, b, c, d.' The equation $ax^2 + bx + c = 0$ is a quadratic with literal coefficients, and is known as the *General Quadratic*. By completing the square the answer is shown to be

$$x = \frac{- b \pm \sqrt{b^2 - 4ac}}{2a},$$

the formula by means of which *every* quadratic can be solved by substitution. Note that if $b^2 - 4ac$ is a perfect square, the roots come out exactly, and the equation could have been solved by the Factor Method. If a, b, c are such that $b^2 - 4ac$ is negative, the square root cannot be found, which means that the roots are imaginary.

IDENTITIES : An identity is a statement of equality which is independent of the values of the letters involved, and $\equiv$ is usually used instead of the usual 'equals' sign $=$. Thus

$$(x + y) (x - y) \equiv x^2 - y^2$$

These are only examples of the more elementary mathematical equation. The equation form is also much used in the sciences. In chemistry, for instance, it is used to indicate the result of chemical reactions. See CHEMISTRY

equator, imaginary line drawn round the earth midway between the earth's N. Pole and S. Pole. It is lat.0°, all other latitudes being measured N or S.

On the equator the sun is directly overhead at noon at the equinoxes.

equinox, see SEASONS

equivalent, term used in chemistry. The equivalent weight of an element is the number of grams of that element which will combine with or replace one gram of hydrogen or 8 grams of oxygen.

Erasmus, DESIDERIUS (1466–1536), Dutch scholar, *b* Rotterdam ; travelled and studied in France, England, Italy and Germany ; became an Augustinian monk 1492 ; one of the greatest Renaissance pioneers of classical learning. By his writings (which offended both Protestants and Roman Catholics) he attacked the outworn traditions and abuses of the Church, and thus hastened on the Reformation. He taught men to seek inspiration directly from the Bible and from the early Christian fathers ; produced a scholarly edition of the NT, and revived interest in the Greek and Latin classics.

erbium, rare earth and element, Er ; atomic weight 167·2 ; atomic number 68.

Erebus, *er'ē-bŭs*, in old Greek tales (*a*) the son of Chaos ; (*b*) region through which souls were supposed to pass on their way to Hades.

Erebus, MOUNT, see POLAR REGIONS

Erfurt, town, Germany ; 14m from Weimar ; noted for manufacturing railway stock and textiles ; pop.167,000.

erg, see MECHANICS

Erie, *ēr'i*, one of the Great Lakes of N. America ; on the Canadian border ; is

240m long. Also a city, Pennsylvania, USA, on L. Erie ; has many important industries, e.g. iron, petroleum ; pop. 117,000.

Erin, *ăr'in*, poetical name for Ireland. *Erin go bragh* (*ăr'in gŭ brŏ*) means ' Ireland for ever.'

Erinoid, see PLASTICS

Eritrea, *er-ē-trā'ä*, former Italian colony in NE. Africa, bordering the Red Sea ; area 45,000sq.m ; pop.600,000 ; administered by the British since 1943. The capital is Asmara.

Erivan, Armenian capital near the Turkish border ; pop.200,000.

ermine, see STOAT

Ermine Street, see BRITAIN

erne, see EAGLE

E'ros, Greek god of love ; the Cupid of the Romans. For his statue see LONDON (PICCADILLY)

Eros, nearest of the minor planets ; it completes its orbit in 642 days ; mean distance from the sun 135,500,000m ; diameter probably *c*20m ; discovered 1898.

ERP, see MARSHALL, GENERAL G. C.

ersatz, *ăr'zäts*, German word now popularly used in English. It means substitute, and is usually applied to synthetic substances, e.g. plastic garments, synthetic foods, etc.

Erse, see GAELIC

Ervine, ST JOHN, *ŭr'vin* (1883–   ), writer and dramatic critic, *b* Belfast. As a dramatist he wrote *The First Mrs Fraser*; author of *The Theatre in My Time*.

Erzurum, district of Asiatic Turkey ; also a town with a great trade with Europe and Asia ; pop.48,000.

Esau, *ē'sö*, son of Isaac. His birthright was stolen by his brother Jacob ; Genesis 27.

escalator, *es'kä-lā-tor*, moving stairway, i.e. an endless belt with steps, the treads of which remain horizontal while moving up or down an incline. The stair is usually electrically driven. *Escalator* is the trade name for this labour-saving device, now commonly used in large stores, and especially at many stations of the London Underground. The largest, at Leicester Square Underground station, is 161ft long, with a perpendicular height of 80½ ft.

escribed circle, see TRIANGLE

Escurial, palace and monastery 26m from Madrid, Spain ; designed for Philip II ; begun 1563. The building 744ft long by 580ft wide, is said to have 11,000 windows. In its handsome church lie the dead kings of Spain.

Esher, town, Surrey ; has remains of Cardinal Wolsey's palace ; pop.44,000.

Eskimos, see POLAR REGIONS

Esperanto, name of an artificial international auxiliary language invented by Dr Zamenhof of Warsaw *c*.1878. In order to make it easier to learn it has 28 letters, rules that have no exceptions, and phonetic spelling.

Esquiline Hill or **Mons Esquilinus**, *es'kwi-*lĭn, highest of the ' Seven Hills ' on which ancient Rome was built.

esquire, see SQUIRE

essay, literary composition, almost always in prose, and generally brief and informal. Notable English essayists include Charles Lamb and William Hazlitt. More recent essayists include Robert Lynd, E. V. Lucas, George Orwell, etc.

Essen, German town ; near the R. Ruhr ; noted for the Krupp steel-works devastated by British and American bombing in World War II. The pre-war pop. was 660,000.

Essex, county in SE. England ; faces the N. Sea ; mainly farming ; co.tn Chelmsford.

Essex, EARL OF (1566–1601), English courtier, *b* Netherwood, Herefordshire ; strikingly handsome and very charming, but conceited and undiplomatic. For long Queen Elizabeth's favourite, he fought at Zutphen and under Drake ; married Sir Philip Sidney's widow ; was opposed to Lord Burghley. He failed to suppress O'Neil's rising against the English in Ireland, and after senselessly plotting against the queen was beheaded. The story of the ring given by Elizabeth as a pledge that she would always protect him is probably untrue. Essex was a poet, master especially of the sonnet.

esters, chemical compounds derived from acids by replacing one or more hydrogen atoms with an alkyl radical or group, for example, ethyl acetate, $CH_3.COO.C_2H_5$. Natural fats are glyceryl esters of the fatty acids. Many esters are liquids with a pleasant smell.

Esther, book of the OT named after Esther, adopted daughter of Mordecai, a Jewish exile. She became queen of the Persian king Xerxes *c*.470BC.

Estonia, see USSR

Étaples, *ä-tä'ple*, popular seaside town near Boulogne, France.

Eternal City, see ROME

ethane, colourless, odourless gas of the paraffin series.

Ethelbert, king of the Anglo-Saxon kingdom of Kent 560–616 ; was overlord of much of E. Britain. A noted lawmaker, his wife Bertha (*d c*.615) was a Christian, and it was she who persuaded her husband to welcome St Augustine and his missionaries. See AUGUSTINE

Ethelred I (*d* 871), King of Wessex and Kent, elder brother of Alfred the Great, with whom he fought successfully against the Danes at Ashdown.

Ethelred II (*d* 1016), King of the English, son of Edgar ; was known as Ethelred the Unready ; succeeded 979, and in constant conflict with the Danes, whom he attempted to buy off by raising danegeld ; ordered the massacre of the Danes 1002.

Ethelwulf (*d* 858), King of the English ; succeeded 839 ; father of Alfred the Great.

ether, *ē'thĕr*, name given to a medium once

thought to exist in all space, including that between atoms and electrons, and regarded as necessary for the explanation of the passage of light, electromagnetic waves, etc. Its existence was never proved, and modern science has no need for this hypothesis.

ethers, organic compounds usually prepared by the action of a dehydrating agent (e.g. concentrated sulphuric acid) on alcohols. Ordinary ether is diethyl ether ($C_2H_5)_2O$, readily inflammable. Its vapour mixed with air explodes easily ; used as an anaesthetic and a solvent. Its rapid evaporation can be used to produce artificial cold.

ethics, *eth'iks,* study (1) of what is *meant* by such statements as ' this is *good,*' ' that is *bad,*' ' one *ought* to do so-and-so,' ' it is *right* to do this,' ' it is *wrong* to do that,' etc. ; (2) how such statements are related to one another.

Ethiopia, *ē-thi-ō'piä,* kingdom of NE. Africa, formerly Abyssinia ; area 350,000sq.m; pop. *c.*12,000,000 comprising Abyssinians and Negro tribes. The country, largely mountainous with hot valleys, has vast forests. Exports are coffee, hides and gold. There is great mineral wealth as yet scarcely developed. When the country was invaded by Italy 1935, the Emperor Haile Selassie I sought refuge in England, and was restored to his throne 1941. The cap., Addis Ababa, is linked by rail with the Red Sea.

Ethiopia may be said to be rushing out of the past, so swift and comprehensive are the modernising reforms of its Emperor. Addis Ababa has now one of the finest hotels in the world, and is linked by air with various towns, including Cairo. The country's legal system has recently been completely overhauled ; witch doctors are being ousted by well-equipped hospitals ; a fine army has been organised ; education has made tremendous strides, and immense stores of gold, iron, coal and petroleum are being exploited with energy and foresight.

Read *Ethiopia,* David Matthew.

ethnology, study of the distribution and development of human races ; their classification into yellow, brown, black, and white ; also tribal and racial customs.

ethyl group, monovalent radical found in many organic compounds, e.g. ethane.

etiquette, *et'i-ket,* correct behaviour ; keeping conventional rules of society, e.g. a man or boy raises his hat to a lady ; a younger person rises when an older person enters a room, etc. Also observing the rules governing polite behaviour at various functions, e.g. weddings, dinners, parties and dances.

Etna, active volcano, Sicily ; 10,758ft.

Eton, *ē't'n,* town, Buckinghamshire, on the R. Thames, 21m from London ; noted for its college, founded by Henry VI. There are over 1,000 boys ; and among

famous Etonians may be numbered Canning, Chatham, Fox, Gladstone, Peel and Wellington, who declared that Waterloo was won on the playing-fields of Eton.

Etruria, *ē-tru'ri-ä,* ancient district of Italy, almost identical with the modern Tuscany ; its enterprising people (the Etruscans) were at the height of their power in the 7th c. BC. They made the first practical use of the arch ; their graves were adorned with elaborate paintings ; they were masters of pottery-making, and of craftsmanship in gold, silver, etc.

Ettrick Water, Scottish R. joining the Tweed near Selkirk. Ettrick was once a forest in this area. The ' Ettrick Shepherd ' was James Hogg, the Scottish poet.

' **Et tu, Brute,**' see BRUTUS, M. J.

Euboea, *ū-bē'ä,* Greek isl. ; *c.*90m long ; noted for its marble ; chief town Chalcis.

eucalyptus or **gum-tree,** *ū-kä-lip'tŭs,* evergreen tree found mostly in Australia. The blue-gum yields the eucalyptus oil used in medicine.

Eucharist, see SACRAMENT

Euclid (Eucleides), Gk mathematician who taught in Alexandria *c.*300BC. He was not the founder of geometry, but the first to arrange earlier discoveries. His works include *Elements of Geometry* (in 13 books), and a collection of problems on the division of areas. His sequence of propositions was almost universally used till this century. He wrote also on optics and the principles of music.

Eugène, PRINCE, *ū-jēn* (1663–1736), Austrian soldier, *b* Paris ; entered the Austrian army, and became Austria's greatest military genius ; fought successfully against the French in Italy ; began an association with the English Duke of Marlborough, 1704, aiding him at Blenheim ; fought also against the Turks ; captured Belgrade ; *d* Vienna.

eugenics, *ū-jēn'iks,* scientific breeding in accordance with fundamental factors that improve physical and mental racial qualities. The science was originated by Sir Francis Galton (1822–1911), and owes much to the researches of the abbé Mendel.

euphemism, see FIGURES OF SPEECH

Euphrates, *ū-frā'tēz,* river flowing *c.*1,800m from Asia Minor through Iraq to join the Tigris. The valley of the ' Two Rivers ' was the scene of the ancient Babylonian civilisation.

euphuism, *ū'fū-izm,* artificial style of writing (late 16th c.) in which excessive use was made of alliteration and classical allusions ; so named from the book *Euphues* (1579) by John Lyly. See FIGURES OF SPEECH

eureka, *ū-rē'kä,* Greek, *I have found* ; see ARCHIMEDES, and note that *Eureka* is the state motto of California.

eurhythmics, *ū-rith'miks*, art of expressing harmony by bodily movements. The crochet is the time unit ; certain gestures represent modifications of regularity in the music. Even young pupils benefit from this joyous self-expression. See DALCROZE, E. J.

Euripides, *ū-rip'i-dēz* (*c*.480–407BC), most tragic of Greek dramatists ; *b* Phyla (Attica) on the day the battle of Salamis was fought. As a youth he was an athlete ; later an artist. His fame rests on his superb plays, perhaps 90 in all, though only 18 survive, among them *Alcestis, Medea* (acknowledged as one of his masterpieces), *Hippolytus, Hecuba, The Trojan Women, Electra.*

EURIPIDES 480–407 B C.

Euripides gives us stories of gods and goddesses, but they act as human beings. His understanding (especially of women) accounts for his peculiar gift of mixing good and evil in his characters so that he has been both condemned and praised. His popularity in our day is largely due to the metrical translations by Professor Gilbert Murray.

Note the following :

'Ἡδύ τοι σωθέντα μεμνῆσθαι πόνων (Sweet is the remembrance of troubles when one is in safety).

Σοφὴν δὲ μισῶ. Μὴ γὰρ ἔν γ' ἐμοῖς δόμοις

Εἴη φρονοῦσα πλεῖον ἤ γυναῖκα χρή. (I hate a learned woman. May there never be in my abode a woman knowing more than a woman ought to know).

Νεικῶν παλαιῶν χρηστὸς ἀμνήμων ἀνήρ (A worthy man is not mindful of past injuries).

Europa, *ū-rō'pă*, in old Greek tales, daughter of Agenor, King of Phoenicia ; carried off to Crete by a white bull ; became the wife of Zeus.

Europe, continent ; area 2,686,000sq.m ; pop.380,416,000 : or, including European Russia, area 4,500,000sq.m ; pop. 511,458,000 ; separated from Asia by the Ural Mts, Caucasus and the Caspian Sea. The *continental shelf* (a region of shallow water) extends 100m W. of Ireland.

The climate of Western Europe is oceanic, with abundant rainfall ; in the Mediterranean region rainfall is often insufficient for agriculture ; Central Europe has very cold winters and hot summers. Among mt. ranges the most remarkable are the Alps ; others are the Carpathians, the Balkan mts. ; Apennines ; Pyrenees ; the sierras of Spain and the Scandinavian highlands. Of rivers, the Volga (*c*.2,300m) is the longest ; others are the Danube, Don, Dnieper, Pechora, Dvina and Rhine. Scandinavia has vast coniferous forests ; in the far north of the continent are immense regions of tundra, and in S. Russia are the steppes. Coal is mined on an immense scale, also iron, especially in Britain, Sweden and Germany ; most metals are found abundantly.

The inhabitants of Europe are chiefly Aryan, at any rate in speech ; and the chief countries, apart from Great Britain, are Austria, Belgium, Bulgaria, Czechoslovakia, Denmark, France, Germany, Greece, Hungary, Italy, Netherlands, Norway, Polahd, Portugal, Rumania, Spain, Sweden, Switzerland, Turkey in Europe, USSR and Yugoslavia. The idea of a United States of Europe has long been discussed. A Pan-European Union was founded 1926, followed by proposals for a European Federation in the N. and W. Winston Churchill advocated the creation of the United States of Europe 1940 ; and (1948) Ernest Bevin proposed a union of Western Europe. The first meeting of the Council of Europe was held at Strasbourg, Aug 1949. During a Consultative Assembly of the Council of Europe (Nov 1950) a European army was discussed at Strasbourg ; and (1951) General Eisenhower became Supreme Commander of W. European forces organised by the Atlantic Treaty Powers.

europium, rare earth and element, Eu ; atomic weight 152·0 ; atomic number 63.

Eurydice, *ū-rid'i-sē*, in old Greek tales, wife of the poet and musician Orpheus. After her death Orpheus charmed Pluto with his lyre to allow Eurydice to return from Hades. Orpheus was told not to look back, but in his eagerness he did so, and thus lost Eurydice for ever.

evacuee, *ē-văk'ū-ē*, word first commonly used during World War II for a person evacuated from an area considered unsafe to an area regarded as less liable to attack (especially from the air) by the enemy. In 1941 over 1,340,000 people were evacuated from London.

Evans, ADMIRAL SIR EDWARD, see MOUNT-EVANS, LORD

Evans, R. IFOR (1899–   ), scholar and

literary critic ; author of *A Short History of English Literature*, etc.

Evans, MARY ANN, see ELIOT, GEORGE

evaporation, *ē-vap'ō-rā-shon*, generally the conversion of a liquid into a vapour without necessarily reaching boiling-point. The evaporation of water in nature is of great importance as the cause of rain and snow, without which life could not be supported.

Eve, *ēv*, wife of Adam ; Genesis 2.

Evelyn, JOHN, *ev'e-lin* (1620–1706), *b* Wotton House, near Dorking (Surrey) ; a wealthy country gentleman who was politically cautious, and as a Royalist lived abroad during the Civil War. Friend of many famous men (e.g. Robert Boyle, Pepys and Charles II), he helped to found the Royal Society, was interested in music, art, navigation, etc., and especially in agriculture and gardening. His book *Sylva* (1664) pleaded for the planting of trees ; his *Terra* (1676) is an attempt to study farming scientifically. He is most famous for his *Diary,* covering over 50 years, and giving valuable details of people, life and events in England, and of his Continental tours.

John Evelyn's *Diary* (found 1817 in an old clothes basket in a country house in Surrey) is full of vivid descriptions of places and events, e.g. the following from his account of the Great Fire of London, 1666 :

Oh, the miserable and calamitous spectacle, such as, haply, the world had not seen the like since the foundation of it, nor can be outdone till the universal conflagration of it. All the sky was of a fiery aspect, like the top of a burning oven, and the light seen above forty miles round about for many nights. God grant my eyes may never behold the like, who now saw above ten thousand houses all in one flame ; the noise and crackling and thunder of the impetuous flames, the shrieking of women and children, the hurry of people, the fall of towers, houses, and churches, was like a hideous storm, and the air all about so hot and inflamed that at the last one was not able to approach it, so that they were forced to stand still and let the flames burn on, which they did for nearly two miles in length and one in breadth. The clouds also of smoke were dismal, and reached upon computation nearly fifty-six miles in length. Thus I left it this afternoon burning, a resemblance of Sodom, or the last day. London was, but is no more.

Everest, highest mt. in the world, rising 29,141ft among the peaks of the Himalayas, and bordering Nepal and Tibet ; named after Sir George Everest (1790–1866), surveyor-general of India.

Though planes have flown over it (first in 1933), Everest has so far defeated climbers. In 1920 the Dalai Lama of Tibet gave permission for attempts to be made from the Tibetan side. Expeditions include those under General Bruce 1920, 1922 and 1924, when G. H. Leigh-Mallory and A. C. Irvine perished at 28,200ft while ' going strong for the top.' Other expeditions include the Hugh Ruttledge expedition 1933 ; Maurice Wilson's lone attempt in which he lost his life 1934 ; E. F. Shipton's 1935 expedition ; the 1936 Ruttledge attempt; and the W. H. Tiltman expedition 1938. Yet another attempt was planned 1947.

' **Everyman,**' see DRAMA

Evesham, *ēv'sham* ; *ē'sham,* town, Worcestershire ; scene of the defeat of Simon de Montfort by Prince Edward (later Edward I) 1265.

evolution, *ē-vō-lū'shon* (Latin *evolvere,* to unroll), theory that the earth took shape *gradually,* and that living things as we now know them are the result of slow and more or less continuous change. This theory is fundamentally different from the old religious belief that God made the world, and everything in it, by a single act of creation, and that hence living things began as we now see them. Increasing knowledge during the last 200 years or so, especially that of the geologist and biologist, has destroyed the old belief, replacing it with the theory that the earth and its life-forms have gradually evolved and are still evolving.

Evolution goes back to the birth of our planet. Modern science suggests that possibly there were originally two stars revolving about each other, one of which exploded, its gaseous mass disrupting to form what are now the planets, these continuing to circle the remaining star, namely the Sun, centre of our present Solar System. Of these planets our earth is one, and its age may be considered to be at least 3,200 million years, and probably much more.

For a long time the new earth's surface was too hot and molten to be stable ; but eventually the crust cooled sufficiently to become more or less solid, and vapour or steam condensed to form oceans and lakes separated by land masses, the present arrangement of land masses being *c.*100,000,000 years old.

The idea of the evolution of life is one of the greatest conceptions of modern times. We owe the theory to many careful and patient observers, among whom the two most outstanding are Jean Baptiste Lamarck (1744–1829), a French scientist, and the English naturalist, Charles Darwin, whose *Origin of Species* (published 1859) created bitter controversy, but eventually won world wide recognition. For a time Darwinism eclipsed the theories of Lamarck, but the principles of the earlier scientist are now considered preferable in some respects to some of Darwin's theories, especially his theory of the survival of the fittest. Briefly we may say that :

Lamarck's view of evolution is that a creature has an inward urge to fulfil its needs and adapt itself to its environment, changing its habits and even its bodily structure to satisfy this urge and this need. Further, that modifications acquired by the parent are transmitted to the offspring.

Darwin's view of evolution is that creatures best adapted to their surroundings or habitat are best able to survive ; and that, therefore, by a process of natural selection due to the struggle for existence, creatures with the best adaptations to their particular environment survive and carry forward their evolutionary changes.

We do not know how life originated on this planet. Many theories have been put forward, but none is completely satisfactory. It seems likely, however, that life began in water, since water comprises 80 per cent of all living things. We may suppose that abundant supplies of oxygen, hydrogen and carbon in the dawn of the earth's long day enabled microscopic living cells (bacteria) to evolve from non-living material, each cell having *chromatin* in the centre, i.e. a compound of carbon, oxygen, nitrogen, and possibly sulphur. We may believe, further, that once life appeared there were many millions of years in which death was unknown, as the only lifeforms inhabiting the earth were simple cells which never died, but reproduced themselves indefinitely by splitting in two.

Later, no doubt, *these single-celled forms became colonies.* Later still, we may suppose, the immensely important advance was made of *division of labour*, i.e. some cells in a colony or organism specialised in one kind of work only, e.g. assimilating food, repairing tissue, etc. It was this specialisation which led to the building up of *complex bodies*, and also to the vital principle of *sex*, now recognised as one of the chief causes of variation in life-forms, and hence a fundamental prerequisite of evolution. By simply breaking in two, a living organism inevitably *duplicated* itself, *but the joining of male and female*

(similar but never identical) made it possible for offspring to differ slightly from the parents, hence variation with its many opportunities for adaptation.

There are today organisms so humble that we find it difficult to say if they are plant or animal, e.g. certain bacteria and the sponges. It seems likely that the first living things gave rise to seacreatures of the plant type, i.e. able to manufacture a form of chlorophyll, using it together with sunlight to break down carbon dioxide and to build up sugars. But other organisms incapable of doing this came into being. These, though incapable of feeding in the manner of plant-forms, were able to feed on the plants themselves. Thus at a very early date there evolved two chief types of living things, plants and animals.

The geologist studying rock formations gains a vivid picture of the gradual development of life—how the giant ferns of the Carboniferous period gave place to trees ; how lowly animal forms developed a sense of direction, producing a head and limbs, developing breathing apparatus, nervous system, etc. ; and how in the Silurian period the first backboned creatures appeared. The pageant moves slowly upward—fish, reptile, bird, mammal, man.

Though geologists prefer to speak of ages and periods, and to avoid the measurement of time in years, we may very roughly indicate the significant changes in the development of life as shown in the Table below.

Evidence in support of the theory of evolution is derived from (1) a comparative examination of different plants and animals, showing that widely different creatures may have many similarities, e.g. the fore-limb of the frog, the wing of a bird, the flipper of a whale, and the human hand, all variations of one fundamental structure, and hence strongly suggesting a common ancestry ; (2) the fact that the bodies of most of the higher animals (*Vertebrates*) possess what are now useless organs, i.e. *vestigial remains* of organs that were *once* useful, e.g. the human body retains a hint of a third eyelid, also the now useless appendix ;

first sea creatures (without backbone)	appeared	*c.* 1,700,000,000 years ago
oldest known fossils		800,000,000
first land animals		500,000,000
coal measures laid down (fishes, giant plant-forms)		300,000,000
huge saurians (dragons of the prime)		280,000,000
first mammals		60,000,000
first man-apes		8,000,000

or again most birds have scales on the legs, a link with their reptile and fish ancestry ; (3) breeders of dogs, pigeons, mice, etc. are able to produce varieties artificially, hence the conclusion that nature may produce variations in the course of generations ; (4) the rocks afford abundant evidence of evolution. Geologists may trace among fossils the gradual development of various creatures, successive strata containing fossils showing advances (or sometimes regressions) in form. Thus, the modern horse, a noble animal, is descended from a far-off ancestor (*eohippus*) no larger than a hare; and there is no doubt that the rocks contain evidence of almost every variation between the emergence of *eohippus* to the horse as we know it today. Also most of the higher creatures show in the egg or before birth a recapitulation of the history of the race. Thus, mammals in embryo have gill-slits at one period before birth, a link with gill-breathing fish of the dim past.

To summarise the *causes* of evolution is no easy task. According to Charles Darwin the cause of survival is bound up with the struggle for existence. Life is always fighting for living-space, for a chance to multiply, and any racial variation tending to give a species an advantage in the struggle is handed down to following generations. Much of this is no doubt true, but the modern form of Lamarck's theories seems, on the whole, preferable, namely that today's life-forms are the product of age-long variation and adaptation, the result of persistent environmental stimulus which, if continuing over many generations, may bring about the appearance of new types.

We cannot leave the story of evolution at the point where life has attained the order known as Primates (see LIVING THINGS), for man himself is the product of variations that have gone before. It would seem that man, as distinct from brutes, has inhabited the earth little more than a few million years. Closely akin to apes and monkeys, and with them descended from some common but remote ancestor, man differs from all other creatures in many significant ways, e.g. in standing erect (even the gorilla prefers as a rule to shuffle on all fours) ; in his ability to speak ; still more his ability to reason. His use of fire and tools, his power to change environment, and, most of all, his awareness of himself, long ago gave him pride of place in the animal world. The male gorilla has a brain of *c*.500cc ; the average human brain, much folded, and hence with a vastly greater surface area) has a volume of not less than 1,480cc).

When man first stood upright (thus gaining full use of his forelimbs), and when his brain outmatched that of any other animal, is not known ; but we have various clues. It has been customary to regard the earliest traces of man

as belonging to the Pliocene period of geological time, but Sir Arthur Keith believes that the beginnings of the species *homo sapiens* (man) date from the Miocene, though he has suggested that the human level was not attained till as recently as *c*.200,000 years ago. Other scientists declare that man was human rather than brutish a million years ago, or more.

That the first decisive cleavage between man and the rest of the Mammalia began, probably, in the Miocene period (say 20–30 million years ago) is supported by discoveries as recent as 1944, namely by skulls found in the Rift Valley, Kenya, by Dr. L. S. B. Leakey. Scientists who have examined these in detail have declared (1947) that these skulls seem to indicate a far-off period when man and the gorilla were in the making ; indeed the race to which these remains belong may have been the one that developed into the gorilla along one branch, into man along another.

The remains of *hominidae* antedate all others by immense ages. The name *Pithecanthropus erectus* (erect ape-man) is given to the creature which, in the Pleistocene period, was apparently evolving along the line that was to lead to man. Remains of a skull of *Pithecanthropus erectus* were discovered in Java 1891, but it is evident that even this primitive ape-man was far advanced beyond the ape. A somewhat similar skull (the so-called Pekin Man) was unearthed in China 1929. The brain-case of the Pekin Man is much thinner than that of the (possibly co-eval) Piltdown skull discovered 1912 at Piltdown (Sussex) which is though to indicate a race of ape-men *c*.5½ft tall, with low, flat heads and overhanging brows. *Homo Heidelbergensis* is the name given to primitive man of the type indicated by a lower jaw discovered near Heidelberg 1907 ; and a race known as Neanderthal may have lived in Europe *c*.25,000–50,000 years ago. Neanderthal man, named from the place (near Düsseldorf) where parts of a skeleton were found 1859, was apparently loose-limbed, had a massive jaw, and was in many ways related to the modern ape, but used fire and made flint weapons. A very similar skull was found on Mt Carmel 1925 ; and (1912) Dr Leakey found in Kenya fossil skulls thought to indicate the presence there of the ancestors of the Negro race. A skull found in London 1935 (possibly 100,000 years old) is certainly older than the Cromagnon skull found in Dordogne (France) ; but even with these relics, there are a number of ' missing links ' in the chain of evidence concerning human evolution. In 1948 an expedition in Kenya found the skull of an ape which, though estimated to be 20,000,000 years old, shows human features. The latest pronouncements on the evolution of *homo sapiens* come from Sir Arthur Keith, and are found in his excellent book, *Essays on Human Evolution.*

Finally, evolution is a process that is still going on, since life is ever on the march. How long this pageant has been moving is beyond our comprehension, but we gain some glimpse of the immense aeons of time that have passed since life began its great adventure if we reduce the earth's 3,000 million years to, say, a day of 24 hours. Then, if 3,000 million years are called 24 hours, we may say that from 00.00 hours to *c.*13.00 hours by the clock, the earth had no living thing. The first fossils date from *c.*19.00 hours, and the coal measures were laid down when the hands of the clock pointed to within 5 minutes of 23.00 hours. Mammals emerged at 23.40 hours ; and the first ape-man rose on his hind legs *c.*23.59 hours.

Read *The Antiquity of Man,* also *Essays on Human Evolution,* Sir Arthur Keith ; early chapters of *The Outline of History,* H. G. Wells ; and a chapter headed *Biology and Human Progress* (by Sir J. Arthur Thomson) in *An Outline of Modern Knowledge.*

See BIOLOGY ; DARWIN, CHARLES ; GEOLOGY ; LIVING THINGS, etc.

Évora, *ev'ō-rä,* city, Portugal ; 70m NE. of Lisbon ; has many Roman remains ; pop.22,000.

Évreux, *ā-vrū,* beautiful old town 67m NW. of Paris.

ewe, see SHEEP

Ewing, SIR JAMES ALFRED, *ū'ing* (1855–1935), engineer and scientist, *b* Dundee ; for a time assistant to Lord Kelvin ; notable for many improvements in electrical apparatus.

examinations, tests designed to discover knowledge or ability, usually by means of oral or written questions.

The passing of certain examinations is regarded as proof that a required standard of knowledge has been attained. Thus, while most schools set internal examinations from time to time to find how much the pupils have learned, there are also external examinations which impose a common standard throughout the country.

In recent years there has been a tendency to distrust written examinations as the sole method of selection and assessment, especially of younger children. Attempts are now being made to standardise the keeping of school records, and these, together with intelligence tests, are being increasingly used to determine to which type of secondary school a child should proceed.

Prior to 1951 MATRICULATION was the ' key ' to a professional career, and was designed to qualify a successful candidate for entrance to a university. Equivalent examinations were the PREVIOUS at Cambridge and RESPONSIONS at Oxford, a similar examination in Scotland being the PRELIMINARY (Prelim.).

At present a complete revision of the examination system is taking place under the guidance of Mr George Tomlinson, Minister of Education. The General and the Higher Schools Certificate are being replaced by the GENERAL CERTIFICATE OF EDUCATION, candidates for which must be 16 or over. This examination can be taken at three levels—general, advanced and higher, the last approximating to University scholarship standard. A student wishing to specialise will take, say, the General Certificate in 3 or 4 subjects, and then proceed to take the Advanced Standard in his special subjects. It is unnecessary to take a subject at the lower level before taking it at the advanced stage.

Apparently it is becoming customary for universities to demand passes in what will be the advanced stage of the examination before admitting students to degree courses—Matriculation being no longer sufficient recommendation for admission in these days of keen competition. Pupils at school are advised by the headmaster ; students who have left school may well apply to one of the correspondence colleges mentioned below.

DEGREES may be obtained by passing examinations while in residence at a university or by external students of London University, the latter being well advised (if unable to attend lectures) to study under the direction of a Correspondence College, e.g. Wolsey Hall, Oxford, or University Correspondence College, Burlington House, Cambridge. For all London degrees (whether taken by internal or external students) it is necessary to pass a preliminary examination ; an Intermediate examination (often referred to as ' Inter '), and a Final (the actual degree) examination. This series of steps applies also to other universities. See UNIVERSITIES

By passing the required examinations a student may take his Bachelor of Arts (B.A.) degree, a preliminary to becoming Master of Arts (M.A.) or Doctor of Philosophy (Ph.D.) or Doctor of Literature (D.Litt.). Other degrees include M.B., Ch.B (Bachelor of Medicine, Bachelor of Surgery) for those who decide to become medical practitioners, and M.D. (Doctor of Medicine). Science students take B.Sc., i.e. Bachelor of Science, with its variations B.Sc. (Eng.), i.e. Bachelor of Science (Engineering) ; B.Sc. (Econ.), i.e. Economics. Law students take the LL.B., i.e. Bachelor of Laws ; and there are also such degrees as Bachelor of Divinity (B.D.) ; Bachelor of Music (B.Mus.), etc. External students may obtain particulars from The Registrar, University of London, W.C.1. The City and Guilds of London Institute conducts a wide range of examinations of nationally accepted standards, the subjects covering textiles, engineering, building, cookery, and handicraft.

Examinations are organised by the Civil Service Commissioners to select, by *competitive* examinations, candidates for vacancies in the various branches of the Civil Service ; also for the commissioned ranks in the Navy, Army, and Air Force, and for the Metropolitan Police. In most cases candidates have to be between 21 and 24 years.

Practical hints : When sitting for an examination try not to worry ; take your time ; write quickly but never scribble ; remember your ' target ' is to impress the examiner with your ability, i.e. what you know and your *method* of expressing it ; read the question—and be quite sure you are doing what the examiner asks, e.g. do not write the life of the Duke of Wellington if the examiner asks for a description of the battle of Waterloo. Give all the relevant information you can. If, say, you are asked for the *results* of Waterloo, tabulate them (*a*), (*b*), (*c*), etc. ; do not confuse results with *causes*. On the whole, use short sentences. Before you begin make a mental note of the average time you can afford per question, and do not seriously exceed this ; always leave time for a final reading and correction of your work ; be sure to read the instructions at the top of the examination paper. Where appropriate, use neat, clear diagrams. Number every answer plainly. In mathematical papers, be sure your answers stand out boldly and that your working is reasoned. Do not give the answer in feet when it should be square yards. Above all—don't worry ! See TECHNICAL EDUCATION ; UNIVERSITIES

Excalibur, see ARTHUR

excavator, *eks-kä-vā'ter*, mechanical device for digging holes, and especially for forming trenches (e.g. for cables, and water-mains) also (usually larger models) for excavating reservoirs, building railway embankments or making cuttings. The commoner type, motor-driven (125hp or more) has a heavy jib which may be luffed or derricked by controlling levers, and either a scoop, grab, or shovel removing up to a ton of earth at a time, or a series of buckets on an endless chain. A variation of the latter type becomes the dredger used in harbours, rivers, canals, etc.

ex-centre, see TRIANGLE

exchange, in money affairs, the transfer of money of one country into that of another, the rates of exchange normally differing very slightly from day to day as the result of trade balances, amount of gold in a country, international loans, etc. In another sense an exchange is a building where merchants meet to transact business, e.g. the stock exchange, the wool, corn and coal exchanges.

Exchequer, *ex-chek'ĕr*, in Norman and later times a government department responsible for collecting the king's revenues ; named from the chequer (or chess) board once used to help in calculating the amounts due. The duties of the Exchequer were taken over 1834 by the Treasury, the Chancellor of the Exchequer being its head.

excise, see CUSTOMS

excommunication, act of excluding a member of a religious body from its fellowship. Pope Innocent III excommunicated King John of England ; Leo X excommunicated Luther ; Pius V excommunicated Queen Elizabeth 1570.

executor, *eg-zek'ūtĕr*, in law a person appointed by a will to carry out the wishes of some person who has died. He must first ' prove ' the will, i.e. receive a probate copy, and then pay funeral expenses, also debts (any to the State coming first) and legacies.

Exeter, *ek'sē-tĕr*, co.tn and cathedral city, Devon ; *c*.9m from the mouth of the R. Exe ; noted for its public school ; pop.74,000.

Exeter College, a college of Oxford University, founded 1314. It is specially associated with Devon and Cornwall. The buildings include the 19th c. chapel, with decorations by Burne-Jones and William Morris, both members of the college, as also was R. D. Blackmore.

exhibition, public show to encourage trade, e.g. the Great Exhibition in a huge glass building (designed by Sir Joseph Paxton), constructed in Hyde Park, London, 1851 ; also such exhibitions (or expositions) as that of Paris 1889, for which the Eiffel Tower was built ; that at Wembley 1924 (British Empire) ; World Fair, Chicago 1933 ; and Glasgow Exhibition 1938.

existentialism, *eks-is-ten'shäl-ism*, fashionable, philosophical cult much talked of 1946–47. A form of modern materialism, its philosophy is based on the theory that man is nothing but the sum of his experiences, that all experience is inexplicable and tragic, and that to be free a man must act, otherwise he is nothing. The cult, ill-defined even in *L'Etre et le Néant* (Being and Nothingness), was originated by Jean-Paul Sartre, a Frenchman whose plays (e.g. *Huis Clos, Mort Sans Sepulture*, and *La Putain Respecteuse*), are supposed to reveal something of the meaning of Existentialism. In *Existentialism*, Guido Ruggiero has brilliantly argued that the cult rests on a false basis.

Exmoor, forest and moorland in W. Somerset and N. Devon ; noted for ponies, also red deer.

Exodus, *ek'sō-dŭs*, second book of the OT. The title means ' going forth.' Exodus gives an account of Israel in Egypt, and of how Moses led the people into the wilderness.

expansion, increase in size ; in physics, that due to heat.

Most solids, liquids and gases expand when heated and contract when cooled (see HEAT), but there are exceptions. Some alloys at ordinary temperatures expand when cooled, dentists making use of this property for ensuring that a metal filling fits tightly into a tooth. Type-metal, by expanding on solidification, gives a sharp edge to the type. Note also that water contracts when cooled from 100° to 4°C, after which it *expands*, forming ice at 0°C, with further expansion during the change. Ice itself contracts normally.

(1) SOLIDS : expansion (and contraction) is less than for liquids and gases, but exerts enormous force if resisted. Thus, an iron cube with edge 1in heated from 0°C to 100°C, would require a force equal to 35 tons to prevent its expansion ; hence the space left between railway lines, and the use of *oval* holes in the fish-plates joining them, otherwise in hot weather the rails would buckle. Similarly, the girders of the Forth Bridge rest on rollers, thus allowing for a linear expansion of 12in ; steam pipes in a boiler are curved to allow for expansion ; metal tyres are shrunk on to a wheel, i.e. put on hot so as to fit tightly when cold, and therefore slightly smaller. Red-hot rivets were once used in shipbuilding, but welding is now replacing this method. Formerly, clocks had to be fitted with compensating pendulums ; nowadays Invar steel is being increasingly used. The reverse of these processes is now widely employed, e.g. engine cylinder-heads are cooled in a refrigerator before being screwed to the cylinder barrels.

The coefficient of linear expansion of a substance is the amount unit length expands when the temperature rises one degree (C or F), i.e. the fractional increase of length per degree rise in temperature. Useful coefficients of linear expansion per degree Centigrade are :

brass	·000018	lead	·000028
copper	·000017	platinum	·000085
glass	·0000085	steel	·000012
iron	·000012	zinc	·00003

These coefficients apply to *all* units of measurement ; thus a bar of iron 1yd long expands ·000012yd if heated 1°. Square (areal) expansion is approximately twice linear expansion ; cubical, 3 times linear, approx.

(2) LIQUIDS : The coefficient of apparent expansion is the fractional increase of volume per degree rise in temperature, neglecting the expansion of the container, i.e. real coefficient = apparent + cubical coefficient of the container ; it is found by heating a liquid in a density bottle, and noting the weight of the liquid expelled, whence apparent coefficient

$$= \frac{\text{weight of expelled liquid}}{\text{weight remaining} \times d}$$

where *d* is the difference in temperature.

(3) GASES, see GAS

experimenting, see HOBBY

exploration, discovery of unknown or little-known regions of the earth. Marco Polo, who journeyed from Venice to China in the 13th c., may be regarded as a pioneer of modern exploration ; Columbus led the way to S. America 1492 ; Cabot to N. America 1497, the year in which Vasco da Gama rounded the Cape of Good Hope, and thus reached India. Sir Francis Drake sailed round the world 1577–80. The Dutch navigator Tasman found Tasmania and NZ ; Captain Cook put Australia on the map *c*.1768, and the interior of the continent was explored by Oxley, Sturt, Eyre, etc. Africa (' the Dark Continent ') was explored in the 19th c. by Livingstone, Stanley, Hannington, Speke, etc., while the search for the NW. and NE. Passages led to much Polar exploration in the 18th and 19th c. The N. Pole was reached by Peary 1909 ; and in the Antarctic, Captain Scott reached the S. Pole a month after Roald Amundsen, who had arrived Dec 1911. Further Antarctic exploration has been done by Shackleton, Commander Byrd and Sir Douglas Mawson.

The Sahara was conquered by Georges Haardt and Louis Audouin-Dubrieuil 1924. Rosita Forbes travelled through the Libyan Desert 1920. Central Asia, almost a closed book 50 years ago, has been explored by Dr Sven Hedin, who crossed the Takla-Makan Desert 1895, and later made a daring journey into Tibet, followed (1904) by a British military expedition that fought its way to Lhasa. C. M. Doughty, Gertrude Bell, R. E. Cheesman, T. E. Lawrence and Rosita Forbes were pioneers in Arabia. Harry St John Philby crossed the singing sands of the Rub'al Khali Desert 1932—1,800m in 90 days, discovering the fabled city of Ubar, and the spot where a gigantic meteorite had fallen.

New Guinea, with its snow-capped mts., almost impenetrable jungles, and poisonous snakes, has been explored by such daring adventurers as C. A. Moncton (1907), D. Mackay and W. S. Little, and (1910–11) Staniforth Smith, who climbed Mt Murray. L. Austen and W. H. H. Thompson explored NW. Papua 1924 ; and between 1930 and 1934 Michael Leahy (in search of gold) made 10 journeys in Dutch New Guinea.

S. America still offers the lure of the unknown to adventurers. Colonel P. H. Fawcett examined the amazing Lake Titicaca, between Chile and Peru, came across an anaconda 85ft long, pushed through Brazilian forests, and (1925) with his son Jack set out in search of a strange race of Indians, and never returned.

' **Explorer II,**' see AVIATION

explosives, mixtures capable of becoming gases almost instantaneously. Though of supreme importance in modern warfare, they are also of great use in peacetime, e.g. in mining, quarrying, etc.

The earliest explosive was gunpowder

(saltpetre, charcoal and sulphur), first used in guns c.1320, and almost the only one known for 500 years. Nitrocellulose and nitroglycerine were discovered 1846. Alfred Nobel invented a means of detonating dynamite. At the beginning of World War I the chief high explosive was lyddite, later largely displaced by trinitrotoluene (TNT), and others ; and improvements in bombs in World War II led to a huge variety of explosives in the form of oil-bombs, phosphorus bombs, block-busters, bombs weighing 10,000lb, and (1945) a wholly new type of explosive, the atom-bomb, first used against the Japanese.

expositions, see EXHIBITIONS

Exton, see NYLON

extra-mural lectures, see UNIVERSITIES

Eyck, HUBERT VAN, *īk* (*d* 1426), Flemish artist ; became court painter at Ghent ; famous for the cathedral altar-piece *Adoration of the Lamb,* completed by his brother Jan. The brothers were pioneers in oil-painting.

eye, organ of vision. A ball *c.*1in in diameter, the human eye has a white outer layer (*sclerotic*) in which, at the front, is a transparent ' window,' the *cornea.* Behind this window is the hole by which light enters, its size (like the stop of a camera) increasing or diminishing according to the light by means of minute muscles in the iris (usually blue, grey, or brown). Behind this is a crystalline lens enabling us to focus objects on the *retina,* a sensitive screen of nerve-ends at the back of the eye. The space between the lens and the retina contains a clear jelly-like substance called the *vitreous humour.*

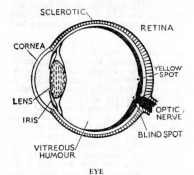

EYE

The structure of the Human Eye

The retina (10 layers of tissue containing a purplish substance which apparently absorbs light and is quickly decomposed by it) is linked with the brain by the optic nerve, the nerve-end forming a blind spot easily discovered if you close your left eye, move this page *c.*6in from your face, and stare at the cross below. The spot will vanish because it is focussed on that part of the retina insensitive to light.

The yellow spot is the portion of the retina where we see objects most clearly ; its sensitiveness to colour is dealt with under LIGHT.

By having two eyes we are better able to judge distance, and to form an impression of the solidity of objects. The image on the retina is inverted, but the brain rectifies this in its interpretation of the stimuli received.

Short-sightedness (*myopia*), due to a defect in the lens, causes an image to be focussed in front of (and not *on*) the retina, hence the need of concave spectacles ; long-sightedness (*hypermetropia*), the reverse, makes convex lenses necessary. *Astigmatism* is due to the lens of the eye having different curvatures in different directions, and is corrected by spectacles with cylindrical lenses.

eyebright, humble meadow-plant (family *Scrophulariaceae*) ; usually only a few inches high. The oval leaves, in pairs, are somewhat hairy and crinkled. The small spikes of flowers are white or pale lilac.

Eylau, *i'low,* town, Germany ; scene 1807 of Napoleon's defeat of the Russians and Prussians.

Eyre, *ār,* lake, S. Australia ; a marsh only in the dry season.

Eyre, EDWARD JOHN, *ār* (1815–1901), explorer, *b* Hornsea, Yorkshire ; emigrated to Australia 1833, where he explored much territory, notably the coast between Adelaide and King George Sound. Later he was governor of NZ.

Ezekiel, *ē-zē'ki-el,* Hebrew prophet and priest carried off from Jerusalem to Babylon by Nebuchadnezzar *c.*597BC.

Ezra, Jewish scribe exiled in Babylon, but allowed *c.*458BC to return with 1,500 men, also women and children, to rebuild the Temple at Jerusalem.

F

F, chemical symbol for fluorine.

f, see FOCAL LENGTH

Fabian Society, *fā'bi-an,* Socialist organisation founded 1884. Named after Fabius Maximus, the Roman general who was noted for his cautious tactics, the society believed, not in violent revolution, but in gradually educating the public to demand Socialism.

Fabius Maximus, *fā'bi-us* (*d* 203BC), Roman general, nicknamed ' the Delayer ' because he avoided pitched battles with Hannibal, and thus paved the way for Scipio's victories. See FABIAN SOCIETY

Fabre, JEAN HENRI, *fä'br* (1823–1915), French student of insects, *b* Sainte-Leone, Aveyron ; at first extremely poor ; became a schoolmaster. Fabre devoted almost all his long life to observing insects, notably wasps and bees, and wrote about them in a way that reveals his sense of the dramatic and his astonishingly careful observation. His motto was : *See for yourself.*

factors, in mathematics, the factors (or measures) of a number are numbers that will divide into it exactly, e.g. the individual factors of 12 are 1, 2, 3, 4, 6, and 12 ; for $3 \times 4 = 2 \times 6 = 1 \times 12 = 12$. A number with factors is a *multiple* of its factors ; *prime numbers* (or *primes*) are numbers with no factors except themselves and 1. The following are prime numbers : 3, 7, 11, 13, 17, 19, 23, 29, 31, 37, 41, 43, 47, 53, 59, 61, 67, 71, 73, 79, 83, 89, 97, 101, 103, 107, 109, 113, 127, 131, 137, 139, 149, 151, 157, 163, 167, 173, 179, 181, 191, 193, 197, 199. The highest known prime number is 2,305,843,009,213,693,951.

The *highest common factor* (HCF) of two or more numbers is the greatest number that divides each exactly, e.g. the HCF of 105, 135, 180 is 15, sometimes called greatest common measure (GCM), or greatest common factor (GCF) ; the least (or lowest) common multiple (LCM) of two or more numbers is the smallest number exactly divisible by each of the numbers, e.g. 48 is a common multiple of 6 and 8, but 24 is the *least* common multiple.

Useful algebraic factors include :
1. $a^2 + ab = a(a+b)$
2. $(a+b)^2 = a^2 + 2ab + b^2$
3. $(a-b)^2 = a^2 - 2ab + b^2$
4. $a^2 - b^2 = (a+b)(a-b)$
5. $a^3 + b^3 = (a+b)(a^2 - ab + b^2)$
6. $a^3 - b^3 = (a-b)(a^2 + ab + b^2)$
7. $(a+b)^3 = a^3 + 3a^2b + 3ab^2 + b^3$
8. $(a-b)^3 = a^3 - 3a^2b + 3ab^2 - b^3$
9. $a^3 + b^3 + c^3 - 3abc = (a+b+c)$ $(a^2 + b^2 + c^2 - ab - bc - ca)$
10. $(a+b+c)^2 = a^2 + b^2 + c^2 + 2bc + 2ca + ab$

11. $a^4 + a^2b^2 + b^4 = (a^2 + ab + b^2)$ $(a^2 - ab + b^2)$
12. $a^2(b-c) + b^2(c-a) + c^2(a-b) = -(a-b)(b-c)(c-a)$
13. $bc(b-c) + ca(c-a) + ab(a-b) = -(a-b)(b-c)(c-a)$
14. $a(b^2 - c^2) + b(c^2 - a^2) + c(a^2 - b^2) = (a-b)(b-c)(c-a)$

It is useful to have proof of (2) above ; this may be shown by the diagram :

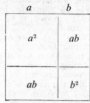

$(a+b)^2$ must equal the sum of the large square (a^2) + the sum of the two rectangles (the area of one being *ab*, hence the area of both is 2*ab*) + the area of the small square, each side of which is *b*, and its area, therefore, b^2. By somewhat similar reasoning we may prove (3) above. See HCF ; MATHEMATICS ; PERMUTATIONS ; REMAINDER THEOREM

Factory Acts, Acts passed to remedy the worst evils created by the rapid growth of the factory system in the 18th and early 19th cs. The first attempt to improve conditions was made by Manchester magistrates who, 1784, forbade pauper children to be employed more than 10 hours a day. The 1819 Act forbade the employment of children under 9 ; later Acts applied only to cotton mills, and were easily evaded ; but by appointing responsible inspectors the 1833 Act did much to limit the hours of work for young people in textile mills. Other important Factory Acts were those of 1840, 1844 (including the fencing of dangerous machinery) ; the Coal and Iron Mines Act, 1850, further regulating labour ; the 1867, 1874 and 1879 Acts ; the 1891 Act, prohibiting the employment of children under 11, raised to 14 in 1920 ; and the 1937 Act, dealing in great detail with labour and hygienic conditions, safety, etc. See SHAFTESBURY, LORD

Faeroes, THE, *fār'ōs* (' sheep islands '), group of Danish islands *c.*200m NW. of the Shetlands. Altogether there are 21 islands, 17 of which are inhabited. Chief industries are sheep farming and fishing. Now linked by air with Denmark and Britain.

fagging, in English public schools, system of allowing older boys and girls (usually 6th form) to order younger boys and girls to do certain duties, e.g. tidying studies and running errands.

Fahrenheit, see THERMOMETER

Fairfax, LORD THOMAS (1612–71), chivalrous and cultured soldier, *b* Denton, Yorkshire ; opposed Charles I ; took a prominent part in the battle of Marston Moor ; became Commander-in-Chief of Cromwell's New Model Army, which he led to victory at Naseby. He refused to sit as one of the king's judges, and helped Charles II to secure the throne 1660.

Fair Isle, one of the islands of the Shetland group ; well known for knitted garments bearing its name.

Faisal I (Faisal al Hussein), *fī'sal* (1883–1933), King of Iraq ; distinguished Arab leader 1914–18 ; installed by the British as king 1921 ; proved to be a diplomatic administrator.

Faisal II (1935–   ), King of Iraq ; came to the throne 1939 when not quite 4, a regent (the Amir Abdul Illah) acting for him during his minority.

Faiyûm, *fī-yoom'*, fertile province of Upper Egypt ; also the name of a town there.

fakir, *fä-kēr'*, religious beggar, chiefly in India ; usually a Mohammedan. Often a fanatic, he may be regarded with veneration for his penances and self-mutilations, e.g. lying on a bed of nails.

Falaise, *fä-lāz'*, town 20m from Caen, France ; birthplace of William the Conqueror.

Falange, THE, Fascist counter-revolutionary political movement in Spain from 1936, i.e. the beginning of the Spanish Civil War. The Falangist Dictatorship has General Franco at its head, and was set up 1942.

Falcon, see HAWK

Falkirk, *föl'kŭrk*, town, Stirlingshire ; ironworks centre ; scene 1298 of Edward I's victory over Wallace, and of the Young Pretender's victory 1746 ; pop.38,500.

Falkland Islands, *fölk'land*, group of *c*.100 islands in the S. Atlantic, noted for sheep ; discovered 1592 ; British since 1771 ; chief town Stanley. Hereabouts (1914) British ships defeated 5 German cruisers.

Fall River, city, Massachusetts, USA ; noted for cotton manufacture ; pop. 115,000.

Falmouth, *fal'mŭth*, port, Cornwall ; has an exceptionally fine harbour ; exports include copper, china clay and granite.

Falstaff, see OLDCASTLE, SIR JOHN

Family Allowance Act, Act which came into operation in Britain 6 Aug 1946, and provided for weekly payments at Post Offices at the rate of 5s for each child after the first.

Fanning Island, British island of the Gilbert and Ellice group. It is a Pacific cable station.

fantasia, *fan-tä'ziä*, in music, a less formal composition, e.g. the fantasias by J. S. Bach.

FAO, short for Food and Agriculture Organisation, a section of UNO. Its

duties are to build up reserves of essential foods, and to arrange world-control of foodstuffs. It was founded 1945. See UNO

farad, unit of electrical capacity. A capacity of 1 farad requires 1 coulomb of electricity to raise its potential 1 volt ; the microfarad is one-millionth of a farad. See ELECTRICITY

Faraday, MICHAEL (1791–1867), scientist, founder of the vast modern industry of electrical engineering, born in London, though of Yorkshire parents ; apprenticed to a bookseller ; but became laboratory assistant at the Royal Institution to Sir Humphry Davy. Faraday, who was deeply religious, became an exceedingly popular lecturer. He experimented for 40 years, and though responsible for highly important discoveries in chemistry (e.g. the liquefaction of gases ; manufacture of glass ; the examination of metallic alloys ; vaporisation of mercury, etc.), is most famous for his pioneer work in electricity. Faraday made his first electric battery 1812. He experimented 1821 with electromagnetism, and 1831 discovered the induction of electric currents. A month or two later he constructed the first dynamo, thus laying the foundations of modern electric light and power. He studied electrochemical decomposition, magnetism and electrolysis.

Faraday's discovery of induction was a momentous one. Again and again he failed to produce an induced current of electricity in an unelectrified wire when current was passing through another wire close by. Eventually he found that as a primary current ceases to flow, an induced current will pass through a second conductor in the *reverse* direction. After this, 10 days of continuous experiment led him to build securely the foundations of modern electrical engineering. He found how to generate current mechanically, and by making the first dynamo paved the way to making electricity a prime mover. Of his many books *The Chemical History of a Candle* is perhaps the best known. See ELECTRICITY

Far East, see MIDDLE EAST

farina, *fä-rē'nä*, starchy preparation, usually maize meal in N. America ; a flour derived from cassava in S. America. Potato starch (used for sizing cotton) is also called farina.

Farjeon, HERBERT, *fär'jŭn* (1887–1946), author, dramatic critic, theatrical manager, *b* London. His sister, Eleanor, has written delightfully fanciful books.

farming, see AGRICULTURE

Farne Isles, 17 islands 2m off the coast of Northumberland ; linked with the story of Grace Darling. Great numbers of seabirds breed there.

Farnese, *fär-nā'sä*, name of a wealthy and famous Italian family whose illustrious members included Alessandro (Pope Paul III), who *d* 1549. The family became extinct 1731, but the Farnese palace (Rome) and works of art remain.

Farnham, town, Surrey ; birthplace of William Cobbett ; pop.24,000.

Farnol, JEFFERY (1878–   ), popular British novelist ; lived for a time in America ; won fame with his delightful book *The Broad Highway*, an exciting romance ; has since published many novels (most of them with some historical background), e.g. *The Amateur Gentleman* ; *Black Bartlemy's Treasure* ; *The Lonely Road ; Heritage Perilous.*

Farnworth, cotton-spinning town, Lancashire ; also has coal mines and ironworks ; pop.29,000.

Farouk, *fa-rook'* (1920–   ), King of Egypt, *b* Cairo, only son of King Fuad ; succeeded 1936.

farthingale, hooped frame supporting a wide skirt, a fashion introduced into Elizabethan England from Spain. A modification was popular in Queen Anne's day, and also (as the crinoline) in George IV's.

Fascism, *fass'-izm*, international political movement, anti-communist and anti-democratic. Fascism began in Italy after World War I under the leadership of Benito Mussolini. Italy was in a state of political chaos and there were threats of socialist revolution or of a complete breakdown of law and order. Mussolini promised to prevent either of these developments by placing the services of his private army of Black-shirts (so called because they wore black shirts ; mostly unemployed and discontented ex-soldiers) at the disposal of all who feared socialism and anarchy. In 1922 200,000 Blackshirts marched on Rome. The incompetent Parliamentary Government collapsed ; Mussolini became Premier, and later Dictator, with the title of Duce (*doo'chay*) or Leader.

The new Fascist Government brought industry and many departments of life under control of the State. Political opposition was suppressed by Black-shirt violence where expedient. Later it became necessary for Mussolini to maintain his popularity in Italy by trying to conquer territories for Italy abroad. In 1935 he went to war with Abyssinia. This involved a breach with the League of Nations, and Mussolini joined hands with Hitler, Nazi Dictator of Germany, who was already defying the League in an effort to regain for Germany what she had lost after World War I. In 1934 Germany and Italy had nearly come to blows over Austria (see DOLLFUSS) ; but in 1936 they both sent help to Franco, which enabled him eventually to establish Fascism in Spain. Fascism still prevails in Spain and in several South American countries. In Italy it was overthrown when Italy was defeated by the Allies in World War II.

During World War II the USSR appealed to communists and democrats throughout the world to sink their differences for the time being and unite in a common war against ' World Fascism,' and Russian propaganda spoke of Nazism as if it were a kind of Fascism.

Nazism and Fascism have much in common. One of the differences between them was that Fascism arose in countries where the Roman Church had political power, and when Fascist parties came to power they shared it with the Church ; whereas in Germany and Austria the Nazis came into conflict with the Church, then did all they could to deprive it of power, and persecuted it when it resisted. Another difference was that Nazis were much more violent against Jews than the Fascists were.

Fascism and Nazism resemble Communism in that they are *totalitarian*, i.e. hold that the interests of individuals must be entirely subordinated to the interests of the State (which means in practice those who hold office under the Fascist, Nazi, or Communist Dictator, as the case may be) and have no sympathy with the (British and American) democratic belief that it is better in the long run to secure agreement in political disputes by making concessions on both sides. But Communism differs from Fascism and Nazism in that it destroys the power and confiscates the wealth of the capitalists, whereas Fascism and Nazism allow the capitalists to keep much of their wealth as long as they do not interfere with the party in politics.

Led by Sir Oswald Mosley, a Black-shirt or Fascist movement existed in Britain before 1939. It used organised violence against political opponents. During World War II the British Union of Fascists was suppressed in order to prevent it from giving help to Hitler and Mussolini ; but since the war it has been active again, especially in London, and in certain conditions it might become a menace to the survival of democracy in Britain.

The name Fascist comes from the Latin *fasces*, i.e. a bundle of reeds and an axe borne before the chief magistrates in ancient Rome as a symbol of authority (the axe), and of strength in unity (the bundle of reeds), and hence applied to *groups* of people. See HITLER, ADOLF ; MUSSOLINI, BENITO ; NAZISM ; POLITICS

Fates, in old Greek tales, three sisters : Clotho, who held a distaff on which was spun the thread of human life ; Lachesis, who spun good and evil into it ; and Atropos, who sat waiting to cut the thread.

Father of Learning, see ARISTOTLE

fathom, measure of length or depth = 6ft approx. ; more exactly 6·08ft, i.e. 0·01 of a cable or 0·001 of a nautical mile ; 1·8288 metres.

fats and oils, esters of glycerol. All are mixtures of several molecules and comprise carbon, hydrogen and oxygen. They occur in plants as vegetable fats and oils, e.g. cotton seeds, sunflower, linseed, palm and olive oil ; and also in animal tissues (adipose tissue), such stores of food containing stearin, palmitin and olein, all found in beef suet, fish livers, butter, margarine and lard. Waxes are esters of alcohols other than glycerin. Fixed oils and fats are used as food and medicines, in soap-making, and as lubricants. See PETROLEUM

fatty acids, group of chemical compounds, namely organic acids with the general formula $C_nH_{2n+1}COOH$; found in living things as free acids, and, more frequently, as gylcerides (esters of glycerol) in fats and oils.

faun, see SATYR

Faust, *fowst,* seems to have been a German scholar of the 16th c. but legends quickly sprang up about him, and by 1587 it was said that he had sold himself to a devil (Mephistopheles) for 24 years, and that after performing amazing feats by means of magic, he died in great terror. This story forms the basis of Christopher Marlowe's *Dr Faustus,* 1604, and (with important alterations) that of Goethe's verse-drama and Gounod's opera. See DRAMA ; GOETHE, J. W. VON ; GOUNOD, F. C.

Faversham, town, Kent ; noted for oyster fisheries.

Fawcett, HENRY (1833–84), politician and economist, *b* Salisbury ; blind at 24, but entered Parliament, becoming known as 'the Member for India.' As Postmaster-General he introduced several postal reforms.

Fawkes, GUY (1570–1606), conspirator, *b* Yorkshire. An ardent RC, Fawkes hoped that when James I came to the throne 1603 much would be done to further the RC cause. Bitterly disappointed, he planned to destroy the Protestant government with the aid of Christopher and John Wright (whom he had known at school), Thomas Winter, Sir Everard Digby (*b* 1578), a wealthy man who supplied the conspirators with funds, Robert Catesby, who became the actual leader of the plotters, Francis Tresham, and others.

Hiring a house close to the Parliament building (London), they tunnelled into the cellars, stored gunpowder there, and prepared to blow up Parliament 5 Nov 1605. Fawkes, on guard on the night of 4 Nov., was ready to fire the train of gunpowder. But Tresham warned his friend, Lord Monteagle, who was in Parliament, not to attend the opening ceremony. Becoming suspicious, Monteagle had the cellars searched. Fawkes was discovered, and after being tortured was put to death 1606. Of the other conspirators, some were executed, others shot in Staffordshire while trying to escape, and a few fled from the country.

Fayum, province of Upper Egypt.

Fe, chemical symbol for iron, from Latin *ferrum.*

Federals, see AMERICAN CIVIL WAR

Federated Malay States, see MALAYA

Felixstowe, *fe'lik-stō,* coastal holiday town, Suffolk.

fellah, *fel'ä* (plural *fellahin*), Arabic word for a peasant or ploughman, especially in Egypt, where the fellahin, descended from the ancient Egyptians, live mostly in mud hovels, and have customs and agricultural methods (e.g. the water-wheel, *sakiya,* and balanced bucket, *shaduf*) of high antiquity.

felony, word used by English lawyers for serious crime or wrong-doing.

felspar, group of opaque crystalline minerals, silicates of alumina with variable amounts of potassium, sodium, or calcium. They occur widely in nature, and form the chief constituents of granite and other primary rocks.

felt, cloth made of wool, hair, or fur by damping, rolling and pressing. Wool is the most suitable material, but hat felts include rabbit, hare and beaver fur. Roofing felt contains cow hair.

felucca, *fe-loo-kä,* vessel of the E. Mediterranean and the Nile ; has lateen sails and oars.

femur or **thigh bone,** *fe'mer,* longest bone in the human body. It is between the pelvis or hip-joint and knee-joint. See SKELETON

fencing, art of using for recreation a foil or other light weapon.

Fenian Movement, *fe'nian,* Irish organisation begun *c.*1847 by O'Mahoney and developed by James Stephens in a terrorist attempt to overthrow the British Government and create an Irish republic. It grew out of the discontent that sprang up among the Irish during the famines of 1840, which compelled thousands of Irish to emigrate to USA, and was responsible for assassinations, insurrections (e.g. that in Canada 1866), and the blowing up of Clerkenwell prison 1867. The name is derived from Feine, legendary Irish warriors.

Fenn, GEORGE MANVILLE (1831–1909), novelist and writer of boys' stories, *b* London ; wrote 200 books, including *Nat the Naturalist.*

fennel, plant (family *Umbelliferae*) with tall and almost solid stem ; leaves (used in cooking) fern-like, and small yellow flowers.

Fens, marshy but fertile district (70m long and 35 wide) in the neighbourhood of the Wash, England. Francis, Earl of Bedford, attempted to drain the area known as Bedford Level 1634, but it was not till 1807 that this was successfully accomplished. Grain, flax and potatoes are widely cultivated, and the region is noted for wild fowl.

Fenton, part of Stoke-on-Trent, Staffordshire ; noted for earthenware.

Ferdinand V (1452–1516), King of Spain ; married (1469) Isabella, sister of Henry IV of Castile, and by conquering Granada eventually became sole ruler of the peninsula outside Portugal. With the discovery of America by Columbus

1492, Spain grew rich and powerful. Ferdinand was acknowledged to be the craftiest king of his day, except Henry VI of England, with whom he was frequently allied. He was the father of Catherine of Aragon.

Fermanagh, *fĕr-man'ä,* county of N. Ireland ; chief town Eniskillen.

fermentation, slow decomposition of organic substances induced by micro-organisms or enzymes (organic nitrogenous substances) of animal or vegetable origin. Alcoholic fermentation of sugar, producing spirit, is caused by yeast ferment, i.e. the growth of minute oval cells, the most favourable temperature being 25–30°C. The action, exceedingly complicated, is the result produced by zymase on sugar. Fermentation is used not only for wines and spirits, but also for motor fuel. Lactic fermentation is caused by the *lactic bacilli.* Fermentation by bacteria includes cellulose fermentation, yielding acetic and butyric acids ; also oxidizing bacteria. Fermentation by moulds includes those resulting from *penicillium.* See PENICILLIN

Fermi, PROFESSOR ENRICO (1901–), Italian physicist ; chose to leave Fascist Italy ; became a naturalised American ; experimented with ' heavy water,' and discovered that by causing slow neutrons to bombard the uranium isotope, vast energy is released, a principle employed in the atom-bomb of 1945.

fern, most highly developed of the flowerless plants (*Cryptogamia*), including those with woody trunks, e.g. tree-ferns and horsetails. True ferns have leaves on the back of which are reddish-brown patches containing thousands of minute capsules (spores or sporangia), each with *c.*64 spores. These grow, not into a fern, but into a small, heart-shaped green scale, below which are the sex organs, the fertilising of which produces a new plant in every respect like the original. Hart's-tongue, maidenhair, common polypody, lady fern and royal fern are well-known varieties.

Fernandez, JUAN, *fer-nän'däth* (*d* 1602), Spanish sailor, *b* Cartagena ; spent his life as a pilot on the Pacific coast of S. America, and discovered the island now bearing his name.

Fernando Póo, *fer-nän'dō pō-ō,* island of Spanish Guinea, 20m from the west coast of Africa ; area 800sq.m ; pop. 34,000 ; exports cocoa.

Ferrara, decaying city, Italy, on the delta of the R. Po ; was the birthplace of Savonarola ; pop.120,000.

ferret, partly domesticated variety of the polecat ; thought to have originated in Africa (though now unknown there). Much used for catching rabbits, it is *c.*14in long, is pale yellow, and has red eyes.

ferric oxide, see IRON AND STEEL

Ferrol, fortified port, Spain ; manufactures linen and cotton ; has a large export trade ; pop.64,000.

ferromagnetic, see MAGNETISM

fertilisers, see MANURES AND FERTILISERS

Festival of Britain, series of local displays and activities (1951) celebrating the centenary of the Great Exhibition, the chief centre being the South Bank Exhibition, London, with its Royal Festival Hall, Dome of Discovery (365ft across), and other attractions.

Festus, PORCIUS (*d* AD62), Roman administrator of Judaea ; heard (in the presence of Herod Agrippa II) St Paul's case, and sent him for trial in Rome (Acts 24–25).

Fettes, SIR WILLIAM (1750–1836), wine and tea merchant, *b* Edinburgh ; left £166,000 to found Fettes College, opened 1870.

Feuchtwanger, LION, *foicht'väng-ĕr* (1884–), German author, *b* Munich ; won success as a dramatist ; famous for his novels, e.g. *The Ugly Duchess* ; *Success* ; and *Josephus* ; but most of all for his *Jew Süss* (1924), a dramatic study of 18th c. Germany.

feudalism, *fū'dal-izm* (late Latin *feudum,* property), social and political system of western Europe which gradually took shape after the fall of Rome, and was widely established between the 9th and the 14th or 15th c. The system was based on the tenure (the holding in *feud*) of land. The king, in theory, was the sole owner, but granted estates to his subjects, e.g. nobles (as tenants-in-chief, etc.) in return for their sworn allegiance (homage) to him, and their promise to render military or adminis-

THE HART'S TONGUE FERN

trative service. In the same way the tenant-in-chief granted land to his mesne lords, they to their vassals, and so down to the serf, a peasant bound to the soil.

Except the king, every holder of land was vassal to an overlord, and was ' his man,' his overlord promising to be ' true lord and protector.'

On the Continent it was more or less understood that the vassal owed loyalty to his immediate overlord only, and thus the overlord might summon his vassals to support him in a rebellion against the king ; but in England the Saxon feudalism, completed by William I, who maintained a strong central government, encouraged the customary belief that loyalty to the king came first. For all that, feudalism gave the overlords (especially among the thegns) great powers, e.g. they ruled the local court of justice.

Feudalism, an extremely complicated system, may be reduced to its lowest terms and shown diagramatically thus :

KING
|
TENANTS IN CHIEF
(Earls, Bishops, Towns, Abbots, Barons)
|
LESSER TENANTS
(holding directly from above)

Its beneficial effects were that it made the holding of land dependent on service ; assured regular and systematic cultivation of the soil, essential for a land then more or less self-supporting ; gave everyone except the serf a definite status in the community superior, say, to the ' wage-slaves ' of the later Industrial Revolution ; was a means of raising armed forces in case of need.

This system was not a good one because society was static, i.e. there was little room for experiment or progress— each had to keep his place in his own class or sphere, hence the theory ' The rich man in his castle, the poor man at his gate ' ; and it was wholly unfitted for municipal development, so that it was impossible to fit the towns into it, the system being designed for an agricultural community only. See MAGNA CARTA ; VILLEIN

Fez, walled city, Morocco ; once one of the two capitals ; on the R. Sebu ; has long been sacred to Mohammedans, and still has beautiful mosques, and the sultan's palace. There is much trade brought by desert caravans, but this is rapidly declining ; pop.144,000.

FFI, see GAULLE, GENERAL DE

Fibreglass, *fī'bēr-*, trade name for a fine flexible glass used for textiles, and also as a sound or heat insulating felt. See GLASS

fibula, see SKELETON

Fichte, JOHANN GOTTLIEB, *fich'te* (1762– 1814), German thinker ; visited Em-

manuel Kant ; wrote on philosophy, notably *On the Notion of the Theory of Science* ; profoundly influenced Schopenhauer ; was a violent German nationalist and at the same time intensely self-centred. Some of his teachings influenced the theory of Nazism in the 20th c.

fiction, see BOOKS

Fid. Def., see MONEY

FIDO, originally short for Fog Investigation Dispersal Operation, later known as short for Fog, Intensive Dispersal of, a name now recognised as descriptive of a method of dispersing fog at an airfield or airport to enable planes to take off or land safely. Experiments began 1942 when, in World War II, it was imperative that bombing Germany should continue even in foggy weather. FIDO was used for emergency landings from 1943, and contributed towards the destruction of Rundstedt's forces in Belgium 1944. The method was to lay pipes along the runways and burn vapourised petroleum—80,000 gallons per hour—thus creating sufficient heat to disperse fog over a wide area.

Field, EUGENE (1850–95), American poet and journalist, *b* St Louis, Missouri ; notable for his charming verses for children.

fieldfare, bird akin to the thrush ; visits Britain in large flocks in winter. It is *c.*10in long, has a chestnut back, ash-coloured head, and black tail. It feeds on grubs, snails and berries.

Fielding, HENRY (1707–54), author, born near Glastonbury ; educated at Eton and Leyden. Amused at Samuel Richardson's novel *Pamela*, he wrote *Joseph Andrews* (1742), primarily intended as a parody of *Pamela* ; *Jonathan Wild* ; *Amelia*; and the immortal *Tom Jones*, one of the greatest novels ever written, and among the first in English literature ; the plot, a masterpiece, the characters (e.g. Squire Western, Sophia and Blifil the hypocrite), vividly alive. Fielding is known as ' the father of the English novel.'

field-marshal, see MARSHAL

field mouse, see VOLE

Field of the Cloth of Gold, name for the meeting-place near Calais between Henry VIII of England and Francis I of France, June 1520, so called from the magnificence displayed.

field scabious, *-skā'bi-ŭs*, hairy plant (family *Dipsacaceae*) ; leaves feather-like at each side of the stalk ; lilac florets in a compact head ; blooms summer and autumn.

fiery cross, charred sticks dipped in goats' blood, and formerly carried from township to township in the Scottish highlands to summon clansmen to fight, especially in the Jacobite rising (1745). The custom is described in Scott's *Lady of the Lake*, canto 3.

Fife, county of Scotland between the firths of Forth and Tay ; richly agricultural ;

has coal mines ; co.tn Cupar ; called the 'Kingdom of Fife,' probably because it was until recently extremely self-contained.

'**Fifteen,**' THE, see JAMES EDWARD

fifth columnist, originally a sympathiser with General Franco in Madrid during the Spanish Civil War (1936), described as such by General Mola when leading four columns of troops against the city ; now a name for one who commits acts of sabotage or works against his country.

fig, Mediterranean tree (though found elsewhere) producing a valuable fruit, particularly in Turkey. Usually *c.*15ft high, it has deeply lobed leaves, downy beneath. The fig is curiously pollinated by one species of wasp only, the grubs of which carry pollen from the male to the female flowers. The tree may produce two crops a year.

THE FIG

'**Figaro, The Marriage of,**' see BEAUMARCHAIS, P.

'**Fighting Téméraire,**' see TURNER, J. M. W.

Figl, DR, see AUSTRIA

figures of speech, or figures of rhetoric, include :

ALLITERATION : repetition of a letter or sound at the beginning of two or more words close together, e.g. *Ru*in seize thee, *ru*thless king (Gray).

ANTITHESIS (placing against), emphasizing one thought by contrast with the next, e.g. *Beauty* for *ashes*, the *oil of joy* for *mourning* (Isaiah).

ASSONANCE, using similar vowel sounds, e.g. The w*oe*s of h*o*peless lovers (Dryden).

EPIGRAM, meaning formerly an inscription only ; now any brief and pointed saying in prose or verse, e.g. *The child is father of the man* (Wordsworth) ; *To scorn delights and live laborious days* (Milton) ; masters of the epigram include Catullus, Martial, Tacitus, Pope, Gray.

EUPHEMISM, saying something less severely than might be expected, e.g. Light-fingered gentry (Thackeray) for *pickpockets* ; not to be confused with *euphuism*, an affected style of writing named after the book *Euphues* (1579) by John Lyly.

IRONY (dissimulation), writing or saying what you do not mean, knowing you will not be taken literally, e.g. ' Clever fellow ! ' addressed to someone who has just made an ass of himself.

METAPHOR and SIMILE (*sim'i-li*), comparisons ; the simile is an acknowledged comparison introduced by *like*, *as*, or *so* (e.g. My heart is *like* a singing bird) ; a metaphor is a compressed simile without *like*, *as*, or *so* (e.g. He is the *black sheep* of the family). Avoid the mixed metaphor where ideas are unsuitably related, e.g. Looking back over the *sea* of life, we observe the years as *milestones*. . . .

METONYMY (*mē-ton'i-mi*) (change of name), using one word to suggest another or others, e.g. *Whitehall* for *the Government.*

ONOMATOPOEIA (*on-ō-mat-ō-pē'iä*) (making the sound echo the sense), a means of suggesting ideas by sounds, e.g. the *crashing* waves ; the *booming* guns ; Orion flying *fast* from *hissing snake* (Spenser).

PERSONIFICATION : giving human qualities to an abstract or inanimate thing, e.g. The *sleepless* pillow ; the *melancholy* trees.

Fiji, *fē'jē,* group of *c.*320 British islands in the S Pacific, *c.*1,100m north of NZ. They are mainly volcanic, and are notable for their pleasant climate and rich vegetation. Exports include sugar, gold and copra ; the capital is Suva on Viti Levu ; total area *c.*7,000sq.m ; total pop.260,000.

films, motion-pictures with sound accompaniment, now the world's most popular entertainment.

The first step in making a film is to write a scenario (the story arranged in scenes). Some scenes may be ' shot ' out of doors ; more frequently they are built up from scale models, with carefully planned lighting effects, and the employment of suitable actors and actresses, the most popular of whom (film-stars) may often be of greater attraction than the story.

Films may be based on short stories, novels, historical foundations (as *King Henry the Fifth* or *Gone with the Wind*) or on scripts specially written for filming. In any case, the producer and director are largely the creators and inspiration of the film. For many years USA (particularly Hollywood) was supreme in the film world, but British film companies have in recent years taken up the challenge, and there are now immense studios in the South of England, notably Denham, Inverheath, Elstree and Shepherd's Bush, London. *Camera work*, an essential part of all film production, is more an art than is sometimes imagined. Much depends on the angle of the shot ; much also as to whether it is a close-up, whether one scene breaks off abruptly or gradually dissolves, and so on. Equally important is *editing*, i.e. arranging the various shots (and there may be many hundreds) in correct sequences so as to build up a continuous and progressive story. Shots need not be taken in the order in which they are projected on the screen, and may have to be arranged, and also ' cut,' i.e. reduced, by an expert. Modern films are usually *c.*8,000ft long ; each picture is *c.*1in × ¾in.

Projection is achieved by throwing on a screen a series of pictures (24 per sec.) so quickly that the eye cannot see the change from one to another, hence the impression of movement. Projectors consist essentially of a powerful arc-lamp of, say, from 25–75 amps ; a focussing lens ; a revolving shutter, usually in the form of a Maltese cross, which, actuated by a sprocket, cuts off the beam of light while one picture is taking the place of the next.

In *sound films* the sound-track runs parallel to the series of pictures, and is *c.*⅛in wide. Sound waves created during the acting of the film are picked up by the microphone, and converted into electric impulses that cause a neon-tube to glow more or less brightly, its light being focussed as a minute spot on the edge of the photographic film. When developed the sound-track appears as a permanent record. Conversely, as the film passes through the projector, greater or lesser amounts of light are directed via the sound-track to a photo-electric cell which causes pulsating current to flow to a low-frequency amplifier and loud-speaker, where the impulses are changed back into sounds. Though largely automatic, these complex machines require skilled operators during running time.

The modern cinema owes its entertainment and instruction to many pioneers, now almost forgotten, among whom may be mentioned Edward Muybridge of Kingston-on-Thames, who as early as 1872 photographically analysed the movements of a running horse ; but the true ' father ' of the film was undoubtedly William Friese-Greene (*d* 1921), an Englishman who in 1890 took ' motion pictures ' of traffic near Hyde Park Corner, London. George Eastman (of USA) began manufacturing a nitro-cellulose film 1889, an immense step forward ; and inventors who improved the cinema-camera include Thomas Alva Edison and also Robert Paul, who (1896) succeeded in projecting moving pictures on a screen, his ' hero ' being a London bootblack. French and German inventors quickly perfected both camera and projector. The USA was the first country to become ' film conscious,' and the Pacific coast with its dry atmosphere and bright sunlight proved ideal for the production of films. Cinemas devoted more or less exclusively to film-shows date from *c.*1914. British film exhibitors were compelled 1927 by Act of Parliament to include at any rate *some* British films at every show—a great encouragement to Gaumont-British and Gainsborough Films.

So-called ' talkies ' or sound films became popular 1929 ; colour films (notably technicolour), passed the experimental stage 1932. The National Repository of Films, to preserve notable films for future generations, was founded 1934. Stereoscopic films were a novelty in 1945. The technicolour sound cartoon was raised to new heights by the creative genius of Walt Disney, whose *Snow White and the Seven Dwarfs* made film history 1938.

The film industry has created hundreds of new occupations, from ' stars ' and producers to scenario-writers, musicians with a knowledge of the technique required, cinema managers, projectionists, technicians of all kinds. Apart from cinemas, of which there are now *c.*5,000 in Britain and *c.*17,000 in USA, churches, clubs and schools are making increasing use of films. Arthur Rank's Junior Clubs interest young people in social life and natural history.

Sound films in colour are now being increasingly used in schools and colleges. They are a great aid in teaching almost all subjects, e.g. English, mathematics, history, science, languages ; and the Ministry of Education's Production Committee has bold and comprehensive plans for the future.

Microfilms of books may now be used by patients unable to turn the pages of an ordinary book. An enlargement of each page is thrown on the ceiling, and a page ' turned ' by pressing a button.

filtration, the separation of undissolved solids from liquids by filtering, e.g. in the laboratory passing through a filter-paper. The clear liquid obtained is the filtrate.

finch, large family of small birds found in temperate zones except Australia ; notable for hard, conical beaks, 9 primary wing feathers, 12 tail feathers ; mainly seed-eaters ; usually seen in flocks.

British finches include HAWFINCH, handsome bird 7in long ; brown back, pinkish breast, yellow-brown head, large blue beak ; GREENFINCH (or green linnet), 6in long ; common song bird, greenish above, yellow below ; nests in hedges, lays 4–6 bluish-white eggs with purplish spots at the larger end ; GOLD-FINCH, 5in long, handsome plumage marked black, white and yellow ; nests in trees ; lays 4–5 eggs (May) bluish-white, speckled at the larger end ; feeds much on thistles ; BULLFINCH, black and grey, the male has a red breast ; lays 5 bluish-white eggs spotted with orange

DIAMONDS

plate 33

The Premier Diamond Mine, Pretoria, Transvaal. It was here that the Koh-i-Noor, the world's largest diamond, was found. (*South African Railways and Harbours*)

plate 34   **GOLD**

Miners leaving the elevator on a Rand gold mine.   (*South African Railways and Harbours*)

OIL   plate 35

Oil derricks along the beach on the coast of California. (*U.S. Information Service*)

plate 36   ALUMINIUM

Top : Aluminium is obtained from bauxite, here being sorted from the earth on top of a mountain in the Gold Coast. (*C.O.I.*). *Bottom :* A worker in Ontario piling aluminium ingots for shipment. (*Canadian National Film Board*)

THE LINNET

or brown ; LINNET, 5½in long, frequents
waste land ; brownish, the male has
a crimson forehead and chest. Nests
.of twigs and wool are generally built in
low bushes. The bluish-grey eggs are
much speckled. See also CHAFFINCH
Fingal's Cave, basaltic formation on the
island of Staffa. See BASALT
finger-prints, impressions used as a means
of identifying persons, no finger-prints
being in all respects alike. The system
was advanced by Sir Francis Galton
1890, and as the print of the thumb and
fingers remains unchanged through life,
the police keep finger-print records of all
criminals at New Scotland Yard, where
the Henry method (devised by Sir
Edward Henry) of grouping them is used.
Finisterre, CAPE, *fin-is-tār'*, extreme west
point of NW. Spain.
Finland, republic (since 1917) between
Sweden and Russia. After ceding to
USSR (1940) *c.*16,000sq.m, the area is
now *c.*130,000sq.m ; pop.4,055,000. The
country is supremely rich in forests,
which makes lumbering, paper and
cellulose manufacturing its most important industries ; crops include rye,
barley, oats, wheat and potatoes. There
are immense herds of reindeer. Exports
include timber and wood for paper-
making. The people are highly educated,
and are mostly Lutherans in religion.
The parliament is known as *Eduskunta.*
The capital is Helsinki (Helsingfors).
' Finlandia,' see SIBELIUS, JEAN
Finsen, NIELS RYBERG (1860–1904), Danish
scientist ; *b* Thorshaon, Faeroe Islands ;
inventor of the Finsen lamp, providing
ultra-violet rays for medical treatment.
fiord, *fi-örd,* usually a narrow but deep inlet
of the sea (often glacier-formed) with
mts. rising steeply from the water ;
particularly associated with Norway,
though this type of waterway is found
in British Columbia, Scotland and NZ.
fir, name of several species of trees, including (*a*) the SPRUCE, found in Britain,
Switzerland, Norway, etc. ; exceedingly
tall, straight and spire-like ; the cones
have papery scales hanging from the
spray ; the timber is much used for
telegraph poles, floor boards, and still
more for pulping into paper ; and (*b*) the
SILVER FIR, tall, stately, but not as regular
as the spruce ; the needle-like leaves
remain for 8 or 9 years ; the cones ' sit '
on the branches. Both trees supply
turpentine.
fire, occurs in nature as volcanic heat,
forest fires, etc., but is used by no
animal except man, in whose life it caused
important changes in prehistoric times,
enabling tribes to migrate to colder
regions. It also led to civilising effects,
e.g. cooking, baking clay for bricks,
pottery, etc., forging weapons. Fire was
early worshipped as a god. The Greeks
believed it to have been stolen from
heaven by Prometheus.
  Before the invention of matches, fire
was artificially made in various crude
ways, e.g. rotating a piece of wood in
a groove, using fire-saws, by striking
flint and steel together, thus igniting
tinder, i.e. half-burned linen and decaying
wood.
  To make a fire in the open, first collect
enough dry wood ; kindle a little paper
and a few twigs, adding more wood ;
keep the fire close together, place logs
on 3 sides, leaving the side to the wind
open. Have your back to the wind when
striking a match. In very windy weather
kindle a small fire in a tin or bucket,
transferring it later.
  Fire brigades were known in Egypt
4,000 years ago. In Britain they were
developed by fire insurance companies.
Horse-drawn fire-engines have now been
largely replaced by motor fire-engines
travelling at 40mph, and supplying up
to 600 gallons of water per min, in some
cases over 3 times this quantity. In
World War II the AFS (Auxiliary Fire
Service) did magnificent work during
German raids.
  For putting out fires the latest advance
is the use of ' wet water,' i.e. water containing an agent which causes it to
penetrate rather than bounce off when
sprayed.
fire brigades, see FIRE
fire damp, combustible gas found in coal
mines, chiefly methane.
fireworks, said to have been brought to
Europe from the Far East in the 13th c.
by returning Crusaders. In manufacture, potassium nitrate (saltpetre) and
chlorate of potash are much used, also
sulphur and charcoal. The colours are
obtained by including salts of metals,
e.g. salts of strontium for red stars, of
sodium for yellow, of copper for blue,
of barium for green. The Catherine
wheel is a paper tube of gunpowder etc.
round a circular piece of wood ; Bengal
lights (used in warfare) give a vivid and
steady flame due to excess of saltpetre ;
rockets (of cardboard) are filled with
gunpowder, together with stars, or an
explosive such as tonite. Wrecked ships
may send up rockets as signals of distress

10

and a rocket apparatus may now be found at *c*.350 places round the British Isles. Roman candles were first used in Italy ; squibs are actually small rockets ; Very-lights, much used in World War I, give brilliant illumination ; Dover flares have over 1,000,000 candle-power. In World War II planes dropped flares over the target before bombing.

First of June, GLORIOUS, naval battle fought 1 June 1794, when Lord Howe defeated the French off Brest.

fish, cold-blooded vertebrate animal living in fresh or sea water, and (with few exceptions) breathing with gills. As a rule the body is ' streamlined ' for speed, and may be considerably flattened vertically, as in the rays, or horizontally, as in the sole and turbot. The surface is covered with scales, the structure of which is sometimes akin to horn, sometimes of a bony texture. Most fish have a two-chambered heart containing venous blood. They move largely by means of the tail and the caudal fin, though other fins may be used. The skeleton may be cartilaginous, as in the sharks and rays, or bony, as in the great majority of species.

Fish breathe by taking in water by the mouth, passing it over plates supplied with blood-vessels, and out through the gills. Most fish are well supplied with teeth, and they have well developed hearing. Sight is good, except in deep-water fish, or those in underground streams, species of which are without eyes. Barbels hanging near the mouth are sensitive organs of touch. Almost all fish are darker above than below, and many have protective colouring, e.g. plaice. Fish generally produce large numbers of eggs—the herring 20,000–30,000, the cod about 8,000,000, but comparatively few young fish reach maturity.

Food fish include herring, salmon, sole, turbot, mackerel, plaice, cod, halibut and haddock. Fish valued at £20,000,000 is landed annually at British ports, and the fisheries of the UK employ *c*.60,000 people.

Fisher, HERBERT A. L. (1865–1940), *b* London ; President of the Board of Education 1916–22, introduced the Education Act 1918 ; a noted historian ; Warden of New College, Oxford, and Vice-Chancellor Sheffield University ; author of *History of Europe* (1935).

Fisher, JOHN (1459–1535), English churchman, *b* Beverley, Yorkshire ; opposed Henry VIII's divorce of Catherine of Aragon ; beheaded for refusing to acknowledge the king as head of the Church.

Fisher of Kilverstone, JOHN ARBUTHNOT, LORD (1841–1920), British sailor, *b* Rambodde, Ceylon ; First Sea Lord 1904–10 and 1914–15 ; substituted the colleges of Osborne and Dartmouth for the *Britannia* ; developed naval ordnance ; created the dreadnought ; introduced oil fuel and submarines into the British navy.

Fishguard, town, Pembrokeshire (Wales) ; port of embarkation for Ireland.

fish-plates, see RAILWAYS

fission of atoms, see RADIOACTIVITY

Fitzger'ald, EDWARD (1809–83), poet, *b* Bredfield House, near Woodbridge, Suffolk ; friend of Thackeray, Carlyle, Rossetti and Tennyson ; also of Swinburne, who brought to light Fitzgerald's greatest poem, a translation of the Persian *Rubáiyát of Omar Khayyám* (1859).

Fiume, *fē-oom'ā*, Adriatic port of Yugoslavia. The modern portion has fine buildings and streets ; industries include paper and tobacco ; pop.54,000.

Five Members, namely John Hampden, John Pym, Denzil Holles, Sir Arthur Hazlerigg and William Strode, whom Charles I tried to arrest, 1642, in the Commons, but found that ' the birds had flown.'

Five Mile Act (1665), part of the *Clarendon Code*. The act forbade ministers expelled from their livings, 1662, to reside within 5m of any corporate town unless they declared on oath that resistance to the king was unlawful.

fives, ball-game associated especially with our universities and public schools, notably Eton, Rugby and Winchester.

Five Towns, see BENNETT, A. ; STOKE-UPON-TRENT

Five-Year Plan, see STALIN, JOSEF ; USSR

flag, piece of coloured bunting hanging from a staff or halyard as a symbol. In the Middle Ages the standard was a large, long flag, often pointed, and usually adorned with heraldic devices. A banner was a large square or rectangle emblazoned with armorial ensigns to show that the bearer was entitled to lead his troops.

National flags evolved slowly. The English white flag with the cross of St George was probably introduced by Richard I.

Our national flag, the UNION JACK, comprises the banner of St George (white with a red cross) for England ; the banner of St Andrew (a white saltire or diagonal cross on a blue field) for Scotland ; the banner of St Patrick (white with a red saltire) for Ireland. The banners of England and Scotland were combined 1603, and confirmed 1707 ; and St Patrick's cross was added at the union with Ireland 1801.

The story of the STARS AND STRIPES (Star-Spangled banner or Old Glory) of USA is uncertain. It now has 6 horizontal white stripes and 7 red ones, indicating the separation of the 13 original states 1776 ; and a blue field with 48 stars (6 rows of 8), one star for each of the 48 states now comprising the Union. Whether the flag was designed by George Washington (taking the idea from the coat-of-arms of the

English family from which he was descended) is doubtful, but there seems some reason to think so.
See PLATE V

Flambard, RALPH (d 1128), chief minister of William Rufus, whom he advised in money matters. He was bishop of Durham 1099.

Flamborough Head, *flam'bŭ-rŭ*, bold chalk promontory on the Yorkshire coast.

flamingo, *flä-ming'gō*, wading bird with rosy or scarlet plumage ; black on the wings ; may stand 6ft high ; has very long, thin legs ; found in large flocks by rivers and lakes in Africa, southern Europe and America.

Flammarion, CAMILLE, *flä-mä-rē-aw*n' (1842–1925), French astronomer, noted for his observations of Mars, and as a popular writer.

Flamsteed, JOHN (1646–1719), astronomer, b Denby, Derbyshire ; appointed to the new Greenwich Observatory ; noted for his catalogue of ' fixed ' stars.

Flanders, now a district of Belgium, namely E. and W. Flanders ; scene of bitter fighting in World War I, hence the Flanders poppy for remembrance.

flannel, highly absorbent soft woollen cloth. The industry, originally centred in Wales, e.g. Welshpool, is now chiefly carried on in Lancashire (especially Rochdale) and in Yorkshire.

flares, see FIREWORKS

flash-point, the lowest temperature at which the vapour of an inflammable liquid explodes when mixed with air.

Flaubert, GUSTAVE, *flō-bār'* (1821–80), French novelist, b Rouen ; lived un-eventfully in the country was the friend of Victor Hugo, Émile Zola, Alphonse Daudet, etc., and inspired Guy de Maupassant. A master crafts-man, he was amazingly painstaking, and combined realism with romance. Among his finest novels are *Salammbô* (an epic of ancient Carthage) ; *L'Educa-tion Sentimentale,* and (most famous of all) *Madame Bovary.*

flavine, *flav'ēn* ; *flā'vēn,* antiseptic dis-covered 1916. A yellow acridine dye, $C_{13}H_{12}N_2O$, it is obtained from oak bark.

flax (*Linum usitatissimum*), plant (family Linaceae) with slender, erect stems c. 18in high, lance-shaped alternate leaves, and bluish-purple flowers c.1in across. Flax is cultivated in Ulster and York-shire, being sown about April or May and harvested August.

Flax provides several useful materials. *Linseed oil* is manufactured from the seeds by crushing ; it is much used in mixing paints, varnishes. After most of the oil has been extracted, the waste is made into *linseed cake,* a rich protein food for fattening farm stock. LINEN (Latin *linum,* flax) is a fabric manu-factured from the fibre of the stalk. One of the oldest textiles, it was used by the ancient Egyptians. It is woven to make (among other things) sheets, fine lawns, cambrics and patterned damask

tablecloths. The chief centres are N. Ireland, Scotland (notably Dunfermline) and Barnsley, Yorkshire.

A new process enables manufacturers to produce damask tablecloths and table-napkins which are immune from gravy stains. The plastic, vinyl butyral, is used.

What is called NZ flax is actually a plant of the lily family. Its long leaves (sometimes 8ft) yield a valuable fibre, known as PHORMIUM, stronger than either hemp or flax.

Flaxman, JOHN (1755–1826), English sculptor, b York ; employed by Wedge-wood as a designer 1775–87. One of the greatest classical sculptors.

F-layer, see APPLETON, SIR E.

flea, sucking insect, a parasite on both man and animals ; the species *Pulex irritans* can leap 200 times its own length.

Fleay, DAVID, see PLATYPUS

Flecker, JAMES ELROY (1884–1915), English poet, b London ; died before he reached the height of his genius for lyrical beauty; noted for *The Golden Journey to Samar-kand,* and the plays *Don Juan* and *Hassan.*

Fleet Air Arm, see AVIATION

Fleet Street, famous London thoroughfare from Ludgate Circus to Temple Bar ; named from the R. Fleet, now flowing unseen to the Thames. Today the name Fleet Street stands for journalism, for it is there that many leading newspapers and magazines are published.

Fleetwood, port at the mouth of the R. Wyre, Lancashire ; noted for trawl-fishing ; has steamer services to Belfast and Isle of Man ; is developing as a holiday resort ; pop.27,000.

Fleming, SIR ALEXANDER, British bacteri-ologist ; discovered penicillin 1929 ; shared the Nobel Prize (medicine) 1945. Sir Alexander Fleming was born in Ayr-shire 1881. He was knighted 1944. See PENICILLIN

Fleming, SIR JOHN AMBROSE (1849–1945), electrical engineer and inventor, b Lan-caster ; most famous for his researches in radio, and for his 2-electrode thermi-onic valve, the essential feature of radio.

Flemings, inhabitants of Flanders. Flem-ish immigrants to England and Wales advanced our woollen and weaving industries.

Fletcher, JOHN, see BEAUMONT AND FLETCHER

fleur-de-lys, see EMBLEMS

flight, see AVIATION

Flinders, MATTHEW (1774–1814), sailor, b Donington, Lincolnshire ; explored the S. Pacific ; proved that Tasmania is an island ; charted the Gulf of Carpen-taria, etc.

Flint or Flintshire, county of N. Wales ; noted for dairy farming. Mold is now the county town.

Flint, town, Flintshire ; formerly the co.tn. ; on the R. Dee.

flint, natural variety of impure silica, SiO_2. Compact, opaque, usually dark grey or

brown, it flakes off in shell-like fractures.
Flint, found in chalk, was much used
by prehistoric man for sharp-edged tools
and weapons, and for fire-making. In
E. Anglia many churches are built of
flints.

Flints in lighters are usually alloys of
cerium or iron.

floating debt, short-term Government
obligation (e.g. Treasury Bills) to cover
a temporary need for ready cash.

Flodden, BATTLE OF, fought between the
Scots led by James IV, and the English
under the Earl of Surrey, 1513. The Scots
were defeated, the king and many nobles
being killed. Flodden, a ridge of the
Cheviots, is *c*.3m SE. of Coldstream.
Read *Marmion*, Sir Walter Scott.

Florence, Italian city on the R. Arno and
in Tuscany ; industries include silk ; is
set in magnificent wooded country, and
has beautiful buildings. e.g. the cathedral
with Giotto's campanile (detached tower),
art galleries, schools, villas, etc. ; was
the home of Boccaccio, Dante, Galileo,
Leonardo da Vinci, Michelangelo and
Petrarch ; pop.371,000.

Flores, one of the 9 islands of the Azores.

Florida, most southerly state of USA, a
peninsula east of the Gulf of Mexico ;
abounds in lakes, rivers and marshes.
Famous for fruit-growing, it produces
also timber and tobacco ; has many
holiday resorts ; cap. Tallahassee. To
the south is a chain of islands stretching
230m and known as FLORIDA KEYS, one
of the chief, KEY WEST, being a holiday
resort and naval station linked by
electric railway (partly across viaducts)
with the mainland.

flowers, see BOTANY

'flu, see INFLUENZA

fluorescence, *floo-ō-ress'ens*, property of
various substances (e.g. paraffin oil,
quinine, sulphate solutions, chlorophyll,
etc.) of absorbing light of one hue (or
wave-length), and emitting light of
another hue, always of a longer wave-
length, i.e. nearer the red end of the
spectrum.

Modern fluorescent lighting consists
of a tubular mercury vapour lamp coated
with fluorescing salts. See ELECTRICITY.
Ultra-violet ' light ' (actually, of course,
invisible) causes the coating to fluoresce ;
such lighting is used in modern schools
and factories.

Fluorescence is not to be confused
with phosphorescence, the property of
some bodies (e.g. living jelly-fish, glow-
worms, decaying wood) of shining coldly
after exposure to light, the result of slow
oxidation.

fluorine, *floo'ō-rēn*, gas and element, F ;
atomic weight 19·00 ; atomic number 9.
Greenish and with a choking smell, it is
the lightest of the halogens, and is
extremely reactive.

fluorspar, calcium fluoride, CaF_2, colourless when pure.

Flushing, port, Netherlands ; on Walcheren I. and at the mouth of the

R. Schelde ; has much shipping and
trade ; pop.23,000.

Flushing Meadows, see UNO

Fly, river of New Guinea. It is *c*.620m
long.

fly, insect (order *Diptera*) with two wings.
The jaws are for piercing or sucking, or
both ; the feet may have pads enabling
the insect to walk on smooth surfaces ;
from the egg comes a white maggot. The
droning sound in flight indicates that the
wings may vibrate 600 times per sec.
Varieties include gnat, house fly (*Musca
domestica*), hornet and bot-fly.

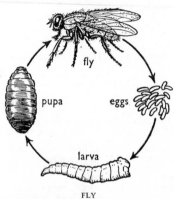

FLY
Life Cycle of the House Fly

Recent investigation suggests that
cephenemyia, a Brazilian fly, holds the
world's speed-record for flight, namely
400ẏd per sec., or over 800mph.

flying bombs, popular name for the German
jet-propelled projectiles (V1) directed
against London and SE. England 1944.

Flying Dutchman, THE, nickname of the
captain of a ghost ship said to sail many
seas, but especially in the region of the
Cape of Good Hope. The legend (which
inspired Richard Wagner's opera) is that
the vessel is doomed never to reach port
because of the wickedness of her captain,
Vanderdecken. See WAGNER, W. R.

flying-fish, mackerel-like fish of tropical
seas ; has long pectoral fins used to sustain a leap out of the water (sometimes
of 200yd) when trying to escape from
enemies.

' Flying Fortress,' see AVIATION

flying-fox, name given to a large bat,
especially in Malaya. The distance from
wing-tip to wing-tip may be 5ft. The
animal feeds on flowers and fruit.

flying lemur, *lē'mĕr*, name for the colugo
of Malaya. The small animal has loose
skin along the sides of the body, and
this acts as a parachute. It lives chiefly
on leaves, and may leap 70yd.

' Flying Scotsman,' see RAILWAYS

flying-wing, see AVIATION

FM, short for so-called frequency modula-
tions of radio waves as used in broad-

casting, a development likely to ensure better reception by diminishing over-crowding of certain wave-lengths ; hence the establishment by the BBC of its first high-power FM transmitter at Wrotham Hill, Kent.

focal length (f), for spherical mirrors $f = \frac{1}{2}r$, where r is radius of curvature ; for all spherical mirrors $\frac{1}{v} + \frac{1}{u} = \frac{1}{f}$ if v = distance of image from mirror, u = distance of object ; for lenses

$$\frac{1}{v} - \frac{1}{u} = \frac{1}{f}.$$

Magnification $= \frac{v}{u}$. See LIGHT

Foch, FERDINAND, *fŏsh* (1851–1929), French soldier, *b* Tarbes ; wrote books on war-fare. In World War I Foch became supreme commander of the Allied forces on the Western front, March 1918.

focus, *fō'kŭs,* point at which converging rays of light (or heat) from a point meet again ; or the point from which diverg-ing rays are considered to emanate. See LIGHT

Foggia, *fŏd'jä,* province in S. Italy ; also its cap., a busy industrial town ; pop. 63,000.

Folkestone, *fōk'stŭn,* port and holiday resort on the Kent coast ; noted for fishing ; has steamer service to Boulogne; pop.36,000.

folk-moot, see LOCAL GOVERNMENT

folk-songs, songs, long unwritten, that have gradually grown into being ; the tunes usually have melody only, i.e. they are not harmonic. Though often simple, folk-songs have a sincerity and freshness that is a great part of their charm. England owes much to Cecil James Sharp for collecting and preserving many of them. See SHARP, CECIL JAMES

Fontainebleau, *faun-ten-blō,* town 37m SE. of Paris ; famous for its beautiful forest of over 40,000 acres, and for its palace, one of the finest in France ; scene of the abdication of Napoleon 1814.

Fontenoy, see AUSTRIAN SUCCESSION, WAR OF

Foochow, *-cho,* Chinese treaty-port and tea-exporting centre ; on the R. Min, 125m NE. of Amoy ; noted for a bridge 800 years old ; pop.400,000.

food, nutritive matter eaten or drunk by animals to sustain life, i.e. for the purpose of growth, work, repair and warmth. It has been estimated that in 70 years the average man drinks 44,000 pints of liquid, eats 265cwt of bread, 8,000lb of meat, and 50cwt of vege-tables ; in all, the contents of 25 one-ton lorries.

Forty-one raw materials *at least* are required to keep the human body healthily active. In the main, diet comprises 3 classes of food : (1) *heat-* or *energy-producing,* i.e. carbohydrates, such as fats, starch, sugars ; (2) *body-building,* i.e. foods rich in protein, e.g. milk, meat, eggs, liver, cheese, fish, peas,

beans, lentils, brown bread, nuts. (3) *protective foods,* including vitamins, e.g. butter, etc., green vegetables, fruit and fish, especially herrings.

The body ' burns ' (oxidises) the food we eat, i.e. changes it into energy or heat, and we may make comparisons of the energy-values of foods by assessing their heat values in Calories—a Calorie being the amount of heat required to raise the temperature of 1 kilogram of water 1°C (approx.). An invalid lying in bed needs at least .1,700 Calories per day ; an office-worker needs *c.*2,400 Calories, a Canadian lumberjack 5,000. A baby weighing 8lb at birth requires 92,000 Calories to double its weight. 1 gram of fat contains 9·3 Calories.

By carbohydrates we mean combina-tions of carbon and water without nitrogen, e.g. sugars and starches, which the body transforms into glucose before ' burning ' them as fuel. By proteins we mean foods that build up or repair living tissue. A protein molecule contains carbon, hydrogen, oxygen and nitrogen ; often sulphur, sometimes phosphorus. From these the body manufactures amino-acids.

Among important human foodstuffs are lean beef (18·4 per cent protein) ; fish, rich in protein and fat (boiled her-ring contains 26 per cent protein), and milk, which is a balanced mixture of water, protein, sugar, fat and mineral matter, all in an easily digestible form. Cream and butter are easily digested forms of fat ; margarine (82 per cent fat) is excellent. Cheese, although in some forms not easily digested, is highly nutritive. Eggs (especially when lightly boiled) are valuable, being rich in protein and fat. Of cereals, oats are rich in nitrogenous matter, hence oatcakes with butter, porridge and milk is an excep-tionally valuable combination of foods. Barley and rice are poor in protein ; wheat contains (in the form of white bread) 51 per cent sugar, starch and dextrin, and only 6·5 per cent protein ; hence, though highly nutritious, bread is by no means the perfect food. Potatoes abound in starch ; green vegetables and some fruits (apart from their vitamin content) are sources of mineral salts, among which are calcium, which (like phosphorus) is essential to bones and teeth, and is therefore particularly im-portant to the growing child. Blood requires salt, iron and iodine.

The following simple key-foods include all the items necessary for a balanced diet : milk, butter, eggs, cheese, whole-meal bread, green or root vegetables, fresh fruit, and (occasionally) liver or herring. Wholesome meals are oatmeal, milk and fruit ; or brown bread, butter, cheese and tomato ; or herring, potatoes (in their jackets), and a green salad. See DIGESTION ; VITAMIN

foot-and-mouth disease, disease of cattle (also sheep and pigs) causing eruptions on the mouth and feet. It spreads rapidly. Infected animals must not be moved out of their area. See AGRI-CULTURE

football, as a rough and tumble game without rules was played in the 3rd c., but the sport did not become a true contest of skill before 1800. Today there are two kinds, Association and Rugby.

ASSOCIATION (or SOCCER) began at Charterhouse, the famous school. A set of rules was first drawn up 1863. The Association Cup was first competed for 1871, and won outright by the Wanderers. It is now usually known as the English Cup. Later this famous trophy was secured by Blackburn Rovers. Aston Villa have won it many times. The first match between England and Scotland, played 1872, ended in a draw. The Football League was founded 1888.

Amateurs play football as a hobby, professionals make their living at the game.

Association is played by 11 players on each side, i.e. goalkeeper, 2 full-backs, 3 half-backs, 5 forwards, known as outside-right, inside-right, centre, inside-left, and outside-left. The field cannot be longer than 130yd or more than 100yd wide ; goalposts should be 8yd apart, the bar being 8ft above the ground. As a rule the game lasts 90 minutes, ends being changed at half-time. The referee is sole judge of fair or foul play. Holding the ball or touching it with the hands is not allowed.

For a *penalty-kick* the ball is placed 12yd in front of the centre of the goal ; a *free kick* may be made in any direction the player chooses. When the ball is kicked or headed into *touch* (i.e. across the *side* of the field) the opposing team is given a *throw-in*—the thrower holding the ball above his head as he stands with his feet on the touch-line. A player is *offside* when there are not at least two opponents between him and the opponents' goal-line.

RUGBY is named from Rugby School (see RUGBY SCHOOL). The first match between England and Scotland was played in the season 1870–71.

Rugby should be played with teams of 15 ; and the field of play should not be more than 110 by 75yd. The goal is 2 upright posts over 11ft high and 18ft 6in part, with a crossbar 10ft above the ground. The idea of the game is to kick the ball *over* the crossbar and between the posts. A *drop-kick* is made by allowing the ball to fall from the hands, and kicking it as it bounces. A *place-kick* is made after placing the ball on the ground. A *punt* is made by dropping the ball from the hands and kicking it *before* it touches the ground. *Tackling* means holding an opponent so that he cannot pass or play the ball. When the forwards of each side close round the ball they form a *scrummage*. A *try* is gained by the player who first

puts his hand on the ball when in his opponents' in-goal ; and a goal is won by kicking the ball over the crossbar from the place-kick or a drop-kick. A goal kicked from a try counts 5 points, a dropped goal 3, and a mark or penalty goal 3 points. A try not converted counts 3 points.

In Rugby League Football or Northern Union (especially popular in N. England and also in Australia) the side has 13, and there are various other modifications.

foot-pound, in physics, practical unit of work. It is the work done in raising 1lb 1ft against gravity.

foot-poundal, in physics, work done by a force of 1 poundal acting through a distance of 1ft.

Forbes, GEORGE WILLIAM (1869–1947), prime minister of NZ 1930–35.

Forbes, ROSITA (1893–), British explorer ; crossed the Libyan desert in native costume 1920 ; made an expedition to Asia ; visited Ethiopia 1924–25. A daring adventurer, her books and lectures have won great popularity.

force, see MECHANICS

Ford, HENRY (1863–1947), born near Dearborn, Michigan, USA ; started life as a farmer, and did not begin manufacturing cars till he was 40. At 60 his business was making 30s profit a second. He became the world's leading industrialist and its second richest man, but his life and genius were not directed towards making money, and he paid his workers higher wages than was customary till prevented from doing so by USA legislation. Ford built up his vast works on the principle that the world needed cheap and efficient cars, tractors and planes. His son, EDSEL BRYANT FORD (1893–1943), identified himself with his father's business, and was at one time the third richest man in USA.

Ford, JOHN (1586–1639), dramatist, *b* Ilsington, Devon ; noted for his play *'Tis Pity She's a Whore*, and as collaborator with Dekker and Webster.

Foreign Legion, see MERCENARIES

Foreign Office, British Government department. It is under the Secretary of State for Foreign Affairs, assisted by a Parliamentary Under-secretary, and is responsible for conducting relations between the British Government and foreign governments, instructing ambassadors and consuls, and keeping close watch upon all political changes abroad likely to affect British interests.

foreign trade, exchange of goods and services among various countries.

forests, popularly thought of as densely wooded areas, but in Scotland a ' forest ' is a wild tract of mountainous country, usually without trees, in which red deer are allowed to roam.

Notable forests in Britain include New Forest, Hampshire, *c.*90,000 acres, chiefly oak and beech ; noted for ponies ; Forest of Dean, Gloucestershire. Traces of the Weald (Kent) and of Sherwood Forest (Nottinghamshire) remain. In Norman times kings delighted in hunting deer, and the Forest Laws were severe.

Afforestation, the scientific planting of trees, is supervised in Britain by the Forestry Commission (1919), responsible for planting large areas (e.g. Scottish Highlands, E. Anglia) with spruce, larch and fir. Much has been done, but more ought to be done, as Canadian and Scandinavian forests are unlikely to be able to supply future demands for timber, and the wood-pulp, from which paper and cellulose are made.

The Imperial Forestry Institute is at Oxford.

Forfar, *för'fĕr,* co.tn, Angus ; noted for linen.

forging, production of iron or steel articles by pressing, rolling and hammering, without raising the metal to meltingpoint. The industry includes the blacksmith's art ; also modern methods of drop or die forging, in which a hammer (weighing 3,000lb or more) presses heated metal into a die. Bolts, nuts, rivets, etc. are now largely made by machine forging. A forging press (for heavy flanged plates and cranks) may exert a pressure of 10,000 tons.

Forli, city of Italy ; south of Ravenna ; noted for silk and iron ; pop.60,000.

formaldehyde, *för-mal'dē-hīd,* gas, HCHO, with irritating smell, first prepared 1867. Very soluble in water (hence formalin, a 40% solution of formaldehyde), it is much used as a disinfectant. Formaldehyde is an important factor in the manufacture of plastics.

formic acid, H·COOH, colourless, fuming liquid, found in ants, the bristles of stinging nettles, etc. ; has a corrosive action, and is used in tanning and electroplating.

Formosa or **Taiwan,** *för-mō'sä,* island off the coast of China, ceded to Japan 1895 but returned 1945 ; area 13,900sq.m ; the east coast has the highest cliffs in the world (6,000ft). The island, famed for its beauty, exports camphor ; cap. Taihoku.

Forster, WILLIAM EDWARD (1818–86), English politician, born of Quaker parents at Bradpole, Dorset ; Member of Gladstone's cabinet 1868 ; played a prominent part in the introduction of the Education Bill 1870, by which School Boards were established.

Fortaleza, *för-tä-lä'zä,* Brazilian port trading in coffee and rubber ; pop. 194,000.

Fort Augustus, Scottish village on the Caledonian Canal ; its fort (1716) is now a Benedictine abbey.

Fort Garry, see WINNIPEG

Forth, Scottish river ; flows 51m to Alloa, where it reaches the Firth of Forth. Its windings are called links. The river is spanned at Queensferry by the Forth Bridge, over 8,000ft long. See BRIDGES

In addition to the railway bridge there is shortly to be a new bridge designed to carry road traffic. It will be 1½m long.

Fort Sumter, island fort in Charleston Harbour, S. Carolina, USA.

Fortunate Islands, in old Greek tales, islands of the blessed, vaguely imagined as beyond the Pillars of Hercules.

Fort William, town near the south end of the Caledonian Canal. It has had a meteorological station since 1889. Here are aluminium works ; also a hydroelectric power station.

' Forty-Five,' THE, see JAMES EDWARD

forum, in ancient Roman towns, an open space where business was done ; particularly the various *fora* of Rome, e.g. Forum Julium, Forum Augustum, Forum Trajanum (the most spacious and splendid), and the Forum Romanum where from very early days the assembly of the people met, and magistrates addressed them from the *rostra*.

Fosdick, HARRY EMERSON (1878–), American preacher and writer.

Fosse Way, see BRITAIN

fossils, see GEOLOGY

Fotheringay, *foth'ering-gä,* village, Northamptonshire ; has ruins of the castle where Mary Queen of Scots was executed 1587.

Foucault, LÉON, *foo-kō* (1819–68), French scientist ; physicist at the Paris Observatory ; noted for determining the velocities of light in air, water and a vacuum, and for his work on electromagnetic fields, but most of all for Foucault's pendulum, which, by consistently bearing to the right, proves that the earth is rotating. Such a pendulum is a permanent exhibit at the S. Kensington Science Museum, London.

Fountains Abbey, ruined Cistercian abbey near Ripon, Yorkshire ; begun *c*.1140 ; destroyed by Henry VIII's orders 1540.

four dimensional space, i.e. space-time, including with the three physical dimensions (length, breadth and height) a fourth dimension, *time*. In the spacetime ' continuum ' (whole) an event is a point, represented by four co-ordinates; the history of the event a line ; the series of events an area. Just as it is mathematically possible to write down equations governing three dimensions, so it is feasible to devise equations for n dimensions. See RELATIVITY

Four Freedoms, popular name for points in a speeech (1941) by President Roosevelt. He referred to the need every nation had for freedom of speech and expression ; freedom to worship God in one's own way ; freedom from want ; and freedom from fear. See ATLANTIC CHARTER ; UNO

Fourth Republic, name for the historical period in France beginning with its liberation from German occupation 1944.

Fowey, *foy,* historic port, Cornwall ; exports china clay ; called Troy Town by Sir A. Quiller-Couch.

Fowler, SIR JOHN (1817–99), English engineer ; built the Metropolitan Railway (London), opened 1863 ; and with Sir Benjamin Baker designed the Forth Bridge.

fox, animal related to the dog. The common British fox (*Vulpes canis*), usually reddish-brown above, white below, has a long bushy tail (' brush '). Notorious for its cunning, the fox devours birds and small animals, and usually lives in a burrow (its ' earth ').

Varieties include the Arctic fox, valued for its glossy white coat in winter, and the silver fox with thick, shining black fur. The latter is now frequently reared in captivity.

Fox hunting, still a popular though cruel sport, is done with hounds and horses. A kennel of hounds may be from 25–75 couples. Notable English hunts are the Quorn, Meynell, Cottesmore, Pytchley and Belvoir.

Read *Reynard the Fox*, John Masefield.

Fox, CHARLES JAMES (1749–1806), statesman, *b* London ; educated Eton and Oxford ; became ' Whig leader ' and opposed Lord North's policy towards American colonists ; later formed coalition with Lord North. He strove for Parliamentary reform, for honest administration, and for restrictions on the power of the king ; was tolerant in all matters relating to Roman Catholics and Ireland. When the Whigs were defeated (1784) Fox stayed out of office and opposed Pitt, the Prime Minister, particularly his policy during the French Revolution. A gambler in his younger days, he was an eloquent orator and had a charming personality.

Fox, GEORGE, see SOCIETY OF FRIENDS

Foxe, JOHN, *foks* (1516–87), English churchman, *b* Boston, Lincolnshire ;

CHARLES JAMES FOX 1749–1806

notable for his book *Acts and Monuments*, better known as *Foxe's Book of Martyrs*, which greatly advanced Protestantism in England.

foxglove, tall, handsome, poisonous plant (*Digitalis purpurea*) often 5–6ft high ; has long broad leaves, whitish below ; a spire of pink and purple bells spotted with purple inside, each bell with 5 sharply-pointed sepals.

Foyle, LOUGH, name of an inlet of the sea between Eire and N. Ireland ; actually the estuary of the R. Foyle.

fractions (Lat. *fractus*, broken), in mathematics, a fraction is part of a whole, e.g. $\frac{3}{4}$, sometimes written 3/4, where 4 is the *denominator*, showing into how many parts a whole is equally divided, 3 the *numerator*, showing how many of those parts are taken. If the denominator is 10, 100, etc. the fraction is a *decimal fraction*, all others are *vulgar fractions* (Lat. *vulgus*, common). In a *proper fraction* the numerator is less than the denominator, e.g. $\frac{5}{7}$; an *improper fraction* has a numerator greater than its denominator, e.g. $\frac{7}{5}$; a *mixed number* is a quantity consisting of a whole number (*integer*) and a proper fraction, e.g. $3\frac{1}{8}$, and may be expressed as an improper fraction, e.g. $\frac{25}{8}$. *To divide one fraction by another*, turn the divisor upside down and multiply, e.g.

$$3\frac{1}{8} \div \frac{5}{16} = \frac{25}{8} \times \frac{16}{5} = 10.$$

Note the following fractions and their equivalent decimals :

$\frac{1}{2}$	= ·5	$\frac{3}{7}$	= ·$\dot4$2857$\dot1$
$\frac{1}{3}$	= ·$\dot3$	$\frac{3}{10}$	= ·3
$\frac{1}{4}$	= ·25	$\frac{3}{20}$	= ·15
$\frac{1}{5}$	= ·2	$\frac{4}{5}$	= ·8
$\frac{1}{6}$	= ·1$\dot6$	$\frac{4}{7}$	= ·$\dot5$7142$\dot8$
$\frac{1}{7}$	= ·$\dot1$4285$\dot7$	$\frac{5}{6}$	= ·8$\dot3$
$\frac{1}{8}$	= ·125	$\frac{5}{7}$	= ·$\dot7$1428$\dot5$
$\frac{1}{9}$	= ·$\dot1$	$\frac{5}{8}$	= ·625
$\frac{1}{10}$	= ·1	$\frac{5}{9}$	= ·$\dot5$
$\frac{1}{12}$	= ·08$\dot3$	$\frac{5}{12}$	= ·41$\dot6$
$\frac{1}{20}$	= ·05	$\frac{6}{7}$	= ·$\dot8$5714$\dot2$
$\frac{1}{40}$	= ·025	$\frac{7}{8}$	= ·875
$\frac{1}{80}$	= ·0125	$\frac{7}{9}$	= ·$\dot7$
$\frac{1}{100}$	= ·01	$\frac{7}{10}$	= ·7
$\frac{1}{1000}$	= ·001	$\frac{7}{12}$	= ·58$\dot3$
$\frac{2}{3}$	= ·$\dot6$	$\frac{8}{9}$	= ·$\dot8$
$\frac{2}{5}$	= ·4	$\frac{8}{11}$	= ·$\dot7\dot2$
$\frac{2}{7}$	= ·$\dot2$8571$\dot4$	$\frac{9}{10}$	= ·9
$\frac{3}{4}$	= ·75	$\frac{9}{11}$	= ·$\dot8\dot1$
$\frac{3}{5}$	= ·6		

See DECIMALS

' **Fram,**' see NANSEN, DR F.; POLAR REGIONS

Framlingham, old Suffolk town on the R. Ore ; has a college founded 1865.

Frampton, SIR GEORGE JAMES (1860–1928), British sculptor who designed statues of Queen Victoria, one of Queen Mary, Peter Pan (Kensington Gardens), and the Edith Cavell Memorial, London.

franc, silver coin, unit of French currency and equivalent to 100 centimes ; its English equivalent in 1946 was officially a half-penny.

France, western European country and republic ; area 212,895sq.m, divided into 90 departments ; pop.42,000,000, including Alsace and Lorraine and those in Algeria.

The 'fair land of France' has an oceanic climate in the west, but continental in the interior, where there are considerable extremes of heat and cold. The Bay of Biscay is notorious for its high winds and rough seas, and the sunny south may be intensely cold in winter, due to the *mistral*, a cold wind that has caused Provençal towns to have narrow, winding streets. Separated from Spain by the Pyrenees, France has a central plateau, with the Maritime Alps in the south rising to Mont Blanc. Farther north are the Jura Alps and the wooded Vosges. The chief rivers are the Seine, Loire, Garonne and Rhône. A land of infinite variety, it has the Bretons in the north-west, pure Celts with customs of their own and great traditions ; the Landes south of the R. Garonne, where shepherds walk about their sandy fields on stilts ; the Loire valley subject to floods ; the R. Rhône generating electric power as it rushes to the Mediterranean.

The departments of France are similar to counties in England.

Note the following *old* provinces or regions of France :

Anjou (area now largely covered by Maine-et-Loire)

Aquitaine (region between the R. Garonne and the Pyrenees)

Artois (extreme NE.)

Brittany (extreme NW.)

Burgundy (wine district including departments numbered 34, 35, 57)

Champagne (region in the NE., including several areas long famous for sparkling wines)

Gascony (region in the extreme SW., bounded by the Atlantic, R. Garonne and the Pyrenees)

Guienne (region of the SW., roughly an extensive area in the neighbourhood of Bordeaux)

Ile de France (N. of Paris)

Normandy (including the departments between Picardy and Brittany)

Poitou (S. of the Loire)

Minerals are not abundant, but Lorraine, Le Creusot and St Etienne are noted for iron ore ; Lille for iron and steel, also linen and cotton. Aluminium and potash are produced ; salt is mined near Nancy, a town manufacturing cotton and also metal goods. Coal is found, but not in sufficient quantities for home use, one of the largest coal-fields being near the Belgian border. Linen is manufactured in the NE., a region where flax is grown on a considerable scale ; and Rouen is known as the Manchester of France, so great is its cotton trade, and Le Havre (importing American cotton) is often styled the Liverpool of France. Sèvres is notable for delicate chinaware ; also Limoges. Lyons has long had a

great reputation for silks, brocades and velvets. Amiens produces clocks and jewellery ; and in the neighbourhood of the French Riviera (where Cannes and Nice are the two most famous tourist centres) are manufactured perfumes and soaps. In addition, France exports cars, wines, glass and chemicals.

Largely agricultural, the land is intensively cultivated by peasants. Besides flax, wheat, oats and barley are grown also buckwheat, maize, sugar-beet, hemp, tobacco and beans. Cider-making is important, but the cultivation of the vine and the manufacture of wines (e.g. champagne, burgundy, bordeaux, moselle) is widespread. Many forest areas still remain, especially of oak, birch, pine, chestnut and (in the south) the cork tree.

The capital is Paris ; towns include Marseilles, with shipping linking France with the East and Far East ; Bordeaux, Nice, Toulouse, Nantes, Strasburg, Toulon, etc. Of much interest are such towns as Reims (or Rheims) with its 13th c. cathedral ; Avignon, a home in the south of the popes from 1309–76 ; Cloyes, where the pitiful Children's Crusade started 1212 ; Calais, an English possession till 1558 ; Crécy, where Edward III won a victory 1346. There is the old fortress town of Metz (Lorraine) ; the Bay of Biscay town of La Rochelle, with its fine harbour ; the busy seaport of Boulogne, the Channel port of Cherbourg.

The French colonial empire includes French India, Indo-China, Cambodia, Algeria, Tunisia, W. Africa and Madagascar.

Known to the Romans as Gaul, the country was for long an important part of the Roman empire, being conquered by Julius Caesar. At Marseilles Agricola went to school as a boy, and even today France has magnificent Roman remains, e.g. the great aqueduct at Nîmes, the amphitheatre at Bordeaux and the ruins at Arles. Later conquered by Clovis, leader of the Franks (or Free Men), the country was called France from *c.* AD870. Charlemagne was crowned Roman Emperor of the West, AD800, ruling not only what is now France but parts of Germany, Spain and Italy, giving the region its first settled and central government. Another great and early ruler was Hugh Capet (*c.*987), his family giving France her kings for 800 years.

English kings for several centuries attempted to link France and England, and to rule both countries, hence the wretched Hundred Years' War in which Henry V won an outstanding success at Agincourt 1415, the struggle being ended at last (1450) in consequence of the successes won for France by Joan of Arc. Gradually France became increasingly powerful, and Cardinal Richelieu made Louis XIII supreme. But the government then, and later, was sadly unrepresentative, and while from Louis XIV's day onwards France won brilliant victories and extended her possessions overseas, the peasantry were oppressed by unjust taxes, leading finally to the Revolution and the Reign of Terror. Louis XVI and his queen perished by the guillotine 1793. After the Revolution came the stirring days of the great Napoleon who almost became master of Europe, but was defeated 1815 at Waterloo. The Franco-Prussian War (1870–1871) caused humiliation and suffering in France, and the country suffered much in, and after, World War I, and still more in World War II, Marshal Pétain surrendering to Nazi Germany 17 June 1940, though General de Gaulle rallied Frenchmen everywhere, founding the Free French Movement, later (1942) known as La France Combattante, his 1944 administration being recognised by the United Nations. While occupied by the Nazis, France was cruelly plundered, and she suffered also from British and American bombing aimed at German-controlled war industries, and especially as a result of Allied invasion on and after D-Day (6 June 1944). In 1946 France adopted a new constitution, Vincent Auriol being President of the Fourth Republic. Fear of Russia caused successive French governments to give a lead in promoting West European co-operation, e.g. (1950) M. Robert Schuman's plan for Iron and Steel : but neutralism (i.e. the desire to avoid war at all costs) was an important factor in French politics.

The government comprises a Chamber of Deputies and a Senate. The president is elected for 7 years, but in practice the executive is too weak, and French cabinets last, as a rule, only for very short periods. This is due also in some measure to the quick temper and emotional instability of the French.

With a genius for enjoying themselves, the French delight in cooking and eating. They love to dine, or to sip their drinks, where they may enjoy the sunshine or find a cool place in the shade. They are highly artistic, and Paris has for centuries been the home of new fashions in feminine apparel and in hair styles. The French have also a genius for music, art and literature. The ballet, the play (especially comedy), dancing, singing are part of French life. Their dramatists include Corneille, Molière, Racine and Voltaire ; their poets, include Alfred de Musset, and the great song-writer Béranger. Among novelists may be mentioned Balzac, Victor Hugo, Alexander Dumas (père and fils), Flaubert, Émile Zola, Guy de Maupassant, Alphonse Daudet, Pierre Loti, Barbusse and Anatole France. France's great musicians and writers of opera, include Berlioz, Gounod, Bizet, César Franck (b Belgium, but lived in Paris) ; Debussy, Saint-Saëns, Fauré ; and the country owes much to the influence and inspiration of the Société Nationale de Musique.

In art the French have a proud tradition, and such names spring to the mind as Poussin, Claude, Watteau, Boucher, Fragonard, Ingres, Corot, Cézanne, Manet, Renoir, Millet and Pissarro, while French artists have often been pioneers of new trends in painting and carving, e.g. Manet of Impressionism, Rodin of a new strength in sculpture.

Since the Revolution, France has employed the metric system of weights and measures ; the unit of the monetary system is the franc.

France, ANATOLE, *fräns* (1844–1924), French writer, *b* Paris ; won lasting fame for the perfect lucidity of his novels and biographies, e.g. Le Livre de mon Ami, Histoire Comique, L'Île des Pingouins, Les Dieux ont Soif, La Révolte des Anges, Thaïs, etc. Resembling Bernard Shaw and H. G. Wells, he is never vicious, and remains a superb master of satire. His novels depict French life with brilliant penetration, and reveal the beauty of a refined intellect.

France, PRESIDENTS OF, see PRESIDENT

franchise, see ELECTION

Francis I (1494–1547), King of France ; noted for his gallantry and splendour ; met Henry VIII of England at the Field of the Cloth of Gold, 1520.

Francis Ferdinand (1863–1914), Austrian archduke and heir to the imperial throne, *b* Graz ; was an opponent of the Greater Serbia movement. While touring Bosnia he was assassinated by a Serbian at Sarajevo, a crime which hastened World War I.

Francis Joseph I (1830–1916), Emperor of Austria, reigned 1848–1916, one of the longest reigns in world history, also one of continual discontent and strife. His grand-nephew, Charles, abdicated 1918.

ST FRANCIS OF ASSISI *c.*1182–1226

Francis of Assisi, *-as-së′zë* (*c.*1182–1226), Italian saint described as the most blameless and gentle of all saints, and known

as ' the little poor man ' ; *b* Assisi,
Umbria. Though the son of a wealthy
cloth merchant, he voluntarily became
poor in sincere imitation of Christ ;
founded the Franciscan order of Grey
Friars ; served lepers ; was tireless in
his ministries to the poor and needy,
and abounding in good humour and
merriment. His devotional book *The
Little Flowers of St Francis* is a delight.

Franck, CÉSAR AUGUSTE, *frängk* (1822–90),
French musician, *b* Liége ; a brilliant
organist and noted composer.

Franco, GENERAL (1893–   ), leader of
the Nationalists (Fascists) in the Spanish
Civil War 1936–39 ; became (1939)
caudillo (i.e. head) of Spain, generalissimo
of the army, and prime minister of the
state. See FALANGE, THE

Franco-Prussian War, struggle 1870–71 between France and Prussia, aided by
Bavaria and other German states.
Napoleon III objected to a German
prince becoming king of Spain. Bismarck then invaded France, compelled
the French to retreat from Alsace-
Lorraine, except the fortress of Metz,
which was surrendered after the notable
victory of the Germans at Sedan.
Bismarck's armies besieged Paris Sept
1870–Jan 1871 ; and, finally, France
gave up Alsace-Lorraine, and paid
£200,000,000. This war led to German
predominance in Europe and upset the
balance of power.

Frankau, GILBERT, *frank'ō* (1884–   ),
British author whose successes include
Peter Jackson, Cigar Merchant. His
daughter, Pamela, is also a writer.

Frankfort-on-the-Main, *frangk'fĕrt*, ancient
and historic city, Germany ; noted for
banking and as the birthplace of the poet
Goethe ; pre-war pop.546,000.

Frankfort-on-the-Oder, busy town, Germany ; long an important centre for
manufacturing machinery, paper and
chemicals ; pop.75,000.

frankincense, fragrant gum tapped from
trees growing abundantly on the Somali
coast and in S. Arabia ; used in religious
ceremonies by the ancient Egyptians,
Persians, and especially by the Jews as
incense.

Franklin, BENJAMIN (1706–1790), one of the
most famous of all Americans. Statesman, scientist, author, he was *b* Boston.
He published a newspaper in Philadelphia ; was author of *Poor Richard's
Almanac*, full of quaint wisdom ; and
was chosen to represent America in
negotiations with England. For 5 years
he lived in London, doing all he could
to prevent the breach between the two
countries. In France he enlisted the
support of Louis XVI for the colonies.
He urged the abolition of slavery ; was
regarded as the most typical of all
Americans, and was one of the first to
give his country a sense of unity.
As a pioneer in science he experimented with electricity, proved that
lightning was a form of electricity ; in-

vented lightning conductors ; studied
weather and earthquakes; discovered the
use of oil for calming rough water ;
investigated artificial fertilisers ; and
made the first bifocal spectacles.

Franklin, SIR JOHN (1786–1847), explorer,
b Spilsby, Lincolnshire ; was a middy
at the battle of Copenhagen; made three
Arctic explorations prior to 1827 ; in
command 1845 of the *Erebus* and *Terror*
which set out to find the NW. Passage,
but never returned. Later expeditions
were sent to search for Franklin's party,
but no traces were found until M'Clintock discovered records of the expedition.

Franks, tribes living near the R. Rhine in
the 3rd c. In the 4th c. they separated
into the Ripuarian and Salian Franks,
the latter under Clovis founding the
kingdom of France. Later, a branch of
these became established in Germany
east of the Rhine.

Fraser River, chief river of British Columbia ; 800m ; noted for salmon.

Fraunhofer, JOSEPH VON, *frown'hō-fĕr*
(1787–1826), German scientist ; discoverer of the Fraunhofer lines, i.e. dark
lines crossing the continuous spectrum
of the sun, and corresponding precisely
to the line spectra emitted by various
gases when suitably excited. The lines
are due to absorption by cooler gases in
the sun's chromosphere, and reveal the
presence of these gases in its outer
envelope. It was in this way that helium
was discovered in the sun before being
found in the earth. See SPECTRUM

Frazer, SIR JAMES (1854–1941), anthropologist, *b* Glasgow ; studied the
mythology and folk-lore of all ages. Of
his books the most famous is *The Golden
Bough.*

Frederick I (*c.*1123–90), German king and
Holy Roman Emperor whose ambition
was to restore the Holy Roman Empire
of Charlemagne. In repeated attempts
to do this he was involved in wars with
Italy, which ended in his defeat at the
battle of Legnano 1176. He died while
leading a crusade against Saladin.
Though a warrior, he was an enlightened
and able administrator, and his memory
is still revered in Germany. He was nicknamed ' Barbarossa,' i.e. ' Red Beard,'
and was traditionally believed to sleep in
a cave at Berchtesgaden.

Frederick II (1194–1250), crowned King of
Germany 1215, and Holy Roman Emperor 1220. He was also King of Sicily,
and the laws he issued there (destroying
feudal privileges) were notable. He was
buried in Palermo cathedral, and is
remembered as being the first to establish
in Europe great nations that were independent of the pope, and also as a
scholar and a patron of science and
literature. He was known in his day as
stupor mundi, i.e. Wonder of the World.

Frederick IX, King of Denmark; succeeded
his father (Christian X), 1947.

Fredericksburg, city of Virginia, USA, on
the R. Rappahannock, 60m from Rich-

mond ; notable for a battle of the American Civil War, when the Confederates under Lee defeated the Federals 1862.

Frederick the Great (1712–86), King of Prussia, *b* Berlin ; son of Frederick William I, who treated him with the utmost severity ; succeeded his father 1740. Though cynical, he declared himself the servant of the people, and proved an expert in administration, setting up an efficient government. In military affairs he built up a disciplined and regimented army, the most efficient in his day. Owing to the claims on Silesia by Maria Theresa, he was involved in the Seven Years' War (1756–63), and though surrounded by more powerful enemies, contrived by superb military tactics, to preserve his boundaries, beginning the enveloping tactics for which Germany later became famous.

An autocrat, he increased his country's wealth, encouraged industry, art and culture, and was as famous for his personal courage as for his tolerance ; but his success laid the foundations of Germany's later wars of aggression.

Read Macaulay's essay, *Frederick the Great*, and Thomas Carlyle's biography of him. See SEVEN YEARS' WAR

Frederick William I (1688–1740) King of Prussia, father of Frederick the Great. A notable administrator, he made Prussia a first-class power in Europe, and had a passion for tall soldiers and for military display.

Frederick William of Prussia (1620–88), called the Great Elector ; at 20 succeeded his father as Elector of Brandenburg ; won renown as a soldier, and created the military spirit of Prussia, which, developed by Frederick the Great, bore fruit in modern Germany's warlike spirit.

Fredericton, capital of New Brunswick, Canada ; noted for lumbering.

freedom of the city, honour conferred on a citizen for some notable service. The Freedom of the City of London is presented only as a high distinction for exceptional service ; those so presented become Freemen.

Free French, patriots who, under General de Gaulle, strove to make France independent of German domination after 1940. Banding themselves to form the Fighting French, they eventually won recognition as representatives of the people, and were able to set up a Provisional Government.

free lance, see JOURNALISM

freeman, originally (as in ancient Greece and Rome) one who was not a slave ; later, in England, a serf or villein who had become free by residing a year and a day in a chartered town ; later still, a man who had a right to share in the government of a city or borough ; now a person of distinction who is honoured by being given the freedom of a city or borough.

Freeman, EDWARD AUGUSTUS (1823–92) historian ; notable for his *History of the Norman Conquest.*

Freemasonry, brotherhood with a religious foundation and world-wide fellowship, numbers perhaps 4,000,000 members who meet at lodges, the oldest being Edinburgh Lodge No. 1, with records going back to 1599. The chief Freemason is the Grand Master.

Freetown, port and cap. Sierra Leone ; has the finest harbour in W. Africa ; pop. 55,000.

free trade or **tariff reform,** principle of international commerce unhampered by government restrictions, tariffs, etc. Free trade was advocated by Adam Smith in his *Wealth of Nations*, and encouraged in the UK by Pitt 1786, but this country believed in protection prior to 1846, when the fear of famine compelled Parliament to adopt the free trade measures advocated by Richard Cobden, John Bright and Sir Robert Peel, all supporters of the Anti-Corn Law League.

By this policy duties on imports are removed so that other countries may freely send their goods here, and until 1914 Britain remained the chief home of free trade. The Tariff Reform League (founded 1903 by Joseph Chamberlain) advocated restrictions on imports ; and the Safeguarding of Industries Act 1921 made articles of the ' key ' industries subject to import duty. Tariffs became general 1931–32, the idea being to prevent British industrialists losing trade because goods imported without duty from other countries were sold at lower prices than those at which we could afford to sell them.

IMPERIAL PREFERENCE is the policy of reducing duties on goods imported from the Dominions, and is not to be confused with EMPIRE FREE TRADE, i.e. duty-free imports and exports within the empire. See COBDEN, R. ; PROTECTION

freezing, change of a liquid to a solid owing to a fall of temperature. Gradual in substances like wax, it occurs suddenly when crystals are formed, e.g. water when it reaches the freezing-point (0°C ; 32°F). The freezing point of helium is -270°C. Most substances take up less space when frozen ; but water expands $c.9\%$ when it becomes ice, hence ice is lighter than water ; hence also the pressure of its expansion in pipes causes bursts.

Freezing mixtures include a mixture of snow and common salt, giving a temperature of $c.-20$°C ; also 10 parts of crystalline calcium chloride to 7 of snow, with a temperature of -55°C. The principle of many freezing machines is that of producing cold by evaporation, as in ammonia refrigerators.

Freiburg, *frī'burch*, historic cathedral town, Baden, Germany ; noted for the manufacture of silk, cotton and paper ; pop.112,000.

French, SIR JOHN, see YPRES, EARL OF

French Guiana, *gē-än'ä,* colony bordering Brazil ; area 34,000sq.m ; notable for timber, cocoa and gold ; cap. Cayenne.

French Revolution, period of upheaval in France 1789–95. The root causes were the approaching bankruptcy of France and the persistence of the feudal system, which prevented the middle class (merchants and traders) having any share in the government, and had reduced the common people to a state of misery. Prior to 1789 the king ruled by means of ministers whom he appointed or dismissed at pleasure ; society was divided into three groups or estates : the *noblesse* or aristocracy ; the clergy ; and the commons. In the towns was a middle class, the *bourgeoisie* (professional men and traders) ; in the country were peasants, i.e. slaves of the landowners (*seigneurs*). While aristocrats and clergy were practically untaxed, money for the king, his court, administration and wars was raised from taxes on the peasantry —the very people least able to afford it.

There had long been unrest. Voltaire, Diderot and Rousseau had stirred thoughts of revolution and taught that the will of the people ought to be supreme. Then, in Louis XVI's day, came wars without profit. France was almost bankrupt ; ministers were incompetent ; taxation was increased.

In desperation a new parliament was called, i.e. the States-General (1789), in which all three estates were represented (aristocrats, clergy and commons), and this became the National Assembly. When the Paris mob stormed the Bastille 14 July, its fall was regarded as the end of the old order of tyranny. France blazed into revolution ; the peasants murdered the *seigneurs,* burned their chateaux (castles or houses), refused to pay taxes, and were in open rebellion.

The whole spirit of the revolution was summed up in the cry *Liberty, Equality, Fraternity.* The revolutionary flag, the *tricolor,* was blue, white and red. At first popular fury was directed against the aristocrats only, but after the death of Mirabeau, 1791, nothing could save the king. Like thousands of other victims of the Reign of Terror (1793–94), Louis XVI was guillotined 1793, followed some months later by his queen, Marie Antoinette, the desire of many being for a republic.

French armies won successes against Austria and Prussia, but at home the various parties in Paris (e.g. Girondist or moderate party, the Jacobin or extreme republican party) were squabbling among themselves. Day after day the tumbrils rolled to the busy guillotine, carrying victims who had been hastily tried and condemned. Charlotte Corday murdered Marat ; Madame Roland, Danton, Robespierre, all perished. Then (1795) came the Directory, an administration of 5 responsible to 2 Assemblies.

The French Revolution stirred all Europe, and pioneered the way for democracy. It shattered the notion that the rich were meant to suppress the poor, and led to government reorganisation not only in France but in many other countries.

Read *A Tale of Two Cities,* Charles Dickens ; *The French Revolution,* Thomas Carlyle.

French W. Africa, federation including :

	area (sq.m)	approx. pop.
Senegal	78,000	1,700,000
Mauritania	322,000	490,000
Fr. Guinea	97,000	4,020,000
Ivory Coast	190,000	3,850,000
Dahomey	47,000	1,350,000
Fr. Sudan	582,000	3,790,000
Niger	483,000	2,160,000

The total area of the federation is approx. 1,800,000sq.m ; the capital is Dakar (Senegal) ; and the chief exports are ground-nuts, palm kernels, cocoa, timber, bananas and gold. Togoland is French mandated territory.

frequency, see WAVE-MOTION

fresco (Italian *fresh*), method of wall-painting with water colours on fresh plaster. The art, known in ancient Crete, Egypt, India and Greece, was at its best in Italy during the 15th c.

fretwork, 3-ply or fine-grained wood (e.g. satinwood, walnut, sycamore or lime) carved in perforated patterns. For all particulars see *Hobbies Weekly.*

Freud, SIGMUND, *froit* (1856–1939), Austrian scientist, *b* Moravia of Jewish parents ; became a doctor, but turned to the study of psychology, and was professor of neurology at Vienna from 1902. The founder of psycho-analysis, whereby various mental disorders are cured by applying his technique for examining the state of the sub-conscious mind, Freud was a pioneer of revolutionary methods now proved to be of supreme value.

friar (French *frère,* brother), name for a member of an order of monks of the RC church who begs, e.g. a Franciscan, Dominican, Augustinian, or Crutched (i.e. Crossed) friar ; often known by the colour of his habit (dress), e.g. Grey Friar (Franciscan), Black Friar (Dominican), White Friar (Carmelite). See MONKS AND NUNS

friction, resistance due to one body moving over another ; depends on the material of the two bodies, and on the perpendicular pressure. The maximum statical friction (when a body is at rest) is greater than the kinetic friction of a moving body. Friction enables the wheels of a tram to ' hold ' to the track up or down hill, and makes possible friction gearing and the friction-drive in cars. It is reduced by the use of lubricants, hence all revolving axles, ball-bearings, etc. are well oiled. See MECHANICS

frictional electricity, see ELECTRICITY

Friendly or Tonga Islands, British islands *c.*400m SE. of Fiji ; pop.40,000. Mostly coral islands (though some are volcanic), they export copra.

Friendly Societies, organisations to which working people contribute small sums weekly to ensure relief in old age and sickness, first formed *c.*1790 ; now closely controlled by the state ; may be any society of this nature, e.g. an industrial insurance society, or Friendly Societies proper, e.g. Independent Order of Oddfellows, or Ancient Order of Foresters.

Friends, see SOCIETY OF FRIENDS

Friesland, *frēz'-,* province of the Netherlands ; low-lying, but has fertile soil.

frigate, *frig'it,* fast sailing vessel, forerunner of the modern cruiser. Larger than a sloop but less than a ship of the line, she carried 25–50 guns on the main and on a raised quarter-deck.

frigate-bird, tropical, web-footed seabird related to the pelican. Including the forked tail, it may be 3ft long ; the hooked bill is longer than the head ; the wing-span often 7ft. The bird catches flying-fish in the air.

Frisian Islands, islands off the coast of the Netherlands ; they include Texel.

Frith, WILLIAM POWELL (1819–1909), artist, *b* Yorkshire ; noted for his pictures depicting crowds of people, e.g. *Derby Day, The Railway Station.*

Frobisher, SIR MARTIN, *frō'bish-ĕr* (?1535– 94), sailor and pirate, *b* Yorkshire. A typical sea-dog of Elizabeth's reign, he made three daring voyages to the Arctic in search of the NW. Passage ; was knighted for his gallantry when fighting against the Spanish Armada, and was mortally wounded when attacking the Spaniards at Brest.

Froebel, FRIEDRICH, *frū'bel* (1782–1852), German educationist ; famous for his kindergarten (garden of children) system.

frog, see AMPHIBIAN

froghopper, see CUCKOO SPIT

Frogmore, royal house, Windsor Park ; also the burial place of Queen Victoria and Prince Albert. See WINDSOR

Froissart, JEAN, *frwä-sär* (1338–1410 ?), French historian, *b* Valenciennes ; was secretary to Philippa, queen of Edward III of England ; visited David II of Scotland ; followed Edward the Black Prince to Gascony ; was present at the battles of Crécy and Poitiers ; is said to have died at Chimay. Froissart is famous for his *Chronicles* of the chief events in England, Scotland, Flanders, France and Spain, 1326–1400, and especially for his vivid descriptions, his interesting details, and his accounts of chivalrous deeds.

Frome, *froom,* town, Somerset.

frontispiece, see BOOKS

frost, sometimes called hoar frost or rime, formation of minute ice-crystals on the ground, and plants, due to condensation of water vapour on surfaces below 32°F. It is injurious to plants, and any screen that reduces radiation is a protection. Frost-bite is due to exposure to severe

cold, the fingers and toes being most easily affected. De-icing of the wings of aircraft is important, since an accumulation of ice increases both weight and air-resistance.

frost-bite, see FROST

Froude, JAMES ANTHONY, *frood* (1818–94), English historian, *b* Dartington, Devon ; author of many historical works, but most famous for his *History of England from the Fall of Wolsey to the Defeat of the Spanish Armada,* a vivid and scholarly panorama, though his accuracy has sometimes been challenged.

fructose or **laevulose,** fruit-sugar, $C_6H_{12}O_6$; occurs (with glucose) in many sweet fruits, and in the nectar of flowers.

Fry, name of a Quaker family, including Joseph Fry (1728–87), founder of J. S. Fry and Sons, cocoa and chocolate manufacturers. See FRY, ELIZABETH

Fry, CHARLES BURGESS (1872–), athlete, *b* Croydon, noted footballer, cricketer, and a delightful writer on sport.

Fry, ELIZABETH (1780–1845), one of the pioneers of prison reform, *b* Earlham, Norfolk. Her maiden name was Elizabeth Gurney. She married Joseph Fry (*not* the Joseph mentioned above) at 20, and became a Quaker minister. Though she organised schemes for aiding the poor, for improving the conditions of lunatic asylums, she is best remembered for her life work in prisons. She began by visiting the Norwich prison ; went on to Newgate (London), where her faith, simplicity and sincerity won the affection of the prisoners. She later toured prisons in England, Scotland, Ireland, France, Holland, impressing every government with the need for reform, and seeing the reforms gradually adopted. Kings listened to her pleadings ; wretched criminals loved her.

Fuad I, *fu-äd'* (1868–1936), King of Egypt from 1922 ; granted a new constitution 1930.

fuchsia, *fū'shä,* flowering shrub introduced into Europe *c.*1788 from S. America, Mexico and NZ ; has funnel-shaped flowers usually red or purple, but often white, cream, or pink ; may grow from 10–12ft in Devon and Cornwall.

fuchsine, formerly called magenta, a red dye prepared from aniline and toluidine.

fuels, sources of heat and energy. All are either mainly carbon or are hydrocarbons, and the result of combustion is the conversion of carbon into carbon dioxide, and the oxidation of hydrogen to form water.

Fuels may be classed as (1) *natural fuels* : solids, e.g. wood, peat, and the various types of coal, as lignite or brown coal, gas-coal, coking, house, or iron-smelting coal and anthracite, the latter being *c.*95 % carbon ; see COAL ; liquid, e.g. petroleum, now increasingly used in industry ; see PETROLEUM ; and natural gas, e.g. the form of marsh gas tapped in Pennsylvania, USA.

(2) *Prepared fuels* : solid—e.g. char-

FUR

(1) *Chinchilla*   (2) *Sable*   (3) *Musquash*   (4) *Mink*

coal, prepared peat which has been improved by the Board of Fuel Research (founded 1917) ; pulverised coal ; gascoke, and metallurgical coke or blastfurnace coke ; coalite and coal briquettes. Liquid—artificial gas fuels, e.g. coal-gas, coke-oven gas, producer gas, now of much importance in industry ; water-gas ; oil-gas, etc.

fugue, *fūg*, piece of music in which a theme is repeated with many variations, all harmonised according to the laws of counterpoint. Bach's fugues are outstanding examples.

führer, *fū'rĕr*, in Germany, a Nazi ' leader ' ; first applied, as *der Führer*, to Hitler when Chancellor of the Third Reich.

Fuji-san or **Fuji-no-yama**, *foo'jĕ sän* ; *-nō-yä'mä*, Japanese sacred mt. and volcano, inactive since 1707 ; rises 12,370ft ; is 60m W. of Tokyo.

fulcrum, see MECHANICS

Fulham, borough of SW. London.

fuller's earth, mixture of hydrated silicates of magnesium and aluminium ; occurs as a soft variety of clay in England and N. America ; often used in soaps.

Fuller, THOMAS (1608–61), witty and learned churchman ; *b* Aldwinkle, Northamptonshire ; noted for his *Worthies of England*.

Fulton, ROBERT (1765–1815), engineer, born in Pennsylvania, USA ; built the steamer *Clermont* at New York 1807, and was thus the first to apply steam successfully to navigation. See SHIPS

fumitory, *fū'mi-tĕri*, field plant (family *Fumariaceae*) with delicate much divided leaves, irregularly-shaped pink flowers set alternately on the stem ; in flower all summer.

Funchal, *foon-shäl'*, capital of Madeira ;

port of call for ships, and a popular health resort ; pop.31,000.

functional tendencies, see ARCHITECTURE

function of a number, in mathematics, an expression which depends for its value on the value of that number. The degree of the function depends on the highest power of the number involved in the expression. For instance, $ax^3 + bx^2 + cx + d$ is a function of the 3rd degree in x, with general coefficients a, b, c, d.

Symbols for a function of x are $F(x)$, $f(x)$ or $Q(x)$.

Fundy, BAY OF, narrowing channel between New Brunswick and Nova Scotia ; noted for strong tides, rising over 50ft.

Fünen, well cultivated Danish island in the Baltic ; cap. Odense.

fungus (plural, *fungi*), large class of simple flowerless plants (*Thallophyta*), such as mushrooms and toadstools ; closely related to seaweeds and bacteria. Fungi contain no starch or chlorophyll, have no roots, but only creeping threads, and obtain carbon from living matter (if parasites) or from decaying matter if saprophytes. Reproduction is by a vast number of spores.

MUSHROOMS (e.g. *Agaricus campestris*), grow best in damp, warm cow or horsedung. Cultivated mushrooms (grown in dark cellars) may be obtained at all seasons. The cap, 3–5in across, is white and silky ; the gills below are first salmon-pink, then dark.

Some TOADSTOOLS are poisonous, e.g. one resembling the mushroom, but with white gills, and a hollow stem inserted in a bulb at the base ; also the fly fungus, its bright red cap studded with white, raised spots ; other fungi include puff-balls ; moulds, e.g. *penicillium* ; also mucor, which grows on damp bread ; yeasts ; rusts, e.g. wheat rust ; smuts ; mildews, as the vine blight and rose mildew.

fur, pelt (or skin covered with hair) of various animals, particularly chinchilla, sable, mink, musquash, ermine, skunk, beaver, seal, bear, also fox, rabbit, mole and squirrel. The chief sources are Canada and Siberia (Australia to a less extent). In Canada the Hudson Bay Company has been collecting and exporting furs since 1670. Most fur-bearing animals are trapped in the wild state, but foxes are now bred in captivity.

furnace, fire heating a boiler ; also an apparatus for smelting ores, e.g. a roasting hearth or a blacksmith's forge, the draught being supplied by bellows ; also the *blast furnace*, largely used for smelting pig-iron. This has a forced draught. Some blast furnaces, over 80ft high, and with air rushing through at a pressure of 10lb per sq.in, reach 1,400°F ; the output of metal may be 2,000 tons a week. There is also the reverbratory furnace, and the Bessemer. The finest steel is smelted in *crucibles.* Electric furnaces develop tremendously high temperatures.

One of the latest developments of the furnace is the fusion of metals by enveloping them in coils carrying high-frequency oscillating current. Intense heat is secured by eddy currents created in the metal.

Furness, region of NW. Lancashire.

Fusan, *foo'săn,* town and port, Korea ; a noted railway terminus ; pop.210,000.

fuse, in electricity, an arrangement to prevent too high a current flowing through a circuit. A fuse is usually a short length of wire of low melting-point (e.g. tin). If the current becomes excessive, the fuse melts, thus breaking the circuit and interrupting the flow.

Be sure to switch off the current before touching any part of the circuit. If some of the bulbs fail to light, examine the fuse-box, and if one of the fuses is without a wire, insert a new piece between the terminals.

fuselage, see AVIATION

fusel oil, by-product of alcohol ; a mixture of butyl and iso-amyl alcohols with organic compounds.

fusion, change from solid to liquid by the action of heat.

fusion, LATENT HEAT OF, see HEAT

fustian (*Fustat*, a suburb of Cairo), cotton or mixed linen fabric, including velvet-like materials, e.g. corduroy and velveteen.

Futurism, see ART

F(x), see FUNCTION OF A NUMBER

Fyfe, HAMILTON (1869–), *b* London ; journalist and author ; won fame as a war correspondent 1914–18 ; editor of several newspapers.

Fyne, *fīn,* sea loch (inlet), Argyll ; noted for herrings.

fyrd, see MILITIA

G

g, see ACCELERATION

gad-fly, two-winged fly, *c.*1in long ; sucks the blood of horses and cattle in summer.

gadolinium, *gad-ō-lin'iŭm,* rare earth and element, Gd ; atomic weight 156·9 ; atomic number 64.

Gadshill, village near Rochester, Kent. Hereabouts (*Henry the Fourth,* part 1) Falstaff was robbed ; and here Charles Dickens died.

Gaea, *jē'ä,* in old Greek tales, daughter of Chaos, and mother of heaven and the sea.

Gaelic, *ga'lik,* language of the Gaels, a Celtic people living in Ireland, the Highlands of Scotland, and Canada, where many of them settled after the Highland Clearances (evictions) of the 19th c. Gaelic is still spoken in SW. Ireland, the West Highlands and Islands, and in Canada ; but it is dwindling fast, and although belated efforts are being made to save it, may soon die out altogether. See CELTI

Gainsborough, town, Lincolnshire ; on the R. Trent ; noted for shipbuilding and engineering ; called St Oggs in George Eliot's *Mill on the Floss.*

Gainsborough, THOMAS (1727–88), artist, *b* Sudbury, Suffolk ; naturally clever with his pencil as a child ; became famous as a portrait painter, first in Bath, then in London, where his sitters included George III, and many of the most famous people of the day. His masterpieces include *The Blue Boy,* sold 1921 for £150,000. One of the original members of the Royal Academy, 1768, but after his *Three Princesses* was given a bad position in the gallery, he never exhibited again, and withdrew his membership.

Gaitskell, RT. HON. HUGH (1906–), economist and politician ; Labour MP for S. Leeds 1945 ; held various ministerial appointments prior to becoming Chancellor of the Exchequer Oct 1950.

Galactic System, see ASTRONOMY

Galápagos, *gä-lä'pä'gōs* (Spanish for *tortoise*), twelve islands with several hundred islets in the Pacific ; owned by Ecuador ; noted for giant tortoises. The islands export guano and orchilla moss.

Galashiels, *gal'ä-shēlz*, town, Selkirkshire ; important for its woollen industry, particularly tweed-making in which it specialises ; also hosiery and footwear.

Galatia, *gä-lā'shi-ä*, anciently a district of Asia Minor, so named after the Gauls who invaded it in the 3rd c. BC ; later a Roman province, home of the Galatians, to whom St Paul wrote an Epistle, possibly from Antioch, *c.*AD53.

Galatians, see GALATIA

Galaxy, another name for the Milky Way, i.e. all the visible stars comprising one vast island group, possibly 50,000 million, among which is our own Solar System. Other galaxies are known to exist, but these are called extra-galatic nebulae as they are beyond the Milky Way, the farthest yet noted being *c.*140 million million light-years distant. See ASTRONOMY

Galba, SERVIUS SULPICIUS (3BC–AD69), Roman emperor for the last few months of his life.

Galen, CLAUDIUS, *gā'len*, 2nd c. Greek doctor, *b* Pergamum ; in great favour with the Roman emperor Marcus Aurelius ; author of 500 medical works ; ranks with Hippocrates as one of the greatest doctors before William Harvey, and as the founder of experimental physiology.

galena or **lead glance,** *gä-lē'nä*, commonest ore of lead ; found as lead sulphide, PbS. See LEAD

Galgacus, see BRITAIN, ANCIENT

Galicia, *gä-lish'i-ä*, (1) region of S. Poland ; has great forest areas ; produces timber, grain and hemp ; noted for petroleum ; (2) a province of NW. Spain.

Galilee, division of N. Palestine ; was a Roman province in the days of Christ ; also lake or inland sea *c.*13m long ; fed by the R. Jordan ; largely surrounded by mountains, and almost 700ft below the level of the Mediterranean. It is known also as the Sea of Tiberius or Lake Gennesaret.

Galileo, *gal-i-lā'ō* (1564–1642), Italian pioneer in science and astronomy ; *b* Pisa ; early showed an inquiring mind and a genius for clear reasoning ; became professor of mathematics at Pisa University, but had to resign because his theories were in advance of his day. In Padua (1592) he made many scientific discoveries, and constructed the first astronomical telescope, hence a revolution in the fundamentals of astronomy.

Galileo noted Jupiter's moons, confirmed Copernicus's theory of the Solar System, and observed sun-spots and several planets. Befriended by Cosmo II, Grand Duke of Tuscany, he was summoned to Rome 1616 to answer charges

GALILEO 1564–1642

of heresy, and again 1633, when, as an old man, he was compelled to declare before the Inquisition that the sun went round the earth. This was required that his scientific discoveries and theories might be discredited, and that the old beliefs of the Church might not be disturbed. After a brief imprisonment he was allowed to return to his home near Florence. Towards the end of his life he was blind.

Galileo ranks as one of the world's master thinkers. When only a youth he observed a swinging lamp in Pisa Cathedral, and was led to deduce the laws relating to pendulums. He discovered that when a body falls, the space through which it passes in equal times increases in the ratio 1, 3, 5, etc. He improved the thermometer, investigated magnetism, and noted the rotation of the sun, and also its inclination. He remains a supreme example of genius shackled by the ignorance and superstition of his time.

In Fahie's *Life of Galileo* we read :
Galileo, first of all men to see the heavens by telescope, was modest and unassuming. Of self-praise so much is recorded of him that when his sight was decaying he used to comfort himself by saying that *of all the sons of Adam none had seen so much as he.*

gall, one of many swellings caused on the leaves of various trees by insects. One of the best-known is the oak-gall, called oak-apple, the result of the gall-fly *Cynips quercus folii* burying an egg, the grub later feeding on the leafy matter. Galls are found on leaves of beech, lime and spruce.

galleon, large Spanish ship (15th–17th c.) ; sometimes with 3 or 4 gun-decks, always with a lofty stem and stern. Galleons were used to carry treasure from the W. Indies. In warfare the galleon was awkward to handle, hence the success of smaller but nimbler English ships.

galley, see SHIPS

Galli-Curci, AMELITA, *gäl'lē koor'che* (1889–), famous Italian soprano.

Gallipoli, *gä-lip'ōlē*, fortified area of European Turkey ; at the mouth of the Dardanelles ; scene 1914–16 of a disastrous British attempt to aid Russia.

gallium, element, Ga, and metal of the aluminium group ; atomic weight 69·72 ; atomic number 31 ; discovered 1875.

Galloway, district of SW. Scotland, comprising shires of Wigtown and Kirkcudbright ; noted for cattle, sheep and especially small, strong horses.

Galloway, MULL OF, most southerly point of Scotland, a promontory over 200ft high.

Gallup, DR GEORGE (1901–), director of the American Institute of Public Opinion, a fairly accurate indication of popular feeling on a variety of matters, political and non-political, public reaction being based on answers to questions put to 1,500 people. A somewhat similar service in Britain, the Social Survey, is a government organisation which does not, however, collect political opinion.

Galsworthy, JOHN, *gölz-wŭr-thi* (1867–1933), author and dramatist, *b* Coombe, Surrey ; educated Harrow and Oxford ; called to the Bar 1890 ; travelled abroad while a young man. He became famous as a writer (1906) with the publication of his novel *The Man of Property*, the first of a long series of brilliant novels portraying the English upper middle-class, the series becoming known later as *The Forsyte Saga*, in which the varying fortunes of the Forsyte family are told in masterly style and with vivid characterisation. Among other Forsyte books are *To Let*, *The White Monkey*, *The Silver Spoon*, *Swan Song*, *Maid in Waiting*, *Flowering Wilderness*.

Galsworthy was also a notable playwright, his first success being *The Silver Box* (1906), a social study of absorbing interest. It was followed by *The Skin Game*, *Loyalties* and *Escape*, which are all masterly studies of social conditions in his day. His books and plays deal with late Victorian, Edwardian and later times, but his art is timeless.

Galvani, LUIGI, *gäl-vä'ni* (1737–98), Italian professor of anatomy, *b* Bologna ; discovered animal electricity. His name is commemorated in the *galvanic* current.

galvanised iron, thin sheets of iron coated with zinc by dipping into molten metal, a method devised *c*.1742. See ZINC

galvanometer, instrument for detecting or comparing small electric currents, the principle depending on the magnetic effect. Sensitive types will record less than a millionth of an ampere by using a beam of light in place of a pointer. See ELECTRICITY

Galveston, city and port, Texas, USA ; has a fine harbour ; notable for its trade in cotton, also oil and timber ; pop.61,000.

Galway, *göl'wä*, farming county, W. Eire ; has a rocky coast ; visited by tourists, especially the wild district of Connemara; co.tn Galway.

Galway, university and co.tn, Galway, Eire ; notable for fisheries ; exports marble.

Gamba, PIERINO (1936–), Italian musical prodigy, who, when only nine, conducted the Royal Opera House orchestra, Rome. He conducted in the Albert Hall (London) when only 11 years of age.

Gambetta, LÉON (1838–82), French statesman, *b* Cahors, Lot ; leader of the party that opposed Napoleon III ; proclaimed the establishment of the 3rd Republic 1870 ; Premier 1881–82.

Gambia, British Crown colony by the R. Gambia, which flows 1,000m in W. Africa. The colony has an area of 4,132sq.m ; the climate is unhealthy ; exports include ground-nuts, also palm kernels, skins, beeswax ; cap. Bathurst.

gambling, betting or staking money (often at odds) against some other person on the outcome of a sporting or other event, in the hope of winning stake money.

English and Scots laws about gambling are obscure. Some forms of organised gambling, especially those in which chance plays a larger part than skill, are illegal ; but betting on horse races and on football is practised on a large scale, and football pools and bookmaking are flourishing major industries.

Those who gamble are lured on to some extent by the excitement of gambling, and by the hope of winning huge sums for relatively small stakes. Few of them realise that mathematically their chances of real success are very low indeed.

Some countries raise funds by means of lotteries, much as many charitable organisations in this country raise funds from raffles, but on a much larger scale. Many people buy numbered tickets, a few of the counterfoils are drawn out of a hat, or otherwise selected by pure chance, and those numbers are declared to be winning numbers. A proportion of the fund raised by the sale of tickets is then distributed as prize money to the holders of the corresponding tickets.

game, birds or animals killed in field-sports, coursing, or shooting ; includes pheasants, partridges, black-game, red grouse, bustard, ptarmigan (Scotland), woodcock, snipe, quail, landrail, wild duck (Scotland), rabbit and hare. A game licence is required before game may be shot, and no-one may kill game during what is called the close season. For partridges this is 2 Feb.–31 Aug. ; pheasants 2 Feb.–30 Sept. ; grouse 10 or 11 Dec.–11 Aug. ; black-game 11 Dec.–19 Aug. Hares are protected from March–July.

Game laws make poaching a finable offence ; and the work of game-keepers is to care for game and to keep trespassers off the estate. A *game-keeper's* ' *museum* ' is his collection of dead birds and animals that prey on game.

gamma-rays (γ-rays), electromagnetic waves up to *c*.1·4/100 millionths cm in length, vibrating over 2×10^{18} times per sec. They result from the explosion of the nuclei of atoms, and are one of the natural ' by-products ' of the atomic disintegration that accompanies radioactivity. See RADIOACTIVITY ; WAVE-LENGTH

Gandhi, MOHANDAS KARAMCHAND, *gän'dē* (1869–1948), known as the Mahatma (saint and wise one), Indian Nationalist leader ; *b* Porbandar ; studied in London ; leader of the Indian Home Rule movement from *c*.1919, his method of ' attacking ' the British Government being that of civil disobedience and non-co-operation ; repeatedly threatened to starve to death if his demands were not agreed to ; attended the Indian Round Table Conference 1931 ; later became vindicator of the Untouchables (out-casts) ; exercised an enormous influence in India. Regarded as a saint, his sincerity was never in question.

In Sept 1947 he used his immense influence to prevent civil strife between Moslems and Hindus in Calcutta by threatening to starve himself to death if it continued. In Jan 1948 he was assassinated by a fanatical Hindu belonging to an organisation which disapproved of Gandhi's desire to see Hindus living peaceably with their rivals, the Moslems. At his funeral Pandit Nehru said : ' Gandhi's journey is ended, but the journey of the Indian people has just begun. Let us march forward under the radiant light of his teachings.'

GANDHI 1869–1948

THE GANNET

Ganges, *gan'jēz*, Indian river rising in an ice-cave among the Himalayas ; flows *c*.1,500m to the Great Delta in the Bay of Bengal, and has among its tributaries the Jumna and Hooghly. The Ganges joins the Brahmaputra at Goalanda. Regarded as sacred by Hindus, it is bathed in (especially at Benares) in the belief that its waters wash sin away.

ganglion, a collection of nerve-cells, e.g. the solar plexus of the sympathetic ner-vous system in the abdomen.

gannet or **solan goose**, seabird *c*.3ft long ; has white plumage except for some black wing feathers and a tinge of buff on the head. The birds arrive in Britain (notably the Bass Rock) in spring, where the females lay one egg each in rough nests on cliff edges.

gantry, see CRANE

Garbett, DR CYRIL FORSTER (1875–   ), English churchman ; Bishop of South-wark 1919 ; of Winchester 1932 ; Archbishop of York 1942 ; author of several books.

garden city, see TOWN PLANNING

gardening, cultivation of the soil either for an ornamental garden, i.e. flowers, bushes, ornamental trees and rockeries, or for a vegetable garden.

The science of gardening is known as horticulture, and prior to the 16th c. it was largely developed by monks who were chiefly concerned with growing vegetables and fruit, and also herbs for medicinal purposes.

Since then gardening has become increasingly popular, and the majority of people living in town or country cultivate gardens, often having both an ornamental and a vegetable garden. The cultivation of an allotment (a rented piece of ground) has grown in popularity in the last 25 years, and was encouraged during World War II by the *Grow More Food Campaign*.

The following gardening books are recommended : *Modern Gardening*, J. S. Dakers ; *Gardening for Pleasure*, G. E. Whitehead ; *Saturday in My Garden*, F. H. Farthing.

Garfield, JAMES ABRAM (1831–81), Ameri-can statesman, *b* Orange, Ohio, USA, of humble parents ; commanded an infantry brigade in the Civil War ; elected Republican president 1881 ; assassinated by a lawyer.

Gargantua, see RABELAIS, F.

gargoyle, *gär'goil*, projecting water-spout (usually of stone) which, in Gothic architecture, is often a grotesque animal or human shape.

Garibaldi, GIUSEPPE, *gä-rē-bäl'dē* (1807–82), Italian revolutionary whose extraordinary feats of generalship helped to liberate Italy from Austrian and Papal rule ; *b* Nice ; joined the Young Italy movement ; fled to S. America, where he proved himself a master of guerilla warfare while aiding Rio Grande to fight the Brazilians ; defended the new Roman republic against the French 1849 ; made a famous march across Italy to reach the Venetian republic, and escaped from the armies of France, Austria, Spain and Naples to USA. Later he bought part of the island of Caprera, where he lived as a farmer, but he was soon again fighting the Austrians. As dictator of the two Sicilies he recognised Victor Emmanuel as king.

GARIBALDI 1807–82

He is justly regarded as a fine statesman, as a courageous patriot whose ' red shirts ' won liberty for all Italy, and as a national hero, ranking with Cavour and Mazzini as a maker of modern Italy.

garlic, plant (order *Liliaceae*) of the onion family ; grows to a height of 2ft ; has an onion-like root and white flowers. Wild garlic (*Allium oleraceum*) is used in cooking.

Garonne, *gä-rön'*, French river ; flows *c.*360m by Toulouse to Bordeaux on the Bay of Biscay.

Garrick, DAVID (1717–79), actor, *b* Hereford ; friend of Dr Samuel Johnson, with whom he set out 1737 from Lich-

field for London, where they arrived with only 4d between them. Having won in 1741 an astonishing success as Richard III, he became owner of Drury Lane theatre, and established a reputation as one of the greatest Shakespearean actors of all time.

Garter, ORDER OF THE, see CHIVALRY

Garvin, JAMES LOUIS (1868–1947), journalist, *b* Birkenhead ; editor of the *Observer* 1908 ; during the inter-war period an influential writer on foreign affairs.

gas, one of the three states of matter (the others being solid and liquid). In a gas, the molecules have least cohesion, hence a gas always occupies all the space in which it is placed. When cooled sufficiently, gases become liquid or solid ; similarly heat may change a solid or liquid to a gas. Vapour is a gas readily made liquid by a small decrease of temperature or increase of pressure, e.g. water vapour.

Gas laws include (*a*) Boyle's law (1662) : *If the temperature of a gas remains constant, its volume changes inversely as the pressure,* i.e. if the pressure (P) is doubled, the volume (V) is halved ; (*b*) Charles's law : *At constant pressure all gases expand by 1/273rd of their volume at 0°C for a rise in temperature of 1°C* ; i.e. the volume of a given mass of gas at constant pressure is directly proportional to the absolute temperature. Actually, gases do not strictly obey these laws, except at higher temperatures. Gay-Lussac's law of gaseous combination states that *when gases combine they do so in a simple ratio by volume to each other and to the gaseous product, measured under the same conditions of temperature and pressure.* This is explained by Avogadro's hypothesis : *Equal volumes of all gases contain equal numbers of molecules under the same conditions of temperature and pressure.*

Common gases include oxygen, nitrogen, hydrogen, carbon dioxide, carbon monoxide, methane, coal-gas, water gas (produced by passing steam over incandescent coke), producer gas from anthracite, coal or coke.

Coal gas is widely used for domestic and industrial purposes. See DIAGRAM p. 285

Certain gases, such as chlorine, mustard, phosgene, etc., are highly poisonous and were used in World War I, but not in World War II. See THERMO-DYNAMICS

Gascony, formerly a province of SW. France; its people, small but lively, were proverbially boastful. See FRANCE

gas engine, type of internal combustion engine which harnesses the power released by explosions of a mixture of gas and air in a closed cylinder. Invented *c.*1860 for use with coal-gas, the gas engine was improved by Nicholas Otto, who introduced the 4-stroke type, i.e. one explosion to every four strokes

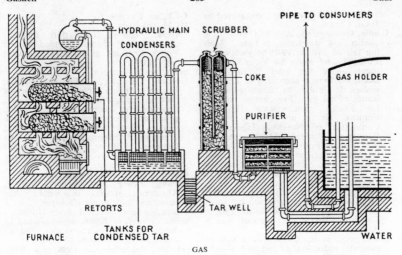

PIPE TO CONSUMERS

HYDRAULIC MAIN   SCRUBBER
CONDENSERS
COKE   GAS HOLDER
PURIFIER
RETORTS   TAR WELL
TANKS FOR   WATER
FURNACE   CONDENSED TAR

GAS

Diagram of the production of coal-gas

of the piston. Sir Dugald Clerk's 2-stroke engine (1886) led to gas-engines developing 5,000 hp.

The most recent advance is the GAS TURBINE, increasingly used since *c.*1936. As the steam turbine is driven by the energy of expanding steam, so the gas turbine has a wheel driven direct by the blast of burning fuel, its simplicity eliminating working parts liable to get out of order. This type has immense possibilities as a marine engine, and for developing electric power. Units producing 10,000hp are now challenging the efficiency of the Diesel engine.

Gaskell, ELIZABETH CLEGHORN (1810–65), author, *b* Chelsea (London), daughter of William Stevenson, but brought up by an aunt at Knutsford, Cheshire. She married William Gaskell 1832, and wrote her first novel *Mary Barton* after the death of her baby son. Her famous story *Cranford* charmingly depicts life in Knutsford, and was written for Charles Dickens' magazine *Household Words.* Her other books include *Sylvia's Lovers* and a vivid biography of her friend Charlotte Brontë.

gas-meter, to read : ignore dial D, which is used only for testing. Read the others in A, B, C order, taking the smaller of two figures if the hand is between them, except when it is between 0 and 9, in which case read 9 ; add 00 after setting down the four readings ; this is the *present* reading of the meter ; subtract previous reading ; this leaves number of cu.ft of gas used since last reading. In the diagram the meter reads 37500cu.ft. See THERM

Gastropoda, see MOLLUSCA

Gates, HORATIO (1728–1806), American soldier ; partly responsible for com-

pelling General Burgoyne to surrender at Saratoga 1777 ; commanded the Southern Army, but was defeated at Camden 1780.

Gateshead, town, County Durham ; faces Newcastle across the Tyne ; notable for iron foundries, shipbuilding, chemicals, etc. ; pop.105,000.

Gath, ancient Philistine city, Syria.

Gatun, see CANALS

Gatwick, *gat'ik*, village, Surrey ; has an airport opened 1936. The circular Martello Air Station is linked by rail with Victoria Station, London.

Gauchos, *gow'chō*, natives of the pampas in Uruguay and Argentina (S. America), partly Indian, partly Spanish. They are daring horsemen, and are skilled with lasso and bolas.

Gaul, old name for France, from the Latin Gallia ; included also the region now known as Belgium and the Netherlands,

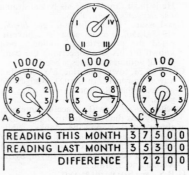

READING THIS MONTH	3	7	5	0	0
READING LAST MONTH	3	5	3	0	0
DIFFERENCE		2	2	0	0

GAS METER

and a part of Germany ; conquered by Julius Caesar.

Gaulle, GENERAL DE, *dĕ gawl* (1890–   ), soldier and statesman, *b* Lille.   After the fall of France 1940 he escaped to England, and while the Vichy Government under the aged Pétain ruled Occupied France according to German wishes, de Gaulle was recognised as the leader of all Free Frenchmen, later of La France Combattante (Fighting France). He set up 1943 the French Committee of National Liberation ; Paris was liberated 1944 by the FFI (Les Forces Françaises de l'Intérieur). De Gaulle became president 1945, but resigned 1946. From 1947 he attempted to rally the French to abolish party differences.

gauntlet, in armour, leather glove (with or without fingers) protected by small metal plates ; introduced in the 13th c. To throw down the gauntlet was a challenge to fight.

gauss, *gows,* in the CGS system, unit of magnetic induction, or the unit of field strength. The present strength of the earth's magnetic field (at Greenwich) is approx. 0·17 gauss. See GAUSS, K. F.

Gauss, KARL FRIEDRICH (1777–1855), German scientist and mathematician who mathematically discovered the planet Ceres, and experimented with electricity and magnetism, hence the *gauss,* the unit of magnetic induction.

Gautier, THÉOPHILE, *gō-tyä'* (1811–72), romantic French author and poet, *b* Tarbes. His writings include *Le Capitaine Fraçasse,* and his ghost-story *La Morte Amoureuse.*

Gaveston, PIERS, *gav'-* (*d* 1312), courtier, favourite and foster-brother of Edward II of England.   Son of a Gascon knight, he ruled the king in all things till the exasperated barons banded together against him. He was beheaded near Warwick.

Gay, JOHN (1685–1732), poet and playwright, *b* Barnstaple, Devon ; befriended by Alexander Pope ; wrote *Shepherd's Week, Fifty-one Fables,* and the much-loved ballad *Black-eyed Susan.* He is most famous for his lyrical drama *The Beggar's Opera,* 1728.

Gay-Lussac, LOUIS JOSEPH, *gā lü-säk'* (1778–1850), French scientist ; investigated the properties of iodine ; best known for his law concerning the combining volumes of gases. See GAS

Gaza, *gā'zä,* town, Palestine, SW. of Jaffa ; now an airport. In the OT (Judges 16) we read that Samson carried away its gates.

gazelle, *ga-zel',* swift, graceful antelope, usually less than 30in high ; light brown above, darker on the flanks, white below ; eyes large and soft ; legs very slender ; horns up to 13in long ; found mostly in desert regions of Egypt, Syria, Arabia and S. Iran.

G.B.S., see SHAW, BERNARD

GC, see DECORATIONS

GCF, see FACTORS

GCM, see FACTORS

Gdynia, *g'dēn'yä,* Baltic port, Poland ; rivals Danzig though founded on the Polish Corridor as recently as 1920 ; pop.78,000.

gears, see MECHANICS

Geddes, SIR ERIC, *ged'is* (1875–1937), British politician ; played an important part in transporting troops 1914–18 ; presided over a committee (1922) which produced proposals (known as the Geddes Axe) for reducing national expenditure. His brother, SIR AUCKLAND GEDDES (1879–   ), held important government posts 1916–24, including that of ambassador to USA.

Geddes, JENNY, see COVENANTERS

Geelong, *jē-long',* port and city, Victoria, Australia ; trades in wool ; has tanneries and paper factories ; is a pleasant summer resort ; pop.41,000.

geisha, *gā'shä,* in Japan, a girl trained to dance, sing, tell witty stories, and so entertain friends invited to a party.

gelatine, colourless, tasteless glue from hides and bones.

gelding, see HORSE

Gelée, CLAUDE, *zhĕ-lā* (1600–82), French painter better known as Claude le Lorrain (from Lorraine, his birthplace) ; noted for classical landscapes.

Gellert, *gel'ĕrt,* hound said to have been given to Llewellyn 1205 by King John. It was slain by Llewellyn who imagined that it had killed his infant son, though actually it had saved the child from a wolf ; tradition says the dog is buried at Beddgelert, N. Wales.

gem, cut and polished precious stone, e.g. diamond, ruby, sapphire, topaz and emerald.   Gem-cutting was carried on in Paris in the 13th c. ; Amsterdam has been a famous centre since the 15th c. ; now London rivals Amsterdam, Antwerp and Paris.

gendarme, *zhän-därm'* (*gens d'armes,* men-at-arms), member of the French military constabulary, mostly under civil control.

General Assembly, (1) annual meeting at Edinburgh of elected representatives of the Church of Scotland to discuss and vote upon church policy for the coming year. (2) See UNO

General Certificate of Education, see EXAMINATIONS

Genesis, *jen'ē-sis,* first book of the OT ; the Hebrew title is *In the Beginning.* Genesis tells the Hebrew story of the Creation ; also stories of the patriarchs, e.g. Abraham and Jacob.

Geneva, *jĕ-nē'vä* (*a*) lake between Switzerland and France ; 45m long ; drained by the R. Rhone, which flows through (*b*) the handsome city of Geneva, cap. of the canton, and beautifully situated by the lake ; notable for its many fine buildings, e.g. the 12th c. cathedral of St Peter, and the imposing palace of the Nations, Geneva being the HQ of the former League of Nations. The city was a great centre of the Protestant faith from Calvin's day (16th c.), and was associated with the foundation of the Red Cross Society ; pop.124,000.

Geneva Convention, international agreement 1906 whereby countries at war undertake to give proper care to the wounded, to respect those who attend them, also vehicles, buildings and hospital ships which show a red cross on a white background.

Genoa, *jen'ō-ä,* city and port, N. Italy ; notable for its docks and harbour, also for shipbuilding, ironworks and textile mills ; birthplace of Columbus ; pop. 661,000.

genre, see ART

gentian, *jen'shan,* name of several plants (family *Gentianaceae*) including the field gentian, found in pastures (notably in Scotland) ; has a short upright stem ; pointed leaves and usually 5-pointed intensely blue flowers.

GENTIAN

geodesy, *jē-od'ē-si,* large scale surveying.

Geoffrey of Monmouth, *jef'ri,* 12th c. English writer of *Historia Britonum, c.*1139. It is a collection of ancient Breton legends.

geography, study of the earth and its life ; comprises *mathematical geography,* dealing with the size of the earth, its place in the universe, seasons and tides ; *cartography,* the science of map-making; *physical geography,* contours, heights and rivers ; *geomorphology,* shapes of landmasses and oceans ; and *climatology,* study of climate and weather. In recent years *human geography,* the study of

man in relation to the earth, has become the most important branch of the science, and all the branches mentioned above are studied with particular reference to their effect on man, and the effect of man's works on nature.

While the German Ratzel believes that environment determines the way in which man evolves, Vidal de la Blanche believes that man is not only influenced by his environment, but that he has some control over it, and that much depends on his mental ability. Here anthropology and archaeology are allied to geography, which goes on to show how different societies and cultures influence each other, and how they are moulded by environment. The study of the growth of towns and nations, and the relations between industry, agriculture, trade, transport, engineering and the earth comprise *political* and *commercial geography.*

Read *The World's Wealth,* W. G. Moore.

geology, science of the history of the earth and its life as recorded in the rocks ; closely allied with or including *petrology* and *mineralogy,* which deal with the minerals of which rocks are composed ; *stratigraphy,* the history and geography of ancient land surfaces ; *palaeontology,* the science of fossils ; *dynamical* and *structural geology,* aspects that deal with the causes and processes of geological change. A geologist requires knowledge of all these sciences, and in the course of his studies he examines borings, mineshafts, rivers, rail and road cuttings, glacial moraines, the weathering of rocks and so on.

Rocks may be classified as (*a*) *igneous* (i.e. fire-formed), (*b*) *sedimentary,* (*c*) *metamorphic* and (*d*) *igneous,* which completes the cycle. No trace of the original igneous rocks is to be found today, but beneath the solid crust of the earth is a ' shell ' of such intense heat that when pressure is exerted locally it readily liquifies and may come to the surface, through vents or fissures, in the form of lava, so that new igneous rocks appear from time to time when lava is ejected from a volcano in eruption.

As the crust of the earth cooled, wind and rain broke down the original rocks, and carried the material to seas and lakes. There it was deposited in layers (strata), either as sand, mud or silts. In time, owing to the pressure of overlying sediments, these hardened, and became level beds of sedimentary rocks. Stresses set up in the underlying rocks gradually folded or warped the strata into mountains or plateaux, on which the work of erosion (weathering) began again. In the process of folding, such sedimentary rocks were sometimes altered in character, becoming metamorphosed, the mineral form and structure being changed. Similar changes are also produced by the heat of igneous rocks flowing over wide areas. The whole process—igneous rock, sedimentation, mountain-building to a higher level, and erosion to a lower level—is called a geological cycle.

Great and long-continued folding processes have built up the Alps, Andes, Himalayas and other ancient mountain chains, and it would seem that all the continents are gradually but continuously being elevated or depressed, e.g. the British Isles, which are sinking along the east coast, rising (an inch or so per century) along the west.

Much of our knowledge about conditions and life in geological ages is derived from a study of *fossils*, i.e. the hard remains of living creatures, e.g. shells, skeletons and leaf-stems, preserved in the rocks ; and it was William Smith (1769–1839), ' the father of geology,' who first pointed out that we may use fossils as a means of ' dating ' various rock strata ; for all but the oldest rocks (formed before life appeared, or when only soft - bodied creatures existed) have fossil remains.

Since William Smith's day geologists have divided time into Eras, Periods, Epochs and Ages, most of them several million years in duration. Such divisions are based on a study of relative phases in the evolution of their typical fossils. Fossils may also enable the geologist to determine the conditions in which various rocks were formed. •

Geological time is usually divided into the following periods :

(*a*) *Pre-Cambrian*, an era no doubt longer than all the later periods put together, since it includes those remote ages in the earth's long history (possibly 3,000 million years) before life of any kind existed, and also the period when whatever life did exist possessed no hard parts and has, therefore, left no traces in the strata then laid down. The terms *Azoic* (without life) and *Eozoic* (the dawn of life) are sometimes given to the pre-Cambrian era.

(*b*) *Palaeozoic* (ancient life). This opened with the Cambrian era, when the warmer waters swarmed with corals and trilobites (creatures somewhat resembling the woodlouse, but often 9ft long). In rocks of the *Silurian* period we find fossils of ancient crustaceans (shrimp-like), and also the first fishes (though not true fishes), a highly important event in evolution, since these creatures were the first backboned animals (*vertebrates*). *Devonian* rocks (the Old Red Sandstone) abound not only in fish but in fossils of spiders, amphibians and land plants of kinds now extinct.

The Devonian was followed by the *Carboniferous* period, a time when what is now Britain was under water, and when immensely thick layers of limestone were laid down. Later the region that is now the N. Sea became the delta of a huge river which left great quantities of millstone grit over areas of N. England and the Midlands. In the swamps of the delta grew forests, the decaying vegetation of which eventually became the coal seams that are of supreme importance to Britain today. Devonian rocks are rich in fish-fossils ; the Carboniferous in fossils of tree-ferns, mosses, horsetails and insects, e.g. mayflies and dragonflies. The last period of the Palaeozoic Era is called the *Permian*.

(*c*) *Mesozoic* (medieval life), an Era that witnessed the appearance of wholly new forms of life. Its three periods are the *Triassic*, *Jurassic* and *Cretaceous*, the last-named being the period when minute sea-creatures (*foraminifera*) with chalky shells died and sank to the ocean bed, thus forming chalk strata. The geologist is enabled to ' date ' the rocks of this period by studying their fossil ammonites and belemnites.

The Mesozoic was the era during which reptiles, birds and the first mammals appeared. It was supremely the age of giant reptiles, e.g. the *plesiosaurus*, a sea-creature with paddles, and such land reptiles as the huge *dinosaurus*, the *brontosaurus* (sometimes 60ft long and weighing *c.*20 tons), and the *atlantosaurus*, possibly 100ft long. The *stegosaurus* (remains of which have been found in Britain and N. America) had a spinal ridge of great leaf-like shields, each *c.*3ft across. One group of dinosaurs developed into bat-like creatures having a kind of web enabling them to leap immense distances. Of these ' flying reptiles,' the *pterodactyl* (*ter-ŏ-dak'til*) was one of the most remarkable, having a wing-span of 20ft. It was not, however, in any scientific sense a bird, the earliest example of which was the toothed *archaeopteryx* (*är-kē-op'tĕr-iks*).

The age of reptiles seems to have come to an abrupt end, probably due to an entirely new environment, and with the dawn of the *Cainozoic* (Recent-life) Era new animal-forms appeared.

(*d*) *Cainozoic* or *Tertiary*, period in which animal life as we know it today made its appearance. It begins with the *Eocene* and *Oligocene*. In the *Miocene* great mountain-building movements were going on which resulted in the formation of the Alps and the Himalayas. All through this period (ending with the *Pliocene*) present-day forms of animal life and vegetation were spreading over the whole earth. It is evident from the fossils of earlier ages that the climate of these latitudes had been much warmer prior to the Tertiary period than it is now, and that in Britain climatic conditions were then not unlike those of the Amazon region today. The new climate conditions brought into being animals with smaller bodies but relatively larger brains, though among giants of the period were the *mastodon*, a mammal not unlike the later mammoth ; also the *dinotherium*, with curved tusks. The Pliocene is of interest to geologists because it is the first geological period in which definite traces of primitive man are found, though Sir Arthur Keith puts such traces back to the Miocene.

The Tertiary is interesting because of its varied climatic conditions, a series of Ice Ages beginning probably 1,000,000 years ago. Wide areas became covered with a thick ice-sheet (similar to that now over most of Greenland), the ice extending at least as far south as London, and also over much of Europe.

(e) *Quaternary* : The Ice Ages bring us out of the Tertiary into the Quaternary period. It seems that for a time warmer conditions returned to the north (not once only, but possibly several times), and that we are now living in a period when the ice is retreating. A modern scientist (de Geer) believes that as recently as 9,000 years ago Stockholm was under a thick sheet of ice. The work of glaciers in carving valleys and moulding the landscape is of great interest to geologists. Glacial moraines, deposits of boulders and of boulder clays, indicate one or other of the Ice Ages.

The pre-history of the earth is a study of great importance, not merely from the academic viewpoint, but in many practical ways. The geologist is able, by a study of rock formation, to determine where and at what depth water may be found, in what localities various ores can be mined, and the regions where oil may be tapped.

Read *Geology in the Service of Man*, W. G. Fearnsides and C. M. B. Bulman ; *The Old Red Sandstone*, Hugh Miller, an old classic, but fascinating and instructive nevertheless.

See ASTRONOMY ; EVOLUTION ; ICE AGE

geometrical progression (GP for short) ; in mathematics, a series of quantities in which each term is obtained by multiplying the preceding one by a constant factor, called the common ratio, e.g. 7, 14, 28, 56, each term (in this case) being twice the preceding. If, in a series of n terms, the common ratio is r, the first term being a, and the sum S, then $S = \dfrac{a(r^n - l)}{r - l}$; if r is less than l, the formula $S = a\dfrac{(l - r^n)}{(r - l)}$ may be used.

Note also l (last or n^{th} term) $= ar^{n-l}$.

S ∞ (sum of an infinite number of terms) $= \dfrac{a}{l - r}$, only true when $r < l$.

GM $= \sqrt{ab}$. See RATIO

geometry, branch of mathematics dealing with the properties of space, a form of exact reasoning based on axioms, basic principles which may be interpreted as either self-evident truths or necessary assumptions. Geometry arose from thinking about the practical ' rules of thumb ' used (perhaps in Egypt) by

early builders and land surveyors ; it was first put in order by Euclid (a Gk thinker) *c*.300BC, and is now regarded as comprising (i) *elementary geometry,* (a) *plane geometry*, dealing with lines, angles and figures, as squares, triangles, circles and their properties ; and (b) *solid geometry*, dealing with the properties of bodies having volume, e.g. cube and pyramid ; (ii) *higher Euclidean geometry*, dealing chiefly with curves resulting from cutting a cone in various ways, thus giving *conic sections*, e.g. the ellipse, parabola and hyperbola. Descartes invented *analytical geometry c*.1637 as a means of expressing the position of a point by co-ordinates, and resolving these into algebraic equations.

Since then new ideas of space have resulted in new systems of geometry (e.g. those of Riemann, Minkowski and Einstein) which have started from the assumption that physical space may not have the exact properties ascribed to it by Euclid. If this is so, it cannot be true that Euclid's axioms really are self-evident.

George, patron saint of England since Norman times ; said to have been George of Cappadocia who was put to death AD303 by Diocletian, but nothing is known of him with certainty except that he was martyred at Lydda, Palestine. Legend says he slew a dragon, and then preached Christianity. His festival is 23 April.

George I (1660–1727), King of Great Britain and Ireland, son of the Elector of Hanover and Sophia, granddaughter of James I of England. He secured the support of the Whigs and the Duke of Marlborough ; succeeded 1714 ; was unable to speak English, and owing to his frequent absences on the Continent he left the government in the hands of Sir Robert Walpole and other ministers, a policy which greatly strengthened the power of the cabinet. Events of his reign include the Jacobite rising 1715 and South Sea Bubble 1720.

George I (1845–1913), King of the Hellenes, *b* Copenhagen, younger son of Christian IX of Denmark ; chosen King of Greece 1862 ; reigned from 1863.

George II (1683–1760), King of Great Britain and Ireland, only son of George I. As Prince of Wales he quarrelled much with his father, whom he succeeded 1772; was influenced for good by his wife Caroline of Anspach ; retained Sir Robert Walpole as premier ; disliked and opposed the elder Pitt ; declared that ' ministers are the king in this country ' ; was the patron of Handel, the musician. Notable events of his reign include the Jacobite rising 1745 ; Wolfe's victory at Quebec 1759 ; Clive's successes in India ; the rise of Methodism under John Wesley.

George II (1890–1947), King of the Hellenes, eldest son of Constantine I ; reigned 1922–23 and 1935–1947.

George III (1738–1820), King of Great Britain and Ireland, grandson of George II, *b* London ; succeeded 1760. Determined from the first to be king in fact as well as in name, he wished to revive the old idea of the Divine Right of kings. Known as ' Farmer George,' he ' gloried in the name of Briton,' and became fairly popular for his homely ways and blameless private life.

Dismissing the Whigs, he ruled as an autocrat through his minister Lord North, premier for twelve years, but he blundered badly in his attitude to the N. American colonists. Owing to frequent attacks of insanity (he became permanently mad 1811) he was compelled to hand over the government to Pitt. His reign witnessed the French Revolution, the defeat of Napoleon by Nelson and Wellington, and the beginnings of the industrial revolution.

George IV (1762–1830), King of Great Britain and Ireland, eldest son of George III, *b* London. As Prince of Wales he lived wildly, drinking, gambling, spending extravagantly. He became Regent 1811, and succeeded 1820, earning the contempt and enmity of all. He was hissed in the streets, and treated his wife, Caroline of Brunswick, shamefully. His utter inability vastly strengthened the power of Parliament. It was said of him that he was ' a bad son, a bad husband, a bad father, a bad subject, a bad monarch and a bad friend.'

George V (1865–1936), King of Great Britain and Ireland, and the British Dominions beyond the Seas, Emperor of India ; *b* Marlborough House, London. Second son of Edward VII and Queen Alexandra, he entered the navy 1877, but gave up the career 1892 on the death of his elder brother, the Duke of Clarence. Created Duke of York that year, he married Princess Victoria Mary of Teck 1893 ; became Prince of Wales 1901 ; succeeded 1910 ; crowned 22 June 1911.

George V shared in all the anxieties of the war of 1914–18, winning the affection of the people. He was critically ill 1928, and enjoyed immense popularity at his Silver Jubilee 1935. His reign witnessed (besides World War I) the first foundations of a system of social security ; winning of votes for women, establishment of the IFS ; the first Labour government (1924) ; the economic crisis of 1931 ; a new Indian constitution 1935.

George VI (1895–   ), by the Grace of God of Great Britain and of the British Dominions beyond the Sea, King, Defender of the Faith (Emperor of India till 1947), *b* York Cottage, Sandringham 14 Dec ; third monarch of the House of Windsor ; second son of George V ; succeeded 11 Dec 1936 on the abdication of his elder brother, Edward VIII. He was crowned 12 May 1937. His illness in 1948 caused great concern.

George VI married Elizabeth Bowes-Lyon (daughter of the Earl of Strathmore and Kinghorne) 26 April 1923. The Queen was born 4 Aug 1900. Their children are PRINCESS ELIZABETH (heiress presumptive to the throne), *b* London 21 April 1926, and PRINCESS MARGARET ROSE, *b* Glamis Castle (Scotland) 21 Aug 1930. See ELIZABETH, PRINCESS

George Cross, see DECORATIONS

George Cross Island, see MALTA

Georgetown, port and cap., British Guiana; situated at the mouth of the Demerara R. ; greatly damaged by fire 1945 ; pop.94,000.

George Town, cap. and port, Penang, Straits Settlements ; exports rice, sugar and tin ; pop.165,000.

Georgia, Atlantic state of USA ; grows wheat on the hills, rice in the plains ; especially notable for cotton, also tobacco ; its forests yield pitch-pine ; the minerals include manganese and bauxite ; named after George II ; founded by James Oglethorpe ; cap. Atlanta.

Georgia, republic of USSR ; is south of the Caucasus Mts ; grows tea, cotton and tobacco ; chief town TIFLIS.

geranium, *je-rā′ni-ŭm,* plant (family *Geraniaceae*) with lobed leaves and five-petalled flowers, one British species being herb robert ; common garden geraniums (so called) are actually varieties of the genus Pelargonium.

German, SIR EDWARD (1862–1936), composer, *b* Whitchurch, Shropshire ; composed orchestral symphonies and songs, also incidental music to several of Shakespeare's plays ; of his operas, *Merrie England* is best-known. His real name was Edward German Jones.

germander speedwell, small plant (often creeping) with stalkless oval saw-edged leaves. The four-petalled bright blue flower with a white centre has two crimson stamens.

GERMANDER SPEEDWELL
The flowers, the leaves and the heart-shaped seed

germanium, element, Ge ; atomic weight 72·60 ; atomic number 32 ; rare, greyish-white metal discovered 1886.

German silver, alloy of *c*.5 parts copper, 2 parts zinc, and 2 parts nickel. Bluish-white, it is much used in the manufacture of cutlery, ornaments, electrical resistances, etc.

Germany, republic of central Europe. Prior to the Nazi régime (1933–45), Germany had an area of *c*.181,700sq.m, having lost Alsace-Lorraine to France and E. Prussia to Poland, while Danzig had become a free city, all as a result of World War I. Hitler compelled Austria to become part of the German Reich 1938, and during World War II other territories, e.g. Danzig, Slovakia, part of Poland, Denmark, Belgium, Netherlands, France, were either incorporated in Germany or occupied by Germans ; but all such territories were lost after World War II. Today the area is *c*.137,000sq.m, with an estimated pop. of 66,000,000. Large areas of Germany itself, many industrial centres and cities, were devastated by British and USA bombing during World War II, and Germany was in effect divided into two parts, the eastern occupied and administered by Russia, the western by Britain, USA and France.

The country comprises (*a*) a northern plain, the soil being somewhat poor, though forests abound, (*b*) the Rhine valley, with exceedingly fertile soil and a climate favouring the vine, (*c*) the southern plateau, generally unsuited to agriculture, except in the many valleys. Here are more forests, also mountains rising to nearly 10,000ft. The famous Black Forest region is in the south-west.

The chief rivers are the Weser, Elbe, Oder and (most important of all) the Rhine. The climate is continental, being somewhat colder in winter and warmer in summer than in England.

Germany's agricultural products include wheat, rye, oats, barley, maize, potatoes, beans, hemp, rape, sugar-beet, flax, tobacco and the vine. The people have brought dairying almost to a fine art. The forests yield timber and wood-pulp in immense quantities. The vast mineral wealth is unusually varied, e.g. iron (but of low grade), manganese, copper, lead, zinc, nickel, sulphur, antimony, cobalt, wolfram, uranium, etc., and also petroleum, the latter being synthetically manufactured on a large scale prior to, and during, World War II. Coal is also found. In no country in Europe was industry more highly developed than in pre-war Germany. Besides the usual manufactures (e.g. iron and steel, textiles and chemicals) the Germans specialised in knitted goods, hosiery, glass, musical and also scientific instruments, all manner of weapons and munitions of war, most of them in advance of those of other countries ; also in toys, clocks, watches and jewellery.

Germany had over 43,000m of railway in 1936, all except *c*.700m being State-owned. From 1933 onwards some thousands of miles of wide motor-roads (*autobahnen*) were built. Ship canals are an important feature, e.g. the Kiel Canal, carrying over 22,000,000 tons of shipping annually, also the Mittelland Canal, opened as recently as 1938. The chief ports include Hamburg, Bremen, Stettin, Königsberg, Kiel (Baltic). The cap., Berlin, on the R. Spree, is still largely in ruins. Other towns include Cologne (famous for its Cathedral and, among other manufactures, eau-de-Cologne), Munich (noted for its beer), Leipzig (world-famous for books and printing), Essen (noted for iron and steel, and the vast Krupp works producing munitions till destroyed by Allied bombing). Much of Germany's heavy industry was centred (prior to 1945) in the valley of the Ruhr, where great destruction was wrought by bombing in World War II.

Long a collection of almost independent states, Germany became to some degree unified as the German Empire after the Franco-Prussian War (1871), but with the abdication 1918 of the Emperor William II (known as the Kaiser), the country became a parliamentary republic. Later, the National Socialist Party (the Nazi party) led by Adolph Hitler won power, Hitler becoming Chancellor 1934. His desire to create a greater Germany led to his annexing one region after another, and ultimately (1939) to war. The Nazi period of German history is known as Dritte Reich, i.e. third Reich, the first being the Holy Roman Empire (962–1806), and the second, the Reich established by Bismarck, 1871–1918. Modern Germany (at the moment controlled by Russia, Britain, USA and France) comprises the following states (*Länder*):

American Zone : Bavaria, Württemberg Baden, Bremen and Hesse.

British Zone : Schleswig-Holstein, North Rhine-Westphalia, Hamburg and Lower Saxony.

French Zone : Rhineland-Palatinate, Baden, Württemberg-Hohenzollern and Saar, the latter voting for economic union with France 1947.

Russian Zone : Brandenburg, Saxony, Saxony-Anhalt and Mecklenburg.

Berlin itself is jointly occupied.

The Germans, a typical Teutonic race, usually have fair hair and blue eyes, especially in Prussia, those in the Rhineland and Bavaria being somewhat darker. Industrious and eminently systematic, they are lovers of music, song, the opera and the cinema, and have produced masterpieces of each. They excel in mechanical ingenuity. As scientists they are pre-eminent, notably in chemistry, and have done much pioneer work in plastics, explosives, synthetic substitutes for rubber, petrol

GERMANY AFTER WORLD WAR II

Western Germany, containing the Ruhr industrial area, consists of the zones occupied by the Western Allies 1945–49 : Eastern Germany is the area occupied by the Russians during the same period. Inside Eastern Germany, Berlin was divided into sectors, each being occupied by one of the four Allied Powers

and food. German doctors have long been world famous. In recent years German roads and architecture have been copied by most of the more advanced countries. In literature they boast a great tradition, e.g. Goethe, Lessing, Schiller, Heine, Hauptmann and Thomas Mann. Among their famous men—to mention only a few—are the musicians Mendelssohn, Bach, Beethoven, Handel (though he lived mostly in England), Gluck, Schumann. The great reformers John Huss and Martin Luther were Germans ; and so were Gutenberg, pioneer of printing, Immanuel Kant the philosopher, Leibnitz and Hegel.

Another name honoured in Germany is that of Frederick the Great, to whom military glory was everything. Unhappily his dreams of consolidating and extending Germany have long been those of the Germans as a people, especially the Prussians, dreams which have twice led to Germany's defeat this century. It is this ambition, coupled with a belief that the Germans are a super-race, that has brought such misery to a brilliantly clever and otherwise friendly people.

In 1949 Western Germany was called upon to build up a new constitution, and Britain and USA hope to see a new Germany taking its place in the Western Union of Europe. But the German problem remained unsolved, largely because the victorious powers (the USA, Great Britain, France and Russia) could not maintain agreement. In Nov 1950, in response to Russian activities in Eastern Germany, the Western Powers began to consider rearmament of Western Germany against possible Russian aggression.

germs, see BACTERIA

Gestapo, *ge-shatä'pō* (short for Geheime-Staats-Polizei), Nazi secret police ; used by the Nazi party in Germany and German-occupied countries to prevent and crush political opposition to Nazi rule ; developed into a terrorist organisation which, even on suspicion, removed political prisoners to concentration camps ; particularly active and brutal 1939–45. See NAZISM

Gesta Romanorum, *jes'tä* (*Deeds of the Romans*), collection of tales from Roman history, probably compiled in the 13th c. ; first printed in English by Wynkyn de Worde *c.*1510.

Gethsemane, *geth-sem'ä-nē*, quiet spot on the slopes of the Mount of Olives, about ¾m from Jerusalem. Christ was arrested in a garden there.

Gettysburg, *get'iz-bŭrg*, town, Pennsylvania USA. Near by was fought July 1863 a battle of the American Civil War, the Federals defeating the Confederates. The battlefield, dedicated by Abraham Lincoln as a national cemetery, has over 5,000 graves and a statue of Liberty. For Lincoln's Gettysburg speech see LINCOLN, ABRAHAM

geyser, *gī-zer*, hot spring sending up water and steam like a fountain ; found only in volcanic regions, and probably the result of water heated by molten lava underground. The most famous geysers occur in Yellowstone National Park, Wyoming, USA (' Old Faithful ' emits a spout of water 150ft high every 63 minutes) ; in Iceland, notably the Great Geyser, 70m from Reykjavik ; and in the neighbourhood of Rotorua, NZ, notable for hundreds of geysers.

GFS, see YOUTH ORGANISATIONS

ghat, *gawt* (Hindu, *path of descent*), flight of steps on a river bank in India ; notably the forty-seven ghats of Benares, used by pilgrims who bathe in the river or burn their dead hereabouts.

Ghats or **Ghauts,** EASTERN AND WESTERN, two ranges of mountains parallel to the east and west coasts of S. India.

Ghent, *gent*, city and port, Belgium ; cap. of E. Flanders ; at the junction of the river Lys and Schelde ; abounds in streams and canals, and has over 200 bridges. The chief industrial city of Belgium, it is noted for its cotton, flax and linen ; has long been famous for its flower shows ; pop.161,000.

ghetto, see JEWS

Ghibellines, see GUELPHS

giant panda, see PANDA

Giant's Causeway, see BASALT

gibbon, see APES AND MONKEYS

Gibbon, EDWARD (1737–94), historian, *b*

Putney ; son of a country gentleman ; was delicate in youth, and though he went to Oxford, had little academic training. Lived for a time at Lausanne (Switzerland), and made a tour of Europe, part of which was spent in Italy. One evening in 1764 he was sitting on the steps of the Church of Ara Coeli, Rome, while barefooted friars were singing vespers there. It was at this moment that he first had the idea of writing his famous book *The Decline and Fall of the Roman Empire*. He toiled at this 1772–87, and when it was complete he felt that his life's work was done. His history, a vivid pageant of prose, remains one of the greatest pieces of literature in our language. His style is superb ; his knowledge and judgment are generally unimpeachable.

As an example of Gibbon's style we take the following description of Mahomet as given in the *Decline and Fall* :

According to the tradition of his companions, Mahomet was distinguished by the beauty of his person— an outward gift which is seldom despised, except by those to whom it has been refused. Before he spoke, the orator engaged on his side the affections of a public or private audience. They applauded his commanding presence, his majestic aspect, his piercing eye, his gracious smile, his flowing beard, his countenance that painted every sensation of the soul, and his gestures that enforced each expression of the tongue. In the familiar offices of life he scrupulously adhered to the grave and ceremonious politeness of his country : his respectful attention to the rich and powerful was dignified by his condescension and affability to the poorest citizens of Mecca : the frankness of his manner concealed the artifice of his views ; and the habits of courtesy were imputed to personal friendship or universal benevolence. His memory was capacious and retentive, his wit easy and social, his imagination sublime, his judgment clear, rapid, and decisive. He possessed the courage both of thought and action ; and although his designs might gradually expand with his success, the first idea which he entertained of his divine mission bears the stamp of an original and superior genius.

Gibbons, GRINLING (1648–1721), English wood-carver, *b* Rotterdam ; discovered by John Evelyn, who introduced him to Sir Christopher Wren. His matchless carvings of fruit, foliage and flowers may be seen in St Paul's, at Chatsworth House and Petworth.

Gibbs, SIR PHILIP (1877–), writer ; war correspondent 1914–18 ; author of many novels, e.g. *The Street of Adventure, The Unchanging Quest, Blood Relations ;* his autobiography, *Pageant of the Years*.

Gibraltar, *ji-bröl'tĕr*, British colony on a rocky headland in the extreme S. of Spain ; *c*.4m long, ¾m wide, and rising 1,396ft. Controlling the western entrance to the Mediterranean through the Straits of Gibraltar (*c*.14m wide at the narrows), it is of supreme importance as a naval and air base. The rock is strongly defended, guns and munitions, etc. being housed in deep tunnels. The town is at the NW. corner of the rock.

Captured 1704 by Sir George Rooke, Gibraltar has been British since 1713. From 1779–83 it resisted a memorable siege when Lord Heathfield defended it successfully for three years seven months against the French and Spanish.

Gideon, *gid'i-on*, Hebrew judge and warrior ; son of Joash ; called by God to deliver Israel from the Midianites ; Judges 6–8.

Gielgud, JOHN, *gēl'gŭd* (1904–), actor and producer of plays, *b* London ; notable for his production of *Hamlet* 1934 ; has acted in many successful stage-plays and films.

Giggleswick, village, W. Yorkshire ; noted for its public school founded 1512.

Gigli, BENJAMINO, *jēl'yee* (1890–), Italian tenor ; first sang at Covent Garden 1930.

Gilbert, SIR HUMPHREY (1539–83), English navigator, step-brother of Sir Walter Raleigh, *b* Dartmouth, Devon. In 1578 he set out to find the NE. Passage, but failed ; he led an expedition 1583 to Newfoundland, planting at St John's the first English colony in America. On the return voyage he sailed in the *Squirrel* (of only 10 tons), the smaller of his two ships, but she sank. Just before she went down the crew of the other vessel (the *Golden Hind*) heard him call, *We are as near heaven by sea as by land.*

Gilbert, SIR WILLIAM SCHWENCK (1836–1911), humorist, *b* London ; became a lawyer, but soon turned to dramatic work, notably burlesques. He won fame by his twenty years' association with Sir Arthur Sullivan, the composer, in the production of Gilbert and Sullivan operas (e.g. *Trial by Jury* (1875), *HMS Pinafore, The Pirates of Penzance, Patience, Iolanthe, Princess Ida, The Mikado, Ruddigore, The Yeomen of the Guard, The Gondoliers*), in all of which Sullivan's charming music and Gilbert's topsy-turvy wit and humour combine to give delightful entertainment. See SULLIVAN, SIR ARTHUR SEYMOUR

Gilbert Islands Colony, island group in the Pacific, including Fanning I., Christmas I., the Gilbert Group of sixteen islands, the nine Ellice Islands and the Ocean I. The total area is 330sq.m ; the whole group belongs to Great Britain.

Gilead, *gil'ē-ad*, mountainous district of Transjordan (E. of the R. Jordan).

Gilgal, *gil'gal* (Hebrew, *stone circle*), OT name for several places, including one near Jericho.

Gillingham, *gil'ing-am*, town, Kent, on the R. Medway ; pop.55,000.

gin, *jin,* intoxicant. A colourless spirit, it is distilled from maize, with a little barley malt, and is flavoured with juniper berries.

ginger, plant of the E. Indies ; has lance-shaped leaves *c.*12in long, and clusters of yellow or blue flowers on a tall, leafless stem. The edible ginger used in cooking is from the underground stem.

gingham, *ging'am,* cotton or linen fabric often woven into stripes or checks.

Giorgione, *jŏr-jŏ'nā* (*d* 1510), Italian painter ; set free Venetian art from its religious fetters, and in place of saints and angels filled his glowing pictures with figures of ordinary men and women, substituting for ' heaven ' the beauty of nature in the world as we know it.

Giotto di Bondone, *jŏt'tō* (*d* 1337), Italian artist, called the father of the Italian Renaissance ; born near Florence. When Pope Benedict XI required proof of his ability, Giotto is said to have drawn a circle with one sweep of his hand. As city architect of Florence, he designed the cathedral campanile (separate bell-tower) ; but he is most famous for his pictures and frescoes, among which are studies of the Virgin and the Son, and of St Francis of Assisi.

Gippsland, *gips'-,* region of SE. Victoria, Australia.

GINGER

The root, the stem and the flowers

THE GIRAFFE

giraffe or **camel'opard,** *ji-räf',* tallest of all animals, sometimes reaching 18-20ft ; remarkable for its long front legs and neck. The two horn-like prominences on its head are covered with skin ; the long tongue is used in tearing down leaves from trees, though the animal very occasionally browses on grass, standing with legs far apart to do so. Light fawn with blotches of darker colour, the giraffe is common in Africa from Ethiopia to the Transvaal.

Girl Guides, sister association to the Boy Scouts. The movement, founded by the Chief Scout, Lord Baden-Powell, was advanced by his sister, Agnes Baden-Powell.

Guides are trained to ' guide ' girls younger than themselves, and one of the ideals is to make them worthy and useful citizens with character, intelligence, and physical and mental well-being. Girls of 8–11 may be Brownies, a group meeting under the leadership of a ' Brown Owl ' ; these may go on to be Recruits, Tenderfoots, or Guides, 11–16 ; girls over 16 may be Rangers ; each patrol has a leader, and a number of patrols make up a company with a captain, who must be over 21 ; a Ranger over 18 may be a lieutenant.

Badges awarded to Guides include those for child-nursing, signalling, star-knowledge, cobbling, toy-making, farming, cycling, dancing, riding, skating and pathfinding. The highest award is the Nurse Cavell Badge for life-saving. The Guide Promise and the Guide Laws are the same as those for Boy Scouts. The movement received a Royal Charter 1923, and now has *c.*1,300,000 members.

Gironde, *zhē-rawnd'*, department of SW. France ; cap. Bordeaux.

Girondists or **Girondins,** *ji-ron'dist*, members of the moderate republican party in the French Revolution. They were named from the district of Gironde, from which the leaders came. Overpowered by extremists (Jacobins) 1793, most of them perished by the guillotine.

Girtin, THOMAS (1775–1802), water-colour artist, *b* Southwark, London ; master of harmonious colouring.
" Had Tom Girtin lived," said Turner, " I should have starved."

Girton College, one of two colleges for women at Cambridge ; founded 1869.

Gisborne, *giz'bĕrn*, port, North I., NZ.

Gisors, BATTLE OF, see DIEU ET MON DROIT

Gissing, GEORGE (1857–1903), novelist, *b* Wakefield ; author of *The Private Papers of Henry Ryecroft.*

Gizeh, *ge'za*, town, Egypt, by the Nile, *c.*3m south of Cairo ; near it are the Sphinx and the Pyramids.

Glace Bay, *gläs*, town and port, Cape Breton I., Nova Scotia ; trades chiefly in coal and iron ; pop.26,000.

glacier, *glas'i-er*, slow-moving river of ice fed by an accumulation of snow. *Ice-sheets*, spread over Iceland, Greenland and Antarctica, travel 5–75ft a day towards the sea, where they break down into icebergs. Where a *glacier* flows along a valley, e.g. the Alps, Himalayas, Alaska, etc., it advances from 1–7ft daily, and ends as the source of a river or lake, e.g. the Rhone glacier. Rock debris left at the sides form *lateral moraines* ; those at the end, *terminal moraines* ; those in the middle, *medial moraines*, where the melting of the ice has formed an ice cavern in which debris is deposited, form *medial moraines.* Ice-erosion of land features is so distinctive that an ice-eroded landscape can be recognised long after the climate has completely changed. Many hills and valleys in Scotland and England have been shaped by prehistoric glaciers during the ' Ice Ages.'

gladiator, *glad'i-ā-tĕr* (Latin *gladius,* sword), professional fighter in ancient Roman times. He fought wild beasts in the amphitheatre, or in various ways engaged in contests with other gladiators. Before a fight in Rome the gladiators marched past the emperor and cried, *Ave Caesar, morituri te salutant*, i.e. ' Hail, Caesar, those about to die salute you.'

Gladstone, WILLIAM EWART (1809–98), statesman, *b* Liverpool of Scottish parents ; Tory member for Newark 1833 ; President of the Board of Trade 1843, when he had a seat in the Cabinet ; Secretary for War and the Colonies in Sir Robert Peel's ministry 1845 ; opposed the Liberals and Palmerston, but later gave up his Tory views. As Chancellor of the Exchequer 1853 he introduced a scheme for abolishing income tax ; violently opposed Palmerston again and

GLADSTONE 1809–98

also criticised Disraeli's proposed Reform Bill.

Gladstone joined Palmerston's Liberal ministry 1859 as Chancellor, the beginning of his most brilliant parliamentary period ; reduced income tax to 4d ; was the most able and active member of the Cabinet ; and was in charge of the rejected Reform Bill 1866. Leader of the Liberals 1867, he succeeded Disraeli as Prime Minister 1868, and passed important measures, e.g. the Irish Land Act and the Education Act 1870. Though disliked by Queen Victoria, he was Prime Minister again 1880–85, 1886, and 1892–94. He raised the Liberal party to great power. He failed to settle the Irish question, and became convinced of the need for Irish Home Rule, but his second Home Rule Bill was thrown out by the Lords 1894. He was eminently a champion of free trade.

With his passion, eloquence and vitality, Gladstone was a great political figure in Britain for over 50 years. A devout churchman and scholar, he wrote learnedly on the relations of State and Church, delighted in the classics, in walking, and in felling trees on his beautiful estate at Hawarden, Flintshire, where his fine library is now available for use by students who, if they wish, may book a room there, and live there for a time with others engaged in research.

Glamis, *gläms*, village, Angus. Near by is Glamis Castle, once the home of Macbeth. The castle, home of the Earl of Strathmore, was frequently visited by Princess Elizabeth in her early years.

Glamorganshire, coastal county, S. Wales ; has iron and coal in the north, but the south, noted for dairy farming, is called ' the Garden of Wales ' ; co.tn

Cardiff. A rich coal seam was found recently.

glands, groups of cells in animals (including man) ' secreting ' (manufacturing) substances essential to normal health. The lymphatic glands filter the lymph before it enters the bloodstream. The ductless glands produce hormones (i.e. extremely complex organic chemicals) which are released into the blood-stream and help to regulate many bodily processes.

Among ductless glands the most important are (i) the *thyroid* gland, comprising a lobe at each side of the windpipe, which produces thyroxine, energising the body, and enabling it to use sugar for energy ; the thyroid requires iodine to keep it active ; (ii) the *parathyroid*, behind the thyroid, which controls the amount of calcium in the blood ; (iii) the two *adrenal* glands, which affect the sex impulses and adapt the body to any sudden emergency by releasing adrenaline ; (iv) the *pituitary*, at the base of the under part of the brain ; this controls the growth of bone, the production of fat, and stimulates other glands ; (v) sex glands, or *gonads*, which secrete in the female *ova*, or eggcells, and in the male the sperm-cells needed to fertilise ova before reproduction can take place.

Glasgow, *glas´gō*, Royal Burgh, the largest city in Scotland ; on the R. Clyde ; great industrial centre for iron, steel, chemicals, shipbuilding (at Clydebank where the *Queen Mary* and *Queen Elizabeth* were constructed), leather, woollens, muslin, distilling, tobacco and furniture. Coal is mined in the neighbourhood. The cathedral is chiefly 13th c. The university was founded 1450. The city has a lord provost, and sends 15 members to Parliament ; pop.1,088,000.

glass, mixture of white sand (see SILICON), sodium carbonate, and calcium carbonate fused together, and forming a fusion of sodium silicate and calcium silicate. There are many varieties, e.g. *Bohemian glass*, a mixture of potassium and calcium silicates ; the addition of lead oxide produces *optical glass* ; *coloured glass* has a minute quantity of metallic oxide or salt, e.g. gold and copper give ruby red ; uranium produces green, and adds also a fluorescent quality (made use of in X-ray screens).

Glass is not in fact a solid, but a *liquid* that has been supercooled without crystallisation occurring. A poor conductor of heat, glass readily cracks when suddenly heated, owing to the strain of uneven expansion. To minimise this, glass may be annealed, i.e. reheated and allowed to cool slowly. Crown glass (for windows) is 72% silica, 11% lime, 17% soda ; flint glass is 55% silica, 10% lead, 35% potash. Glassware is still blown at the end of long tubes by skilled craftsmen ; but most processes in its manufacture are now performed by machinery.

Glass was known in Thebes 3400BC ; the Romans used window glass in the 3rd c. AD. There were glass windows in Wearmouth Abbey (County Durham) AD764, but it was long before windows became common in Britain. Recently, plastics have challenged glass ; thus, from 1925 urea-formaldehyde plastics (amino-plastics) have been made in vastly increasing quantities for many purposes.

The uses to which varieties of glass are put today are countless. Fibreglass Ltd produce continuous filament for glass-wool (much used in insulation) and for dress material rivalling silk. Beautiful, delicate, hanging in abundant and graceful folds, it is also fireproof, and may be woven into lengths of many hues. Glass wicks and filters are other products of the modern glass-maker's skill. Toughened (annealed) glass is made to withstand tremendous strains without breaking ; and Vitrolite is now finding its way into the modern house, especially for kitchen walls and sinks. Glass furniture is gaining in favour, and Pilkington Brothers Ltd manufacture glass ' bricks ' now incorporated in many schools to give as much sunlight as possible.

Glastonbury, town, Somerset ; rich in historic remains. Its ruined abbey is on the site of an earlier building which, according to legend, was founded by Joseph of Arimathea, who is supposed to have planted the famous Glastonbury thorn, said to have bloomed every Christmas Day. The town is supposed to be the Avalon of the King Arthur legends.

Glauber's salts, see SODIUM

glee, see SINGING

Glen Coe, *-kō´*, desolate valley, Argyllshire ; 10m long ; scene 1692 of the massacre of the MacIans (a *sept* or branch of the MacDonalds) by government troops, the excuse being that the MacIans had not made submission in time to William and Mary, and were, therefore, rebels.

Glen Coe is often spelt, less correctly, Glencoe.

Glendower, OWEN (*c.*1359–1416), Welsh rebel, claimed descent from the old Welsh princes ; champion of Welsh independence, boldly resisting English domination.

Read Shakespeare's *King Henry the Fourth*.

Glengarry (*a*) valley of the R. Garry, Inverness-shire, (*b*) a Highland bonnet or cap.

Glenmore, valley 60m long, Inverness-shire. Here is the Caledonian Canal.

gliding, see AVIATION

Globe Theatre, see SHAKESPEARE, WILLIAM ; THEATRE

Glorious First of June, see FIRST OF JUNE, GLORIOUS ; HOWE, LORD

Glossop, *-ŭp*, cotton-manufacturing and coal-mining town, Derbyshire ; pop. 20,000.

' Gloster Meteor,' see AVIATION

Gloucester, *glos′tĕr*, co.tn, Gloucestershire; on the R. Severn ; manufactures machinery, matches and chemicals ; has flour mills ; noted for its 11th c. cathedral ; pop.62,000.

Gloucester, DUKE OF (1355–97), known as Thomas of Woodstock, son of Edward III ; helped to crush the peasant rising 1381 ; became the chief opponent of Richard II's favourites ; for a time more or less ruled England ; murdered at Calais.

Gloucester, H.R.H., DUKE OF (1900–   ), 3rd son of George V, married Lady Alice Scott ; appointed Governor-General of Australia 16 Nov 1943, assumed office 30 Jan 1945.

Gloucester, HUMPHREY, DUKE OF (1391–1447), son of Henry IV of England ; wounded at Agincourt ; protector for the young Henry VI.

Gloucestershire, county of central England; includes the Cotswold Hills and Forest of Dean ; is mainly agricultural, but has two mining districts ; co.tn Gloucester.

glow-worm, female of the beetle *Lampyris noctiluca*. Though the male becomes fully developed, the female remains wingless and grublike, and has spots giving out a greenish-white light.

Glubb, JOHN BAGOT (1897–   ), known as Glubb Pasha, British soldier in Iraq etc. ; did important work with the Arab Legion in World War II.

Gluck, CHRISTOPH, *glook* (1714–87), German composer, born in Bavaria ; called the father of opera ; famous for the exquisite music of *Orfeo ed Euridice* (his masterpiece), and that of *Iphigénie en Aulide*, in which a few singers and a chorus express varying emotions and dramatic situations.

glucose or **dextrose** or **grape-sugar**, crystalline sugar, $C_6H_{12}O_6$, which occurs in certain sweet fruits and honey. The human body changes sugars and carbohydrates into glucose before converting them into energy. Glucose is commercially produced from starch, and is a perfect energy-giving food.

glue, impure gelatine prepared in various ways, e.g. boiling the skins of animals or fish ; also made from rubber, or by mixing and heating quicklime and linseed oil.

glutton, see WOLVERINE

glycerine or **glycerin** or **glycerol**, *glis′ĕr-ēn, -in, -ol*, $CH_2OH.CHOH.CH_2OH$, sweetish syrup. A by-product of soap manufacture, it has three hydroxyl groups and a high boiling-point, and is colourless and odourless. Used in preparing the explosive nitroglycerine, its esters, with fatty acids, are glycerides. Those of the higher fatty acids (e.g. stearic, palmitic, etc.) are common in vegetable and animal fats and oils.

glycogen, *glī′kō-jen*, the form in which the body stores carbohydrates manufactured from glucose and starch in the liver.

glycol or **ethylene glycol**, $CH_2OH.CH_2OH$, sweet, colourless liquid ; much used in car radiators to prevent freezing.

GM, see GEOMETRICAL PROGRESSION

G-man, USA slang for ' Government man,' i.e. a detective who is a special agent of the Federal Bureau of Investigation.

GMT, see TIME

gnat, *nat*, small two-winged insect related to the mosquito ; nine species occur in Britain, all passing the larval stage in stagnant water, all blood-sucking.

gneiss, *nīs*, rock comprising various mixtures of quartz, felspar and mica in layers.

gnu, see WILDEBEEST

Goa, Portuguese colony on the west coast of India ; is *c*.250m south of Bombay ; produces rice, fruits, betel-nuts, iron and manganese.

goat, horned animal akin to the ox, sheep and antelope. The male has a strong odour and is usually bearded. The wild goat belongs to Iran, Asia Minor and N. Africa ; domesticated varieties are widespread. The milk, free from tubercular infection, is rich in fat and casein. The Angora and Cashmere varieties yield silky hair.

Gobelin, JEAN, *gō-blan′* (d 1476), French dyer, b Reims ; made and dyed exquisite tapestries.

Gobi or **Sha-mo**, *gō′bē*, desert area of *c*.30,000sq.m in central Asia, mainly in Mongolia and Turkistan. Part is waterless, but some regions have sufficient scrub to support the flocks and herds of wandering tribes.

God, supreme being in, and creator of, the universe ; and as such worshipped by mankind. Primitive races are vividly aware of powerful beings or spirits, and in some primitive religions many gods are supposed to exist. More advanced races adopt the idea of one all-sufficient being, a belief taught by Christ, who gave us the idea of God the *father*, unseen, but known by the inward spirit of man. Christians believe that the perfection of all goodness, God's loving nature, is revealed in Christ's earthly life. In their view there can be ultimately no contradiction between science and religion. Science seeks to discover truth, and like faith must bring us to a belief in something not only beyond but also within ourselves, so that conscience is the voice of God urging us towards goodness.

Godalming, *god′al-ming*, charming old town, Surrey. Here is Charterhouse, the well-known boys' public school.

Godavari, *gōdä′vărē*, sacred river, India ; flows 700m, from the W. Ghats, across the Deccan, to the Bay of Bengal.

Godfrey, Count of Bouillon, *-bwee-yŏn* (d 1100), led a crusade 1096, and laid siege to Jerusalem, which he ruled until his death. He was a French nobleman.

Godiva, LADY, *gō-dī′vă*, wife of the 11th c. Leofric of Mercia, who, according to legend, promised not to continue his harsh treatment of the people of

Coventry if his wife rode naked through the town. She did so, covered by her long hair. Coventry has a bronze statue of Lady Godiva.

Godolphin, 1ST EARL OF, *gō-dol'fin* (1645–1712), English politician ; shared in the exile of Charles II, who subsequently made him First Lord of the Treasury. From 1702–10 he was mainly responsible for directing the country's affairs as the leader of Queen Anne's administration.

'God Save the King,' see ANTHEM

Godwin (*d* 1053), English earl. He was the most powerful man in the kingdom in the reign of Edward the Confessor, who married his daughter. Godwin, who opposed the Normans, was the father of Harold II, Sweyn and Tostig.

Godwin, MARY WOLLSTONECRAFT (1759–1797), writer, *b* London ; notable as a pioneer of women's rights, especially in education and independence ; her daughter, Mary, was Shelley's second wife.

Godwin-Austen or K2, world's second highest mt., and the highest in the British Empire (28,250ft). A peak of the Himalayas, it is named after Henry Godwin-Austen (1834–1923), a noted mountaineer.

Goebbels, DR JOSEPH, *gŭ'belz* (1897–1945), Nazi Propaganda Minister of Germany 1933–45. He committed suicide in the last days of the Nazi régime.

Goering, HERMAN WILHELM, *gŭr'ing* (1893–1946), German politician, *b* Rosenheim ; supported Hitler ; prime mover in many of the National Socialist (Nazi) bids for power ; commanded the German air force (*Luftwaffe*) ; a Field Marshal from 1938 ; condemned to death at the Nuremberg Trials, but took his own life in prison.

Goethe, JOHANN WOLFGANG VON, *gŭ'tĕ* (1749–1832), German thinker and writer, *b* Frankfort-on-Main of good family ; studied law ; became the trusted minister of Charles Augustus, Duke of Saxe-Weimar, and remained at Weimar till his death, though his visit to Italy 1786–1788 stirred again his romantic spirit.

As a scientist he was a pioneer of the theory of evolution and of a new theory of colour. He was critic, soldier, financier, philosopher, statesman and writer, his writings including lyrical poetry which ranks among the greatest of its kind. His prose includes *Götz von Berlichingen,* founded on robber legends of the Rhine. This greatly influenced romantic literature, and inspired Sir Walter Scott ; also *Hermann Und Dorothea.* His greatest work is *Faust,* completed a few weeks before he died. All his life he sought knowledge, and died calling for ' Light ! More light ! ' Note : *Geteilte Freud' ist doppelt Freude,* i.e. Joy shared is joy doubled.

Gog and **Magog,** legendary British giants. Carvings of them were made for the Guildhall (London) 1708.

Gogol, NIKOLAI VASSILIEVITCH, *gŏ'gŏli* (1809–52), writer, born in Poltava; known as the father of the Russian novel ; author of *Taras Bulba,* a Cossack romance ; *The Government Inspector,* a brilliant satire ; and *Dead Souls,* somewhat in the manner of Charles Dickens.

Goidels, Celtic tribe which early invaded Britain, driving the inhabitants to western Ireland ; their speech developed into the Irish and Scottish Gaelic and the Manx dialects. See CELTI

gold, metallic element, symbol Au (Latin *aurum*) ; atomic weight 197·2 ; atomic number 79 ; specific gravity 19·3 ; bright yellow in colour ; melting-point 1,063°C ; good conductor of heat and electricity ; not corroded by air or water ; extremely malleable, and may be beaten into sheets (gold-leaf) so thin that 254,000 make 1in. Gold occurs in ' nuggets ' or as grains in rock or sand, and is mined in S. Africa (chiefly in the Transvaal), USA, Canada (where output is rapidly increasing), USSR, Mexico, Australia, India, etc ; 40 tons of sea-water contain about 1gr.

Regarded as a precious metal from the earliest times, gold is too soft to be used pure even for ornamental purposes, and is usually alloyed with copper or silver. Pure gold is 24 carat ; standard gold 22 carat. A bar of gold weighs 200oz troy.

A country is said to be on the *Gold Standard* when it will discharge its debts abroad by exporting gold ; this was abandoned by Britain 1931. At the moment the USA has the largest gold reserves. See MONEY ; RAND

Gold Coast, British colony, W. Africa, comprises with Ashanti, the Northern Territories, and Togoland, a total area of *c.*92,000sq.m ; has 334m of coastline ; pop.4,000,000. The region is now healthier than it was. A new constitution was inaugurated and the first free elections held 1951.

The Gold Coast became British in the 19th c. after the Portuguese had exploited it for gold and slaves. A harbour was opened at Takoradi 1928 ; exports include gold, manganese ore, diamonds, but chiefly cocoa, amounting to 50 % of the world total ; cap. Accra. ASHANTI (under British protection since 1896) has an area of *c.*24,000sq.m ; pop. 600,000 ; notable for cocoa, mahogany, gold, also rubber and gum copal ; chief town Kumasi. NORTHERN TERRITORIES, under British protection since 1901, produce maize, millet, yams, ground-nuts, tobacco, indigo and livestock ; chief town Tamale. TOGOLAND, under mandate to France and Britain, was formerly a German colony ; area 43,000sq.m.

golden calf, image made by Aaron during the travels in the wilderness of the Hebrews ; worshipped as an idol while Moses was on Mt Sinai (Exodus 32).

Golden Fleece, see JASON AND THE GOLDEN FLEECE

Golden Gate, channel, California, USA ; links San Francisco Bay with the Pacific ; crossed by an immense bridge 6,600ft long.

Golden Gate Bridge, see BRIDGES

' **Golden Hind,**' see DRAKE, SIR FRANCIS

Golden Horn, beautiful opening of the Bosphorus separating Galata from Istanbul.

Golden Rule, name sometimes given to Christ's words (Matt. 7) : *Whatsoever ye would that men should do to you, do ye even so to them.*

' **Golden Treasury, The,**' see PALGRAVE, F. T.

goldfinch, see FINCH

goldfish, small fish of the carp family ; introduced into Britain in the 17th c. ; feeds on raw meat or crushed vermicelli.

gold rush, see KLONDIKE

Goldsmith, OLIVER (1728–74), poet, author and dramatist, born in Ireland ; spent his boyhood in the village of Lissoy, W. Meath ; was always at the bottom of the class at school. He grew up to be careless of money, and was continually in debt. Though too idle to study or work hard, he was kindly, simple, friendly and good-humoured. After failing in his studies of medicine at Edinburgh, he wandered for two years in Flanders, France, Switzerland and Italy, playing his flute to earn his food and lodging. Returning 1756, he lived in a garret near St Paul's, London, for three years. Meanwhile, he won the affection of Dr Samuel Johnson and Sir Joshua Reynolds, and became famous for his prose work, *The Letters of a Citizen of the World* (supposed to be a Chinese philosopher's view of the English) ; *The Vicar of Wakefield,* a delightful novel ; his poems, *The Traveller* and *The Deserted Village* (written with Lissoy in mind) ; and his plays, *The Good Natur'd Man* and *She Stoops to Conquer.*

Dr Johnson's epitaph for him, *Nullum quod tetigit non ornavit,* i.e. He touched nothing that he did not adorn, is true, for all his writings have grace and charm.

golf, popular game. It is one of the national games of Scotland, its HQ at St Andrews. Golf is played on a course laid out on links, i.e. sandy ground by the sea, or over land set with obstacles, and provided with 18 (or sometimes 9) holes on as many greens. The idea is to go round the course in as few strokes as possible. In singles, one player plays another ; in a foursome, two players with one ball (taking alternate strokes) play another two. The clubs include driver, brassie, spoon, various irons, mashie, niblick, putter; an attendant who carries the clubs is a caddie.

Golgotha (Hebrew, *skull*), hill outside Jerusalem, scene of Christ's crucifixion.

Goliath, *gō-lī'ath,* Philistine giant of Gath ; slain by David with a sling (1 Samuel 17).

Gomorrah, see SODOM AND GOMORRAH

Goncourt, EDMOND DE, *gawn-koor'* (1822–1896), and his brother JULES DE GONCOURT (1830–70), French novelists who wrote several books jointly, e.g. *Madame Gervaisais.*

gondola, *gon'dō-lä,* long, low, flat-bottomed boat used on the canals and lagoons of Venice ; the decked prow and stern are raised ; there is a curtained cabin for passengers. It is propelled by standing gondoliers.

Gondomar, COUNT OF, *gōn-dō-mär'* (1567–1626), Spanish diplomat ; ambassador to England 1613–22 ; favoured a match between Charles (afterwards Charles I) and the Spanish Infanta ; largely responsible for the execution of Sir Walter Raleigh.

Gonville and Caius College, *gon'vil, keez,* college of Cambridge University, usually known as ' Caius.'

Good Friday, see CALENDAR

Good Hope, CAPE OF, headland of S. Africa, *c.*30m south of Cape Town.

Good King Wenceslas, see WENCESLAS

Goodwin Sands, sandbank *c.*5m off the Kent coast.

Goole, W. Yorkshire port on the R. Ouse ; has docks, shipbuilding yards and flour mills, also much timber trade ; pop. 20,000.

goose, name of various birds closely related to ducks and swans ; British wild geese include the bean goose, and the grey-lag, from which our domesticated varieties are descended.

gooseberry, fruit of the shrub (genus *Grossularia*), related to the red and black currant ; it is cultivated for its fruit, from which a sauce eaten with goose was once made. The fruit is now used to stew or to make tarts, or for jam making.

Goossens, name of a famous family of English musicians, including Eugène (1845–1906), for ten years conductor of the Carl Rosa company ; his son Eugène (1867–   ), also a noted conductor for the Carl Rosa company and the British National Opera Company ; also *his* son Eugène (1893–   ), conductor and composer.

gopher wood, *gō'fẽr,* timber of which Noah's ark was built (Genesis 6) ; probably cypress.

Gordian Knot, in old Greek tales, a knot of bark made by Gordius King of Phrygia when fastening the pole to the yoke of a sacred wagon. An oracle declared that whoever loosed the knot would rule Asia. Alexander the Great did so by *cutting it with his sword*—a prompt way of dealing with a difficulty.

Gordon, ADAM LINDSAY (1833–70), poet, born in the Azores ; brought up in England; had a passion for horse-racing. At twenty he was sent to Australia, where he earned a precarious living. His poems, breathing the very spirit of Australia, are known as *The Bushman's Bible.* He has a memorial in Westminster Abbey. Possibly his most famous verse is :

Life is mostly froth and bubble ;
Two things stand like stone :
Kindness in another's trouble,
Courage in your own.

Gordon, GENERAL CHARLES GEORGE (1833–1885), British soldier, *b* Woolwich ; distinguished himself at the siege of Sebastopol ; earned the nickname ' Chinese ' Gordon for his skilled command of Chinese troops in the Taiping rebellion 1863 ; proved a capable administrator during two years in the Egyptian Sudan, where 1877–80 he was governor-general. He helped with colonial administration in India and Palestine, and when the Mahadi (a religious leader) had gathered rebellious Sudanese around him in Egypt, Gordon had the task of evacuating Egyptian troops and employees. This he did. Finally, with one British officer only, he was trapped in Khartoum, where British forces, long delayed, arrived two days after he had been overwhelmed and murdered.

Though impatient and headstrong, Gordon was the finest type of Christian soldier, a great lover of the Bible, courageous, mystical, and a genius in dealing with backward peoples.

Gordon riots, riots in London, June 1780, headed by Lord George Gordon (1751–1793) in an attempt to repeal the Catholic Relief Act of 1778. The riots are described by Charles Dickens in *Barnaby Rudge*.

Gorgons, in old Greek tales, ugly sisters (Medusa, Euryale and Stheno) with snakes instead of hair. To look at them was to be turned to stone, but Perseus killed Medusa by striking her while looking at her *image* in his shield.

Gorgonzola, town near Milan, Italy ; noted for cheese.

gorilla, see APES AND MONKEYS

Gorki, third city of USSR, formerly Nijni-Novgorod ; pop.650,000 ; at the junction of the Volga and Oka *c*.250m NE. of Moscow ; manufactures chemicals ; famous till 1932 for its great annual fair. The city was renamed after the Revolution in honour of Maxim Gorki.

Gorki, MAXIM (1868–1936), Russian author, *b* Nijni-Novgorod ; ran away to become cook's boy on a Volga steamer ; travelled far and wide in Russia, and knew what it was to be desperately poor. He won fame with his short stories of vagabonds. His long novels are less successful, but *Mother* (1907) was filmed, and his play *The Lower Depths* is impressive though gloomy throughout. He became increasingly ' the spokesman of the workers,' and wrote much about Socialist doctrines. The best of his writings are *Childhood, In the World* and *Reminiscences of My Youth,* superb descriptions of life in Russia before the Revolution. Read (in translation) *Childhood,* Elizabeth Gow.

GORSE

Görlitz, *gŭr'lits,* manufacturing town, Silesia ; pop.95,000.

gorse or **whin,** prickly shrub (family *Leguminosae*) of heaths ; the yellow flower has a large petal, two narrow ' wings,' and a small ' keel.' The BROOM, closely related, is similar, but the flowers are larger and more golden.

Gort, FIELD-MARSHAL VISCOUNT (1886–1946), British soldier ; won the VC in World War I ; in World War II was Commander-in-Chief of the British Expeditionary Force, and had to evacuate Dunkirk 1940 ; Governor of Malta 1942–44 ; later High Commissioner for Palestine.

goshawk, see HAWK

Goshen, *gō'shen,* region of the Nile delta ; home of the Israelites when they first dwelt in Egypt.

Gospels (OE *god-spel,* good news), first 4 books of the NT, said to have been written by Matthew, Mark, Luke and John. They give us ' portraits ' of Christ, and interpretations of his life and teaching.

Gosse, SIR EDMUND WILLIAM, *gos* (1849–1928), poet and critic, *b* London ; an authority on French literature, which he did much to bring before the British public ; biographer (e.g. of Thomas Gray, Ibsen, Swinburne) ; also reviewer and journalist.

Göteborg, *yŭ-te-bor'y,* one of the chief towns of Sweden ; a port and also the terminus of the Göta canal ; industries include shipbuilding, sugar-refining and textiles ; pop.326,000.

Gotha, *gō'tä,* town, Germany ; *c*.15m from Erfurt ; has many industries ; pop. 46,000.

Gotham, *gō'tham,* Nottinghamshire village notable from the 15th–16th c. for its ' wise men ' who, according to tradition, are said to have forbidden King John to ride across their meadows, afterwards pretending to be mad so as to escape punishment.

Gothic, see ARCHITECTURE

Goths, Teutonic tribe which attacked the Roman empire from the E. and NE. in the 3rd c., finally destroying it, and

301

advancing into France, Spain and Germany.

Göttingen, *gŭt'ing-en,* town, Prussia (Germany) ; noted for chemicals, scientific instruments, books and its university (founded 1734) ; pop.40,000.

Gottland, *gŏt'-,* Baltic island belonging to Sweden.

Gounod, FRANÇOIS CHARLES, *goo-nō'* (1818-1893), French composer, b wrote the tune for the hymn *There is a green hill,* and also much church music ; most famous for his operas, including *Irene,* and his magnificent interpretation of Goethe's *Faust,* in which the *Jewel Song* and the *Soldier's Chorus* are exceptionally fine.

gourd, trailing plant ; species include *vegetable marrow* ; also the *melon* or *water melon* ; *pumpkin* (a great favourite in USA) weighing perhaps 20lb (some have reached 80lb) ; the *squash* ; also the *cucumber,* first known in Britain in the 16th c. The *gherkin* is a young or small gourd.

GOURD

Govan, *gŭv'an,* suburb of Glasgow, S. of the R. Clyde, it is noted for shipbuilding and engineering.

Gower, JOHN (*d* 1408), poet, and friend of Chaucer. Little is known of his life. He wrote several long poems, of which *Confessio Amantis* (a collection of stories) is the best.

Goya y Lucientes, FRANCISCO JOSÉ DE, *gō'yä ē loo-thē-en'tes* (1746-1828), Spanish artist ; born near Saragossa ; painted realistic scenes, and was famous for portraits, and for his horrifying drawings of scenes in the Spanish civil wars of his time.

Gozo, see MALTA

GP, see GEOMETRICAL PROGRESSION

Gracchus, GAIUS SEMPRONIUS, *grak'ŭs* (153-121BC), and his brother TIBERIUS SEMPRONIUS (163-133BC), famous Roman reformers who proposed that public lands should be shared as small holdings among the poor, that colonies should be founded for the poor ; they also advocated certain army reforms, a monthly dole of corn to all citizens. Both perished during riots.

Grace, WILLIAM GILBERT (1848-1915),

cricketer, b Downend, Gloucestershire, captained the English teams against Australia. Tall, broad and bearded, he was a superb batsman and a skilful bowler ; scored 54,000 runs in first-class cricket ; took over 2,800 wickets.

grafting, see PLASTIC SURGERY

Grafton, 3RD DUKE OF (1735-1811) statesman of the FitzRoy family ; First Lord of the Treasury (1766) under Pitt ; later he was Lord Privy Seal.

'Graf Zeppelin,' see AVIATION

Graham, JOHN, see DUNDEE, VISCOUNT

Grahame, KENNETH, *grā'am* (1859-1932), author, b Edinburgh ; 30 years in the service of the Bank of England ; loved for his whimsical sketches of childhood, *The Golden Age,* and his children's classic *The Wind in the Willows,* later dramatised by A. A. Milne as *Toad of Toad Hall.*

Graham's Land, region in the Antarctic ; part of the British colony of the Falkland Islands. Hope Bay is a base for important whaling activities.

grammar, branch of learning concerned with language, especially with the rules of correct speech (including pronunciation), writing (including spelling) and the study of the relations of words to one another.

One of the most important writers on English grammar was the late H. W. Fowler, whose *Dictionary of Modern English Usage* is still the best authority in all discussions on nice points of pronunciation, spelling, and the correct use of words. It should, however, be fully realised that any language is a living thing and therefore continually changing. What was unimpeachable English some years ago need not necessarily be correct or desirable today ; and while a knowledge of grammar is important we should remember that academic rules are not to be reverenced to the exclusion of custom and the idiom of the times.

Each language has its own grammar, and in English grammar we may consider either words or sentences, *parsing* the former, *analysing* the latter. To parse a word is to say what part of speech it is, and to give various other particulars. There are eight parts of speech, and these may be briefly (and therefore inadequately) summarised as follows :

1. NOUN, name of a person, place, or thing, e.g. *boy, Julius Caesar, London, family, loveliness, truth.* A noun may be Singular or Plural in Number, i.e. one or more than one ; it may be Common (e.g. *man*) or Proper (e.g. *John Smith*) or Collective (e.g. *flock, crew, audience*) ; it may be Concrete, i.e. a word standing for a tangible thing, or Abstract, i.e. words standing for intangible things, as *history, beauty, music, hardness,* etc. In English there are four Genders, namely Masculine (male), Feminine (female), Common, i.e. of either sex, as *parent,* and Neuter, i.e. neither sex, as *stone, pain,* etc. Note that in Latin only a

few nouns are of the Common Gender, and that in very many cases nouns that are Neuter in English are Masculine or Feminine, e.g. *mensa* (a table) is Feminine. French grammar has Masculine and Feminine Gender only, hence we have *la gare*, the railway station, which is Feminine, and *le livre*, the book, which is Masculine.

2. PRONOUN, a word used in place of a noun, as the Personal Pronouns, *I, thou, he, she* ; the Demonstrative Pronouns, *this, that, such, one* ; the Relative or Conjunctive Pronouns, *which, who, that, as* ; the Interrogative Pronouns, *who? which? what?* The Personal Pronouns are so called because they stand for three persons : (*a*) the First Person, i.e. the person speaking, e.g. *I, me* ; *we, us* ; (*b*) the Second Person, i.e. the person spoken to, e.g. *thou, thee* ; *ye, you* ; (*c*) the Third Person, i.e. the person or thing spoken of, e.g. *he, him* ; *she, her, it* ; *they, them.*

3. ADJECTIVE, word that describes a noun or adds to its meaning, e.g. *good, five, many, black.* Adjectives of quality and some of quantity may appear in one of three forms, e.g. *tall, beautiful,* adjectives of the Positive Degree ; *taller, more beautiful,* adjectives of the Comparative Degree ; *tallest, most beautiful,* adjectives of the Superlative Degree. Sometimes such adjectives take different forms, e.g. *good, better, best.*

4. VERB, a word that tells us what the subject of a sentence does, or what is done to it, e.g. *Birds fly,* where *fly* is the verb, and *birds* is the subject. A verb may be Transitive, in which the action passes from subject to object, e.g. *He* hit *the nail,* or Intransitive if it merely denotes a state or if the action does not pass from subject to object, e.g. *She sings sweetly.* A verb is in the Active Voice when the subject does something *to* something, e.g. *John shot a rabbit,* or Passive Voice, when the subject suffers something to be done to it, e.g. *A rabbit was shot by John.*

A singular subject requires a singular verb ; similarly the verb must agree with the Person of the subject, hence a verb is finite when limited by number, person, etc. ; the form known as the Infinitive is not subject to these limitations, and usually appears after the word ' to,' e.g. *to be, to run,* etc.

To conjugate a verb we have to take note not only of person and number but also of Tense, the Tense of a verb indicating either the time of action or the degree of completeness. Thus, *he sees* is Present Tense ; *he saw* Past Tense ; *he will see* Future Tense. Each tense may have one of four forms of completeness : Indefinite, e.g. *I see, I saw, I shall see* ; Continuous or Imperfect, e.g. *I am seeing, I was seeing, I shall be seeing* ; Perfect, e.g. *I have seen, I had seen, I shall see* ; Perfect Continuous, e.g. *I have been seeing,*

I had been seeing, I shall have been seeing.

The Imperative Mood (used only in the Present Tense and in the Second Person) expresses a command or an entreaty ; the Subjunctive Mood expresses a purpose, wish, condition or doubt. In French verbs the person and tense are indicated by the endings of the words, e.g. *je parle,* I speak, *ils parlèrent,* they spoke, *il parlait,* he was speaking, etc. There are four conjugations of French regular verbs (i.e. those ending in *-er, -ir, oir* and *-re*), but many verbs are irregular—as, indeed, every schoolboy knows, e.g. the verb *être,* to be.

5. ADVERB, a word used to modify a verb or an adjective. Adverbs may be grouped as those of (*a*) time, e.g. *now, then, always* ; (*b*) of place, e.g. *up, near, here* ; (*c*) of manner, e.g. *slowly, cleverly*; (*d*) of degree, e.g. *much, merely, only* ; (*e*) of certainty or doubt, e.g. *possibly, perhaps.*

6. PREPOSITION, word usually placed before a noun in English to show the relative position of subject or object, e.g. *after, at, beside, beyond, into, off, on, over, under,* etc.

7. CONJUNCTION, a word that joins words or sentences, e.g. *and, but, so, however,* etc. Note also the Correlatives, i.e. conjunctions invariably used in pairs, e.g. *either . . . or.*

8. INTERJECTION, an exclamation expressing emotion, e.g. *hurrah !*

Besides parsing words the grammarian may analyse a sentence. He defines a sentence as a complete thought put into words. It must have a Subject about which something is said. What is said about the subject is the Predicate—Latin *praedicare,* to say about. A Clause is a group of words which does not contain a finite verb.

In English grammar there are three kinds of sentences : (*a*) Simple, containing one subject and predicate, e.g. *Ships convey food,* where the subject is the word *ships,* the predicate the words *convey food* ; (*b*) Compound, i.e. comprising two or more simple sentences, joined by a conjunction ; (*c*) Complex, a sentence in which there is a principal clause and one or more subordinate clauses.

If a noun is the subject of a sentence it is said to be in the Nominative Case ; if it is the object of a sentence it is in the Objective Case. The Possessive Case is (in English) often indicated by the apostrophe, e.g. *The man's hat.*

In Latin grammar the student is required to know six cases, namely : Nominative, answering (as in English) the question *who* or *what* ; Vocative, i.e. the case of the person or thing addressed, e.g. *Domus,* O house ; Accusative, answering *whom* or *what* ; Genitive, answering *to* or *for whom* or *what,* and Ablative (a case peculiar to Latin) answering such questions as *by*, *with*, or *from whom* or *what*.

There are five declensions of Latin nouns, known by the endings of their Genitives, namely (singular) *-ae*, *-i*, *-is*, *-ūs* and *-ei*.

Such matters as punctuation, the normal order of words in sentences, purity of diction, figures of speech, the laws of metre in poetry, the origin and growth of language and especially of some particular language with its many borrowings, are other aspects of grammar.

Read *The King's English* and *Modern English Usage* (Fowler) ; *Our Living Language*, Grattan and Gurrey.

Grammar School, see EDUCATION

gramophone, *gram'ō-fŏn*, instrument, developed from Edison's phonograph, 1877, for reproducing recorded sounds. The sounds are recorded as variations in a continuous groove on a disc or drum. The disc is rotated and a needle resting in the groove is made to vibrate by the irregularities of the groove which were caused by the original recording. These vibrations are transferred to a diaphragm (a flexible disc which acts as a transmitter) and then to an amplifier which increases the sound.

The electric gramophone or radio-gram was invented *c.*1925.

An instrument using cheap paper records and played by light-rays has recently been invented by Fernando Crudo of Buenos Aires. But more important, perhaps, is the recent invention of Marvin Camras, a son of Russian parents in USA, who has perfected a wire ' record ' which will play for two hours, while longer wires give a continuous programme lasting eight hours. Comparable to the Marconi-Stille Magnetic Recorder once used by the BBC for reproducing programmes, the mechanism comprises a fine wire magnetised in response to the vibrations of a microphone. When passed again between the poles of a magnet it reproduces sounds faithfully, and may be used, not only as a new type of gramophone, but as a type of Dictaphone.

A recent innovation is the use of coloured plastic records, ruby for classical music, black for popular tunes, etc.

Grampians, *gram'pi-anz*, mts. forming the Highlands of Scotland ; they include Ben Nevis, 4,406ft.

gram-weight, see MECHANICS

Granada, *grä-nä'dä*, formerly a Moorish kingdom of S. Spain, now a province. The cap., Granada, over 2,200ft above sea-level, has a cathedral and a university ; pop.181,000.

Granby, JOHN MANNERS, MARQUIS OF (1721–70) ; commander of British soldiers in Germany in the Seven Years' War ; responsible for brilliant victories.

Grand Banks, region of somewhat shallower water SE. of Newfoundland ; area *c.* 500,000sq.m ; rich in fish, notably cod.

Grand Coulee Dam, see DAM

Grand National, see AINTREE

Grand Rapids, city, Michigan, USA ; noted for lumbering and aircraft ; pop. 164,000.

Grand Remonstrance, the Long Parliament's statement to Charles I, 1641 ; it complained of misgovernment and suggested remedies.

Granicus, *grä-nī'kŭs*, river flowing to the Sea of Marmora ; gave its name to a battle 334BC in which Alexander the Great defeated the Persians. See ALEXANDER THE GREAT

granite, *gran'it*, primary, fire-formed crystalline rock, a mixture of felspar, quartz and mica. Though costly, it is much used as building stone, e.g. Cornish, Aberdeen, and the red Peterhead granites.

Grant, JAMES AUGUSTUS (1827–92), soldier and explorer, *b* Nairn ; wounded at the relief of Lucknow ; with John Hanning Speke explored the sources of the Nile 1860–63.

Grant, ULYSSES SIMPSON (1822–85), American soldier and statesman ; born near Clermont, Ohio ; served in the American Civil War ; was a brilliant strategist ; amply justified Abraham Lincoln's faith in his ability by the way he commanded all the armies of the North, compelling the Confederates (under Lee) to surrender 1865. Grant was Republican president of the USA 1868–76, but died in poverty. Simple, direct, honest, he was a stern disciplinarian and an enlightened administrator.

Grantchester, village, Cambridgeshire ; immortalised by Rupert Brooke :
Stands the church clock at ten to three ?
And is there honey still for tea ?

Grantham, town, Lincolnshire, noted for agricultural machinery, plastics, etc. ; pop.22,000. Sir Isaac Newton attended the grammar school.

Granville, SECOND EARL, *gran'vil* (1815–91), English statesman, *b* London ; entered Parliament as a Whig ; led the Liberals in the House of Lords from 1855 ; a supporter of Gladstone.

grape, see VINE

grapefruit, citrus fruit resembling the orange, though larger ; has a thick yellow skin, acid, refreshing taste, and is the fruit of an evergreen tree sometimes called shaddock or pomelo. Grown in parts of Asia, and especially in Florida, California and the W. Indies, it became a favourite in USA *c.*1895, though scarcely known in Britain before 1920.

grape-sugar, see GLUCOSE

graph, *graf* (Gk *graphein*, to write), diagram usually drawn on squared paper (*a*) as a method of solving algebraic and other problems, especially where a function *y* is expressed in terms of another function *x*, thus producing a curve representing an equation ; and (*b*) as a chart showing variations in temperature, rise or fall of imports or exports, etc.

graphite, *graf'īt*, mineral, a crystalline form

of carbon ; often wrongly called lead (as in ' blacklead ' and ' lead-pencil ') ; found in Ceylon and N. America, also Cumberland ; another name is plumbago. Graphite is used as a lubricant.

Grasmere, village, Westmorland, by L. Grasmere. Here is Dove Cottage, Wordsworth's home 1799–1813, now a museum ; Wordsworth and Hartley Coleridge are buried in the churchyard.

grass, plant found all over the world except in the coldest areas of the Polar Regions ; c.4,000 varieties are known, most of them growing only a few inches high, though Indian bamboos are sometimes 100ft. Stems of grasses are rounded or flattened ; those of sedges are 3-cornered. Grasses produce many seeds.

The wild grasses of our fields and meadows include annual meadowgrass, sheep's fescue, wood melic, perennial rye-grass : cereals, such as wheat, barley, rye, millet, maize and rice are cultivated grasses. Esparto is made into ropes and paper. In N. America vast, treeless grasslands are known as *prairie*; similar regions are known as *steppes* in Russia. In S. America grasslands may be *pampas*, especially notable for pampas grass with silky white plumes 10ft high or (in tropical regions) as *savannas*, known locally as *llanos* (*lä′nōz*) in Venezuela, *campos* in Brazil. The temperate grasslands of SE. Africa are known as the *veld* (*felt*).

grasshopper, insect common in Britain. Its chirp is caused by rubbing the edges of its straight wings.

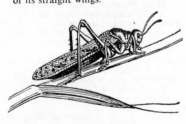

THE GRASSHOPPER

The LOCUST, similar but usually larger, is found in N. America, Asia and Africa, where swarms of countless millions often destroy crops. Such swarms are now attacked from the air by spraying various chemicals from aircraft. See PLATE 9

grass snake, see SNAKE

Gratian, *grā′shi-an* (AD359–383), Roman emperor from AD375. He sternly repressed heathen worship, and was assassinated at Lyons.

Grattan, HENRY (1746–1820), Irish statesman, reputed Ireland's greatest orator, and therefore styled the ' Irish Demosthenes ' ; with the Ulster Volunteers secured Irish legislative independence 1782.

Gratz, town, Austria ; manufactures machinery ; pop.208,000.

grave accent, see ACCENT

Gravelines, *gräv-lēn′*, port, France, c.12m from Dunkirk.

Graves, ALFRED PERCEVAL (1846–1931), Irish author, b Dublin ; noted for his poem, *Father O'Flynn*, for *The Irish Song Book*, and as a leader of the Celtic revival in Ireland.

Graves, ROBERT RANKE (1895–   ), author, son of A. P. Graves ; wrote *Goodbye to All That* ; *Lawrence and the Arabs* ; *I, Claudius* ; *Claudius the God* ; the two last being vivid portrayals of the Roman empire 10BC–AD54.

Gravesend, Kentish port on the R. Thames; has much trade, also iron-foundries, shipbuilding, etc. ; pop.35,000.

A wide area below the town is likely to be developed as the world's biggest flying-boat terminal.

gravitation, tendency of one body to be attracted by another. According to Sir Isaac Newton's law of gravitation, the force of attraction between two bodies (masses) varies inversely as the square of the distance between them, and is proportional to the product of the masses of the two bodies. Thus, the force of attraction (in dynes) between two masses, m_1 and m_2 (in grams), separated by a distance d (in cm) is given by the formula $F = \dfrac{km_1m_2}{d^2}$ where

k is the gravitational constant, i.e. $6 \cdot 65 + 10^{-8}$ CGS units. The acceleration due to gravity (g) for falling bodies on the earth is 981cm per sec. per sec., roughly 32ft per sec. per sec., and varies slightly from place to place.

Newton's law holds good for practical purposes, but for radiant matter, it requires correction, as shown by Einstein, whose theory of Relativity explains gravitation on the basis of the geometrical properties of space. See MATTER ; RELATIVITY

Gray, THOMAS (1716–71), poet, b London ; travelled for three years on the Continent with Horace Walpole ; professor of modern history, Cambridge, from 1768. Shy and rather melancholy, he was a sincere friend and an admirable letter-writer. His exquisite poems include *A Distant Prospect of Eton College*, *The Death of a Favourite Cat* (which belonged to Walpole), *The Progress of Poesy* ; and, most famous of all, *Elegy Written in a Country Churchyard* (Stoke Poges, Buckinghamshire, where he is buried).

Gray's exquisite verse is illustrated by this stanza from his *Elegy* :

Full many a gem of purest ray serene
    The dark unfathom'd caves of ocean
        bear :
Full many a flower is born to blush
        unseen,
    And waste its sweetness on the
        desert air.

As a craftsman Gray was exceedingly painstaking, and the story that he spent a whole day debating whether or not to delete a comma, though possibly exaggerated, may have some truth in it. See WOLFE, J.

grayling, fresh-water food fish of the salmon family ; fairly common in British rivers ; *c*.10in long ; has a many-rayed dorsal fin.

Gray's Inn, one of the Inns of Court, Holborn, London.

Great Barrier Reef, series of coral reefs stretching for 1,200m off the coast of Queensland (Australia). It is still growing in extent, and is one of the wonders of the world ; an under-water garden of rainbow hues, abounding in many-coloured fish.

Great Bear (*Ursa Major*) group (constellation) of seven stars sometimes called either the Plough or Charles's Wain ; two of these seven stars (a, b) are known as the Pointers because they point almost (but not quite) to the Pole Star ; the Little Bear (*Ursa Minor*) is nearer the Pole Star.

THE GREAT BEAR CONSTELLATION

(a) *and* (b) *are the Pointers*

Great Bear Lake, lake, NW. Territories Canada ; drained by the Great Bear R. As a result of Canadian skill and enterprise the Great Bear L. region has been producing considerable quantities of uranium and uranium minerals since *c*.1930. In spite of being in the remote and intensely cold far North, uranium and radium ores are now produced on such a scale that the lead of the Belgian Congo and other sources of supply has been challenged. The present emphasis on atomic energy makes the uranium deposits in the Great Bear region of supreme importance.

The famous Eldorado Radium Mines at La Bine Point here blast radium ore from the frozen earth, and send the concentrate by plane to Port Hope, Ontario, over 4,500m away.

Great Britain, see BRITISH ISLES

Great Commoner, THE, see PITT, WILLIAM

Great Council, see PARLIAMENT

' **Great Eastern,'** see SHIPS

Great Exhibition, see EXHIBITIONS

Great Ferghana Canal, see UZBEKISTAN

Great Fire, see WREN, SIR C.

Great Ice Barrier, see POLAR REGIONS

Great Karroo, lofty plain, Cape Province, S. Africa ; notable for sheep.

Great Lakes, five lakes between Canada and USA. They are : Superior (world's largest), Michigan, Huron, Erie and Ontario ; total area *c*.98,000sq.m. All the lakes are ice-bound in winter. The chief ports are Toronto, Hamilton and Fort William (Canada) ; Chicago, Milwaukee, Detroit, Cleveland, Erie and Buffalo (USA).

Great Orme's Head, headland of Caernarvonshire.

Great Plague, see PLAGUE

Great Pyramid, see ARCHITECTURE

Great Salt Lake, lake, Utah, USA ; over 4,000ft above sea-level. There is so much salt in the water that fish cannot live in it.

Great Seal, seal kept by the Lord Chancellor, and affixed to public Acts of State. Since the union of England and Scotland (1707) it has been the Seal of Great Britain. See PRIVY SEAL

Great Slave, river, Canada ; flows 265m to the Great Slave L.

Great Slave Lake, lake, NW. Territory, Canada ; area 11,000sq.m.

Great Wall of China, defensive rampart begun *c*.215BC. It is 1,500m long, averages 20ft high, and was intended to keep out Mongol tribes. The wall was useful against the Japanese 1937.

' **Great Western,'** see SHIPS

Greater Antilles, see ANTILLES

grebe, *grēb*, diving bird with curiously lobed feet, legs far back, and small tail ; found on British rivers and ponds ; varieties include great-crested grebe and little grebe, known also as dabchick.

Grecians, see BLUE COAT SCHOOLS

Greco, EL, *el grā'ko* (*d* 1614), Spanish artist, notable for portraits and for his religious

THE LITTLE GREBE

11 *d*

paintings, which have a unique rhythmic design.

Greece, kingdom of SE. Europe, bounded by Albania, Bulgaria, Yugoslavia and Turkey, and also by the Aegean and Ionian Seas ; total area *c*.50,270sq.m, comprising (*a*) the mainland, *c*.41,450 sq.m, namely Central Greece, Thessaly, Peloponnese, Macedonia, Epirus and Thrace ; and (*b*) a large number of islands (e.g. the Aegean and Ionian Is., Crete, Sporades, Cyclades), their total area being *c*.8,820sq.m ; total pop. 8,000,000. The north and south regions of the mainland are joined by the narrow isthmus of Corinth, now cut by a canal.

Though mountainous the country has exceedingly fertile valleys watered by short rivers, and as the climate is warm and sunny, the people very successfully cultivate a variety of fruits, especially olives and currants (currants are one of the chief exports ; our word *currant* comes from *Corinth*). Tobacco is grown on a large scale, also vines, figs and oranges. The mineral wealth is considerable, e.g. chrome ore, magnesite, iron pyrites, lead, iron and marble, that from Paros being exceptionally fine.

The capital of Greece is Athens, and other large towns include Piraeus (the port of Athens), Thessalonika, Volos, Cavalla ; also (in Crete) Candia and (in the Ionian Is.) Corfu. Greece has much shipping trade, especially between the islands and along the rocky coast of the mainland.

Education, though not highly developed, is compulsory and free. The people speak modern Greek, a language differing considerably from ancient Greek, although basically the same. They have preserved the love of liberty for which their forerunners were famous, proof being given as recently as World War II, in which the Greek army and Greek guerillas gallantly resisted both Fascist and Nazi invaders.

The country suffered shockingly during World War II, being occupied by Italy, Germany and Bulgaria. Famine and civil war added to her troubles, and even in 1948 she remained a crippled state in spite of much assistance. The children suffered much from TB, and from lack of education ; but with aid from UNESCO conditions are now improving.

Three years of civil war (Government forces against guerillas) ended in 1949, the year in which British troops began to be withdrawn. From 1948 to 1949 USA Aid to Greece amounted to over 470 million dollars.

Conquered by the Romans 146BC, Greece was later a part of the Byzantine Empire till AD1204, and was conquered by the Turks in the 15th c., remaining under Turkish rule till 1821, when she won independence.

The glory that was Greece goes back to *c*.700BC. Ancient Greece comprised a group of more or less independent states, e.g. Thessalia, Epirus, Boeotia, Aetolia, Acarnania, Attica, Corinth, Argolis, Achaea, Elis, Messenia, Laconia (or Sparta), Arcadia, all jealous of each other, though sometimes groups united to expel a foreign aggressor, e.g. Darius, the Persian king, defeated at the battle of Marathon 490BC, and his son, Xerxes, whose fleet was destroyed at Salamis, 480BC, his army being almost annihilated at Plataea 479BC.

Flushed with triumph after these outstanding victories, and inspired by Pericles, Athens became the centre of a powerful confederacy, so that the age of Pericles (*d* 429BC) is regarded as the greatest in the history of Greece. Solon and Themistocles had encouraged crafts and trade, and these were now flourishing. Athens had many merchant princes, the city (with its port) being the emporium of the then-known world. Slaves were employed to make (almost on mass-production lines) articles intended for the great and ever growing export trade.

The arts flourished, e.g. architecture, the ruins of ancient Greece being evidence of the supreme splendour that has passed away, though the Greeks were ignorant of the principles of the arch. Sculpture achieved a perfection never since attained ; Pheidias, the greatest of Greek sculptors, completed his statue of Athene in Athens *c*.438BC. It was Pheidias who raised the magnificent temples on the Acropolis (see PLATES 66, 67), and it was in his time that Sophocles and Euripides were producing some of the world's greatest dramas. Greek literature is an inspiration today, and such names as Homer ; the tragedians Aeschylus, Sophocles and Euripides; the comic poet Aristophanes; the historians Herodotus, Thucydides and Xenophon ; the orators Isocrates, Aeschines and Demosthenes recall the greatness of the past.

'You Greeks,' an old Egyptian said, ' are always children.' They were restlessly inquisitive, hence their wonderful progress in philosophy. The works of Plato and Aristotle are still closely studied by philosophers ; and it should be noted that some of these ancients (from Thales to Aristotle) had a conception of science which, in its basic principles, was often startlingly similar to some of our most modern theories of matter and energy. In mathematics, astronomy, music the ancient Greeks were daring and eminently logical thinkers.

Greek youth delighted in games and sports, hence the Olympic Games, held every four years. In religion the Greeks believed in a great number of gods and goddesses, and the highly imaginative Gk mind attempted to explain all manner of natural phenomena by stories (myths) of these supposed beings. Their gods and goddesses included Zeus, Aphrodite, Hera, Pallas Athene, Ares, Hermes and a host of inferior deities, e.g. nymphs, sirens, dryads inhabiting woods and lakes etc. Typical hero-gods were Hercules and Perseus.

From c.1000BC the people of Greece were styled Hellenes, i.e. the people of Hellas or Greece ; hence Hellenism means the culture of ancient Greece, a term used today for reproducing in modern life something of the artistic and literary ideals of the best age of Greece.

Read *The Ancient World*, T. R. Glover; *What Happened in History*, Gordon Childe ; *Greek Science*, Benjamin Farrington ; *Hellenic Travel*, W. A. Wigram.

Greek, language that developed from the Indo-European group of languages. See LANGUAGE

Ancient (or classical) Greek comprises several dialects, namely (a) *Ionic*, notable for its melodiousness, Old Ionic, or epic, being the language of Homer, New Ionic that of Herodotus ; (b) *Attic*, the standard form of classical Greek, its chief difference from Ionic being in its contraction of vowels. This, the language of Aeschylus, Sophocles, was the parent of the Hellenic language (*Koine*) which overran the ancient world, and later was the language of the NT, often now called NT Gk. (c) *Aeolic*, the dialect in which Sappho wrote ; (d) *Doric*, spoken in the Peloponnese and elsewhere and used in literature for Doric passages (songs) in Athenian tragedies.

What is sometimes called *Greek proper* includes variations extending to the 2nd c. AD ; *late Greek* is that commonly spoken to the end of the 16th c. ; *Middle Greek* to the end of the 15th c. *New* or *Modern Greek* may be (a) *Romaic* (Demot'ic) i.e. the common speech of Greeks today, or (b) *Neo-Hellenic* (Katharev'usa) which attempts to purify demotic by reviving old idioms and forms.

The melodious vowels of Greek, the richness of inflexional forms (notably in the verb), and the ease with which compounds can be made, made ancient Greek both precise and flexible : it was an ideal language for expressing fine shades of meaning, for composing scientific terms, and for imaginative writing.

The Greek alphabet (as from 403BC) is:

capitals	minuscules	Greek names	English equivalent
A	α	Alpha	a
B	β	Beta	b
Γ	γ	Gamma	g
Δ	δ	Delta	d
E	ε	Epsilon	e (in *let*)
Z	ζ	Zeta	z
H	η	Eta	ee
Θ	θ	Theta	th (in *thin*)
I	ι	Iota	i
K	κ	Kappa	k
Λ	λ	Lambda	l
M	μ	Mu	m
N	ν	Nu	n
Ξ	ξ	Xi	x
O	ο	Omicron	o (in *not*)
Π	π	Pi	p
P	ρ	Rho	r
Σ	σ, ς	Sigma	s
T	τ	Tau	t
Υ	υ	Upsilon	u
Φ	φ	Phi	ph
X	χ	Chi	ch (in *loch*)
Ψ	ψ	Psi	ps
Ω	ω	Omega	o (in *note*)

See LANGUAGE

Greek literature, see GREECE

Greek Patriots, sometimes called simply Partisans ; five groups of guerillas fighting against Axis armies in World War II. They did much for Greece, but finally caused civil war, 1944.

Green, JOHN RICHARD (1837–83), historian, b Oxford ; became a clergyman ; suffered from ill-health ; greatly helped in his writing by his wife. Green wrote *Making of England* and *Conquest of England*, but is most famous for his *Short History of the English People* (1874) in which, for the first time, stress was laid more on religious and social movements than on kings and wars.

greenfinch, see FINCH

Greenland, Danish possession almost wholly in the Arctic, and north-east of N. America ; may be regarded as the world's largest island (area 827,300sq.m). All but 34,000sq.m are perpetually covered with snow and ice ; pop.17,000, chiefly Eskimos and some Danes. Known to the Norsemen, Greenland was rediscovered by John Davis 1585. The USA acquired the right to establish air bases there 1941.

Greenock, *grin'ŭk*, port, Renfrewshire ; on the Firth of Clyde ; c.22m from Glasgow ; has excellent docks and much foreign trade. Industries include shipbuilding, engineering, spinning and sugar-refining ; pop.79,000.

Greenwich, *gren'ich*, historic borough of SE. London ; is on the Thames ; has engineering works, the Royal Naval College and the Royal Observatory, through which the longitude 0° passes, and from which Greenwich Mean Time is broadcast ; pop.63,000.

It should be noted that the fog and smoke and illuminations of London have compelled the staff of the Royal Observatory to seek new quarters, and that before long the Observatory will be housed in the 15th c. castle of Hurstmonceux, Sussex. The change will make no difference to the world's time system however ; Hurstmonceux is on the Greenwich meridian.

Greenwich Mean Time, see TIME

Greenwood, ARTHUR (1880–), English politician ; Labour MP 1922 ; Deputy Leader of the Labour Party from 1935.

Gregg, JOHN R., see SHORTHAND

Gregory, name of sixteen popes, including

Gregory I (see below) ; Gregory VII (or Hildebrand) deposed by the emperor Henry IV (*d* 1085) ; Gregory IX, friend of St Francis of Assisi (*d* 1241) ; Gregory XIII (*d* 1585), notable for his reform of the calendar.

Gregory I (*d* 604), pope and saint. The story is told by Bede that Gregory saw slaves on sale in Rome, and learned that they were Angles from Deira, ruled by Aella. He replied, ' They have the faces of angels. Their country shall be saved from God's anger (*de ira Dei*), and Alleluia shall be sung in Aella's kingdom.' Hence his sending (597) of St Augustine to Britain. His name is preserved in ' Gregorian chant.'

Grenada, *grē-nä'dä*, island of the British W. Indies ; cap. St George's.

Grenfell, JULIAN (1888–1915), soldier-poet; killed in World War I ; best remembered for his poem *Into Battle*.

Grenfell, SIR WILFRED THOMASON (1865–1940), medical missionary in Labrador from 1892 ; author of a stirring autobiography *A Labrador Doctor* ; was among the great adventurers of his day, making the well-being of the hardy fishermen of this inhospitable region his life-ministry.

Grenoble, *gre-nō'bl*, city, France ; 60m from Lyons ; noted for kid gloves and buttons ; pop.102,000.

Grenville, GEORGE, *gren'vil* (1712–70), English statesman ; Prime Minister 1763–65 ; notable for passing the American Stamp Act 1765 ; nicknamed ' Gentle Shepherd ' by Pitt.

Grenville, LORD (1759–1834), statesman ; supported Pitt ; with Fox formed (at Pitt's death 1806) a coalition ministry which ended 1807.

Grenville, SIR RICHARD (*d* 1591), sailor of an old Cornish family ; twice colonised Roanoke I. for Sir Walter Raleigh ; second-in-command of a squadron in the Azores, where his ship was cut off by fifty-three Spanish galleons, which he fought till mortally wounded, an incident immortalised in Tennyson's poem *The Revenge* :

And the sun went down, and the stars came out far over the summer sea,
And never a moment ceased the fight of the one and the fifty-three.
Ship after ship, the whole night long, their high-built galleons came,
Ship after ship, the whole night long, with her battle-thunder and flame ;
Ship after ship, the whole night long, drew back with her dead and her shame.

Gresham, SIR THOMAS (*d* 1579), *b* London ; made a huge fortune as a merchant ; founded the Royal Exchange, which was visited by Queen Elizabeth 1570. ' Gresham's Law ' is that *bad money drives out good*.

Gretna Green, village, Dumfriesshire, where (1770–1940) many runaway young English couples were married by the blacksmith. As Scots law now requires that one of the two shall have resided in Scotland at least twenty-one days, such romantic runaway marriages do not occur.

Grey, CHARLES, 2ND EARL (1764–1845), statesman, *b* Fallodon, Northumberland ; Whig leader ; Prime Minister 1830 ; passed the Reform Act 1832.

Grey, LADY JANE (1537–54), beautiful and accomplished daughter of Henry Grey, Duke of Suffolk ; married Guildford Dudley, son of the Duke of Northumberland 1553 ; succeeded Edward VI, her cousin, and was queen for nine days ; executed with her husband on Tower Hill.

Grey Friars, see MONKS AND NUNS

Grey of Fallodon (1862–1933), Liberal statesman, known as Sir Edward Grey before being created Viscount ; Foreign Secretary 1905–16 ; consistently favoured understanding with France ; lessened Anglo-Russian hostility ; a sincere lover of peace ; failed to avert World War I, perhaps because he did not make a bold declaration that Britain would fight. He was an earnest supporter of the League of Nations ; died at Fallodon, Northumberland.

VISCOUNT GREY OF FALLODON 1862–1933

Viscount Grey, partly blind towards the end of his life, was the finest type of English country gentleman, and a lover of nature, as shown by his books, e.g. *The Charm of Birds*.

Grey Owl (*d* 1938), N. American naturalist, claimed to be the son of an American father of Scottish descent and an Indian mother ; had a great love of birds and animals, and a remarkable knowledge of beavers, about which he wrote in his popular nature books.

Grid System, method of supplying electricity in England, Scotland and Wales. The Central Electricity Board was formed 1927, and gradually old generating stations were taken over or new ones built, power being mainly transmitted along overhead steel-cored aluminium wires supported on pylons, transformers being, in the main, of the 3-phase type. The control centres are London, Glasgow, Newcastle, Leeds, Manchester, Birmingham and Bristol. One highly beneficial result has been the transmission of electricity to rural areas. New generating stations are now being built, and the total generating capacity of the Grid is c.14,000,000 kilowatts, say 18,750,000hp.

Great hydro-electric undertakings generating for the public include the British Electricity Authority, Grampian Electricity Supply Company, and the North of Scotland Hydro-Electric Board. Britain hopes to build 30 power-stations by 1953. The Grid programme includes extensions and constructions totalling £200,000,000. The biggest power-station at present is at Barking ; it has 10 boilers and 12 turbines.

The Central Electricity Board was abolished by nationalisation in 1947.

See PLATES 42–44

Grieg, EDVARD, grēg (1843–1907), Norwegian composer, b Bergen ; notable for *Peer Gynt*, an orchestral piece, and for much exquisite music.

Grimm, JAKOB (1785–1863), and his brother Wilhelm (1786–1859), German students of Teutonic language and mythology ; best known as joint authors of *Grimm's Fairy Tales.*

Grimsby, port, Lincolnshire ; south of the Humber ; chiefly notable for its trawl and other fishing ; pop.78,000.

Grindelwald, -vält, tourist resort, Switzerland.

groat, English coin minted 1351, valued at 1d, but later at 4d ; issued again in Henry VII's reign ; revived as a silver coin 1836 ; not used since 1887 ; also a foreign coin.

grog, see RUM

Groningen, chrō'ning-en, town, Netherlands ; has a university (1614) ; manufactures woollen goods ; rope-making ; sugar refining ; pianos and furniture ; pop.129,000.

Groote Schuur, grō'ta shoor, former home of Cecil Rhodes, and now the official home of the Prime Minister of the Union of S. Africa. It is c.3m from Cape Town.

gross, grōs, a dozen dozen articles, i.e. 12² or 144.

Grotius, HUGO, grō'shi-us (1583–1645), Dutch author, whose legal knowledge, tolerance, and humane disposition led him to write his famous book *De jure belli et pacis,* 1625, the foundation of modern international law.

Grouchy, EMMANUEL, MARQUIS DE, groo-shē' (1766–1847), one of Napoleon's most trusted generals ; fought at Hohenlinden and Wagram, but at Waterloo he misunderstood his orders and failed to bring his corps on to the battlefield in time to give Napoleon badly-needed help.

ground-nut (pea-nut, monkey-nut, or earth-nut), name of the fruit of a pea-like annual plant which, after flowering, buries its fruit

in the ground ; much cultivated in tropical countries for its food-value and for its oil (used in making margarine). A wool-like protein fibre is now made from ground-nuts. Known as ARDIL, this synthetic fabric may be combined with natural wool or cotton and with rayon.

Dr George Washington Carver, the Negro scientist who d 1943, found 300 ways of using ground-nuts.

Ground-nuts are now grown on a large scale in Kenya and Tanganyika (see PLATE 10, *top*). The African ground-nut scheme, proposed 1946, was a disastrous failure, its annual report (1949) showing liabilities amounting to £23,000,000. A total loss of £36,000,000 was sustained when the original scheme was abandoned in favour of an experimental project.

groundsel, plant (*Senecio vulgaris*) with yellow flowers, often drooping, and partly enclosed in a green cup. It has a hairy stem, and feather-like, dark, glossy leaves.

Group Movement, see OXFORD MOVEMENT

grouse, game bird found chiefly in N. Britain, especially on Scottish moors ; lays 6–14 reddish-yellow eggs blotched with brown ; may be shot Aug. 12–Dec. 10. The *black grouse* has a lyre-shaped tail ; it is sometimes known as *blackcock.* The black grouse, extremely shy, is found in flocks of 40–50 ; *ptarmigan* (tär'mi-gan), or white grouse, grey in summer, white in winter, is found on Scottish mountains.

THE BLACK GROUSE

Grub Street, old name for a street in London, E.C., once the home of many poor writers.

Guadalajara, gwäthä-lä-hä'rä (a) province of Spain ; (b) city, Mexico ; pop. 144,000.

Guadalcanal, see SOLOMON ISLANDS

Guadalquivir, gwädäl-kwiv'ēr, river of Spain ; flows 360m to the Gulf of Cadiz.

Guadeloupe, gwä-dĕ-loop', French colony of seven islands in the W. Indies. All are subject to earthquakes. Products include sugar and bananas ; cap. Basse-Terre.

Guadiana, *gwä-thē-ä′nä,* river, Spain ; flows *c.*380m to the Gulf of Cadiz ; of little use to shipping.

Guam, see LADRONE ISLANDS

guano, *gwä′nō,* excreta of birds, found chiefly in Peru, Chile and Pacific islands. It provides a manure rich in phosphates and ammonia, but has now been largely superseded by artificial fertilisers.

Guatemala, see CENTRAL AMERICA

guava, *gwä′vä,* sweet, pear-shaped fruit with yellow or red pulp and kidney-shaped seeds. The small tree (a native of the W. Indies) has square branches and white flowers.

Guayaquil, *gwīä-kēl,* largest city, Ecuador. A busy port exporting cocoa, quinine and coffee ; was much damaged by an earthquake 1942 ; pop.200,000.

Guedalla, PHILIP, *gwē-dal′a* (1889–1944), British author ; a barrister for 10 years, but turned to writing books in which he combined historical accuracy with vividly portrayed characters, e.g. *The Duke* (a life of Wellington) ; *The Queen and Mr Gladstone, The Hundred Days, Mr Churchill,* etc.

guelder rose, *gel′dĕr,* small tree (family *Caprifoliaceae*) common in Britain ; has lobed leaves with toothed edges, clusters of creamy flowers surrounded by larger white blooms ; bright red berries.

Guelphs, *gwelfs,* political party which from the 11th–14th c. defended the independence of Italy and the supremacy of the pope, and were opposed by the Ghibellines, who supported the German Emperors.

Guernsey, one of the Channel Islands ; grows grapes, tomatoes, etc. ; noted for its breed of cows ; occupied by the Germans in World War II.

Guiana, *gē-ä′nä,* region on the NE. coast of S. America ; (*a*) BRITISH GUIANA, British Crown Colony ; area *c.*90,000 sq.m ; pop.365,000 ; notable for mountain scenery and waterfalls ; · produces sugar-cane, rum, timber and rice ; minerals include gold, diamonds, manganese and bauxite ; cap. Georgetown. (*b*) FRENCH GUIANA, or CAYENNE, *kä-en′,* area *c.*35,000sq.m ; cap. Cayenne ; includes various isls., e.g. Devil's Isle. (*c*) NETHERLANDS GUIANA (between the other two) has an area of *c.*55,000sq.m; cap. Paramaribo. Netherlands Guiana is also known as Surinam.

All the Guianas have abundant tropical vegetation, and are noted for medicinal barks. See NETHERLANDS ; RALEIGH, SIR W.

Guienne, *güe-en′,* formerly a province of SW. France. See FRANCE

Guildford, *gil′fĕrd,* co.tn, Surrey. A cathedral is being built ; pop.45,000.

guilds, groups of craftsmen and merchants, some in England being founded as early as the 12th c. Organisations of the kind were common in Europe (e.g. Germany

and Italy) during the Middle Ages, each association watching over its own interests. Merchants guilds had rules for honest dealing, buying and selling ; the craft guilds ensured that reasonable prices were charged, and that the standard of workmanship was high— due, in part, to the widespread system of apprenticeship. Many guilds have remained to this day in the form of companies, e.g. the weavers', fishmongers' and saddlers'.

guillemot, *gil′ē-mot,* seabird of the auk family ; has a dark head, back and wings but is white below. The legs are placed well back ; the short wings are pointed. The guillemot lays one egg on a rocky ledge, and is fairly common along British coasts.

guillotine, *gil′ō-tēn,* French beheading machine named after Joseph Ignace Guillotin (1738–1814), who proposed the idea 1789, the first guillotine execution taking place 1792. The machine comprised two upright posts with grooves guiding a heavily weighted knife with a slanting edge, an improvement on the Scottish ' maiden ' and the Halifax gibbet.

Also the name of a machine used by printers and book-binders for cutting and trimming paper.

guinea, *gin′i,* former gold coin of English currency ; the guinea changed value as sterling fluctuated, but was fixed 1717 at 21s. Gold guineas are no longer used, but it remains customary to charge for professional services and certain articles in ' guineas,' i.e. multiples of 21s.

guinea fowl, bird of the pheasant family, though more like a small turkey ; occurs wild in S. and Central Africa. Slate coloured, it is widely domesticated for its eggs and delicate flesh.

Guise, *gēz,* industrial town, France ; on the R. Oise.

Guise, DUKE OF, *gēz,* title of various members of a famous French family, including François, 2nd Duke (1519–63), a noted general, more or less ruler of France in the reign of Francis II ; also Henri, 3rd Duke (1550–88), assassinated by order of the king (Henry III).

guitar, *gi-tär′,* stringed instrument. The modern Spanish form with six strings is much used as an accompaniment to the voice.

Gulf Stream, warm ocean current issuing from the Gulf of Mexico ; flows round Florida as a deep blue ' river ' travelling *c.*65m a day ; gradually becomes a NE. drift of slightly warmer water E. of Greenland and Iceland and round the British Is. Winds blowing across the surface are warmed and take up moisture, but it is doubtful if its effect on the temperature of W. Europe is as great as geographers once believed.

gull, order (*Laridae*) of seabirds usually grey and white, with webbed feet and long wings. British species include the *black-headed* gull, having a red beak

THE COMMON GULL

and in summer dark brown head and neck ; *herring gull*, with yellow beak and red legs ; *kittiwake*, differing from other members of the species by having no hind toe ; lays 2–3 pale buff eggs spotted and blotched with brown ; *skua* ; also *tern*, with long wings and forked tail, lays buff or greenish eggs blotched with black or brown.

' Gulliver's Travels,' see SWIFT, JONATHAN

gum-tree, see EUCALYPTUS

gun, weapon, including small-arms, e.g. rifle, revolver ; also field guns and mortars.

The basic principle is that a missile is projected from the barrel by the pressure of gases resulting from an explosion.

Early types of guns fired cannon balls and chain-shot, the first great advance in design being the breach-loading type. Modern guns fire shells carrying explosives, e.g. aircraft cannon, howitzers. The modern rifled barrel has helical grooves to impart rotary motion to the shell or bullet, thus adding greatly to the stability of the projectile in flight, and increasing the accuracy of the gun. Rapid fire is attained by feeding bullets automatically into the breach, e.g. revolver, machine-gun (with belt feed), Bren, Sten and Lewis gun. In World War II the Tommy gun was much used, and aircraft carried guns which, if firing through the propeller, were synchronised so that the projectile always missed the blades. Anti-aircraft guns (AA) are designed to fire at a steep angle, and, like many other modern guns, are automatically sighted.

Guns are likely to be superseded by weapons of the rocket type. As these have no recoil, a heavy launching base is not required. The VI and V2 weapons were of this kind.

Ordnance, i.e. cannon, has developed from a simple type of gun said to have been first used at the battle of Crécy, 1346.

gunpowder, oldest known explosive ; a mixture of approximately 75% saltpetre, 15% charcoal (usually made from alder, willow or dogwood) and 10% sulphur. Gunpowder was known in the 6th c. in China ; used by Khubla Khan 1230 ; investigated by Roger Bacon ; first employed in warfare at Crécy 1346 ; led to a new type of warfare. See EXPLOSIVES.

Gunpowder Plot, see FAWKES, GUY

Gunter, EDMUND (1581–1626), churchman and scientist ; inventor of Gunter's chain used in surveying. The chain is 22yd long, and has 100 links.

Gurkha, *goor'kä*, native race of Nepal. Gurkha regiments have an outstanding record of service with the British Army in India.

gurnard, *gŭr'nĕrd*, sea-water fish with a large, ugly head ; has feelers on the underside ; found in British waters, and esteemed as good table fish.

Gurney, ELIZABETH, see FRY, ELIZABETH

Gurney, JOSEPH JOHN (1788–1847), born in Norfolk ; member of a banking family ; became a Quaker minister ; helped his sister, Elizabeth Fry, in her work of prison reform.

Gustavus II or Gustavus Adolphus, *gŭs-tā'-vŭs* (1594–1632), King of Sweden from 1611, known as the Lion of the North, *b* Stockholm ; made peace with Denmark and Russia. He was both a wise and enlightened administrator, and a courageous and brilliant soldier. Gustavus became the champion of Protestantism ; won remarkable victories in the Thirty Years' War, notably that against Tilly (in command of the Catholic forces) at Breitenfeld 1631 ; and died fighting at the victorious battle of Lützen 1632.

Gutenberg, JOHANNES, *goo'ten-berg*, (*c*.1398–1468), German printer ; pioneer in Europe of printing by movable types, *c*.1454 ; *b* Mainz. See PRINTING

Guthrum (*d* 890), Danish leader ; defeated by Alfred at Ethandune 878, and made the peace of Wedmore, by which the Danish occupation of E. England was reorganised.

gutta-percha, *per'-ka*, substance very much like rubber, but less elastic ; obtained by tapping trees in Malaya and Java ; used as an electric insulator, especially for submarine cables, and formerly as a covering for golf balls of the kind known consequently as *guttie-ba's*.

Guy, THOMAS, *gī* (1644–1724), printer and philanthropist ; made a fortune partly in S. Sea stock, and founded Guy's Hospital, London, 1721.

Gwynn, NELL, *gwin* (1650–87), popular name for Eleanor Gwynn, English actress who excelled in comedy ; captivated Charles II, with whom she lived from 1669.

gymnastics (Greek *gymnos*, naked), cult of

physical fitness greatly favoured by the ancient Greeks. Prussia revived the idea during the war against Napoleon ; and the German system, with its apparatus (e.g. trapeze, horizontal bars and vaulting horse) was popular till challenged by the Swedish system in which little or no apparatus is required. Gymnastics, a feature of the Nazi Youth movement, were encouraged in Britain, and ' keep fit classes ' were first organised by the Government in 1937.

The Women's League of Health and Beauty (leader Prunella Stack) enjoyed great popularity for some years before the beginning of World War II.

Gypsies, wandering race (calling themselves Romany men, *rom'-*) which came from India into W. Europe (Spain, Italy and Hungary) *c.*1400, professing to be pilgrims from *Egypt* (hence the name). There are perhaps 45,000 in Britain. Mostly law-abiding, they are expert judges of horses. They usually live in a caravan (*vardo*), tell fortunes, and lead a care-free life. Read George Borrow's *Romany Rye.*

gypsum, see CALCIUM

gyr-falcon, see HAWK

gyro-compass, see COMPASS

gyroscope, *jī'rō-skōp,* instrument consisting of a heavy wheel rotating at very high speed, and mounted so as to move freely in any direction. Its properties are (*a*) that its axis remains fixed in space as long as the wheel rotates, i.e. it refuses to turn with the motion of the spinning earth ; and (*b*) precession, i.e. when a force tends to alter the direction of its axis, the wheel turns about an axis at right angles to the axis about which the force is applied. Adaptations of the gyroscope are used as stabilisers in ships, submarines, aircraft and in the gyro-compass. In aircraft they are the ' heart ' of the ' automatic pilot.'

H

H, chemical symbol for hydrogen.

h, see QUANTUM THEORY

Haakon, *haw'kon,* name of several kings of Norway, from Haakon I (915–61) to Haakon VII, *b* 1872, became King of Norway on its separation from Sweden 1905 ; married Princess Maud, daughter of Edward VII. He was exiled during during World War II.

Haarlem, *här'lem,* town, Netherlands ; noted for tulips ; linen factories ; science academy ; printing ; pop.150,000.

Habakkuk, *hab'ă-kŭk,* OT prophet, possibly of the 7th c. BC, when Judah was invaded by the Chaldeans.

Habeas Corpus, *hā'bē-as kör'pŭs* (Lat. ' that you should have the body in court ') ; famous writ in English law. In earlier times prisoners were frequently kept in English prisons without trial. The passing of the Habeas Corpus Act 1679 made it a law that every prisoner should appear in court within two days of being imprisoned, and the cause of his detention stated. Habeas Corpus is thus one of the chief safeguards of personal liberty. It cannot normally be suspended except by Act of Parliament.

Haber, FRITZ, *hä'bĕr* (1868–1934), German chemist ; discovered a synthetic method of manufacturing ammonia ; from which is derived the modern method of making nitrates for fertilisers. See AMMONIA

Haddington, co.tn, E. Lothian, on R. Tyne ; has grain market ; Knox Memorial Institute ; it is the probable birthplace of John Knox.

Haddingtonshire, see LOTHIANS, THE

haddock, valuable food fish, *c.*2ft long ; has a black line and a black patch rather like a thumb imprint, at each side of the body ; feeds (chiefly on molluscs and spawn) in shoals ; caught in trawl nets ; may be eaten fresh, or, split and smoked, as Finnan haddock.

Haddon Hall, baronial mansion, Derbyshire, on the R. Wye, 2m from Bakewell ; has a 12–15th C. chapel and a famous Long Gallery. The hall, associated with Dorothy Vernon's elopement with Sir John Manners, partly inspired Sir Walter Scott's *Peveril of the Peak.*

Hadow Report, see EDUCATION

Hadrian, *hā'dri-an* (AD76–138), Roman emperor : brought up by the Emperor Trajan, whom he succeeded AD117 ; aimed to consolidate rather than to extend the empire ; travelled far and wide, visiting Britain AD122, when *Hadrian's Wall* (73m long) was built from the Solway to the Tyne ; traces, with its 17 major forts, still remain. Hadrian was responsible for many reforms, including direct taxation and a regular civil service ; also for many magnificent buildings.

Haeckel, ERNST HEINRICH, *hek'el* (1834–1919), German scientist and thinker, *b* Potsdam ; supported Darwin's theory of evolution ; disbelieved in a personal god.

haematite, *hēm'ă-tīt,* natural ferric oxide, Fe_2O_3 ; a valuable blood-coloured ore of iron free from phosphorus.

haemoglobin, see BLOOD

hafnium, rare metallic element, Hf ; atomic weight 178·6 ; atomic number 72.

Hagana or **Haganah,** Jewish military organisation opposing the ' Stern Gang ' in Palestine, but responsible for many skirmishes with the Arabs after World War II.

Hagar, see ISHMAEL

Hagen, *hä'gen,* Ruhr town, Germany ; manufactures textiles ; tanning, distilling and brewing ; pop.152,000.

Haggai, *hag'ā-ī (c.*520BC), OT prophet ; urged the Jews to rebuild the Temple.

Haggard, SIR RIDER (1856–1925), English novelist, *b* Bradenham, Norfolk ; lived for a time in S. Africa, where he was secretary to the Governor of Natal, 1875 ; returned to England, where he was a lawyer and farmer ; knighted 1912. He is best known for his thrilling stories which show his knowledge of Africa, e.g. *Jess, She, Ayesha, Allan Quatermain,* and *King Solomon's Mines,* the hero of which, Allan Quatermain, was actually the bold Frederick Courteney Selous (1851–1917), who explored Matabeleland, and other regions, and was a noted big-game hunter.

haggis, dish once a favourite in England, but now considered a Scot's national dish, comprising chopped lungs, heart, liver of a sheep, with suet, oatmeal, onion, seasoned with pepper and salt, all boiled in a sheep's stomach.

Hague, see THE HAGUE

Hai, see AI

Haider Ali, *hī'där (c.*1720–82), ruler of Mysore ; proclaimed himself sultan after dethroning the rajah ; allied with the Nizam of Madras ; fought the British at Chengam, and was defeated 1767 ; marched on Madras 1779, being defeated by Sir Eyre Coote, who, aided by the fleet, overcame his force in several battles, 1780–81.

Haifa, *hī'fä,* busy port, Palestine ; has an excellent modern harbour, also rail and air services (the latter to Egypt) and a pipeline from Mosul. There are many flourishing industries ; pop.145,000.

Haig of Bemersyde, DOUGLAS HAIG, 1ST EARL (1861–1928), British general, *b* Edinburgh ; descended from the 17th laird of Bemersyde (Berwickshire). Douglas Haig fought in Egypt and S. Africa ; was in command of the 1st Army (1915) in World War I, later succeeding Sir John French as Commander-in-Chief of British troops in France. He was promoted Field-Marshal 1917, and much criticised for his trench warfare, but showed great skill in driving back the Germans 1918. He founded the British Legion, and was buried at Dryburgh Abbey.

Hail Columbia, see ANTHEM

Haile-Selassie I, *hī'lē se-läs'ē* (1891–   ), Emperor of Ethiopia from 1930 ; introduced western reforms, including (1931) a new parliamentary system ; found refuge in England when Ethiopia was attacked by Italy 1936–40 ; restored 1941.

Haileybury College, *hä'li-beri,* Hertford-

shire ; originally a training school for cadets in the E. India Company ; became a public school 1862.

Hainault, *e-nō',* province, Belgium, noted for its rich coalfields and iron mines ; fertile soil ; cap. Mons.

Haiti, *hā'ti,* republic in the W. of Haiti Island, which is the 2nd largest island of the W. Indies ; area 10,204sq.m ; pop.3,000,000. Haiti, which is very fertile, produces timber, cocoa, cotton, hides, sisal, sugar (cane), but its prosperity has been hampered by many revolutions. French and Creole French (a debased French) are spoken ; cap. Port-au-Prince. UNESCO is now improving conditions, e.g. health, farming, education, etc. The remainder of the island is the Dominican Republic.

hake, *hāk,* food fish of the cod family ; *c.*3ft long ; dark grey above, lighter below ; particularly common off the coast of Cornwall.

Hakluyt, RICHARD, *häk'loot (c.*1553–1616), English geographer and churchman ; *b* London, of a Hereford family ; chaplain at the British embassy in Paris ; later Archdeacon of Westminster ; encouraged the colonisation of Virginia ; wrote *Divers Voyages Touching the Discovery of America* ; most famous for *The Principal Navigations, Voyages, and Discoveries of the English Nation,* an intensely interesting chronicle of adventures.

Hakodate, port, Japan ; has a large harbour ; pop.207,000.

halberd, weapon much used by English foot soldiers in the 16th c. It was a long pole with a metal point and axehead.

halcyon days, *hal'si-on,* period of calm. Alcyon is Gk for kingfisher, the ancient Greeks believing that in autumn the bird laid eggs on the sea, which remained calm till they were hatched.

Haldane, JOHN BURDON SANDERSON, *hōl'dän* (1892–   ), scientist, son of John Scott Haldane and nephew of 1st Viscount Haldane ; served in World War I ; reader in biochemistry Cambridge University 1922 ; professor of biometry University College, London, 1933 ; notable for his writings, e.g. *Science in Everyday Life.*

Haldane, JOHN SCOTT (1860–1936), *b* Edinburgh, brother of 1st Viscount Haldane ; a brilliant biologist, he related the effect of industrial occupation to physiology ; director of the Mining Research Laboratory, Birmingham ; publications include *Organism and Environment* and *The Philosophical Basis of Biology.*

Haldane of Cloan, RICHARD BURDON, 1ST VISCOUNT (1856–1928), Scottish barrister, philosopher, and later the statesman whom Earl Haig declared to be the greatest Secretary of State for War Britain ever had ; reorganised and partly mechanised the British army in time for World War I ; resigned in Cabinet crisis 1915 ; did great work in education ; wrote much as a philosopher ; Lord Chancellor in the first Labour Government.

half-life period, see RADIOACTIVITY

halibut, *hal'i-būt,* largest of the flat fishes, usually 4–5ft long ; brown above ; common in the N. Atlantic and the N. Sea ; excellent food fish. The liver provides halibut oil, extremely rich in vitamin A.

Halicarnassus, Greek town (now Budrum) of Asia Minor, where Herodotus was born, and where the Mausoleum stood, one of the seven wonders of the ancient world.

Halidon Hill, battlefield, near Berwick-on-Tweed, where the English under Edward III defeated the Scots under Sir Archibald Douglas 1333.

Halifax, (1) town, W. Yorkshire ; noted for worsted (woollen) goods and carpets; also dyeing ; pop.89,000 ; (2) cap. Nova Scotia ; a busy winter port with much W. Indian and S. American trade. Halifax is a terminus of the CPR ; pop.70,000.

Halifax, CHARLES MONTAGUE, EARL OF (1661–1715), Whig statesman ; helped to found the Bank of England 1694 ; Prime Minister 1697 ; reformed the coinage and introduced Exchequer Bills.

Halifax, EARL OF (1881–), British statesman ; *b* Yorkshire ; educated Eton and Oxford ; Unionist member for Ripon 1910–25 ; President of the Board of Education 1922–24 ; Minister of Agriculture 1924–25 ; Viceroy of India 1926–31, holding that office with distinction ; President of the Board (now Ministry) of Education 1932–35 ; succeeded his father as Viscount 1934 ; Foreign Secretary 1938 ; British Ambassador to the USA 1940 ; created Earl 1944.

Halifax, GEORGE SAVILE, 1ST MARQUIS OF (1633–95), British statesman ; brilliant orator ; offered the crown to William of Orange.

Hallam, HENRY (1777–1859), historian, *b* Windsor ; noted for his *View of the State of Europe During the Middle Ages,* and his *Constitutional History of England.* His son, ARTHUR HENRY (1811–33), *b* London, died in Vienna, and was commemorated by Lord Tennyson in *In Memoriam.*

Halle, *häl'e,* city, Saxony (Germany) ; noted for its saltworks, railways and university ; pop.220,000.

Hallé, SIR CHARLES, *hal'ā* (1819–95), British musician, born in Westphalia ; founded the Hallé Orchestra, Manchester.

Hallelujah Chorus, see HANDEL, G. F.

Halley, EDMUND, *hal'i* (1656–1742), astronomer, born near London ; made a star-map of the S. hemisphere ; was a friend of Newton ; became Astronomer Royal at Greenwich 1719 ; investigated trade-winds and the earth's magnetism ; famous for his discovery of the comet named after him. See COMET

Hall of Fame, handsome building, New York, in which the names of famous Americans are enshrined, e.g. Benjamin Franklin, Abraham Lincoln, William Penn and George Washington.

halo, see AUREOLE

halogens, *hal'ō-gens* ; *hā'lo-,* group of non-metallic elements (fluorine, chlorine, bromine, iodine) having closely related properties ; all are salt-producers and form halides.

Hals, FRANZ (*c.*1580–1666), Dutch artist, probably *b* Antwerp ; noted for his portraits, including his famous *Laughing Cavalier,* which is included in the Wallace Collection, London ; and *The Burgomaster and his Wife,* exhibited in the National Gallery, Edinburgh.

Hälsingborg, industrial port, Sweden ; has a large trade ; pop.69,000.

hamadryad, another name for the king cobra of India, Malaya and the Philippines ; may be 14ft long ; is yellowish with black bands ; fierce and poisonous.

Haman, *hā'man,* chief minister of Ahasuerus, King of Persia, in the 5th c. BC. His story is told in the OT book, Esther.

Hamburg, city, Germany ; on the R. Elbe ; had vast industries, e.g. shipbuilding, milling, sugar-refining, chemicals. Its modern quarters were handsomely planned, but suffered severely from bombing in World War II ; pop. 1,384,000.

Hamelin, *hä'melin,* romantic old fortress town, Germany ; on the R. Weser ; noted for the manufacture of iron goods and paper ; scene of the legend of the Pied Piper ; pop.26,000.

Hamilcar, see HANNIBAL

Hamilton, (1) mining town, Lanarkshire ; on the R. Clyde ; pop.38,000 ; (2) a city, Ontario, called ' the Birmingham of Canada,' noted for iron, cotton and woollen goods ; on L. Ontario ; pop. 174,000 ; (3) cap., Bermuda ; (4) a town, NZ ; pop. 28,000.

Hamilton, DUKE OF, title of the premier dukedom of Scotland ; borne by families of Hamilton and Douglas-Hamilton since 1643.

Hamilton, EMMA, LADY (*c.*1761–1815), Emma Lyon, probably of Ness, Cheshire ; of humble birth, beautiful and witty ; married Sir William Hamilton, English ambassador at Naples. Lord Nelson fell in love with her 1793 ; their child, Horatia, was *b* 1801. Lady Hamilton, the subject of almost 50 portraits by Romney, gambled her fortune away a few years after Nelson's death, and died at Calais. See NELSON, LORD

Hamilton, JAMES, 1ST DUKE (1606–49), Scottish supporter of Charles I ; led an army into England 1648, but defeated at Preston by Cromwell, and was executed a year later.

Hamitic, see LANGUAGE

Hammer of the Scots, see EDWARD I

Hammond, WALTER REGINALD (1903–) cricketer, *b* Dover ; played for England against Australia ; captained the English team 1938–39 and 1946 ; established new records in test matches ; an excellent batsman ; head of batting averages 1933–39.

Hammond organ, see ORGAN

Hammurabi, *häm-u-rä'bē* ; *-pē* (*d* 2080BC), King of Babylon ; built up a vast and well-ordered empire ; noted for his wise administration and his code of laws, the earliest known.

Hampden, JOHN, *ham'den* (1594–1643), son of William Hampden of Great Hampden, Buckinghamshire. His mother was a relative of Oliver Cromwell. Hampden became a lawyer ; inherited his father's estate, entered Parliament 1621 ; was imprisoned 1627 for refusing to pay a forced loan raised by Charles I ; but is most famous for his bold refusal to pay Ship Money.

English ports had previously paid sums of money towards the expense of the navy, especially in time of war, but when (1635) Charles called on the *inland* towns to contribute in time of peace, Hampden denounced the tax as an act of tyranny, and refused to pay the 20s demanded, at once becoming a popular hero.

He was one of the Five Members 1642 whom the king tried to arrest. In the Civil War he raised a regiment, and fought at Chalgrove Field (Oxfordshire), where he was severely wounded, dying six days later.

Hampshire (Hants, for short), county of England with coastline on the English Channel ; includes the I. of Wight, which is distinct for administrative purposes ; famed for trout streams, agriculture, cattle and horse rearing. Has fertile valleys, hills and woods, including New Forest ; among principal towns are Portsmouth, Winchester (co.tn), Bournemouth and Southampton.

Hampton, *ham'tŭn* ; *hamp'-*, village, Middlesex ; included in Twickenham ; noted for Hampton Court, a palace built near the Thames by Cardinal Wolsey *c.*1515 ; has over 1,000 rooms, and beautiful gardens, including the famous Maze and a vine planted 1768.

Hampton Court Conference, meeting 1604 at Hampton Court, when the Puritans appealed in vain to James I for changes in the Prayer Book ; the king accepted, however, their proposal for a new translation of the Bible, which took shape as the Authorised Version of 1611.

Hamsun, KNUT (1859–   ), Norwegian author ; started as a clerk, then became farm-worker, schoolmaster and tram conductor in USA ; won fame with his novels *Sult, Hunger* (1899), a description of slow starvation, *Growth of the Soul.* Nobel Prize for literature, 1920.

hand, measure of length ; 4in ; used especially in measuring the height of horses.

Handel, GEORGE FREDERICK, *han'dl* (1685–1759), composer, *b* Halle, Lower Saxony (Germany), son of a surgeon who dis-

HANDEL 1685–1759

couraged his musical genius during childhood ; visited Italy for three years ; given a post by the Elector of Hanover (later George I of England) ; came to England 1710, and was naturalised 1726. Though by then famous, especially for his operas, he was twice bankrupt owing to the bitter opposition of the Prince of Wales.

Turning to oratorio, of which he became the matchless composer, he wrote *Saul* and also *Israel in Egypt*, 1739, *L'Allegro* 1740, and in 23 days composed *The Messiah* (1741), his most famous work. *Judas Maccabaeus* was completed 1747. By 1753 he was blind. His works include 41 operas, 27 oratorios, many cantatas, chorals, and much organ, orchestral and chamber music.

Handel's *Messiah* remains his greatest work, and we do not wonder that its composer afterwards declared that the famous *Hallelujah Chorus* came to him as a gift. ' I did look up and saw all heaven opening before me, and the Great God himself.' The first performance of this oratorio took place at the New Music Hall, Dublin, 13 April 1742, and so many tickets were sold that the ladies were asked to ' leave their hoops at home ' (i.e. not to attend in the extremely wide skirts which were then fashionable), so that more people could be packed in the hall. The performance realised £400, an amazing sum in those days. Even after over 200 years the *Messiah* remains a great favourite, and is sung by many church choirs at Christmas, the Huddersfield singers being world-renowned.

The custom of standing during the singing of the *Hallelejuah Chorus* dates from the first performance in England (London 23 March 1743), when, at the first notes, George II and all others present rose, and remained standing to the end. Read *Handel*, Newman Flower.

handicrafts, see HOBBY

Hanford, town, Washington State, USA, site of atomic energy piles ; pop.60,000.

Hangchow, *hang'chow*, town and treaty port *c.*118m SW. of Shanghai, China ; noted for silk, gold and silver ware ; pop.600,000.

Hankow, *hän'kō*, Chinese river treaty port on the Yangtse R. ; noted for exporting tea ; pop.800,000.

Hanley, one of the ' Potteries ' of Staffordshire ; birthplace of Arnold Bennett ; pop. (with Stoke) 251,000.

Hannibal, military genius and bitter enemy of Rome. His father, Hamilcar Barca, a Carthaginian soldier and statesman, was the leader of the Carthaginians against the Romans in the First Punic War (see PUNIC WARS) ; later he led an army to Spain, where after nine years of fighting and statesmanship he created an empire. He was killed in battle 228BC.

As a boy Hannibal promised his father to spend his life fighting the Romans. He became leader of his father's army when only 25 ; to reach Italy he marched through Spain, then over the Pyrenees, across S. Gaul (now France), and over the Alps, a feat which is amazing for its daring and for the skill with which it was accomplished. The Romans, who had imagined that no enemy could ever come that way, sent army after army in an effort to hold Hannibal back, but yet he advanced, and eventually reached S. Italy, where, 216BC, he defeated a Roman army of 90,000 at Cannae.

His brother, Hasdrubal (who had been fighting against the Romans in Spain) marched into N. Italy 207BC, hoping to join forces with Hannibal, but in a battle along the banks of the R. Metaurus he was killed, and his army defeated—a disaster which even the skill and daring of Hannibal could not overcome. The Romans beat his generals in Spain and Sicily, and crossed the Mediterranean to Carthage (N. Africa), where the Carthaginians were overwhelmed at Zama 202BC

Even then, remembering his promise, Hannibal continued to stir up enemies against Rome, though he had fled to Bithynia, Asia Minor. Finally, 183BC, finding that it was impossible to destroy the power of Rome, he committed suicide by taking poison.

Hannington, JAMES (1847–85), English missionary, born in Sussex ; consecrated first bishop of Equatorial E. Africa ; murdered by Mwanga, King of Uganda, on his way to Uganda ; distinguished for his strength of character and individuality.

Hanno the Great, Carthaginian leader who, after the Carthaginian defeat at Zama 202BC, went to Rome to sue for peace.

Hanoi, *hă-noi'*, capital of the French protectorate of Tonkin, French Indo-China, known since 1946 as the republic of Viet-Namh ; pop.124,000.

Hanover, *han'ōvĕr*, (1) former province of Germany ; mainly agricultural. Its Elector succeeded Queen Anne as George I of England 1714. (2) The cap. of the province ; on the R. Leine ; one of the largest cities of Germany, and a great railway centre ; pop.355,000.

Hansard, official parliamentary report, so named because Luke Hansard (1752–1828) and his sons printed the *Journals* of the House of Commons from 1774. Hansard is now available weekly.

Hanseatic League, *han-sē-at'ik*, union of towns in NW. Germany for trade and for the defence of their ' liberties ' i.e. trading privileges ; founded 1241. At one time the League included 64 towns with a common fleet, army and government. It was much depleted in the Thirty Years' War, and finally included only Bremen, Lübeck and Hamburg.

Hansford-Johnson, PAMELA (1912–), English novelist and critic ; her books include *The Trojan Brothers*.

hansom cab, see ROADS

Hants, postal abbreviation for Hampshire. See HAMPSHIRE

Hanway, JONAS (1712–86), English traveller, b Portsmouth ; said to have been the first man to carry an umbrella in London.

Hapsburg, *häps'bur*ch, name of a famous European family derived from Habichtsburg or Hawk's Castle, built near the Rhine 1028 by Werner, Bishop of Strasbourg. One of his descendants was elected Holy Roman Emperor 1273 as Rudolf I. The family added largely to their landed possessions thereafter ; and Maximilian I (1459–1519) won new power and greatness by marrying Maria of Burgundy.

His grandson (Charles V) was Holy Roman Emperor and also King of Spain ; Charles's son was Philip II of Spain. The death of Charles II of Spain 1700 brought about the War of the Spanish Succession, ending 1714 in the establishment of the Bourbons.

Hapsburgs ruled as Holy Roman emperors without a break to the death of Charles VI 1740, when the male line became extinct, but the claims of Charles's daughter, Maria Theresa, caused the War of the Austrian Succession ; her descendant, Francis II, known (1804) as Emperor of Austria, abandoned the title of Holy Roman Emperor 1806. Hapsburgs ruled in Austria-Hungary till 1918.

hara-kiri, often incorrectly written harakari, act of ceremonially committing suicide by slashing open the stomach ; long practised by the Japanese.

Harcourt pentane lamp, see CANDLE-POWER
Hardanger, *här'dängĕr,* beautiful fiord
(inlet) on the SW. coast of Norway.
hard currency, relative term in Britain for
currency in short supply issued by
countries which can offer goods in great
demand, e.g. the dollar and the Swiss
franc. See DOLLAR
Hardicanute (1019–42), son of Canute,
whom he succeeded as King of Denmark
1035 ; ruled England cruelly and unsuccessfully from 1040 until his death.
Hardie, JAMES KEIR (1856–1915), British
Labour leader ; *b* Lanarkshire ; at first
a miner ; founded one of the first
Socialist publications, *Labour Leader* ;
entered Parliament 1892 ; helped to
found the Scottish Labour Party 1888,
and the Independent Labour Party
1893 ; leader of Labour Party in House
of Commons 1906–15. He was a man
of sterling qualities and high integrity.
Harding, WARREN GAMALIEL (1865–1923),
29th President of the USA, elected
1920 when America resented President
Wilson's association of the USA with
European events, and wished to adopt an
isolationist policy.
hardness of water, see CALCIUM
Hardwick Hall, great house near Chesterfield, Derbyshire, named after Bess of
Hardwick, wife of George, Earl of
Shrewsbury ; begun *c.*1590, it is noted
for its many windows and works of art.
Hardy, THOMAS (1840–1928), English
author and poet, *b* Upper Bockhampton,
near Dorchester ; studied as an architect, but turned to writing. His novels,
all with a hint of the futility of human
life, include *Under the Greenwood Tree*
(1872), *Far from the Madding Crowd,*
The Return of the Native, The Mayor of
Casterbridge, The Woodlanders, Tess of
the D'Urbervilles, Jude the Obscure. In
them is the humour and pathos of the
people he knew and loved in his own
Wessex country. Something of the same
sad sincerity belongs to his poems, and
also to his masterpiece, his epic-drama
The Dynasts, which paints a picture of
man fretting himself against unchanging
forces.
    Hardy's ashes repose in Westminster
Abbey ; his heart is at Stinsford, near
Dorchester.
Hardy, SIR THOMAS MASTERMAN (1769–
1839), British vice-admiral, *b* Kingston,
Dorset. In command of the *Victory* at
Trafalgar (1805), when Lord Nelson
died in his arms.
hare, see RABBITS
harebell, British plant of slender stem and
drooping bell-shaped blue flower, found
also in Africa and America.
harem, *hä'rem,* in Mohammedan countries,
that part of a house or palace where the
women live. The *Koran* allows a man
4 wives (the Sultan having 7), and each
wife has her own apartments.
Harewood, 6TH EARL OF, *här'-* (1882–1947),
member of the Yorkshire family of Lascelles ; served in World War I ; married

Princess Mary (Princess Royal) 1922.
Harfleur, *är-flür',* coastal fortress village,
France ; scene of a victory 1415 by
Henry V of England.
Hargreaves, JAMES (*d* 1778), handloom
weaver near Blackburn, Lancashire, who
invented a carding-machine, and later
(1766) the spinning-jenny, which vastly
increased the rate of cotton production
and revolutionised the industry ; was
persecuted by fellow workers who
thought his invention would upset
labour conditions ; he opened a spinning
mill in Nottingham, but died comparatively poor.
Harlech, *här-lech,* historic town on the
coast of Wales (Merionethshire) ; its
castle was captured 1468 by the Yorkists,
hence the song, *The March of the Men*
of Harlech.
Harlem, Negro quarter of New York, USA.
Harley Street, London street between Marylebone Road and Cavendish Square ;
noted for the consulting rooms of
medical specialists.
harmattan, *här-ma-tan',* hot, dusty wind in
W. Africa ; blows October–March.
harmonic progression, in mathematics, a
progression the reciprocals of whose
terms are in arithmetic progression. The
simplest arithmetical progression (A.P.)
is, 1, 2, 3, 4, 5 etc., and the simplest
H.P. is the reciprocals of these, i.e.
1, $\frac{1}{2}$, $\frac{1}{3}$, $\frac{1}{4}$, $\frac{1}{5}$ etc. The sum $1 + 2 + \ldots$
$+ n$ is $\frac{1}{2}n(n + 1)$; but there is no simple
formula for the sum of *n* terms. The
name reminds us that the terms vary as
the lengths of strings vibrating to the
harmonics of a fundamental note. See
ARITHMETICAL PROGRESSION
harmony, see SOUND
Harmsworth, HAROLD, see NORTHCLIFFE,
LORD
Harold I (*d* 1040), son of Canute, and half-
brother of Hardicanute, with whom he
shared the kingdom till 1037, when
Harold ruled all England.
Harold II (*c.*1022–66), son of Earl Godwin ;
controlled his brother-in-law, Edward
the Confessor ; had great military
talents. After shipwreck in Normandy
1063 he was compelled by Duke William
to promise to aid him to become king
of England at Edward's death. When
Harold became king 1066, his banished
brother, Tostig, landed in the north with
Harold Hardrada of Norway. Harold
defeated them at Stamford Bridge (Yorkshire), but meanwhile William of Normandy had landed, and Harold was
killed during the battle of Hastings.
Haroun-al-Raschid, *hä-roon-äl-ra-shĕd*
(763–809), Caliph of Bagdad from 786 ;
notable as a soldier, for the prosperity
and magnificence of his reign, and as
the central figure in *The Arabian Nights.*
harp, musical instrument evolved from the
twanging of a bow-string ; much
favoured in ancient Egypt. The triangular form is now most common, its
43 strings being plucked by the fingers
or with a plectrum.

Harpenden, town, Hertfordshire. The Rothamsted Agricultural College is nearby.

harpoon, see WHALE

harpsichord, -*kord*, 16th c. musical instrument in great favour 17th–18th c. Forerunner of the piano, its strings were plucked (not *struck*) when a key was depressed. The SPINET, a similar keyboard instrument common 16th–18th c., had 5 octaves.

harpy, in old Greek tales, a monstrous bird with a woman's head.

harrier, see HAWK

Harriman, WILLIAM AVERELL (1891–   ), American administrator ; dealt with Lend-Lease from 1941 ; ambassador to Moscow 1943, US Secretary of Commerce 1946.

Harris, southern part of the Long Island, Outer Hebrides, Scotland ; its wool is woven into ' Harris tweeds.'

Harris, JOEL CHANDLER, see UNCLE REMUS

Harrisburg, cap. Pennsylvania, USA ; noted for lumbering, also iron and steel ; pop.84,000.

Harrison, BENJAMIN (1833–1901), 23rd President of the USA ; elected 1888.

Harrison, JOHN (1693–1776), clockmaker, born in Yorkshire ; invented the gridiron compensation pendulum ; awarded £20,000 for his ship's chronometer, the most accurate then known.

Harrogate, health resort, W. Riding, Yorkshire ; noted for chalybeate and sulphur springs ; pop.49,000.

Harrow-on-the-Hill, town, Middlesex ; noted for its church, and still more for its public school, founded by John Lyon 1571 ; pop.216,000.

Harrow School, English public school founded by John Lyon ; granted a charter 1571 ; became the chief rival of Eton and Winchester towards the end of the 18th c. Famous men educated at Harrow include Byron, Peel, Palmerston and Winston Churchill.

hartal, *här-tal'* (in India), the closing of shops and businesses as an act of mourning or as a protest against some political situation.

Harte, FRANCIS BRET, *härt* (1839–1902), American author, *b* Albany, New York State, USA ; had only 3 years' schooling ; at 18 was a gold-miner in California, also professor of literature in California University 1870–71 ; won fame with his stories of pioneer life in America, all full of humour and pathos ; and with his poems, including *The Luck of Roaring Camp* ; was popular as a lecturer ; spent his last years in Britain ; consul in Glasgow 1880–85 ; lived in London from 1885.

hartebeest, *härt'ē-bēst*, exceptionally swift S. African antelope, *c*.4ft high at the withers ; reddish colour ; has turned-back horns.

Hartford, cap., Connecticut, USA ; a noted banking centre ; pop.166,000.

Hartlepool, *hart-le-pool'*, port, County Durham; has much trade in coal and iron;

pop.15,000 ; close by is W. Hartlepool, with a similar although larger trade ; pop.64,000.

Harty, SIR HAMILTON (1879–1941), composer, *b* County Down ; attained international fame as a conductor ; director of the Hallé Orchestra 1920–33 ; later of the London Symphony Orchestra.

Harvard, JOHN, *här'věrd* (1607–38), English Puritan, *b* Southwark London ; went 1637 as a minister to Charlestown, Massachusetts, USA ; bequeathed his books and half his estate to found a college, now America's oldest and most famous university. This is at Cambridge, 3m from Boston (USA). Finely equipped and with *c*.5,000 students, Harvard includes medical, law, arts, and science schools, also facilities for studying engineering, business, mining and forestry.

Harvard University, see HARVARD, JOHN

harvest mouse, see MOUSE

Harvey, WILLIAM (1578–1657), physician, *b* Folkestone ; studied medicine at Padua, where his attention was drawn to the valves in blood-veins ; appointed physician at St Bartholomew's Hospital, London 1609 ; in a lecture to the College of Physicians 1616 announced his theory of the circulation of the blood, the greatest advance in physiology since Aristotle's day. His book expanding the theory (1628) is the basis of all modern physiology. Harvey's discoveries were at first ridiculed by the medical world, and he was for many years unpopular. He lived however to see his views widely accepted. As physician to Charles I, he had charge of the two young princes at the battle of Edgehill. See BLOOD

Harwell, site of the atomic energy experimental station near Didcot, Berkshire ; established 1946. There are two piles, the larger, known as BEPO, being started up in July 1948. It has since produced valuable radio-isotopes used in the UK and overseas. Recent experiments include studies of the effects of neutrons and gamma-rays on various materials. The beta-spectrometer separates electrons of different energy. See SELLAFIELD

Harwich, *här'ij*, port, Essex ; a packet station for the Continent ; noted for its docks and harbour.

Harz Mountains, *härts*, mt. range in N. Germany ; rich in silver and iron ; a favourite tourist centre.

Hasdrubal, *haz'drū-bäl* (d 207BC), Carthaginian soldier, brother of Hannibal ; killed at the battle of Metaurus. See HANNIBAL

hashish, see HEMP

Hastings, seaside town, Sussex ; noted for its esplanade and gardens ; has a Norman castle ; pop.49,000. The postwar reconstruction of the town includes a 2-decker thoroughfare, one street level for shops, the other for traffic. See HASTINGS, BATTLE OF

Hastings, BATTLE OF, fought 14 Oct 1066 ; changed the course of English history, for in the morning England was Saxon, by nightfall Norman, Saxon Harold II being dead with an arrow through his eye, and the Norman Duke William (William the Conqueror) being ruler. The scene was a hill *c*.6m from Hastings, later called Senlac.

William, Duke of Normandy, landed at Pevensey shortly after Harold had defeated a Norwegian army at Stamford Bridge, Yorkshire. Harold marched south, grouped his private soldiers (or house-carls) round him, his other soldiers (most of them poorly armed) in companies protected by stakes. At first the battle went well for the Saxons, who fought bravely and kept their ranks closed ; but a number gave chase to a few of William's men who were retreating, and William at once ordered others to pretend they were running away. The Normans then turned and attacked. Even then the house-carls on the hill held their ground, but towards evening Norman arrows fell in showers, the ranks drew back in disorder, and Harold was killed. For a vivid description of the battle read John Richard Green's *Short History of the English People*, chapter 2. See BAYEUX TAPESTRY

Hastings, FRANCIS-RAWDON, 1ST MARQUIS (1754–1826), British soldier and administrator ; *b* Ireland ; fought in the American War of Independence 1775–83 ; appointed Governor of Bengal 1813. As Commander-in-Chief in India, he planned the campaigns which established British rule ; responsible for an enlightened policy and for important reforms.

Hastings, WARREN (1732–1818), one of the founders of the British Empire in India ; became a writer in the E. India Company ; supported Lord Clive ; appointed first Governor-General of India 1773. Bitterly opposed by Sir Philip Francis, he carried out excellent reforms, acted as an able administrator, dealt boldly with Haidar Ali, and may be said to have saved British power in India from destruction. He had opportunity to enrich himself but never did so.

Unhappily Sir Philip Francis persuaded Edmund Burke to attack Hastings' honour. He was impeached 1786 (the year after his return from India), and a trial lasting over seven years began 1788. Eventually the House of Lords acquitted him unanimously.

Hathaway, ANNE, see SHAKESPEARE, WILLIAM

Hathor, *hä'thör*, ancient Egyptian goddess, daughter of Ra ; represented as a cow.

Hatto II (*d* 970), Archbishop of Mainz (Germany). He is associated with the legend of the Mouse Tower at Bingen, where he is said to have been killed by rats or mice.

Hatton, SIR CHRISTOPHER (1540–91), Elizabethan courtier, *b* Northamptonshire ; Lord Chancellor 1587.

hauberk, protective coat of chain mail worn in Norman times.

Hauptmann, GERHART, *hawpt'män* (1862–1946), German dramatist and poet ; *b* Silesia ; notable for his realistic plays, e.g. *Die Weber, Und Pippa Tanzt* ; Nobel prize for literature, 1912.

Hausa, *howsa*, warlike Negro race in Central Sudan, whose language is largely spoken in areas between the Mediterranean and the Gulf of Guinea.

hautboy, *hō'boi, ō'boi*, woodwind instrument from which the modern oboe is descended ; greatly favoured by Handel, who used it in orchestral pieces.

Havana, *hä-van'ä*, port and cap., Cuba (W. Indies) ; has a good harbour ; noted for the manufacture of cigars ; pop.659,000.

Havelock, SIR HENRY, *hav'lok* (1795–1857), soldier, born near Sunderland ; saw military service in Burma and the Afghan war. During the Indian Mutiny he relieved Lucknow with aid from Sir James Outram.

Haverfordwest, port and cap. Pembrokeshire.

Havre or **Le Havre,** *ä'vr*, commercial port, France, at the mouth of the R. Seine ; noted for shipbuilding, ironworks and milling ; pop.107,000.

Hawaii, *hä-wī'ē*, name of a group of 24 volcanic islands in the N. Pacific, formerly known as the Sandwich Is. The Hawaiian islands, have an area of *c*.6,420sq.m ; pop.520,000. The islands include Oahu and Molokai (see DAMIEN, FATHER). The climate is excellent, and tropical vegetation is abundant ; products include rice, cane sugar, pineapples and coffee. The islands, discovered 1778 by Captain Cook, are popular with tourists, and the craters of active volcanoes are a source of interest to them. Hawaii belongs to the USA, which has here the great naval base of Pearl Harbour, attacked by Japanese planes 7–8 Dec 1941 ; cap. Honolulu (on Oahu).

Hawarden, *här'den*, town, Flintshire. Hawarden Castle was Gladstone's home.

hawfinch, see FINCH

Hawick, *haw'ik*, town, Roxburghshire ; noted for tweeds and hosiery.

hawk, name of several British birds of prey. (*a*) The (male) SPARROW-HAWK (12–16in long) has slate-blue plumage above, greyish-brown with darker bars below, blue beak, yellow legs and feet, and short wings ; makes a deadly swoop on its quarry, i.e. small birds, young rabbits and poultry ; the 5–6 rounded, bluish-green eggs are spotted. (*b*) The GOSHAWK, now rare, has bluish-grey plumage above, white barred with brown below. (*c*) The HARRIER (so-named because it *harries* or attacks small birds) has long wings and legs but a small beak.

Closely related to hawks are FALCONS, which include kestrels and kites, all with curved beaks, short, pointed wings, long toes ; the JER-FALCON or GYR-FALCON, found in N. Europe, Asia and America, occasionally visits Britain in winter. A

THE SPARROW-HAWK

native British falcon is the PEREGRINE
FALCON, usually found in wild districts ;
lays 3–4 eggs (reddish-brown and
mottled) on sea cliffs ; the male (known
as a *tiercel*) is *c*.15in long, the female
perhaps 18. The MERLIN, smallest of
British falcons and exceedingly swift, has
greyish-blue plumage with pale yellow
underparts spotted with brown ; though
c.11in long, it weighs only 6oz ; nests on
the ground in heather ; lays 4 eggs,
reddish, mottled with brown. The
KITE, now very rare, is *c*.25in long ; has
reddish-brown plumage above, blackish
stripes below ; a forked tail of reddish
feathers. The KESTREL (often called
windhover because it hovers almost
motionless before plunging to the attack)
is reddish-brown with bluish spots or
bars on the back, fawn or chestnut breast.
The nest is in tall trees or on old towers ;
lays 5 reddish-brown eggs.

    HAWKING or FALCONRY (now out of
fashion but still practised) is the sport
of hunting with trained hawks or falcons,
chiefly peregrine falcon, goshawk, or
sparrow-hawk. Known in China 2000BC,
it was much practised in Britain from
Saxon times to the 17th c., and was most
popular as a royal pastime in Queen
Elizabeth's day. The birds, trained when
young, were first blindfolded and almost
starved, and then taught to return to the
wrist after making a capture.

Hawke, LORD (1705–81), admiral, *b*
London ; famous for his brilliant victory
at the battle of Quiberon Bay 1759, when
he defeated the French and removed all
possibility of invasion in the Seven
Years' War.

hawking, see HAWK

Hawkins, SIR JOHN (1532–95), sailor, *b*
Plymouth. He was the first Englishman
to trade in slaves, rounding them up
(1562) in W. Africa, and sailing with

them to S. America and the W. Indies ;
plundered Spanish ships, and was rear-
admiral in the fight against the Armada
1588.

Haworth, *how'erth*, village, W. Yorkshire ;
home of the Brontë sisters.

hawthorn, *may* or *whitethorn*, small bushy
tree much used in hedges. The branches
bear many sharp thorns ; the trunk is
grey and rough ; the flowers have five
white petals, though some hawthorns
have red flowers ; the bright red berries
appear in autumn, and are called haws.

Hawthornden Prize, THE, see DRUMMOND,W.

Hawthorne, NATHANIEL (1804–64), Ameri-
can novelist, *b* Salem, Massachusetts.
His many books include *The Scarlet
Letter, Twice Told Tales,* and *Tanglewood
Tales* (a book of Greek myths).

Hay, IAN (1876–   ), pen-name of John
Hay Beith, soldier, novelist, playwright.
His novels include *Pip* (1907) and *A Knight
on Wheels.* Among his plays is *A Damsel
in Distress.*

Haydn, FRANZ JOSEPH, *hī'd'n* (1732–1809),
Austrian composer, born near Vienna,
where, though poor, he received musical
training. He won fame with his
oratorios, e.g. *The Creation.* He composed 150 symphonies, 77 quartets,
c.40 trios, much religious music, many
songs, and the Austrian national anthem,
composed (Vienna) 1797.

    Haydn may be said to have originated
the modern form of the symphony,
sonata, etc.

    After Haydn had heard his own
Creation for the last time Beethoven
kissed his hand.

Hayes, town, Middlesex ; builds aircraft ;
pop.61,000 with Harlington.

Haye Sainte, see WATERLOO, BATTLE OF

hay-fever, catarrhal affection of the mucous
membrane of the eyes, nose, mouth and
air passage, due to the irritation set up
by the pollen of grasses and plants ; it
troubles many people in summertime,
and causes sneezing and headache.

hazel, large shrub of Europe, N. Africa
and Asia ; the British hazel, sometimes
30ft high, has a leaf similar to the alder,
but with a point at the tip ; the catkins
are golden-green in February, the nut
(known as filbert or cob-nut), is in a
' cup ' with jagged edges. Water diviners
use the pliable branches when searching
for hidden springs. The WITCH HAZEL,
a small tree, has oval leaves, and yellow
flowers appearing in late autumn. See
ILLUSTRATION, p. 321

Hazlitt, WILLIAM, *haz'lit* (1778–1830),
writer, *b* Maidstone, Kent ; early became friendly with Coleridge, Wordsworth and Charles Lamb ; had a stormy
and unhappy life and a quarrelsome
nature ; travelled much on the Continent ; was a parliamentary reporter
and dramatic critic ; wrote on philosophy and Shakespeare ; had a wide
knowledge of art ; in later years suffered
from ill-health and poverty, but died
saying, ' Well, I've had a happy life.'

A shrewd literary critic, Hazlitt is most famous as an essayist, e.g. his essays *Going a Journey, The Feeling of Immortality in Youth.*

H-bomb, popular name for a type of atomic bomb not generally known until 1950. The advantage of the hydrogen bomb over the uranium or plutonium bomb is that there is apparently no limit to its size. By its very nature, the plutonium bomb cannot exceed a comparatively small volume without spontaneous explosion, but the H-bomb may contain almost any quantity of heavy hydrogen, since in any case it requires a plutonium explosion to release its energy. The fission of uranium is a breaking-down process—using heavy atoms ; that of the H-bomb is a building up process beginning with the second lightest atom known, namely, that of heavy hydrogen.

HCF, short for highest common factor, i.e. the highest number that will divide exactly into 2 or more numbers, e.g. 8 is the HCF of 32, 48, 56, thus :

$$32 = 2 \times 2 \times 2 \times 2 \times 2 \text{ or } 2^5$$
$$48 = 2 \times 2 \times 2 \times 2 \times 3 \text{ or } 2^4 \times 3$$
$$56 = 2 \times 2 \times 2 \times 7 \qquad \text{ or } 2^3 \times 7$$
$$\therefore \text{ HCF} = 2 \times 2 \times 2 \text{ or } 2^3$$

To find the HCF of 2 large numbers keep on dividing till the *last divisor,* e.g. to find the HCF of, say, 2613 and 10868, we may work as follows :

```
2613)10868(4
     10452
      416)2613(6
          2496
          117)416(3
              351
               65)117(1
                  65
                  52)65(1
                     52
                     13)52(4
                        52
```

$\therefore$ HCF = 13 (i.e. last divisor). Note that time and space are saved by setting out the sum as follows :

6	2613	10868	4
	2496	10452	
1	117	416	3
	65	351	
4	52	65	1
	52	52	
		13	

He, chemical symbol for helium.
head, in physics, depth of a liquid.
head-hunters, see DYAKS
health, normal condition of the body, dependent to a large degree on (*a*) wise eating of suitable foods in a varied diet ; (*b*) sufficient sunlight ; (*c*) plenty of fresh air ; (*d*) regular exercise, e.g. walking and games ; (*e*) enough sound sleep, say 8–12 hours a day for young people, according to age—a younger child needs more sleep than children of, say, 12–14 years of age ; (*f*) correct clothing, i.e. light enough to allow the free circulation of air, but warm enough to retain heat in winter ; (*g*) personal cleanliness, i.e. frequent use of soap and water ; (*h*) due care in regularly emptying the bowels ; (*i*) avoidance of infection ; (*j*) temperance in drinking intoxicants and in smoking.

PUBLIC HEALTH is State supervision in relation to the collection of refuse, child welfare, drainage, food inspection, provision of clinics and notification of infectious diseases, these matters being superintended by a local medical officer. The Ministry of Health (set up 1919) is concerned with all such matters, and with housing, etc. NATIONAL HEALTH INSURANCE schemes date from Lloyd George's National Health Insurance Act of 1911, and provide free medical treatment, sickness benefits for all insured persons, the whole being revised by Sir William Beveridge, whose Social Insurance Scheme was made known 1941. In 1948 the Labour Government introduced a National Health Insurance scheme whereby members of the medical profession are paid a minimum salary by the Government to treat patients who come within the bounds of the scheme. Patients do not now pay doctor's fees for professional services, but have to pay a fixed weekly contribution out of their income (whether medical treat-

HAZEL
The catkins, the leaf and the nuts

ment is being received or not) so that they may have medical treatment when, and as often as, it is needed. Doctors may of course accept patients who still wish to pay for professional services. These are called private patients.

hearing, see EAR

heart, see BLOOD

heat, form of energy (see MATTER) ; flows from bodies at a higher temperature to those at a lower ; generally causes expansion of solids, liquids, gases (see EXPANSION) ; these contract when cooled, but an important exception is water.

Heat travels in several ways. (*a*) *By conduction* : Metals are good conductors, water and air bad conductors. (The insulating value of woollen clothing is due to the presence of particles of air trapped by the fibre, thus preventing escape of body-heat.) In conduction the molecules of a substance pass on heat-energy to one another without moving out of their place. (*b*) *By convection* : That is to say, the molecules *move*, carrying heat energy with them, as in liquids and gases, a principle made use of in domestic hot-water systems, where hot water rises and flows round the system of pipes. (*c*) *By radiation,* i.e. by *wave-motion* : The waves do *not* heat the medium through which they travel, but will pass through empty space, and heat the object on which they fall. Thus glass transmits much of the radiant heat from a white-hot body, less from a red-hot body, and scarcely any from a body at, say, 100°C ; so that a glass-house allows the heat of the sun to *enter*, but does not allow the warmth within to *escape*. Dull, dark metal surfaces make the best *radiators* of heat ; highly-polished metal surfaces make poor radiators.

Heat causes *evaporation* of a liquid into a vapour (without necessarily reaching boiling-point). See BOILING-POINT

The difference between heat and temperature is that heat is the *quantity* or *amount* of heat in a body, whereas temperature is the *difference* in heat-levels. The latter determines the direction of flow ; thus 1,000cc of water at 10°C has more heat than 10cc of water at 15°C ; the spark from a flint may be 1,000°C, or more, but it contains so little heat that it will not burn your hand while still red-hot.

The scientific unit of heat is the *calorie*, i.e. the amount of heat that will raise the temperature of 1 gram of water 1°C. The *British Thermal Unit* (B.Th.U.) is the quantity of heat that will raise the temperature of 1lb of water 1°F. A *therm* is 100,000 B.Th.U., a unit much used by coal-gas companies who undertake that each cu.ft of gas supplied will (usually) produce 500 B.Th.U. of heat. The *thermal capacity* of a body is the number of heat units that will raise its temperature 1°. The *specific heat* of a substance is the ratio :

$$\frac{\text{thermal capacity of the substance}}{\text{thermal capacity of the same weight of water}}$$

(see SPECIFIC HEAT). *Latent heat of vaporisation* of a substance is the quantity of heat that will change unit mass of liquid into vapour without change of temperature. For water its value is 536 calories per gram at normal pressure, or 970 B.Th.U. per lb. *Latent heat of fusion* of a substance is the quantity of heat that will change unit mass of a solid into liquid without change of temperature. For water (as ice) its value is 80 calories per gram, or 144 B.Th.U. per lb. *Water equivalent* of a body is the weight of water that has the same thermal capacity as the body. For the effects of heat on a gas, see GAS.

Heat may be produced in various ways, e.g. (*a*) by light and other electromagnetic waves, as in the absorption of sunshine ; (*b*) from mechanical energy, as when a bicycle pump becomes hot ; (*c*) from chemical energy, as when concentrated sulphuric acid is added to water ; (*d*) from electrical energy, e.g. the filament of an electric lamp ; (*e*) by molecular energy, e.g. a vapour changing into a liquid.

Mechanical equivalent of heat is the amount of work which, if converted entirely into heat, produces unit quantity of heat. Its value is 4·2 joules (or $4·2 \times 10^7$ ergs) per calorie, or 778ft-lb per B.Th.U., or 1,400 ft-lb per lb deg. C. See ELECTRICITY ; THERMODYNAMICS ; THERMOMETER ; ZERO

heath or **heather,** names for moorland shrubs (family *Ericaceae*) including (*a*) *cross-leaved heath* with leaves in whorls of four on a stem ending with a cluster of pink bells ; (*b*) *bell heather*, with rich purple bells close together on upper part of stem ; (*c*) *ling*, with purple, pink or (rarely) white deeply lobed flowers—the

CROSS-LEAVED HEATH

A stem of leaves and flowers, and (*left to right*) *the pistil, flower, stamen and a leaf*

more abundant heather in Britain. All heathers are pollinated by bees, and flower July–Sept.

Heathfield, GEORGE AUGUSTUS ELIOTT, LORD, *hĕth-* (1717–90), general, born in Roxburghshire ; fought at Dettingen and in the Seven Years' War ; most famous for his superb defence of Gibraltar (1779–83), during the War of American Independence.

Heathrow, *hĕth-ro'*, trans-Atlantic and trans-Continental airport, Middlesex, opened for civilian services 1946. Now known as London Airport, near Hounslow, it is 2½m long, and when complete will be one of the world's largest and busiest air terminals.

Heaviside, OLIVER (1850–1925), scientist, *b* London ; developed long-distance telephony ; suggested what is now known as the Heaviside (or Heaviside-Kennelly) layer, i.e. a level of the atmosphere (*c.*60m above the earth), thought to comprise ionised air particles which reflect radio waves, thus preventing them from going off into space.

Heaviside-Kennelly layer, see ATMOSPHERE ; HEAVISIDE, O. ; RADIO

heavy water, popular name for deuterium oxide, D_2O, present in ordinary water to the extent of *c.*1 part in 5,000 ; specific gravity 1·1 ; freezing point 3·82°C ; boiling-point 101·42°C.

DEUTERIUM, D, or heavy hydrogen, is an isotope of hydrogen ; atomic weight 2. Only a few litres of heavy water were available in USA in 1940, but by 1945 large quantities had been produced for experimental work on atom bombs.

Hebe, *hē'bē*, in old Gk tales, goddess of youth, daughter of Zeus, and wife of Heracles.

Hebrew, see JEWS

Hebrews, EPISTLE TO THE, NT letter by an unknown writer urging the Jews to remain loyal to Christ.

Hebrides, *heb'ri-dēz*, sometimes called Western Islands, *c.*500 islands off the west coast of Scotland ; grouped as OUTER HEBRIDES, including Lewis-Harris (the Long Island), N. and S. Uist, etc., and INNER HEBRIDES (including Skye, Mull, Iona and Staffa) ; noted for magnificent and rugged scenery. Cattle and sheep rearing, fishing and weaving are the chief occupations of the inhabitants, numbering *c.*80,000. ' Hebrides ' is by origin a mistake in an ancient manuscript for the correct form (*Ebudes*) of the ancient Latin name.

Hebron, *hē'bron*, ancient town, Palestine, *c.*20m from Jerusalem ; pop.25,000.

Heckmondwike, W. Yorkshire town 8m from Huddersfield ; noted for carpet and blanket weaving.

Hecla, highest active volcano in Iceland (5,100ft).

Hector, in old Gk tales, son of Priam, King of Troy, and husband of Andromache ; killed by Achilles while defending Troy against the Achaeans ; figures prominently in Homer's *Iliad*.

Hecuba, *hek-yū-bä*, in old Gk tales, wife of Priam, King of Troy, and mother of Hector, Paris and Cassandra.

hedgehog, mammal, common in Britain ; *c.*10in long, excluding its short tail. It is covered with spines, and when it rolls itself up into a ball presents a thorny problem to its attackers ; sleeps through the winter ; produces 4–6 young at a time ; feeds on insects, worms, snails and slugs.

THE HEDGEHOG

hedge sparrow, see ACCENTOR

Hegel, GEORG WILHELM FRIEDRICH, *hā'gel* (1770–1831), German thinker, *b* Stuttgart ; his system of philosophy inspired Karl Marx, and although valuable and important in itself, was to some extent a source of Fascist and Nazi ideas.

Heidelberg, *hī'del-bŭrg*, famous university city, Germany ; on the R. Neckar ; noted for its book trade ; long associated with Calvinism ; pop.73,000.

Heine, HEINRICH, *hī'ne* (1797–1856), German lyric poet, *b* Düsseldorf of Jewish parents ; settled in Paris 1830 ; married a rich lady ; paralysed and blind in his last years.

Hejaz, *he-jäz*, region of Arabia between Nejd and Tihama. It borders the Red Sea.

Helen, in old Gk tales, the beautiful wife of Menelaus, King of Sparta. She was carried off to Troy by Paris. This caused the Trojan war.

Helicon, *hel-i-kon*, mt. in Greece ; 5,736ft ; regarded anciently as sacred to Apollo.

helicopter, type of aircraft likely to be used on a large scale within a few years. It is a development of the autogyro, a propeller-driven plane with the addition of a rotor to enable it to descend or ascend almost vertically. This type of aircraft was enormously improved by Raoul de Pescara (*d* 1937) ; and today the helicopter has no wings and no forward-acting propeller, being entirely

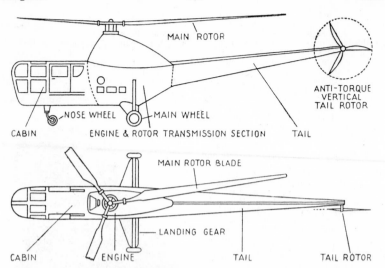

MAIN ROTOR

ANTI-TORQUE
VERTICAL
TAIL ROTOR

NOSE WHEEL   MAIN WHEEL

CABIN   ENGINE & ROTOR TRANSMISSION SECTION   TAIL

MAIN ROTOR BLADE

LANDING GEAR

CABIN   ENGINE   TAIL   TAIL ROTOR

PARTS OF A HELICOPTER

(*top*) *a side view of the machine*
(*bottom*) *the machine viewed from above*

power driven by horizontal rotating blades. By increasing the pitch of the rotor perpendicular lift is obtained. A small propeller in the tail counteracts the reaction of the main rotor, and also serves as a rudder.

The first helicopter night-mail began experimentally 1949, linking Peterborough and Norwich, and carrying 450lb of mail per flight.

Heligoland, rocky island in the N. Sea, *c*.35m from the mouth of the R. Elbe ; area 130 acres ; strongly fortified by the Germans, to whom it was ceded by the British 1890; occupied by the British 1945.

Its fortifications and U-boat pens were blown up 1947, and what remains of the island is likely to become a bird sanctuary.

heliograph, *hē′li-ō-graf* (Gk *helios,* sun, *grapho,* I write), instrument with a mirror by means of which sunlight (or an artificial light) may be flashed long distances, and used to send messages by Morse ; now largely superseded by radio.

heliometer, telescopic instrument first used for measuring the diameter of the sun, later for that of stars and star-clusters.

Heliopolis, *hē′li-op′ō-lis,* ancient town, Egypt, *c*.10m from Cairo.

Helios, *hē′li-os,* in old Gk tales, god of the sun, later identified with Apollo, and sometimes called Hyperion.

heliostat, *hē′li-ō-stat,* astronomical clockwork instrument designed to move a mirror with the apparent velocity of the sun, thus keeping the instrument trained continuously on it for telescopic or spectroscopic examination.

helium, *hē′li-ŭm* (Gk *helios,* sun), element

and inert gas, He, atomic weight 4·002, atomic number 2, discovered spectroscopically 1868 in the sun by Sir Norman Lockyer, and among gases obtained by heating cleveite by Sir William Ramsay 1894 ; found in natural gases in N. American oil-fields, and in the atmosphere (one part in 200,000) ; has 92 per cent the lifting power of hydrogen, and, being non-inflammable, was once much used for inflating airships.

Many new uses have been found for helium in recent years. Being exceedingly penetrating, it is used to relieve sinus trouble ; is combined with anaesthetics ; improves the welding of metals.

The production of helium since 1940 is largely due to C. W. Seibel of USA.

Hellas, at first a small district of Thessaly (Greece) inhabited by Hellenes ; later the name for all Greece, all the inhabitants of which are still called Hellenes. See GREECE

hellebore, plant (family *Ranunculaceae*) found in Britain and the Mediterranean region ; source of various narcotics, i.e. drugs that produce sleep.

Hellenes, see GREECE

Hellespont, *hel′is-pont,* old name for the Dardanelles.

helmet, defence for the head, e.g. that worn by the Greeks, Romans, Assyrians, Egyptians, Etruscans, some being richly ornamented. The pointed Norman helmet usually had a nose-guard ; the 14th c. type (bascinet) was light, and sometimes had a visor, i.e. a protection for the face. The 18th c. helmet used by cavalry was rather like the Gk type.

In modern warfare metal helmets are worn (sometimes camouflaged) by soldiers, and also by ARP wardens, members of the AFS, etc. The dispatch-rider's *crash helmet* is a unique type.

Helmholtz, HERMANN VON, *helm'hōlts* (1821–94), German scientist, *b* Potsdam ; notable for his work on the sense-organs, the conservation of energy and the theory of colour.

Helots, *hel'ot*, slaves of the lowest grade in ancient Sparta.

Helsingfors, see HELSINKI

Helsinki, *hel'sin-kē*, fortified port and cap., Finland ; on the Gulf of Finland ; noted for its Baltic trade ; has a famous university ; is sometimes called Helsingfors ; pop.355,000.

Helvellyn, *hel-vel'in*, mt. in Cumberland ; 3,118ft.

Hemans, FELICIA DOROTHEA, *hē'manz* (1793–1835), poet, *b* Liverpool ; best remembered for *The Homes of England* and *Casabianca*.

Hemel Hempstead, town, Hertfordshire, scheduled (1946) for development as a satellite of London ; pop.21,000.

Hemingway, ERNEST (1898–), American novelist, *b* Illinois ; notable for introducing into novel-writing a new style of prose narrative, tough, matter-of-fact, deliberately unsensational. Among his best-known novels are *A Farewell to Arms, Death in the Afternoon, Men without Women, In our Time*, and especially *For Whom the Bell Tolls*, a story of the Spanish Civil War, filmed 1943.

hemlock, poisonous plant (order *Umbelli-*

THE HELLEBORE

ferae) ; has white flowers in umbrella-like clusters ; behind each cluster are three small leaves, all turned to one side. The stem, covered with purple blotches, is smooth and ribbed ; the seed-vessels are short and round ; the leaves fern-like.

hemp, name of several plants, fibres of which are used for making ropes, twine, sails, sacks, etc. Varieties are grown in India, Africa, Russia, Italy. An intoxicating drug (bhang) is made from Indian hemp, and may be drunk, eaten, or smoked. In Arabic the name is hashish.

henbane, see POISONOUS PLANTS

Henderson, ARTHUR (1863–1935), British politician ; Chairman of the Labour Party 1908 ; President of the Board of Education 1915 ; Cabinet Minister 1916–17 ; Home Secretary 1924 ; Foreign Secretary 1929. His son, ARTHUR, was Air Minister 1947.

Hendon, residential town, Middlesex ; noted for boating ; manufactures aircraft and has flying schools ; a noted airport ; pop.138,000.

Hengist, said to have been the first Anglo-Saxon chief to invade England, landing *c*.AD450 at Ebbsfleet, Kent, with his brother Horsa.

Henley, WILLIAM ERNEST (1849–1903), poet, playwright and journalist, *b* Gloucester ; contributed to many magazines ; best known for his poems, including *Invictus ; England, My England*, and *The Passing*.

Henley-on-Thames, town, Oxfordshire ; noted for its yearly regatta.

Henrietta Maria, *hen-ri-et'ä mä-rē'ä* (1609–1669), youngest daughter of Henry IV of France ; married Charles I of England 1625 ; bravely supported her husband in the Civil War ; left England 1644, but returned 1660.

henry, unit of electromagnetic inductance, named after Joseph Henry (1799–1878), American scientist who discovered electromagnetic induction at the same time as Michael Faraday. See ELECTRICITY

Henry, name of various emperors of the Holy Roman Empire, including : Henry IV (1050–1106), ruled from 1056 ; a diplomat and soldier ; was an opponent of feudal power and of the power of the pope ; Henry VI (1165–97) hoped to make Italy the centre of his empire, but failed.

Henry I (1068–1135), King of England, *b* Selby, Yorkshire, son of William the Conqueror ; secured the throne 1100 in the absence of his elder brother, Robert of Normandy, who after a rebellion was Henry's prisoner for the rest of his life. Though Henry's private life was depraved, he earned, as king, the title of the Lion of Justice ; founded the *Curia Regis* or royal court ; governed wisely ; kept a check on the barons ; established travelling judges, and saw the life of the nation improve. He married Matilda, daughter of Malcolm of Scotland.

Henry II (1133–89), King of England from 1154 ; first of the Plantagenets, being the son of Matilda, daughter of Henry I, and her second husband, Geoffrey Plantagenet, Count of Anjou.

Succeeding Stephen, he married Eleanor, the divorced wife of Louis VII, and thus ruled over half of France. Vigorous and kingly, he compelled the Welsh princes to do homage, and made Scotland, for a brief period, part of his vast domain. In his day the Great Council was frequently summoned, the nobles were firmly controlled, and an attempt made to control the clergy by the *Constitutions of Clarendon*, but this led to Thomas Becket's opposition, and his murder 1170. We may say that Henry II gave England constitutional law. His disobedient sons caused him much unhappiness in later life.

Henry III (1207–72), King of England, *b* Winchester ; succeeded his father (John) 1216 when only nine years old, the country being ruled during his minority by the Earl of Pembroke, later by Hubert de Burgh.

Henry III began to reign 1227. Though a devout Churchman, a scholar, and a brave soldier, he was wholly incompetent as a king. He filled offices of state with Frenchmen, and his neglect of the principles of *Magna Carta* impelled the great barons, headed by Simon de Montfort, to make him accept the *Provisions of Oxford* 1258. Later, civil war broke out, and after victory at Lewes 1264 Montfort was defeated and slain at Evesham 1265, with the result that Henry's son, later Edward I, became ruler in fact, and put into practice the very principles for which Montfort had died.

Henry IV (1367–1413), King of England, son of John of Gaunt. He was known as Henry of Bolingbroke, also as Earl of Hereford and Duke of Lancaster, and was thus the first of the Lancastrians. Banished 1398 by Richard II, he returned to depose Richard 1399, becoming king with the consent of Parliament, which chose him rather than Roger Mortimer. Rebellions were raised by Owen Glendower in Wales, and by the Percys, 1403, 1405 and 1408.

Henry V (1387–1422), King of England ; *b* Monmouth, son of Henry IV, whom he succeeded 1413. Shakespeare gives us a vivid but perhaps too fanciful a picture of the prince as ' Madcap Hal.' He was well trained in warfare, and came to the throne with a high sense of responsibility and a conviction that he was divinely destined to rule France.

After suppressing a Lollard insurrection, Henry found an excuse for invading France 1415, captured Harfleur (Normandy), and with only 8,000 men won a brilliant victory at Agincourt. Invading France again, he took Rouen 1419, and by the *Treaty of Troyes* (1420) compelled the mad king, Charles VI, to acknowledge him as regent and also as heir to the throne. He married the Princess Catherine. But the various French factions united in opposing him, and he died at Vincennes while still trying to subdue the country. Though idolised by the people, Henry was not a great statesman.

Henry VI (1421–71), King of England 1422–61, son of Henry V, whom he succeeded when only nine months old, England being ruled by the Duke of Bedford, N. and E. France by the Duke of Gloucester. Henry grew up to be pious, gentle and scholarly (he founded Eton, and also King's College, Cambridge), but was frequently insane, and was no match for his active and ambitious queen, Margaret of Anjou.

His reign saw (*a*) the wretched French war result in the defeat of the English, mainly as a result of the inspiration given by Joan of Arc, till only the Calais district remained ; and (*b*) the Wars of the Roses from 1445, the battle of Towton (1461) ending in a Yorkist victory, Edward IV being proclaimed king. Captured at Tewkesbury, Henry was put to death 1471.

Henry VII (1457–1509), King of England, son of Edmund Tudor ; was the first of the Tudor kings ; represented the house of Lancaster through his mother, a descendant of John of Gaunt, father of Henry IV. Henry was *b* Pembroke Castle ; exiled in Brittany ; landed Milford Haven (Wales) 1485, defeating and killing Richard III at Bosworth (Leicestershire) 22 Aug. He married Elizabeth of York, eldest daughter of Edward IV, thus uniting the two contending parties and bringing the Wars of the Roses to an end. He crushed various rebellions, e.g. those of Lambert Simnel and Perkin Warbeck ; made peace with France ; and diplomatically married his daughter Margaret to James IV of Scotland.

Beginning to reign after a long period of bitter strife, Henry VII succeeded in uniting the country, in reducing the power of the barons by imposing heavy fines, taking away their retainers, and allowing no-one but himself to make or use guns. Though much may be said against his unconstitutional methods of demanding subsidies and forced loans, he nevertheless succeeded in advancing commerce, securing foreign markets, and in giving England a prosperity previously unknown. He fostered trade and exploration by granting a charter to Cabot, discoverer of N. America ; he encouraged building, art and the New Learning ; he called Parliament frequently at first.

Henry VIII (1491–1547), King of England, *b* Greenwich, son of Henry VII ; became king 1509 ; married Catherine of Aragon (Spain), widow of his brother Arthur (who *d* 1502).

With the help of Cardinal Wolsey, Henry strove to keep ' the balance of power' in Europe ; defeated the Scots at Flodden 1513 ; and met Francis I of France at the spectacular ' Field of the Cloth of Gold ' 1520. He was given the title of *Fidei Defensor* (Defender of the Faith) by the pope, but quarrelled with him over the divorce of Catherine of Aragon and his wish to marry Anne Boleyn, resulting in (*a*) Wolsey's dismissal ; (*b*) the break with Rome (see REFORMATION) by which Henry was accepted as head of the Church in England, no further payments being made to Rome. Henry closed the monasteries 1536–39, taking their revenues, and crushing a Catholic insurrection (the Pilgrimage of Grace) protesting against these acts.

Careful to arrange that Parliament legalised whatever changes he made, Henry kept supreme authority in his own hands. He had his useful minister Thomas Cromwell executed 1540.

HENRY VIII 1491–1547

In his youth Henry was handsome, fond of sport, and versed in the ' New Learning ' of the Renaissance ; but later he became corpulent, cynical and cruel. He married in all six wives : (1) Catherine of Aragon (mother of Queen Mary); (2) Anne Boleyn (mother of Queen Elizabeth), executed 1536 ; (3) Jane Seymour (mother of Edward VI) ; (4) Anne of Cleves ; (5) Catherine Howard, executed 1542 ; and (6) Catherine Parr, who outlived him.

Henry advanced the Reformation, encouraged learning, controlled the nobles, increased maritime enterprise, laid the foundations of the navy, and established England as an important European power.

Henry IV (Henri Quatre) (1553–1610), first of the Bourbon kings of France ; known as Henry of Navarre because, after his mother's death 1572, he was King of Navarre, once a kingdom of Spain.

Henry became King of France 1594 at a time of bitter strife between Huguenots and Catholics. Often compared with Elizabeth of England, he had few religious principles but stood for tolerance, and issued the *Edict of Nantes*, 1598, giving the Huguenots freedom of worship. He supported the German Protestants ; united a disordered France ; and with the help of his famous minister the Duc de Sully, reorganised the nation's finance and administration. He made valuable commercial treaties ; and though immoral won the affection of his people, and came to be regarded as the greatest and most essentially French of all the kings of France.

Henry, O. (1862–1910), pen-name of William Sydney Porter, American author born in N. Carolina ; famous for his stories of life in New York and Texas, all full of surprise and humour.

Henry of Navarre, see HENRY IV (HENRI QUATRE)

Henry the Lion (1129–95), German prince, Duke of Bavaria and Saxony ; a great soldier and an enlightened ruler ; married Matilda, daughter of Henry II of England, and was thus the ancestor of the electors of Hanover and kings of Great Britain.

Henry the Navigator (1394–1460), Portugese prince, *b* Oporto ; noted for sending out many ships to discover details of W. Africa and the Azores.

Henty, GEORGE ALFRED (1832–1902) *b* Trumpington, Cambridge ; famous as a writer of boys' stories.

Hepworth, BARBARA (1903–), sculptor, *b* Wakefield. Her style is somewhat akin to that of Henry Moore.

Hera, *hē'rä*, in old Greek tales, queen of heaven, wife of Zeus.

Heraclitus, *her-ä-klī'tūs* (*c.*540–475BC), Gk thinker who declared that all things flow, and that change is the only reality.

Herat, *her-ät'*, town, Afghanistan ; of great importance as a military base ; manufactures leather and woollen goods; has supplies of oil ; pop.85,000.

Herbart, JOHANN FRIEDRICH (1776–1841), German thinker, *b* Oldenburg ; did much to make education scientific.

Herbert, SIR ALAN PATRICK (1890–), contributor to *Punch* ; MP (Independent) for Oxford University, 1935–48 ; author of *Holy Deadlock*, leading to the reform of the Marriage Acts 1937, and of much humorous verse ; popular broadcaster.

Herbert, GEORGE (1593–1633), clergyman and poet, *b* Montgomery ; noted for his book, *The Temple*, containing some of the finest religious verse in our language.

herb paris, see POISONOUS PLANTS

herb-robert, plant (family *Geraniaceae*) of the roadside ; has an unpleasant smell ; stem *c.*12in high ; deeply-cut leaflets, green at first, but red in autumn ; reddish-purple five-petalled flowers.

Herculaneum, *hŭr-kū-lā'nē-ŭm,* ancient town, Italy ; buried under 40–100ft of hot ash when Vesuvius erupted AD63 and 79. Large areas have been excavated since 1719, and many treasures brought to light.

Hercules, *hŭr'kū-lēz,* hero of many old Gk tales ; son of Zeus. Immensely strong, he strangled two serpents while in his cradle. Being told by the oracle at Delphi to serve Eurystheus, King of Tiryns, he performed twelve famous labours : slaying the Nemean lion ; destroying the many-headed Hydra of Lernae ; capturing alive the Arcadian stag, and, later, the Erymanthian boar ; cleansing the stables of Augeas by running two rivers through them ; exterminating the Stymphalian monsters; capturing the mad bull of Minos, King of Crete, and also the man-eating horses of Diomedes ; securing the girdle of the queen of the Amazons ; seizing the oxen of Geryon, and the three golden apples from the garden of the Hesperides ; and bringing Cerberus, the three-headed dog, from Hades. Other mighty deeds include those done while with the Argonauts, and his rescue of Hesione from a sea-monster.

heredity, *hē-red'i-ti,* reappearance of similar characteristics of mind or body of the parent in the child, or the passing on of characteristics from one generation of animals or plants to another. Thus a musician's son may (or may not) *inherit* a love of music ; or the offspring of a wholly black rabbit and a wholly white rabbit may have partly white and partly black fur. Heredity is thought to be due, in part, to *chromatin* in the germ-cells during sexual reproduction.

Modern theories of heredity owe most to G. J. MENDEL (1822–84), an Austrian monk who found by experiment that by crossing pure-bred peas having yellow seeds (Y) with pure-bred peas having green seeds (G) he got *all* Ys ; but that when *these* Ys were crossed with one another, they gave 75% Y and 25% G. Why ? Mendel's answer was that character Y is ' dominant,' character G ' recessive,' i.e. Y asserts itself over G when both are combined in the same plant. (See diagram)

Herefordshire, *her'ē-fĕrd-,* county of W. England, on the borders of Wales ; especially noted for cattle ; co.tn Hereford, on the R. Wye ; noted for its cathedral and ruined castle ; also for roses and farm produce ; pop.31,000.

Hereward the Wake, *her'ē-wörd,* English hero who raised rebellions against William the Conqueror. Little is actually known of him, but Charles Kingsley's novel *Hereward the Wake* is a stirring romance.

Hergesheimer, JOSEPH, *hŭr'ges-hī-mĕr* (1880–), American writer, *b* Philadelphia, author of *The Bright Shawl, Cytherea, The Limestone Tree, Tropical Winter,* and (possibly his best novel) *Java Head,* notable for its variety of convincing characters.

Heriot, GEORGE, *herry-ot* (1563-1624), rich goldsmith (Scott's ' Jinglin Geordie ') *b* Edinburgh, where he founded Heriot's

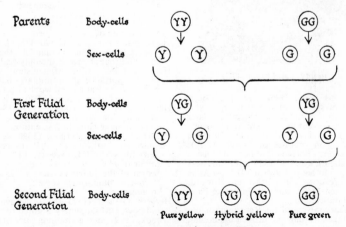

ANALYSIS OF MENDEL'S EXPERIMENT

Note that pure *yellow,* pure *green have sex-cells* Y, Y *and* G, G ; *while* hybrids *yellow-green, green-yellow both have sex-cells* Y, G *and* Y, G. *Yellow being dominant, it asserts itself in both hybrids as well as in the pure yellow.*

Hospital, built 1628–59, but used as a school since 1885. A portion of the funds support the Heriot-Watt College (1887).

Hermes, *hŭr'mēz,* in old Gk tales, winged messenger of the gods ; also the god of eloquence, good fortune, and of cunning ; known to the Romans as Mercury.

hermit or **anchorite,** one who lives alone for religious meditation. English hermits sometimes lived in a room (cell) in a church. St Simeon Stylites (AD388–459) lived for thirty years on top of a pillar near Antioch.

Hermitage, THE, Russia's largest and finest museum and art gallery. It is at Leningrad, and was begun *c.*1760.

Hermon, mt. of Syria and Lebanon ; *c.*10,000ft high.

Herne Bay, holiday town on the I. of Thanet, Kent.

Herodotus, *hē-rod'ō-tŭs* (d 424BC), first Gk historian, though strictly a Persian, having been born at Halicarnassus, Asia Minor, a Gk city under Persian rule. He travelled in Persia, Egypt, Italy, Sicily and around the Black Sea ; lived for a time in Samos, and then in Athens, where he was a friend of Sophocles. His fame rests on his fascinating histories, the story of the struggle between the Greeks and Persians, but including much besides, e.g. accounts of his travels, of famous people, curious beliefs and customs. He is rightly styled the Father of History.

Herod the Great, *her'ŭd* (74–4BC), King of Judaea ; captured Jerusalem 37BC, and later governed Palestine for the Romans. His son HEROD ANTIPAS, governor of Galilee, beheaded John the Baptist, and shared in the trial of Jesus.

heron, *her'on,* bird akin to the stork ; has long legs, and long straight beak ; its plumage is usually bluish-grey and white. Found in most parts of the world, especially in the tropics, the heron's food includes frogs and fish. In Britain the common heron (*Ardea cinerea*) frequents lonely streams, lakes and marshes ; is *c.*3ft long ; has a crest of blackish feathers, and nests in colonies (heronries) in tall trees.

Hero of Alexandria, 2nd c. mathematician and scientist ; a pioneer in experiments with steam pressure.

Herrenvolk (German, master race), name claimed by the Nazis for the German (and other Nordic) people, on the false assumption that they were superior to other races.

Herrick, ROBERT (1591–1674), poet, *b* London ; apprenticed to his uncle, a goldsmith ; became vicar of Dean Prior, Devonshire, where his housekeeper was Prudence Baldwin (the ' Prue ' of his poems), and where he died. One of our greatest lyric writers, he has left us exquisite poetry in his *Hesperides,* e.g. *Gather ye Rosebuds,* and *Cherry-Ripe.*

herring, valuable food fish of the Atlantic and especially the N. Sea ; usually *c.*12in long ; swims in shoals in search of minute sea creatures ; lays 30,000 eggs ; is generally caught in a drift-net or seine. When cured, herrings are called bloaters; if split and smoked, kippers.

Herriot, ÉDOUARD, *e-rē-ō'* (1872–　　), Fr. statesman ; *b* Troyes ; formed a Radical Socialist government 1924 ; Premier 1932 ; author of several books.

Herschel, SIR JOHN, *hŭr'shel* (1792–1871), son of Sir William Herschel. A brilliant mathematician and astronomer, he surveyed the stars systematically 1822–33 and 1834–38, identifying 500 nebulae and nearly 4,000 double stars.

Herschel, SIR WILLIAM (1738–1822), German astronomer, *b* Hanover, but came to England when 19, where, after some success as a musician, he studied astronomy with a series of improved telescopes. He raised the number of known nebulae from 180 to 2,500 ; discovered Uranus 1781 ; calculated its period of rotation ; was private astronomer to George III ; lived at Slough (near Windsor), where he was greatly helped by his remarkable sister, CAROLINE HERSCHEL (1750–1848), who discovered 5 comets, and added 561 stars to the catalogue compiled by Flamsteed.

Hertford College, *har'-,* one of the colleges of Oxford University ; founded *c.*1283.

Hertfordshire, often written Herts, county of England watered by the rivers Lea and Colne ; co.tn Hertford, noted for corn, malt and flour.

Hertz, HEINRICH RUDOLF, *herts* (1857–94), German scientist, *b* Hamburg ; famous for his discovery of the propagation of electromagnetic (radio) waves. By *Hertzian waves* we mean radio waves with a frequency from above 3×10^7 cycles per sec. (short waves) to below $1 \cdot 5 \times 10^5$ cycles per sec. (long waves of 2,000 metres). See WAVE-MOTION

Hertzian waves, see WAVE-MOTION

Hertzog, JAMES BARRY, *her'tsŏch* (1866–1942,) S. African statesman of German-Dutch descent; advocated Dutch supremacy in S. Africa ; Premier 1924 ; formed a national government with General Smuts 1933, Hertzog again being premier.

Hesiod, *hē'si-od* (*c.*700BC), Gk poet, notable for his *Works and Days,* partly a manual of agriculture, partly an essay on the dignity of labour ; also *Theogony,* the story of the creation. Two of his sayings are :

　　Work is no disgrace : it is idleness which is a disgrace. (῎Εργον οὐδὲν ὄνειδος, ἀεργίη δέ τ᾿ ὄνειδος.)

　　Evil planned harms the plotter most. (Ἡ δὲ κακὴ βουλὴ τῷ βουλεύσαντι κακίστη.)

Hesperides, *hes-peri'dēz,* in old Gk tales, nymphs who guarded the golden apples of Hera in gardens vaguely described as being in the Far West.

Hess, DAME MYRA (1890–　　), English

12

pianist ; has toured USA and Europe ; excels in her interpretation of Bach and Mozart.

Heston-Isleworth, *-ĭzl'werth,* town, Middlesex ; noted aviation centre ; pop.95,000.

heterodyne, in radio, the effect produced in a receiver by the interference of two alternating currents of slightly different frequencies, the resultant lower beat-frequency being more easily amplified.

Hewlett, MAURICE (1861–1923), English author of romantic novels, e.g. *The Queen's Quair.*

hexagon, in geometry, plane figure with six sides. See AREA

hexameter, see VERSE

Hexham, *hex'am,* town on the R. Tyne, Northumberland ; noted for its 12th c. church and ruins of a 7th c. monastery.

Heysham, *hā'sham,* port and holiday town, Lancashire ; has regular cross-channel services to Ireland ; pop.25,000.

Heywood, *hā'wood,* Lancashire town noted for cotton and woollen goods ; pop. 23,000.

Hezekiah, *hez-ē-kī'ä,* King of Judah 725–697BC ; strove to abolish idolatry and to restore the worship of Jehovah.

HF, see YOUTH ORGANISATIONS

Hg, chemical symbol for mercury ; Lat. *hydrargyrum.*

Hiawatha, see AMERICAN INDIANS

hibernation, *hī-bĕr-nā'shon,* going to sleep for the winter, as do bats, squirrels, dormice, frogs and snakes ; such creatures then draw on stores of fat laid up in their bodies. Some, however, sleep in summer, chiefly certain shellfish and fresh-water fish (e.g. African mud-fish), as they cannot live actively in dry weather. A summer sleep is called *aestivation.*

Hibernia, *hī-bŭr'ni-ä,* name given by Latin writers to Ireland.

hickory, tree belonging to N. America, but grown in Britain. The large leaves are divided into leaflets ; the fruit is a nut, one species producing the pecan. The timber is very tough.

hide, see DOMESDAY BOOK

Hiero I, *hī'ē-rō,* Tyrant of Syracuse 478–467BC. Hiero II, King of Syracuse 270–216BC, was an ally of the Romans.

hieroglyphics, *hī'ĕr-ō-glĭfĭk* (actually sacred characters or signs), name for the early picture-writing of the ancient Egyptians (and also of the Mexicans, etc.). Hieroglyphics were known in Egypt before 2600BC ; one style, *hieratic,* being used by the priests, the other, *demotic,* by others. The signs remained undeciphered prior to the discovery of the Rosetta Stone 1799. See ALPHABET

Higher School Certificate, see EXAMINATIONS

highest common factor, see FACTORS ; HCF

Highland Mary, girl immortalised by Robert Burns, and generally thought to have been Mary Campbell, who died at Greenock 1786.

Highway Code, THE, group of provisions for the guidance and safety of all who use British roads. These are published by His Majesty's Stationery Office in the form of a booklet, *The Highway Code.* This advises all road users to be courteous and careful ; to know and observe the signs and signals used for regulating traffic ; to be sure *you* are fit to use the road—alcohol, even in small amounts, lowering alertness and the sense of caution, hence driving under the influence of drink (regarded in law as a very grave offence) means danger for yourself and for others. See ROADS

highwaymen, robbers on British (or other) roads, particularly from the 17th–19th c. e.g. Claude Duval (1643–70), Dick Turpin (1706–39), Will Nevison (1639–1684).

High Wycombe, *wī'kŭm,* town, Buckinghamshire ; noted for furniture ; pop. 39,000.

Hill, OCTAVIA (1838–1912), social reformer, *b* Wisbech, Cambridgeshire ; did much to improve the homes of the poor, and to preserve common land and historic sites.

Hill, SIR ROWLAND (1795–1879), reformer, *b* Kidderminster ; a pioneer in school administration, but most famous for his introduction of the Penny Post 1840. He was Secretary to the Post Office 1854–64, and was responsible for the present system of money orders.

Hilton, JAMES (1900–   ), British writer ; author of *Lost Horizon* (1933), *Random Harvest, So Well Remembered* ; *To You, Mr Chips.*

Hilversum, holiday town, Netherlands ; noted for carpet and blanket making, and its radio station ; pop.81,000.

Himalayas, *hi-mä'lä-yä,* him-ä-lä-yä, i.e. 'the abode of snow,' vast mt. range N. of India ; includes the highest peaks in the world, e.g. Everest, 29,141ft, Godwin-Austen (K2), 28,250ft. The range is over 1,500m long. Rivers include Indus, Ganges and Brahmaputra.

Himmler, HEINRICH (1900–45), German Nazi leader ; in command of police and Gestapo from 1936.

Hinckley, *hingk'li,* town, Leicestershire ; manufactures boots and hosiery.

Hindenburg, PAUL VON, *hin'den-burch* (1847–1934), German general and statesman ; served in the Austro-Prussian and the Franco-Prussian wars ; defeated the Russians at Tannenberg in World War I, and later was in supreme command of all the German forces. The idol of the German people, he worked in the closest harmony with General Ludendorff 1914–18, and remained a noble figure even in his last years when Adolf Hitler was his greatest opponent, and when the Nazi party was shaping the destiny of Germany. He was President of the German Republic 1925, and again 1932, being succeeded 1934 by Hitler.

Hindhead, *hīnd'hed,* beautiful district, Surrey.

Hindley, *hind'li,* town, Lancashire ; noted for cotton and coal ; pop.22,000.

Hindu, *hin'doo,* popularly any non-European inhabitant of India ; more strictly one descended from Aryans who migrated in prehistoric times from the NW. to the Ganges district, later spreading south. Hinduism, the religion of the Hindus, of whom there are *c.*255,000,000 in India, is a mixture of Brahmanism and Buddhism, the worship of a host of gods and goddesses. The teaching, largely found in the *Upanishads,* includes reverence for the Brahman, and the rigid observance of the caste system. Commonly the Hindus worship Vishnu or Siva ; an honoured place is given to the cow ; and often extreme self-denial is practised.

Hindu Kush, *-koosh,* lofty mt. range separated by the valley of the Indus from the Himalayas. Some of the peaks rise to 23,000ft.

Hindustani, *hin-doo-stä'nē,* language spoken almost throughout India ; contains a large mixture of Arabic and Persian words. A variation spoken by Indian Mohammedans is called Urdu.

Hinsley, CARDINAL (1865–1943), eminent RC, born near Selby, Yorkshire ; travelled much on missionary work in Africa ; appointed Archbishop of Westminster 1935.

Hippocrates, *hī-pok'rä-tēz* (*b c.*460BC), Gk physician, called the father of modern medicine, born on the island of Cos ; practised as a doctor in Thrace ; said to have died at a great age. His clinical histories are models of their kind, and he regarded medicine and surgery as sciences. He wrote learnedly on many aspects of diseases and their remedies. The ideals he gave his profession remain to this day.

Hippolytë, *hi-pol'i-tē,* in old Greek tales, Queen of the Amazons.

Hippolytus, *hī-pol'i-tŭs,* in old Greek tales, son of Theseus.

THE HIPPOPOTAMUS

hippopotamus, large mammal, often weighing 4–5 tons, now found only in Central Africa, though common in Britain in the Pleistocene period. The hippopotamus, which may be 14ft long, has blackish or slate-coloured hide, and a very large head with eyes and nostrils so placed that they are above water when the remainder of the animal is submerged. It lives on vegetable matter, will lie in streams or lakes for many hours, and is closely related to the pig and peccary.

hire-purchase, system of hiring goods or services which remain the vendor's property until an agreed number of instalments has been completed. Once open to much abuse, the system was amended 1938 by an Act sponsored by Miss Ellen Wilkinson.

Hirohito, *hē-rō-hē'tō* (1901–   ), Emperor of Japan ; succeeded to the imperial throne 1926 ; travelled much in Europe as a young man, and did much to introduce Western ideas into his country. How far he was directly responsible for Japan's entry into World War II is not clear, but he and his country suffered complete defeat 1945.

Hiroshima, port, Japan ; more or less destroyed by an atom-bomb 1945, and the pop. of 344,000 largely wiped out.

John Hersey's 30,000-word report on the first city to be destroyed by an atom bomb caused a stir in Sept 1946. It was broadcast by the BBC a few weeks later, and did much to make the world realise the sheer horror and frightful suffering that will be wrought by atomic warfare.

Hispaniola, island of the W. Indies, now divided into Haiti and Santo Domingo, the latter known also as the Dominican Republic. See HAITI.

Hitchin, old town, Hertfordshire ; has much trade in corn and malt ; noted for straw-plaiting, and for its lavender.

Hitler, ADOLF, *hit'lĕr* (1889–1945), Führer (leader) and Chancellor of the Third Reich (i.e. Third German Empire, founded 1934) ; founder of the National Socialist (or Nazi) Party, *b* Austria ; an orphan at 15 ; wounded in World War I ; became a political revolutionary ; joined the German Workers' Party ; studied the principles of propaganda, and by impassioned speeches aroused new hopes among a bewildered people. Hitler wrote *Mein Kampf* (My Struggle) 1925–27, outlining startling new political theories and German ambitions, a work planned while he was in prison for his part in a rising 1923 against the democratic government.

Appointed Chancellor of the Reich by von Hindenburg 1933, he became Führer 1934, confirmed later by a bogus referendum, in which votes were secured by intimidation. Allying himself with Mussolini, Dictator of Italy, Hitler assumed supreme command of the German army 1938. He welded a divided people into a united nation incorporating Austria ; had visions of world domination ; overran Czechoslovakia ;

HITLER 1889–1945

and attacked Poland without provocation 1939, thus bringing about World War II. He narrowly missed assassination 1944 ; and perished May 1945. Read *The Last Days of Hitler*, H. Trevor-Roper, and see AUSTRIA ; WORLD WAR II.

Hittites, *hit-īts*, ancient inhabitants of Asia Minor and Syria ; attained a high degree of civilisation *c.*2000BC, but vanished *c.*700BC. Traces of the Hittite empire have been brought to light since 1880, and many treasures have been unearthed at Carchemish. Their picture-writing is even now only partly understood.

Hobart, *hō'bärt*, cap., Tasmania ; has a fine harbour. The many industries include shipbuilding, iron founding and milling ; pop.72,000.

Hobbes, THOMAS (1588–1679), English philosopher, *b* Malmesbury ; noted for his book *Leviathan*, in which he argues that without a government commonly obeyed by all, men in seeking to defend their own lives and liberty destroy the life and liberty of others, whence a war of all against all that makes life ' nasty, brutish, and short.' The only remedy for this is that each man should ' be contented with so much liberty against other men as he would allow other men against himself,' and set up a central authority (the Sovereign or government) to see that this promise is respected. A number of people united in this way forms a Commonwealth, and so long as the Sovereign is recognised and obeyed by everybody peace will continue. Once government has been established in this way everybody ought to support it as the only alternative to the war of all against all.

Hobbes also held that as there cannot be two sovereigns in one Commonwealth, the Church must obey the State. For this reason he has sometimes been called a Fascist ; but in fact he is one of the founders of English democratic politics. The chief fault of the views put forward in *Leviathan* is that no provision is made for control of the Sovereign by the subjects. It looks at politics too much from the point of view of the government. This one-sidedness was corrected by Locke.

Hobbs, JOHN BERRY (1882–), cricketer, *b* Cambridge ; member of the ground staff at the Oval 1903. One of England's greatest batsmen, he scored 197 centuries by 1934, played in 41 test matches against Australia ; was unsurpassed as a fieldsman at cover point.

hobby, recreation, pastime, a spare-time occupation.

There are, for example, outdoor hobbies, e.g. gardening. Anyone interested in this might well take *Gardening*, 6d monthly, or *Gardeners' Chronicle*, 6d weekly, and might decide to specialise in growing flowers or vegetables or fruits, or perhaps to concentrate on a rock garden with its great variety of Alpine and other plants.

Natural history affords hours of enjoyment, giving us a reason for going into the country at all seasons, studying birds and animals, or perhaps making a special study of trees or plants. A friend of the compiler collected no less than 647 botanical specimens found within a few miles of his Yorkshire home. That someone should broadcast 1946 in praise of snails goes to show that even grown men choose strange hobbies sometimes.

Associated with naturalists, very often, is the art of bird photography. Cherry Kearton photographed big game, and there is infinite pleasure (for those with infinite patience) in the photographing of birds in their natural haunts ; out of such photographs one may build up an entertaining and instructive lecture, illustrated (of course) with your own slides. Any kind of photography is worth following up, but the wise photographer does not dabble in many branches or snap anything on sight from sheep in a field to Uncle George in the back garden. He concentrates. He becomes an expert in cloud photography, still life, interiors, trick photography, village customs, church architecture, etc.

The mention of church architecture suggests that one of the most interesting of all hobbies is the study of your own immediate neighbourhood—your own town or city, together with the villages within, say, cycling distance. Collecting facts and figures relating to local industries and farming, knowing the history of the region, its notable people and old-time oddities, studying its folk-lore is all well worth while ; and it should be noted that as a rule much of village interest centres in and around the church. Even gravestones have supplied some people with a jolly pastime, that of collecting curious epitaphs.

But then some people will collect anything. Here, indeed, is the secret of a great many hobbies, e.g. stamp collecting, or collecting the autographs of famous people or BBC stars or famous cricketers. One may collect photographs, postcards and information about, say, footballers, notable men and women, ships, trains or planes. Whatever the information you gather, it is a good idea to have some simple but handy system of keeping the material. One may store it in box-files, labelling each box appropriately, e.g. AIRCRAFT (diagrams of, 1946–52) or BRITISH LOCOMOTIVES (newspaper cuttings) ; or one may paste items of interest on plain postcards, arranging these in some sort of order, and storing them upright in a box or drawer. One public speaker thus collected over 5,000 funny stories, and very useful they were whenever he had to prepare a speech.

Many people collect valuable or beautiful objects, e.g. brassware, copperware, drinking glasses of, say, the 17th and 18th c., old china, first editions of books, sporting prints, coins and medals. Such hobbies become more fascinating the more you learn about them, and an experienced and therefore discerning collector derives more pleasure from his hobby than a somewhat indifferent amateur.

'Making things' is a hobby, and a very good one. Meccano is a toy for young children, but it may be a serious hobby for a youth or a man, enabling him to study the principles of engineering, and even aiding him in perfecting useful inventions. Similarly, running a model railway, or building model locomotives to scale, is an occupation calling for skill in craftsmanship. Consult, for example, The Meccano Magazine 9d monthly. There is also Aeromodelling, a pastime for those with skilled fingers.

Painting, sketching, bookbinding, bee-keeping, writing to a pen-friend, running a school or club magazine, these are only a few examples of a vast variety of hobbies. In a wider sense, a hobby may be a cultural pastime, e.g. the study of, or delight in, say, music, art or poetry. Embroidery and wood-carving may be raised from a hobby to an art ; or one may devote all one's spare time to mastery of the piano or the violin, or listen regularly and critically to the BBC's Third Programme. Acting in local plays or producing plays gives scope for those who have ability in this direction ; and as youth matures into manhood it often happens that hobbies merge gradually into service, so that the

young man who once delighted to go to see a play gradually finds himself ' running the show ' in aid of some local charity.

Hobson, THOMAS (d 1631), Cambridge carrier who would not allow a horse out of his stables except in its proper turn, hence the saying, Hobson's choice, i.e. no choice at all.

hockey, exclusively amateur outdoor game, with rules drawn up at Wimbledon 1883. The Hockey Association was formed 1886 ; and the game has been increasingly played by women and girls since 1895. Each member of 2 teams of 11 has a stick with a curved blade. Normally the game lasts 70min, and is played on a ground 100yd × 55yd, the goals being 4yd wide and 7ft high.

Hofer, ANDREAS, hō'fĕr (1767–1810), Tirolese patriot who led a secret agitation in favour of linking the Tirol with Austria ; shot at Mantua.

Hoffmann, ERNST (1776–1822), German author, b Königsberg, composed, painted and wrote romantic books with remarkable grace. Offenbach's opera The Tales of Hoffmann is based on some of Hoffmann's stories.

Hogarth, WILLIAM, hō'garth (1697–1764), artist, b London ; famous for his hatred of cruelty and the social evils of his day, which his remarkable pictures (e.g. A Rake's Progress, Marriage à la Mode) did much to bring to popular notice. He was a fine colourist, and revolutionised English art by introducing the small picture, and what might be called the ' conversation piece.'

Hogben, LANCELOT (1895–), scientist and author, b Southsea ; professor at London and Aberdeen ; devised a world language, Interglossa ; most famous for his Mathematics for the Million, Science for the Citizen.

Hogg, JAMES (1770–1835), poet and sheep-farmer, known as the Ettrick Shepherd ; b Ettrick, Selkirkshire ; won success with The Queen's Wake, 1813, a series of admirable ballads. Besides poetry (e.g. Bonny Kilmeny) he wrote several novels, e.g. The Brownie of Bodsbeck and The Confessions of a Justified Sinner, the latter an original and revealing study of Protestant religious psychology.

Hogmanay, Scottish name for New Year's Eve, when gifts are exchanged, delicacies given to children, and there is much festivity.

Hohenlinden, hō-en-lin'den, village, Bavaria (Germany) ; scene of a French victory over the Austrians 1800.

Hohenzollern, hō-en-tsŏl'ern, German family named from a castle near the source of the Danube. Members were electors of Brandenburg, kings of Prussia, and (1871–1918), German emperors, William II being the last of the line.

Hokkaido, hŏk'kī-dō, region of Japan, sometimes called Yezo, area 34,277 sq.m, including the Kurile Is.

Holbein, HANS, *hōl'bĭn* (1497–1543), German artist, *b* Augsburg ; met Erasmus at Basel, and at his suggestion came to England, where he was befriended by Sir Thomas More, and later won the patronage of Henry VIII, of whom he painted several portraits. His rich colour, his delicate and accurate draughtsmanship, his insight into the character of his sitters, make him one of the world's most famous artists. He died in London of the plague.

Holborn, *hō'bĕrn*, London borough including the British Museum, London University and Lincoln's Inn.

Holderness, *hōl'der-ness*, corn-growing region of E. Yorkshire.

Holinshed, RAPHAEL, *hol'inz-hed* (*d* 1580), English chronicler about whose life little is known, though his *Chronicles of England, Scotland and Ireland* (1577) supplied Shakespeare with material for some of his historical plays.

Holland, see NETHERLANDS

holly, bush or small tree common in Britain ; has prickly leaves near the ground, but those above may be without spines. The flowers (pink outside, white within) appear in May ; the berries are poisonous ; in winter they turn deep red.

hollyhock, tall garden flower (native of China), often 8–10ft high, with large, rough, rounded leaves, and a spike of white, pink, purple, or yellow flowers.

Hollywood, district west of Los Angeles, California, USA ; noted for its film industry situated here largely because of the fine climate and brilliant sunshine.

Holmes, OLIVER WENDELL, *hōmz* (1809–94), American writer and poet, *b* Cambridge, Massachusetts. He had abundant good humour, a vivid imagination, and wide sympathies, all reflected in his wise and witty books, e.g. *The Autocrat of the Breakfast Table* 1858, *The Professor at the Breakfast Table*, *The Poet at the Breakfast Table*.

holmium, rare earth and element, Ho ; atomic weight 163·5 ; atomic number 67.

Holstein, *hōl'shtīn*, formerly a Danish duchy ; later a province of the former Prussian state of Germany.

Holtby, WINIFRED (1898–1935), *b* Yorkshire ; writer, journalist, critic ; author of *Mandoa, Mandoa* ; *Land of Green Ginger* ; *Anderby Wold* ; *South Riding*. Her life-story is told by Vera Brittain in *Testament of Friendship*.

Holy Alliance, THE, organisation established after the downfall of Napoleon (1815) by the rulers of Russia, Austria and Prussia to check revolutionary outbreaks in Europe.

Holy Communion, see SACRAMENT

Holy Grail, THE, see ARTHUR

Holyhead, *holi'hed*, port of Anglesey, N. Wales ; has a steamer service to Eire.

Holy Innocents' Day, festival of the Christian Church, 28 Dec., in memory of the massacre of children by Herod (Matthew 2).

Holy Island, see LINDISFARNE

Holy Land, name sometimes given by Christians to Palestine.

Holyoke, city, Massachusetts, USA ; noted for textiles and paper ; pop.54,000.

Holy Roman Empire, created by Charlemagne, who was crowned emperor by the pope at Rome 800, Charlemagne's empire comprising France, Germany, and part of Italy. It fell to pieces after his death, but was revived in the 10th c. by Otto the Great, Duke of Saxony, though France was not included.

Gradually the idea grew up that the emperor must be elected by German princes (known as Electors). Long struggles took place between the pope and various emperors, and in 1250, when Frederick II died, the empire was in a state of chaos. By 1346, when Charles of Bohemia was emperor, the empire comprised little more than Germany ; in the 14th c. Albert of Hapsburg became emperor, and from then till its fall 1806, after Napoleon's conquests in Germany, the empire was continuously governed by Hapsburgs, the most famous being Charles V, the last, Francis.

Holyrood, at first an abbey founded (Edinburgh) 1128 by David I ; a palace added in the 15th c. was the chief home of Scottish sovereigns of the Stuart line. More recently Holyrood has become a temporary home of royalty when visiting Scotland.

Holy Thursday, see ASCENSION

Holy Week, see CALENDAR

homage, declaration of loyalty, especially by a feudal tenant to his lord when receiving property, or of a knight to a king.

Homburg, holiday town, Germany ; has given its name to a type of soft felt hat for men.

home counties, see SHIRE

Home Guard, civilian defence force, totalling *c.*2,000,000, raised 1940 in Britain for defensive purposes. The HG rendered good service in World War II, especially during the flying-bomb attacks on S. England. When first formed it was known as the LDV (Local Defence Volunteers).

Home Office, government department with buildings in Whitehall, London. It is under the control of the Home Secretary, who is responsible in England and Wales for prisons, criminal lunatic asylums and approved schools ; appoints stipendiary magistrates and recorders ; directs the Metropolitan Police ; administers the Factory and Shop Acts ; deals with the creation of new peers. In Scotland the functions of the Home Office belong to the Scottish Office.

Homer, *hō'mĕr*, Gk epic poet, whose works are the oldest European poetry we have, and some of the noblest.

Smyrna, Argos, Colophon, Salamis (in Cyprus), Rhodes, Chios and Athens all claim to have been his birthplace, but it has been seriously suggested that there never was such a man as Homer, and that the two great Homeric epics (the *Iliad* and the *Odyssey*) were first put together as collections of traditional ballads, and received their final form between 800 and 500BC. There is much, however, to support the belief that a poet, Homer, did exist in ancient Greece, but there is no evidence that he was blind, as is sometimes supposed.

Sung by bards or wandering minstrels, the Homeric poems became known over the whole Greek-speaking world long before the 6th c. BC. The text was edited for recitation at the national festival in Athens as far back as *c.*540BC, and Plato (*d* 347BC) refers to Homer as the educator of Greece. In recent times William Hazlitt declared : *The multitude of things in Homer is wonderful, the splendour, the truth, the power, the variety.*

The *Iliad*, an epic poem in 24 books, deals with 51 days in the 10th and last year of the siege of Troy (Ilium) by the Greeks, especially with the wrath of Achilles. Achilles is sulking in his tent because he considers that the share of the spoils allotted to him is too small. Fighting begins again, and without Achilles the Greeks are hard pressed by the Trojans, especially Hector. In the fighting Patroclus, the friend of Achilles, is killed by Hector. Mad with grief Achilles leaves his tent, takes on Hector, and kills him, after which the eventual destruction of Troy is certain. The *Odyssey*, also in 24 books, relates the wanderings (during 10 years) of Odysseus (Ulysses) on his way home after the fall of Troy. Among his adventures are his meetings with the Cyclops, with the enchantress Circe, and with the Sirens, and his safe return home to Penelope, his wife, in Ithaca.

Translations of Homer are many, those into English including translations by Lord Derby, Alexander Pope, and George Chapman, by whose masterly version John Keats was greatly moved when he first read it (see Keats' sonnet ' Much have I travelled '). But no translation can ever reveal to the full what has been termed Homeric grandeur and Homeric laughter. It can merely hint at the ' wide expanse that deep-browed Homer ruled as his demesne,' or enable us (as Keats continues) ' to breathe its pure serene.' Nevertheless, magnificent as the *Iliad* and *Odyssey* undoubtedly are, it is true that ' even Homer sometimes nods.' His dramatic power and fire are unrivalled, his imagery is not unlike that of the Bible ; and his metaphors and similes are world renowned and quoted almost every day.

As an example of Homer's style we may consider these lines from the *Iliad,* where Andromache, looking from the walls of Troy, sees her husband's body desecrated by Achilles :

Then from the house she rushed, like one distract,

With beating heart ; and with her went her maids.
But upon the tow'r she reach'd, where stood the crowd,
And mounted on the wall, and look'd around,
And saw the body trailing in the dust,
Which the fleet steeds were dragging to the ships,
And sudden darkness overspread her eyes ;
Backward she fell, and gasp'd her spirit away.
Far off were flung the adornments of her head,
The net, the fillet, and the woven bands ;
The nuptial veil by golden Venus given,
That day when Hector of the glancing helm
Led from Eëtion's house his wealthy bride.
The sisters of her husband round her press'd,
And held, as in the deadly swoon she lay.
But when her breath and spirit returned again,
With sudden burst of anguish thus she cried :
' Hector, oh woe is me ! to misery
We both were born alike ; thou here in Troy,
In Priam's royal palace ; I in Thebes,
By wooded Placos, in Eëtion's house,
Who nurs'd my infancy ; unhappy he,
Unhappier I ! Would I had ne'er been born !
See TROY

Home Rule, term generally used with reference to Ireland, the self-government of which was long debated between Liberals and Conservatives. The Home Rule party came into prominence after Gladstone's Land Act and his Disestablishment of the Irish Church, its great leader eventually being Charles Stewart Parnell, who made it the vital issue of British politics in the 19th c. Gladstone's first Home Rule Bill 1886 was followed by bills of 1893, 1913. Ireland (Eire) has more or less had self-government since 1922. Gladstone also spoke of some degree of Home Rule for Scotland, and the same has been promised by the Labour Party for many years. So far nothing has been done. An unofficial plebiscite held experimentally at Kirriemuir in 1949 declared overwhelmingly in favour of Home Rule for Scotland on the model of Northern Ireland.

' **Home, Sweet Home,**' see PAYNE, J. H.

Homildon Hill, hill, Northumberland ; scene of a Scottish defeat by Hotspur 1402.

Homs, *hŏms,* city, Syria ; trades in oil and cotton ; pop.60,000.

Honan, *hō-nan',* province of China ; watered by the Yellow R.

Honduras, see CENTRAL AMERICA

honey, see BEE

honeysuckle, twining shrub (family *Capri-*

HONEYSUCKLE

foliaceae) with blue-green oval leaves in opposite pairs ; the flower is trumpet-like, yellow to purple outside, pale yellow inside after fertilisation by hawk-moths.

Hong Kong, British Crown Colony comprising various islands off the SE. coast of China, especially one with an area of 32sq.m, first occupied by the British 1841 ; also British Kowloon ; total area of the colony 391sq.m. The cap., Victoria, has a superb harbour, and is linked by rail with Canton and Hankow. A university was opened 1912. The immense trade includes camphor, coal, cotton, flour, hides, iron and oil. The colony was liberated from the Japanese 1945 ; and civil war in China led to British reinforcements in Hong Kong 1949. In 1951 US citizens were advised to leave ; pop. (1947) 1,600,000.

Honi soit qui mal y pense, *o-nē swä′ kē mäl ē päns,* old French, meaning ' Cursed be he that thinks ill of it ' (i.e. of what I am doing) ; motto of the Order of the Garter ; said to date from the time of Edward III.

Honiton, town, Devon, noted for pillow-lace since the 16th c.

Honorius, FLAVIUS, *hō-nō′ri-ŭs* (384–423), Roman emperor, *b* Constantinople ; failed to prevent the Goths from destroying Rome. He ruled from AD395.

Honours, see UNIVERSITIES

Honshu, *hon′shoo,* largest of the Japanese islands. See JAPAN

Hood, SAMUEL (1724–1816), British admiral ; defeated De Grasse in the W. Indies 1782 ; aided Admiral Rodney to destroy the Fr. fleet at Dominica ; captured the Fr. fleet at Toulon ; created a viscount 1796. Several British warships have been named after him, one being HMS *Hood,* the battle-cruiser destroyed by the German ' pocket battleship ' *Bismarck* in the North Atlantic, May 1941, shortly before the *Bismarck* herself was sunk.

Hood, THOMAS (1799–1845), poet, *b* London ; edited several popular magazines ; went abroad after becoming bankrupt, but eventually paid his creditors in full. He had great sympathy for the poor, as we realise when reading *The Song of the Shirt* (*Punch,* 1843), the story of a needlewoman struggling to keep herself and two children on 7s a week ; or his poem *The Bridge of Sighs.* He is best remembered for his clever puns and humorous verses.

Hooghly, tributary of the R. Ganges, India ; flows 145m via Calcutta to the Bay of Bengal ; noted for its tidal wave.

hookah, type of tobacco pipe common in the Near East and India. Smoke passes through a vase of water, and thence along a flexible tube to the smoker. The Persian nargileh is somewhat similar.

Hook of Holland, village of the Netherlands ; linked by steamer service with Harwich.

Hoover, HERBERT CLARK (1874–   ), 31st President of USA, born in Iowa of Quaker ancestry ; became a mining engineer ; during and after World War I did fine work in relieving distressed Europe. Republican President 1928–32, he was defeated, when he stood for a second term, by Roosevelt.

hop, twining plant of temperate Europe, Asia and N. America. The stems rise to 15 or 20ft ; the rough leaves are heart-shaped and have toothed edges ; the male flowers are green ; the female develop into cone-like heads.

In England hops are chiefly grown in Kent. The cultivation of hops for brewing beer was introduced from Flanders *c.*1524.

Hope, ANTHONY (1863–1933), pen-name of Sir Anthony Hope Hawkins, novelist, *b* London ; author of many popular satires, and especially noted for *The Prisoner of Zenda,* a Balkan romance.

Hopkins, HARRY (1890–1946), American social worker ; special adviser to President Roosevelt ; Director of Lease-Lend from 1941.

Horace (QUINTUS HORATIUS FLACCUS), *hor′is* (65–8BC), Roman poet, *b* Venusia in S. Italy, son of a freed slave ; fought under Brutus ; introduced 39BC by Virgil to Maecenas, patron of several literary geniuses, and spent his last years on a farm near Tivoli. A plump, easy-going man, he lived in comfort, but in his poems he reveals his kindly wisdom, his gentle and often humorous satire. He is famous for his exquisitely expressed thoughts, still frequently quoted. Expert in many different metres (all Greek in origin), he took Greek models for his immortal odes, for which he is most famous.

As an example of one of the odes we may take that in which Horace speaks to his young friend Licinius Maurena. Licinius, having been successful, is anxious to go still further and to be a somewhat violent supporter of one political party. To him Horace gives wise counsel :

Tempt not the deep ; nor while you fly
The storm, Licinius, steer too nigh

The breakers on the rocky shore ;
Hold fast, contented evermore,
The way of Peace, the Golden Mean :
That bounded space which lies between
The sordid hut and palace hall.
Read *The Odes of Horace*, translated
by Lord Dunsany.

Horatius, *hŏ'rā-shŭs,* actually Horatius
Cocles, Roman hero (blind in one eye),
who, with two companions, is said to
have held a bridge over the Tiber against
an Etruscan army led by Lars Porsena,
who was attempting to restore the exiled
Tarquin. The story, largely legendary,
is finely told in Macaulay's *Lays of
Ancient Rome.*

Horeb, *hŏ'reb,* mt., Arabia, where Moses
drew water from the rock. Its other
name is Sinai.

Hore-Belisha, RT. HON. LESLIE (*be-lēsh'ä*
(1895–   ), barrister who became
Minister of Transport 1934, introducing
pedestrian crossings and the familiar
Belisha beacons ; Secretary of State for
War 1937–40 ; Minister of National
Insurance 1945.

hormones, *hor'mōn,* complex chemical substances produced by the ductless glands,
e.g. insulin. See GLANDS

hornbeam, British tree now much used for
making hedges. When allowed to grow
naturally it may become 70ft high ; its
leaves are dark green and have toothed
edges ; its flowers appear as yellow catkins ; its timber is hard, heavy and
white.

hornblende, mineral, chiefly magnesium
silicate with some iron ; found in many
igneous rocks.

hornbook, type of lesson-book used in
schools *c.*1450–1750. Usually a flat
piece of wood with a handle, it had the
alphabet, numerals and the Lord's
prayer, covered with transparent horn.

Hornchurch, residential town, Essex ;
pop.85,000.

hornet, largest of British wasps ; *c.*1in
long ; reddish in colour ; common in
S. England and in most parts of Europe.

Hornsey, *horn'si* ; *-zi,* London borough ;
includes Alexandra Palace, home of
television.

Hornung, ERNEST WILLIAM, *hŏr-nŭng* (1866–
1921), novelist, *b* Middlesbrough ; lived
for a time in Australia ; noted for his
stories of Raffles, the gentleman burglar.

horoscope, see ASTROLOGY

Horrocks, JEREMIAH (1619–41), astronomer,
b Liverpool ; observed the transit of
Venus 1639 at Hoole, Lancashire.

Horsa, see HENGIST

horse, handsome and useful domesticated
animal, long the friend of man ; for
centuries (as a pack-horse) used for
carrying goods ; almost the only means
of transport and travel in Britain before
railways.
 The shire horse, descended from the
old English war-horse, is the largest in
the world ; may stand 17 hands (a hand
being roughly 4in) ; the Clydesdale is
named from that district in Scotland ; the

E. Anglian shire horse is called a Suffolk
Punch ; carriage horses include Cleveland (Yorkshire) bay (bay meaning
reddish-brown or chestnut). Saddle
horses for riding include racehorses bred
from Arabian sires ; all thoroughbreds
are descended from one of three famous
horses, and their names and history are
recorded in the *General Stud Book.* The
hunter is usually a black or chestnut
thoroughbred ; the hackney or nag has
changed little since the 14th c. Ponies
are small horses, e.g. Shetland ponies
with shaggy hair, and the half-wild
ponies on Dartmoor, Exmoor and in the
New Forest. Some ponies are still used
in coal and salt mines. Wild horses are
now found only in Mongolia, the mus-
tangs of N. America being regarded as
domestic horses that have become wild
since being taken there by the Spaniards
in the 16th c. A male horse kept for
breeding is a stallion ; a female, a mare ;
a male horse not kept for breeding is a
gelding ; a young mare is a filly, a young
male horse a colt ; the offspring of a male
ass and a mare is a mule.
 All horses are descended from a prehistoric animal (*eohippus*) no larger than
a hare, with five toes on each foot, but
by evolution these have been reduced to
one toe only, and the remains of two,
i.e. the splint-bone just above the fet-
lock (see EVOLUTION).
 Famous horses include Black Bess
(traditionally, but incorrectly, said to have
been ridden by Dick Turpin) ; Bucephalus, tamed by Alexander the Great ;
Napoleon's horse, Marengo ; and the
fabled Pegasus, the winged horse of
Apollo.
 Horse racing has been popular in
England for centuries, especially since
the introduction of the Grand National
at Aintree (Liverpool) 1839. Notable
racecourses are at Newmarket, Ascot,
Goodwood, York, Doncaster, etc. Racing is always associated with betting, and
the mechanical ' tote ' has been in use
since 1929.

horse chestnut, see CHESTNUT

Horse Guards, see LONDON

horse-power (hp), British unit of power,
actually more than the working power
of a good horse ; defined as the work
done at the rate of 550 foot-pounds per
sec., or as the power required to raise
33,000lb one foot in one minute. It is
equivalent to 746 watts.

Horsham, town, Sussex. Christ's Hospital
(the Blue Coat School) is 2m SW. of it.

Horst Wessel, see WESSEL, HORST

Horst Wessel song, *hŏrst vess'el,* by Horst
Wessel (*d* 1930), regarded after 1933 as
the official Nazi rallying song.

horticulture, scientific gardening (Lat.
hortus, a garden, *cultura,* cultivation).
The Royal Horticultural Society has its
HQ at Vincent Square, Westminster,
S.W.1. See GARDENING

Horus, *hŏ'rŭs,* hawk-headed Egyptian sun-
god, son of Osiris.

12 a

HORSES

(1) *Suffolk Punch* (2) *Clydesdale* (3) *Hunter* (4) *Racehorse* (5) *Shetland Pony*

Hosea, *hō-zē'ä,* one of the lesser Hebrew prophets ; lived *c.*700BC. His book in the OT teaches that God requires loving-kindness rather than sacrifice.

hospital, institution for the treatment of diseases and injuries, for training doctors and nurses, and for medical research. Famous London hospitals include St Bartholomew's (founded 1123), St Thomas's (1200), Guy's, King's College, and there are hospitals specialising in children's ailments, consumption, eyes, skin, etc. Britain's hospitals were nationalised July 1948.

Hotchkiss, BENJAMIN BERKELEY (1826–85), American inventor of quick-firing Hotchkiss gun, an early type of machine-gun.

Hôtel des Invalides. *ō-tel dä za*n-*vä-lēd,* hospital and house for wounded soldiers, established in Paris by Louis XIV, 1670 ; notable for its dome, beneath which Napoleon lies.

hôtel de ville, *-dĕ vēl,* French for town-hall.

Hotspur, see PERCY, SIR HENRY

Hottentot, *hot"n-tot,* Negro inhabitant of S. Africa, so-called by early Dutch settlers. 'Hottentot' meant 'jabberer' or 'quacker,' a reference to the peculiar clicking sounds of the Hottentot language. Hottentots, including two chief tribes (*a*) Khoikhoi, and (*b*) Bushmen, are usually *c.*5ft 3in in height. A primitive people, they live in portable beehive huts, believe in magic and witch-doctors, and have ceremonial dances.

Houdini, HARRY, *hoo-dē'ni* (1873–1926), stage name of Ehrich Weiss, American entertainer and conjurer, son of a Hungarian-Jewish rabbi ; became a locksmith ; appeared on the variety stage as the world's greatest expert in escaping when handcuffed and tied with ropes, performed many astonishing tricks.

Houghton, LORD, *hō't'n* (1809–85), originally Richard Monckton Milnes, poet, *b* London ; notable as a friend of literary men.

house, a building built to be lived in ; varies in many cases according to requirements imposed by the climate and to the materials available, e.g. Eskimos build houses of blocks of snow, called *igloos* ; Red Indians use tent poles covered with animal skins, etc., to form *wigwams* ; houses made of mud are found throughout the East, in S. Africa and Central America. The Mindanao *tree-house,* built at the top of a tree, is reached only by ladder. Other varieties are the Russian *log house,* the Swiss *chalet,* built of wood, usually with an outside stair.

'*House*' implies *something built to last.* In Britain houses are of many styles and sizes, although most are built of stone or brick. There are mansions and cottages, villas and flats ; detached and semi-detached houses, i.e. houses either standing by themselves or attached to others.

Some people prefer to live on a river, and they inhabit houseboats.

The Roman ' villa ' differed from the villas known to us. It was in fact a comfortable farm-steading built round an open courtyard, and (as we may see from many excavated sites) had central heating and beautiful tessellated floors. In recent years there has been a tendency towards living in flats, i.e. a number of dwellings under one roof. Great blocks of flats are now a feature of London and most other cities. Some are known as *service flats,* e.g. meals are served from a central kitchen. New York *skyscrapers* rise to remarkable heights, e.g. the Empire State Building, 1,248ft, with 102 storeys, and room for 80,000 people.

Lawyers in England term a house (with garden and outbuildings) a *messuage.*

We need to keep in mind the ideal that every man, woman and child has the right to good housing conditions, e.g. warmth, light, ventilation, sanitation and comfort. Therefore all sound slum-clearance and progressive town-planning schemes should be encouraged. The shortage of houses after World War I led to an Act (1919) which stimulated the building of reasonably good houses, and local housing schemes were still further advanced by an Act of 1923 ; this, and other measures, brought about the great new housing areas that later sprang up in and around most of our towns and cities. An Act of 1931 did something to improve houses in rural areas, but was by no means sufficient. The devastation caused by bombing in World War II brought about an acute shortage of houses, and at the same time drew attention to the need for better houses, in the planning of which it was recognised that women architects should be called upon to design the rooms and kitchens, putting in them as many labour-saving devices as possible. Since *c.*1935 in USA and *c.*1945 in Britain, *prefabricated houses* have been available, i.e. houses assembled in a few days, the parts having been manufactured elsewhere on mass-production lines, e.g. the ' Portal house,' named after Lord Portal.

A house may be *owned* or *rented.* In England an owner pays rates, while a tenant (one who does not own the house in which he lives) pays rates besides a rent to the landlord. In Scotland rates are often shared between tenant and landlord. Rent days may be weekly or monthly, but are usually quarterly ; in England the *Quarter Days* are Lady Day, 25 March ; Midsummer Day, 24 June ; Michaelmas Day, 29 Sept. ; Christmas Day, 25 Dec. In Scotland they are Candlemas (2 Feb.), Whitsunday (15 May), Lammas (1 Aug.), Martinmas (11 Nov.) ; the ' Removal Terms ' being 28 May and 28 Nov. See ARCHITECTURE ; TOWN PLANNING

household gods, see LARES ET PENATES

House of Commons, see PARLIAMENT

House of Lords, see PARLIAMENT

Houses of Parliament, see LONDON

Housman, ALFRED EDWARD (1859–1936), English poet ; best known for his books of verse, *A Shropshire Lad, Last Poems,* and for his learned editions of the Latin poets Juvenal and Manilius. He was Professor of Latin at Cambridge for many years.

Housman, LAURENCE (1865–   ), brother of A. E. Housman ; notable as an artist, also for fanciful poems, plays and stories.

Houston, *hoo'sst'n,* railway-manufacturing city, Texas, USA ; pop.385,000.

Houston, LADY, *hooss-* (*d* 1936), inherited a fortune of over £5,000,000 from her husband, Sir Robert Houston, a Liverpool shipowner. Intensely patriotic, she enabled Great Britain to win the Schneider Trophy outright 1931, and defrayed the expenses of the Houston Mt Everest expedition 1933.

Hove, holiday town near Brighton, Sussex; pop.58,000.

Howard, CATHERINE (*d* 1542), 5th wife of Henry VIII ; executed on Tower Green (London).

Howard, CHARLES, 2ND LORD HOWARD OF EFFINGHAM (1536–1624), largely responsible for the defeat of the Spanish Armada.

Howard, JOHN (1726–90), reformer, *b* Hackney, London ; inherited considerable wealth ; lived mostly at Cardington, Bedfordshire ; famous for the reforms he brought about in prisons. Howard wrote *The State of the Prisons of England and Wales* (1777). He visited prisons in France, Germany and the Netherlands, and was notable for his work in connection with the plague, and in investigating conditions in hospitals.

Howard of Effingham (*d* 1573), son of the 2nd Duke of Norfolk ; Lord High Admiral 1554–73 ; crushed the Wyatt rebellion. For his son, see HOWARD, CHARLES

howdah, *how'dä,* elaborate seat on the back of an elephant ; often with an ornamental roof.

Howe, JULIA WARD, (1819–1910), poet, *b* New York ; did much towards emancipating American slaves ; wrote *The Battle Hymn of the Republic.*

Howe, RICHARD, EARL (1726–99), admiral, *b* London ; shared in Hawke's action in Quiberon Bay 1759 ; famous for his defeat of the French at ' the glorious first of June,' 1794, and as a master of naval strategy.

Howitt, MARY, *how'it* (1799–1888), author ; wrote many tales for children, and translated Hans Andersen's fairy-tales.

Howitt, WILLIAM (1792–1879), author, *b* Heanor, Derbyshire ; wrote many popular books, including *Rural Life in England.* For his wife, see HOWITT, MARY

howitzer, *how'it-sĕr,* type of gun discharging its projectile at a high angle.

Howrah, *how'rä,* town linked with Calcutta, India ; noted for jute ; pop.225,000.

Hoylake, holiday town, Cheshire, 8m from Birkenhead ; pop.25,000.

hp, see HORSE-POWER

H.P., see HARMONIC PROGRESSION

Hucknall, mining town, Nottinghamshire ; pop.21,000.

Huddersfield, prosperous town, W. Yorkshire, on the R. Colne ; noted for woollen cloth, coal and iron ; pop. 124,000.

Hudson, river of USA ; flows *c.*300m in New York State.

Hudson, HENRY (*d* 1611), English explorer, of whose early life little is known. He attempted to discover the NW. Passage to China, 1607, 1608, 1609 (when he surveyed the N. American coast from Virginia to the Hudson river), and 1610, when he discovered the bay and strait named after him. He was caught in the ice, and in the following June was set adrift in an open boat with his son and seven loyal followers. He was never heard of again. Hudson led the way to the great fur-trading and whaling industries of N. America.

Hudson, WILLIAM HENRY (1841–1922), author and naturalist, born near Buenos Aires (Argentine) ; came to England 1874, where he remained poor and almost unknown till late in life. Hudson wrote charmingly and with exact knowledge about the English countryside, e.g. *British Birds, Birds in London, Hampshire Days, Adventures among Birds, The Book of a Naturalist.* A bird sanctuary and a statue of *Rima* (by Epstein) in Hyde Park form a memorial to Hudson, whose epitaph is : *He loved birds, and green places, and the wind upon the heath, and saw the brightness of the skirts of God.*

Hudson Bay, large opening of N. Canada ; joined by Hudson Strait to the Atlantic ; is ice-bound in winter, but has the growing port of Churchill.

Hudson Bay Company, English trading company founded 1670, and covering the area of N. America watered by rivers flowing into Hudson Bay ; now a limited liability company ; trades in furs ; has depots at Winnipeg.

Hué, see ANNAM

Huggins, SIR WILLIAM (1824–1910), English astronomer ; invented a means of photographing star-spectra. See SPECTROSCOPE

Hughes, THOMAS, *hūz* (1822–96), *b* Uffington, Berkshire ; educated at Rugby under Dr Arnold ; became a county court judge ; best remembered for his popular book, *Tom Brown's Schooldays* (1857), an account of his life at Rugby.

Hugo, VICTOR MARIE, *hū'gō* (1802–85), French author, playwright and poet, *b* Besançon. He was poor as a young man, but quickly attracted attention by his poetry (on which his claim to greatness very largely rests), and won increas-

ing fame with his play *Hernani* (1830) ;
later with his romantic novels, e.g. *Notre
Dame de Paris*, the story of an ugly
hunchback, Quasimodo ; *Les Misérables*,
and *Les Travailleurs de la Mer*. His
stories for children were widely popular,
and after being exiled for a time he spent
his last years in Paris, accepted as the
Grand Old Man of French literature.

Huguenots, *hū'gĕ-not*, French Protestants,
especially in the 16th and 17th cs., when
their Church numbered many nobles and
humbler folk, except in Paris and the
North, where the people, like the king
and most of his court, remained staunch
RC. The Huguenots were persecuted
as heretics by Francis I and Henry II.
In Charles IX's reign there were bitter
religious wars, but even the Massacre of
St Bartholomew 1572, when thousands
were slaughtered in the streets of Paris,
left the Huguenots uncrushed. Henry IV
gave them liberty of conscience by the
Edict of Nantes (1598). Cardinal
Richelieu was tolerant ; but in Louis
XIV's day severe persecution again took
place, and the *Edict of Nantes* was revoked 1685, a step which compelled
thousands of Huguenots to seek refuge
in England, Holland and Germany,
taking their skill with them.

hula-hula, native dance of the Hawaiian
Is. ; performed by women and girls
wearing grass skirts and garlands ;
accompanied by singing and drumming.

Hull, busy and progressive Yorkshire port
on the Humber estuary ; has great
docks ; notable for ship-repairing, rope
and canvas making, sugar refining, milling, oil refining. It has very extensive
fisheries, and was at one time famous
for whaling ; exports products of the
W. Riding of Yorkshire and Midlands,
e.g. woollen and cotton goods, and has
a vast trade with the Baltic ports ;
suffered severely from German bombing
1940–44 ; birthplace of William Wilberforce. Its university college was opened
1928. Work on rebuilding the centre
of the city has been long delayed. The
official name is Kingston-upon-Hull ;
pop.287,000.

Hull, CORDELL (1871–), *b* Tennessee,
USA, Secretary of State for USA from
1933 ; attended the war conference,
Moscow, 1943 ; responsible for co-
operation between USA and the Soviet.
He received the Nobel Prize 1945.

Humber, estuary of the E. coast of England;
separates Yorkshire from Lincolnshire ;
receives the waters of the rivers Ouse,
Trent, Derwent, Wharfe and Nidd.
Plans for a bridge (one mile long) were
passed 1946.

Humboldt, BARON VON, *hum'bōlt* (1769–
1859), German scientist ; *b* Berlin ;
expert in mining, geology, languages,
economics and science ; made important weather observations ; travelled
much abroad, especially in S. America,
and at 76 began his famous *Kosmos*, an
amazing encyclopedic account of the

physical universe. His elder brother,
KARL WILHELM (1767–1835), was an
authority on languages.

Hume, DAVID (1711–1776), philosopher
and historian, *b* Edinburgh ; notable
for his *Treatise on Human Nature* ;
attacked superstitions and was regarded
by many as a wicked atheist. He was
one of the three greatest philosophers
of the 18th c., the other two being
Berkeley and Kant.

humerus, see SKELETON

humming bird, one of a family of 500 species
found mainly in tropical S. America,
the smallest being 2¼in long. Usually
vividly coloured, the humming sound is
caused by the rapid vibration of its wings
as it darts from flower to flower. It
feeds on minute insects. Its nest of moss,
hair and leaves is a deep cup ; two eggs
only are laid.

humus, see SOIL

Hundred Days, period between Napoleon's
return from the island of Elba to his
surrender after Waterloo, 1815.

Hundred Years' War, long series of wars
between England and France. The wars
began 1338 when, claiming the French
crown and wishing to add to his possessions, Edward III invaded France. He
won the battles of Sluys 1340 ; of
Crécy 1346 ; and captured Calais about
the same time. The English victory at
Poitiers 1356 led to the Treaty of
Brétigny, Oct 1360, when it was agreed
that King John of France (who had been
made a prisoner) should be released, but
that Edward III should keep his possessions in N. France.

The Black Prince had been ruling
Aquitaine with aid from John of Gaunt.
When war broke out again 1369, he
fought a losing campaign and had to
give ground. There was a truce from
1390–95, and peace was made when
(1397) Richard II married a French
princess ; but trouble began again
1399, though actual fighting did not
break out till 1403. Henry IV of England joined forces with the French Duke
of Burgundy, and in 1413 yet another
truce was arranged ; but Henry V
invaded France 1415, and won the battle
of Agincourt ; and by the *Treaty of
Troyes* (signed 1420) he was declared
heir to the throne of France. Meanwhile he ruled as regent for the mad
king, Charles VI ; but all this was
hateful to many thousands of Frenchmen, and though Henry V entered Paris
as conqueror 1422, English successes
were actually at an end.

A new spirit arose in France once
Joan of Arc had defeated the English
at Orleans 1429. The French regained
Paris 1436, and after many defeats the
English were at last driven out of the
country, with the exception of Calais.
The war may be said to have ended with
the capture of Bordeaux by the French
1453.

Hungary, inland European country at

present under an Allied Control Commission ; included in the Axis Powers in World War II, being occupied by Germany 1944, but liberated 1944–45 ; area (1946) 36,000sq.m ; pop.10,000,000. Hungary is largely a vast and exceedingly fertile plain with rich coal and oil fields. The people are chiefly Magyars ; cap. Budapest, on the Danube. See AUSTRIA

Hungry Forties, see CORN LAWS

Hunmanby Hall, Methodist girls' school founded near Filey, E. Yorkshire, 1928.

Huns, Asiatic warrior race which, in the 4th c. invaded S. Russia, subdued the Ostrogoths, and later under their great leader, Attila, swept across Central Europe until defeated at Châlons 451.

Hunt, LEIGH (1784–1859), writer, born near London ; with his brother edited *The Examiner* ; imprisoned for libelling the Prince Regent ; friend of Keats, Shelley, Lamb and Hazlitt ; wrote poetry (e.g. *Abou Ben Adhem*) and essays full of humour. He was charming in manner, but wholly unbusiness-like.

Hunt, WILLIAM HOLMAN (1827–1910), artist, b London. He, Millais and Rossetti formed the Pre-Raphaelite Brotherhood. His unconventional pictures attracted much notice, e.g. *The Shadow of Death,* and, most of all, *The Light of the World.*

Huntingdon, co.tn of Huntingdonshire ; on the R. Ouse ; birthplace of Oliver Cromwell.

Huntingdonshire, English county NE. of the Fens ; co.tn Huntingdon.

hurdling, race (usually 120, 220, or 440yd) with hurdles 10yd apart, and, in the longer races, 2ft 6in high.

Hurlingham, district of SW. London ; noted as the world HQ of polo.

Huron, *hū′ron,* one of the Great Lakes, N. America ; 207m long ; has many islands. See GREAT LAKES

hurricane, cyclonic storm, N. Atlantic, frequently developing near the W. Indies. It is highly destructive to property. A similar wind in the N. Pacific is called a typhoon. It occurs mostly in the Philippines and along the coast of E. Asia.

Hurstmonceux, see GREENWICH

huskies, see POLAR REGIONS

Huskisson, WILLIAM (1770–1830), statesman ; a supporter of Pitt ; was President of the Board of Trade, and largely responsible for abolishing the navigation laws ; did much to encourage free trade ; killed at the opening of the Liverpool-Manchester Railway.

Huss, JOHN (d 1415), early Bohemian reformer ; entered Prague University, where he became a rector. Stirred by the teaching of John Wycliffe, he demanded the abolition of many corrupt practices in the Church. Invited to the Council of Constance 1414, he was betrayed by the Emperor Sigismund, who had offered him safe conduct, and was burnt as a heretic. His martyrdom paved the way for Martin Luther and the Reformation.

Hutton, LEONARD (1917–), English

cricketer ; first played in county cricket 1934 ; scored 364 runs (1938) against Australia, and played in the earlier of the disastrous series of Test Matches 1948.

Huxley, ALDOUS (1894–), author and scientist ; won fame with his witty and penetrating *Chrome Yellow* 1921 ; notable for essays, short stories and novels revealing a cynical outlook, especially his *Brave New World* (1932) ; published *Grey Eminence* 1941.

Huxley, JULIAN SORELL (1887–), biologist, brother of Aldous ; brilliant in his pioneer work, and as a writer of popular scientific books ; associated with J. B. S. Haldane and H. G. Wells (*Science of Life*) ; Honorary Lecturer at King's College 1927 ; well known as a lecturer, broadcaster and author, e.g. *The Stream of Life, At the Zoo, Evolution* (1942) ; responsible for many educational films.

Huxley, THOMAS HENRY (1825–95), scientist ; grandfather of Aldous and Julian Huxley, b Ealing ; had only two years' schooling ; was four years aboard a navy survey ship in the Torres Straits ; became a bold supporter of the theory of evolution, and was all his life an outspoken advocate of freedom of thought. An expert in biology, he was author of *Man's Place in Nature,* and also of many scientific essays ; responsible for political, social and moral reforms.

Hwang-ho, see YELLOW RIVER

hyacinth, *hī′ä-sinth,* bulbous flowering plant (family *Liliaceae*) of Switzerland, Spain and Italy ; introduced into Britain 1596. Fragrant bell-shaped flowers grow on a leafless stalk.

Hyacinthus, in old Greek tales, a beautiful youth accidentally killed when playing quoits with Apollo. Hyacinths sprang up from his blood.

hybrid corn, see MAIZE

Hyde, *hīd,* town, Cheshire ; notable for cotton ; pop.29,000.

Hyde, EDWARD, EARL OF CLARENDON (1609–74), English statesman ; a devoted Royalist in the Civil War ; Lord Chancellor after the Restoration. His daughter, Anne, married James, Duke of York, and was the mother of Queen Anne.

Hyde Park, see LONDON

Hyderabad, extensive native Indian state in the Deccan ; noted for cotton, cane sugar and rice ; also its cap., a walled city with a pop. of 729,000.

Hydra, *hī′drä,* in old Greek tales, a nine-headed monster inhabiting a swamp near Lernae ; slain by Hercules.

hydra, fresh-water tube-like creature $c.\frac{1}{2}$in long ; its mouth is surrounded with minute tentacles with which it captures its food.

hydrangea, *hī′dran-jĕ-ä,* garden or greenhouse plant introduced into Britain from China ; notable for masses of white, pink or blue flowers.

hydrate, compound containing combined water ; generally applied to salts containing water of crystallisation, e.g. copper sulphate crystals contain five molecules of water with every molecule of copper sulphate. Water can be removed only by heating or by the action of a dehydrating agent.

hydraulics, *hī-dro'liks,* practical application of the principles of the science of hydromechanics, i.e. in the main, the use of water in motion as in canals, rivers, or in hydraulic machinery, as machines operated by fluid pressure, e.g. hydraulic jack, elevator, crane, ram and press.

The principle of the hydraulic press is based on Pascal's law of fluid pressures. See MECHANICS

hydride, chemical compound of two elements only, of which one is hydrogen, e.g. cuprous hydride, Cu_2H_2.

hydrocarbons, chemical compounds of carbon and hydrogen only. They occur in a remarkably large variety of forms, and may be grouped (*a*) paraffins, C_nH_{2n+2}, characterised by lack of chemical activity, and known as saturated hydro-carbons, e.g. marsh gas ; (*b*) olefines, C_nH_{2n}, the ethylene series ; these, like the third group (*c*) the acetylenes, C_nH_{2n-2}, are reactive, and form derivatives by replacement and direct addition. There are also cyclo-paraffins, polymethylenes, benzene hydrocarbons, etc.

The sources of hydrocarbons are chiefly (*a*) natural deposits of petroleum and (*b*) coal-tar ; their uses are varied and of increasing importance. See PETROLEUM

hydrochloric acid, see CHLORINE

hydrocyanic acid, *hī-drō-sī-an'ik,* prussic acid. It is an intensely poisonous liquid with a smell of bitter almonds.

hydrogen, *hī-drō-jen,* colourless, odourless, tasteless gaseous element, H ; atomic weight 1·0080 ; atomic number 1 ; valency 1 ; boiling-point $-252·7°C$; though not poisonous does not support respiration ; as the lightest element known, it has been used for filling zeppelins and balloons, but is dangerous because extremely inflammable ; burns in air to form water ; combines with oxygen in sunlight ; forms compounds with halogens, sulphur, phosphorus, nitrogen and carbon, also with some metals to form hydrides ; is present in the sun, and is involved in sunspots. In the laboratory hydrogen may be obtained by the action of zinc and dilute sulphuric acid. The oxy-hydrogen blow-pipe gives a temperature of 2,800°C ; if the flame impinges on lime an intense white light (limelight) is produced.

HYDROGEN PEROXIDE, H_2O_2, is a viscous liquid with strong oxidising properties ; it is also a powerful bleaching agent. It is usually met in solution as 10 vols or 20 vols, meaning that 1 vol of the solution will give 10 or 20 volumes of oxygen on decomposition.

HYDROGEN CHLORIDE, HCl, is a colourless gas which dissolves in water to form hydrochloric acid.

hydrogenation, chemical reaction involving the addition of hydrogen, in presence of a catalyst, to a substance.

hydrolysis, *hī-dröl'i-sis,* chemical decomposition of a compound by water, as the part-decomposition of salts of weak acids by water, the water also being decomposed.

hydrophone, *hī'drō-fōn,* instrument for detecting sounds under water, e.g. the propellers of an enemy submarine ; first used in World War I.

hydroponics, *-pon'iks,* cultivation of plants without soil, the method being to supply the roots with the necessary salts in solution ; also known as tank-farming.

hydrostatic paradox, see MECHANICS

hydrostatics, science of the forces and pressures of liquids at rest. See MECHANICS

hydroxide, compound of an element, usually a metal, with hydrogen and oxygen, as in sodium hydroxide, NaOH, the oxygen and hydrogen being usually regarded as connected, and hence forming the hydroxyl group.

hyena, *hī'-ēnä,* carrion-eating animal related to civets and dogs, but cat-like in appearance, with powerful teeth and jaws, sloping back, short tail. It has a queer laughing howl. Found in Asia and Africa, it was common in Britain in prehistoric times.

hygiene, see SALUS

hygrometer, *hī-grom'ētĕr,* instrument for finding the dew-point, and also the amount of water-vapour in the air.

Hylas, *hī'las,* in old Greek tales, a beautiful youth who sailed with the Argonauts and fell in love with a water-nymph.

Hylea, see AMAZON

Hymen, *hi'men,* in old Greek tales, god of marriage ; son of Bacchus and Aphrodite.

Hymenoptera, *-me-nop'tĕr-ä,* large order of insects with (as a rule) four transparent wings, e.g. ant, bee and wasp.

Hypatia, *hī-pā'shia (d 413),* daughter of Theon of Alexandria ; wrote on mathematics, and is said to have been murdered for attempting to cause the Roman governor of Egypt to persecute Christians. Read Charles Kingsley's *Hypatia.*

hyperbola, *hī-pŭr'bŏlä,* in mathematics, section of a cone (see CONE), i.e. the locus of a point moving so that its distance from a fixed point (*focus*) bears a constant ratio, greater than unity, to its distance from a fixed straight line (*directrix*). There are two branches to this curve.

hyperbole, *hī-pŭr'bō-lē,* deliberate exaggeration in speech or writing, as Milton's lines in *Paradise Lost* :

So frowned the mighty combatants that hell

Grew darker at their frowns.

Hyperion, *hī-pēr'i-on,* in old Greek tales, one of the Titans (giants).

hyperspace, see FOURTH DIMENSION

hypnotism, *hip'nō-tizm,* artificial means of causing a person to become unconscious.

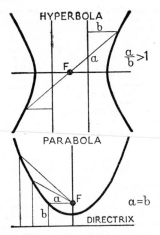

THE HYPERBOLA AND PARABOLA

First known as mesmerism, after Friedrich Anton Mesmer (1733–1815), a German doctor, it was once largely trickery or, at best, haphazard ; but now hypnotism is scientifically employed by psychoanalysts for the examination of neurotic patients, and for removing hidden fears, and rectifying distorted views due to disorders of the subconscious mind.

By inducing a kind of sleep the hypnotist gains control over the subject he has hypnotised. Lunatics are the most difficult subjects to influence. If the subject is willing to receive impressions, the hypnotist may order him to do this or that, the subject readily and accurately obeying as long as the suggestion is not contrary to his deepest convictions. Post-hypnotism is that in which the subject, while hypnotised, receives a command to do something at a future time, and duly does it when the time comes, even though not then under active hypnotic influence. Thus, a man told by the hypnotist to drink a glass of water next day at 4 pm will obediently do so, imagining all the time that he is doing it of his own free-will.

An amazing feature of hypnotism is that the subject not only believes whatever the hypnotist wills him to believe, but reverts to the past in a remarkable way. Thus, a full grown woman told, when under hypnotic influence, that she is a year old, will begin crawling instead of walking ; and a man who has written books, if persuaded by the hypnotist that he is only eight years old, will write a sentence in a schoolboy style, making the mistakes in spelling that a small boy might be expected to make.

Following Mesmer came James Braid of Manchester, Bernheim of Nancy, Forel of Zurich. A very remarkable exponent of hypnotism in our own day is Peter Casson of Bridlington, Yorkshire, who (when only 24) startled the BBC by hypnotising men and women he could not see. His success in a television programme (1946) was so great that the BBC authorities were afraid to allow him to appear again, since not only his audience but actually members of the staff were under his control.

hypo-, *hī'pō-*, in chemistry, prefix meaning ' containing less oxygen.' Hypo is also used as a trade name for sodium thiosulphate, $Na_2S_2O_3$, employed in photography.

hypocaust, *hip-ō'köst*, shallow heating chamber or channel under baths or a house, particularly in Roman times. Examples are to be seen in the ruins of many Roman villas in Britain.

hypotenuse, *hī-pŏt'e-nūz*, in mathematics, the side of a right-angled triangle opposite the right-angle. *The square on the hypotenuse equals the sum of the squares on the other 2 sides.* The best-known proof of this proposition is that devised by Pythagoras, a Gk mathematician of the 6th c. BC. Long before his time, Egyptian builders (without being able to prove it) knew that a triangle, e.g. of sides 3, 4 and 5 units contained a right angle ($3^2 + 4^2 = 9 + 16 = 25 = 5^2$), and used this fact in building.

hyrax, *hī'raks*, hoofed animal which, in spite of its small size (*c.*20in long) is related to the horse and elephant. Rather like a rabbit, it has brown fur, and is found in Africa and Arabia. It is the cony of the Bible.

hyssop, *his'ŭp*, evergreen shrub of the Mediterranean region ; has lance-shaped leaves and purplish flowers. The Bible hyssop was actually the caper plant.

COAL   *plate 37*

An example of a British pithead at St Helens, Cumberland, showing trucks and elevator.
(*Picture Post Library*)

plate 38   COAL MINING

Coal is still the life-blood of industry. *Top :* Inside a coal mine. (*Photo Illustrations, Scotland*).
Bottom : Working at the coal-face, Ashington Colliery, Northumberland. (*Fox Photos Ltd*)

COAL DISTRIBUTION

plate 39

Top : How the coal is transported from the coal-face. (*Photo Illustrations, Scotland*).
Bottom : Scene in Sheffield, one of Britain's greatest steel cities ; the smoky atmosphere is
typical of a coal-and-steel economy. (*Topical Press*)

plate 40   COLLIERIES : OLD AND NEW

Top : Broadsworth Main Colliery. (*Aerofilms Ltd*). *Bottom :* The colliery of the future, an architect's model for development at Rothes, Fife. (*National Coal Board*)

I

I, chemical symbol for iodine.

i, see IMAGINARY NUMBER

iambic pentameter, see METRE

iambus, see METRE

Ibadan, *ē-bä'dän,* largest town, W. Africa. It is in S. Nigeria ; pop.390,000.

Iberia, *ī-bēr'iä,* name given by the Greeks to the SW. peninsula of Europe, now Spain and Portugal ; also, anciently, the region S. of the Caucasus, now known as Georgia.

Iberian peninsula, *ī-bēr'iän,* from the Gk name *Iberia,* given by them to the SW. peninsula of Europe ; known to the Romans as *Hispania* ; now comprising Spain and Portugal, i.e. countries south of the Pyrenees.

ibex, *ī'beks,* animal of the goat family ; includes the Alpine ibex, now almost extinct, with curving horns over 40in long ; other varieties are the Arabian, Ethiopian and Asiatic species.

ibis, *ī'bis,* tall wading bird rather like a stork, but with a long curved beak. The glossy ibis visits Britain occasionally. The Egyptian ibis was once sacred.

Ibn Sa'ud, *ib'n sood* (1880–   ), Arab ruler of Saudi Arabia from 1932 ; an able administrator, a brilliant soldier. Crowned King of Hejaz 1926, he united his territory into an Arab confederation, and (1930) set about modernising his country, e.g. installing radio stations and encouraging the use of motor transport. One of the founders of the Arab League (1945).

Ibsen, HENRIK (1828–1906), Norwegian, *b* Skien ; lived at Bergen and, later, at Oslo ; famous for his many plays, e.g. *The Pretenders, Pillars of Society, The Doll's House, Ghosts, An Enemy of the People, The Master Builder, The Wild Duck, When We Dead Awaken* and *Peer Gynt.* Of these, the first and last were at once popular successes ; the others were too unusual in matter and style to win immediate applause.

Ibsen broke what were then the accepted conventions of dramatic art, and more than that, he attacked existing social institutions and Christianity with all the ardour of a revolutionist.

Icarus, see DAEDALUS

ice, water in a solid state. Pure water freezes at 0°C or 32°F at normal atmospheric pressure, and from 4°C downwards it expands as the temperature decreases ; ice is therefore lighter than water, its specific gravity being ·918. Sea water becomes ice at $c.-2$°C.

ICEBERGS, broken portions of glaciers, are found chiefly in the N. Atlantic ; roughly 8/9ths are below the surface. The *Titanic* was sunk 1912 by an iceberg.

Vessels of the USA Coast Guard now form an Ice Patrol in spring, and broadcast the movements of bergs.

Ice Age, see GEOLOGY

Iceland, volcanic island in the N. Atlantic ; area *c.*40,000sq.m ; pop.132,000. Chiefly a bare plateau, its snow-covered volcanoes include Hecla, which is active. Though trees are few, mosses and heather are plentiful, and root crops are grown in the valleys. Exports include ponies, sheep and fish ; also sulphur. There are many hot springs. The island, long associated with Denmark, has been an independent republic since 1944 ; cap. Reykjavik. The Icelandic parliament is the oldest in Europe, and is called the *Althing.* British troops and USA marines garrisoned Iceland during World War II.

iceland spar, crystalline variety of calcite, $CaCo_3$; found in Iceland ; employed in various optical instruments.

Iceni, *ī-sē'nī,* ancient British tribe in E. Anglia at the Roman invasion of Britain ; revolted under Boadicea AD61, but crushed.

' Ich Dien,' see WALES, PRINCE OF

ichneumon fly, *ik-nū'mon,* one of *c.*6,000 species of membrane-winged flies, 1,200 being known in Britain. Most ichneumon flies lay eggs in caterpillars, the grubs feeding on the tissue.

ichthus, see EMBLEMS

ICI, short for Imperial Chemical Industries Ltd, a British chemical combine formed 1926 when Nobel Industries Ltd, United Alkali Co. Ltd, British Dyestuffs Corporation Ltd, and Brunner Mond & Co. Ltd became one firm with a capital of £74,479,000, and *c.*70,000 employees, thus forming the largest research group in the British Empire. The company manufactures heavy chemicals, organic chemicals, pharmaceutical products, non-ferrous metals, sporting ammunition, paints, resins, plastics, leathercloth, building products, fertilisers, and petrol from coal.

icon or **ikon,** *ī'kon,* in the (Greek) Orthodox Church, a representation in mosaic and painting (but never sculptured) of Christ, the Virgin or one of the Apostles ; often richly ornamented. Hence *iconoclast,* i.e. a breaker of idols.

iconoclast, see ICON

Iconoscope, trade name for a cathode-ray tube used in television to transmit a scene in the form of electrical impulses.

Ida, *ī'dä* (*d* 559), King of Bernicia ; his capital was Bamborough.

Idaho, *ī'dä-hō,* NW. state of USA. Idaho is mostly rugged mountain ranges with deep canyons, but some wheat is grown. Gold, silver and lead are mined ; cap. Boise.

identity card, card required to be carried

345

in World War II (and after) by all British civilians, and to be shown on any official demand. The card gives the full name of the owner, postal address, and has a code number.

Ides, in the Roman calendar, the 13th day of the month, except in March, May, July, Oct., when the Ides fell on the 15th.

idiom, an expression with a meaning all its own, usually peculiar to the language. Thus : I'll see you *Monday week* is idiomatic, since the words *Monday week* have actually no meaning apart from their idiomatic use, i.e. *a week after Monday.* Similarly, the French say *tout le monde* (actually *all the world*), where we should say *everybody.*

idyll, *id'il* ; *ī'dil* (Greek *eidyllion*, little picture), usually a short poem, often about the country. Tennyson (*Idylls of the King*) used the term for separate poems comprising what is almost an epic.

If, *ĕf,* French island in the Gulf of Marseilles ; has a castle (Château d'If) used as a prison.
    Read *The Count of Monte Cristo.*

ignis fatuus, see WILL-O'-THE-WISP

ignition, *ig-ni'shon,* setting alight or strong heating. *Ignition-point* is the temperature at which a substance begins to burn, i.e. at which combustion takes place.

iguana, *i-gwä'nä,* large tree lizard of tropical regions, notably Central and S. America, also W. Indies ; *c.*5ft long, greenish with brown bands ; has a kind of fringe along the back, and a sagging pouch under the chin.

IHS, symbol used in Christian worship from early times ; may stand for Gk IHΣOYΣ (Jesus) (the third letter being Latinised) ; or for the initial Lat. words, *Jesus Hominum Salvator,* i.e. Jesus Saviour of Men, or *In Hoc Signo* (*vinces*), i.e. In this sign (thou shalt conquer).

ikon, see ICON

Il Duce, see DUCE

Île de France, see FRANCE

ilex, *ī'leks,* alternative name for the common holly ; also the American plant (*Ilex paraguayensis*) from the leaves of which yerba maté (Paraguay tea) is made. The holm-oak is sometimes called ilex, but it does not actually belong to that genus, although its proper name is *Quercus ilex.*

Ilford, town, Essex ; noted for making paper and photographic materials ; pop.180,000.

Ilfracombe, *-koom,* holiday town on the N. Devon coast.

Iliad, see HOMER

Ilium, see TROY

Ilkeston, mining town, Derbyshire ; manufactures hosiery and lace ; pop.30,000.

Ilkley, *ilk'li,* W. Yorkshire town and spa on the R. Wharfe.

illinium, rare earth and element, Il ; atomic weight 146·0 (?) ; atomic number 61.

Illinois, *ili-noi',* state of USA between the rivers Ohio and Mississippi ; has

immense level and fertile prairies. Noted for wheat, flour-milling and pork-packing, it produces oil and coal ; cap. Springfield, but Chicago is the largest city.

ILP, see INDEPENDENT LABOUR PARTY

image, see LIGHT

imaginary number, in mathematics, a number with negative square, e.g. $\sqrt{-1}$. The symbol is *ι*. This is not to be confused with an incommensurable number, i.e. a number that cannot be expressed exactly as a proper fraction, e.g. π or $\sqrt{2}$.

imago, *i-mā'gō,* name for a perfect or an adult insect after passing the larval and pupal stages.

immigration, see EMIGRATION

Immingham, Lincolnshire port on the Humber ; its great docks were begun *c.*1912. Immingham exports much coal from the Midlands.

immunisation, see VACCINATION

impeachment, trial of a minister of state or high public official on charges of bad administration, the House of Commons acting as accusers, the House of Lords as judges ; notable impeachments in history include those of Lord Bacon and Warren Hastings.

Imperial Airways, see AVIATION ; BRITISH OVERSEAS AIRWAYS CORPORATION

Imperial Chemical Industries Ltd, see ICI

Imperial Preference, see FREE TRADE

Imperial War Museum, see LONDON

impetigo, *impi-tī'gō,* inflammation of the skin marked by isolated blisters which form crusty scabs. Sometimes called ' scrum pox.'

Impressionism, see ART

Inca, *ing'ka,* native tribe of Peru with a remarkable and ancient civilisation. Inca actually means *lord.* The last of the Inca chiefs, Atahualpa, was murdered by the Spaniards 1533. The Inca empire, destroyed in Pizarro's conquest of Peru, covered an area 2,000m long and 500m wide. The cap. was Cuzco, over 11,000ft above sea-level. There were many roads with cuttings and bridges ; the people, skilled farmers, made terraces (*andenes*), from which the Andes probably take their name. Masters of building, textile-weaving, pottery-making, etc., the Incas were sun-worshippers. Many of their fine fortresses, temples and palaces remain and have been excavated.

incense, sweet-smelling gums burnt in religious ceremonies over charcoal or in a censer ; anciently employed by the Jews, Greeks and Romans, also in the RC church today.

in-centre, see TRIANGLE

Inchcape Rock or **Bell Rock,** rock off the east coast of Scotland, near the mouth of the R. Tay. It is 500yd long and 100yd wide, and has had a lighthouse since 1807. Formerly a bell warned sailors. It is the subject of a well-known poem by Robert Southey.

inclined plane, see MECHANICS

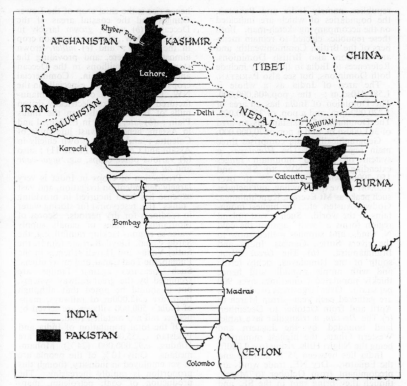

AFGHANISTAN   KASHMIR   CHINA

Khyber Pass

TIBET

Lahore

IRAN

BALUCHISTAN

Delhi

NEPAL

BHUTAN

Karachi

Calcutta

BURMA

Bombay

Madras

—— INDIA

■ PAKISTAN

CEYLON

Colombo

income tax, money paid to the Government on earned or unearned income, calculated according to earnings, and family circumstances, e.g. a married man with children will pay less income tax than a single man who earns the same amount.

A minimum living allowance is granted in all cases, but after this has been met, tax is deducted. In the case of unearned income (e.g. dividends from shares held in companies) tax is deducted at the highest rate, i.e. (1948) 9s. in the £.

indenture, see DEED

Independence, DECLARATION OF, document adopted by Congress 4 July 1776 (Independence Day) by representatives of 13 American states, repudiating allegiance of Americans to the British Crown.

Independent Labour Party, usually styled ILP, British Socialist organisation founded 1893 at Bradford, Yorkshire ; early associated with Keir Hardie, Ramsay MacDonald and Viscount Snowden. The ILP was dissolved 1948.

index, in mathematics, a number showing how many times a given number is multiplied by itself, e.g. 5^4, where 4 is the index, showing that 5 is to be raised to the 4th power, i.e. $5 \times 5 \times 5 \times 5 = 625$; $5^2 = 5 \times 5$, i.e. 25, and is read *five*

squared ; $5^3 = 5 \times 5 \times 5$, i.e. 125, and is read *five cubed.* Indices are much used for large numbers, e.g. the age of the earth (possibly 3,000 million years) might be written 3×10^9 ; also for extremely small quantities, e.g. $1/10{,}000$th $= 10^{-4}$. The latter is an example of negative indices ; note that $\frac{1}{10} = 10^{-1}$; $\frac{1}{100} = 10^{-2}$; $\frac{1}{1000} = 10^{-3}$, etc.

Note also that

$$a^m \times a^n = a^{m+n}$$
$$a^m \div a^n = a^{m-n}$$
$$(a^m)^n = a^{mn}$$
$$a^0 = 1$$
$$a^{-n} = \frac{1}{a^n}$$
$$a^{\frac{1}{n}} = \sqrt[n]{a}$$
$$a^{\frac{m}{n}} = \sqrt[n]{a^m} \text{ or } \left(\sqrt[n]{a}\right)^m$$

India, general name for that triangle of Asia roughly S. of Afghanistan and Tibet, and in part between the Arabian Sea on the W. and the Bay of Bengal on the E. Before 1947 this region (larger than Europe) constituted Britain's Indian Empire, consisting of 11 provinces with a measure of self-government, five large areas directly under British rule, and some 500 native states. In 1947 India was divided into two self-governing republics, namely India and Pakistan, the boundaries of which are indicated on the accompanying sketch-map. Both these republics elected to remain members of the British Commonwealth, and are therefore also British Dominions. References to India in this entry include both Dominions, but see also PAKISTAN.

The area of India as a whole is 1,581,410sq.m ; the pop.406,000,000. The Dominion of India has an area of 1,220,000sq.m, and a pop. of 337,00,000. The Dominion of Pakistan has an area of 361,000sq.m, and a pop of 70,000,000.

Geographically India comprises three main regions : (a) The *Himalayas*, a system of parallel mountain ranges extending 1,500m NW. to SE., and 150–200m wide. This rises to over 10,000ft above the snowline, and includes such peaks as Mt Everest, Kunchinjunga, Godwin-Austen, etc., the highest mountains in the world. Such a vast upland region forms a ' wall ' against the cold N. winds, and supplies melted snow to the rivers Sutlej, Ganges, Indus and Brahmaputra. (b) The *Great Plain*, south of the Himalayas, richly fertile and with ample rainfall, and hence thickly populated (sometimes over 900 per sq.m). Over large areas two harvests are gathered each year—from March to April and from October to December. (c) The *Deccan*, a triangular lava table-land bounded by the Eastern and Western Ghats, the highest mountains being the Nilgiri Hills, rising to c.9,000ft.

India lies between 35°N latitude and the Equator. Dry NE. trade winds are predominant from October to March, though they bring rain in the SE. and in Ceylon. The northern plains are hot in April and May. After mid-June the SW. monsoon ' bursts ' with thunderstorms along the W. coast, and spreads over almost all India by July, bringing 90% of the annual rainfall in three months. Since c.300,000,000 people depend on the land for their livelihood, the Indian *ryot* (peasant or farmer) awaits the coming of the monsoon as anxiously as the Egyptian *fellah* watches for the rising of the Nile. Should the monsoon fail disastrous famines result, e.g. that of 1877 when 5,000,000 people in India died of starvation.

Plant and animal life is everywhere abundant and varied. The Himalayas abound in deer, yak, bears, elephants, monkeys and tigers, and the Tarai jungle is notable for its big game. The Great Plain has monkeys, panthers, leopards, hyenas, jackals, elephants, deer, etc., and also snakes and crocodiles. In the Deccan (especially in the Nilgiri Hills) are forests including teak, ebony, satin-wood, sandalwood, palm and bamboo.

Though India has over 150,000,000 cattle (chiefly for milk and for use as beasts of burden), the people for the most part live on (a) *rice*, a plant requiring considerable heat and much water—hence rice is the chief crop of the Lower Ganges and the coastal areas of the Deccan ; (b) *wheat*, grown largely in the N. and NW., also a cool-season crop in the tropics ; and (c) *millet*, grown almost everywhere, and providing the staple food of millions in the Deccan and on the Indus Plain. Commercial crops include (a) *cotton*, especially in the NW. Deccan, much of it now manufactured in the hydro-electrically driven mills of Bombay ; also on the Indus Plain ; (b) *jute*, raised in E. Bengal and in Assam, hence the vast jute mills of Calcutta ; and (c) *tea*, grown chiefly in Assam and Ceylon (see PLATE 11) ; also (d) various other crops, e.g. *sugar-cane* and *oil seeds*.

Production of crops in India is very largely dependent on irrigation, and vast expense has been incurred in providing ' tanks ' (i.e. reservoirs) for storing water in readiness for dry periods. Scores of thousands of miles of canals supply water to regions lacking rainfall, e.g. the Sarda Canal, Lloyd Barrage (Sind), the Sutlej Valley and Haveli schemes in the Punjab, the Thal Canal, and many others. Such measures against famine are seconded by the great railway systems, but it should be noted that although there are c.42,000m of railways, many of India's 500,000 villages are served by neither rail nor metalled road.

Of the total population of India and Pakistan c.255,000,000 (i.e. 65%) are Hindus, c.92,000,000 (24%) Mohammedans. Only 10% of the people are as yet employed in industry, though this proportion is rapidly increasing. The production of coal, petroleum, manganese, monazite, tungsten, etc., also of jute, cotton and a host of other textiles is carried on. Mica and salt are mined. To some extent cars and aircraft are manufactured. It is interesting to note that the British Commonwealth's largest steel works are at Jamshedpur (Bihar), a town with a population of 140,000. Here over a million tons of steel are produced yearly. India is now manufacturing aluminium.

But progress in industry and also in government is still hampered (a) by the existence of many differing and opposed religious groups ; (b) by the caste system, possibly evolved from a colour-bar introduced by fair-skinned invaders from the north c.4,000 years ago, and now dividing the population into groups, many of them associated with some particular occupation, ranging from the high-caste Brahmin through 2,000 lower degrees to the 50,000,000 people in the depressed classes whose occupations are styled unclean, and whose very shadows are held to defile other Hindus ; (c) by the fact that over 220 languages are spoken, e.g. Western Hindi, spoken by 71,000,000, Bengali, Bihari, Teluga, Marathi, Tamil, etc. ; (d) by the fact that a vast number of the peasants are in debt to money-lenders ; and (e) by the bitter hatreds of various opposing sections of the community.

In many ways India is an epitome of what is meant by the phrase ' the gorgeous East.' Under blue skies and amid luxuriant vegetation are ' rose-red cities half as old as time,' besides countless palaces, temples and mosques, e.g. the Taj Mahal at Agra ; the temples of Ahmedabad and Allahabad ; the Jane temple at Khandagiri ; the rock or cave temples of Karli, Ellora, Ajanta and Elephanta. There is the Golden Temple of Amritsar ; the Pearl Mosque, lofty Kutab Minar, and the Jumma Musjid of Delhi—once proud of its peacock throne studded with priceless jewels. At Benares is the Monkey Temple ; at Calcutta the Burmese Pagoda ; at Mysore the stone Bull ; at Lucknow the Palace of Light. Gwalior has a famous fort and palace. India is a land where religious pilgrimages are made by millions, e.g. to Benares ; where snake-charmers and holy men (*fakirs*) lie on spikes, hoping thereby to gain heaven's blessing. Immortalised by Rudyard Kipling in *The Jungle Book*, India is the home of legend and mysticism.

The Portuguese were in India late in the 16th c., and British interests began with the formation in 1600 of the East India Company, which had ' factories,' i.e. trading stations, on the E. coast. Charles II gave the company the island of Bombay 1668, and a station was set up at Calcutta 1690. Meanwhile the Mogul Empire, founded by Mohammedans in the 16th c., was breaking up. Extended by Akbar the Great, it had reached its peak in the reign of Sha Jehan, builder of the Taj Mahal. When attacked by the Maratha war lords the empire crumbled, and in the chaos which followed the French took Madras, and seemed about to secure immense and widespread power when Robert Clive won a victory at Arcot 1751 which turned the tide. From that time British influence increased.

Clive's pioneer work was carried on by Warren Hastings who, as Governor of Bengal from 1772–85, increased the area of British territory, improved the laws and revenue system, and defeated Hyder Ali's invasion of the Carnatic, 1780. Lord Cornwallis overhauled the East India Company, and the Marquis Wellesley not only raised British prestige but made favourable alliances with Native States. To Lord William Bentinck were due still further reforms, notably the abolition of suttee, i.e. the burning of widows ; and Lord Dalhousie introduced railways, telegraphs and cheap postal services as well as adding to the area under British rule.

The Indian Mutiny of 1857 led ultimately to the abolition of the East India Company, its administration being taken over by the British Government ; and in 1876 Queen Victoria was proclaimed Empress of India. Far-reaching reforms were begun by Lord Curzon, who (1899–1905) established the rate of 15 rupees to the £1, and improved irrigation, transport, the legal system, education, agriculture, banking and the army. At the Coronation Durbar of George V (1911) it was announced that the seat of government was to be Delhi, not Calcutta.

That India should wish to be self-governing (as, say, Canada or Australia) was understandable, but the basic difficulty all along was the fact that the country was not united. What is known as Indian Nationalism took shape 1886 when the Indian Congress Party was formed. This demanded a native parliament, and opposed British rule. The movement was led by young Hindu students, and later (1906) the Moslem (or Muslim) League was founded. The desire for Home Rule was intensified by Gandhi, who began a civil disobedience campaign. In 1929 the Viceroy (Lord Irwin) announced that ultimately India would reach Dominion status, his promise following the publication of the report made by the Simon Commission (1927) in which an All-Indian Council was recommended, the princes being represented there. This led to a Round Table Conference in 1930, but Gandhi and the Indian Congress still demanded complete independence, and further attempts to solve the problem of government were unavailing because of disagreement among Marathas, Sikhs, Indian Christians, etc., and because Gandhi wished to include outcasts among the Hindus. An Act of 1935 proposed to give India control of practically everything except defence and external affairs, the Governor, however, retaining supreme authority for emergency, but the Hindus and Moslems of Congress were still disunited, and the princes opposed both. As Gandhi and his lieutenant, Nehru, were at loggerheads with the Princes, Indian federation appeared as remote as ever.

During World War II new difficulties arose. The Moslem League, convinced that they could never work with Hindus, demanded a separate Moslem state, to be called Pakistan, while the Hindu party (Mahasabha) asked for majority rule. The British Government made generous offers in 1940 for increasing Indian representation on the Executive Council, and later (1942) Sir Stafford Cripps offered complete independence after World War II, promising a new constitution formulated by Indians themselves by means of a Constituent Assembly. But even this proposal broke down when Congress claimed an *immediate* Indian Cabinet. Rebellion resulted, and Gandhi and Nehru were arrested with all the Congress leaders.

Field-Marshal (later Viscount) Wavell, who became Viceroy of India 1943, found no way out of the difficulty, but soon after securing a majority in the election of 1945 the British Labour Government appointed Louis Mountbatten (now Earl Mountbatten) as Wavell's successor, and it was he who, as last Viceroy, brought the long period of negotiation to an end. It was agreed that complete independence be granted from July 1947, the two British Dominions of India and Pakistan coming into being at the same moment. After this historic new departure, great social changes took place, notably the virtual disappearance of wealthy hereditary Princes as rulers of States. Though retaining their titles they were liable to lose their power at any moment.

The capital of the Dominion of India continues to be Delhi, that of Pakistan is Karachi, in the province of Sind.

Read *India*, Lady Hartog (Nelson) ; *What about India?* L. F. Rushbrook Williams (Nelson) ; *Indian Pageant*, F. Yeats Brown ; *The Discovery of India*, J. Nehru. The latter, written in prison, is the work of India's most brilliant author.

Indiana, *indi-an'ä,* thickly populated state of USA to the west of Ohio. It is richly agricultural, and at the same time wealthy in minerals, e.g. oil, coal and natural gas ; cap. Indianapolis.

Indianapolis, *-ap'ō-lis,* cap., Indiana, a state of USA. A great railway centre, it has manufactures including iron, textiles and canned meat ; pop.387,000.

Indian Civil Service, service in which British and Indians had judicial, medical and other appointments prior to 1947.

Indian Congress, see INDIA

Indian corn, see MAIZE

Indian Forestry Service, see FORESTS

Indian ink, ink made from lamp-black mixed with thin glue ; first manufactured in China.

Indian Mutiny, revolt of native regiments against British rule in India. Among many causes may be noted those which actually brought about open warfare, namely (*a*) the British Government's order to send Bengal regiments overseas in spite of the belief by high caste Hindus that they must never leave India ; and (*b*) issuing of cartridges greased with the fat of pigs or cows, the pig being regarded as unclean by Mohammedans, the cow sacred to Hindus.

Mutiny broke out among the Sepoy regiments at Meerut, 1857. Delhi was attacked, as also the British in Lucknow and Cawnpore, though fighting was largely confined to Hindustan. Sir Henry Havelock was too late to relieve Cawnpore, but Delhi was held, the Lucknow garrison reinforced, and the revolt stamped out by Sir Colin Campbell.

Indian National Congress, founded 1885, stood at first for unity among Indians,

general improvement, and co-operation between Britain and India. It was associated 1916 with the Muslim League (formed 1906). Congress came under the leadership of Gandhi 1920, and in 1927 demanded independence for India, a demand modified 1932. Dominion status for India, defined as the goal of the British Government on several occasions, was reaffirmed 1940, but Congress rejected the proposals of Sir Stafford Cripps 1942, and progress towards a working agreement was delayed by disunity among the Indians themselves, though approached 1946. See INDIA

Indian Nationalism, see INDIA

Indian Ocean, ocean between Africa and Java, Australia, etc ; swept by monsoons ; has many coral islands.

Indian rope trick, see ROPE TRICK

indiarubber, see RUBBER

indigo, *in'di-gō,* blue dye, once exported from India, and manufactured from a pea-like plant, but since *c.*1890 manufactured synthetically from naphthalene.

indium, white metallic element, In, discovered with the spectroscope 1863 ; obtained pure by electrolysis of chloride ; atomic weight 114·76 ; atomic number 49.

Indo-China, land area between the Gulf of Siam and the China Sea ; almost completely tropical. French Indo-China (286,000sq.m) comprises Cochin-China, Laos, Tonkin, Annam and Cambodia ; the administrative cap. is Saigon. Indo-China was invaded by the Japanese July 1941.

Indo-Gangetic Plain, see INDIA

Indonesia, *in-dō-nē'si-ä,* name covering two regions of Dutch influence (*a*) the United States of Indonesia, which (from *c.*1949) now comprise the Indonesian Republic (now recognised as exercising authority over Java, Sumatra, Madura and Borneo), with the Great E., i.e. the islands between Celebes and New Guinea ; and (*b*) the Kingdom of the Netherlands, which includes Dutch possessions in the W. Indies, Surinam and Curaçao. Together (*a*) and (*b*) form the Netherlands Indonesian Union, a draft agreement on which was reached (1945) by Dutch and Indonesian delegates at Cheribon, Java.

From Aug 1950 the Republic (of 10 provinces) had a People's Representative Council.

Indore, native principality of Central India ; cap. Indore, a growing city with pop. of 204,000.

inductance, see ELECTRICITY

induction, see FARADAY, MICHAEL ; MAGNETISM

induction coil, electrical instrument consisting of (*a*) a core of soft iron wires insulated from each other ; (*b*) a primary coil of a few turns of thick insulated copper wire ; (*c*) a secondary coil of many turns of thin insulated copper wire, the ends forming a spark-gap ;

(d) a make-and-break, usually a spring and a soft iron armature ; (e) a source of electricity, say a battery.

When current flows the core becomes magnetised, attracting the armature, and thus breaking the circuit ; when no current flows the armature returns to its normal position by the action of the spring, thus closing the circuit and again allowing current to flow, the action being repeated. The rapidly changing electric field due to the breaking of the primary circuit induces a high voltage between the ends of the secondary coil so that a spark leaps across the gap ; a condenser is usually included, thus reducing sparking at the make-and-break and causing the secondary current (pulsating, but always in the same direction) to increase in voltage. Such coils are now much used for coil ignition in cars, a distributor being included to direct the current, in correct sequence, to the sparking-plugs ; also once widely used for operating X-rays where a high voltage was required, though a high voltage transformer and valve rectifier are now used.

A similar principle is found in the *transformer*, a type of induction coil without an interrupter. This apparatus reduces or increases voltage (a conversion known technically as ' stepping ' down or up). Transformers are much used for converting current that, for economy, is distributed long distances at dangerously high voltages to voltages more suitable for general use, e.g. the Grid System may distribute a current of 1 amp. at 132,000 volts, this being stepped down to a current of 600 amps. at 220 volts by means of a transformer ; but this can only be done with alternating current (AC).

Indulgence, Declaration of, declaration made by James II, 1687, without the consent of Parliament, giving religious liberty to Roman Catholics and Dissenters, thus setting aside the *Test Act.*

indulgencies, see Luther, Martin ; Reformation

Indus, river of India, flowing 1,700m from Tibet to the Arabian Sea ; Karachi is on its delta. The Lloyd barrage is at Sukkur.

Industrial Revolution, a process of social and economic change, especially in England and Scotland, c.1750–1850, when changes occurred in industrial *method* (from handwork to work by power-driven machinery), in industrial *organisation* (from work at home to work in factories), and in *scope,* i.e. from production for local needs to large-scale production to supply world markets. This process was accompanied by an enormous increase of population, a rise in the standard of living, and the occurrence of many difficulties of readjustment of existing political and social institutions to altered conditions.

Such changes were due to (a) im-portant textile inventions, e.g. Kay's flying shuttle (1733) ; Hargreaves' spinning jenny (1764), improvements by Arkwright and Crompton ; (b) the invention of power-driven machinery due to James Watt's steam-engine, later applied to the machines already mentioned ; (c) inventions making possible the production of the machinery necessary for industrial expansion, e.g. Smeaton's blast-furnace (1760), Cort's iron puddling process (1783), and later improvements in steel manufacture ; (d) the advance in methods of transport, hence speed in bringing raw materials to the factories and the export of manufactured goods, e.g. the building of canals (notably 1760–1830), better roads, the invention of the steamship (say 1820 onwards), and the spread of railways from c.1825.

In c.100 years Britain changed from being mainly an agricultural country with a few small towns and a pop. (1750) of only 6,000,000, to a largely industrial community of 18,000,000 in 1850, and 36,000,000 c.1900. The inventions meant increased speed in production, hence the replacement of hand methods in the home by mechanical means in factories built, first by streams supplying water-power, later on or near coalfields where steam power was available. Fear of unemployment caused many riots (e.g. the Luddites 1811–12) and the smashing of machinery, but the ultimate effect of machinery was to make goods cheaper, to increase the demand, and to cause more (not less) employment.

The Industrial Revolution, however, *did* cause a great change in the distribution of population. There was a drift to the towns, where conditions were thoroughly bad. Competition for work was keen, working hours long, not only for men but for women and children, most of whom at one time toiled 18 hours a day. Eventually various reforms brought about improvements, e.g. the Factory Acts. The rapid growth of the new industrial areas (long unrepresented in Parliament) led to the Reform Bill of 1832.

The drift of population towards industrial areas created a labour problem in agriculture, and a revolution in farming, e.g. enclosure (1760–1830) of fields, rotation of crops, improved methods of breeding cattle. Better transport led to the quicker importation of cheap food from overseas, which brought a great depression in British agriculture, notably 1875–1900.

We may say that the Industrial Revolution continued into the 2nd half of the 19th c., and even (with the introduction of electricity) into the present century.

inertia, see Matter ; Mechanics

Infanta, title given at one time to a Spanish or Portuguese princess ; masculine, *Infante.*

infantile paralysis (poliomyelitis), inflammation of the grey matter of the spinal cord. Patients may be treated while in an ' iron lung,' which induces respiration when the patient cannot breathe for himself. The curative method introduced by Sister Elizabeth Kenny, an Australian nurse, is now recognised as being possibly one of the best treatments so far discovered, provided it is introduced during the initial stages of the disease.

There was a serious outbreak of the disease 1947, from which many people died, others became paralysed for life, but many patients recovered. Treatment by injecting grape-sugar and liquid silver (a discovery made by a German doctor, 1947) is another remedy claimed to be effective if given in the early stages.

infection, transmission of a disease, actual contact being unnecessary. The common cold is an infectious disease. If a disease is communicated only by contact with a diseased person it is called ' contagious.' Infection (the entry of bacteria into the body) may occur as the result of (*a*) air-borne bacteria entering by nose or throat, (*b*) bacteria in food and drink (alimentary tract), or (*c*) bacteria entering via the skin (i) through a wound, (ii) by injection. Air-borne diseases include tuberculosis, mumps and whooping cough ; water-borne diseases include typhoid, cholera, etc. Contagious diseases include diphtheria.

inflation, monetary condition of a country in which the amount of money the people have to spend is greater than the amount of goods that can be bought in the shops; always indicated by rising prices and lowering values of money.

influenza, often called 'flu ; an infectious disease generally causing a high temperature, inflammation of the respiratory organs, headache and depression ; possibly caused by a virus. Injections against influenza are only partially successful.

Information, CENTRAL OFFICE OF, British Government department succeeding the Ministry of Information 1946 ; prepares publicity for Government departments.

infra-red rays, electromagnetic waves or heat rays longer than the red waves of the visible spectrum ; invisible to the human eye, but much used in long-distance photography, and in instruments enabling planes and ships to steer through fog.

Inge, WILLIAM RALPH, *ing* (1860-   ), Dean of St Paul's 1911–34. Through his writings, often pessimistic, he earned the title of ' the gloomy dean.' His many books include *Outspoken Essays* and *God and the Astronomers*.

Ingleborough, mt. of W. Yorkshire (Pennines) rises 2,370ft ; noted for Ingleborough Cave.

' Ingoldsby Legends,' see BARHAM, R. H.

Inkerman, *ingk-ĕr-män'*, village near Sebastopol ; scene 1854 of the defeat of the Russians by British and allied forces during the Crimean War.

Inland Revenue, BOARD OF, department of the British Government which collects taxes, death and stamp duties, etc. ; founded 1694.

Innocent, name of 13 popes, among them Innocent III (1160–1216), who greatly enhanced the papal authority, and compelled King John of England to accept Stephen Langton as Archbishop of Canterbury.

Innsbruck, old ʼand beautiful town at the head of the Brenner Pass (Austrian Tirol) ; a popular tourist centre ; makes cloth, glassware and stained windows ; pop.56,000.

Inns of Court, English legal societies in London, e.g. Lincoln's Inn, Inner Temple, Middle Temple and Gray's Inn. They have the exclusive right of calling candidates to the English Bar. Founded in the 13th c. each has its own library, dining-hall and chapel.

King's Inn, Dublin, and the Faculty of Advocates, Edinburgh, are the Irish and Scottish equivalents.

inorganic, see CHEMISTRY

inquest, inquiry called by a coroner when a person has died suddenly, or as the result of violence, or in suspicious circumstances, etc. The court has a jury, and witnesses may be called. In Scotland such investigations are conducted privately by the Procurator-Fiscal. Under the English system evidence given at a coroner's inquest will probably appear in the newspapers, and may therefore influence the minds of jurors serving at any trial, e.g. a murder trial, later on. This seems undesirable, particularly as evidence is taken at coroner's inquests that would not be admissible in an ordinary court.

Inquisition, cruel court of the RC Church from 1248–1835, though less cruel from the 17th c. onwards. Its purpose was to try and to condemn heretics, and though set up in Italy, Germany and France, it was most powerful and lasted longest in Spain, where hundreds of thousands of victims were tortured, and where Thomas de Torquemada (1420–98) as Grand Inquisitor, was most notorious.

insect, creature sharing with the crab, lobster, etc. the peculiarity of having the skeleton outside. Insect means ' cut in,' i.e. the body is in three parts—head, thorax, abdomen, the connection between the thorax and abdomen being sometimes extremely slender. The external skeleton is of brittle material, *chitin*. All species have six legs attached to the thorax. Most adults have wings, and can fly, but there are exceptions.

Growth, as a rule, begins with the egg, from which comes the *larva* (sometimes called a grub, or, in moths and butterflies, a caterpillar). This becomes a *pupa*, from which the perfect insect emerges, the whole series of changes being known as *metamorphosis*. Some insects, however, emerge from the egg in adult form (*nymphs*), and moult

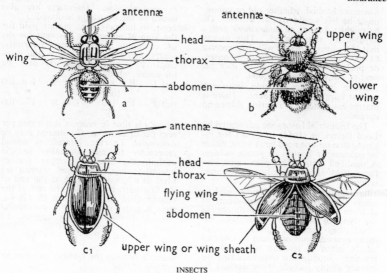

INSECTS

(a) *the Tsetse Fly* (*diptera*) (b) *the Humble Bee* (*hymenoptera*)
(c₁) *the Dytiscus Beetle* (*coleoptera*) (c₂) *as* (c₁) *but showing flying wings*

several times ; some adults lay eggs from each of which many insects are hatched.

In proportion to their size and weight insects are remarkably muscular, e.g. the wings of the common housefly vibrate over 300 times per sec, and a flea's jump is equivalent, weight for weight, to a man's leap over St Paul's. The insect eye is compound, and all sense organs are highly developed.

Some moths are 11in across, but most insects are very small.

It seems that insects have developed little in the last few million years, and while over 500,000 species have already been scientifically described, there are thought to be at least 4,000,000 species.

Many insects are useful to mankind, e.g. bees for honey and in fertilising plants ; but some insects are responsible for much damage to crops, and for carrying disease, e.g. the bluebottle fly, the house fly and the mosquito. The control of harmful insects is receiving increasing attention from entomologists and biologists. On the other hand, insects are often used to destroy unwanted plants : thus, vast areas of E. Australia (*c.*60,000,000 acres) were infested 1925 with prickly-pear, but the menace was overcome by importing eggs of the insect *Cactoblastis cactorum*, the larvae of which ate over 15,000,000,000 tons of prickly-pear.

Read *The Biological Control of Insects*, Hugh Nicol ; *Social Life in the Insect World*, J. H. Fabre ; *An Insect Book for the Pocket*, Edmund Sandars.

insectivorous plants, *in-sek-tiv′ŏr-ŭs*, plants that imprison insects in their leaves or flowers, and dissolve them. British species include sundew and bladderwort.

insomnia, see SLEEP

instinct, see ZOOLOGY

insulator, *in′su-lā-tĕr*, may be (*a*) a non-conductor of electricity, e.g. glass, porcelain, rubber, and many varieties of plastics, (*b*) a heat insulator of great importance in heating systems. Clothes are, in part, insulators. It is worth noting that the thin walls of modern prefabricated houses are sometimes better heat insulators than brick or stone walls. See ELECTRICITY ; PLATE 45

insulin, crystalline substance produced in the pancreas ; actually a hormone controlling the amount of sugar in the blood. Dr F. G. Banting discovered *c.*1923 a method of manufacturing insulin (the trade name) from the pancreas of sheep or oxen. This is used in cases of diabetes, when prescribed amounts are injected into the body.

insurance, provision against loss, injury, illness, or old age ; also of making sure that when we die there will be money for those we leave. We may insure against fire by paying a small annual sum (the premium) to some insurance company which, in its turn, promises to pay the value of our house should it be accidentally destroyed by fire. Or we may ' take out ' a policy of *life insurance*, e.g. a young man might choose to insure himself for £1,000 at death, which means that every year he would pay the company a sum of money to insure that whenever he died, whether old or young, those he left would receive £1,000. Or he might take out an *endowment policy* payable at, say, age 65. This means that if he lives to 65 he will then receive £1,000 (and perhaps more, if bonuses, or profits, are added) ; if he dies his next of kin will receive £1,000.

Other insurances include insurance against burglary and accident. There is marine insurance, i.e. insuring ships and cargoes.

The Industrial Insurance advocated by Lord Beveridge (1944) is a plan for insuring that no-one need be in want, either in sickness or health, in youth or age. A modified form of his plan came into force 1948 as a compulsory insurance scheme.

intelligence tests, tests now much used to assess the IQ (intelligence quotient) of children of 11+ in order to determine the type of secondary education for which they are best suited ; also in many examinations of young people and adults, often in relation to vocational training. Intelligence tests requiring no literary ability include those devised by Dr. Ballard ; also various developments of the original Binet tests. Possibly the most commonly used tests (at any rate for school children) are the Moray House Intelligence Tests, the most recent series being individual and not for groups.

Inter-American Highway, see ROADS

interdict, *inter-dikt'*, form of punishment by the RC Church (*a*) *general*, as when public worship, burial, etc. are forbidden, e.g. Pope Innocent III's interdict on England 1208 ; and (*b*) *local*, when it applies only to some diocese or parish. Similar punishment of a person is usually called *excommunication.* Interdicts are also issued by the Courts in Scotland.

interest, in business, etc., money paid for the loan of money, or payment for the use of capital ; may be paid quarterly, yearly, etc. The sum lent is the principal (P) ; and interest (I) may be (*a*) *simple*, when

(i) $I = \dfrac{P \times r \times t}{100}$ (ii) $T = \dfrac{I \times 100}{P \times r}$

(iii) $P = \dfrac{I \times 100}{r \times t}$ (iv) $R = \dfrac{I \times 100}{P \times t}$

where t is time *in years*, r is the rate per cent per annum ; or (*b*) interest may be *compound*, i.e. the interest is added repeatedly (usually annually) to the capital, the amount gaining further interest ; thus, compound interest on £100 at 6% would be £6 at the end of the first year, £6 3s 6d at the end of the second, then £6 7s 4d, then £6 11s 6d, etc. A sum invested at 5% compound interest doubles itself in approx. 14 years. For compound interest

$$\text{Amount} = P \times \left(1 + \frac{r}{100}\right)^n$$

where n denotes the number of years or periods of time.

Interglossa, see LANGUAGE

Interlaken, *-läken*, beautiful town and health resort between lakes Thun and Brienz, Switzerland.

internal combustion engine, engine in which fuel is burned in the cylinders, as opposed to the steam engine, in which fuel is burned in a furnace and steam conveyed to the cylinders, with, of course, loss of heat during transmission.

Among fuels employed in internal combustion engines are (*a*) *coal gas* and similar gases, including producer gas, water-gas, and gas from blast furnaces. In every case the gas is mixed with air

---

INTERNAL COMBUSTION ENGINE

Fig. A *The side view of a four-cylinder Engine partly in section ; and* Fig. B *The transverse section through one of the cylinders* (1) *Crank Shaft end bearings* (2) *Crank Shaft middle bearings* (3) *and* (4) *Crank Pins* (5) *Pistons* (6) *Gudgeon Pins* (7) *Connecting Rods* (8) *Water Jackets* (9) *Water Uptake* (10) *Circulating Water Pump* (11) *Cam Shaft* (12) *Chain Sprockets* (13) *Cams* (14) *Valve Tappet Rollers* (15) *Valve Tappets* (16) *Valve Caps* (17) *Valve Springs* (18) *Tappet Screw Adjustment.*

Fig. C *The four-stroke cycle* (a) *Induction. The Piston descends, drawing the mixture of Air and Fuel through the Inlet Valve* (1) *Sparking Plug* (2) *Inlet Valve (open)* (3) *Exhaust Valve (closed)* (4) *Piston* (5) *Cylinder* (6) *Connecting Rod* (7) *Crank Pin* (b) *Compression. The Piston goes up, compressing the charge : both Valves are closed* (c) *Firing. The Piston is forced down on the working stroke as the compressed charge is fired by an electric spark : both valves are closed* (d) *Exhaust. The Piston rises again, forcing burnt gases out of the cylinder through the open Exhaust Valve.*

Fig. D *A Poppet Valve in a side-Valve arrangement* (1) *Valve Stem* (2) *Sleeve* (3) *Valve Head* (4) *Collar or Disc* (5) *Spring* (6) *Cam.*

Fig. E *A diagram of a very simple form of Carburetter* (1) *Fuel* (2) *Needle Valve* (3) *Float Chamber* (4) *Float* (5) *Fuel Level* (6) *Jet* (7) *Throttle* (8) *Mixture to Engine.*

Fig. F *Diagrammatic view of a Coil-Ignition system* (1) *Distributor's Casing* (2) *Spark Gap* (3) *Rotor Arm or Rotating Distributor* (4) *Condenser* (5) *Cam* (6) *Spring Contact* (*the old-fashioned type is used in this diagram for lucidity of illustration*) (7) *Moving Contact Point (earthed)* (8) *Coil* (9) *Switch* (10) *Battery* (11) *Cylinder* (12) *Sparking Plug* (13) *Earth.*

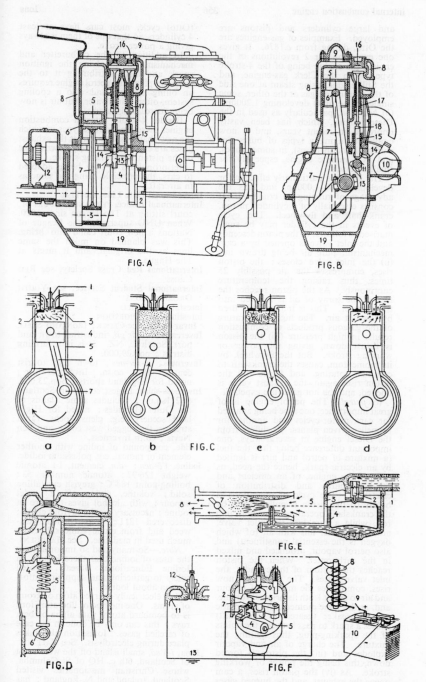

FIG. A

FIG. B

FIG. C

FIG. D

FIG. E

FIG. F

INTERNAL COMBUSTION ENGINE

and large cylinders and pistons are employed. Examples of gas-engines are the Otto, dating from *c.*1876. It gives one explosion for 2 revolutions of the engine, the engine being of the 4-stroke type ; also the Clerk gas-engine, and the Still engine, using steam at one side of the piston and gas at the other, some single-engine units developing 1,200hp ; (*b*) *heavy oil*, particularly as used in the Diesel engine, which has been vastly improved in recent years, and is now employed in many types of buses (including London buses), in some planes, and as a marine engine, especially for smaller vessels.

The Diesel is particularly effective for developing 100–1,000hp, and has the advantage of running on crude oil. It consists essentially of a cylinder, piston, crank-shaft and fly-wheel. The cycle of events in the cylinder may be summarised as follows: (i) the piston descends and the inlet valve is opened by a cam mechanism, pure air being drawn in ; (ii) the inlet valve closes ; the piston rises, compresses the air possibly 25 times, thus raising the temperature enormously. As the piston reaches the top, a fine spray of oil is injected into the cylinder. This is immediately fired by the hot air. The high temperature of the gaseous products of combustion results in high pressure (iii) the piston is thrust down, giving the power or working stroke. But the fly-wheel, by its momentum, causes the crankshaft to continue rotating, and hence (iv) the piston rises again, the exhaust valve is opened, and the hot gases are expelled.

(*c*) *petrol* : The petrol engine is of great importance, one type being adapted for cars, motor-cycles and another for propeller-driven planes. It differs from the Diesel engine in several ways, one important difference being that the fuel (a mixture of petrol and air) is ignited by an electric spark, hence the need, as part of the engine, of an efficient and reliable source and distribution of electricity. The cycle of operations is briefly (i) the piston is pulled down by the crankshaft operating the connecting rod, while a cam lifts the inlet valve, and the cylinder fills with air (of which oxygen is the essential constituent) and also petrol vapour, produced and mixed in the carburetter. When the piston reaches the bottom of the cylinder, the inlet valve closes. The piston (ii) now rises, compresses the mixture of vapour and air to about 1/6th its original volume, and, at the same moment, the automatic contact-breaker (geared to the shaft) causes a spark to pass between the points of the sparking-plug, thus igniting the mixture. The charge of air and vapour explodes and (iii) the piston is forced down, this being the power or working stroke. As (iv) the piston rises, a cam opens the exhaust, and the burned gases are expelled. As this is a 4-stroke

(Otto) cycle, most cars have at least 4 cylinders, so that one of them is always giving a power stroke.

In addition to the carburetter and mechanism for supplying the ignition spark and also distributing it to the sparking-plugs, the petrol engine requires an oiling system, and also a cooling system, often using water, but air is now being increasingly used.

Besides 4-stroke internal combustion engines there are 2-stroke types in which the new charge is drawn in as the exhaust gases are expelled, and every downstroke of the piston is a working stroke.

Jet-propulsion is now being adapted to cars, the principle being the same as in aircraft.

International Date Line, see TIME
International Justice, PERMANENT COURT OF, court sitting at The Hague since 1920. When UNO superseded the League of Nations a new court came into being. This was planned on much the same lines as the original, and it meets at The Hague.
International Red Cross Society, see RED CROSS
International Student Service, see YOUTH ORGANISATIONS
intestate, see WILL
intestines, see DIGESTION
' **Invar** ' **steel**, see CLOCK; IRON AND STEEL
Invercargill, -*kär'gil*, industrial town and port, South I., NZ. It is in a farming district ; pop.29,000.
Inverness, *in-vĕr-nes'*, town and tourist centre, also co.tn, Inverness-shire ; noted for Highland sports ; pop.23,000.
Inverness-shire, largest county in Scotland (4,211sq.m) ; includes some islands of the Outer Hebrides ; noted for Highland scenery, e.g. glens, lochs, rapid streams, the rugged west coast, and Ben Nevis ; co.tn Inverness.
iodide, compound of iodine with another element or radical, e.g. potassium iodide.
iodine, *ī'ō-dēn* ; -*dīn*, element, I ; atomic weight 126·92 ; atomic number 53 ; boiling-point 184°C ; greyish crystalline solid ; volatile, giving off a violet vapour ; with alcohol gives tincture of iodine ; necessary for the thyroid gland ; discovered 1811 ; prepared from seaweed and from crude Chile saltpetre ; much used in medicine. See HALOGENS

Note.—So many and so important are the uses of iodine that there is now an Iodine Educational Bureau devoted solely to gathering and supplying information about iodine.
ion, *ī'on*, electrically charged atom or group of atoms. One method of liberating ions is to bombard atoms with alpha or beta rays ; this can only be done in the case of rarefied gases. Ionisation also takes place during electrolysis. See VALENCY
Iona, *ī-ō'nä*, small island off the west coast of Scotland, 6th c. HQ of St Columba, whose Christian missionaries visited Scotland, Ireland and N. England ; has a restored 12th c. cathedral.

Ionian Islands, 40 mountainous islands (including Corfu and Cephalonia) in the Ionian Sea between Greece and Italy. Grapes are cultivated. The islands have belonged to Greece since 1863.

Ionian Sea, sea between Greece and Italy ; actually part of the Mediterranean.

Ionic order, see ARCHITECTURE

ionic theory, see ELECTROLYSIS

Iowa, *ī'ōwä,* fertile state of USA. It is west of the R. Mississippi, and is noted for cereals and cattle ; cap. Des Moines.

ipecacuanha, *ip-ē-kak-ū-an'ä,* Brazilian plant, the dried roots of which are used in medicine.

Iphigenia, *ifi-jē-ni'ä,* in old Greek tales, daughter of Agamemnon and Clytemnestra.

Ipswich, co.tn, Suffolk ; on the R. Orwell ; makes agricultural implements ; birthplace of Cardinal Wolsey ; pop.89,000.

IQ, see INTELLIGENCE TESTS

Iran, *ē-rän',* kingdom known also as Persia ; mostly a high, dry plain south of the Caspian Sea ; area 628,000sq.m ; pop.15,000,000. There are few rivers, and the land to the east is desert, hot in summer, cold in winter. Crops include wheat, cotton, sugar and fruits, all dependent on irrigation ; also gums, tobacco, opium, silk. Carpets and shawls are made. Oil is found in immense quantities, and there are other minerals, few of which are worked to any large extent. The cap. is Tehran, where (1943) President Roosevelt, Stalin and Churchill met for an important conference.

Cyrus founded a Persian empire 537BC, and the country was conquered AD639 by Arabs. (Between these dates lived Cambyses (*c.*529BC) ; Darius, who made war on the Greeks ; and Xerxes, finally beaten by the Greeks at Salamis, Persia being later conquered by Alexander the Great. The magnificent ruins of ancient Susa and Persepolis have been brought to light in recent years.) In modern times, both Britain and the Soviet Union have influenced the development of Iran, especially under Reza Shah Pahlevi, succeeded 1941 by Mohammed Reza Pahlevi.

Iraq, *ir-äk',* kingdom formerly (and sometimes still) called Mesopotamia, i.e. ' the land between the two rivers (Euphrates and Tigris). Bordered by Arabia and Iran, with an area of *c.*117,000sq.m and a pop. of 3,600,000, the country has great possibilities and is not yet fully developed. The Basra to Baghdad railway is linked with Europe, and there are also air lines and desert buses to Baghdad. Irrigation is insufficient, but wheat, barley, rice, dates and cotton are grown. The chief export is oil, two important pipelines (1,150m) being completed 1935. The terminals are Haifa (Palestine) and Tripoli (Syria). The country was freed from Turkish rule by the British 1914–18, and the first parliament of the new kingdom was opened 1925. The cap. is

Baghdad, the ancient city of the caliphs, e.g. Haroun al Raschid of *The Arabian Nights.* The city is on the R. Tigris, and is a great trading centre. See ASSYRIA ; BABYLONIA ; UR

Ireland, large island west of England and Wales ; area 32,408sq.m ; consists largely of a central plain with much bogland and many loughs (lakes), e.g. Neagh, Erne, Allen, Derg, and drained by slow rivers, e.g. Barrow, Liffey, Boyne and Shannon. The northern and western coasts are rugged, and Achill I. (Co. Mayo) has cliffs 2,000ft high. Mountains include those of Mourne (Co. Down), reaching 2,796ft at the peak of Slieve Donard ; the Wicklow Mts (3,039ft) ; and Macgillicuddy's Reeks (3,414ft). The climate, as a whole, is equable, the rainfall considerable.

IRELAND

Showing the boundary between Ulster and the South

Ireland grows much the same crops as those of England, but flax is an important product of the north, hence the great linen industry in Belfast and neighbouring towns. A land of green pastures (poetically ' the Emerald Isle '), Ireland has cattle, sheep, pigs, poultry and horses, particularly hunters, in large numbers. Huge quantities of potatoes are grown, especially for home consumption. There is much dairy farming. Coal, copper, salt and marble are mined, but not in large quantities. N. Ireland is noted for its shipbuilding yards and whisky distilleries ; Dublin, in Eire, is a centre for brewing stout. Exports include dairy produce, cattle and linen. The Shannon hydro-electric power station (near Limerick) provides cheap power for the greater part of Eire ; and Foynes, in the Shannon estuary, is the air station for trans-Atlantic air liners.

Ireland is divided politically into (*a*) the independent democratic republic of Eire, constituted 1922, but known till 1937 as the Irish Free State (IFS), with its own cap. (Dublin), parliament and president (see DAIL EIREANN) ; pop. 3,000,000 ; and (*b*) Northern Ireland (Ulster), which has a separate parliament, though returning 13 members to the House of Commons, London. The executive power is vested in the governor. The pop. is 1,300,000 ; cap. Belfast.

Known to the Romans as *Hibernia*, Ireland is the home of a Celtic people who adopted Christianity in the time of St Patrick (i.e. the 5th c.), and are now mostly RC, except in Northern Ireland, which is chiefly Protestant. The Norman kings of England attempted to rule Ireland, and Henry II compelled the Irish to submit, but English rule in the 15th c. was confined to 600sq.m only, those 'beyond the Pale,' as it was called, owning no allegiance to the English crown. Henry VIII styled himself King of Ireland ; Cromwell ruthlessly put down rebellions, and from 1801–1920 Ireland was united with Great Britain. See CELTI

Ireton, HENRY (1611–51), soldier, born near Nottingham. A Parliamentarian in the Civil War, he fought at Marston Moor and Naseby ; was one of the judges at the trial of Charles I ; died in Ireland when Lord Deputy for Cromwell.

iridium, *i-rid'ium*, rare metallic element, Ir ; silvery ; harder than platinum, and one of the heaviest substances known (specific gravity 22·4) ; atomic weight 193·1 ;

THE IRIS

atomic number 77 ; discovered 1804 ; used as an alloy for the tips of pen points ; some of its solutions are rainbow coloured, hence the name (from Iris, goddess of the rainbow).

Iris, *i'ris*, in old Greek tales, goddess of the rainbow.

iris, plant (family *Iridaceae*), found by ponds, streams ; has tall sword-shaped leaves. The yellow iris (June, July) has a short tube folding back into three yellow sepals with black streaks, and three pale yellow petals.

Irish Sea, sea between Ireland and N. England ; greatest width (E. to W.) c.150m.

Irkutsk, district of central Siberia, USSR. The cap. Irkutsk, a fine city, has a pop. of 250,000.

IRO, see DISPLACED PERSONS

iron, see IRON AND STEEL ; MAGNETISM

Iron Age, last of the three prehistoric ages known as Stone, Bronze and Iron ; occurred at different times in different regions. It is only vaguely defined, but may be placed roughly as beginning in Europe *c.*4000BC, though sometimes regarded as the period 1000–500BC.

iron and steel, metals of great importance today, steel being actually a variety of iron :

(1) IRON, Fe (Lat *ferrum*) ; atomic weight 55·85 ; atomic number 26 ; melting-point (when pure) *c.*1,535°C. A greyish-white element, is malleable (easily hammered into shape), also easily magnetised, but does not remain magnetised ; has two common oxides (*a*) red or ferric oxide (Fe_2O_3), and (*b*) black or magnetic oxide (Fe_3O_4) ; quickly oxidizes in air, forming *rust*, i.e. mainly ferric oxide (Fe_2O_3) ; is found in meteorites ; occurs richly in the earth in various ores, always with impurities, e.g. silicon, sulphur, carbon and phosphorus. It was known 6,000 years ago, but the so-called Iron Age was roughly 1000–500BC.

Iron was used by the Greeks 600BC. Prior to AD1600 it was smelted with charcoal, hence the destruction of forests in England, e.g. Forest of Dean and the Weald, where iron was smelted by prehistoric tribes. Coal-smelting became general in the 18th c.

Today the production of iron includes the following processes (*a*) *roasting*, a preliminary purifying process, (*b*) *smelting*, chiefly in large quantities in a blast furnace, producing masses known as pigs, (*c*) *resmelting* the pig-iron in a cupola furnace to form cast iron, (*d*) *reheating* the pig-iron and *puddling* in a reverbratory furnace to produce wrought (or malleable) iron after balls of iron (blooms) have been welded and rolled.

Prior to 1939 the finest cast iron would stand a strain of 15lb per sq.in, but research by the British Cast Iron Research Association has resulted in ACICULAR IRON capable of standing a strain up to 60lb per sq.in, and having a glass-like surface.

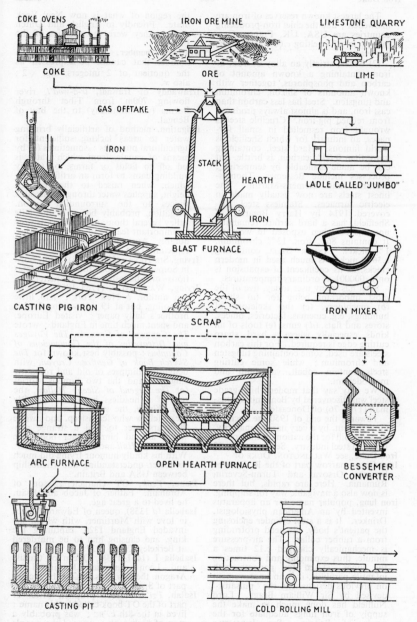

COKE OVENS

IRON ORE MINE

LIMESTONE QUARRY

COKE

ORE

LIME

GAS OFFTAKE

IRON

STACK

HEARTH

IRON

BLAST FURNACE

LADLE CALLED "JUMBO"

CASTING PIG IRON

SCRAP

IRON MIXER

ARC FURNACE

OPEN HEARTH FURNACE

BESSEMER CONVERTER

CASTING PIT

COLD ROLLING MILL

IRON AND STEEL PRODUCTION

The largest known reserves of iron are in Sweden ; and the chief iron-producing countries are USA, UK, France, Germany ; in all smelting c.60,000,000 tons per year.

(2) STEEL, strictly an alloy of iron, or iron containing a known amount of carbon and phosphorus, together with known amounts of silicon, chromium and tungsten. Steel has less carbon than cast iron, and is almost always produced from refined pig-iron. Crucible steel is wrought iron resmelted in small furnaces, an industry for which Sheffield is world famous. Hard steel, containing more than 0·60% carbon, is brittle, but can be made malleable by tempering ; processes include Bessemer, Thomas-Gilchrist and Siemens-Martin. The finest steels are now usually made in electric furnaces. Stainless steel, discovered 1914 by Harry Brearley of Sheffield, has a hard surface remaining untarnished when exposed to weather. It contains 86% iron, 13% chromium, 1% nickel. ' INVAR ' STEEL, containing c.36% nickel, is much used in modern clocks, as its coefficient of expansion is only ·000001 at ordinary temperatures.

Steel has many uses today, five of the most important being for (a) ships, (b) machinery, (c) the skeletons of buildings, e.g. cinemas, factories, offices, stores and flats, (d) guns, (e) tools of all kinds, especially where a hard, sharp cutting edge is required. For this carbon steels are used, some containing tungsten and chromium ; while some cutting steels contain cobalt, vanadium and molybdenum.

We may say that modern high-grade steel was discovered by Benjamin Huntsman (1704–76) of Doncaster.

Towards the end of 1950 the Socialist Government, by a very narrow majority, passed a Bill for the nationalisation of the iron and steel industry. See PLATES 49–52

Iron Duke, see WELLINGTON, DUKE OF

Iron Gates, narrow part of the R. Danube between Orsova and Turnu-Severin, Rumania. Here are rapids, but there is now also a navigable way for shipping.

iron lung, popular name for an apparatus invented by an American physiologist, Drinker. It is a steel cylinder enclosing the patient's body, his head protruding from a rubber collar. The air-pressure is mechanically changed c.12 times a minute, thus expanding and contracting the lungs. Used for patients with infantile paralysis, it is an improvement on previous designs, e.g. the ' pulsator ' devised by Sir William Bragg. Lord Nuffield has done much to make the supply of iron lungs adequate for the needs of Britain. See INFANTILE PARALYSIS.

Ironsides, see CIVIL WAR

irony, see FIGURES OF SPEECH

Iroquois, ir'ō-kwoi, group of N. American Indians, of whom the Mohawks were the chief tribe. Their territory was in the region of what is now New York State. Friendly to English and Dutch settlers, they were the enemies of the French.

irrational number, in mathematics, a number that cannot be expressed as the quotient of 2 integers, e.g. $\sqrt{2}$; also π.

Irrawaddy or **Irawadi,** ir-ä-wod'i, river flowing 700m from Tibet through Burma (via Mandalay) to the Bay of Bengal.

irrigation, method of artificially bringing water to areas lacking sufficient for agricultural purposes ; sometimes (a) by means of canals, from which water is led off to fields or farms, or (b) by building dams to form an artificial lake, which, when raised to the required height, supplies water through controlled sluices to the surrounding region. Irrigation, probably begun in the Nile valley several thousand years BC, is now an important feature of many countries, notably Australia, India, Egypt and especially USA. See DAM

Irving, SIR HENRY (1838–1905), actor, born in Somerset ; famous for his interpretations of Shakespearean characters.

Irving, WASHINGTON (1783–1859), American author, b New York ; had little schooling, but at 19 was writing for his brother's daily paper ; visited Europe, and spent much time in England ; wrote *The Conquest of Granada, The Voyages and Discoveries of the Companions of Columbus* ; possibly best known for *The Sketch Book of Geoffrey Crayon,* with delightful glimpses of old and romantic England, and the two famous stories (a) *The Legend of Sleepy Hollow,* the tale of a headless horseman, (b) *Rip Van Winkle,* the story of a happy-go-lucky fellow who fell asleep, and awoke 20 years later to find a strange new world around him. Other books are *Bracebridge Hall* and *Tales of a Traveller.* With his kindly humour Irving did much to foster understanding and friendship between USA and Britain.

Isaac, ī'zăk, OT character ; son of Abraham. Father of Jacob and Esau, he lived to a great age.

Isabella (d 1358), queen of Edward II, but in love with Mortimer, with whom she invaded England 1326, capturing the king, and causing him to be murdered at Berkeley Castle 1327.

Isabella I (1451–1504), Queen of Castile and Leon ; married Ferdinand of Aragon, the pair thus uniting the greater part of Spain.

Isaiah, ī'zī'ä, Hebrew prophet, writer of part of the OT book called by his name ; lived in the 8th c. BC ; was probably a man of high rank ; warned the people that punishment would come from Assyria because of their neglect of Jehovah. His prophecies are notable for their exquisite imagery and poetry.

Consider, say, the concluding verses of the 40th chapter of Isaiah :

FLAGS OF THE WORLD

UNITED NATIONS

ARGENTINE

AUSTRALIA

CANADA

EGYPT

FRANCE

INDIA

NEW ZEALAND

NORWAY

PAKISTAN

TURKEY

UNION OF SOUTH
AFRICA

U.S.S.R

UNITED KINGDOM

U.S.A.

YUGOSLAVIA

(*United Nations Association*)

Plate V

Plate VI   WEDGWOOD

In 1774 Josiah Wedgwood discovered a white porcelain bisque of great delicacy and capable of receiving a colour throughout its whole substance. This material he named 'Jasper.' *Above :* Designed in 1780, this celebrated vase is made of blue Jasper with white Jasper embossments made separately and applied by hand. It depicts the Judgment of Paris. (*Josiah Wedgwood & Sons Ltd.*)

JAPANESE PORCELAIN   *Plate VII*

With its harsh but pleasing colours, this Kioto brush-holder is a brilliant example of late
nineteenth-century Japanese ceramic art.

Plate VIII   TAPESTRY

H.M. The Queen's coat of arms, impaling the Royal Arms with those of Bowes-Lyon. Its bright colours and formal design make this a particularly suitable subject for depiction in tapestry. (*By gracious permission of H.M. The Queen ; R. Cruickshank, Esq., Edinburgh Tapestry Co.*)

TAPESTRY   *Plate IX*

The Phoenix, another tapestry showing how effectively bright colours and sharp outline can be used in this medium. (*R. Cruickshank, Esq., Edinburgh Tapestry Co.*)

1

3

5

COLOUR IN PRINTING

White light can be separated into three main groups of different colours (see *Plate I*)—those associated with yellow, those with red, and those with blue. Red with yellow gives orange ; yellow with blue, green ; and so on. In the ' four-colour ' printing process a full range of colours is obtained by photographing the coloured original four times : (*a*) through a blue filter. (*b*) through a green filter, (*c*) through a red filter, (*d*) with no filter. From each of these negatives a printing plate is made, and these plates are inked as follows : (*a*) in yellow, (*b*) in red, (*c*) in blue, (*d*) in black. In printing, the paper receives first an impression of the yellow plate. On it impressions of the red, blue, and black plates are then successively superimposed.

Opposite : Impressions of (1) yellow plate ; (2) red plate ; (3) red on yellow ; (4) blue plate ; (5) blue on red and yellow ; (6) black plate. *Above :* Printing completed by superimposition of black on blue, red and yellow.

The picture itself is taken from O. S. Nock, *Scottish Railways* (Nelson).

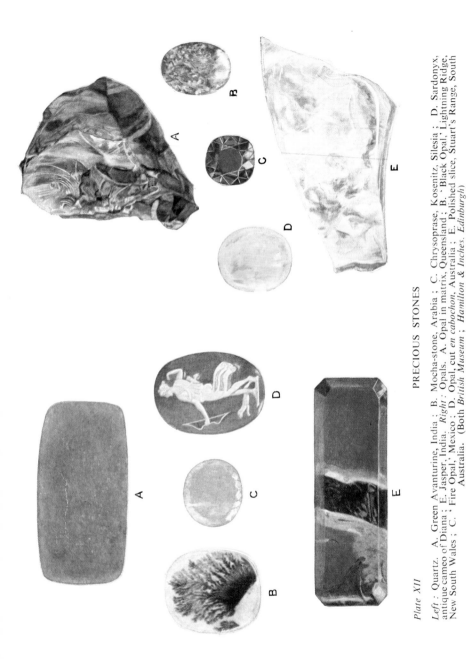

Plate XII

PRECIOUS STONES

Left : Quartz. A. Green Avanturine, India ; B. Mocha-stone, Arabia ; C. Chrysoprase, Kosenitz, Silesia ; D. Sardonyx, antique cameo of Diana ; E. Jasper, India. *Right :* Opals. A. Opal in matrix, Queensland ; B. 'Black Opal,' Lightning Ridge, New South Wales ; C. 'Fire Opal,' Mexico ; D. Opal, cut *en cabochon*, Australia ; E. Polished slice, Stuart's Range, South Australia. (Both *British Museum ; Hamilton & Inches, Edinburgh*)

Why sayest thou, O Jacob, and speakest, O Israel : *My way is hid from the Lord, and my judgment is passed over from my God?*

Hast thou not known, hast thou not heard, that the everlasting God, the Lord, the Creator of the ends of the earth, fainteth not, neither is weary? There is no searching of his understanding.

He giveth power to the faint, and to them that have no might he increaseth strength. Even the youths shall faint and be weary, and the young men shall utterly fall ; but they that wait upon the Lord shall renew their strength ; they shall mount up with wings as eagles; they shall run and not be weary, and they shall walk and not faint.

' I Serve,' see PRINCE OF WALES

Ishmael, *ish'mā-el,* Bible character ; son of Abraham ; banished with his mother, Hagar, to the wilderness (Genesis, 16–25). Mohammed traditionally claimed descent from Ishmael.

isinglass, *ī-zing-glas,* gelatine made from the dried swimming bladder of sturgeon and other fish.

Isis, *ī'sis,* part of the Thames flowing through Oxford.

Isis, Egyptian goddess ; mother of Horus : worshipped also in Greece, Italy and Roman Britain.

Islam, *iz'lām,* name in the *Koran* for the Mohammedan religion.

island, *ī'land,* area of land surrounded by water. Continental islands comprise the same type of rock as the mainland ; oceanic (separated by deep water) are usually either of coral or volcanic origin. The largest islands are Greenland (827,300sq.m), New Guinea (330,000 sq.m), Borneo, Baffin Land, Madagascar, Sumatra, Great Britain, Honshu or Honshiu (Japan), Celébes.

Isle of Man, island in the Irish Sea ; area *c.*230sq.m ; pop.50,000. The island, a favourite holiday centre, is noted for beautiful scenery, but it is also agriculturally prosperous, and has mines producing iron, lead and slate. The people (a mixture of Celts and Norse) formerly spoke Manx, i.e. a Celtic language. The legislature, called the Tynwald, comprises (*a*) the Council, (*b*) the House of Keys ; cap. Douglas.

Isle of Wight, *-wīt,* island separated from Hampshire by the Solent ; area 147 sq.m ; has a delightful climate, hence its many holiday and health resorts.

Islington, borough of London ; adjoins Finsbury. As recently as last century, Islington was a village in green fields.

Ismailia, *is-ma-lē'yä,* town, Egypt ; on the Suez Canal.

Ismail Pasha, *is-mä-ēl'* (1830–95), Egyptian ruler ; planned great schemes for improvement, but found himself in debt, and hence sold his shares in the Suez Canal Company to Disraeli 1875.

isobars, see CLIMATE

Isocrates, *ī-sok-rä-tēz* (436–338BC), Greek orator ; famous for his *Panegyricus,*

praising Athens as the leading city of Greece. He is notable for his clear, smooth style.

Note : Πολλῶν ἡ γλῶττα προτρέχει τῆς διανοίας. In many, the tongue outruns the sense.

Isolationism, political policy in USA, especially after World War I, of isolating America from European affairs, hence reluctance on the part of USA to enter World War II prior to the attack on Pearl Harbour by the Japanese.

isomerism, *ī-som'ĕr-izm,* in chemistry, the phenomenon of chemical compounds having the same molecular formula but different properties ; thus, the isomers butane and isobutane have the formula C_4H_{10}, but the difference between them is due to a different arrangement of the atoms in the molecules. Isomerism is frequently met with among carbon compounds. In certain cases, called stereoisomerism, it is necessary to have three-dimensional formulae to account for the existence of isomers.

isoprene, see RUBBER

isosceles triangle, see TRIANGLE

isothermal lines, see CLIMATE

isotopes, *ī'sō-tōps,* substances with identical chemical properties but different atomic weights ; thus, there are 8 isotopes of lead, all with 82 electrons and 82 protons, but each with a different number of neutrons. Bromine is a mixture of 2 isotopes with atomic weights 79 and 81 ; isotopes of uranium are U-235, U-238, U-239. Actually isotopes are atoms with the same atomic number but different atomic mass. The name was invented by the British scientist, Frederick Soddy. Recently greatly increased use has been made of radio-isotopes, e.g. those made in the atomic pile at Oak Ridge. Radio-sodium is used in medicine. Other radio-isotopes are used in agriculture and industry.

The Harwell Pile, Berkshire, has been producing valuable radio-isotopes since 1949, many of them for export. See MATTER ; RADIOACTIVITY ; SODDY, F.

Israel, STATE OF, see JEWS ; PALESTINE

Israelites, see JEWS

Issus, ancient port of Asia Minor ; here Alexander the Great defeated Darius 333BC.

Istanbul or **Stambul,** *ē-stan-bool',* city and port of Turkey, Europe, formerly cap. of the Turkish Empire ; on a headland in the Sea of Marmora and between the Golden Horn and the Bosphorus. Galata, with its arsenals and docks, and Pera are suburbs. The palace of the sultan (Seraglio) has fine buildings and a famous ' high door.' Of the 379 mosques, St Sophia is the most famous ; much of the city is crowded with mean and narrow streets, but some areas are modern. Industries include leather goods, perfumes, tobacco pipes and gold and silver embroideries ; pop.850,000.

Founded as BYZANTIUM by the Greeks, the city was known as CONSTANTINOPLE from AD330, when it was rebuilt by the Roman Emperor Constantine. It was later the cap. of the Byzantine Empire, or Eastern portion of the Roman Empire, i.e. S. Italy, and what we now call the Balkans, Turkey in Asia, Greece and Egypt.

The Byzantine Empire fell 1453 when the Turks captured Constantinople ; its scholars fled westwards, and thus brought to Europe the ' New Learning ' that led to the Renaissance.

isthmus, *iss'mŭs,* narrow neck of land uniting either two continents (e.g. Panama and Suez), or a peninsula to the mainland, e.g. the isthmus of Corinth.

Italy, formerly a kingdom, but a republic since the abdication of Umberto II (1946) ; area *c.*193,000sq.m ; pop. 46,000,000 ; comprises a European peninsula S. of the Alps between the Adriatic and Tyrrhenian Seas ; has a ' backbone ' of mts. (the Apennines) S. of the fertile plain of Lombardy. The rivers include Po, Adige, Arno and Tiber, and among the lakes are L. Como and L. Maggiore.

The climate is generally warm, so that, in addition to cereals (including wheat), grapes, olives, chestnuts, rice and flax are raised. The silkworm is cultivated on a large scale. Oranges and lemons are grown. Italian wines are famous, and in considerable demand. Though lacking in mineral wealth, Italy produces sulphur, iron pyrites, mercury, lead, zinc and aluminium. Marble is quarried. Manufactures include woollens, cotton, silks, rayon, hemp, linen, motor cars, chemicals and works of art, e.g. pottery, glass (especially Venetian) and mosaics.

Italy has long been favoured by tourists for the sake of its beautiful scenery and for its historic sites and art treasures; Venice, Rome, Milan, Naples and the I. of Capri have their individual attractions. There are the excavated cities of Pompeii and Herculaneum, the glorious buildings of Pisa and Turin. There is St Peter's at Rome and St Mark's in Venice. In Florence, home of some of the greatest art treasures in the world, Dante was born and Savanarola was burned ; Columbus and Mazzini were born at Genoa ; Galileo at Pisa ; Cicero at Arpinum. At Cremona, Stradivari made his superb violins ; at Cannae, Hannibal won his greatest victory (216BC).

A land of artists, musicians, poets, reformers, Italy has Rome, on the R. Tiber, as its capital, once the heart of the vast Roman Empire (see ROME). Remains of its ancient splendour may be seen in countless forms—amphitheatres, temples, aqueducts, villas, triumphal arches, roads, antique pottery, ornaments and sculptures.

The Roman empire, which may be said to have ended *c.*AD489, was followed by the Gothic kingdom of Italy ; and the country was conquered and divided by the Byzantine Empire, the Lombards, the Franks, and, later, invaded by French and German kings, and those of the Austro-Spanish line. Italy broke up into many small city-states, often republican and intensely democratic during the Middle Ages, but ruled after the Renaissance mainly by foreign kings (especially Austrian and Spanish) or by the Pope. Then, in the 19th c., arose leaders like Mazzini, Cavour and Garibaldi, who sought to unite the country into a single kingdom. (This process is known as the Risorgimento or national awakening.) Victor Emmanuel was at last proclaimed sole ruler 1861. To the mainland Sardinia and Sicily were added ; but scarcely had the kingdom won freedom from foreign domination than it came under the Fascist rule of the dictator, Mussolini, 1924. Industry revived. Government was as corrupt as ever but more efficient. Education was made more thorough. A great navy was built, and vast building schemes were inaugurated. Mussolini (*Il Duce*), dreaming of a new Roman empire, invaded Ethiopia (the king of Italy being declared Emperor of Abyssinia 1936). With immense tracts of Libya S. of the Mediterranean, i.e. Libia Italiana, area *c.*810,000sq.m, Mussolini extended his dominions in Europe by conquering Albania after five days of warfare 1939. In World War II Italy sided with Germany, but was compelled to sue for an armistice 1943. Rome fell 4 June 1944, so Mussolini's gains were soon lost.

From 1948 Signor de Gasperi was head of a Coalition Government, and by 1951 Communism seemed to be weakening.

The people of Italy, chiefly RC, speak Italian, a language derived directly from Latin. Great Italians, besides those already mentioned, include Petrarch, Boccaccio, Ariosto, Machiavelli, Tasso, Leonardo da Vinci, Michelangelo, Titian, St Francis of Assisi and Verdi.

The island of SARDINIA, part of Italy, is 170m long, and has an area of 9,300 sq.m. The cap. is Cagliari. Timber, wine and minerals are produced, and there are fisheries, including sardines, named from the island.

SICILY, separated from Italy by the Strait of Messina (2m broad) has an area of 9,940sq.m. It is mountainous, and has Mt Etna, an active volcano. The valleys are exceptionally fertile. Wheat and fruit are grown, and there are sardine fisheries. Sulphur is exported. The largest city is Palermo.

Ithaca, *ith'ä-kä,* old name for the small Ionian island now called Thiaki. Ithaca was the fabled home of Ulysses (Odysseus).

Ivan, *i-văn',* name of several Russian rulers, e.g. Ivan IV (1530–84), the first Russian ruler to call himself Tsar, and to conclude a treaty with England.

ivory, hard, fine-grained, creamy white substance derived from the tusks of the hippopotamus, walrus and elephant. The best is obtained from the tusk of the elephant, that from the African elephant being the finest of all. A single tusk sometimes weighs 200lb. Ivory is used for ornamental purposes, billiard balls, etc.

Ivory Coast, colony of French W. Africa ; the people are mostly Negroes ; products include coffee and palm-oil.

ivy, evergreen that winds round trees (often killing them) and climbs up walls to a great height, clinging by means of rootlets. It has glossy five-lobed leaves, yellow-green flowers and small black berries. See POISONOUS PLANTS

Iwojima, *ē-ō-jē'mä*, Japanese island 660m from Tokyo ; captured by Americans March 1945.

Ixion, *iks-i'on*, in old Greek tales, King of Lapithae, Thessaly ; condemned for misdemeanour to be bound to an ever-turning wheel.

Izmir, *iz-mēr*, town, Turkey ; formerly called Smyrna ; pop.185,000. It is a notable naval base on the Aegean Sea.

Izvestia, official daily paper of the Supreme Soviet of Russia. It was founded 1917.

J

J, see MECHANICAL EQUIVALENT OF HEAT

jackal, *jak'awl*, brownish animal akin to the dog and wolf. The Egyptian breed is *c*.50in long and 16in high at the shoulder ; the Asiatic somewhat smaller. In both the tail is short and bushy. Jackals feed mostly on carrion. They herd together in packs.

jackdaw, see CROW

Jackson, *jak'sŭn*, cap. Mississippi state, USA ; pop.62,000.

Jackson, ANDREW (1767–1845), seventh President of the USA (1828–36).

Jackson, THOMAS JONATHAN (1824–63), American soldier, known as Stonewall Jackson after the first battle of Bull Run, where, as Confederate (southern states) leader in the Civil War, he showed indomitable courage and stern discipline. He was General Lee's most trusted supporter.

Jacksonville, *-vil*, commercial town and railway centre, Florida, USA ; has great river trade (St John's R.), and is a tourist centre ; pop.173,000.

Jacob, *jā'kŭb*, OT character, younger son of Isaac. He stole the blessing and inheritance intended for his brother Esau. He had a vision at Bethel of a ladder set up from earth to heaven ; journeyed to Haran ; owned many flocks and herds. He was later known as Israel. Among his sons was Joseph, who caused his aged father to settle in Egypt (Genesis 25–49).

Jacob, NAOMI (1889–), English novelist ; had a varied career and a hard life ; fought for women's rights ; supporter of the Labour Party. Her books include *A Passage Perilous*.

Jacobins, *jak'ōbins*, revolutionary extremists in Paris during the French Revolution, who did much to bring about the death of the king, roused the working class against the middle classes (who had been in the forefront of the first phase of the Revolution), and directed the Reign of Terror. The Jacobin Society ended 1794 with the death of Robespierre.

Jacobites, *jak'ō-bīts*, those who, after 1688, refused to accept William and Mary as rightful rulers of Britain, and supported the claims of James II and his descendants. See JAMES EDWARD

Jacobs, WILLIAM WYMARK (1863–1943), *b* London ; won fame with his humorous stories and novels, almost all about seafaring men, e.g. *The Skipper's Wooing*, *A Master of Craft*.

Jacquard, JOSEPH MARIE, *ja-kärd*, *jhä-kär'* (1752–1834), French inventor, *b* Lyons ; fought in the Revolution ; invented a loom which completely changed the weaving industry.

jade, *jād*, mineral, a silicate of magnesia. It is usually green, but sometimes yellowish or white ; found in NZ, Siberia, and especially in China, where skilled craftsmen carve exquisite jade ornaments.

Jaffa, port, Palestine. Though old, much of it has been recently rebuilt. Jaffa exports oranges, olive oil and wool. It is called Joppa in the Bible ; pop.94,000.

Jagger, CHARLES SARGEANT (1885–1935), sculptor, born in Yorkshire ; notable for several war memorials, especially that of the Royal Artillery at Hyde Park Corner, London. His brother, David, won fame as a portrait-painter.

jaguar, largest of the spotted cats of Central and S. America, and of the Argentine. The jaguar (*Felis onca*), a powerful, tree-climbing beast, is over 4ft long ; hunts monkeys, small animals, alligators, and sometimes attacks domestic animals.

Jain, *jīn*, follower of the Indian religion, Jainism, founded in the 6th c. BC. Jains eat no animal food and take care never to kill any creature. Their temples are among the finest examples of Indian architecture.

Jamaica, *jä-mā'kä*, British island in the Caribbean Sea, 90m S. of Cuba. One of the W. Indies, its area is 4,450sq.m ; pop.1,238,000. The name means 'land of wood and water,' and Jamaica has beautiful scenery with fertile valleys and mts. rising to 7,388ft. The tropical climate is healthy. There is excellent pasture. Products include timber, dyes, fruits, nuts, maize and Indian corn ; the chief exports are sugar (see PLATE 12), rum and coffee.

Discovered 1494 by Columbus, and formerly Spanish, the island has been British since 1655. It was once the HQ of pirates. The capital is Kingston.

jamboree, see BOY SCOUTS

James, *jāmz*, saint and apostle ; a fisherman, and a son of Zebedee, he was put to death by Herod Agrippa AD44 (Acts 12). Also James, son of Alphaeus ; and James, possibly the brother of Jesus.

James I and VI (1566–1625), King of Great Britain, *b* Edinburgh ; son of Mary Queen of Scots and Lord Darnley : ruled first as James VI of Scotland ; succeeded Elizabeth as King of England 1603.

King James asserted the Divine Right of Kings, and came into conflict with Parliament. He failed to please either the Protestants or the Roman Catholics, the latter organising the Gunpowder Plot 1605. Controlled for a time by the Duke of Buckingham, his foreign policy involved Great Britain in the Thirty Years' War.

Though deceitful and tactless, James was learned and sincerely religious ; a witty Frenchman described him as 'the wisest fool in Christendom.' Through weakness and what he called 'kingcraft' he led the way to the Civil War of Charles I's reign.

James II and VII (1633–1701), King of Great Britain and Ireland, younger son of Charles I ; as Duke of York he escaped to France in the Civil War ; was Lord High Admiral for a time when his brother (Charles II) was king, but had to resign (under the *Test Act* of 1673) because he openly confessed himself a RC. His second marriage (to Mary of Modena), a Catholic, did not improve his popularity, but he succeeded Charles II 1685.

His reign saw Monmouth's rebellion collapse at Sedgemoor 1685 ; the brutal policy of Judge Jeffreys ; James's *Declaration of Indulgence* 1687 ; the acquittal of the Seven Bishops 1688, the year in which his son (James, later known as the Old Pretender) was born. The possibility of a continuation of the Stuarts led the Whigs to invite William of Orange and his wife, Mary, daughter of James, to become king and queen. William landed at Torbay 1688, and James fled to France, where, after feeble attempts to regain the throne, he died.

It should be noticed that although James II was tactless, politically blind, often obstinate, he was ahead of his times in desiring religious tolerance, and wished to govern wisely. See JACOBITES

James I (1394–1437), crowned as King of Scotland 1424, after release from imprisonment in England from 1406. His stern rule provoked anger among the nobility, and in 1437 he was murdered at Perth. He was a poet, and *The Kingis Quair* (i.e. *The King's Book*), a long love-poem in Scots, is probably his work.

James II (1430–60), King of Scotland, son of James I ; ruled from 1437 ; killed at the siege of Roxburgh Castle.

James III (1451–88), King of Scotland ; succeeded his father, James II, 1460. His reign was marked by many rebellions ; like his grandfather, James I, he was murdered.

James IV (1473–1513), King of Scotland ; led a rebellion against his father, James III ; ruled from 1488. Brilliant but erratic, he was a popular king ; he married Margaret, daughter of Henry VII of England ; quarrelled with Henry VIII, and was killed at Flodden.

James V (1512–42), King of Scotland ; son of James IV, whom he succeeded before he was two ; governed from 1530 ; his daughter was Mary Queen of Scots, born just seven weeks before her father's death.

James Edward (1688–1766), son of James II of England, hence a Stuart prince. He was known as the Old Pretender ; *b* London ; hurriedly taken to France, living there with his exiled father ; claimed the English throne, and raised an unsuccessful rebellion, the Fifteen (1715) ; *d* Rome.

His son CHARLES EDWARD (1720–88) was the Young Pretender (' Bonnie Prince Charlie '), *b* Rome ; hero of the Forty-Five (rebellion of 1745), when he gathered many Highlanders in Scotland, captured Edinburgh, defeated the government troops at Prestonpans (9m from Edinburgh), invaded England as far as Derby, but was crushingly defeated near Inverness at Culloden Moor 1746. Becoming a fugitive, he was gallantly defended by loyal Scottish friends, notably FLORA MACDONALD (1722–90), who enabled him (disguised as Betty Burke) to escape to France. He *d* Rome.

James, HENRY (1843–1916), *b* New York ; became a naturalised British subject ; famous for over 40 novels written in masterly style, and with attention to the psychological development of character, e.g. *The American*, *The Turn of the Screw*.

James, WILLIAM (1842–1910), American psychologist, brother of Henry James.

Jameson, SIR LEANDER STARR (1853–1917), *b* Edinburgh ; known as ' Dr Jim ' when administrator of Rhodesia ; led the ' Jameson Raid ' 1895 to help the Uitlanders of Johannesburg ; after surrendering to the Boers was imprisoned by the British ; Premier of the Cape Legislative Assembly 1904–8.

Jameson, STORM (1897–   ), novelist, *b* Whitby, Yorkshire ; author of *The*

Lovely Ship, Farewell to Youth, Cloudless May, The Other Side.

Jamestown, ruined village, Virginia, USA ; at the mouth of the James R. ; site of the first English settlement (1607).

jam music, see JAZZ

Jamshedpur, see INDIA

Japan, called Nippon Koku, i.e. Land of the Rising Sun, empire comprising 4 large islands (Honshu, Shikoku, Kyushu and Hokkaido or Yezo) and *c*.4,200 smaller islands off the east coast of China and in the N. Pacific Ocean, total area *c*.148,000sq.m ; pop.74,000,000. Before World War II Japanese possessions included Formosa, part of Manchuria, Korea (85,000sq.m), Manchukuo, etc.

Japan is mountainous (Fuji-san, the sacred mountain is 12,370ft) and has many volcanoes. It is subject to severe earthquakes. The coast is indented ; the valleys are fertile, but much of the land is unproductive. The climate is generally moist, with hot summers and very cold winters.

Mainly agricultural, Japan grows rice, wheat, potatoes and tobacco. The immense forests product timber, and the country is noted for lacquer trees, camphor and mulberry ; there is an abundance of fruit trees, e.g. orange and loquat. Flowers are many and varied.

Minerals include gold, silver, copper, lead, tin, iron, chromite and petroleum. Silk, cotton, earthenware, lacquered ware, paper, toys and fancy goods are manufactured.

The cap., Tokyo, has a pop. of over 4,800,000. Other towns include Osaka, Kyoto, Nagoya, Yokohama. The people have recently made rapid strides towards European standards of education, and have largely remodelled their towns in accordance with Western ideas. The Japanese are highly artistic. Their religions include Shintoism and Buddhism. The Emperor (Mikado) was until recently regarded as a divine being. Foreigners were not allowed in the country prior to 1853, and a form of feudalism persisted till 1868. Wars were fought for more living space, 1894 against China, 1904 against Russia ; and a dispute with China over Manchuria led to the bitter Sino-Japanese war 1937, Japan taking Manchukuo, and continuing to attack China (especially from the air) till World War II, when, after raiding Pearl Harbour (1941), she caused the USA and her allies to declare war. Though the Japanese had considerable successes at first (e.g. Singapore and the Philippines), the USA mounted a huge attack, culminating in the destruction of Hiroshima and Nagasaki, Aug 1945, when atom-bombs were dropped. Unconditional surrender to the United Nations meant the end of the Sino-Japanese war also. After the war Japan was occupied by Allied forces.

Prior to 1945 Japanese mandated territories (the whole area being known as Nanyo) included the Marshall Islands, Carolines and Ladrones.

A tremendous change in Japanese outlook has recently taken place. The Japanese have declared their determination never to go to war again, and restitution is now being made to China, Burma and India. The people are able to manufacture goods for peace but not for war, and under USA guidance are being trained in the principles of democracy. In January 1951 President Truman sent Mr J. Foster Dulles to study political conditions in the Pacific area, and to consider the possibilites of a Japanese peace treaty with a view to incorporating Japan into a Pacific bulwark against Russian aggression.

Japan, SEA OF, sea between Korea and Russia ; almost tideless, but has dangerous shallows.

Japheth, *jā'feth,* one of the sons of Noah (Genesis 10).

japonica, *jä-pon'ik-ä,* ornamental wall plant introduced into Britain from Japan in the 18th c. ; has white, orange, or red flowers often appearing in spring before the foliage.

Jarrow, *jär'rō,* port, Co. Durham ; on the R. Tyne ; noted for shipbuilding, iron and coal ; home of Bede, who died here AD735 ; pop.26,000.

Jason and the Golden Fleece, *jā'sun,* subject of an old Greek tale. Jason's father, Aeson, King of Iolcus, had been removed from his throne by his wicked halfbrother Pelias. As Jason was the rightful heir, Pelias sent him on the dangerous (and apparently impossible) errand of bringing back the Golden Fleece.

Jason set out with many heroes— called Argonauts because they sailed in a marvellous ship, *Argo,* built by Argos, one of the heroes—and after an eventful voyage they reached Colchis. But King Aeëtes forbade Jason to take the fleece from the grove of Mars till he had tamed two fire-breathing oxen with brass feet, ploughed a field with them, and sown it with dragon's teeth, every one of which would spring up as a warrior and fight. In spite of all these difficulties, Jason succeeded with the aid of the king's daughter, Medea, a sorceress, who fell in love with him. He and Medea eventually reached Iolcus, where Pelias was murdered.

jasper, crystalline variety of quartz ; may be red, brown, or black ; sometimes streaked ; takes a high polish.

Jassy, *yäs'ē,* trading city, Rumania ; pop.105,000.

Java, see NETHERLANDS

Java Sea, *jä'vä,* shallow strait between Java and Borneo.

jay, see CROW

jazz, syncopated dance music, based on African music taken to America by slaves. The melody is secondary to the rhythm and colour. Introduced from USA to Britain *c*.1918, jazz led *c*.1935 to *swing music,* largely based on simple harmonics, and making much use of the guitar, piano, percussion instruments and saxophone. It has a slight melodic theme. Other variations have given us *jam music* and *rippling rhythm*.

The great feature of jazz is that it allows for much extemporisation. What is termed authentic jazz has always either two or four beats to the bar, and throughout there is a steady and unvarying pulse supplied by percussion instruments. Its weakness (as in swing music) is that so often the extemporisations are nothing more than melodic cliches, e.g. such rhythmic devices as the rubato or ' hold-off ' effects, staccato interjections of the trumpets, flamboyant and pretentious openings and conventional endings.

That jazz is popular proves that it makes a strong appeal, but nevertheless it is merely a phase in musical history ; it appeals to sentiment alone, and requires of the listener no great effort of attention; it is not creative to any considerable degree, since it is actually built up on a series of formulae and conventions.

Jeans, SIR JAMES (1877–1946), scientist and author ; elaborated a tidal theory of the creation of the solar system ; wrote fascinating books on astronomy, e.g. *The Universe Around Us, The Mysterious Universe, The Stars in their Courses.*

Jedburgh, *jed'bŭ-rŭ,* royal burgh, co.tn, Roxburghshire ; has a ruined abbey founded 1118 ; famous for woollens, particularly tweeds.

jeep, small open car capable of being driven over rough ground ; much used by Americans in World War II.

Jefferies, RICHARD, *jef'riz* (1848–87), born near Swindon ; an accurate and observant naturalist, also a superb writer of prose, e.g. *The Gamekeeper at Home, Wild Life in a Southern County.* Read also *Wood Magic, Bevis,* and his autobiography, *The Story of My Heart.*

Jefferson, THOMAS (1743–1826) American statesman, born in Virginia ; chief author of the *Declaration of Independence* 1776. After being ambassador to France, he became Secretary of State under George Washington, 1790, and leader of the Democratic party. He stood for the independence of the various states, and was opposed by Alexander Hamilton, who believed in centralised rule. Twice President of the USA (1801–9), Jefferson was responsible for establishing the cap. of the USA at Washington ; introduced successful financial measures ; made further expansion of USA possible by adding the Louisiana Territory ; and believed wholeheartedly in government of the people by the people.

Jeffreys, GEORGE, *jef'riz* (1648–89), better known as Judge Jeffreys ; notorious for his treatment of people involved in the so-called Popish Plot, in the trials of the Rye House plotters, and of rebels in the Monmouth Rebellion 1685 ; died in the Tower of London.

Jehoiakim, *jē-hoi'ä-kim,* King of Judah ; reigned 608–597BC (2 Kings 23).

Jehoshaphat, *jē-hosh'ä-fat,* King of Judah c.873–849BC ; renowned for his justice and piety.

Jehu, *jē'hū,* King of Israel 842–815BC ; noted for his furious driving as a charioteer.

Jellicoe, 1ST EARL, *jel'i-kō* (1859–1935), admiral ; b Southampton ; commander of the Grand Fleet 1914–16, when, after the battle of Jutland, he became First Sea Lord, and combated the U-boat menace.

jellyfish, popular name for various *hydrozoa* in the sea, one species being bell-shaped, the mouth fringed with tentacles. A stinging species in British waters is c.7in across, but in the tropics similar kinds may be several feet in diameter ; the Mediterranean PORTU-GUESE MAN-OF-WAR is a jellyfish with a blue bladder filled with gas.

JELLYFISH

Jena, *yä'nä,* historic town near Weimar, Germany ; scene of the defeat of the Prussians by the French, 1806 ; associated with Schiller, Luther and Goethe ; famous for its university (1548) ; long known for the Zeiss optical works ; pop.53,000.

Jenner, EDWARD (1749–1823), doctor, b Berkeley, Gloucestershire ; famous as the discoverer of vaccination, a preventive measure against what was then the scourge of smallpox ; received grants from Parliament of £10,000, and later £20,000. See VACCINATION

Jennings, SARAH, see MARLBOROUGH, DUKE OF

Jephthah, *jef'thä,* OT Judge of Israel (Judges 11, 12).

jerboa, *jer-bō'ä,* mouse-like animal of E. Europe, Asia and N. Africa ; c.6in long, with a tufted tail ; hops much as the kangaroo ; lives in burrows ; feeds on roots. Said to be the original ' desert rat ' of World War II.

Jeremiah, *jer-ē-mī'ä,* Hebrew patriot and prophet of the 7th c. BC ; born near Jerusalem ; urged his countrymen to seek aid from Egypt against Assyria ; saw his people taken into captivity ; often spoken of as 'the weeping prophet,' but the OT book of Lamentations is probably not all his work.

jer-falcon, see HAWK

Jericho, *jer'i-kō,* ancient city and modern village, Palestine, *c.*15m NE. of Jerusalem. The OT story of the walls falling down when the Israelites had encompassed the city seven times is confirmed by modern archaeologists.

Jeroboam, *jer-ō-bō'äm,* name of two kings of Israel : Jeroboam I, ruled 937–915BC, son of Nebat ; Jeroboam II, ruled 781–740BC, son of Joash ; led Israel to victory against the Syrians.

Jerome, JEROME K. (1859–1927), humorous writer, *b* Walsall, especially famous for *Three Men in a Boat* ; wrote the play *The Passing of the Third Floor Back.*

Jersey, *jĕr'zi,* largest of the Channel Islands ; noted for Jersey cattle and early potatoes ; has been English since 1066 ; cap. St Helier.

Jersey City, city separated from New York, USA, by the Hudson R. ; noted for its varied manufactures and as a railway centre ; has relics of an early Dutch colony ; pop.301,000.

Jerusalem, see PALESTINE

Jesse, OT character ; father of David (1 Samuel 16) ; hence Jesse window, a church window, showing the descent of Jesus from Jesse.

Jesuits, see LOYOLA, IGNATIUS

Jesus, see CHRIST

Jesus College, name of two colleges : one at Oxford (founded 1571), the other at Cambridge (founded 1496). Both have a high proportion of Welsh students ; Jesus, Cambridge, is famous (or notorious) for a sometimes ungraceful style of rowing invented by Steve Fairbairn, the well-known ' coach.'

jet, variety of lignite ; intensely black ; takes a high polish ; found at Whitby, Yorkshire ; also in Bavaria, France, Germany, etc ; used for ornaments.

jet-propulsion, see AVIATION

Jews, nation of *c.*11,000,000 ; much persecuted, with no country of their own until recently, but treasuring great traditions.

A Semitic race, the Jews are sometimes called Hebrews (their language being Hebrew) or Israelites because they claim descent from Jacob, later named Israel. They regard Abraham as the ' father of their nation,' and it was he who *c.*2000BC journeyed from Ur of the Chaldees to SE. Palestine (now called Israel). For long the Israelites were slaves in Egypt, being led, after 40 years in the desert, to the borders of Canaan (or Palestine) by Moses, there becoming a powerful nation notable for their prophets, e.g. Amos, Isaiah, Jeremiah, and their kings Saul, David, who built the fortified city of Jerusalem, and his son, Solomon, who *c.*1000BC raised the Temple on the hill known as Zion. The N. part of the kingdom was overthrown 721BC ; the S. *c.*586BC ; the Temple was destroyed AD70 by the Roman emperor Titus. The Jews were robbed of national life AD130 by the Emperor Hadrian, and from that time they became a scattered people making their homes first in Greece, Egypt, Italy, and later in almost every country in the world, notably Russia, USA (which has now over 5,000,000 Jews) and the UK.

The Jews had been farmers in their own land, but they became men of business, especially money-lenders. They lived as a rule in a Jewish neighbourhood known as a *ghetto (get'ō)* or Jewry ; and were often shockingly ill-treated by Christians, as we read in Shakespeare's play *The Merchant of Venice,* where Shylock voices the cry of all Jews. They were severely persecuted in England in the 12th c. ; in Russia 1882 ; but the most terrible persecution began *c.*1933 when Hitler declared that Nazi Germany must have no trace of Jewish blood.

' Zionism ' is a world-wide movement of Jews towards making Palestine the home of the Jewish nation again ; from 1919 to 1948 Palestine was administered as a mandated territory by Great Britain. A limited number of Jews were allowed to settle in the country, and it was hoped that ultimately it would be possible to establish an independent state in which Jews and Arabs would live together peaceably. In May 1948 the British withdrew. Arabian armies invaded Palestine from Egypt, Iraq, Transjordan and Syria ; but the Jews proclaimed the State of Israel, obtained for it a useful measure of American and Russian recognition, and resisted successfully.

The Jews' most precious book, *The Talmud,* is based on the OT. Much of what we know of the Jews of Christ's day comes from JOSEPHUS (*jō-sē'fŭs*), historian of the Jews, *b c.*AD37. In NT times, as before, the Jews worshipped one God, Jehovah or Yahweh ; were fanatically religious, regarding themselves as God's chosen people, and all other nations as Gentiles ; dreamed of a Messiah who should deliver them from Roman oppression ; and had many religious groups or sects, e.g. the well-to-do *Sadducees* ; also the *Pharisees,* who thought religion meant keeping the laws of Moses. Their teachers were *rabbis.* The chief council was the *sanhedrin (san'e-drin),* a committee of 71, with a high priest as chairman. Their churches (then as now) were styled *synagogues (sin'a-gogs).* See PALESTINE

Jew's harp, old musical instrument held between the teeth, the musician plucking a steel tongue and controlling its vibrations with his lips.

Jezebel, *jez'ē-b'l,* wife of Ahab, King of Israel. Cunning and unscrupulous, she was thrown from a window by order of Jehu. See 1 Kings 18, 19, 21.

Jezreel, anciently a town, Palestine, c.11m from Nazareth ; home of King Ahab in OT times.

Jibuti, see SOMALILAND

Jinnah, MOHAMED ALI (1876–1948), Indian lawyer and politician ; President of the Muslim League 1916, 1920, 1934 ; appointed first Governor-General of Pakistan 1947.

jinriksha, see RICKSHAW

Joab, jŏ'ab, OT soldier ; nephew of David. See 2 Samuel 2, 1 Kings 2.

Joad, DR CYRIL EDWIN MITCHINSON, jŏd (1891-), popular writer on philosophy ; became well-known to the general public as a member of the BBC Brains Trust team ; head of the department of philosophy and psychology, London University, since 1930 ; his books include *Common Sense Ethics, Mind and Matter, Is Christianity True? The Mind and Its Workings* and *After Dinner Philosophy.*

Joan of Arc (1412–31), French heroine and saint (St Joan) ; lived 19 years and won lasting fame.

She was born in the village of Domrémy when almost all the N. of France was in the hands of the English and their allies, the Burgundians. The traditional story is that at 16 this farmer's daughter heard voices bidding her deliver France from the English. Although her father was angry with her, and although the parish priest laughed, she at last persuaded a soldier to take her to Charles VII, whose court was then at Chinon. In some mystic way Joan recognised the king among a crowd of courtiers, and her sincerity impressed him so much that he gave her leave to lead soldiers to Orleans, then besieged by the English.

With a suit of shining armour, a white horse, a sword, and a white and gold banner with a portrait of Christ, she rode at the head of the king's armies, and drove the English from Orleans 1429, doing in 8 days what the French had hitherto been unable to do in 7 months.

Her triumph put new heart into all Frenchmen, inspiring them to fight as never before. Known as the ' Maid of Orleans,' Joan became the spirit of reconquest, and after other successes had the joy of seeing Charles VII crowned at Reims, July 1429.

The Maid of France then wished to return to her own village, but the king would not allow her ; she led other armies, was wounded in the attack on Paris, betrayed by the worthless king, who made a secret truce with his enemies, and captured by the Burgundians, who sold her to the English. She was tried by the Inquisition. A council of French churchmen at Rouen decided that her voices had not been from God but from the devil. Finally, 30 May 1431, she was tied to a stake in the market-place

and burned as a witch, an Englishman giving her a wooden cross to hold in her last moments. Her faith eventually brought to an end the miserable Hundred Years' War.

Such is the traditional account. How much is true, how much merely legendary, it is impossible to say ; but it must be mentioned that Margaret Murray has made out a very strong case for thinking that Joan was in fact a member of the persecuted witch-cult (see WITCHCRAFT).

Joan of Arc was made a saint 1920. Her story is told in *Saint Joan,* a play by Bernard Shaw.

Job, jŏb, book of the OT, its hero, Job, being a prosperous and righteous man who, though severely tried by misfortunes of every kind, remains loyal to God, and keeps his faith. The author of this poetic drama is unknown. The patience of Job is proverbial.

Joel, one of the lesser prophets of the OT. His book was written c.500BC or later. He lived in Jerusalem.

Joffre, JOSEPH JACQUES CÉSAIRE, zhawf'r (1852–1931), French general ; in charge of a battery during the siege of Paris 1870 ; Commander-in-Chief of the French armies in World War I, but resigned 1916. A man of simplicity and sincerity, he was so much beloved by his countrymen, and especially by his soldiers, that they called him Papa Joffre.

Johannesburg, yō-han'es-bŭrg, town, Union of S. Africa ; in the Transvaal ; associated with gold production at Witwatersrand ; linked by air with London ; pop. 728,000 (including 324,000 Europeans) ; city of gold and skyscrapers ; declared to be the richest town of the S. hemisphere ; has 350,000 gold-miners.

John, saint and apostle ; son of Zebedee ; kinsman of Jesus ; fisherman on the Sea of Galilee ; with his brother James was one of Christ's first disciples. To him Christ committed the care of his mother. Tradition says that John lived to a great age at Ephesus.

It was long supposed that John, ' the beloved disciple,' wrote the Gospel of St John, stressing the divine nature of Christ, but this is now questioned by scholars. It is also regarded now as extremely doubtful if St John wrote the prophetic Book of Revelation (the last book of the NT), evidently the work of an exile in the island of Patmos.

John, name of twenty-three popes, including John VIII (d 882) ; John XII (d 964) ; and John XXII (d 1334), who resided at Avignon, and introduced a new system of taxation.

John (1296–1346), King of Bohemia ; killed at Crécy.

John (1167–1216), King of England, son of Henry II ; nicknamed Lackland ; rebelled against his father ; plotted against his brother, Richard I, while Richard was abroad ; reigned from 1199, and proved himself wholly incapable. Involved in a war with France, he lost Normandy, earned the contempt of the barons, and was compelled by them to set his seal to *Magna Carta*, at Runnymede, 1215.

John was responsible for the murder of his nephew, Arthur, Richard I's son and legitimate heir. He quarrelled with the pope (Innocent III) over the election of Stephen Langton as Archbishop of Canterbury, and was excommunicated.

John II (1319–64), King of France from 1350 ; known as The Good ; defeated and captured by the Black Prince at Poitiers 1356 ; died in captivity in London.

John III (1624–96), King of Poland, actually John Sobieski ; ruled from 1674 ; proved to be a capable soldier ; fought against the Turks, whom he defeated at Vienna 1683, and liberated Hungary, but was continually busy with intrigues.

John (1545–78), Spanish soldier known as Don John of Austria ; crushed the Turks at Lepanto 1571.

John, AUGUSTUS (1878–   ), artist, *b* Tenby, Pembrokeshire ; notable for his portraits.

John Bull, imaginary person supposed to be a typical Britisher ; stands for the spirit of the British people. The name was first used *c*.1712. John Bull is pictured as a sturdy, weather-beaten English farmer, often with a bulldog at his feet.

John of Gaunt, *gawnt* (1340–99), 4th son of Edward III, *b* Ghent (known in England as Gaunt) ; created Duke of Lancaster when 22 ; supported Edward the Black Prince when fighting in Acquitaine ; married Blanche, daughter of the former Henry Duke of Lancaster ; made repeated attempts to become King of Castile (Spain) ; loyally supported the young king, Richard II, over whom he had much influence.

A wise and moderate counsellor, he had great influence in the politics of the day. In his last years he banished his own son, who later returned as Henry IV. John of Gaunt championed John Wycliffe and the Lollards, and was the patron of Geoffrey Chaucer.

John o' Groat's House, spot near Duncansby Head, Scotland, regarded as the most northerly point of the British Isles ; named, it is said, from an octagonal house built by a Dutchman, Groot or Groat, *c*.1600. It had eight doors so that (according to the story) each of the builder's quarrelsome sons could enter by his own.

John the Baptist, last of the prophets to foretell the coming of Jesus, whom he actually baptised in the R. Jordan ; lived chiefly in the desert ; warned people to repent of their sins ; rebuked Herod Antipas, Governor of Galilee, for marrying Herodias ; beheaded *c*.AD28. He was called the Baptist because he baptised his followers. See Matthew 3, 11, 14 and 21.

Johnson, AMY (1905–41), aviator ; won fame by a solo flight from England to Australia in 19 days, 1930 ; married J. A. Mollison, the noted airman who, 1932, made the first solo E.–W. flight across the N. Atlantic.

Johnson, ANDREW (1808–75), American statesman, *b* N. Carolina ; 17th President of the USA, 1865.

Johnson, SAMUEL (1709–84), often referred to as Dr Johnson ; *b* Lichfield, Staffordshire ; almost blinded, as a child, by smallpox, and was awkward in his movements, having odd twitchings. Although the poorest, he was the cleverest scholar at Oxford.

After being a schoolmaster at Edial, near Lichfield, he travelled to London 1737 with David Garrick. He tried to earn a living by writing, but often went hungry ; published two periodicals, *The Rambler* and *The Idler* ; earned £100 in a week by writing a novel, *Rasselas* ; was twice arrested for debt, but was aided by Samuel Richardson. Johnson founded a club attended by Sir Joshua Reynolds, Edmund Burke, Oliver Goldsmith, etc., and from 1762 received a government pension of £300 a year. He wrote *Lives of the Poets*, and published a scholarly edition of Shakespeare's plays.

Dr Johnson's greatest literary achievement was his *English Dictionary*, at which he toiled in a house in Gough Square, London. As early as 1747 he outlined his plan to Lord Chesterfield, but his lordship took little notice of the unknown scribbler. When, after seven years, the great and immediately popular work was complete, Lord Chesterfield hastened to congratulate Johnson, who replied in a celebrated letter (see CHESTERFIELD).

We happen to know much of Dr Johnson's faults, his mode of dress, his ways of life, his difficulties and triumphs, and his manner of speech (he was, perhaps, the greatest and best talker England has ever had) because a Scotsman, JAMES BOSWELL (1740–95), took careful notes of almost everything Johnson did or said. Boswell, a lawyer, *b* Edinburgh, wrote a famous *Life of Dr Samuel Johnson* (published 1791), one of the most vivid and fascinating biographies in any language, a living portrait of a rude, ungainly figure with a kind heart, a mighty genius, and an unconquerable spirit.

The following sayings are typical of Johnson :

When two Englishmen meet, their first talk is of the weather.

A man is generally better pleased when he has a good dinner upon his table, than when his wife talks Greek.

When you see a Whig you see a rascal.

Sir, let me tell you, the noblest prospect which a Scotchman ever sees is the high road that leads him to England !

When a man is tired of London he is tired of life.

Johnston, SIR HARRY HAMILTON (1858–1927), explorer, *b* London ; made expeditions to various regions in Africa ; discovered the okapi 1900.

Johore, state in the south of the Malay peninsula ; about the size of Wales ; cap. Johore Bahru. Under British administration, it is noted for rubber, palm-oil and pineapples, etc.

Jonah, *jō′nä,* Hebrew prophet whose story is told in the OT book of Jonah with much symbolism ; probably a parable to show that God is more than a national deity.

Jonathan, OT character, son of Saul ; won renown as a soldier when fighting the Philistines ; chiefly remembered as the great friend of David (1 Samuel 13, 14, 18, 20, 23, 31, and 2 Samuel 1).
  Note (2 Samuel 1) : *Saul and Jonathan were lovely and pleasant in their lives, and in their death they were not divided.*

Jones, EDWARD GERMAN, see GERMAN, EDWARD

Jones, SIR HAROLD SPENCER (1890–   ), Astronomer Royal since 1933 ; author of fascinating books, e.g. *Worlds without End, Life on other Worlds.*

Jones, INIGO (1573–1652), architect, *b* London ; introduced the Palladian style of architecture into England from Italy.

Jones, PAUL (1747–92), American sailor and adventurer ; born in Scotland ; engaged in the slave trade ; settled in Virginia. In the war of American Independence he harassed British shipping, and engaged in a memorable fight off the Yorkshire coast 1779. It was in this engagement that, asked if he would surrender, Paul Jones replied (even though his ship was sinking) : *I have not yet begun to fight.*

jonquil, *jong′kwil* (*Narcissus jonquilla*), garden plant with spear-like leaves, and 2–6 fragrant yellow flowers clustered at the top of a leafless stem.

Jonson, BEN (1573–1637), dramatist, *b* Westminster (London) ; served in Flanders ; became an actor ; produced his first play, *Every Man in His Humour,* 1598. Favoured by James I, for whom he wrote 30 masques, he was noted for his classical comedies (in which he humorously ridicules contemporary life), e.g. *Volpone, The Silent Woman, The Alchemist.* He combined learning with literary charm in his plays and poems. Two well-known poems of his are, *Drink to me only,* and his epitaph on Shakespeare. Though favoured by noble lords in earlier life, he later lost much of their patronage, but for long he was the ruling spirit of the Mermaid Tavern, and the somewhat quarrelsome friend of Chapman, Beaumont, Fletcher, Donne and Shakespeare. He died in poverty, and his tomb in Westminster Abbey has the famous epitaph, *O Rare Ben Jonson.*

Joppa, see JAFFA

Joseph, *jō′zef,* son of Jacob ; *b* Haran, Iraq (Mesopatamia) ; sold by his jealous brothers to merchants, who sold him again to Potiphar, a high official in the court of Pharaoh. Owing to skill in interpreting dreams, and other services, Joseph became Prime Minister of Egypt, where, later, Jacob and his family settled (Genesis 37–50).

Joseph, husband of Mary, the mother of Jesus. A native of Bethlehem, he was a carpenter, and is thought to have died before Christ began his ministry.

Joseph of Arimathea, *ari′mä-thē-ä,* wealthy Jew who was a secret disciple of Jesus. Christ was buried in a tomb that had been prepared for Joseph. See GLASTON-BURY

Josephine (1763–1814), married the Viscount de Beauharnais, who was guillotined 1794. She became the wife of Napoleon Bonaparte (1796), and thus Empress of France. She was divorced by Napoleon 1810.

Josephus, see JEWS

Joshua, *josh′ū-ä,* OT soldier ; leader of the Israelites after Moses ; conquered Canaan. Also the name of the OT book giving an account of his life and death.

Josiah, *jō-sī′ä,* King of Judah *c.*639–608BC ; did much to rid the land of idolatry.

joule, in physics, unit of work, i.e. work done in 1 second by an electric current of 1 ampere flowing through a resistance of 1 ohm ; hence 1 joule = 10^7 ergs, or 3,600,000 joules = 1 KWH (kilowatt-hour), or 4·2 joules = 1 calorie or 0·738 foot-pound.

Joule, JAMES PRESCOTT, *jool* (1818–89), scientist, *b* Salford (Manchester) ; studied electricity and magnetism, and was a pioneer in developing the steam engine. He is most famous for his investigation of the relationship between energy and heat, hence his determination of the mechanical equivalent of heat. The *joule* is named after him. See ELECTRICITY

journalism, writing for newspapers or magazines. A journalist may secure regular employment with some provincial or national newspaper, or be on the staff of some magazine. Probably one of the best ways of entering the profession is by becoming first a junior reporter for a provincial paper, then a sub-editor and later an editor. Excellent opportunities for advancement exist for young men and girls ; proficiency in writing verbatim shorthand is necessary if large scale reporting work is desired.
  If not on the staff of a periodical one may become a FREE LANCE journalist, i.e. a regular or occasional contributor to some periodical. Freshness of ideas and clarity of style are vitally important. Much practical help will be found in *The Authors' and Artists' Year Book* (A. & C. Black). Work submitted to editors must be typed on one side of the paper only. State the number of words. There is little market for verse. Prose

JUNIPER

A landscape of Juniper bushes

contributions include news items, humorous articles, articles giving information or views on topics of the moment ; also *fiction*, notably the short story (see SHORT STORY).

Articles accompanied by first-class photographs always receive attention.

Jove, alternative name for Jupiter. See JUPITER

Joyce, JAMES (1882–1941), author and scholar, *b* Dublin ; notable for his psychological interest in his characters, best illustrated in his amazing novel *Ulysses*, the story of twenty-four hours told in 1,000 pages. The book caused a sensation 1922. Others of his less violent books are in simpler style, and have much beauty.

JP, see JUSTICE OF THE PEACE

JTC, short for Junior Training Corps, at one time commonly known as the OTC, i.e. Officers Training Corps. An organisation for training boys at Public Schools for the army, the JTC was completely reorganised 1950–51, being renamed CCF (Combined Cadet Forces), providing training for young people prior to their entry into the navy, army and air forces.

Juan Fernandez, *hwän fŭr-nän′däth*, group of mountainous islands 400m off the coast of Chile ; noted for seals ; Alexander Selkirk (the original Robinson Crusoe) was marooned on one of the islands for four years.

Judaea, *joo-dē′ä*, region in southern Palestine. See PALESTINE

Judah, *joo′dä*, Jacob's 4th son ; his tribe (settled in southern Palestine) became the greatest of the twelve tribes of Israel, and from it sprang the House of David.

Judas Iscariot, *is-kär′i-ot*, one of Christ's twelve apostles. A man of ability, he betrayed Christ to the priests for a reward of 30 pieces of silver, later returning the money and hanging himself.

Judas Maccabaeus, *mak-ä-bē′ŭs* (*d* 160BC), leader of the Jews in their struggle against the Syrians. He was successful until overwhelmed at Elasa, where he was slain.

judge, one who presides over a court of law to hear civil and criminal cases, and is empowered to do so by the State.

Judges, BOOK OF, book of the OT telling the story of the Hebrews from the death of Joshua to the birth of Samuel, a period of, say, 300 years. Judge here means a leader, e.g. Samson, Jephthah and Gideon.

Juggernaut, *jug′ĕr-nŏt*, name of a Hindu idol drawn, on festival occasions, from its temple in the province of Orissa (India). It is popularly believed that fanatics throw themselves under the heavy wheels, though this is questioned. Nevertheless, *juggernaut* has come to mean anything which crushes people or things.

ju-jitsu, *ju-jit′soo*, Japanese form of wrestling now popular in Europe and USA. The idea is to apply leverage to your opponent's limbs so that he must submit.

Julian, *joo′li-än* (331–363), Roman emperor, known as Julian the Apostate, *b* Constantinople. The nephew of Constantine the Great, he was highly successful in fighting in Gaul and against German tribes ; proclaimed emperor by his soldiers, and ruled from 361 ; died while retreating after an invasion of Persia ; attempted unsuccessfully to blend Christian principles with paganism.

Juliana, *-ä′nä* (1909–), Queen (1948) of the Netherlands ; only child of Queen Wilhelmina ; married Prince Bernhard of Lippe 1937 ; she has four children, all daughters, the first of which was *b* 1938.

Jumna, swift-flowing tributary of the Ganges (India), which it joins after flowing 80m via Delhi and Agra.

jumping, in athletics, includes high jump, long jump and pole vault.

Juneau, *joo′nō*, port and cap., Alaska ; has paper mills, and is a centre for the fur trade, fishing and mining.

Jung, PROFESSOR C. G., *yung* (1875–), Swiss psychologist, *b* Basle ; has greatly advanced the science ; has stressed the importance of early memories ; author of many books.

Jungfrau, *-frow*, peak of the Alps rising 13,671ft.

juniper, *joo'ni-pĕr*, small, bushy, slow-growing evergreen similar to the yew ; the leaves are awl-shaped ; the cones round and like dark blue berries ; the timber is deep red.

Junius, LETTERS OF, series of letters on public affairs published in *The Public Advertiser* (London), 1769–72. The author (sometimes signing himself Junius or Philo Junius) remains unknown, though it has been suggested that he was actually Sir Philip Francis, a violent Whig, or possibly Burke or Earl Temple. Savage attacks on George III, the government, Sir William Draper and others, the letters created a sensation.

junk, Chinese sailing ship with high forecastle and stern, and a large square sail, usually of matting.

Juno, *joo'nō*, in old Roman tales, a goddess, called Hera by the Greeks.

Jupiter or **Jove,** *joo'piter*, in old Roman tales, god of rain, thunder, growth of the fields ; known to the Greeks as Zeus ; regarded also as the god of hospitality, truth and justice, and as the god of war.

Jupiter, see ASTRONOMY

Jura, wooded mt. range (France and Switzerland) 200m long.

jurisprudence, see LAW

jury, in English law a group of twelve citizens who listen to evidence in a court of law. All must agree, i.e. the verdict must be unanimous. Generally, any man or woman between the ages of 21 and 60 (except doctors, lawyers and ministers of religion) may be called to sit on a jury in a civil or criminal case. A coroner's jury may number from twelve to twenty-three. See INQUEST

In Scotland a jury comprises twelve citizens in civil cases, fifteen in criminal, and the verdict is decided by a majority.

Jusserand, JEAN, *zhus-rän'* (1855–1932), French diplomat and author ; noted for his books dealing with English life and literature, e.g. *English Wayfaring Life in the Middle Ages, Piers Plowman.*

Justice of the Peace, unpaid magistrate ; acts much as a judge at the trial of those brought before him for minor offences ; may award punishment, usually fines. If the offence is serious he hands the case to a higher court. Justices sit on the Bench, i.e. in the local or county court ; meet at petty sessions ; also sit on Quarter Sessions, i.e. county courts that meet four times a year. Often written JP.

justiciar, *jūs-tish'i-ĕr*, chief justice ; in the 12th and 13th c. was often the king's chief minister.

Justinian I, *jūs-tin'ian* (483–565), Roman Emperor ; nephew of Justin I, and co-ruler with him of the Eastern Roman empire, and emperor 527, his reign lasting 38 years. His military conquests, though spectacular, were of doubtful value, but he succeeded in winning back Italy from the Goths. He spent vast sums on building the church of St Sophia, Constantinople (Istanbul). His claim to lasting fame is his collection of Roman civil law, revised and codified by committees set up by him 528–534. Known as *Corpus Juris Civilis,* this has remained the foundation of the law for all Western Europe, except England.

jute, fibre from two plants grown chiefly in Bengal and Assam. Jute grows 5–10ft high, and after its inner bark has been steeped in water, it is beaten out and manufactured, largely in Calcutta (India) and Dundee (Scotland), for cordage, sail-cloth, tarpaulin, and also for making carpets.

Jutland, peninsula, Denmark ; area 11,430 sq.m ; gave its name to the battle of Jutland (1916) during World War I, the British gaining a somewhat unsatisfactory victory.

Juvenal, *joo'vē-näl* (*d* AD140), Latin poet ; lived from the reign of Nero to that of Antonius Pius. In his sixteen satires he gives us a picture of the corrupt manners and customs of his age, though there is no doubt that there was another side to the picture. His brilliant style is forceful, and his writings are adorned with phrases often quoted today, e.g. *Mens sana in corpore sano,* i.e. A sound mind in a sound body ; *Probitas laudatur et alget,* Honesty is commended, and starves ; *Nemo repente fuit turpissimus,* No one ever reached the climax of vice at one step ; *Quis custodiet ipsos custodes?* Which may be freely translated : Yes ; but who will protect us from our protectors ?

juvenile offenders, boys or girls under the age of seventeen found guilty of some crime. If a first offence (i.e. if convicted for the first time), they may be released from court, and placed under the care of a probation officer in the hope that with encouragement they will reform. Otherwise they may be sent to an Approved School, or awarded corporal punishment, or they (or their parents) may be fined. Children under 14 cannot be sent to prison.

Much has been done in recent years to give juvenile offenders a fair chance. Special juvenile courts are held to consider their cases. Many schools have unofficial courts at which minor misdemeanours are dealt with.

Read *Juvenile Delinquency,* A. E. Jones.

Juxon, WILLIAM (1582–1663), English churchman ; Bishop of London 1633 ; was a friend of Charles I, whom he attended at his execution. It was to Juxon that Charles gave the one word, ' Remember.'

K

K, chemical symbol for potassium (*kalium*).

'k' method, see RATIO

K2, see GODWIN-AUSTEN

Kaaba, *kä'bä*, shrine of the Great Mosque, Mecca. It is *c*.50ft high, 40ft long, and 30ft wide. Within it is the Black Stone, probably a meteorite, *c*.7in long. This is kissed by all devout Mohammedans who make the pilgrimage to Mecca. See MOHAMMED

Kabul, *caw'b'l*, cap. Afghanistan ; mostly built of mud ; pop.120,000.

Kaffirs, *kaf'ēr*, those Bantu-speaking negroid natives of S. Africa who are not Moslems ; more especially the tribes that migrated from equatorial Africa into the region east of the Drakensberg Mts shortly before Europeans arrived there. It includes the Zulu-Kaffirs. The people, tall, dark brown and flat-nosed, are fine hunters and warriors (using knobkerries and oval leather shields, etc.). They live in kraals, i.e. cattle-enclosures surrounded by huts, often of wattle and daub with thatched domes. They believe in witchcraft and ancestor-worship, but they have been considerably civilised.

Throughout the 19th c. there were wars against the Kaffirs (1809, 1834, 1846, 1858 and 1877).

Kagawa, *kä-gä'wä* (1888–), Japanese Christian ; founded the Labour Federation ; supported by General MacArthur after Japan's defeat in World War II.

Kagoshima, *kägō-shē'mä*, Japanese port ; pop.182,000 ; noted for silk and cotton.

Kaiser, THE, see WILLIAM II (1859–1941)

Kalahari Desert, *kälä-hä'rē*, upland region with scrub, N. of the Orange R., S. Africa; supports cattle.

Kalat, *kä-lät'*, state of Baluchistan, Pakistan.

kaleidoscope, *kä-lī'dō-skōp*, optical instrument devised by Sir David Brewster *c*.1816. It comprises a tube with two (sometimes three) mirrors set lengthways, and a number of coloured bits of glass. Multiple reflections give an endless variety of patterns. Popular as a toy, it is also useful to designers.

Kalends, first day of the month in ancient Roman times.

Kalgoorlie, gold-mining town, W. Australia; *c*.375m E. of Perth.

Kalinin, *käl-ē'nen*, river port, USSR ; on the R. Volga ; noted for textiles and leather ; pop.160,000.

Kaliningrad, see KÖNIGSBERG

Kalmar, manufacturing town and port, Sweden ; pop.23,000.

Kalmucks, Mongolian race in Central Asia ; mostly Buddhist. Many are still wanderers with herds of cattle and horses.

kalong, see BAT

Kamet, *kä'met*, peak of the Himalayas, 25,447ft.

Read *Kamet Conquered*, F. S. Smythe.

Kanara, *kün'ärä*, W. coast region (Goa to Malabar), India ; has a heavy rainfall.

Kandahar, *kün-dä-här'*, one of the chief commercial towns of Afghanistan ; in British hands during the wars of 1839–42 and 1879–80 ; pop.51,000.

Kandy, former cap. Ceylon ; noted for its Buddhist temple ; pop.51,000.

kangaroo, pouched animal found only in Australia and New Guinea ; notable for its very long and powerful hind legs, the long tail, on which it partly rests, and the small head with erect ears. The fur may be reddish, grey or black. Kangaroos vary in size from that of a rabbit to over 5ft in length. They feed in companies on grass and roots ; are timid, and when alarmed take leaps as long as 30ft. The young (born one at a time) live in a pouch in the front lower half of the mother's body.

Similar, but smaller, is the *wallaby*.

Kansas, *kan'zäs*, state of USA ; noted for its prairies ; exports pork and beef (mostly canned). The cap. is Topeka.

Kansas City, twin towns, USA, the larger (state of Missouri), noted for meat packing ; pop.400,000 ; the smaller in Kansas ; pop.121,000.

Kant, IMMANUEL, *känt* (1724–1804), German thinker, b Königsberg ; at first extremely poor ; appointed professor of philosophy at Königsberg 1770. He lived uneventfully, and never travelled more than 40m from Königsberg, but he gathered many friends and admirers. He is remembered for his books *The Critique of Pure Reason, The Critique*

KANT 1724–1804

of Practical Reason, and *The Critique of Judgment.* These books (and Kant's other writings on Ethics) turned philosophy upside down and raised problems that have not yet been solved.

Concluding his *Critique of Pure Reason,* Kant says, ' Two things fill the mind with ever-increasing wonder and awe : the starry heavens above me and the moral law within me.'

Kant's philosophical writings are often very difficult to understand ; but there is no doubt of their supreme importance.

kapok, *kā'pok,* tall, evergreen tree native of the W. Indies. The leaves have 5–8 leaflets ; the yellow flowers are coated with silky wool much used for stuffing cushions and furniture.

Karachi, *kä-rä'chē,* port, airport and cap. (since 1947) of the British Dominion of Pakistan ; formerly capital of Sind ; a great railway centre on the delta of the R. Indus ; pop.360,000.

Karakoram, *kärä-kō'rŭm,* range of the Himalayas reaching to Tibet ; crossed by a pass at 18,000ft.

Karelia, *kä-rä'liä,* republic of USSR, between L. Ladoga and the White Sea. A portion was taken from Finland (to whom it officially belonged) by Russia 1939, after some fighting.

Karlsruhe, *kärls'roo-e,* cap., Baden, Germany ; great manufacturing centre, especially of machinery, railway stock, etc. ; heavily bombed in World War II ; pop. (1939) 190,000.

Karnak, modern Arabic name for the site of the ancient city of Thebes, its ruined temples (Karnak and Luxor) being near the R. Nile, Upper Egypt. See PLATE 65.

karri, tall gum-tree of Australia, its hard wood being much used for paving roads.

Karroo, *ka-roo',* wide plains (Great and Little), Cape Province, S. Africa ; usually covered with stunted bushes on which sheep graze.

Kashmir or **Cashmere,** native Indian state N. of the Punjab ; area 84,000sq.m ; noted for magnificent scenery with mts., forests, gorges, lakes ; exports shawls woven from the soft hair and under-fleece of goats.

Katanga, *kä-täng'gä,* region of the Belgian Congo ; produces copper and uranium.

Katrine, LOCH, *kat'rin,* loch (lake) in the Trossachs of Scotland, which supplies Glasgow with water. Its magnificent scenery is described in Scott's *The Lady of the Lake.*

Kattegat, part of the N. Sea between Denmark (Jutland) and Sweden. It is dangerous to shipping.

katydid, kind of grasshopper common in America ; named from the fanciful idea that its chirping sounds like the words, *Katy did.*

Kaunas, *kow'nas,* cap., Lithuania (USSR) ; on the R. Niemen ; pop.125,000.

kauri pine, *kow'ri,* coniferous tree of NZ and Queensland ; may be 150ft high ;

yields a yellow, smooth-grained timber much used in joinery and cabinet-making ; also hard resin.

kayak, *kī'ak,* Eskimo boat with a wooden frame covered with skin ; usually for only one person. It may be 18ft long, and is propelled with a double paddle.

Kaye-Smith, SHEILA (1889–), English writer whose books are mostly about the peasantry of Sussex ; she won fame with her novel *The Tramping Methodist,* 1908, and has written *Sussex Gorse, Green Apple Harvest* and *The Hidden Son.*

Kazan, *kä-zän,* historic city, USSR ; pop.400,000 ; noted for textiles and chemicals.

KC, see BARRISTER

Kea, *kä'ä,* olive-green NZ parrot remarkable for having changed its habits since the introduction of sheep. Formerly it lived on fruit and seeds, but now it attacks sheep, and is therefore shot at sight.

Kean, EDMUND (1787–1833), actor, *b* London ; notable for his mastery of tragedy, as in Shylock or Richard III. Coleridge said that to see him was like reading Shakespeare by flashes of lightning.

Kearton, CHERRY (1871–1940), naturalist and photographer, born in Yorkshire ; pioneer of animal photography. He filmed big game in their natural haunts ; had many exciting adventures ; author of *Wild Life Across the World.*

Keats, JOHN (1795–1821), English poet, *b* London. As a schoolboy he was always ready to fight, always generous and fond of reading. An orphan at 15, he studied to become a doctor, but, having a small private income, devoted all his attention to literature, numbering among his friends Leigh Hunt, William Hazlitt, Shelley and Joseph Severn (1793–1879) the painter.

His first volume, *Poems,* appeared 1817, containing the famous sonnet *On First Looking into Chapman's Homer. Endymion,* a long poem which Keats described as ' a feverish attempt rather than a deed accomplished,' was published 1818, and scorned by the critics. About this time Keats had a breakdown in health, due in part to overstrain after nursing his brother Thomas, and partly because of an unhappy love affair. His poems, *Hyperion, Lamia, The Eve of St Agnes, To Autumn, To a Nightingale, On a Grecian Urn,* and his superb ballad *La Belle Dame sans Merci* appeared 1820 ; also in this year he showed signs of consumption. He travelled to Italy with Joseph Severn, and died Rome, being buried there under a stone with an epitaph chosen by himself : *Here lies one whose name was writ in water.*

John Keats has a unique place among English poets. He lived for, and he wrote only, what was beautiful, believing with all his heart that ' A thing of beauty is a joy for ever.' His poetry does not preach, nor does it teach ; it is simply an expression of emotion, but an exquisite and sensitive expression, full of imagery and the music of words. In it is much of the pure Greek spirit.

From *Endymion* come the famous lines :

A thing of beauty is a joy for ever :
Its loveliness increases ; it will never
Pass into nothingness, but still will keep
A bower quiet for us, and a sleep
Full of sweet dreams, and health, and quiet breathing.

Keble, JOHN, *kē'bl* (1792–1866), churchman and poet, born in Gloucestershire ; vicar of Hursley (Hampshire) for his last 30 years. He was a pioneer of the Oxford Movement, but most famous for his book *The Christian Year,* and his many hymns, e.g. *Sun of my Soul.*
Keble College, Oxford, was founded 1870 as a memorial.

keep-fit classes, see GYMNASTICS

Keighley, *kēth'li,* town, W. Yorkshire ; manufactures worsted goods and textile machinery ; pop.52,000.

Keith, SIR ARTHUR, *kēth* (1866–   ), *b* Aberdeenshire, anthropologist ; professor of the Royal College of Surgeons 1908–33 ; knighted 1921 ; author of many learned and also popular works, e.g. *Antiquity of Man, Essays on Human Evolution.*

Keller, HELEN (1880–   ), courageous American, born in Alabama State ; lost the senses of sight, smell and hearing at 19 months, and was dumb. In the care of Anna Sullivan, her teacher, she learned to speak, read and typewrite. Later she studied at Boston, graduating with honours 1904. She made a complete success of life in spite of severe handicaps, as shown by her books, e.g. *The Story of My Life, Midstream,* etc.

Kellermann, FRANÇOIS (1770–1835), French general ; led ' Kellermann's charge ' at the battle of Marengo (1800) ; fought in the Peninsular War and at Waterloo.

Kellogg, FRANK BILLINGS (1856–1937), American statesman, born in New York State ; USA ambassador to Britain 1923–25 ; chiefly remembered for the well-intentioned Briand-Kellogg pact (1928) to outlaw war.

Kells, BOOK OF, exquisite 8th c. Irish illuminated MS of the Gospels, now in Trinity College, Dublin. It was written in the monastery at Kells, a market town of County Meath.

kelp, ash of burnt seaweed, containing soda, potash and iodine.

Kelvin, WILLIAM THOMSON, LORD (1824–1907), British scientist and inventor, *b* Belfast ; appointed Professor of Natural Philosophy at Glasgow University when only 22, and remained there for fifty-three years, becoming a world-renowned figure in science.
A pioneer in scientific theories, Kelvin investigated the age of the earth, molecular dynamics, the wave theory of light, diffusion of gases ; while, on the practical side, he made countless improvements to electrical instruments, particularly those for recording and measuring electric current, e.g. the mirror galvanometer and the household electric meter. He vastly improved telegraphy, and was largely responsible for the successful laying of the Atlantic cable 1857. The improved compass, more accurate tables for finding a ship's position at sea ; standardised electric units ; experiments with the Leyden jar (leading Hertz to his discovery of radio) were all due to his amazing industry and imaginative experiments. He was created Baron Kelvin of Largs 1892.

Kemal Ataturk, *ke-māl' ā-tā-türk* (1880–1938), President of the Turkish republic 1923 to his death, and virtually dictator for 16 years. Having led the Turks to victory against the Greeks, he boldly destroyed the time-honoured caliphate, and introduced new ideas and customs into a revitalised nation. See TURKEY

Kempenfelt, RICHARD (1718–82), sailor, *b* Westminster, son of a Swede in British service. As a rear-admiral he defeated the French fleet off Ushant 1781. While his ship the *Royal George* was being repaired at Portsmouth, she overturned because all the guns had been carelessly crowded together on one side of the ship. In consequence Kempenfelt and 800 men perished.
Read Cowper's *Loss of the Royal George*

Ken, THOMAS (1637–1711), churchman, *b* Berkhampsted, Hertfordshire ; was one of the seven bishops who refused to read the *Declaration of Indulgence* ; best remembered as a writer of hymns, e.g. *Awake my Soul* and *Glory to Thee, my God, this night.*

kendyr or **kendir,** strong fibre used in Asiatic Russia in place of cotton and hemp.

Kenilworth, town, Warwickshire, noted for its castle, immortalised by Scott in his novel *Kenilworth.*

Kennedy, MARGARET (1896–   ), British novelist and playwright ; won fame with her novel *The Constant Nymph* (1924), since dramatised and filmed with great success. She also wrote *Escape Me Never, The Midas Touch.*

Kennington, district, London (Lambeth) ; has Kennington Oval, the ground of the Surrey County Cricket Club.

Kenny, SISTER ELIZABETH, see INFANTILE PARALYSIS

Kensington, royal borough of London with various museums, including the Victoria and Albert ; also Kensington Gardens.

Kensington Gardens, see LONDON

Kent, English county bordered by the R. Thames, Sussex, etc. ; has the N. Downs and the Weald ; co.tn Maidstone. Kent is especially famous for hop-growing ; coal is mined near Dover. The county has long been famous for cricket.
Kent was also the name of an Anglo-

The key signatures shown above (left to right) are those of the Keys of G, D, A, E, B ;
F, B Flat, E Flat, A Flat, D Flat.

Saxon Kingdom, ruled in the 6th c. by Ethelbert.

Kent, EDWARD AUGUSTUS, DUKE OF (1767–1820), British prince, b London, 4th son of George III, and father of Queen Victoria.

Kent, DUKE OF (1902–42), 4th son of George V of England ; created duke 1934 ; married Princess Marina of Greece and Denmark. He was killed in a flying accident. His children are Prince Edward (b 1935), now Duke of Kent ; Princess Alexandra (1936), and Prince Michael (1942).

Kent's Cavern, limestone cave near Torquay, Devon ; first explored 1825 ; found to have remains of Stone Age man, also bones of mammoth, rhinoceros, grizzly bear and lion.

Kentucky, state of USA, S. of the R. Ohio. It is noted for tobacco, also wheat, maize and various minerals, e.g. petroleum and coal ; cap. Frankfort. See MAMMOTH CAVE

Kenya, kĕ-nyä', British colony and protectorate in equatorial E. Africa ; area 224,960sq.m ; pop.4,000,000. Though wide regions are unproductive, Kenya is being vigorously developed, e.g. irrigation, communications (including the Great N. Road), soil conservation, agriculture. Cereals are grown ; the forests yield cedar. Gold, sodium and carbonate are mined. Kenya is the world's chief source of pyrethrum seed. The capital is Nairobi, on the Uganda railway ; other towns include Mombasa, noted for its fine harbour.

Kepler, JOHANN (1571–1630), German astronomer ; was assistant to Tycho Brahe. A brilliant mathematician and a pioneer of knowledge, he is most famous for his three laws of planetary motion : (a) each planet moves in an ellipse with the sun at one of its foci ; (b) the areas enclosed by lines drawn from the focus to two successive points on the planet's path are proportional to the time taken in travelling along them ; (c) the squares of the periodic times of the planets are proportional to the cubes of their mean distances.

Keppel, VISCOUNT (1725–86), English sailor; accompanied Lord Anson on his voyage round the world 1740–44 ; admiral 1778.

keratin, complex organic substance of the protein type found in animal horns and hoofs.

Kerensky, ALEXANDER FEODOREVITCH, ker'en-skē (1881–   ), Russian politician. A brilliant socialist leader, he was Premier of the 1917 coalition government of Russia, but was driven from Petrograd by Lenin, and escaped to England. His books include The Crucifixion of Liberty.

kerosene, actually paraffin oil, a mixture of hydrocarbons obtained from petroleum.

Kerry, county in the province of Munster, Eire ; mostly mountainous or bog ; cap. Tralee.

kestrel, see HAWK

Keswick, kez'ik, town, Cumberland ; on the R. Greta.

ketones, kē'tōns, series of organic chemical compounds formed by (a) the oxidation of secondary alcohols ; (b) distillation of calcium salts of fatty acids ; and (c) the action of certain reagents on acid chlorides, e.g. C_2H_5COCl.

Kettering, town, Northamptonshire ; noted for boots and shoes ; pop.35,000.

Kew Gardens, see BOTANIC GARDENS

key, in music, a group of notes which agree in melodies and harmonies with one note (the keynote or ' tonic '), from which is named the tonality of a given scale. Every note in the scale has two such groups of notes or keys, the Major and the Minor. The practice of composing music in definite keys came in during the 16th c. and during the 20th there have been signs that it may be abandoned.

See DIAGRAM above

Keyes, LORD (1872–1945), British admiral ; in command of the Dover Patrol during World War I, and responsible for shipping thousands of troops across the Channel in spite of German submarines ; planned the raid on Zeebrugge 1918 ; raised to the peerage 1943.

Keynes, JOHN MAYNARD, kānz (1883–1946), economist, b Cambridge ; became Lord Keynes 1942 ; author of highly important works on economics, e.g. The General Theory of Employment, Interest and Money, in which are proposals for control of credit and currency ; for a time a director of the Bank of England ; negotiated the American Loan Agreement of 1945. See ECONOMICS

Keys, HOUSE OF, part of the Parliament of the I. of Man ; consists of 24 members elected by the people.

Key West, see FLORIDA

khaki, buff fabric for military uniform in the British army. First used in India 1848, it gives valuable camouflage to the troops, and was named from a Hindu word for dust.

khan, kän, oriental word for lord ; first adopted by Jenghiz, the Mongol ruler. Cham is a variant.

Kharkov, chär'kof, former cap. of the Ukraine (USSR) ; pop.833,000 ; great trading centre, notably agricultural produce and machinery, especially tractors.

Khartoum, *kär-toom'*, cap., Anglo-Egyptian Sudan ; near the junction of the Blue and White Nile. The town (pop.46,000) is of great commercial importance. Here General Gordon was killed 1885.

khedive, *ke-dēv'*, title (1867–1914) of the Viceroy of Egypt ; first granted to Ismail Pasha.

Khibiny, che-*bi'nē*, town, Kola peninsula, USSR ; produces apatite for phosphate fertilisers.

Khiva, *kē'vä* ; chē'-, region of Uzbekistan, USSR ; includes the finest cotton lands in Russia.

Khyber Pass, *kī'bĕr*, pass between India and Afghanistan, 33m long and in places only 15ft wide.

kiang, *ki-ang'*, wild ass of Tibet ; reddish brown except the head and under parts, which are cream.

Kicking Horse Pass, pass over the Rockies, Canada. The CPR crosses the Rockies by this route.

Kidderminster, town, Worcestershire ; noted for carpets ; pop.35,000.

kidneys, organs in man and animals which take waste material from the blood in the form of urine. The average weight is 4½oz. They are placed one at either side of the lumbar spine.

Kiel, *kēl*, Baltic port, Germany ; noted for its harbour and dockyards ; pop. 272,000. See CANALS

Kiel Canal, see CANALS

Kiev, *kē-ef*, cap. of the Ukraine ; on the R. Dnieper ; trades in grain ; manufactures glass ; said to have been founded 5th c. AD ; scene of fierce fighting in World War II ; pop.850,000.

Kildare, county in the province of Leinster, Eire ; co.tn Naas.

Kilima Njaro, *kil-ē-män-järō*, mt., Tanganyika ; rises 19,321ft, and is the highest point in Africa.

Kilkenny, county in the province of Leinster, Eire ; also its co.tn.

Killarney, town, County Kerry, Eire. Near by are the three famous lakes in wild and beautiful scenery.

Killiecrankie, mountain pass, Perthshire. Hereabouts (1689) Claverhouse (Bonnie Dundee) defeated a force sent by William III to subdue the Jacobites, but was himself killed in the battle.

Kilmarnock, town, Ayrshire ; manufactures carpets, woollens, boots and shoes ; pop.41,000.

kilowatt, see WATT

kilt, knee-length pleated skirt worn by men ; worn by Assyrian soldiers, by mountaineers in the Balkans (commonly of white linen), but usually associated with regiments of the Scottish Highlands, each having its own tartan, i.e. a distinctive design of woven coloured stripes. All Highland regiments wear the kilt. The pouch hung in front of the kilt is a *sporran*.

Kimberley, *kim'bĕr-li*, town, Cape Pro-

vince, S. Africa. Its growth since 1870 is due to the De Beers diamond mines. Besieged by the Boers 1899–1900, it was relieved after 124 days ; pop.56,000. See PLATE 33

kimono, *ki-mō'no*, loose robe worn by men and women in Japan. Highly decorative and very comfortable, it is tied with a sash.

Kincardineshire, *kin-kär'din-*, Scottish county on the east coast ; co.tn Stonehaven.

Kinchinjanga, *kin-chin-jung'gä*, peak of the Himalayas, 28,146ft.

Kinder Scout, mt., Derbyshire, highest point (2,088ft) of the Peak District.

kinetic energy, see MECHANICS

kinetics, branch of mechanics dealing with the effect of motion and mass, and with velocity and acceleration.

The kinetic theory of gases assumes that all the molecules of a gas are perfectly elastic, and are in constant and rapid motion.

king, ruler, especially among Teutonic races, the chief of a tribe early being known as a king. Anglo-Saxon chiefs governed small kingdoms. In Norman times the power of the king was enhanced. Royal power in England was great in Tudor times, though even then Parliament was gaining control, and by the end of the Stuart period Parliament was supreme. Today the king, though beloved, gathering to himself the proud tradition of his subjects, and being their most honoured representative, has little actual authority, government being in the hands of the Prime Minister, the Cabinet, and the two Houses of Parliament.

Government by a king is called monarchy, and may be either despotic (absolute) or constitutional. A constitutional monarchy is one in which the king rules in accordance with a recognised constitution ; an absolute monarchy one in which the king rules as he pleases. See KINGS AND QUEENS

King, WILLIAM LYON MACKENZIE (1874–1950), Canadian Liberal statesman ; Minister of Labour 1909–11 ; Prime Minister of Canada 1921 ; re-elected 1935 ; concluded *Odensburg Agreement* (1940) with President Roosevelt, and the *Hyde Park Declaration* 1941 ; retired 1948. He held office for 21 years, i.e. longer than any other British political leader, and strove tirelessly to weld together Canada, Britain and the USA.

king-crab, see CRAB

King Edward VII Land, region of the Antarctic SE. of Ross Sea.

kingfisher, bird belonging to the same family as the hornbills. The common kingfisher of Britain (*Alcedo ispida*), one of the handsomest of British birds, is c.7in long, has a very sharp-pointed beak ; is brilliant green on the head, sides of the neck, and short wing-coverts, all spotted with blue, and dark green merging to bright blue on the

THE KINGFISHER

back ; its throat is white. Often seen perching on a branch overhanging a stream, it preys on small fish. The nest is usually in a tunnel in a river bank ; the eggs are pale and unspotted.

The LAUGHING JACKASS of Australia and New Guinea is a species of kingfisher. It is usually brown, black, and white, and gives a peculiar gurgling cry at dawn and dusk.

King George V Land, region of the Antarctic due S. of Tasmania.

King-Hall, COMMANDER STEPHEN (1893–), British sailor ; served with the Grand Fleet 1914–17 ; intelligence officer Mediterranean Fleet 1925–26, Atlantic Fleet 1927–28 ; Independent Labour MP 1939 ; founded the *National News-Letter* 1936 ; well-known broadcaster.

Kinglake, ALEXANDER WILLIAM (1809–91), born near Taunton. He wrote *Eothen*, a charming and lively account of his travels in the Balkans and the Middle East.

king-maker, see WARWICK, EARL OF

Kings, BOOKS OF, two books of the OT containing a history of the Hebrew kings from Solomon (*c.*970BC) to the end of the monarchy 586BC.

kings and queens :

OF ENGLAND

Saxons and Danes	Began to reign
Egbert	827
Ethelwulf	839
Ethelbald	858
Ethelbert	858
Ethelred	866
Alfred the Great	871
Edward the Elder	901
Athelstan	925
Edmund	940
Edred	946
Edwy	955
Edgar	958

Edward the Martyr	975
Ethelred the Unready	979
Edmund Ironside	1016
Canute	1017
Harold I	1035
Hardicanute	1040
Edward the Confessor	1042
Harold II	1066

Normans	
William I (The Conqueror)	1066
William II	1087
Henry I	1100
Stephen (and Matilda)	1135

Plantagenets	
Henry II	1154
Richard I	1189
John	1199
Henry III	1216
Edward I	1272
Edward II	1307
Edward III	1327
Richard II	1377

Lancastrians	
Henry IV	1399
Henry V	1413
Henry VI	1422

Yorkists	
Edward IV	1461
Edward V	1483
Richard III	1483

Tudors	
Henry VII	1485
Henry VIII	1509
Edward VI	1547
Mary I	1553
Elizabeth	1558

OF GREAT BRITAIN

Stuarts	
James I (James VI of Scotland)	1603
Charles I	1625
Commonwealth (Oliver Cromwell) (Richard Cromwell)	1649
Charles II (restored)	1660
James II	1685
William III and Mary II	1689
Anne	1702

House of Hanover	
George I	1714
George II	1727
George III	1760
George IV	1820
William IV	1830
Victoria	1837

House of Saxe-Coburg-Gotha	
Edward VII	1901

House of Windsor	
George V	1910
Edward VIII	1936
George VI	1936

OF SCOTLAND

Kenneth I	844
Donald I	860
Constantine I	863
Donald II	879
Constantine II	900
Malcolm I	942
Indulphus	954
Duff	962
Culen	967
Kenneth II	971
Constantine III	995
Kenneth III	997
Malcolm II	1005
Duncan I	1034
Macbeth	1040
Malcolm III (Canmore)	1057
Donald Bane	1093
Duncan II	1094
Donald Bane (restored)	1095
Edgar	1097
Alexander I	1107
David I	1124
Malcolm IV	1153
William the Lion	1165
Alexander II	1214
Alexander III	1249
Margaret of Norway	1285
John Baliol or Balliol	1292
Robert the Bruce	1306
David II	1329
Robert II (Stuart)	1371
Robert III	1390
James I	1406
James II	1437
James III	1460
James IV	1488
James V	1513
Mary Queen of Scots	1542
James VI (James I of England from 1603)	1567

King's College, college of Cambridge University, founded 1441 by Henry VI. Its chapel is one of the finest examples of Perpendicular (15th c.) architecture.

King's College, college of the University of London, established 1829 for training in literature and science ; engineering was added later ; then a medical department, which developed into King's College Hospital 1839. A theological department was added 1847 ; evening classes started 1856. There is now a department for training teachers.

King's College School, English public school founded 1829 as a junior department of King's College, London.

King's Counsel, distinction conferred on eminent barristers and advocates. They must ask for leave before they may act against the Crown, but this is never refused. A KC is entitled to wear a silk gown, hence *to take silk* means to become a KC. See BARRISTER

King's County, see OFFALY

King's Cross, district of N. London. King's Cross station is the terminus of the London and North-Eastern Railway (now part of British Railways).

Kingsford-Smith, SIR CHARLES EDWARD (1897–1935), Australian airman ; made a record-breaking flight from Australia to England 1929, and (1930) the return flight in 10½ days.

Kingsley, CHARLES (1819–75), English churchman and writer, *b* Holne, Devon ; for long rector of Eversley, Hampshire. He is famous for his novels *Yeast* and *Alton Locke*, in which he gives vivid pictures of London's poor ; but best remembered for *Westward Ho !* a thrilling historical tale of adventure in Queen Elizabeth's day. Other books of his are *Hypatia*, a novel of early Christianity, *Hereward the Wake*, mingling history and romance, *The Heroes*, in which he tells again many Gk tales, and *The Water Babies*.

King's Lynn, town and port, Norfolk ; on the R. Ouse ; pop.23,000.

King's Prize, see BISLEY

King's School, see CANTERBURY

Kingston, cap. and largest port, Jamaica ; pop.109,000.

Kingston-upon-Thames, town, Surrey ; 12m from London ; a new power station was opened 1948 ; pop.36,000.

Kingstown, port and holiday town, County Dublin, Eire ; linked by steamer with Holyhead ; in Irish, Dun Laoghaire.

King Willow, see WILLOW

Kinross, co.tn, Kinross-shire, a county of Scotland between Perthshire and Fifeshire.

Kipling, RUDYARD (1865–1936), author and poet, *b* Bombay, India. At six he was in the care of a relative at Southsea (Hampshire), and apparently not very happy there. He was educated at United Services College, Westward Ho (Devon), a school immortalised in his story *Stalky and Co.*, in which Kipling himself appears as ' Beetle.' From 1882–89 he was a journalist in India, writing *Departmental Ditties*, and prose, e.g. *Plain Tales from the Hills. The City of Dreadful Night* appeared 1891, the year in which his novel, *The Light that Failed*, was published. His best-known volume of verse is *Barrack Room Ballads*; and 1894–95 came what are perhaps his most successful works, the two *Jungle Books*, full of humour, fascination, thrill and a rare fancy ; Mowgli, Bagheera, etc. have an assured place in our literature. His inimitable *Just so Stories* reveal Kipling in his happiest mood.

Another excellent book was *The Seven Seas* ; others were *Kim* and *Captains Courageous*, later filmed. Mention must be made of his two happy interpretations of the spirit of old England in *Puck of Pook's Hill* and *Rewards and Fairies*, both written after he had bought Bateman's, a 17th c. house at Burwash, Sussex. Among his poetry is the hymn, *Recessional*, beginning *God of our fathers, known of old*.

Kipling was great as a writer of verse and prose, a master of words, of haunting melody and of vivid description. His writing has been decried as propaganda in favour of imperialism, but after World War II there was a renewed recognition of its value as literature.

Kirkcaldy, *kŭr-kä'dĭ, -kŏl'dĭ,* town and port, Fife ; called the ' lang toon ' because of its great length ; birthplace of Adam Smith, the economist ; noted for its fine harbour ; manufactures linoleum and textiles ; pop.47,000.

Kirkcudbright, *kŭr-koo'brĭ,* co.tn, Kirkcudbrightshire, a county of SW. Scotland.

Kirkstall Abbey, see LEEDS

Kirkstone, pass between L. Ullswater and Ambleside, Westmorland.

Kirriemuir, small town, Angus ; birthplace of J. M. Barrie, who called it Thrums.

Kitchener of Khartoum, HORATIO HERBERT, EARL (1850–1916), British soldier, born in County Kerry, Ireland ; major of cavalry in Egypt, where he saw much fighting ; Commander-in-Chief of the Egyptian army (1892) ; this campaign (1898) resulted in the recovery of the Sudan after the decisive victory at Omdurman, enabling him to enter Khartoum. He was raised to the peerage on his return to England.

Having dealt swiftly with the Boers in the S. African war, Kitchener was British agent (the Sirdar) in Egypt 1911–14. Appointed Secretary for War at the outbreak of World War I, he recruited a new army of over 1,000,000 men, showed remarkable foresight and thoroughness, but failed to appreciate the full significance of new tactics, and was in part responsible for our defeat at Antwerp and in the Dardanelles. In an attempt to establish understanding with Russia, he sailed in the cruiser *Hampshire* from Scapa Flow, and was lost at sea when the vessel struck a mine.

kite, see HAWK

kittiwake, see GULL

kiwi, *kē'wĭ,* bird found only in NZ. Peculiar for its very small wings, its feathers look like stiff hairs. It is unique in having its nostrils at the tip of the beak. About the size of a small hen, it is unable to fly. Another name is *apteryx* (Gk for ' wingless ').

Klondike, river, Yukon Territory, Canada ; joins the R. Yukon near Dawson City ; scene of the 1896 gold rush. See YUKON

Knaresborough, *närz'bŭ-rŭ,* historic town on the R. Nidd, W. Yorkshire ; noted for its petrifying well.

knight, at one time a soldier who had received military distinction ; now a distinction granted by the king to men who have rendered conspicuous service to the community, e.g. inventors, discoverers, merchants, donors of charitable gifts and authors. The king, or his representative, lays the royal sword on the shoulder of the man thus honoured, a symbolic act known as the *accolade.* A knight is addressed as ' Sir ' ; his wife is a dame, though popularly known as ' Lady.'

There are many British orders of knighthood, e.g. the Order of the Garter, the Bath, St Michael, and St George, etc. The Order of the British Empire (instituted 1917) is for those who have given distinguished service in the colonies, etc. The Scottish order of knighthood is that of the Thistle ; that of Ireland is the Order of St Patrick.

In origin, knighthood was a preparation of youth for service in war. At its highest and best it had a strong religious motive. The novice spent the night before receiving knighthood in prayer, his armour being placed on the altar of the church. This was known as the *vigil.* The ceremony of conferring knighthood took the form of a service after a ceremonial bath. In theory, at least, the knight was chivalrous and high-minded, going forth to right wrongs, protect women, and do good ; he was also, in theory, a member of a great brotherhood who, though they might fight each other, observed the rules of knighthood ; thus some of John of Gaunt's knights when fighting the Spaniards, who were aided by the French (1389), were taken ill with dysentery, and were invited by the enemy to recover in a camp behind their lines. They went, were shown every kindness by the French, and then returned to take up arms against their late hosts as vigorously as ever.

Sometimes a knight was dubbed (created) on the field of battle. Military knighthood decayed during the Hundred Years' War ; and the tournament was discouraged by Edward III and Henry V, except on rare spectacular occasions.

Knight, ERIC, *nīt* (1897–1943), born in Yorkshire ; lived much in USA ; author of many clever books, e.g. *The Flying Yorkshireman* ; *Lassie, Come Home.*

Knight, DAME LAURA, English painter ; daughter of Charles Johnson of Nottingham. She won fame with her pictures depicting the circus and stage, and first exhibited at the Royal Academy 1903.

Knights Hospitallers, group of knights who, in the Middle Ages, provided shelter and care for sick and wounded, and especially for pilgrims to Jerusalem. The idea survives in the St John Ambulance Association. See NURSING

Knights of the Round Table, see ARTHUR

Knights Templars, military and religious order of knighthood founded at Jerusalem 1118 for the defence of pilgrims to the Holy Land (Palestine), and named after the palace in Jerusalem known as Solomon's Temple. The order had HQ in London, hence the Inner and Middle Temple, near the Strand, and the Temple Church there.

Knockmealdown, mt. range of S. Eire ; highest point 2,609ft.

Knossos, see AEGEAN ART

knot, in cordage, a loop or series of loops. Some of the most useful types are (*a*) *reef,* for joining two ropes of the same thickness ; the only knot used in First

Aid bandaging ; (*b*) *sheet-bend*, for joining ropes of different thicknesses ; (*c*) *bowline*, quickly unfastened, but forms a loop that will not slip ; (*d*) *clove-hitch*, useful for fastening a line to a post, etc. ; holds fast under strain ; (*e*) *sheep-shank*, for shortening a rope without having to cut it ; (*f*) *granny*, often used, but unreliable.

knot, nautical measure of speed, *not* of distance. One Admiralty knot is one nautical mile *per hour*.

In 1945 the RAF adopted the knot and the nautical mile as standard measures of speed and distance.

knout, *nowt*, whip, usually of leather thongs (sometimes interwoven with wire) used in Russia, till abolished by Tsar Nicholas I (1796–1855), for punishing criminals.

Knox, COLONEL FRANKLIN (1874–1944), USA Navy Secretary, who built up the modern Atlantic and Pacific fleets, and was thus partly responsible for ultimate victory in World War II.

Knox, JOHN, *noks* (*c.*1505–72), Scottish reformer, born near Haddington ; was the companion of the martyr George Wishart, who inspired Knox to adopt the Protestant faith. Captured by the French troops which took St Andrews castle 1547, Knox was sent by them to the galleys, but was released 1549. He did much to advance the Reformation by his vigorous preaching at Berwick and Newcastle ; was influenced by Calvin during his visit to Switzerland ; returned to Scotland 1559, and with the support of various Protestant nobles began his life's work of abolishing papal authority in Scotland, and replacing the RC religion with a form of Calvinism (Presbyterianism) in spite of Mary Queen of Scots. He helped to bring about various Acts confirming Scotland's adherence to Protestantism.

John Knox was not only a great religious reformer but also, for Scotland, the spirit of the Renaissance, doing much to establish a sound democratic education, and evolving a practical scheme which, under Church guidance, provided scholars with an extensive schooling.

Contrary to popular opinion, this fearless preacher, often regarded as narrow-minded, was actually more enlightened than most men of his day. He was certainly rough in speech, harsh in judgment, and on fire with a determination to make Scotland Calvinist, but he was more tolerant and practical than many of his contemporaries, and had a streak of humour that saved him from being wholly fanatical.

Knutsford, *nŭts'fĕrd*, town, Cheshire ; immortalised as Cranford by Mrs Gaskell.

koala, small animal (usually *c.*2ft long) often spoken of as the Australian bear, though it is not a bear but a kangaroo. It lives among eucalyptus (or blue gum)

THE KOALA

trees, the leaves of which provide it with food.

Kobé, *kō'be*, port, Japan ; on Osaka Bay ; has many industries ; pop. 967,000.

Koch, ROBERT, *kawch* (1843–1910), German bacteriologist ; ranks with Pasteur as a pioneer of that science ; discovered the organisms causing tuberculosis and cholera ; found the antidote to anthrax.

Koh-i-noor, see DIAMOND

kohl, *kōl*, antimony or lead sulphide used by women in eastern countries for darkening eyebrows and eyelashes.

Koine, see GREEK

Komati, river of SE. Africa ; flows into Delagoa Bay.

Königsberg, *kŭnichs-berch*, city and port, Germany ; near the mouth of the R. Pregel ; pop.368,000. Now called Kaliningrad.

Koo, DR WELLINGTON (1888–   ), Chinese statesman, b Shanghai ; educated in USA ; Minister to Britain 1921 ; Prime Minister and Minister of Foreign Affairs 1926–27 ; prominent in the League of Nations ; Ambassador in London ; a very able and distinguished diplomat ; retired 1946.

Köpenick, *kŭ'penik*, manufacturing district of Berlin.

kopje, *kop'i*, name in S. Africa for a flat-topped hill, somewhat similar to a tor in Cornwall.

Koran, see MOHAMMED

Korea, name by which Chosen is now commonly known. It was Japanese from 1910. After World War II that part of Korea which lies S. of the 38th parallel was occupied by American, that part which lies N. of it by Russian troops. Both sides evacuated their troops 1948. In June 1950 N. Korean Communists invaded S. Korea. U.N. forces aided S. Korea. China intervened against them and bitter fighting ensued. See CHOSEN

Kosciusko, *kos-i-ŭs'kō,* highest mt. (7,328ft) in Australia. It is in New S. Wales, and in winter the range (extending to Victoria) is one of the most exciting ski-ing regions in the world.

Kosciusko, TADEUSZ (1746–1817), Polish patriot ; led a revolt against the Russians 1794 ; captured Warsaw. He was taken prisoner, but worked always for the freedom of Poland. He is buried at Cracow.

Kossuth, LOUIS, *kosh'oot* (1802–94), Hungarian patriot ; demanded independence for Hungary 1848, and became Regent of Hungary. His armies were defeated 1849 by Serbs and Croats, and he spent his last years in exile.

Kowloon, see HONG KONG

kowtow, *kō'tow,* Chinese form of worship, greeting, or homage. The person who kowtows kneels and bows his head to the ground.

kraal, *kräl,* Dutch word for a group of huts encircled by a stockade ; hence a Hottentot or Kaffir village.

Krakatoa, see VOLCANO

Krefeld - Uerdingen, *krä'felt ĕr'ding-en,* Rhineland town (Germany) ; manufactures machinery, chemicals and textiles ; pop.169,000.

Kreisler, FRITZ, *krīs'lĕr* (1875–   ), Austrian violinist and composer ; toured USA when only 14 ; displayed an amazing technique ; interpreted classical music (and his own delightful studies) with extraordinary success ; owned two violins by Stradivarius.

Kremlin, see MOSCOW

Krishna, four-handed god of the Hindus, especially of the lower classes. His story is told in the epic of the *Mahabharata.*

Kronje, PIET ARNOLDUS, *kron'i* (1840–1911), Boer soldier ; captured the Jameson raiders 1896 ; defeated by Lord Roberts 1900 ; exiled to St Helena for a short time.

Kronstadt, *krōn'shtät,* port of Leningrad ; at the mouth of the R. Neva ; has extensive docks.

Kropotkin, PRINCE PETER, *kro-pŏt'kin* (1842–1921), Russian revolutionary, *b* Moscow ; fled to England ; author of social studies, e.g. *Mutual Aid, The Conquest of Bread.*

Kruger, STEPHEN JOHN PAUL, *krŭ'gĕr, kroo'-* (1825–1904), Boer politician, born of an old Dutch family in Cape Colony ; deeply religious but narrow-minded ; hated the British. As President of the Transvaal he encouraged the Boer War.

Kruger National Park, region of 9,000sq.m in NE. Transvaal ; said to have 500,000 animals, e.g. leopards, buffaloes, hippopotami, giraffes and deer ; founded by Kruger 1897 ; owes much to Stevenson-Hamilton, responsible for the Reserve 1902–46.

Krugersdorp, gold-mining town, Transvaal.

Krupp, *krŭp,* name of a German family of iron and steel manufacturers, the founder being Friedrich Krupp (1787–1826), *b* Essen. An enormous business was built up by Alfred Krupp (1812–87), who introduced the Bessemer process. The Krupp works, the largest of their kind in the world, produced immense quantities of arms and munitions during the two World Wars. The works were destroyed by Allied bombing *c.*1943–45.

krypton, element, Kr ; one of the inert rare gases ; found in the atmosphere (one portion in *c.*670,000) ; atomic number 36 ; atomic weight 83·7 ; discovered 1898.

Kubelik, JAN, *koo'be-lik* (1880–1940), Czech violinist, *b* Prague. His son is a well-known conductor.

Kubla or **Kublai Khan,** *koo'blī chän'* (1216–94), Chinese emperor, founder of the Mongol (or Yuen) line of rulers ; succeeded 1259 ; conquered all China by 1279 ; made his capital at what is now Pekin. A wise and enlightened monarch, he established Buddhism as the national religion. His magnificent court, visited by Marco Polo, inspired Coleridge's poem, *Kubla Khan.*

kudu, African antelope ; *c.*4½ft at the shoulder ; reddish brown with white stripes ; has an upright mane and twisted horns.

Kuibyshev, *kwē'bi-shef,* formerly Samara, city, USSR ; on the R. Volga ; important railway centre ; pop.400,000.

Ku-Klux-Klan, see SECRET SOCIETIES

Kumasi, chief town, Ashanti ; pop.45,000.

kunzite, peach-coloured gem which is remarkably fluorescent. It was recently discovered in California.

Kuomintang, *gwō'min-tang,* Chinese Nationalist party founded by followers of Sun Yat Sen.

Kurdistan, region S. of Armenia ; home of the Kurds, a Mohammedan people mostly pastoral nomads.

Kuriles, volcanic islands linked with the Aleutians, and handed to Russia by a secret pact at Yalta, 1945.

Kuwait, see ARABIA

KW, see ELECTRICITY

Kwangtung, province of S. China ; cap. Canton.

KWH, see ELECTRICITY

Kyles of Bute, channel between the I. of Bute and the coast of Scotland ; noted for its fine scenery. (*Caol* in Gaelic means 'narrow,' hence Kyles the 'Narrows.')

Kyoto, former cap. of Japan ; on the I. of Honshu ; pop.1,090,000.

L

Labour, see CAPITAL ; ECONOMICS ; MARX, H. KARL ; POLITICS ; PROFIT-SHARING

Labour and National Service, MINISTRY OF, department of the British Government founded as the Ministry of Labour 1916 ; extended 1939 ; deals with the administration of Employment Exchanges, Factory Acts ; settlement of industrial disputes ; administration of Trade Boards Acts ; collection and publication of facts and figures relating to labour, employment ; responsible for the administration of unemployment insurance ; gives advice to juveniles as to employment.

The Control of Engagements Order (1947) made it obligatory for men and women of certain age-groups to obtain full-time employment from their nearest Employment Exchange or Appointment Offices. Exemption was granted only to married women, and to those whose circumstances made exemption imperative. The Control of Engagements Order was withdrawn 1950.

Labour Exchange, see EMPLOYMENT EXCHANGE

Labour Party, see PARLIAMENT ; PARTY ; SOCIALISM

Labours of Hercules, see HERCULES

La Brabançonne, see ANTHEM

Labrador, area of *c.*120,000sq.m in the extreme E. of N. America. A dependency of Newfoundland, it is noted for cod, herring, salmon and iron ; the pop. is chiefly Eskimo ; cap. Battle Harbour.

A proposal was made (1947) in the Quebec Parliament for the building of a dam 10m long across the Strait of Belle Isle. It was suggested that this would turn the cold Labrador Current back towards the Arctic, and thus keep the R. St Lawrence ice-free all the year, possibly also ridding the Newfoundland Banks of icebergs and fog. Read *A Labrador Doctor,* Sir Wilfred Grenfell.

Labuan, island (area 35sq.m) in the Straits Settlements (Malaya) ; produces camphor, sugar and rubber ; invaded by the Japanese in World War II.

laburnum, tree commonly found in gardens in Britain ; has pendants of sulphur yellow flowers in structure rather like those of the sweet pea, though smaller. The seeds are contained in a pod, and are highly poisonous.

labyrinth, *lab'i-rinth,* maze of passages (usually underground) ; e.g. the Labyrinth constructed *c.*2300BC near Lake Moeris, Egypt, and discovered by Sir Flinders Petrie ; also that on the island of Crete, said to have been built for King Minos, and to have been the home of the Minotaur.

lac, Indian word for 100,000 ; used especially of rupees.

Laccadive Islands, *lak'ä-dīv,* 14 islands included in the province of Madras (India) ; pop.19,000.

lace, patterned open-work fabric, usually woven from cotton thread ; now chiefly machine-made ; but hand-made lace is more valuable. The chief types (all of which may be made by machinery) include (*a*) *needle-point,* a kind of twisted braid on a fabric foundation ; examples are Venetian and Brussels, the latter usually having an arrangement of stars or flowers ; (*b*) *machine-made* ; (*c*) *pillow,* which, when made by hand, is worked on a bobbin (called a pillow). Lace was first made by machinery at Nottingham *c.*1768 ; elaborate styles include Mechlin and Honiton.

Lacedaemon, see SPARTA

Lachesis, see FATES

Lackland, see JOHN (1166–1216)

lacrosse, *lä-cros',* outdoor game ; called ' baggatiway ' by North American Indians who played it in Canada ; now Canada's national game. Introduced to Britain 1876, it gained popularity but has never actually rivalled hockey.

The game is played twelve-a-side ; each player has a hickory stick (the ' crosse '). The stick is about four feet

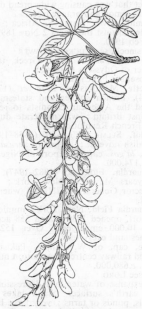

LABURNUM

long, is curved at the top and strung with a triangular net made of catgut. Near the bottom point of the triangle, which is about one and a half feet from the top of the stick, is a ledge of catgut on which the ball rests when it is caught in the net. Players throw the ball to each other, and ' tackle ' as in hockey.

The object is to get the ball into the opponents' goal. The field is from 100–150yd long, with goals 6ft high joined by a cross-piece 6ft wide.

The English Lacrosse Union was founded 1892. County Championships and inter-Varsity matches are played in winter and spring.

lactic acid, CH₃CH(OH)COOH, organic acid discovered 1780 ; obtained by fermenting sugar, tartaric acid, decaying cheese, sour milk and chalk ; there are several natural forms, one being responsible for muscular fatigue.

Ladoga, *lad'ō-gä,* lake (125m long, 80m wide) *c.*25m from Leningrad. It is the largest lake in Europe.

Ladrone or **Marianne Islands,** 14 islands besides Guam (the largest, which came under USA control 1898), the others being part of Nanyo, i.e. Japanese mandated territory.

ladybird, popular name for a flying beetle of which there are over 2,000 species, 40 of them common in Britain. Usually red or yellow, it has a varying number of black or white spots. The larva feeds on plant-lice. One species was introduced into California 1889 to combat an insect that was causing widespread damage to lemon and orange trees.

Ladysmith, town, Natal, S. Africa ; defended against the Boers 2 Nov 1899 to 28 Feb 1900.

lady's smock, see CUCKOO FLOWER

Laertes, *lā-ûr'tēz,* in old Greek tales, father of Odysseus (Ulysses).

laevulose, see FRUCTOSE

Lafayette, MARQUIS DE, *lä-fä-yet'* (1757–1834), French soldier and statesman ; aided the American colonists to revolt against Britain ; was moderate during the French Revolution.

Lagerlöf, SELMA, *lä'gēr-lūf* (1858–1940), Swedish novelist ; author of *Jerusalem.*

Lagos, *lä'gos,* cap. and port of Nigeria ; pop.174,000.

La Guardia, FIORELLO (1882–1947), for 12 years Mayor of New York ; was Director General of UNRRA when he died.

La Guardia Field, New York's municipal airport, opened 1939 ; area 558 acres ; has 10,000 employees. Over 152,000 planes land every year.

Lahore, cap. of W. Punjab, Pakistan ; noted railway centre ; has cotton mills ; pop. *c.*680,000.

laird, see LORD

lake, expanse of water in a depression of the earth's surface. Small lakes are pools, ponds or tarns ; very large lakes are sometimes called seas. Famous lakes include the Caspian Sea (area *c.*170,000sq.m) ; Victoria Nyanza (Africa) ; Aral Sea ; Chad (Africa) ; Nyasa ; Tanganyika ; Baikal (Siberia) ; Great Bear and Great Slave. Lake Titicaca (Bolivia and Peru) is 12,500ft above sea-level.

The Great Lakes of N. America include Superior, Huron, Erie, Michigan, Winnipeg, Ontario, etc. ; and the English Lake District (in Cumberland, Westmorland and N. Lancashire) includes Windermere, Rydal Water, Ullswater, Thirlmere, Coniston Water, situated among beautiful mt. peaks.

Among Scottish lakes (known as *lochs*) are Loch Lomond and Loch Katrine ; Irish lakes (*loughs*) include the lakes of Killarney and Lough Neagh. The largest lake in Wales is L. Bala.

Lake District, mountainous region of NW. England, chiefly Cumberland and Westmorland, but also N. Lancashire. Mts. include Scafell Pike 3,210ft, Helvellyn 3,118ft, Skiddaw 3,054ft ; lakes include Windermere 10¼m long ; Ullswater 7½m ; Coniston, Bassenthwaite, Derwentwater, Wastwater, Thirlmere (supplying Manchester with water), Crummock Water, Buttermere, etc. A favourite tourist centre and beloved by mountaineers, it is associated with Wordsworth, Coleridge, Southey and Ruskin.

lake-dwelling, prehistoric settlement, usually either (*a*) an ' island ' of logs, stones and brushwood, a little distance from the shore of a lake, as occasionally found in Scotland and Ireland ; or (*b*) pile-dwellings, i.e. a series of piles driven into the bed of the lake to support a platform on which rectangular huts were built. This type was common in Italy, Austria, Germany and Switzerland, also Scotland, Ireland, in the so-called Stone Age and Bronze Age. The colony was sometimes reached only by boat, but more often was linked to the shore by a narrow bridge of planks. Such settlements were cut off from attack by wild animals.

Lake Success, see UNO

Lamaism, form of Buddhism mixed with magic, and controlled (in Tibet and Mongolia) by many priests, chief among whom are the Dalai Lama, who lives in a palace near Lhasa, and the Tashi Lama, each supposed to be a previous lama returned to earth. The latest Dalai Lama, a boy, was installed in 1940. Lama means Superior One.

Lamarck, JEAN BAPTISTE, *lä-märk* (1744–1829), French naturalist born in Picardy ; won fame with his *Flore Française* at 34, embodying a new classification of plants ; later studied animal life, and was a pioneer of the theory of evolution. He died blind and poor. He is especially noted for his book on invertebrates, i.e. backboneless animals.

The importance of Lamarck's pioneer work in laying the foundations of the evolutionary theory cannot be overrated, and it may be noted that after being eclipsed by Darwin's theory, based on the struggle for existence, Lamarck's theories, with modifications, are now in the ascendency. See DARWIN, C. ; EVOLUTION

La Marseillaise, see ANTHEM

Lamartine, ALPHONSE MARIE DE, *lä-mär-tĕn'* (1790–1869), French poet and historian, born in Burgundy. For a time entered politics, but was too honest and too much an idealist to succeed. As a poet he has been compared with Cowper (*Méditations, Harmonies,* etc.), and as a historian his books include *Histoire de la Révolution.*

Lamb, CHARLES and MARY, brother and sister famous in English literature.

Charles Lamb (1775–1834), *b* Crown Office Row, Inner Temple, London, attended Christ's Hospital (a school), where he was the friend of Samuel Taylor Coleridge. For 33 years he was a clerk in E. India House. He bravely supported his parents and his sister, Mary (1764–1847), who, under the strain of trying to add a few shillings to their income while at the same time running the home, had a nervous breakdown, and when mentally unbalanced stabbed her mother to the heart. Mary remained in the care of her brother except when an inmate of an asylum at Hackney.

Charles added to his earnings by contributing to various publications, and with Mary wrote *Tales from Shakespeare* (1807). Other books include selections from the Elizabethan dramatists ; these prove him a most able critic. From 1820 he wrote essays for the *London Magazine,* signing them Elia. He retired from the E. India Office 1825 with a pension of £450 a year. Even in his retirement he had many anxieties over his sister, to whom he was touchingly devoted to the end. After suffering much ill-health and adversity, he *d* Edmonton, but Mary lived on nearly another 13 years.

The story of this lovable brother and sister is one of the most tragic and yet beautiful in literature. Charles forgot his irksome employment, his sorrows and anxieties, in hospitality to his many friends and in the joy of writing. His wit, humour, sympathy, fancy, gentleness, knowledge and courage are all in his famous *Essays of Elia,* possibly the finest in our language, and still loved and admired, especially *Christ's Hospital Five and Thirty Years Ago, Mrs Battle's Opinions on Whist, A Chapter on Ears, My Relations, Grace before Meat, Dream Children, Dissertation on Roast Pig, Popular Fallacies, The Superannuated Man,* etc. Elia was the name of one of Lamb's office fellows.

As an example of Elia's style consider this paragraph from *The Praise of Chimney-Sweepers* :

In one of the state-beds of Arundel Castle, a few years since—under a ducal canopy encircled with curtains of delicatest crimson, with starry coronets interwoven—folded between a pair of sheets whiter and softer than the lap where Venus lulled Ascanius—was discovered by chance, after all methods of search had failed, at noonday, fast asleep, a lost chimney-sweeper. The little fellow, having somehow confounded his passage among the intricacies of those lordly chimneys, by some unknown aperture had alighted upon this magnificent chamber ; and, tired with his tedious explorations, was unable to resist the delicious invitement to repose which he there saw exhibited ; so, creeping between the sheets very quietly, laid his black head upon the pillow, and slept like a young Howard.

Charles Lamb is remembered also as a poet, and still more as a most charming letter-writer.

The following are examples of his wit and humour : *Half as sober as a judge* ; *The greatest pleasure I know is to do a good action by stealth, and have it found out by accident* ; '*Presents,' I often say, 'endear Absents.'*

Lambeth, borough of London S. of the Thames ; here is Lambeth Palace, London home of the Archbishop of Canterbury.

Lammermuir, range of hills in Berwickshire, and E. Lothian.

lamp (electric), see ELECTRICITY; LIGHTING

lamp-black, actually soot, i.e. almost pure amorphous carbon ; much used in manufacturing printers' ink and other inks.

Lampeter, town, Cardiganshire ; has St David's College.

lampoon, satire ; generally an attack (a few lines of prose or verse) on the character of some well-known person.

lamprey, *lam'pri,* curious eel-like creature found in salt and fresh water ; three species are known along British coasts, one *c.*3ft long. The lamprey has no jaws, but a powerful sucker with horny teeth.

lamps, see LIGHTING

Lanarkshire, *lan'ĕrk-,* county of SW. Scotland, sometimes called Clydesdale ; densely populated ; co.tn Lanark, noted for cotton-spinning, hosiery, etc. ; but chiefly for its mines and a variety of industries directly or indirectly dependent on coal.

Lancashire, English county W. of Yorkshire and the Pennine Chain ; has a great coalfield in the south, where a huge population is gathered in the ' cotton towns '—Manchester, Bolton, Bury, Rochdale, Wigan, etc., with Liverpool as a port ; cap. Lancaster.

Lancaster, co.tn, Lancashire ; 4m from the mouth of the R. Lune ; noted for spinning, engineering, and especially linoleum ; pop.48,000.

Lancaster, DUKE OF, see JOHN OF GAUNT

Lancaster, HENRY DUKE OF (*d* 1361), English soldier ; a descendant of

Henry III ; commanded an army in Scotland 1336 ; saw much fighting in N. France ; won fame at Sluys. His daughter, Blanche, married John of Gaunt.

Lancaster Sound, channel linking Baffin Bay and Barrow Strait (N. America).

lancers, square dance in five figures ; invented in Paris 1836 ; popular in Britain from *c*.1850 ; has since lost popularity.

landes, *länd*, marshy or sandy region along the coast of the Bay of Biscay ; hence the department of Landes, SW. France.

Land Girl, see WOMEN'S LAND ARMY

Landor, WALTER SAVAGE (1775–1864), poet, *b* Warwick ; noted as the author of various books, including *Imaginary Conversations*.

landrail, see CORNCRAKE

Landseer, SIR EDWIN (1802–73), painter of animals, *b* London ; especially famous for his portrayal of dogs and deer, e.g. *The Highland Shepherd's Chief Mourner* ; *Dignity and Impudence*. He designed the lions in Trafalgar Square. Landseer catered for Victorian tastes : his painting is now regarded much less favourably.

Land's End, most westerly point of England, a granite headland in Cornwall.

Lanfranc, *lan'frangk* (d 1089), Norman churchman, *b* Italy ; entered the Benedictine abbey of Bec ; made Archbishop of Canterbury 1070 ; rebuilt the cathedral ; crowned William II (1087) ; was a great scholar, and did much to improve Church life.

Lang, COSMO GORDON (1864–1945), English churchman ; canon of St Paul's 1901 ; Archbishop of York 1908 ; Archbishop of Canterbury 1928 ; crowned George VI (1937) ; author of *The Miracles of Jesus*.

Langland, WILLIAM, 14th c. poet, probably *b* Shropshire ; believed to have written the famous poem *The Vision of Piers Plowman* 1360–99, giving vivid word-pictures of life in Chaucer's England, with a denunciation of those who oppress the poor, the greed of friars, bribery in Church life, and a description of the misery caused by wickedness and disease. The poem is alliterative (e.g. ' a *f*air *f*ield *f*ull of *f*olk '), and tells how Piers Plowman guides pilgrims to seek St Truth.

Langley, SAMUEL PIERPONT (1834–1906), American scientist and inventor. A pioneer of aviation, he built a motor-driven model plane 1896 which made the first recorded flight for a heavier than air machine.

Langton, STEPHEN (d 1228), English churchman and statesman ; made a cardinal 1206. Though elected Archbishop of Canterbury, he was not allowed to come to England until the pope threatened to depose King John. As archbishop, he opposed the king, and did much to aid the barons to draw up *Magna Carta* 1215. Langton was famous as the author of many religious books.

language (Lat. *lingua*, tongue), communication of thought by speech, also by writing or printing.

The origin of language remains largely an unsolved mystery. Various theories have been put forward, but precisely how man came to individual consciousness of himself and his world, and acquired the unique ability to exchange ideas, is still a puzzle. In some way he eventually learned to attach meaning to various sounds, combined sounds into words, and words into sentences expressing complex thoughts and emotions, a process outlined in masterly style by Professor R. A. Wilson in *The Miraculous Birth of Language* (1937).

The main language groups are (*a*) *Hamitic*, from which many African languages are derived, (*b*) *Semitic*, parent of Hebrew, Phoenician, Arabic, etc., (*c*) *Ural-Altaic*, giving such variations as Hungarian, Finnish, Mongol, Chinese, Japanese, etc., and (*d*) *Indo-European* or *Aryan* (or *Indo-Germanic* group), possibly first spoken in Babylon, Central Asia, N. and S. Russia, and by 2000BC developed into a variety of languages, namely (i) *Armenian*, (ii) an *Asiatic group*, e.g. Old Indian, Old Persian, Sanscrit, etc., and (iii) the *European group*.

Modern English comprises a mixture of many Indo-European languages, among which Norse, Anglo-Saxon, Norman-French, Celtic, Latin and Greek are predominant. In its present form it owes much to the Bible and to Shakespeare ; its spelling and pronunciation remain traditional rather than phonetic.

It should be noted that Latin, the language of the Romans, is of great importance even today because it is largely the foundation not only of English but also of French, Italian, Spanish and other so-called *Romance languages*. Like Greek, it is the basis of thousands of scientific words ; but our ' borrowings ' from other languages are many, e.g. from Russian, Mexican, Hebrew, N. American, Dutch, Hindustani, etc. While many words are introduced into the language every year, other words are falling into disuse, or becoming obsolete, or undergoing a change in meaning.

Normally a language ' grows ' slowly, but many artificial languages, such as *Esperanto*, have been invented, the idea being to produce a world-language by means of which language-differences may be eliminated, but so far none has been adopted for this purpose. In 1942 Lancelot Hogben produced *Interglossa*, founded on common scientific roots. Much has been done in recent years to extend the influence of English, but its spelling, pronunciation and idiom are perhaps too complex for it to become a world favourite, though a simplified form, *Basic English*, is now well established, its 850 words doing the work of *c*.20,000.

By *dialect* we mean a local variation of the standard language, e.g. W. Yorkshire and Cockney. Education tends to discourage dialect in Britain, but much is being done (e.g. by the production of dialect plays) to preserve these vividly expressive variations of ' the king's English.'

Read *The English Language*, L. Pearsall Smith ; *Romance of Words*, Ernest Weekley ; *What a Word!* A. P. Herbert ; and consult *The King's English*, H. W. and F. G. Fowler. See SLANG

Langue d'oc, old French dialect used by the troubadours S. of the R. Loire.

lanoline, fat obtained from purified woolgrease ; much used as a basis for creams and ointments.

Lansbury, GEORGE (1859–1940), politician; entered Parliament 1910 ; chairman of the National Labour Party 1927–28 ; leader of the Parliamentary Labour Party 1931–35 ; was a staunch believer in pacifism, and tried hard to persuade governments to settle disputes in conference.

lanthanum, element and rare earth ; La ; atomic weight 138·92 ; atomic number 57.

Lao-tse, *low'dzŭ*, Chinese thinker ; said to have lived *c.*600BC. Little is known of him, but tradition says he left the city of Chow when a very old man, and after passing through the N. gate of the province was never seen again. Lao-tse was the founder of Taoism. One of the three great religions of China, it is based on reason and virtue as set out in the *Tao-te-King*, the ' Bible ' of Taoism, and praises benevolence, righteousness and the acceptance of life as we find it.

La Paz, *la päs*, city, Bolivia ; here is the seat of the government ; pop.300,000.

La Pérouse, COMTE DE, *pā-rooz* (1741–88), French sailor ; set out 1785 on a voyage round the world, doubled Cape Horn, reached China and then Botany Bay, after which he vanished, his wrecked ship being found on a coral reef of the New Hebrides.

lapis lazuli, *lap'is laz'ū-lī*, rare mineral prized for its brilliant blue colour. Actually sodium aluminium silicate, it contains sulphur. It has been used for ornamental purposes from the earliest times. Found in China, Siberia, Iran and Chile.

Laplace, PIERRE SIMON, MARQUIS DE, *lä-pläs'* (1749–1827) French mathematician ; published papers on the integral calculus before he was 20 ; won fame with his brilliant astronomical theories as set out in *Exposition du système du Monde* (1796) and *Mécanique Céleste*, a work taking rank with Newton's *Principia*. Recognised as the greatest mathematician of his day, he is remembered for his famous nebular hypothesis, his studies of the motions of Jupiter and Saturn and of the moon and tides. He invented the Laplace differential equation.

Lapland, cold northern region in Norway, Sweden, Finland and Russia ; has huge forests ; also rich iron mines. It is the home of the Lapps, many of whom are nomads. They are short and ungainly, and number *c.*35,000 apart from those in Alaska.

La Plata, *lä plä'tä,* city, Argentine ; noted for meat-packing ; pop.200,000. The La Plata R. is an estuary *c.*200m long.

Lapps, see LAPLAND

lapwing, see PLOVER

larch, tall, cone-bearing tree, sometimes 100ft high ; sheds its tufts of needle-like leaves early in winter. The larch, with downward sweeping branches, grows in Britain, and especially in Italy, where it is tapped for its turpentine. The timber makes pit-props.

lard, fat of the pig, especially that surrounding the kidneys and stomach ; when refined it is white and of the consistency of butter.

lares et penates, *la'rēz et pē-nä'tēz,* Latin words which may be translated *household gods*, i.e. home, and everything that makes for home. In ancient Rome *lares* were gods or ancestors ; *penates*, gods guarding the house.

largo, in music, a slow, dignified movement.

lark, name of many closely-related birds, seven of which are found in Britain, though only two breed here—(*a*) SKYLARK, *c.*7in long ; brown, streaked with black above, yellowish white below ; builds a nest of dry grass in a hollow in the ground ; lays 3–5 eggs blotched grey and brown ; feeds mostly on insects and seeds ; loved for its fine singing ; admired for its ability to soar to great heights ; praised by Shelley and Wordsworth ; (*b*) WOODLARK, similar but smaller.

All larks have a long, straight claw on the hind toe, and long, pointed wings.

THE SKYLARK

La Rochefoucauld, FRANÇOIS DUC DE, *lä räsh-foo-kō'* (1613–80), French author ; was for a time a soldier ; plotted much as a courtier ; noted for his letters and memoirs, but most famous for his 700 maxims expressing great wordly wisdom in a subtle and polished style, e.g. *Le vrai moyen d'être trompé, c'est de se croire plus fin que les autres*, i.e. The surest way to be cheated is to think oneself cleverer than other people.

La Rochelle, *lä rō-shel'*, town and port, W. coast of France ; noted for shipbuilding and sugar-refining ; associated with the Huguenots ; pop.48,000.

larva (Latin *mask*), term in biology for a creature between the egg and the adult if its shape and general characteristics are different from those of the perfect creature, e.g. the caterpillar is the larva of the butterfly ; the tadpole the larva of the frog. Many larvae live in water before changing to winged insects.

LARVA

The Caterpillar of the Privet Hawk Moth and the Frog Tadpole

laryngitis, *lar-in-jī'tis*, inflammation of the larynx, or voice organ, causing hoarseness or loss of voice and possibly coughing.

larynx, *lar'ingks*, in human beings, the upper portion of the *trachea* or windpipe ; its front cartilage forms the Adam's apple. Inside the expanded airpassage, which goes up behind the root of the tongue (*epiglottis*), are the *false vocal cords*, two folds of mucous membrane immediately above the *true vocal cords*, which are of an elastic tissue. In speaking, air comes up the larynx, causing a musical note as a result of the vibrations of the true vocal cords, the pitch and character of the note being governed by muscles (controlled by nerves) varying the elasticity of the cords. The musical note is articulated into words partly by the tongue and lips.

La Salle, RENÉ, *lä säl* (1643–87), French explorer ; charted the St Lawrence 1669 ; explored the Ohio and Mississippi ; claimed the country around for the King of France (Louis XIV) and named it Louisiana.

lascar, Indian native sailor, or (more strictly) an Asiatic seaman who was

before 1947 a subject of British India. He is usually employed as a deck hand.

Lashio, town in the Shan States, Burma ; terminus of the Burma Road (from Chungking) built in World War II.

Laski, HAROLD J. (1893–1950), economist, *b* Manchester ; professor of political science, London University 1926 ; noted for many brilliant books, e.g. *The Foundation of Sovereignty, Grammar of Politics, Democracy in Crisis, Rise of European Liberalism* ; was closely associated with the Labour Party.

Las Palmas, port, Grand Canary, Canary Is. ; a refuelling station for oil-burning ships ; pop.124,000.

Lassalle, FERDINAND, *lä säl* (1825–64), German Socialist, *b* Breslau ; founder of the German Socialist movement.

lasso, *lass-oo'* (Spanish *lazo*, snare), cord or thong with a slip-noose ; may be 30–100ft long ; much used by Americans for noosing horses and cattle.

latent heat (Latin *latens*, hidden), quantity of heat required to effect a change of state of one gram of a substance from solid to liquid (latent heat of fusion) or from liquid to vapour (latent heat of vaporisation) without change of temperature. The quantity of latent heat required to transform ice at freezing point to water is as much as would raise the same quantity of water 80°C in temperature. The latent heat of vaporisation of water at normal atmospheric pressure is 536·2 calories per gm.

If the evaporation of a liquid occurs without heat being supplied from an outside source, the necessary heat is taken from the substance itself, and cooling results. On a small scale the evaporation (due to a large surface aided by draught) from wet muslin draped over a milk bottle helps to keep milk cool in hot weather. The same effect is secured with a porous earthenware cover, and with skin water carriers used in hot countries. See HEAT

latent image, see PHOTOGRAPHY

lathe, *lāth*, machine by means of which wood, metal and plastics may be rotated while a shaped tool is held against the surface to produce cylindrical form. Most lathes, especially the heavier types for metalwork, are power-driven ; some (as employed by jewellers) are capable of handling exceedingly small pieces of wood or metal ; others deal with masses weighing 200 tons.

A slight adaptation of the principle of the lathe is the boring machine (horizontal or vertical), e.g. for guns, also cylinders for internal combustion engines.

There are also screw-cutting attachments.

Latimer, HUGH (*d* 1555), martyr, born near Leicester ; became one of the most popular preachers of the Reformation period, and had the support of Henry VIII because he favoured the king's divorce from Catherine of Aragon.

Found guilty of heresy in Mary's reign, he was burned at the stake with Nicholas Ridley at Oxford, his last words being :

Be of good cheer, Master Ridley, and play the man ; we shall this day light such a candle by God's grace in England as, I trust, shall never be put out.

See RIDLEY, NICHOLAS

Latin, one of the Indo-European group of languages (see LANGUAGE) ; has much in common with Greek. Originally spoken by the Latini, inhabitants of the plain of Latium, Italy, it had become the language of the Romans by the 3rd c. BC. Later it broke up into a variety of languages, and gave rise to French, Spanish, Italian and Portuguese, etc.

Latin has long been studied (with Greek) by students. Though by no means as subtle or poetic as Greek, Latin is an excellent medium for historians and orators, and was used in the Courts of W. Europe till the end of the 17th century. A vast number of English literary, scientific and commercial words are of Latin origin.

As a written language, Latin covers three main periods : (*a*) the earlier literature of the Republic, 240–70BC, with such writers as Terence, Scipio and Lucilius ; (*b*) the Golden Age, say 70BC–AD14, including the Ciceronian and Augustan periods, and the works of such men of genius as Lucretius, Ovid, Cicero, Julius Caesar, Sallust, Virgil, Horace and Livy ; (*c*) a period of decline, about AD14–524, which however includes such great writers as Tacitus and Juvenal.

Latin League, see LATIUM

latitude, imaginary circle round the earth, parallel to the equator (which is latitude 0°), and either N. or S. of it, the poles being 90°N or S. All places on the same parallel (or parallel of latitude) are the same distance from the equator ; and on the average the distance of 1° of latitude is approx. 69·16m.

Latium, now a department of Italy in the region of Rome ; anciently a wide area inhabited by Latins, the Latin League comprising 30 states or towns ; destroyed by Rome *c.*338BC.

Latvia, see USSR

Laud, WILLIAM (1573–1645), Archbishop of Canterbury from 1633, *b* Reading, Berkshire. Though genuinely pious and courageous, he reverenced tradition and hated Puritanism, hence his support of Charles I, his belief in the Divine Right of kings, his ruthless policies against Dissenters, and his attempts to make all worship uniform. Impeached for high treason by the Long Parliament, he was committed to the Tower, and executed on Tower Hill. He shares with the Earl of Strafford much of the blame for the Civil War, and made the blunder of attempting to force people to do what conscience forbade.

laudanum, *lŏd′năm,* poisonous alcoholic tincture of opium ; taken to relieve pain.

Lauder, SIR HARRY (1870–1950), Scottish singer and comedian, *b* Portobello ; immensely popular for his blend of humour and sentiment ; wrote and composed his own songs, e.g. *I Love a Lassie* ; knighted 1919 ; autobiography *Roamin' in the Gloamin'* published 1928.

laughing gas, nitrous oxide, N_2O ; colourless and rather sweet ; used in dentistry. See NITROGEN

laughing jackass, see KINGFISHER

laurel, see BAY TREE

Laurie, ANNIE (1682–1764), Scottish girl immortalised by her rejected lover, William Douglas, in a famous song, somewhat altered and set to music by Lady Scott (1810–1900).

Laurier, SIR WILFRED (1841–1919), Canadian statesman, born in the state of Quebec ; Prime Minister 1896, the first French Canadian to hold that office. His slogan was *Canada first.*

Lausanne, *lō-zan′,* city, Switzerland ; near L. Geneva ; much favoured by tourists ; has long been an educational centre ; scene 1932 of a reparations conference ; pop.93,000.

Lausanne, TREATY OF, 1923, attempt between the three powers—France, Britain and Italy—to settle with Turkey various Near East questions, including the mandated states of Palestine, Iraq and Syria. This was followed (1932) by a conference of European Powers, at which it was agreed to end payment of World War I debts.

lava, see BASALT

Laval, PIERRE, *lä-väl′* (1883–1945), French politician ; Prime Minister 1931–32, later Minister for Foreign Affairs. In World War II he was Hitler's pawn after the fall of France, compelling the French to collaborate with Germany. For this he was tried 1945, and sentenced to death.

lavender, shrub with a thick stem branching into a bushy head *c.*2ft high ; has downy-green leaves with rolled edges ; spikes of mauve flowers, from which oil of lavender (the basis of lavender-water) is distilled.

Lavery, SIR JOHN, *lā′veri* (1856–1941), portrait painter, *b* Belfast.

Lavoisier, ANTOINE LAURENT, *lä-vwä-zi-ā* (1743–94), French chemist, *b* Paris ; appointed to many offices, e.g. advising on the manufacture of gunpowder, and various economic reforms, public health and currency, while at the same time experimenting in chemistry and physics. His fame rests on his various discoveries, including the true nature of combustion, disproving the phlogiston theory ; and (with Laplace) the discovery of the composition of water. During the Revolution he was guillotined by an ignorant tribunal which declared : *France needs no more scientists.*

law, word with several meanings : (*a*) *natural laws* which, in a general sense, nature always obeys ; (*b*) *law of the land,* i.e. a group of rules by which order and justice are maintained. These vary in different countries, e.g. in Britain motorists must drive on the *left* of the road, in USA on the *right* (the point is that if everyone obeys the law of the road there will be no collisions) ; (*c*) *civil law*, governing the way in which citizens should treat one another ; (*d*) *canon law*, laws that have been made by churchmen ; (*e*) *statute laws*, those made by Parliament ; (*f*) *by-laws*, regulations or orders made by a corporation, company or trade ; (*g*) *criminal law*, dealing with crimes against people or property.

A country's laws form its *legal system.* The *legislature* (in Britain) is Parliament, which has the right to make and unmake laws. Judges in law courts declare the law, the police see that alleged lawbreakers are brought to trial.

Great law-givers include Moses, Hammurabi, King Alfred. The laws of most European countries and of USA are based on those of the Romans.

Law, BONAR (1858–1923), politician, born in New Brunswick, Canada ; entered the British Parliament as a Conservative 1900 ; leader of the party 1911 ; Chancellor of the Exchequer, under Lloyd George ; attended the Peace Conference 1919 ; Prime Minister for a short period from 1922 ; a man of unquestioned honesty.

law agent, see NOTARY

lawn tennis, variation of the old game of tennis, known in England in Chaucer's day, and in favour in the 16th c. Tennis, being extremely complicated and for the nobility only, was adapted (as lawn tennis) in the 19th c. for popular play, its code of laws being issued 1875, and the first championship played at Wimbledon 1877. The Lawn Tennis Association was founded 1888, and the Davis Cup instituted 1900.

Notable tennis champions include W. Tilden, F. J. Perry, Mlle S. Lenglen, Helen Moody and Dorothy Round.

The Wightman Cup is the women's equivalent of the Davis Cup.

Lawrence, DAVID HERBERT (1885–1930), English poet and novelist, born in Nottinghamshire ; travelled in Italy, Australia and Mexico ; wrote many novels (e.g. *Sons and Lovers*), several plays, and was noted as a poet, especially for his description of nature.

Lawrence, DR ERNEST (1901–   ), American scientist famous for his research into atomic structure ; awarded the Nobel prize for his invention of the cyclotron ; has applied physics to biology and medicine, especially to the treatment of cancer ; experimented in the artificial production of radium ; associated with the development of the atom-bomb of 1945.

Lawrence, SIR HENRY (1806–57), soldier and administrator, *b* Ceylon ; fought in the Burmese, Afghan and Sikh wars ; in command at Lucknow during the Indian Mutiny, where he held out for six weeks, but died of wounds.

Lawrence, LORD (1811–79), soldier and administrator, *b* Richmond, Yorkshire ; Lieutenant-Governor of the Punjab ; responsible for many reforms ; won the favour of the Sikhs ; captured Delhi during the Indian Mutiny (1857) ; Governor-General of India (1864), when he introduced wise policies.

Lawrence of Arabia (THOMAS EDWARD LAWRENCE) (1888–1935), British soldier and administrator, born in a Welsh village near Snowdon ; travelled much in Syria.

During World War I he turned aside from excavating Hittite ruins to become head of the military intelligence department in Egypt. Given the rank of colonel 1916, he organised an Arab Bureau, and became director of the Arab army against the Turks, planning and carrying out many daring raids. He co-operated with General Allenby in Palestine, holding Damascus until Allenby arrived.

Lawrence attended the Peace Conference 1919 ; was regarded as having a more intimate knowledge of Middle East problems than any other living man, and was styled the ' uncrowned king of Arabia.'

After being at the Colonial Office, he became a private in the RAF (1922). He later entered the Tank Corps, but returned to the RAF as Aircraftsman Shaw. He was killed in a motor-cycle accident.

Lawrence published a translation of Homer's *Odyssey* ; also *The Seven Pillars of Wisdom*, one of the most remarkable books of this century. Read *Lawrence and the Arabs*, Robert Graves.

Layamon, *lä'a-mon, lä'yä-*, English poet who lived *c.*1200 ; wrote *Brut*, the first English poem after the Norman conquest. This traces the history of Britain to the 7th c.

Lazarus, name of two NT characters ; (*a*) the brother of Mary and Martha at Bethany (mentioned in John 11, where we read that Jesus raised him from the dead) ; (*b*) a beggar in the parable of Dives and Lazarus (Luke 16).

LCC, short for London County Council. See LONDON COUNTY COUNCIL

LCM, in mathematics, short for least common multiple, i.e. the least number into which two or more numbers will divide without remainder, e.g. 24, 36, 75 :

$$24 = 2 \times 2 \times 2 \times 3 \quad \text{or } 2^3 \times 3$$
$$36 = 2 \times 2 \times 3 \times 3 \quad \text{or } 2^2 \times 3^2$$
$$75 = 3 \times 5 \times 5 \quad \text{or } 3 \times 5^2$$
$$\therefore \text{LCM} = 2 \times 2 \times 2 \times 3 \times 3 \times 5 \times 5$$
$$\text{or } 2^3 \times 3^2 \times 5^2$$

i.e. 1,800. See FACTORS

Leacock, STEPHEN (1869–1945), economist, *b* Hampshire ; went to Canada as a child ; became professor of political economy ; author of many books on economics, but more famous as a writer of humorous short stories.

lead, metallic element, Pb ; atomic weight 207·21 ; atomic number 82 ; occurs in nature mainly as lead sulphide, PbS, i.e. the mineral galena, found chiefly in USA, Australia, Spain ; extracted by roasting in a reverbratory furnace. A soft, silvery metal, its melting-point is 327°C ; specific gravity 11·3.

Being easily manipulated, lead is much used by plumbers, especially for piping. Its compounds, all poisonous, include LEAD DIOXIDE, PbO_2, a dark brown powder ; LITHARGE (lead monoxide), PbO, a crystalline, reddish-yellow solid, used in manufacturing flint-glass, various glazes, varnishes, etc. ; RED LEAD, Pb_3O_4, a scarlet powder used as a pigment ; WHITE LEAD (basic lead carbonate, $2PbCO_3.Pb(OH)_2$), much used in making paint. As an alloy, lead is mixed with antimony to make shot and type-metal ; four parts of tin to one part of lead (together with a minute quantity of antimony) forms PEWTER, once commonly used for drinking cups, dishes, etc. LEAD ACETATE (sugar of lead), $(CH_3COO)_2Pb.3H_2O$, a crystalline soluble salt, is used in dyeing ; LEAD TETRA-ETHYL is the anti-knock agent in ' ethyl ' petrol.

Lead is the final result of the radio-activity of uranium. Its atom has 82 outer electrons and 82 protons, but there are also 8 isotopes, the two most abundant being (a) 208 times the weight of the hydrogen atom, and (b) 206 times the weight of the hydrogen atom.

lead glance, see GALENA

leaf-insect, straight-winged insect with wing-covers (especially in the female) closely resembling leaves in shape and colour ; found mostly in tropical regions.

League of Nations, see UNO ; WILSON, T. W. ; WORLD WAR I

Leamington, lem', fashionable health resort, Warwickshire ; has medicinal springs ; pop.34,000.

Leap year, see CALENDAR

Lear, EDWARD (1812–88), writer and artist, b London ; most famous for his humour, e.g. *Book of Nonsense Rhymes* (with quaint drawings), and *More Nonsense Rhymes.* See LIMERICK

Least Common Multiple, see LCM ; FACTORS

leather, tanned skin or hide of an animal, e.g. cow, ox, horse, or the skins of smaller animals, e.g. sheep, deer, goats, also of marine creatures, such as seals, crocodiles and sharks ; also lizards etc.

Prior to the 19th c. tanning was usually a lengthy process (one or two years), but for sole leather it now takes three to six months. After soaking, leather is then (if necessary) steeped in slaked lime, or some other chemical, to remove hair. It is then delimed and tanned, possibly with a liquid containing tannic acid from oak-bark or chestnut extract, sumach, gambier ; or alum may be used in a tawing process, especially for glacé-kid and calf kid. We have also chrome-

tanned leathers, now much in favour (e.g. for boot soles). These are soaked in a solution of chrome alum or chromium sulphate, the process being completed in a few days only.

Chamois leather is prepared from the skins of sheep and deer, usually by an oil process. So-called Morocco (for book-binding) is usually goatskin tanned with sumach, and may (or may not) have come from N. Africa. Patent leather is leather covered with varnish.

Artificial leather may be, say, American leather-cloth, which is actually cloth with an oily pigment in it ; or vegetable leather, a kind of caoutchouc dissolved in naphtha and smeared on linen.

See PLATE 16 (*bottom*)

leather-jacket, see CRANE-FLY

leaves, see BOTANY

Lebanon, see SYRIA AND LEBANON

Leblanc, NICHOLAS, *lĕ-blän'* (1742–1806), French chemist ; founded the Leblanc process of producing soda artificially, a method now replaced by the Solvay process.

Lebrun, ALBERT, *lĕ brün* (1871–1950), French statesman ; President of the Republic 1932, forming a national government.

Lecky, WILLIAM EDWARD (1838–1903), historian, born near Dublin ; author of several important books, the most famous being *The History of England in the 18th Century.*

Leclanché cell, see ACCUMULATORS AND BATTERIES

Le Creusot, *lĕ krŭ-zō,* town, France, 55m from Dijon ; noted for iron and coal ; pop.33,000.

Lee, ROBERT EDWARD (1807–70), American soldier ; became Commander-in-Chief of the Confederate army in the American Civil War ; showed great courage and skill, winning many victories (e.g. Bull Run 1862, Chancellorsville 1863) ; but the Federals had superior forces, and he surrendered to General Grant at Appomattox Court House 1865.

Leeds, city, W. Yorkshire ; on the R. Aire ; associated with woollen goods, tailoring, also leather, printing and engineering ; has a university (founded 1904). KIRKSTALL ABBEY is within the boundary ; pop.493,000.

Leeds, THOMAS OSBORNE, 1ST DUKE OF, (1628–1712), wished to maintain Clarendon's policy of intolerance towards the RC faith or that of Dissenters ; was among those who invited William of Orange to England.

Leek, silk-manufacturing town, Staffordshire.

Leeuwenhoek, ANTON VAN, *lā'ven-huk* (1632–1723), Dutch scientist ; first to observe bacteria through the microscope and to describe red blood corpuscles. See BACTERIA

Leeward Islands, British colony among the W. Indies ; total pop. c.108,000 ; they include (a) ANTIGUA, the seat of the government, noted for sugar ; cap.

St John ; (*b*) BARBUDA, popular with sportsmen for its deer-stalking and tarpon fishing ; (*c*) ST KITTS, producing sugar and cotton ; cap. the port of Basseterre ; also the Is. of Nevis and Anguilla ; (*d*) MONTSERRAT, discovered by Columbus 1493 ; has been British since 1784 ; largely mountainous and subject to hurricanes ; exports cotton-seed, cotton and limes ; chief town Plymouth ; (*e*) British Virgin Is.

left or **left wing,** term used loosely in politics to cover those parties which favour a rapid rather than a slow rate of progress ; nowadays usually means the Socialist party and its supporters. The term seems to have come from the National Assembly at Versailles 1789, when the more moderate party sat on the right, extremists on the left. See PARLIAMENT

legatee, see WILL

Leghorn, *le-gorn'*, port, Tuscany, Italy ; noted for shipbuilding ; is 12m from Pisa ; popular with tourists ; pop. 129,000 ; gave its name to the Leghorn fowl, a good egg-laying breed of poultry. (Leghorn is the English name ; the Italian is Livorno.)

legion, chief unit of the Roman army ; originally *c.*3,000 men, but increased by Servius Tullius to 4,200, i.e. 3,000 troops with heavy arms, 1,200 with light. From the time of Marius (157–85BC) a legion consisted of 6,000 men, and was divided into thirty maniples (or companies), each commanded by two centurions. A legionary soldier's arms comprised helmet, shield, cuirass, sword, dagger and the *pilum,* a kind of javelin.

legislature, body of people in a country with power to make laws, e.g. (in theory) the king and the two Houses of Parliament in the UK ; two Houses of Parliament in Australia or Canada ; the President and Congress in USA.

Le Havre, see HAVRE

Leibniz, GOTTFRIED WILHELM, *lip'nitz* (1646–1716), German mathematician and philosopher, *b* Leipzig ; became doctor of law ; was president of the Berlin Academy. He is notable as the discoverer of the differential and integral calculus ; also for his philosophy, which may be summarised as the theory that this world is the best possible, and that everything is for the best.

Leicester, *les'tĕr*, historic co.tn and city, Leicestershire. A great industrial centre, it is noted for hosiery, boots, shoes, lace and rubber goods. Leicester is on the R. Soar ; pop.257,000. Among its many ancient buildings are the ruins of the abbey where Cardinal Wolsey died.

Leicester, ROBERT DUDLEY, EARL OF (*d* 1588), son of the Duke of Northumberland, he was brother-in-law of Lady Jane Grey. He married Amy Robsart 1550, for whose death he was supposed to have been responsible. Present at the siege of St Quentin 1557, he com-

manded an expedition to the Netherlands 1585, was in command of the forces at Tilbury in Armada year, and died suddenly at Cornbury, Oxfordshire.

For thirty years a favourite of Queen Elizabeth, Leicester was also one of her suitors. He entertained her lavishly at Kenilworth, and was renowned for his magnificence, but he was disliked as a statesman, and was an incompetent soldier. Vain and unscrupulous, he was a patron of literature and architecture, and showed favour to the Puritans.

Leicestershire, Midland county of England ; noted for farming, mining and hunting ; co.tn Leicester.

Leigh, *lē*, town, Lancashire ; has silk and cotton factories, coal mines and iron foundries ; pop.45,000.

Leighton, LORD FREDERICK, *lā'tun* (1830–1896). Victorian painter, *b* Scarborough, Yorkshire. His pictures are ' classical ' subjects, and are very refined in treatment. They appealed strongly to Victorian taste, but are less highly thought of nowadays. Leighton was made a peer one day and died the next.

Leinster, *len'stĕr*, province of Eire, separated from Connaught by the R. Shannon.

Leipzig, *lip'sik*, city, Saxony (Germany) ; long noted for its university, libraries, museums, music festivals, trade in books, and for printing, bookbinding and paper-making. Its fair, one of the greatest in the world, has been held since *c.*1170 ; pop.702,000.

Leith, see EDINBURGH

Leitrim, *lē'trim*, county of Eire, in the province of Connaught ; co.tn Carrick on Shannon.

Leix, *leks*, county of Eire, known as Queen's County prior to 1922 ; it is in the province of Leinster ; co.tn Maryborough.

Leland, JOHN, *lē'land* (*d* 1552), antiquary, *b* London ; searched the records of abbeys and colleges for items of antiquarian interest ; noted for his *Itinerary,* a record of an antiquarian tour in England and Wales.

Lely, SIR PETER, *lē'li* (1618–80), portrait painter, born near Utrecht ; lived in England from 1641.

lemming, rodent, rather like a vole, found in Norway, Lapland, Siberia and N. America. The European lemming,

THE LEMMING

WATER FOR POWER   *plate 41*

Great volumes of water race through the Canadian landscape. When harnessed by dams
like this one at Barret Chute they provide power for Canadian industries.
(Canadian National Film Board)

plate 42   HARNESSING THE WATER

Top : To harness this source of power requires constructional work costing hundreds of thousands of pounds. This picture shows work in progress on the Loch Sloy Dam, Dumbartonshire. (*North of Scotland Hydro-Electric Board*). *Bottom :* Spillway of the Chickamauga Dam, U.S.A. (*U.S. Information Service*)

POWER FROM WATER

plate 43

One great advantage of power-from-water is that it does not create dirt. *Top :* Three 17,400 h.p. water-driven turbine generators at Tongland Power Station. (*English Electricity Co.*). *Bottom :* Tongland Power Station : an external view. (*British Electricity Authority*)

plate 44   POWER FOR DISTRIBUTION

Power is distributed by a grid or network of transmission cables. *Top :* 487 ft. high steel pylons carry the grid across the Thames. (*British Insulated Callender's Cables Ltd*). *Bottom :* A modern grid control room. (*G.E.C.*)

ELECTRICITY

plate 45

A 530,000 volt arc jumping a string of insulators under test.
(*Steatite and Porcelain Products Ltd*)

plate 46   ATOMIC POWER—

By splitting the atom, science has given man a new source of almost incalculable power. This
1,000,000 volt electric generator at Oxford is used in connection with atomic research.
(*Sport and General Press*)

—GOOD OR ILL ?   *plate 47*

Explosion of an atom bomb. (*London News Agency*)

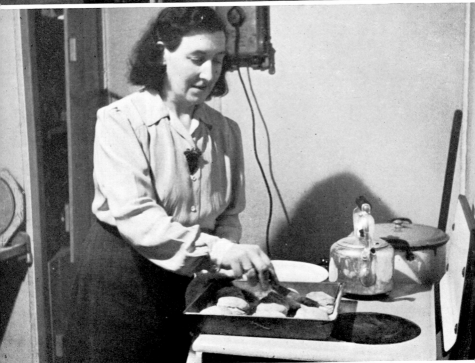

plate 48 USES OF ELECTRICITY

Electricity in the laboratory—and in the home—(*Top : I.C.I.   Bottom : Picture Post Library*)

chiefly brown, with black and white patches, is thick-set and short ; feeds on plants and is destructive to crops ; makes burrows. The most curious feature of the lemming is the occasional mass-migration that takes place, when millions of lemmings hurry westwards to the Gulf of Bothnia or the Atlantic, and swim out to sea till drowned. See MIGRATION

Lemnos, Greek island in the Aegean Sea ; produces wines and fruits.

lemon, fruit of a small evergreen tree, native of the E. Indies ; has oblong leaves and fragrant white flowers. The fruit contains *c.*7% citric acid ; the skin (made into candied peel by immersion in boiling sugar) is valuable for essence of lemon, an essential oil. Lemon juice is especially rich in vitamin C.

lemon sole, see SOLE

lemur, *lē'mĕr,* animal, one of the Primates (apes, monkeys and men) ; has a fox-like rather than a monkey type of face, and a bushy tail. There are many species, the largest being roughly the same size as a fox, the smallest no larger than a mouse. The true lemur is found only in Madagascar, but variations are common in Africa and India. Lemurs live wholly in trees (except when going from one copse to another), and are night-feeders, hence their large eyes.

Lena, *lē'nä,* river of Siberia ; flows *c.*2,800m to the Arctic Ocean.

Lend-Lease, wartime financial arrangement authorised by USA 1941–45 ; supplies were sent to the Allied Nations on the understanding that they would, in return, forward what they could to USA. Supplies issued by USA were valued at over 50,000,000,000 dollars. See WORLD WAR II

length, MEASURE OF, see WEIGHTS AND MEASURES.

Lenin, VLADIMIR ILYICH ULIANOV (1870–1924), founder of the USSR ; *b* Simbirsk ; early became a disciple of Karl Marx, whose Communist ideals he planned to execute at the earliest opportunity. A lawyer in St Petersburg (now called Leningrad), he was banished to Siberia, and met Trotsky in London 1902, the beginning of a momentous collaboration.

Lenin edited the first illegal Socialist newspaper; continuously stirred Russian workers by his propaganda, leading them to establish local soviets (councils) ; organised with Trotsky the Russian Revolution Nov 1917 ; became dictator of the new union of soviets, and restored order out of chaos with the aid of the Red Armies (red, symbol of revolution). He concluded a trade agreement with Britain 1921. He died of creeping paralysis. His embalmed body is in Red Square, Moscow.

Undoubtedly brutal and ruthless in his methods, Lenin was a practical idealist wholly without personal ambition. He had amazing organising

LENIN 1870–1924

ability, and was a pioneer in scientific development.

One of the first statesmen to realise the value of expert knowledge and technical ability, he destroyed an age-old system in Russia and lived to see the successful operation of a new form of government. See MARX, H. KARL

Leningrad, university city, great railway centre, and chief port, USSR ; on the delta of the R. Neva (Gulf of Finland) ; has a huge foreign trade ; pop. (1939) *c.*3,200,000 ; founded (as St Petersburg) by Peter the Great 1703, and was the Russian cap. till 1917. The name was then changed to Petrograd, and again 1924 to Leningrad. Leningrad is linked with the Volga by canal ; notable for magnificient buildings and its October 25th Street ; besieged by the Germans for ten months ending Jan 1943.

Lens, *läns,* town, N. France ; noted for mining, iron and steel ; pop.34,000.

lens, see LIGHT

Lent, see CALENDAR

lentil, plant (family *Leguminosae*), particularly common in Mediterranean countries ; resembles vetch ; has oblong leaflets and also tendrils ; its small blue flowers are like those of the pea. The fruit, in pods, is one of the most nutritious of all foods, and contains 25·7% protein ; 1% fat ; 59·2% carbohydrates ; 14·1% ash and water.

Leo, name of 13 popes, including Leo I (*d* 461), who succeeded in saving Rome from the invading Vandals ; Leo III (*d* 816), who crowned Charlemagne ; Leo X (1475–1521), a great patron of learning and art during the Renaissance.

Leofric (*d* 1057), Saxon earl, succeeded his father as Earl of Mercia ; was the husband of Lady Godiva.

Leominster, *lem'in-stĕr, lem'stĕr,* town, Herefordshire ; noted for hops and cider.

14

León, *lā-ōn,* old kingdom of N. Spain ; now a province.

Leonardo da Vinci, *lā-ōn-är'dō dä vēn'chē,* (1452–1519), artist, sculptor, inventor, scientist and pioneer, one of the world's outstanding geniuses, born in the village of Vinci, near the R. Arno, Italy ; extremely handsome and remarkably strong. As a youth he was exceptionally musical. He wrote poetry. At 18 he was apprenticed to Verrocchio, a sculptor and artist.

Between the ages of 30 and 47 he was in the service of Duke Ludovico Sforza of Milan, leading an exceedingly busy and varied life, e.g. inventing weapons, carving statues (including an equestrian statue of the duke), painting world-famous pictures, including his mural painting, *The Last Supper.* Later he moved to Florence, about which time he painted his portrait, *Mona Lisa,* now ranked among the greatest of European paintings, the mystical smile lending charm and mystery. He was military adviser to Cesare Borgia ; competed as an artist with Michelangelo ; and in 1516 accepted an invitation from Francis I to work in France, where he died.

LEONARDO DA VINCI 1452–1519

As a scientist Leonardo da Vinci had views of astronomy far beyond those of the astronomers of the time ; realised that many rocks had been laid down in water ; understood the classification of animals and the fundamental laws of gravitation, heat and light ; noted the working of the heart, and perceived that the blood circulates continuously, thus building up the tissues ; held that the search for perpetual motion was vain ; rediscovered the principles of pressures in liquids ; investigated wave-motion and the propagation of sound in air ; invented a heavier-than-air machine, and was a pioneer of the principles of mechanical flight ; constructed water-mills, breech-loading cannon, a swimming-belt, a smoke stack, a mincing-machine and a conical rifle bullet ; experimented with explosives and also with steam, which he suggested as a motive force for ships. In his pictures he reveals not only imagination and skill in breaking away from tradition, but his understanding of people. His use of colour and line are almost unsurpassed. For him the world was crowded with secrets about which he was curious to the end.

Leonidas, *lē-on'i-das* (*d* 480BC), King of Sparta from *c.*490BC ; remembered for his heroic defence of the pass of Thermopylae against the Persians, almost every man perishing.

leopard, *lep'ėrd,* flesh-eating animal, sometimes called panther ; common in Africa, Iran, India and China. The leopard (*Felis pardus*) is of the cat tribe, and has a yellowish body (often 4ft long) covered irregularly with black circles or spots. It climbs trees, hunts antelopes, monkeys, and smaller animals, but rarely attacks man. There is the *clouded leopard* of SE. Asia, and the *snow leopard* (or *ounce*). The so-called leopard of India, the cheetah, belongs to a different species. The *panther* (*c.*7ft long) is a ferocious spotted cat of Africa, S. Asia and Java.

Leopold I (1790–1865), younger son of Francis, Duke of Saxe-Coburg-Gotha ; married Princess Charlotte, daughter of George IV of England ; accepted (1831) an invitation to become King of the Belgians ; ruled wisely. As uncle of Queen Victoria, he gave her much advice on statecraft.

Leopold III (1901–) King of the Belgians, son of King Albert ; married Princess Astrid of Sweden 1926, who was killed in a motor accident 1935. Leopold succeeded his father 1934. In World War II he gave orders for his army's resistance to cease, which caused a good deal of anguish to the Belgian people, but whether it was actually open to him to do anything else is questionable. In 1945 Liberals and Socialists demanded Leopold's abdication. He returned 1950 with Catholic and clerical support ; but feeling ran high and he agreed that his son, Baudouin, should be crowned in September 1951.

Leopoldville, see BELGIAN CONGO

Lepanto, BATTLE OF, naval engagement 1571 between the Holy League, under Don John of Austria with *c.*200 ships, and a Turkish fleet of 275 ships off Lepanto, a harbour of Greece, 12m NE. of Patras. The last sea fight between oared galleys, the battle resulted in the complete defeat of the Turks.

leprosy, disease in which large spots on the face and limbs become ulcers, and leave white scars ; or, in another form, an extensive ulceration with decay of the nervous system. Gangrene of the limbs often follows, or the patient may die of pneumonia. No remedy was known before the 20th c., but now treatment may (if begun in time) prove successful, e.g. injections of chaulmoogra oil or hydrocarpus oil. A still more recent discovery is sulphetrone, first produced 1950 by British chemists, and now being tested in leper settlements overseas. Mentioned in the Bible (e.g. Leviticus 13), leprosy was prevalent in Asia and Europe long ago. In Europe, during the Middle Ages, lepers were compelled to wear a distinctive dress, to sound a bell or clapper, and to live apart in lazarettos. Their existence must have been utterly wretched. Many churches of Britain still have peep-holes in the chancel so that lepers might take part in the sacrament without entering. In Scotland the modern place-name Liberton means *lipper-town*, i.e. the settlement in which the lepers had to live in medieval times. Leprosy is common in the E. Indies, Malaya, over large areas of Asia, and along the African coasts, but it is now rare in most European countries, and is scarcely known in Britain, though isolated cases do occur. The RC Church has done fine work for lepers ; the devotion of Father Damien at Molokai being a shining example.

Lesbos, see MITYLENE

Leslie, DAVID (1601–82), Scottish soldier ; assisted the Parliamentarians at Marston Moor 1644, but later opposed Cromwell, and was defeated at Dunbar 1650.

Lesseps, FERDINAND DE, *le-seps'* (1805–94), French engineer ; entered the consular service ; organised a company 1858 to build the Suez Canal ; undertook 1879 the construction of the Panama Canal, but failed. See CANALS

Lesser Antilles, see ANTILLES

lesser celandine or **pilewort,** see CELANDINE

Lessing, GOTTHOLD EPHRAIM (1729–81), German dramatist and critic, born in Saxony ; set a new fashion by writing *Miss Sara Sampson,* 1755, a domestic play based on an English rather than a French model. He founded a national German literature ; noted for his *Laokoon,* a book that did much to revive an appreciation of art.

Letchworth, see TOWN PLANNING

Lethe, *lē'thē* (Gk *forgetfulness*), in old Greek tales, river of the underworld. Once the souls of the dead drank of its waters they forgot their earthly life.

lettres de cachet, *let'r dē kä-shä',* letters signed by the kings of France (especially Louis XIV), who thus sent many people to imprisonment for life without trial.

Letts, Indo-European race speaking a language similar to Lithuanian, and now numbering *c.*75% of the pop. of Latvia. Generally tall and robust, they tend to be blue-eyed and blonde.

leucocyte, *lū'cō-sīt,* white blood-corpuscle.

Levant, *lē-vant'* (French *levant,* rising, i.e. Orient), name given to the E. Mediterranean region generally, say Asia Minor, Syria, Palestine and Egypt.

The LEVANT COMPANY was an English trading association 1592–1825, importing such things as currants, spices, carpets, shawls and raw silk.

Leven, *lē'ven,* loch, Kinross-shire. Mary Queen of Scots was imprisoned in a castle on one of its islands.

Leverhulme, WILLIAM HESKETH LEVER, 1ST VISCOUNT, *lē'věr-hūm* (1851–1925), manufacturer, *b* Bolton, Lancashire ; began a soap-making business which eventually became world-wide ; built the model town of Port Sunlight near the R. Mersey ; was in co-partnership with his thousands of employees.

Leverrier, URBAIN JEAN JOSEPH, *lē-ve-riā'* (1811–77), French astronomer ; shares with the English astronomer, John Couch Adams, the distinction of having discovered the planet Neptune.

levers, see MECHANICS

Levi, *lē'vī,* OT character, 3rd son of Jacob, with whom he emigrated to Egypt. His descendants, known as Levites, were frequently priests among the Israelites. The OT book *Leviticus* deals with the customs and duties of the priests.

Lewes, *lū'is,* co.tn, Sussex ; on the R. Ouse ; has remains of a Norman castle. Hereabouts Simon de Montfort took Henry III prisoner 1264.

Lewis, northern part of the Long Island, Outer Hebrides (Scotland) ; the southern part, known as Harris, is noted for Harris tweeds.

Lewis, CECIL DAY (1904–), British poet and author. His publications include *Collected Poems, The Friendly Tree.*

Lewis, CLIVE STAPLES (1898–), tutor of Magdalen College, Oxford ; author of the brilliant and searching *Screwtape Letters, The Problem of Pain, That Hideous Strength,* and other books.

Lewis, SINCLAIR (1885–1951), American writer, born in Minnesota State ; won instant fame with his fine novel *Main Street* (1920), followed by *Babbit,* a name which has clung to the type of businessman—successful, smug and stupid—which forms the central figure in the book. Other vigorous and critical studies of defects in modern American life (especially in the Middle W.) include *Elmer Gantry, Anne Vickers, Dodsworth* (later filmed), and *Martin Arrowsmith.* Lewis was the first American to be awarded the Nobel Prize for Literature, and he has done much to reveal weakness in American society.

Lewis, WYNDHAM (1884–), British novelist and artist, *b* Maine, USA ; notable for his revolutionary art compositions of planes and wedges, symbolic, he declared, of mass-production and a machine-ruled world ; famous for his satires, e.g. *The Apes of God, Time and Western Man,* and other critical books.

Lewisham, borough of S. London.

lewisite, poison arsenical gas in the form of a heavy, oily liquid with the odour of geraniums ; blisters the skin.

Lexington, town, Massachusetts, USA ; scene 1775 of the first battle of the American War of Independence.

Leyden, *lī'den*, town, Netherlands ; noted for cloth and yarn, etc. The university, founded 1575, has long had a famous medical school ; pop.77,000.

Leyden jar, see ELECTRICITY

Leyland, MAURICE (1900–), cricketer, *b* Harrogate ; brilliant left-handed batsman ; has played against Australia.

Leys School, THE, *lēz*, English public school, Cambridge ; founded by Wesleyans 1874.

Lhasa, *lăs'a*, chief city, Tibet ; home of the Dalai Lama, whose palace is a fortress dominating the city. Lhasa, a place of pilgrimage for Buddhists, has many temples ; pop.20,000.

liana, *lē-ä'nä*, general name for long tropical climbing plants ; usually they kill the trees that support them.

Lias, in geology, lowest division of the Jurassic system ; chiefly clay, sand and limestone ; found in Britain from Devon to Yorkshire ; rich in fossils of reptiles.

libel, see SLANDER AND LIBEL

Liberal Party, see PARLIAMENT

Liberia, *lī-bēr'iä*, independent Negro republic, W. Africa ; north of the Gulf of Guinea ; area *c.*43,000sq.m ; pop. 2,500,000 ; exports include rubber, palmkernels and coffee ; cap. Monrovia.

Liberty Bell, bell, cast in England 1752, recast in America 1753, with the inscription ; *Proclaim liberty throughout the land, unto all the inhabitants thereof* ; and rung at Philadelphia 4 July 1776 to celebrate American Independence.

Liberty, Equality, Fraternity (*Liberté, Egalité, Fraternité*) : motto of the French Republic at the Revolution 1792.

Libia Italiana, see LIBYA

libra, see MONEY

Libya, former Italian colony (*Libia Italiana*) in N. Africa ; established 1938–39 ; area *c.*810,000sq.m. Towns include Benghazi, Derna and Homs. Its conquest by the British Eighth Army was completed 1942–43.

licence, in law, permission or authorisation to do or possess something, e.g. a licence to sell tobacco or patent medicines, drive a car or possess a gun.

lichen, *lī'ken*, division of fungi, each individual being actually a dual growth comprising a colony of algae and a colony of fungi. They grow on rocks by the sea and on moors and mountains ; on the bark of trees and on stone walls. The plant body (often a thin scale or disc) is fungus ; the small green algae (within the fungus) manufactures food for both. The algae could not live alone; the fungus could not live without the algae. The so-called reindeer-moss is actually a lichen ; and possibly the ' manna ' gathered by the Israelites was an edible lichen.

Lichfield, cathedral city, Staffordshire ; birthplace of Dr Johnson.

Licinius (*d* 324), Roman emperor ; persecuted Christians.

Lick Observatory, observatory built for the University of California at the expense of James Lick (*d* 1876). It is on a peak of Mt Hamilton, California, 4,280ft above sea-level, and is noted for its large refracting telescope.

lictor, in ancient Rome, an officer who walked before the higher magistrates, and carried an axe buried in a bundle of rods (*fasces*), symbol of the magistrates' power to administer corporal punishment. See FASCISM

Liebig, JUSTUS, *lē'bich* (1803–73), German chemist ; improved the chemistry of agriculture ; increased soil productivity by the use of new fertilisers ; investigated many organic compounds ; discovered aldehyde and chloroform.

Liechtenstein, *lich'ten-shtīn*, principality between Austria and Switzerland ; area *c.*60sq.m ; pop.10,000 ; cap. Vaduz.

Liége, *lē-āzh*, handsome city, Belgium, on the R. Meuse ; centre of a rich coalfield ; produces iron and steel ; pop. 151,000.

lifeboat, boat used for rescuing sailors or passengers by air when in danger ; it may be (*a*) an open boat carried for emergency use by ships ; (*b*) rubber dinghy, carried by aircraft, and easily inflated ; (*c*) rescue boats that go out from the shore to vessels in distress, particularly (in Britain) those maintained by the Royal National Lifeboat Institution, founded 1824, and responsible for the rescue of over 74,000 lives round our shores. Lifeboat pioneers include William Wouldhave (inventor of the self-righting boat), and Henry Greathead, who built the first lifeboat, launched Newcastle-on-Tyne 1789.

A lifeboat must be strong and exceptionally seaworthy. The British type is built of English oak, Canadian rock elm and red cedar, Burma teak and Honduras mahogany. She must be able to empty water almost as quickly as it is shipped, hence the metal flaps in her sides (scuppers), allowing decks and cockpits to empty in 12 seconds. She must be capable of floating even when full of water, so there are 70–120 aircases in the body. She must travel in bad weather, so that water-tight engines are necessary. These develop up to 120hp. The largest boats (51ft long, 26½ tons) are capable of travelling 300m at 9 knots, and bringing back 100 people. The Institution maintains 6 types of motor lifeboat.

Lifeboat crews are rightly honoured for their courage and endurance in face of peril and hardship.

Liffey, river, Eire ; flows *c.*50m to Dublin Bay.

Lifford, co.tn, County Donegal, Eire ; on the R. Foyle.

light, electromagnetic radiation which makes the source visible to the eye, though the term is extended also to slightly shorter (ultra-violet) and slightly longer (infra-red) wavelengths not registered by human eyes.

The sun, stars, a candle flame, are seen by their own light ; the planets and all earthly objects such as hills, pins and people, by reflected light.

Newton's corpuscular or emission theory of light regarded light as being composed of material particles sent out in all directions by luminous bodies ; it has however given place to a much more complex explanation, namely that light consists of quanta of energy moving as in waves, hence the wave (or undulatory) theory supposes that waves varying in length from approximately $3 \cdot 85 \times 10^{-7}$ metres to $7 \cdot 6 \times 10^{-7}$ metres may, under normal conditions, be perceived by the eye, but that waves between $3 \cdot 85 \times 10^{-7}$ metres and 1×10^{-7} metres (ultra-violet), and, similarly, waves longer than $7 \cdot 6 \times 10^{-7}$ metres (i.e. the infra-red rays) are invisible, though their heat effect may be *felt*.

For practical purposes, however, we may consider light as a *ray* or *beam*. A ray of light incident on a flat reflecting surface (e.g. a plane mirror) is reflected so that the reflected and incident rays make equal angles with the normal to the mirror at the point of incidence. The incident ray, its reflected ray, and the normal to the mirror at the point of incidence are in the same plane. The image appears as far behind the flat mirror as the object is in front, but it is laterally inverted, i.e. the left hand becomes the right hand.

For spherical mirrors and also for lenses (according to the 'Real-is-Positive' sign convention)

$$\frac{1}{v} + \frac{1}{u} = \frac{1}{f}$$

where v is distance of image, u distance of object, and f focal length, all distances being measured from the mirror or lens ; distances of real foci, images, or objects being positive ($+$), distances of virtual foci, images, or objects being negative ($-$). Note that for spherical mirrors the focal length is $\frac{1}{2}r$, where r is radius of curvature. Or we may say that for lenses

$$\frac{1}{v} - \frac{1}{u} = \frac{1}{f}$$

where distances are measured from the lens, those measured in the direction of the incident light being negative numbers. The focal length of a converging lens is negative, and of a diverging lens positive, when using this convention.

Lenses include the following types : (*a*) plano-concave ; (*b*) double concave ; (*c*) plano-convex ; (*d*) double convex ; (*e*) concavo-convex (convex meniscus) ; (*f*) convex-concave (concave meniscus). Lenses are of glass or plastic.

For practical purposes light may be

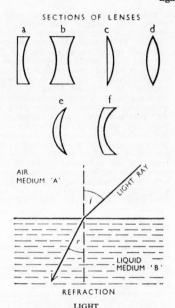

SECTIONS OF LENSES

REFRACTION

LIGHT

(*above*) *Sections of Lenses*
(*below*) *Refraction of Light*

regarded as travelling in straight lines unless passing from one medium to another, when it is *refracted* (i.e. turned from its normal course). If passing to a denser medium it is refracted *towards* the normal, if to a less dense medium *away from* the normal. The index of refraction is called μ (mu) ; and a ray of light travelling, say, from air to glass would be expressed $_a\mu_b$. If i and r are angles of incidence and refraction respectively, the general formula for refraction is

$$\mu_b = \frac{\text{velocity of light in medium A}}{\text{velocity of light in medium B}} \text{ or } \frac{\text{sine } i}{\text{sine } r}$$

When the eye and object are in a line perpendicular to the reflecting surface

$$\mu = \frac{\text{real depth}}{\text{apparent depth}}$$

The critical angle is the greatest angle of incidence (i.e. between ray and normal to boundary) in the denser medium for the light to emerge into the rarer medium

$$_a\mu_b = \frac{1}{\text{sine of critical angle in medium B}}$$

When what we call 'white' light passes through a glass prism it is dispersed. Viewed through a suitable optical instrument the resulting band is seen as a *spectrum*, i.e. an arrangement of colours, namely, red, orange, yellow, green, blue, indigo and violet (see SPECTRUM). We are aware of these colours by means of the sensitive ' curtain,' the retina, at the back of the eye (see EYE), which comprises nerves ending in minute cones or rods arranged in three groups. Each of these groups responds to a broad band of visible wavelengths whose maximum sensitivities lie in the red, green, or violet parts of the spectrum. Any pure colour of a particular wavelength will excite one, two, or three of these groups of receptors to a particular degree. It seems that the perception of colour by the brain is the result of the particular extent of the response in combination. Thus, yellow light from incandescent sodium vapour, which is mono-chromatic, i.e. of one wavelength, will excite the ' red ' or ' green ' receptors about equally, with the result that the brain perceives yellow. Now if a mixture of red and green light is received by the eye in equal amounts, the same two groups of receptors are excited in the same way, and the brain will again note the resulting mixed light as yellow. The same effect is attained if all wavelengths from red to green are received, most yellows in nature being ' mixed ' yellows of this sort.

Colour in nature and paint is always due to subtraction from the ' white ' light falling on an object. A geranium is red because it absorbs from ' white ' light the yellow-green-blue end of the spectrum and returns only the red to the eye. You may have noticed that in light lacking red (e.g. sodium light) the geranium appears black.

The velocity of light in a vacuum is 186,282m.p.sec or 3×10^{10} cms per sec. This has been shown by several experiments, notably those made by the American, Albert Michelson (1852–1931).

Michelson also measured the velocity of light in water directly. The result obtained by him confirm the theory that

$$_a\mu_w = \frac{\text{velocity in air}}{\text{velocity in water}}$$

For polarisation of light see POLARISATION. See also RELATIVITY ; WAVE-MOTION

Light Brigade, see BALACLAVA

lighter, large, flat-bottomed boat used for loading or discharging vessels in port, or for carrying cargo over a short distance ; sometimes provided with steam, or other power, but usually towed.

lighthouse, lofty, tower-like building with a powerful lamp used to guide ships at sea ; may be on a rock or reef or on the coast. The earliest known example was the Pharos at Alexandria, built c.283–247BC ; one of the most famous lighthouses today is the Eddystone.

Nowadays the light is usually derived from the vapour of a mineral oil burned under pressure as an incandescent gas, the lamp being surrounded by lenses and reflecting prisms, sometimes moved by clockwork, and often floated in mercury.

LIGHTSHIPS, ships moored near some shoal or dangerous point, show a warning light to vessels. Most of them are now self-acting, the lamp being switched on or off by the effect of dusk or dawn on a selenium ' eye.'

British lighthouses and lightships are maintained by Trinity House.

The development of radar since 1940 has already entirely revolutionised methods of piloting ships in darkness and fog, and it seems likely that there will soon be no need of either lighthouses or lightships.

lighting, as old almost as civilisation ; began no doubt with fire-light and blazing torches, followed by simple lamps in which a wick floated in oil, and by candles. The oil lamp with an Argand burner came into use c.1783, and gave a white light superior to any other then known. Gas lighting was invented by William Murdoch 1792, Pall Mall (London) being illuminated by gas 1807. Welsbach's incandescent gas-mantle greatly improved gas illumination. Sir Humphry Davy made possible the once popular arc-lamp ; and the pioneers of the modern electric lamp were Thomas Alva Edison and Sir J. W. Swan, who first employed fine carbon filaments, later tungsten.

Later still the vacuum bulb was improved by filling it at very low pressure with an inert gas, e.g. argon, to increase illumination. The gaseous pressure decreases the tendency of the metal to vaporise, and hence enables a higher temperature to be used. The percentage of electrical energy turned into light increases with increase in the temperature of the filament. The coiling and re-coiling in the coiled-coil type of filament reduces loss of heat by radiation, and thus enables the higher temperature to be attained with less watts. A brilliant effect is obtained with krypton, and great use is now being made of discharge tubes, e.g. the sodium vapour lamp, the mercury vapour lamp, etc. Fluorescent lighting is now in great favour. See FLUORESCENCE

lightning, see THUNDER AND LIGHTNING

lightning conductor, see THUNDER AND LIGHTNING

lightship, see LIGHTHOUSE

light-year, reckoned as 6,000,000,000,000 miles ; but see also PARSEC.

lignite, partly-formed coal, usually brownish and of a woody nature ; contains a higher proportion of hydrocarbons than ordinary coal.

lignum vitae, vī′tē, tree (a native of Jamaica) with clusters of blue flowers ; notable for its extremely hard and heavy wood.

Ligny, lē-nyē′, village, Belgium ; 9m from Charleroi ; scene of Napoleon's fruitless victory over the Prussians 1815 during the Waterloo Battle.

Liguria, ancient division of NW. Italy ; now a department including Genoa.

Li Hung-Chang, *lē-* (1823–1901), Chinese statesman ; attempted to make China a great military nation, and did much to foster trade with the West.

lilac, tree (native of Asia and E. Europe) common in Britain ; has heart-shaped leaves, and pyramids of white or purple flowers ; the wood is much used for inlaying.

Lilienthal, OTTO, *lēl'yen-täl* (1848–96), German pioneer in aircraft ; demonstrated the value of cambered wings ; killed while gliding.

Lille, *lēl,* French city, 66m south-east of Calais ; important railway and canal centre ; a great manufacturing town (e.g. linen, cotton, tobacco, sugar, etc.) ; pop.189,000.

Lilliburlero, satirical song, the words by Wharton, the tune by Purcell. It is said to have ' sung James II out of three kingdoms.'

Lilliput, see SWIFT, JONATHAN

Lily, see AIRSTRIP

lily, bulbous plant (family *Liliaceae*) common in temperate climes. From erect and leafy stems spring large, showy, funnel-shaped flowers ; species include the Madonna or St Joseph's lily (pure white and fragrant).

lily-of-the-valley, British plant with underground creeping stem. The small white fragrant bell-flowers bloom in spring.

Lima, cap. Peru ; pop.523,000 ; a great commercial and industrial centre. Its port is Callao.

lime, see CALCIUM

LIME

The leaves and the flowers

lime or **linden,** handsome British tree often found in city streets. In May ruby red buds appear, opening to show emerald green heart-shaped leaves ; the flowers are yellowish and fragrant. The fine-grained timber is much used for carving. A different tree (the W. Indian lime) produces the citric acid from which lime juice is obtained.

Limerick, county in the province of Munster, Eire. The co.tn is the city and port of Limerick, on the R. Shannon ; noted for flour, bacon, lace ; pop. of the town 43,000.

limerick, nonsense verse of five lines. The origin of the name is doubtful. Limericks were popularised by Edward Lear (1812–88), but more recent limericks are usually more complex, e.g.

There was a young fellow called Wright, Whose speed was far greater than light.
> He set off one day
> The Einsteinian way,
And returned on the previous night.

lime water, see CALCIUM

Limoges, *lē-mōzh',* town and important railway centre, France, 251m SSW. from Paris ; has many industries ; famous for its enamel ware ; pop.108,000.

limpet, see MOLLUSCA

Limpopo or **Crocodile River,** river of S. Africa ; flows 800m to the Indian Ocean.

Lincoln, *lin'kŭn,* city and co.tn, Lincolnshire, on the R. Witham ; famous for its 13th c. cathedral ; noted for agricultural machinery and flour milling ; also its races ; pop.66,000.

Lincoln, ABRAHAM (1809–65), American statesman, born in a log cabin in the woods of Kentucky, USA. He was a farmer's son. His mother taught him to read, but she died when he was only nine. The father's second wife, a kind, sensible woman, helped the growing boy, who was eager to learn. Too poor to buy books, Lincoln borrowed them, e.g. *The Pilgrim's Progress, Aesop's Fables,* etc. ; studied far into the night ; early won a reputation for his love of fairplay, hence his nickname, Honest Abe. At seventeen he was tall, odd-looking, broad, and strong ; had piercing eyes and dark hair ; was respected for his skill in wrestling and in lifting heavy weights.

Lincoln worked in a store at twenty-one, but studied law in his spare time. Later he practised as a lawyer in Springfield, Ohio. He was elected to Congress 1846.

The question of slavery arose in 1854. At that time most of the American slaves worked on cotton plantations in the south. Their owners were ready to fight for the right to use slaves on their plantations, but Abraham Lincoln worked for the abolition of slavery, and in a political campaign 1858 he and Stephen A. Douglas were rivals for a seat in the Senate ; and their debates aroused immense interest. Douglas was

ABRAHAM LINCOLN 1809–65

elected, but it was Lincoln whose speeches had stirred the country most ; so much so that when Douglas and he were candidates for the presidency (1860) Lincoln won, becoming sixteenth president 1861.

The southern states strove to gain separation from the northern states, and there was all the heartbreak of the American Civil War. But Lincoln stood resolutely for union of south and north and for the abolition of slavery. He issued (1 Jan 1863) his famous *Proclamation of Emancipation* : *I do order and declare that all persons held as slaves . . . are and henceforward shall be free.*

In spite of mistakes, setbacks, disappointments, Lincoln (the gaunt giant with the queer jaw and overhanging eyebrows) never lost faith in the righteousness of his cause. He made many famous speeches, the most famous of all being delivered Nov 1863 when dedicating the battlefield of Gettysburg as a cemetery :

Fourscore and seven years ago our fathers brought forth on this continent a new nation conceived in liberty and dedicated to the proposition that all men are created equal. Now we are engaged in a great civil war, testing whether that nation, or any nation so conceived and so dedicated, can long endure. We are met on a great battlefield of that war. We have come to dedicate a portion of that field as a final resting-place of those who here gave their lives that that nation might live.

It is altogether fitting and proper that we should do this. But, in a larger sense, we cannot dedicate, we cannot consecrate, we cannot hallow, this ground. The brave men, living and dead, who struggled here have consecrated it far above our poor power to add or detract.

The world will little note nor long remember what we say here, but it can never forget what they did here. It is for us, the living, rather to be dedicated here to the unfinished work which they who fought here have thus far so nobly advanced.

It is rather for us to be here dedicated to the great task remaining before us—that from these honoured dead we take increased devotion to that cause for which they gave the last full measure of devotion ; that we here highly resolve that these dead shall not have died in vain, that this nation, under God, shall have a new birth of freedom, and that government of the people, by the people, for the people, shall not perish from the Earth.

The war dragged on till 1865 (see AMERICAN CIVIL WAR), but Lincoln finally succeeded in uniting north and south as well as setting 4,000,000 slaves free. Almost immediately after peace was declared, a drunken madman (John Wilkes Booth) shot Lincoln and killed him ; but Honest Abe had done his work.

Lincoln College, college of Oxford University ; founded 1427 ; attended by John Wesley.

Lincolnshire, large eastern county of England, between the Humber and Wash ; mostly low-lying ; chiefly agricultural, noted especially for wheat and barley ; co.tn Lincoln.

Lincoln's Inn, legal centre, one of London's Inns of Court. Its 16th c. gateway is in Chancery Lane ; the gardens in Lincoln's Inn Fields (west of the Inn) were formerly the scene of many duels.

Lind, JENNY (1820–87), Swedish singer, known as the Swedish nightingale ; *b* Stockholm ; first appeared in England 1847 ; was probably the world's greatest soprano.

Lindbergh, COLONEL CHARLES (1902–), American aviator and scientist ; made the first solo flight from New York to Paris 1927 ; did much to develop air schemes. His infant son and heir was kidnapped and murdered 1932.

linden, see LIME

Lindisfarne or **Holy Island,** small island some miles off Berwick ; has the ruins of a monastery, and associations with St Aidan and St Cuthbert, 7th c. Christian missionaries.

Lindrum, WALTER (1899–), Australian billiards player ; came to England 1931 ; achieved (1932) a world's record break of 4,137. He is left-handed, and remains the greatest player of the day.

Lindsay, VACHEL (1879–1931), American poet, *b* Illinois ; his vagabond life is revealed in many of his poems.

Linear Measure, see WEIGHTS AND MEASURES

linen, see FLAX

ling, food fish found in the N. Atlantic ; may be 4–6ft long ; is grey or black above, greyish below. The female produces 12–30,000,000 eggs a season.

ling, see HEATHER

Linklater, ERIC (1899–), Scottish author, *b* Dounby, Orkney ; served in the Black Watch ; studied medicine ; was assistant editor of the *Times of India* ; visited USA 1928–30 ; noted for his brilliant satire *Juan in America* ; wrote also *Magnus Merriman* which, though full of humour, reveals the author's hatred of humbug ; also *Poet's Pub* ; *The Cornerstones*, etc., and various War Office publications, e.g. *The Defence of Calais* ; *The Highland Division.* Read also his *Private Angelo.*

Linlithgow, *lin-lith'gō*, co.tn, W. Lothian or Linlithgowshire ; has ruins of a palace, birthplace of Mary Queen of Scots.

Linnaeus, CARL, *li-nē'ŭs* (1707–78), naturalist, born in Sweden ; travelled much on the Continent ; was professor of botany at Uppsala 1741 till his death ; author of many scientific works, the greatest being *Genera Plantarum.* To Linnaeus we owe the present system of giving two Latin names to animals and plants, and though his systematic classification of plants has been revised, it formed a foundation for all later work. The Linnaean Society was formed 1788.

linnet, see FINCH

linotype, machine invented by a German watchmaker, and introduced into Britain *c.*1890. Somewhat like a huge typewriter, it has matrices that are arranged in line-order by an operator who depresses appropriate keys. The typemetal is automatically cast line by line, thus enabling newspaper printing to be done extremely rapidly. See PRINTING

linseed, see FLAX

Lin Yutang (1895–), Chinese scholar ; author of *My Country and My People*, with introduction by Pearl Buck.

lion, largest animal of the cat genus ; now found only in Africa and SW. Asia, but once common in England ; may be 9ft long, including the tail, and weighs as much as 500lb. It is tawny yellow, but the mane of the male may be brown or (like the tuft of the tail) black. The lion lives 30 years in the wild state. Closely resembling the tiger, it hunts at night. The female produces 2 or 3 cubs a year.

Lion Heart, see RICHARD I

Lipari Islands, *lēp'ä-rē*, group of 7 Italian islands N. of Sicily. All are volcanic, notably Stromboli.

Lippe, *lip'e*, minor state of Germany ; cap. Detmold.

Lippi, FILIPPO (*d* 1469), known as Fra (i.e. brother) Lippo Lippi, Italian artist,

b Florence ; famous for his *Coronation of the Virgin* (in the Academy, Florence), *Madonna and Child*, etc. His figures are all intensely human. He is the subject of a poem by Robert Browning.

liquefaction of gases, changing a gas to a liquid : (*a*) by cooling below the critical temperature ; (*b*) by cooling and increasing pressure ; (*c*) by pressure alone (if the gas has a fairly high critical temperature).

liquid air, air cooled below the boiling-point of its various gases ; appears as a pale blue liquid, which largely consists of liquid oxygen ; boiling-point $-182\cdot9°$C; first produced 1885 ; much used in the commercial production of oxygen from the atmosphere by fractional distillation, the nitrogen being used as a fertiliser, and also for the synthetic production of ammonia and nitric acid.

Liquid Measure, see WEIGHTS AND MEASURES

liquorice, *lik'or-iss*, plant (family *Leguminosae*) of S. Europe, Asia, Africa, with bluish flowers ; the root yields liquorice.

Lisbon, *liz'bŭn*, city and cap., Portugal ; pop.705,000 ; on the R. Tagus ; exports fish, fruit and wines ; devastated by an earthquake 1755 ; has an airport at Sacavem.

Lisburn, cathedral city, County Antrim, N. Ireland ; noted for linen goods.

Lismore, port, New S. Wales, Australia ; noted for saw-mills and sugar refining.

Lister, LORD (1827–1912), surgeon, *b* Upton, Essex ; long associated with Edinburgh and Glasgow ; from 1866 until almost thirty years later investigated the causes of septic poisoning after surgical operations ; insisted on cleanliness, and showed that inflammation was due to bacteria ; led the way to modern methods of preventing bacteria entering wounds, i.e. to *asepsis.* See ANTISEPTICS

Liszt, FRANZ, *list* (1811–86), Hungarian pianist and composer ; became the foremost figure in the musical world of his day, and was styled the prince of pianists. At Weimar, where he settled 1849, he conducted at the Court Theatre, made the town the centre of musical life in Germany, and composed much of his best music. He introduced a new technique into pianoforte playing and invented the symphonic poem. Among his compositions for the piano are *Études de Concert*, the *Hungarian Rhapsodies*, etc., while his orchestral compositions include the *Dante* and the *Faust Symphonies.*

Litany, see PRAYER BOOK

literature, see ENGLISH LITERATURE

litharge, see LEAD

lithium, element, Li ; specific gravity 0·534, hence it is the lightest solid known ; atomic weight 6·94 ; atomic number 3 ; silvery white metal found in various rare minerals.

lithopone, see BARYTES

Lithuania, see USSR

litmus, soluble substance prepared from

lichens ; much used as an indicator of chemical change ; is turned red by acids, blue by alkalies.

Littoria, see PONTINE MARSHES

Litvinoff, MAXIM, *lit-vĕ'nŏf* (1876–), Russian statesman ; Soviet representative in London 1918. As Commisar for Foreign Affairs in Moscow, signed various treaties of non-aggression 1933 ; did much to draw Britain and America closer to the Soviet. Later he was replaced by Molotov.

liver, see DIGESTION

Liverpool, city and port on the R. Mersey, Lancashire ; pop. *c.*800,000 ; has 37m of quays, a floating landing-stage, spacious docks, warehouses and an overhead railway ; imports sugar, fruit, oil, grain and cotton ; has a vast trade and passenger service with USA ; noted for shipbuilding, engineering, flour, tobacco and chemicals. Its unfinished cathedral, consecrated 1924, and designed by Sir Gilbert Scott, will be the largest in England. A Roman Catholic cathedral now being built will be the biggest in the world when complete. Liverpool University was founded 1903. At Speke, close by, is an airfield, also a penicillin factory.

Liverpool and Birkenhead are linked by the Mersey Tunnel, opened for traffic 1934. The tunnel, 3m long, cost *c.*£8,000,000. At its lowest depth it is 170ft below the bed of the river. Liverpool is the world's first radar port, shipping in the Mersey being guided by radar since 1948.

Liversedge, *-idj*, town, W. Yorkshire ; noted for cotton, worsted and chemicals.

Livingstone, town, formerly the capital of N. Rhodesia.

Livingstone, DAVID (1813–73), Scottish missionary and explorer, *b* Blantyre, Lanarkshire ; began work in a cotton mill at 10 ; studied Latin, botany and zoology in spare time ; became a doctor ; was ordained a missionary 1840 ; sent to Bechuanaland (Africa) by the London Missionary Society.

He taught the natives for 9 years, and then began his famous African travels : he crossed the Kalahari Desert and reached L. Ngami ; made an expedition down the R. Zambesi, discovering the Victoria Falls ; explored east and central Africa, discovering L. Nyasa, and reached Zanzibar 1864 after seeing much of the horrors of the slave-trade ; set out in search of the sources of the Nile, arrived at L. Tanganyika, discovered L. Moero and L. Bangweulu ; journeyed up the west coast of Tanganyika to Ujiji (1869), reached Nyangwe (on the R. Lualaba) 1871, and returned to Ujiji, where he was found by H. M. Stanley, who had been sent in search of him by the *New York Herald.* Stanley greeted the explorer with the famous and very polite words, ' Dr Livingstone, I presume ? ' Stanley had arrived in the nick of

DAVID LIVINGSTONE 1813–73

time, for Livingstone's stores had gone, but he refused to return with Stanley, and continued his search for the source of the Nile.

One morning his faithful native attendants found Livingstone kneeling by his bed ; he had died while at prayer. His body was carried to the coast, and finally buried in Westminster Abbey.

In 33 years Livingstone travelled 30,000m in ' darkest Africa,' the land he loved, and where many of the native tribes almost worshipped him. His books include *Missionary Travels and Researches in Africa.* He exposed the evil of the slave-trade, which was later suppressed. Read *Livingstone The Liberator* by J. I. MacNair.

living things, CLASSIFICATION OF, method of naming and arranging plants and animals. Living things (apart from germs) are either plants or animals. The animal kingdom is divided into sub-kingdoms known as *phyla* ; these into *classes* ; *classes* are divided into *orders* ; *orders* into *families* ; *families* into *genera* ; each genus (singular of *genera*) into *species.* An animal (or plant) has two Latin names (*a*) the *genus* (with a capital letter), (*b*) the *species* (beginning with a small letter) e.g. *Canis familiaris* for the domestic dog, which belongs to the *Phylum,* Vertebrata ; *Class,* Mammalis ; *Order,* Carnivora ; *Family,* Canidae ; *Genus,* Canis. In the same way *Ranunculus acris* is the bitter buttercup ; *Ranunculus repens,* the creeping buttercup ; and we might write *R. acris* or *R. repens* for short. This method of classification is largely due to Carl Linnaeus (1707–78), the famous Swedish naturalist.

Modern biologists have other ways of classifying living things, e.g. classification according to the functions of various organs, or based on embryology, etc.

Briefly, the plant world is divided into two great divisions, seed-bearing and non-seed-bearing plants ; the former includes flowering plants, of which the two divisions are (a) Monocotyledons, having only one seed-leaf, and (b) Dicotyledons, having two seed-leaves. In (a) the central axis of the root system is very short, and there is a tuft of roots, all of equal thickness ; and the parts of the flower are in 3's or multiples of 3 ; but in (b) there is a central main root with thinner side roots, and the parts of the flower are in 4's or 5's, or multiples of those numbers. In (a) the leaves have parallel veins ; in (b) the leaf has a main vein or main veins with lesser veins making a network.

The animal kingdom comprises at least three great divisions (a) Protozoa, i.e. single-celled creatures, approaching bacteria in form, (b) Invertebrates, 18 phyla of animals without backbone, and totally differing from (c) Vertebrates, which have a backbone and central nervous system, a phylum to which belong (among others) fishes, amphibians reptiles, birds and mammals, the latter (which, among other things, suckle their young) including monkeys, apes and men.

Livy (59BC–AD17), Roman historian. Titus Livius was born at Padua, and died there. He seems to have been a person of note, and was in favour with the Emperor Augustus. His life's work (on which he spent 40 years) was his *History of Rome*, in 142 books, of which only 33 (with parts of others) remain. Although uncritical, he was superb in his descriptions of battles, sieges, and heroic figures. The work, fascinating even today, tells the story of Rome and the growing empire as a romantic prose epic.

Among others of his remarks is : *Horridum militem esse debere* ; *non caelatum auro et argento, sed ferris et animis fretum . . . Virtutem esse militis decus*, i.e. The soldier should be fear-inspiring, not decked with gold and silver, but relying on his courage and his steel . . . Valour is the soldier's adornment. (*History*, Book 9).

lizard, scale-clad reptile, usually with 4 legs, and always with movable eyelids. Most lizards are only a few inches long, but some are 3ft or more ; c.1,500 species are known, including the iguana, common in the W. Indies and S. America ; the Australian frilled lizard ; the chameleon, etc. There are two British species : (a) COMMON LIZARD, c.6in long, brown above, which feeds on insects among

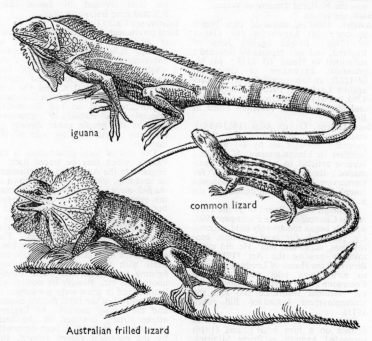

iguana

common lizard

Australian frilled lizard

LIZARDS

Like the Crocodile the Iguana *uses its tail as a weapon ; the* Common Lizard *is found in Britain ;* Frilled Lizards *raise their frills when brought to bay : they normally move on four feet but use only two feet when running quickly.*

dry heaths, etc. ; (*b*) SAND LIZARD. Lizards usually lay eggs ; but the British slow-worm (actually a lizard) produces fully formed young.

llama, *lä′mä,* domesticated breed of the guanaco, an animal (*c.*4ft at the shoulder) found only in S. America (Peru to Patagonia). Resembling the camel, but without the hump, the llama, usually white, is used as a beast of burden, and for its milk.

Llanberis, *hlan′-,* village and noted beauty spot, Caernarvonshire ; has slate quarries.

Llandaff, *hlan-daf′,* cathedral city, now part of Cardiff. The cathedral was damaged by bombing in World War II.

Llandovery, *hlan-,* town, Carmarthenshire. Its public school was founded 1848.

Llandudno, *hlan-dud′nō,* holiday seaside town, Caernarvonshire ; pop.20,000.

Llanelly, *hlä-neth′li,* port, Carmarthenshire ; noted for tin-plate, copper-refining and chemicals ; pop.38,000.

Llangollen, *hlan-goth′len,* village on the R. Dee, Denbighshire. Hereabouts is the lovely Vale of Llangollen, home of the the ' Ladies of Llangollen,' i.e. Eleanor Butler and Sarah Ponsonby, who lived together about fifty years, Sarah dying 1831. Their house (*Plas Newydd*) is now the National Theatre of Wales.

llanos, see GRASS

Llewelyn, *hlū-el′in,* name of two Welsh princes : (*a*) LLEWELYN THE GREAT (*d* 1240) ; fought against John of England, and was repeatedly defeated ; submitted to Henry III 1237 ; (*b*) his grandson, LLEWELYN AP GRUFFYDD (*d* 1282), at first successful in his wars against England ; became independent 1265, but was taken prisoner by Edward I, and after a further rebellion killed at Builth.

Lloyd George, DAVID, *loid-* (1863–1945), statesman, *b* Manchester of Welsh parents ; brought up by his uncle (a cobbler) in Llanystumdwy, N. Wales ; became articled to a solicitor at Portmadoc ; Radical MP (when only 27) for Carnarvon Boroughs 1890 ; opposed Joseph Chamberlain and denounced the S. African War.

President of the Board of Trade 1905, he was Chancellor of the Exchequer 1908, when he began remarkably bold reforms, e.g. proposals for land taxation, coal royalties, super-tax, etc. He did much towards passing the Act (1911) for depriving the House of Lords of the right to turn down bills passed by the Commons ; was largely responsible for the National Insurance Bill and the Unemployment Insurance Bill (both 1911).

Early in World War I he placed British finance on a firm basis ; and (1916) succeeded Asquith as Prime Minister, giving the country new hope, inspiring munition workers, encouraging support from USA, and energising the national war-effort. He attended the Peace Conference 1919 ; resigned the Premiership 1922 ; became leader of a few Liberals, and urged the country to use its natural resources. To within a few months of his death he remained a vigorous critic of any government in power. He was raised to the peerage as Earl Lloyd George.

Often spoken of as ' the Welsh Wizard,' Lloyd George had deep and broad sympathies with the people. He was a born orator, and had all the passion and wit of the Celtic race. He served his country superbly in war, but his later years—though he never failed to advocate the interests of the farming community—were less glorious.

Lloyd George, MEGAN, daughter of David Lloyd George ; Independent Liberal MP from 1929.

Lloyd's, *loidz,* London HQ of marine insurance ; founded as Lloyd's Coffee House *c.*1690 ; keeps a register of all shipping, classified according to seaworthiness. Lloyd's is now in Leadenhall Street.

loach, British fresh-water fish *c.*4in long ; dark green above.

load, see MECHANICS

Lobengula (*d* 1894), Matabele king from 1870 ; accepted British protection 1888, but later revolted, his forces being defeated near Bulawayo 1893.

lobster, see CRUSTACEAN

local government, in the UK, administration of affairs in a parish, borough, or county. It is closely related to central government, i.e. the government of the whole country by Parliament (see PARLIAMENT). Both local and central government in the UK and the self-governing parts of the British Commonwealth are based on two democratic principles : (*a*) election of representatives by the people either directly or indirectly ; and (*b*) the rule of the majority.

The unit of local government is the PARISH, which may be traced back in England to the Anglo-Saxon settlement, or township, with its meeting known as the *folk-moot.* Today the parish has lost the great importance it once enjoyed, but since 1894 every parish must hold a *parish meeting,* and if the parish has a pop. of 300 or more, it may elect a *parish council* of from 5–15 members. This committee is responsible for the oversight of the local school or schools, and deals with matters relating to, say, lighting the streets, the water supply, allotments, etc., though its powers are limited, and in some ways are subject to the approval of the rural district council and the county council. In England affairs strictly confined to the local church have, since 1919, been dealt with by the *parochial church council,* this appointing a new vicar, etc. Any parishioner may attend, even if not a member of the Church. There is also the *vestry meeting,* held at Easter, the vicar being chairman. Such a meeting elects churchwardens, etc. In Scotland the right of a congregation to choose its own minister has been recognised since the seventeenth century.

In Anglo-Saxon, Norman and later times the vestry meeting was much more important than now, once completely controlling parish affairs ; the court baron (after 1066) governed the manor, i.e. the district under the control of the local lord ; and the folk-moot governed the township. By 1555 the duty of repairing roads fell on the parish ; and laws passed 1572, 1597 and 1601 gave the care of the poor into the keeping of the parish, the parish vestry having also the care of the church, the aged, the sick, the business of apprenticing children, the duty of collecting rates, and keeping law and order (which meant appointing a constable), so that the vestry meeting of today is only, so to speak, the ghost of the important local committee it was formerly.

For long Britain was mainly rural (open country) rather than industrial with large centres of population, so that for centuries affairs beyond the control of the parish devolved on the shire, later usually called a county, hence the COUNTY COURT, in which the sheriff (i.e. the *shire-reeve*—an officer appointed by the king to see that matters were carried on in accordance with the king's wishes) was supremely important. The sheriff had to make up accounts annually, and pay the balance to the king's exchequer. In England he is now of little importance, and is indeed ranked below the lord-lieutenant, an official first appointed in Tudor times, his business being with military affairs, though he may also be the chief magistrate. He may keep his office for many years, while the sheriff is appointed annually. Other important members of the county council are the coroner (see CORONER), and the justice of the peace (who writes JP after his name), first appointed 1344. His duties now include not only keeping the peace, but such matters as granting licences for the sale of intoxicants, etc.

In Scotland the sheriff is the county-court judge, and his court is known as the Sheriff Court.

The modern county council comprises councillors elected for 3 years. In England a quarter of the council are county alderman. The Local Government Boundary Commission issued (1948) a report suggesting that, outside London, England should be regarded for government purposes as 47 counties administered by county councils and local councils, together with 17 large towns (or groups of towns) known as ' all-purpose ' authorities.

A county council has many duties, from protecting wild birds to managing the police force, various types of schools, etc. The county council issues county registration numbers for cars, and receives a share of the tax paid by the owners. Its meetings are governed by a chairman, and it is advised by experts, e.g. the medical officer of health, the county surveyor, the chief constable, and the director of education.

But many affairs of a given area are controlled not by the county council but by the TOWN COUNCIL. It is a common practice to speak of towns and cities, but it is more correct to speak of BOROUGHS, of which there are two kinds, (*a*) larger, older, or more important ones, namely *county boroughs*, and (*b*) smaller, newer, or less important ones, namely *boroughs*. *Borough* comes from the OE word *burgh*, possibly a fortified place. Years ago a town became a borough by securing (usually for a payment) a document from the lord of the township or from the king granting certain privileges, among them the right to elect its own officers. Members of a borough were called *burgesses*. The Scottish form of ' borough ' is ' burgh.'

Today every borough has its representatives called councillors. The councillors elect the aldermen, and the aldermen and councillors annually elect (or re-elect) the mayor or lord mayor. The Scottish equivalent of ' alderman ' is ' bailie ' ; of ' mayor,' ' provost ' ; of ' lord mayor,' ' lord provost.'

To be an *elector* (i.e. one who may take a share in choosing a councillor) you must be 21, a British subject, and must reside normally in that district or own property there, thus having your name on the register of local government electors.

A candidate for the local council is first nominated by two electors of the ward for which he hopes to be chosen as its representative. He is chosen or rejected according to a secret vote by ballot (see ELECTION). Formerly local elections were held in November, but since 1949 they have taken place in April (or May) in England, on the 1st and 2nd Tuesdays of May in Scotland. Members of a local council may be grouped into various committees, e.g. those dealing with transport, highways and sewers, finance, electricity, rating, markets, water, museums, libraries, watch and health. The money required for carrying out these and other public services is derived (*a*) from the local rates, and (*b*) from various government grants.

A MAYOR wears a fur-lined robe and a gold chain on civic occasions. He is chairman of the council, and a member of all committees. When he sits in council or goes in procession the mace is laid on the table or carried before him as a sign of authority. He is addressed as Mr Mayor ; referred to as ' the worshipful Mayor of . . .' and in court is called ' Your Worship.'

A large borough may become a county borough, in which case its mayor

becomes a LORD MAYOR ; such a town has its own Social Welfare Committee for dealing with the poor ; also its own sheriff.
Read *His Worship the Mayor*, W. E. Tate (Nelson) ; *Local Government in England and Wales*, W. Eric Jackson.

Locarno, town, Switzerland ; scene of a meeting of representatives of Britain, France, Germany and Italy, 1925, when a pact was signed guaranteeing the peace of Europe ; denounced by Germany 1936.

loch, see LAKE

Lochaber, *loch-ä'bĕr*, mountainous district of Inverness-shire ; centre of a great hydro-electric power scheme.

Locke, JOHN (1632–1704), English philosopher, *b* Wrington, Somerset ; long associated with the Earl of Shaftesbury, who, when he fled to Holland after being accused of treason, was accompanied by Locke. In Holland, Locke was a friend of William of Orange, with whom he returned to England. His last years were spent in the home of Sir Francis Masham at Oates, Essex.
As a philosopher, Locke is famous for his *Essay Concerning Human Understanding*, in which he raises problems that later attracted the attention of Berkeley and Hume. As a thinker he is notable for his plain common sense.
His political philosophy follows up the work of Hobbes. Locke's greatest contribution here is his insistence that the Government must periodically obtain popular sanction for what it has done. This principle has been embodied in the political systems of Great Britain and America.

Locke, WILLIAM JOHN (1863–1930), British novelist, born in Barbados ; author of *The Beloved Vagabond* ; *Simon the Jester*.

Lockhart, JOHN GIBSON, *lok'ĕrt*, see SCOTT, SIR WALTER

locomotives, see RAILWAYS

locus, *lō'kus* (Latin *place* ; plural *loci*), line, straight or curved, traced by a point according to certain conditions ; e.g. the locus of the point P, if always 1cm from the line AB, is a line parallel to AB and 1cm distant.

P
. - - - - - - - - - -

A———————————B

Or, let O be a fixed point. If the point P moves so as always to be the same distant from O, its locus will be the circumference of a circle.

locust, see GRASSHOPPER ; PLATE 9

lodestone, see MAGNETISM

Lodge, SIR OLIVER (1851–1940), scientist, *b* Penkhull, Staffordshire ; professor of physics at University College, Liverpool 1880–1900 ; first Principal of Birmingham University 1900–19. A pioneer in the use of electromagnetic waves and of practical radio, he wrote popularly on science, e.g. *Man and the Universe* ; *Modern Problems* ; *Ether and Reality* ;

Science and Human Progress. After the death of his son Raymond, he was deeply interested in spiritualism.

Lodz, *luj*, town, Poland ; noted for textile industries ; pop.497,000.

loess, see CHINA

Lofoten Islands, *lō-fō'ten*, islands off the NW. coast of Norway.

Logan, peak of the Rocky Mts ; rises 19,850ft, and is the highest mt. in Canada.

logarithms. We know that, say, $25 = 5^2$ and that $125 = 5^3$; and it is reasonable to assume that any number between 25 and 125 can be represented by some power of 5 between 2 and 3, i.e. 5 to the power *2 and a decimal*. These powers are called logarithms.
In general terms, if $a = b^c$ then c is the logarithm (log) of a to the base b. Written briefly this is $c = \log_b a$; also a is called the anti-logarithm (antilog) of c to the base b.
From $a = b^c$ it follows that $b = a_c^{\frac{1}{c}}$ (by taking the cth root of both sides), which gives $\log_a b = \frac{1}{c}$. Hence

$$\log_b a \times \log_a b = c \times \frac{1}{c}, \text{ i.e. } 1.$$

The laws of logarithms are the same as the laws of indices (or powers) though they appear in another form. They should be memorised as follows :

$$\log_x(ab) = \log_x a + \log_x b$$
$$\log_x\left(\frac{a}{b}\right) = \log_x a - \log_x b$$
$$\log_x(a^n) = n \times \log_x a$$
$$\log_x \sqrt[n]{a} = \frac{1}{x} \times \log_x a$$
$$\log_a 1 = 0$$
$$\log_b a \times \log_a b = 1$$
$$\log_x b \log_b a = \log_x a$$

John Napier (1550–1617), a Scottish mathematician, published his discovery of natural logarithms 1614. They were calculated to the base e, which is the expansion of $\left(1 + \frac{1}{n}\right)^n$ when n is indefinitely big ; its value is approximately 2·718. (The value to 10 decimal places is actually 2·7182818284.) Natural logarithms are of great value in advanced mathematical investigations.
Logarithms used in numerical calculations are called common logarithms, and are to the base 10. The great advantage of using logarithms is that multiplication and division are reduced to simple addition and subtraction, the finding of power of numbers (e.g. $1·07^{21}$) becomes a sum in multiplication, and the extraction of roots (e.g. $\sqrt[17]{2·95}$) becomes a sum in division. Tables of logarithms, together with instructions for using them, are printed in most algebraic text-books, usually to 4 decimal figures, the decimals being called the

mantissae (singular, *mantissa*) of the logarithms, and an integer preceding them being known as the *characteristic*. The latter is to be found by a simple method of inspection. Books of tables to 7 decimal figures are also published. Numerical calculations worked out with the help of logarithms are only approximate ; but the approximation is sufficiently close for practical purposes. Obviously the results arrived at with 7-figure tables are more accurate than those worked with the 4-figure tables.

logic can be defined as an investigation of the ' validity ' of different ' forms of reasoning.' But what do we mean by that ? Consider the following statements :

1 ' All pantaps are angaraptic '
2 ' George is a pantap '

Now, we have not the least idea what is meant by ' pantap ' or by ' angaraptic.' But we do know that *if* both the statements are true, then *it must also be true* (3) *that* ' George is angaraptic.' We know *that* not because of anything to do with ' pantaps ' or ' angaraptic,' but simply because we see that the *form* of argument used in arriving at or ' inferring ' statement (3) from statements (1) and (2) is sound ; or as a logician would say, ' valid.'

The form of argument used above comes out more clearly if we express the same reasoning in general terms (as in algebra) :

(1) All A is B
(2) C is A
Therefore—
(3) C is B.

The study of forms of reasoning and of their validity is what is known as ' logic.' This branch of philosophy remained more or less as its founder Aristotle left it until quite recently, when Bertrand Russell and others began to widen its scope.

Loire, *lwär*, longest river of France ; rises in the Cevennes, and flows *c*.610m to the Atlantic.

Loki, in old Norse tales, spirit of mischief.

Lollards, religious sect. Followers of John Wycliffe, they were Church reformers in the 14th and 15th c. Regarded as heretics, they opposed Mass, ecclesiastical endowments, etc. Many died for their faith ; all prepared the way for the Reformation.

The Lollards (named from the Dutch *lollen*, to sing) became a political party, and since they attacked not only the indolence of the clergy but also their riches, they may be regarded as pioneers of much more recent Socialist teaching.

Lombards, Teutonic tribe that invaded and settled in Italy in the 6th c., became one with the Italians, and by the 13th c. were noted as bankers and merchants. They traded much with England, hence Lombard Street, London, where many of them founded foreign banks.

Lombard Street, see LOMBARDS

Lombardy, division of N. Italy ; largely a well-watered plain.

Lombok, island of the Netherlands E. Indies ; is mountainous and volcanic ; has been Dutch since 1894, and is now part of E. Indonesia.

Lomond, *lo'mund*, largest loch (lake) in Scotland ; 23m long ; area *c*.27sq.m. Ben Lomond rises to the East.

London, port and cap. of the UK and of the British Empire ; on the R. Thames ; comprises : (*a*) *City of London* (one sq.m), under the jurisdiction of the Lord Mayor of London ; (*b*) *administrative county of London*, area 120sq.m, with the city of Westminster, royal borough of Kensington, and 26 other boroughs, all governed since 1888 by the London County Council (LCC) ; and (*c*) *Greater London*, area *c*.700sq.m ; estimated pop.9,000,000.

Beginning as a collection of dwellings round the ' Pool ' (an expansion of the Thames) in the Celtic period, London became important with the building of the first bridge in Roman times. Fortified by the Romans and Normans, it was a busy trading-centre in the 12th c., and later famous for guilds and livery companies. Trade expanded in the 16th c., when the Merchant Adventurers, Muscovy Company and E. India Company, etc. were founded. The Great Plague 1665, from which *c*.70,000 people died, brought business almost to a standstill ; the Great Fire 1666 (said to have begun near London Bridge) rendered 100,000 people homeless, destroyed old St Paul's, the Guildhall, over 80 churches and 13,000 houses, but to some extent cleared the way for Sir Christopher Wren, and other architects, to replace timbered houses with buildings of brick and stone. *The Monument* (a fluted column 202ft high) commemorates the Fire. The later growth of the Empire increased the trade and business of the cap. which, in 1801, had a pop. of 1,200,000, and in 1901 over 6,580,000. Bombed by the Germans in World War I, London suffered still more severely in World War II, first from high-explosives and incendiaries, later from flying bombs (V1 and V2) ; causing altogether 29,890 deaths, and the destruction of over 1,000,000 houses.

The county of London alone has 8,000 streets, 2,000 churches, 20,000 shops ; the *Port of London* (from Teddington to the sea) has 4,200 acres of docks, with an annual trade worth £500,000,000. The chief *docks* are Victoria and Albert, Tilbury, and W. India. Centre of the nation's commerce, banking and insurance, London's manufactures include engineering, shipbuilding, brewing, printing, pottery, chemicals, tailoring, silk-weaving, manufacture of boots and shoes, paper and furniture. The great *railway stations* include King's Cross, Euston, St Pancras, Charing Cross, Victoria, Liverpool Street, Paddington and Waterloo, and there is the remarkable system of the *Underground* or *Tube*, with tunnels linking 250 stations by electric trains, on which 3,000,000 passengers travel every day. The system is governed by the London Passenger Transport Board, which also operates buses, coaches and trams, thus transporting, in all, over 12,000,000 people per day.

Croydon and Northholt are important airports ; also Gatwick and Heathrow, the latter (now named London Airport) being the largest in the British Isles.

The county of London returns 62 Members to Parliament ; Greater London over 100.

Interesting sights of London are :

AIR MINISTRY, Adastral House, Kingsway. The windows display models and photographs of aeroplanes.

ART GALLERIES : (*a*) *Burlington House*, Piccadilly ; (*b*) *Tate Gallery*, Millbank ; (*c*) *Wallace Collection*, Hertford House, Manchester Square ; (*d*) *National Gallery*, Trafalgar Square, founded 1824, has one of the finest collections in the world ; (*e*) *National Portrait Gallery* (behind the National Gallery), with over 3,800 portraits of famous British men and women from 1400 to our own day ; opened 1896.

BUCKINGHAM PALACE, London home of the King and Queen ; begun 1703 for John Sheffield, Duke of Buckingham, bought by George III ; rebuilt 1825–36.

THE CENOTAPH, Whitehall, designed by Sir Edwin Lutyens as a memorial to ' The Glorious Dead ' of World War I and II ; scene of the annual Remembrance Day ceremony.

CLEOPATRA'S NEEDLE, Thames Embankment ; is the oldest monument in London. It is wrongly named, as this huge stone obelisk was carved in Egypt 1,500 years *before* Cleopatra's day, say *c*.1475BC. It was brought to England 1878, and had an adventurous voyage. It is 68ft high ; weighs 180 tons.

COVENT GARDEN (near the Strand), London's chief fruit, vegetable and flower market. The name is a corruption of *convent* garden.

DOWNING STREET, Whitehall, named after Sir George Downing, Secretary to the Treasury in the 17th c. ; No. 10 is the official London home of the Prime Minister.

EMBANKMENT (or Victoria Embankment), runs by the Thames from Blackfriars Bridge to Westminster ; is noted for handsome plane trees ; has many monuments, e.g. *Royal Air Force Memorial*. It is dominated by *Shell-Mex House.*

HOUSES OF PARLIAMENT, Westminster, on the banks of the Thames ; designed by Sir Charles Barry to replace an old building burned down 1834 ; completed *c*.1850. The clock tower is 316ft high ; its largest bell, *Big Ben*, weighs over 13 tons. The Houses cover 8 acres and cost over £3,000,000 to build. The *House of Lords* is a gilded room where 550 lords

sit ; before the throne is the *Woolsack*, the Lord Chancellor's seat, a reminder that, formerly, England's prosperity depended largely on wool. In the *House of Commons* is the Speaker's chair, with Government and Opposition benches right and left ; debate may continue only as long as the Mace is on the table. Attached to the Houses of Parliament is the historic *Westminster Hall*, begun by William II ; its 14th c. oak roof, of exceptional interest, rises 90ft above the hall and is 238ft long, 67¼ft wide.

A new House of Commons has been built to replace the one much damaged in a raid during World War II. The architect is Sir Giles Gilbert Scott ; there are seats for 939 people. The building is air-conditioned.

HYDE PARK, area 360 acres, has a lake (the *Serpentine*) ; is noted for its many wild fowl, also *Rotten Row*, a sand track much used by riders.

KENSINGTON GARDENS, between Hyde Park and Kensington Palace, include the famous *Round Pond*, much used for model yachting, and Sir George Frampton's statue of *Peter Pan.*

LONDON BRIDGE, built by John Rennie and his two sons, opened 1831, replacing an old bridge with 19 arches, many houses, and fortified gates, above which were displayed the spiked heads of traitors.

LORD'S CRICKET GROUND, HQ of English cricket, belongs to the Marylebone Cricket Club (MCC). The nearest station is St John's Wood.

THE MALL, tree-lined avenue from Admiralty Arch to Buckingham Palace.

MANSION HOUSE, home of the Lord Mayor since 1753, faces the Bank of England.

MARBLE ARCH, north corner of Hyde Park ; designed by John Nash ; stands near the site of the old *Tyburn gallows* where rebels and highwaymen were hanged prior to 1783. The Tyburn (a stream) now flows underground.

ROYAL MINT, Stepney, begun 1810, a building where our coins are minted ; may be visited free if application is made to the Deputy Master ; over 4,000,000,000 coins have been struck since 1900.

MUSEUMS include (*a*) *Natural History Museum*, Cromwell Road, S. Kensington ; (*b*) *Victoria and Albert Museum*, close by ; famous for books, photographs, carpets, examples of the goldsmith's and silversmith's craftsmanship ; (*c*) *Geological Museum*, Exhibition Road ; SW7 ; (*d*) *South Kensington Science Museum* ; (*e*) *Imperial War Museum*, Lambeth Road, Southwark, founded 1920 ; (*f*) *London Museum*, notable for Roman antiquities ; (*g*) *United Services Museum*, Whitehall ; (*h*) *British Museum*, Great Russell Street, Bloomsbury ; a building designed by Sir Robert Smirke (1781–1867), begun 1828 ; notable for its huge circular reading room, with a dome 140ft in diameter and 106ft high ; has 50m of book-shelves and over 4,000,000 books. The museum collection began with natural history specimens collected by Sir Hans Sloane (1660–1753) ; the treasures now include sculptures from ancient Greece, Rome, Nineveh and Egypt ; also illuminated MSS, pottery, metalwork and precious stones.

PICCADILLY, famous street, with *Piccadilly Circus*, where *Eros*, Sir Alfred Gilbert's winged archer, stands.

PUBLIC RECORD OFFICE, Chancery Lane.

REGENT'S PARK, area 470 acres, opened 1838.

ST JAMES'S PALACE, handsome brick building begun in Henry VIII's day. Here slept Charles I before walking to execution. *St James's Park*, near by, is noted for its water-fowl.

ST PAUL'S CATHEDRAL, replacing a Norman church destroyed 1666, is Sir Christopher Wren's masterpiece. Built 1675–1710, it is in Renaissance style. The dome, rising 365ft, is almost 150ft in diameter, and crowned with a golden cross. The cathedral, 515ft long, has a west front approached by steps 180ft wide. In the south tower hangs Great Paul, a bell weighing 17 tons. In the interior of the church there are many monuments in memory of famous people, including Wellington, Nelson, General Gordon, Dr Johnson, Turner and Sir Christopher Wren, whose epitaph has the words : *Si monumentum requiris circumspice*, i.e. If you would see his monument, look around you. The high altar was damaged by a German bomb Oct 1940.

TOWER OF LONDON, covers 13 acres, has been a fortress, palace and prison. Close by the Thames, built for William I, has walls 12–15ft thick and contains a notable chapel. Bones, supposed to be those of Edward V and his brother (princes in the Tower) were found here. Other towers include St Thomas's above *Traitor's Gate*. Instruments of torture and old armour and weapons are to be seen in the museums ; and the priceless *Crown Jewels* are in a strong-room. In the Tower we meet the Yeomen of the Guard (or Beefeaters) in scarlet and gold uniforms. *Tower Hill*, close by, reminds us of many executions there, e.g. Sir Thomas More, Thomas Cromwell, the Earl of Surrey, etc.

TRAFALGAR SQUARE, has *Canada House, South Africa House, Admiralty Arch*, the *National Gallery, St Martin's-in-the-Fields*, and, in the centre, *Nelson's Monument*, a column 145ft high. The huge lions below were designed by Sir Edwin Landseer. There are memorials to Admiral Beatty and Admiral Jellicoe.

WATERLOO BRIDGE, completed 1945, replaces John Rennie's bridge of 1817.

WESTMINSTER ABBEY, new in the 8th c. was rebuilt in Norman style by Edward the Confessor. The west towers (225ft high, are 18th c., and much of the building was restored in the 19th c. The church is 530ft long ; the interior of the nave, 166ft long, is 100ft high. *Henry VIII's Chapel*, an exquisite example of its period, is notable for its roof like ' a web of stone.' The House of Commons met in the *Chapter House* 1289–1547, and coronations have been held in the Abbey since the time of King Harold. The tombs and monuments include those of some of our greatest men and women. Included in the famous *Poet's Corner* (south transept) are memorials to Chaucer, Milton, Shakespeare, Burns, etc ; elsewhere are the tombs of Sir Isaac Newton, Henry V, Queen Elizabeth, Edward the Confessor and Edward I, whose chair has been used at the coronation of all our kings since his day. Beneath is the *Stone of Scone* which he stole from Scotland. There is also the tomb of the *Unknown Warrior*, a tribute to those who fought in World War I ; and the Battle of Britain Memorial, dedicated 1947.

WHITEHALL, first known as York Place, became Henry VIII's property after Cardinal Wolsey died. For the next 150 years it was a royal palace, the court moving to St James's 1698, after the palace had been destroyed by fire. The name now refers to a wide road from Trafalgar Square towards the Houses of Parliament. Here are the *Horse Guards*, two mounted troopers of the Household Cavalry. The *Changing of the Guard* occurs c.10.30am and 4pm. In the rear is the *Horse Guard's Parade* where, on the King's birthday, the ceremony of Trooping the Colours is performed.

ZOOLOGICAL GARDENS (better known as the Zoo), occupies 37 acres of Regent's Park.

Books about London include : *London* (in the *King's England Series*), Arthur Mee ; *Guide to London* (Ward Lock) ; *Guide to London*, H. V. Morton ; *London, An Encyclopaedia*, William Kent.

London, city and port, Ontario, Canada ; noted for chemicals and machinery ; pop.81,000.

London, JACK (1876–1916), American writer, *b* San Francisco ; led a roving and adventurous life from whaling to taking part in the Klondike gold rush 1897, and tramping through USA and Canada. He is best known for his outdoor books, e.g. *Call of the Wild* ; *The Sea Wolf* ; and *White Fang*. Read *Sailor on Horseback*, Irving Stone.

London County Council (LCC), body administering an area of 117sq.m ; constituted 1888 ; comprises a chairman, 20 aldermen, 129 councillors ; the rateable value of its property is c.£54,000,000 ; offices : County Hall, Westminster Bridge, London, SE1.

Londonderry, *lŭn-dŭn-der'-i*, county of

Northern Ireland. The co.tn, London-derry (better known as Derry), is on Lough Foyle. It was besieged 1689 by James II.

London plane, see PLANE

London University, university founded 1836 reorganised 1900. It has had imposing new quarters, Bloomsbury, since 1936 ; differs from Oxford and Cambridge in that all degrees are open to *external* students ; provides courses in theology, arts, laws, music, medicine, science, engineering, economics, political science ; has *c*.15,000 internal and nearly 20,000 external students.

Longchamp, WILLIAM DE, -*shamp* (*d* 1197), churchman, born in Normandy ; appointed Bishop of Ely and Chancellor of England by Richard I ; was haughty, quarrelsome and contemptuous of everything English. Although imprisoned, he escaped to France.

Long Eaton, town, Derbyshire ; noted for lace ; pop.26,000.

Longfellow, HENRY WADSWORTH (1807–82), American poet, *b* Maine ; studied law ; travelled much in Europe and was inspired by the history, legend and romance of the countries he visited. Professor of foreign languages at Maine and Harvard, he settled (1843) at Craigie House, Cambridge, Massachusetts, where most of the remainder of his life was spent.

Longfellow's poetry, never profound, and without the brilliance of that of Keats or Shelley, is homely, simple and full of sweetness and gentleness, e.g. *The Village Blacksmith* ; *A Psalm of Life* ; *The Rainy Day.* His narrative poetry includes *Evangeline* ; his dramatic works include *The Golden Legend.* His many translations (e.g. from the German Norse and Spanish) introduced America to European lore and legend in a happy way ; but his greatest work is *The Song of Hiawatha.* This Red Indian saga, full of action and melody, was set to music by Coleridge-Taylor. See AMERICAN INDIANS.

Longford, county of Leinster, Eire ; also its co.tn, 76m from Dublin ; has tanneries, corn mills.

Long Island, island SE. of New York State ; washed by East R. and Long I. Sound ; area 1,682sq.m. Here is Brooklyn, Long I. City and Coney I.

longitude, *lon'ji-tūd,* angular distance east or west of a chosen meridian, i.e. an imaginary line circling the earth and passing through the poles. The standard meridian (0°) is generally regarded as that passing through Greenwich. Places east of Greenwich have noon 4min earlier for each degree of longitude, places west 4min later for each degree of longitude.

Long Parliament, name given to the English Parliament 1640–53. It was dissolved by Cromwell, but later restored, finally ceasing 1660. Some of its members (143 Presbyterians) were forcibly ex-cluded 1648, the remaining members being nicknamed the Rump.

loom, see WEAVING

Loos, ANITA (1893–), American woman writer who caused a sensation (1925) with the publication of her social satire *Gentlemen Prefer Blondes.*

Lope de Vega, *lō'pā dā vā'gä* (1562–1635), Spanish dramatist and poet ; fought in the Spanish Armada 1588 ; spent his last years as a priest. Born at a time when Spanish drama was formless and lifeless, Lope de Vega created a new and vigorous literature, producing nearly 2,000 plays and religious dramas (mostly founded on the history of Spain).

loquat, *lō-kwot',* Chinese and Japanese bush or small evergreen tree. The fruit is sometimes called the Japanese quince.

Loran, see RADAR

lord, baron or peer of the realm ; son of a duke or marquis, or the eldest son of an earl ; feminine, *lady.* The Scots ' laird ' is the same word, but means ' landowner ' or ' proprietor.'

Lord Chief Justice, in England a judge who ranks next to the Lord Chancellor.

Lord High Chancellor, see CHANCELLOR

Lord Justice Clerk, next judge in Scotland after the Lord President.

lord mayor, see LOCAL GOVERNMENT

Lord President of the Court of Session, highest judge in Scotland ; also sits as Lord Justice General to try criminal causes.

lord provost, see LOCAL GOVERNMENT

lords-and-ladies, see POISONOUS PLANTS

Lord's Cricket Ground, HQ of the MCC (Marylebone Cricket Club), now in St John's Wood, London, NW ; founded by Thomas Lord (1757–1832), and moved to its present site 1814. See CRICKET

Loreto, *lō-rā'tō,* town near the Adriatic coast of Italy. It is a famous place of pilgrimage for Roman Catholics.

Loretto School, public school, near Mussel-burgh, *c*.6m from Edinburgh ; founded 1827.

Lorient, *lō-rē-än',* naval base, France, 30m from Vannes ; once associated with French E. India ; pop.46,000.

Lorne, LORD, see ARGYLL

Lorraine, *lō-rān',* district of France N. of Alsace ; belonged to Germany 1871–1919.

lory, see PARROT

Los Angeles, city, California, USA ; noted for exporting fruit, and still more as the HQ of America's film industry ; centre of a mining district ; pop.1,504,000.

Lossiemouth, holiday town and port, Morayshire.

Lot, OT character ; nephew of Abraham, whom he accompanied to Canaan (Genesis 13). He escaped the destruction of Sodom, but his wife, looking back, was changed into a pillar of salt (Genesis 19).

Lothians, THE, old district of Scotland ; now includes the shires of Haddington (E. Lothian), Edinburgh (Midlothian) and Linlithgow (W. Lothian).

Loti, PIERRE, *lō-tē'* (1850–1923), French

writer, *b* Rochefort ; joined the navy ; author of many novels, mostly with a melancholy sentiment, two of the best being *The Iceland Fisherman* and *Madame Chrysanthemum.*

lotus, genus of plants including the bird's foot trefoil ; popular name for the water-lily ; also a name for the jujube-tree, possibly referred to in legends of the *lotus-eaters,* said to have lived in N. Africa.

loudness, see PHON

lough, see LAKE

Loughborough, *lŭf'bŭ-rŭ,* town, Leicestershire ; on the R. Soar ; makes hosiery, electrical apparatus and church bells ; pop.33,000.

Louis, *loo'is ; loo'i,* name of 18 kings of France, including the Holy Roman Emperor, Lewis I (or Louis I), who *d* 840 ; Louis VI (1078–1137) ruled from 1108 ; was the great rival of Henry I of England.

Louis VII (1120–80), King of France from 1137 ; rival of Henry II of England.

Louis IX (1214–70), King of France, known as St Louis ; ruled from 1236 ; directed the 7th crusade, eventually reaching Palestine ; compelled Henry III (of England) to renounce his claims to Normandy, Anjou, Maine and Poitou.

Louis XI (1423–83), French king ; ruled from 1461 ; had an unlovable nature ; encouraged the middle classes to oppose the nobility ; was a skilled administrator. He governed as an autocrat, taxed the peasants, paved the way for commercial expansion ; largely united a rebellious country.

Louis XII (1462–1515), French king. As duke of Orleans he led an unsuccessful revolt ; ruled from 1498 ; gained control, for a time, of Italy ; married (as his 2nd wife) Mary Tudor, sister of Henry VIII of England.

Louis XIII (1601–43), French king, son of Henry of Navarre and Marie de' Medici ; succeeded 1610. Possessed of a weak character, he was trained, even as a spoilt child, to intrigue. His country suffered civil war till the rise of Richelieu, who completely controlled the king.

Louis XIV (1638–1715), King of France ; son of Anne of Austria and Louis XIII ; succeeded, 1643, when only five, the country being governed by his mother and by Cardinal Mazarin. Louis began to rule when Mazarin *d* 1661. When the ministers of state assembled to ask to whom they were to be responsible (i.e. who was to be chief minister), the king replied, ' To me.'

Though it is doubtful if he ever declared ' l'État, c'est moi,' Louis was for 72 years supreme in France, responsible to a large extent for an outstandingly glorious period. He was vigorous, capable, a born administrator, a genius in choosing ministers of state, a fine soldier, an astute politician in international affairs, and the inspiration of art, learning and building.

LOUIS XIV OF FRANCE 1638–1715

His wars include the Dutch War and the War of the Spanish Succession. For 50 years he was the most influential figure in European affairs, and he considerably enlarged his country's boundaries. In later life he persecuted the Protestants, and revoked the *Edict of Nantes,* but for much of his long reign France enjoyed religious toleration and internal peace, a remarkable contrast to the former civil wars. She was thus able to make commercial and industrial progress, to foster the arts as never before, to build palaces (e.g. that at Versailles), erect monuments, make magnificent roads, dredge harbours and exploit all her resources.

With his ministers Colbert and Louvois, Louis ruled as a great king, earning the title ' Le Roi Soleil ' ; but it should be noted that there was little personal liberty, and that the government was dependent on one man, Louis, alone.

Louis XV (1710–74), French king, great-grandson of Louis XIV ; ruled from 1723, but was controlled by Cardinal Fleury ; did little to improve France after the disastrous Seven Years' War. His private life was scandalous. Apparently he saw misfortune coming to France, for he is credited with saying, *Après moi, le déluge,* i.e. after me, the flood.

Louis XVI (1754–93), French king, *b* Versailles, succeeded his grandfather, Louis XV, 1774 ; married Marie Antoinette, who persuaded him to dismiss the finance minister, Jacques Necker, the subsequent breakdown in finances hastening the Revolution 1789. Living in luxury, and unable to appreciate the trend of affairs, Louis was compelled to flee to Varennes 1791, but was taken back to Paris, tried (as Louis Capet) by the Jacobins, and guillotined.

LOUIS XVI OF FRANCE 1754–93

His queen, Marie Antoinette (1755–1793), was also guillotined. Daughter of the Empress Maria Theresa, she was *b* Vienna. She married Louis 1770. Living carelessly, she dominated her husband and was to blame for much of the bad government. Overfond of pleasure, indiscreet, vain, she was nevertheless charming.

Louis XVIII (1755–1824), King of France, brother of Louis XVI ; entered Paris 1814 ; fled when Napeolon escaped from Elba, and returned 1815, pursuing a moderate policy.

louis d'or, *loo-i dör,* French gold coin used 1640 (time of Louis XIII) to 1795 ; valued at *c.*16s.

Louisiana, state of USA. It is west of the lower Mississippi ; noted for forests ; cultivates maize, rice, cotton ; named in honour of Louis XIV ; cap. Baton Rouge.

Louis Philippe, *loo'ē' fē-lēp'* (1773–1850), King of the French ; after 1793 fled to Switzerland, and found refuge in USA and England ; returned to France at the revolution of 1830 ; steered a middle course, but became increasingly unpopular, and finally escaped to England at the revolution of 1848, dying in Surrey.

Louisville, *loo'is-vil,* city and river port, Kentucky, USA ; on the R. Ohio ; a great railway centre ; noted for tobacco, meat-packing, petroleum, etc. ; pop.319,000.

Lourdes, *loord,* town, south of France ; visited by RC pilgrims who worship in the Grotto of Our Lady of Lourdes.

Lourenço Marques, *lō-ren'sō mär'kes,* cap. and port, Portuguese E. Africa ; pop. 48,000.

Louth, *low*th, county in the province of Leinster, Eire ; co.tn Dundalk.

Louvain, *loo-va*n, town, Belgium ; an important railway junction ; noted for

its university and cathedral ; suffered severely in World Wars I and II ; pop. 39,000.

Louvre, *loo'v'r,* magnificent building, Paris; originally a palace, now a museum with priceless art treasures.

lovebird, see PARROT

Loveday, ALAN (1928–), NZ violinist ; early showed remarkable promise as a musician. With help from friends and the NZ Government, came to England where he was trained by Albert Sammons ; played as a soloist at the Albert Hall when only 18.

Lovelace, RICHARD (1618–58), English poet ; a Royalist, he was imprisoned, and there wrote *To Althea from Prison,* beginning, *Stone walls do not a prison make.*

Low, PROFESSOR A. M. (1888–), Scottish scientist ; inventor of a new type of petrol engine, a form of television, radio-torpedo control devices ; an expert in acoustics and matters relating to aviation ; author of scientific works, e.g. *Science in Industry* ; *The Future* ; *Life and Its Story* ; *The Wonder Book of Invention* ; *Low's Book of Home Experiments* ; and many books for boys.

Low Countries, name sometimes given to the Netherlands ; may or may not include Belgium.

Lowell, *lō'el,* city, Massachusetts, USA ; 26m from Boston ; produces cotton and woollen goods ; pop.101,000.

Lowell, JAMES RUSSELL, *lō'el* (1819–91), American poet and author, *b* Cambridge, Massachusetts ; descended from English Puritans ; American ambassador in London from 1880 ; wrote against slavery. He was author of *Biglow Papers* ; *My Study Windows* ; and many others.

Lowestoft, *lōs'toft,* port and holiday town, Suffolk ; noted for its quaint narrow streets (scores) and its great fish market ; has a large fishing fleet ; shipbuilding yards ; pop.42,000.

Lowther Hills, range between Lanarkshire and Dumfriesshire.

Loyola, IGNATIUS, *lō-yō'lä* (1491–1556), Spanish saint and mystic ; was a page at the court of Ferdinand and Isabella ; became a chivalrous knight ; dedicated himself to the RC Church ; compiled a series of spiritual exercises by which men were to find grace and joy and to live rightly ; had a vision on the way to Rome ; founded the Society of Jesus (Jesuit Order) ; declared a saint 1622.

His life and preaching, his romantic personality, and his practical organisation of a growing community did much to strengthen the RC Church, even when Protestantism was gaining ground. Members of the Society of Jesus later became known as Jesuits, their enthusiasm sometimes leading them to believe that the end justified the means, hence various corrupt practices. Founded 1534 for the reconversion of Protestants and other heretics and the spread of the RC faith, the society became immensely powerful. It has several schools and colleges in Britain.

Lubbock, SIR JOHN, see AVEBURY, LORD

Lübeck, *lū'bek,* city, Germany, north of Hamburg ; trades with the Baltic ; noted for shipbuilding and chemicals ; pop.225,000.

Lucan, *lū'kän* (AD39–65), Roman poet, born in Spain ; conspired against the Emperor Nero, and was compelled to commit suicide. He is noted for his *Pharsalia,* an epic of the war between Caesar and Pompey.

Lucas, EDWARD VERRALL (1868–1938), English author ; wrote much for *Punch* ; noted for his charming travel books, e.g. *A Wanderer in London* ; *A Wanderer in Holland,* but chiefly for his essays, his anthology *The Open Road,* and his biography of Charles Lamb.

Lucca, city, near Pisa, Italy ; manufactures silk, jute, cotton ; refines olive oil ; pop.82,000.

Lucerne, beautiful lake, Switzerland ; area 44sq.m ; also a town by the lake ; a famous tourist centre ; pop.55,000.

lucerne, see ALFALFA

Lucian, *lū'shan,* 2nd c. writer, born in Syria. Though Greek was not his native language, he wrote excellent Greek prose. He is noted for his various dialogues giving pictures of the manners of his age. He made fun of the romances of his day and satirized contemporary religions in his *True Histories.*

Lucknow, city, India, *c.*200m NW. of Benares ; noted for articles of silver, gold, ivory, and for silks, muslin and shawls ; pop.387,000. Besieged during the Indian Mutiny from July 1857 to March 1858, Lucknow was finally relieved by Sir Colin Campbell.

Lucretius, *lū-krē'shi-ŭs* (d 55BC), Latin poet of whose life scarcely anything is known, though his hexameter poem *De Rerum Natura* (On the Nature of Things) is a masterpiece. Written to dispel ignorance and superstition, it proves that Lucretius had theories of the nature of light, the atomic basis of matter, and of evolution comparable with our most advanced knowledge.

The idea of the famous poem *Vitai Lampada* (Sir Henry Newbolt) may be traced to Lucretius :

Sic rerum summa novatur
Semper, et inter se mortales mutua vivunt.
Augescunt aliae gentes, aliae minuuntur, Inque brevi spatio mutantur saecla animantum
Et quasi cursores vitai lampada tradunt.

This has been translated : Thus the sum of things is ever being replenished, and mortals live one by one and all by give and take. Some races wax and others wane, and in a short space the tribes of living things are changed, and like runners hand on the torch of life.

Lucy, SIR THOMAS, see SHAKESPEARE, WILLIAM

Luddites, named after Ned Ludd of Leicestershire, rioters from 1811–16 who attempted to destroy machinery in Nottingham, Derby, Lancashire and Yorkshire because they thought it responsible for unemployment.

Ludendorff, ERIC VON (1865–1937), German soldier ; won the battle of Tannenberg 1915 ; joint-commander from 1916 with Hindenburg ; became a staunch supporter of the Nazis 1923.

Ludlow, *lŭd'lō,* town, Shropshire ; has a ruined castle.

Ludwigshafen, *loot'vichs-häfen,* town and river port, Bavaria, Germany ; on the R. Rhine ; trades in coal and timber ; famous for chemicals, dyes, fertilisers ; pop.143,000.

Luftwaffe, *luft'väf-e,* name of the air force of the Third German Reich. The word means *air-weapon.*

Lugano, lake, Switzerland and Italy ; 16m long ; also a city on its north shore (Switzerland).

Luke, saint and evangelist ; possibly a physician of Antioch. Though not a Jew, he was a follower of St Paul. He may have been the author of the *Acts of The Apostles* and of *St Luke's Gospel,* probably *c.*AD60.

lumen, unit of luminous flux, defined as the quantity of light falling on one sq.ft of the inner surface of a sphere of 1ft radius, at the centre of which is one standard candle.

luminous paint, phosphorescent paint that shines in the dark after exposure to sunlight ; may be mainly calcium sulphide or barium sulphide.

Lundy, island off the coast of Devon ; area 1,050 acres. *Lundy* means island.

Lune, English river flowing 45m mostly through N. Lancashire to the Irish Sea.

lungs, breathing organs. They are two large, spongy organs in the thorax, the right with three lobes, the left with two, both linked by the bronchial tubes with the *trachea* (or windpipe), thence through the *larynx* to the mouth and nose. Air enters by the mouth or nose, passing down to the lungs, lined with minute air-sacs or cells where certain changes take place, namely, water and carbon dioxide are given up from the blood, and at the same time the blood takes up oxygen. Therefore, air breathed out contains carbon dioxide and water.

This process is made possible by the veinous blood from the right side of the heart passing through thin capillaries in the air-cells while on its way through the lungs to the left side of the heart, coming as it does in close contact with air breathed in.

Each lung has a delicate membrane (the *pleura*) which forms a closed sac, the outer surface of which lines the inside of the thorax, the inner surface covering the outer part of the lung. Oil in the sac allows the lung to expand or contract without friction. The muscles causing expansion or contraction of the lungs include the diaphragm, the muscles between the ribs, the neck muscles, which are used in an emergency, e.g. during an attack of asthma.

A normal and healthy man inhales from 14–18 times a minute, say *c.*30cu.in of air, though oxygen alone is of use to him. The lungs have a capacity of *c.*100cu.in. In fish, respiration is accomplished by means of gills.

lupin, garden plant ; has tall spikes each of which has numerous flowers shaped like those of the pea family. The colours range from all shades of blue and mauve to yellow, pink and white. The leaves are shaped somewhat like the spokes of a wheel.

Lusaka, cap., N. Rhodesia.

'Lusitania,' see SHIPS

lute, stringed musical instrument of eastern origin ; said to have been brought to Europe by returning crusaders. Its pear-shaped body, built up of staves of wood, has usually four or six strings.

lutecium, *lū-tē'shi-ŭm*, element, Lu ; atomic weight 174·99 ; atomic number 71 ; one of the rare earths.

Luther, MARTIN (1483–1546), German Protestant reformer, *b* Eisleben ; son of a peasant ; became a monk. After reading the Bible he believed men could find God for themselves, so that he came to doubt the principles of the RC faith and to question the pope's authority, especially his right to issue indulgences, which amounted to forgiveness for sin.

As professor of philosophy at Wittenberg University, Luther began to preach so boldly that he made a stir in Germany; and (1517) he nailed to the door of All Saints Church, Wittenberg, a list of 95 objections to Pope Leo's sale of indulgencies. For this he was summoned to the council at Leipzig, and declared an outlaw of the Church. Later (1521) he was ordered to appear before the Diet of Worms. When friends tried to dissuade him from going, he replied : ' Though there be as many devils in Worms as tiles on the roofs, yet will I go.'

Facing his accusers, he said, ' Here I stand. I can do no other. So help me, God.'

It was a great moment in history and in the story of the Reformation. Luther was in danger of his life, but friends (not enemies) kidnapped him, the Elector of Saxony found him a refuge in Wartburg Castle, where Luther translated the Bible from Latin into German.

Luther married Katherina von Bora, a nun. He was buried at Wittenberg. He was a skilled musician and a great lover of dogs.

LUTHERANISM, the Protestant faith founded by Luther, today numbers *c.*60,000,000 members, 4,000,000 in USA. See REFORMATION

Lutine Bell, bell salvaged from a French ship, wrecked 1790. The bell now hangs in Lloyd's (London), and is tolled when important news is to be announced.

Luton, town, Bedfordshire ; makes ladies' hats, also cars ; has dye-works ; pop. 109,000.

Lutterworth, see WYCLIFFE, JOHN

Lutyens, SIR EDWIN (1869–1944), architect, *b* London ; responsible for the Cenotaph, Whitehall ; the new Government House, Delhi ; Liverpool RC Cathedral ; and other buildings.

Lützen, see GUSTAVUS II

Luxembourg, palace in Paris. Designed 1615 for Marie de' Medici, it was remodelled 1836, and is now noted for its art treasures and beautiful gardens.

Luxemburg, *lŭk'sem-bŭrg*, grand duchy between Germany and France ; area 999sq.m ; pop.300,000 ; has rich iron mines ; overrun by Germany 1940, when the Grand Duchess Charlotte fled to England, returning 1945 ; cap. Luxemburg ; pop.57,000.

Luxor, town on the Nile, 418m from Cairo, Egypt ; visited by tourists for its magnificent ruins (Luxor and Karnak) on the site of the ancient city of Thebes.

Luzon, see PHILIPPINES

Lw'ow, *lvuf,* trading city, Ukraine ; noted for fairs ; pop.219,000.

lyceum, *lī-sē'um,* educational institution, named from the Lyceum, near Athens, where Aristotle taught his pupils.

Lycurgus (*d c.*800BC), reputed founder of the laws of Sparta.

Lydia, *lid'i-ä,* ancient country of Asia Minor ; was exceedingly wealthy in the time of Croesus ; conquered in the 6th c. BC by Cyrus.

lye, *lī,* by-product in the manufacture of soap ; very important as a source of glycerol.

Lyell, SIR CHARLES, *lī'el* (1797–1875), Scottish geologist ; styled the ' father of modern geology ' ; supported Darwin's evolutionary theories.

Lyly, JOHN, *li'li* (*d* 1606), writer, *b* Kent ;

THE LYNX

the first Englishman to write prose fiction, e.g. *Euphues, The Anatomy of Wit* ; and *Euphues, His England*, love-stories written in a very affected style which came to be known as ' *euphuism*.'

lymph, see BLOOD

Lympne, *lim*, village, radio station and airport, Kent.

Lynd, ROBERT (1879–1949), writer, *b* Belfast ; noted as an essayist ; always shrewd and witty.

Lynn, city, Massachusetts, USA ; noted for boots and shoes ; pop.98,000.

lynx, forest animal of the cat family ; may be 36in long not including its short tail ; has tufted ears, bearded cheeks, and is heavily built. It climbs trees and preys on birds and animals ; found in Europe, Tibet and N. America.

Lyons, *lī'-ŭnz*, historic city, France, where the Rhône and Saône meet ; famous for silk weaving, also dyeing and printing ; pop.561,000.

Lyons, JOSEPH ALOYSIUS (1879–1939), Australian statesman ; Tasmanian Premier 1923–29 ; Premier of Australia 1939 ; did much to put the country's finances on a firm footing.

lyre, *līr*, stringed musical instrument of ancient and medieval times. It was especially favoured by Greek minstrels, who used it to accompany verses sung or recited ; hence *lyric* verse.

lyre-bird, Australian bird roughly the same size as a pheasant ; so named because its remarkably long tail-feathers suggest the shape of a lyre. In the courting season the male struts and dances before the female.

lyric poetry, see POETRY

Lysander, *lī-san'dĕr* (*d* 395BC), Spartan commander ; defeated the Athenians in the naval battle off Aegospotami 405BC, later capturing Athens ; accompanied Agesilaus in his campaign against the Persians ; killed at the battle of Haliartus.

Lyte, HENRY FRANCIS (1793–1847), born near Kelso (Scotland) ; wrote many hymns, among which *Abide with me* is the most famous.

Lytham St Anne's, *lith'm*-, seaside holiday resort, Lancashire ; pop.30,000.

Lytton, EDWARD GEORGE BULWER, 1ST LORD, *lit'ŭn* (1803–73), statesman and writer, *b* London ; entered Parliament when only 26 ; Colonial Secretary for a short period ; best remembered for his many novels, e.g. *Pelham* ; *Eugene Aram* ; *Rienzi* ; *The Last Days of Pompeii* ; *The Last of the Barons* ; revived interest in the historical romance.

M

Maas, see MEUSE

Maastricht, *mäs'tricht*, town, Netherlands ; on the R. Maas ; manufactures pottery, glass, textiles ; pop.73,000.

Mac, Gaelic, *son* ; common in Scottish names. Thus MacAllister represents Gaelic *MacAlasdair*, i.e. ' the son of Alexander.'

McAdam, J. L., see ROADS

MacArthur, GENERAL DOUGLAS (1880–), USA soldier and far-sighted statesman ; Commander-in-Chief of the SW. Pacific Area from 1942 during World War II ; was brilliantly successful in ' hopping ' across the islands from Australia towards Japan, receiving the surrender of that country 1945, and guiding it during its early post-war reconstruction period. His commando troops in the Philippines attracted world-wide admiration. In 1950 MacArthur was in command of the United Nations troops in Korea. After repeated reverses he drove the North Koreans back to the Chinese frontier, but when the Chinese communists intervened was himself driven back behind the 38th parallel. In April 1951 he was relieved of all his commands by President Truman for failing to comply with directives which had forbidden him to make pronouncements on political matters. See KOREA

Macassar, port of Celebes, an island of the Netherlands E. Indies ; exports macassar (vegetable) oil ; pop.87,000.

Macaulay, ROSE, English novelist, notable for her witty revelations of modern society. Her novels include *Told by an Idiot* (1923) ; *Orphan Island*.

Macaulay, THOMAS BABINGTON (1800–59), politician and historian, *b* Rothley Temple, Leicestershire ; had an amazing vocabulary even as a child of four ; wrote an epic at ten, and a history of the world at twelve. Possessing an exceptionally good memory, he became a lawyer ; entered Parliament 1830 as a Whig ; made notable speeches in favour of the Reform Bill ; was appointed legal adviser to the Supreme Council in India, and was responsible for introducing European literature and science into higher education in India, and drawing up a new penal code. Created Lord Macaulay 1857, he died two years later and was buried in Westminster Abbey. Macaulay won fame with (*a*) his *Essays*, e.g. those on Milton, Clive and Warren Hastings ; (*b*) his poetry, notably his *Lays of Ancient Rome* (1842), so vivid

that the past lives and throbs in them again ; also his poem *The Armada* ; and (*c*) his famous *History of England from the Accession of James II*, a work marred by his Whig prejudices, but nevertheless admired for its picturesque style.
' I wish,' said Lord Melbourne once, ' that I could be as cocksure of one thing as Macaulay is of everything.'

Macbeth (*d* 1057), nephew of Malcolm II of Scotland ; Commander-in-Chief of the army of King Duncan, whom he murdered and succeeded 1040 ; slain by Duncan's son, Malcolm III. His life is the basis of Shakespeare's play, *Macbeth*.

Maccabees, name of a notable Jewish family of the 2nd c. BC. Mattathias, a priest, refused to offer pagan sacrifices when ordered to do so by the Syrians. He and his sons (John, Simon, Eleazar, Jonathan and Judas, known as Judas Maccabaeus) stirred up a revolt, and thus succeeded in preserving the Jewish laws and religion.

Macclesfield, town, Cheshire ; noted for silk ; pop.35,000.

McCracken, ESTHER (1902–), dramatist, *b* Newcastle-on-Tyne ; well-known broadcaster since 1935 ; wrote *The Willing Spirit* ; won fame with her play *Quiet Wedding* (1938). Other plays include *Quiet Week End* and *No Medals*.

MacDonald, FLORA, see JAMES EDWARD

MacDonald, JAMES RAMSAY (1866–1937), statesman, *b* Lossiemouth (Scotland) ; was a journalist before becoming Secretary of the Labour Party 1900 ; entered Parliament 1906 ; Leader of the Labour Party 1911–14, and again 1922 ; formed Britain's first Labour government 1924 ; Prime Minister again 1929 ; formed a Coalition National Government 1931, of which he was Prime Minister until 1935. A sincere advocate of international peace, he failed to realise the practical necessity of preparing for war with Nazi Germany.

Macduff, Scottish hero, partly legendary ; said to have lived in the 11th c. and to have conspired with Malcolm Canmore to overthrow Macbeth ; appears in Shakespeare's play *Macbeth*.

Macedonia, *mas-ē-dō′niā*, in ancient times a kingdom on the Aegean Sea ; noted for gold, silver, salt and vineyards ; raised to power by Philip II (359–336BC) and his son, Alexander the Great. It is now a region in Greece, Bulgaria and Yugoslavia.
After World War II the Renovation Party rebelled in an attempt to secure independence.

McGill University, Canadian university founded 1821 ; named after James McGill of Montreal (*d* 1813) ; noted for engineering and medicine.

Macgillycuddy's Reeks, *mä-gil′i-kŭd-iz rēks*, mountains in County Kerry, Eire.

Machiavelli, NICCOLÓ, *mä-kiä-vel′lē* (1469–1527), Italian statesman and author,

b Florence ; employed on diplomatic missions ; was impressed by the unscrupulous but successful methods of Cesare Borgia. His fame rests on two of his many books, the *Discourses* and *The Prince*. These deal with the principles of government. Machiavelli believed that individuals should live rightly, but that craftiness is necessary in state affairs.

Mackail, DENIS (1892–), author ; won fame as a novelist and humorist ; his books include a life of Sir J. M. Barrie. Read *Our Hero*.

McKenna, REGINALD (1863–1943), British politician, lawyer and banker ; entered Parliament as a Liberal 1895 ; Chancellor of the Exchequer 1915, taxed amusements, and put duties on cars and films.

Mackenzie, river of Canada ; flows 2,300m from the Rocky Mts to the Arctic Ocean.

Mackenzie, COMPTON (1883–), writer, *b* W. Hartlepool ; author of *Sinister Street* (a psychological study of schoolboy life) ; *Windsor Tapestry*, and various novels.

mackerel, food fish common in British waters ; from 14–18in long ; the back is bluish-green barred with black ; the female lays 300,000–650,000 floating eggs. Mackerel are caught chiefly with seine and drift nets.

McKinley, mt. Alaska ; height 20,300ft.

McKinley, WILLIAM (1843–1901), American statesman ; *b* Ohio ; advocated Protection ; saw the successful passing of the McKinley Act 1890 ; 25th President of USA 1896 ; was cordial towards Britain.

Maclaren, IAN, pen name of John Watson (1850–1907), born in Essex ; preached for 25 years in Liverpool ; author of *Beside the Bonnie Brier Bush.*

Macmahon, MARSHAL, *mäk-mä-awn′* (1808–1893), French soldier ; won the battle of Magenta 1859 ; lost the battle of Sedan in the Franco-Prussian war ; President of France 1873–79.

MacNeice, LOUIS, *mak-nēs′* (1907–), poet ; lecturer in Greek at Bedford College, London, from 1936 ; has translated the *Agamemnon of Aeschylus.*

Madagascar, tropical island 240m from the SE. coast of Africa ; area 228,000 sq.m ; pop. 4,000,000 ; became a French Protectorate 1896 ; exports gold, cattle, rubber and beans ; cap. Antananarivo.

Madcap Hal, see HENRY V

madeira, *mä-dēr′ă*, wine made from grapes grown in the Madeira Is.

Madeiras, see PORTUGAL

Madison, JAMES (1751–1836), American statesman, born in Virginia ; helped to draw up the constitution of the USA ; President 1808 and again 1812.

Madonna (Italian, *my lady*), name given to the Virgin (the Mother of Christ) as portrayed in art, e.g. portraits by Raphael, Leonardo da Vinci, Titian and Murillo.

Mad Parliament, met 1258 at Oxford ; protested against Henry III's extravagances, and drew up the *Provisions of Oxford.*

Madras, *mä-dräs'*, province, India ; forms the larger part of the Deccan ; cap. Madras, a city on the Coromandel coast. The city, which has a fine harbour, and exports cotton, hides, indigo, tea, etc., grew up on the site of a trading station founded 1640 by the East India Company ; pop.777,000.

Madrid, *mä-drid'*, cap. Spain ; on a dry plain 2,400ft above sea-level ; can be bitterly cold or fiercely hot ; noted for magnificent buildings, including the bull-ring. Suffered from air attacks during the Spanish Civil War, 1937–38 ; pop. 1,172,000.

madrigal, see SINGING

Madura, town in Madras Province, India ; noted for its immense temple ; pop. 240,000.

Madura, see NETHERLANDS

Maecenas, GAIUS, *mē-sē'nas (d* 8BC),wealthy and cultured Roman ; friend of the Emperor Augustus, and of Virgil and Horace ; a patron of art and literature.

maelstrom, *mäl'strom*, whirlpool ; named from the Maelstrom off the coast of Norway (Lofoten Is.), an area of strong currents menacing shipping.

Maesteg, *mīs'teg*, iron and coal mining town, Glamorganshire ; pop.23,000.

Maeterlinck, COUNT MAURICE, *mä'tĕr-lingk* (1862–1949), Belgian writer and dramatist, *b* Ghent. His plays include *La Princesse Maleine* ; *Pelléas et Mélisande*; *The Abbot of Setubal* ; *Les Aveugles*, and *L'Oiseau bleu* (*The Blue Bird*). Among many famous books are those on bees and ants. Much of his work is mystical.

Mafeking, town in the north of Cape Province, S. Africa ; besieged by the Boers Oct 1899 to May 1900, being gallantly defended by (Lord) Baden-Powell till relieved.

magazines, see NEWSPAPERS

Magdalen College, *maud'lin*, one of the richest and most famous of the colleges of Oxford University ; founded 1458 ; noted for its chapel, lofty tower and choral services.

Magdalene College, *maud'lin*, college of Cambridge University, founded 1542. In the library is the MS of Samuel Pepys' diary, Pepys being a former student.

Magdeburg, city, Germany. A railway junction on the R. Elbe, it is noted for beet-sugar refining, for iron-works and engineering ; pop.334,000.

Magellan, FERDINAND, *mä-jel'an* (*d* 1521), Portuguese sailor ; took service in Spain ; embarked 1519 with a fleet of five ships to find a western route to the Moluccas, then known as the Spice Is. He sailed down the east coast of S. America ; crushed a mutiny while resting in Patagonia ; entered the strait now known as Magellan Strait, 1520 ; battled through storm, and went on for 98 days across the Pacific, so naming it because there he enjoyed calm weather. He was the first to sail the Pacific, though not the first to see it. He reached the island of Cebu (one of a group now known as the Philippines), and was killed on a neighbouring island by the natives. His squadron proceeded, one ship with 31 men at last reaching Spain, the first to circumnavigate the globe.

Maggiore, LAGO, *mä-djō'rä*, lake, 38m long, between Switzerland and Italy.

magic, widely practised among primitive tribes, is the supposed art of influencing the course of natural events (such as the weather, the growth of crops, the fertility of animals, etc.) by performing appropriate spells, incantations, and other rites and ceremonies, of which the secret is known only to a chosen few (' medicinemen,' ' witch-doctors,' etc.).

Magic is normally practised for the supposed good of the community. Among primitive peoples the witch-doctor is responsible for performing the appropriate rituals for obtaining rain when it is needed, for promoting an abundance of crops, etc. He may also undertake in return for payment to work magic for private individuals, and in this way magic begins to be used for doing harm to others. When belief in magic begins to die out, it is this ' private magic ' that lingers on : traces of it remain in England even now. The witch-doctor is also responsible for training his successor. His magical ' knowledge ' (i.e. knowledge of the proper ceremonies) is kept secret from ordinary people, and this makes the witch-doctor extremely powerful so long as most people believe that magic really obtains results. In many primitive communities the ' king ' is little more than a witch-doctor. Knowledge of magic was probably the earliest source of kingly power. The witchcraft widely practised in W. Europe until modern times seems to have been a survival of pre-Christian religions. The witches (men and women, but mostly women) were grouped in ' covens ' of 13, and met on various occasions to worship their god with rites intended to promote fertility. The god was thought to be present in the body of the master of the coven : to Christians he was the ' Devil.' The witch-religion was extremely widespread, and in the 15th c. there began a grim struggle between it and the Christian churches. In the 17th c. the witch-cult was finally suppressed. Read Margaret Murray, *The Witch Cult in Western Europe.*

magic square, arrangement of consecutive figures in a square so that the rows, columns, and usually the diagonals add up to the same number, e.g. in the square illustrated, all the totals are 34. Magic squares are of great antiquity,

1	15	14	4
12	6	7	9
8	10	11	5
13	3	2	16

and were once much in favour with astrologers.

Maginot Line, *mä-zhē-nō*, series of defences built along the eastern border of France ; named after André Maginot (1877–1932); proved useless in World War II, German forces entering France largely via Belgium and Holland.

magistrate (Latin *magistratus*), in ancient Rome, official concerned with administering the law, either e.g. a consul, censor, praetor, aedile, quaestor, or tribune of the plebs (people).

Today a magistrate is concerned with affairs of civil government ; thus, in England, a magistrate is usually a justice of the peace or the mayor of a borough. Magistrates sit in local courts and hear cases relating to minor offences.

In Scotland a magistrate is the provost or a bailie of a burgh.

Magna Carta (Lat. *great charter*), document to which King John of England was compelled to set his seal 15 June 1214.

As a result of his misgovernment, the barons (also the clergy and common people) united to put an end to tyranny. Largely guided by Stephen Langton, Archbishop of Canterbury, they drew up a charter based on the ' good laws of Edward the Confessor,' and on a charter of Henry I (1100). The king met the barons either on an island in the Thames or nearby in the meadow of Runnimede (a spot near Staines), and there promised to abide by the provisions of the charter.

In the main, *Magna Carta* was a restatement of old principles, e.g. no man may be punished without fair trial ; punishment must be proportionate to the offence ; justice (i.e. fair trial) must not be denied or delayed. It stated that the laws must be kept by the king, and that demands by the king beyond his customary rights could not be made without consent of the Great Council, duly summoned in recognised form, i.e. the king was unable to tax the people without the consent of Parliament.

Magna Carta, often referred to as ' the Charter of English Liberties,' may be summed up as a document making law superior to the power of the king.

magnesium, element, Mg ; light, silvery metal ; atomic weight 24·32 ; valency 2 ; atomic number 12 ; melting-point 651°C ; specific gravity 1·75 ; widely distributed in various compounds, e.g. magnesite, dolomite, etc. ; is found also in chlorophyll (in plants) ; prepared by electrolysis ; burns in air with an intensely white flame to form magnesium oxide, MgO, hence its use in fireworks, flashlights, etc. Magnesium becomes explosive when mixed with potassium chlorate (e.g. in incendiary bombs) ; may be found in water as the sulphate known as Epsom salts, $MgSO_4.7H_2O$, and in the chloride of sea-water, a cubic mile of sea-water containing about 6,000,000 tons of magnesium ; much

used in various light alloys, especially in aircraft, also in various magnesium-manganese alloys.

magnetic declination, London (1950) = 8° 55′W.

magnetic dip, London (1947) = 66° 45′.

magnetic mine, German invention first used in World War II ; so constructed that the approach of iron or steel caused an explosion. The menace of these mines led the British to degauss their vessels, i.e. encircle the hull with a copper band which was electrically energised.

magnetic storm, disturbance associated with sun-spots and the aurora borealis ; affects the earth's magnetic conditions, and interferes with radio communication.

magnetism, force, not yet fully understood, that gives iron, steel (and also nickel and cobalt) the property of attracting iron. Magnetism was known long ago as a property of the *lodestone*, a magnetic variety of natural black iron oxide (magnetite), Fe_3O_4, which, if freely suspended, points roughly north and south ; hence, no doubt, the beginning of the mariner's compass (see COMPASS). Substances strongly attracted by a magnet are ferromagnetic ; those weakly attracted are paramagnetic.

A *magnetic field* is the area where magnetic forces act. If lines are drawn in this area to show the direction of the forces (called lines of force), such lines will crowd together where the field strengthens. The earth is a magnet, and by *terrestrial magnetism* we mean its magnetic field. This varies according to time and place, but, in the main, the field is such as would be caused by a powerful magnet lying in the centre, its south pole pointing roughly to the geographic north. A magnetised needle free to swing horizontally or vertically will set itself in the direction of the magnetic north and south, and at an angle to the horizontal, termed *magnetic dip*. The vertical plane of such a needle is the magnetic meridian. In London the compass pointed *c*.9° west of north in 1950. This, called the magnetic variation at London, is diminishing by *c*.0·1 % per year.

Magnets are (*a*) *permanent*, of bar or horseshoe and various other shapes, or (*b*) *temporary electromagnets*. The points at which a magnet appears to have its magnetic force centred are termed *poles*. That pole which seeks to point north, if free to move, is called the north-seeking pole, the other is the south-seeking or south pole. Like poles repel ; unlike attract. Unit magnetic pole (the *weber*) is defined as that pole which, when placed 1cm from an equal like pole in air, repels it with a force of 1 dyne. Since, also, the force between magnetic poles varies inversely as the square of the distance apart, it follows that $F = \dfrac{m_1 m_2}{d^2}$ in air, where m_1, m_2 are

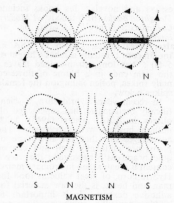

MAGNETISM

Diagram showing how (above) unlike poles attract, and (below) like poles repel

the pole strengths in webers, d is their distance apart in cm, and F the force between them in dynes.

Magnetic field strength is defined as the force in dynes on unit north pole placed there, and the unit is called the *gauss.* In a field of 1 gauss, unit pole experiences a force of 1 dyne. A pole of strength m webers in a field of H gauss experiences a force of mH dynes. At the moment, the strength at Greenwich of the earth's magnetic field in a horizontal direction is a little under 0·2 gauss.

The approach of a magnet to an unmagnetised piece of magnetic material causes the latter to become a magnet by INDUCTION. In the case of soft iron the induced magnetism is lost when the magnet is removed, hence soft iron is used for electromagnets (temporary), but steel for permanent magnets.

A solenoid (i.e. a helical coil of wire in which a current is flowing) sets up a magnetic field with a north and south pole. If a soft iron bar is placed inside the solenoid it becomes a magnet by induction as long as the current flows, the induced magnetism in the iron being much greater than that due to the coil. This is the principle in ELECTROMAGNETS, in some of which miles of wire are used, and currents of 5,000 amps employed. Since all that is required to make these magnets is the switching on of the current, and since merely switching off demagnetises them, electromagnets of

giant size are used for transporting tons of scrap-metal about iron foundries and engineering works. In its simplest form it is also an electromagnet that rings the household bell armature.

It is not easy to explain the phenomenon of magnetism. The theory is that in an unmagnetised bar of iron or steel the atoms (each being actually a minute electric circuit) have their planes at *all* angles, whereas in a magnetised bar these confused circuits are regimented into line so that all lie at right angles to its length. In the first, the energies cancel each other ; in the second they produce a cumulative effect, magnetism.

Professor Blackett has recently accounted for the presence and strength of terrestrial magnetism by publishing a new theory : That a rotating sphere of considerable size *must* become a magnet. The theory is supported by examination of the magnetic strength of the sun and a star in the constellation Vigo, the velocity of their spin multiplied by their mass giving the same magnetic ratio as that of the earth.

magneto, *mag-nē'tō*, might be described as a small dynamo-with-ignition coil, i.e. the dynamo-generated current is 'broken' when at its maximum. Magnetos, once used for ignition in various internal combustion engines, e.g. cars, tractors and aircraft, have been largely superseded by the coil and battery circuit.

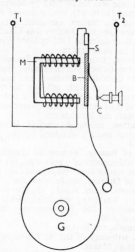

THE ELECTRIC BELL—A SIMPLE APPLICATION OF THE PRINCIPLE OF MAGNETISM

Connected with the terminals T_1, T_2, *there is a push-button (not shown in the diagram).*
By pressing this button the circuit is closed, whereupon by induction the magnet M becomes
magnetised so that the iron bar B is momentarily attracted to the poles of the magnet, thus
causing the gong G to be struck. At the same time this movement of the bar breaks the
circuit at contact C. The magnet then ceases to attract the bar B and the spring S reasserts
itself, renewing contact at C and—provided that the button is still being pressed—allowing
the same sequence of events to go on repeating itself.

magnetophone, *-fōn,* German invention somewhat similar to the Marconi-Stille magnetic recorder-reproducer. First used by the BBC 1946, it is a thin strip of plastic tape impregnated with a magnetic material. It gives perfect reproduction. See GRAMOPHONE

magnetron, invention which has greatly aided the development of radar. Though the cavity magnetron, designed by Professor J. T. Randall, and shown at Birmingham University early in 1940, is only a few inches high, electrons are given an immense speed, thus producing short radio waves with an intensity 1,000 times that of any known before.

Magnificat (Lat. *doth magnify*), name of the canticle or hymn beginning *My soul doth magnify the Lord* (Luke 1).

magnolia, tree or shrub (2–80ft high) native of tropical Asia ; has large fragrant, tulip-shaped flowers, white, pink, purple, or sometimes yellow.

magpie, see CROW

Magyars, *moji'ars,* a race of people who formerly lived beyond the Ural Mts, but moved into the plain of the Danube AD889, where they still live in the country which is now Hungary. Magyar is the dominant language in Hungary.

maharajah, *mä-hä'rä-jä,* Indian title meaning *great king* ; held by highest ranking Hindu princes or rajahs ; feminine *maharani.*

Mahdi, *mä'dē,* Messiah or leader whose coming is expected by Mohammedans. The title was taken 1843 by Mohammed Ahmed (1848–85), who gathered followers in the Sudan, occupied Khartoum (where General Gordon was killed), and was later defeated 1885 by Lord Wolseley.

Mahé, see SEYCHELLES

mahogany, more correctly Spanish mahogany (which yields valuable timber of great durability, hardness and beauty), a massive tree with ash-like leaves and reddish-yellow flowers. The red-brown wood is of great value to cabinet-makers.

Mahomet, see MOHAMMED

Mahrattas, *mä-rat'ä,* warlike Hindus of Central India ; subdued by the British 1843.

maid of honour, unmarried daughter or granddaughter of a peer who, for two or three weeks at a time, attends the queen.

Maid of Orleans, see JOAN OF ARC

Maidstone, co.tn, Kent ; on the R. Medway ; has many industries and is in the centre of the hop-growing district ; pop.46,000.

mail-coach, see ROADS

Main, tributary of the R. Rhine, which it joins at Mainz.

Maine, *mān,* NE. state of USA ; has mts., lakes and forests ; cap. Augusta.

Mainz, *mīnts,* town, state of Hesse (Germany) ; on the R. Rhine ; has much trade ; noted for its cathedral ; pop. 159,000.

Mais, STUART PETRE BRODIE (1885–), English writer and popular broadcaster, televiser, and author of travel books,

essays and novels ; his books include *Delight in Books* (BBC talks) ; *A Modern Columbus* ; *There'll Always Be An England.*

maize, cereal grass, known in USA as Indian corn ; usually reaches a height of 5–6ft ; has long, strap-shaped leaves ; the stem ends in a plume of flowered male spikes, pollen falling on the female spikes below.

In recent years hybrid corn, a scientifically bred maize, has superseded all others in USA, where (1945) 3,000 million bushels were harvested. The advantages are that the new type of plants are uniformly high and can be quickly and easily harvested ; the protein content is greater than in ordinary maize. Hybrid corn, of great value as food for man and beast, is the raw material for adhesive dextrin. It is important in making penicillin, sulpha-products and synthetic vitamin C. The stalk plays a part in the manufacture of plastics, wallboards, nitro-cellulose and synthetic rubber.

Majorca, see BALEARIC ISLANDS

Majuba Hill, *mä-joo'bä,* height of the Drakensberg Mts, Natal ; scene of a British defeat by the Boers 1881.

Malabar, *mal'ä-bär,* coastal region of the Deccan, SW. India ; noted for teak, rice and coffee.

Malacca, portion of the Malay Federation ; between Singapore and Penang ; area 640sq.m ; British since 1825 ; produces rice, coconuts and rubber.

Malachi, *mal'ä-kī,* 5th or 4th c. BC Hebrew prophet ; regarded as author of the last book of the OT.

malachite, *mal'ä-kīt,* basic copper carbonate ; found in the Urals.

Malaga, *mal'ä-gä ; mä'lä-gä,* port, S. Spain ; exports wine etc. ; manufactures textiles ; pop.257,000.

Malan, DANIEL FRANÇOIS (1874–), S. African statesman ; as leader of the Nationalist Party 1933, advocated an independent republic ; Prime Minister 1948. His policy of 'apartheid' (racial segregation), 1950, provoked criticism.

malaria, see MOSQUITO

Malaya, *mä-lā'ä,* peninsula of S. Asia, 700m long ; comprises Siam (see SIAM) ; the Netherlands E. Indies (see NETHERLANDS), and four British settlements : (*a*) *Singapore,* island at the south of the peninsula, area 220sq.m ; pop.720,000 ; founded 1819 by Sir Stamford Raffles ; the port of Singapore, a great British naval base with a floating dock and air-station, was captured by the Japanese 1942, and restored to the British 1945 ; it exports most of the world's cultivated rubber : (*b*) *Penang,* including part of the mainland (Province Wellesley) and Penang I. (area 110sq.m) ; produces rice, tapioca and rubber : (*c*) *Malacca* (see MALACCA) : (*d*) *Labuan* (see LABUAN) ; also various *Federated Malay States* on the mainland under British rule, e.g. Perak, Selángor, Negri Sembilan and Pahang, total area 27,540sq.m ; pop.271,000 ; chief town Kuala Lumpur. There is also the state of *Johore* (far south of the peninsula) ; cap. Johore Bahru ; and the states of Kedah, Perlis and Kelantan.

The British Government is planning to give Malaya self-government within the British Empire ; and since 1948 the Federation of Malay has had Kuala Lumpur as its capital. Singapore remains a British colony. Since 1943 Communists have caused much political unrest.

In 1949 Malayan bandits were causing widespread panic, and in Feb 1950, 350,000 volunteers mobilised in an anti-bandit campaign. Communists later destroyed a rubber factory at Singapore. See PLATE 8 (*bottom*)

The products of Malaya as a whole include rubber, rice, coconuts, pineapples (especially canned), oil-palm, tea, also tin, gold, wolfram, tungsten, phosphates, petroleum and timber.

Malcolm, *mal'kŭm*, name of four Scottish kings : Malcolm I (*d* 954), ruled from 943, known as Malcolm Canmore ; Malcolm II (*d* 1034), king from 1005 ; Malcolm III (*d* 1093), son of King Duncan I ; fled when his father was slain by Macbeth, but became king 1057 ; Malcolm IV (1141–65), ruled from 1153.

Maldive Archipelago, *mal'dĭv*, group of British islands. *c.*400m SW. of Ceylon. The climate is unhealthy. The products include dried fish, cowrie shells and tortoise-shell.

Mall, THE, see LONDON

mallard, wild duck common in Britain. The male has a glossy green head and neck, chestnut breast, wings with violet hues, yellowish beak, red feet and legs.

Malleus Scotorum, see EDWARD I

Mallory, GEORGE LEIGH (1887–1924), British mountaineer ; member of the 1922 and 1924 Everest Expeditions. With Andrew Irvine (*b* 1902) he made the final attempt on the peak of Everest, in which both perished.

mallow, roadside and waste-ground plant. Common mallow, 1–3ft high, has 5-pointed leaves, those near the root sometimes blotched with purple ; the 5-petalled flower is mauve. Another common species is the MARSH MALLOW with hoary down on the stem ; 3–5 lobed leaves ; bluish flowers ; blooms Aug.–Sept.

Malmesbury, WILLIAM OF, *mämz'bĕri* (*d c.*1143), monk noted for his English chronicles *Gesta Regum* and *Historia Novella*, covering the Norman period.

Malmö, port, Sweden, facing Copenhagen ; trades in timber ; pop.160,000. Its modern theatre is one of the finest in Europe.

Malory, SIR THOMAS, 15th c. English writer, author of our most important prose work before Elizabethan times, namely, *Morte d'Arthur*, a summary of the legends of King Arthur. See ARTHUR

Malplaquet, *mäl-plä-kä'*, village of NE. France ; scene of Marlborough's defeat of the French 1709.

malt, *mölt*, grain (usually barley) after being processed for use in brewing or distilling. It is first thoroughly cleansed and saturated with water, then strained and spread on a malt floor. There the temperature begins to rise and it is allowed to germinate sufficiently before it is put into a malt-kiln (an oven) to dry. It is afterwards mashed. Malt, a rich body-builder, is also used for medicinal purposes.

Malta, *möl'ta*, British island, naval base and garrison in the Mediterranean, *c.*60m from Sicily ; is 17m long ; area *c.*90sq.m; pop.286,000 ; close by is the smaller island of GOZO, part of the British colony.

Though treeless, Malta is fertile ; among its products are potatoes, onions and cummin seed. The cap., VALLETTA, has a magnificent harbour, and is a port of call for ships to and from the East. It was heavily bombed during World War II, over 1,900 people being killed, and 5,300 houses destroyed, besides 23,000 seriously damaged. Malta, indeed, became the most frequently bombed spot in the world after 1940, having 3,339 alerts, and being awarded the George Cross 1942. It has since often been called George Cross Island.

St Paul was shipwrecked on Malta AD58. The island became the property of the Knights of St John 1530, and was besieged without success by the Turks 1565. It has been British since 1814.

The island now has a 50,000-ton floating dock.

Malthus, THOMAS ROBERT (1766–1834), English economist, *b* Surrey ; educated

MALTHUS 1766–1834

Cambridge ; published 1797 his *Essay on the Principle of Population*, a work in which he sought to show by economic reasoning that every increase in the food supply leads necessarily to a further increase of the population ; and that the operation of this 'iron law' of economics must inevitably defeat any attempt to raise the general standard of living. In Britain during the 19th c. the population increased rapidly, so did the supply of imported foodstuffs (especially wheat from America), and the gloomy doctrines of Malthus came to be generally disregarded by economists. After World War II the inadequacy of the world's food supply to support its expanding population caused a revival of interest in Malthusian economics.

maltose, crystalline sugar, $C_{12}H_{22}O_{11}$, formed in malt by the enzyme, diastase, acting on starch ; may be converted by the enzyme, maltase (which occurs in yeast etc.), into glucose.

Malvern, low hills, Worcestershire - Herefordshire ; also a holiday town (actually Great Malvern), Worcestershire ; also a public school (Malvern College) opened 1865.

Malwa, union of *c*.39 Indian native states at Gwalior 1948.

Mamelukes, *mam'e-lūks*, military ruling class of medieval Egypt. Their origin goes back to the 13th c. custom of the Seljuk Turks, then masters of Egypt, of carrying off young men from other territories, training them as soldiers, and making them bodyguards for the sultan. From 1250 to 1517 these Mamelukes (i.e. *slaves*) governed Egypt. They were wiped out 1811 when many Mameluke chieftains were treacherously massacred by Mehemet Ali.

mammoth, prehistoric elephant-like animal; had woolly hair and huge curved tusks, often 8–10ft long ; fed on pine-needles. Fossilised remains have been found in N. Europe, especially Siberia, and mammoth bones were discovered under Regent Street, London, 1921.

Mammoth Cave, Kentucky, USA, limestone cavern discovered 1809 ; is *c*.4m long. There are many avenues, domes and passages. The cave is noted for stalagmites ; also for blind fish in the lakes and streams.

Managua, *mä-nä'gwä*, cap., Nicaragua ; shattered by an earthquake 1931 ; pop.120,000.

Manaos, *mä-nä'ŭs*, river port, Brazil ; on the Rio Negro, a tributary of the Amazon ; exports rubber ; pop.90,000.

manatee, or sea-cow, aquatic mammal *c*.8ft long ; somewhat resembles a seal. It has no external hind limbs ; the eyes are small ; the skin wrinkled. The manatee is common near the coast of W. Africa and S. America.

Manchester, city, Lancashire ; on the R. Irwell ; pop.685,000 ; linked with Liverpool and the sea by the Manchester Ship Canal (*c*.35m), and is therefore an inland port ; distributes the products of the Lancashire cotton industry ; manufactures clothing, machinery and chemicals. Its University (opened 1903) was founded 1851 as Owen's College. The Roman name was Mancunium.

Manchester, city, New Hampshire, USA ; noted for cotton ; pop.78,000.

Manchester Ship Canal, see CANALS

Manchukuo, see MANCHURIA

Manchuria, Chinese territory of 500,000sq.m (pop.43,000,000) ; it is north of Korea, and produces a large variety of crops, including soya beans ; is rich in minerals ; has much lumbering. The exports include soya beans, millet, maize, coal, sulphate of ammonia, wool and skins. The capital is Mukden. From 1930 Japan occupied much of the region as Manchukuo. Since 1945 Communists have controlled large areas. See CHINA

Mandalay, river port, Upper Burma ; on the R. Irrawaddy ; pop.148,000. The city is famous for gongs, swords, gold, silver and ivory. See BURMA

mandarin, name given by foreigners to a Chinese military or civil official. Mandarin is the language spoken by Chinese officials.

Mandated Territory (British), see BRITISH COMMONWEALTH OF NATIONS

M and B, see SULPHONAMIDES

Mandeville, SIR JOHN, *man'dē-vil*, 14th c. author of a book of supposed travels. He was possibly Jehan de Bourgogne, a doctor in Liége. Most of the adventures and pretended eye-witness accounts are fantastic.

mandoline, *man'dō-lin*, musical instrument with pear-shaped body and short neck. Of the lute class, it may have 4–5 pairs of strings tuned in unison.

mandrake, plant found in Mediterranean regions and among the Himalayas. It

MAMMOTH

has purple or white flowers, and a divided root, which was thought to look something like a human form, and was said to shriek when the plant was uprooted from the ground.

mandrill, large baboon of the W. coast of Africa ; has vermilion nose, blue cheeks, purplish hinder-parts with red buttocks, brown fur and yellow beard. It lives largely on insects.

Manet, ÉDOUARD, *mä-nā* (1832–83), French artist, *b* Paris. He aroused hostility and bitter resentment over his interpretation of *Olympia* which he treated in a novel way, endeavouring to give purity of outline ; greatly influenced the development of French art.

manganese, element, Mn ; atomic weight 54·93 ; atomic number 25 ; specific gravity 8·0 ; melting-point *c*.1,260°C. A reddish-white metal, hard and brittle, it is prepared from pyrolusite (natural manganese dioxide, MnO_2) by reduction with carbon, and is much used as a hardening constituent in many alloys, e.g. the very tough manganese steel containing up to 13% manganese, and for manganin, an alloy of 83% copper, 13% manganese and 4% nickel, especially useful for resistance coils. Manganese dissolves in dilute acids. Its chief compounds are permanganates of sodium and potassium. POTASSIUM PERMANGANATE, dissolved in water, gives a purple solution used as a disinfectant. Manganese dioxide, a black powder, is used as a depolariser in the Leclanché cell, and as a laboratory catalyst for preparing oxygen by the action of heat on potassium chlorate.

mange, see MITES

mango, evergreen tree, native of the E. Indies ; often grows 60ft high ; has lance-shaped leaves ; the yellow and green flowers mature into kidney-shaped fruits.

mangrove, tree of tropical swamps. The trunk has roots above the water. The seed germinates before falling, and sends out stems and roots while still hanging from the branch.

Manhattan, see NEW YORK

manicurist, see CHIROPODY

Manila, cap. and chief port of the Philippines ; pop. *c*.685,000.

manila hemp, fibre from a plant of the banana family, now grown in most tropical regions ; makes excellent ropes.

Manipur, *mŭn'ē-poor*, native state, India, east Assam.

Manitoba, province of Canada, between Ontario and Saskatchewan. Its lakes include Winnipeg and Manitoba. Formerly known as the Red R. Settlement, the province is noted for cereals, and produces coal, iron and gold ; cap. Winnipeg.

manna, food of the Israelites when in the wilderness (Exodus 16); possibly the sweet sap of a shrub *Alhagi maurorum* or *Tamarix mannifera.* See LICHEN

Mannerheim, GUSTAV, *-hīm* (1869–1951),

Finnish soldier and statesman ; defended Finland against the Soviet armies 1939 ; President of Finland 1944–46.

Mannheim, *man'hīm,* town, Baden (Germany) ; pop.280,000 ; notable for iron, machinery, glass, earthenware and woollen goods.

Mannin, ETHEL (1900–), author, *b* London ; writer of many unconventional novels, e.g. *Martha* ; *Red Rose* ; *The Blossoming Bough.*

Manning, CARDINAL (1808–92), English churchman ; went over to the Church of Rome 1851 ; Archbishop of Westminster from 1865 ; a cardinal from 1875 ; had much sympathy with working folk.

manometer, *mä-nom'e-tĕr,* instrument (usually a U tube holding a liquid) for measuring the pressure of a gas, vapour or liquid.

manor, see LOCAL GOVERNMENT ; VILLEIN

manor-house, see ARCHITECTURE

Mansfield, town, Nottinghamshire ; manufactures hosiery, boots and shoes and textiles ; pop.50,000.

Mansfield, WILLIAM MURRAY, EARL OF (1705–93), Scottish lawyer who became Lord Chief Justice of England. He gave the famous decision that a slave was free once he set foot in England.

Mansion House, THE, see LONDON

mantis, straight-winged insect of S. Europe and the tropics. One species (the praying mantis) rests with the forelegs raised as if in prayer.

Mantua, *man'tūä,* city east of Milan, Italy ; birthplace of Virgil ; pop.43,000.

Manu, *man'oo,* in Hindu legends, the first man ; hence the father of mankind.

Manucol, trade name for the recently discovered sodium alginate (derived from seaweed) which stabilises emulsions and suspensions, e.g. if mixed with medical preparations there is no need to shake the bottle before use.

manures and **fertilisers,** substances added to the soil to supply what may be lacking. Plants extract from the soil various ingredients as their food, and these must be replaced if the soil is not to be impoverished. This may be done by the method of rotation of crops, or by using organic manures, e.g. humus from the farmyard, i.e. decayed straw and animal excreta rotted down ; also by the use of decayed vegetable matter, e.g. the gardener's compost heap, and by ploughing back into the soil certain green crops, especially mustard, clover, and so on.

Artificial manures and fertilisers include (*a*) phosphates, readily obtained from bones and rock salt treated with sulphuric acid, or basic slag (from steel furnaces) treated with citric acid ; (*b*) nitrogenous fertilisers, as those derived from nitrate of soda, a deposit imported first from Chile *c*.1831, or with sulphate of ammonia, once a by-product of gas-works, and later manufactured by extraction from the air, and now sold

1 *Railway*   2 *Main Road*   3 *Minor Road*   4 *River*

MAP

Above is a picture of the view from a point on the main road near Auch, looking north towards Ben Dorain (Argyll). Below is a map of the same area, showing how the shape of hills and valleys is represented on the map by contour-lines. In this map the vertical interval between adjacent contours is 250ft. Notice also the scale, which is shown in the top left-hand corner of the map.

in the form of sulphate of ammonia ; and (c) potash fertilisers, e.g. sulphate of potash and muriatic of potash. See AGRICULTURE ; NITROGEN

Maoris, *mow'ris,* natives of NZ. Polynesians, they may have emigrated from Hawaii, and now number c.80,000. Their tribal dances still persist. The Maoris are represented in the NZ Parliament, and there is no discrimination against them.

map, an accurate detailed reproduction, either flat or in relief, of all or part of the earth's surface or of the sky. Maps are drawn to scale ; that is to say, one inch on the map is equivalent to one mile, or ten miles or whatever may be decided beforehand, on the earth's surface. The scale is governed by the size of map required and the use to which it will eventually be put.

Nowadays, as well as political maps showing boundaries, and maps showing oceans, rivers and mountains, etc., maps are used to represent such things as the distribution of population ; housing ; arable land ; coal ; industries ; and climate.

During World War II specially prepared maps were used a great deal for tracking purposes, i.e. giving accurate positions of aircraft and shipping while they were travelling, so that the direction of their routes could easily be ascertained.

maple, tree closely related to the sycamore ; common in Europe, Asia and N.

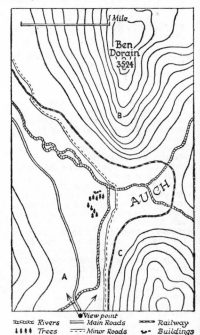

Rivers ― *Main Roads* ― *Railway*
Trees ― *Minor Roads* ― *Buildings*

STEEL   *plate 49*

Steel-works at Newcastle, Australia, showing ore-unloading bridges and blast-furnaces.
(*Australian News and Information Bureau*)

plate 50   STEEL INDUSTRY

Top : Inspecting a steel-furnace. (*Keystone Press Agency*).   *Bottom left :* A Bessemer converter blowing-off. (*C.O.I.*).   *Bottom right :* A Bessemer converter tilted to pour out the molten steel after its purification. (*E.N.A.*)

STEEL PLATES

plate 51

Steel plates on the cooling banks in the Dorman Long steel plate mills. On the left a great magnet is seen lifting the plates. (*E.N.A.*)

plate 52   **STEEL FOR SHIPS**

A Clydesider moving down the slipway after launching.   (*Scottish Council : Development and Industry*)

MODERN SEA TRANSPORT

S.S. *Queen Elizabeth.* (*Cunard White Star*)

plate 53

plate 54   RAIL AND DOCK

Top : The *Flying Scotsman* leaving Edinburgh (Waverley) on its daily non-stop run to London (King's Cross). (*British Railways*). *Bottom :* Avonmouth Docks, Bristol, showing the Royal Edward Dock and the Oil Basin. (*E.N.A.*)

CARGOES   *plate 55*

Top : Cargoes being handled at the dockside. (*Port of London Authority*). *Bottom :* Imported
timber in the railway-yards adjoining Bo'ness Docks, West Lothian. The Forth Bridge can
be seen in the background. (*British Railways*)

plate 56   SYDNEY HARBOUR BRIDGE

One of the world's greatest bridges. The main span is 1,650 feet.
(*Australian News and Information Bureau*)

America, the maple leaf being the emblem of Canada. Has broad leaves, greenish or red small flowers and winged fruit. In N. America two varieties are tapped for their sap, i.e. maple sugar.

Maquis, *mä-kē,* French underground resistance movement against the Germans during their occupation of France in World War II.

Marat, JEAN PAUL, *mä-rä* (1743–93), French revolutionist, *b* Switzerland ; became a distinguished physician, practising successfully in London ; studied electricity and optics ; but became increasingly the enemy of those who ruled the mob, and was fearless in denouncing them. Marat did much to foster the French Revolutionary spirit. He suffered from a skin disease, and could write only when in his bath, where he was stabbed to death by Charlotte Corday.

Marathon, BATTLE OF, *mar'a-thon,* decisive victory of the Greeks over the Persians, 490BC. The battle was fought on the plain of Marathon, *c.*20m from Athens, the Greeks being led by Callimachus and Miltiades. Of the Persians, under Darius, 6,000 were killed, though the Greeks lost less than 200.

A runner, Pheidippides, who carried news of the victory to Athens, dropped dead on arrival there. It is in commemoration of this feat that a severe long-distance race is known nowadays as a Marathon.

marble, limestone (a form of calcium carbonate, $CaCO_2$), usually crystalline and very hard ; capable of taking a high polish ; much used by sculptors.

Marble Arch, THE, see LONDON

Marcellus, MARCUS CLAUDIUS (*d* 208BC), Roman soldier in the 2nd Punic War ; captured Syracuse 212BC ; was five times consul.

March, ROGER MORTIMER, 1ST EARL OF (*d* 1330) ; rebelled against Edward II ; finally captured by Edward III, and hanged.

Marches, borders of a country, especially (in the Middle Ages) the frontier area between Wales and England. The marches were governed by specially appointed wardens.

Marconi, GUGLIELMO (1874–1937), Italian inventor ; developed the theories of Maxwell and Hertz in a practical way, and achieved a long series of improvements in radio. He transmitted signals across the English Channel 1899 ; founded a commercial service between Britain and America 1903 and invented a new radio valve 1910. In World War I he perfected a directional aerial. Marconi used microwaves, and introduced the beam system. He shared the Nobel prize for physics 1909, and was made a marquis 1929.

Marcus Aurelius, *-au-rē'li-us* (AD121–180), Roman emperor, enlightened, wise, capable ; *b* Rome ; succeeded Antoninus Pius AD161, for a time sharing his high office with Lucius Verus. A thinker rather than a man of action, he protected the empire from enemies (e.g. the Parthians, Germans and Dacians), but did not excel as a military commander. He fostered art, science and literature, administered justice, lived a saintly life, and left a collection of practical *Meditations* still greatly treasured.

mare, see HORSE

Mare, WALTER DE LA (1873–), English poet, *b* Charlton, Kent ; author of much that is exquisite and fanciful. A skilled craftsman in words, his books of verse include *Songs of Childhood* ; *Peacock Pie* ; *Motley* ; *Bells and Grass.* Other books include *The Three Mulla-Mulgars* ; *The Memoirs of a Midget* ; *The Lord Fish* ; *On the Edge.*

Marengo, village, N. Italy ; scene 1800 of Napoleon's victory over the Austrians.

Mareth Line, German defensive positions in Tunisia in World War II, overcome by the British 8th Army in March 1943.

Margaret (1283–90), Queen of Scotland. Known as the Maid of Norway, she was the daughter of Eric II of Norway, and became queen (in name) 1286. She was to have married Edward II of England, but died at Orkney.

Margaret (1553–1615), known as Marguerite of Valois, daughter of Henry II of France. She married Henry of Navarre, afterwards Henry IV.

Margaret of Anjou, *-än-zhoo* (1430–82), married Henry VI of England 1445 ; played a prominent part in the wars of the Roses.

Margaret Rose, PRINCESS, see GEORGE VI

margarine, see MILK

Margate, holiday town and port, Kent ; pop.25,000.

Marianne Islands, see LADRONE ISLANDS

Maria Theresa, *mä-rī'ä te-rē'zä* (1717–80), Empress of Austria, daughter of the Emperor Charles VI, whom she succeeded 1740. Her claims to the Hapsburg inheritance were challenged by Charles Albert of Bavaria, and Silesia was taken from her by Frederick the Great of Prussia. There followed the wars of the Austrian Succession and the Seven Years' War, but Maria Theresa (with her husband Francis of Lorraine) encouraged her people, ruled wisely, showed great bravery and consolidated her possessions. She was the mother of Marie Antoinette.

Marie Antoinette, see LOUIS XVI

Marie Louise, *mä-rē' loo-ēz'* (1791–1847), *b* Vienna ; married Napoleon I (as his 2nd wife) 1810. She was a daughter of the Emperor Francis I.

marigold, name of various garden plants, especially *Calendula officinalis,* with oblong leaves and large orange or lemon flowers.

marionettes, *mä-ri-ō-nets',* small figures worked by wires or strings by an unseen producer, and made to ' act ' or dance on a miniature stage. Known to the Greeks and Romans, they were exceedingly popular in France 16th–18th

15

century. Recently interest has revived
in puppet shows, a somewhat similar
entertainment.

Read *Vagabonds and Puppets*, Walter
Wilkinson.

Marius, GAIUS, *mā-rī'ŭs* (157–86BC), Roman
general ; related to Julius Caesar.
Driven from Rome by Sulla, he fled to
Carthage, returning to aid Cinna's
revolution. He was seven times consul,
and reformed the army.

Mark, saint and Jewish evangelist ; apparently a Levite of Cyprus. Accompanying
Paul and Barnabas on their first missionary journey, he was later with Peter in
Rome. He wrote the second Gospel, and
may have died in Egypt.

Mark Antony (MARCUS ANTONIUS) (*d* 30BC),
Roman soldier and orator ; related to
Julius Caesar, who gave him several high
offices. He was consul 44BC. After
Caesar's assassination he roused Rome
to drive out Brutus and Cassius, and with
Octavian and Lepidus ruled the empire.
While in Egypt he fell in love with
Cleopatra, but married Octavian's sister.
In the battle of Actium 31BC he was
defeated ; and later, wrongly imagining
that Cleopatra had taken her own life,
he committed suicide.

Marlborough, town near the Marlborough
Downs, Wiltshire ; notable in the old
coaching days ; now has a famous public
school (Marlborough College) founded
1843.

Marlborough, JOHN CHURCHILL, DUKE OF
(1650–1722), soldier and diplomat, *b*
Ashe, near Axminster. He married
Sarah Jennings, who later had much
power over Queen Anne.

Churchill proved his abilities as diplomat and soldier in the service of James II
but, as a supporter of the Church of
England, he did not approve of James's
policy. He therefore aided William III
to secure the crown, and for this was
created Earl of Marlborough.

After 1690, he lost favour with William
for a time ; but when Anne became
queen he was in supreme command of
the Dutch and English forces allied
against Louis XIV of France. In spite
of countless difficulties, he won a series
of brilliant victories : Blenheim 1704
(for which he received an estate at
Woodstock, where he built Blenheim
Palace) ; Ramillies 1706 ; Oudenarde
1708 ; Malplaquet 1709. Not so well
known but most brilliant of all was the
stratagem by which he forced the ' Ne
Plus Ultra ' Line 1711. Further victories
were impossible because his wife was
dismissed by Anne and because the
Tories opposed the war ; despite his
successes in the field, he was recalled and
tried for misuse of public money.

' The Victorious Duke of Marlborough '
was a master of strategy. Other generals
of the time used their skill to evade
battle ; he used his to bring the enemy
to battle and made it his object to destroy
the opposing force. He took more care

THE DUKE OF MARLBOROUGH 1650–1722

of his men than any former general, and
remains one of the greatest yet most
puzzling of all Englishmen.

Marlborough's wife, Sarah Jennings
(1660–1744), had an immense influence
on the affairs of her day. She became a
Whig 1706 ; had a violent temper, and
from 1710 used her biting wit against the
Queen and the Tories.

A vivid biography of Marlborough has
been written by his descendant, Winston
Churchill.

Marlowe, CHRISTOPHER, *mär'lō* (1564–93),
poet and dramatist, *b* Canterbury ;
friend of Sir Walter Raleigh ; killed in a
tavern brawl at Deptford.

An outstanding literary genius, Marlowe made blank verse popular in
English drama ; wrote the first great
English tragedy ; composed the first
great English historical drama, and was
undoubtedly the inspiration of Shakespeare. His chief plays are *Tamburlaine
the Great* ; *Doctor Faustus* (notable for
its superb poetry) ; *The Jew of Malta* ;
Edward the Second. As a poet he is best
remembered for his *Hero and Leander*,
and the lyric *Come, live with me and be
my love.*

marmoset, small squirrel-like monkey of
Central and S. America ; has thick fur ;
lives in trees.

marmot, rodent akin to the squirrel ; often
14–24in long. The coarse fur is yellowish-
brown. Marmots live in a burrow, and
are found in the Alps, Pyrenees and in
N. America, where they are called
woodchucks.

Marne, river of France ; joins the R. Seine
at Charenton.

Marquesas, *mär-kā'säs,* group of volcanic
French islands in the Pacific.

Marrakesh, town, Morocco ; pop.241,000 ;
important trading centre, and former
capital.

marrow, see GOURD

Marryat, CAPTAIN FREDERICK (1792–1848), British sailor and novelist, *b* Westminster ; ran away to sea and joined the navy ; saw much fighting. He was the author of exciting novels, e.g. *Frank Mildmay* ; *Peter Simple* ; *Mr Midshipman Easy* ; *Masterman Ready* ; *The Settlers in Canada* ; *Children of the New Forest.*

Mars, see ASTRONOMY

Marsa'la, port, Sicily ; exports wine ; pop.63,000.

Marseillaise, LA, see ANTHEM

Marseilles, *mär-sälz,* city and Mediterranean port, S. France. Its many industries include soap manufacturing, shipbuilding, milling, printing and chemicals ; it has a thriving export trade and many passenger services, notably with N. Africa and (especially since the opening of the Suez Canal) with the East and Far East. The greatest port in France, its pop. is *c.*640,000. Much of the older part of the city was destroyed by the Germans 1942–44.
The French national anthem (the *Marseillaise*) takes its name from this city.

marshal, originally an official who regulated ceremonies. An Earl-Marshal is an officer of state in England, and is in charge of the College of Arms. A Field-Marshal of the Army and Marshal of the Royal Air Force correspond in rank to an Admiral of the Fleet in the Navy. These are the three highest ranks in H.M. Forces.

Marshall, GENERAL GEORGE C. (1880–), USA soldier and diplomat ; became US Chief of Staff 1939 ; was special envoy to China ; appointed Secretary of State (US Foreign Secretary) 1947, and drew up the Marshall Plan for Europe, a post-war attempt to unite the nations of Europe with Britain and USA by a common economic understanding. Often referred to as ERP (European Recovery Programme), the Marshall Plan offered aid to European countries not dominated by Russia, and included a 4-year reconstruction plan. In 1948 the first goods supplied to Britain and her dependencies were delivered, part of an allotment valued at over £330,000,000. Britain's economic recovery had been maintained so successfully that in Dec 1950, two years before the date originally planned, Britain ceased to receive Marshall Aid. During the whole period, Britain had received Aid to the extent of over £200,000,000.

Marshall Islands, atolls and lagoon islands of the N. Pacific, east of the Carolines. Copra is exported.

Marshalsea, old London prison, Southwark, attached to the Marshalsea court ; rebuilt 1811 ; in use for debtors till 1849 ; immortalised by Charles Dickens in *Little Dorrit.*

marsh mallow, plant with thick tooth-edged oval leaves and large, rosy flowers ; an extract from the roots was at one time used with other ingredients in making the spongy sweetmeat known as marsh mallow.

marsh marigold, handsome spring flower like a large buttercup ; grows by ponds or slow streams. The flower (without petals) has five yellow sepals ; the leaves, dark above, lighter below, are roughly heart-shaped.

Marston, JOHN (*d* 1634), English dramatist ; quarrelled with Jonson and Dekker ; wrote *Antonio and Mellida* ; *The Dutch Courtezan.*

Marston Moor, region near York ; scene of a Parliamentarian victory over the Royalists 1644.

marsupial, lower order of mammals, the young being carried in a pouch under the mother's body, e.g. kangaroo, bandicoot, wombat and opossum.

Martello towers, 74 defensive towers erected on the south and east coasts of England when Napoleon threatened invasion.

marten, savage animal of the weasel tribe ; climbs trees ; has a reddish-brown fur and long, bushy tail. The only British species (found in lonely areas) is the pine marten, *c.*20in long.

Martha, NT character ; sister of Lazarus and Mary ; showed hospitality to Jesus. See Luke 10 ; John 11–12.

Martial, *mär'shal,* 1st c. Roman writer ; *b* Spain ; noted for his epigrams. One of his sayings (from *Epigrammata*) is : *Non amo te, Sabidi, nec possum dicere quare* : *Hoc tantum possum dicere, non amo te,* i.e. I do not love you, Sabidius, and I cannot say why ; this only I can say, I do not love you.

martin, see SWALLOW

Martinique, *mär-ti-nēk',* French island of the W. Indies ; has Mt Pelée, a volcano which caused terrible destruction 1902, destroying St Pierre. The capital is Fort de France ; products include fruits, sugar, coffee, rum and cotton.

Marvell, ANDREW (1621–78), poet, politician, scholar and wit ; born in Yorkshire ; MP for Hull, 1669. After the Restoration he wrote bitter pamphlets against the government. A friend of Milton, he is remembered for his lyrics about gardens etc.

Marx, H. KARL (1818–83), violent prophet of international revolutionary socialism. A German, Marx was *b* Trèves ; expelled from Paris as a dangerous person, and in Brussels (1847) drew up the manifesto of the Communist Party. Two years later he settled in London, where he died. He was the author of *Capital* and founder of the (Communist) First International. See page 429.
For an account of Marxism, see COMMUNISM

Mary, Mother of Jesus, saint referred to by Roman Catholics and some others as the Blessed Virgin Mary.

Mary I (1516–58), Tudor Queen of England, daughter of Henry VIII and Catherine of Aragon ; succeeded Edward VI 1553.

MARSUPIALS

(1) *Opossum*   (2) *Red Kangaroo*   (3) *Bandicoot*   (4) *Wombat*

KARL MARX 1818–83

A devout RC, she married Philip II of Spain 1554 ; restored the old religion, and enforced the laws against heretics (Protestants), 300 of whom went to the stake as martyrs, for which she gained the epithet ' Bloody Mary.' She was involved in a war against France, and lost Calais 1558.

According to Holinshed (*Chronicles*), one of Mary's last sayings was : ' When I am dead and opened, you shall find *Calais* lying in my heart.'

Mary II (1662–94), Queen of England, daughter of James II and Anne Hyde ; married William, Prince of Orange 1677, living with him in Holland till proclaimed joint sovereign of England 1689.

Mary of Guise (1515–60), queen of James V of Scotland, whom she married 1538 ; mother of Mary, Queen of Scots. Mary of Guise was the daughter of the Duke of Guise, and she played an important part in Scottish politics, allying Scotland with France.

Mary, PRINCESS ROYAL AND COUNTESS OF HAREWOOD, only daughter of King George V and Queen Mary ; married Viscount Lascelles 1922, who was known later as the Earl of Harewood ; created Princess Royal 1931. She is greatly interested in and is president of the Girl Guides ; during World War II she was appointed Commander-in-Chief of the ATS.

Mary, QUEEN MOTHER (1867–   ), queen of George V. A daughter of the Duke of Teck, she was *b* Kensington Palace (London) ; betrothed to the Duke of Clarence (eldest son of Edward VII), but after his death, married his brother, the Duke of York (later George V) 1893 ; crowned queen 22 June 1911 ; enjoyed with her husband great popularity at

their Silver Jubilee 1935. Since the death of her husband (1936) she has lived quietly, although not entirely out of the public eye, for she still attends many London functions ; her only daughter is Mary (Princess Royal), *b* 1897 ; her eldest son is the Duke of Windsor, followed by King George VI, the Duke of Gloucester and the late Duke of Kent.

Mary, Queen of Scots (1542–87), *b* Linlithgow, daughter of James V of Scotland ; became queen when only a few days old. At five years she was sent by her French mother to France ; at sixteen she married the Dauphin, Francis II, the king's eldest son ; was Queen of France 1559–60 ; became a widow 1560.

Mary returned to Scotland 1561 to find the people unfriendly towards her and a religious stir being caused by John Knox, Protestant reformer and harsh opponent of the RC faith. She married her cousin, Lord Darnley, who proved to be weak minded and worthless, so she turned for advice to her Italian secretary, David Rizzio, a skilled musician. This angered Darnley, who took part in the plot to murder Rizzio, accomplished (Holyrood Palace, Edinburgh) 1566. Mary's son (afterwards James VI of Scotland, James I of England) was *b* 1566. Darnley was killed in an explosion (Kirk o' Field, Edinburgh) 1567, which was evidently the result of a plot by the 4th Earl of Bothwell (1536–78), whom Mary subsequently married.

The rebellion of many Scottish nobles who were angry at Mary's marriage, led to a skirmish at Carberry Hill, Mary being captured and Bothwell escaping to Norway, where he died. Compelled to abdicate while imprisoned in Loch Leven Castle, Mary escaped after nine months, but her followers were defeated at Langside 1568. She fled to England, where Queen Elizabeth, a Protestant, kept her prisoner for almost twenty years.

At this time a plot, called the Babington plot, was being hatched against Queen Elizabeth, the facts of which have never come to light, so there is a great deal of doubt about the accepted story, which is as follows :

Anthony Babington, a young Catholic devotee of Mary's, and at one time a page in her household, was plotting to murder Queen Elizabeth—a plot which Philip of Spain approved and which he called the ' holy enterprise.' Sir Francis Walsingham, a clever statesman of Queen Elizabeth's, discovered this plot ; he discovered, too, that Mary had been in league with Babington and had corresponded with him (this has been the subject of much controversy). When the English Parliament heard about it, they decided that Mary must be tried for plotting to kill Queen Elizabeth. The trial was held at Fotheringay Castle (Mary's prison), where, after a vain attempt to defend herself, she was found guilty. Her penalty was death, but Queen Elizabeth was for long unwilling to sign the death-warrant. Eventually a death-warrant was dispatched before Queen Elizabeth could change her mind, and Mary was hastily executed, a tragic end to a fascinating but unhappy queen.

Whatever may have happened in reality, the account of Mary's part in the plot is based more on assumption than actual fact.

Maryland, state, USA ; south of Pennsylvania ; founded 1634, and named after Henrietta Maria, queen of Charles I ; cap. Annapolis.

Marylebone, *mär'li-bōn,* north-west borough of London.

Masaryk, THOMAS, *mä'sä-rēk* (1850–1937), Czechoslovak statesman and patriot ; worked ceaselessly for Czech and Slovak political freedom after World War I. President of Czechoslavakia 1919, 1927, 1934, he was the author of important books. His son, JAN MASARYK (1886–1948), was also a distinguished patriot, and was Foreign Minister in the exiled government (London) from 1940. He took his own life when the Communists came to power.

Masefield, JOHN (1878–   ), poet and author, *b* Ledbury, Herefordshire ; sailed round Cape Horn ; led a sailor's life with the White Star Line ; had a hard struggle in USA ; began a literary career with *Saltwater Ballads* ; won fame (1911) with his narrative poem *The Everlasting Mercy.* Among his poems are *The Widow in the Bye-Street* ; *The Daffodil Fields* ; *Dauber* ; *Lollingdon Downs* ; *Reynard the Fox* ; *Right Royal.* His many plays include *The Tragedy of Nan* (dialect) ; *Good Friday* ; *The Trial of Jesus.* He has also written several novels. Masefield succeeded Robert Bridges as Poet Laureate 1930.

Masham, LADY (*d* 1734), favourite of Queen Anne. She was Abigail Hill before she married Lord Masham. Eventually she replaced the Duchess of Marlborough at court, and influenced the queen in favour of a Tory government.

Mashonaland, *mä-shō'nä-,* east part of S. Rhodesia.

Mason, ALFRED EDWARD WOODLEY (1865–1948), English novelist ; author of *The Four Feathers.*

masque, *mask,* 17th c. dramatic entertainment with dances and music, the plot and character-study being of less importance than scenery and song. Some of the best masques were written by dramatists, e.g. Beaumont, Chapman and especially Ben Jonson (e.g. *The Sad Shepherd*) ; and one of the finest is *Comus* by John Milton.

Mass, Roman Catholic celebration of the Eucharist or Holy Communion ; name also used for solemn and dignified music composed for the service. See SACRA-MENT

mass, see MATTER ; MECHANICS ; RELATIVITY

Massachusetts, *mä-sä-choo'sets,* state of USA, north of Connecticut and on the Atlantic seaboard ; founded 1620 by the Pilgrim Fathers ; notable for fine scenery ; grows much fruit ; cap. Boston.

Massawa, town and port on a coral island in the Red Sea ; on the coast of Eritrea ; noted for pearls ; captured by the British April 1941.

Massinger, PHILIP (1583–1640), dramatist ; lived chiefly in London. His most notable play is *A New Way to Pay Old Debts,* masterly in plot but stilted in style.

Mastersingers, see WAGNER, W. R.

masurium, *mä-sū'ri-ŭm,* rare element, Ma ; atomic weight 100·0 (?) ; atomic number 43 ; discovered by X-ray spectrum analysis 1925.

Matabeleland, *matä-bē'lē-,* west district of S. Rhodesia. The Matabele rebelled 1896, but were pacified by Cecil Rhodes, who met their chiefs in the Matoppo Hills.

Matapan, cape in S. Greece ; hereabouts a British fleet sank an Italian squadron 1941.

match, splinter (usually of aspen or white pine) with a ' head ' easily ignited by friction, often of potassium chlorate, phosphorus, etc. Matches are manufactured at the rate of 1,000,000 an hour by machinery, especially in Baltic countries. The ' safety match ' was invented *c.*1855 ; and two-headed matches were invented a few years ago.

mathematics, science (or group of sciences) dealing with number, quantity and magnitude. *Pure mathematics* includes arithmetic, algebra, trigonometry, the calculus, geometry ; while *applied mathematics* includes a host of sciences, e.g. statics, dynamics, electricity, optics, molecular physics, astronomy, etc.

Matilda (*d* 1083), wife of William the Conqueror, whom she married 1053.

Matilda (1102–67), Queen of England, daughter of Henry I ; married Geoffrey of Anjou (1128). With Robert, Earl of Gloucester, she defeated Stephen at Lincoln 1141, and was crowned in London, but the civil war continued, and Matilda returned to Normandy.

Matlock, town, Derbyshire ; noted for fine scenery and its medicinal springs.

Matoppo Hills, see RHODES, C. J.

Matriculation, see EXAMINATIONS

matter, ' stuff ' of which physical things are made, i.e. anything that has the properties of inertia and mass. The possession of inertia means that force is required to move it, or (if moving) to stop it ; owing to its mass it attracts other matter, and therefore has weight. Note that weighing only *compares* masses, and that although mass is constant, weight varies. Thus, a body weighing 191lb at the equator weighs 192lb at the N. or S. Pole, because the poles are 26m nearer the centre of the earth ; similarly a weight of 1lb on the earth would (by our standards) be less than 3oz on the moon, a smaller body.

Matter may be (*a*) an element (see ELEMENT), (*b*) a compound, or (*c*) a mixture. These may be in the form of solid, liquid or gas.

The ultimate nature and structure of matter remains a mystery. The ancient Greeks dimly perceived the basic principles of the Atomic Theory, e.g. Democritus (470–360BC) ; but John Dalton (1764–1844), an English chemist, was the first to outline a scientific explanation of it, namely, that all matter is composed of extremely minute particles, atoms, that may exist (*a*) as elements, i.e. substances comprising only one kind of atom, the number of kinds, and hence the number of elements, being about 92, or (*b*) as compounds, formed by the chemical union of the atoms of two or more elements, e.g. water, comprising two atoms of hydrogen combined with one atom of oxygen. Such a union of atoms forms a molecule, i.e. the smallest particle into which a compound can be broken up without losing its essential nature.

A drop of water is still water if only, say, 0·1cm in diameter, or even 0·0001cm; but if we take a single molecule of water and split *that*, we have water no longer but two atoms of hydrogen and one of oxygen, each element having different properties from the compound, water.

All the atoms of an element are identical in chemical behaviour, but no two elements have atoms of the same weight ; thus, if we take the atomic weight of oxygen as 16, that of hydrogen is 1·0078, of copper 63·57. These differences in weight are due to the structure of each atom.

Mental pictures of the atom are always imperfect, and therefore to be used with caution. One, suggested by the Danish scientist Niels Bohr, is of the atom as virtually a minute Solar System, having electrons revolving round a central nucleus, their orbits incredibly small, their speeds unimaginably great, rarely less than 20,000mps. Modern scientists believe that every atom consists of a small heavy nucleus approx. 10^{-12} cm in diameter, round which is a ' large ' empty space *c*.10^{-8} cm in diameter, in which electrons revolve. Each electron has a negative charge (or *is* a negative charge) of electricity, and the total negative charges of the electrons normally equal the positive charge of the nucleus (called the atomic number Z). The electrons have a mass of 1/1,840 of a hydrogen atom.

But the nucleus itself need not be simple. It may be complex, comprising particles of (*a*) positively charged protons, (*b*) neutral neutrons, each with a mass nearly equal to that of a hydrogen atom. The simplest atom of all is that of hydrogen, which contains one proton and one electron. Next in simplicity comes

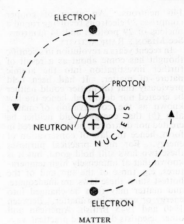

MATTER

The Structure of a Helium Atom

the helium atom, which has a nucleus of two protons and two neutrons, with two electrons revolving round it. Normally an atom has as many electrons as protons ; and when they are numerous they revolve round the nucleus in groups at different distances from it.

Removal or addition of electrons from or to the outer envelope may occur without altering the chemical properties of a substance, simply changing it positively or negatively. Should electrons in the outer layers drop to an inner layer light is emitted. If electrons in the inner layer move still nearer the nucleus, X-rays are emitted. Only by alteration of the nucleus do we bring about chemical change in the nature of the atom. In radioactive elements (all with heavy, complicated nuclei) disintegration of the nucleus occurs spontaneously, together with the emission of γ-rays (gamma rays, resembling light rays), α-particles (alpha particles, positively charged helium atoms) and β-particles (beta particles, electrons). The result is a new element.

The fact that many atoms have weights that are integral multiples of one unit suggests that all elements ought to be integral multiples of the unit. It has been discovered that this is actually true, and that where the atomic weights are not whole numbers, this is due to a mixture of atoms having identical chemical properties but different atomic weights. These variant forms are called isotopes. One of uranium's isotopes was used in making the first atom bomb, and its separation from others was one of the most difficult problems scientists had to solve. See ISOTOPE

We may then picture the simplest atom (hydrogen) as having one electron revolving round one proton, whereas one of the uranium isotopes has 92 electrons revolving round a nucleus of 92 protons and

146 neutrons. An atom of copper comprises 29 electrons revolving round a nucleus of 29 protons and 34 neutrons. See MESON ; RADIOACTIVITY

In recent years a revolution in scientific thought has come about as a result of further investigation into the atomic nature of matter. It had been held previously that (a) matter could neither be created nor destroyed, hence the law known as the conservation of mass ; also (b) that energy could neither be created nor destroyed, but only altered in form, hence the law of conservation of energy. For most practical purposes these two laws still hold good, but it is known that at immensely high temperatures, e.g. those of the sun and of the hottest stars, these laws are inadequate, and matter may then be changed into energy or energy into matter. Between 1940 and 1945 British, American and other scientists discovered practical ways of converting matter directly into energy, thus bearing out Einstein's prediction (1905) that the amount of energy, E, equivalent to a mass, m, is given by the equation $E = mc^2$, where c is the velocity of light. Hence, if a mass of 2·2lb were wholly converted into energy, it would be equal to 25,000,000,000 kilowatt hours of energy, say, roughly the total electric power generated in USA in two months. See MECHANICS

Matterhorn, peak of the Alps between Switzerland and Italy, 6m from Zermatt ; 14,780ft high.

Matthew, saint and apostle. A Jewish tax-collector, he became a disciple of Jesus, and may have been martyred fifteen years after Christ's crucifixion. That he actually wrote the Gospel of St Matthew is doubtful.

Matto Grosso, state of Brazil ; noted for dense forests.

Maugham, SOMERSET, *mawm* (1874–), British author and dramatist, *b* Paris ; qualified as a doctor ; wrote novels with extremely clever plots, e.g. *Of Human Bondage* ; *Cakes and Ale* ; *The Moon and Sixpence.* He was outstandingly successful as a writer of short stories. As a dramatist, his plays reveal technical perfection and are pervaded with delightful irony and wit ; among the best are *Caesar's Wife* ; *East of Suez* ; *Our Betters* ; *The Letter* ; *The Breadwinner* ; *Then and Now.*

Maundy Thursday, Thursday before Easter, when a religious ceremony of washing the feet of poor people was performed in England by the reigning monarch till the time of William III. The custom of giving money to certain poor people is still maintained.

Maunu Loa, see VOLCANO

Maupassant, GUY DE, *mō-pä-sä̈n* (1850–1893), French writer, one of the world's greatest masters of the short story, *b* Normandy ; died in an asylum. His characters are vividly alive. Apart from his novels (e.g. *Une Vie* ; *Bel-ami*), he

wrote *Boule de Suif* ; *Sur l'Eau* ; *Clair de Lune* ; *Yvette* ; *Contes et Nouvelles.*

Mauretania, name of several ships, the newest (launched 1938) having a tonnage of 33,000.

Mauritania, *mau-ri-tā'nia*, part of the Federation of French W. Africa ; area over 320,000sq.m.

Mauritius, *mau-rish'ius*, island of the Indian Ocean ; area 720sq.m ; has been a British colony since 1810. Its fertile valleys produce sugar, aloes, coconuts and vanilla, but crops are sometimes damaged by cyclones ; cap. Port Louis. Dependencies include Rodrigues and many coral islands.

Maurois, ANDRÉ, *mō-rwä* (1885–), French writer. As an interpreter in World War I, he was in close touch with the British, hence his successful book, *Silences du Colonel Bramble* ; but his fame is largely due to his astonishing series of biographies, graphic as fiction, and revealing intimate knowledge of the times, e.g. the lives of Shelley (*Ariel*), Disraeli, Byron, Voltaire. Notable, too, are his *Essai sur Dickens* ; *Études Anglaises* ; *A History of England* ; *The Art of Living* ; *Battle of France* ; *A Time for Silence* ; and his autobiography *I Remember, I Remember,* followed by *Call No Man Happy.*

mausoleum, tomb or sometimes a cenotaph, usually of considerable size, so named from the huge tomb of King Mausolus who died in Asia Minor 353BC. His monument, erected by order of his widow Artemisia, was one of the Seven Wonders of the ancient world.

mavis, see THRUSH

Mawson, SIR DOUGLAS (1882–), explorer, *b* Bradford, Yorkshire ; went to Australia as a youth ; joined Sir Ernest Shackleton's Antarctic expedition 1908 ; led the Australian expedition 1911–14 ; discovered King George V Land ; led the 1929–31 expedition ; wrote *Home of the Blizzard.* See POLAR REGIONS

Maxim, SIR HIRAM (1840–1916), American inventor (e.g. improved electric lamps and pumps) ; noted especially for the Maxim automatic gun.

Maximilian I (1459–1519), Emperor of the Holy Roman Empire from 1493 ; *b* Vienna ; added considerably to his wide possessions, but later lost many of his gains.

may, see HAWTHORN

Maya, *mä'yä*, ancient race of Central America. Their descendants now live in Mexico, Guatemala, Honduras, and are of Indian stock. The ancient Mayas had an astonishing degree of culture from *c*.200BC to *c*.AD900, possibly due to Asiatic or Egyptian emigrations. Their temples were built on huge stone platforms ; they sacrificed to many gods ; had an elaborate calendar of eighteen months, each with twenty days, and a hieroglyphic writing awaiting fuller interpretation.

The language is still spoken in Yucatan, where the finest Maya ruins may be seen.

Mayfair, fashionable district of W. London, north of Piccadilly.

' **Mayflower,**' see PILGRIM FATHERS

mayfly, popular name for a species of ephemera, the larva of which lives under water ; the perfect insect (appearing in May) lives only for a few days, sometimes only a few hours.

Mayo, *mä'yō,* county of Eire in the province of Connaught ; co.tn Castlebar.

mayor, see LOCAL GOVERNMENT

maypole, in early times, a tall pole decorated with garlands and coloured ribbons round which people danced during May day festivities ; many English villages still have maypoles.

Mazarin, CARDINAL, *maz-ä-ra*n (1602–61), Sicilian who became a statesman in France ; succeeded Richelieu 1643. By subtle diplomacy he made advantageous treaties which vastly enhanced the prestige of France, and laid the foundations of Louis XIV's brilliant reign.

Mazzini, GIUSEPPE, *mät-sē'nē* (1805–72), Italian patriot, *b* Genoa ; founded the Young Italy movement for the reorganisation of the country on nationalist and democratic lines ; lived as an exile in Marseilles, Switzerland and England. His writings were the inspiration of those who wished to make Italy a republic ; associated with Garibaldi and Cavour.

Of this bold pioneer it has been said that he had a vision of a regenerated Italy while awaiting execution, that, escaping death, he lived to see his dreams come true ; but in fact Italy became a monarchy ruled by the House of Savoy. That was achieved rather by Cavour than by Mazzini.

MC, see DECORATIONS

MCC, see CRICKET

meadowsweet, plant of damp places. The leaves, dark above, have white down below. The stem has two stipules where the leaf-stalk joins it ; the fragrant, creamy white flowers are in clusters on short, branching stalks.

Meander, ancient name for the R. Menders or Menderez of Asia Minor ; has so many turns that ' to meander ' now means ' to wander about.'

measles, contagious disease characterised by fever and pink spots. One attack usually gives the patient life-long immunity.

meat, flesh of any animal considered as food, e.g. venison, the flesh of the deer ; or veal, the flesh of a calf ; more commonly that of the ox (beef), sheep (mutton or lamb), and pig (bacon, ham or pork). Since *c.*1860 meat-packing has become an important industry, especially in USA and Australia, also Argentina. Frozen meat is exported to refrigerators.

Meath, county of Eire in the province of Leinster ; co.tn Trim.

Mecca, see ARABIA

Meccano, *mek'a-nō,* constructional model engineering first marketed 1901 by Frank Hornby (*d* 1936). The *Meccano Magazine,* first issued 1916, now priced 9d monthly, circulates throughout the English-speaking world. The first Hornby (clockwork) train appeared 1916, and was followed by electrically operated models.

mechanical equivalent of heat (J) in physics, the amount of work obtainable by the complete conversion of unit quantity of heat into mechanical work, or the mechanical energy that must be expended to raise unit weight of water 1°C. Hence $J = 4.2$ joules (approx.), or 4.2×10^7 ergs per calorie. Electrical energy in joules $=$ amperes $\times$ volts $\times$ seconds (IVt). Note that 3,600,000 joules $= 1$ KWH (kilowatt-hours). See HEAT

mechanics, science of the action of force on bodies ; comprises (*a*) statics, where force produces rest ; (*b*) dynamics, where force produces motion ; (*c*) hydrostatics, dealing with liquids at rest ; (*d*) hydrodynamics, dealing with liquids in motion ; (*e*) pneumatics, concerning gases in motion. Considered mathematically and with reference to the laws of motion, these sciences comprise theoretical mechanics ; applied mechanics deals with machines.

The fundamental laws of mechanics were first clearly stated by Sir Isaac Newton in his *Principia.* They are :

(*a*) *A body continues in a state of rest or of uniform motion in a straight line unless made to alter that state by an outward impressed force.* (This is the principle of inertia.)

(*b*) *The rate of change of momentum is proportional to the impressed force, and takes place along the line of action of the force.*

(*c*) *To every action there is an equal and opposite reaction.*

Momentum is the product of mass and velocity.

MEADOWSWEET

If a unit force (F) is so chosen that unit force gives unit acceleration (a) in unit mass (m), then $F = ma$. If m is 1 gram mass, and a is 1cm per sec. per sec., the unit of force is called a dyne, i.e. a dyne is the force that produces an acceleration of 1cm per sec. per sec. in a mass of 1 gram. If 1lb mass and 1ft per sec. per sec. are used, the unit of force is the *poundal*.

The weight of a body is the force exerted on it by the attraction of the earth, i.e. gravity. All bodies in a vacuum fall (at one place on the earth's surface) with the same acceleration, g, $c.$32ft per sec. per sec., or (more exactly) 981cm per sec. per sec., as demonstrated dramatically by Galileo when he dropped a cannon-ball and lead shot from the leaning tower of Pisa.

It follows from the definition of a dyne (as given above) that the force on 1 gram mass due to gravity is (approx.) 981 dynes, because the acceleration is (approx.) 981cm per sec. per sec. This is the ' weight ' of a gram mass, and is usually known as gram-weight ; therefore 981 dynes = 1 gram-weight. Similarly, 32 poundals = 1lb-weight. It is important to note that g varies slightly with latitude. See also MATTER

The gram-weight and the pound-weight are sometimes used as force units ; and since $F = ma$ and $W = mg$, therefore

$$\frac{F}{W} = \frac{a}{g}$$

where W = weight and g = acceleration due to gravity.

VELOCITY AND ACCELERATION : Velocity is the rate of change of distance with time, and is said to be uniform if a body travels equal distances in equal intervals of time. Acceleration is the rate of change of velocity with time, and is said to be uniform if the velocity changes by equal amounts in equal intervals of time. If a body starting from rest obtains equal increases of velocity, the space it describes will be proportional to the square of the time, and for such a body

$$v = u + at$$
$$s = \frac{u + v}{2} t \text{ or } ut + \tfrac{1}{2}at^2$$
$$v^2 = u^2 + 2as$$

where u = initial velocity, v = final velocity, a = acceleration, t = time, and s = distance.

PARALLELOGRAM OF FORCES : A force may be represented in magnitude and direction by a straight line drawn to scale. The resultant of two or more forces is the single force which would have the same effect. To find the resultant for two inclined forces meeting at a point, we employ the method of parallelogram of forces, i.e. (in Fig. 1) if OA and OB represent two forces, their resultant is represented by the diagonal OD of the parallelogram OADB ; and if two sides of a triangle OA and AD represent the magnitude and direction of two forces acting at a point, OD represents their resultant. See Fig. 2.

ENERGY : The energy of a body is its capacity for doing work. Position energy (not strain energy) may be due to the body's shape or position, hence potential energy (mgh) where h is the height of its position above the datum level, g the acceleration due to gravity. If due to the body's motion it is kinetic energy ($\tfrac{1}{2}mv^2$), where m is mass, v velocity of body, and h is height above the ground. Both formulae are measures of the work done by the body before reaching a position or state of rest.

Normally, energy is never destroyed, but is converted into another form (see MATTER) ; thus, chemical energy is turned into heat in combustion, heat to mechanical energy in heat-engines ; electrical energy to heat energy in electric fires, ovens, irons, etc.

LEVERS : A lever is a rigid bar turning freely on a fixed point, the fulcrum. Levers are of two orders according to the relative position of power (P), fulcrum (f), weight (W), as shown in Figs. 3 and 4. If a and b = length of arms, P = power, W = weight, then $bP = aW$, i.e. the moment of force is the product of force and arm. But note that the ' arm ' is the perpendicular from the fulcrum to line of action of force, e.g. a bicycle crank is *not* always the arm.

WHEELS : The wheel and axle constitute a lever of the first order, with the radius of the axle (a) and the radius of the wheel (b) as the two arms. Thus, if a is 2in and b is 20in, a weight of 50lb at A can be balanced by an effort of 5lb at B, since $50 \times a = 5 \times b$. If the 50lb weight represents the friction between the axle and the wheel-bearing, it is clear that with a sufficiently thin axle the effort at the rim of the wheel needed to overcome it will be very small.

Mechanical advantage is

$$\frac{\text{resistance of load}}{\text{effort}} ;$$

velocity ratio is

$$\frac{\text{distance effort moves}}{\text{distance load is moved in same time}} ;$$

so that, for levers, velocity ratio is

$$\frac{\text{effort arm}}{\text{load arm}} .$$

PULLEYS, mechanical devices for reducing effort, are of various kinds. Fig. 5 may be regarded as an illustration of the simplest pulley, where effort = load ; but if we have a system of pulley-blocks and tackle (Fig. 6) in which there is one fixed pulley and one movable

MECHANICS

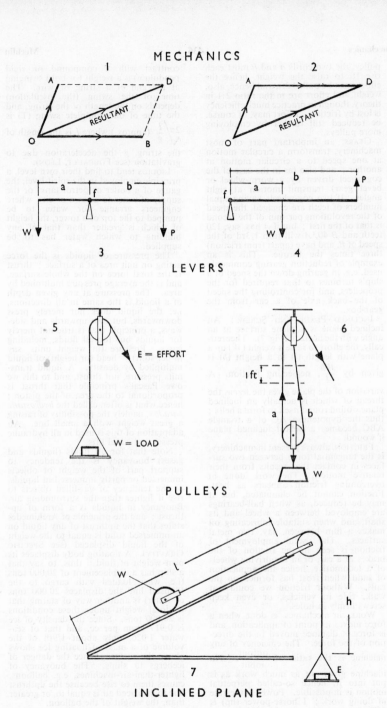

1

RESULTANT

2

RESULTANT

LEVERS

3

W   f   P

a   b

4

f

a   b

W   P

5

E = EFFORT

W = LOAD

6

1 ft

a   b

W

PULLEYS

7

W

l

h

E

INCLINED PLANE

pulley, the two cords *a* and *b* must each rise 1ft to raise the weight, hence the effort must be pulled 2ft, and hence, also, weight and effort are in the ratio 2:1 in theory, though in practice much efficiency is lost by friction. Effort may, of course, be reduced still further by employing more pulleys.

GEARS, an important part of most machinery, transform a circular motion at one speed to a circular motion at another ; and also (as in the case of the cog-wheel driven by a worm-wheel or bevel gear) transmit motion at right angles. If two cog-wheels having equal numbers of teeth are engaged, the speed of the revolutions per min of the second is that of the first ; but if *A* has, say, 120 teeth and *B* 40, *A* will turn 1/3rd of the speed of *B*, and have (apart from friction) three times the torque. This is an example of reduction gearing commonly used, e.g. in gearing down the speed of a ship's turbines to that required for the propellers, and for controlling the speed of the back axle of a car from the gear-box.

INCLINED PLANE AND SCREW : An inclined plane is a plane surface at an angle with the horizon (Fig. 7). Theoretically, the effort to raise a weight (*W*) up a plane with length (*l*) to a height (*h*) is given by $\frac{Wh}{l}$, neglecting friction. A variation of the plane gives the *screw*, the thread of which is actually an inclined plane wound round itself to form a helix ; thus the hypotenuse AC of a triangle ABC becomes a helical inclined plane if wound.

FRICTION, always present in machinery, is the tangential force between two surfaces in contact that results from their relative motion. The work done in overcoming friction appears as heat. Friction cannot be eliminated, but it may be reduced, as when ball-bearings are employed between a wheel and its shaft, and when suitable lubricating oil makes a film between, say, two metal surfaces. The useful employment of friction is seen in the friction of the brakes of a car, or in the driving wheels of a locomotive, hence the application of sand when frost has formed on the rails. Without friction we could not walk, ride in vehicles, or even keep screws firmly in holes.

WORK, in mechanics, is done when a force moves its point of application, and is force × distance moved in the direction of the force. The efficiency of any machine is the ratio of $\frac{\text{output}}{\text{input}}$. No machine gives out as much work as is put into it, hence so-called perpetual motion is impossible. Power is the rate of doing work ; 1 horse-power (hp) is 550ft-lb per sec., or 33,000ft-lb per min.

PENDULUMS. A simple pendulum (in contrast with a compound or rigid pendulum) is a weight (or bob) swinging at the end of a string or wire. The time of the swing (the oscillation) depends on the length of the string, and the time of one complete swing (T) is $2\pi\sqrt{\dfrac{l}{g}}$ (approx.) where *l* is the length of the string, *g* the acceleration due to gravitation (see FOUCAULT, LÉON).

LIQUIDS tend to find their own level, a principle employed in the spirit-level, the gauge of a boiler or petrol tank, or the supply of water to a town or city, where engineers arrange for water to be pumped to the top of a tower, the height of which is greater than that of any building to which water has to be supplied.

The pressure of liquids is the force acting on unit area of a surface ; thrust is the total force on the whole surface, and is the average pressure multiplied by area. The pressure at any given depth of a liquid is the same in all directions, i.e. the liquid does not merely press downwards, but also upwards and sideways, a principle that is true not merely for liquids but for all fluids, including gases. Pressure (in weight units, say lb per sq.ft) = head (or height) of liquid multiplied by density. A liquid transmits pressure, not thrust, and to this we owe Pascal's principle that thrust is proportional to the area of the piston ; hence what is often called the *hydrostatic paradox*, namely the possibility of raising a great weight with a small one. An adaptation of this is used in all hydraulic presses and canal lifts.

Note that for all fluids (liquids and gases) buoyancy is the tendency to support part of the weight of objects immersed or partly immersed in liquids, or the tendency of gas-filled objects to rise if lighter than the surrounding air. Buoyancy in liquids is a form of upthrust ; and the principle of Archimedes states that the upthrust of any liquid on an immersed solid is equal to the weight of the liquid displaced (see SPECIFIC GRAVITY). A floating body displaces its own weight of fluid ; thus, to say that a ship has a displacement of 20,000 tons (i.e. when loaded with cargo to the Plimsoll line she displaces 20,000 tons of water) is another way of stating that its total weight under these conditions is 20,000 tons. Since the density of ice is 0·917 gram per cc, and that of sea-water 1·026, only about 1/9th of the volume of a mass of floating ice shows above the surface, hence the danger of icebergs to ships. The buoyancy of lighter-than-air-machines, e.g. balloons, causes them to rise because the upthrust due to displaced air is equal to, or greater than, the weight of the balloon.

Mechanics' Institutes, see BIRKBECK, G.

Mechlin, *mek'lin*, town, Belgium ; noted for (Mechlin) lace ; pop.60,000.

Mecklenburg, minor state of Germany ; cap. Schwerin.

medal, piece of stamped metal to commemorate a notable occasion or an important person. See DECORATIONS

Medea, in old Greek tales, daughter of Aeëtes, King of Colchis. With her magic she helped Jason to steal the Golden Fleece.

Medes and Persians, see MEDIA

Media, ancient country south of the Caspian Sea. Becoming a nation *c.*700BC the Medes captured Nineveh 606BC ; but Cyrus of Persia became ruler of the Medes and Persians *c.*500BC. The law of the Medes and Persians (Daniel 6) was regarded as being unalterable.

median, see TRIANGLE

Medici, CATHERINE DE', *dä med'ē-chē* (1519–89), *b* Florence, married Henry II of France 1533. For forty years she dominated France. Ambitious and crafty, she plotted the massacre of the Huguenots 1572.

Medici, LORENZO, DE' (1448–92), styled the Magnificent, wealthy Italian who, though immoral and crafty, raised Florence to fame as a city of art and literature.

Medici, MARIE DE' (1573–1642), *b* Florence ; married Henry IV of France ; regent for her son Louis XIII. Ambitious and unscrupulous, she had supreme power (being aided by Cardinal Richelieu) till her son exiled her.

medicine, science and practice of treating disease. Great pioneers in the art of healing include Hippocrates, a Greek born *c.*460BC, and the Roman doctor, Galen, on whose knowledge and methods little advance was made from *c.*200BC to *c.*AD1200. In 16th c. medicine Paracelsus of Switzerland and Ambroise Paré of France are important figures. Then came William Harvey who published (1628) his account of the circulation of the blood. Dr Hunter (1728–93) laid the foundations of modern pathology. The use of the microscope led to still further advances, especially in histology (the study of cells) ; later to bacteriology, and hence the work of Louis Pasteur, and that of Lord Lister, who demanded cleanliness, and introduced antiseptics.

Surgery (or operative therapeutics) has made immense strides since Lord Lister's day ; and since Sir James Young Simpson's discovery of chloroform. The invention of X-rays (widely used since the beginning of the 20th c.) has been invaluable. Today X-rays enable surgeons to locate the exact centre of the trouble. Loss of blood is now reduced to a minimum ; instruments are sterilised ; wounds (lesions) are kept free from infection ; cutting operations are often by-passed by manipulative surgery.

The commonest treatments prescribed by medieval practitioners were bloodletting and the administration of herbal drugs, the nature of which was at that time by no means perfectly understood.

Gradually, however, medicine has developed into one of the most exact of the applied sciences. It has long been necessary for some members of the profession to specialise, with the result that the general practitioner hands over many of his cases to the specialist for expert diagnosis (ascertaining the nature of the disease) and treatment. Moreover, preventive medicine is recognised today as of great importance ; hygiene is taught in schools, public clinics have been established ; hence also improved sanitary conditions, correct diet, keep-fit classes, all intended to *prevent* illness by building up rightly nourished, sensibly used bodies in a healthy environment.

Modern medical practice is aided by many new and powerful drugs. e.g. penicillin, sulphonamides, and by plastic surgery, radiology (employing radium salts, ultra-violet light, X-rays, etc.), and the application of psychology to the treatment of neurotic cases. In May 1950 the King and Queen inaugurated the new National Institute of Medical Research at Mill Hill.

As a career medicine offers great opportunities in general practice, as a consultant or specialist, in scientific research, and there are excellent government appointments. Such careers are now open to women as well as men. University courses take at least five (more usually six or seven) years.

As a result of the National Health Service Act (1946) the Minister of Health assumed responsibility for health centres, hospitals, etc. from July 1948 ; doctors in Britain are now paid out of national funds, patients thus receiving (if they choose) free advice and treatment. All employed persons must now pay a weekly contribution to the scheme.

medicine-men, see MAGIC

Medina, see ARABIA

Medina Sidonia, DUKE OF, *mä-dē'nä sē-dō'niä* (1550–1615), incapable Spaniard chosen by Philip II to take charge of the Armada 1588.

Mediterranean Sea, sea between S. Europe and N. Africa ; area *c.*1,145,000sq.m ; joined with the N. Atlantic by the Strait of Gibraltar ; linked by the Suez Canal with the Indian Ocean ; is almost tideless. Anciently it was believed to be in the middle of the world. Its partial control by the Axis in World War II for a time enhanced the difficulties of the United Nations.

medlar, tree found in Britain. In the wild state it has spines, but in orchards it is spineless ; has lance-shape leaves, downy on the underside ; white flowers (May), and round, green fruit.

Medusa, see PERSEUS

Medway, river of Kent ; flows 70m to the mouth of the Thames.

Mee, ARTHUR (1875–1943), journalist ; editor of *The Children's Encyclopaedia*, first published 1908 ; founded *The Children's Newspaper* 1919 ; author of many books, e.g. *1,000 Beautiful Things*. He also produced *The Children's Bible*, etc. He died before completing *The King's England* series of county books.

Shrewd, businesslike and a giant for work, Arthur Mee never lost his sense of wonder or the ability to make others share it to the full. His life story is finely told in *Child of Wonder* by his friend Sir John Hammerton.

megaparsec, see ASTRONOMY ; PARSEC

megger, see ELECTRICITY

Megiddo, *mē-gid'ō*, town, Palestine ; captured by General Allenby 1918.

'Mein Kampf,' see HITLER, A. ; NAZISM

Mekong, *mā'-*, river ; flows 2,800m from Tibet and the borders of Siam to the China Sea.

Melbourne, *mel'běrn*, city and cap., Victoria, Australia ; on the R. Yarra ; noted for shipping, iron founding, flour and woollen mills, etc. ; prospered after the gold rush of 1851 ; named after Lord Melbourne ; pop.1,170,000.

Melbourne, WILLIAM LAMB, 2ND VISCOUNT (1779–1848), English politician ; entered Parliament 1806 as a Whig ; was Prime Minister 1834, and again 1835–41. He is chiefly notable for the tactful way in which he aided the young Queen Victoria.

melodrama, see DRAMA

melon, see GOURD

Melos, volcanic island of Greece, one of the Cyclades. Also known as Milo.

Melrose, town, Roxburghshire ; near the R. Tweed ; has a ruined abbey.

Read Scott's *Lay of the Last Minstrel*.

melting-point, constant temperature at which a solid changes to the liquid state.

Useful melting-points include :

		°C
bismuth		271·0
butter		33·0
copper		1,084·0 (approx.)
glass	from	800·0
gold		1,063·0
ice		0·0
iron		1,500·0 (approx.)
lead		327·0
mercury		–39·0
paraffin wax		55·0 (approx.)
phosphorus (white)		44·0
platinum		1,750·0
sulphur		113·0
tin		231·0
tungsten		3,400·0

Melton Mowbray, town, Leicestershire ; noted for pies and cheese. It is a great centre of fox-hunting and horse-breeding.

Melville, HERMAN, *mel'vil* (1819–91), American author, *b* New York ; went to sea at 18, some of his adventures giving him details for his masterly whaling story *Moby Dick*.

Members of Parliament, see PARLIAMENT

Memel, *mā'mel*, town and port, Lithuania ; pop.50,000 ; annexed by Hitler 1939.

Memphis, *mem'fis*, anciently the capital of Lower Egypt, 14m south of Cairo ; noted for its impressive ruins.

There is also a Memphis (Tennessee) in USA ; pop.293,000.

Menai Strait, *men'ī*, channel between Caernarvonshire and Anglesey, Wales ; spanned by a suspension bridge (1826), and the Britannia tubular bridge built 1850.

Mr F. O. Harber of Bangor has drawn up a scheme for building three dams across the Straits, the middle one to have turbines generating *c.*70,000,000 units of electricity annually, and thus supplying power and light to N. Wales.

Mencius, *men'shi-ŭs*, 4th c. BC Chinese teacher of the principles laid down by Confucius. As a social reformer he was greatly ahead of his age.

Mendel, GREGOR (1822–84), Austrian monk, founder of modern scientific investigation of the laws of heredity. See HEREDITY

Mendelssohn, FELIX, *men'del-sōn* (1809–47), German composer, *b* Hamburg, son of a Jewish banker ; played the piano in public at nine, began composing at eleven, and by the time he was twenty had given the world his E flat octet, two symphonies, three piano quartets, two sonatas, his superb overture to *A Midsummer Night's Dream*, and many songs and musical pieces. Greatly acclaimed in Britain, he produced his oratorios *St Paul* 1836, and *Elijah* 1846. Genius as he was, he suffered from too much popularity, and much of his work is merely sentimental.

Mendips, low limestone hills, Somerset.

Menelaus, *men-ē-lā'ŭs*, in old Greek tales, King of Sparta, brother of Agamemnon, and husband of Helen. The Trojan War was caused by Paris, son of Priam, carrying off Helen.

Menin, Belgian town. The MENIN GATE (at Ypres) is on the Menin road, and is a memorial to those who fell in battle at Ypres 1914–18.

Men of the Trees, see TREES

mensuration, generally regarded as that branch of mathematics which deals with the measurement of lines and figures, e.g. circles, triangles, ellipses, pyramids and spheres.

menthol, organic compound of the terpene group. It is derived from various peppermint plants.

Mentone, *men-tō'nē*, seaside health resort on the Riviera, S. France.

Mentor, in old Greek tales, the faithful and prudent friend of Ulysses. The word now stands for a wise counsellor.

Menuhin, YEHUDI, *men-ū'hin*, *yehoody* (1916–   ), violinist, *b* New York ; studied under Georges Enesco ; made gramophone records (1934) of sonatas, one of his sisters (Hephzibah) accompanying at the piano. He played at the Albert Hall (London) 1938, and (1943) raised over £25,000 for charities.

Menzies, ROBERT GORDON, Australian statesman ; Prime Minister 1939–41.

While Labour governed he watched with anxiety the spread of Communism, but in Dec 1949 he led the successful Liberal-Country Party, and again became Prime Minister.

mepacrine, see MOSQUITO

Mercantile Marine, shipping carrying cargo or passengers, i.e. the Merchant Navy. A career in the Merchant Navy offers good prospects, full details of which may be obtained from the General Secretary, National Maritime Board. It is usual to enter the service via a training ship (e.g. HMS *Conway*, near Birkenhead, or HMS *Worcester*, Greenhithe) or by way of Pangbourne Nautical College. There is a School of Navigation at Southampton. For cadetships apply to the chief shipping firms.

Mercator, GERARDUS, *měr-kā'těr* (1512–94), Flemish geographer.

mercenaries, soldiers who hire their services to any king or prince who will pay them, e.g. the Scots Guards in France from the 15th to the 18th c., or the Foreign Legion, organised in France 1831.

mercerisation, process discovered by John Mercer (1791–1866), an English chemist, whereby cotton or other goods receive a silky appearance.

Merchant Adventurers, name of a 14th c. trading company of English cloth exporters with HQ in London. Incorporated 1407, they had a vast trade with Antwerp. The company dissolved 1808.

Merchant Taylors' Company, London company of traders founded in the 14th c. Their public school in London was founded 1561. Another Merchant Taylors' School was founded at Liverpool 1618.

Merchiston Castle School, *měr'chis-tŭn*, public school founded Edinburgh 1833.

Mercia, large kingdom of England in Anglo-Saxon times ; eventually included all the country from the Thames to the Humber, except E. Anglia ; founded *c.*582 ; conquered by Egbert 825.

Mercury, in old Roman tales, the god of trade ; also the messenger of the gods ; identified with the Greek Hermes.

Mercury, see ASTRONOMY

mercury or quicksilver, element and metal, Hg ; normally in the form of a silvery liquid ; atomic weight 200·61 ; atomic number 80 ; specific gravity 13·6 ; melting-point −39°C ; boiling-point 357°C ; found as cinnabar (natural mercuric sulphide, HgS) in Spain, Italy, Mexico and S. America ; obtained from the ore by roasting in air. Its many compounds are poisonous, e.g. mercurous chloride (calomel) ; mercuric chloride (corrosive sublimate) ; mercuric fulminate, which explodes when struck. The alloys (known as amalgams) are used in dentistry. Mercury is much used in scientific instruments, e.g. barometers, thermometers, vacuum pumps, in discharge lamps, also formerly for silvering mirrors.

mercury vapour lamp, lamp, much used in street lighting, artificial sun-ray treatment, etc. ; emits greenish light when an electric current passes through mercury vapour, and gives ultra-violet radiation. See ELECTRICITY

Meredith, GEORGE, *mer'e-dith* (1828–1909), poet and novelist, b Hampshire. A genius with a style usually too involved to win popularity, he wrote *The Ordeal of Richard Feverel* ; *The Egoist* ; *Diana of the Crossways*.

meridian, see LONGITUDE

Merino, see SHEEP

Merionethshire, county of N. Wales ; noted for rugged scenery ; co.tn Dolgelly.

Merlin, see ARTHUR

merlin, see HAWK

Mermaid Tavern, London tavern (Cheapside) from *c.*1529 to the Great Fire, 1666; believed to have been frequented by Shakespeare, Jonson, Beaumont, Fletcher and other dramatists and wits.

Merrilies, MEG, gypsy character in Sir Walter Scott's *Guy Mannering*, based on Jean Gordon of Carlisle.

Mersey, *mŭr'zi*, river flowing 70m from Derbyshire to the Irish Sea. On its estuary is Liverpool, linked with Birkenhead by (*a*) a railway tunnel, opened 1886 ; (*b*) a tunnel for vehicular traffic, opened 1934. This, slightly under 3m long, reaches 170ft below the river bed, and cost *c.*£8,000,000.

Merthyr Tydfil, *mŭr'thěr tid'vil*, town, Glamorganshire ; has iron and steel works and coal mines ; pop.65,000.

Merton College, college of Oxford University, founded 1264. Its buildings, among the oldest in Oxford, include a fine chapel and a 14th c. library.

mesmerism, see HYPNOTISM

meson, name recently given to part of the nucleus of an atom. There are two types : (*a*) the pi-meson with a mass of 286 times that of the electron, and (*b*) the mu-meson with a mass of 216 times that of the electron.

Mesopotamia, *mes-ō-pō-tā'miä*, anciently the region between the Euphrates and Tigris ; scene of fighting 1918 when the British took it from the Turks ; now largely included in Iraq. See BABYLONIA ; IRAQ

mesotron, sometimes called the heavy electron, X-particle, a particle of matter with a charge of the same magnitude as the electron, but a mass *c.*150 times larger, i.e. intermediate between that of the electron and the neutron and proton.

Messiah, see CHRIST

Messina, *me-sē'nä*, city and port, Sicily ; largely rebuilt since its destruction 1908 by an earthquake ; pop.214,000.

Messina, STRAIT OF, channel separating Sicily from Italy.

messuage, see HOUSE

metabolism, *mē-tab'ō-lizm*, chemical changes continually going on in living tissue, i.e. *anabolism*, the building up of tissues from simpler substances, and *catabolism*, the breaking down of complex substances into simpler ones.

metals, elements possessing, as a rule, certain characteristics, e.g. metallic lustre, malleability, ductility and high specific gravity. They are good conductors of heat and electricity, take a brilliant polish, have chlorides that are true salts, and oxides that are basic, though all metals have not these characteristics. Among the best-known metals are aluminium, antimony, barium, calcium, *chromium*, cobalt, copper, gold, iridium, *iron*, lead, magnesium, *manganese*, mercury, *molybdenum*, *nickel*, platinum, potassium, radium, silver, sodium, tin, *tungsten*, *vanadium*, and zinc, those in italics being ' ferrous ' (i.e. used in the manufacture of steel), the others being ' non-ferrous.' A mixture of two or more metals is an alloy, e.g. steel or brass ; gold or silver dissolved in mercury forms an ' amalgam.'

The art and science of producing metals and their alloys is called metallurgy. A metal is usually obtained (often by roasting) from an ore, e.g. aluminium comes from the mineral bauxite, iron from haematite, lead from galena, mercury from cinnabar, and silver from argentite.

ALLOYS play a tremendously important part in industry today. There are, for example, scores of steel alloys, each perfected for a particular purpose ; the aluminium alloys include duralumin, the result of the so-called age-hardening whereby an alloy is left several days to gain hardness and strength ; the aluminium alloy RR59 (nickel, copper, silicon, magnesium, titanium, iron and aluminium) after ageing and heat-treatment has a tensile strength of 30 tons per sq.in, and is used for pistons in aircraft. Magnesium alloys are in great demand ; copper and copper alloys are required in almost all electrical apparatus ; brass is another useful alloy, and bronze has many uses, notably leaded bronze for high-speed bearings. Cobalt with chromium and tungsten gives stellite, used for cutting-tools. Lead-tin alloys give solders ; brass supplies the solder for brazing. Much use is made in the motor-car industry of CAPILLARY JOINTING, e.g. two steel parts with a copper disc between them are passed through an electric furnace containing hydrogen but no oxygen. Welding of plates in shipbuilding is now replacing the use of rivets.

In recent years CLAD METALS have been winning popularity, e.g. the ' three-ply ' Alclad, i.e. duralumin with an extremely thin coat (above and below) of pure aluminium, the final product being strongly resistant to corrosion from weather and salt water. Metal-spraying (especially zinc, cadmium and aluminium) is increasing ; radioactive metals will undoubtedly play a vital part in the dawning Atomic Age. See ORE ; and also PLATES 34, 36, 49–56, 58, 59, 61 Read *Metals in the Service of Man*, W. Alexander and A. Street.

metamorphosis, *met-ă-mŏr´fō-sis*, term used in biology for the changes a creature passes through in its life-history, e.g.

the metamorphosis of the butterfly : egg, caterpillar, pupal or chrysalis stage, imago or perfect insect.

metaphor, see FIGURES OF SPEECH

Metaurus, *mē-tau´rŭs*, river of Italy (Umbria).

Metaurus, BATTLE OF, fought near the R. Metaurus 207BC, when two Roman consuls finally defeated Hasdrubal, the Carthaginian, thus destroying Hannibal's last hope of conquering Rome.

Metcalf, JOHN, see ROADS

meteorites, see SHOOTING STARS

meteorology, see CLIMATE

meteors, see SHOOTING STARS

Methodism, see WESLEY, JOHN

methyl alcohol, see ALCOHOL

methyl group, univalent radical CH_3 ; e.g. methyl alcohol, once produced by distilling wood, now made synthetically ; methylated spirit is ordinary alcohol rendered unfit for drinking by the addition of methyl alcohol.

metol, crystalline organic compound, a salt of $CH_3NH.C_6H_4OH$, used as a developer in photography.

metre (Gk *metron*, measure), any particular form of poetic rhythm determined by the number and kind of *feet* it contains.

Prosody is the group of rules (sometimes very successfully broken) governing the *form* of poetry, e.g. the arrangement of feet in any one line, *each foot having one accented syllable*. Many kinds of metre are employed in English poetry, the commonest foot being the *iambus*, which has the accent falling on the second of two syllables, and is the basic unit of the metres used in the sonnet, ode, epic, lyric, and also in blank verse. The iambus appears in such words as at-*tack*. The reverse of the iambus is the *trochee*, i.e. an accented syllable followed by an unaccented one, e.g. *ho*-ly. The *spondee* (somewhat rare in English poetry) has both syllables accented. Where the poet needs a more swiftly-flowing verse he may use the *anapaest*, each foot having two unaccented syllables followed by an accented syllable, e.g. in-ter-*vene*. The dactyl is an accented syllable followed by two unaccented syllables, e.g. *mer*-il-ly.

A *stanza* is a group of lines, and the various types of lines include the *tetrameter*, i.e. having four feet and therefore (as a rule) four accents, the *hexameter* with six, and so on.

Much English verse is in iambic pentameters, e.g.

The *gen*-ius *calls* thee *not* to *pur*-chase fame.

Dactylic Hexameters (six feet to the line) have a dactyl as the fifth foot : other feet may be dactyls or spondees, e.g.

Homeward se|renely she|walked with| God's bene|diction u|pon her.

What is often called *common metre* is verse written in lines alternately of eight and six feet, e.g.

O sleep it is a gentle thing
Beloved from Pole to Pole,

a form much used in old English and Scottish ballads and in many hymns. In *long metre* all the lines have eight feet. The iambic hexameter is sometimes called an Alexandrine, e.g. the last line of a Spenserian stanza : *As one for knightly giusts and fierce encounters fit.* Though blank verse and free verse (*vers libre*) do not employ *rhyme* (except incidentally), lyric verse derives not a little of its music from rhyme, i.e. similarity of sound at the ends of two or more lines. The words *birth* and *earth* rhyme because they sound much alike, and such rhymes are known as masculine, i.e. the rhyming portion in each word is one syllable in length. A feminine rhyme has two or more rhyming syllables, e.g. en*ded*, sus*pended*. Feminine rhymes are often employed in humorous verse, and Robert Browning sometimes used them with startling but rather grotesque effects, but as a general rule only masculine rhymes are used in dignified poetry. Most of Milton's poems and Shakespeare's plays are in unrhymed iambic pentameters, e.g. *Friends, Romans, countrymen, lend me your ears* ; rhymed iambic pentameters are known as *heroic verse*. See POETRY

metric system, see WEIGHTS AND MEASURES

Metz, *mets ; mes,* town, France, on the R. Moselle ; once famous as a fortress ; pop.70,000.

Meuse or **Maas,** *mūz ; mäs,* river flowing 575m from France and through Belgium and the Netherlands to the N. Sea.

Mexborough and **Swinton,** towns, W. Yorkshire, near Sheffield ; noted for pottery, iron, glass, coal ; combined pop.28,000.

Mexico, republic south of the USA, from which it is divided by the Rio Grande del Norte. A tapering land-area of *c.*770,000 sq.m between the Atlantic and Pacific, Mexico is largely a plain bounded by the Eastern and Western Sierra Madre mts. There are various volcanoes, among which is one that erupted 1943. The country produces cereal crops, also sugar, coffee, pepper, cotton, tobacco, tropical fruits, sisal (for hemp), and vast quantities of timber, notably mahogany, ebony, and also rubber. The minerals include silver, gold, petroleum, copper, lead and zinc ; pop.21,000,000.

The early inhabitants, Aztecs, were conquered by the Spaniards in the 16th c., but interesting remains of old civilisations may be seen, especially the pyramids. Mexico has been a republic since 1867. The language is Spanish ; the religion RC. The cap., Mexico City (pop. 1,464,000) stands 7,000ft above sea-level.

Mexico, GULF OF, extension of the N. Atlantic west of Cuba ; largely surrounded by USA and Mexico.

Mexothone, *mek'sō-thōn,* recently discovered substance which, when dusted or sprayed on the soil, destroys harmful weeds and leaves crops unharmed.

Meynell, ALICE CHRISTIANA, *men'el (d* 1922), English poet, essayist and critic.

Mg, chemical symbol for magnesium.

Miami, *mi-am'i,* holiday town and winter resort, Florida, USA ; linked by air with the W. Indies ; pop.172,000.

mica, *mī'kä,* name of a group of minerals easily cloven into thin transparent plates, especially potassium hydrogen aluminium silicate, $KH_2Al_3(SiO_4)_3$; mined in India and USA.

Micah, *mī'kä,* OT prophet, probably 8th c. BC.

Michaelangelo, see MICHELANGELO

Michaelmas Day, see CALENDAR

Michelangelo, *mī-kel-an'jē-lō* (1475–1564), Italian sculptor, poet and painter, ranks among the superb figures in world history ; played with a mallet and chisel as a baby ; carved his matchless *Pietà* (the Madonna with the dead Christ across her knees) 1498 ; suffered because of attacks from jealous sculptors and the political factions of his day ; created his magnificent *David* out of a piece of discarded marble.

MICHELANGELO 1475–1564

As an artist Michelangelo worked for four years lying on his back to adorn the ceiling of the Sistine Chapel (Rome). He spent another three years painting the *Last Judgment* there, the largest fresco in the world. Honest, generous and kindly to those who treated him fairly, he was ferocious towards enemies. Kings and popes begged him to serve them. He lived (like the figures he painted and struck from living marble) as a giant among men.

Michelson, ALBERT ABRAHAM, *mī'kel-sŭn* (1852–1931), American scientist ; associated with E. W. Morley (1838–1923) in the famous Michelson-Morley experiment (1887) interpreted as disproving the existence of ether, hence Einstein's theory of Relativity.

Michigan, *mish'i-gan,* 3rd largest of the Great Lakes. It is in USA ; area 22,400sq.m.

Michigan, north state of USA ; has many lakes ; possesses hydro-electric power. Lansing is the capital but Detroit is the largest city.

micro-, in the metric system, one-millionth ; otherwise used for ' very small.'

microbes, see BACTERIA

microchemistry, chemical investigation in which exceedingly small quantities of solids or liquids are used ; thus, while a chemist as a rule may deal with several grammes of a substance, or with litres or milli-litres of a liquid, the microchemist may deal with quantities only 0·0001 of these. Pioneers of this branch of investigation include the French scientist François Vincent Raspail (1794–1878) ; Kuhlmann, an Austrian manufacturer of chemical balances ; Emich and Pregl, the latter (1912) devising a method of discovering the relative amounts of carbon and hydrogen in two milligrams of an organic substance ; also Chamot in America, Feigl in Vienna. The science has advanced enormously in recent years.

microfarad, see FARAD ; ELECTRICITY

microfilm, very small film, especially one used for storing as a photographic record of e.g. valuable books or documents.

micrometer, instrument for measuring lengths to a high degree of accuracy ; often in the form of a micrometer screw gauge.

micro-micron, written $\mu\mu$, i.e. one-millionth of a micron or 10^{-12} metre.

micron, written μ ; one-millionth of a metre.

microphone, instrument of which there are various types, e.g. that used in telephones, where a diaphragm is in contact with loosely packed granules of carbon. The vibration of the diaphragm under the influence of sound waves compresses the granules, and changes the electrical resistance in sympathy with the vibrations. This principle is used in radio. Another type depends on changes in the electrical capacity of a condenser. In the ' hot wire ' microphone, now extensively used, a thin strip of platinum is kept heated by an electric current. Sound waves cause variations in temperature, hence equivalent variations in electric resistance.

microscope, generally an optical instrument consisting of a combination of lenses enabling the observer to see minute objects considerably enlarged. The modern instrument owes much to the invention in the 18th c. of the achromatic lens by Chester Moor Hall and John Dolland. An earlier (17th c.) pioneer was the Dutchman Leeuwenhoek. Strain on the eyes is reduced by using the binocular microscope having two eyepieces ; the use of quartz lenses enables

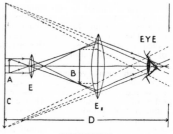

MICROSCOPE

The image B *of object* A *produced by the first lens* E *acts as an object for the eye-lens* E_1, *which then forms the final image* C *at a distance of distinct vision* D *from the eye*

objects to be viewed with ultra-violet light, even though as small as 1/240,000th in ; and still greater magnification is obtained with polarised light.

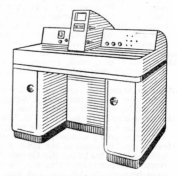

THE MAGNETIC ELECTRON MICROSCOPE

Magnification up to 100,000, and even much more, is obtained by the electron microscope invented *c.*1940, in which streams of electrons are controlled by magnetic fields.

Read *Beyond the Microscope,* Kenneth M. Smith.

Micro-Zoo, popular name for an arrangement by which many people may see enormously magnified creatures of microscopic size, e.g. the Micro-Zoo in the Buhl Planetarium, Pittsburgh, USA.

Midas, *mi'das,* legendary King of Phrygia. Granted his request for a touch that would turn everything to gold, he found it a curse rather than a blessing. Having offended Apollo, he was given the ears of an ass.

Middle Ages, usually regarded as the period from the 5th to the 15th c. ' The DARK AGES ' is usually taken to mean *c.*AD400–*c.*AD1000.

Middle East, term generally indicating the countries of S. Asia between the eastern boundaries of Iran to Burma, especially SW. Asia. The NEAR EAST is regarded as extending from and including Turkey to Persia, Egypt being included ; the FAR EAST is E. Asia, e.g. Siam, China, Japan, etc.

Note that during World War II the British Middle East command included Egypt, Palestine, Arabia, Syria, Iraq, Persia. In ordinary usage the phrase Middle East often has this meaning, perhaps justified by the fact that the countries in question stand culturally and strategically between Europe and Asia.

Middlesbrough, port, N. Yorkshire. South of the R. Tees, it is a centre of the Cleveland mining district ; produces iron and steel ; noted also for ship-building ; pop.141,000.

Middlesex, county of S. England, and practically a suburb of London.

Middleton, town, Lancashire ; manu-factures cotton, silk, iron and chemicals ; pop.28,000.

Middleton, THOMAS (*d* 1627), dramatist ; contemporary of Dekker and Rowley. Of his many plays, *Women Beware Women* is perhaps the best.

Midlands, counties of England between Yorkshire and the R. Thames, and be-tween E. Anglia and the Welsh border.

midnight sun, phenomenon due to the inclination of the earth's axis. The sun may be seen above the horizon for twenty-four hours a day for six months in the year at the N. and S. poles. On (and north of) the Arctic Circle it may be seen at midnight on 21 June, and on (and south of) the Antarctic Circle it may be seen at midnight on 21 Dec. Tourists often call the north of Norway the Land of the Midnight Sun.

Midsummer Day, see CALENDAR

Midway Islands, group of small USA islands 1,200m from Hawaii ; scene of a fierce battle with the Japanese June 1942.

mignonette, *min-yun-et'*, favourite garden plant (family *Resedaceae*) since *c.*1752 ; has alternate leaves ; fragrant flowers with cream petals and numerous red stamens.

migration, *mī-grā'shŭn*, annual mass-move-ment of animals, birds and fish from one region to another and back.

Migration is most easily observed in birds. Indeed, the birds of Britain are grouped as migratory or resident, the latter remaining all the year round (though individuals or flocks may move from one locality to another), the former visiting these islands in their breeding season or in search of more abundant supplies of food.

It seems that, as a rule, birds breed in the colder of any two districts they may inhabit, hence swallows come north from Africa to lay their eggs in Europe, including Britain. Some birds (e.g. quail) wait for a favourable wind before beginning their journeys, but many birds (e.g. swallows, cranes and wild duck) begin their long migratory flights almost to the hour. Naturalists are agreed that

usually puffins arrive on and depart from our shores with remarkable punctuality, and swifts arrive and depart almost on the same dates every year, no matter what the weather may be.

By ringing birds and by long and patient observation many details of migration have come to light in recent years, and it is now possible to trace the main routes of a great many migratory birds, including the amazing track of the golden plover, which in spring flies from the Argentine over the USA to the far north, returning in autumn from Labrador, etc., via 2,400m of ocean to S. America. In good weather the ocean flight is apparently made non-stop. Other golden plovers are known to fly from Alaska to Hawaii, a distance of 2,000m with no resting-place between. Even these flights are exceeded by the Arctic tern, which flies from the Arctic to the Antarctic, a distance of over 10,000m.

How these astonishing journeys are completed remains a mystery. Nor do we know in what way birds keep their courses at night and over wide areas of the sea. It is believed that they have a sense of direction almost wholly lost or never developed in man. The reason for migration is not altogether plain. Climate, and hence the supply of food, may have something to do with it ; and possibly geological changes over a long period of time have gradually separated the breeding grounds and the feeding places, the birds meanwhile retaining the habit of laying eggs in one and feeding in the other, a habit which, in the course of many thousands of years, has entailed even longer flights annually. It is perhaps wisest to admit that much about migra-tion is still a puzzle.

Apart from bird migration we may note that of fish, the salmon being a good example ; an even more remark-able example being the eel, which descends rivers to breed far out in the sea. Among migratory animals the buffaloes of N. America were once conspicuous, their yearly processions between Canada and Mexico being a most interesting feature of their habits. Still more dramatic is the occasional migration of the lemming. It occurs possibly once in five or twenty years ; and when it happens, millions of Scandinavian lemmings (small rodents) form a gigantic mass-movement, rush-ing across Norway and Sweden till they reach the sea, into which they plunge and then continue swimming till they are drowned.

Read *The Story of Migration*, E. A. R. Ennion.

Mikado, *mi-kä'dō*, title formerly given by Europeans to the emperor of Japan.

Milan, *mi'lan*, first city of Lombardy, N. Italy ; pop.1,265,000 ; famous for its beautiful white marble cathedral, and for other fine buildings, e.g. the opera house (La Scala) ; also for its pictures and books ; manufactures textiles, cars and porcelain.

mile, measure of length ; may be (*a*) *mile statute* (the ordinary mile), i.e. 8 furlongs ; 80 chains ; 320 rods, poles or perches ; 1,760yd ; 5,280ft ; 63,360in ; also 1/3rd of a league. A mile is 1·6093 kilometres, hence (roughly) 5 miles = 8 kilometres. To change mph to ft per sec. multiply by 1·4667 ; (*b*) *geographical mile,* i.e. the length of one minute of lat., a distance of 6 046ft at the equator and 6,108ft at the Poles, the *mean* length being taken as 6,076·8ft ; (*c*) *the nautical mile* for measuring distances at sea is for practical purposes 6,080ft, i.e. 10 cables, a cable being slightly over 600ft.

Miletus, *mī-lē'tŭs,* anciently the chief city of the Ionian colonies of Greece.

Milford Haven, Atlantic opening on the coast of Pembrokeshire. North is Milford, a naval base and trawler-fishing port.

militia, *mi-lish'ä,* companies of civilians trained for home defence only ; a development of the OE FYRD, i.e. army, first mentioned in the Anglo-Saxon Chronicle *c.*600. This, reorganised by Alfred the Great, declined after the Norman Conquest, and in Edward I's time was known as the militia. The Home Guard (HG) of World War II had much in common with the highly organised militia of Queen Elizabeth's reign, and the militia that defended the east of England from the French and Dutch *c.*1666.

milk, liquid food. Cow's milk contains 87% water, 3·5% albuminoids (albumin, casein), 5% lactose or milk-sugar, nearly 4% fat ; milk of goats and asses is excellent, but for infants human milk is the ideal, and this contains *lecithin* which stimulates brain-development.

Cow's milk heated before delivery in order to destroy bacteria, especially those of bovine tuberculosis, is known as *pasteurised* ; tuberculin-tested (TT) milk comes from cows regularly examined and found free from tuberculosis ; partly dehydrated milk becomes condensed milk ; if *all* the water is evaporated the residue is powdered or dried milk. A champion milking cow will produce its own weight of milk in 10–12 days. See PLATE 18

Milk products include : (*a*) CURD ; (*b*) WHEY, separated from curd by the addition of rennet, an acid substance from the stomachs of calves ; (*c*) CHEESE, made from curd ; varieties include Cheddar (from Somerset), Cheshire, Stilton, Gorgonzola ; (*d*) CREAM, the fat of milk ; (*e*) BUTTER, once made from cream by churning in farm dairies, but now manufactured on a large scale in factories ; should contain 80% fat and some casein. Butter substitutes include MARGARINE, made from coconut-oil, palm-oil, etc., also hydrogenated oil, e.g.

fish-oils from which the unpleasant taste has been removed.

The first milk bar in England was opened in Fleet Street, London, by an Australian in 1935.

A process of making butter without churning and in 5 minutes instead of *c.*45 was made known 1946. It involves the use of carbon dioxide under pressure.

Heating milk by means of radio frequency is now proving effective in killing disease bacteria.

Milky Way, see ASTRONOMY

Mill, JOHN STUART (1806–73), economist and thinker ; *b* London ; read Greek at three, Latin at four ; was for 38 years in the E. India office ; advocated the rights of the working man, also woman's right to vote ; author of *Principles of Political Economy* ; *System of Logic* ; *On Liberty.*

Millais, SIR JOHN EVERETT, *mi-lā'* (1829–96), British artist, *b* Southampton ; painted many exceedingly popular pictures, e.g. *The Carpenter's Shop* (showing Christ at work) ; *The Blind Girl* ; *The North-West Passage.*

millennium, period of 1,000 years. The word is often used for an imagined future paradise on earth.

miller's thumb, see BULLHEAD

millet, grain from a variety of cultivated grasses, especially *Panicum miliaceum,* the seed of which is much used for poultry in Europe, but as human food in India. See DURRA

Millet, JEAN FRANÇOIS, *mē-yä* (1814–75), French artist, son of peasant parents ; won fame with his country scenes, e.g. *The Winnowers* ; *The Angelus* ; *The Gleaners* ; *The Man with a Hoe.*

Mill Hill School, public school (London) founded 1807, for the sons of Nonconformists.

millibar, unit of atmospheric pressure. A bar is the pressure of a million dynes per sq.cm, or of a column of mercury 29·53in or 750mm high. A millibar is 1/1,000th of this.

Millikan, ROBERT ANDREWS (1868–), American scientist ; gained the Nobel prize (1923) for his work on electrons.

Milne, ALAN ALEXANDER (1882–), British author ; won fame with *When We Were Very Young,* featuring a little hero, Christopher Robin ; followed by *Winnie-the-Pooh* ; *Now We Are Six* ; *The House at Pooh Corner* ; as a playwright he is known by *Mr Pim Passes By* and *The Dover Road.*

Milnes, R. M., see HOUGHTON, LORD

Milo, *mī'lō,* famous athlete of ancient times, probably *b* S. Italy. He gained prizes at the Olympic games, and is credited with carrying a heifer on his shoulders and eating it the same day.

Milocarian Cup, silver trophy presented to the AAA (Amateur Athletic Association) by the Milocarian Club 1946 ; may be competed for by schools and colleges annually by boys between the ages of 15 and 17.

Miltiades, *mil-tī'ä-dēz* (*d c*.488BC), Athenian soldier ; one of the generals responsible for the bold policy by which the Greeks won victory at Marathon.

Milton, JOHN (1608–74), poet, *b* Bread Street, Cheapside, London ; son of a Puritan. At Christ's College, Cambridge, he was nicknamed ' The Lady.' During the Commonwealth he was Latin Secretary to the Committee for Foreign Affairs. He went blind 1652. His first marriage (1641) was unsuccessful. His wife left him (1643), but two years later they were reconciled. She died 1654. He married again 1656, and a third time 1663, his last wife showing more affection than the other two, or his three daughters. He died in London.

MILTON 1608–74

Of his many pamphlets, his *Areopagitica*, a defence of the freedom of the Press, is the greatest. As a learned poet, his mind stored with classic lore, he has left us majestic and intensely beautiful poems, e.g. *L'Allegro* and *Il Penseroso* ; *Lycidas* (an elegy on his friend Edward King) ; various sonnets, including *On His Blindness* and *To the Lord General Cromwell* ; and also his *Samson Agonistes*, a tragedy in the Greek manner, in which blind Milton takes blind Samson for his hero.

But his fame rests on his two epics *Paradise Lost* and *Paradise Regained*, among the finest of their kind in modern European literature. *Paradise Lost*, a poem in twelve books, was begun 1658 and published 1667. It was, however, the fruit of an inspiration that had blossomed as early as 1640. Milton received only *c*.£10 (and his widow another £8) for this long poem dealing with man's disobedience and his loss, thereby, of Paradise. The poem is full of grand imagery and sonorous sounds, e.g.

Now came still evening on, and twilight gray
Had in her sober livery all things clad ;
Silence accompanied, for beast and bird,

They to their grassy couch, these to their nests,
Were slunk, all but the wakeful nightingale ;
She all night long her amorous descant sung ;
Silence was pleas'd ; now glow'd the firmament
With living sapphires : Hesperus that led
The starry host rode brightest, till the moon,
Rising in clouded majesty, at length
Apparent queen unveil'd her peerless light,
And o'er the dark her silver mantle threw.

Paradise Regained, in four books, is less successful.

One other of Milton's achievements remains : his masque *Comus*, a masterpiece of its kind. Presented at Ludlow Castle 1634 before the Earl of Bridgewater, it is a pastoral entertainment. Comus, a god, waylays travellers and tempts them to drink a magic potion which changes their faces into those of wild beasts. A lady benighted in a forest falls into the clutches of Comus, but is rescued by her brothers with the aid of Sabrina, goddess of the R. Severn.

Milwaukee, city and port, Wisconsin, USA; on the west shore of L. Michigan ; trades in coal, timber, flour, iron, steel, leather and electrical goods ; pop. 587,000.

mimosa, plant, shrub or tree of the family *Leguminosae*, particularly common in America. The leaflets are often sensitive, folding at a touch ; and the small flowers are yellow.

minaret, slender tower of a Mohammedan mosque. It has a balcony (sometimes several balconies) from which priests call the people to prayer.

Minch, channel east of the Outer Hebrides ; also the LITTLE MINCH, west of Skye.

mind, sometimes defined as that part of you with which you feel and think. This is a bad definition. Your mind is not a *part* of you in the same sense as your nose and your hands are parts. Your mind is *you* altogether, in so far as you think, feel or know what you are doing. Thus a better definition of mind would be : *man considered as a being which feels, thinks, remembers, knows, decides.*

We have no knowledge of any activity of mind that does not seem somehow to be connected with physiological processes in the living body, especially with those processes which occur in the brain. It is also a fact that certain brain injuries produce certain well-known disorders of the mind. This being so, people sometimes talk of mind as something which happens or exists in the brain ; but mind cannot be so easily explained away. When something is explained scientifically or in any other way, it is explained *by* a mind *for* a mind. The mind giving an explanation, so to speak, stands outside the explanation. Thus all minds can be explained in this way *except* that mind which is giving the explanation. See BRAIN ; PSYCHOLOGY

Mindanao, *min-dä-nä'ō,* island of the Philippines ; area *c.*37,000sq.m. Some miles off is the greatest known ocean depth, 35,410ft.

Minden, town, Westphalia, Germany ; scene of a battle (1759) in which the British and Hanoverians defeated the French ; pop. *c.*32,000.

mine, (*a*) excavation in the earth from which salt, coal or ores are brought to the surface ; (*b*) an explosive in various forms, e.g. one buried in the ground and exploded by electricity, or a type exploded by pressure or movement, as the booby-trap, much used by the Germans 1940–45 ; also the sea-mine exploding on contact, and the magnetic mine detonated when iron or steel approach. Mines were also dropped by parachute during World War II.

miner's safety lamp, see DAVY, SIR H.

Minerva, Italian goddess of wisdom, identified by the Romans with Athena.

minium, red lead, Pb₃O₄.

mink, flesh-eating animal of the weasel family, but resembling the pole-cat ; has valuable, soft, glossy fur, shaded yellowish to dark brown, and a bushy tail. It is found in Poland, Finland, Siberia and N. America.

Minneapolis, *min-ē-ap'ō-lis,* university city, Minnesota, USA ; on the R. Mississippi ; manufactures metal goods and cars ; pop.492,000.

Minnesota, state of USA, west of Wisconsin, and chiefly noted for wheat and for its rich iron deposits ; cap. St Paul.

minnow, fresh-water fish, 3–6in long, common in British rivers.

Minoan period, see AEGEAN CIVILISATION

Minorca, see BALEARIC ISLANDS

Minos, *mī'nos,* in old Greek tales, king and lawgiver of Crete, and a son of Zeus. Recent excavations on the island reveal traces of his great palace, and of the labyrinth where the fabled Minotaur lived.

Minotaur, *mīn'ō-taur,* in old Greek tales, a monster with a man's body and a bull's head ; dwelt in a labyrinth belonging to King Minos of Crete ; devoured young men and maidens ; was slain by Theseus with the help of Ariadne.

Minsk, *mēnsk,* cap. Byelorussia (White Russia) ; has many and varied manu-factures ; pop.240,000.

minstrel, singer or performer on some musical instrument, or both, in the Middle Ages ; often a poet who sang his own songs much as the Anglo-Saxon scop or gleeman did. The minstrel, or jongleur, belongs especially to the Norman period and to later times. Many were attached to nobles ; others wandered freely from great house to great house.

Mint, ROYAL, see LONDON

minuet, *min-ū-et',* dance in 3–4 time ; originated in Poitou ; reached Paris

1650. Hence also a musical com-position of the same form.

minutes, official record of the meeting of a committee. Minutes of the previous meeting are read by the secretary, and, if passed by the members, are signed by the chairman as a faithful record.

Mirabeau, HONORÉ, COMTE DE, *mē-rä-bō* (1749–91), French statesman and author ; had a stormy youth ; lived wildly ; but was a great orator, and strove, without success, to avert the Revolution by making the king and queen leaders of a new order of justice and civic govern-ment.

miracle plays, see DRAMA

mirage, optical illusion frequently seen in hot countries. When air immediately above, say, the sand of a hot desert becomes heated, it is less dense than cooler air at a higher altitude. Since a ray of light passing from a medium that is less dense to one that is more so is refracted, an observer may see images in the sky, apparently below him, often looking much like lakes. A somewhat similar effect on a small scale may some-times be observed if we look along a road on a hot day. An inverted mirage is occasionally seen over the sea near the coast. This is due to warm air overlying cold.

mirrors, reflecting surfaces, usually of bronze in ancient Egypt, Greece and Rome ; later of silver. Glass was first used for mirrors in Venice *c.*1300. Modern mirrors are backed with a precipitate of silver salt. For spherical mirrors (concave or convex), see LIGHT

Mishna, collection of Jewish interpretations of the laws of Moses ; compiled *c.* AD200.

missionaries, Christian men or women who go overseas to carry the message of the Gospel to the heathen. Home mis-sionaries do similar work in our cities.

Ever since the days of St Paul, the Christian Churches have been very active in the field of missionary effort. Modern missionary movements are largely due in Britain and America to the Baptists and Wesleyans, to the Church of England, and the Church of Scotland and the British and Foreign Bible Society. In Africa and India British missions have not only spread knowledge of Christian beliefs : they have also inaugurated the whole process of educa-tion, and have done much to improve medical and sanitary conditions.

Great missionaries include, besides St Paul and St Augustine, William Cary (1761–1834), a cobbler, who became the first Baptist missionary and laboured in India ; Robert Morrison, another cobbler, who translated the Bible into Chinese ; John Williams, evangelist of the S. Seas ; Robert Moffat (1795–1883), who taught the Bechuanas ; David Livingstone ; Bishop Crowther, a Negro ; Bishop Selwyn, who carried the Gospel to the Maoris of NZ ;

MIRAGE

Looking towards the Bedouin tent in the middle of the desert, the traveller sees it mirrored in what appears to be a pool of water. This water however is only an illusion. It is a mirage formed by the reflection of light from a layer of hot air at ground level.

Bishop Patteson, martyred in Melanesia ; James Hannington (1847–85), who died in Uganda ; James Chalmers, killed by cannibals 1901 ; John G. Paton, known as the Apostle of the New Hebrides ; Father Damien, who served the lepers on Molokai ; and Albert Schweitzer (*b* 1875), the German doctor, thinker, and musician who went to the Congo 1913.

Mississippi, river of USA. With the Missouri (2,900m), it flows 4,500m to the Gulf of Mexico, and is navigable for 2,000m. It frequently floods vast areas.

Mississippi, state of USA ; has 85m of coastline on the Gulf of Mexico ; noted for cotton, also maize, sugar cane and great forests ; cap. Jackson.

Mississippi Scheme, see SOUTH SEA BUBBLE

Missouri (river), see MISSISSIPPI

Missouri, central state of USA ; rich in minerals, e.g. coal, zinc, lead, iron, etc. ; cap. Jefferson City.

mistletoe, evergreen plant (*Viscum album*) of the family *Loranthaceae.* Found in Europe and Asia, it grows on various trees, e.g. black poplar and apple, as a type of parasite, but feeds also on carbohydrates made in the leathery leaves. It has green flowers and white berries ; once regarded as sacred by the Druids, and associated with magic in old tales.

mistral, cold dry wind experienced chiefly in winter in the Rhône valley.

Mitcham, town, Surrey ; actually a south-west suburb of London ; noted for its fair and its common ; pop.55,000.

Mitchell, MARGARET, American writer, author of *Gone with the Wind* (1936), a novel of the American Civil War. She died 1949.

Mitchell, REGINALD (1895–1937), *b* Stoke-on-Trent, designer of the *Spitfire* fighter plane, an immense advance in aircraft performance, and a vital factor in winning the Battle of Britain, 1940. See AVIATION

mites, small creatures, often resembling minute spiders, though without waists. As parasites they cause diseases, e.g. mange.

Mitford, MARY RUSSELL (1787–1855), writer, *b* Alresford, Hampshire ; noted for her charming sketches of country life and characters in *Our Village.*

Mithradates VI (131–63BC), King of Pontus, i.e. a region south-east of the Black Sea ; ruled from 121BC ; waged three wars against Rome, over-running the Roman province of Asia, but defeated by Pompey.

Mithraism, pagan religion which competed with Christianity. See ZOROASTER

Mitylene, *mit-ē-lē'nē*, Greek island in the Aegean Sea ; also called Lesbos ; produces olives, grapes and raisins ; chief town Mitylene ; pop. of the island *c.*178,000.

Mn, chemical symbol for manganese.

moa, flightless bird that became extinct a few centuries ago ; formerly inhabited NZ, and was sometimes 12ft high.

Moabites, inhabitants of Moab, east of the

Dead Sea, an ancient Semitic people frequently at war with the Israelites, but conquered by David, though they regained their independence.

The MOABITE STONE, discovered 1868, has an inscription in Hebrew script of *c.*850BC.

moat, deep trench, usually filled with water, surrounding and protecting a castle.

Mobile, *mō-bēl'*, city, Alabama, USA ; has many industries including shipbuilding ; pop.79,000.

mocking bird, thrush-like bird of N. America and the W. Indies. It has a long tail, short wings, black and white plumage. It is so named because it readily imitates the cries of other birds.

Modder, river of S. Africa ; flows 186m through the Orange Free State and Bechuanaland to the R. Vaal.

model-building, see HOBBY

Modelcraft, see HOBBY

Model Parliament, see PARLIAMENT

Modena, *mō'dā-nä,* city, N. Italy ; manufactures terracotta and silk; pop.113,000.

Modern School, see EDUCATION

modulus, term used in mathematics in connection with logarithms. To change a logarithm as devised by John Napier from the base *e* to the base 10, multiply by $\dfrac{1}{\log_e 10,}$ which is equivalent to 0·4343, this being known as the modulus. Also a term used in mechanics. A modulus of elasticity is the ratio of stress to strain. See LOGARITHMS

Moffat, ROBERT (1795–1883), Scottish missionary ; went to S. Africa 1816 ; ministered in Bechuanaland. His daughter married David Livingstone.

Moffatt, JAMES (1870–1944), *b* Glasgow, chiefly known for his translation of the Bible into modern English. See BIBLE

Mogul, form of Mongol ; name given to the empire founded in India *c.*1526 by Baber, a Mohammedan conqueror. The empire was greatly extended by his grandson Akbar, but fell to pieces 1707.

mohair, fleece of the Angora goat. Its manufacture has been carried on at Bradford (Yorkshire) since 1848. It is used for heavy cloths and plushes. There are Angora goat ranches in west USA.

Mohammed or **Mahomet** (*d* 632), Arab prophet, founder of Mohammedanism (or Islam), *b* Mecca *c.*570. Deeply religious, he believed that God revealed new truths to him in visions, and so he began to preach.

As a result of his new doctrine he had to flee from Mecca, but he returned within eight years as conqueror of Arabia. He died of fever, and was buried at Medina. At the time of his death all Arabia had accepted his religious teaching. Mohammed's faith was based on that of the Christians, but he believed that he had received further revelations, and his religious system, now the faith of some 209,000,000 people, chiefly in Arabia, Central Asia, N. and E. Africa, India and Malaya, stressed the worship of one god only : *There is no God but Allah, and Mohammed is his prophet ;* also the unity of God, the reality of the Resurrection, of the Day of Judgment, and of heaven as a happy place, hell as a place of torment. Prayers must be said daily.

Mohammed declared that 'whithersoever ye turn, there is the face of God,' but later the custom arose of always turning the face towards Mecca, the Holy City of the Moslems. The Moslem is called to prayer by the muezzin (or crier). There is no Sunday or Sabbath, but every Friday a sermon is preached in the mosques at the midday services in addition to the usual prayers. Every Mohammedan aspires to make the pilgrimage to Mecca, preferably in the twelfth month of the year, and to visit the Kaaba (see KAABA). Giving alms is part of the Mohammedan religion ; fasting is strictly observed in the ninth month (Ramadan).

The divine revelations which Mohammed claimed form the basis of the Mohammedan ' Bible,' i.e. the *Koran,* purporting to contain revelations by the angel Gabriel. Its 114 chapters are called *Suras.* On its teaching Moslems base their religious life, but a great wealth of Moslem religious matter has grown up in addition to the *Koran,* the 7th c. edition of which is in rhymed prose, and is certainly the finest example of Arabic literature.

Mohawks, warlike N. American Indian tribe now settled in Canada.

Mohicans, *mō'i-kan,* extinct N. American Indian tribe. At one time living in what is now Pennsylvania and New England, their villages were often stockaded, and the men wore mantles of feathers.

Read *The Last of the Mohicans,* Fenimore Cooper.

Möhne Dam, dam 850yd long, 150ft thick, in the Ruhr valley, Germany ; breached by RAF Bomber Command crews under Wing-Commander Guy P. Gibson, 16 May 1943.

moidore, old Portuguese gold coin worth roughly a guinea ; not minted after 1732.

Moiseiwitsch, BENNO, *mwa-si-vitch* (1890–), Russian pianist, *b* Odessa ; first played in London 1909 ; best known for his interpretations of Chopin.

molasses, by-product in the manufacture of sugar ; a thick, brownish syrup.

mole, common British animal, *c.*6in long, with thick grey or black fur much like velvet ; has exceptionally long claws, and burrows rapidly in search of worms and grubs, throwing up heaps of soil. Its underground nest has many tunnels. The mole is harmless.

molecule, see CHEMISTRY ; ELEMENT ; MATTER

Molière, JEAN-BAPTISTE, *moll-yare* (1622–1673), French dramatist and actor, *b* Paris ; founded a theatrical company which, after many struggles in the provinces, won success in the cap., and secured the patronage of Louis XIV. Molière made an unfortunate marriage, but in spite of difficulties and disappointments and all the duties of a theatrical manager he wrote plays bubbling over with humour, all of them satires on the manners and beliefs of his day.

Forsaking Italian models, Molière created a new drama for France and for the world. Among his masterpieces are *Les Fourberies de Scapin* ; *Le Tartuffe* ; *Don Juan* ; *Le Misanthrope* ; *Georges Dandin* ; *L'Avare* ; *Le Bourgeois Gentilhomme* ; *Les Femmes Savantes* ; and *Le Malade Imaginaire*. His ridicule of pretence, hypocrisy, bores and superstition made him many enemies, but he is now acknowledged as one of the greatest of all French dramatists.

Mollusca (Latin *molluscus*, rather soft), name for cold-blooded, soft-bodied, limbless creatures without a bony skeleton, almost all with a protective shell ; comprise (I) bivalves with two shells ; (II) univalves or Gastropoda (' stomach-foots ') with one shell.

(I) A *bivalve* has usually a foot by which it is attached to a rock ; feeds by opening its shells and taking in water, e.g. (*a*) OYSTER, edible varieties found along British coasts including those at Whitstable Kent ; lays as many as 1,800,000 eggs May–Aug. ; for pearl oyster, see PEARL : (*b*) COCKLE, found near marine low-water mark : (*c*) MUSSEL, also edible : (*d*) LIMPET, with a shell like a small chalk tent ; clings tightly to a rock etc., but roams at high tide : (*e*) SCALLOP, has two many-coloured, fan-shaped shells ; common on our sea-shores : (*f*) RAZOR-SHELL or SOLEN, burrows deeply in wet sand : (*g*) TEREDO, powerful boring shell-fish, long the enemy of wooden vessels ; said to have given Brunel the idea for the Thames tunnel. See page 450.

(II) *Gastropoda :* marine examples include (*a*) WHELK, which, like all this group with one shell only, has a curious rippling movement of its soft ' foot,' and a spiral shell into which the body retreats : (*b*) PERIWINKLE (or WINKLE) similar, but smaller : (*c*) COWRY, abundant in the Pacific.

Land examples include (*a*) GARDEN SNAIL, with a spiral shell that may be 2in high ; hibernates in winter ; can live long without food ; leaves a silvery trail of mucus ; will climb over a razor blade without injury ; its tongue may have 12,000 ' teeth ' : (*b*) SLUGS, actually closely related to snails, but have a flat and only partly formed shell *under* their soft mantle.

Molluscs include also Cephalopoda, i.e. varieties of CUTTLE-FISH ; those in British waters, *c.*8in long, have a body like a bag, and a mouth with eight short and two long tentacles. They swim backwards jerkily ; protect themselves by a ' smoke-screen,' i.e. an inky fluid. So-called cuttle-fish ' bone ' is actually an inside shell. The OCTOPUS of British seas is greyish-brown, with eight tentacles and a parrot-like beak ; in deep oceans is found the GIANT SQUID, sometimes weighing ten cwt, its tentacles 30ft long. A small and beautiful variety is the NAUTILUS.

Read *British Shells*, F. Martin Duncan.

Moloch, *mō'lok*, fire-god of the Canaanites, to whom human sacrifices were made. His images were of brass.

Molokai, *mō-lō-kä'ē*, Hawaiian island. Its leper settlement was the scene of Father Damien's sacrificial service 1873–89.

Molotov, VYACHESLAV MIKHAILOVICH, *mōl'ō-tof* (1890–), Russian politician. Became a Communist 1906 ; was a member of the All-Russian central executive 1927 ; was later Minister for Foreign Affairs, till succeeded by Andrei Vyshinsky in 1949.

Moltke, COUNT VON, *mōlt'ke* (1800–91), Prussian soldier and one of the creators of the German empire ; *b* Parchim in Mecklenburg ; wrote various notable war-histories ; conducted three campaigns : (1) a war between Prussia and Denmark 1864 ; (2) a war (1866) against Austria and her allies, in which Austria was crushed after six weeks by his remarkable strategy ; (3) the Franco-Prussian war 1870. Moltke replaced Napoleon's tactics with an entirely new system.

Moluccas or **Spice Islands,** *mō-lŭk'äz*, group of Dutch islands in the E. Indian Archipelago ; they produce tortoise-shell and cloves.

molybdenum, *mo-lib-dē'nŭm*, white metallic element, Mo ; atomic weight 95·95 ; atomic number 42 ; specific gravity 9·1 ; melting-point 2,620°C ; found as the mineral molybdenite, MoS_2, in Australia and Norway ; used in making steel for high-speed lathes.

momentum, see MECHANICS

Mona, *mō'nä*, Roman name for the island of Anglesey.

Monaco, *mon'ä-kō*, principality on the Mediterranean coast of France ; actually a town with a miniature harbour ; pop.23,000, but visited by upwards of 2,000,000 a year ; noted for its casino at Monte Carlo.

monad, any element with a valency of one.

Monaghan, *mon'ä-gan*, county, Eire, in the province of Ulster ; co.tn Monaghan, *c.*50m from Dublin.

monastery, see MONKS AND NUNS

Monel metal, trade name of an alloy comprising 67% nickel, 28% copper, and small amounts of manganese and iron ; withstands corrosion, and is used for turbine blades and laundry fittings ; introduced *c.*1905.

Monet, CLAUDE, *mō-nä* (1840–1926), French artist, *b* Paris. Developing Turner's art, he was a pioneer of Impressionism, and a student of the changing effects of light and colour.

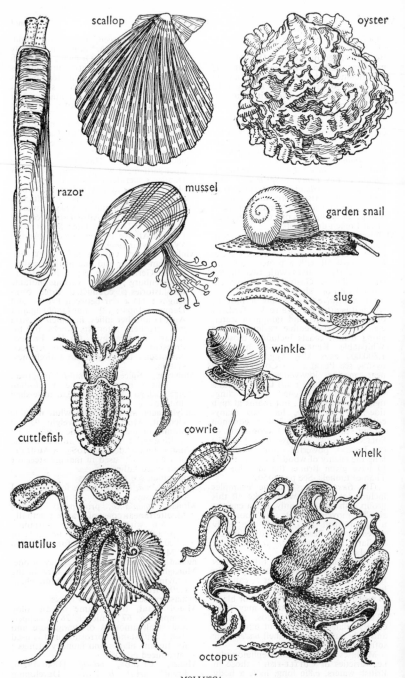

scallop

oyster

razor

mussel

garden snail

slug

cuttlefish

winkle

cowrie

whelk

nautilus

octopus

MOLLUSCA

Some examples of sea Mollusca ; the only exceptions shown here are the Garden Snail and the Slug, which are both land varieties.

He used pure colour in small patches, e.g. rendering green, not by mixing it on the palette, but with dabs of yellow and blue.

money, token used as payment for goods or service, which affords a basis for comparing the value of commodities as well as being a general medium of exchange ; has practically replaced the ancient system of *barter* which served primitive peoples where each man or family was self-supporting.

Later division of labour meant that a smith, for example, might wish to barter his plough-share for a farmer's wheat, but if the farmer did not require a new plough-share, exchange was impossible, so that the more useful system of exchanging a *token* for the wheat was introduced so that the farmer was able to buy articles that he needed with his token (money). Shells, stones, rice and gunpowder have all been used as a medium of exchange, but generally precious metal has been employed in the form of coins stamped for a king or government. Eventually goldsmiths (the first bankers) began to issue receipts that could at any time be exchanged for gold ; thus, instead of a merchant A carrying £100 in gold to B, A might give B a receipt for £100 which B could change into gold when he chose to present it to the goldsmith. Thus began the *credit system*, leading to the issue of more notes of credit than the goldsmiths actually possessed, on the assumption that *all* their creditors would not happen to want *all* their money on one day ; hence modern banking, whereby banks issue more money in the form of notes, and later of bank 'deposits,' than their actual gold reserves ; also our present system of paying by cheque, a simplification of business transactions.

Prior to 1914, gold sovereigns and half-sovereigns were *legal tender* in Britain (i.e. they could be used for purchasing goods), but now £1 and 10s notes are issued by the Treasury (and by the Bank of England since 1928). Gold, silver, bronze, cupro-nickel (proposed for British coinage 1946) is ' *standard money.*'

The commodity used as standard money must be in general a *medium* of exchange ; a *measure* of value ; a *store* of value, i.e. it must not deteriorate with time. Also it must be portable and hard to counterfeit.

After World War II a World Bank was organised (1947) by the United States, an attempt to assist international trade.

Countries try to keep a balance between the amount of money available and the amount required for purchasing commodities. Too much money causes *inflation*, i.e. increase in prices and the cost of living. The theory of money, of great interest to economists, has been dealt with by R. G. Hawtrey, *Currency*

and Credit ; J. M. Keynes, *Treatise on Money* (1930) ; Geoffrey Crowther, *Outline of Money*.

COINAGE, the metal money of a country, was perhaps first used by the Chinese and Greeks *c.*700BC. The earliest Greek coins were of electrum (alloy of gold and silver) ; Croesus, King of Lydia (561–546BC) is said to have first issued gold coins. The coinage of Philip II of Macedonia and his son Alexander the Great became the chief international coinage of the ancient world, and led to the Roman bronze *as* and silver *denarius* (first struck 269BC). The first English gold coin (noble) was minted 1344 ; the early British shilling (Anglo-Saxon *scylling*), once worth 5d, was first minted 1504. The florin, issued 1849, was known till 1852 as the ' graceless florin ' because the letters DG (*Dei gracia*) were omitted. Today British coins bear the date, name of the reigning monarch, and the inscription D G BR (*or* BRITT) OMN REX FID DEF, i.e. *By the Grace of God King of Great Britain, Defender of the Faith* ; FID DEF is short for *Fidei Defensor*, the title given by Pope Leo X (1521) to Henry VIII for his defence of the sacraments of the Church. British coins prior to 1949 bear also the letters IND IMP, i.e. *Indiae Imperator* (Emperor of India).

' *Sterling* ' (i.e. standard British weight and genuine quality, e.g. the pound sterling, 123·274 grains of 22 carat gold) probably comes from the old silver penny, once stamped with a starling. Our ' £ s d ' stand for £, short for *libra*, a Roman unit of weight ; *s* for *solidus*, a silver coin 1/20th of a *libra* ; *d* the Roman *denarius*. Cupro-nickel was substituted for silver in British coinage 1947. Farthings (Anglo-Saxon *a fourth*) are stamped with a wren—our smallest bird on our smallest coin. Our nickel-brass 3d-bit shows the plant thrift (sea-pink), a hint that we should be thrifty.

The side of a coin (or medal) bearing the head is the *obverse* ; the other is the *reverse*. On British coins the king's head faces left or right in successive reigns. George VI faces left. The portrait of Britannia on our coins is said to have been drawn 1665 by Philip Rostier, his model being Frances Stewart, Duchess of Richmond.

The collection and study of coins and medals is *numismatics*. . See COST OF LIVING ; DOLLAR AREA ; FLOATING DEBT ; HARD CURRENCY ; INFLATION ; SURTAX ; TAXES, etc.

Mongolia, see CHINA

Mongols, wandering peoples of Central Asia. One of their emperors conquered China 1234, and among his descendants was Kublai Khan ; other Mongol conquests extended to Hungary and India. The Mongols are a yellow race with slant eyes and prominent cheekbones.

The word MONGOLIAN denotes also

the whole of the yellow race, one of the great divisions of mankind.

mongoose, small, flesh-eating animal. The Indian mongoose, with grey fur and a bushy tail, is notable for its ability to kill snakes, including the cobra.

Monk, GEORGE (1608–70), Devon soldier who helped to win the battle of Dunbar. He was also a sailor, and fought the Dutch. He became Duke of Albemarle, and after Cromwell's death did much to restore the exiled Charles II to the throne.

monkey, see APES AND MONKEYS

monkey-nut, see GROUND-NUT

monkey-puzzle tree, popular name for the Chilean pine, introduced into Britain 1796.

monks and **nuns,** men and women who choose to live in a monastery or nunnery. A monk (Greek *monos,* alone) hopes to escape the temptations of life by living with men only ; a woman who ' takes the veil,' i.e. becomes a nun, seeks a good life by living with women only ; and both, in theory, lead a life of prayer and devotion, vowing to remain poor, unmarried and obey those in authority.

Life in 4th c. monasteries was harsh, but the strict rules gradually relaxed till, between 1020–1120, reform was needed. New monasteries were built by religious enthusiasts, and for long the monasteries were of great importance. Monks translated books, kept records of historical events, cared for the poor, ministered to the sick and dying and built beautiful churches. Many (especially in later years) took an active part in politics. As the monasteries grew rich and owned land, the earlier religious zeal waned, monks became idle and careless. They were denounced by the Lollards, and Henry VIII brought about the final dissolution of the monasteries in Britain, the lesser in 1536, the greater 1539. As a result, many of the monks were in great distress ; the common people had to be relieved by the newly created poor laws, land was enclosed, the wealth of the monasteries went to the State, and the removal of abbots from the House of Lords made way for newly created peers.

In the 14th or 15th c. a typical English or Scottish monastery was a group of buildings with a church and usually cloisters (to the south), dormitories, kitchens, a chapter-house, library, parlour, an infirmary for old or sick monks, a frater or dining-hall and a gate-house.

A day in the life of a monk in a Benedictine monastery began with a two-hour service at midnight, another service at 6am, a 3rd at 7.45am, followed by breakfast (a little dry toast and a cupful of wine or beer), a service at 8.30am ; then a meeting in the chapter-house where a chapter of St Benedict's *Rules* was read, offenders punished, monastery business discussed. The monk might then walk in the cloister till 10am, when Mass was celebrated.

Dinner was at 11am, after which there was a short time for recreation (conversation or playing bowls). In the afternoon the monk might work in the fields, or copy a book till *c.*6pm, when he attended Vespers. A light supper was served *c.*7pm, and after a meeting in the chapterhouse the monk retired to bed at 8pm.

A monastery governed by an abbot was called an abbey ; one governed by a prior, a priory. Officials included a precentor, responsible for the musical portion of the church services ; a sacrist, in charge of the vestments, plate, etc., and a cellarer, responsible for food and drink.

Monastic orders include :

Benedictines or *Black Monks* (wearing a black habit), founded by St Benedict, *d* 543 ; *Cluniacs,* a revised form of the Benedictines, founded by St Bruno at Cluny, France ; *Cistercians* (Grey or White Monks), founded 1098 by Robert of Citeaux, France, e.g. Melrose, Tintern, Fountains ; *Austin Canons* or *Canons Regular* or *Augustinians,* also known as *Black Canons* ; *Praemonstratensians* ; *Gilbertines,* an order in which monks and nuns lived (apart from each other) in one monastery ; *Franciscans* or *Grey Friars,* founded 1209 by St Francis of Assisi ; *Dominicans* or *Black Friars,* founded 1215 by St Dominic (1170–1221) of Spain; *Carmelites* or *White Friars* ; *Carthusians,* the monks, living in separate cells, being allowed to talk only once or twice a week.

monk's hood, see ACONITE ; POISONOUS PLANTS

Monmouth, DUKE OF, *mon'mŭth* (1649–85), son of Charles II, *b* Rotterdam. Being a Protestant, various plots were formed to secure the succession for him. He landed in Dorset 1685 and raised a rebellion, but was defeated at Sedgemoor and later executed.

Read *Lorna Doone,* R. D. Blackmore.

Monmouth, GEOFFREY OF, see ARTHUR

Monmouthshire, county politically linked with Wales ; has important coal mines. The county hall is at Newport.

monocotyledon, see BOTANY

Monomark, trade-name for a system by which a person or firm may register a series of letters, or letters and figures, as an identification mark, especially useful when mailing confidential letters.

monopoly, exclusive right to manufacture or sell certain goods ; often granted in Queen Elizabeth's day, and encouraged by Lord Burghley, James I and Charles I. Today the word indicates the control of the supply of a commodity by one firm, or group of firms, with the danger of raising the price, since there can be little or no competition ; or fixing a price, and leaving the demand to adjust itself. See ECONOMICS

monotheism, see RELIGION

monotype, machine for setting up metal type ; invented 1887 by an American lawyer, and used by *The Times* 1909. The linotype produces a slug or solid line of type, but the monotype produces lines comprising separate letters so that alterations can be made without having to re-set the whole line. The process is performed by two machines : (1) a kind of typewriter with keys which cause holes to be punched in a roll of paper ; (2) a casting machine which, guided by this, casts single letters and automatically arranges them in correct order. See PRINTING

Monro, HAROLD, *mŭn-rō'* (1879–1932), English poet, *b* Brussels ; responsible for the *Georgian Poetry* series (edited by Edward Marsh).

Monroe, JAMES (1758–1831), American statesman, *b* Virginia, of which he was twice governor ; elected President of the USA 1816, and again 1820 ; famous for the ' MONROE DOCTRINE,' i.e. no outside interference in the affairs of N. and S. America. See TRUMAN, HARRY S.

Mons, town, Belgium ; noted for mining ; scene of the first and last battles of World War I ; pop.25,000.

Mons Esquilinus, see ESQUILINE HILL

monsoon, see ATMOSPHERE ; INDIA

Monster Petition, see CHARTISM

Montagu, LADY MARY WORTLEY (1689–1762), married Edward Montagu, ambassador at Constantinople 1712. Beautiful and accomplished, she is famous for her vivid letters, full of satire and wit. These are descriptive of travels in Europe, Asia and Africa, and especially Turkey.

Montaigne, MICHEL EYQUEM DE, *mon-tăn'* (1533–92), French essayist, born at the Château de Montaigne in Périgord ; inherited his father's estates, where he built a tower, and there, among his books and in privacy, wrote his immortal *Essays.* Among the greatest ever penned, they are racy and full of learning, giving us word-pictures of himself, a kindly and thoughtful onlooker of the bitter strife of his day.

Of his *Essays* Montaigne writes : *Comme quelqu'un pourroit dire de moy, que j'ay seulement faict icy un amas de fleurs estrangieres, n'y ayant fourny du mien que le filet à les lier,* i.e. As one might say of me that I have only made here a collection of other people's flowers, having provided nothing of my own but the cord to bind them together.

Montana, state of USA bordered by Canada ; is rich in copper, coal, lead, silver and petroleum ; cap. Helena.

Mont Blanc, *mŏn blän' (white mt.),* highest peak of the Alps, 15,782ft. At present a tunnel for vehicular traffic is being bored. It will be 7½m long, and will link France and Italy.

Montcalm, LOUIS JOSEPH, *mont-käm'* (1712–59), French soldier, born near Nîmes ; appointed 1756 in command of French forces in Canada ; defended Fort Ticonderoga against the British, but defeated and mortally wounded at Quebec during the fight against General Wolfe.

Mont Cenis, *mon se-nē',* mt. (11,755ft)

between France and Italy ; with a pass (*c.*7,000ft high) ; and a tunnel 7¾m, opened 1871.

Monte Carlo, see MONACO

Monte Cassino, *mŏn'tä kä-sē'nō,* monastery, 45m north-west of Naples, Italy ; founded by St Benedict, AD529 ; scene of fierce fighting in World War II.

Monte Cristo, *-krēs'tō,* Italian island, 26m south of Elba ; immortalised by Dumas (père) in *The Count of Monte Cristo.*

Montenegro, see YUGOSLAVIA

Monte Rosa, mt. between Italy and Switzerland ; 15,217ft.

Montesquieu, BARON DE, *mon-tes-kū'* (1689–1755), French writer ; inherited wealth from his uncle ; ordered his estates on the lines of an English landlord. He is notable for his book *Esprit des Lois* (Spirit of Laws) which greatly influenced political and social thought in the 18th c.

Montessori, MARIA, *mon-tes-sō'rē* (1870–), Italian educationist ; author of *The Montessori System,* a method largely based on a sense of touch.

Montevideo, *mon-tē-vid'ē-ō* ; *mon-tē-vidä'ō,* cap. Uruguay ; pop.770,000 ; has a fine harbour ; exports meat (packed and frozen), wool, hides and eggs.

Montezuma, name of two Aztec rulers : Montezuma I, who reigned from 1437, extending the empire ; and Montezuma II (1466–1520), last Aztec ruler of Mexico, killed by his own followers when more or less a prisoner of Cortes.

Montfort, SIMON DE, *mont'fĕrt (d* 1265), statesman, youngest son of the Earl of Leicester ; married the sister of Henry III ; had a great love of justice and strong religious convictions, hence his nickname ' Earl Simon the Righteous.' With the barons, Montfort compelled the king to accept the Provisions of Oxford 1259, but after the Mise of Amiens 1264 he took up arms against Henry, capturing him at Lewes, and (1265) calling a Parliament to which representatives of the towns were sent for the first time. Deserted by many of the barons, he was defeated and killed at Evesham.

Montgolfier, JOSEPH MICHEL (1740–1810), French inventor, who, with his brother Jacques Étienne, was a pioneer in the development of balloons.

Montgomery, BERNARD LAW (1887–), general, born in County Donegal, Ireland. In World War II he drove the Germans out of N. Africa, shared in the liberation of France 1944, and the allied victories against Germany's western front. He believes in 100% physical and mental fitness ; is a teetotaller and a non-smoker, also a devout churchman who reads his Bible daily. He was made a Field-Marshal 1944 ; later Viscount Montgomery of Alamein. Read *Montgomery,* Alan Morehead.

Montgomeryshire, county of N. Wales ; oats are grown and ponies reared. The county offices are at Welshpool.

month, 1/12th of a calendar year ; has 31 days except April, June, Sept. and Nov., which have 30, and Feb. with 28 (but 29 in Leap Year) ; a *lunar month* is sometimes regarded as being 28 days, but the actual length depends on the precise meaning given to the term, e.g. the *synodical month*, i.e. the time taken by the moon to make a complete revolution relative to some point, is 29 days 12 hours 44 minutes 2·8 seconds, and the *tropical month* is 27 days 7 hours 43 minutes 4·7 seconds.

Montpellier, town, France ; 6m north of the Mediterranean ; centre of a winemaking district ; pop.91,000.

Montreal, largest city in Canada ; is on an island in the R. St Lawrence (Quebec), and stands finely on Mt Royal. A great railway centre, it is noted for shipping, its harbour, flour mills and railway engineering ; pop.903,000.

Montrose, port, Angus ; trades with the Baltic ; yarn making, fishing and rope making ; popular holiday resort.

Montrose, JAMES GRAHAM, 1ST MARQUIS OF (1612–50), Scottish soldier ; took part in drawing up the National Covenant 1637. As a supporter of Charles I, led the Scottish clans to several victories, but was defeated by David Leslie at Philiphaugh. After attempting to raise a rebellion 1650, he was hanged. Montrose, a gay, courageous, and brilliant leader, was also a poet, and was styled the ' finest gallant of the realm.' Read his biography by John Buchan.

Montserrat, see LEEWARD ISLANDS

Monument, THE, see LONDON

Moon, see ASTRONOMY

moonstone, colourless semi-precious stone ; actually felspar.

Moore, GEORGE (1852–1933), Irish author with perfection of style and a remarkable mingling of realism and imagination. His books include *The Brook Kerith* (1916) ; *Esther Waters.*

Moore, SIR JOHN (1761–1809), soldier, *b* Glasgow ; adopted a system of light infantry of great use in the Peninsular War, where he was left in supreme command. While assisting the Spaniards against Napoleon's superior forces, he fell back on Corunna, and was killed when his troops were about to embark. His burial is immortalised in Charles Wolfe's poem beginning ' Not a drum was heard.'

Moore, THOMAS (1779–1852), poet, *b* Dublin. His Eastern poem *Lalla Rookh* was immensely popular in his day, but he is best remembered now for his graceful, simple and passionate songs, e.g. *Irish Melodies, National Airs* ; and his life of Byron.

Moore, THOMAS STURGE (1870–1944), English poet, *b* Hastings. A woodcarver, he was also an author of books on art criticism. His *Collected Poems* were published 1932.

moorhen, see WATER HEN

Moors, word generally indicating N.

African peoples whether Arab or Berber. They have been Mohammedans since 647, and from the 8th c. were settled in Spain, where their art and science were in advance of those in the rest of Europe. Their rule in Spain ceased 1492.

moose, largest of the deers ; may stand 7ft and weigh over 1,000lb. Roaming in N. America to the Arctic regions, it has large antlers, travels almost silently through forests, and is hunted for sport and for its flesh.

THE MOOSE

moot, Anglo-Saxon for a meeting of freemen, e.g. folkmoot and shiremoot.

moraines, see GLACIER

moralities, see DRAMA

moratorium, period fixed by law during which a debtor may legally delay payment of a debt ; usually used only in an emergency to avert a financial crisis.

Moravia, *mŏ-rā'viă*, part of Czechoslovakia. See CZECHOSLAVAKIA.

Moravian Church, Protestant Christian sect strongly evangelical and missionary ; has *c*.3,000 members in Britain.

Moray or Elginshire, north-east county of Scotland ; has 32m of coastline on Moray Firth ; co.tn Elgin.

mordant, solution used for fixing dyes in fabrics ; of two kinds (*a*) basic metal hydroxide for acidic dyes ; and (*b*) acidic mordants for basic dyes. See DYES

Mordecai, character in the OT book *Esther* ; discoverer of Haman's plot to destroy the Jews.

More, SIR THOMAS (1478–1535), statesman, author, lawyer, politician, lover of the fine arts, *b* London ; educated at Oxford, where he was caught up by the spirit of the Renaissance, and studied Latin, Greek, French, theology and music. For a time he lived almost as a monk, and wore a hair shirt. An MP

1504, he was knighted 1521 ; regarded favourably by Henry VIII. Appointed Speaker of the House 1523, he succeeded Cardinal Wolsey as Lord Chancellor, but resigned over the question of the king's divorce from Catherine of Aragon. For refusing to acknowledge Henry VIII as head of the Church in England he was sent to the Tower and beheaded.

As an author, More is best remembered for his book *Utopia* (1516), the story of life on an imaginary island with a perfect political organisation. The name comes from two Greek words meaning *nowhere*.

More's eldest daughter, Margaret (1505–44), married William Roper. She was one of the most learned women of her day.

Morecambe, *mör'kam,* holiday town, Lancashire, on Morecambe Bay ; includes Heysham ; combined pop.37,000.

morganatic marriage, union of a member of a royal or princely family with some person of lower rank.

Morland, GEORGE (1763–1804), artist, *b* London ; particularly noted for his country scenes, e.g. *The Inside of a Stable.*

Morley, woollen manufacturing town, W. Yorkshire ; pop.36,000.

Morley, VISCOUNT (1838–1923), Liberal author and statesman, *b* Blackburn, Lancashire ; writer of fine studies of Burke, Rousseau, Voltaire, Cobden and Cromwell. He was Liberal MP for Newcastle-on-Tyne 1883 ; became Chief Secretary for Ireland ; had much to do with Gladstone's Home Rule Bill ; and was Secretary of State for India 1905–10. As an author, he excelled in his *Life of Gladstone* and his *Recollections* ; as a statesman he was responsible with Lord Minto for the Minto-Morley reforms in India, leading towards self-government.

Mormons, popular name for a sect founded USA by Joseph Smith (1805–44), author of *The Book of Mormon,* which, he claimed, had been revealed to him in a vision. The sect now numbers *c.*600,000.

Morocco, country, NW. Africa ; total area *c.*183,000sq.m, pop.7,500,000, the nominal ruler since 1927 being Sultan Sidi Mohammed.

Morocco comprises three zones : Tangier (an international zone) ; a Spanish zone (cap. Tetuan) ; and a French zone (cap. Marrakesh). The chief products include cereals, many kinds of seeds (e.g. linseed), fruits, cork, iron, phosphates, and especially Morocco leather and eggs. To these gypsum and petroleum may soon be added.

morphine, *mör'fēn,* though styled ' God's own medicine ' by Dr William Osler because of its merciful relief of pain, morphine, an alkaloid found in opium, may soon be replaced by DEMEROL, discovered 1939 by two German doctors.

Morris, WILLIAM (1834–96), poet and lover of beauty, *b* Walthamstow ; inherited a comfortable income. With Burne-Jones and Rossetti he helped to develop the ' Pre-Raphaelite ' style in art.

In attempting to furnish his home (Red House, Bexley Heath) he began a campaign for producing more beautiful furniture, wall-papers and crockery. He wrote poetry, e.g. his epic *The Life and Death of Jason* ; *The Earthly Paradise,* etc. ; founded the Kelmscott Press for printing beautiful books ; became a Socialist ; opposed Capital because it meant mass-production, and mass-production meant that the worker had no joy in his work ; lived solely (as he said) to make the earth a happy and beautiful place.

Morris dance, country dance possibly borrowed from the Moors of Spain ; popular in Tudor England, especially for May Day celebrations. The lilting tunes are usually in two-four or four-four time.

Morrison, HERBERT (1888–   ), English politician. From errand boy, shop assistant, he became Labour MP 1923 ; chairman of the National Labour Party 1929 ; Home Secretary 1940 ; Lord President of the Council 1945.

Morse, SAMUEL FINLEY BREESE (1791–1872), born in Massachusetts, USA ; first a portrait painter ; later devoted himself to perfecting the electric telegraph, succeeding 1844 in sending the message by wire from Washington to Baltimore : *What hath God wrought?* He invented the Morse code:—

mortar, mixture of clean sand, freshly burned lime or cement, and water. Plaster is slaked lime mixed with sand. Plaster of Paris (sometimes added to ordinary plaster for walls and ceilings) is a form of calcium sulphate, and is made by heating gypsum to *c.*120°C and adding water. It is so named because gypsum is found in large quantities near Paris.

mortgage, *mör'gij,* method of borrowing money. The borrower (*mortgagor*) by deed conveys his property to the lender (*mortgagee*), and agrees to pay back the sum advanced (with interest) in a stated time. If he fails, the mortgagee may sell the property to recover the amount of the money he lent, and any interest which is owing on it. If a borrower repays the money, the lender by deed re-conveys the property to him.

Mortimer's Cross, battle of the Wars of the Roses, fought 1461 in Herefordshire, the Yorkists winning.

Mortlake, parish, Surrey, close to Richmond ; noted as the finish of the annual Oxford and Cambridge boat race on the R. Thames ; pop.24,000.

mortmain (French *mort,* dead ; *main,* hand), legal term for lands that had passed into the possession of corporations or (especially in feudal times) of the Church, and had thus ceased to be liable for Death Duties, as the owner never died. The *Statute of Mortmain* 1279 forbade bequests of this kind.

Morton, HENRY VOLLAM (1892–), British author ; noted for his books on London ; also his series *In Search of England* ; *In Search of Scotland* ; *In Search of Ireland* ; *In Search of Wales* ; *In Search of South Africa* ; also *In the Steps of the Master* ; *In the Steps of St Paul.*

Moscow, *mos'kō,* city, USSR. Anciently the cap., it gave place 1703 to St Petersburg (now Leningrad), but became the cap. again 1918. On the R. Moskva it has the Kremlin, an old, grim, palace of the czars, now the HQ of the Soviet government, and is noted also for its great churches. Like London, Moscow has an underground railway. The manufactures include textiles, leather goods, chemicals and machinery.

In the famous Red Square is the tomb of Lenin, whose embalmed body lies in a glass case. Since 1932 the building of the Palace of the Soviets has continued, a vast pile that will eventually be the tallest building in the world, rising 1,365ft, including a stainless steel statue of Lenin 325ft high.

Rebuilding the city on modern lines began 1935, many buildings being moved overnight, e.g. number 24 Gorki Street, weighing 23,000 tons, was moved 150ft. Flats are a feature of the city. The people of Moscow burnt the city 1812 to defeat Napoleon, and in World War II the Germans almost captured it. The pop. is estimated at 4,500,000.

Moscow Agreement, THE, international agreement arrived at in an eleven-day conference at Moscow, Dec 1945, which dealt, among other things, with the preparation of peace treaties after World War II ; Far-Eastern questions ; an Allied Council for Japan ; and the establishment of a UNO commission for the control of atomic energy.

Moscow Declarations, THE, agreement reached 1943 that the USSR and USA were united in their combined effort to defeat Germany.

Moselle, *mō-zel',* river of France ; flows 320m from the Vosges through Lorraine and Germany to the Rhine. The river gives its name to a wine.

Moses, law-giver and leader of the Jews *c.*1250BC : younger brother of Aaron. Hidden as a baby among bulrushes by the Nile, he was adopted by Pharaoh's daughter. Having killed an Egyptian taskmaster he fled into Midian, but returned to lead the Israelites out of slavery in Egypt. He guided them forty years in the desert, but died without entering the Promised Land (Palestine). To him we owe the Ten Commandments.

Moslem League, see INDIA

Mosley, SIR OSWALD, *mō'zli* (1896–), English politician. At first a Conservative MP, he became an Independent, and later led the British Blackshirts, a body similar to Mussolini's Fascists. He was imprisoned during the early years of World War II.

mosque, *mosk,* Mohammedan place of worship, usually with a central dome and several minarets, a court and a lake for ceremonial washing. Within are carpets but no seats, and a niche indicating the direction of Mecca.

mosquito, *mŭs-kē'tō,* winged insect of the gnat family. Some twenty kinds are found in Britain. The egg is laid in stagnant water, and the creature does not leave the water till it becomes a perfect insect. The female attacks human beings by sucking the blood, and is dangerous because it may leave behind germs of yellow fever, or malaria, sometimes called intermittent fever or ague. Dr Walter Reed (1851–1902) of USA discovered that yellow fever is due to the mosquito *Stegomyia fasciata* ; other pioneers were William Gorgas, Jesse Lazear, and Carlos Finlay (*d* 1915). Sir Ronald Ross (1857–1932), a British doctor, traced malaria to the mosquito

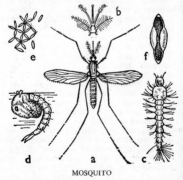

MOSQUITO

The malaria-carrying Anopheles : (a) *the female* (b) *head of the male* (c) *the larva* (d) *the pupa* (e) *the egg mass* (f) *the egg*

anopheles. Oil is now poured on pools and marshes in tropical countries, thus imprisoning the mosquito larvae, and greatly reducing the menace of disease.

Malaria, at one time the cause of 3,000,000 deaths a year, was formerly treated with doses of quinine ; later, atebrin, known also as mepacrine, was used ; but since 1945 paludrine has been the world's most potent remedy.

A still more recent remedy is chloroquine, the activity of which is three times that of mepacrine. In 1947 the discovery of pentaquine (SN 13,276) was announced. It is believed to be a positive cure for malaria.

mosses, elementary class of flowerless plants comprising, with liverworts, the class Bryophyta. They reproduce by means of spores, and contain green colouring matter (chlorophyll). One of the most useful mosses is sphagnum or bog-moss, recently found to be valuable in the treatment of flesh wounds.

Mosul, *mō'sool,* town, Iraq ; faces the ruins of Nineveh across the R. Tigris ; has oil-wells and a pipeline to Haifa ; pop.260,000.

Motherwell, town, Lanarkshire ; noted for coal mines and engineering works ; pop. *c.*68,000.

moths, see BUTTERFLIES AND MOTHS

Motley, JOHN LOTHROP (1814–77), American historian, *b* Dorchester, Massachusetts, USA, *d* Dorchester, England ; author of two famous books, *Rise of the Dutch Republic* (1856) and *History of the United Netherlands.*

motor-car, see INTERNAL COMBUSTION ENGINE ; MOTOR VEHICLES

motor vehicles, self-propelled vehicles, usually petrol-driven or run on heavy oil. It was the invention of the internal combustion engine by Daimler 1884 that made the modern car possible.

The use of heavy oil in a type of Diesel engine followed experiments *c.*1928, and now many commercial vehicles (buses and lorries) run on crude oil, which is cheaper than petrol, and gives from 2–3 times the mileage per gallon.

Private cars, using petrol, have been vastly improved in recent years. For the principle of the engine, see INTERNAL COMBUSTION ENGINE. Usually there are four gears ; the synchromesh, working on cone clutches, being one of the latest types. A clutchless and gearless car has been evolved recently, the driving element being a centrifugal pump, the vanes of which control variable speeds.

Moulmein, *mōl-mān',* port, Burma ; exports teak and rice ; pop.65,000.

mountain, elevation of the earth's crust higher than a hill, at least 1,000ft above sea-level. Mountains are due to folding of the earth's crust during cooling, or to volcanic eruptions which build up cones.

MOUNTAINEERING is a thrilling sport, the Alps offering exceptional hazards to adventurous climbers, though Scotland and the English Lake District are by no means to be despised. The British Mountaineering Council was formed 1944 to help lovers of climbing in England, Wales and Scotland, and the secretary, J. E. Q. Barford, has prepared an excellent book, *Climbing in Britain,* dealing with every aspect of mountaineering in these islands. See EVEREST

mountain ash, see ROWAN

Mountbatten of Burma, LOUIS, 1ST EARL (1900–), statesman and naval officer, great-grandson of Queen Victoria ; served in the Navy in World War I, responsible for the reconquest of Burma after Japanese invasion in World War II, and created Earl Mountbatten of Burma 1946 ; succeeded Lord Wavell as last Viceroy of India 1947, and was first Governor-General of the new Dominion.

Mountevans, 1ST BARON (1881–), Admiral, R.N. Joined British Antarctic expedition 1909 ; returned in command of expedition after the death of Captain Scott 1913 ; commanded HMS *Broke* 1917 when that ship with HMS *Swift* engaged and defeated six German destroyers. Became London Regional Commissioner for Civil Defence 1939. Author of *Adventurous Life* (1946).

Mount Vernon, estate, Virginia, USA. Here, near the R. Potomac, is George Washington's home and grave.

mouse, small rodent of which three species are found in Britain : (*a*) house mouse (*Mus musculus*), brown, with long ears, is 4–5in long including the tail ; (*b*) harvest mouse, one of our smallest mammals, and the only one with a tail used for holding on to grasses, etc. when climbing ; is orange-brown above, white below ; builds a round nest in standing corn ; (*c*) long-tailed field mouse, much like the house mouse, but with a longer tail. See DORMOUSE

Mozambique, see PORTUGAL

Mozart, WOLFGANG AMADEUS, *mō'tsärt* (1756–91), celebrated German-Austrian musician, *b* Salzburg (Austria). Greatly interested in music when only three ; made a musical tour (playing the harpsichord) at six, and a second at seven, when he played his own compositions on the violin and organ, amazing both Paris and London. He wrote his first oratorio when only ten, and received his composer's degree at fourteen. Mozart married, 1782, but his wife was a poor housekeeper, and he himself was careless and too generous. His sharp tongue made him many enemies, and he lived in poverty. He died when only thirty-five, and was buried in a pauper's grave.

One of the world's most astonishing musical geniuses, Mozart excelled in almost every kind of composition. His 626 works include piano concertos, church music, chamber music, string quartets (notably his G minor), 41 symphonies, e.g. the *Jupiter* symphony, and many operas, e.g. *The Magic Flute, The Marriage of Figaro, Don Giovanni,* etc. His *Requiem Mass* was still unfinished when he died.

MP, short for Member of Parliament. See PARLIAMENT

Mr Speaker, see PARLIAMENT

mu, see LIGHT ; REFRACTIVE INDEX

muezzin, mosque official who, from a minaret, calls Mohammedans to prayer five times a day.

Mukden, *mook-den'*, chief town, N.E. China ; pop.863,000.

mulberry, tree or shrub with heart-shaped leaves and spikes of greenish-white, wind-fertilised flowers. The fruit, in appearance rather like the raspberry, may be black, white or red. Silkworms feed on the leaves.

Mulberry Harbour, see D-DAY ; WORLD WAR II

mule, machine used for mechanical spinning. Invented 1779 by Samuel Crompton, it is used especially in the cotton industry.

mule, see HORSE

Mülheim, *mūl'hīm*, town, Germany, on the R. Rhur ; pop.137,000.

Mull, island of the Inner Hebrides ; has rocky coasts and rugged mts. ; only town Tobermory. Off the Ross of Mull (its SW. promontory) lies Iona, where St Columba landed. In Tobermory Bay lies a wreck of the Spanish Armada.

Mullah, *mŭl'ä*, Mohammedan law-expert. The so-called ' mad Mullahs ' were fanatics who led risings against the British in India 1897–98, and in Somaliland 1899–1910.

mulligatawny, *mŭli-gä-taw'ni*, soup made with curry powder, boiled fowl or meat, and rice.

Multilateral School, see EDUCATION

Multiple Proportions, see CHEMISTRY

multiple stores, see SHOP

multiplication, actually a quick method of adding ; the number multiplied is the *multiplicand* ; the result of multiplying is the *product*. See table below.

Mumbles, district of Glamorganshire ;

includes Mumbles Head and the village of Mumbles. Oystermouth stands on Swansea Bay. The Mumbles lifeboat has rendered conspicuous service.

mummy, see EMBALMING

mumps, contagious disease causing a swelling of the salivary glands, etc. It is painful in the early stages, but one attack usually gives immunity.

Münchhausen, BARON VON, *mungch'hau-zen* (1720–97), German cavalry officer about whom impossibly wonderful tales were told.

mungo, short, fine woollen fibre made from rags and cloth-cuttings. See SHODDY

Munich, *mū'nich*, cap., Bavaria (Germany) ; on the R. Isar ; pop.761,000 ; long famous for its handsome buildings, and as a centre of culture ; noted for stained glass and scientific instruments. Here the Nazi programme may be said to have originated, and here (1938) a conference was held at which Hitler insisted on including the Sudeten region (Czechoslovakia) in the Reich, promising to make no further demands. Munich was severely bombed during World War II. See CHAMBERLAIN, NEVILLE

Munster, one of the four provinces of Eire.

Münster, *mŭn'stĕr*, manufacturing town, Germany ; pop.143,000.

Munthe, AXEL, *moon'te* (1857–1949), Swedish doctor and writer ; practised in Paris and Rome ; retired to the I. of Capri, where he wrote several books, the most famous being *The Story of San Michele*, 1929.

Murcia, *mŭr'shi-ä*, city, Spain ; pop. 205,000 ; noted for rearing silk-worms.

Murdock, WILLIAM (1754–1839), Scottish inventor, born in Ayrshire ; became assistant to James Watt ; remembered as a pioneer in gas-lighting. See COAL-GAS ; LIGHTING

Murillo, BARTOLOMÉ ESTEBAN, *mū-ril'ō* (1617–82), Spanish painter, *b* Seville ; died from a fall while painting an altarpiece in Cadiz ; notable for religious pictures and scenes of everyday life.

MULTIPLICATION TABLE

times	2	3	4	5	6	7	8	9	10	11	12	13	14	15	16	17	18	19
2 is	4	6	8	10	12	14	16	18	20	22	24	26	28	30	32	34	36	38
3 is	6	9	12	15	18	21	24	27	30	33	36	39	42	45	48	51	54	57
4 is	8	12	16	20	24	28	32	36	40	44	48	52	56	60	64	68	72	76
5 is	10	15	20	25	30	35	40	45	50	55	60	65	70	75	80	85	90	95
6 is	12	18	24	30	36	42	48	54	60	66	72	78	84	90	96	102	108	114
7 is	14	21	28	35	42	49	56	63	70	77	84	91	98	105	112	119	126	133
8 is	16	24	32	40	48	56	64	72	80	88	96	104	112	120	128	136	144	152
9 is	18	27	36	45	54	63	72	81	90	99	108	117	126	135	144	153	162	171
10 is	20	30	40	50	60	70	80	90	100	110	120	130	140	150	160	170	180	190
11 is	22	33	44	55	66	77	88	99	110	121	132	143	154	165	176	187	198	209
12 is	24	36	48	60	72	84	96	108	120	132	144	156	168	180	192	204	216	228
13 is	26	39	52	65	78	91	104	117	130	143	156	169	182	195	208	221	234	247
14 is	28	42	56	70	84	98	112	126	140	154	168	182	196	210	224	238	252	266
15 is	30	45	60	75	90	105	120	135	150	165	180	195	210	225	240	255	270	285
16 is	32	48	64	80	96	112	128	144	160	176	192	208	224	240	256	272	288	304
17 is	34	51	68	85	102	119	136	153	170	187	204	221	238	255	272	289	306	323
18 is	36	54	72	90	108	126	144	162	180	198	216	234	252	270	288	306	324	342
19 is	38	57	76	95	114	133	152	171	190	209	228	247	266	285	304	323	342	361

Murman, *moor-män'*, *c*.200m of the north coast of the Kola Peninsula, Russian Lapland. MURMANSK, with an ice-free port, is the terminus of the Murmansk railway ; pop.120.000. In World War II British and American ships, at great hazard, landed supplies here for Russia.

Murray, *mŭr'i*, river of South Australia. Of its 1,250m some 1,200m form the boundary between New S. Wales and Victoria. It is the continent's most important waterway.

Murray, PROFESSOR GILBERT (1866–), British scholar, son of an Australian statesman, *b* Sydney, New S. Wales ; regius professor of Greek at Oxford ; noted for his verse translations of various Greek plays by Euripides, Sophocles, Aeschylus ; author of *A History of Ancient Greek Literature*, and also of books on modern politics.
Read *Greek Studies*.

Murray, SIR JAMES AUGUSTUS HENRY (1837–1915), Scottish scholar, born in Roxburghshire ; editor of the *Oxford English Dictionary*.

Murrumbidgee, tributary of the R. Murray ; flows 1,350m in New S. Wales.

Murry, JOHN MIDDLETON (1889–), author and literary critic, *b* London.

Muscat, only port of a region of Arabia (Muscat and Oman) ; pop.20,000.

Muscat and Oman, see ARABIA

muscatel, kind of grape ; also a sweet wine.

muscle, elastic body tissue with which (in the higher animals) movement is performed ; is either voluntary, i.e. controlled by the will, or involuntary. Voluntary muscles, attached to bones by tendons, comprise fibres about 1in long and 0·002in in diameter. When stimulated by a nerve they contract. Involuntary muscles include the heart, muscles of the stomach, intestines, bladder, all under the control of the sympathetic ganglia.

Muscovy, old name for Russia.

Muses, in old Greek tales, daughters of Zeus who presided over the arts, e.g. Clio, muse of history ; Calliope, of epic poetry.

museums, LONDON, see LONDON

mushroom, see FUNGUS

music, form of self-expression closely related to dancing, poetry and drama ; named from the nine muses of Greek mythology. It is perhaps the oldest of all the arts, since we can scarcely imagine a time when some form of singing or rhythm was unknown to primitive man, but it is also an art which has developed more recently than most others.

Music is a combination of (*a*) tones, (*b*) rhythm. It exists as an art the world over, but music as we now know it began in Europe in the Middle Ages, a development of simple Greek melodies and of the elementary diatonic scale (or modes). Starting with plain-song in the RC Church, it was elaborated by combining two or more melodies which could be sung together, and this gave rise to the highly diversified method of counter-

point in vocal and instrumental writing (1500–1700). Vocal melodies were elaborated in the madrigal ; instrumental music developed into pieces for combinations of wood-wind, stringed, brass (e.g. trumpets), and percussion instruments, as employed in orchestras. At the same time we find dance tunes and songs *outside* the Church, from which instrumental music was developed for its own sake, hence the suite, sonata or symphony. After the time of Bach the emphasis was on harmony rather than on counterpoint, and instrumental music became still more elaborate. Sonatas, quartets, concertos, symphonies were composed by the great ' classical ' exponents of form, e.g. Haydn, Mozart and Beethoven, and some of the world's best operas were written during this period.

From Beethoven onwards music tended to become more emotional and individualistic in the hands of the Romantics, e.g. Schumann, Chopin, Berlioz and Liszt ; and Wagner revolutionised the opera. Programme music later became highly popular, and at the beginning of the 20th c. Schönberg broke away from tradition by abandoning the usual key-system. Other less startling experimenters included Delius.

The music of the 20th c. sometimes differs in many ways from that of preceding centuries. There has been a revival of primitive musical forms (jazz) ; swing music (so called *c*.1935), i.e. a phase of jazz with a simple harmonic basis and a melodic theme above. Like all forms of jazz, this type gives great possibilities of improvisation, so that musicians have much freedom for impromptu flourishes and variations, a type much played by dance-bands. Modern music has complexities and forms evolved by highly skilled pioneers, and shows many changes due to improvements or inventions of instruments. Thus the church organ has its variation, the cinema organ, with its wide range of ' effects ' ; the Hammond (electric) organ gives great possibilities ; the saxophone and ukelele (a form of guitar) are much in evidence ; also electric and ether-wave instruments, e.g. thermin and trautonium.

It should be noted that music has reached the masses this century as never before, owing to radio broadcasts and sound-films, for many of which music is specially written ; hence greater technical skill on the part of the rank and file of musicians is required, and possibly there is more critical listening on the part of music-lovers, though this is open to question.

Notable musicians include Bach, Beethoven, Brahms, Chopin, Debussy, Delius, Elgar, Gounod, Grieg, Handel, Haydn, Liszt, Mendelssohn, Mozart, Palestrina, Rimsky-Korsakov, Rossini, Schubert, Schumann, Sibelius, Strauss, Stravinsky, Tchaikovsky, Verdi and

Wagner. To these we may add the names of such modern musicians as Vaughan Williams, Benjamin Britten, Michael Tippett, Arnold Bax, Shostakovitch, Prokofiev and William Walton.

The lives of the great composers are told briefly in a series of Pelican books *You and Music*. A useful book is *Music in England*, Eric Blom. *Stories of Great Music*, John Horton, is an excellent introduction to many famous works ; and there is also *The Pursuit of Music*, by Sir Walford Davies. As an introduction to music and singing, *Youth and Music*, Dr Desmond Macmahon, is useful, especially for those who wish to organise the musical side of Youth Clubs. It includes a chapter on jazz and swing.

Youth community song books include those published by Boosey and Hawkes Ltd, who also publish books of instruction for the playing of various instruments, e.g. violin, trumpet and drums. There is also *The National Youth Song Book*, edited by Dr Desmond Macmahon; and for all details of musicians, instruments, musical terms, etc., consult *The Oxford Companion to Music*, Percy A. Scholes, or *Everyman's Dictionary of Music*, Eric Blom.

For advice as to music as a career, apply to a music teacher, or write to the secretary, Royal Academy of Music ; the Royal College of Music, or the Royal Scottish Academy of Music.

The following are some of the commoner terms, signs and abbreviations, used in music :

accelerando, becoming gradually quicker

adagio, slow

andante, moderately slow or graceful ; literally ' going '

animato, i.e. animated, with spirit

a tempo, in time. Common time is shown as 𝄴 i.e. four crochets to the bar, or 𝄵 two minims to the bar

clef, sign at the beginning of a stave showing the position of middle C,

e.g. 𝄞 G, or treble clef ;

 𝄢 F or bass clef

crescendo, written ◁ , gradually increase in tone

DC, i.e. *da capo* (from the beginning) ; hence the player returns to the beginning of the movement till he comes to the double bar marked *Fine*

decrescendo, written ▷ , i.e. becoming softer

diminuendo (*dim.*) gradually decreasing in tone

flat, written ♭, lowers the pitch of a note by a semitone

forte (*f.*), loudly or strongly

forte-piano (*f.p.*), loud, then soft

fortissimo (*ff.*), very loud

legato (*leg.*), smoothly ; opposite of the *staccato* style (shown by a dot above

or below the note, e.g. ♪♪), showing that the notes are to be detached from one another

loco (*lo.*) i.e. return to the proper pitch after having played an octave higher or lower

mezzo-forte (*mf.*) moderately loud

mezzo-piano (*mp.*), moderately soft

natural (written ♮), restores a note that has been sharpened or flattened to its original pitch

octave, written commonly 8va, and may indicate (*alta*) that the music is to be played an octave higher, or (*bassa*) an octave lower

piano (*p.*), softly

piano-forte (*pf.*), soft, then loud

pianissimo (*pp.*), very softly

pianississimo (*ppp.*), as softly as possible

rallentando (*rall.*), gradually slower

repeat (indicated thus ‖: or thus :‖ and placed at the beginning and end of a passage, means that the portion so marked is to be played again

rest, i.e. a pause, written thus if the value of a semibreve ▬ , this also indicates a whole bar's rest ; thus for the value of a minim ▬ , and hence ⌐ = crochet ⌐ = a quaver ⌐ = a semiquaver and ⌐ = a demisemiquaver. The sign ⌢ over a note or rest indicates that it is to be held longer than its normal length ; placed over a double bar it means : conclude after a repeat

sharp, written ♯ , raises the pitch of a note a semitone

slur, written ⌢ , i.e. play the notes in a smooth (*legato*) manner

tie, written ⌢ or ⌐ , i.e. play the notes below as one

tremolando (*trem.*), in a trembling manner

See JAZZ ; OP. ; SOUND ; YOUTH ORGANISATIONS

musk, plant (family *Scrophulariaceae*) cultivated in greenhouses in Britain ; has yellow flowers and soft-haired leaves that formerly gave a peculiar fragrance but now, for some unknown reason, rarely (if ever) do so.

musk deer, greyish-brown deer, *c.*20in high, found in Central Asia ; hunted for musk, a substance taken from its stomach glands, and used in making perfumes.

musk-ox, shaggy ox with brown hair and flattened horns ; roams over the extreme north of Canada.

musk rat, animal akin to the mole and shrew. From 10–16in long, it has webbed feet and valuable fur ; found in Russia and the Pyrenees.

Muslim League, see INDIA

muslin, fine cotton fabric used for dresses and curtains ; largely made in India.

musquash, N. American animal akin to the beaver ; trapped for its fur ; lives much in water, and has partly-webbed hind feet.

Musselburgh, *mŭs'l-bŭ-rŭ,* town, Midlothian, practically a suburb of Edinburgh.

Musset, ALFRED DE, *mŭss-ā'* (1810–57), French poet, dramatist, and story-writer, *b* Paris ; was passionate and witty. His poems include the lyrical *Les Nuits* ; and among his plays are *Un Caprice* and *Les Caprices de Marianne,* his greatest comedy.

Mussolini, BENITO, *moos-sō-lē'nē* (1883–1945), Prime Minister and Duce (or Dictator) of Fascist Italy 1922–43. A blacksmith's son, he became a teacher, then a manual worker in Switzerland, where he organised strikes. In Italy he identified himself with an anti-Bolshevist movement ; joined the Socialist Society ; founded *Il popolo d'Italia* ; fought in World War I ; built up the Fascist party, which, growing powerful in the disordered country after 1918, marched on Rome 1922, the King (Victor Emmanuel) inviting Mussolini to become Premier and Dictator.

Having secured supreme power, Mussolini united Italy in a remarkable way ; he extinguished opposition, strengthened the central government, encouraged trade, carried out some social reforms, and began the rebuilding of wide areas of Rome 1932. His efforts to solve the problem of unemployment led to rearmament and to an attempt to build up a colonial Empire. Mussolini attacked and conquered Abyssinia 1935–36 ; in 1937 sent Italian troops to Spain to help Franco, the Fascist leader, to overthrow the democratically elected Spanish government. Meanwhile he had allied himself with Hitler. He was present at the Munich conference 1938. At Easter 1939 he invaded Albania. After the collapse of French resistance 1940 he declared war on France and Britain. In October 1940 he attacked Greece. In the end he failed miserably as Hitler's ally ; resigned office 1943, and was executed by Partisans.

Mustafa Kemal, *ke-mäl'* (1880–1938), Turkish statesman, *b* Salonica ; succeeded after World War I in recovering lost territory for Turkey ; formed a republic 1923 after abolishing the sultanate. He abolished the caliphate 1924, and set about modernising the country on Western lines.

mustang, see HORSE

mustard, name of various plants, including the British species, black, white and wild mustard (charlock). The mustard of

MUSSOLINI 1883–1945

commerce is a blending of the seeds of the black and white varieties coloured with turmeric.

Mutiny of the ' Bounty,' see ' BOUNTY '

Mycenae, see AEGEAN CIVILISATION

Myers, ELIZABETH (1912–47), novelist, *b* Manchester ; author of *A Well Full of Leaves,* etc.

myopia, see EYE

Myrmidons, *mŭr'mi-dons,* in old Greek tales, soldiers who gave unquestioning obedience to Achilles.

Myron, Greek sculptor of the 5th c. BC ; among his famous works is the *Discobolus.*

myrrh, *mŭr,* gum resin oozing from a small tree of Arabia and Abyssinia ; used as a medicine and perfume. It was one of the gifts of the Wise Men to the child Jesus.

myrtle, *mŭr'tl,* evergreen shrub, native of W. Asia ; introduced into Britain 1597 ; has bright oval opposite leaves, fragrant white flowers, and purple berries.

Mysore, *mī-sōr',* native state of the Deccan, India ; cap. Mysore, with pop.151,000.

mystery plays, see DRAMA

myth, *mith,* story handed down by word of mouth from ancient times ; usually about the adventures of gods or goddesses or of some hero ; often providing what was once regarded as an explanation of natural phenomena, e.g. the myth of Persephone ' explains ' why flowers fade in autumn on the assumption that they are mourning her departure to the underworld. All races have their myths, those of the ancient Greeks, Romans, Egyptians, Scandinavians and Celts being some of the most fascinating.

N

N, chemical symbol for nitrogen.

Na, chemical symbol for sodium ; Latin *natrium*.

Naaman, *nā'ä-man*, Syrian general of whom we read in the OT that he was cured of leprosy by Elisha (2 Kings 5).

nabob, *nā'bob*, title of a native ruler, or a person of rank, in India.

Naboth, *nā'both*, OT character ; executed by the orders of Jezebel, wife of King Ahab, because he refused to part with his vineyard (1 Kings 21).

Nabulus, see SHECHEM

Nagasaki, port, Kyushu, Japan ; pop., 1940, *c*.212,000. The city was destroyed by an atom-bomb, 9 Aug 1945.

Nagoya, town, Honshu, Japan ; pop. 1,328,000 ; manufactures silk and cotton goods, also clockwork.

Nagpur, *näg'poor*, chief city, Central Provinces and Berar, India ; pop. 302,000 ; serves the cotton area of the Deccan.

Nahum, *nā'hŭm*, OT prophet who, in the 7th c. BC, prophesied the fall of Nineveh.

Nairn, county of Scotland ; has a coastline on Moray Firth ; co.tn Nairn.

Nairobi, *nī-rō'bē*, town and cap. Kenya ; on the Kenya-Uganda railway ; coffee is grown in the neighbourhood ; centre for big game shooting ; pop.52,000. See PLATE 11 (*top*)

Namaqualand, region in the north-west of Cape Province ; has poor pasture.

Namur, *nä-mūr'*, city, Belgium ; 35m south-east of Brussels ; pop.32,000.

Nancy, *nän-see*, city, France. 220m east of Paris ; an important railway centre ; pop.121,000.

nankeen, yellowish cotton fabric said to have been first made at Nanking, China.

Nanking, *nan'king*, capital of China after 1928, though Chungking and Hankow became temporary capitals during the war with Japan. Nanking is on the Yangtse-Kiang ; pop.1,700,000. The walls are 20m round. The city is linked by rail with Shanghai (192m).

Nansen, DR FRIDTJOF, *nän'sen* (1861–1930), Norwegian Arctic explorer ; reached lat.86°N by a sledge journey from the *Fram* 1895. He wrote *Farthest North*, one of the most thrilling of all books on Arctic exploration.

Nantes, *nants*, city, France, on an island in the R. Loire ; a port though 35m from the sea ; noted for shipbuilding, and the manufacture of wood pulp ; pop.195,000.

Nantes, EDICT OF, proclamation issued 1598 by Henry IV of France, giving a degree of liberty to the Huguenots (Protestants) ; revoked 1685 by Louis XIV.

naphtha, *naf'thä*, name of a variety of hydrocarbons obtained from paraffin oil,

coal-tar and petroleum ; much used for cleansing and in soap-making.

naphthalene, *-lēn*, white, crystalline solid derived from coal-tar, familiar in the form of moth-balls ; a hydrocarbon, $C_{10}H_8$, it is used in making organic dyes.

Napier, *nā'pē-ěr*, port, North Island, NZ ; damaged by earthquake 1931 ; wool is exported ; pop.21,000.

Napier, SIR CHARLES JAMES (1782–1853), British soldier. In the war against Sind he won a decisive victory at Hyderabad 1844, and is *said* to have cabled a dispatch : *Peccavi* (Latin *I have sinned*).

Napier, JOHN (1550–1617), mathematician, born near Edinburgh ; suggested the present notation for decimals, and invented logarithms.

Napier, ROBERT CORNELIS, 1ST BARON, (1810–90), noted British soldier ; planned the attack on Lucknow during the Indian Mutiny. In the Abyssinian campaign 1867 he successfully stormed Magdala. He was commander-in-chief in India 1870–76.

Naples, *nā'plz*, city and port overlooking the Bay of Naples, west coast of Italy, one of the most beautiful bays in the world. Above is Mt Vesuvius. Exports include wine and olive-oil ; pop.995,000. The Italian proverb *Vedi Napoli, e poi muori*, popularly translated, ' See Naples, and die,' suggests that so beautiful is Naples and its bay that we ought not to die without seeing it.

napoleon, former French gold coin issued by Napoleon I ; worth *c*.15s 10d.

Napoleon Bonaparte, *nä-pō'lē-ŭn bō'nä-pärt* ; *-bau-nä-pär'tä*, (1769–1821), Emperor of the French, known as Napoleon I ; *b* Ajaccio, Corsica, of an old Italian family ; was a lieutenant in an artillery regiment when only sixteen ; lived in France, and during the French Revolution showed his military genius at the siege of Toulon, compelling the British and Spanish to withdraw. He also helped to defeat the Austrians.

A born leader of men, Napoleon became the idol of his French soldiers. After marrying Josephine de Beauharnais, he was given command (1796) of the French army in Italy, his success there astonishing and alarming all Europe. Few leaders had ever moved armies so swiftly or taken such risks. By 1797 he had beaten the Italians and Austrians, triumphs that made him the greatest figure in France. He returned to Paris as the hero of the hour, bringing priceless treasures (pictures, statues, jewels) for the French museums and art galleries.

In control of the Directory, Napoleon built a strong and ambitious France. He dreamed of conquering Europe and

NAPOLEON 1769–1821

establishing an empire in Africa and
Asia. The French fleet sailed 1798 from
Toulon for the invasion of Egypt, where
Napoleon defeated the Egyptians at the
battle of the Pyramids, compelled Cairo
to surrender, and began to establish an
outpost of the new French empire.
But his plans were frustrated by Lord
Nelson, who destroyed the French fleet
at the battle of the Nile, thus cutting off
Napoleon's supplies.

Returning to France, Napoleon reorganised French affairs, crossed the
Alps, marched into Italy, captured
Milan, defeated rebellious Austrians at
Marengo (1800), was proclaimed Emperor 1804, and crowned himself in
Notre Dame, Paris. He made his
brothers kings of the countries he had
conquered. Picking a quarrel with
Britain, which he described as ' a nation
of shopkeepers,' he boastfully declared
that he would invade the country. This
he was prevented from doing by Lord
Nelson, who scattered the French fleet
at Trafalgar 1805.

Virtually a dictator, Napoleon bullied
smaller nations, imprisoned the pope,
crushed Austria at the battle of Austerlitz, conquered Prussia by a victory at
Jena 1806, and defeated Russia ; but in
doing all this he made many formidable
enemies, hence Spain dared to revolt,
and with British help, fought the
Peninsular War. Austria again rebelled
1809. Determined to starve us into submission, Napoleon planned what was
called the Continental System, by which
he forbade trade between European
countries and Britain. He persuaded
the Tsar of Russia (Alexander I) to be
a party to this arrangement, but eventually the Tsar declared that he would
trade with Britain (1810), whereupon
Napoleon invaded Russia, reached
Moscow, and began the terrible retreat
of 1812, only c.1,000 of his Grand Army
of 600,000 surviving the ordeal.

Prussia and Austria defeated Napoleon
at Leipzig, and he was eventually compelled to abdicate 1814, being banished
to the island of Elba. Making a dramatic
escape, March 1815, he landed in France,
gathered a new army, and began the
stirring Hundred Days, ending in June,
when he was finally defeated by Wellington and Blücher at Waterloo. He was
banished to St Helena, where he died,
being buried (1840) in the Hôtel des
Invalides, Paris.

Napoleon's brothers included JOSEPH
(1768–1844), King of Spain 1808 ;
LUCIEN (1775–1840), made an Italian
count ; LOUIS (1778–1846), King of
Holland 1806 ; JEROME (1784–1860),
King of Westphalia (part of Germany).

Napoleon I had one child, FRANCIS
CHARLES (1811–32), Duke of Reichstadt,
King of Rome and known as Napoleon
II. The child's mother was Napoleon's
second wife, Marie Louise.

NAPOLEON III (1808–73), son of Louis
Bonaparte, became emperor 1852 ;
lived in recklessly magnificent style ;
gave up the throne after the French had
been defeated in the Franco-Prussian
War, and found refuge in England,
where he died.

Napoleon III, see NAPOLEON BONAPARTE

Narcissus, in old Greek tales, a beautiful
youth, for love of whom Echo pined
away. Narcissus, in love with his own
reflections was changed into a flower,
the narcissus.

narcissus, genus of bulbous plants (family
Amaryllidaceae) including the daffodil,
jonquil ; all much cultivated by gardeners.

Nares, SIR GEORGE, see POLAR REGIONS

Narvik, ice-free port, NE. Norway ; scene
of fierce attacks by British shipping
against the Germans 1940.

narwhal, see WHALE

Naseby, village, Northamptonshire ; scene
1645 of a Parliamentary victory over the
Royalists.

Nash, PAUL (1889–1946), water-colour
artist ; notable for his pictures of World
War I and World War II.

Nash, RICHARD (1674–1762), man of
fashion, better known as Beau Nash.
A notorious gambler, he was the lion
of society at Bath.

Nashville, *nash'vil*, cap. Tennessee, USA ;
manufactures cotton and tobacco ; has
a big timber trade ; also two universities ; pop.167,000.

Nasmyth, JAMES, *nā'smith* (1808–90),
engineer, *b* Edinburgh ; patented the
steam-hammer 1842.

Nassau, port and cap. of the Bahamas ;
pop.29,000 ; exports sponges and fruit.

Natal, see UNION OF SOUTH AFRICA

National Anthem, see ANTHEM

National Book League, see BOOKS

National Convention, name of the French
parliament 1792–95 representing the
Revolutionary spirit of the people. It
replaced the old legislative assembly,
proclaimed France a republic, con-

demned Louis XVI to death, and in diplomacy and military power counted for much in the affairs of Europe.

national debt, total sum of money which the government of a country owes to those from whom it has borrowed, either at home or abroad. In its present form, it is due largely to the expenses of warfare. The British National Debt may be said to date from the founding 1694 of the Bank of England. *Funded debt* is now understood to mean permanent debt on which interest alone is paid without any attempt to clear the debt as a whole. *Floating debt* includes treasury bills.

In World Wars I and II the government borrowed money in the form of *redeemable debt*, i.e. money it undertakes to repay within a specified number of years. In both wars Britain incurred heavy debts abroad, particularly with the USA.

national emblems, see EMBLEMS

National Gallery, see LONDON

National Health Insurance, see HEALTH

National Health Service Bill, Bill brought forward (1946) by the Labour Government as part of their nationalisation plan. It provided (as from 1948) for free medical and dental attention throughout the British Isles ; the nationalisation of hospitals (hitherto supported largely by voluntary contributions) ; prohibition of the sale of doctors' practices ; and the division of the country into regional hospital boards and health centres, the Minister of Health being responsible for the whole service. The Bill aroused much controversy, and a section of the medical profession bitterly opposed it.

The National Insurance Bill (1946) was based on the Beveridge Plan (see BEVERIDGE, LORD). The scheme did not come into full operation till 1948, though the payment of Family Allowances operated as from August 1946. The basis of the plan is that every man over the age of 18 and working for an employer now pays 4s 11d weekly, every woman 3s 10d, thus securing a national fund from which payments are made when required, e.g. *unemployment benefit* —26s weekly for a breadwinner, 7s 6d weekly for his eldest child, and 5s weekly for each of the others. *In sickness* a married man receives 49s 6d, including 7s 6d for his eldest child. A *widow's pension* (once only 10s a week) is now 26s weekly ; 33s 6d weekly if she has a child of school age ; an *orphan's guardian* receives 12s weekly ; *maternity allowances* (i.e. payments to mothers at the birth of a child) is 36s for 13 weeks ; and *retirement pensions* are 26s weekly for an insured man, and 16s for his wife.

Men and women who do not work for an employer (e.g. traders, artists, doctors) pay 6s 2d weekly (women 5s 1d) ; and people who have a private income pay 4s 8d (women 3s 8d).

That the scheme is, in general, sound is beyond question, but that it is abused by many is also undeniable.

Read *National Health Insurance in Great Britain,* 1911–46, R. W. Harris.

National Insurance, see NATIONAL HEALTH SERVICE BILL

nationalisation, control by the nation or State rather than by individuals ; especially the acquisition and management by the State of industry and transport. Nationalisation is one of the main policies of the Labour Party (Socialists) who advocate State-control of industry, including mines, railways, civil aviation, banks, hospitals and road-haulage. The British Labour Government (elected 1945) quickly nationalised the Bank of England, railways (as from 1 Jan 1947), coal mines, etc. In 1950 the Labour Government succeeded by a narrow majority in nationalising iron and steel. Soviet Russia nationalised on a much vaster scale after 1917. See CAPITAL ; ECONOMICS ; UNITED KINGDOM

National Physical Laboratory, research centre at Teddington (Middlesex). The grounds cover 50 acres. Precise standards are maintained, and special problems are investigated in the 16 large and many smaller buildings.

National Portrait Gallery, see LONDON

National Savings Certificates, securities guaranteed by the State, and of special value to the small investor. The National Savings Movement, formed 1916, encourages thrift. Prior to 1 April 1947 certificates bought for 15s were in 10 years worth £1 0s. 6d, equivalent to compound interest at £3 3s 5d per annum, free of income tax. Such certificates (up to a maximum of 500, cost £375) could be bought at a Post Office, bank, National Savings Centre, or through one of over 200,000 Savings Groups in schools, factories, offices, clubs, etc., the latter encouraging regular weekly saving. There is also an issue of £1 Saving Certificates, these being worth £1 3s after 10 years. The 8th issue (1947) comprised 10s certificates, of which 1,000 may be held by any one person, though the maximum for the £1 certificates is 250.

national theatre, see THEATRE

National Trust, THE, society founded 1895 to preserve historic buildings and areas of natural beauty in Britain, the latter including areas in the Lake District, Derbyshire, Exmoor, Blakeney Point (with its wild life), the Farne Is., etc. The society buys land or buildings, or receives them as gifts or bequests, and ensures that they are open to all.

National Union of Students, see YOUTH ORGANISATIONS

natural gas, gas issuing from the ground, often in association with oil-wells, and especially in some regions of the USA, where it is used for lighting and heating ; is usually largely methane and ethane.

nautch girl, see DANCE

nautical terms, see SHIPS

nautilus, see MOLLUSCA

Navarino, bay on the south-west coast of Greece, giving its name to a naval battle 1827 in which combined fleets of Britain, France and Russia destroyed the Turkish and Egyptian navies, and thus heralded Greek independence.

Navarre, formerly (11th–17th c.) a kingdom between France and Spain.

navicert, *nav'i-sŭrt,* certificate, issued during World War II, allowing goods to be imported by neutral countries.

navigation, art of steering a ship or plane from one point to another. Ships were at one time navigated only along the coast, then by means of the stars or a compass, later with the aid of charts, a sextant, and a chronometer (an accurate type of clock) ; now both ships and planes are being increasingly directed by radar.

Navigation Act, see CROMWELL, OLIVER

navy, collection of ships either (*a*) for commerce, as the merchant navy, or (*b*) for warfare. The first navy of note was that of Athens, largely built up by Themistocles ; other early navies were those of Rome, Carthage, Venice, Genoa, Spain, Holland, Tudor England, Prussia, Russia and France.

The wars of the 18th c. saw the building of fleets of ships solely for fighting, and the transition from sailing vessels to ironclads took place gradually after the battle of Trafalgar 1805, the USA later building a navy which became immensely powerful in the 20th c.

The (BRITISH) ROYAL NAVY may be said to have begun with King Alfred, and is proud to be regarded as the senior service. The battle of Sluys, 1340, established English sea-power in the Middle Ages. Guns were first used in the 14th c. Ships of war were built on a large scale in Tudor times, and the defeat of the Spanish Armada 1588 gave England command of the seas. Enlarged and improved in Cromwell's day, the British Navy was long in competition with that of the Dutch. James II did much to strengthen our navy and better its administration. Lord Anson had a great influence for good, as also had succeeding admirals, e.g. Hawke, Boscawen, Rodney, Howe, Hood, and especially Nelson.

In more recent times Lord Fisher introduced bigger guns and the use of torpedoes and dreadnoughts. Oil has now largely replaced coal as fuel. Britain made immense strides in World Wars I and II, in both defeating the German submarine menace, and in the latter overcoming the magnetic mine. The Navy now has aircraft carriers, and is making use of radar on an increasing scale.

Builders of British warships include Cammell Laird (Birkenhead, on the R. Mersey) ; John Brown of Clydebank, Glasgow ; W. Denny of Dumbarton ; Harland and Wolff of Belfast and Glasgow ; Vickers-Armstrong at Barrow-in-Furness and Newcastle-on-Tyne. Navy ships are also built at Cowes, Southampton and Greenock.

Of special interest are the giant naval craft of the *King George V* class, each with a displacement of 35,000 tons. These ships are 739ft long ; beam 103ft ; driven by Parsons geared turbines developing 110,000hp. They have a crew of 1,900 and carry 10 14-in guns ; 16 5·25in and 6 multiple pompoms. With an almost equal displacement, *Nelson* and *Rodney* (1925) were fine examples of British capital ships, each 660ft long ; beam 106ft ; armoured with 14 and 16-in plates ; carrying 9 16-in guns ; 12 6-in ; 2 torpedo-tubes (24·5in), and having a wartime crew of 1,640. In 1948, however, these and other capital ships (including *Queen Elizabeth, Valiant,* and the battle cruiser *Renown*) were scrapped.

Larger still is HMS *Vanguard,* with a displacement of 45,000 tons, a floating fortress costing £11,000,000 to build and over £650,000 a year to keep at sea.

British fleet aircraft carriers include the new *Ark Royal* (laid down 1943) of which few details are yet available, though it is known she has Parsons geared turbines (4 shafts), and an anticipated speed of 32 knots. Aircraft carriers of the *Implacable, Indefatigable* type have a displacement of c.23,000 tons, a crew of 2,000. Both these vessels were completed 1944 ; also the *Indomitable* (length 760ft). Of the *Illustrious* class (e.g. *Victorious* and *Formidable*) the ships are 753ft long, 95ft in beam ; have a draught of 24ft ; develop 110,000hp ; a speed of 31 knots, and carry a great many guns.

During World War II British naval losses included the fine capital ships *Barham, Hood, Prince of Wales, Repulse, Royal Oak* (torpedoed at Scapa Flow, 1939), and the aircraft carriers *Ark Royal, Courageous, Eagle* and *Glorious,* the latter sunk in action with the German *Scharnhorst* and *Gneisenau* off Norway, 1940.

The immense USA Navy includes capital ships of the *Montana* class, displacement 58,000 tons (65,000 when fully loaded) ; length 903ft. Estimated to cost at least £27,000,000 each, the vessels were ordered 1940, but it is known that important changes in design have been incorporated since the keels were laid, due to advances in air tactics and the use of atom bombs.

USA ships of *Iowa* class have a displacement of 45.000 tons ; length 800ft ; crew of 2,700. The guns include 9 16-in ; 20 5-in ; 80 40mm AA, besides 4 or more aircraft and 2 catapults. The heavily armoured *South Dakota* class are of 35,000 tons displacement, the boilers of the *Washington* and *North Carolina* working at a pressure of 600lb per sq.in. The *Colorado* class includes two ships of 32,000 tons each. The world's biggest aircraft carriers belong to the USA Navy, e.g. *Coral Sea* (1946), *Franklin D. Roosevelt* and *Midway*, each of 45,000 tons, 986ft in length, 136 in beam ; carrying 137 aircraft, including large bombers of the latest type. These super-vessels have a hp of 200,000, a speed of 33 knots, and a complement of over 4,000 officers and men. Among USA landing-craft are the LSM 293 type.

Future naval warfare will certainly include homing torpedoes, improved and high-speed submarines, supersonic aircraft ; rockets largely replacing shells ; increased radar range-finders, and atomic bombs, the latter probably confined to ports, docks and stores. See RANK; SHIPS

Naxos, Greek island of the Cyclades ; noted for wine and marble.

Nazareth, town, Galilee, Palestine ; *c.*65m north of Jerusalem ; was the early home of Jesus ; present pop.13,000. Read *In the Steps of the Master*, H. V. Morton.

Nazism, political creed of the NSDAP (National Socialist German Workers' Party) or Nazi Party, which brought Hitler to power in 1933, and through which Hitler ruled Germany 1933–45.

Nazism was first propounded by Hitler in *Mein Kampf* (*My Struggle*), a book which he wrote in prison 1923–24. Its main features were as follows : A nation that does not fight for its existence must soon perish. Nothing weakens the nation so much as racial impurity, i.e. an admixture of aliens (especially Jews). The German nation is a Masternation, destined to rule the world. In order to fulfil its task, the German nation must ruthlessly get rid of all the Jews by whose presence its life is defiled (and of course all their wealth must be handed over to faithful supporters of the Nazi Party) : it must also rid itself of all, especially communists and pacifists, inside Germany who resist the fulfilment of Germany's historic mission. According to *Mein Kampf* it is likewise Germany's task to unite German Austria with the Fatherland. After that she must conquer ' living-space ' in Eastern Europe. The real enemy is not France or Britain—Hitler always hoped that it would be possible for Nazi Germany to come to terms with France and Britain—but Russia : both because Russia is the home of Communism and because Germany has no mountains or seas to defend her eastern frontier against Russia, a larger and equally expansive power. With Italian Fascism, Nazism was at first in conflict over Austria (1934–36) : but from 1936 until 1944 Facism and Nazism were hand-in-glove with one another.

Nazism throve on the conditions pre-vailing in Germany between the two World Wars. Those who feared and hated Communism—especially the great industrialists and the impoverished middle-class—rallied increasingly to Hitler, while the socialist side of Nazism appealed powerfully to Germany's unemployed. In 1928 the Nazi Party had only 12 seats in the Reichstag (Germany's Parliament) : in 1930, 107 ; in 1932, 230.

In 1932 it became increasingly evident that democratic government had failed, and that only Hitler could stem the rising tide of Communism. The Nazi doctrine that Germany must become once more a great military power, and the fact that only the Nazi Party was able to unite large sections of the German people had recommended it to the chiefs of the German army ; and early in 1933 they persuaded Hindenburg, the President, to make Hitler Chancellor of Germany. At once he began to carry out in practice what he had been preaching ever since 1920.

Having obtained emergency powers, he suppressed the parliamentary opposition, and launched a fearful persecution of democrats, Jews and Communists. Meanwhile, he ordered full-scale rearmament. In June 1934 he ' liquidated ' a conspiracy inside the Nazi Party itself, led by the revolutionaries Roehm and Strasser. The Nazi Party ceased then to be in any sense a revolutionary party ; but it still appealed to unemployed workers for whom there now was plenty of work in Germany's war factories. From 1934 until 1945 Nazism was absolutely supreme inside Germany ; anybody who even whispered against it was beaten up by Nazi thugs, robbed, murdered, or thrown into a concentration camp.

Once supreme inside Germany, Hitler proceeded to carry out his schemes of conquest. In 1936, German troops reoccupied the Rhineland ; this was contrary to the post-war treaties, but Britain and France weakly did nothing to enforce them. In 1938 Nazi Germany seized Austria, and at Munich obtained British and French approval for the seizure of certain Czechoslovak frontier-lands, on the grounds that these territories were largely inhabited by people of German blood. In 1939, Germany finally overran Czechoslovakia (March) and invaded Poland (September). For what happened afterwards, see WORLD WAR II.

Neagh, *nā*, lough (lake), N. Ireland, the largest in the British Is. ; area 153sq.m.

Near East, see MIDDLE EAST

Neath, town, 8m from Swansea, S. Wales ; industries include coal, iron, copper and chemicals ; pop.33,000.

Nebo, *nē'bō*, mt., sometimes called Pisgah, near the Dead Sea, Palestine. From its summit Moses viewed the Promised Land (Deuteronomy 34).

Nebraska, central state of USA ; has sand-hills in the north-west, but has been made more productive by irrigation; cap. Lincoln.

Nebuchadnezzar, *neb-ū-kad-nez'ĕr,* name of two kings of Babylon : NEBUCHADNEZZAR I, ruled 1146–1122BC ; NEBUCHADNEZZAR II, ruled 605–562BC, made Babylon the wonder city of the world ; captured Jerusalem and Tyre.

nebulae, see ASTRONOMY

Necker, JACQUES (1732–1804), French minister of finance ; amassed a fortune as a banker ; revealed the sorry plight of French finance to Louis XVI, and was dismissed from his post. After being recalled, he was again dismissed and once again recalled.

nectarine, see PEACH

needlework, one of the oldest of the crafts ; has long flourished in the East, where exquisite work is still done. Italian needlework was rivalled in the 17th c. by that of English needlewomen, whose art was revived at the end of last century.

Negeb, *neg'eb,* mostly desert region of Israel, S. of Tel-Aviv. Beersheba is the most important town. The Jews are hoping soon to supply the area with piped water, and thus make it productive.

Negri Sembilan, see MALAYA

Negroes, members of a race long resident in equatorial Africa between the Sahara and the territory of the Hottentots and Bushmen. Negroes are characterised by long arms and legs, brown, red-brown, or blackish-brown skin, woolly hair, thick lips, and flattened noses. Many of their 1,000 languages are made up of one-syllable words ; their dwellings are usually huts ; their weapons were at one time (and in some areas still are) spears, bows and throwing knives ; many tribes still believe in magic.

In the 16th c. there began what William Wilberforce later described as the ' odious traffic in human flesh,' i.e. the shipping of thousands of Negroes from Africa (especially the west coast) to the W. Indies and N. and S. America to work in the cotton fields as slaves. Descendants of Negro slaves number over 12,000,000 in USA alone today, and though most of them still work in cotton, sugar and rice plantations, or as unskilled employees in towns, they are capable of taking advantage of education, and some have become famous.

Nehemiah, *nē-hē-mī'ă,* reputed author of the the OT book of *Nehemiah* ; lived in the 5th or 4th c. BC. He was governor of Judea, and rebuilt the walls of Jerusalem.

Nehru, PANDIT, *nā'roo* (1889–   ), son of Pandit Motilal Nehru ; studied in England ; called to the Bar ; President of the Indian Congress Party ; first Prime Minister of the Dominion of India from 1947. As Gandhi's successor, he has an immense influence in India. A Socialist in politics, he is an accomplished scholar and the author of several important books, e.g. *Discovery of India.*

In 1950 he signed an agreement with the Prime Minister of Pakistan—an attempt to settle E. and W. Bengal minority problems ; and later that year and in 1951 sought to prevent war between China and the United Nations.

Nehru, PANDIT MOTILAL (1861–1931), Indian agitator and close supporter of Gandhi ; devoted his later years to demanding immediate dominion status for India.

Nejd, see ARABIA

Nelson, cotton and engineering town, Lancashire ; pop.38,000.

Nelson, river of Canada ; flows c.400m from L. Winnipeg to Hudson Bay.

Nelson, town, S. Island, NZ ; associated with sheep-farming.

Nelson, HORATIO, VISCOUNT (1758–1805), admiral, *b* Burnham Thorpe, Norfolk ; entered the navy as a boy ; made a captain 1779. Under Admiral Hood he was largely responsible for the capture of Bastia and Calvi, Corsica, 1794, but lost his right eye. At the battle of St Vincent 1797 he successfully disobeyed orders by turning out of the line to capture four Spanish ships, for which he was knighted. He lost his right arm in an engagement off Teneriffe. At the battle of the Nile in Abukir Bay 1798 he destroyed the French fleet, and was created Lord Nelson. In the attack on Copenhagen 1801, under Sir Hyde Parker, he was engaging the Danish forts and ships when Parker signalled him to retire, but Nelson, putting his telescope to his blind eye, continued the fight, and was highly successful. For this he was created a viscount.

From 1803 Nelson sailed in the *Victory* on the look-out for the French

NELSON 1758–1805

when Napoleon was planning an invasion of England. Following Villeneuve to the W. Indies, he learned that the French fleet had doubled back. Nelson arrived in European waters before the enemy, made a brief visit to England, and having planned his attack with his captains (the plan being known as the 'Nelson touch'), met the French off Cape Trafalgar (Spain), and fought his last battle, destroying the French, putting an end to Napoleon's plan for invasion, and also winning the last great naval battle in which sailing ships were employed. He died on board the *Victory* after exclaiming ' Thank God I have done my duty.' He was buried in St Paul's.

One of the greatest of all naval commanders, Nelson was bold but calculating. He demanded obedience, but was sympathetic towards his seamen, and instituted many reforms in the navy. As a man he was pompous. Though married, he lived much with Lady Hamilton, by whom he had a daughter, Horatia. Nelson's Column, Trafalgar Square, London, is a national tribute to him. See TRAFALGAR

Nelson, THOMAS, see PRINTING

Nelson's Monument, see LONDON

Nemesis, *nem'ē-sis,* in old Greek tales, daughter of Night, and goddess of vengeance.

Nen, river flowing 90m to the Wash, England.

neodymium, *nē-ō-dim'iŭm,* rare earth and element, Nd ; atomic weight 144·27 ; atomic number 60.

neon, element, Ne. An invisible inert gas, atomic weight 20·183, atomic number 10, it occurs in the atmosphere as one part in 55,000. At low pressures it emits a rich orange glow when subjected to an electric discharge, and is used in neon-signs, glass tubes having electrodes, usually of iron.

neon lighting, see ELECTRICITY

Nepal, *ne-paul',* independent country between India and Tibet ; area *c.*54,000 sq.m ; pop.5,600,000 ; cap. Katmandu. Though exceedingly mountainous, the country has fertile valleys (producing rice, timber and oilseeds) amid the Himalayas. Slavery existed till 1926.

Neptune, in old Roman tales, god of the sea, counterpart of the Greek Poseidon. His palace was supposed to be under the sea, and his symbol was a trident.

Neptune, see ASTRONOMY

neptunium, radioactive element, Np ; discovered while investigating atomic fission 1940–45 ; atomic weight 239·0(?); atomic number 93.

Nero (AD37–68), Roman emperor, step-son of the Emperor Claudius, whom he succeeded AD54, taking the names Nero Claudius Augustus Germanicus. With Seneca as his tutor, he showed much promise, and to the end was a patron of art. He was generous to the poor, but fell under the sway of Poppaea Sabina,

whose evil influence, together with his fits of madness, impelled him to sensual and cruel acts.

Giving himself up to a life of idle luxury, Nero ruled as a tyrant. That he actually ' fiddled ' while Rome was burning AD68 (as was once believed) is untrue, but he chose to blame the Christians for the fire, and persecuted them without mercy. He issued absurd decrees ; caused his mother and wife to be murdered ; and finally roused such hatred that, deserted by all, he committed suicide.

Nerva, MARCUS COCCEIUS (*d* AD98), Roman emperor from AD96 ; a wise ruler.

nerves, see NERVOUS SYSTEM

nervous system, complex arrangement of nerves, nerve-cells and ganglia, which (especially in the higher animals, including man) control and co-ordinate movement, and give awareness of environment. In man the system comprises (*a*) *central nervous system,* i.e. the brain, spinal cord, and the nerves reaching to almost every part of the body, the brain being largely concerned with sensations and movement ; and (*b*) *the sympathetic system,* regulating purely automatic functions, e.g. the activity of the glands. This is mostly distributed as a fine network, but becomes more dense in certain areas, where it forms a ganglion or *plexus.*

Nerves are built up of nerve-cells (*neurones*), and each neurone has (*a*) a short *dendron,* and (*b*) a longer *axon.* What we call a nerve is actually a double fibre containing a sensory (or an *afferent*) nerve carrying incoming impulses to the spinal cord or brain, and thus keeping us aware of what is happening in the body or beyond it, especially by means of special senses (e.g. sight, sound, touch, taste, smell, temperature, etc.), and also a motor (or an *efferent*) nerve which carries outgoing impulses to muscles, causing them to contract.

Thus, a nerve in the foot having received a stimulus (say a prick) carries this ' news ' to the cord and brain, and another nerve carries an ' order ' to such muscles as are required to cause the foot to be raised. In this case the action is reflex, i.e. the impulse passes by dendrons from the afferent to the efferent nerve, and the action is automatic. Doctors often locate a nerve lesion by tapping the knee and noting how swift or violent is the immediate reflex action (a kick). The speed at which an impulse travels along the nerves is from 115–265ft a sec. A lecturer may make 30 movements of the speech organs every second. The body is continually adjusting its mechanism as a result of stimuli from the nerves, and such adjustments are involuntary. When voluntary decisions have to be made, however, these are carried to the higher brain, where control is exercised according to emotion or logical reasoning.

The spinal cord is the column of nerve cells and fibres from the base of the skull to the first lumbar vertebra, i.e. it runs through the spinal column, and consists of white matter outside (nerve fibres) and, inside, of nerve cells. In all, 31 pairs of nerves are given off. See BRAIN

Ness, LOCH, lake, also a river, Inverness-shire. The Loch Ness ' monster,' declared by some to be ' prehistoric,' has caused widespread interest by its supposed appearances since 1934.

Nestor, in old Greek tales, King of Pylos. One of the Argonauts in his youth, he fought in the Trojan war when an old man.

netball, game commonly played out of doors, usually by women or girls. The ground (similar to a hockey-pitch) may be 100ft by 50ft ; the goals are upright poles with an iron ring 15in in diameter carrying an open net 10ft above the ground. The ball (as used in Association football) must pass through the net to score. The game is played in two periods of 15min each. A side may be five or seven players. No player may run while she holds the ball, but has to ' pass ' to one of her team as soon as possible.

Netherlands, kingdom comprising what is called Holland, i.e. 13,514sq.m beside the N. Sea and between Belgium and Germany, together with regions over-seas, all, however, regarded as a unit, since the Dutch do not refer to colonies, but think of the Netherlands, at home and abroad, as one kingdom.

HOLLAND is largely a region of low-lying country (*polderland*), much of it reclaimed from the sea by building immense dams or dikes, and by drainage canals and pumping machinery, formerly powered by windmills, now mostly by steam. After World War I the Dutch set about the gigantic task of draining the Zuyderzee. The polder south of Wieringen (50,000 acres) was opened up first. A second area was completed during World War II, though further development was prevented by the Nazi invasion.

With a rich soil, many rivers (e.g. Rhine, Maas, Yssel, Schelde), a genial climate, and the industry of the pains-taking Dutch, Holland produces many crops, including flax, hemp, oats, barley, sugar-beet, and especially bulbs, for which the land is world-famous, its fields of tulips and hyacinths being a pageant of colour in spring. Farming and fishing occupy *c.*22 per cent of the 9,300,000 people, but the country is primarily industrial, manufacturing bricks, margarine, cocoa, chocolate, cotton, linen, damasks and other textiles, confectionary, glassware, chemicals, per-fumes, also rayon, radio equipment and fertilisers. Amsterdam is noted for diamond-cutting.

Holland, a kingdom, has a States-General (Parliament) comprising (*a*)

Eerste Kamer (first chamber) of 50 members elected for 6 years, and (*b*) Tweede Kamer (second chamber), comprising 100 members elected for 4 years by popular vote. During World War II Holland was overrun by German armed forces, and as an occupied country she suffered terribly, though the spirit of the people remained unbroken, and sabotage was actively carried on against the Nazis.

The cap. is Amsterdam ; other towns include Rotterdam, Utrecht, Groningen, Haarlem, Tilburg and Nymegen.

The Dutch have long been famous for their courage and their love of inde-pendence, hence their bitter wars against Spain. They have also been a great and daring seafaring nation. In art the Dutch have excelled in portraits and studies of interiors ; among their famous artists are Rembrandt, Franz Hals and Vermeer. The Dutch have also a notable literary inheritance.

The Netherlands overseas comprises the Dutch E. Indies, Dutch Guiana or Surinam, and Dutch W. Indies (total area *c.*774,000sq.m).

The most important of the DUTCH E. INDIES is *Java*, area *c.*50,000sq.m, pop.44,000,000 (the most densely popu-lated region in the world). Java has active volcanoes in its mt. chain, a hot and (in parts) unhealthy climate, im-mense teak forests, and a mixed pop. (including *c.*600,000 Chinese besides the Malayans) chiefly engaged in cultivating coffee, tea, sugar, sago, tobacco, and especially rubber. Among the chief towns are Batavia and Samarang. *Madura* is another densely populated island noted for copra, teak and rice. *Sumatra,* an island of 163,000sq.m, is separated from Java by the Strait of Sunda. The island has heavy rainfall and tropical heat, hence its exceptionally varied and interesting plant and animal life. There are huge forests, and coal and gold are mined. The exports include rice, tobacco, maize and pepper. Also included among the Dutch E. Indies is part of the island of *Borneo* ; also Bali and Lombok. The adminis-trative cap. for all the Netherlands E. Indies is Batavia.

DUTCH GUIANA or SURINAM is an area of 55,000sq.m on the north coast of S. America. See GUIANA

The DUTCH W. INDIES are a group of six islands, including Curaçao.

See also INDONESIA

net personalty, English legal term for the movable property (money and goods) left by a testator (one who has died and made a will), *less* any charge for debts.

nettle, common plant of waste places and lanes. The STINGING NETTLE has minute green flowers, and leaves armed with fine stinging hairs containing formic acid. The ' DEAD ' NETTLE has a square stem, and (in spring) white or red

THE STINGING NETTLE

flowers. The ' dead ' nettles belong to a different family (*Labiatae*) from that of the stinging nettle (*Urticaceae*).

Neuchâtel, *nū-shä-tel'*, town, Switzerland, noted for watches and jewellery ; pop. 24,000 ; overlooks L. Neuchâtel, over 24m long.

neutralisation, in chemistry, the interaction of an acid and a base, with the formation of a salt.

neutron, see CHADWICK, SIR J. ; MATTER ; RADIOACTIVITY

Nevada, *ne-vad'ä,* state of USA. It is east of California, and though much of it comprises barren mt. ranges, it is rich in minerals. Silver was found there 1859. The capital is Carson City.

Neville's Cross, battle 1346 in which the English defeated the Scots near Durham.

Newark, *nū'ĕrk,* manufacturing city, New Jersey, USA ; pop.428,000.

Newark-on-Trent, town, Nottinghamshire. In its castle (now a ruin) King John died.

Newbolt, SIR HENRY (1862–1938), British poet and author ; won fame with his book of verse *Admirals All.* His poems are mostly about English seamen, e.g. *Drake's Drum,* though *Vitai Lampada* is immensely popular. His books include *The New June.*

New Brunswick, east coast province of Canada ; noted for vast forests, and for its wood pulp industry. Natural gas and oil have been found, and minerals are mined ; cap. Fredericton.

Newburn, town, Northumberland ; noted for iron, steel and coal ; pop.20,000.

Newbury, town, Berkshire ; scene of fighting in the Civil War 1643 and 1644.

Newcastle, town, New S. Wales, Australia ; on the Hunter R. ; centre of a great coal-mining area ; largest centre for iron and steel production south of the equator ; pop.128,000.

Newcastle, THOMAS PELHAM-HOLLES, DUKE OF (1693–1768), English Whig politician ; Prime Minister 1757–62.

Newcastle, WILLIAM CAVENDISH, DUKE OF (1592–1676), English royalist ; supported Charles I, but was defeated at Marston Moor 1644.

Newcastle-under-Lyme, town, Staffordshire ; on the R. Lyme ; noted for brewing and tanning ; pop.65,000.

Newcastle-upon-Tyne, city, Northumberland, 8m from the N. Sea ; noted for shipbuilding and repairing ; also for iron, steel, armaments, engineering and chemicals ; has a vast export trade. The ruins of a 12th c. castle remain ; there are six bridges across the Tyne ; pop.283,000.

Newchwang, town and port, Manchuria ; pop.166,000 ; opened for foreign trade 1858, but ice-bound in winter.

New College, despite its name, one of the oldest colleges of Oxford University, founded 1379 by William of Wykeham. It is always referred to as ' *New*-College,' never as ' New.'

Newcomen, THOMAS, *nū-kum'en* (1663–1729), engineer, *b* Dartmouth ; invented an improved (steam-condensing) pumping engine 1710.

New Coventry, name of an industrial town planned 1950 as an Australian memorial to Britain's dead in two world wars. It is at Rooty Hill, near Sydney.

New Deal, name for President F. D. Roosevelt's comprehensive measures (1932 onwards) to improve American social conditions and to promote the economic recovery of American farming and industry after the terrible slump of 1929–31. National Industrial Recovery Administration (NRA) included huge schemes designed to create work for vast numbers of unemployed workers. For the first time in USA history the Government intervened in industrial affairs and introduced national schemes of pensions, unemployment and sick pay ; Trade Unions became more important. The New Deal attempted to control inflation and to reduce surplus products. It included trade agreements with foreign countries. There was much criticism of Roosevelt's methods, but he certainly introduced a new era of prosperity, though the experiment was cut short by World War II. See POLITICS ; TVA

New Delhi, see DELHI

Newdigate Prize, prize awarded yearly at Oxford University for an English poem on a set subject. Valued at £21, the prize was founded by Sir Roger Newdigate, *d* 1806. Very few indeed of the prizewinners have later been famous as poets.

New England, name at one time given to the American states of Connecticut, Maine, Massachusetts, New Hampshire, Rhode I. and Vermont.

New Forest, delightful wooded district, Hampshire ; noted for its ponies.

Newfoundland, *nū-fŭn-land'* ; *nū-fownd-,* island of N. America, and the oldest English colony. It was discovered 1497 by John Cabot, who received £10 as a reward. It is off the north-east coast of Canada ; area (without Labrador) 42,000sq.m ; pop.309,000 ; has a rugged and bleak coast where hardy fishermen are engaged in cod fishing. Inland are great forests ; lumbering and wood-pulping are important industries. Various minerals are mined (including iron) ; cap. St John's. Much of the interior is yet unknown ; a number of English schoolboys explored new areas a few years ago. In March 1949 Newfoundland became Canada's 10th province.

New Guinea, *gin'i,* Pacific island, second largest in the world ; area 330,000sq.m ; under Netherlands (West) and British control (from Australia) in the East. The climate is tropical ; products include coconuts, coffee, cocoa, sago, rubber and kapok. Gold is mined in the Owen Stanley Mts (reached by plane). The south-east portion of the island (90,000sq.m) is PAPUA, much of it still unexplored, though the Fly R. makes a waterway to the interior ; cap. Port Moresby. The island was for a time in Japanese hands in World War II.

New Hampshire, Atlantic state, USA. Some 75 per cent of its area (over 9,000 sq.m) is forest. The region is known as the Switzerland of America ; cap. Concord.

Newhaven, port, Sussex ; has a regular steamer service with Dieppe, France.

New Haven, port and city, Connecticut, USA ; noted for fire-arms, clocks, etc. Here is Yale University ; pop.160,000.

New Hebrides, *heb'ri-dēz,* group of *c.*30 British-French islands in the S. Pacific. They produce copra, coffee, cotton, cocoa and timber ; cap. Vila. The people (Melanesians) are still cannibals.

New Jersey, Atlantic state, USA ; produces timber, fruits, fish, etc. ; notable for copper, petroleum and textiles ; cap Trenton.

New Learning, see RENAISSANCE

New Life Movement, see CHINA

Newlyn, Cornish fishing village beloved by artists.

Newman, CARDINAL (1801–90), *b* London John Henry Newman, among the founders of the Oxford Movement, won fame as a great Anglican preacher, but entered the RC Church 1845. He was made a cardinal 1879. He wrote the hymn *Lead Kindly Light,* and the poem *The Dream of Gerontius.*

Newmarket, town, Suffolk ; HQ of English horse-racing.

New Mexico, mountainous southern state of USA ; cap. Santa Fé.

Newnham College, *nŭn'am,* college for women at Cambridge, founded 1871.

New Orleans, *aur'lē-anz,* city and port, Louisiana, on the R. Mississippi ; America's chief cotton centre ; pop. 495,000.

New Plymouth, *plim'ŭth,* town in N. Island, NZ ; associated with cattle-rearing and dairying ; pop.20,000.

Newport, town, and cap., I. of Wight.

Newport, port, Monmouthshire ; on the R. Usk ; has much shipping (e.g. coal, iron, etc.) ; noted for its transporter bridge ; pop.89,000.

New South Wales, state, Australia, south of Queensland ; area over 309,000sq.m ; pop.2,930,000 ; well served with roads, railways and air-lines ; largely agricultural (especially wheat, maize, oats, rice, fruits) and sheep farming (wool being the chief product) ; notable for coal, copper, silver, lead, and especially (since 1851) gold ; chief towns : Sydney, cap., Broken Hill and Newcastle.

newspapers, daily or weekly publications recording events ; may also give comments, generally on the latest political events (in the form of a *leader*), also having contributed articles of wide interest, letters from readers, and perhaps critical notes on art, drama, music and broadcast features, together with financial and commercial news and comments. As a rule the price is small, but if the circulation is large (some great British papers exceed a daily circulation of 2,000,000 copies) a huge revenue is derived from advertisements. A page in a national daily may cost over £1,000 ; an announcement in the Births, Marriages and Deaths column of, say, the *Manchester Guardian,* costs *c.*1s 6d a line.

Apart from minor news-sheets, newspapers may be said to date from the 18th c., their development being at first retarded by the Stamp Act (1712) which raised the price.

The popularity of periodicals reflecting current events was increased by writers like Bolingbroke and Dean Swift, founders of the political leading article, and by the essays of Addison and Steele ; but the first British journalist was Daniel Defoe, and the first newspaper worthy of the name was *The Review,* founded 1704. *The Times,* founded by John Walter 1785, eventually became the world's most famous newspaper, its ' lay-out ' being the model for all others, and its system of gathering news out-rivalling the government post, so that *The Times* was first with news of the victory at Waterloo, 1815. The USA was a pioneer in newspapers with a popular appeal, often, however, serving news more attractively than truthfully, and publishing much sensational material. In Britain two newspaper pioneers of outstanding influence were Lord Northcliffe, founder 1896 of the *Daily Mail,* and Sir George Newnes, who introduced a new type of weekly periodical, e.g. *Tit-Bits.* The 20th c. has seen the rise of great Sunday newspapers, e.g. *Sunday Times, Sunday Pictorial, Sunday Dispatch, Sunday Graphic, News of the World* ; also newspapers making a special feature of photographs, e.g. the *Daily Mirror,* the *Daily Sketch,* and Edward Hulton's popular *Picture Post,* founded 1938. A unique weekly, *The Children's Newspaper,* was founded 1919 by Arthur Mee.

The editorial department of a modern newspaper receives news by post, telephone, telegram, cable, teleprinter and radio ; from correspondents and reporters, and from various news agencies, e.g. Reuters, founded (in London) 1851, and the Press Association, the Central News, and the Exchange Telegraph. Type is now set up with linotype machines ; circular stereotype plates are employed on giant rotary presses using 100 miles of paper a day, and printing, folding and counting 50,000 copies an hour, sometimes even more.

In all but totalitarian states the freedom of the Press (i.e. a newspaper's right to print its own or its readers' views) is jealousy guarded. In return for their freedom newspapers undertake a vital responsibility : they must give the people *facts,* for in a democracy the people will vote foolishly if ill-informed. In Britain some newspapers feed their readers entirely on items of trivial importance, and make large profits thereby. By others the highest standards of British journalism have been successfully maintained.

Newspapers have long had a great influence in politics and in moulding public opinion. Among great London dailies are *The Times,* the *Daily Express, Daily Herald,* the *Daily Mail,* the *Daily Mirror,* the *Daily Telegraph,* and the *News Chronicle.*

Scotland has *The Scotsman,* the *Glasgow Herald* and the *Bulletin.*

Famous English provincial newspapers are the *Manchester Guardian,* the *Yorkshire Post,* the *Birmingham Post* and the *Sheffield Daily Telegraph.*

Closely associated with newspapers are magazines and journals, some weekly, others monthly. Lists of such publications may be found in, say, *Whitaker's Almanack,* and among some likely to be of special interest to youth are the following, those with an asterisk being particularly suitable for girls :

> *Aero Modeller*
> *Amateur Cine World*
> *Amateur Photographer*
> *Boy's Own Paper*
> *Children's Newspaper*
> *Countryman*
> *Discovery*
> *Flight*
> *Geographical Magazine*
> **Housewife*
> *John o' London's Weekly*
> *Listener*
> *Meccano Magazine*
> *Picture Post*
> **Queen*
> *Radio Times*
> *Railway Magazine*

> *Reader's Digest*
> *Sailplane and Glider*
> *Scout*
> **Vogue*
> ** Woman and Beauty*
> ** Woman's Own*
> *Woodworker*

New Statesman, THE, see PASSFIELD, LORD

Newstead, *nu'sted,* village, Nottinghamshire ; its abbey was once the home of Lord Byron. He and his friends scandalised and shocked society by their wild Newstead parties.

newt, see AMPHIBIAN

Newton, SIR ISAAC (1642–1727), scientist, *b* Woolsthorpe, Lincolnshire ; educated at Grantham School and Trinity College, Cambridge. Elected to a fellowship at Cambridge, he lived there for 30 years, and was so absent-minded that he had to be cared for by friends. MP for Cambridge University for two brief periods, he became Warden of the Mint (London) 1695, and Master 1699. President of the Royal Society 1703 till his death, he was knighted 1705 ; and buried in Westminster Abbey.

Newton was brilliant as an astronomer, physicist and mathematician. He discovered the laws of gravitation, and the story that he was led to consider the subject by the fall of an apple is very possibly true. The Newtonian laws are not destroyed but only extended by Einstein's theory of Relativity, which owes everything to Newton's *Principia,* a book published 1687 because of Edmund Halley's persuasion, and at his expense.

Newton's assertions that every particle of matter attracts every other particle with a force varying directly as the product of their masses, and inversely as the square of their distance, is the basis of all modern knowledge of matter

NEWTON 1642–1727

RADAR   *plate 57*

Top : Plotting aircraft by radar, showing (*left*) the Plan Position Indicator and (*right*) the
Range-Finder. (*Wireless World*). *Bottom :* Close-up of a Range-Finder. When the radar
beam in its rotation encounters an object a 'response' appears on the line of light shown in
the picture. The two smallest spikes of light indicate single a/c at *c.* 50 and 55 miles.
(*Crown Copyright : Controller, H.M.S.O.*)

plate 58   THE AIR AGE

Top : Prestwick Airport, almost the only one in Britain that remains fog-free all through the year. (*B.O.A.C.*). *Bottom :* A Vickers *Attacker* fighter powered by a Rolls-Royce Nene turbo-jet engine. (*Vickers Ltd*)

CIVIL AVIATION

plate 59

Top : The B.O.A.C. Speedbird Constellation aircraft *Bangor II* in flight. *Bottom :* The B.O.A.C. Speedbird Solent class flying boat *Southampton* at her moorings. (Both *B.O.A.C.*)

plate 60   POSTAL COMMUNICATIONS

Without a world-wide intercommunication men would be unable to co-operate in the production of all the things they need. *Top :* The International Telephone Exchange switchboard;
Bottom left : the Post Office driverless underground train, London; *right :* A G.P.O.
linesman on maintenance duties. (*P.M.G.*)

and energy, and his application of these, and other principles, to the movements of the planets, laid the foundations of modern astronomy.

But Newton was supreme in other fields. He was the first to realise the significance of the spectrum. He explained light on the corpuscular theory which, after being discarded, is now, with very considerable modifications, accepted. With Leibniz he shares the honour of working out the differential calculus. He advanced optics, and invented the reflecting telescope. He discovered the binomial theorem and the use of fluxions. Of him it has been said : *No other man presents a record of devoted service in the cause of science with such conspicuous genius and success.*

To the end Newton remained singularly modest ; about himself he said : ' I do not know what I may appear to the world, but to myself I seem to have been only like a boy playing on the seashore, diverting myself in now and then finding a smoother pebble or a prettier shell than ordinary, while the great ocean of truth lay all undiscovered before me.'

See RELATIVITY ; SPECTRUM

New Year's Day, see CALENDAR

New York, state of USA ; has several mt. ranges and picturesque lakes ; rich in minerals, and a great industrial region ; cap. Albany.

New York, largest city of USA ; built on Manhattan I. (13½m long and 2¼ wide) at the mouth of the Hudson R. and also on other islands where the Hudson and East R. open into Long I. Sound, north of Sandy Hook ; has a magnificent harbour with wharves and docks for Atlantic liners ; includes BROOKLYN (facing Manhattan, with which it is linked by fine bridges across East R.), also JERSEY CITY, linked with New York by railway tunnels under the R. Hudson.

Having no room for horizontal expansion, the city has in parts expanded vertically, so that the ' skyscraper ' buildings of Manhattan rise to 300ft, and have, in some blocks, 60 storeys. The older portion is irregularly laid out : the more recent has streets east and west, avenues north and south. Many are known by numbers, e.g. 5th Avenue, the finest ; others have more ordinary names, e.g. Wall Street and Broad Street, both centres of American finance. Broadway eventually becomes the highroad to Albany. Buildings between streets are known as *blocks* ; and notable examples include the City Hall and Court House, of white marble ; the American Museum of Natural History (Manhattan Square) ; St Patrick's RC Cathedral ; Astor Library ; Columbia University ; bridges include the famous suspension bridge across East R. ; also the Brooklyn and Manhattan bridges. There is a great network of railways, among them three trunk lines.

The city, noted for its huge hotels,

is the commercial and business capital of USA. It has many manufactures ; pop. (city proper) 7,455,000 ; Greater New York has a pop. of 11,690,000.

New Zealand, country of the British Commonwealth ; comprises N. Island (area 44,281sq.m) ; S. Island (58,092 sq.m), and Stewart and Chatham islands, total area 103,415sq.m ; pop.1,794,000. Separated by Cook Strait, the two main islands, between lat.34° and 47° S, are largely mountainous, but no point is very far from the Pacific Ocean, so that the climate is excellent—moist, mild and sunny. The scenery is superb. Mt Cook (S. Island) is the highest point (12,349ft) ; and the neighbourhood of Rotorua (N. Island) is famous for its volcanoes, geysers and hot springs, the most remarkable of their kind in the world.

NZ has great forests, especially of giant tree-ferns and Kauri pine which yield valuable resins. Agriculture is progressive, and includes sheep farming, vast flocks pasturing in the province of Canterbury ; from it comes the frozen ' Canterbury lamb ' imported by the UK. Other exports are wool and butter ; and coal, gold and iron are mined. Manufactures include textiles, leather, furniture, chemicals and rubber goods.

Excellent roads are a feature of the islands ; railways are still being developed, also civil aviation. Hydroelectric power is cheap. The capital is Wellington (N. Island) ; other important towns include Auckland, Hamilton, Christchurch, Dunedin. The country is a sportsman's paradise ; there are over 850,000 acres of beautiful scenery specially reserved.

First sighted by Tasman 1642, NZ was explored by Captain Cook 1769. The region became a British colony 1841, a dominion 1907. It is governed by a Governor-General, an executive council, and a legislature of two Houses. The natives of NZ, the Maoris, number c.80,000. A Polynesian race, they are said to have reached the country no more than 500 years ago or so ; they are highly developed both physically and mentally, and enjoy equal rights with the white inhabitants, almost all of whom are British. New Zealand is almost the only country in the world where a ' colour problem ' has been solved to the satisfaction of both ' colours.'

See PLATES 17, 19

Ney, MICHEL, *nā*, (1769–1815), one of Napoleon's marshals ; captured Mannheim 1799 ; distinguished himself at Jena and Eylau ; fought in Spain ; saved the remnants of the French army in Napoleon's retreat from Moscow 1812 ; went over to Louis XVIII after Napoleon was sent to Elba.

When Napoleon returned, Ney deserted the king, and commanded part of Napoleon's army at Waterloo, where he plunged into the fighting like a junior officer. Later he was arrested by the restored Royalist government and shot as a traitor. Ney was nicknamed the ' bravest of the brave.'

Ni, chemical symbol for nickel.

Niagara Falls, *nī-ag'ä-rä,* portion of the R. Niagara (N. America) between L. Erie and L. Ontario. The falls are (*a*) American, 1,080ft wide and 167ft high ; and (*b*) Canadian or Horseshoe, 3,100ft wide and 158ft high. They are visited by many tourists. A hydro-electric power station supplies electricity over a wide area.

Niagara Falls is also a town, Ontario, Canada ; also a town, USA (pop. 78,000) ; both towns are near the falls.

Nicaea, *nī-sē'ä,* ancient city of Asia Minor where the Nicene Creed was drawn up in AD325.

Nicaragua, see CENTRAL AMERICA

Nice, *nēss,* city and holiday resort of the French Riviera ; exports olive-oil ; pop.184,000 ; noted for its carnival ' The Battle of Flowers.'

Nicholas, *nik'ō-läs,* the original ' Santa Claus,' 4th c. saint of Asia Minor ; said to have been buried at Bari, Italy ; regarded as the patron of travellers, seafarers, merchants and children.

Nicholas I (1796–1855), Tsar of Russia from 1825 ; increased Russian territory.

Nicholas II (1868–1918), Tsar of Russia from 1894 till his abdication 1917. He was murdered by Bolshevik revolutionaries.

Nichols, BEVERLEY (1899–   ), English author of *The Fool Hath Said, Down the Garden Path,* etc.

Nicias, *niss'i-äs* (*d* 413BC), Athenian general in the Peloponnesian War ; in command of an expedition to Sicily 415BC, but defeated by the Spartans.

nickel, element and metal, Ni ; resembles iron and is silvery white ; atomic weight 58·69 ; atomic number 28 ; specific gravity 8·9 ; melting-point 1,435°C ; is magnetic. The chief source of nickel is Ontario, Canada. Nickel dissolves readily in dilute nitric acid ; is in great demand for use in alloys, especially nickel steel, plantinoid, etc. and for nickel plating. It is alloyed with copper for coins. Nickel silver is an alloy of nickel, copper and zinc ; nickel steel contains 3·5% nickel (approx.). As nickel strongly resists corrosion, it is much used for armour-plating, in the manufacture of guns, aircraft, etc., and (as nickel-chrome) for wire.

Nicobars, see ANDAMANS AND NICOBARS

Nicodemus, NT character. A Pharisee, he was a secret disciple of Christ (John 3, 7, 19).

Nicolson, HAROLD (1886–   ), British politician (National Labour MP 1935), author and critic.

nicotine, see TOBACCO

Niemen, *nyä'm'n,* river flowing 500m through USSR, Poland, to the Baltic.

Niemöller, PASTOR MARTIN, *nee'mĕ-ler* (1893–   ), German Lutheran clergyman ; sent to a concentration camp for his resistance to Nazi paganism, released 1945 ; one of the great religious figures of modern times. Now Bishop of Hesse-Nassau.

Nietzsche, FRIEDRICH, *neet'shĕ* (1844–1900), German prophet of hatred and violence ; long suffered from ill-health, and died insane ; denounced Christianity, and put forward a theory of supermen ; author of *Good and Evil* ; *The Will to Power,* etc. His writings imbued Germany with nationalism and a desire for military conquests.

Niger, *nī'jĕr,* river of W. Africa ; flows 2,600m from French Guinea, and through Nigeria to the Gulf of Guinea, entering by a delta with many mouths ; navigable for 1,000m.

Nigeria, *nī-jēr'iä,* British colony and protectorate, W. Africa ; area (including Cameroons) 372,000sq.m ; pop. 21,000,000. Conditions have vastly improved in recent years ; swamps have been drained, railways built, airports opened. The exports include tin ore, iron ore, bauxite ; palm-kernels, palm oil, ground-nuts and cocoa. There is a large coalfield. The cap., Lagos, is a busy port. See IBADAN

nightingale, bird of the thrush family ; visits England (as far north as Yorkshire) April–August ; is *c.*6in long ; russet brown above, brownish white below. The nest of leaves and grass is built near the ground. Noted for its beautiful song heard especially at night, the nightingale is sometimes called *philomel* (after Philomela in old Greek tales) by English poets.

THE NIGHTINGALE

Nightingale, FLORENCE, see NURSING

nightjar, migratory insect-eating bird visiting Britain in summer ; somewhat resembles the swift, but is grey, spotted and barred with yellow and brown ; lays two marbled eggs on the bare ground, often near heather.

nihilism, see TURGENEV, I. S.

Nike, *nī'kee,* in old Greek tales, goddess of victory ; called Victoria by the Romans.

Nile, African river flowing *c.*4,000 miles, hence it is the second longest in the world ; it rises in L. Victoria Nyanza, flows north as the White Nile, and is joined at Khartoum by the Blue Nile. At Aswan British engineers constructed, 1902, an immense dam with 180 sluices to regulate the flood waters. Without the annual flooding, supplying water for agriculture and leaving behind a rich silt, Egypt would be a desert ; but the true explanation of this flooding was not found till the 19th c., when John Hanning Speke and Sir Samuel Baker proved that it is caused by the seasonal rains of the interior, i.e. in Uganda and Ethiopia. At Cairo the river rises 25ft June–Sept. It enters the Mediterranean by a delta. A scheme is now being examined for increasing and further regulating the flow, one plan being the turning of L. Uganda into a gigantic reservoir. See LIVINGSTONE, DAVID ; SPEKE, J. H.

Nile, BATTLE OF, fought 1798 between the British fleet (under Lord Nelson) and the French fleet in Abukir Bay (Egypt), resulting in the defeat of the French. Nelson's victory cut off Napoleon and his army in the Middle East. This encouraged other countries to ally themselves against France.

Nilgiri Hills, see INDIA

nimbus, see AUREOLE

Nîmes, *nēm,* city, France, 25m from the Mediterranean ; exports silk and wine ; notable for its superb Roman remains ; pop.104,000.

Nimrod, OT character ; a notable hunter and warrior (Genesis 10).

nine-points' circle, see TRIANGLE

Nineveh, *nin'e-ve,* ancient city, Assyria ; by the Tigris. Its ruins face the modern city of Mosul. Nineveh was famous for its temples, palaces and gardens, especially in the time of Sennacherib (*c.*700BC). See ASSYRIA

Ningpo, city, China ; on the R. Yung ; near the site of a former city said to have been founded *c.*2200BC. Once a treaty port (from 1842), it is noted for carpets and lace, also for carved woodwork ; pop.300,000.

Niobe, *nī'ō-bē,* in old Greek tales, wife of Amphion, King of Thebes, and mother of 12 children. When they were slain she was turned to stone, but her tears continued to flow.

niobium, element, Nb ; atomic weight 92·91 ; atomic number 41 ; rare metal. Also known as columbium.

Nippon, native name for Japan.

Nirvana, see BUDDHISM

nitrate, see NITROGEN

nitric acid, see NITROGEN

nitrocellulose, name for a group of nitric acid esters of cellulose, including celluloid and gun-cotton. See CELLULOSE

nitrogen, inactive gaseous element, N, forming *c.*75·5% by weight and 78·06% by volume of the atmosphere ; atomic weight 14·008 ; atomic number 7 ; boiling-point −195·8°C ; colourless and odourless ; supports neither combustion nor (although not poisonous) respiration ; combines with hydrogen and oxygen on sparking, and with some metals when heated, thus forming nitrides.

The chief natural compound is nitre or saltpetre, but nitrogen is now largely obtained from the air. Active nitrogen, thought to be atomic nitrogen, is more reactive than ordinary nitrogen.

Nitrogen forms five oxides with corresponding acids, of which NITRIC ACID is the most important. Known also as *aqua fortis,* nitric acid, HNO_3, is corrosive, and is a powerful oxidising agent. It acts on most metals, generally giving off oxides of nitrogen. It may be prepared by distilling a nitrate (usually potassium or sodium nitrate) with concentrated sulphuric acid, or by the oxidation of ammonia and air over heated platinum. The salts of nitric acid are valuable fertilisers, nitrogen in this form being essential to the soil. Nitrogen is an essential in plant and animal tissue.

What is known as the NITROGEN CYCLE may be summarised thus : Plants (with the exception of the pea and bean family) are unable to use nitrogen in the air, but lightning causes nitric acid to reach the soil along with rain. There it forms nitrates, and is absorbed by plants through the roots. As a plant decays, and as animal dung decomposes (the animal having fed on nitrogenous material of plant origin), ammonia is formed. This is attacked by bacteria in the soil, where it becomes a nitrite, i.e. a salt of nitrous acid ; further attack by bacteria produces nitrates, which are again absorbed by plants, and thus the cycle goes on, part of the nitrogen going back to the air. It is estimated that over every sq.m of the earth's surface there are about 20,000,000 tons of nitrogen. Plants need nitrogen, in compound form, to produce proteins.

NITRIC OXIDE, NO, is a colourless gas ; NITROUS OXIDE or LAUGHING GAS, N_2O, is used as a mild anaesthetic by dentists. NITROGEN PEROXIDE, NO_2, is a dark brown gas with a pungent smell. Nitrogen compounds are much used in the manufacture of explosives. Nitrobenzene, $C_6H_5NO_2$, is a pale, yellow, liquid with an odour of bitter almonds. See AMMONIA

nitrogen cycle, see NITROGEN

nitroglycerine or glyceryl trinitrate, $C_3H_5(NO_3)_3$, heavy oily liquid that explodes violently as a result of shock or detonation ; forms the basis of dynamite.

nitrous oxide, see NITROGEN

nizam, *ni-zam',* viceroy or chief administrator in the Mogul Empire (India) ;

particularly the title of the hereditary ruler of Hyderabad, who abdicated 1948.

Noah, *nō'ä,* OT character ; father of Shem, Ham and Japheth ; built an ark, and survived the flood (Genesis 6–9).

Nobel, ALFRED, *nō-bel'* (1833–96), Swedish chemist, *b* Stockholm ; invented dynamite 1866, also claimed over 120 other inventions, chiefly explosives ; formed the Nobel's Explosives Company, England, 1871, and was responsible for vast improvements in mining and armaments. A large part of his immense fortune was devoted to founding the Nobel prizes (first awarded 1901) for exceptionally fine work in physics, chemistry, medicine, literature, and for any work that promotes international peace. The prizes (valued at about £8,500 each) are awarded yearly.

noble, old English gold coin of Edward III's day valued at *c.*6s 8d.

node, see SOUND

noise, see SOUND

Nonconformists, name given to *c.*2,000 clergy of the Church of England who resigned their livings 1662 rather than accept the terms of the Act of Uniformity. The name is now given to all Dissenting religious groups, e.g. Baptists, Congregationalists, Methodists, Presbyterians, etc.

nones, 5th (but in Mar., May, July and Oct. the 7th) day of the Roman month.

nonjur'ors, *c.*400 clergymen (and a few other members) of the Church of England who declared they could not take the oath of allegiance to William and Mary, 1689.

Nordenskiold, NILS, *noor-den-shüld* (1832–1901), Swedish explorer ; made several Arctic voyages, notably that of the *Vega,* 1878–80, when he sailed the North-East Passage.

Nore, THE, sandbank at the mouth of the R. Thames ; has had a lightship since 1731.

Norfolk, English county, north of Suffolk ; has a N. Sea coast of 90m ; also sand dunes and woods ; notable for fruit-growing and market-gardening ; co.tn Norwich.

Norfolk, see WILLIAMSON, HENRY

Norfolk, island *c.*930m from Australia ; area 13sq.m ; chief town Kingston ; governed from Australia.

Norfolk, port and naval base, Virginia, USA ; industries include shipbuilding, textiles and chemicals ; pop.144,000.

Norfolk, DUKE OF, title created 1483. John Howard, 1st duke, made Earl Marshal by Richard III, was killed at Bosworth 1485. Thomas Howard, 4th duke (1536–72), was executed for his share in the Ridolfi plot. Henry Fitzalan-Howard, 15th duke (1847–1917), took part (as Earl Marshal) in the coronations of Edward VII and George V. The principal seat of the family is at Arundel Castle, Sussex.

' Norge,' see POLAR REGIONS

Norman, MONTAGU, LORD (1871–1950),

banker, *b* London ; governor of the Bank of England 1920 ; advised a return to the gold standard 1925 ; Privy Councillor 1923 ; created Lord Norman 1944.

Norman architecture, see ARCHITECTURE

Normandy, ancient Channel province of France between Picardy and Brittany. The name is still used for a district covered by five departments. Its people, the Normans (i.e. Northmen) with Scandinavian blood, early spoke French and conquered the district round about. Duke William eventually invaded England 1066, and after the battle of Hastings brought about the Norman conquest thus enriching the population with a love of adventure, great military, legal and administrative powers and a devotion to the Church. The Normans brought a knowledge of Norman-French, and a love of chivalry, besides the distinctive style of Norman architecture. See ARCHITECTURE

Normanton, stone-quarrying and coal mining town, W. Yorkshire.

Norrköping, *naur'chŭ-ping,* town and port, Sweden ; industries include textiles and shipbuilding ; pop.72,000.

Norse, the old language of Norway, carried to Iceland, Greenland, Orkney, Shetland and the Hebrides, during the period (8th–13th c.) when seafaring Norsemen (i.e. Northmen, Vikings, or Scandinavians as a whole) set out from Norway and Denmark, to raid other lands or settle there, e.g. England (as ' Danes ') in the 9th c., also Iceland, Greenland, Normandy, and apparently even N. America.

North, LORD (1732–92), English statesman; Prime Minister for George III, 1770–82, and again for some months in 1783. He encouraged George III to oppose the Whigs, and was partly responsible for the loss of our American colonies.

Northallerton, town, N. Yorkshire ; scene of the Battle of the Standard 1138.

North America, continent ; area 8,350,000 sq.m ; pop.163,000,000 ; includes Alaska, Canada, Mexico, Newfoundland, Labrador and USA.

Northamptonshire (often written Northants), midland county of England ; co.tn Northampton, on the R. Nene. The town, noted for boots and shoes, has pop.92,000.

North Atlantic Pact, treaty signed by representatives of Great Britain, USA, Canada, Norway, Denmark, France, the Benelux countries, and Italy in the belief that by guaranteeing mutual aid they may thus deter any other nation from making war on any one of the nations concerned. The Treaty came into force in Sept 1949. See EUROPE

North Borneo, see BORNEO

North Cape, headland in N. Norway, usually regarded as Europe's most northern point.

North Carolina, *kä-rō-lī'nä,* state of USA ; crossed west by the forested Appalachian Mts, which rise to 6,000ft ; cap. Raleigh.

Northcliffe, ALFRED CHARLES WILLIAM HARMSWORTH, VISCOUNT (1865–1922), pioneer of modern newspaper production ; launched the *Daily Mail* 1896 ; created Lord Northcliffe 1905 ; Viscount 1917 ; owned the *Evening News* and *Weekly Dispatch.* His brother, HAROLD HARMSWORTH (1868–1940), controlled the *Daily Mirror,* and later the *Daily Mail* and was created Viscount Rothermere 1919.

North Dakota, *dä-kō'tä*, NW. state of USA ; mostly prairie ; cap. Bismarck.

North-East Passage, sailing route to China by the north of Europe and Asia ; long sought by Arctic explorers ; discovered by Nils Nordenskiold 1878–80. See POLAR REGIONS

Northern Ireland, see IRELAND

northern lights, see AURORA BOREALIS

Northern Rhodesia, see RHODESIA

Northern Territory, state of Australia ; area 523,620sq.m ; pop.5,200 ; cap. Darwin. Largely pastoral, but farming and the mineral wealth (especially gold) await further development.

North Foreland, chalk promontory, Kent.

Northmen, see NORMANDY

Northolt, town, Middlesex ; noted for its airport.

North Pole, see POLAR REGIONS

Northrop, JACK, see AVIATION

North Sea, shallow portion of the Atlantic east of the British Is. ; area *c.*190,000 sq.m ; maximum breadth *c.*420m ; noted for cod, especially on the Dogger Bank.

North Shields, see SHIELDS

North Uist, *yoo'ist* ; *oo'eeshtch*, island of the Outer Hebrides ; pop.2,800, chiefly engaged in fishing and cattle-rearing.

Northumberland, county of NE. England ; separated from Scotland by the Cheviot Hills and the R. Tweed ; has an important coalfield ; administrative HQ Newcastle-on-Tyne.

Northumbria, kingdom of Anglo-Saxon Britain between the Humber and Forth, and east of the Pennines. Prior to AD600 it comprised the kingdoms of Bernicia (between the Tyne and Forth), and Deira, the region from the Tyne or Tees to the Humber. The most notable ruler was King Edwin, who married Ethelburga, a daughter of the King of Kent. He welcomed the Christian missionary Paulinus, and became a Christian 627. He was killed at Hatfield Chase (Yorkshire) 633. Edinburgh was named after him.

North-West Frontier, i.e. of Britain's former Empire in India. It is between Afghanistan and the Punjab, and is now part of Pakistan ; the capital of the province is Peshawar.

North-West Passage, see POLAR REGIONS

North-West Territories, region of Canada, area *c.*1,310,000sq.m ; pop.12,000. The area, north of lat.50°N, is notable for its mineral wealth, e.g. gold, lead, radium and uranium (Great Bear L. District) and petroleum ; also for its fur trade ; administered from Ottawa.

Northwich, salt-producing town, Cheshire. Mining has caused the ground to sink, hence many of the houses are aslant.

Norway, Scandinavian kingdom *c.*1,100m long and 250m wide ; area *c.*124,500 sq.m ; pop.3,000,000. Noted for its rugged coast with many deep, narrow inlets (fiords) and small islands, the country is mountainous, and its swift streams generate hydro-electric power. Rich in forests, it produces wood pulp and timber, exporting also fresh and canned fish, whale-oil, furs and iron ore. Norway is notable for its merchant fleet and for shipbuilding.

The country is ruled by a king and his Storting (parliament). Known as the ' Land of the Midnight Sun,' it is much visited by tourists, and was the home of the Vikings who, 1,000 years ago, raided England, and of Eric the Red who is believed to have sailed as far as N. America. The cap. is Oslo ; other towns include Bergen, Trondhjem, Stavanger, etc.

The people, hardy and resourceful, inherit a great tradition. Famous Norwegian authors are Ibsen, Björnson, Hamsun, Undset, etc.

During World War II the Germans occupied the country from 1940. King Haakon VII found refuge in England while Quisling ruled Norway under German direction.

The Norwegian Arctic areas include Svalbard (Spitsbergen), while the Antartic areas include e.g. Biland, Bouvet Island, etc.

Norwich, *nor'idge*, famous old city and co.tn, Norfolk, on the R. Wensum ; noted for its handsome cathedral ; manufactures textiles, mustard, boots and shoes, etc. ; pop.103,000.

Norwood, SIR CYRIL (1875–   ), English educationist ; headmaster of Harrow 1926–34.

nose, part of the body through which we breathe, and with which we smell. It is lined with vessels that warm and moisten air before it passes to the lungs ; also *cilia* or fine hairs preventing impurities reaching the lungs, hence the importance of breathing through the nose. It has the *olfactory region,* i.e. an area where the nerve of smell branches into the moist mucous membrane, thus enabling smells to be distinguished. Many animals and birds (especially flesh-eaters) have a much more highly developed sense of smell than man, but even we can easily detect the presence of 3/100,000,000th of a grain of musk.

notary, *nō'täri*, in England, usually a solicitor ; in Scotland a law agent. He is appointed to certify that some formality of the law has been observed in his presence.

Notre Dame, *nau-tr däm'*, (French *Our Lady*, i.e. the Virgin Mary), name of many French churches, notably Notre Dame de Paris, on the site of a 7th c. church. The present building, dating from 1163, is a noble example of Gothic architecture. It has 37 chapels, much old glass, and a spire 315ft high.

Nottingham, city and co.tn, Nottinghamshire ; pop.281,000 ; on the R. Trent ; noted for hosiery, lace, bicycles and tobacco ; has a castle (now a museum). There is also a university.

Nottinghamshire, midland county of England, largely in the valley of the R. Trent ; has remains of Sherwood Forest ; is a great cricketing county ; noted as a source of gypsum.

Nova Lisboa, see PORTUGAL

Nova Scotia, *nōvǎ skō'shǎ,* province on the east coast of Canada ; area 21,000sq.m ; pop.578,000 ; linked with New Brunswick by an isthmus only 13m wide ; noted for apples ; also produces coal, iron and steel ; cap. Halifax, at the terminal of the CPR. Nova Scotia was largely colonised in the reign of James I and VI by Scotsmen, hence the name (New Scotland) ; British since 1713.

Novaya Zemlya, *no'vǎ-yǎ zem-lyǎ,* Russian islands in the Arctic ; area 30,000sq.m.

novel, form of prose fiction in which the writer portrays characters whose thought and emotions are revealed as the action of the plot unfolds, hence its inevitable and close association with the drama of real life.

The name is derived from Boccaccio's *Novella Storia,* and its history in Britain and America may be traced from the stories of Defoe, Richardson, Fielding, Smollett and Sterne to the great novelists of the 19th c. Sir Walter Scott was among the pioneers of the romantic novel ; Jane Austen gave us novels dealing with manners rather than adventures ; the psychological and sociological novels of modern times include those of various French and Russian novelists. See BALZAC ; DICKENS ; DOSTOIEVSKI ; ENGLISH LITERATURE ; SCOTT, SIR WALTER ; TOLSTOY ; ETC.

Novello, IVOR, (1893–1951), actor and dramatist, *b* Cardiff ; composed the song *Keep the Home Fires Burning* ; has won success on the films ; produced *The Dancing Years* ; *Perchance to Dream,* etc.

novocaine, synthetic drug much used as a local anaesthetic ; has largely replaced cocaine.

Noyes, ALFRED, *noiz* (1880–), English poet, born in Staffordshire ; has written much musical verse, e.g. *The Loom of Years* ; *Drake* ; *Forty Singing Seamen* ; *A Salute from the Fleet* ; *Ballads and Poems* ; and the notable epic *The Torch Bearers.* Many of his poems were set to music by Sir Edward Elgar.

NRA, see NEW DEAL

NS (New Style), see CALENDAR

Nubia, district of the Anglo-Egyptian Sudan.

nuclear physics, branch of physics dealing with the nucleus of the atom, and with radiations from radio-active substances. Its study led to atomic fission.

Nuffield, WILLIAM RICHARD MORRIS, VISCOUNT (1877–), *b* Cowley, Oxfordshire. From being a cycle repairer he became a manufacturer of motor-cycles, then of light cars. Later he founded at Cowley, near Oxford, the firm of Morris Motors Ltd, which by 1926 was manufacturing yearly over 100,000 cars on mass-production lines. He created a large motor combine with subsidiary companies abroad. He also manufactured many aeroplanes. Created a viscount 1938, he has given away huge sums, e.g. £2,000,000 (1936) for medical research at Oxford University.

Nuffield College, see OXFORD

Nullarbor Plain, remarkable limestone region (*c.*100,000sq.m) in the south of S. Australia and W. Australia. Here are sandhills in what was once the sea bed. The Transcontinental Railway (linking Kalgoorlie with Port Pirie) runs across the plain for 328m in a straight line without crossing a river and without a tree being in sight.

Numbers, book of the OT, containing accounts of two numberings (i.e. countings) of the Israelites.

numerals, see ROMAN NUMERALS

numerator, see FRACTIONS

numismatics, see MONEY

Nunc Dimittis, *nungk di-mit'is,* opening words (Latin) of Simeon's song, *Lord, now lettest Thou Thy servant depart in peace* ; Luke 2.

Nuneaton, *nŭn'ē-tŭn,* town, Warwickshire ; manufactures textiles ; pop.46,000.

nuns, see MONKS AND NUNS

Nuremberg, *nŭ'rem-bŭrg,* old city, Bavaria (Germany) ; 95m north of Munich ; notable for quaint buildings, handsome churches and art collections ; manufactures toys, watches, chemicals ; pop. 431,000. The ' Nuremberg Laws ' were a code of laws persecuting Jews. The city was bombed during World War II.

After World War II Nuremberg was the scene of the trial of Nazi war criminals. Twenty-one of them were accused of having waged aggressive war, and being responsible for war crimes on a vast scale during the war. The crimes were described as the result of cold and criminal calculation, and the prisoners were accused also of wantonly murdering and torturing as well as deliberately pillaging occupied territories. It was revealed by the commandant of the concentration camp at Auschwitz that in that camp alone 2,500,000 people were exterminated between 1940 and 1943, besides 500,000 who died of disease and starvation. The Tribunal included Lord Justice Lawrence (President of the Council and Sir Norman Birkett for Britain, and representatives for USA, France and Russia. Over 400 open sessions were held, and 38,000 affidavits were signed by 155,000 people.

Prisoners sentenced to death were : Goering, Ribbentrop, Keitel, Kaltenbrunner, Rosenberg, Frank, Frick, Streicher, Sauckel, Jodl, Seyss-Inquart, Bormann. Hess, Funk and Raeder were sentenced to life imprisonment ; others to 20, 15 and 10 years' imprisonment. Schacht, von Papen and Fritzsche were acquitted. Sentences were delivered 30 Sept 1946.

nursing, skilled care of the sick or injured ; may be said to have become a science and profession as a result of the fine pioneer work of Florence Nightingale (1820–1910), *b* Florence, Italy. Taking 37 nurses with her, she organised at Scutari a hospital for the wounded in the Crimean War, becoming known as 'The Lady of the Lamp' from her custom of visiting the tents, lamp in hand, at night. (Read Longfellow's *Santa Filomena.*) Later she trained nurses at St Thomas's Hospital, London, and raised nursing to a noble and skilled profession.

FLORENCE NIGHTINGALE 1820–1910

The National Nursing Association was founded 1874 by the Order of St John of Jerusalem ; the British Nurses' Association was founded 1887 ; the international Red Cross (for the care of war victims, e.g. wounded, prisoners, etc.) was founded 1864, see RED CROSS. The Royal Army Medical Corps (RAMC was founded 1898 ; the Voluntary Aid Detachments (known as the VAD) were organised in World War I to provide extra help in hospitals.

For nursing as a career for girls, write for particulars to the Ministry of Labour and National Service, who will give full

THE NUTHATCH

information regarding general and specialist nursing. For boys, the Ministry of Labour has a useful pamphlet, Male Nursing, No. 45 in the series *Careers for Men and Women.*

nut'hatch, climbing bird found more commonly in S. England. It is *c.*5in long, grey above, with white throat and yellow underparts. It runs up and down trees, nests in a hole, and feeds on insects.

nutmeg, tree, a native of Malaya ; may be 30ft high ; has yellow flowers. Its seed is the nutmeg used for flavouring.

Nyasa, *nya'ssa,* lake of E. Africa ; drained by the Zambesi ; 360m long ; discovered by Livingstone 1859. See LIVINGSTONE, DAVID

Nyasaland, British Protectorate in Central Africa ; area 47,950sq.m ; pop. 2,183,000 ; produces coffee, tobacco, cotton and tea ; government cap. Zomba.

nylon, *nī'lon,* plastic textile evolved after patient research by the American chemist W. H. Carothers, and his collaborators, working on discoveries made by Emil Fischer, a German chemist.

The process, greatly improved and extended since 1932, consists of combining carbon chains with amide groups, the thread being an artificial silk twice as strong as natural silk and much more elastic. Exton is a similar product. These synthetic fibres are among the most remarkable chemical achievements of the century.

Recent experiments have shown that nylon suitably treated with acrylic resin has its durability increased by 35–50%, a discovery of great importance to the hosiery trade. See PLASTICS

Nymegen, *nī-mā'gen,* town, Netherlands ; pop.94,000.

nymphs, in old Greek tales, immortal maidens, as nereids and naiads dwelling in the sea or streams, dryads in trees, oreads in mountains.

O

O, chemical symbol for oxygen.

Oahu, see HAWAII

oak, slow-growing forest tree. The common British oak, often 100ft high and over 25ft round the trunk, has deeply lobed leaves, dark and glossy green. The leaves of *Quercus sessiliflora* have stalks unlike those of *Quercus pedunculata*, which have very small stalks. The fruit (an acorn) does not appear till the tree is *c.*70 years old. Many oaks live 1,000 years, some considerably more. Oak-galls are homes for the grubs of gall-flies. Mistletoe sometimes grows on oaks, the Druids formerly cutting it down with golden knives. The fine-grained timber of the oak (once in great demand for ships) is largely used in building, and for church furniture.

THE OAK

Oak-Apple Day, 29 May, birthday of Charles II, also the day (1660) he landed at the Restoration. It commemorates his escape from the battle of Worcester by hiding in the Boscobel oak, 1651.

Oakham, *ōk'am*, co.tn, Rutland. Its county hall, formerly the banqueting hall of a 12th c. castle, has a remarkable collection of horseshoes. The public school was founded 1584.

Oakland, city, California, USA ; cans fruit ; noted for textiles and iron goods ; pop.302,000.

Oak Ridge, see TENNESSEE

oakum, hempen fibre made from old ropes; formerly used for caulking wooden ships, i.e. sealing the seams. Picking oakum was once a common employment in prisons and workhouses.

oasis, *ō-ā'sis*, fertile spot in a desert, often with a lake. Groves of date palms are usually found at an oasis, especially in the Sahara.

oast-houses, *ōst*, buildings for drying hops Usually round, with a conical roof, they are a feature of the landscape in Kent.

Oates, CAPTAIN LAWRENCE EDWARD GRACE, *ōts* (1880–1912), British soldier and explorer ; served as an army captain in the S. African war ; sailed with Captain Scott on his Antarctic expedition 1910, and made the journey to the Pole with him. Being crippled with frostbite on the return journey, he went out to die, hoping to make it easier for the others to get back to their depot. He thus earned the title of ' a very gallant gentleman.' See POLAR REGIONS

Oates, TITUS (1649–1705), *b* Oakham, Rutland ; worthless fellow who declared he had discovered a Popish Plot 1678 to overthrow the Protestant faith in England, and by this means caused *c.*36 innocent people to be executed. Though condemned to life imprisonment, he was later released and pensioned. See POPISH PLOT

oats, cultivated cereal grown in Europe as far as latitude 70°N ; usually sown in drills with phosphates ; harvested when pale yellow, the average yield being 40–60 bushels an acre. Oats are largely employed for feeding livestock, but ground oats are used (as oatmeal) for human consumption, especially as porridge, which has a high percentage of fat and albuminoids.

Obadiah, *ō-bă-dī'ă*, 5th c. OT prophet, author of the book that bears his name.

Oban, *ō'ban*, port, Argyllshire ; tourist centre for the W. Highlands of Scotland.

Oberammergau, *ō-běr-äm'ĕr-gow*, village of Upper Bavaria (Germany), famous since 1633 for its Passion Play, presented periodically in a theatre. Resembling the miracle plays of the Middle Ages, it is in 18 acts, and is given by 600 performers before 4,000 spectators. It depicts the last hours of Christ, and is intensely moving.

Oberon, *ō'běr-on*, king of the fairies in various old German tales ; also a fairy character in Shakespeare's *Midsummer Night's Dream.*

Obi, *o'bē*, river, W. Siberia ; flows 2,250m to the Arctic Sea.

observatory, building where astronomical, meteorological, magnetic and other observations are scientifically made. The Royal Observatory, Greenwich, was founded 1675. (Its HQ are now at Hurstmonceux, a village in Sussex.) Because of the clear atmosphere, there are several observatories in west USA, e.g. the Lick Observatory on Mt Hamilton ; the Yerkes Observatory (Wisconsin) ; and the observatory on Mt Palomar (California), for which a 200in reflecting telescope has recently been constructed. The Mt Wilson Observatory was built 1905 (California).

obsidian, hard, black, shining rock, actually a natural glass formed by volcanic action.

O'Casey, SEAN (1884–   ), Irish dramatist, *b* Dublin ; mingles reality and symbolism ; noted for *Juno and the Paycock, Ash Leaves and Lavender,* etc.

occupational therapy, recently developed science and art of treating certain diseases or injuries by assisting the patient to do useful work, especially weaving, toy-making and carpentry. It is designed to bring muscles into play which need exercise.

ocean, *ō'sh'n,* large body of water. The oceans are : Atlantic (area 31,530,000 sq.m, greatest depth 30,143ft) ; Arctic (5,541,600sq.m) ; Indian (28,350 000 sq.m) ; Pacific (63,986,000sq.m), greatest depth 35,410ft off Mindanao. The term Southern Ocean is now used for the Antarctic, i.e. the waters south of a line joining the extremities of Africa, NZ, and S. America. The total area of sea water is 141,050,000sq.m.

Oceania, *ō-shē-ä'niä,* south and central Pacific Ocean, with Australia, NZ, and many islands, e.g. Fiji, New Guinea, Polynesia, Marquesas, Hawaii and Samoa.

Oceanus, *ō-sē'ä-nŭs,* in old Greek tales, god of the ocean, and father of all things.

ocelot, *os'e-lot,* wild cat of tropical America; *c.*3ft long ; has tawny fur beautifully marked.

Ochils, *ō-chils,* mts., Scotland, from Stirlingshire to the Firth of Tay.

O'Connell, DANIEL (1775–1847), born in County Kerry, Irish patriot (known as the Liberator) ; won the right for Catholics to sit in Parliament, and was elected MP 1830. A gifted and eloquent speaker, he was opposed to violence.

O'Connor, THOMAS POWER (1848–1929), Irish journalist and politician ; founded *T.P.'s Weekly* ; became MP 1880, and was for a time ' father ' of the House.

octagon, in geometry, plane figure with 8 sides and angles.

octane, hydrocarbon, C_8H_{18}, of the paraffin series ; this is the 100 octane spirit known as aviation spirit.

Octavia, *ok-tā'viä (d* 11BC), sister of the Roman emperor Augustus, and wife of Mark Antony, who deserted her for Cleopatra. See AUGUSTUS

octopus, see MOLLUSCA

ode, among the Greeks, a poem intended to be sung to musical accompaniment, e.g. the odes of Pindar ; in more recent times an elaborate lyric with a heroic or passionate theme. Horace wrote the finest Latin odes ; and in English literature the odes of Gray, Keats, Milton, Shelley, Swinburne, Tennyson and Wordsworth are among the noblest. See POETRY

Odense, *ō'then-sä,* port, Denmark ; Hans Andersen was born in a house there, now a museum ; pop.92,000.

Oder, *ō'der,* river ; flows *c.*550m from Czechoslovakia to the Baltic.

Odessa, Black Sea port of the Ukraine, USSR ; on the R. Dniester ; notable for its export of wheat, sugar and wool. The pop. of 604,000 includes many Jews.

Odyssey, see HOMER

Oedipus, see SOPHOCLES

Offa (*d* 796), King of Mercia from 757 ; became overlord of all England, except Northumbria. OFFA'S DIKE is an earthwork along the Welsh border.

Offaly, county of Eire in the province of Leinster ; formerly called King's County ; chief town Tullamore.

Offenbach, JACQUES, *ŏf'en-bäch* (1819–80), French composer, *b* Cologne ; notable for his many comic operas, and the tuneful *Tales of Hoffmann.*

Ogden, C. K., see BASIC ENGLISH

Oglethorpe, JAMES EDWARD (1696–1785), English soldier and politician ; founded the American colony of Georgia 1733.

Ogpu, *og'poo,* state security department of USSR. It exists for the discovery and abolition of all revolutionary activities.

Ohio, state of USA. It is north of the R. Ohio, a tributary (*c.*970m) of the Mississippi ; produces corn crops, cattle and sheep ; has coal, oil and natural gas ; cap. Columbus.

ohm, *ōm,* unit of electrical resistance ; that resistance through which a potential difference (PD) of 1 volt will produce a current of 1 ampere ; defined as the resistance of a column of mercury 106·3cm long, 1sq.cm cross-section, at 0°C. Note : the total resistance

(R) *in series* : $R = r_1 + r_2 + r_3$

in parallel : $\dfrac{1}{R} = \dfrac{1}{r_1} + \dfrac{1}{r_2} + \dfrac{1}{r_3}$

specific resistance (S) of a wire : $R = \dfrac{S}{A}$

where R = resistance in ohms, *l*=length in cm, A = cross-sectional area in sq.cm. Note : If E is EMF (volts), C is current (amps), R is resistance (ohms), then $R = \dfrac{E}{C}, C = \dfrac{E}{R},$ and E = C × R. This is known as Ohm's Law. See ELECTRICITY

Ohm, GEORG SIMON (1787–1854), German scientist ; discovered 1827 what is now called Ohm's Law. See OHM

oil of vitriol, concentrated sulphuric acid, H_2SO_4.

Oise, *wäz,* river flowing *c.*185m from the Ardennes (Belgium), through France, to join the R. Seine.

Oka, tributary of the R. Volga (USSR), which, after *c.*960m, it joins at Gorki.

okapi, *ō-kä'pi,* rare giraffe-like animal of Central Africa ; about as large as a mule. Purplish, it has short yellow legs striped horizontally with black ; discovered 1900 by Sir Harry Johnston.

O'Kelly, SEAN THOMAS, (1882–   ), president of Eire 1945.

Okinawa, island 325m from Japan ;

stoutly defended by the Japanese till overcome by American troops April 1945.

Oklahoma, state of USA between Kansas and Texas ; largely prairie, with a slight rainfall. Minerals include oil, coal and natural gas ; the chief town is Oklahoma City, notable for cotton, cattle, horses, etc., and canning ; pop. (Oklahoma City) 204,000.

Olaf, name of five kings of Norway. Olaf I (963–1000) built the first Christian churches in Norway. Olaf II (995–1030) became Norway's patron saint.

Old Age Pensions, (now officially known as Retirement Pensions), are payable to men over 65, to women over 60, who have retired from regular employment, while those employed after these ages become eligible, men at 70, women at 65. A further condition is that the person desiring a retirement pension must have made a minimum number of contributory payments. The standard rates are 26s a week for all insured persons and widows, 16s for married women who qualify on their husbands' contributions. Full particulars can be obtained from the National Assistance Board.

Old Bailey, Central Criminal Court, London.

Oldbury, ōld'beri, town, Worcestershire ; manufactures chemicals, bricks, iron and steel ; pop.36,000.

Oldcastle, SIR JOHN (d 1417), English soldier ; hanged for sharing in a Lollard conspiracy ; popularly thought to have been the original of Shakespeare's Falstaff in King Henry the Fourth.

Oldenburg, ōl'den-burch, minor German state ; cap. Oldenburg.

Oldham, town near Manchester, Lancashire ; noted for cotton-spinning, etc. ; pop.111,000.

Old Sarum, see ELECTION ; REFORM ACTS

Old Trafford, suburb of Manchester ; has the famous Lancashire cricket ground.

olefines, ō'lē-fīns, unsaturated hydrocarbons that burn with a luminous but smoky flame, e.g. the gas, ethylene, C_2H_4. The general formula for olefines is C_nH_{2n}, n being any whole number except one.

Oliphant, PROFESSOR MARCUS, ol'i-fant (1901– _), b Adelaide, Australia ; pioneer in atomic research ; specialist on the effect of electricity on gases and also on nuclear physics ; associated with the development of radar and the atom-bomb of 1945.

olive, ol'iv, evergreen tree of the Mediterranean region, usually c.20ft high. In the wild state it has spiny branches, but is without spines when cultivated. The flowers are white. From the plumlike fruit, olive oil is pressed.

Olives, MOUNT OF, also called Olivet, mt. near Jerusalem ; rises 2,680ft ; once noted for its olive trees ; associated with the life of Christ.

Olivet, see OLIVES, MOUNT OF

Olivier, SIR LAURENCE (1907– _), British actor immensely successful on stage and screen ; especially noted for his film title parts in Henry the Fifth and Hamlet.

Olympia, ō-lim'piä plain in the Peloponnese, Greece ; scene of the famous Olympic Games.

Olympic Games, athletic contests (e.g. running, boxing, wrestling, etc.) immensely popular in ancient Greece from the 8th c. BC, and held every four years at Olympia. The Olympic Games were revived in 1894 as an international festival, the last world contest being held in London 1948. The next Olympiad will be held at Helsinki in 1952. The Games now include gymnastics, hockey, football, wrestling, weightlifting, running, shooting, etc.

Olympus, ō-lim'pŭs, highest peak of a mt. range between Thessaly and Macedonia (Greece) ; rises 9,794ft. Its summit was believed by the ancient Greeks to be the home of gods and goddesses.

Omagh, ō'mä, co.tn, Tyrone, N. Ireland.

Omaha, ō'mä-hŏ, city, Nebraska, USA ; on the R. Missouri ; noted for railway plant, smelting, etc. ; pop.224,000.

Omar Khayyam, ō'mär chī-yäm' (d 1111 or 1123), Persian, b Nishapur ; won fame as a mathematician, but is best remembered as a poet, especially for his long poem (in quatrains) the Rubáiyát, brilliantly translated into English by Edward FitzGerald 1859.

Omdurman, Nile city, Anglo-Egyptian Sudan ; faces Khartoum ; a great trading centre ; scene 1898 of a British victory over the Egyptians ; pop. 105,000.

Omsk, city, Siberia, USSR ; on the Trans-Siberian Railway ; pop.281,000.

onager, on'ä-jĕr, wild ass of the steppes of Central and W. Asia ; has sandy hair, short legs and a black stripe down the middle of the back.

Onega, ō-nē'gä, second largest lake in Europe ; area 3,800sq.m ; is north-east of L. Ladoga, Russia.

O'Neill, EUGENE (1888– _), American dramatist, b New York,; won fame with his one-act play Anna Christie ; Nobel prize-winner 1936.

O'Neill, HUGH, ō-nēl' (d 1616) ; as second Earl of Tyrone, led risings against the English ; died in Rome.

onion, vegetable akin to the leek and garlic, its bulbous root being useful in cooking. It is exported from Madeira, Brittany, and especially Spain and Portugal.

Ontario, on-tār'io, province, Canada, north of the Great Lakes ; area over 412,000sq.m ; produces wheat, maize, timber (especially for pulp and paper), but is most notable as Canada's chief manufacturing area ; cap. Toronto.

Ontario, smallest of the Great Lakes of N. America ; area 7,540sq.m.

onyx, on'iks, kind of agate with alternate milk-white and black or coloured layers ; much used for cameos.

Oolite, *ō'o-līt,* geological name for the upper and middle divisions of the Jurassic rocks ; largely deposits of limestone with marine fossils.

op., short for Lat. *opus,* ' work ' ; used especially for more serious musical works. In theory, a musician's works are arranged in order of composition, hence, a piece of music by Bach styled Op.6 may be assumed to have been written after Op.5 ; but actually there is much confusion, and the rule is often broken. If a work has many separate parts it may be subdivided, e.g. Op.1, No.2, etc.

Op. post. means a work posthumously published, i.e. published after the composer's death.

opal, *ō'pal,* gem ; actually hydrated silica, the finest having a bluish or yellowish tint. It is found in Australia, Guatemala, Hungary, Japan and Mexico. See PLATE XII

opera (Lat. *opera,* works), drama allied with music ; became more than a mere concert with the production of *Orpheus* (1762) by Gluck, a German musician, though Italy was the original home of opera. German composers developed opera along increasingly dramatic lines, so that when the Italian Verdi, who had written *Il Trovatore,* 1853, in the Italian manner, came to write *Otello* (1887), he did so with all the dramatic power of the German tradition.

British composers have never excelled in this art. Among the few who have written successful operas are Purcell (*Dido and Aeneas, c.*1680) ; Balfe, e.g. *The Bohemian Girl* ; Wallace (*Maritana*); Edward German (*Merrie England*) ; Dame Smyth (*The Wreckers*) ; Vaughan Williams (*Hugh the Drover*) ; and Benjamin Britten, noted for *Peter Grimes* and *The Rape of Lucretia.*

Italian opera writers include Rossini (*The Barber of Seville*) ; Verdi (*Rigoletto, La Traviata, Aïda,* etc.) ; Mascagni (*Cavalleria Rusticana*) ; Puccini (*La Bohème, Tosca* and *Madame Butterfly*).

French opera writers include Gounod (*Faust*) ; Bizet (*Carmen*) ; Saint-Saëns (*Samson and Delilah*).

German opera writers include Mozart (*The Marriage of Figaro, The Magic Flute,* etc.) ; Weber (*Der Freischütz*) ; Wagner (*The Flying Dutchman, Tannhauser, Lohengrin, The Mastersingers of Nuremberg, Parsifal,* and the *Ring* operas) ; Strauss (*Der Rosenkavalier*).

Russian opera writers include Mussorgsky (*Boris Godunov*) ; Borodin (*Prince Igor*).

Grand opera now usually means opera in the grand and impressive manner, and also without *spoken* dialogue. It is in contradistinction to comic operas, which may be comic in the popular sense, or may simply be of less importance musically. In Britain light opera (best illustrated by, say, *The Mikado,* of Gilbert and Sullivan) has long been popular ; but in France *opera comique* means, usually, any opera, comic or tragic, which contains spoken dialogue. Read *Opera Tunes to Remember,* Florence M. Clark (Nelson) ; *Opera,* Edward J. Dent.

Ophir, *ō'fĕr,* probably SE. Arabia ; mentioned in the OT as a source of gold for Solomon.

opium, dried milky juice from the partly ripened seeds of the opium poppy. It is used medicinally to give sleep or relieve pain. The opium poppy has been cultivated in China since the 8th c. AD, and the dangerously unhealthy habit of smoking opium became a craze there in the 18th c. By exporting Indian opium, the British caused the Opium War 1839–40, when the Chinese tried to prevent its importation. China ceased to grow opium, and Britain to export it, 1917.

Oporto, Portuguese port ; on the R. Douro ; centre of a wine-producing region, hence *port* ; noted also for textiles ; pop.263,000

opossum, *ō-pos'ŭm,* animal of N. and S. America. The only marsupial outside Australia, it has a slender body, a long snout, and a tail used in climbing. The opossum usually lives in trees.

Oppenheim, E. PHILLIPS, *op'en-hīm* (1866–1946), British author of many novels with exciting plots.

Oppenheimer, DR J. ROBERT, *op'en-hīm-ĕr,* American scientist, *b* New Mexico ; directed the final stages of the atombomb of 1945 ; author of *Quantum Mechanics.*

optophone, see SELENIUM

opus, see OP.

oracle, see PROPHET

Oran, *ō-rän,* port, Algeria ; trades in cereals, esparto and iron ore ; pop. 195,000.

Orange, chief river of S. Africa ; flows *c.*1,300m from Basutoland to the Atlantic.

Orange, title derived from a small district in SE. France formerly ruled by the princes of Orange, from whom was descended indirectly William the Silent, founder of the Dutch Republic ; also his grandson William III of England.

orange, fruit of an evergreen citrus tree 25–30ft high, with glossy leaves, white flowers (see PLATE 6, *bottom*). The fruit is actually a berry, comprising ten or more pulpy carpels in a thick rind containing oil glands. Oranges are grown for export in USA (especially Florida and California), S. Africa, Australia and Palestine ; varieties include the sweet orange (*Citrus aurantium*) ; bergamot (yielding perfume) ; Seville or bitter orange, used for marmalade ; mandarin; tangerine (from Tangier), blood orange ; Jaffa ; and the seedless navel orange of S. America.

Orange Free State, see UNION OF SOUTH AFRICA

Orangemen, members of an Irish society to repress Catholic emancipation.

Originally they were supporters of William of Orange.

oratorio, sacred musical composition in which a story is more or less dramatically unfolded (without scenic effects) by principal singers, choir and orchestra. Great composers of oratorios include Scarlatti, an Italian of the 17th c. ; Bach ; Handel, composer of *Saul, Israel in Egypt, Samson, Judas Maccabaeus* and *The Messiah,* his masterpiece. Others are Haydn (*The Creation*) ; Mendelssohn (*Elijah*), and, in recent years, Sir Edward Elgar, famous for *The Dream of Gerontius,* and William Turner Walton's masterpiece *Belshazzar's Feast.*

orchid, *aur'kid,* family of plants with showy flowers, often vividly coloured and curiously marked. Some 5,000 species are known, and they are found in many parts of the world, more especially in tropical areas, notably the forests of Brazil and E. Indies, where extraordinary specimens have been dis-

ORCHIS

(top) the Early Purple Orchis, (bottom) the Spotted Orchis : an individual flower, the style and stamens

covered, many mimicking insects, spiders and snakes. The flower of the orchid has two lateral petals with a lower one between them which is lip-like in appearance. Some orchids grow in the ground, others (*epiphytes*) on trees. Handsome and curious orchids may be seen at Kew. Our British flowers, purple orchis, spotted orchis and lady's slipper, are hardy varieties of orchid.

orchis, plant related to the orchids of tropical climes. Species in Britain include (*a*) EARLY PURPLE ORCHIS, and (*b*) SPOTTED ORCHIS, a plant of damp woods and chalky banks, having a pale purple flower (June, July) with spots. Orchis is the name given to other British orchids that mimic insects but are not of this genus, e.g. the BEE ORCHIS, a plant of limestone districts.

Orczy, BARONESS, *aur'ksi,* pen-name of Mrs Montagu Barstow, an Anglo-Hungarian writer who won fame 1905 with the publication of *The Scarlet Pimpernel,* a thrilling romance of the French Revolution. This was followed by a host of exciting stories, e.g. *Beau Brocade, I Will Repay, The Elusive Pimpernel,* and *Will-o'-the-Wisp.* In 1946 her memoirs were published under the title of *Links in the Chain of Life.* She died 1947.

ordeal, ancient form of trial based on the assumption that God protects the innocent ; hence, especially in Anglo-Saxon times (*a*) ordeal *by battle* ; (*b*) ordeal *by fire,* the accused walking over hot ploughshares or carrying a hot iron to prove his innocence ; (*c*) *by hot water,* i.e. plunging the arm into boiling water, and being judged guilty if scalded; and (*d*) *being flung into a pond or river* (often bound), and regarded as guilty if able to float, a test often applied to persons suspected of witchcraft.

ordnance, see GUN

ore, mineral containing sufficient metal to make the extraction of it a profitable undertaking. An average of 1oz of gold is obtained from a ton of rock, but lead, tin, zinc, etc. may amount to 50% of the mineral with which they are found. Britain, the Urals (USSR), Scandinavia, N. America, etc. are rich in iron ; valuable ore deposits are found in Rhodesia, Mexico, and near the Great Lakes, USA ; Cornwall has deposits of almost every common metal. Note that :

This ORE—gives—this METAL	
argentite	silver
bauxite	aluminium
cassiterite	tin
cinnabar	mercury
copper pyrites	copper
galena	lead
haematite	iron
magnesite	magnesium
pentlandite	nickel
zinc blende	zinc

Oregon, Pacific state of USA ; has important industries, e.g. gold, silver and copper ; grows wheat and fruits ; raises farm stock ; cap. Salem.

Orel, *ŏr-yŏl',* town, USSR ; on the Oka somewhat north of the Ukraine ; also a river flowing 130m to the R. Dnieper.

Orestes, *ō-res'tēz* in old Greek tales, son of Agamemnon and Clytaemnestra.

organ, musical instrument with pipes of various lengths blown by wind, and controlled by the keyboard, the tone depending on a series of stops (e.g. *diapason, viol,* etc.). Large organs actually comprise two or more instruments (such as great organ, swell and solo), which may be played separately or in combination, the action of the whole being either pneumatic or electric. The CINEMA ORGAN has, in addition, a variety of ' effects,' e.g. bells and drums. A pipeless or ELECTRONIC ORGAN was invented 1930, and developed by Compton, Hammond, etc. The Hammond organ has ninety-one small discs. These by revolving at various speeds between the poles of a magnet cause alternating currents of different frequencies, which are converted into sounds and amplified. In 1949 the BBC installed at Maida Vale a pipeless organ, the ' Electrone.' The largest of its kind, it has great tonal content and variety.

organic, see CHEMISTRY

organ pipes, see SOUND

Oriel College, *ō'ri-el,* college of Oxford University, founded 1326. One of its most famous members was Cecil Rhodes.

Orient, see ANATOLIA

Orinocco, see RALEIGH, SIR WALTER

Orinoco, *ō-ri-nō'kō,* river of S. America ; rises near the Brazilian frontier, its source being discovered 1944 ; flows *c.*1,600m mostly through Venezuela to the Atlantic, entering by a large delta.

oriole, *ōr-i-ōl',* bird about the size of a thrush. It has yellow, green and black plumage ; short legs ; long wings. The golden oriole (golden with black on wings and tail) visits Britain while migrating.

Orion, *ō-rī'on,* in old Greek tales, a giant and hunter blinded by the King of Chios. After his death he was given a place in the sky, hence the constellation of Orion, including the Orion nebula.

Orissa, *ō-ris'ä,* province of the Dominion of India, since 1936 ; south of Bihar ; largely agricultural ; chief city Cuttack.

Orkneys, *ŏrk'niz,* 90 islands, north of Caithness, Scotland ; total area *c.*375 sq.m ; pop.21,000. Twenty-nine islands are inhabited, the largest is Pomona ; between it and Hoy (second largest) is Scapa Flow, where the German fleet was scuttled June 1919 ; cap. Kirkwall.

Orleans, *aur-lā-än,* city, France ; on the R. Loire ; manufactures machinery, hosiery, etc., but is most famous as a trading centre ; scene of Joan of Arc's first success against the English 1429 ; pop.71,000.

Orleans, DUKE OF, title borne by various members of the French Bourbon family, including (*a*) CHARLES (1391–1465), who married the widow of Richard II of England ; taken prisoner at Agincourt 1415, he was ransomed 1440, and was one of the greatest French poets of the Middle Ages ; (*b*) PHILIP II (1674–1723); and (*c*) LOUIS PHILIPPE (1747–93), who was guillotined.

Orlon, trade name since 1950 for a textile similar to nylon but more like wool. It is exceedingly durable. See PLASTICS

Ormskirk, town, Lancashire. Industries include rope-making and iron-founding.

ornithology, see BIRDS

Orpen, SIR WILLIAM (1878–1931), artist, *b* Dublin ; made a notable series of pictures of World War I ; famous for portraits, and a lover of brilliant colours.

Orpheus, *ŏr'fūs,* in old Greek tales, son of Calliope ; famed for his extraordinary skill on the lyre, animals and even trees following when he played. His wife was Eurydice.

Orpington, town, Kent ; gave its name to a breed of poultry ; pop.50,000

Orsova, *ŏr'shō-vo,* one of the chief towns on the R. Danube (Rumania) ; near the Iron Gates.

orthocentre, see TRIANGLE

OS (old style), see CALENDAR

Osaka, *ō'sä-kä,* second city and a port, Japan ; on Honshu I. ; has notable shipbuilding yards, and produces textiles and glassware. Tea is grown in the vicinity ; pop.3,252,000.

Osborne House, house in the I. of Wight. It was the favourite residence of Queen Victoria, who died there 1901.

Osbourne, SAMUEL LLOYD, see STEVENSON, R. L.

osier, *ō'zhĕr,* shrub or low tree of the willow family found in damp places. The narrow leaves are silvery beneath ; the catkins are golden yellow. Slender, pliant osier twigs are used for basket-making.

Osiris, *ō-sī'ris,* Egyptian god, husband of Isis, father of Horus ; became the god of resurrection, judge of the dead, and lord of the underworld.

Oslo, port, city, and cap., Norway ; on the south-east coast ; has a fine modern harbour ; manufactures textiles, paper, iron and steel goods ; formerly called Christiania ; under German rule 1940–1945 ; pop.275,000.

osmium, white metal and element, Os ; atomic weight 190·2 ; atomic number 76 ; melting-point 2,700°C (approx.). With specific gravity 22·5, it is the heaviest substance known.

osmosis, *os-mō'sis,* in chemistry, the passage of a solvent through a semi-permeable membrane from a solution of lower osmotic pressure to one of higher osmotic pressure.

Osnabrück, *os-nä-brük',* city in Western Germany, an important railway junction ; manufactures paper and textiles ;

THE OTTER

pop.94,000 before World War II, during which time it was severely bombed.

osprey, os'pri, bird c.24in long ; has dark brown back and wings ; throat, crown and underparts whitish. The osprey soars to great heights, hunts fish, and nests in high trees or cliffs. Once common in several parts of Britain, the osprey is now probably extinct, although a few were still known in N. Scotland at the beginning of the century.

Ossett, town, W. Yorkshire ; makes woollen cloth and shoddy.

Ossian, Irish hero and poet ; a great figure in Gaelic lore.

Ostend, holiday town and port, Belgium ; has a ferry service with Dover, and many railway connections ; severely bombed in World War II ; pop.55,000.

Ostia, ancient ruined city, once the port for Rome.

ostrich, largest living bird ; may be 8ft high. The wings, useless for flight, are an aid in running. The plumage of the male is black with some white feathers, but the female is grey. Ostriches, now scarce in the wild state, are found in desert regions in Africa and Arabia. Since 1867 ostrich farms have been established in S. Africa, USA and Australia. The birds' feathers are used for decorative purposes, e.g. trimming ladies' hats and for making fans.

Oswald (d 642), formed Northumbria from the kingdoms of Bernicia and Deira. He was killed while fighting Penda, King of Mercia, and is remembered for his efforts to promote Christianity.

Oswestry, town, Shropshire ; has tanneries and woollen mills.

Otago, ō-tä'gō, district of S. Island NZ ; cap. Dunedin.

Otley, town on the R. Wharfe, W. Yorkshire ; makes printing machinery and worsteds.

Ottawa, federal cap.; Canada, on the Ottawa R. ; has handsome New Parliament buildings, erected 1916–20 ; is the home of the Governor-General ; has a large trade in lumber and paper. An imperial economic conference met at Ottawa 1932. Pop.155,000.

otter, animal found in Britain, America, etc. It is c.24in long ; has thick and valuable fur, webbed feet, and a tail usually 18in long. The otter makes a burrow near a stream ; feeds on fish ; and is hunted in Britain (with otter hounds) May–Oct.

Otterburn, village, Northumberland, 16m south of the Scottish border. Its wild moors were the scene of the moonlight battle of Otterburn (or Chevy Chase) 1388, when the Scots defeated the English. The *Ballad of Otterburn* is often confused with this Scottish victory.

Ottoman Empire, Moslem empire founded in Turkey c. AD1300 by Orkhan, ruler of the Ottomans, a nomad tribe which settled in Turkey c.1230. The Ottoman Empire succeeded the Seljuk empire, which had fallen to pieces after driving out the Crusaders (13th c.) : and it was itself overwhelmed out of Central Asia by a Mongol invasion led by Tamburlane the Great 1402.

Making an astonishing recovery, the Ottoman Turks captured Constantinople 1453, thus destroying what was left of the Greek or Byzantine Empire (see CONSTANTINE THE GREAT ; CRUSADES). It will be remembered that one of the main impulses of the 15th–16th c. Renaissance in Western Europe was the new knowledge of ancient Greek literature broadcast by refugee scholars from Constantinople.

From 1452 to 1699, the Ottoman Empire was a threat to Christianity in Central and SE. Europe. At Kossovo in 1389 the Ottomans had defeated a Serb-Hungarian army. During the 15th c. they were held up for a time by the Hungarian national hero John Hunyadi (1387–1456), and by his son Matthias Corvinus (1443–90), who became King of Hungary : but in battle at Mohács 1526 they destroyed the ' flower of Hungarian chivalry,' and by the end of the 16th c. had overrun most of Hungary, with the exception of Transylvania. In other directions their rule embraced the Mediterranean and extended eastwards as far as Persia.

Hungary was finally redeemed from Ottoman rule by Austria 1699 ; Greece by a national insurrection 1821–29 ; Serbia and the modern countries Rumania and Bulgaria by the Treaty of San Stefano with Russia 1878. Egypt came fully under British control 1904. In Turkey itself the Sultan Abdul Hamid (Abdul the Damned) was deposed 1908 by the Young Turk Revolution, and the Ottoman Empire came to an end 1920, being replaced by a republic, under the Treaty of Sèvres.

Ottomans, members of the Ottoman (i.e. Turkish) empire. Ottoman is derived from Osman, a 13th c. Turkish leader.

Oudenarde, *ow-de-när'de,* town, Belgium ; scene of Marlborough's victory over the French 1708.

Oudh, see AGRA AND OUDH

ounce or **snow leopard,** animal of the mountainous regions of Central Asia ; may be 7ft long ; has grey, woolly fur with large spots.

Oundle, *own'dl,* town, Northamptonshire ; has a famous public school, founded in the 16th century.

Ouse, *ooz,* name of several English rivers, e.g. Yorkshire Ouse (60m), which joins the Humber ; Great Ouse, flowing 160m to the Wash.

Outram, Sir JAMES, *oo'tram* (1803–63), soldier, born in Derbyshire ; took part in the Afghanistan campaign 1839, and made a famous ride of 350m from Kalat to Karachi. He defended Hyderabad 1843, and helped to defend Lucknow during the Indian Mutiny.

ouzel, name of several birds of the thrush family, among them the RING-OUZEL, a kind of large moorland blackbird, visiting Britain in summer. There is also the water-ouzel, better known as the dipper. See DIPPER

Oval, THE, ground of the Surrey County Cricket Club, Kennington Park Road, London, S.E. ; opened 1846. See CRICKET

Ovid, *ov'id* (43BC–AD17), Roman poet, b Sulmo ; studied law in Rome, also rhetoric ; visited Athens ; toured Asia Minor ; married three times ; lived a life of pleasure in Rome till banished to a town on the Danube AD9.

Ovid's poems include *Amores* ; *Ars amatoria* ; *Remedia Amoris* (an apology for having offended the Emperor Augustus with *Ars amatoria*) ; *Heroides* ; *Medea* (a tragedy which is lost) ; *Fasti,* all in elegaic couplets ; and his famous *Metamorphoses,* a series of delightful romantic tales. His poetry, full of beauty, imagination and action, has had an immense influence on English literature, especially on that of Elizabeth's day.

Note the following sayings from the works of Ovid :

Cetera quis nescit? i.e. The rest who does not know ?

Tempus edax rerum, i.e. Time the devourer of all things.

Medio tutissimus ibis, i.e. You will go most safely in the middle.

Oviedo, *ō-vyā'thō,* city, Spain ; 60m north-west of Leon ; manufactures textiles ; noted for its university ; pop.51,000.

Owen, ROBERT (1771–1858), social reformer. At 19 he managed a Manchester cotton mill with 500 hands. He imported raw cotton from USA ; was a pioneer of better houses and education for workpeople ; founded a model village at New Lanark, and advanced Socialism and the co-operative movement.

Owens, JOHN (1790–1846), Manchester merchant, founder of Owens College, opened 1851.

THE BARN OWL

owl, night-flying bird of prey, usually with large eyes adapted to seeing in the dark, and encircled with feathers. The plumage is soft, the wings short Owls fly almost noiselessly, and hunt small rodents.

Among British owls are (*a*) BARN OWL, tawny above, white below ; sometimes known from its cry as the ' screech-owl ' ; (*b*) LONG-EARED OWL, with erect tufts of feathers above the eyes ; found in groups, especially among pine woods ; (*c*) SHORT-EARED OWL, yellowish with brown tufts ; visits Britain in winter ; (*d*) TAWNY OWL (or brown or wood owl), reddish above, barred below ; well known for its hooting cry ; nests in hollow trees. All species lay whitish eggs.

oxalic acid, poisonous solid $(COOH)_2$. Its presence in rhubarb leaves makes them poisonous.

ox-eye, plant resembling a large daisy ; has tall, stiff stem, and feathery leaves without stalks.

Oxford, city and co.tn of Oxfordshire ; on the R. Thames, here called the Isis. One of the oldest and most beautiful cities in England, its High Street (known as the ' High ') is among the most famous and graceful in Europe. The cathedral is partly Norman. There are remains of the town walls.

Oxford's long history goes back at least to Saxon times. The *Provisions of Oxford* were drawn up here 1258 ; here were Charles I's HQ during part of the Civil War ; Latimer and Ridley were burned at the stake in Broad Street 1555, Cranmer 1556. Industries include printing, especially of educational works; also car and aeroplane manufacture, the Morris works being at Cowley, close by.

Oxford has for long been famous as a seat of learning, and among its museums and libraries may be mentioned the Ashmolean Museum and the Bodleian Library.

The pride of the city is its university. Oxford has many stately colleges, their buildings set about with beautiful gardens. The colleges (with dates founded) are as follows : All Souls 1437, Balliol 1266, Brasenose 1509, Christ Church 1532, Corpus Christi 1516, Exeter 1314, Hertford 1874, Jesus 1571, Keble 1870, Lincoln 1427, Magdalen 1458, Merton 1264, New College 1379, Oriel 1326, Pembroke 1624, Queen's 1340, St John's 1555, Trinity 1554, University 1249, Wadham 1612, Worcester 1714, St Edmund's Hall 1269 ; there is also St Catherine's Society (1868), Campion Hall, St Benet's Hall, and St Peter's Hall. The women's colleges are : Lady Margaret Hall 1878, Somerville 1879, St Hugh's 1886, St Hilda's 1893, and St Anne's Society 1879. Diploma courses in sociology are taken at Nuffield College and Ruskin College.

Entrance to the university is gained by passing the special entrance examination known as Responsions, or equivalent. It is possible to win scholarships giving the student free, or partly free, education ; otherwise the cost of taking a degree in arts, divinity, law, music, or medicine, together with other expenses, may approach £1,000. Full particulars from the Assistant Registrar, University Registry, Oxford.

Oxford and Asquith, HERBERT HENRY ASQUITH, 1ST EARL OF (1852–1928), *b* Morley, Yorkshire. Son of a woollen manufacturer, Asquith became a lawyer, and entered Parliament as a Liberal 1886. As Chancellor of the Exchequer (1905), he reduced the national debt, planned a scheme for old age pensions, and made important alterations in income tax. He followed Campbell-Bannerman as Prime Minister 1908–16, and was created an earl 1925. He is remembered also for his bold and successful handling of the House of Lords crisis, settled by the Parliament Act 1911. He served the Liberal party and his country with honour and devotion.

He used the famous phrase *wait and see* 1910 when being questioned about the Finance Bill.

Oxford Movement, religious revival of the 19th c., largely due to E. B. Pusey, John Keble and Newman. It sought to introduce more elaborate ritual into church worship, and was popularised by *Tracts for the Times*, published from 1834. Anglocatholicism is a lasting result of the Oxford Movement. Several of the leaders of the movement went further, and, like Newman, joined the Church of Rome.

Oxfordshire, county of England ; north of the R. Thames ; noted for its pastureland, but has many important manufactures ; co.tn Oxford.

Oxford University, see OXFORD

oxgang, see BOVATE

oxidation, chemical term for the process by which the percentage of the electronegative part of a compound is increased. Methods of oxidation include (*a*) adding oxygen to an element or compound, (*b*) removing hydrogen. A common example is the formation of rust, due to the oxidation of iron.

oxide, compound of two elements, one of which is oxygen.

Oxonian, from *Oxonia*, Lat. form of Oxford ; a native of Oxford or a member of Oxford University.

Oxus, river of Asia flowing 1,500m from the Pamir plateau to the Sea of Aral. It is now called Amu Darya.

oxygen, gaseous element, O, one of the most widely distributed in nature ; comprises 21% by volume and 23% by weight of the atmosphere ; is essential to almost every form of life (anaerobic bacteria are possibly the only exception) and to combustion. Oxygen was discovered 1774 by Joseph Priestley. Its atomic weight, 16·0000, is now taken as the atomic weight standard. Its atomic number is 8.

An odourless and invisible gas, it may be obtained by heating (*a*) various metallic oxides. e.g. those of silver, gold, mercury, platinum ; (*b*) higher oxides or peroxides of metals, e.g. barium, lead ; or (*c*) salts rich in oxygen, e.g. chlorates, especially potassium chlorate. In the laboratory, manganese dioxide, as catalyst, is mixed with potassium chlorate and heated, and the gas collected over water ; industrially, oxygen is prepared by the liquefaction of air and fractional distillation. Liquid oxygen is used as the airman's oxygen supply in high-flying planes ; the gas mixed with either hydrogen or acetylene is used in the oxy-hydrogen or oxy-acetylene blowpipe for welding.

OZONE, O_3, produced by silent electric discharge on oxygen, or by the electrolysis of sulphuric acid, has more energy than oxygen. An unstable allotropic form of oxygen, it is a bluish gas, exceedingly active chemically, converting sulphur, phosphorus and arsenic into their highest oxy-acids, and liberating halogens from their hydracids. It may possibly exist as a layer of the upper atmosphere.

oyster, see MOLLUSCA

P

P, chemical symbol for phosphorus.

Pacific Highway, see ROADS

Pacific Ocean, largest of the world's oceans ; covers a third of the earth's surface ; area 63,986,000sq.m ; greatest depth 35,410ft off Mindanao; remarkable for its many islands, e.g. the Aleutians, the Kuriles, the Philippines and the innumerable volcanic and coral islands, chiefly in the South. Control of the Pacific was won from the Japanese by the USA navy during the later stages of World War II.

pacifism, *pas'i-fizm*, belief that war in any circumstances (even against oppression and injustice) is wrong.

Pactum serva, see EDWARD I

Paddington, borough of London. Its station is the terminus of the former GWR.

paddy, see RICE

Paderewski, IGNAZ JAN, *pä-de-ref'skē* (1860–1941), Polish pianist and patriot. During World War I he won support in USA for the creation of a free and united Poland, and later accompanied the British mission to Warsaw 1918, and was President of the new republic 1919. He was broken-hearted when Poland was overrun in World War II, and declared he would not play again till his country was free.

Padua, city of N. Italy ; notable for its cathedral and churches ; famous in the Middle Ages for its university ; pop. 163,000.

Paganini, NICOLO, *pägä-nē'nē* (1784–1840), brilliant Italian composer and violinist, *b* Genoa ; toured Europe ; a pioneer of stopped harmonics.

Page, WALTER HINES (1855–1918), American ambassador to Britain 1913–18 ; advocated America's entry into World War I.

pagoda, *pä-gō'dä*, in India and E. Asia, a tower-like building, especially Buddhist erections in China or Japan having an odd number of roofs. The pagoda at Kew is of Chinese pattern.

Pahang, mountainous Malay state (British), soon to achieve self-government ; produces gold and rubber. See MALAYA

Paignton, *pān'tun*, seaside resort, Devon ; noted for cider; pop.24,000.

Paine, THOMAS (1737–1809), writer and reformer, *b* Thetford, Norfolk ; defended the American colonists in their fight for independence ; supported the leaders of the French Revolution in his book *The Rights of Man*. He wrote *The Age of Reason*, an attack on religion.

Read *Tom Paine*, W. E. Woodward.

Painlevé, PAUL, *pan-lě-vä'* (1863–1933), French thinker, scientist, statesman and aviation expert ; was Prime Minister 1917, and again 1925.

painting, as a form of art, began thousands of years ago. Stone Age men ornamented bone weapons and the walls of their caves (as we may see in France and Spain). Very little Greek and Roman painting has come down to us, but Europe treasures many pictures painted since *c*.AD1300.

Christianity has long inspired European artists ; and from the 12th–16th c. the works of the Italian artists (Giotto, Donatello, Bellini, Giorgione, Titian, Raphael, Michelangelo and Leonardo da Vinci) also of Dürer (German) were almost always religious.

Gradually *portrait-painting* became popular ; Holbein was a master of it in the 16th c. The 17th c. Dutch artists became notable for their *genre* (*zhän'r*) pictures, i.e. scenes from everyday life ; Rubens (Flemish) and Rembrandt were genre artists. *Landscape painting* began in Italy and reached a high level with Canaletto (18th c.).

Hogarth stands out as one of the earliest British artists with an individual style; others (of the 18th c.) were George Romney, Sir Joshua Reynolds, Sir Henry Raeburn and Thomas Gainsborough ; landscapes and seascapes were favourites with George Morland, John Crome, Thomas Girtin, John Cotman, David Cox, John Constable and (greatest of all) Turner. In the 19th c. Holman Hunt, Dante Gabriel Rossetti and Ford Madox Brown revived the style of the Italian artists before Raphael, calling themselves the *Pre-Raphaelites* ; other famous British artists of this period include William Morris, Lord Leighton, Sir Edwin Landseer and G. F. Watts. Our modern artists include Sir William Orpen, Frank Brangwyn, C. R. W. Nevinson, Sir John Lavery, C. W. Furse, Augustus John, Frank O. Salisbury, Dame Laura Knight, Rex Whistler, Sir A. J. Munnings, etc.

Towards the end of the 19th c. many European artists rebelled against tradition, declaring that painting had become merely pretty, hence such movements in the 20th c. as *Impressionism*, which may be said to have begun with James McNeill Whistler and the French artists Edouard Manet and Claude Monet. This was advanced by Renoir, Pissaro, Cézanne, etc., who perfected new and striking techniques in colour and lighting. Among the greatest of the Impressionists was the Scottish painter William MacTaggart. There followed *Post-Impressionism*, then *Cubism* (*kū'bizm*), in which straight lines and geometrical patterns predominated, the Spanish artist Picasso being a pioneer of this innovation.

Other modern art forms include *Futurism* (originating in Italy *c.*1910) in which grotesque shapes were supposed to express the artist's mental state ; also *Surrealism*, which deliberately gave up the attempt to depict the ' real ' of waking hours, and tried to express abstractions (e.g. hatred) by representing the scenery and appearances of things in dreams. Surrealism is not altogether unrelated to modern tendencies in music.

A British artist whose picture is hung in the Royal Academy of Arts (founded 1768 by George III) may be an Associate, or may be elected as one of the forty-two Members (each with R.A. after his or her name). The Royal Academy holds a famous exhibition in May. An art-master will give advice to those contemplating art as a career.

Read *Vision and Design*, Roger Fry ; *What is Art?* D. S. MacColl ; *European Painting and Sculpture*, Eric Newton. Biographies of modern painters are given in a Penguin series, *Modern Painters*, edited by Sir Kenneth Clark.

See PLATES XIII–XVI

Paisley, town, Renfrewshire ; world-famous for spinning cotton thread ; noted for Paisley shawls since *c.*1780 ; pop.92,000.

Pakistan, British Dominion in India, the formation of which was discussed by the Muslim League 1940, and which actually came into being July 1947. The area is not yet finally defined, but includes two distinct regions : (*a*) the western zone, namely Sind, the W. Punjab, the North-West Frontier provinces and Baluchistan ; and (*b*) a region 1,000m distant, namely East Bengal. The total area is *c.*362,000sq.m, and it should be noted that there is no corridor between the two zones, and their only means of communication between Karachi, the Pakistan capital, and Dacca, cap. of E. Bengal, being the overland air routes and the sea route round S. India, a distance of 3,000m. Of the pop. of *c.*70,000,000 over half live in E. Bengal. The people are largely Muslims. The creator of the new Dominion was Mohamed Ali Jinnah, its first Governor-General, who died soon after the Dominion came into being, and whose grave (near Karachi) has already become a place of pilgrimage. In spite of many differences, it seems likely that Pakistinis will achieve unity of purpose, striving to carry on the work so ably begun by Mr Jinnah. See INDIA

Palace of the Soviets, see USSR

palanquin, *pal-an-kēn'*, in India and China, a conveyance for one person ; actually a form of litter carried by two or (more usually) four bearers.

Palatinate, region of Germany W. of the Rhine.

palatine, see SHIRE

Palatine Hill, one of the seven hills of ancient Rome.

Pale, THE, portion of Ireland (after 1172)

where Anglo-Norman rule was supreme. It was largely in the east, and was so called from the 15th c.

Palembang, town, Sumatra, Netherlands E. Indies ; pop.109,000.

Palermo, city, port and cap., Sicily ; noted for its beautiful palace. Manufactures chemicals and machinery ; exports include lemons and tobacco ; pop.452,000.

Palestine, formerly British mandated territory in Asia east of the Mediterranean ; since 1948, the independent state of Israel ; area *c.*10,400sq.m ; pop.1,740,000, chiefly Jews and Arabs ; comprises the hill country of Galilee and Judea, the five plains (including the Jordan valley), Beersheba and desert. The chief river, the Jordan, flows into the Sea of Galilee (L. Tiberias), over 690ft below sea-level, and into the Dead Sea, area 405sq.m. Having no outlet, the Dead Sea (1,286ft below sea-level) is exceedingly buoyant owing to the great salt content, therefore there is no possibility of a swimmer sinking.

Palestine is largely agricultural, with a temperate climate and fertile soil over a considerable area (though water is scarce) ; it produces wheat, barley, millet, potatoes, also olives, oranges (notably Jaffa oranges), figs and grapes. Its ports include Haifa, Jaffa, the modern Tel Aviv, Gaza, Acre ; other towns include Hebron, Nablus, and the cap., Jerusalem, with pop.155,000. Captured by General Allenby 1917, Jerusalem was Moslem from AD637 to 1517, when it was in Turkish hands. Being the holy city of the Jews, it still retains its ancient walls. Here stood the Temple built by Solomon *c.*980BC, destroyed by Nebuchadnezzar 586BC, rebuilt 515BC, and again by Herod (completed AD29), and finally reduced by Titus AD70. Part of its outer wall is known as the ' Wailing Wall.'

Other historic sites of Palestine (the Holy Land) recall the OT and the NT, especially the life of Christ, e.g. Bethlehem, with the Church of the Nativity, and also Nazareth.

After World War I Palestine was a British Mandated Territory under the League of Nations. There was continual friction and sometimes fighting between Jews and Arabs. Jews were being allowed to settle down in the country, and the Arabs did not see why they should be expected to make room for them. The British Mandate came to an end 1948, and Palestine was invaded by the Arab states (Egypt, Iraq, Syria, Transjordan). The Jews fought back successfully, and with help from the USA managed to establish the National State of Israel. The new State was formally recognised by the UK in 1949, but it had been invaded (1948) by Syrian, Lebanese, Arab and Egyptian troops, and though large areas were allotted to Arabs, Israel remained politically unsettled. See JEWS

Palestrina, GIOVANNI, *pa-lăs-trē'nä* (*d* 1594), Italian composer ; improved church music ; composed many madrigals, but most famous for his splendid Masses.

Palgrave, FRANCIS TURNER, *pöl'gräv* (1824–1897), poet, *b* London ; famous for his anthology, *The Golden Treasury of English Songs and Lyrics*, first published 1861, and since brought up-to-date many times.

palimpses, see BRASS

Palissy, B., see POTTERY

Palk's Strait, *pauk,* channel (40m wide) between Ceylon and India.

palladium, *pa-lā'di-ŭm,* element, Pd ; atomic weight 106·7 ; atomic number 46 ; specific gravity 11·9 ; white metal resembling platinum. Mined in Ontario, it is now used in making jewellery.

Pallas or **Pallas Athene,** see ATHENA

palm, *päm,* family of trees (*Palmae*) found in tropical and sub-tropical regions. There are *c.*1,100 species, including coconut, date, betel, sago and rattan palms. All are tall and unbranched, sometimes rising to 150ft, and crowned with large feather-shaped or fan-like leaves. Many palms are valuable not only for their fruit or nuts, but for their leaves (used in thatching and basket-making), their fibre, including copra (the dried kernel of the coconut), and various juices from the trunk.

palmer, *päm'ĕr,* old name given to a Christian who had visited the Holy Land (Palestine). He was so called from the custom (especially in crusading times) of bringing back a palm staff or branch.

Palmer, JOHN, see ROADS

Palmerston, VISCOUNT, *päm'er-stŭn* (1784–1865), *b* Hampshire ; entered the Commons 1807. He separated from the Tories, and was Foreign Secretary 1830–41 and again 1846–51. He was Prime Minister 1855 and suppressed the Indian Mutiny. Resigning 1858, he was Prime Minister again 1859 till his death. Palmerston, who had charm of manner and was a great sportsman, was always resourceful, but he was ' showy,' and on the whole more of a politician than a statesman.

palmistry, see PROPHET

Palm Sunday, see CALENDAR

Palmyra, ruined town 150m north-east of Damascus, Syria.

Palomar Observatory, see OBSERVATORIES ; TELESCOPE

Paludrine, see MOSQUITO ; QUININE

Pamir, plateau known as ' The Roof of the World ' ; *c.*13,000ft high ; links the Himalayas with the Hindu Kush.

pampas, see GRASS

pan-, as a prefix, is derived from a Greek word meaning ' all.' Thus ' Pan-slavism ' is a political movement aiming at co-operation among *all* the Slav nations.

Pan, in old Greek tales, the god of shepherds. He had the horns and legs of a goat ; played on a simple musical instrument made of reeds of various lengths (known as Pan's pipes), and often surprised and frightened travellers by appearing suddenly, hence the word *panic.*

Panama (republic) see CENTRAL AMERICA

Panama Canal, see CANALS

Panama, ISTHUMUS OF, land link between Central and S. America ; from 40–110m wide.

Pan-American World Airways System, vast system of air-lines across the Atlantic, Pacific, etc. ; has operational HQ at La Guardia Field, New York, USA. The company's giant airliners have normally a cruising speed of 340 mph over distances approaching 3,000m. The 1948 airliners powered with gas-turbines incorporate the latest achievements in aircraft construction. The Clipper service is unrivalled, passengers being able to breakfast on the east coast of USA and reach Los Angeles, after crossing the continent, in time for lunch at 12.30. The Rainbow Clippers fly well above the weather.

The 4-engined double-decked Pan American Stratocruiser carries 80 passengers (on day trips) ; has an operational range of 3,500m, flies at 30,000ft ; is over 110ft long with a wing-span of 141ft ; total gross weight 135,000lb.

Pancake Day, see CALENDAR

panda, name of two somewhat related animals, (*a*) small brown cat-bear of Assam and the Himalayas ; (*b*) giant panda, an exceedingly rare animal of Tibet ; bear-like in appearance ; has a white face and body, black legs, and black rings round the eyes ; may weigh over 20st. It is very slow in its movements, and feeds on bamboo.

Pandora, in old Greek tales, the first woman. As the wife of Epimetheus, she inquisitively opened a box, and let out all the evil spirits that vex mankind. Happily, however, she closed it in time to keep hope from escaping.

pangolin, *pang-gō'lin,* toothless animal found in S. Asia and in Africa ; may be 2–3ft long, somewhat lizard-shaped, and covered with horny plates. It rolls into a ball when attacked, and feeds on termites at night.

Pankhurst, MRS, see ELECTION

Pan's pipes, see PAN

pansy, plant of the family *Violaceae.* The oblong leaves are cut and lobed ; the flowers purple, whitish, or yellow, or a mixture of these. The plant is sometimes called heartsease or love-in-idleness.

Pantellaria Island, strongly fortified island in the Sicilian Narrows ; formerly Italian ; captured by the Allies June 1943.

Pantheon, see ARCHITECTURE

panther, see LEOPARD

pantomime, originally the art of acting without words, common in ancient Greece, and still more popular with the Romans ; now applied to the acting of children's fairy stories such as *Cinderella,*

PANDAS

(1) *Panda (the Cat Bear)*   (2) *The Giant Panda*

Jack and the Beanstalk, in which there is music, dancing, humour, frequent scene changes, and always finishing with the reconciliation of hero and heroine, who we are told ' live happily ever after.' Pantomimes are generally performed during the Christmas season to provide entertainment for children.

Panzer (German, iron-clad), name given in World War II to the German armoured division.

Papal State, see VATICAN

Papen, FRANZ VON, *pä'pen* (1879–   ), German politician ; Chancellor of Germany 1932 ; tried for war crimes 1945–46 ; acquitted.

paper, material used mainly for writing or printing on ; evolved from leaves, thin strips of bark and papyrus (see PAPYRUS). The method of making paper introduced into Europe by the Moors in the 11th c. is believed to have originated in China. The first English paper-mill was established in the 16th c., and in the 19th c. hand-made was mainly ousted by machine-made paper, which alone could satisfy the enormous demand for paper for books, and, still more, for newspapers (newsprint).

Today cheap paper is a cellulose product, made sometimes from grasses (e.g. esparto), more often from spruce, pine, or poplar. Forests in N. America and Scandinavia supply the timber, which is cut into chips, boiled (or digested) with alkaline or acid liquids under pressure, bleached, and finally produced in rolls often 4m long. More expensive (and more enduring) papers are made from cotton fibre (almost pure cellulose), cotton and linen rags, straw, bamboo and flax ; or from various mixtures of these, often with china clay ; but hand-made paper is still the best.

papers, see NEWSPAPERS

papier mâché, *pä-pyä mä-shä* (French, pulped paper), hard but light substance made from paper-pulp mixed with glue, size, clay and water, and moulded into a variety of articles.

Papin, DENIS, *pä-pan'* (1647–1712), French scientist ; studied boiling-points and pressures ; made the first piston-driven steam engine.

Papua, see NEW GUINEA

Papworth, village settlement, Cambridge, for tuberculosis patients ; opened 1917 ; has many village industries.

papyrus, *pä-pī'rŭs* (plural *papyri*), kind of paper made in ancient Egypt from reeds (*Cyperus papyrus*) growing by the Nile. These were laid in strips at right angles, moistened, beaten flat and polished (see PAPER). Papyri continued in use until *c.*AD400. A papyrus roll 135ft long with writing in praise of Rameses III (*d* 1170BC) is preserved in the British Museum.

Pará or **Belem,** *pä-rä'*, town and port, NE. Brazil, on the estuary of the Pará R., and cap. of a large rubber-producing region ; exports rubber ; pop.309,000.

parable, see ALLEGORY

parabola, *pa-rab'ō-la*, in mathematics,

section produced by cutting a cone parallel to the slanting edge ; also the locus of a point, the distance of which from a fixed point (*focus*) is always equal to its distance from a fixed straight line (*directrix*). The curve traced by a projectile *in vacuo* is a parabola.

Paracelsus, *par-ä-sel'sŭs* (1493–1541), Swiss medical pioneer ; *d* Salzburg, Germany ; did much to bring new knowledge and methods to healing. See ALCHEMY

parachute, umbrella-shaped device of silk, nylon, or Egyptian cotton by means of which a person or object may be safely dropped from a great height owing to the resistance to the air the parachute affords. As safety devices parachutes are carried in planes. In modern warfare, stores, ammunition, tanks and lifeboats are often dropped by parachute, and paratroops descend behind the enemy lines to disrupt communications.

The terminal velocity of a mandropping parachute is about that reached by a man jumping from a height of 10ft.

The parachute proper is usually pulled open by a miniature parachute which opens first ; but for dropping troops from low levels the parachutes are temporarily attached to a device in the aircraft which pulls them open as the paratrooper jumps.

paraffin series, hydrocarbons with the general formula C_nH_{2n+2} ; including (*a*) the gases methane, ethane, propane and butane ; (*b*) liquids that form the chief constituents of mineral oils, e.g. paraffin oil or kerosine, derived from the distillation of petroleum ; and (*c*) such solid forms as paraffin wax.

Paraguay, *par'ä-gwä* ; *pä-rä-gwī'*, river of S. America ; flows 1,800m to the R. Paraná.

Paraguay, republic of S. America. Situated between Brazil and Argentina, it has no coastline ; area *c.*61,000sq.m ; pop. 1,100,000. Largely a plain with much grassland and vast forests, it has many swamps. Exports include cattle, meat, hides, timber (mainly cedar) ; agriculture remains somewhat primitive ; yerba maté (native tea) is grown ; freed from Spanish domination 1811 ; cap. Asuncion.

parallel, see LATITUDE

parallel, in, see ELECTRICITY

parallelogram, see QUADRILATERAL FIGURE

parallelogram of forces, see MECHANICS

parallel straight lines are straight lines in the same plane running in the same direction. By definition they never meet, no matter how far they are produced : but for practical purposes two straight lines which meet at infinity, or at a very great distance, may be regarded as parallel lines.

paramagnetic, see MAGNETISM

Paraná, river of S. America ; flows 2,000m to the estuary of the R. Plate.

Parana, town, Argentina ; trades in timber, meat and wool ; pop.78,000.

parasite, animal, plant, or bacterium living on some other creature, usually with harmful results to the 'host,' though sometimes the result is mutually beneficial, in which case the association is called symbiosis. Among animal parasites are the flea and liver-fluke of sheep. Plant parasites include dodder, mistletoe (though only partially), and such fungi as the 'rust' of wheat, potato-blight, mildews, moulds and toadstools. Disease bacteria (e.g. that causing malaria) are parasites.

paratroops, see PARACHUTE

pariah, *pä-rī'ä*, out-caste of S. India ; a Hindu of the lower class without caste, sometimes styled an 'untouchable.'

Paris, in old Greek tales, son of Priam, King of Troy, and Hecuba ; by carrying off Helen (wife of Menelaus of Sparta) he caused the Trojan war.

Paris, *par'is* ; *pä-rē'*, city and cap., France ; on the R. Seine and two islands in the river ; pop.2,900,000 ; of Greater Paris 4,890,000.

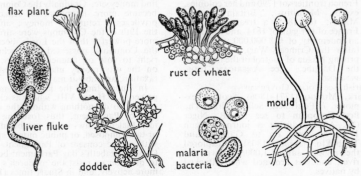

flax plant

rust of wheat

mould

liver fluke

dodder

malaria bacteria

PARASITES

Examples of the Parasites that affect plant and animal life

One of the most beautiful cities in Europe, Paris has handsome boulevards, spacious squares and many parks, e.g. the Champs Elysées and the Bois de Boulogne. Notable public buildings include the Eiffel Tower, originally 985ft high ; the Louvre, a magnificent museum and art gallery ; the Palais de Justice and Conciergerie ; the Panthéon ; the Invalides, where Napoleon is buried ; the famous Sorbonne (a university) ; the Arc de Triomphe and many churches, the most famous being the historic Notre Dame, a 12th c. cathedral. The ancient walls and the Bastille have vanished. The city, long a favourite with tourists, has countless cafés, restaurants and dance halls and more theatres than any other city in the world, e.g. the Opera House, Théâtre Français ; Odéon ; Thèâtre de la Gaîté. There are thirty bridges over the Seine, the most famous being the Pont Neuf. Paris, largely rebuilt since the 17th c., is finely planned. Its airport is Le Bourget.

Industries include the making of jewellery, cabinet work, silks and woollens, tapestries, lace, embroidery, scientific instruments and chemicals.

Paris is named from the Parisii, a tribe inhabiting the banks of the Seine when Caesar conquered Gaul. The city was besieged by the Germans in the Franco-Prussian War of 1870–71. In World War II the government moved to Vichy, remaining there till the city was liberated from Nazi occupation by the FFI (Forces Françaises de l'Intérieur) and Allied troops 1944.

Paris, TREATIES OF, international treaties signed in Paris : (*a*) 1763, a treaty by which, after the Seven Years' War, France surrendered to Britain all American possessions except Louisiana, Britain restoring Guadaloupe, Martinique and St Lucia ; also Goree (in Africa) in exchange for Senegal ; and Spain recovering the Philippines and Havana but surrendering Florida to Britain ; (*b*) 1814, a treaty restoring the French frontiers of 1790 and her colonies, except Mauritius ; Britain gaining Malta ; (*c*) 1815, a treaty depriving France of her gain of 1814, and imposing an indemnity of £28,000,000 ; (*d*) 1856 (after the Crimean War), a treaty depriving Russia of control of the mouth of the Danube. See AMERICAN INDEPENDENCE

parish, see LOCAL GOVERNMENT

Park, MUNGO (1771–1806), Scottish explorer, *b* Foulshiels, Selkirkshire. The first European to see the R. Niger (W. Africa) during a journey begun 1795, he went on to Gambia and Timbuktu. Again (1805) he explored the region, sailed 1,000m down the river, and was drowned when attacked by natives.

Parker, SIR HYDE (1739–1807), British sailor ; did good service in the American War of Independence ; the fleet-commander whose cautious signals Nelson pretended not to see at the Battle of Copenhagen 1801.

Parliament (French *parler*, to speak), legislature of Britain and other self-governing parts of the British Empire ; evolved during 1,000 years, whereas the USA system of government was designed by a few men in a few months. The Parliament of the United Kingdom was formed 1707 by the Act of Union, which amalgamated the Parliaments of England and Scotland. The English parliamentary tradition goes back to Anglo-Saxon times, when the council of a Saxon or English kingdom was called the *witan* or *witenagemot*, i.e. an assembly of wise men, a kind of council of chiefs who, as a rule, advised the king in matters of government. In Norman times the king was advised by the *Great Council*, a committee that met only when required by the king. At first it comprised lords (or barons), abbots and bishops ; but in the 13th c. knights of the shires and burgesses from the towns joined the assembly, sometimes at York and Winchester as well as in London. Simon de Montfort was the first to summon (1265) a Parliament in which were men chosen (i.e. *elected*) by the boroughs or towns as their representatives. Edward I summoned the so-called Model Parliament 1295, not so much to receive its advice as to tell it what he wanted. Nevertheless, the Model Parliament had features not unlike those of Parliament as we know it. It consisted of two knights from every shire ; two burgesses from every city and borough ; and a number of churchmen, all in addition to the lords, so that Edward's Parliament represented the nobles, the Church and the people. In early days the several Estates of the Realm met together, but in the 13th c. they began to meet as two bodies, i.e. the House of Lords and the House of Commons, the Lords doing most of the business, the Commons merely agreeing and receiving orders to find money, etc. Gradually the Commons became more important by exacting privileges in return for money ; and in the 19th c. the Commons were already more powerful than the Lords, because the Commons possessed the exclusive right to vote on financial matters, i.e. on the way money may be raised by taxation, and how it may be spent. In Tudor times the king had much power, e.g. Henry VIII, who was clever enough to do nothing without the consent of Parliament, thus fostering the idea that new laws could not be made, or taxes imposed, or public money spent without the consent of Parliament. In Queen Elizabeth's day Parliament began to question or resist the monarch's will more actively, and in Stuart times (1603 onwards) Parliament felt strong enough to check the king at every point by refusing to vote money unless he did as the majority of the members wished. As James I and Charles I could not agree with their Parliaments they tried to rule without them ; this led to the Civil War, and ultimately (1694) to the *Triennial Act*, which enjoined that no Parliament could sit for a period longer than three years ; a *Septennial Act* was passed 1716, by which, if it chose to do so, Parliament might sit for seven years, a limit reduced to five years 1911, though in exceptional circumstances (e.g. in World War I) a Parliament may remain as long as seems to it desirable. By the *Parliament Act* of 1911 the House of Lords became subordinate ; and now, although the Lords can *hinder* a Bill for two years, it cannot *prevent* the Bill becoming law. If the House of Commons passes a Bill three times, it becomes law even if the House of Lords does not agree ; hence, in part, our claim to be a democratic people (see Politics).

Much as a school meets for terms, so Parliament meets for *sessions*, each lasting about a year ; a session is opened by the king, or his representative, and each is *prorogued*, i.e. temporarily concluded till, finally, Parliament is *dissolved*, i.e. disbanded, whereupon a new House of Commons must be elected. The House of Lords is not affected by elections, because its members are members for life. The House of Lords consists of Peers of the United Kingdom ; 16 Scottish Peers ; 24 English bishops ; and 2 English archbishops. Members of the House of Commons now receive £1,000 a year.

In the House of Commons the Speaker (always addressed as Mr Speaker) is the chairman, and no-one may speak without his permission. On his right sit the members of the government, on his left members who are in opposition.

For the method by which Members of Parliament are elected to the House of Commons see Election. Party Members are grouped into various parties, e.g. *Conservative and Unionist Party* (usually called *Conservatives*), generally wishful to maintain traditional government, often reluctant to make sweeping changes, but, on the whole, much more ready to do so now than formerly. This party has evolved from the *Tories*, a nickname earned in the days of Charles II, the name Conservative being used from *c.*1830.

The *Liberal Party* began as the *Whigs*, and was the strongest in England for fifty years or so after 1714. (The name is said to come from Whigamore, the name of a group of Scottish Covenanters.) The Whigs, becoming known as Liberals *c.*1832, may be said to believe in the rights of the common people, and to stand for *all* rather than for a class. They desire progress and reform, and are willing to bring about freedom of trade and better education. The Liberal Party has become much less important than the Labour Party (see below). Its last great service to the nation was the great programme of social and constitutional reforms carried out under Lloyd George and Asquith 1907–14.

The *Labour Party* is an important group that desires to see business and industry controlled by the State (or nation) instead of by individuals or firms, believing that in this way there would be equal chances of success for all, and that we should all be co-operating with, instead of competing against, each other. The Labour Party (which did not become notable till the 20th c.) was first represented in Parliament 1900. It became the official Opposition 1923, and won a substantial majority 1945.

At the General Election of 1950 Labour was again returned, but with a majority of only 8 ; in the 1945 Election Labour had had a majority of 186. The total number of votes (1950) was 28,769,477.

In a *General Election* the electors (see Election) return to Parliament 625 Members of the House of Commons. If, say, 350 were Conservatives, 25 Liberals, and 250 Labour, the new Government would be Conservative, having a majority, and the Cabinet would be composed of Conservatives. The Labour Party would then become the Opposition, their business being to criticise and often oppose measures proposed by the Government.

The *Cabinet* is virtually a small committee gathered round the Premier (Latin *primus*, first) or Prime Minister. Members of the Cabinet are called Cabinet Ministers, and act as heads of Government departments, e.g. Minister of Transport, Minister of Health, Chancellor of the Exchequer, Secretary of State for Foreign Affairs, First Lord of the Admiralty ; all are chosen by the Prime Minister. Our first Prime Minister was Sir Robert Walpole, who held office 1721–42. See Politics. For a description of the Houses of Parliament see London.

Read *The Point of Parliament*, Sir A. P. Herbert.

Parliament Act, law of 1911 by which (*a*) the House of Lords is unable to reject or amend a money bill, and cannot interfere with a measure passed three times by the Commons, (*b*) the normal life of the House of Commons is regarded as from seven to five years.

Parliament, Houses of, see London

Parma, town N. Italy ; noted for silks and woollens ; has a famous cathedral and university ; pop.123,000.

Parma, 3rd Duke of (1545–92), Italian soldier. A brilliant military commander, he was Governor-General of the Netherlands for Philip II of Spain from 1578.

Parnassus, mt. in Greece ; rises 8,069ft, and was anciently sacred to Apollo, the Muses and Dionysus.

Parnell, CHARLES STEWART, *pär-nel'* (1846–1891), Irish politician; entered Parliament 1875 ; strove to secure Home Rule for Ireland. He might well have succeeded, but was driven from public life when it became known that he was implicated in a divorce suit brought by Captain O'Shea against his wife.

Parr, CATHERINE (1512–48), 6th wife of Henry VIII ; *b* Kendal Castle, Westmorland ; survived the king.

Parr, THOMAS (*d* 1635), known as Old Parr ; claimed to have lived in ten reigns (Edward IV to Charles I) ; died London at the reputed age of 152.

Parramatta, second oldest town, New S. Wales, Australia ; the centre of a fruit-growing region ; manufactures cloth.

parrot, common name for highly intelligent birds with an upper and lower hooked bill. Usually brightly coloured, they nest in holes in trees, are largely fruit-eaters, but they also eat seeds and nuts.

The parrot, found chiefly in tropical regions, is usually long-lived. It makes an interesting pet. The order includes : (*a*) PARAKEET, usually much smaller, and with a long tail ; (*b*) BUDGERIGAR, an Australian parakeet ; (*c*) MACAW, a large S. American parrot with gorgeous plumage, chiefly red, blue and yellow ; (*d*) COCKATOO, a native of Australia ; has a crest of feathers on the head ; the largest cockatoos are black, but most are white, sometimes with yellow or red ; (*e*) LORY, found only in Australia, New Guinea, and neighbouring islands ; its food includes the nectar of flowers ; (*f*) LOVEBIRD, a native of S. and Central America.

It is well known that parrots can be trained to talk, but of course they do not understand what they are ' saying.'

Parry, SIR CHARLES (1848–1918), composer, *b* Bournemouth ; noted for his setting to music of Blake's *Jerusalem.*

parsec, taken as approx. 3¼ light-years, say *c*.19,000,000,000,000 miles ; the Kilo-parsec is 1,000 parsecs ; the Mega-parsec is 1,000,000 parsecs.

Parsees, see ZOROASTER

Parsifal, see WAGNER, W. R.

parsnip, plant (family *Umbelliferae*) found in a wild state in Britain, and also much cultivated as a vegetable.

Parsons, SIR CHARLES (1854–1931), British engineer ; notable as the inventor of the marine steam turbine. See SHIPS

Parthenon, see ARCHITECTURE

Parthia, ancient name for a region now to the north of Iran. The capital was Ctesiphon.

Partick, western area of Glasgow ; on the R. Clyde ; pop.54,000.

Partisans, war-time bodies of guerillas or irregular troops raised from the civil population in a country occupied by enemy forces. Partisans did much to harass the Germans in World War II, especially in Yugoslavia, Greece, France, Italy and Poland.

partridge, game bird of which two species

THE GREY PARTRIDGE

are common in Britain : (*a*) the grey partridge, the egg being pale brown, and (*b*) the French partridge, distinguished by its bright red legs and beak, and its handsome plumage. Partridges feed on grain, seeds, insects, etc. They may be shot 1 Sept.–1 Feb.

part-song, an unaccompanied song for three or more voices singing different parts.

party, in politics, a group of people whose views are in common and who put forward a programme of government.

In Great Britain there are two important political parties. Before 1924 the two great parties were the Conservative and the Liberal Parties ; now they are the Conservative and the Labour Parties. One important difference between these parties is that the Labour Party demands that necessary changes should be carried out as quickly as possible, whereas the Conservatives prefer gradual development. At elections the British people choose between these two policies as presented to them by the candidates. If in a General Election the Labour Party gains a majority in the House of Commons, a Labour Government is formed. If, on the other hand, the Conservatives win a majority, a Conservative Government is formed. Everything that the Government intends is openly criticised by the Opposition in the House of Commons, and in order to pass an Act the Government must obtain, after discussion, the approval of a majority of Members. Normally a British Cabinet can rely on the support of its own Party, which of course is in a majority in the House of Commons ; if the Cabinet does not obtain that support it has to resign and a General Election is held.

The British system of political parties is a typical two-party system. The same system exists in the United States where the two parties are the Democratic and the Republican Parties. Of these the Republicans are traditionally the more conservative.

In some Continental countries, where elections are governed by the principle of proportional representation, three or more important parties exist. At first sight a *many-party system* seems to be advantageous, inasmuch as it provides for the representation of varying shades of political opinions ; but under this system it often happens in practice that after an election no single party has in parliament a majority over all the rest, with the result that no government which can be formed is strong enough to govern effectively. Recent French political history illustrates this weakness very clearly.

When this happens in a democratic country (see POLITICS), people begin to think that democracy is no good, and give their support to those forces (such as Communism and Fascism) which seek to abolish democratic government and democratic liberties. This is what happened in Germany between 1925 and 1932, leading to the establishment of Hitler's Nazi dictatorship.

Once in power, Communists and Nazis and other anti-democratic movements normally establish what is known as the *one-party system* ; all other parties are banned, and the country is governed thereafter by representatives of the victorious anti-democratic party, which elects its own members, and therefore is in no way subject to popular control. This is the system which obtains in Russia (see POLITICS).

Pascal, BLAISE (1623–62), French thinker, scientist, stylist and monk ; entered a monastery 1654.

Pascal was a brilliant scientist and mathematician ; he wrote treatises on conic sections, experimented on atmospheric pressure, and founded the science of hydrodynamics. He was also one of the finest prose writers of France, and was an outstanding defender of Christianity. His books include the *Pensées*.

pasha, *pä'shä* ; *pä-shä'*, Turkish title for governors of provinces and high military or naval commanders.

Passfield, SIDNEY JAMES WEBB, 1ST LORD (1859–1947), *b* London ; became an authority on sociology, economics and municipal government ; was a member of the Fabian Society ; responsible for improved poor law administration ; founded *The New Statesman* 1913 ; entered Parliament 1922 ; raised to the peerage 1929 ; author of books on socialism, etc. He married Beatrice Potter (who died 1943), an authority on social, industrial and unemployment problems ; together they wrote *The History of Trades Unionism* ; *Industrial Democracy* ; *English Local Government* ; *Soviet Communism*.

passion flower, climbing plant found chiefly in the warmer regions of America ; notable for its large, showy, saucer-like flowers (blue, purple, red, white, or yellow) with a peculiar arrangement of stamens and anthers.

Passion Play, see OBERAMMERGAU

Passover, ancient Jewish feast still observed by Jews at the beginning of the harvest ; named from the fact that the destroying angel passed over the thresholds of the Israelites in Egypt (Exodus 12) but smote the first-born of the Egyptians. The Passover, also called the feast of unleavened bread, was observed by Christ the night before his crucifixion.

passport, permission to travel in a foreign country. British passports are granted by the Foreign Office.

Pasteur, LOUIS, *päs-tŭr* (1822–95), French scientist, *b* Dôle ; won fame as a chemist ; found the cause and cure of an epidemic in silk-worms then ruining the French silk industry ; studied bacteriology and the causes of infectious diseases ; discovered the value of antiseptic and aseptic methods, later developed by Lord Lister.

Pasteur found a vaccine to prevent anthrax, and instituted the pasteurisation of milk. The Pasteur Institute, Paris, founded 1888 in his honour, is the home of notable investigations in the prevention and cure of disease. See ANTISEPTICS

pastimes, see HOBBY

Paston, name of a Norfolk family. The famous *Paston Letters* (written to, or by, members of the family, and *c*.1,200 in all) give interesting details of the period 1422–1509.

Patagonia, southern region of S. America belonging to the Argentine and Chile.

patent, *pat'n't*, document issued by the Crown (i.e. the government) giving the holder the sole right, for a period, to manufacture or make use of an invention. An inventor in Britain may apply to the Patent Office, 25 Southampton Buildings, London, W.C.2 for a provisional patent, protecting him for six months, or the patentee may lodge (i.e. send) a complete specification, usually with drawings, costing £6 in fees, giving him a monopoly for four years. It is advisable to employ an expert in drawing up the specification. For the fifth year a payment of £5 is required, for the sixth £6, etc. to the sixteenth year, when the monopoly normally ceases.

Pater Noster, *pä'tĕr nos'tĕr* ; *pat'-* (Latin *Our Father*), Latin name for the Lord's Prayer ; also given to the larger beads of a rosary.

pathology (Greek *pathos*, disease, *logos* discourse), study of diseases, a branch of biology including the structural changes due to disease of the body and misfunctions of the mind (psychopathology).

Patiala, most important of the Sikh states, India ; its cap. Patiala (pop.70,000), manufactures carpets.

Patmos, small rocky island in the Aegean Sea ; area 12sq.m. St John was probably banished to this spot, and may have written the *Book of Revelation* here.

Patna, *pŭt′nä,* town on the R. Ganges, India ; has a large trade in oil-seeds, rice and cotton ; pop.176,000.

Patras, *pä-träs′,* port on the Gulf of Patras, Greece ; trades in wine, currants, raisins, lemons and olive oil ; pop. 67,000.

patriarch, *pā′tri-ärk,* head of a family or tribe, especially among the Jews, who used the word for the great ' fathers ' of their race, e.g. Abraham, Moses, etc. The title was also given later to the bishops of Alexandria, Rome and Antioch.

patrician, *pä-trish′an,* member of the aristocratic ruling class in ancient Rome, and thus opposed to the plebs or plebeians. Originally only patricians could take priestly office or give legal decisions. The senate was composed almost exclusively of patricians till *c.*300BC.

Patrick, patron saint of Ireland ; died, it is said, 17 March AD493, having done much to convert the Irish to Christianity.

Pau, *pō,* town 60m east of Bayonne, France ; visited for its fine mt. scenery; pop.39,000.

Paul, ST, apostle, first called Saul, *b* Tarsus, Cilicia, possibly about the time Jesus was born in Judea. A Jew and also a Roman citizen, he was at first a merciless opponent of Christianity, but was impressed by Stephen, and, while on the road to Damascus, intending to seek out Christians and put fetters on them, he was converted.

A change of heart and mind and loyalty was accompanied by a change in name (Saul becoming Paul), and by devoting the remainder of his life to preaching the gospel of Jesus. Paul made three great missionary journeys : (*a*) to Cilicia ; (*b*) to Greece ; (*c*) over much the same ground as (*b*), but with his HQ at Ephesus. In all, as a faithful evangelist, he did much to establish the Christian belief in Europe and Asia. Arrested in Jerusalem, he appealed unto Caesar, was tried in Rome, and executed there, possibly *c.*AD67.

We read of St Paul's preaching and travelling in the NT (Acts), and there also are his letters (epistles), e.g. the first and second Epistles to Timothy, and the Epistle to Titus, also the famous Epistles to the Romans, Galatians and Corinthians.

Read *In the Steps of St Paul,* H. V. Morton.

Paulinus, *paul-ī′nŭs* (*d* 644), *b* Rome, became a monk ; sent by Pope Gregory the Great to help St Augustine to convert the English ; baptised Edwin, King of Northumbria, 627, and became the first Archbishop of York.

Paulinus, GAIUS SUETONIUS, Roman general ; governor of Britain AD59–62 ; conquered the Iceni led by Boadicea.

Pavia, *pä-vee′a,* university city, northern Italy ; known as ' the city of a hundred towers ' ; noted for its cathedral ; pop.52,000.

pax Romana, i.e. Roman peace, name given to the period AD98–180 (death of Marcus Aurelius), when the Roman empire enjoyed peace.

Paxton, SIR JOSEPH (1801–65), born in Bedfordshire ; was head gardener at Chatsworth House ; won fame as architect of the Crystal Palace, built for the Great Exhibition 1851.

PAYE, short for *pay as you earn,* i.e. payment of income tax not as an annual (or twice-yearly) sum, but by deduction from a weekly wage or monthly salary. See TAXES

Payne, JOHN HOWARD (1791–1852), American actor and dramatist, *b* New York ; remembered as the homeless writer of *Home, Sweet Home.*

Pb, chemical symbol for lead, from the Latin *plumbum.*

PD, see ELECTRICITY ; POTENTIAL DIFFERENCE

pea, cultivated climbing plant (family *Leguminosae*) with white flowers, and a single row of seeds (peas) in a pod. These when removed from the pod and cooked provide a tasty vegetable either fresh (green peas) or dried. The pea is rich in sugar and farinaceous matter (proteins).

Very similar, the SWEET-PEA, cultivated for its fragrant white, pink, red, or purple flowers, was introduced into Britain *c.*1700.

Peace, river of W. Canada ; flows *c.*1,000m into the Great Slave L.

Peace with Honour, see BERLIN, CONGRESS OF

peach, small fruit tree (family *Rosaceae*), native of Asia ; has pink, red, or white flowers. The ripe fruit has a velvety skin, and is pale yellow and crimson in colour. The NECTARINE, smaller, is a variety.

Peach, LAWRENCE DU GARDE (1890–   ), author and dramatist ; won fame with his hundreds of radio plays, especially a series giving a dramatic history of England, and his dramatised Bible stories. His publications include *Practical Plays for Stage and Classroom, The Castles of England, Famous Men of Britain, Famous Women of Britain, The Path of Glory,* and many films and stage plays ; also a special series of one-act plays for youth groups.

peacock or **peafowl,** large bird of the pheasant family. A native of India and SE. Asia, it is kept in Britain for ornamental purposes. The hen lays 25–30 eggs. The peacock is notable for gorgeous plumage ; on its head it has a crest like a coronet, and when erected and opened like a fan its tail feathers display magnificent colours and large eye-like spots.

Peak District, mountainous region, Derbyshire. Its highest points include Kinder Scout (over 2,080ft) and Black Tor.

pea-nut, see GROUND-NUT

pear, tree of the genus *Pyrus.* Cultivated varieties include bergamot and jargonelle.

The trees are often trained as espaliers against walls that have southern exposures.

pearl, shimmering form of calcium carbonate built up inside their shells, layer by layer, by various molluscs, including mussels and clams, but particularly by oysters. This is the result of irritation set up by a parasite or foreign body which the oyster entombs in mother-of-pearl. Cultured pearls are produced by deliberately placing a grain of sand in an oyster, a method long practised by the Japanese. Pearl oyster beds are found in the Persian Gulf, and off the coasts of Ceylon, Australia and Mexico. Rose-tinted pearls are exported from the Bahamas.

Pearl Harbour, inlet 6m west of Honolulu, Hawaii. It is a great Pacific naval base for the US fleet ; and it was a sudden and unexpected Japanese attack (7 Dec 1941) on Pearl Harbour that brought the USA into World War II. Every American battleship and most of the American aircraft in the Hawaiian area were damaged, also various airfields, by Japanese carrier-borne aircraft. Of naval personnel 2,117 were killed, 960 missing and nearly 900 wounded.

Pearson, Sir CYRIL ARTHUR (1866–1921), *b* Somerset ; founded the *Daily Express* 1900 ; became blind ; opened St Dunstan's Hostel. See BLINDNESS

Peary, ROBERT EDWIN (1856–1920), American explorer ; made a memorable Arctic sledge journey 1891–92, and discovered that Greenland is an island. After several attempts, reached the N. Pole 1909. See POLAR REGIONS

peat, substance comprising decomposed vegetable matter, largely compressed mosses. Cut and dried, it is used as fuel, notably in Ireland (where half of Britain's 6,000,000 acres of peat are found) and in the north of Scotland.

peccary, *pek'äri,* animal like a small pig ; found in flocks in N. and S. America. The flesh is like pork but not so fat.

pedal triangle, see TRIANGLE

Peeblesshire, lowland county, Scotland ; co.tn Peebles, noted for tweeds.

peel, small castle or tower on the borders of Scotland and Wales ; once used as a place of refuge during border raids.

Peel, JOHN (1776–1854), huntsman, born in Cumberland ; hero of the song *D'ye ken John Peel?* by John W. Graves, written *c.*1828.

Peel, SIR ROBERT (1788–1850), statesman, born near Bury, Lancashire. A Tory, he entered Parliament 1809 ; was Secretary for Ireland at twenty-four. As Home Secretary 1822 he was responsible for many reforms, including the abolition of the death sentence for a number of crimes, and the formation of the Metropolitan Police (called ' peelers ' or ' bobbies ' after him) ; leader of the Tories 1827 ; supported Catholic emancipation ; opposed the Reform Bill ; formed a short-lived government

SIR ROBERT PEEL 1788–1850

1834 ; a second 1839 ; and a third 1841, which imposed income tax on incomes over £150, introduced the Bank Charter Act 1844, reduced tariffs, and increased the education grant. Though still a Tory, he came to believe in free trade, and proposed the repeal of the Corn Laws 1845, which he carried.

At first disliked but later respected by Queen Victoria, Peel was a progressive Conservative.

peerage, those who succeed to titles, namely (in Britain) dukes, marquises, earls, viscounts and barons. A peer is created by letters patent as a reward for valuable service to the State, and by being raised to the peerage he has a seat in the House of Lords.

peewit, see PLOVER

Pegasus, *peg'ä-süs,* constellation of four stars making a square. See BELLEROPHON

Peierls, DR RUDOLPH (1907–   ), German-Jewish scientist, *b* Berlin ; escaped from Nazi persecution to England ; closely associated with the atom-bomb of 1945.

Peiping or **Peking** or **Pekin,** *bä-ping'* ; *pē-king',* former capital of China ; pop. estimated at *c.*1,300,000. An ancient walled city, it was the capital of Kubla Khan's empire. It fell into Japanese hands during the Sino-Japanese War 1937–45, and in 1947 was besieged by the Chinese Communists.

Pekin, see PEIPING

Pelée, *pě-lā',* volcano in the island of Martinique. Its eruption 1902 destroyed the town of St Pierre. See VOLCANO

Peleus, *pē'lēūs,* in old Greek tales, King of the Myrmidons in Thessaly ; husband of Thetis and father of Achilles.

Pelham, HENRY, *pel'am (d* 1754), English statesman ; Whig Prime Minister 1743–

PENGUINS

(1) *King Penguins*   (2) *Blackfooted Penguin*
(3) *Gentoo Penguin*   (4) *Adelie Penguin*
(5) *Rockhopper Penguin* (6) *Ringed Penguin*

1754 ; opposed to Carteret's war policy, and did much to reduce national expenditure.

Pelias, in old Greek tales, King of Iolcus ; sent Jason to bring back the Golden Fleece.

pelican, large web-footed bird ; wing-span 10–15ft ; feeds on fish caught in its huge bill, the lower part of which has a pouch of naked skin ; found in temperate and tropical regions.

Pelion, *pē'li-on,* mt. range of Greece ; associated with many Greek tales.

Peloponnese, THE, anciently S. Greece ; now called the Morea.

Peloponnesian War, *pel-ō-po-nē'shan,* war waged 431–404BC between Athens and Sparta, ending in the capture of Athens by Lysander ; its history was written by the Athenian Thucydides.

Pelorus Jack, see WHALE

pelvis, structure, comprising two bones, that carries the weight of the human body and joins the trunk to the legs.

Pembroke, MARY, COUNTESS OF (1561–1621), sister of Sir Philip Sidney, *b* Ticknell Palace, Worcestershire ; married Henry Herbert, 2nd Earl of Pembroke. A learned woman, she encouraged Ben Jonson and Spenser, and to her Sir Philip Sidney dedicated his *Arcadia.* Her epitaph (by Ben Jonson ?) begins : *Underneath this sable hearse Lies the subject of all verse.*

Pembroke, WILLIAM HERBERT, 3RD EARL OF (1580–1630), statesman, *b* Wilton, Wiltshire. Pembroke College, Oxford, was named after him. He was a friend of Shakespeare.

Pembroke College, college of Oxford University, founded 1624 by James I. Dr Johnson was an undergraduate there.

Pembroke College, college of Cambridge University, founded 1346 ; its chapel was designed by Sir Christopher Wren.

Pembrokeshire, county, Wales ; has a much indented coast ; noted for coal, iron and lead. The county offices are at Haverfordwest.

pemmican, dried lean meat pounded into a paste ; first used by American Indians. It is included by explorers in their stores.

pen, instrument for writing with ink. Quills were used until the first steel pens became commercially successful, largely as a result of Joseph Gillott's inventions *c.*1830. Birmingham is now the chief centre for the manufacture of steel pens. Fountain pens were invented by Waterman 1883.

penal servitude, *pē'nal,* punishment which, in Britain, replaced transportation 1853. Penal servitude may be from five years to a life-sentence. Prisoners sentenced to penal servitude are known as convicts. Convict prisons include Dartmoor, Parkhurst, Broadmoor (for criminal lunatics), Aylesbury and Peterhead.

Penang, see MALAYA

penates, see LARES

Penda (*d* 654), pagan King of Mercia ; defeated and killed Edwin, King of Northumbria at Hatfield Chase 633, also Oswald of Northumbria 642.

pendulum, see MECHANICS

Penelope, *pē-nel'ō-pē,* in old Greek tales, wife of Odysseus (Ulysses). During her husband's absence at Troy she refused to marry till she had completed a piece of embroidery which she secretly unwove at night.

penguin, *pen'gwin,* flightless bird found only south of the equator, and chiefly in the Antarctic. The plumage is white or grey below, black above ; young birds have mole-grey fur which is later replaced by feathers. The birds stand erect on webbed feet, have thick, slightly curved beaks, and use their wings as paddles. They are found in huge colonies. Varieties include the ' king ' and ' emperor ' penguins.

Read *The Worst Journey in the World*, by Apsley Cherry-Garrard.

penicillin, *pen-i-sil'in*, product of the mould *Penicillium notatum*, now employed with exceptionally beneficial results in curing certain diseases, such as those due to pneumococcal and streptococcal infection ; first investigated 1929 by Professor Sir Alexander Fleming, who happened to notice that a mould growing on agar-jelly produced a substance (penicillin) that destroyed staphylococci (pus-forming) bacteria.

His pioneer work was advanced 1938 by bacteriologists at Oxford University (e.g. Sir Howard Florey and Dr Chain), who made the important discoveries (*a*) that as a dry salt preparation, penicillin is a powerful antiseptic, preventing the growth of certain bacteria even when diluted to one part in 150,000,000 ; (*b*) that it has practically no toxic (poisonous) effect on human beings when administered in large or small doses ; (*c*) that once in the blood-stream it attacks disease bacteria by way of the white corpuscles, increasing their ability to destroy 'enemy' bacteria ; (*d*) that unlike the sulphonamide drugs, penicillin does its work whether disease bacteria are present in large or in small numbers, not by killing them but by preventing multiplication, though we do not understand *how* ; (*e*) that it is, therefore, not only an antiseptic but also a chemotherapeutic (i.e. chemical-healing) substance of unique possibilities, capable of medicinal uses as a preventive as well as a cure.

Production was at first limited to very small amounts, but with the aid of experts in USA, Imperial Chemical Industries and others, it was possible 1943 to treat fifteen trial patients. Later, penicillin was reserved for war casualties only. Now production is on a vast scale, and doctors and surgeons have a new and powerful weapon with which to fight disease. Unfortunately, penicillin has no action on the tubercle bacillus.

Read *Miracle Drug*, David Masters.

peninsula, projecting piece of land almost surrounded by water e.g. the Italian, Balkan and Malay peninsulas. The base (if narrow) is called an isthmus.

Peninsular War, struggle between Britain (as the ally of Spain and Portugal) against France 1808–14 in the Iberian peninsula (Spain and Portugal) ; undertaken as part of the British attack on Napoleon, and largely directed by the Duke of Wellington. Features of the war were the retreat of Sir John Moore to Corunna, where (1809) his army was embarked, though he was killed ; Wellington's victory at Talavera 1809, and his subsequent falling back to the lines of Torres Vedras, covering Lisbon (Portugal) ; the capture by the French of Badajoz and Ciudad Rodrigo ; the capture of Almeida by Wellington, also

Albuera, both 1811, and his victory at Salamanca 1812, leading to his capture of Madrid. Later, after victory at Vittoria 1813, he drove the French into France, and finally to Toulouse, when Napoleon's abdication ended the war.

Penn, WILLIAM (1644–1718), *b* London ; became a Quaker minister, and for some of his writings was imprisoned in the Tower of London. After travelling and preaching in Germany and Holland he received 1681 a grant of land in America (north of Maryland), which was named Pennsylvania. There he established a Quaker colony, founded and named Philadelphia, and made treaties of friendship with the Indians.

Penn, a devout and upright man, was a friend of James II, and a great democrat.

Pennines, *pen'īns*, range of mts. (England) from the Scottish border to the Trent, the southern portion being the Peak. Often called the ' backbone of England,' the Pennines rise to 2,930ft at Cross Fell. Other heights are Whernside, Ingleborough and Mickle Fell.

Pennsylvania, *pen-sil-vā'nia*, state of USA. It is south of New York State, and is noted for coal, iron and steel, petroleum; named after William Penn, its Quaker founder 1681 ; cap. Harrisburg.

pentameter, see METRE

pentane, highly inflammable liquid, C_5H_{12}, one of the hydrocarbons of the paraffin series ; a constituent of petroleum.

Pentecost, *pen'tē-köst*, Greek word meaning fiftieth, i.e. the 50th day after the Jewish Passover ; celebrated by Christians on Whitsunday as the anniversary of the coming of the Holy Ghost (Acts 2).

Pentland Firth, strait between the Orkneys and the Scottish mainland. Its strong currents make it dangerous for ships.

Pentland Hills, range of hills (Midlothian) near Edinburgh. The highest point is *c.*1,900ft.

Pentonville, see PRISON

penumbra, see SHADOW

Penzance, town and popular health resort, Cornwall ; has a fine harbour ; noted for fishing.

pepper, climbing plant with broad leaves and bright red berries. When ground, the berries make black pepper or (if without the skin) white pepper. Pepper comes from the E. Indies, especially Sumatra.

pepsin, enzyme produced in the stomach, where, mixed with acid, it changes proteins into peptones. See DIGESTION

Pepys, SAMUEL, *pēps* (1633–1703), civil servant, *b* London ; entered the Navy Office, where he remained during the plague 1665. Regarded with favour by the Duke of York (later James II), Pepys greatly improved the efficiency of the navy and of naval administration. He was elected MP for Harwich, and twice imprisoned on suspicion of being implicated in the Popish Plot. He was president of the Royal Society 1684.

Pepys, therefore, in his lifetime was a busy and successful public servant. Long after his death he won fame by the publication 1825 of his *Diary*, secretly written in shorthand and bequeathed to Magdalene College, Cambridge. The diary reveals his weaknesses, his inquisitiveness, his keen observation of people and events, and his fund of humour. A vivid picture of the years 1660–69, it is one of the most fascinating records in our language. A typical entry is :

12 Aug 1667 To St James's, where we find the Duke gone a-hunting with the King. To my bookseller's, and did buy Scott's *Discourse of Witches.* After dinner, all alone, to the King's playhouse, and there did happen to sit just before Mrs Pierce, and Mrs Knippe, who pulled me by the hair. The play being done, I took the women and Mrs Corbett, who was with them, by coach, it raining. Then home, and my wife come ; and so, saying nothing where I had been, we to supper and pipe, and so to bed.

Perak, see MALAYA

per cent or **percentage** (Latin *centum*, hundred), in commercial arithmetic, used for *in every hundred* ; thus 5% is $\frac{5}{100}$ or $\frac{1}{20}$ or 0·05. Note :

$66\frac{2}{3}\% = \frac{2}{3}$ $20\% = \frac{1}{5}$
$50\% = \frac{1}{2}$ $12\frac{1}{2}\% = \frac{1}{8}$
$33\frac{1}{3}\% = \frac{1}{3}$ $5\% = \frac{1}{20}$
$25\% = \frac{1}{4}$ $2\frac{1}{2}\% = \frac{1}{40}$

Also the following percentages of £1 :

13s 4d = $66\frac{2}{3}\%$ 2s 6d = $12\frac{1}{2}\%$
10s 0d = 50% 2s 0d = 10%
6s 8d = $33\frac{1}{3}\%$ 1s 0d = 5%
5s 0d = 25% 6d = $2\frac{1}{2}\%$
4s 0d = 20% 3d = $1\frac{1}{4}\%$
1d = 0·416%

perch, fresh-water fish common in British rivers ; has a humped back that is dark green, paling to white below, with dark bands ; may be 9–12in long ; weight 2–3lb.

Percy, Sir HENRY (1364–1403), eldest son of the 1st Earl of Northumberland ; named Hotspur from his impetuous gallantry in fights against the Scots, e.g. Otterburn 1388. Though a friend of the Prince of Wales (later Henry V), he rebelled against Henry IV.

Percy, THOMAS (1729–1811), scholar, *b* Shropshire ; published the famous *Reliques of Ancient English Poetry*, 1765. He was bishop of Dromore 1782.

Père-Lachaise, *pār lä-shāz'*, famous Paris cemetery of over 210 acres. Many notable people are buried there, including Abélard and Héloïse, Balzac and Molière.

perennial, herbaceous plant that lives several years ; thus distinguished from plants that live only one year (annuals) or two (biennials).

perfume, see SCENT

Pergamum, ancient city of Asia Minor ; *c.*50m north of Izmir.

Pericles, *per'i-klēz* (490–429BC), Athenian statesman who inspired the Greeks to love beauty, to think boldly, to seek after learning, and to work together rather than quarrelling among themselves. An aristocrat, he believed in the commonsense of the common people. One of the world's great orators, he was soldier, thinker and leader. For thirty years he ruled Athens, making her supreme among the states of Greece. He improved her laws, saw that her fleets were unmatched, urged others to raise temples, and inspired a love of drama, philosophy and art, especially architecture, so that the age of Pericles was the most brilliant in the history of Greece. As an old man he directed the Peloponnesian war for two years. His Funeral Oration at the burial of a number of Greek soldiers is memorable, as these few sentences show :

PERICLES 490–429 B.C.

'Such is the Athens for which these men, in the assertion of their resolve, nobly fought and died ; and well may every one of their survivors be ready to suffer in her cause. If a test of worth be wanted it is to be found in their closing scene. None of these allowed either wealth, with its prospect of future enjoyment, to unnerve his spirit, or poverty with its hope of a day of freedom and riches, to tempt him to shrink from danger. Thus choosing to die resisting rather than to live submitting, they fled only from dishonour, but met danger face to face, and after one brief moment, while at the summit of their fortune, escaped not from their fear, but from their glory.

'So died these men as became Athenians. You, their survivors, must determine to have as unfaltering a resolution in the field.'

periodic table, see ELEMENT

periscope, optical instrument (for seeing round corners) in various forms : (*a*) a tube (usually collapsible) by which light is twice reflected at right-angles by mirrors, a type used in trench fighting in World War I ; (*b*) submarine periscope, enabling an observer below water to scan the horizon : the inclusion of a lens or lenses gives magnification also ; (*c*) a form enabling medical students to observe an operation, details being reflected to a vertical screen.

Perm, city of USSR ; on the R. Kama ; has many industries ; pop.240,000.

permanganate, salt of permanganic acid, $HMnO_4$; often used briefly for potassium permangate, i.e. permanganate of potash, $KMnO_4$, a soluble salt which, in solution, is an oxydising agent.

permutations, in mathematics, method of finding in how many ways a number of objects may be arranged. Thus, the 3 letters *abc* may be arranged *abc*, *acb*, *bac*, *bca*, *cab* and *cba*, i.e. 6 ways, or factorial 3 (written 3 ! i.e. $3 \times 2 \times 1$) if all the letters are used each time. We may arrange 7 things in factorial 7 ways, i.e. $7 \times 6 \times 5 \times 4 \times 3 \times 2 \times 1 = 5,040$ ways. If we take not all but only *some* of the objects, the number of permutations of *n* different objects taken *r* at a time is

$$_nP_r, \text{ i.e. } \frac{n!}{(n-r)!}.$$ *Combination* of *r* different objects selected from *n* objects is by

$$_nC_r, \text{ i.e. } \frac{n!}{r!(n-r)!}.$$

Pernambuco or **Recife,** *pŭr-nam-bū'kō* ; *rā-sē'fe*, port, Brazil ; noted for cotton, tobacco and rum ; also for its handsome buildings ; pop.530,000.

Péron, JUAN DOMINGO, *pā-ron'*, (1895–), Argentine statesman ; trained as a soldier ; was anti-democratic during World War II ; elected President 1946 ; proving a shrewd and vigorous reformer.

Perpendicular, see ARCHITECTURE

perpetual motion, ideal long searched for by alchemists who believed a machine could be constructed which, once set going, would go on working usefully for ever. We now know this to be impossible, for inertia and friction cannot be overcome except by energy, and no machine can produce more energy than is put into it. Radioactive substances may continue to emanate energy for centuries, but even these fail to make good their losses.

Persephone, *per-sef'on-ē*, in old Greek tales, daughter of Zeus and Demeter (Ceres). Carried to the underworld by Pluto, she was sought by her mother, and at last permitted to return to earth for six months every year. At her departure flowers drooped and birds ceased to sing (autumn) ; when she returned the earth was lovely and happy again. The myth is a poetic explanation of the seasons. The Romans knew her as Proserpine.

Persepolis, ruined city, once the capital of the ancient Persian empire ; *c.*35m north-east of the modern Shiraz ; destroyed by Alexander the Great 331BC.

Perseus, *pŭr'sūs*, in old Greek tales, son of Zeus and Danae ; sent by King Polydectes to secure the head of Medusa. Perseus succeeded, and on his way home saved Andromeda from a sea-monster. He turned Polydectes to stone by showing him Medusa's head, and became King of Argos.

Persia, see IRAN

Persian Gulf, portion of the Indian Ocean between Iran and Arabia.

persimmon, *per-sim'un*, American tree with a pulpy reddish-yellow fruit, delicious when thoroughly ripe ; also the fruit itself.

PERSIMMON

The leaves, the flowers and the fruit : (*top right*) *a staminate flower and* (*bottom right*) *a pistillate flower*

personalty, see NET PERSONALTY

perspective, in drawing and painting is, in its simplest form, the representation of objects or scenes on a flat surface in such a way that they appear to have length, breadth and depth, an art wholly unknown to, say, the ancient Egyptians. Hence lines that appear to recede from the observer are drawn in such a way that, if extended, they would meet at the ' vanishing-point,' which may be on, above, or below the eye-level.

Perth, city and cap., W. Australia ; on the Swan R. ; became important during the gold rush *c.*1890 ; its port is Fremantle ; total pop.230,000.

Perthshire, central county of Scotland ;
has fine mt. scenery ; co.tn Perth, on
the R. Tay ; noted for dyeing and
distilling ; pop.35,000.

Peru, *pā-roo'*, republic of S.
America, largely west of Brazil and Bolivia ; area
482,000sq.m ; pop.7,000,000. Its mts.
include the Andes, parallel to the
Pacific. Much of the country is little
known. Trade has recently been improved by building more roads and
establishing airways. The chief exports
are cotton, copper, petroleum, vanadium
and sugar. Varieties of zebu are now
reared, and there is much stock-raising.
Maize is grown, also tea, rubber and
quinine.
Conquered by Pizarro in the 16th c.,
Peru had long been the home of the
Incas. The cap., Lima (pop.523,000), is
the burial place of Pizarro.
Read *Conquest of Peru,* W. H. Prescott.

Perugia, *pā-roo'jä*, city on the R. Tiber,
Italy ; of great antiquarian interest ;
manufactures textiles ; pop.82,000.

Peshawar, *pe-shä'wär*, important town and
military station of the North-west
Frontier Province, Pakistan ; guards the
Khyber Pass ; trading centre and railway junction ; pop.130,000.

Pestalozzi, JOHANN HEINRICH, *pes-tä-lōt'sē*
(1746–1827), Swiss educationist, born
Zürich ; the first teacher to consider the
child as more important than the subject
taught.

Pétain, HENRI PHILIPPE, *pā-ta*n' (1856–
), French soldier, *b* Cauchy-à-la-
Tour ; held important commands in
World War I ; became a marshal 1918.
In World War II, as an old man, he
surrendered Occupied France to the
Germans 1940, and was a pawn in
Hitler's hands. He was imprisoned for
life 1945.

Petchora, river of USSR, flows *c.*1,000m
from the Urals to the Arctic Ocean.

Peter (*d c.*AD68), saint and apostle ; at
first called Simon. Like his brother
Andrew he was a fisherman. Loyal but
impetuous, he became one of Christ's
disciples, and was the ' rock ' (Greek
petros) on which Christ founded his
Church. After the Ascension he spent
his life preaching, notably in Asia
Minor. He is believed to have been
crucified in Rome. Of the two so-called
Epistles of Peter the second is almost
certainly *not* his. According to Roman
Catholics, Peter was the first pope.

Peter II (1923–), former King of
Yugoslavia ; son of King Alexander I ;
married Princess Alexandra of Greece
1944 ; became King 1941 ; dethroned
1945.

Peterborough, cathedral city, Northamptonshire ; on the R. Nene ; trades in malt,
coal and agricultural produce ; pop.
44,000.

Peterhead, port on the coast of Aberdeenshire ; noted for its herring fisheries.

Peterhouse, oldest of the Cambridge colleges ; founded 1257.

Peterloo, MASSACRE OF, dispersal by the
military of a mob in St Peter's Field,
Manchester, which had met (1819) to
demand parliamentary reform. Several
people were killed, and the incident
caused indignation throughout the
country.

Peter Pan, title of a play by Sir J. M. Barrie ;
also the name of its chief character—
' the boy who wouldn't grow up,' so
' Peter Pan ' is used to mean ' young in
spirit.' The story of the play is found
in *Peter and Wendy* ; and in Kensington
Gardens (London) is Sir George
Frampton's statue of Peter Pan because
in *The Little White Bird* Barrie wrote :
' He (Peter Pan) escaped from being a
human when he was seven days old . . .
and flew back to the Kensington
Gardens.' See BARRIE, SIR JAMES
MATTHEW

Peter the Great (1672–1725), greatest of
Russian tsars, *b* Moscow ; ruled a
vast barbarian country from 1689, and
forcibly introduced many advantageous
reforms as a result of his travels abroad,
including England. Among his civilising
efforts were reforms in the press, education and Church ; the reorganisation of
the army and navy ; the introduction
of European customs (notably in dress),
and his encouragement of foreign trade.
He enlarged his borders. He founded
the new capital, St Petersburg, now
Leningrad.
A fierce and brutal tyrant, he was a
giant in stature and in mental abilities.

Peter the Hermit (*d c.*1151), priest at Amiens
when Pope Urban II inspired the first
crusade 1095. He led a band of crusaders from Cologne to Constantinople.

Pethick-Lawrence, LORD (1871–),
Labour statesman ; Secretary of State
for India 1945–47.

Petition of Right, statement drawn up by
Wentworth, Pym and others in
Charles I's 3rd Parliament 1628. The
king promised not to raise money without Parliament's consent and not to imprison anyone for refusing to pay an
illegal tax.

Petrarch, *pē'trärk* (1304–74), Italian poet,
b Arezzo (Tuscany), but went to Avignon
as a child. Inspired by his love for a
beautiful woman, Laura, whose identity
remains a mystery, he wrote a Latin
epic *Africa* (the life of Scipio Africanus)
that won great applause. He is remem-

THE FULMAR PETREL

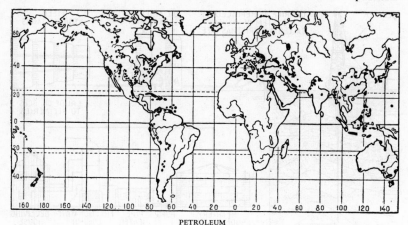

PETROLEUM
A Map of World Sources of Petroleum

bered as a lyric poet, the first to make the sonnet popular ; and though he lived in an ignorant age, he was the herald of the Renaissance.

petrel, name for a number of seabirds, including the fulmar, shearwater and the stormy petrel or Mother Carey's chicken. The latter breeds in Britain (chiefly Scotland), and is swallow-like. Black, except for a white patch in front of the tail, it nests on cliffs, and lays one egg. The petrel family also includes the albatross.

Petrie, Sir FLINDERS, *pē'tri* (1853–1942), English Egyptologist and pioneer of practical archaeology ; brought to light the everyday life of ancient Egypt, especially through his excavations at Naucratis, Daphnae, Coptos, Abydos and Memphis. See ARCHAEOLOGY

petroleum, inflammable mineral oil, usually dark brown or greenish (not unlike a heavy lubricating oil) ; a complex mixture of hydrocarbons with small quantities of sulphur, nitrogen, water, silica, etc. The chief sources are N. America (which supplies *c.*63% of the total world output), Rumania, Poland, USSR, Iran (Persia), Burma and the E. Indies. The N. American supplies include those in Canada, where vast sources are as yet unexploited, e.g. those at Vermilion Field and in the oil-bearing sands of NE. Alberta.

Crude petroleum is not found in underground lakes, as is sometimes imagined, but soaked into sand or soft sandstone. With it are vast quantities of methane, and it is the pressure of this gas (often 500lb per sq.in) that drives the oil to the surface when a well is bored. Drilling the bore may take years, and the well may be 3,000ft deep.

As crude petroleum is a mixture of variously-sized molecules, it is possible by fractional distillation to extract its chief components. This is done in various ways, one of which is by heating the oil under pressure (to prevent boiling), and pumping it into the base of a tower where, as the pressure is released, the lighter molecules rise to the top as petrol or gasoline, somewhat heavier molecules are drawn off about half-way up as illuminating oil, and below this gas-oil and fuel-oil are tapped. Thus, crude USA petroleum by distillation gives (*a*) 35% petrol for cars, planes, etc ; (*b*) 10% paraffin for oil lamps ; (*c*) 15% gas-oil, used in gas-works ; and (*d*) 38% fuel-oil used (i) in Diesel engines in the form of a fine spray, especially for driving ships, and now in a new type of internal combustion engine, and (ii) as a source of lubricating oils, e.g. Essolube and Mobiloil ; also for producing wax and asphalt. American petroleum is rich in paraffins ; Russian in cyclic hydrocarbons, i.e. compounds of carbon and hydrogen only, e.g. benzine.

The first notable production of petroleum on a commercial scale was the drilling of Drake's well, Pennsylvania (1859). Since then production has increased, until now *c.*300,000,000 tons are raised every year. A plant for refining crude oil from coal has been working in England at Bolsover, near Chesterfield, for some years, and synthetic petroleum is produced in USA and Germany, the former having rich supplies of methane, a natural gas.

Oil was discovered in Brazil 1946 ; it has also been found very recently in Peru. Drilling for natural gas, and possibly oil, is going on near Dalkeith (Scotland) ; and since 1945 USA experts have been searching for oil off the coast of California (see PLATE 35), Florida and Texas ; deposits are located by the aid of radar and gravimeter.

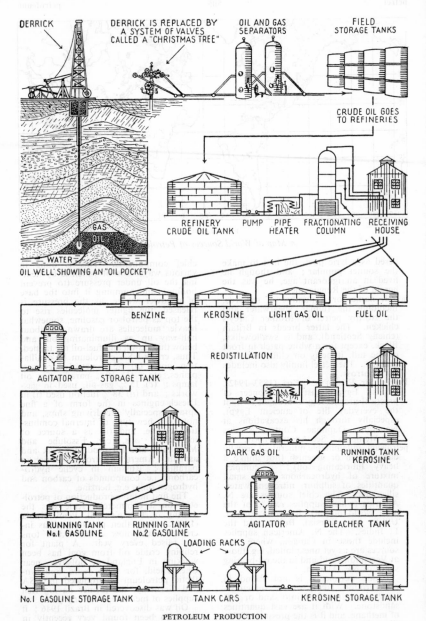

DERRICK

DERRICK IS REPLACED BY A SYSTEM OF VALVES CALLED A "CHRISTMAS TREE"

OIL AND GAS SEPARATORS

FIELD STORAGE TANKS

CRUDE OIL GOES TO REFINERIES

GAS
OIL
WATER

OIL WELL SHOWING AN "OIL POCKET"

REFINERY CRUDE OIL TANK   PUMP   PIPE HEATER   FRACTIONATING COLUMN   RECEIVING HOUSE

BENZINE   KEROSINE   LIGHT GAS OIL   FUEL OIL

AGITATOR   STORAGE TANK

REDISTILLATION

DARK GAS OIL   RUNNING TANK KEROSINE

RUNNING TANK No.1 GASOLINE   RUNNING TANK No.2 GASOLINE   AGITATOR   BLEACHER TANK

LOADING RACKS

No.1 GASOLINE STORAGE TANK   TANK CARS   KEROSINE STORAGE TANK

PETROLEUM PRODUCTION

Most of the other very numerous Crude Oil by-products are obtained through a process of distillation identical or similar to the one represented above

Petrol, severely rationed in Britain during and after World War II, was derationed at Whitsuntide 1950.

It is obvious that eventually the world's supply of oil must become exhausted, but the supply of methane is still enormous ; and supplies of liquid hydrocarbons in the Rocky Mts, in Indiana, Kentucky, Pennsylvania, W. Virginia, etc. are estimated to contain 92 billion barrels. This is insignificant when compared with the amount of petroleum that can be derived from coal deposits, an estimate 1943 indicating that this source alone is sufficient to supply all the petroleum needed for 1,000 years.

Among notable oil pipe-lines is that from the oilfields of N. Iraq to the ports of Haifa and Tripoli, the total output (when the new lines are completed) being *c*.10,000,000 tons a year ; the Big Inch pipe from Texas to Baltimore, i.e. 1,388m ; that from the Mackenzie R. basin to refineries on the Alaskan Highway.

Pumping petroleum from England, under the English Channel, to a Continental base was one of the most astonishing engineering feats of World War II.

pets, domesticated or tame birds and animals. Care and consideration are essential if a pet is to be happy. City dwellers ought not to keep, say, a spaniel unless ample provision is made for him to run freely in the country. The housing of birds in small cages is a cruel practice and should be discontinued, though most cage-birds may live happily in an aviary large enough for them to fly about.

Many pets may be bought at local live-stock stores ; dogs from local breeders. It is wise to seek the advice of an expert when purchasing. If pets cannot be procured locally, write to one of the London stores, where many kinds of animals may be bought. Useful books include *The Boy's Own Book of Pets and Hobbies.* Weekly publications include *Cage Birds and Bird Fancy* ; *Our Dogs, Dog World, Fur and Feather,* etc.

Points to note :

Dogs should run *c*.10m a day ; must have water *always* handy ; need two good meals a day ; raw meat once or twice a week ; the name and address should be on the collar. *Cats* should be fed twice a day. They need plenty of milk, and ought to be kept indoors at night. *Cavies* or *guinea-pigs* are best housed in a bottomless hutch that can be moved about a lawn. They need water twice and a handful of oats once a day. *Mice* should always be kept in pairs, and should have a large cage (which must be dry). Feed them once or twice a day on canary or millet seed and oats, and a small piece of bread dipped in milk ; lift by the middle of the tail. *Rabbits* need a hutch 18in above the ground, the floor of which should be tarred. Feed them on bran and oats, with a handful of vegetables either green or root ; raise by holding the flesh behind the shoulders (*not* by the ears) and support their legs. *Tortoises* may eat lettuces in the garden but will certainly *not* kill beetles. Keep two, not one alone. *Budgerigars :* do not keep in cages, but in an aviary protected from draughts and hot sun. *Canaries,* if kept in a cage, should not hang near the ceiling, where the air is too hot for them.

Money may be made by breeding and selling many pets, especially budgerigars, canaries, rabbits and dogs.

petty sessions, local courts in England presided over by Justices of the Peace, or sometimes by stipendiary magistrates. They try cases of minor offences (e.g. riding a cycle without a lamp after lighting-up time). There is no jury.

Pevensey, village, Sussex. William the Conqueror landed hereabouts 1066.

pharaoh, *făr'ō,* ancient Egyptian title meaning king. In all about thirty Dynasties (or families) of Pharaohs ruled ancient Egypt for over 3,000 years before even the Roman Empire came into existence. The earliest Pharaohs were thus almost as remote from the ' ancient ' Greeks in time as those Greeks from ourselves.

Pharisees, see JEWS

pharmacy, *făr'mă-si,* trade and practice of preparing and compounding medicines, and of making up (i.e. dispensing) doctors' prescriptions. Only such doctors, chemists or druggists (technically pharmaceutical chemists or pharmacists) as are members of the Pharmaceutical Society (founded 1841) are allowed to practise in this way. Intending students should write for details of examinations to the Secretary, Pharmaceutical Society of Great Britain.

Pharos, *fā'ros,* western point of Alexandria (Egypt) ; site of the ancient Pharos or lighthouse, once one of the Seven Wonders of the World. Built *c*.260BC in the reign of Ptolemy II, it was probably *c*.500ft high.

Pharsalus, town of ancient Greece ; scene of fighting between Rome and Macedonia 197BC, and of the defeat of Pompey by Julius Caesar, 48BC.

pheasant, *fez'ant,* domesticated game-bird related to partridges and poultry ; possibly introduced into Britain by the Romans. The plumage of the male is brilliant, its long tail being wedge-shaped. Pheasants feed on insects, snails and berries ; the female lays *c*.12 eggs in April. Pheasants may be shot from 1 Oct. to 31 Jan.

Pheidias, *fī'di-as* (*d* 432BC), one of the greatest of Greek sculptors ; *b* Athens ; appointed by Pericles to superintend the building of the Parthenon on the Acropolis ; famous for his statue of Athena. See SCULPTURE

Pheidippides, see MARATHON, BATTLE OF

phenol or **carbolic acid,** *fē'nol,* white, solid

coal-tar product, C_6H_5OH ; has a carbolic smell and is used as a disinfectant and in the manufacture of various plastics, especially bakelite.

Philadelphia, *fil-ă-del'fiă,* ancient city, Lydia, Asia Minor.

Philadelphia, port and third largest city of USA ; pop.1,935,000 ; on the Delaware R., Pennsylvania ; noted for leather goods, carpets, tobacco, chemicals and sugar. Here, 1776, the Declaration of Independence was signed, and here is the Liberty Bell.

philately, see STAMP COLLECTING

Philemon, friend of St Paul, who wrote a letter to him about Philemon's slave, Onesimus.

Philip, name of two saints : (*a*) the Apostle, associated with Jesus in feeding the five thousand (John 6) ; and (*b*) the evangelist mentioned in Acts 8.

Philip, name of six kings of France, among them PHILIP II (1165–1223), who enlarged his borders, and won the battle of Bouvines 1214 ; PHILIP IV (1268–1314), developed the central administration of the country, and defied the pope (Boniface VIII) ; PHILIP VI (1293–1350), ruled from 1328, and in the Hundred Years' War suffered defeat at Sluys 1340 and Crécy 1346.

Philip II (382–336BC), King of Macedonia, father of Alexander the Great ; made war on Thrace and Thessaly. By winning the battle of Chaeronea 338BC against combined opposition he became master of Greece ; was assassinated while preparing an expedition against Persia. Philip, who made the Macedonian army the finest fighting force in the ancient world, was also a brilliant statesman.

Philip II (1527–98), King of Spain, *b* Valladolid ; married Mary, Queen of England, 1554 ; ruled from 1556. Regarding himself as the champion of RC religion, he dispatched the Armada 1588 against England. He lost control of the Netherlands, and failed in all his schemes.

Philippa of Hainault, *e-no'* (*d* 1369), Dutch queen of Edward III of England, whom she married 1328. She established a company of Flemish weavers at Norwich ; is famous for her intercession on behalf of the burghers of Calais 1347.

Philippi, *fi-lip'ī,* ancient city of Macedonia, near the R. Gangas. Here Octavian (later the first Roman Emperor) defeated Brutus 42BC ; and later St Paul established a Christian church, the one addressed by him in the *Epistle to the Philippians.*

Philippines, *fil'i-pēns,* commonwealth of islands (the chief being Luzon and Mindanao) in the Pacific, *c.*500m southeast of Asia ; total area 114,400sq.m ; pop.16,000,000. The exports (largest customer USA) are tropical products, e.g. sugar, Manila hemp, coconuts and timber. Discovered 1521 by Magellan, the islands were later governed by USA

till 1946, and were the scene of fierce fighting between Japanese and American troops in World War II ; cap. Manila (in Luzon), pop.623,000.

Philistines, *fil'is-tīn,* ancient and warlike people of Palestine, especially in and around Gaza, Ashkelon and Gath ; fought the Israelites ; were subdued by Sennacherib *c.*700BC.

Phillpotts, EDEN (1862–), British author and dramatist, *b* India ; has written many novels (some with Devon as a background). His plays include *The Farmer's Wife.*

philomel, see NIGHTINGALE

philosophy, the systematic study of the *principles* underlying our knowledge, our experience and our conduct. A philosopher is one who seriously devotes himself to philosophical studies. In considering (for example) our scientific knowledge, he does not content himself (as scientists do) by trying to answer the question ' What do we know ? ' ; he goes on to ask himself the more difficult question ' How do we know it ? ' In considering conduct he does not ask himself ' Is it wrong to tell lies ? ' but (for example) ' Can I tell a lie, and at the same time reprove other people for doing so, without contradicting myself ? And if not, why not ? '

The branch of philosophy that deals with principles of conduct is called *ethics,* that which deals with the principles of knowledge *epistemology* or *theory of knowledge.* Other important branches of philosophy are those that deal with the theory of the state (*philosophy of politics*), with the principles of correct reasoning (*logic*) and with the principles of art (*aesthetics*).

In all these studies the philosopher finds that underlying our knowledge and our ordinary practice there are many concealed assumptions—principles of thought and action so much taken for granted that normally we hardly bother to think about them : e.g. the assumption that, for example, an electric light cannot possibly be both ' off ' and ' on ' at the same moment ; in other words that is must be *either* ' on ' *or* ' off,' not both. It is not the philosopher's business to *prove* that such basic assumptions are ' true ' or ' false,' or even that they are ' correct ' (which is not quite the same thing). He cannot *prove* such assumptions because, like everybody else, he has to make those very assumptions in order to prove anything at all. His business is to find out what exactly the basic assumptions are : and to point it out to other people if he finds that the basic assumptions which they are using contradict one another.

People do not always thank him for doing this ; but it is a very necessary and important task.

Among the world's greatest philosophers are the Greeks : Socrates (*c.*470–399BC), Plato (*c.*427–347BC) and

Aristotle (384–322BC) ; the Frenchman, Descartes (1596–1650) ; Leibniz, a German (1646–1716) ; Locke, an Englishman (1632–1704) ; Berkeley, an Anglo-Irishman (1685–1753) ; Hume, a Scotsman (1711–76) ; Kant (1724–1804) and Hegel (1770–1831), both Germans. The most important British philosophers of the 20th c. are Bertrand Russell (Earl Russell), A. N. Whitehead (*d* 1947) and R. G. Collingwood (*d* 1942).

philosopher's stone, substance which the alchemists sought for in vain as a means of turning base metals into gold. See ALCHEMY

Phiz, see BROWNE, H. K.

phlogiston, *flō-jis'ton,* substance once supposed to be part of any material that would burn, a theory widely held till Lavoisier (1743–94), the French chemist, showed that combustion occurs only in the presence of oxygen.

Phoebe, see PHOEBUS

Phoebus, *fē'bŭs,* Greek name for Apollo, the sun god, Phoebe being the Greek name for Artemis, the moon goddess.

Phoenicia, *fē-nish'iä,* anciently a region of Asia Minor, north of Palestine. A narrow coastal strip, its towns included Tyre and Sidon. The Phoenicians, the greatest sailors of the ancient world, were the founders of Carthage. Their finest period was *c.*1200–700BC, when they colonised many areas, and exported purple dye, also glass and metal.

Phoenix, *fē'niks,* cap., Arizona, USA ; pop.65,000.

phoenix, legendary Egyptian bird with red and gold plumage. It was said to live 500 years and then throw itself into a fire, rising again from the ashes.

Phoenix Park, large and beautiful park, Dublin ; scene 1882 of the murder by terrorists of Lord Frederick Cavendish.

phon, *fon,* unit of loudness. The sound of a watch ticking at a distance of 3ft is taken as 30 phons, that of an aeroplane engine as 120. Each phon (after the first) is 26% louder than the one below.

phonetics, *fō-net'iks,* science of speech-sounds ; deals with the way in which sounds are formed, and employs special signs to indicate sounds accurately.

phormium, see FLAX

phosgene, poison gas with a smell like musty hay.

phosphates, *fos'fāts,* salts of phosphoric acid ; of great importance to plant and animal life, the chief being phosphates of sodium, calcium and magnesium. For phosphatic manures see MANURES AND FERTILISERS

phosphorescence, see FLUORESCENCE

phosphoric acid, *fos-for'ik,* H_3PO_4, crystalline, easily-soluble solid.

phosphorus, *fos'for-us,* non-metallic element, P ; atomic weight 30·98 ; atomic number 15 ; melting-point 44·1°C ; boiling-point 280·5°C ; named from the Greek meaning *light-bearer,* due to its property of giving a bluish-green light in the dark ; essential to all living plants and animals, and is abundant in bone and egg-shells ; occurs naturally as a complex phosphate of calcium in the excreta of birds ; is prepared by reduction of a phosphate in an electric furnace. Two forms are (*a*) white (or yellowish) phosphorus, the commoner ; a waxy and highly inflammable poisonous solid that must be kept under water, as it quickly catches fire in air ; (*b*) red phosphorus.

Phosphorus sulphide is used in making matches. Phosphates are important fertilisers.

photo-electric cell, device that reacts to light by a change in electrical resistance produced when light falls on certain light-sensitive elements. (It can therefore be used for measuring light-changes.) The photo-electric effect is the emission of electrons from a metal surface when light of suitable wave-length falls on it. If the metal surface is used as a cathode, with another plate as anode, and both are enclosed in a vacuum, the electrons are repelled from the cathode, and a current flows as a result across the gap. The rate of emission of electrons is proportional to the intensity of the light, hence the application of the principle to sound films.

A selenium cell fulfils a similar function, but does not depend on photo-electricity.

photo-finish, see PHOTOGRAPHY

photography, *fō-tog'rä-fi,* from Greek *phôs,* light, *grapho,* I write, art and process of producing permanent pictures by the action of light ; requires (*a*) a camera ; (*b*) a method of fixation.

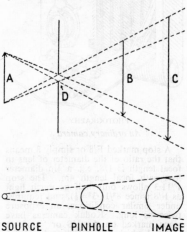

SOURCE   PINHOLE   IMAGE

THE PRINCIPLE OF THE PINHOLE CAMERA

A : *Object* D : *Pinhole* B, C : *Images. The image of the source is circular if the pinhole is circular. The image at C is larger than the image at B and as the image becomes larger the definition becomes poorer.*

Much may be learned by experimenting with a Pin-hole Camera, i.e. a light-tight box with a minute hole in one side, say 1/50in in diameter. An image will be thrown clearly at the back, and may be viewed from behind if the back of the camera is, say, of ground glass or tissue-paper. If a lens (e.g. one from a cheap telescope) is used, and a hole made at the top of the box so that the observer can see inside (having his head and the box covered by a heavy cloth) it is possible to slide a card backwards and forwards till a clear image is secured. The more distant the object, the nearer the card must be to the lens.

Cameras require : (a) a lens ; (b)—except in the simple box-camera—a focussing arrangement ; (c) a stop to regulate the amount of light ; (d) a shutter to regulate the time of exposure ; (e) a sensitized plate or film which ' holds ' the image after exposure, though the mystery of the ' latent image ' is still only partially explained. Refinements of these principles give the complex modern camera.

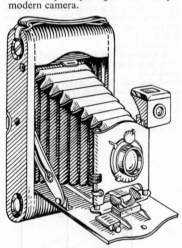

PHOTOGRAPHY
An ordinary camera

A stop marked F/8 or simply 8 means that the ratio of the diameter of lens to focal length is 1/8, e.g. a ½in diameter lens with focal length 4in. The stop F/11·3 allows only half as much light as F/8 (since $8^2/11·3^2=\frac{1}{2}$), and requires, under similar conditions, an exposure twice as long. Kodak cameras have stops marked on the US or ' uniform system,' which shows F/4 as 1 ; F/5·6 as 2 (i.e. requiring twice the exposure of F/4) ; F/8 is marked 4 (4 times the exposure of F/4).

The modern film is coated with gelatine in which crystals of silver bromide are suspended, the silver bromide (AgBr) having specks of silver sulphide from the sulphur in the gelatine. It seems that light somehow ' prepares ' a single speck of the grains of AgBr. When immersed in the developing solution, the bromide at the ' prepared ' spot deposits silver, and the chemical change spreads to all the grains in which the change started. Where more light fell during exposure, more grains are affected, and the consequent deposit of silver is denser. The unaffected AgBr is removed during subsequent immersion in a fixing solution. The result is a *negative*—dark where the subject was light and transparent where the subject was dark. The fixing solution is usually ' hypo ' (sodium thiosulphate), and the ' hypo ' is finally washed off to prevent it slowly combining with the silver.

Printing reverses the negative, and on a somewhat similar principle to that outlined above provides us with a permanent picture of the objects photographed.

Colour photography is now becoming possible for the amateur, but though there are a number of processes for producing a colour transparency, to be viewed against the light or projected on a screen, the opaque colour picture can only be produced as yet by a very complicated process.

Photography has many practical applications. e.g. the cinema ; photographing distant objects with a telephoto lens ; use of ultra-violet light and infra-red waves for observing details the eye cannot see ; X-ray work, of great value in surgery and industry ; recording star spectra and the movements of stars ; micro-photography, which has increasing possibilities in the study of bacteria ; aerial photography ; surveying (photogrammetry), etc.

The word *photography* was first used by Sir John Herschel 1840. Pioneers were William Talbot, Joseph Petzval (who first used the portrait lens 1841), D. O. Hill, Frederick Scott Archer, inventor of the collodion plate, George Eastman (USA), who first sold dry plates 1880, Louis Daguerre (1789–1851), the Frenchman who invented the silver plate process, and Clerk Maxwell, who evolved a 3-colour process 1861.

The latest camera now enables the photographer to take, develop and fix a picture within 60 seconds. The invention is not actually new, but an improvement on an earlier method known as tintype photography.

Since 1947 most racecourses have installed the photo-finish camera for recording and determining the winning horse.

photometer, *fō-tom'ē-tẽr,* instrument for measuring the candle-power, or luminous intensity, of a source of light, by comparison with a standard. The laboratory standard is the Harcourt-Pentane lamp of 10 international candlepower. The

Rumford shadow photometer and the Bunsen grease-spot photometer are useful for simple measurements. The Lummer-Brodhun and various types of flicker photometers have advantages over the simpler types.

photosphere, *fō'tō-sfēr,* luminous outer surface of the sun.

phototelegraphy, *fō'tō-tē-leg'rǎfi,* system of transmitting pictures by electric wire or radio, the principle involving a positive photographic print on celluloid film which is placed in a transparent cylinder rotated while a minute spot of light focussed on the film passes through it to a photoelectric cell. The current thus set up is amplified, and used to alter a carrier current either along a wire or as a radio wave. At the receiving end the varied impulses operate an electrically controlled light-valve which modifies the intensity of a beam of light moving across a photographic film. This reproduces a replica of the original photograph. The system has been used since 1928 for reproducing newspaper photographs, plans, diagrams, phototelegrams and blue prints, the scanning of a picture of 60sq.in taking *c.*6 minutes.

Phrygia, *frij'iä,* ancient country of Asia Minor, chiefly along its western shore ; existed as a kingdom till early in the 7th c. BC.

phylactery, *fi-lak'těri,* strip of parchment with sayings from Exodus 13 and Deuteronomy 6, the strip being kept in a small calf-skin case tied to the forehead or left arm, a custom among the Jews from the 3rd c. BC. Modern Jews sometimes wear a phylactery on an undergarment.

physical training (often briefly PT), method of assisting one to ' keep fit ' by regular exercises, including a form of drill (or Swedish drill), and possibly organised games and gymnastics ; now a part of the school curriculum, army training and youth activities. The idea is to develop or keep in a healthy and vigorous condition various muscles and organs, to encourage deep and regular breathing, and the co-ordination of mind and body. See GYMNASTICS

physician, one who is qualified to diagnose and treat ailments of human beings, whether the illness be mild or serious ; to perform small operations, and to administer drugs.

A qualified physician generally has the degree of M.B., Ch.B. (Bachelor of Medicine and Bachelor of Surgery) or its equivalent.

If a qualified physician wishes to specialise he enters on a period of further study, and when he has written a thesis which has been accepted by the examining body he receives the degree of M.D. (Doctor of Medicine).

physics, *fiz'iks,* branch of science dealing with the laws and nature of the material and physical universe, e.g. heat, light, sound, electricity, magnetism, matter and energy. It has made immense and

revolutionary advances this century, especially in concepts of the atomic structure of matter and the release of atomic energy.

physiology, *fiz-i-ol'ō-ji,* branch of the science of biology ; deals with the normal functions (but not particularly the structure) of animals and plants. Human physiology has advanced enormously since Harvey's discovery (17th c.) of the circulation of the blood. More recent advances include the complex workings of the various glands, metabolism (the breaking down of food), micro-organisms and embryology. An excellent book giving the latest results of investigations is *Human Physiology,* Kenneth Walker.

pi (π), *pī,* symbol for the ratio of the circumference of a circle to its diameter, i.e. $3 \cdot 141592653 \dots$; roughly $\frac{22}{7}$, or antilog. $0 \cdot 4972$. For practical purposes it may be assumed that $\pi = 3 \cdot 142$; $\pi^2 = 9 \cdot 8696$; $\sqrt{\pi} = 1 \cdot 7725$. As a matter of interest here is π worked out to 127 places : $3 \cdot 14159265358979323846264338$ $3279502884197169399375105820974944 5$ $92307816406286208998628034825342117$ $0679821480865132723066470938446 +$.

See CIRCLE ; TRIGONOMETRY

pianoforte, *pi-an-ō-fōr'tē* (Italian soft-loud), musical instrument of the percussion type. A development of the harpsichord, the pianoforte (or piano) dates from the early 18th century. The instrument may be upright or horizontal (called a grand, boudoir grand, slightly smaller, or a very small baby grand). The neo-Bechstein or Siemens-Bechstein is an electric variety, and *c.*1925 an American (J. H. Hammond) invented a new type of instrument in which sounds persist long after the wire is struck. There are also two-manual instruments.

Piave, *pyä'vä,* river of NE. Italy ; flows 125m to the Adriatic Sea.

Picardy, *pik'ěr-di,* province of France before the Revolution ; had a coastline on the English Channel.

Picasso, PABLO RUIZ, *pē-käs'sō* (1881–) modern Spanish painter, *b* Malaga. His remarkable pictures first caused a stir in this country *c.*1910.

Piccadilly, see LONDON

Piccard, AUGUSTE (1881–), Swiss doctor ; became a professor at Brussels University ; made remarkable balloon ascents (reaching over 54,000ft, 1932) in his investigation of the stratosphere ; planner of deep-sea exploration in a special spherical diving-chamber.

picric acid, poisonous yellow crystalline solid used as an explosive and as a dye. The liquid is an excellent remedy for flesh burns.

Picts, name for people who once lived in N. Scotland, and made continual attacks on the Romans from the 3rd c. AD. They were never wholly subdued. See CELTI

Piedmont, *pēd'mont,* region of NW. Italy ; chief city Turin.

PIGS

(1) *African Warthog*   (2) *Wild Sow*
(3) *Large White Boar*   (4) *Large Black Sow*

Pietermaritzburg, *pētĕr-mär'its-bŭrg*, cap., Natal, S. Africa. An important railway junction, it is the seat of the provincial government ; pop.56,000.

pig, wild or domestic animal with flat snout, tusks in upper and lower jaw, four toes to each foot, though only two touch the ground ; pendent ears and coarse bristles. Wild pigs include the European wild boar. Domestic varieties include white, middle white, and black. The female is called the ' sow ' ; the male, the ' boar.' The plural of pig is pigs or swine. The flesh is pork (forbidden food to the Mohammedan and Jew), or (if cured) bacon. Related to the pig is the African wart-hog, with pads (or warts) above the eyes.

pigeon, *pij"n*, name for various species of birds, including the British wild pigeons, e.g. turtle-dove, a summer visitor ; stock dove, with plain grey plumage ; wood-pigeon, a larger bird with a white patch at each side of the neck ; and blue rock pigeon, found along the coasts of Scotland and Ireland. From the latter are descended the countless domesticated varieties, e.g. pouter (with an enormous crop) ; carrier ; runt ; barb ; fantail ; tumbler ; Jacobin (with a kind of hood) and trumpeter. The homer is now used for carrying messages in peace or war.

Pigeon flying and racing, now a popular sport, was introduced into Britain *c.*1871. Some pigeons fly 2,000yd a minute, and some have flown 1,000m in one flight. Pigeon post has long been used as a wartime emergency, e.g. in the siege of Paris 1870–71.

Pigeons lay 1–2 white eggs ; eat a vast amount of corn and make a cooing sound.

pike, freshwater fish found in British rivers ; may be nearly 4ft long and weigh 40lb ; is olive grey above, thickly spotted in lighter tints ; silvery below.

Pilate, PONTIUS, Roman procurator (governor) of Judea AD26–36 ; handed Christ over to the Jews for crucifixion.

pilchard, fish similar to the herring ; found in the English Channel and the Mediterranean ; if caught before full-grown it is a sardine, so named from the island of Sardinia.

pilewort, see LESSER CELANDINE

pilgrim, one who makes a journey to visit some place considered sacred, e.g. the ancient Greeks who journeyed to the shrines of Apollo at Delphi and of Diana at Ephesus. Mohammedans who visit Mecca, and members of various Indian sects who visit shrines of Rama and Krishna are pilgrims.

Among Christians, pilgrimages to Palestine (the Holy Land), and especially Jerusalem, began in the second c. AD, and the custom was greatly encouraged by the pilgrimage made 326 by St Helena, mother of the Emperor Constantine, who claimed to have found the Holy Sepulchre at Jerusalem. From the 8th c., Christian pilgrims were allowed to pass road-tolls free. Many wore a scallop as a badge. Today pilgrimages are still made to the tomb of Thomas Becket (Canterbury), to St Albans, and to Lourdes (S. France).

Pilgrimage of Grace, rebellion in the North of England 1536–37 as a protest against the dissolution of the monasteries by Henry VIII, and because the introduction of sheep-farming was causing less employment. The leaders were Robert Aske, Lord Darcy and Sir John Constable with 30,000 rebels and a banner displaying the five wounds of Christ. All the leaders were executed.

Pilgrim Fathers, name given to a group of Puritans who, with their wives and families (in all *c.*100), sailed 1620 to N. America in order to enjoy liberty of conscience there, i.e. to worship God as they felt they ought, a right they were denied in England in the reign of James I.

Their leaders were William Brewster of Scrooby (Nottinghamshire) and William Bradford (Yorkshire). The company had intended to use two ships, but one (the *Speedwell*) proved unseaworthy, so they all sailed together in the *Mayflower*, a double-decked brigantine with a high stern, and of no more than 150 tons.

Leaving Plymouth in September, the colonists landed at what is now Plymouth (Massachusetts) in December. Winter came. They had little food. Menaced by wild animals and by Red Indians, they suffered greatly, half their number dying in the first few months. More colonists joined them two years later, and another 98 in 1623.

Among the Pilgrim Fathers was Miles Standish (1584–1656), a Lancashire man whose courage and commonsense did much to maintain security. We read of him in Longfellow's poem, *Miles Standish*, though the poet is incorrect in saying that Standish hoped to marry Priscilla Mullins, the wife of John Alden, another of the Pilgrim Fathers.

The sailing of the *Mayflower* had a great influence on America. The region, secured for the colonists by Sir Edwin Sandys in Sir Walter Raleigh's colony of Virginia, became the home of an increasing number of families, and was known as New England. On the whole, the colonists were deeply religious, high-minded, hard-working and lovers of learning. See BRITISH COMMONWEALTH OF NATIONS ; PURITANS

Pilgrim's Way, ancient track of 120m supposed to have been used by pilgrims to the tomb of St Thomas of Canterbury ; runs over the N. Downs from Winchester via Farnham, Burford and W. Malling.

Pilgrim Trust, society founded 1930 by Edward Stephen Harkness of New York to help to preserve buildings of historic interest in the UK, also to keep the countryside fair, and to encourage a love of music and art.

pillars, see ARCHITECTURE

Pillars of Hercules, old name for two rocks at the entrance to the Mediterranean, namely Calpe (Gibraltar) and Abyla (Ceuta).

pillory, instrument of punishment used in Britain from the 13th c. to 1830. It consisted of a post with a crosspiece through which the culprit's head and hands were thrust. Standing thus, the victim was usually jeered at, though not always, for sometimes the crowd regarded him as a hero, e.g. Daniel Defoe, sentenced 1703 for his famous plea for religious toleration.

pilot, *pī'lŭt,* seaman holding a licence to navigate a vessel through dangerous waters. Also one who flies aircraft.

Pilsen, *pil'zen,* town, Bohemia (Czechoslovakia) ; manufactures beer ; pop. 115,000.

Pilsudski, JOSEPH CLEMENS, *pil-sut'skē* (1867–1935), Polish statesman ; strove to free Poland from the domination of Russia ; became Premier 1926, ruled as a dictator, and encouraged friendly alliances and foreign trade.

pimpernel or **poor man's weatherglass,** plant (family *Primulaceae*) with slender, square stem on the ground ; opposite stalkless leaves ; bright scarlet flowers open in the morning in clear weather ; often called the scarlet pimpernel.

pina cloth, see PINEAPPLE

Pindar (*d* 443BC), last and greatest of the Greek lyric poets, *b* Cynoscephalae (Boeotia) ; knew and loved the old Greek tales ; is said to have excelled on the lyre. Famous in his lifetime, he was greatly honoured, and regarded almost as divine.

Pindar wrote choral songs, carnival songs, dancing songs and dirges, but almost all his poems are lost except his *epinikia,* i.e. odes written to celebrate the victors in athletic contests such as the Pythian Games. His poetry, the very spirit of Greece, is full of music and vivid metaphor. The metres of his odes are complex.

pine, genus of cone-bearing trees, especially the Scots pine (wrongly called Scots fir), a handsome tree of Scottish and Scandinavian mountains ; has a rugged, reddish trunk perhaps 100ft high. The egg-shaped cones grow singly or in pairs. The timber is valuable, and the tree yields turpentine. See page 514.

pineapple, tropical plant with a cluster of sharply-toothed, sword-like leaves springing from the ground, and a centre leaf-cluster beneath which the berries grow together into a juicy fruit with a spiny skin. The fruit is exported from Hawaii and Puerto Rico. See PLATE 8 (*top*)

PINA CLOTH, *pē'nyä,* made from the leaf fibres, is worn in Brazil, Malaya and the Philippines.

pine marten, see MARTEN

Pinero, SIR ARTHUR WING (1855–1934), dramatist, *b* London ; noted for his *The Second Mrs Tanqueray* and *The Gay Lord Quex.*

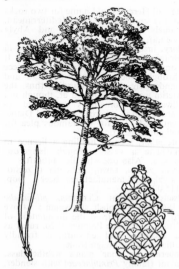

THE SCOTS PINE

The pine needles (leaves), the tree and the cone

pin-hole camera, see PHOTOGRAPHY

Pinkie, BATTLE OF, fought 1547 near Musselburgh, Scotland ; the English defeated the Scots. The cause was the attempt by the Protector Somerset to force Mary Queen of Scots to marry Edward VI. In this project he was unsuccessful.

pinnace, light vessel used as a tender for a warship ; formerly a sailing ship, now usually driven by steam or oil.

pipe and tabor, combination of musical instruments formerly played by one musician, especially at morris dances. The pipe had three holes ; the tabor was a kind of drum *c.*6in deep and 12in across, hanging from his left wrist and beaten with a stick.

pipe-fish, see SEA HORSE

pipette, *pi-pet'*, glass tube for transferring (by suction) small quantities of liquid from one vessel to another ; may be designed to transfer a given quantity, or graduated for varying amounts.

pipit, *pip'it*, perching bird similar to the lark, and sometimes called titlark. Varieties include the meadow pipit (*Anthus pratensis*), the commonest ; tree pipit, visiting Britain April–Sept.; and rock pipit, the only British song-bird living among rocks by the coast.

Piraeus, port for Athens, the chief in Greece. Modernised since 1929, it has pop.290,000. The ancient town was built in the age of Pericles (5th c. BC).

pirates, see BUCCANEERS AND PIRATES

Pisa, *pē'zä*, city, Italy, on the R. Arno, its port being Leghorn. Manufactures include silks and ribbons ; pop.72,000.

Pisa is chiefly famous for its magnificent cathedral with a separate *campanile* (bell-tower) leaning 16ft out of the perpendicular. The campanile, built 1174–1350, is 179ft high.

Pisgah, see NEBO

pistol, firearm used with one hand only ; dates from *c.*1500. The pistol had first a wheel-lock, then a flint-lock. It was greatly improved in the age of duelling, and horse-pistols were carried by travellers in the days of highwaymen. An improved form of pistol was the revolver ; the Colt revolver was invented 1835 in the USA. An automatic is a magazine pistol which goes on firing so long as the trigger is pressed : a revolver fires only single shots.

pistole, French name for a 16th c. Spanish gold coin worth *c.*17s.

Pitcairn Island, British island almost midway between Australia and America ; first occupied 1790 by mutineers from the *Bounty*. It is 2½m long. See also ' BOUNTY '

pitch, *pich*, may be (*a*) coal-pitch ; (*b*) wood-pitch ; (*c*) bitumen ; see BITUMEN.

Coal-pitch is the residue after distilling coal-tar. A mixture of hydrocarbons, it is black and lustrous, and though apparently solid is actually a very thick liquid, the soft variety melting at *c.*40°C, the hard at 100°C. From it are made asphalt, roofing felt, varnishes, lacquer, etc.

pitch, in music, denotes the place in the scale occupied by one note relatively to others : thus the note A is of ' higher pitch ' than G, B than A, C than B♭, etc. The pitch of a note depends on the frequency of vibration. Orchestras now usually take A as 439, or sometimes as 444, vibrations per sec.

pitchblende, *pich'blend*, oxide of uranium, U_3O_8, an ore, containing traces of radium. A pitch-like substance, it is found in the North-west Territories, Canada, in Colorado, E. Africa, Germany and Cornwall.

pitcher-plant, insect-eating plant found chiefly in the E. Indies and China. The leaves end in a hanging pitcher, the interior of which has smooth sides and a liquid that dissolves insects falling into it. Fine specimens may be seen at Kew.

Pitman, SIR ISAAC, see SHORTHAND

Pitt, WILLIAM (1708–78), 1st Earl of Chatham, one of the greatest of all British statesmen. MP for Old Sarum (a pocket borough) 1734, he opposed the Whig Sir Robert Walpole. He was strongly disliked by George II ; was Paymaster-General 1746–55, when he refused to accept the customary sums appropriated by former paymasters. An opponent of corrupt political practices, he formed a coalition with Newcastle, 1757, in the Seven Years' War, and became the dominant figure in British politics.

Immensely popular, Pitt saw that Britain must be supreme at sea, and was the first of our statesmen to realise the vast possibilities of a world-wide empire. He directed the policy that enabled Wolfe to win Canada, and Clive to lay the foundations of British India ; made famous speeches in the House of Commons ; stood for the people against George III ; created Earl of Chatham 1766, and thus ceased to be ' The Great Commoner ' ; lived to see much of his good work destroyed by lesser men, and made his last speech in Parliament a few days before he died. He was the father of the Younger Pitt.

Pitt, WILLIAM (1759–1806), son of the 1st Earl of Chatham ; known as William Pitt the Younger ; *b* Hayes, Kent ; had the Elder Pitt's genius for oratory, and by his first speech in Parliament 1781 earned from Edmund Burke the tribute that he was not a chip off the old block, but the old block itself.

Pitt advocated many reforms. He was Chancellor of the Exchequer in Shelburne's government, and the bitter enemy of Charles James Fox. His formation of a ministry 1783 at the age of twenty-four was regarded by his opponents as a boyish prank. He was supported by a large majority 1784 ; did much to restore economic prosperity after the war with America ; fostered commercial expansions ; and reorganised the E. India Co. He introduced free trade, and though unsuccessful in his dealings with Ireland, built up British influence abroad, and organised a coalition against France. A brilliant administrator, he made the office of prime minister that of head of the cabinet, responsible to the people rather than to the king, and was therefore more democratic than his Whig rivals.

Pittsburgh, *pits'bŭrg,* university city, Pennsylvania, USA ; famous for its coal and natural gas ; a great centre for steel manufacture, metal goods, earthenware, etc. ; pop.665,000.

pituitary gland, see GLANDS

Pius, *pī'ŭs,* name of 12 popes, among them : Pius V (1504–72), pope from 1566 ; excommunicated Queen Elizabeth ; strengthened the work of the Inquisition ; Pius IX (1792–1878), elected 1846 ; Pius XI (1857–1939), became pope 1922 ; Pius XII (1876–), elected pope 1939.

Pizarro, FRANCISCO, *pee-thä'ro* (1475–1541), Spanish conqueror ; sailed to Panama, heard of the vast wealth of the Incas of Peru, and with only 168 followers dared to invade their country. After inviting their usurping ruler, Atahualpa, to his camp, he routed the latter's army of 40,000, and treacherously executed Atahualpa 1533. He then conquered the remainder of the country, but was assassinated. Greedy for power and wealth, he was a detestable character whose one virtue was courage.

Read *History of the Conquest of Peru,* W. H. Prescott.

place-names, in Britain may be traced to early times, e.g. the Anglo-Saxon period, and (in England) to *Domesday Book.* Note :

Celtic place-names, e.g. *afon* = river (Avonmouth) ; *dwr* = water (Calder ; Derwent) ; *esk* = water ; *pen* = hill ; *dun* = a hill-fort (Dundee) ; *llan* = church or sacred enclosure, as in many Welsh towns ; *cwm* = a depression in the hills.

Anglo-Saxon or OE : *-ham, -ton, -worth, -garth, -burgh* have the idea of an enclosure (Birmingham, Kenilworth, Edinburgh) ; *stead* = town (Hampstead).

Norse, Danish : *-by, -thorp* or *-throp* or *-trop* = village (Whitby, Burnham-Thorpe, etc.) ; *-toft* = a homestead (Lowestoft) ; *-thwaite* = forest clearing (Crossthwaite) ; *-garth* = enclosure ; *beck* = stream ; *-foss* = waterfall (High Force) ; *ford* = a river crossing (Hereford) ; *-wick* = creek (Warwick) ; *scar* = cliff (Scarborough) ; *ness* = headland (Caithness).

plague, *plāg,* name once given to any epidemic, e.g. the Black Death in the 14th c., the Great Plague of London, 1665, in which over 100,000 people died. It is now given only to bubonic plague, a disease caused by *bacillus pestis.*

The ten plagues of Egypt (Exodus 7–12) prior to the release of the Israelites by Pharaoh were : turning the water of the Nile into blood ; swarms of frogs ; gnats ; flies ; pestilence among cattle ; boils on man and beast ; destruction by thunder and hail ; swarms of locusts ; darkness ; death of the first-born of man and beast among the Egyptians. See BLACK DEATH

plaice, *plās,* valuable food fish of the N. Atlantic and N. Sea ; begins life as a ' round ' fish, but later becomes flat, the right side brown with red or orange spots, the left white.

plaintiff, *plān'tif,* in English law, one who brings another person (defendant) to court, and seeks relief against him. In Scotland a plaintiff is called the pursuer, and the other party is known as the defender.

Planck, MAX, *plängk* (1858–1947), German scientist, *b* Kiel ; awarded the Nobel prize for physics 1918 for his Law of Radiation.

Planck discovered that radiant energy is sent out in ' packets ' (quanta). Unlike the smallest unit of electricity, the charge of an electron, the unit of radiant energy, is different for every wavelength on which it is emitted. The quantum of energy = $h\nu$ where ν is the frequency of the radiation, and h a universal constant now known as PLANCK'S CONSTANT. Planck's theory has had enormous success in explaining facts of atomic physics, spectra, distribution of radiant energy with wavelength from the sun. See QUANTUM THEORY

plane, tall tree (often 70ft) found in Britain. The handsome Oriental plane is common in city streets. The ash-grey bark flakes off, forming yellowish patches ; the leaves are thin and shaped like a hand. This tree thrives in London.

planetarium, *plan-ē-tār'iům,* circular building with a dome representing the night sky. On the interior surface of this a complicated projector throws points of light to represent various planets, stars and constellations, all capable of being speeded up so that in a few minutes the movement of a night or a century or more may be watched by several hundred spectators. Planetaria are to be found in Germany and USA. Recently the Minister of Education announced that a planetarium for Britain is to be established at South Kensington, London.

planets, see ASTRONOMY

plankton, *plangk'ton* (Greek *planktos,* wandering), minute animal- or plant-life in water. Plankton include diatoms, algae, foraminifera and radiolaria, etc. They form the food of many fish.

Plankton may be (*a*) plant life, greenish in colour, or (*b*) animal forms. In the main (*a*), known as phytoplankton, is the food on which (*b*) feeds, the latter, known as zooplankton, being itself the food of many sea creatures, from the herring to the blue whale.

By adding suitable nutrient salts to the waters of small lochs in Scotland, scientists have recently increased the amount of plankton, and therefore increased the number of fish.

Plantagenets, *plan-taj'e-nets,* kings of England 1154–1399, namely : Henry II, Richard I, John, Henry III, Edward I, Edward II, Edward III, Richard II. Sometimes called Angevins because Henry II inherited the French lands of Geoffrey of Anjou, they are better known as Plantagenets from Geoffrey's custom of wearing a sprig of broom (Latin *planta genista*) in his helmet.

plantain, plant (order *Plantaginaceae*) varieties of which include (*a*) greater plantain, with egg-shaped leaves ; green flowers (June, July) in spikes, (*b*) ribwort plantain, the narrow leaves (like the juicy stems) being ribbed ; has minute white flowers (with yellow stamens) forming a cone.

plants, see BOTANY

plants and nitrogen, see NITROGEN

Plas Newydd, see LLANGOLLEN

Plassey, *plǎs'ē,* name of a battle fought 1757 between the British under Clive, and troops (including some French soldiers) of the Nawab of Bengal, Suraj-ud-Dowlah. Here Clive won a victory by which he dethroned the nawab, and replaced him with Mir Jaffir. The site of the battle (*c.*95m north of Calcutta) was washed away by the R. Bhâgirathi *c.*1800.

plastics, name of many compounds that are a paste during manufacture, but hard, tough, insulating material when moulded.

These have been adapted to so many uses in recent years that we may be said to live in the Plastic Age.

Plastics include two chief types, (*a*) *thermoplastic materials,* which may be remoulded (when heated) any number of times, e.g. cellulostic plastics, natural resin and wax compositions, bitumastic products, and the glass-like plastics, as vinyl, styrene, etc ; (*b*) *thermosetting plastics,* which, once heated and moulded become insoluble and heat-resisting, including the phenolic and amino-plastics, and coloured casein products.

The industry dates from 1865, when cellulose acetate was discovered, and derives from the discoveries of Professor Leo Hendrik Baekeland, a Belgian chemist who first produced the plastic known as ' Bakelite,' a mixture of formaldehyde and phenol (carbolic acid). Modern plastics are manufactured largely from cellulose, acetone, phenols (coal-tar by-products), formaldehyde (produced synthetically from methane), casein (an extract of milk) and glycerine. All are varieties of carbon compounds. Everyday plastic articles include ornaments, as ' Erinoid ' casein plastics ; aircraft accessories, often of cellulose acetate ; innumerable ' Bakelite ' products such as electric switches, telephones, ' Vacuum ' flasks ; and plastic planes, the latter giving immense possibilities in the production of cheap aircraft. Since 1932 great developments have been made in the production of plastic textiles, e.g. nylon thread made of material derived from coal, air and water. This is twice as strong as natural silk, and USA and Britain are building up huge industries in this connection. ICI (Imperial Chemical Industries Ltd), British Industrial Plastics Ltd, British Xylonite Ltd, Bakelite Ltd, British Celanese Ltd, Celluloid Corporation, USA, are only a few of many companies producing vast quantities of plastics. As recently as 1950 yet another new plastic fibre was becoming popular, namely Orlon, which has the ' feel ' of wool. See ORLON, and also PLATE 32

Surprising new possibilites are the result of the discovery of SILICONES, a family of synthetic resins, the basis of which is petroleum, brine and sand. Silicone vapour is used for waterproofing garments. Other silicones are heat-resisting to a remarkable degree.

Read *Plastics,* V. E. Yarsley and E. G. Couzens.

plastic surgery, branch of surgery dealing with the repair or restoration of damaged or lost parts of the body ; sometimes called *grafting* or *skin grafting,* and may be said to date from the experiments of the French surgeon Reverdin, *c.*1867. Among famous British specialists today is Sir Harold Gillies.

Skin to cover an open wound may be taken from, say, the abdomen with a Padgett dermatome, a razor-edged instrument that cuts a strip of skin 1/70in thick, and rolls it on a drum. Holes are punctured in this thin living film, which is then bound in position.

The science also includes the making of artificial limbs and parts of the body of plastic materials, e.g. building up a plastic ear, nose, part of a jaw, a thumb, etc., usually so skilfully moulded and coloured that it is almost indistinguishable from natural flesh.

Great use is now being made of the rare metal tantalum. Experience shows that it undergoes no change when buried in human flesh.

Plataea, *plä-tē'ä,* city of ancient Greece ; scene of the decisive battle in which the Greeks finally defeated the Persians 479BC.

Plate River, estuary (*c.*170m long and 138m wide at the mouth) between Argentina and Uruguay ; its finest harbour is Montevideo. Hereabouts (Dec 1939) was fought the battle of the R. Plate, resulting in the scuttling of the German pocket battleship *Admiral Graf Spee.*

platinum, hard, silvery, metallic element, Pt ; atomic weight 195·23 ; atomic number 78 ; specific gravity 21·4 ; melting-point 1,750°C. It is superior to gold in its resistance to corrosion. Found chiefly in USA, the Ural Mts, Brazil, S. Africa and Australia, it is much used as a catalyst in chemistry, also by jewellers, and in electrical instruments, its coefficient of expansion being almost that of glass.

Plato, *plä'tō* (*d* 347 BC), Greek philosopher, one of the greatest of all time. He was an aristocrat, and from his youth was the embodiment of Athenian civilisation, versed in poetry, music, drama, oratory and the art of thinking. A pupil of Socrates, whom he reverenced, he opened a school in the garden of Academeus, about a mile from Athens, hence the word *academy* (a place of learning). There, except for a year when he visited Syracuse, he spent the rest of his life, his pupils including Aristotle and Demosthenes. He was *c.*80 when he died.

Plato's works, apart from his *Epistles,* are in the form of 35 *Dialogues,* among which the most notable are *Theaetetus, Parmenides, Timaeus, Philebus, Critias, Phaedrus, Phaedo, Symposium, Gorgias, Protagoras,* and (most famous of all) the *Republic.* In the earlier dialogues he expounds views which were undoubtedly held by Socrates ; but in the later ones he uses Socrates as a mouthpiece for his own teachings. In all he proceeds by question and answer, always asking what the speaker means precisely by the word or phrase he uses, bit by bit clearing away muddled thinking and misconceptions. This method of reasoning is known as dialectic. It is especially suitable in philosophy, which does not teach new truths, but rather enables us to understand more fully things that we knew already.

One of his most famous ' pictures ' of mankind is that of men sitting in a cave, their backs towards a fire. They see, not reality, but only the shadows of reality cast on the wall before them.

Plato believed that we know truth because of inborn experience. Like most great philosophers, he believed in God, and for him God meant goodness. The world's debt to Plato is incalculable. He taught men to think clearly, to inquire into everything, and to change their minds as they came on new truths. ' Time,' he said, ' will teach you to abandon much of what you now consider to be right.' Note also, ' When men speak ill of thee, live so that nobody will believe them.'

platypus or **duckbill,** *plat'i-,* remarkable web-footed, egg-laying Australian animal *c.*18in long. It has a snout like the bill of a duck. The first platypus to breed in captivity (1944) was kept by David Fleay, the Australian naturalist.

THE DUCKBILLED PLATYPUS

Plauen, *plow'en,* town, Saxony (Germany) ; manufactures textiles ; pop.110,000.

Plautius, AULUS, see BRITAIN

play, see DRAMA

Playfair, LYON, 1ST BARON (1818–98), British scientist, born in India ; created a peer 1892 ; made important investigations into steam-coal and the gases of blast furnaces.

plebiscite, *pleb'i-sīt* (Latin *plebs,* people, *scitum,* decree), decision made, not by the representatives only of a country, but by the people themselves ; in effect, a mass vote on some urgent question of national importance, e.g. the plebiscite of the entire German people for the annexation of Austria 1938.

Pleiades, *plē'yä-dēz,* in old Greek tales, seven daughters of Atlas who, pursued by Orion, were changed into doves and placed among the stars, hence the constellation of the Pleiades, mentioned in Job 38.

pleurisy, *plur'isy,* inflammation of the *pleura,* i.e. the lining of the lungs. It is the result of bacterial infection, usually after exposure to a chill.

Plimsoll, SAMUEL (1824–98), *b* Bristol ; MP for Derby 1868 ; pioneer of the Merchant Shipping Act 1876 ; caused the Plimsoll line (the safety load-line) to be painted on all British merchant ships, thus obviating overloading.

Plinlimmon, mt., N. Wales, near the source of the R. Severn ; rises 2,462ft.

Pliny the Elder, *plin'i* (*d* AD79), Roman writer, *b* Como (Novum Comum) ; killed during an eruption of Vesuvius. His most famous book (in 37 parts) is a so-called natural history, a collection of notes on the universe as a whole, various places, animals, plants, and on medicine, minerals, painting and sculpture.

Pliny the Younger (*d* c.AD113), Roman writer, nephew of Pliny the Elder. He was *b* Como (Novum Comum). His *Letters* include those to the Emperor Trajan, some with references to the treatment of Christians. One letter gives an account of the eruption of Vesuvius AD79.

Pliofilm, trade name for a packing material first commercially produced in Britain 1949.

plough, *plow,* farming implement for cutting furrows in the soil, thus turning it over so as to expose it for weathering. Ploughs may be drawn by horses, oxen, or tractors. It is believed that the plough (possibly little more than a pointed stick) was the earliest, or one of the earliest, of all inventions.

Ploughing by radio has already been done in England, the plough being subject to remote control.

Plough, THE, see GREAT BEAR

Plovdiv, *plov'dif,* city and important trading centre, Bulgaria ; pop.113,000.

plover, *pluv'ĕr,* name of a large family of British birds, including : (*a*) GOLDEN PLOVER, c.11in long, with greyish-black plumage spotted with yellow above and black below ; more common in the

north than in the south ; (*b*) GREY PLOVER, similar to the golden, but without the yellow spots ; common near the coast in winter ; (*c*) GREEN or COMMON PLOVER, better known as LAPWING or (from its cry) PEEWIT ; dark green on back and crest, with black throat and white underparts ; about the size of a pigeon ; feeds on snails, worms and insects ; lays eggs on bare ground, their colour and patches matching the soil. See MIGRATION

plum, fruit tree (family *Rosaceae*). The common plum (*Prunus domestica*) found wild in Britain, is used as a stock on which some 200 other varieties are grafted. The most important plum is the Victoria.

plumbago, see GRAPHITE

Plutarch, *ploo'tärk* (*d* AD120), Greek writer, *b* Chaeronea (Boeotia) ; lived for a time in Rome, where he won the favour of the emperors Trajan and Hadrian. He wrote about 60 essays with the title *Opera Moralia,* in which he deals with health, astronomy and marriage in a delightful and learned manner ; but he is most famous for his series of 46 biographies known as *Plutarch's Lives.* These contrast or compare famous Greeks and Romans from Theseus and Romulus to Alexander the Great and Julius Caesar. They are of great value historically, and are written in a vivid style.

Pluto, ancient Roman name for the god of the underworld ; married Persephone.

Pluto, name given to an operation of World War II in which pipelines were laid (1944) from England to France to supply oil to the allied armies approaching Germany. After D-Day over 170,000,000 gallons of oil were supplied by Pluto.

Pluto, see ASTRONOMY

plutonium, radioactive element, Pu ; atomic weight 239·0(?) ; atomic number 94 ; used in the production of atomic energy. Its discovery was announced 1945. See HARWELL ; RADIUM ; SELLAFIELD

Plymouth, *plim'ŭth,* city and port, Devon, at the mouth of the R. Plym ; has a magnificent harbour ; includes DEVONPORT with its natural harbour and naval station on the Tamar estuary ; has been famous for shipping for many centuries. It was on Plymouth Hoe that Drake played bowls (1588) before helping to beat the Armada ; and from Plymouth (1620) sailed the *Mayflower.* The city has much trade, great fisheries and important chemical works. It was severely damaged by German raids in World War II ; pop.181,000.

plywood, board made of three (or more) layers of thin wood, the grain of each sheet at right angles to the next, all glued or cemented under pressure. Special lathes are used for peeling logs, thus securing large unjointed areas (sometimes 84in square). Though light, plywood has remarkable strength.

THE GOLDEN PLOVER

pneumatic wave-controller, *nū-mat'ik*, the mechanical device, partly rubber, devised in World War II to act as a floating breakwater. A mammoth pontoon, each unit was 200ft long, 25ft high, with a weight of over 700 tons, including the concrete keel.

pneumonia, *nū-mō'nia*, inflammation of the lungs.

Po, longest river of Italy; flows *c*.415m through Piedmont, Lombardy, etc. to the Adriatic, entering by a delta.

Pocahontas, *pō-kä-hon'täs* (*d* 1617), daughter of the American Indian chief Powhattan; fell in love with Captain John Smith, pioneer in Virginia, and is said to have saved his life. Thinking Smith was dead, she married John Rolfe, and came to England 1616.

pochard, diving duck; visits Britain in winter (though a few pairs nest in marshes). It has reddish-brown head and back, and grey sides.

pocket-boroughs, see REFORM ACTS

Pocock, GUY (1880–   ), author and editor, *b* Hampstead; with the BBC 1934–40; author of novels, essays and anthologies, notably (with Sir Arthur Quiller-Couch) the *King's Treasuries of Literature*; also many English books for schools.

Poe, EDGAR ALLAN, *pō* (1809–49), American author and poet, *b* Boston, Massachusetts; drank heavily, took opium, and died in poverty. He had a remarkable mastery of words, as shown not only in his poetry (e.g. *The Bells*) but also in his brilliant short stories, among which is *The Murders of the Rue Morgue*, interesting as one of the first detective stories ever written. His tales of horror are strangely fascinating.

poet laureate, official national poet. The first English poet laureate was Ben Jonson; others were Lord Tennyson (from 1850), Alfred Austin (1896), Robert Bridges (1913), and John Masefield (1930). See BAY TREE

poetry, language used in such a way as to express *everything* that is involved in an experience—*feeling* (i.e. physical sensations), *emotion* and *thought*. One difference between poetry and prose is that in poetry the expression of feeling and emotion is fundamental. Another is that in prose no use is made of *metre*. Much prose indeed is rhythmical, but in prose the rhythm undergoes continuous development. In poetry certain basic rhythms (or variations of them) are repeated over and over in accordance with a definite scheme or pattern, this pattern of rhythms being what is called the metre. The metrical pattern may be 'closed' or 'open.' Read aloud the following lines, and you will see what is here meant by a 'closed-pattern metre':

> Yet this inconstancy is such
>   as you too shall adore :
> I could not love thee, dear, so much
>   loved I not honour more.

Here line 3 has recognisably the same rhythm as line 1; line 4 the same as line 2. The 'closing' of the pattern is effected by *rhyme*: (line 4) *more* rhymes with (line 2) *adore*; (line 3) *much* with (line 1) *such*. Together the four lines form one self-contained unit of the metre, called a *stanza*; and each new stanza is marked off from the one before it by a change of rhyme.

In some metres the pattern is 'open.' An example is the *blank verse* used by Milton in *Paradise Lost*:

> Of *man's first* disobed*ience* ‖ *and* the *fruit*
> of *that* forbidden *tree* ‖ whose *mor*tal
>   *taste*
> brought *death in*to the *world* ‖ and *all*
> our *woe* . . .

Here the unit is a single line of ten syllables. Five of these ten are stressed; and there is a break of rhythm (the 'caesura') in every line, somewhere between stress no. 2 and stress no. 4 (here marked ‖). There is no rhyme, and no 'closing of the pattern.' Notice that Milton varies the basic rhythm freely: if he did not, the metre would soon become monotonous and dull. Blank verse allows the greatest freedom; but it is extremely difficult to write blank verse really well.

Poetry is much more imaginative than ordinary prose. It has to be so in order to express to the full not only thought but also the feeling and emotion from which it springs. Feeling is expressed in poetry by making, so to speak, a 'picture' of the experience, as in these lines from a poem about the campaign in Italy in World War II:

> The Irno Bridge : the spring wind from
>   the town
> shifts rubble-dust across ; ghost-walking
>   yet,
> sharp dust of murdered houses ten
>   months down.
>   (George Campbell Hay)

Here phrases like 'the spring wind' and 'ghost-walking yet' express, no doubt, a shuddering sensation *felt* by the poet as he looked at the Irno Bridge. 'Sharp dust' expresses its grittiness to *touch*, 'murdered houses' the poet's *emotion*. In other words, the 'picture' contains not only things seen, but things heard and felt and thought. By subsequently imagining and *putting into words* (and metre) the various elements of an experience the poet expresses its many aspects, i.e. he becomes more fully aware of all that was involved in it; and anybody who reads the poem comes likewise to be more fully aware of all that has been involved in similar experiences of his own. In this way poets and readers of poetry come to enjoy their experiences more fully.

Poetry has many forms, the most

important being ballad, epic, lyric and dramatic. A ballad is in form a song, often fairly lengthy, which tells a story in some very simple closed-pattern metre, like *Sir Patrick Spens, Chevy Chase*, etc. An *epic* is always a very long poem in an open-pattern metre. The greatest of all epics are the earliest, Homer's *Iliad* and *Odyssey*, Greek epics which tell the legends of the Siege of Troy and of the Homecoming of Odysseus afterwards. Virgil's *Aeneid* is more sophisticated. In it he celebrates the greatness of the newly-founded Roman Empire as foreshadowed in the wanderings of Aeneas (legendary Trojan founder of Rome). Another epic is Dante's *Divine Comedy*. It has for its subject a journey through Hell, Purgatory and Paradise. Yet another is Milton's *Paradise Lost*, its subject being the Fall of Man as told in Christian and Hebrew legend.

Lyric poetry is best defined as the poetry of personal or private feeling and emotion. It is a spontaneous outburst, often intensely moving. The metres of lyric poetry are infinitely varied ; they are often fairly simple, but sometimes extremely complex ; generally they are ' closed-pattern ' metres, and in English lyric poetry rhyme is normally employed. Among the most notable lyric poets are Keats, Shelley, Burns and Donne. More formal than the simplest lyric poetry is the *sonnet*, a poem of 14 lines, with rhymes. More formal and more complex is an *ode*, distinguished by its elaborate stanza. A familiar example is Keats' *Ode to a Nightingale*.

Dramatic poetry is poetry spoken by actors in a play. The supreme examples of poetic drama are possibly the *Agamemnon* of Aeschylus, and Shakespeare's *King Lear*.

Read Palgrave's *Golden Treasury* and the *Oxford Book of English Verse*. For books about poetry, read Wordsworth's Preface to the Introduction of *Lyrical Ballads*, and A. E. Housman's *The Name and Nature of Poetry*.

Poets' Corner, see LONDON

pogrom, deliberate massacre on a large scale, especially of Jews in Russia, e.g. the pogroms of 1881, 1903, 1905 ; later applied to Nazi persecutions of the Jews.

Poincaré, RAYMOND, *pwan-kä-rä* (1860–1934), French statesman ; became Prime Minister 1912, President 1913. During the difficult and dangerous days of World War I he guided the fortunes of France with a masterly hand. Retiring from the presidency 1920, he was Prime Minister again 1922–24, being largely responsible for the occupation of the Ruhr by French and coloured troops. He was Prime Minister yet again 1926–29.

Pointers, THE, see GREAT BEAR

points, see RAILWAYS

poison, substance which, when it enters the body, and finds its way into the bloodstream, seriously affects health or causes death. Common poisons include laudanum, arsenic, belladonna, prussic acid and strychnine. These, and others, should be distinctly labelled and (if in liquid form) should be sold in blue or green bottles with ribbed sides, so that one may tell at sight or (in the dark) *by touch* that the contents are dangerous. They may only be bought from a pharmaceutical chemist after the name and address of the purchaser has been recorded and his signature obtained.

Poison gases used in warfare include mustard (dichlorodiethyl sulphide), lewisite (chlorovinyl dichlorarsine), arisen and chlorine.

See also POISONOUS PLANTS

poisonous plants common in Britain include : (*a*) BELLADONNA or DEADLY NIGHTSHADE, with fleshy rootstock ; may be 3–4ft high ; has drooping, bell-shaped purple flowers and shining black berries ; (*b*) CUCKOO-PINT or LORDS-AND-LADIES or WAKE ROBIN, has

POISONOUS PLANTS
(*left to right*) Foxglove, Hemlock and Cuckoo-Pint (*top left*) the fruits of the Cuckoo-Pint and (*bottom*) a spike of flowers

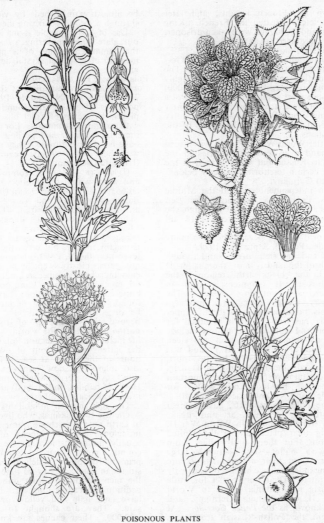

POISONOUS PLANTS

(*top left*) *Monkshood*   (*top right*) *Henbane*
(*bottom left*) *Ivy*   (*bottom right*) *Deadly Nightshade*

arrow-shaped leaves often blotched with purple, a flowering stem with a large (often spotted) cowl, inside which are purple flowers, fertilised by trapped insects ; later has bright red berries ; (*c*) FOXGLOVE ; (*d*) HEMLOCK ; (*e*) HENBANE, with funnel-shaped yellow flowers veined with purple ; the fruit is a capsule with a lid ; (*f*) HERB PARIS, has oval leaves and yellow flowers ; the fruit is a black berry ; (*g*) MONKSHOOD, with toothed leaves and dark blue hood-shaped flowers.

Most fungi are poisonous, and so also is ivy.

Poitiers, *pwä-tyä'*, town, France, *c.*60m from Tours ; noted for its cathedral and university ; scene of an English victory over the French 1356, at which the Black Prince won distinction ; pop. 42,000.

Poitiers, BATTLE OF, fought 1356 between the English, led by Edward the Black Prince, and the French, led by King John II. In this battle of the Hundred Years' War the English archers shot

18

down the French knights, and later completely defeated the French. King John and 2,000 men were taken prisoner. See HUNDRED YEARS' WAR

Poitou, see FRANCE

Poland, republic between USSR and Germany ; area 1939 c.150,000sq.m. The population today can only be roughly estimated (possibly it is 30,000,000) because very great numbers of Poles died or were driven out of the country during World War II, when the country suffered shockingly at the hands of the Germans.

After World War II Poland was forced to hand over certain territories in the east to Russia, but was awarded in the west certain territories formerly belonging to Germany.

An independent state in the Middle Ages, Poland was partitioned between Russia and Germany 1795, though she enjoyed independence from 1918 till again divided 1939.

World War II began when Germany invaded Poland, September 1939.

Poland has rich forests, and though much of the land is poor, there is fertile soil in the ' black-earth ' region of the south-east. It is intensely cold in winter, and hot in summer. The country, mainly agricultural, produces cereals, potatoes and sugar-beet. Upper Silesia has iron ; Galicia is noted for its oil and salt. Manufactures include cotton, woollen goods, iron and steel, and before World War II Poland was making increasing use of her new port, Gdynia, on the Baltic, and of Danzig. The capital is Warsaw ; other important towns are Breslau, Lodz (noted for textiles) and Krakow (the old capital).

The Poles, mostly RC, have a great tradition in literature, art and music. They fought valiantly in World War II, taking their place among the United Nations, but their land suffers from being a buffer state between large powers, and their ambition to secure lasting independence has been repeatedly frustrated. Their only outlet for trade (Danzig and Gdynia) prior to World War II cut through Germany, and was known as the *Polish Corridor*. At present the Polish-Russian frontier is roughly the boundary proposed 1919 by Lord Curzon, known as the *Curzon Line*.

polarisation, in electricity, occurs in various primary cells, and is the formation at the positive pole of hydrogen, which causes a fall in the EMF.

Polarisation of light occurs when light passes through certain crystals, a part of its radiation being absorbed. This is not readily observable, but if such light is passed through a second polariser, suitably arranged, the light may be extinguished altogether. Light reflected from a smooth surface (the sea, a smooth road and a shop window) is partially polarised, and this reflected light may

be almost extinguished by viewing it through a second polarising medium.

Use of this principle is made to cut out glare when motoring. *Polaroid* is the commercial name of a polarising medium of a special crystal deposit on glass.

Polaroid, see POLARISATION

Polar Regions, coldest areas of the earth. They circle the N. and S. Poles, the positions of which are found by explorers by means of exact observations with accurate instruments. For centuries these inhospitable and perilous regions have lured adventurers. They are dealt with here as (I) Arctic regions, and (II) Antarctic regions :

(I) ARCTIC REGIONS, comprise land and water within the Arctic Circle, i.e. lat.66½°N. The Arctic Ocean (including Barents Sea, White and Kara Seas) has an area of c.6,000,000sq.m. The chief islands are Greenland, Banks Land, Ellesmere Land, Novaya Zemlya, Wrangell I. and Spitsbergen. The cold is usually intense, but often the climate (even near the N. Pole) is comparatively mild, areas mostly swept by bitter winds enjoying a brief summer so kindly that as far north as Ellesmere Land primroses, buttercups and dandelions have been found. Admiral Peary declared that he once found a bee on the ice ½m beyond the north tip of the most northerly land in the world. Animal life includes white foxes and Polar bears ; the latter spend 95 out of every 100 hours of their lives at sea. There are also migratory snow buntings, Arctic skuas, Arctic terns, whales and seals. Herds of reindeer (or caribou) are found in N. America and Siberia.

The only human inhabitants of the Arctic are the Eskimos, who live in huts of earth on a whalebone framework, or in igloos made of blocks of snow, usually hotter inside than we in this country could bear. Eskimos are primitive people who delight in songs, stories and dancing. From time to time the men set out on long hunting expeditions or trading journeys. Eskimos have lank hair and yellow or brown skin. They are thought to number c.32,000. Their canoes are known as kayaks ; their dogs (called huskies) never bark but only howl.

Arctic exploration may be said to date from the search for the NW. Passage, i.e. a sailing route round the north of N. America. John Cabot, who began the search for this route to China, was followed by John Davis, who explored the coasts of Greenland and Labrador, and by Henry Hudson, whose name is preserved in Hudson Bay. Baffin reached 77° 45′ N, 1616, the highest latitude attained for 236 years, and he also discovered Baffin Bay and Ellesmere Land. Sir William Parry (1820) sailed farther west along the coast of N. America than anyone had ever done before. James

Clark Ross found the N. Magnetic Pole in Boothia Peninsula 1831, its true position being located 1945.

In command of the *Erebus* and *Terror*, Sir John Franklin sailed far along the NW. Passage 1845, but failed to return, and it was M'Clintock, a Scotsman, who found the only document with news of the Franklin expedition, a scrap of paper proving that Franklin had perished 1847. Even then the full story of the *Erebus* and *Terror* could not be told, but bit by bit explorers came upon relics which showed that Franklin had actually reached a point from which it was possible to reach the Pacific, but it was not till 1905 that Roald Amundsen (in the *Gjoa*) conquered the Passage.

Meanwhile, search had been made for the NE. Passage to China by way of Norway and Siberia, the 16th c. English pioneers being Sir Hugh Willoughby and Richard Chancellor. There was also the Dutchman, William Barents, who made important discoveries about 1596, though they cost him his life. The Swedish explorer Nils Nordenskiold sailed the *Vega* out of the Atlantic into the Pacific via the NE. Passage 1879.

The N. Pole men (those who attempted to sail or sledge farthest north) are the adventurers who thrill us most, e.g. Elisha Kane and Charles F. Hall, and Carl Weyprecht and Julius Payer who together were caught in the ice and carried across the Arctic Ocean. A great name in Arctic exploration is that of Sir George Nares, *b* 1831. He reached a point (1875) within 400m of the Pole.

The story of the *Jeannette* is a tragedy, but it was the beginning of a remarkable achievement. It was in this ill-fated ship that George Washington de Long, an American, sailed north 1879, the leader and eleven of his companions being starved to death after the *Jeannette* went down off the bleak coast of Siberia. The consequences were surprising, for some years later bits of the wreck were picked up off the coast of Greenland, giving Dr Nansen (a Norwegian) the idea of steering the *Fram* into the Arctic ice in the hope that she would be carried by the drift of the Arctic currents across, or near, the N. Pole. Sailing 1893, he moored his ship to an ice-floe, drifted for thirty-five months, and reached a higher latitude than had then been attained. Nansen and his friend Frederick Johansen undertook a sledging expedition of fifteen months which brought them very near the Pole. Finally, Nansen met Frederick Jackson, who had been sent to the Polar Region by the English newspaper proprietor, Lord Northcliffe, a meeting of two explorers on the white roof of the world that was as dramatic in its way as that of Livingstone and Stanley in the heart of Africa.

The first explorer to reach the N. Pole was Admiral Robert Edwin Peary, an American, who fought his way north eight times, and more than once took his wife with him. Their daughter, Marie (*b* 1893) was the first white child born beyond the Arctic Circle. Peary faced innumerable dangers and suffered many privations, but at 52 he sailed on till he reached 80°N, made five marches of 25m each, taking on his last journey 3 Eskimos, a Negro and 40 dogs, thus, on 6 April 1909, a white man and a black man stood together at the N. Pole.

Since then the N. Pole has been conquered by air. Though Solomon Andrée, a Swede, failed 1897 to reach the Pole by balloon, the American Richard Byrd flew over the N. Pole, as did Roald Amundsen in the airship *Norge*, both in 1926. Aircraft between America and parts of Europe now cross the Arctic as a matter of course.

During 1937–38 a number of Russian scientists landed by plane within a mile or so of the N. Pole, and in 7 months drifted on an ice-floe 900m to the Greenland Sea. They made valuable investigations into weather conditions and submarine life.

(II) ANTARCTIC REGIONS, differ from the Arctic in that the Antarctic is mainly a continent buried in ice and snow, the Arctic largely a sea, wide areas of which are frozen. Antarctica, the sixth biggest land-mass in the world, has 14,000m of coastline, an area of *c*.5,000,000sq.m, including Graham Land Peninsula (700m south of S. America), Wilkes Land, S. Victoria Land and Ross I. The coasts of the Weddell Sea and Ross Sea (fringed by the Great Ice Barrier) are fairly well known ; the interior is chiefly a huge plateau *c*.9,000ft above sea-level, with ice often over 1,000ft thick. Huge glaciers move slowly towards the coast, e.g. the Beardmore Glacier ; and there are mt. ranges 13,000–15,000ft high. On Ross I. is Mt Erebus, an active volcano. Buried under the snow are rich seams of coal discovered 1908, proving that at one period the S. Pole was a warm region rich in forests, though now the coldest and strongest winds on earth blow over this white wilderness.

Exploration of the Antarctic is perhaps even more dangerous and difficult than that of the Arctic. We may claim Captain Cook as a pioneer, since he was the first navigator to cross the Antarctic Circle (lat.66½°S) 1773. William Smith discovered the S. Shetland Is. 1819 ; and four years later James Weddell (a Scotsman) found the bay known by his name. Charles Wilkes, an American, put Wilkes Land on the map 1840, and James Clark Ross, commanding a British expedition, discovered the Great Ice Barrier and Ross Sea. The famous *Challenger* crossed the Antarctic Circle 1874, the first steamer to do so.

Sailing in the *Discovery*, Sir Robert Falcon Scott reached Ross I., 1902, and later discovered King Edward VII Land.

Within a few years he was to die near the S. Pole. The story begins with Roald Amundsen, who left Norway in the *Fram* 1910, and began his remarkable dash to the S. Pole 20 Oct 1911, arriving 16 Dec. It was in 1910 that Scott left London in the *Terra Nova*, and after wintering in Ross I., set out with sledges for the Pole in Oct 1911. In spite of immense difficulties, he and four companions (Wilson, Bowers, Oates and Evans) fought their way steadily over the ice till they reached the Pole 17 Jan 1912, to find that Amundsen had planted the Norwegian flag there 32 days before.

It was a bitter disappointment to the tired adventurers, and the journey back was heartbreaking. Evans died. Then, on his birthday (17 March) Captain Oates walked out of the tent and laid down his life in the hope that his companions, no longer burdened by the presence of a sick man, might reach the depot where supplies awaited them. But Scott, Wilson and Bowers were caught in a blizzard, and perished ten days later. In Captain Scott's *Diary* is a vivid account of those last hours, and in one of his letters, written only a few hours before he died, are the brave words:

Had we lived, I should have had a tale to tell of the hardihood, endurance and courage of my companions which would have stirred the heart of every Englishman. These rough notes and our dead bodies must tell the tale.

Meanwhile (1908) Sir Ernest Shackleton had left NZ, sailing in the *Nimrod*. He ascended Mt Erebus, climbed the Beardmore Glacier, and reached farther south than anyone of his day. Sir Douglas Mawson sailed south in the *Aurora* 1911, returning 1914, the year in which Sir Ernest Shackleton left England in the *Endurance* in an attempt to cross the Antarctic from Weddell Sea to Ross Sea. His ship was crushed in the ice, and the explorers succeeded in reaching home 1917 only because of the skill and audacity of their leaders. Shackleton led yet another expedition 1921. He sailed in the *Quest*, but died early in the voyage, and was buried on the island of S. Georgia. His book, *The Heart of the Antarctic*, and Sir Douglas Mawson's *The Home of the Blizzard*, make thrilling reading.

Sir George Wilkins flew (1929) as far in one hour as Scott and his sledging party had travelled in a month a few years before ; both Wilkins and Richard Byrd flew over the S. Pole. For all that, vast areas of the Arctic and Antarctic remain to be explored patiently mile by mile, and no doubt many secrets await discovery in these regions of perpetual snow.

As a result of a flight (1945) of the RAF aircraft *Aries*, the position of the N. Magnetic Pole has been established in the neighbourhood of Bathurst I., i.e. 300m west of its former position.

Interest in the Antarctic was suddenly intensified 1947 when about nine nations sent out, or prepared to send out, expeditions ; and when the Argentine laid claim to a vast region. Many countries are, at the moment, anxious to control wide areas, partly to secure whaling rights, partly to establish meteorological stations. The possibility of coal-mining near the S. Pole is as yet remote, but may be realised one day, and there are rumours of rich supplies of uranium, the element necessary for producing atomic energy. Scientists suggest that the winds of Antarctica may one day be harnessed, thus supplying radiant energy for light and power.

Discovery II sailed 1950 on an 18 months' voyage in the S. Indian Ocean, one purpose being to examine conditions in the Antarctic convergence (where cold and warm waters meet), which determines weather in the Southern hemisphere.

polder, in the Netherlands, low-lying region that has been reclaimed from the sea.

polecat, ferocious British animal of the weasel tribe ; *c.*17in long, with a short, bushy tail. The fur, generally blackish-brown, is yellowish below ; the tips of the ears and the lips are white. The polecat lives in deserted rabbit holes, and preys on animals, birds and frogs.

Poles, see POLAR REGIONS

police, organisation of men (and since 1920 some women) responsible for maintaining public order, liberty and the security of life and property. The number of policemen (or constables) and policewomen in Britain is approximately 74,000, including *c.*17,000 members of the London Metropolitan Police Force, founded 1829 by Sir Robert Peel, and now with HQ at New Scotland Yard. The Metropolitan Police are directly responsible to the Home Office, whereas police in the provinces are supervised by county or borough councils. Most of the members of the Force are constables, who wear the familiar dark blue uniform, but others are detectives, who wear plain clothes.

police court, court presided over by a magistrate. It is the court to which offenders are first brought, and it deals with minor offences. More serious cases are sent up to a higher court.

Polish Corridor, see POLAND

Politburo, small sub-committee of the central committee of the USSR Communist Party ; controls administrative power.

political economy, see ECONOMICS

political party, see PARTY

politics (Gk *polis*, city or city-state ; hence *politēs*, member of the *polis*, i.e. a citizen ; hence *ta politika*, politics) comprises all affairs transacted by or on behalf of a *body-politic*, i.e. in any country, the whole body of citizens acting together for a common purpose. ' Politics ' is also the name of that branch of studies which inquires into the nature and functions of bodies-politic.

It is sometimes thought that politics includes all activities connected with the business of governing a country, but this is not the case. In England, many of the powers now belonging to Parliament were formerly exercised by the king as his prerogatives, but since the reign of James II the Royal Prerogatives have become fewer. Apart from purely ceremonial functions almost the only trace of them now surviving is the King's Prerogative of Mercy, i.e. his right to pardon condemned persons without first consulting his Ministers. Nowadays he rarely has occasion or opportunity to intervene in politics. This is what we mean when we say that the King is ' above politics.'

Government in Britain is carried on by the King's Ministers acting in the King's name ; but Ministers are not free to do just as they please, being answerable to the House of Commons, which is elected by the electorate (i.e. the whole body of voters) every five years, or more frequently if necessary. In order to be re-elected, Ministers have to satisfy Parliament, and also a majority of the ordinary citizens, that they are governing the country well, and that the policy put forward by their party is the better one. If they cannot convince a majority of the voters that these things are so, then the opposing party will be returned to power at the next elections.

Once elected, a party is said to have obtained a *mandate*, i.e. popular backing, for the programme proposed by it at the time of the General Elections. Towards the end of its term in office, doubts may arise as to whether the party in power still has popular backing for some of the measures which it recommends.

The House of Lords, however, has certain limited powers of interference by which it can delay enactment of the measures in question until the next elections, thus enabling the electorate to think again. This being so, the party in power will itself think twice before using its majority in the House of Commons to carry measures which may prove to be beyond the scope of its existing mandate.

Thus we see that in Britain the citizens or members of the body-politic have altogether a very large say in the business of carrying on the King's government. Next it is necessary to find out what classes of the population have at any given time possessed the right to vote, for strictly speaking only those who possess that right are members of the body-politic.

In Britain before 1832 (first Reform Act) not very many people except certain classes of property-owners enjoyed the *franchise* (right to vote), and it was then comparatively easy for large land-owners to coerce or bribe a proportion of the voters. The Royal Prerogative was scarcely more extensive than it is now, and power was concentrated in the hands of a few important families. This state of affairs is known as *oligarchy* (Gk *oligarchia*, rule by the few). Since 1918 everybody over 21 (including women) has been allowed to vote. Government is therefore ultimately controlled by the electorate, and the electorate comprises the whole of the adult population, hence the government of Britain is now very largely democratic (Gk *dēmokratia*, government by the people).

Soviet Russia is another country which claims to possess democratic government. In Russia all over 18 years of age may vote, but only those appointed by the Communist Party are allowed to offer themselves as candidates in the elections. This is known as the *one-party system*. Under it the citizens have no choice between alternative policies. Moreover, the Soviets (assemblies) elected in this manner have very little say in matters of government, the country being governed largely by the self-appointed inner councils of the Communist Party, itself a small minority among the Russian people. Thus the claim that democracy prevails in Russia is largely unfounded.

Like Britain, the USA has two parties (Democrats and Republicans). In a few states Negroes are debarred—illegally—from voting, but generally speaking the franchise is unlimited. Laws are made by Congress, an elected legislative assembly closely resembling Parliament. Supreme executive authority (power to get things done) is vested in the *President*, who is elected by the people to hold office for a four-year term. As Chief Executive, the President is in a position similar to that of the British Prime Minister, but with one very important difference : as leader of the majority party in the House of Commons, the Prime Minister can almost always carry his measures in the face of opposition (if not, he resigns and another takes his place), but even urgent policies recommended by the President of the USA in time of crisis may be defeated by a hostile majority in either House of Congress—this is particularly likely to happen in the second half of the pre-sidential term of office. Thus the government is often in a far weaker position in the United States than it ever is in Britain. Nevertheless, the people of the USA have effective control over the activities involved in governing the country, and the USA is therefore a genuinely democratic country.

It is clear that the successful working of such a system depends on the existence of an agreed body of rules, laying down how things are to be done in carrying on government, and universally obeyed by those concerned. This body of rules is known as the *Constitution*. In the USA the Constitution is embodied in a single written document. It is very difficult to carry amendments to the American Constitution, and as social conditions change it is sometimes equally difficult to secure general agreement as to how the existing rules are to be interpreted in situations unforeseen by those who formed the Constitution.

Broadly speaking, it is by judicial re-interpretation rather than by amendment of the Constitution that the American body-politic provides opportunities for constitutional development. This important activity is regulated by the Supreme Court. Judges of the Supreme Court are appointed by the President, but once appointed they are no longer subject to any form of political control. The consequences are summed up in the words of Justice Hughes : *the Constitution is what the judges say it is.* This being so, there have been many occasions on which the Supreme Court, when called upon to say whether certain enactments of Congress are in accordance with the Constitution, have acted as protectors of power and privileges of vested interests, especially American ' Big Business.' American democracy was gravely strained in 1932–33 by Supreme Court opposition to President Roosevelt's New Deal at the time of the Great Industrial depression. Confident of popular support, Roosevelt prepared to coerce the Supreme Court, and it is doubtful what would have happened if he had persisted. As it was, vacancies occurred in the Supreme Court, and Roosevelt secured a favourable majority by filling the empty places with his own nominees.

Unlike the Constitution of the United States, the British Constitution is not embodied in any single written document. When a constitutional difficulty arises in Britain, it has to be thrashed out in Parliament, both sides appealing to the works of learned writers, to the pronouncements of statesmen, and to the practical needs of the country. The last great constitutional crisis in Britain was in 1910–11 over the question of reforming the House of Lords, and it was only after a General Election that agreement was ultimately reached.

In this review of three contemporary political systems only a few of the most important points have been dealt with, but the foregoing discussion is enough to give some idea of the nature of the questions considered in the study of politics. See COMMUNISM ; DEMOCRACY ; FASCISM ; NAZISM ; PARTY ; SOCIALISM

polka, round dance in 2–4 time (the rest being on the second beat) ; said to have been invented *c.*1830 by a Bohemian servant girl.

pollination, see BOTANY
polling day, see ELECTION
poll tax, *pōl*, tax on every poll (i.e. head). It was introduced into England 1377, and again 1380, when it led to the Peasants' Revolt. Poll taxes were levied in England 1513 and 1641 and there were three between 1688–98.
Pollux, see CASTOR AND POLLUX
polo, one of the oldest outdoor games, probably originating in Persia ; first played in England 1869, and extremely popular with British officers in India. A ball game similar to hockey, it is played with a mallet by players mounted on ponies. It is very expensive, and has never been a poor man's sport.
Polo, MARCO, *pō'lō (d c.*1324), Venetian traveller and explorer, son of Nicolo Polo, himself a traveller. Marco accompanied his father and uncle on a journey to China via Acre, Persia, the Pamir plateau (never again crossed by a European for about 500 years), and the Gobi desert, to the residence of Kublai Khan. They arrived 1275, Marco being then about 19. For 17 years he lived in and travelled about China in the emperor's service, grew immensely rich, and visited Tibet, Burma and S. India. When he returned to Venice his wealth impressed everyone but his stories were discredited. While in prison (having been captured in a naval fight against Genoa) he dictated his famous book of travels.
polonium, *pō-lō'ni-ŭm*, radioactive element, Po, known as Radium-F ; atomic weight 210 ; atomic number 84. Polonium breaks down to lead, its activity decaying to half the original value in 136 days.
Poltava, town, Ukraine, USSR ; once famous for its wool fairs ; pop.105,000.
polyanthus, name for cultivated varieties of primula of many colours, originally thought to have been derived from crossing the cowslip and primrose. The ' Giant ' polyanthus is particularly hardy and prolific.
polygon, in geometry, a plane figure bounded by more than 4 straight sides, e.g. pentagon (5 sides), hexagon (6) heptagon (7) octagon (8), nonagon (9), decagon (10). If regular, polygons are equiangular and hence equilateral. The area of a regular ploygon of *n* sides, each of length *a*, may be found from the formula : area $= \frac{n}{4} \cot \frac{180°}{n} \cdot a^2$.
polymerisation, in chemistry, the union of two or more molecules of the same compound to form single molecules, the second compound having the same atomic composition, but a molecular weight two or more times higher.
Polynesia, *pol-i-nē'zia*, name for the coral or volcanic islands of the Pacific, i.e. islands and groups of islands within 30°N and 30°S of the Equator, and between longs. 135°E and 135°S.
polyp, *pol'ip*, generally regarded as a

simple animal in the form of a hollow tube, e.g. the hydra.

polytheism, see RELIGION

pomegranate, *pom'gran-it,* tree common in W. Asia ; has lance-shaped leaves, clusters of red flowers, and yellow fruit with many seeds.

Pomerania, *pom-ĕr-ā'nia,* district of the former German state of Prussia.

Pomona, *pō-mō'nä,* largest island of the Orkneys ; here are Kirkwall, Stromness and Scapa Flow.

Pompeii, see VESUVIUS

Pompey the Great, *pom'pi* (106–48BC), English name for Gnaeus Pompeius, Roman soldier and statesman. Popular with his soldiers, he overthrew the democrats in Africa, cleared the Mediterranean of pirates and brought the east into subjection. With Crassus and Julius Caesar he formed a ' Triumvirate ' which for a time governed the Roman world, thus anticipating the Roman Empire as instituted by Augustus 31BC. He fell out with his associates, and was defeated by Caesar at Pharsalus 48BC. He fled to Egypt, where he was assassinated. See CAESAR, JULIUS

Pondicherry, French possession on the east coast of India ; cap. Pondicherry.

pons asinorum, *ponz as-i-nō'rŭm,* Latin for ' asses' bridge,' nickname of the 5th proposition in the first book of Euclid, i.e. *that the angles at the base of an isosceles triangle are equal.* The proposition is so called because some students fail to get beyond it.

Pontefract, town, W. Yorkshire ; grows liquorice ; has the ruins of a castle where Richard II died or was murdered. Shakespeare calls it Pomfret ; pop. 20,000.

Pontianak, cap. of the self-governing territory (within the Dutch Empire) of W. Borneo. It is on the west coast ; pop.45,000.

Pontine Marshes, *pon'tin,* formerly an unhealthy region south of Rome ; now drained, and known as Littoria.

Pontypridd, *ponti-prēth',* town, Glamorganshire ; noted for iron and coal ; pop. 40,000.

pony, see HORSE

Poole, town on the Dorset coast. It is a noted yachting centre, also a flying-boat terminus ; pop.70,000.

Pools, THE, see GAMBLING

Poona, town *c.*120m south-east of Bombay, India ; manufactures cotton, silk and paper. An important military station, it is the seat of the government of the Bombay Presidency during the wet season ; pop.258,000.

Poor Clares, see CLARE

Poor Law, system of aiding the poor begun in England 1601 when overseers of the poor were appointed in every parish in England. Boards of Guardians, established 1834, were responsible for workhouses and for the relief of the poor. These were abolished 1930 when their work was taken over by county and other councils through Public Assistance committees, all under the direction of the Ministry of Health.

Poozoodoung, town on the R. Irrawaddy, Burma. It is near Rangoon, and has what is claimed to be the largest rice mill in the world.

pope (Gk *papas,* father), Bishop of Rome, head of the Roman Church, claims to be Christ's Vicar on earth ; is elected on the death of the reigning pontiff by the college of cardinals ; lives in the Vatican, Rome (see VATICAN) ; has temporal power over the Vatican State ; was declared 1870 to be infallible, i.e. his decisions in matters of faith and morals cannot be questioned by Roman Catholics.

In the Middle Ages popes wielded immense power, Innocent III (1198–1216) being almost an emperor ; but this supremacy was questioned by Mussolini and Hitler *c.*1933, and much friction between the RC Church and the State followed.

The only Englishman ever to be pope was Nicolas Breakspear, who became Adrian IV 1154.

Rivals to the popes in Rome ruled at Avignon, France, 1309–79.

See CHURCH ; REFORMATION ; ROMAN CATHOLIC CHURCH

pope, ONLY ENGLISH, see ADRIAN IV

Pope, ALEXANDER (1668–1744), poet, *b* London ; a cripple from childhood. As the son of a prosperous linen-draper he did not lack money. He was a son devoted to his mother. Nicknamed ' the wicked wasp of Twickenham,' he was quarrelsome and venomous, but he had many friends, including Jonathan Swift.

His poetry appeals rather to the mind than the heart. Among his best poems are *Essay on Criticism* (written when he was 23) ; *The Dunciad ; Essay on Man ;* a collection of satires, and his translation of Homer's *Iliad* and *Odyssey.* He is best remembered for his epigrams, e.g. *To err is human, to forgive divine.*

Poperinghe, *pō-pĕ-rang',* town, Belgium, 6m west of Ypres. Here (1915) Toc H was founded.

Popish Plot, *pōp'ish,* imaginary conspiracy 1678 said to have been aimed at assassinating the king (Charles II) and a massacre of all Protestants. Actually no such plot ever existed, but Titus Oates, and others, gave false information leading to the arrest and execution of many people. See OATES, TITUS

Poplar, dockland borough of E. London.

poplar, name of a number of soft-timbered trees, including the white poplar, which has alternate leaves, dark green above, white below. All the catkins of one tree are either male or female. The Lombardy poplar is straight and tall as a church spire ; the black poplar has heart-shaped leaves.

Popocatepetl, *pō-pō-kätä'petl,* volcano, Mexico ; rises 17,520ft. (The Aztec name means *smoking mountain.*)

THE BLACK POPLAR

poppy, plant (family *Papaveraceae*) with many species, including the British field poppy with petals round a pepper-pot seed-vessel in a ring of black stamens ; has rough leaves and stem. The opium poppy has white or purple flowers ; the juice yields opium. Poppies were adopted as emblems of Flanders in World War I.

population, number of people in a village, town, city, county or other area ; found by taking a State census, usually every 10 years (as in Britain since 1801, except 1941). The density of population per sq.m (generally reckoned as so many per 1,000) depends, in part, on the use made of mineral wealth and industries ; in Britain there has been a drift to manufacturing and commercial areas since the beginning of the Industrial Revolution, a feature now being controlled by the planning of new towns of moderate size.

Census figures, especially in Europe, show a steady decline in the birthrate (i.e. the number of live births per 1,000 people every year) this century the average family being smaller than formerly, though recently the birthrate has begun to rise.

In round figures the population in Great Britain and Ireland was in

1801	16,345,000
1851	27,535,000
1901	41,600,000
1931	44,790,000
1951	53,000,000 (approx.)

The present population of England and Wales is (approx.) 43,500,000 ; of Scotland 5,200,000 ; of Ireland 4,300,000. The births in Great Britain and Ireland were (1937) 723,779, i.e. 15·3 per 1,000,

and (1947) 1,030,900, i.e. 20·7 per 1,000 ; the deaths were (1937) 597,789, i.e. 12·6 per 1,000, and (1947) 600,706, i.e. 12·1. There are (approx.) 8,500,000 children in England and Wales, and 1,200,000 in Scotland.

About 4,000 people are killed on the roads of the UK every year, and 22,000 die of tuberculosis. The average family in England and Wales was 4·83 in 1851, 3·72 in 1931. A census was taken in the UK in April 1951.

For world population today, the population of each continent, and for the number of people speaking various languages see EARTH. Note that the (estimated) population of

USSR	is	175,000,000
USA	is	135,000,000
Germany	is	69,000,000
UK	is	49,000,000
Brazil	is	41,500,000
France	is	41,000,000

The world's largest cities include London (pop. estimated at *c*.10,000,000) ; New York (USA), 7,454,995, with Greater New York, 11,690,520 ; Tokyo (Japan), *c*.7,000,000 ; Berlin (Germany), 4,250,000 (i.e. before World War II) ; Moscow (USSR), 4,137,000 ; Shanghai (China), 3,418,000 ; Chicago (USA), 3,384,000 ; Leningrad (USSR), 3,191,000 ; Osaka (Japan), 3,000,000 (approx.) ; Paris (France), 2,792,000.

The pop. of the British Commonwealth is (approx.) 540,000,000, comprising *c*.70,000,000 white people, 360,000,000 native races in India and Ceylon, 40,000,000 black people, 6,000,000 Arabs, 6,000,000 Malayas, 1,000,000 Chinese, etc.

One of the most important factors in population is the numbers of people in different age-groups. At present in the UK there are more people under than over 50 years old, but later in the century there will probably be more people over 50 than under it, which means that younger people will have to work harder to maintain the higher age-groups, and also to wait longer for promotion.

porcelain, see POTTERY

porcupine, animal found in S. Europe, S. Asia, Africa and America. The common porcupine found in Europe and Africa has black and white quills, and is *c*.27in long. It feeds at night on roots and vegetables. The American porcupines have quills which are shorter and barbed at the end. None shoots out its quills in self-defence, though popularly supposed to do so. When attacked, a porcupine rushes at its enemy backwards. See page 530.

porphyry, *pör′fi-ri*, fire-formed rock, e.g. the green variety found in Peloponnesus and near Dublin, and the famous red variety obtained from Egyptian quarries by the Romans.

porpoise, see WHALE

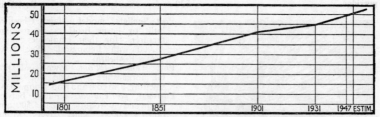

INCREASE OF POPULATION IN GREAT BRITAIN AND IRELAND

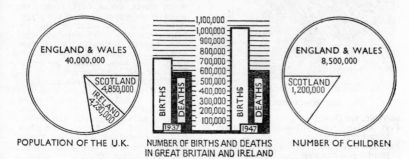

POPULATION OF THE U.K.

NUMBER OF BIRTHS AND DEATHS IN GREAT BRITAIN AND IRELAND

NUMBER OF CHILDREN

POPULATION OF SIX GREAT COUNTRIES OF THE WORLD

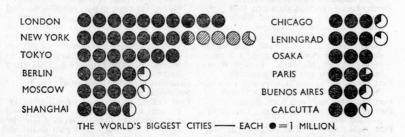

THE WORLD'S BIGGEST CITIES —— EACH ● = 1 MILLION

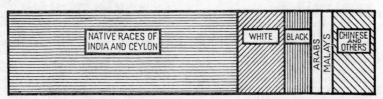

POPULATION PROPORTIONS OF BRITISH COMMONWEALTH

18 a

THE PORCUPINE

porridge, see OATS
Port Arthur, Soviet-Chinese naval base, Manchuria.
Port-au-Prince, *por-tō-prans'*, port and cap. Haiti ; pop.145,000.
portcullis, see ARCHITECTURE
Port Elizabeth, port, Cape Province, S. Africa ; exports wool and hides ; pop.125,000.
Portland, city, Oregon, USA. It is a growing port ; has iron foundries ; pop. 305,000.
Portland, port and city, Maine, USA ; pop.73,000.
Portland, ISLE OF, peninsula, Dorset ; linked with the mainland by Chesil Bank ; the extremity is known as PORTLAND BILL. The naval harbour, PORTLAND ROADS, is protected by huge breakwaters.
Portland vase, ancient glass urn 10in high and 7in round ; once used for human ashes ; has Greek figures in white enamel on a dark blue background. Found near Rome *c.*1640, and long owned by the Portland family, it is now in the British Museum. Broken by a lunatic 1845, it was cleverly restored.
Port Louis, *loo'i ; loo'is,* cap. and port of the island of Mauritius ; pop.57,000.
Port Moresby, cap. and port, Papua.
Port of Spain, port and cap., Trinidad ; pop.105,000.
Port Said, *sä-ēd',* town, Egypt, at the north end of the Suez Canal ; a coaling station ; pop.178,000.
Portsmouth, *pörts'müth,* city, naval base, and port, Hampshire, includes Portsea, Landport, Southsea, etc. ; linked by floating bridge with Gosport. The royal dockyards cover over 300 acres. Nelson's *Victory* is moored here, and here the *Royal George* went down. In Spithead roadstead 1,000 ships may anchor. Charles Dickens was born at Portsmouth ; pop.210,000.
Portsmouth, city, Virginia, USA ; has a naval station ; pop.50,000.

Port Sunlight, model village, Cheshire ; built by Lever Brothers, soap manufacturers, for their employees ; pop. 43,000 with Bebington. See SOAP ; TOWN PLANNING
Port Talbot, *töl'büt,* town and port, Glamorganshire ; noted for copper smelting, also coal and iron ; pop.40,000.
Portugal, *pört'chū-gal,* republic between Spain and the Atlantic ; area 34,500sq.m ; pop.7,954,000 ; chief rivers Minho, Douro, Tagus, Guadiana. Though largely mountainous, Portugal grows much wheat, maize, oats, barley, rice, potatoes and especially olives and grapes ; its exports include wines (notably port from Oporto) ; also sardines, cork, iron, textiles, wolfram, tin, antimony and salt. Portugal was a monarchy till 1910. The cap., Lisbon, is on the R. Tagus, and has a fine airport.
Portuguese overseas possessions include (*a*) the *Madeiras,* a group of fertile islands in the Atlantic, area 314sq.m ; pop.250,000 ; cap. Funchal ; the islands have an excellent climate, and produce Madeira wine ; (*b*) *Azores,* see AZORES ; (*c*) *Cape Verde Islands,* see CAPE VERDE ; (*d*) *Portuguese W. Africa* (i.e. Angola and Portuguese Guinea) ; area *c.* 502,000sq.m ; pop.4,400,000 ; the future cap. is Nova Lisboa ; (*e*) *Portuguese E. Africa* or *Mozambique,* area 297,657sq.m ; pop.5,081,000 ; cap. Lourenço Marques. The region abounds in minerals, and exports sugar, maize, cotton, copra and gold.
Portuguese-man-of-war, see JELLY-FISH
Portuguese West Africa, see PORTUGAL
port wine, rich, red wine from grapes grown in Portugal ; exported from Oporto, after which it is named.
positron, positive electron, i.e. an electric charge equal and opposite to the electron and of the same mass ; discovered 1932 by G. D. Anderson ; found (*a*) in cosmic rays ; (*b*) when various elements are bombarded by neutrons. Its collision with a negative electron results in annihilation, hence its importance in atomic disintegration, e.g. the atom bomb of 1945.
possessive case, see APOSTROPHE
postchaise, see ROADS
Post Office, government organisation replacing earlier systems of conveying messages by special servant or by carrier. The first inland post in Britain was established 1635 ; a Post Office for the three kingdoms and the colonies was set up 1710 under a Postmaster General. The mail-coach system (coaches carrying mails, i.e. letters) began 1784, and by 1836 the distance from London to York (197m) was covered in 20 hours. In 1837 the cost of sending a letter from London to Edinburgh was 1s 3½d, but Sir Rowland Hill inaugurated the penny post 1840. Air mail was instituted 1919 ; and in World War II Airgraphs were used for messages to or from men and women

in the Forces abroad. These were written on forms specially provided, photographed and reduced mechanically, flown to their destination, enlarged, and delivered within a few days.

Besides dealing with letters, stamps, parcels (a service begun 1883), the GPO (General Post Office) has its telephone and telegraph services. It derives a large revenue from licences, including radio (or wireless) licences. It pays out Old Age and various other pensions, and since 1861 has had a savings bank department dealing with *c*.21,350,000 deposit accounts and transacting business to the value of £1,780,000,000 per annum. Money orders were first issued 1792. Cash on delivery (COD) was instituted 1926. In all, Post Office business includes the handling of over 6,230,000,000 letters every year ; *c*.257,330,000 parcels ; 75,000,000 telegrams ; 2,175,000,000 local telephone calls ; postal orders to the value of *c*.£100,000,000 ; and its total transactions with the public usually exceed £3,150,000,000.

Careers in the Post Office are many. They include engineering (assistant engineers rising to *c*.£550–575 a year, with major posts at £950 and over) ; and traffic superintendents.

See PLATE 60

Post-War Credit, compensation to be paid, when conditions allow, to all affected during World War II by the demand for reduction in income tax relief. Some payments have already been made. Post-War Credits cannot be paid until claimants are 65 years of age in the case of men and 60 in the case of women.

potassium, silvery metallic element, K ; atomic weight 39·096 ; atomic number 19 ; valency 1 ; melting-point 62·04°C ; first isolated by Sir Humphry Davy 1807 ; produced by the electrolysis of fused caustic potash ; reacts violently with water, producing hydrogen, which ignites and burns with a violet flame ; is slightly radioactive, emitting β-rays.

Potassium occurs in nature as silicates, and as the oxalate and tartrate in plants, sheep's wool, sea-water and salt deposits. Potassium compounds include POTASSIUM CARBONATE (or potash), K_2CO_3, prepared from wood ashes ; POTASSIUM BICARBONATE, $KHCO_3$, white, soluble salt ; POTASSIUM BROMIDE, KBr, used in photography ; potassium hydroxide (or CAUSTIC POTASH), KOH, much used in making soft soap ; potassium sulphate, a useful fertiliser ; POTASSIUM NITRATE (known as nitre or saltpetre), KNO_3, a powerful oxidising agent used in gunpowder and fireworks. Huge potash deposits were found (1950) near Whitby in Yorkshire.

potassium permanganate, see MANGANESE
potato, plant (*Solanum tuberosum*) that grows wild in S. America. When cultivated it may be 2–3ft high ; the flowers are white, reddish, purple, or bluish ; the fruit is white with a purplish skin when ripe. The underground tuber has ' eyes ' which are actually leaf-buds. Popularly believed to have been introduced into England *c*.1585 by Sir Walter Raleigh, the potato is rich in starch but deficient in nitrogen.

potential difference, *pō-ten'shal*, in electricity, written PD ; measured in volts. If two points have a different electrical potential (EMF) a current of electricity will flow between them when they are joined by a conductor.

potentiometer, *pō-ten-shi-om'ē-tĕr*, name for an instrument for comparing the EMFs of electric cells. By an application of the same principle a proportion (variable in a ' variable potentiometer ') of the potential difference (PD) available from one electrical circuit may be applied to another.

Potomac, *pō-tō'mak*, river of USA ; flows *c*.365m to Chesapeake Bay.
Potosi, *pō-tō-sē'*, town, Bolivia ; stands 13,000ft above sea-level ; pop.36,000.
Potsdam, industrial town, Germany ; *c*.16m from Berlin ; noted for sugar refining, chemical works, etc. ; prior to 1939 the population was 136,000.
Potsdam Conference, meeting, July 1945, at which USA, USSR and Britain agreed (at Potsdam, Germany) to discuss future policy in Germany. Serious differences afterwards developed between the Western Powers and Russia, and the agreement reached at Potsdam ceased to be very effective.
Potteries, name often given to N. Staffordshire, especially to the towns of Stoke-on-Trent, Burslem and Hanley, noted for pottery. See BENNETT, E. A.
pottery, objects of baked clay ; may be earthenware which is porous if unglazed ; chinaware or porcelain if glazed. Glaze is usually applied as a coating to so-called ' biscuit-ware,' after which the article is ' fired ' to a temperature of 900–1,000°C. The base of glaze is usually white lead, though leadless glazes are now used. See PLATE IX

Pottery was made many thousands of years BC, e.g. for cooking, storing and for the ashes of the dead. The potter's wheel was probably first used in Egypt. Famous potters include Bernard Palissy, a French pioneer who died 1589, and Josiah Wedgwood (1730–95), the Burslem potter who brought new beauty to porcelain. Coalport, Sevres, Dresden, Worcester, Derby, Minton and Doulton are among the names of fine chinaware.
Pouishnoff, LEFF, *pweesh'noff* (1891–   ) Russian pianist ; first played in London 1921 ; compositions include *The Musical Box, Petite Valse.*
poultry, domestic fowls, ducks, geese, turkeys, etc. Hens may be classed as (*a*) layers, e.g. Ancona, Leghorn and Minorca ; (*b*) table birds, e.g. Orpington, Plymouth Rock and Rhode Island Red. Fowls are believed to be the domesticated descendants of a bird still

found wild in the Indian jungle. Ducks, possibly domesticated from the mallard, include the Aylesbury duck ; turkeys, descended from wild breeds in N. America, are, like ducks, geese and chickens, fattened for Christmas. Read *Poultry Farming*, edited by Alan Thompson.

Pound, ADMIRAL SIR DUDLEY (1877–1943), British sailor ; First Sea Lord 1939 ; believed that captains of ships should act on their own initiative and not wait for orders. He did much to discount the activities of U-boats.

Pound, EZRA (1885–   ), poet, born Idaho, USA.

poundage, see TONNAGE AND POUNDAGE

poundal, British unit of force=that force which, acting on a mass of 1lb, will impart to it an acceleration of 1ft per sec. per sec. ; equal to 13,825·5 dynes ; 1lb weight=32 poundals.

Pounds, JOHN (1766–1839), crippled cobbler, *b* Portsmouth ; founder 1820 of Ragged Schools, i.e. schools for very poor children. The Ragged School Union (1844) carried on and enlarged his work, and was supported by the Earl of Shaftesbury.

pound sterling, British unit of money worth 20 shillings or 240 pence. In the expression ' £1 stg,' ' £ ' stands for *Libra,* Latin for ' pound.'

power, see MECHANICS

Poznan, *pŏz'näni,* town, Poland ; pop. 272,000.

praefect, see PREFECT

Praetorian Guard, *prē-tō'rian,* household troops of a Roman emperor ; numbered 9 cohorts, say 9,000 men, in the time of Augustus.

Prague, *präg,* cap. Czechoslovakia, formerly the cap. of Bohemia ; on the R. Moldau ; manufactures chemicals and textiles, etc. ; has the castle of the former kings of Bohemia ; also three universities. Prague was the scene of bitter fighting May 1945 ; pop. *c.*900,000.

prairie, see GRASS

prairie dog, *prär'i,* N. American animal similar to the marmot ; lives in colonies in burrows ; is *c.*12in long ; has brown fur ; feeds on grasses and roots.

praseodymium, *prä'zē-ō-dim'iŭm,* rare earth and element, Pr ; atomic weight 140·92 ; atomic number 59.

'Prav'da,' Russian daily newspaper founded 1912. It gives little but Russian news. The title means ' truth,' and the periodical is, of course, Communist.

prawn, see SHRIMP

Praxiteles, *praks-it'e-lēz,* 4th c. BC Greek sculptor, probably *b* Athens ; best known of his surviving works is a statue of Hermes with the infant Dionysus. See SCULPTURE

Prayer Book, authorised service book of the Church of England, partly developed from medieval service books, partly a product of the Reformation, which demanded services in English, not in Latin. The first authorised service in English,

the *Litany* translated by Archbishop Cranmer, was later revised by him in the reign of Edward VI. This was followed by the second *Prayer Book* 1552, revised in Elizabeth's day, and again 1661. In some Anglican churches the Prayer Book is used in a revised form, drafted in 1929.

praying mantis, see MANTIS

praying-wheel, instrument used by Buddhists in Tibet. It consists of many repetitions of written prayers (sometimes, 1,000,000) wound on cylinders, and turned by hand, water or wind.

precentor, see MONKS AND NUNS

precipitation, may be (*a*) water deposited by the atmosphere as snow or rain, or (*b*) in chemistry, the formation of an insoluble substance in a solution as the result of chemical action, e.g. in a solution of sodium carbonate and calcium chloride, a precipitate of calcium carbonate results.

précis, *prā'sē,* condensation of the essentials of a piece of writing ; i.e. a precise summary of a longer statement.

prediction, see PROPHET

prefabrication, term in general use from *c.*1940 (especially in USA) for the method of assembling houses (also ships, etc.) by putting together standardised parts after delivery from a mass-production factory. Prefabricated houses have been built on a large scale in Britain since 1945.

prefect, one who has a position of authority in a school, and who shares the responsibility of keeping order. The ancient Roman *praefect* was an official chosen by superior authority, and not by the people.

Preliminary, see EXAMINATIONS

Premier, see PARLIAMENT ; PRIME MINISTER

premium, *prē'mi-ŭm,* may be (*a*) regular payment by an insured person to the company of which he is a policy holder, or (*b*) a sum above a nominal or fixed price, e.g. when £100 of stock stands at £110, it is at a premium of £10.

Pre-Raphaelites, see PAINTING

Presbyterians, see CHURCH

Prescott, WILLIAM HICKLING (1796–1859), American historian, *b* Salem, Massachusetts ; lost an eye while at Harvard, and for the remainder of his life was almost blind. With determination and patience and the aid of secretaries he wrote among other scholarly works his stirring *History of the Reign of Ferdinand and Isabella,* also *Conquest of Mexico, Conquest of Peru,* two of the most fascinating histories ever written.

President, head of a republic, university or society ; also (especially in USA) of a company ; in British administration, head of a council or a government department, e.g. the President of the Board of Trade. The President of the USA, elected every four years, is chosen by ballot among the electors (representatives) of each state, the result being announced 6 January.

Presidents of the USA since 1901 :

1901, 1905	Theodore Roosevelt	(R)
1909	Taft	(R)
1913, 1917	Woodrow Wilson	(D)
1921	Harding	(R)
1923, 1925	Coolidge	(R)
1929	Hoover	(R)
1933, 1937 1941, 1945	F. D. Roosevelt	(D)
1945, 1949	Truman	(D)

R = Republican   D = Democrat

Pressburg, see BRATISLAVA

press-gang, group of men who at one time ' raided ' a port, kidnapped seafaring men, and compelled them to join the navy ; dates from 1355 (Edward III). The custom was at its worst in the 18th c. and persisted till 1815. As a rule the press-gang landed from a warship, seized likely men, and brutally carried them off, much as described in the novels of Smollett and Marryat.

pressure (mechanics), force acting on unit area of a surface, i.e. head of liquid × density.

Prester John, partly legendary figure said to have been a Christian ruler of Ethiopia in the 12th c. Many stories have been told about him, including the thrilling adventure tale by John Buchan.

Preston, town and port, Lancashire ; on the estuary of the R. Ribble ; most notable for its great cotton industry and engineering works ; pop.120,000.

Prestonpans, holiday town, E. Lothian ; scene of Prince Charlie's victory, 1745. Read Scott's *Waverley.*

Prestwich, cotton town, near Manchester, Lancashire ; pop.32,000.

Prestwick, town, Ayrshire, on the Firth of Clyde ; airport for trans-Atlantic aircraft and one of the best and most suitable airports in the British Isles. It is almost completely fog-free. See PLATE 58 (*top*)

pretender, term often used for one who makes a false claim to the throne, especially the Pretender, Lambert Simnel ; the Old Pretender, i.e. James Edward, son of James II of England ; and the Young Pretender, i.e. Charles Edward, grandson of James II. See JAMES EDWARD

Pretoria, cap. Transvaal, and administrative capital of the Union of S. Africa. A handsome city, it has great steel industries, and seems likely to develop commercially in the near future ; pop. 226,000.

preventive men, see SMUGGLING

Priam, in old Greek tales, King of Troy ; father of Hector, Paris and Cassandra ; slain at the capture of Troy by Neoptolemus.

prickly-pear, see INSECTS

Pride, THOMAS (*d* 1658), English Parliamentarian ; distinguished himself at Naseby. What is known as *Pride's Purge* occurred 1648 when Colonel Pride, with a body of soldiers, prevented

the attendance of *c.*140 Members of Parliament, the remainder, known as the Rump, afterwards condemning Charles I.

Priestley, JOHN BOYNTON, *prēst'li* (1894–), author and dramatist, *b* Bradford (Yorkshire) ; won fame with his novel *The Good Companions* (1929), which, like *Angel Pavement,* has something of the humour and vivid characterisation of Dickens. His plays include *Laburnum Grove* and *Dangerous Corner.*

Priestley, JOSEPH (1733–1804), chemist, *b* Birstall, Yorkshire ; became a Presbyterian minister in Leeds and Birmingham. He is notable for his experiments in electricity and for his discovery of hydrocholric acid, nitric oxide, sulphur dioxide, and, most important of all, of oxygen 1774. He died in Pennsylvania, USA. Priestley lacked a scientific training, and his belief in the phlogiston theory prevented his making the most of his pioneer work on oxygen.

prime minister or **premier,** head of the British government ; he is the king's chief adviser ; has the confidence of a majority in the House of Commons ; is leader of his political party ; selects the members of his Cabinet ; lives at the official residence, 10 Downing Street, London, and at *Chequers,* a house in Buckinghamshire. Sir Robert Walpole (1721–42) is usually regarded as the first prime minister. See PARLIAMENT

British premiers since 1902 :

1902	Arthur J. Balfour (Conservative)
1905	Sir H. Campbell-Bannerman (Liberal)
1908	H. H. Asquith (Liberal)
1916	David Lloyd George (Coalition)
1922	A. Bonar Law (Conservative)
1923	Stanley Baldwin, later Earl Baldwin (Conservative)
1924	J. Ramsay MacDonald (Labour)
1924	Stanley Baldwin (Conservative)
1929	J. Ramsay MacDonald (Labour, then National)
1935	Stanley Baldwin (Conservative with National Labour and Liberal)
1937	Neville Chamberlain (Conservative with National Liberal and Labour)
1940	Winston Churchill (Coalition)
1945	Clement Attlee (Labour)

prime number, number without factors, except itself and one. See FACTORS

primrose, plant (family *Primulaceae*) that flowers in spring ; has a rosette of green, crinkly leaves, above which grow pale yellow flowers of two kinds : (*a*) the ' pin-eyed ' primrose, with the stigma at the mouth of the funnel, the anthers half-way down, and (*b*) ' thrum-eyed,' with the stigma below the anthers.

Primrose Day, see DISRAELI, B.

Primus stove, *prī'mŭs,* apparatus for cooking, especially in the open air ; burns paraffin vapour without a wick, and

THE PRIMROSE

gives an intensely hot flame. The paraffin is vaporised by pressure.

Prince Consort, see VICTORIA

Prince Edward Island, province of Canada, in the Gulf of St Lawrence, area *c*.2,180 sq.m ; pop.95,000 ; offers excellent prospects for field crops, as the soil is exceedingly rich. Fox-farming is important. The province has been British since 1763. The cap., Charlottetown, has a good harbour.

Prince of Wales, title conferred in Britain on the king's eldest son, the heir apparent ; first borne by the son of Edward I, who 1301 was invested with the principality of Wales, and later became Edward II. The plume (3 feathers) of the Prince of Wales has the motto *Ich Dien* (German *I serve*), adopted 1346 by Edward the Black Prince.

Princetown, village, Devon ; has a large convict prison.

printing, art or practice of impressing letters, characters or illustrations on paper, cloth and other materials by mechanical means ; one of the most important inventions in history ; has resulted in the production of books, magazines and newspapers in greater numbers and at lower prices than could ever have been produced by hand.

The basic idea of movable types is said to have come from China. Metal types were first used *c*.1440, possibly due to Laurens Janszoon Coster of Haarlem, but generally associated with Johann Gutenberg (1400–68), a German, *b* Mainz, who set up a printing press *c*.1448 and printed a Bible 1455. The invention was brought to England 1476 by William Caxton (1422–91). Caxton was employed by Edward IV in commercial negotiations abroad, and found time to study the new art of printing at Cologne. His own translation of *Le Recueil des Histoires de Troye*, 1474, was probably printed at Cologne or Bruges, and was followed by an account of the game of chess. Caxton set up a printing press in Westminster, where (1477) he issued the first book printed in England, *The Dictes and Sayinges of the Philosophers*, and, 1481, his first illustrated book, *The Mirror of the World*. Altogether, he published ninety-six books, including the works of Cicero, Chaucer, Malory, etc., and was followed by his foreman, Wynken de Worde. The first Scottish press was set up 1505 by Andrew Miller at Edinburgh, the home of some of the finest printing in the world. The first printing press of America was established at Cambridge, Massachusetts, in 1638. The first weekly paper was published 1622, the first daily in 1702.

Prior to the 19th c. printing required (*a*) a flat-bed, i.e. the type was arranged in a horizontal *forme* on which the paper was pressed, so taking an impression from the raised and inked type ; (*b*) type arranged by hand, each letter picked up individually and arranged in lines in a composing-stick by the compositor, who inserted metal blanks to make spaces between the words. Flat-bed printing is still essential when printing from movable type on cut sheets. Speed has been gained by the introduction of rotary printing, i.e. the use of cylinders carrying curved plates (*electrotypes*), thus allowing paper from reels to be fed through much more quickly than by printing one sheet at a time. A pioneer of this improvement was Thomas Nelson (1822–92), son of the founder of Thomas Nelson and Sons Ltd, printers and publishers of this encyclopedia. His rotary press (1850) may be seen in Edinburgh at Thomas Nelson's printing works. Speed was also increased by the introduction *c*.1886–89 of the Monotype, Linotype and Intertype, machines rather like typewriters, enabling the operator to set up lines of metal type by pressing a series of keys. When assembled into pages, such type may be used for actual printing, or for making moulds for the production of stereotypes.

Newspapers are now printed on giant rotary presses, e.g. those of Messrs Hoe of New York, some delivering papers at the rate of 96,000 per hour, all ready counted, folded and bound into parcels. Cheap books and magazines are produced (with illustrations and coloured covers) in a single operation.

Illustrations are of many kinds. *Lineblocks* are drawn by an artist. The illustration is then photographed, and also, as a rule, reduced in size. A copy of the negative is made on zinc by an etching process, e.g. nitric acid eating away the parts of the zinc not required to carry ink. The zinc is then attached to a block of hard wood. *Half-tone blocks* are much used in newspapers and magazines, especially for reproducing photographs and wash-drawings. These are photographed through glass screens ruled at right angles with lines 60–65 or 100–125 per inch, and even 130–150 per inch, the copy thus being made up of minute dots, close together where the picture is dark, farther apart where it is light. This is processed on copper for fine work, zinc for coarser, and etched with perchloride of iron, and finally made into a block. The *three-colour process* for reproducing coloured pictures is based on the fact that any hue may be obtained by mixing in correct proportion yellow, magenta and blue-green. The picture is photographed through a half-tone screen and then (i) with a blue filter, (ii) a green filter, (iii) a red filter. The blocks are processed much as for half-tone, and are used to print separate pictures, yellow, red and blue, in that order. In the direct method no half-tone screen is used. Other processes are photogravure, photo-lithography, off-set and collotype, also the very recently invented method of printing eight colours in a single operation. See PLATES X, XI

Priscilla, see AQUILLA

prism, in mathematics, solid figure bounded by two parallel faces and any number of other faces perpendicular to them. The shape of the two equal faces determines the type of prism, one instance being the triangular prism. Incidentally, a cylinder is (mathematically) a special case of a prism, its volume being $\pi r^2 l$. The area of a prism is the area of the base $\times$ its distance from the opposite face.

prism, in optics, a block of glass or transparent plastic, usually of triangular section ; especially the prism used for breaking light into its colour spectrum.

prison, place of detention for criminals ; if on modern lines, has usually two blocks of cells running parallel, and *c.*16ft apart, all doors opening on to the central corridor, and each cell with 800–1,000cu.ft of air-space. Furniture includes a bed, table and stool. There is electric light. The warder may observe the prisoner without opening the door. The governor of the prison is responsible in England to the Home Secretary, in Scotland to the Secretary of State for Scotland.

At one time prisons in this country and abroad were vile places, where prisoners were herded together irrespective of age or sex. Among English pioneers of prison reform were John Howard and Elizabeth Fry, whose work led in the 18th and early 19th c. to great improvements, and to the building (1842) of what was then a model prison at Pentonville. Today the old cruelties have given place to systems in which the prisoner is encouraged to lead a better and more useful life. Daring experiments have been made recently in the moral rebuilding of prisoners, notably at Wakefield prison.

Prisoners sentenced to more than one month's imprisonment may be allowed their freedom after 5/6th of the period has been completed if their conduct has been good. Convicts are persons sentenced to penal servitude for three years or more. They, too, may earn remission of their sentences, coming out on what is called ticket-of-leave. Borstal institutions are not actually prisons but reformatory schools, though under the management of the Prison Commissioners.

During the Nazi regime in Germany (say 1934–45), many thousands of Germans and some millions of Jews were herded together in concentration camps, prisons of the worst possible type, the prisoners often being tortured, and sometimes starved to death. Among the worst Nazi prison camps were Belsen, Buchenwald and Dachau.

Privy Council, *priv'i,* in the British constitution, a council which theoretically advises the king on matters of government, though in practice its duties have been taken over by the Cabinet, which in name is a committee of the Privy Council. All actual and former Cabinet Ministers are members of the Privy Council (that is why they are called Right Honourable). The council supervises the granting of municipal charters, and its Judicial Committee is the final Court of Appeal from the Colonial and Ecclesiastical Courts. It gives effect to its decisions by Orders in Council.

Privy Purse, money from the Civil List granted to the king and queen for their personal use ; approximately £110,000 per year for the king, £70,000 for the queen.

Privy Seal, in the UK, the royal seal, kept by the Lord Privy Seal for State documents not sufficiently important to be sealed by the Great Seal.

probability, in mathematics, method of estimating the chances of an occurrence of any one of a number of possible events ; thus, if an event may happen in a ways and fail in b ways, and all these ways are equally likely to occur, the probability of a certain happening is $\dfrac{a}{a+b}$, and of its failing $\dfrac{b}{a+b}$.

probate, *prō'bit,* in England, the official acknowledgment that a will is genuine. When a will is admitted to probate it is filed at Somerset House, London, or at one of the District Probate Registries, where officials make an official copy, known as ' the probate,' which the executor of the will receives, and is acknowledged by all as proof of the will. No property may be administered by an executor without first obtaining probate.

proconsul, in ancient Rome, a magistrate invested with the power of a consul, and in charge of an army or the administration of a province.

Procter, ADELAIDE ANN (1825–64), poet, *b* London ; wrote *Legends and Lyrics,* including *The Lost Chord.*

producer gas, carbon monoxide, CO, mixed with nitrogen ; manufactured by passing air over red-hot coke. Introduced *c.*1878, its calorific value is low, but as it is cheap it is much used for illumination and power.

product, see MULTIPLICATION

profit, gain made in a business transaction, e.g. that made by a trader ; usually reckoned on the cost price (CP) of goods, and frequently stated as so much *per cent.* Thus, a retailer who buys articles at, say, 2s each, and sells (selling price, or SP) at 2s 6d, makes a profit of 6d on 2s, i.e. 25 %. Loss (similarly calculated) is incurred when SP is less than CP. In trading (especially for income tax purposes) profit is sometimes reckoned on SP, not CP.

profit-sharing, plan for industry and business in which employees receive, in addition to the usual rate of wages, a certain proportion of any profits made by the concern, though they are in no way responsible for losses. In theory it is an excellent scheme, presupposing that employees will give better service, and that there will be a sense of unity between managers and workers ; in practice, however, the idea has not, as a rule, worked well on a large scale, though there are certain exceptions, e.g. the Ford motor works, Lever Brothers, and a number of gas-producing companies. Socialists and trade-unionists are suspicious of the idea, since employees have difficulty in bargaining for their rights ; but it would seem that, with good will, some variation of these principles ought to be, at least, a partial solution to modern labour problems. The ' Co-op ' is a form of profit-sharing concern.

Progressives, name given 1889 to a party of the London County Council, comprising councillors holding advanced views ; now often used by a group of councillors of any town or city council to suggest that they are younger and more go-ahead than others.

Prohibition, *prō-i-bish'ŭn,* legislation forbidding the sale or consumption of intoxicants in a given area ; especially the Prohibition experiment tried in USA under the Eighteenth Amendment (passed 1918, repealed 1933). Though well-intentioned, this led to unfortunate consequences, e.g. the smuggling of spirits, giving rise to what was known as bootlegging and racketeering.

proletariat, *-tār'i-at,* indirectly from Lat. *prolas,* offspring, in Marxian economics means that section of the population which has the minimum wage required to support the workers, their wives and children. A working-class which received less than this amount in wages would fail to reproduce itself and would therefore cease to exist. In general, the term is used so vaguely that it is better avoided in serious discussion of political questions.

prologue, *prō'lŏg* (Greek *pro,* fore, *logos,* word), preface or introduction, especially one spoken before a play, e.g. the

explanation given at the beginning of Shakespeare's *King Richard III.* An EPILOGUE is a short address in prose or verse that *concludes* a play. Used by Shakespeare, and common from the 17th to 18th c., it is rarely employed today.

promenade concerts, see WOOD, SIR H.

Prometheus, *prō-mē'thūs,* in old Greek tales, god of fire. Varied stories are told of him, one being that he stole fire from heaven, for which Zeus chained him to a rock.

Proms, THE, see WOOD, SIR H.

Prontosil, see SULPHONAMIDES

propaganda, term now used for the means (e.g. by newspaper articles, presentation of news, public speeches, broadcasting) whereby the people of a country are persuaded to approve some system, idea or creed. In wartime this becomes an influence for maintaining morale at home, and a weapon for attacking the enemy by undermining faith in their government. Most countries had Ministers of Propaganda in World Wars I and II, and in the latter both Hitler and Mussolini made great use of this method of influencing public opinion. Impartial dissemination of news and views leaves the public free to draw their own conclusions ; propaganda is always in danger of attempting to force certain views on the public by publishing a one-sided version of the truth and witholding such items as do not contribute to the effect desired.

Propaganda (and control of education) are indispensable weapons of the totalitarian state.

prophet, *prof'et,* one who claims to foretell the future. The Greek idea of a prophet was that of interpreter of hidden meanings, and those whom we call the OT or Hebrew prophets announced to the people the will of God, but did not necessarily reveal the future.

Prophecy in the sense of claiming to predict goes back to ancient times, e.g. the seer or soothsayer who pretended to read the future by supernatural means, often while in a trance, or by divination. Crystal-gazers have long professed to see the future by gazing in crystal spheres during self-hypnotism ; fortune-tellers may use cards or (as palmists) ' read ' the future in our hand. There are still credulous people who believe in palmistry as a form of magic ; but the truth is that while nothing of our future is revealed in the lines of our hand, much of our past and of our nature may be gathered from a scientific examination. Divination by omens is an old form of foretelling the future, e.g. regarding the flight of birds as a sign of fortune or misfortune, due to superstitions which unfortunately still exist. Even today some newspapers have their humbugs who pretend to foretell the future by reading the stars or by some other absurd method.

The ancient Greeks believed in oracles, usually some priest or priestess who spoke as the mouthpiece of the god he or she represented, e.g. the Oracle of Apollo at Delphi, on the slopes of Mt Parnassus, the priestess (Pythia) sitting on a tripod. Her utterances were deliberately obscure and could usually be interpreted in different ways.

Clairvoyants (French *clair*, clear, *voir*, to see) claim to be able to see what is happening at a distance too great for ordinary sight. This may be true, as some people are truly psychic.

proportion, see RATIO

proportional representation, form of election of representatives. In one form a second ballot is held if no candidate receives an absolute majority ; in another the elector numbers the various condidates in order of preference, known as the alternative vote.

Proportional representation provides for the expression of varying shades of opinion ; but in some countries which have experimented with it, especially in France, it has led to the existence of many parties, and so to much political instability. See PARTY

proposition, see THEOREM

prose, see POETRY

Proserpine, see PERSEPHONE

Protagoras, *prō-tag'ō-ras* (*d* 411BC), Greek thinker, *b* Abdera ; was a teacher in Athens ; drew up new colonial laws for Pericles. Accused of disbelief in the gods, he fled from Athens, and was drowned. His most famous saying is *Man is the measure of all things.*

protection, in economics, the attempt to encourage a country's industries by imposing duties on imported goods. Prior to 1932 Britain practised a policy of free trade, but since then forms of protection have been introduced, chiefly to foster trade within the Commonwealth and to minimise unemployment.

protector, in English history, title given to a ruler, usually when the king was a child or youth, or unable to govern, e.g. the dukes of Bedford and Gloucester during the minority of Henry VI ; the Duke of Somerset during the minority of Edward VI. Cromwell was styled Lord Protector from 1653.

proteins, *prō'tēns* ; organic compounds found especially in cheese, eggs, fish and lean meat. Essential to human diet, they contain carbon, hydrogen, oxygen, nitrogen and sometimes sulphur and phosphorus. By hydrolysis they yield amino-acids. Plants build up proteins from nitrogen compounds, but animals derive them from vegetable matter. See AMINO-ACIDS

Protestants, see CHURCH

protoactinium, see RADIOACTIVITY

protocol, in diplomacy, a rough draft or memorandum often regarded as a basis for a final convention or treaty, e.g. the London Protocol of 1852 ; also an

agreement between employers and employees giving details of a peaceful adjustment of differences.

proton, particle of an atom with a positive charge, and a mass nearly equal to that of a hydrogen atom, i.e. *c.*1,800 times the mass of an electron. The mass of an atom is almost all due to the protons and neutrons of which the atom nucleus is built. See ELEMENT ; MATTER

protoplasm, *prō'tō-plazm*, living substance constituting the cells of animals and plants ; comprises carbon, hydrogen, oxygen, nitrogen, sulphur, phosphorus and sometimes other elements.

protractor, instrument used for measuring angles.

Proust, MARCEL, *proost* (1871–1922), French author, *b* Paris ; notable for a series of novels with the collective title *A la Recherche du Temps Perdu*, i.e. *Remembrance of Things Past.* His books show mastery of detail, and his psychological analysis of character once aroused much comment ; all are rich in thought and poetic style. His theme is the disintegration of aristocratic French society.

Provence, *prō-väns'*, province of S. France prior to the Revolution ; famous in the 12th c. for its dialect (provençal) poetry revived last century.

proverb, brief wise saying, usually well known ; described by Cervantes as ' a short sentence drawn from long experience ' ; vividly expresses the homely wisdom and well-tried everyday philosophy of ordinary folk ; e.g. *There's many a slip 'twixt the cup and the lip* ; *a stitch in time saves nine* ; *all that glitters is not gold.* Sometimes one proverb cancels anothers, as *Many hands make light work*, and *Too many cooks spoil the broth.*

Proverbs, BOOK OF, book of the OT. The full title is *The Proverbs of Solomon, son of David*, but it seems that while Solomon gathered many Hebrew sayings well known *c.*1,000BC, this collection includes proverbs by others, e.g. Agur and King Lemuel.

Providence, cap. and port, Rhode I., USA ; pop.253,000.

Province Wellesley, see MALAYA

Provisions of Oxford, see HENRY III

provost, *prov'ust*, chief magistrate of a Scottish burgh, i.e. the equivalent of an English mayor. Aberdeen, Dundee, Edinburgh, Glasgow and Perth have each a lord provost. In some colleges (e.g. Eton, King's College, Cambridge, and the Queen's College, Oxford) the head is styled a provost.

prune, plum (especially if grown in France, Portugal or California) that has been slowly dried, preferably in the sun.

Prussia, one of the former federated states of Germany ; area 113,750sq.m ; pop. (1939) over 41,000,000 ; includes much of the Rhine valley. Its people have long been imbued with a military spirit, and its king became the first German emperor 1871. Rich in coal and iron, it has great industrial centres, e.g. Essen, Frankfort, Dusseldorf, with Berlin, the capital. The state was abolished by the Allies after World War II.

psalm, *săm* (Greek *psalmos*, a twanging of the strings of a harp), a sacred song intended to be sung to a harp or psaltery. The OT *Book of Psalms* is a collection of 150 Hebrew poems or songs of praise, many of them said to have been written by David. The Prayer Book version of the *Psalms* is the *Psalter*.

psaltery, *söl'teri*, ancient stringed instrument, much like a simple harp ; used in Palestine and Greece.

Psyche, *sī'kē* (Greek *soul*), in old Greek tales, a maiden so beautiful that the jealous Aphrodite sent Cupid to make her fall in love with the meanest of men ; but Cupid himself fell in love with Psyche. The story of their separation and reunion is one of the greatest in classical mythology.

psychiatry, *sī-kī'ă-tri*, science of treating certain mental disorders. It owes much to such pioneers as Freud and Jung, and made great advances during World War II. Psychiatrists are now helping to ensure that employees are suited to their work.

psychology, *sī-kol'ō-ji* (Greek *psyche*, soul or mind), science of the mind in any of its aspects. The science examines consciousness and behaviour, and has to do with perception, reason, memory, emotion and the will. The psychologist endeavours to analyse mind into its simplest components, but this is difficult, for how can he observe a process in his own mind while it is actually taking part in that observation ? How is he to know precisely what goes on in another mind ?

Yet broad fundamentals of thinking, feeling and acting, and their interplay, can be inferred partly from accumulated introspection (self-examination) and partly from behaviourism, i.e. from studying the behaviour of others, and regarding it as an index of mental processes.

The study of the unconscious and subconscious, especially as elaborated by Sigmund Freud, has led in recent years to new discoveries, and new methods of mind-healing by means of auto-suggestion. See BRAIN ; PSYCHOTHERAPY

psychotherapy, *sī-kō-ther'ăpi*, branch of applied psychology dealing with the alleviation, or cure, of mental disorders not due to actual disease of the brain or nervous system, i.e. functional, not organic. The types of treatment may be summarised as (*a*) *persuasion*, the physician appealing to the patient's reason and will ; (*b*) *suggestion*, the physician indirectly giving the patient interests, hope, or belief, likely to assist in curing his mental disorder, sometimes when the patient is awake, sometimes by hypnotic suggestion ; (*c*) *analysis* (or *psychoanalysis*) in which the physician

attempts to explore the patient's mental and emotional life, discovering complexes and deeply hidden repressions ; (*d*) *re-education*, an attempt to restore mental processes to normal activity. See BRAIN ; PSYCHOLOGY

Pt, chemical symbol for platinum.

ptarmigan, see GROUSE

pterodactyl, see GEOLOGY

Ptolemy, *tol'ē-mi*, name of 14 kings of Egypt, among them : Ptolemy I (367–283BC), a general of Alexander the Great ; called Soter (Saviour) for aiding Rhodes 304BC ; his son, Ptolemy II (*d* 246BC), established Egypt's naval power, and built a canal from the Nile to the Red Sea ; his son Ptolemy III (*d* 221BC) raised Egyptian sea-power to its greatest glory. Ptolemy XII, who ruled 51–47BC, shared the kingdom with his sister Cleopatra, as also did Ptolemy XIII.

Ptolemy, 2nd c. AD Egyptian scientist ; is thought to have lived chiefly at Alexandria ; notable for (*a*) his astronomical system (the Ptolemaic system), which, though based on his belief that the earth was the centre of the universe, lasted till the time of Copernicus ; (*b*) his mathematics, including the foundations of plane and spherical trigonometry ; (*c*) his geography, greatly in error, but sound enough to enable him to construct a map of the world remarkably accurate in some respects.

publican, in ancient Roman times, a contractor for public business, especially for collecting taxes.

Public Health, see HEALTH

Public Record Office, see LONDON

public school, type of school so called because it is controlled by a Board of Governors and not owned as private property. Many of these schools are ancient foundations, and have considerable endowments. The original 7 are Winchester, Eton, Shrewsbury, Westminster, Merchant Taylors, Rugby and Harrow, but there are now *c*.200 of these schools for boys and 230 for girls. Traditionally they prepare pupils for the university and the professions, and in the past our administrators both at home and in the empire have been drawn mainly from these schools. In this way public schools have exercised a deeper influence on our social life and customs than any other part of our educational service, and are often regarded as the outstanding English contribution to education. Many though not all, of these schools are resident, and the fees are high, so that only the wealthy can afford to send their children to them.

There is now a movement to throw open the public schools to a much wider section of the population, and many, e.g. Christ's Hospital, Mill Hill, etc. have arrangements whereby they take a number of scholarship children from county schools. Normally, entrance is obtained by means of the Common Entrance Examination, which all candidates must pass. The schools lay great stress on the importance of character development as well as the acquisition of knowledge. Headmasters of the Boys' Public Schools are members of the Head-masters' Conference, and the boys may, on leaving school, become members of the Public School Old Boys' Association.

Particulars of the schools will be found in the *Public Schools Year Book*, and a useful summary in *Whitaker's Almanack*.

Public Schools Exploring Society, organisation founded 1932 by Surgeon-Commander Murray Levick ; has been responsible for pioneer work in Finnish-Lapland forests, Newfoundland (where a party of boys mapped the headwaters of the Gander R.), etc.

Public Trustee, government official (at the Public Trustee Office, Kingsway, London, WC2, opened 1908) through whom the State acts as executor or trustee for wills and other settlements. A testator having no other person whom he can appoint trustee of his will may nominate the Public Trustee as such.

publishing, see BOOKS

Puccini, GIACOMO, *poot-chē'nī* (1858–1924), Italian composer, *b* Lucca ; famous for his operas, e.g. *La Bohème, Tosca, Madame Butterfly*.

Puck, mischievous but friendly fairy of English folk-tales ; known also as *pucca, pojke, pook*, of Irish, Swedish, German and other tales. Puck figures in Shakespeare's *A Midsummer Night's Dream*, and in Rudyard Kipling's *Puck of Pook's Hill*.

Puebla, *pwā'blä*, town, Mexico ; manufactures cotton and woollen goods ; pop.137,000.

Puerto Rico, *pwer'tō rē'kō*, island of the W. Indies under USA control ; noted for sugar, tobacco, coffee, cotton, maize, sweet potatoes, yams ; cap. San Juan, a port with pop.170,000.

See PLATE 7 (*top*)

puffin, seabird of the auk family found in Britain and the Arctic ; has black and white plumage, and a large bill striped red and orange in summer.

Puget Sound, *pū-jit*, opening on the Pacific coast of Washington state, USA.

THE PUFFIN

pugilism, see BOXING

Pulitzer, JOSEPH, *pū'lit-sĕr* (1847–1911), journalist of Jewish descent, *b* Budapest ; made a fortune in the newspaper world of USA. By his will he left the Pulitzer prizes for original work in music, drama and literature, including newspaper work.

pulleys, see MECHANICS

Pullman, GEORGE MORTIMER (1831–97), American inventor ; introduced the first Pullman sleeping-car, also corridor trains and dining-cars.

pulse, see BLOOD

puma, large, tawny, flesh-eating animal of the cat family ; *c.*4ft long ; is known in N. America as the panther or mt. lion, in S. America as the cougar. The animal, usually friendly to man though deadly to horses and cattle, is capable of leaping 40ft horizontally and 20ft into the air.

pumice, grey, porous lava.

pump, mechanism for moving liquids or gases, especially water, oil or air. Features common to most pumps are a piston working within a cylinder, and a system of non-return valves.

The lift pump, of which the usual village pump is a typical example, reduces the air pressure at each stroke of the piston working in a pipe going down to the water supply. Air pressure forces the water up in an endeavour to fill the partial vacuum created, and later strokes lift the water to the spout.

The force pump, of which the fire-engine pump is an example, forces water to a height limited only by the ability of the pump and hose to withstand the pressure. An air reservoir acts as a cushioning spring to obviate water coming in spurts at each stroke of the pump.

Air pumps are used for inflating tyres or giving forced air-jets for laboratory purposes.

Various types of pumps are used on motor-car and in aircraft engines : (*a*) to force lubricating oil round the engine, or (*b*) to deliver fuel to the engine. A common fuel (petrol) pump is of the diaphragm type. A disc-like diaphragm of metal sufficiently flexible to be capable of 'bulging' is moved rapidly backwards and forwards by an electric motor, or other means, thus changing the volume of space at one side, where the fuel passes by. Valves do the rest.

Vacuum pumps, operating on several principles, are used for exhausting electric light bulbs and radio valves.

A variation of the pump gives the *vacuum brake* used on most railway trains and street cars. By pumping air *out* from one side of a piston, air pressure on the other operates the brakes by moving the piston.

The principle of the centrifugal pump is that of setting water spinning at high speed. The axial-flow pump, more or less a propeller revolving at high speed in a tube, is highly efficient.

pumpkin, see GOURD

Punch, illustrated British weekly journal famous since 1841 for its humour, satire and criticism, especially of political matters and social customs.

punch, alcoholic drink made of spirits, fruit-juice, spice, sugar and hot water.

Punch and Judy, puppet play usually performed by a travelling entertainer who is hidden by a screen. With his hands he moves the various ' actors ' (e.g. Punch, or Punchinello ; Judy, his wife ; and others), and makes them ' talk ' as he does so. Toby, his dog, is one of the ' actors.' The show became popular in England c.1700.

Punic Wars, *pū'nik*, three wars fought between the Romans and their rivals, the Carthaginians, whose capital was the flourishing city of Carthage, N. Africa, now in ruins, but once a large port and the centre of an empire in Africa and Spain.

The First Punic War was fought in Sicily (much of which belonged to the Carthaginians) 264–241BC ; the Second chiefly in Spain and Italy. Rome itself was threatened when (c.218BC) the Carthaginian general, Hannibal, took his army over the Pyrenees and across the Alps to Italy (see HANNIBAL) ; but after his victory at Cannae 216BC Hannibal failed to press home his advantage, and Rome won the war. The Third Punic War came to an end when Scipio Africanus Minor captured Carthage 146BC, the city and its neighbourhood then becoming a Roman province.

It may be added that although Scipio destroyed Carthage, the city was rebuilt, became famous for its Christians, and flourished till finally destroyed by the Arabs 698AD.

Punjab, province shared between India and Pakistan. Punjab means ' five rivers,' and here are the Indus, Jhelum, Ravi, Chenab and Sutlej. The products include wheat, indigo, sugar, cotton and tea. There are many canals. The area is almost 100,000sq.m ; the pop. 28,000,000 ; the chief cities are Amritsar (India) and Lahore (Pakistan).

punkah, *pung'kä*, large mechanical fan as used in India. It usually hangs from the ceiling, and is worked by a coolie, or by an electric motor.

pupa, *pū'pä* (plural *pupae*), chrysalis, or resting stage, in the life of an insect which changes from a caterpillar or grub to the perfect adult insect.

puppets, figures or dolls made to ' act ' and ' talk ' by a performer or performers. They were known to the Greeks in the 5th c., and have long been popular in the East, notably in Japan. Shadow-plays and marionettes (in which the figures are moved by strings) are variations. See PUNCH AND JUDY

Purbeck, ISLE OF, peninsula, Dorset ; 12m long, 8m wide ; has chalk hills.

On the SE. coast is Swanage, port and town ; inland is Corfe Castle.

Purcell, HENRY (1658–95), English composer, possibly the most important in the history of English music ; became organist at Westminster Abbey 1679 ; composed the first entirely musical English opera (*Dido and Aeneas*) ; organist at the Chapel Royal 1682 ; wrote music for Shakespearean songs (e.g. *Full Fathom Five*) ; noted for his magnificent *Te Deum* and *Jubilate*. His exquisite songs and graceful music remain popular even now.

purchase tax, tax levied in Britain 1940, and applied to a large variety of goods, e.g. furniture (though *not* on utility furniture), also on cars, calendars, etc.

Puritans, see CHURCH

Purley, town, Surrey ; pop. (with Coulsdon) 50,000.

pursuer, see PLAINTIFF

Pushkin, ALEXANDER SERGEYEVITCH (1799–1837), Russian poet and author. His romantic poems are in the style and spirit of Byron, and of these his *Eugene Onegin* is the most famous, closely followed by *Boris Godunov*, works which greatly influenced later Russian writers.

Putney, London district on the R. Thames. It is the starting-point of the annual Oxford and Cambridge boat race.

putting the weight, event included in most athletic meetings. The competitor must ' put ' (but not throw) a weight of 16lb, the record distance attained being 58ft 4⅞in, by J. Fuchs (USA) 1949.

putty, mixture of fine dry whiting or powdered chalk, linseed oil and white lead.

Pygmalion, *pig-mā'li-on*, in old Greek tales, a king of Cyprus who made a statue in ivory of a beautiful maiden, which Aphrodite brought to life so that he could marry her. Bernard Shaw's drama, *Pygmalion* (1914), is the story of a professor of phonetics who educates a Cockney flower-girl and takes her to a State function, where she is accepted as a society lady. He falls in love with her, and we are then left to suppose that he marries her.

Pygmies, *pig'mi*, according to Homer, an imaginary race of people only a few inches high ; now used vaguely for negroid races of small stature in equatorial Africa and SE. Asia, notably the Malay Peninsula, the Philippines and New Guinea.

Pym, JOHN, (d 1643), statesman, born in Somerset ; entered Parliament 1614 ; supported the *Petition of Right* 1628 ; opposed the tonnage and poundage proposals of Charles I, and in the *Grand Remonstrance* 1641 proposed that ministers should be responsible to Parliament and not to the king. He was one of five members Charles tried to seize 1642.

pyorrhoea, *pī-o-rē'a*, discharge from the gums, due to infection of the membrane surrounding the teeth.

pyramid, *pir'ä-mid*, solid figure usually (but not always) with a square base and triangular sides meeting at the vertex. If the base is a triangle, the figure is known as a tetrahedron. The volume of any pyramid is $\frac{1}{3}$ area of base × perpendicular height. See AREA ; VOLUME

Pyramids, name given to large quadrangular constructions erected by the ancient Egyptians as burial places for their kings. The Pyramids (there are about 70 altogether) which are best known are those three (Cheops, Mycerinus and Chephren) at Gizeh, which stand in the Western desert in close proximity to Cairo. The largest of these pyramids is the Great Pyramid of Cheops, which covers an area of thirteen acres and measures approximately 770ft in length. See ARCHITECTURE

Pyramus, *pir'ă-mŭs,* in ancient Babylonian tales, a youth who loved Thisbe *(thiz'bē),* the two whispering to each other through a hole in a wall. Their parents refused to allow them to marry, so they agreed to meet under a mulberry bush. Thisbe arrived first, but was frightened by a lion. Pyramus, finding Thisbe's veil stained with blood from the lion's jaws, assumed that she had been killed, and took his own life, as did Thisbe when she returned and found that Pyramus was dead. The story, told by Ovid in his *Metamorphoses,* is used with comic effect by Shakespeare in his play, *A Midsummer Night's Dream.*

Pyrenees, *pir'ē-nēz,* mts. separating France from Spain. The highest point is 11,200ft, and the snow-line *c.*9,000ft.

pyrites, *pī-rī'tēz,* compound of a metal with sulphur or arsenic, especially iron pyrites, FeS_2, and copper pyrites, $CuFeS_2$, chiefly mined at Huelva, Spain ; also in Japan, Norway, Italy and USSR.

pyrometer, *pī'rom-ētĕr,* type of thermometer named from the Greek *pyr,* fire, *metron,* measure ; designed to measure

very high temperatures. Varieties include (a) *thermoelectric thermometer,* based on the current set up when two different metals are joined, and one junction is heated ; (b) *platinum-resistance thermometer* ; and (c) the *optical pyrometer,* in which the appearance of a glowing surface (e.g. the interior of a furnace) is compared with a lamp-filament interposed in the field of view. There is also (d) the radiation pyrometer used in conjunction with a thermocouple.

Pythagoras, *pī-thag'ō-ras,* 6th c. BC Greek mathematician, b Samos ; held that number is the basis of the universe, and that the qualities of things are simply their mathematical properties as apprehended by us. He made important discoveries in the theory of acoustics, for example that in music the pitch of a note is determined by the frequency of vibrations. He also elaborated the theory of arithmetical, geometrical and harmonical proportions, and devised a well-known proof of the theorem that the square on the hypotenuse of a right-angled triangle is equal to the sum of the squares on the other two sides.

Pythagoras was also the founder of a religious brotherhood holding mystical beliefs. To him is attributed the doctrine of transmigration of souls.

Pytheas, *pith'ē-as,* 4th c. BC Greek traveller and astronomer ; said to have voyaged as far north as Thule, i.e. probably the Orkney Is.

Pythias, see DAMON AND PYTHIAS

python, see ANACONDA ; SNAKE

pyx, *piks,* may be (a) a vessel or chalice in which the Blessed Sacrament is kept ; or (b) a very small locket worn round the neck of a priest, and used for carrying the Sacrament to sick people.

Q

QED, short for the Latin *quod erat demonstrandum,* i.e. 'which was to be demonstrated.'

QEF, short for the Latin *quod erat faciendum,* i.e. 'which was to be done.'

QMG, see QUARTERMASTER

quadrant, instrument once used by navigators for taking altitudes ; now replaced by the sextant.

quadratic equation, see EQUATION

quadrilateral figure, *kwod-ri-lat'ĕr-ăl,* in geometry, any 4-sided figure, e.g. (a) *trapezium* with 4 unequal sides, no two of which are parallel ; (b) *trapezoid,* having the 4 sides unequal, but 2 of them parallel ; (c) *parallelogram,* 4-sided figure with opposite sides parallel and therefore

equal ; if the sides are all equal and one angle is not a right angle, the figure is a *rhombus* ; if the adjacent sides are unequal it is a *rhomboid* ; (d) *rectangle,* 4-sided figure with the opposite sides parallel and therefore equal, and one of its 4 angles a right angle ; (e) *square,* 4-sided figure with two adjacent sides equal, one of the four angles being a right angle. See AREA ; RECTANGLE ; TRIGONOMETRY; also page 542

quadrille, *kwo-dril'* (Italian *squadra,* a square), 18th c. dance in which four couples stand in a square.

quaestor, *kwēs'tor* lower magistrate of ancient Rome. At one time the quaestor investigated cases of murder ; later the

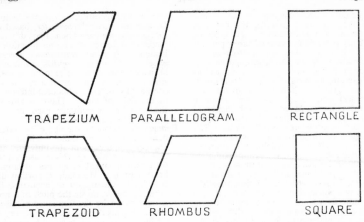

TRAPEZIUM   PARALLELOGRAM   RECTANGLE

TRAPEZOID   RHOMBUS   SQUARE

QUADRILATERAL FIGURES

quaestores classici were officials responsible for the financial administration of the fleet, the *quaestores urbani* having charge of the treasury.

quagga, see ZEBRA

quail, game bird about the size of a thrush, and much like the partridge in shape and colour ; visits Britain ; lays 7–10 buff eggs with brown blotches in a grass-lined hollow.

Quakers, see SOCIETY OF FRIENDS

Quantocks, *kwon'toks,* range of hills in Somerset.

Quantum Theory, *kwon'tum,* principle in physics closely associated with Relativity, and formulated by Max Planck (1858–1947). Prior to this theory it was thought that a particle of matter, or a system of electrons, with an energy-level *a,* reached a higher level A by *continuous variation,* much as a car which accelerates from 40–60mph may be said to move at every speed between these limits. But the Quantum Theory asserts that a particle or a system of electrons is capable of making an instantaneous ' leap ' from one energy-level to another. What is known as Planck's constant (*h*) enables us to calculate such sudden variations. A quantum is *energy* × *time,* i.e. *action* ; and the quantum of action, 6.55×10^{-27} erg-secs, is the ' brick ' of which the universe is built.

According to classical mechanics it should be possible for, say, an electron to circle round its nucleus in an orbit of *any* size, and for the orbit to increase gradually and continuously as the atom is ' fed ' with energy, either by heat or electricity. We now know that the atom cannot increase gradually in this way, but that the electron can only occupy one of a number of orbits of increasing size. As each orbit represents an increase of energy, this means the atom can only take in energy in definite ' packets ' (quanta). Similarly, when energy is given

up or radiated, the process occurs in jumps as the electron drops back from orbit to orbit. Radiation (light or sometimes X-rays) is sent out in ' packets.'

It might be expected that changes in energy levels or orbits of the electron would represent equal amounts of energy. This is not so. The constant in the process is something new in physics—the result of dividing the energy ' packet ' (quantum) by *v,* i.e. the frequency of the radiated (or absorbed) energy. In symbols :

$$e = hv \quad \text{or} \quad \frac{e}{v} = h$$

where *e* = energy quantum, *v* = the frequency, and *h* = the constant in the process, now known as Planck's constant. See PLANCK, MAX ; WAVE-MOTION

Quarter Days, see HOUSE

quartermaster, in the army, an officer responsible for living quarters, and for the supply of rations, stores and ammunition ; a quartermaster general (QMG) is an officer in charge of the supply departments of the army.

quarter-staff, weapon once much used for defence and duelling by English peasants. It was a pole 6–8ft long, tipped with iron at both ends ; it is often mentioned in stories of Robin Hood.

quartet, see SINGING

quartz, see SILICON

Quatre Bras, *kä-tr brä,* village of Belgium ; scene 1815 of a battle between Wellington and Napoleon's general, Ney, the former securing a dearly-bought victory. The battle of Waterloo was fought the next day.

Quebec, province of Canada ; area 594,860 sq.m ; pop.3,332,000 ; famous for its vast forests, from which timber is obtained for making paper, etc. Fertile soil makes for good farming. Minerals include molybdenum.

The cap., Quebec, is a fine city and port

on high ground above the R. St. Lawrence; it is a great tourist centre, and has a large trade in timber, wood-pulp, grain and textiles. On the Plains of Abraham nearby Wolfe captured Quebec 1759, thus securing Canada for Britain. This area is now a public park ; pop.151,000.

' Queen Elizabeth,' see SHIPS ; and PLATE 53

' Queen Mary,' see SHIPS

Queen's College, college of Oxford University ; founded 1340 by Robert de Eglesfield.

Queens' College, college of Cambridge University ; founded 1448 by Margaret of Anjou, queen of Henry VI.

Queen's County, former name for an inland county, Eire, now known as Leix.

Queensferry, town and port at the south end of the Forth Bridge (W. Lothian) ; also a town at the north end (Fife).

Queen's Hall, London, concert hall ; opened 1893 ; had two halls, the larger seating over 3,000 people ; famous for Sir Henry Wood's promenade concerts till destroyed by a bomb 1941. A new hall is now being completed close to Broadcasting House.

Queensland, state, Australia, including the whole NE. part of the continent ; area 670,000sq.m ; pop.1,072,000. The crops include wheat, maize, sugar, rubber and fruit ; wool is exported on a large scale ; coal and gold are mined ; cap. Brisbane.

Queen's University, university of Belfast (N. Ireland), founded 1909 ; non-residential.

Queuille M. HENRI, ke-nē (1884–), French Radical Socialist ; Prime Minister 1948.

quern, ancient form of grain-mill, usually of two flat stones, the upper one (with a wooden handle) being revolved as it rests on the lower. Querns, referred to in Deuteronomy 24, are still used in remote parts of Ireland and Scotland.

' Quest,' see POLAR REGIONS

Quetta, cap., Baluchistan ; damaged by a severe earthquake 1935. It commands the Boland Pass, and hence the road to Kandahar ; pop.60,000.

Quiberon, port, France, on the Bay of Biscay coast. The battle of Quiberon Bay 1759 saw the defeat of the French by Lord Hawke.

quicklime, calcium oxide, CaO ; prepared by heating limestone in a kiln ; used for making builder's mortar ; combines with water to make slaked lime, $Ca(OH)_2$, i.e. calcium hydroxide. See CALCIUM

quicksilver, see MERCURY

Quiller-Couch, SIR ARTHUR, kooch (1863–1944), known also as ' Q,' b Cornwall ; won fame with his novel Dead Man's Rock 1887. His other stories (often in the style of Robert Louis Stevenson) include The Blue Pavilions, The Delectable Duchy, The Ship of Stars and Fort Amity. He wrote Poems and Ballads ; compiled the immensely popular Oxford Book of English Verse, and similar anthologies. As a critic of fine literary judgment he published On the Art of Writing, On the Art of Reading, etc. His delightful story Troy Town describes his beloved Fowey, Cornwall.

Quilpie, kwil'pi, town, W. Queensland, Australia ; noted for its house-to-house supply of hot water drawn from an artesian well.

Quilter, ROGER (1877–), English composer, b Brighton ; set various Shakespearean songs to music ; noted for orchestral pieces, e.g. A Children's Overture. He composed the music for Where the Rainbow Ends.

quince, tree or shrub of the family Rosaceae; introduced into Britain c.1573 ; may be 5–20ft high. The fruit is yellow and pear-shaped.

quinine, kwi-nēn', organic substance derived from the bark of the tree Cinchona succirubra of the Andes, Java and S. India. The crystalline solid has a bitter taste. It is much used in medicine, and was once the chief remedy for malaria, now replaced by paludrine.

quinquireme, see SHIPS

Quintilian, kwin-til'ian (d AD97) Roman orator, b Calagurris, Spain ; founded a school of rhetoric (public speaking) in Rome, and wrote a notable book, The Institutes of Oratory.

Quirinal, kwir'i-nal, one of the seven hills on which Rome is built. It is crowned with a 16th c. palace. See PLATE 75 (top)

Quisling, MAJOR VIDKUN, Norwegian who, when Germany invaded Norway (April 1940), accepted the post of chief of the new Nazi-appointed government ; quisling now means traitor.

Quito, kē'tō, cap., Ecuador ; pop.211,000. Over 9,000ft above sea-level, it was formerly the Inca capital. The city suffered severe earthquake damage Aug 1949.

quod erat demonstrandum, see QED

quod erat faciendum, see QEF

quoits, koits, outdoor pastime played in Scotland and N. England since the 15th c. The player throws two iron rings (weighing c.9lb each) a distance of c.18yd in an attempt to encircle an iron pin embedded in clay.

quotient, see DIVISION

quo vadis, kwō vä'dis, Latin whither goest thou? The novel Quo Vadis? by the Polish writer Henryk Sienkiewicz, published 1895, deals with the persecutions of Christians in Nero's day.

R

R34, R38, R101, etc., see AVIATION
Ra, chemical symbol for radium.
Ra, *rä*, ancient Egyptian sun-god. From the Vth dynasty Egyptian kings bore a Ra-name, e.g. Amen-Ra.
R.A., see PAINTING
Rabat, *rä-bät'*, walled capital and port, French Morocco ; pop.84,000 ; manufactures leather and carpets.
Rabaul, *rä'bowl* ; -*vowl*, former administrative capital, New Britain ; damaged by volcanic eruptions 1937, and bombed so heavily in World War II that it was not rebuilt.
rabbi, see JEWS
rabbits and hares, animals of the order *Rodentia* (gnawing mammals), both common in Britain. The wild RABBIT, generally brownish in colour, has a white stubby tail, breeds 5–7 times a year ; and lives in a burrow, usually one of many forming a warren. The fur (coney) is a cheap substitute for better qualities. Since *c*.1850 rabbits have been a serious pest in Australia. Domestic varieties include the Angora, Flemish Giant and Belgian hare.
The wild HARE, similar to the rabbit, has long and powerful hind legs, is larger (being *c*.24in long), with very long ears ; is tawny red in colour, and lives in a ' form,' i.e. a grass hollow.
Rabelais, FRANÇOIS, *rä-be-lā* (*d c*.1554), French thinker and writer, born near Chinon ; was monk, doctor, scientist, scholar, lawyer, architect and educationist, but known above all as the rebellious and good-humoured author of *Gargantua* and *Pantagruel*, stories of giants written with the immense laughter of a man tremendously in love with life, and impatient with the customs and doctrines of the Middle Ages.
RAC, short for Royal Automobile Club.
raccoon, flesh-eating American animal related to the bear ; is *c*.24in long, with a tail *c*.10in long. A heavy animal, it has thick greyish fur, lives in holes in trees, and hunts at night.
racehorse, see HORSE
Rachel, *rä'chel*, in the OT, favourite wife of Jacob, and mother of Joseph and Benjamin.
Rachmaninoff, SERGEI, *räch-mä'ni-nof* (1873–1943), Russian composer and pianist, *b* Novgorod ; later lived in USA. His *Prelude in C sharp minor*, perhaps his best known musical piece, was written when he was only 20. His symphonies and piano concertos are deservedly popular.
Racine, JEAN, -*sēn*, (1638–99), French tragedian; wrote plays in classical style; sometimes called the Sophocles of France. His dramas include *Britannicus*, *Mithridate*, *Iphigènie*, *Phèdre* and *Athalie*.

His work is superb in construction, dialogue, poetical expression and swiftness of action.
rack, instrument of torture by means of which the victim's limbs were stretched until dislocated ; known to the Egyptians and Romans ; used in England in the 16th century.
rackets, game for two or more players using racquets 30in long. The asphalted 4-walled court is usually 63ft by 31½ft, and the service line is 9½ft from the ground. The ' short line ' is 38ft from the front wall. The court is divided into right and left, with service ' boxes ' 8ft square. The game is somewhat similar to fives and squash rackets, the latter being played by two players on a smaller court.
racon, see ELECTRONICS
radar or radiolocation, *rā'där*, Radio, Angle, Direction And Range. Name given to a radio invention capable of finding range and direction of airborne objects, and later applied to all adaptations of the original invention.
Experimental work in the early stages was conducted by Sir Edward Appleton and M. A. F. Barnett, two Cambridge physicists, and later by M. A. Tuve and G. Bright, two American scientists. Some time later a small group of radar pioneers adapted radar so that it could be used as a weapon of defence in the event of warfare. This small group was headed by the Scottish scientist Sir Robert Watson-Watt. Experimental work was soon sufficiently advanced for the Air Ministry to become actively interested, and by the time radar became a workable project, stations were being

THE RACCOON

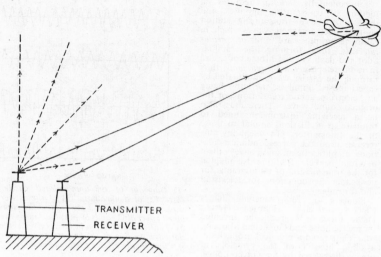

THE PRINCIPLE OF RADAR

Radio energy is sent out in pulses from the transmitter and is reflected in pulses from the plane to the receiver. See also Plate 57.

built all round the coast of Britain to ensure overall coverage for the British Isles.

At the beginning of World War II service personnel were trained as operators and mechanics so that they could operate and maintain these radar installations, which consisted of transmitter and receiver apparatus.

On striking an object within a certain radius the transmitted energy is reflected back to its starting point, where it is picked up by a receiver. After going through various processes in the receiver it appears as a luminous 'response' on a cathode-ray oscilloscope. When the operator sees 'responses' he is able to find the range, direction, number of aircraft and, in some cases, height, long before the aircraft themselves can be seen or heard ; these 'responses' are pin-pointed and can be tracked for long distances, which in World War II provided Fighter Command with much vital information.

Another form of radar was Ground Control Interception (GCI) which played a very important part in assisting fighter pilots to destroy enemy aircraft, and proved to be a most successful answer to Germany's night attacks. Searchlights and anti-aircraft guns too were fitted with radar devices which enabled them to be automatically directed to the required position.

By the introduction of highly sensitive centimetre equipment, extremely accurate plots of shipping could be obtained. The magnetron valve (now being used in many ways for safer peacetime shipping and navigation) was the most important feature of this new equipment, and it was not long before further modifications and improvements in radar resulted in suitable equipment being installed in aircraft. This provided pilots with visual ' moving maps ' of country otherwise invisible to the eye because of darkness or cloud, and made precision bombing of unseen targets possible. 'Loran' (LOng RAnge Navigation), unlike other forms, employs long radio waves. A newer adaptation of the radar principle has enabled successful weather observations to be carried out. See PLATE 57

Radcliffe, *rad′klif,* town near Manchester (Lancashire) ; noted for cotton and paper ; pop.25,000.

radian, *rā′dian,* in mathematics, 57·2958 degrees, i.e. 57° 17′ 44·8″ (approx.), or log. 1·7581. Note, π radians = 180°, defined as an angle subtended at the centre of a circle by an arc equal in length to the radius. See TRIGONOMETRY

radiant energy, see PLANCK, MAX

radiation, see HEAT ; LIGHT ; QUANTUM THEORY

radical, in chemistry, group of atoms in a compound unaffected by reactions that change the remainder of the molecule, e.g. ammonium, NH_4, a univalent radical ; and such hydrocarbon radicals as ethyl, C_2H_5.

radio, word which is now replacing *wireless.* It includes various methods of signalling or of conveying sounds and pictures through space by means of electromagnetic waves without the use of connecting wires.

Fundamentally, radio requires a method of transmitting impulses, and there must be a transmitting station emitting electromagnetic waves which, in radio telegraphy, are sent *at various intervals*, thus forming the familiar ' dot and dash ' of the Morse code, and in radio telephony are *continuous*, thus forming the carrier wave, modulated by superimposed impulses, the latter being an ' electromagnetic translation ' of the original sound wave. There must also be a receiving instrument tuned to resonate to oscillations similar to those of the transmitter. In telephony this receiver produces corresponding oscillations, amplifies them, and conveys them to a loudspeaker. Radio is also adapted for the transmission of photographs for newspaper reproduction, for television and for radar.

Pioneers of radio include James Clerk - Maxwell ; Heinrich Hertz ; David Edward Hughes, who invented the microphone, and Guglielmo Marconi, who made radio a practical proposition, availing himself of the principle of tuning discovered by Sir Oliver Lodge, and, as early as 1901, sending the 3 dots (S in Morse) from Poldhu, Cornwall, to St John's, Newfoundland, an historic achievement. The discovery that a current will pass in one direction only from one crystal to another, or from a crystal to a metallic point (nicknamed cat's whisker) led to the early crystal sets.

Thus far radio telegraphy was possible. Radio telephony, requiring a continuous carrier wave, was due to the pioneer work of Thomas Alva Edison, Sir J. J. Thomson, and, most of all, to Sir Ambrose Fleming, inventor of the thermionic valve.

In radio telegraphy the transmitted signal merely gives a noise in the receiver's telephones. Interruption of the signal can thus be made to give corresponding long and short signals representing ' dashes ' and ' dots ' of the Morse code. Later, the great advance was made that enabled speech and music to be transmitted, and received by radio. This depends on the use of a modulated carrier wave. The carrier wave is a radio signal that increases and decreases (like a wave) millions of times a second. In ' modulating ' the wave is made to increase and diminish at audio-frequencies. In the receiver only the audio-frequencies affect the loud-speaker, and the note is heard corresponding in frequency to the modulation. Today, radio employs a multitude of valves, e.g. the screened grid valve, the variable *mu* (ensuring volume control), etc. See THERMIONIC VALVE. Radio-telephonic messages were first transmitted from England to Australia 1924, an achievement of special interest because it proved that electromagnetic waves followed the curvature of the earth, and did not fly off

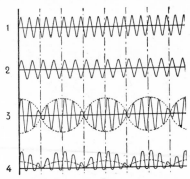

RADIO WAVES

(1) *Diagram of an unmodulated carrier wave* (2) *of a pure note* (3) *of the carrier wave modulated with a pure note—the combined effect of* (1) *and* (2)—(4) *the same wave as* (3) *after rectification in the receiver : the dotted wave line of* (4) *represents the wave that finally affects the loud-speaker.*

into space. This is due to the presence (c.60–100m above the surface) of the Heaviside layer (named after Oliver Heaviside) and the Appleton layer (named after Sir Edward Appleton), perhaps 150m above the earth. To Marconi we owe also BEAM-RADIO, i.e. the transmission of a narrow pencil of waves in one direction only, a principle rapidly developed since c.1935, and especially since 1940, the use of directed microwaves being the foundation of radar, used for ship and plane ' spotting ' in World War II, and now adapted to civilian flying and shipping. See RADAR

In radio-telephony the first necessity is the creation of electromagnetic waves, those between 200 and 2,000 metres being most commonly used, their frequencies varying from 300,000 per sec. to several millions per sec. The transmitter passes current through a series of valves, negative electrons surging or ceasing alternately through a screen (or grid), the frequency of their movement (oscillation) being controlled by a coil of wire and a variable condenser. An aerial receives electric impulses which are radiated into space, and are ' picked up ' by the receiving apparatus if it is tuned to resonate or respond to the frequency of the incoming waves. The receiving circuit is usually tuned by a movable condenser. See PLATES 61, 63 (*top left*)

British BROADCASTING may be said to have begun 15 June 1920, when the voice of Dame Melba was transmitted from a Marconi station at Chelmsford, Essex. The British Broadcasting Corporation (BBC) began as the British Broadcasting Company 1922. Today it receives a large revenue from licences. These were first issued 1927, and cost 10s per year till 1946, when the price was raised to £1. The number of licenced listeners in Britain is c.11,000,000. See FM

TELEVISION owes much to many pioneers, but most of all to J. L. Baird. The BBC began regular television broadcasts 1936. See BAIRD, J. L.; and PLATES 62, 63

British broadcasting has made rapid strides since the end of World War II, e.g. the advances at Tatsfield, Surrey, which is the BBC's receiving and frequency-measuring station ; the equipment of Kingswood Warren, an old mansion on the London–Reigate road, HQ since 1948 of the BBC Research Department ; and the erection of the new Sutton Coldfield television transmitter (the most powerful in the world), its aerial mast rising 750 feet. In accordance with the Copenhagen Conference of 1948, BBC wave-lengths were altered in 1950, though the long wave (1,500 metres) remained.

Apart from television, broadcasting includes time-signals, news, weather reports, talks, features, drama, the Children's Hour, running commentaries on sport and notable events, variety, music, debates, appeals for charity, etc. The BBC's weekly journals include *Radio Times*, first issued 1923, and *The Listener* (1929).

Among the RADIO COLLEGES (recognised by Marconi and on the Air Ministry List) are those at Calmore, Southampton and Colwyn Bay.

World communications have been greatly advanced in range and efficiency by Cable and Wireless Ltd, entrusted by the British government with the maintenance of over 350,000m of cables and radio circuits, thus linking the Empire with almost every country in the world, transmitting not only messages but also pictures (see PHOTOTELEGRAPHY), and perfecting in recent years the direct printer, a device that automatically receives electric impulses, translates them, and types messages ready for delivery.

radioactivity, disintegration (i.e. breaking down) of various elements of high atomic weights, with the emission of invisible rays ; discovered by the French scientist Henri Becquerel c.1896. The study of radioactivity was greatly advanced by Lord Rutherford and Professor Soddy.

Radiations include *alpha rays,* i.e. the expulsion of an alpha particle, which comprises a doubly positively charged helium atom ; also *beta radiation,* the beta particles being lighter electrons carrying a negative charge, often accompanied by the emission of *gamma rays* which, unlike the alpha and beta particles, are non-corpuscular, being very short waves that have great penetrating power.

During the process of radioactivity the element changes its nature. Thus, uranium becomes radium, then radon, then polonium ; finally lead. It is impossible to say when any one atom of a radioactive element will disintegrate, but we may calculate how long it will take *half* the atoms to break down, hence we usually speak of the *half-life period,* which may be a fraction of a second or millions of years, e.g. the half-life of uranium is 5,000,000,000 years, that of radium C^1 is c.0·001sec. Often the ' daughter ' of a ' parent ' radioactive atom is also radioactive.

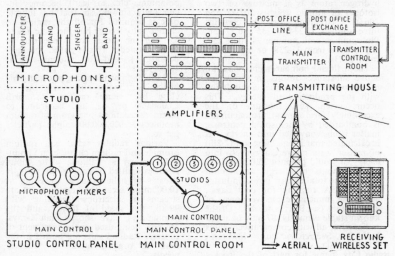

B.B.C. TRANSMISSIONS
How a Broadcast travels from the Studio to the Listener

ISOTOPES OF LITHIUM

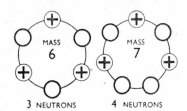

MASS 6 — 3 NEUTRONS   MASS 7 — 4 NEUTRONS

RADIOACTIVITY

The hydrogen nucleus is known as the *proton.* Uncharged particles with approximately the mass of the proton are called *neutrons.* A particle with the mass of an electron but a positive charge is a *positron.* An isotope of natural hydrogen, called heavy hydrogen or deuterium, has a nucleus called a *deuteron.* An ATOM consists of a small heavy nucleus, approximately 10^{-12}cm in diameter, surrounded by a 'large' region 10^{-8}cm in diameter, in which electrons move with immense speed. The nucleus carries a number of positive charges, each $1 \cdot 6 \times 10^{-19}$ coulombs in size, and each electron carries one negative charge of the same size, the number of electrons circling the nucleus being equal to the number of positive charges on the nucleus, so that the atom, as a whole, has a charge of zero. In many cases elements having identical chemical properties have slightly differing atomic masses. Such atoms are called *isotopes.* Ordinary lead of atomic weight 207·19 times that of the hydrogen atom is a mixture of two isotopes of atomic weights 207·77 and 206·08. Uranium normally contains three isotopes, U-234, U-235 and U-238. Plutonium, atomic number 94, mass 239, is produced from U-238, or more often from U-239.

The artificial bombardment of radioactive substances results in the *fission of atoms,* i.e. their partial annihilation with the production of energy. This occurs when, say, thorium or the exceedingly rare element protoactinium is bombarded by high-speed neutrons, matter being converted into energy. It is calculated that if one kilogram (2·2lb) of matter were converted *entirely* into energy, it would produce 25,000,000,000 kilowatt hours of energy, an amount equal to the total electric power industry in the USA running for *c.*60 days ; hence the immense explosive power of atom bombs (see PLATES 46, 47). Of the known stable elements, 87 may be made radioactive, all with comparatively short half-lives. See ATOMIC PILE ; MATTER ; RADIUM ; SELLAFIELD

Radio City, name for part of the Rockefeller Centre, New York ; comprises Radio City Music Hall, the largest indoor theatre in the world (seats 6,200), and also four other giant buildings, e.g. the RCA building (850ft high) in which are the HQ of the National Broadcasting Company.

radio colleges, see RADIO

radiogram, see GRAMOPHONE

radio heat, method of heating by induction. Articles are placed between plates charged with alternating current. Short wave radiations cause molecular friction inside. The invention is now applied in hundreds of ways, e.g. coating iron with a film of tin, setting plastic glues between layers of ply-wood, manufacturing superhard steels, etc.

radio-isotopes, see ISOTOPES

radiolocation, see RADAR

radio-pictures, see PHOTOTELEGRAPHY

radio-therapy, *-ther'ä-pi,* treatment of disease by using radioactive substances, e.g. radium salts ; also, the ionisation due to protons and X-rays. Radioactive phosphorus is used in treating diseases of the white blood cells.

radio waves, see WAVE-MOTION

radium, element, Ra ; one of a group of *c.*40 radioactive elements ; atomic weight *c.*226 ; atomic number 88 ; discovered 1902 by M. and Mme Curie ; found in small quantities in pitchblende. Its activity is due to the disintegration (or breaking down) of its atomic nuclei by the emission of alpha and beta particles and gamma energy radiation. After emitting an alpha particle, radium becomes radon. Radium B (atomic weight 214, atomic number 82) becomes radium C (atomic weight 214, atomic number 83) after the emission of a beta particle. The rate of disintegration of radium as a whole (from radium, radon, polonium, etc. to lead) becomes increasingly slower, so that an infinite time is required for all the radium to change into lead ; but the time taken for *half* the atoms to change can be exactly stated. This is called the half-period (T), and for radium this is 1,600 years.

Radium emanations fog photographic plates, and ionise and warm the air close by. Pure radium is worth £3,000,000 per oz, and according to recent calculations one gram of radium produces 35,000,000,000 alpha particles per sec.

Various radium salts, e.g. radium bromide and radium chloride, are popularly known as radium. The alpha particles emitted by radium are actually streams of helium nuclei travelling at 10,000m per sec. ; the beta particles are streams of electrons travelling with 99·8% the speed of light ; and the gamma rays, waves shorter than X-rays, are now being used in the treatment of cancer. Radium salts are buried in the flesh or organs, often in 'radium needles.'

Akin to radium are other naturally radioactive elements, e.g. *uranium,* U ;

heaviest natural element known ; a hard, white metal ; atomic weight $c.238$; atomic number 92, parent of radium ; found in the Great Bear Lake region, Canada and the Belgian Congo ; half-life $c.5,000,000,000$ years ; when impure comprises three isotopes, U-234, U-235 and U-238. From U-238 comes the element *plutonium*, a surprise for the scientists who, until recently, had imagined that there were 92 elements only. With atomic number 94, atomic weight 239, plutonium is of great importance in the production of atomic energy. *Thorium*, Th, is a radioactive element ; atomic number 90, atomic weight $c.232$; disintegrates with the emission of an alpha particle ; its oxide is found in Britain, but particularly in Brazil and India. *Protoactinium*, Pa, atomic weight 231, atomic number 91, is exceedingly rare in nature. *Polonium*, Po, named by Madame Curie after her native Poland, has atomic weight 210, atomic number 84 ; also known as radium F, as it is one of the stages from radium to lead. *Radon*, Rn, is a radioactive inert gas and element, atomic weight 222, atomic number 86 ; emits alpha particles. Another natural radioactive gas is *actinium emanation*, atomic number 86 ; its half-life is 3·9 sec. ; sometimes called actinon.

The amount of lead assumed to exist in the crust and interior of the globe has provided scientists with a method of calculating the age of the earth based on the rate of radium disintegration, the figure being $c.3,000,000,000$ years. See CYCLOTRON ; MATTER and especially RADIOACTIVITY. Refer also to CURIE, P. ; GREAT BEAR LAKE ; PITCHBLENDE

radium F, see POLONIUM

radius, *rā'di-ŭs*, in geometry, half the diameter of a circle. See CIRCLE

Radley College, public school near Oxford (but in Berkshire) founded 1847.

Radnorshire, *rad'nĕr-*, county of Wales ; co.tn Presteigne.

radon, see RADIOACTIVITY

Raeburn, SIR HENRY, *rā'bĕrn* (1756–1823), Scottish painter, born near Edinburgh ; excelled in portrait painting, of which he painted $c.1,000$. Raeburn is widely regarded as the greatest Scottish painter after Allan Ramsay and McTaggart.

RAF (Royal Air Force), British military air service ; governed by the Air Council, the president of which is the Secretary of State for Air.

The RAF was founded 1 April 1918 as a result of the amalgamation of the Royal Flying Corps and the Royal Air Service, two pioneer bodies which, in World War I, achieved remarkable success with little experience, crudely constructed aircraft developing only 80hp, and a small body of daring pilots. The RAF is the youngest of the three British armed forces, but in spite of this has a great and glorious tradition behind it. Its motto is *Per Ardua Ad Astra*

which may be translated : By steep high places to the stars.

At the outbreak of war in 1939 the Royal Air Force was inadequately equipped both with trained pilots and machines, and although men *were* being trained to pilot aircraft, and planes *were* being built, Great Britain at that period of the war had only a few fully trained, experienced pilots and some rather out-of-date Spitfires to defend her from the enemy.

In 1940, after the capitulation of the French army, the onslaught came, and on 11 August the Luftwaffe (Air Force) began the attack that was to pave the way for the invasion of Britain. Germany's savage attack was concentrated on the south-eastern counties of Great Britain. German aircraft came over in great numbers and were met by a mere handful of courageous fighter pilots who gallantly rose to meet the challenge. Every day for almost two months ' dog-fights ' between British and German planes took place over the south-east corner of Great Britain, often over the English Channel. Although vastly outnumbered by their opponents, the few British pilots proved the superiority of their fighting tactics, and the Hurricanes and Spitfires proved to be much more airworthy than the new German planes. Britain's losses were small ; Germany's very heavy.

After this great battle the Royal Air Force increased even more rapidly, and bombers were being sent in large numbers to attack shipping which had been gathered for the invasion of Britain. Germany's marshalling yards were bombed ; her factories, communications and war-time installations were wrecked by us. The Royal Air Force also protected convoys and waged a bitter war against U-boats which were trying to blockade Britain. After a grim struggle the Air Force succeeded in accounting for many of the U-boats, and the blockade menace ended. Close co-operation was maintained between the Air Force and the army in Italy and Normandy, also between the Air Force and the navy in sea-warfare ; in short, the Air Force was in all theatres of war where its help was needed most.

The maximum strength of bombers during the war was 7,700, and of fighters 6,900. Members of the Canadian, Australian, New Zealand and American Air Forces greatly assisted the Royal Air Force in its tremendous task, as did the survivors of the Dutch, Belgian, Norwegian, French and other Air Forces.

The Women's Auxiliary Air Force was founded 1939 and then numbered 1,700 ; in 1943 it had grown in number to 182,000. These women worked as aircraft mechanics, parachute packers, radio mechanics, meteorologists, radar operators/mechanics, clerks, storekeepers, etc., and released many men who were needed abroad. The WAAF also have a good record of foreign service.

For girls and boys who are air minded and who wish to join the regular Air Force there is the Air Training Corps (ATC) for boys, and the Girls' Training Corps (GTC) for girls. These corps give valuable training for future service life.

On 11 Jan 1949 a memorial window (designed by Hugh Easter) was unveiled at the Rolls-Royce Factory, Derby, in memory of the Battle of Britain Pilots. See BATTLE OF BRITAIN

raffia, split leaves of the raffia palm of tropical Africa and S. America ; after being dyed it is much used for weaving. Raffia provides excellent and inexpensive training in handicraft for young children.

Raffles, SIR STAMFORD (1781–1826), British administrator, born at sea off Jamaica ; founded (1819) the settlement of Singapore ; was the first president of the Zoological Society, London.

ragged robin, untidy-looking plant of damp places ; has a tough green and red stem, lance-shaped leaves in pairs ; flowers on short stalks, the pink petals deeply cleft.

Raikes, ROBERT, *rāks* (1735–1811), *b* Gloucester. A pioneer of prison reform, he is best remembered as the founder (in Gloucester) of the first Sunday School 1780.

rail, name of several varieties of British birds, including the water-rail (11in long), found among marshes and fens. The plumage is olive brown above, grey below. The beak is red. The rail nests among sedges.

railcars, see RAILWAYS

railways may be said to have begun in the Newcastle district *c.*1676 when wagons or trams of coal were hauled by horses along wooden rails. The first steam traction was due to Richard Trevithick (S. Wales) 1804 ; the first passenger railway employing steam was the Stockton and Darlington, opened 1825, its locomotive (*Locomotion*) designed by George Stephenson. *Locomotion*, weighing 7 tons, had a maximum speed of 8mph. The opening of the Liverpool and Manchester Railway, 1830, made railway history, George Stephenson's *Rocket* hauling a load of 17 tons at what was then regarded as the amazing speed of 29mph.

At first there was much opposition to steam railways. Farmers feared that crops would be burned by sparks from the chimneys ; devout people declared that God had never intended men to travel so quickly ; landowners refused to allow the track to cross their estates, or consented only on payment of large sums as compensation ; owners of stage-coaches opposed the innovation, but the work of building a vast railway system went on, and by 1913 British railways, owning nearly 24,000m of permanent way, were regularly carrying

*c.*1,600,000,000 passengers a year, and 568,000,000 tons of freight.

From 1922 until 1947 our chief railways were the Great Western ; London and North Eastern ; London, Midland and Scottish ; and the Southern.

Under the Transport Act 1947 the railways were nationalised, and a single railway system was formed 1 Jan 1948 under the title British Railways.

The standard gauge for British (and most other) railways is 4ft 8½in, measured between the *insides* of the rails. Rails, rolled from steel ingots, are commonly 60ft long, though rails twice as long are coming into use. The rail-joint is secured by fish-plates with holes slightly larger than the bolts, thus providing for expansion and contraction. A gradient exceeding 1 in 200 is considered steep on main lines. The outer rail on a curve is raised to counteract the train's tendency to leave the rails when travelling at speed, owing to the effect of centrifugal force. Points are used for transferring rolling stock and locomotives from one line to another ; the control is usually at the signal-box, where a system of electric control is now replacing that of the heavy hand-lever. Arm-signalling has undergone considerable change in recent years, and is being replaced by electric signalling devices, notably by colour-light signals. Since 1949 Doncaster has had an all-electric self-operating signal-box.

Steam locomotives are classed according to the arrangement of their wheels. Thus, the ' Pacific ' class with 4 leading bogie wheels, 6 coupled driving wheels, and 2 trailing wheels, is designated 4-6-2. Similarly, British locomotives of the ' Atlantic ' class are 4-4-2 (for express and ordinary trains) ; a ' Mikado ' is 2-8-2 ; a ' Mogul ' 2-6-0. The *Cock o' the North* (formerly L & NE) was originally of the ' Mikado ' class, (166 tons), but was rebuilt as a 4-6-2 in 1944. Passenger locomotives have usually large driving wheels, 6ft 2in to 6ft 9in diameter ; freight locomotives have small wheels 4ft 7in to 5ft 3in diameter. General purpose engines, suitable for passenger or freight traffic, and having wheels 5ft 8in to 6ft 2in diameter, are now finding increasing favour. The first streamlined locomotive and train in Britain was the *Silver Jubilee* (L & NE) 1935 ; and as a typical passenger train of pre-war days we may take the LMS *Coronation Scot*, hauled by one of the streamlined ' Pacific' locomotives, e.g. *Coronation, Queen Elizabeth, Queen Mary, Princess Alice* or *Princess Alexandra*. *Coronation* (like the others) is of the 4-6-2 ' Pacific' type, hauling a train weighing 297 tons (exclusive of locomotive and tender) Euston–Glasgow (401·4m) in 6½ hours at an average speed of 61·8 mph. The tender carries 10 tons of coal and 4,000 gallons of water. Steam pressure is

250lb per sq.in. The train, originally painted blue and silver, was withdrawn on the outbreak of war in 1939. The engines had their streamlining removed in 1946.

The *King George V* locomotive (4-6-0) weighs 135 tons 14cwt, and has a tractive effort of 40,300lb.

In 1938 the new streamlined 'Pacific' *Mallard* attained a speed of 126mph on a test run, hauling a load of 240 tons.

There are now *c.*2,500m of electrified track in Britain, the former SR owning a large proportion. Since 1942 this region has been operating a new electric locomotive, a box-type cab with two 6-wheel bogie-trucks. The boiler, electrically fired, supplies steam to heat the passenger coaches. Acceleration with a 1,000-ton freight train is 24mph in 100 secs., and a speed of 75mph is maintained with heavy loads. Much attention has been given recently to the development of *diesel railcars* which burn heavy oil, some of these travelling 75–80mph. Scientists and engineers are now working on plans for operating railways by atomic energy, and there are indications that electrification may be widely extended, and that new sources of power may be employed ; nevertheless it seems likely that coal will be retained for some considerable time, especially since the American invention (1945) of a new method of using this fuel. The latest power unit for locomotives is a *gas-turbine* burning atomised coal that has been cleansed from cinder, and is sprayed into the furnace. Great possibilities lie in this invention.

Luxurious British trains have included the *Cheltenham Flyer* (GW) ; *Coronation* (LNER) ; *Coronation Scot* (LMS) ; *Golden Arrow* (SR) ; and among other notable trains is the *Flying Scotsman.* The world's longest regular non-stop run was made by the LNER, when prior to the outbreak of war in 1939 the *Flying Scotsman* made its daily run in summer in both directions without intermediate stop between King's Cross and Edinburgh (392·7m). This non-stop running was resumed in 1948, and during the period of diversion following the flood damage in SE. Scotland in that year an actual non-stop run of 408·5m was achieved by the *Flying Scotsman* when working over the temporary route.

A new type of locomotive ordered 1947 is intended to be jet-propelled. It is designed to draw 18 coaches (about 575 tons) at 90mph, the power-unit being a gas-turbine driving a generator. Running costs are expected to be low, and the fuel will be cheaper than diesel oil.

The railway colours of the six regions of British Railways are now : *Eastern,* dark blue ; *London Midland,* maroon ; *North Eastern,* orange ; *Southern,* dark green ; *Scottish,* light green ; *Western,*

chocolate. British Railways own 19,790 locomotives ; and passenger trains run over 241,000,000m a year.

Notable railways overseas include the first empire railway, built in British Guiana 1848 ; the Australian railways, including the Transcontinental, crossing the Nullarbor Plain, the longest dead straight track in the world (328m) ; the NZ railways with the famous ' K ' class of 4-8-4 locomotives hauling heavy trains up steep inclines ; the Canadian Pacific which has been operating since 1885, and links Vancouver and Montreal (2,898m) ; the Canadian National Railway, with its famous 4-8-4 locomotives weighing 350 tons ; the USA railways covering 250,000m, and including the *Pennsylvania Ltd* (New York–Chicago), *Broadway Ltd,* with a run of 980m, and *Twentieth Century Ltd,* comprising 12 Pullmans, covering 960m at an average speed of 60mph, drawn by a ' Hudson ' locomotive (4-6-4) of unusual appearance. The USA Union Pacific has a streamlined diesel engine drawing 3 cars at 110mph from New York to Los Angeles. The USA boasts the two longest locomotives in the world, *Black Boy,* with a wheel arrangement of 4-8-8-4, the overall length being 85ft 3in, the indicated hp 7,000, and a locomotive on the Chesapeake and Ohio Railway. This is 154ft long. Among Soviet trains is the mammoth *A. Andreev,* a 4-14-4 locomotive weighing 328 tons, and capable of hauling a train of 2,500 tons over heavy grades. Some French trains now run on pneumatic tyres, e.g. the Paris–Strasbourg train.

Read *The Railway Magazine,* and *Scottish Railways,* O. S. Nock (Nelson). For model railways, read *Meccano Magazine.* Consult also *Whitaker's Almanack* for the most recent railway facts and figures. See PLATES 54, 55

rain, see ATMOSPHERE ; CLIMATE

rainbow, colour effect caused by refraction of light by drops of rain. The observer with his back to the sun sees a series of concentric rings of colour produced by light being broken (as by a prism) into the colours of the spectrum (red, orange, yellow, green, blue and violet). . See PLATE I

raisin, *rä′zn,* dried grape ; largely imported from California, France, Spain, Australia, Asia Minor, Greece and Turkey, the latter being the chief source of the sultana, a seedless variety.

rajah, *rä′jä,* Indian title for king, though often applied to native princes and nobles. The feminine is ranee.

Rajasthan, union of various Indian states (1947) once part of Rajputana.

Rajputana, former British agency, India : area over 132,000sq.m. It is south of the Punjab, and though fertile in the south is sandy and ill-watered in the north. Of its 23 states, 15 joined to make the Union of Rajasthan in 1947.

Raleigh, SIR WALTER, *ral′i* ; *raw′li* (*d* 1618),

soldier, sailor, courtier, pioneer, poet, historian, born (probably *c.*1552) Hayes Barton, near Budleigh Salterton, Devon ; accompanied his half-brother, Sir Humphrey Gilbert, on a voyage of discovery 1578, and reached the W. Indies. He helped to crush a rebellion in Ireland 1580, and became one of Queen Elizabeth's favourite courtiers.

Knighted 1584, he was given 40,000 acres in Munster 1586, where he was regarded as a good landlord, and was among the first to grow tobacco and potatoes in Britain. His marriage with Elizabeth Throgmorton displeased the queen, who banished him from court. Raleigh's arrogance and greed made him exceedingly unpopular, but he won new favour with the queen by his famous voyage 1595 to the Orinoco (his search for El Dorado, a land supposed to be fabulously rich in gold and jewels), the adventure being brilliantly described in his book *The Discovery of Guiana.*

With the Earl of Essex he shared in the Cadiz expedition. He was MP for Dorset 1597, and assisted in suppressing Essex's rebellion, but at the accession of James I (1603) he was charged with plotting against the king, and after an unfair trial was condemned to death. Reprieved when on the scaffold, he was confined in the Tower of London till 1616, when he prepared another expedition to the Orinoco, hoping to return with gold which was badly needed by the king. Raleigh promised not to fight the Spaniards, but a fight ensued, and on his return he was basely arrested, charged again with treason, and executed.

It is undoubtedly true that Raleigh had not the influence on history which some writers have attributed to him, but he played an important part in British colonisation. Having received permission 1584 to found a colony across the Atlantic, he fitted out an expedition which planted itself in what is now N. Carolina, probably on Roanoke I. This colony, which he named Virginia after the virgin queen, Elizabeth, was the first of several inspired by him, and though all his attempts at colonisation failed, his efforts bore rich fruit in later years. The story that Raleigh won the favour of Queen Elizabeth by placing his jewelled cloak across a puddle is probably *only* a story.

ram, see SHEEP

Ramadier, PAUL (1888–   ), French Socialist statesman ; Prime Minister 1947.

RAMC, see NURSING

Rameses, *ram'ē-sēz,* name of eleven kings (Pharaohs) of ancient Egypt, among whom the most important was Rameses II (1300–1225BC). The 4th king of the XIXth dynasty, and styled Rameses the Great, he made war against the Hittites 1296BC ; built vast temples, tombs. etc., at Thebes, Abu Simbel and Karnak.

Ramillies, see SPANISH SUCCESSION, WAR OF

Ramsay, ALLAN, *ram'zi* (1713–84), Scottish portrait-painter ; travelled widely in France and Italy ; settled in London 1756 ; painted portraits of many of the great men and women of his day, one of his best portraits being that of Jean Jacques Rousseau (now in the National Gallery of Scotland). Ramsay's painting is distinguished not quite so much by its technical capacity as by its remarkable intellectual integrity and clarity of vision.

Allan Ramsay the painter was the son of ALLAN RAMSAY the poet (1686–1758), whose *Evergreen* and other collections of Scottish poetry did much in the period following the Union of Parliaments to keep alive in Scotland love of Scottish poetry and of the Scottish language.

Ramsay, SIR WILLIAM (1852–1916), noted chemist, *b* Glasgow ; discovered krypton, zenon and neon, the latter giving rise to neon lighting ; also (with Lord Rayleigh) discoverer of argon ; most famous for his discovery of helium, a product of radium emanation.

Ramsgate, fishing port and holiday town, Kent ; pop.33,000.

Rand or **Witwatersrand,** *rand* ; *wit-wä'tĕrs-ränt,* gold-mining region, Transvaal, S. Africa. The gold-bearing reefs extend *c.*40m, and have been mined since *c.*1886. Johannesburg is the centre of the goldfield said to be the richest in the world. See PLATE 34

ranee, see RAJAH

Rangers, see GIRL GUIDES

Rangoon, *rang-goon,* chief city and port, Lower Burma ; pop.400,000. It is 20m from the mouth of the Rangoon R. ; and near is the famous 6th. c. Shwe Dagon Pagoda, a place of pilgrimage for Buddhists. Rangoon exports teak, rice, petroleum, ivory and cotton.

Rangoon suffered much at the hands of the Japanese, who occupied it for a time in World War II.

Ranjitsinhji, KUMAR SHRI, *run-jĕt-sing* (1872–1933), Indian prince ; became Maharaja of Nawangar 1906 ; served in World War I ; helped to found the Chamber of Princes ; best known in Britain as a famous cricketer.

Rank, JOSEPH ARTHUR (1888–   ), shares in the management of a great milling firm ; best known for his influence in the British film industry, controlling companies with assets of over £50,000,000 ; chairman of seventy or more companies, including Odeon Theatre, Ltd and the Gaumont Picture Corporation.

Ransome, ARTHUR, writer of boys' books, e.g. *Peter Duck.*

rape, plant of the cabbage family (*Cruciferae*) ; grown as fodder or for its seeds, from which vegetable oil is extracted.

Raphael, *raf'ā-el* (1483–1520), Italian artist, *b* Urbino ; a contemporary of Michelangelo and Leonardo da Vinci ; was also an architect and a designer of tapestries and goldplate ; excelled in story-pictures and portraits ; blended colour to perfection. Appointed chief architect of St Peter's (Rome) 1514, he also adorned with paintings many walls of the Vatican.

Raphael, rich and immensely popular, was the handsome and lovable friend of kings, popes and common people. His many famous paintings include *Cupid and Psyche* ; the *Madonna della Sedia*, a classic ideal of peasant motherhood : the *Sistine Madonna* ; and his unfinished *Transfiguration*.

In Raphael the spirit of the Renaissance blossomed fully, but his lack of deep spiritual qualities led eventually to the art-school of the Pre-Raphaelites, i.e. English artists who from *c*.1850 revived sincerity in painting, e.g. Rossetti, Millais and Burne-Jones.

rare earths, elements (atomic numbers 57–71) similar in chemical properties, and all exceedingly rare. They include lanthanum, cerium, samarium, europium gadolinium, terbium, holmium, erbium and thulium.

raspberry, common weak-stemmed shrub (family *Rosaceae*) of Europe ; much cultivated for its fruit, actually a collection of drupes.

Rasputin, GREGORY, *räs-pu'tĕn* (*d* 1916), Russian fanatic who, though born poor in Siberia, eventually exercised immense influence, and was the actual power behind the government till he was murdered for intrigues with Germany.

rat, fierce animal (rodent) with a naked and scaly tail ; usually lives in a hole in the ground ; found the world-over except in very cold regions. The two varieties in Britain are (*a*) the black rat, with greyish hair above, pale yellow below ; and (*b*) the brown rat, larger and more heavily built. Rats carry a flea sometimes infested with the bacteria of bubonic plague.

RATS
The Brown Rat and the Black Rat

England alone is believed to have at least 50,000,000 rats, and the damage for which they are directly responsible is estimated at £100,000,000 a year.

rates, see HOUSE

ratio, in mathematics, the relation with regard to size of one quantity to another of the same kind, e.g. one length may be twice as great as another, one sum of money one third of another, one speed may be half as great as another, one weight three-fifths of another. In general one quantity divided by another gives the ratio of the 1st to the 2nd. Thus the ratio of £10 to £6 $= \frac{10}{6}$ or $\frac{5}{3}$, usually written 5 : 3, the 5 being known as the *antecedent*, the 3 as the *consequent*.

A numerical ratio should generally be expressed as between 2 integers in their lowest terms. As shown above (i.e. $\frac{10}{6} = \frac{5}{3}$), the terms of a ratio can be divided by a common factor, e.g. 40 : 60 = 2 : 3, each term being divided by the common factor 20 ; similarly they can be multiplied by a common factor, e.g. $\frac{5}{6} : \frac{3}{4} = 10 : 9$, each term being multiplied by the LCM of the denominators (12). Similarly also the ratio $\frac{1}{7} : \frac{1}{8} : \frac{1}{9} = 72 : 63 : 56$.

To divide, say £1, in the ratio 7 : 5, it is clear that there must be 7 + 5 or 12 equal shares in 2 groups of 7 and 5. Hence the shares are $\frac{7}{12} \times$ £1 and $\frac{5}{12} \times$ £1, i.e. 11s 8d and 8s 4d. Similarly, to divide (say) a flock of 235 sheep into three groups in the ratio $\frac{1}{3} : \frac{1}{4} : \frac{1}{5}$, this ratio must first become 20 : 15 : 12, giving 47 small groups. Hence the groups will contain (*a*) $\frac{20}{47} \times 235$, (*b*) $\frac{15}{47} \times 235$, and (*c*) $\frac{12}{47} \times 235$ sheep respectively, i.e. 100 sheep, 75 sheep and 60 sheep.

If the antecedents of 2 ratios be multiplied, also their consequents, the ratios are said to be compounded, and the result is the compound ratio of the original ratios ; thus, $ax : by$ is the compound ratio of $a : b$ and $x : y$. If $a : b$ is compounded with itself it gives $a^2 : b^2$, which is called the duplicate ratio of $a : b$. Similarly $a^3 : b^3$ is the triplicate ratio of $a : b$. Likewise $\sqrt{a} : \sqrt{b}$, of $a : b$, is called the sub-duplicate ratio of $a : b$; and $\sqrt[3]{a} : \sqrt[3]{b}$ the subtriplicate ratio.

What is known generally as the ' k ' method is extremely useful in establishing the truth of many propositions on ratio. For example, if
$(a : b) = (c : d) = (e : f)$
prove that each ratio $=$
$(a + c + e) : (b + d + f)$
Let $\frac{a}{b} = \frac{c}{d} = \frac{e}{f} = k$
Then $a = bk$, $c = dk$, $e = fk$ (i)
$\therefore$ by addition $a + c + e = k(b + d + e)$
$$\therefore k = \frac{a + c + e}{b + d + f}$$
Also we can prove that each ratio $=$
$$\left(\frac{pa^n + gc^n + re^n}{pb^n + gd^n + rf^n} \right) \frac{1}{n}$$

19

From (i) $pa^n = pb^n k^n$, $gc^n = gd^n k^n$, $re^n = rf^n k^n$

$\therefore$ by addition $pa^n + gc^n + re^n = k^n$ $(pb^n + gd^n + rf^n)$

$\therefore k^n = \dfrac{pa^n + gc^n + re^n}{pb^n + gd^n + rf^n}$

$\therefore k = \left(\dfrac{pa^n + gc^n + re^n}{pb^n + gd^n + rf^n}\right)\dfrac{1}{n}$

If the ratios of a to b and c to d are equal, the fact may be written either as $a : b = c : d$ or $a : b :: c : d$. The latter form is read ' a is to b as c is to d,' but is seldom used. These four quantities are said to be proportionals or in proportion, and a and d are called the *extremes*, b and c the *means*. Writing the ratios as fractions and cross multiplying, it follows that $ad = bc$. Hence when four quantities are in proportion the product of the extremes is equal to the product of the means. It also follows that the two ratios may be reversed, the *extremes* exchanged, or the *means* exchanged, thus

$a : b = c : d$

$\therefore \quad b : a = d : c$

and $\quad d : b = c : a$

also $\quad a : c = b : d$

If any 3 of the quantities a, b, c, d are known, the 4th can be found from $ad = bc$. Quantities are said to be in *continued proportion* when the 1st is to the 2nd as the 2nd is to the 3rd, as the 3rd is to the 4th, and so on. If a, b, c, d . . . are such numbers, then $\dfrac{a}{b} = \dfrac{b}{c} = \dfrac{c}{d}$ . . . When this is true, a, b, c, d . . . are in Geometrical Progression.

In the simple case of $a : b = b : c$ it follows that $b^2 = ac$, whence $b = \pm \sqrt{ac}$ so b is the Mean Proportional of a and c, and has the value of $\pm \sqrt{ac}$, which is also the Geometric Mean between a and c. Note also that c is the Third Proportional to a and b, and has the value $\dfrac{b^2}{a}$

Exercises on ratio and proportion are of very frequent occurrence in numerical work, and are named *simple* when two units are concerned ; otherwise they are *compound*. The two ways of manipulating ratio and proportion are (*a*) unitary method, and (*b*) method of ratio.

As an example of the unitary method note :

If 9 articles cost £54, how much will 17 cost?

9 articles cost £54

$\therefore$ 1 article costs $\dfrac{£54}{9}$

$\therefore$ 17 articles cost $\dfrac{£54}{9} \times 17 = £102.$

As an example of the method of ratio note :

If 5 men reap a field of 40 acres in 4 days of 9 hours a day, in how many days of 8 hours each will 6 men reap 64 acres?

First write the units in a row, *the answer unit being last.* Copy the actual number in the sum thus :

men	acres	hr. per day	days
5	40	9	4
6	64	8	x

Begin by writing $\dfrac{4}{1}$. This $\dfrac{4}{1}$ is to be multiplied by a fraction from each column as a ratio. In the first column the change from 5 men to 6 would tend to lessen the number of days in which the work could be completed ; in the 2nd column the change from 40 acres to 64 would tend to increase the number of days ; in the 3rd column the change from 9 hours per day to 8 tends to increase the number of days. Hence the result is found thus $x = \dfrac{4}{1} \times \dfrac{5}{6} \times \dfrac{64}{40} \times \dfrac{9}{8}$ which cancels to 6 days.

rationing, generally means equal sharing of goods, especially food, in times of shortage, e.g. to troops cut off from supplies, explorers when food is running out, but used, in particular, for a system adopted in, say, Britain, during World War I to ensure that all (rich and poor alike) could buy at least a minimum amount of essential foods.

During and since World War II British civilians have had *ration books* (buff for adults, blue for juniors, green for a small child) with pages of *coupons* or *points* for various foodstuffs, e.g. meat, eggs, cheese, bacon, sugar, tinned fruits, sweets, etc. From time to time the Ministry of Food makes known the coupon or points value of a commodity. Bread rationing in force 1946–48. As recently as Dec 1950 the meat ration was diminished.

See also CLOTHING COUPONS; DOCKET; UTILITY

Ratisbon, city, Bavaria ; also known as Regensburg ; on the R. Danube ; pop.81,000.

rattan, genus of palm, especially of India ; has feathery leaves 3–4ft long. The stems are used for making canes, walking-sticks and cane-bottomed chairs.

Rattigan, TERENCE (1912–   ), playwright, *b* London ; his plays include *The Winslow Boy.*

rattlesnake, see SNAKE

raven, see CROW

Ravenna, *rä-ven'ä*, city, Italy, 6m from the Adriatic ; noted for its ancient walls and many churches, including a cathedral. Dante's tomb is here. The manufactures include lace, silk and glass ; pop.82,000. See PLATE 68 (*bottom*)

Rawalpindi, *rä-wul-pin'dē*, town, Punjab, Pakistan ; trades with Kashmir ; pop. 181,000.

Rawtenstall, town, Lancashire ; has coal mines, also cotton and woollen mills ; pop.29,000.

ray, name for various fish with flattened bodies, broad fins and eggs in horny cases (often called mermaids' purses).

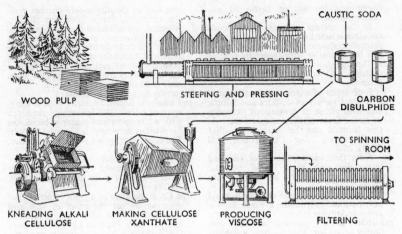

CAUSTIC SODA

CARBON DISULPHIDE

WOOD PULP

STEEPING AND PRESSING

TO SPINNING ROOM

KNEADING ALKALI CELLULOSE

MAKING CELLULOSE XANTHATE

PRODUCING VISCOSE

FILTERING

STAGES IN THE PRODUCTION OF RAYON

The skate is one of the commonest rays. See SKATE.

Ray, JOHN (1627–1705), English naturalist. The Ray Society was founded (1844) in his honour.

Rayleigh, LORD, *rā'li* (1842–1919), scientist, *b* Essex ; he was notable for his investigations in electro-magnetics, atomic weights of gases and wave-motion ; joint discoverer with Sir William Ramsay of argon.

Raymond, ERNEST, *rā'm'nd* (1888–   ), English novelist. His books include *Tell England* ; *The Jesting Army* ; and *The Kilburn Tale.*

rayon, name adopted to replace the unsuitable term ' artificial silk ' for manufactured fibres. The raw materials are chiefly cotton linters (very short fibres covering the cotton seed) or purified wood pulp ; the resulting fibres can be woven into a great variety of fabrics, and, in the form of rayon staple fibre, can be mixed with cotton and wool.

The two principal types of rayon are made by the viscose and acetate processes. In the former, developed by Courtaulds Ltd, cellulose is made into sheets, and treated with caustic soda to form alkali cellulose, later treated with carbon disulphide to form cellulose xanthate. This is dissolved in dilute caustic soda, giving viscose solution. After an important period of ripening, the viscose is forced under even pressure through minute holes into a spinning-bath containing dilute sulphuric acid ; this regenerates cellulose in the form of

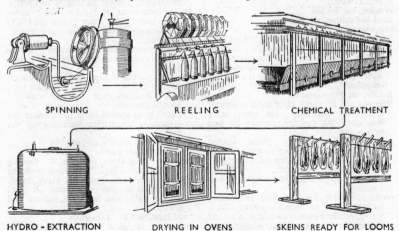

SPINNING

REELING

CHEMICAL TREATMENT

HYDRO - EXTRACTION

DRYING IN OVENS

SKEINS READY FOR LOOMS

FURTHER STAGES IN RAYON PRODUCTION

continuous threads of rayon of any desired fineness.

In the acetate process, the original cellulose is acted on by acetic anhydride, forming cellulose acetate. A solution of this in acetone is ' dry-spun ' by forcing it through fine holes, evaporating the acetone, and collecting the continuous threads.

Both types of rayon can be produced in a great variety of colours and effects, and used either as continuous filaments or in the form of short staple fibre ; in this form it can be spun with other textile fibres. See CELLULOSE ; and PLATE 26

Note that various kinds of seaweed (especially one kind found on the Scottish coast) are now being made into rayon.

Synthetic fibres based on casein, vinyl polymers and polyamides are now known commercially as nylon.

razorbill, British seabird of the auk family ; *c*.17in long ; has greenish-black plumage above, brown throat, white below. The beak is large and flattened.

Reade, CHARLES (1814–84) author ; *b* Oxfordshire ; wrote a number of plays, but is better known for his novels, e.g. *Peg Woffington* ; *It is Never Too Late To Mend* ; *Hard Cash* ; and (most famous of all) *The Cloister and the Hearth.* A masterly story of life in the 15th c., the latter is generally regarded as one of our most notable historical novels.

Reading, *red'ing,* co.tn, Berkshire ; noted as an agricultural centre, also for seeds, biscuits and engineering. Its university dates from 1926. An aerodrome was opened (at Woodley) 1929 ; pop.109,000.

Reading, city, Pennsylvania, USA ; centre of a coal and iron mining district ; pop.110,000.

reading, see BOOKS

Real-is-Positive, see LIGHT

reasoning, see BRAIN

Réaumur, RENÉ DE, *rā-ō-mūr'* (1683–1757), French scientist, *b* La Rochelle ; notable as the inventor of the Réaumur thermometer, on which the boiling-point of water is 80°. See THERMOMETER

' Recessional,' see KIPLING, RUDYARD

Recife, see PERNAMBUCO

Recorder, in England, chief legal officer of a city or borough. He must be a barrister. At quarter sessions he acts as a judge.

rectangle, in geometry, plane 4-sided figure in which the angles are all right angles, and the opposite sides parallel ; area = length × breadth. See AREA ; PARALLELOGRAM ; QUADRILATERAL FIGURE

rectifier, device for changing alternating current (AC) to direct current (DC). Valve rectifiers usually consist of a heated filament and a second electrode acting as anode in a glass bulb free of air and similar to radio receiving valves. During one half of the alternating current cycle the electrons, freed from the glowing filament, are attracted to the anode, and carry the current, but during the other half of the cycle the anode is at a negative potential, hence the electrons cannot flow across. Metal rectifiers have replaced valve rectifiers for many purposes when only a small current is required.

recurring decimal, see DECIMALS

red admiral, British butterfly with a wing-span of *c*.3in. The fore-wings are black with white spots and a scarlet band. the hind-wings brown with a scarlet border. The caterpillar, green with yellow spines, feeds on nettles.

Red Army, see USSR

Redcar, holiday town on the N. Yorkshire coast ; noted for its fine sands ; pop. 24,000.

Red Cross, emblem of a great international organisation for the relief of sick and wounded in war and during famines and plagues ; founded by Henri Dunant (1828–1910), a Swiss who witnessed the suffering of casualties in the battle of Solferino 1859. Between 1864 and 1907 over fifty governments agreed to the principles of the International Red Cross Society. The HQ are at Geneva. In World Wars I and II the organisation did fine work in distributing food and other parcels to prisoners of war. See NURSING

Redditch, *red'ich,* town, Worcestershire, 15m from Birmingham ; manufactures pins and needles, cycles and motor cars, etc. ; pop.25,000.

Red Flag, symbol of international Socialism, also the national flag of USSR since 1917.

redpoll, British song-bird related to the linnet. A winter visitor, its plumage is reddish-brown above ; the bird has a crimson crown, pink breast, white underparts ; feeds on insects and seeds.

Red River, river of N. America ; flows 700m into L. Winnipeg ; also (in USA) a tributary of the Mississippi ; length 1,600m.

Redruth, *-rooth,* town, Cornwall ; centre of a tin and copper mining district ; pop. 35,000.

Red Sea, part of the Indian Ocean between Arabia and NE. Africa ; *c*.1,200m long and 100–200m wide ; linked with the Mediterranean by the Suez Canal. Possibly so named from the minute red organisms sometimes seen among the reefs.

Redskins, see AMERICAN INDIANS

Red Square, see LENIN ; MOSCOW

redstart, migratory song-bird visiting England Apr.–Sept. The cock bird has bluish-grey plumage with a black throat and bright reddish underparts. It nests in old walls, and feeds on insects and grubs.

' red tape,' see BUREAUCRACY

reduction, *rē-dŭk'sh'n,* in chemistry, the process opposite to oxidation ; thus reduction means removing oxygen from

THE REDSTART

THE REDWING

a compound, or the addition of hydrogen, or the decrease in the percentage of the electronegative part of a compound. This actually involves the addition of one or more electrons to the atom, or group of atoms, whereas oxidation is the removal of one or more electrons.

redwing, British song-bird related to the thrush, which it greatly resembles in appearance. It feeds on insects ; has a clear, loud song, and is a winter visitor to Britain.

redwood, see SEQUOIA

reed-bunting, see BUNTING

reefing, partly furling a sail. A sail has a number of short pieces of rope called reefing points. By tying them round the boom or yard-arm the sail is shortened, thus reducing the sail-area presented to the wind.

reel, Scottish national dance for two or more couples, usually to the accompaniment of bagpipes or the fiddle. It is circular, with quick, gliding movements, and often a graceful forming of the figure eight.

reeve, see VILLEIN

referendum, in politics and civics, method of deciding an issue by referring it, not to the representatives of the people (e.g. a Parliament) but to the people themselves. Thus Switzerland decided by a referendum 1920 to join the League of Nations. In USA many affairs in individual states are decided by a referendum, as also in Australia.

Reform Acts, formerly known as Representation of the People Acts, measures extending the franchise (right to vote in Parliamentary elections). The first, or great, Reform Act was passed in 1832,

having been introduced by Lord John Russell. Prior to this, many large industrial towns had no MP, while some of the so-called rotten and pocket-boroughs (e.g. Old Sarum, little more than a heap of ruins) had two. The 1832 Reform Act abolished many of the pocket-boroughs, gave the vote to town dwellers who paid an annual rent of £10, and created twenty-two new boroughs.

Later Reform Acts were those of 1867 when Disraeli extended the vote to householders rated for poor relief, to lodgers, thus increasing the electoral role from 1,353,000 to 2,243,000 ; Gladstone's third Reform Act 1884, when 2,500,000 voters were added to the register ; the Act of 1918, which gave the vote to women over 30, and made various other changes, the electorate of the UK being increased to over 21,500,000 ; and the Act of 1928, giving the vote to practically every man and woman of 21 and over. See ELECTION

Reformation, *ref-or-mā'shon,* religious and political revolution or reconstruction in Europe ; may be said to have begun in the 14th c. with John Wycliffe in England, John Huss in Bohemia, though it did not become an irresistible force till the 16th century.

For long Europe had been Catholic. Men were taught that the will of God could be known only as it was interpreted by the Church, i.e. by the pope in Rome and by the priests ; but pope and priests alike were far from being spiritual ; indeed, the Church had become largely political ; it also demanded the payment of heavy dues, and had accumulated vast wealth. Rivalry between opposing popes (those of Avignon 1378–1449 being antagonists of those at Rome) led to doubts about papal authority, and the New Learning and the more critical spirit fostered by the Renaissance (see RENAISSANCE) caused still further dissatisfaction, and still more questioning of the practices of the Church.

All this unrest came to a head when Pope Leo X attempted to raise money by selling indulgences (pardons for sin) on a large scale and at higher prices than had been done before. This roused Martin Luther (1483–1546), the great German reformer, who nailed to the door of a church at Wittenberg (1517) a list of ninety-five criticisms of indulgences.

The striking of this match set all Europe ablaze. Luther's followers became known as Protestants because they *protested* against the doctrines and practices of the Roman Church ; they held that all the guidance needed for right living was to be found in the Bible. This guidance, of course, could be variously interpreted, as it was in many forms of Protestantism, e.g. the beliefs of the Swiss reformer, Zwingli, and those of John Calvin (1509–64), who founded a new faith (Calvinism) in Switzerland, 1536, from which sprang the Huguenots of France, and the Presbyterian Church of Scotland—a development of Calvinism taken there by John Knox.

In England the Reformation was hastened by Henry VIII's quarrel with the pope over the divorce of Catherine of Aragon, which led to Henry's repudiation of papal authority ; and by the general wish of the middle classes for independence from all foreign control. In consequence came the suppression of the monasteries 1536–39, and (later) the Protestant reforms of Edward VI and Elizabeth. See BIBLE ; CHURCH ; LUTHER, MARTIN

reformatory, see APPROVED SCHOOLS

refraction of light, so-called ' bending ' of a ray of light passing from one medium to another, e.g. air to water or glass. If an incident ray (AP) in air enter, say, a denser medium, glass, at the point of incidence (P), the refracted ray (PB) is refracted towards the normal, i.e. a line (QR) perpendicular to the refracting medium. The refractive index of a medium (μ) is the ratio of the sine of the angle of incidence (APQ) to the sine of the angle of refraction (BPR) when light is refracted from air (or a vacuum) into the medium.

The chief scientific application of the principles of refraction is in the lens (the basis of telescopes, microscopes and cameras) ; the correction of optical defects in the eye ; and the prism, the basis of all spectroscopic instruments. In nature, refractive effects often pass unnoticed, but examples include the foreshortening of objects under water, mirages, the apparent wavy motion of distant objects viewed through intervening rising air on a hot day. See LIGHT ; REFRACTIVE INDEX

refractive index (μ), in physics, is given by

$$a^{\mu}b \quad \frac{\text{velocity of light in medium A}}{\text{velocity of light in medium B}}$$

or

$$\frac{\sin i}{\sin r}$$

where i = angle of incidence, r = angle of refraction.

refrigeration, method of keeping things cold artificially in order to prevent them from going bad, e.g. food, milk, flowers, blood-plasma for surgical use, etc. A refrigerator may induce cold by alternately expanding and compressing air or ammonia ; or carbonic acid or sulphurous acid may be vaporised and recompressed to liquid form. On a large scale, meat is chilled, and thus is preserved for weeks ; and in recent years the domestic refrigerator has won increasing favour.

' Quick-freezing,' i.e. reducing the temperature to 30° below zero almost instantly, preserves the flavour and vitamins of fruits and vegetables indefinitely.

regelation, *rē-je-lā'shon*, term first used by Faraday for freezing caused by removing pressure. Two blocks of ice under pressure melt slightly. When the pressure is removed the water thus formed immediately freezes again (i.e. regelation takes place), and the blocks are united. Regelation accounts for your ability to make a snowball—the particles of ice melt slightly under the pressure of your hands, and become ice when the pressure is released.

Regensburg, see RATISBON

regent, *rē'jent*, one who rules for a sovereign e.g. the Earl of Pembroke in the early years of Henry III ; James Stuart, Earl of Moray, appointed regent after the abdication of Mary Queen of Scots 1567 ; ' Prinny,' i.e. the Prince Regent (later ' George ' IV) who ruled when George III was old and incapable.

Regent's Park, see LONDON

Reggio, *red'jō*, two cities of Italy (*a*) on the Strait of Messina, noted for gloves and silks ; pop.120,000 ; (*b*) northwest of Bologna, noted for cheese, silkworms and leather goods ; pop.93,000.

Regillus, *rē-jil'ŭs*, in ancient times, a lake east of Rome, where the Romans defeated the Latins 496BC.

Read *Lays of Ancient Rome*, Lord Macaulay. See TARQUIN

Regina, *rē-jī'nă*, cap., Saskatchewan ; trades in grain ; pop.58,000.

regional planning, method of developing an area so as to preserve its natural beauty and make full use of its resources, e.g. the schemes now in operation in many parts of Russia and Italy, and such schemes as that of the Tennessee Valley in USA.

Rehoboam, *rē-hō-bō'am*, Jewish king whose reign began *c.*937BC ; son and successor of Solomon (1 Kings 12 and 14 ; 2 Chronicles 12).

Reich, *rīch*, German word meaning empire. The First Reich was the Holy Roman Empire 962–1806 ; the Second (established by Bismarck) 1871–1918 ; the Third was established by Adolf Hitler 1934, the National Socialist (Nazi) régime being the Dritte Reich. The federal legislature consisted 1919 of the Reichstag with proportional representation from the whole nation, and a Reichstat representing separate states.

Reid, THOMAS MAYNE, *rēd* (1818–83), British novelist, born in County Down, Ireland ; author of thrilling tales, e.g. *The Rifle Rangers, The Scalp Hunters*.

Reigate, *rī'gāt*, town, Surrey ; adjoins Redhill ; has many caves ; pop.42,000.

Reign of Terror, see FRENCH REVOLUTION

Reims or **Rheims**, *rēmz* ; *rans*, city, France, on the R. Vesle, *c.*100m northeast of Paris. An important railway centre, it is famous for its noble Gothic cathedral, the scene of the coronation of most of the kings of France. The cathedral was much damaged in World War I. Reims is noted for textiles and champagne ; pop.117,000.

reindeer, see DEER

Reith, LORD, *rēth* (1889–   ), at one time Director General of the BBC ; chairman of Imperial Airways 1938 ; first chairman of the British Overseas Airways Corporation.

Relativity, THEORY OF, mathematical explanation of various laws of physics as put forward by Professor Albert Einstein (*īn'stīn*) (1879–   ), born of Jewish parents, Ulm, Germany. He won fame at twenty-six, and has since been honoured by almost every country in the world. He received the Nobel Prize for physics 1921. A lover of music, an expert violinist, he was a bitter opponent of Nazi principles, taking refuge in England 1933, and later in USA.

Einstein's two outstanding contributions to modern science are the *Restricted Principle of Relativity* (1905) and the *General Principle of Relativity* (1915). These dispose of the theoretical universal medium (the *ether*) by means of which light, radio waves, etc., were at one time believed to travel. As early as 1881 the famous Michelson-Morley experiment was made to discover the speed with which the earth moves through the ether. In the experiment no trace of motion whatever could be detected. The obvious conclusion was that the earth must carry the ether along with it. But other experiments made at that time, and many astronomical facts, prove that the earth does *not* carry the ether along with it. How could this contradiction be overcome ? All the experiments depended on the speed of light, and in his *Restricted Principle of Relativity*, Einstein astonished physicists by declaring that no matter what our relative speed (whether we are approaching the source of light, travelling from it, or at rest) our measurement of the speed of light remains constant,i.e. *c*.186,000 miles per second. He showed also that as the whole universe is in motion there is no absolute or stationary point with which to compare the speeds of moving bodies ; and that measuring instruments and clocks in any portion of space-time conform to the nature of the motion of that portion.

J. W. N. Sullivan puts the argument thus (*An Outline of Modern Knowledge*) : ' We begin to see that the principle is not a mere contradiction in terms if we reflect that a velocity is the ratio of two measurements, a measurement of length and a measurement of time. Einstein says that length and time-lapse are relative conceptions—they vary with the state of motion of the observer. The distance between two events (say, two flashes of light) is not the same for observers who are moving relatively to one another. Nor is the time-lapse between these events the same for all observers. But all observers reach the same value for the velocity of light.'

This can be explained if we revise our ideas of Euclid, whose geometry is not the only one possible. A straight line, for example, is *not* the shortest distance between two points *if the points are on a curved surface*. All the angles in a triangle of three stars are not necessarily equal to two right angles. A Polish mathematician, Minkowski (*d* 1908), revised geometry, and the German geometer, George F. B. Riemann (1826–66), carried on his work, giving us a non-Euclidean (or Riemannian) geometry for the universe in which space and time are combined to form a four-dimensional *continuum*, i.e. length, breadth and height together with time. In this continuum a Euclidean ' straight line ' may well be a spiral. There is no such thing as *the distance between two points*, or *the time between two events*. In the first case time, and in the second case, space, must be taken into consideration. Space and time measurements, being relative, vary according to the motion of the observer or of any automatic measuring apparatus, but the variations are not haphazard ; they take place in such a way that, whatever his motion, each observer finds the same velocity for light.

In the space-time continuum the ultimate speed in the universe is *c*. 186,000m per sec. According to Newtonian theory, if a radioactive particle A travels at 160,000m per sec. towards B, which is travelling towards A, with a speed, say, of 140,000m per sec., the two approach with the sum of these velocities (300,000m per sec.), a speed greater than that of light. Einstein says this is impossible, for their total speeds can never exceed *c*.186,000, a principle associated with the law *that the mass of a body in motion increases with its speed*. In actual practice this increase in mass can hardly be measured until a body is travelling at high speeds ; thus, an electron escaping from a radioactive substance is only $\frac{1}{4}$th greater in mass when travelling at half the velocity of light ; even at $\frac{9}{10}$ths maximum velocity (167,000m per sec.) its mass is only 2·5 times greater ; but these considerations lead to the conclusion that mass is energy, or that matter is essentially a form of motion.

Einstein's theories introduce modifications into Newton's theory of gravitation —that a body travels in a straight line until halted or deflected by some force outside itself. Einstein declares that planets or electrons move as they do because that is the inevitable ' shape ' of the continuum.

In the main, Relativity may be taken as proved by various experiments ; among them that made during a solar eclipse (1919) when a ray of light, passing near the sun, was found by photography and subsequent calculation to have been ' bent ' out of ' the straight ' to the precise amount previously estimated by Einstein. Spectroscopic observations of the sun have further proved the correctness of certain principles of Relativity, e.g. atoms in the sun ought to vibrate less quickly than those on earth, their light having a longer wave-length in consequence ; this has been confirmed ; also the motion of the planet Mercury has brought striking proof of the way in which Einstein's theory explains many difficulties.

A puzzling feature of Relativity is that its space is finite, which makes us ask : *Then what is beyond the bounds of space?* Part of the answer is that the space of, say, a sphere is limited in the sense that there is only so much of it, boundless in the sense that an insect might creep over it for ever without coming to the end of it.

Relativity has been advanced by Sir Arthur Eddington, and we are now faced with such bewildering concepts as the possibility that both space *and time* are curved, which means that our knowledge of the universe can no longer be expressed in words, but only in mathematical signs. Note that while Relativity fits in with much of our latest knowledge of physics, it does not answer *all* our questions, and has so far not been altogether satisfactorily applied to electromagnetic forces, though atomic fission has proved the correctness of Einstein's formulae concerning speed and energy.

In 1929 Einstein made known his Unified Field Theory, and recently he announced an extension of it, the result of over 30 years' work. The revised Unified Field Theory supplies a series of equations for chemical, cohesive and electrical forces, etc., reduced to interrelated formulae for cosmic space, time, matter, energy and gravitation.

religion, in its primitive form, arises from fear of what is not understood, hence animism, the belief that, e.g. the wind or a disease is a spirit, leading to the idea that misfortune may be ' bought off ' by magical rites or by offerings. The root idea is that man is more than body or mind, and that his soul or spirit is aware of the spirit which formed and sustains the universe and all its life.

Polytheism is the belief in *many* gods ; monotheism the belief there is only *one* god. The great religions of the world are ethical i.e. they demand a certain standard of goodness from those who believe, though this inward and spiritual quality of character is often confused with mere outward appearances, so that performing required religious rites takes the place of essential goodness. It may be argued according to logic and reason that there is no god and that man is only a clever animal ; but religion is fundamentally more than reason, and is based on feeling or intuition as well as on the writings or teachings of great religious pioneers.

The chief religious groups of the world are : Mohammedans (210,000,000), following the teaching of the 7th c. Mohammed ; found chiefly in Arabia, N. and E. Africa, central Asia and India ; Buddhists (150,000,000), chiefly in India, Ceylon and Japan, with a variety (Lamaism) in Tibet ; followers of Confucius and Lao-Tsze (350,000,000) found chiefly in China ; Jews (16,000,000) ; also various other non-Christian religions (210,000,000). Christians, including Roman Catholics, Protestants and Coptic Christians number c.700,000,000. They are followers of Jesus Christ ; the Cross is their symbol and the Bible their sacred writings.

Read *Comparative Religion*, A. C. Bouquet ; *God and Human Progress*, John Hadham.

remainder, see DIVISION

remainder theorem, in mathematics, theorem which states that if any rational and integral function of x is divided by $x-a$, the remainder is the same function of a. If the divisor is $x+a$ the remainder is the same function of $-a$. Thus :

(1) Find the remainder when $x^3-3ax^2+4a^2x-a^3$ is divided by $x-a$. Wherever x occurs in the dividend substitute a.

This gives $a^3-3aa^2+4a^2a-a^3$

or $a^3-3a^3+4a^3-a^3 = a^3$.

This is the remainder.

(2) Find the remainder when $x^3+4ax^2+6a^2x+a^3$ is divided by $x+a$. In the dividend substitute $-a$ for x. This gives

$-a^3+4a(-a)^2+6a^2(-a)+a^3$

or $-a^3+4a^3-6a^3+a^3$

$= -3a^3 =$ remainder.

This principle can be applied generally.

(I) Find remainder when $2x^3+4x^2-9x+7$ is divided by $x-2$.

Substitute $x = 2$ in the expression.

Then remainder

$$= 2 \times 2^3 + 4 \times 2^2 - 9 \times 2 + 7$$
$$= 2 \times 8 + 4 \times 4 - 9 \times 2 + 7$$
$$= 16 + 16 - 18 + 7$$
$$= 21.$$

(II) Find remainder when $2x^3+4x^2-9x+7$ is divided by $x+2$.

Substitute $x = -2$ in the expression.

Then remainder

$$= 2 \times (-2)^3 + 4 \times (-2)^2 - 9 \times (-2) + 7$$
$$= 2 \times (-8) + 4 \times (+4) - 9 \times (-2) + 7$$
$$= -16 + 16 + 18 + 7$$
$$= 25.$$

(III) Find remainder when $2x^3-3x^2+5x-42$ is divided by $x-3$.

Substitute $x = 3$ in the expression.

Then remainder

$$= 2 \times 3^3 - 3 \times 3^2 + 5 \times 3 - 42$$
$$= 2 \times 27 - 3 \times 9 + 5 \times 3 - 42$$
$$= 54 - 27 + 15 - 42$$
$$= 0.$$

Since the remainder in (III) is 0, it follows that the divisor is a factor of the dividend. Hence the *Factor Theorem* : *If any rational and integral function of x vanishes when x = a, then x − a is a factor of the function.* Likewise, if the function vanishes when x = − a then x + a is a factor.

This is one of the most important practical uses of the Remainder Theorem.

Rembrandt, *rem'brant* (1606–69), Dutch artist, *b* Leyden ; became rich but died in poverty ; famous for portraits, particularly of old people, outdoor scenes, and for his remarkable etchings. All his work is characterised by contrasts in light and shade, his shadows having a peculiar deep glowing red. Among his many pictures are *The Anatomy Lesson* ; a portrait of himself (now in the National Gallery) ; *The Night Watch* ; *The Adoration of the Magi* ; *The Three Trees.*

Remembrance Sunday, Sunday nearest to 11 Nov., the day (1918) on which World War I ended.

Remus, see ROMULUS

Renaissance, *rĕ-nā'sans* (French from *re*, again, *naître*, to be born), name for the awakening of Europe in the 15th c., the Dark Ages and the Middle Ages giving place to a revival of learning, i.e. a transition from a period of comparative stagnation to a new, wider, and infinitely more vital way of life and thought.

The Renaissance, ushered in by Petrarch and Boccaccio in Italy, was given a great impetus by the capture of Constantinople by the Turks 1453, for many of the city's leading scholars sought refuge in Italy, bringing with them their knowledge of ancient Greek and their love of learning.

Study of the classics opened up new visions to a Europe long befogged by monkish learning only. While the Renaissance in Italy, fostered by wealthy merchant princes and especially by Pope Leo X, blossomed in art and literature, it led to new studies in France and Germany. The Reformation (see REFORMATION) was one result of the new spirit of inquiry which stimulated men's minds, and led to the translation of the Bible into German and English. Equally important was the discovery of printing which enabled more and cheaper books to be read, with the result that knowledge was transmitted and received by means of the printed word.

In England the Renaissance came by way of scholars who, after studying in Padua, Bologna and Florence, returned to Oxford and Cambridge to impart to students an enthusiasm for the classics. Sir Thomas More and Henry VIII encouraged this New Learning, and schools and colleges were founded for teaching subjects previously unknown.

The result of all this was that whereas for centuries men had meekly accepted the dogmas of the Roman Church, there was now a questing attitude of mind. Copernicus and Galileo gave men a new conception of the universe ; alchemy gradually developed from a kind of magic into a more exact science ; Sir Isaac Newton laid the foundations of modern physics ; William Harvey brought to anatomy and medicine the principle of the circulation of the blood. Breaking away from Latin, the language in which the Bible and books of almost every kind had long been written, gave rise to a new realisation of the beauty and possibilities of one's own language, hence German, French and Italian literature, and the wealth of English poetry and drama of the Elizabethan period. This did much to foster national pride. By closing the ports of the E. Mediterranean, the Turks had prevented merchants from importing wares from the East and Far East, e.g. gold, silk, spices and sugar, so Portuguese, Spanish, Dutch and English sailors gradually found new trade routes ; America was discovered, and commercial expansion in the form of colonies began, the trend being westwards. In architecture, also, the Renaissance brought a revival of the classic style.

Renan, JOSEPH ERNEST, *rĕ-nän'* (1823–92), French historian and thinker, *b* Brittany. A noted student of Hebrew, he wrote a famous book, *Vie de Jésus,* on the beginnings of Christianity.

Renfrewshire, *ren'froo-,* county of SW. Scotland ; has the industrial area of the Clyde, e.g. Paisley, Greenock and Port Glasgow ; co.tn Paisley.

Rennes, *ren,* town, France ; 232m south-west of Paris ; pop.99,000.

Rennie, JOHN (1761–1821), born in E. Lothian ; improved the steam engine, but won his greatest fame as a builder of canals, docks and bridges.

His son Sir John Rennie (1794–1874) completed London Bridge 1831.

repertory theatre, see THEATRE

repression, see BRAIN

reptile (Latin *reptilis,* crawling), class of back-boned, lung-breathing, cold-blooded animals, usually laying eggs, though these are sometimes hatched in the parent's body ; includes snakes, lizards, alligators, crocodiles, tortoises, turtles and the tautera of New Zealand.

Repton, village, Derbyshire. Its public school (1556) includes part of a 12th c. monastery.

republic, form of political constitution. A kingdom or monarchy is ruled by the hereditary ruler, i.e. one who rules because his father ruled before him, as in Britain. In a republic, e.g. France or the USA, there is no king, his place being taken by a president chosen by representatives of the people. In recent years several republics, e.g. Germany, Italy, Spain, have been governed by dictators. Other republics include Poland Switzerland, Turkey, USSR (the Soviets) and China. Kingdoms include

Belgium, Denmark, the Netherlands and Sweden.

Republican, see DEMOCRAT

requiescat in pace, see R.I.P.

reredos, *rēr'dos,* in churches, the screen or wall behind the altar. At first a curtain or tapestry, it later became a permanent feature, often of richly carved stone, adorned with niches and figures of saints and angels.

reservoir, *rez'ĕr-vwör,* construction for storing water for household or industrial use ; usually formed by building a concrete dam across a valley, water being conveyed to a town or city along pipes. The service reservoir at Littleton (1925) is one of many used by the (London) Metropolitan Water Board ; its capacity is 6,750,000,000 gallons, water being raised from the Thames by centrifugal pumps. See DAM

resin, substance consisting of carbon, hydrogen and oxygen ; usually of vegetable origin, e.g. gum from a tree, especially the pine. It is used for varnishes, lacquer-work and waxes. Amber is fossilised resin.

resistance (electrical), ratio of the potential difference between the ends of a conductor to the current flowing through it. The unit is the ohm. See ELECTRICITY ; OHM

res'onance, vibration in one body caused by vibration in another. Thus, one tuning-fork may cause another close by to vibrate in unison if they are of the same frequency. Resonance has special reference to the *amplification* of vibrations, e.g. when a tuning-fork is held over a pipe, closed at one end, its length being a quarter the wave-length of the tuning-fork, then resonance occurs.

Electrical resonance is the basis of radio reception, since the natural frequency of oscillation of the receiving circuit is made to correspond to the frequency of the incoming waves.

respiration, see LUNGS

Restitutor Orbis, see AURELIAN

Restoration, THE, in English and Scottish history almost always means the restoration of Charles II, 1660, and the re-establishment of the Church of England. Cromwell with his Ironsides put down all rebellions in favour of the exile, but after Cromwell's death, George Monk (Duke of Albemarle) arranged for Charles to return. He was proclaimed king 8 May 1660, and arrived in London 29 May.

By the Restoration period we mean the period after 1660 when the severe Puritan way of life gave place to a love of amusement, often of indecency ; when literature was more frivolous ; and when Congreve and Wycherley were the chief dramatists.

Retford, town on the R. Idle, Nottinghamshire ; has a large agricultural trade. Its grammar school was founded 1552. The full name is East Retford.

retina, see EYE

Reuter, PAUL JULIUS, BARON DE, *roi'tĕr* (1816–99), *b* Kassel, Germany ; became a naturalised British subject ; notable as the founder of Reuter's news agency, which began with a pigeon-post, and was moved to London 1851.

' Revenge, The,' see GRENVILLE, SIR RICHARD

Revere, PAUL, *rē-vēr'* (1735–1818), soldier, *b* Boston, Massachusetts, USA ; took part in the ' Boston Tea Party ' 1773. In 1775 he rode by night from Charleston to Lexington to warn the colonists of the approach towards Concord of British troops, an exploit related in Longfellow's poem *Paul Revere's Ride.*

revolver, see PISTOL

Reykjavik, *rā'kyä-vēk,* port and cap., Iceland ; exports fish and skins ; pop. 41,000 ; site of a British airport in World War II.

Reynaud, PAUL, *rā-nō'* (1878–   ), French politician ; Prime Minister 1940.

Reynolds, SIR JOSHUA, *ren'ŭldz* (1723–92), artist, *b* Plympton, Devon ; possibly England's greatest portrait painter ; lived in Leicester Square, London, from 1760, painting portraits of all the famous people of his day. The first President of the Royal Academy, he was a friend of Dr Johnson and of Oliver Goldsmith.

Reynolds, QUENTIN JAMES (1902–   ), American journalist, foreign correspondent and author.

rhea, *rē'a,* running bird of S. America. It is akin to the ostrich, which it closely resembles, though it is smaller. The plumage is grey. The bird is captured by horsemen who throw a ' bolas,' i.e. a cord with a weight at each end.

Rheims, see REIMS

rhenium, *rē'ni-ŭm,* rare metal and element, Re ; discovered 1925 ; atomic weight 186·31 ; atomic number 75.

rheostat, *rē'ō-stat,* variable electrical resistance ; much used for starting and regulating electric motors, so avoiding excessive current when the motor is first started and is gathering speed.

rheumatism, *roo'mă-tiz'm,* term given vaguely to almost any disease causing an ache and inflammation in the joints, but applied more accurately to *rheumatoid arthritis.* Since 1949 Compound E has been increasingly used in the treatment of rheumatism. Compound E, now known also as Cortisone, is being manufactured increasingly from the seed of a tropical vine.

Rhine, *rīn,* historic river of W. Europe ; flows *c.*800m from Switzerland, through Germany, passing Cologne and Dusseldorf, enters the Netherlands and reaches the N. Sea by a large delta. Among its tributaries is the R. Ruhr, flowing in a region noted for its coal and iron. After World War I Allied troops occupied the left bank of the Rhine till 1930 ; in World War II the United Nations crossed the Rhine 1945.

The RHINELAND, a province of Germany, is largely industrial.

RHINOCEROSES
(1) *Indian Rhinoceros*   (2) *African Rhinoceros*

rhinoceros, *rī-nos'ĕr-os*, massive hoofed animal, notable for having a horn (or two horns) in the middle of the face ; has thick skin ; is heavy and clumsy in appearance. The Indian variety may be 5ft high at the shoulder, but is timid ; the African has two horns and hairless skin. The white rhinoceros, the largest, is found in S. Sudan, the Congo, and in the Zambesi. All live in swamps, and feed on grass and leaves. Remains of rhinoceroses have been found in Britain.

Rhode Island, *rōd*, Atlantic state of USA. Though the smallest, it is the most densely populated ; cap. Providence.

Rhodes, *rōdz*, island of the Aegean Sea ; area 550sq.m. It was once famous for its huge statue of the sun-god Helios, known as the Colossus. Occupied by the Knights of St John 1309–1523, it became Italian 1922, Greek in 1946 ; noted for grapes, sponges and wine ; cap. Rhodes.

Rhodes, CECIL JOHN (1853–1902), administrator who hoped to build up an all-British Africa ; *b* Bishop's Stortford, Hertfordshire ; went to Africa at seventeen for health reasons ; was educated at Oxford ; amassed a huge fortune from the Kimberley diamond mines ; secured Bechuanaland for the British, and extended British territory by gaining concessions from Lobengula, chief of the Matabele. Rhodes was Prime Minister of the Cape 1890, and after a war with the Matabele added still further areas to British possessions. With Dr L. S. Jameson he planned the Jameson Raid 1895 against the Boers, for which he was compelled to resign the premiership 1896. His bravest act was to go unarmed into Matabele country during a rebellion, and make peace with the leaders in the Matoppo Hills, where, later, he was buried.

Rhodesia is named after this great empire-builder who, though intolerant, impulsive and unscrupulous was courageous and utterly selfless. Much of his fortune was bequeathed to Oxford University, the Rhodes Scholarships for British, German and American students being worth *c*. £400 a year each.

Rhodes, WILFRED (1877–   ), cricketer, *b* Kirkheaton, Yorkshire ; won fame as a left-handed slow bowler ; played for Yorkshire for thirty years, and often for England against Australia.

Rhodesia, *rō-dē'sia*, territory of Africa comprising (*a*) NORTHERN RHODESIA, i.e. the region north of the R. Zambesi, area *c*.290,000sq.m, mostly over 3,000ft above sea-level ; produces copper, cobalt, timber, tobacco, and has great herds of cattle ; cap. Lusaka ; (*b*) SOUTHERN RHODESIA, area *c*.150,000sq.m south of the Zambesi. The country is rich in minerals, e.g. gold, silver, coal, chrome, asbestos, mica, iron, tin and tungsten. Cattle are raised, fruits grown, tobacco cultivated ; cap. Salisbury.

Both N. and S. Rhodesia are in the British Empire ; total pop.3,000,000, mostly native. Rhodesia is named after Cecil Rhodes.

rhodium, *rō'di-ŭm*, rare metal and element,

Rh ; atomic weight 102·91 ; atomic number 45 ; discovered 1804 ; found in nickel-copper ores.

rhododendron, rō'dō-den-dron (Gk rhodon, rose, dendron, trees), evergreen shrub or tree (family Ericaceae), native of the E. Indies, China, Japan and in temperate districts of America. The species Rhododendron Maxinuur, now common in Britain, grows on Alleghany Mountains. The large bushy flowers may be pink, white, lilac or scarlet.

rhomboid, see QUADRILATERAL FIGURE

rhombus, see QUADRILATERAL FIGURE

Rhondda, hron'thǎ, valley district, Glamorganshire ; is a thickly populated coalfield ; pop.120,000.

Rhône, rōn, river (c.500m) rising in a glacier, Switzerland, and flowing, via Lyons (where it is joined by the Saône) through France to the Mediterranean ; supplies hydro-electric power ; linked with several canals.

rhubarb, a plant (family Polygonaceae) with large leaves, fleshy roots and stalks that are edible when cooked. The roots of Chinese rhubarb have medicinal properties.

Rhyl, hril ; ril, holiday town, Flintshire.

rhyme, see POETRY

Rialto, bridge across the Grand Canal, Venice ; built 1591.

Ribble, river ; flows c.75m from the Pennines to the Irish Sea.

ribbon development, the erection of buildings along main roads, especially those leading out of towns and cities, thus extending the ' built-up ' areas where motorists have to drive slowly, and encroaching on the beauty of the countryside. Ribbon building was a bad feature between World Wars I and II. More recent town planning avoids ribbon development where possible. See ROADS

ribs, in the human body, twelve pairs of curved bones from the back bone, the upper seven attached to the sternum, the next three attached to the seventh rib and the lower two unattached at the front, hence the name ' floating ' ribs.

ribwort plantain, see PLANTAIN

rice, fruit or grain of a cultivated variety of grass, the seeds having separate husks and growing in plumes. Immense quantities are harvested in China and India, the Mediterranean countries (notably Egypt), USA and Brazil.

Though rice may be raised in somewhat hilly country, it is chiefly grown in lowland rice-fields (paddy fields) submerged by water (either by direct rainfall or by means of irrigation), and is sown under water. When fully grown, the grass may stand from 1ft–6ft high, with large, pointed leaves. Rice requires a temperature of 60–80° F to ripen, and the husk (paddy or padi) is removed by hulling. Polished rice is of much less food value than unpolished, as polishing removes the bran and germ. Polished rice is deficient in vitamin B, and those

who have little else to eat may suffer from a deficiency disease called beri-beri.

During World War II a revolution in rice occurred, due to the investigations of Gordon Harwell and Eric Huzwnlaub. Their ' converted rice ' retains its vitamin B content, and is therefore much superior to rice milled and polished in the ordinary way. See PLATE 1 (top)

Richard I (1157–99), King of England, known as Richard Coeur de Lion or Lion Heart ; 3rd son of Henry II ; made Duke of Aquitaine (France). Like his brothers, he was rebellious, rising against his father 1188. Though king from 1189, he remained chiefly on the Continent, setting out 1191 after demanding exceedingly heavy taxes.

Tall and broad, a fine, courageous soldier, Richard was cruel, treacherous and unfitted for anything but warfare. He quarrelled with Philip, and Leopold of Austria, and though he captured Acre (Palestine) he failed to free Jerusalem. He did, however, compel Saladin to make a three years' truce, and then set out for England, where Prince John was plotting against him. In an attempt to take a short cut overland, he was captured near Vienna by Leopold, and handed over to the emperor, Henry VI, who imprisoned him in Dürenstein castle till a heavy ransom was paid 1194. Tradition says that Richard was found by his minstrel, Blondel.

Leaving England in the care of the justiciar, Hubert Walter, Richard returned to Aquitaine to fight Philip, and died from a wound received while besieging the castle of Chalus.

Richard II (1367–1400), King of England, b Bordeaux, son of Edward the Black Prince, and grandson of Edward III, whom he succeeded 1377. The country was governed by the earls of Gloucester and Arundel during Richard's youth, but it was the young king who ended the Peasants' Revolt 1381.

With the help of his uncle, John of Gaunt, Richard became a ruler rather than a puppet 1390. He proved wise and peace-loving, and won the esteem of the French and Irish ; but suddenly (1397) his desire for revenge led him to have Gloucester murdered, Arundel arrested, and their supporters exiled, after which he ruled as a tyrant, taxed the people heavily, and thus caused the Duke of Lancaster to lead a rebellion. Richard, captured at Flint 1399, was imprisoned at Pontefract where he died or was murdered.

Shakespeare's play King Richard the Second is one of his greatest tragedies, and Richard of Bordeaux, a modern play, gives a fine interpretation of Richard's character.

Richard III (1452–85), King of England, son of Richard Duke of York, and a brother of Edward IV, at whose death (1483) he became king. The rightful heir was Prince Edward, but he and his brother vanished, and it would seem that the princes were murdered in the Tower of London by Richard's orders.

Many conspiracies were hatched against Richard ; and, finally, the Earl of Richmond (Henry Tudor) landed at Milford Haven, raised a rebellion, and defeated the king, who fell fighting at Bosworth, 1485.

Richard showed evidence of being an able statesman, and there seems little reason to suppose that he was as deformed as some historians have declared.

Richardson, SAMUEL (1689–1761), writer, born in Derbyshire ; became a prosperous printer in London ; wrote his first novel *Pamela* 1740 when he was over fifty. This was followed by *Clarissa Harlowe* and *Sir Charles Grandison.* All are in the form of letters, and the first two, though wordy and sentimental, are notable in the development of the English novel.

Richelieu, CARDINAL, rē-shĕ-lyŭ (1585–1642), for many years the virtual ruler of France, born poor in Paris ; became a churchman ; won the favour of Marie de' Medici. Richelieu was Secretary of State to Louis XIII, who never liked him, but found he could not do without him. Made a Cardinal 1622, and created Duke 1631, he was hated by many, but exposed all the plots against him, and quickly became the most powerful man in the kingdom, largely by means of his clever system of spies.

As a statesman Richelieu believed in building up a strong monarchy. He robbed the nobles of power ; crushed the Huguenots at La Rochelle 1629, but gave them religious freedom ; extended commerce but taxed the people heavily ; founded the French Academy 1635, and by stifling local government prevented political evolution. He died immensely rich. Though able and courageous, he was cruel, calculating, and mean. His character is well revealed in *The Three Musketeers* by Dumas.

Richmond, -mŭnd, historic town, N. Yorkshire ; on the R. Swale ; famous for a castle with a superb Norman keep.

Richmond, town, Surrey, on the R. Thames. Here are remains of Sheen Palace where Queen Elizabeth died 1603 ; also a famous Deer Park ; pop.34,000.

Richmond, cap. and port, Virginia, USA ; on the James R. ; manufactures tobacco, iron and paper ; besieged in the Civil War, being taken by Grant 1865 ; pop.193,000.

rickets, serious disease in children causing curvature of the bones due to their gradual softening. The disease is due solely to lack of vitamin D, which disables the child from properly absorbing calcium and phosphorus, both necessary for building strong bones. Treatment consists of sunbaths, since ultra-violet rays enable the skin to manufacture its own supply of vitamin D.

A course of halibut oil or cod-liver oil is also valuable, the oil being rich in this vitamin.

rickshaw or **jinricksha,** Japanese carriage (for one person) drawn by a coolie who holds the shafts. Rickshaws are common in India and S. Africa.

Ridge, WILLIAM PETT (1860–1930), novelist, born near Canterbury ; author of many humorous books, e.g. *Mord Em'ly,* *'Erb,* etc. descriptive of London life.

riding, see YORKSHIRE

Ridley, NICHOLAS (*d* 1555), martyr, born in Northumberland ; appointed Bishop of London ; was one of the bishops who prepared the first *Prayer Book* (1548) ; supported Lady Jane Grey. Accused of heresy in Mary's reign, he was burned with Hugh Latimer at Oxford. See LATIMER, HUGH

Riemann, GEORG, rē'män (1826–66), German mathematician, possibly the greatest of the 19th c. ; notable for his development of functions, and especially of the non-Euclidean geometry (Riemannian geometry) without which the work of Einstein would have been impossible. See RELATIVITY

rifle, fire-arm with a grooved barrel giving a rotary motion to the bullet or cartridge, thus replacing the older smooth-bore type. The Lee-Enfield (weight 8lb 14½oz) is 3ft 8½in long, has a calibre of ·303, and a muzzle velocity of 2,440ft per sec. It allows a range up to 2,000yd, or even 2,800. The Garand rifle (invented by John C. Garand) is semi-automatic.

Riga, rē'gä, port and cap., Latvia, USSR ; at the mouth of the R. Daugava (Dvina) ; exports grain, timber and flax ; pop. 400,000.

Riga, gulf of the Baltic Sea.

right-angle, in mathematics, 90° ; 3 signs ; 1 quadrant ; ¼ circumference. See ANGLE

right-angled triangle, see PYTHAGORAS

Riley, JAMES WHITCOMB (1853–1916), American poet, born in Indiana ; best remembered for his poems for children.

Rimsky-Korsakoff, NICHOLAS, rim'ski-kör'sä-köf (1844–1908), Russian composer ; famous for his operas, e.g. *The Snow Maiden,* for his orchestral compositions, and as a composer of songs.

ring-ouzel or **mountain blackbird,** -oo'zl ; British song-bird of the thrush family ; has black feathers edged with white or grey and a white patch under the throat. A summer visitor, it often nests among heather.

ringworm, contagious disease of the skin due to fungoid growth which most commonly infects the scalp. It is now treated with doses of thallium acetate and exposure to X-rays.

Rio de Janeiro, rē'ō dä zhä-nā'rō, cap. and chief port, Brazil ; has a magnificent harbour ; exports coffee ; also sugar and hides.

On Corcovada Mt above the harbour stands an impressive figure (125ft high) of Christ the Redeemer, dedicated 1931 to mark the centenary of Brazilian independence ; pop.1,903,000.

Rio Grande del Norte, *rē'ō gran'dā del nawr'tā,* river flowing from Colorado, USA, through Mexico to enter the Gulf of Mexico after *c.*1,800m.

R.I.P., short for the Lat. *requiescat in pace,* i.e. may he (or she) rest in peace.

Ripon, *rip'on,* cathedral city, W. Yorkshire; on the R. Ure. Fountains Abbey is close by.

rippling rhythm, see JAZZ

Rip Van Winkle, see IRVING, W.

river, channel by which rainfall reaches the sea ; may have a main stream with a number of tributaries. The line bounding the area drained is called the watershed. The right bank is the side on your right as you look in the direction the river is flowing. A river rises at its source, and empties at the mouth, sometimes through several mouths forming a delta, e.g. the Nile. A mt. torrent may flow at 18–20mph. Navigable rivers are of great importance to commerce and transport ; if tidal, as the lower Thames, ships may have to wait for high tide to reach a port. Swift rivers (sometimes with waterfalls) may be used for generating electric light and power, e.g. those of Scotland, Norway, Finland and the R. Niagara. All rivers carry mud, etc. to the sea, the Mississippi depositing enough sediment yearly to form a mass of one sq.m 260ft thick, i.e. nearly 500,000,000 tons of solid matter and dissolved salts.

The world's longest rivers include :

River	flows into	miles
Missouri-Mississippi	Gulf of Mexico	4,500
Amazon	Atlantic	4,000
Nile	Mediterranean	4,000
Yangtse	N. Pacific	3,400
Yenisei	Arctic Ocean	3,300
Congo	Atlantic	3,000
Lena	Arctic Ocean	2,800
Mekong	China Sea	2,800
Obi	Arctic Ocean	2,700
Amur	N. Pacific	2,600
Hoangho	N. Pacific	2,600
Niger	Gulf of Guinea	2,600
Volga	Caspian Sea	2,400
Mackenzie	Arctic Ocean	2,300
Yukon	Bering Sea	2,000
Rio del Norte	Gulf of Mexico	1,800
Sao Francisco	Atlantic	1,800
St Lawrence	Atlantic	1,800
Danube	Black Sea	1,725
Euphrates	Persian Gulf	1,700
Indus	Arabian Sea	1,700
Brahmaputra	Bay of Bengal	1,680
Ganges	Bay of Bengal	1,500

riveting, method of joining metal plates, especially in building ships and making boilers. For long the method was that of heating rivets to redness and hammering with hydraulic or electric machinery, the contraction of the cooling rivet ensuring a water-tight joint. Riveting is now being replaced by welding.

Riviera, *rē-vyē'rä,* Italian name for a narrow strip of coast along the Gulf of Genoa, partly in N. Italy, partly in the South of France. The district, backed by mountains, is mild and sunny, noted for flowers, and much favoured by rich tourists and invalids who stay at Nice, Mentone, Monaco, San Remo and Monte Carlo.

Rizzio, DAVID, see MARY, QUEEN OF SCOTS

RN (Royal Navy), see NAVY

roach, fresh-water fish found in nearly all British rivers ; may weigh up to 3½lb ; is silvery, with red fins ; affords good sport to the angler, but is not very good to eat.

road accidents, see ROADS

roads, highways for traffic ; found in all civilised countries ; facilitate travel and transport ; often began as tracks made by primitive tribes using pack-animals for carrying burdens. The invention of wheeled vehicles (known to the Sumerians 3500BC) led to wider tracks. The Romans were famous as builders of a vast system of highways (usually of stone) radiating from Rome. See BRITAIN

The first serious attempts to improve roads in Britain were the Turnpike Acts of George III's reign. These provided for tolls (i.e. payments) to meet the cost of maintaining the highways. Road-building was improved by John Loudon McAdam (1756–1836), a Scottish engineer who used layers of cubical fragments of stone ; Thomas Telford (1757–1834), another Scotsman, famous as a builder of bridges and harbours, was responsible for over 1,000m of roads in Scotland. There was also the remarkable Yorkshireman, John Metcalf (1717–1810), known as Blind Jack of Knaresborough, and General Wade who built military roads in the Scottish Highlands 1726–40. The coming of motor traffic has led to great improvements in road surfaces, e.g. tar-macadam and concrete ; elimination of dangerous corners ; also the construction of fine, wide by-pass roads, i.e. roads that skirt villages and towns so that ' through ' traffic is unimpeded ; also (notably first in Germany) junctions and crossroads with two levels designed to obviate collisions. Most of our greater highways (class I roads) have the familiar white (or yellow) line or studs, and many have two ' lanes ' of traffic in each direction, i.e. fast and slow. The Road Fund is now derived from taxation on motor vehicles. Britain has *c.*180,500m of roads ; USA *c.*3,000,000m.

Road transport was at one time entirely horse-drawn, e.g. carts, wagons, or a variety of carriages, such as cabs with two or four wheels ; hackney carriages drawn by hackneys (a cross between a race-horse and a cart-horse) ; the chase (a light four-wheel carriage) ; postchaise, a covered four-wheel carriage hired for long journeys, and drawn by relays of horses from one posting-house to another ; the phaeton (four-wheel carriage with two horses) popular in the 18th c. ; the hansom cab, designed by J. A. Hansom c.1834.

England's first *stage-coach* ran from Coventry to London 1659, and had inside and outside passengers. Stage-coaches were drawn by two or eight horses, and travelled along bad roads often infested with highwaymen. Travelling from London to Manchester 1754 took 4½ days. The first *mail-coach* (carrying letters as well as passengers) was run by John Palmer 1784 at an average speed of 6mph ; by 1835 there were 700 mail-coaches in the UK. For a vivid description of coaching days read *David Copperfield* by Charles Dickens and *The English Mail Coach* by Thomas de Quincey.

London's first bus (short for *omnibus*, Latin for ' for all ') appeared 1829. Owned by George Shillibeer, it was horse-drawn and carried 22 passengers. The first motor buses were seen in London 1904. Steam vehicles on the roads date from the 18th c., pioneers being Richard Trevithick (1804) and Goldsworthy Gurney ; but by 1896 motor vehicles were in competition, and by 1911 London alone had 3,500 commercial motor vehicles. There are now over 3,000,000 motor vehicles on the roads of Britain. British transport was nationalised 1948.

Traffic lights at busy corners (red for *halt*, amber for *caution*, green for *all clear*) were first used c.1930. The weight of a passing vehicle depresses a pad set in the road, this sending an electric impulse to controlling mechanism, where an intricate arrangement of cams and relays operates the lamps, giving preference (in some types) to the busiest stream of traffic.

Among remarkable roads is the Inter-American Highway, extending nearly 17,000m from Alaska to the Argentine, 16 countries sharing the expense. Parts of it include the famous Alaska Highway, the Andean Highway (Peru) completed 1944, also the Pacific Highway, 1,500m from Canada to Mexico. Another great motor road of N. America is that from Atlantic City (USA) to the Pacific coast, 3,200m. A motor-coach service now links Damascus (Syria) with Baghdad (Iraq), coaches with 18 wheels conveying 36 passengers across 500m of desert in 30 hours, though the journey used to take 20–25 days.

An unfortunate result of thoughtless building after World War I resulted in ' ribbon development ' along many of our roads, including the great arterial roads. Building houses and shops *along* a main highway is now giving place to planning satellite towns *away from* the main highways.

Road accidents have increased enormously since the introduction of motor

traffic, deaths now averaging over 6,000 a year in the UK, mostly due to excessive speed, hence the speed-limit of 30mph in built-up areas. All who use the road —walking, cycling, motoring—should know the *Highway Code* and obey the rules. Only by so doing can we keep death off the road.

An excellent book to read is *The Road Goes On*, C. W. Scott-Giles ; another is *British Roads*, Geoffrey Boumphrey (Nelson). Study also *The Highway Code*.

Roanoke, *rō'ă-nōk*, city, Virginia, USA ; has railway works and flour mills, etc. ; pop.69,000.

Roanoke Island, see RALEIGH, SIR WALTER

Roaring Forties, region of the S. Pacific and Atlantic between 40° and 50° southern latitude, where boisterous winds (known to sailors as the Brave W. Winds) blow, carrying rain to the west coast of Tasmania, NZ and S. Australia.

Roberts, FIELD-MARSHAL EARL (1832–1914), British soldier, *b* Cawnpore ; saw much fighting during the Indian Mutiny, sharing in the relief of Lucknow, and winning the VC (1858) during an action at Khudaganj. He took part in various expeditions ; was commander of the Punjab Frontier Force 1878 ; distinguished himself in the Afghan War (1879) by his entry into Kabul, and still more by his march of 300m to the relief of British troops at Kandahar 1880, where he won a remarkable victory.

Commander-in-Chief in India 1885, Roberts greatly improved the defences of the NW. Frontier. He became Lord Roberts of Kandahar and Waterford 1892. The defeat of the Boers in S. Africa was in a high degree due to the brilliant measures taken by Roberts, who relieved Mafeking, and returned home to be made an Earl.

In World War I he spent two days reviewing Indian troops in France. He was a fine type of soldier, a superb horse-man and a born leader of men.

Robeson, PAUL (1898–   ), Negro actor and bass singer, born in New Jersey, USA.

Robespierre, MAXIMILIEN DE, *rō'bes-pēr* (1758–94), known as the Incorruptible, and one of the chief figures of the French Revolution, *b* Arras ; became a judge ; believed passionately in the principles of Jean-Jacques Rousseau ; dressed as a dandy. As a leader of the Jacobins, he became head of the Committee of Public Safety, and was associated with Danton in the Reign of Terror, being responsible for much of its bloodshed. His desire to bring about a perfect state ended in the worst features of the Revolution, and his own death by the guillotine.

robin, song-bird of the thrush family. The upper parts are greenish-brown ; breast red, and bright eyes black. The nest may be in a grassy bank or an old kettle, pot or boot, and comprises

THE ROBIN

leaves and moss, lined with hair and feathers. The robin lays 5–7 whitish eggs with pale red freckles ; feeds on insects, worms and berries ; delights to live near human habitations ; sings for most of the year ; is the subject of many legends, e.g. that its breast is red because it tried to pull the thorns from Christ's crown while he hung on the cross.

Robin Hood, character in many English ballads and romantic legends ; said to have been an outlaw with HQ in S. Yorkshire and Sherwood Forest, and to have robbed the rich to help the poor. He gathered a company of archers dressed ' in Lincoln green ' as camouflage. Popularly believed to have been the Earl of Huntingdon (*d* 1247) he may have been a citizen of Wakefield in the 14th c. Among his company were Little John and Maid Marion.
Read *Ivanhoe*, Sir Walter Scott.

robot, see CAPEK, K.

Rob Roy (1671–1734), nickname given to Robert Roy MacGregor, Stirlingshire cattle farmer, who became leader of a band of outlaws. Though imprisoned and sentenced to transportation 1722 he was pardoned 1727, after which he settled at Balquhidder, Perthshire. His story is told in Sir Walter Scott's novel, *Rob Roy.*

Robsart, AMY (*d* 1560), married Robert Dudley (later Earl of Leicester) 1550 ; found dead at Cumnor Place, near Oxford, Dudley being suspected of killing her. She is the heroine of Sir Walter Scott's novel, *Kenilworth.*

roc, imaginary bird of Oriental tales, e.g. the giant bird (which fed its young on elephants) mentioned in *The Arabian Nights' Entertainments.* It carried Sinbad the Sailor to the valley of diamonds.

Rochdale, town, Lancashire ; noted for cotton and woollen goods, especially flannel and calico. The co-operative movement began here ; pop.81,000.

Rochelle, see LA ROCHELLE

Rochester, city, Kent ; on the R. Medway ; famous for its cathedral and Norman castle ; manufactures cement ; pop. 35,000.

Rochester, city and port, New York State, USA ; manufactures photographic appliances ; pop.325,000.

rock crystal, see SILICON

Rockefeller, JOHN DAVISON, *rok'ĕ-fel-ĕr* (1839–1937), American business-man, *b* Richford, New York ; formed the Standard Oil Company, and by 1911, when he retired from business, was probably the richest man in the world ; gave huge sums to charities, e.g. medical research and social organisations.
His son was John D. Rockefeller, Junior (1874–   ).

Rockefeller Centre, see RADIO CITY

' **Rocket,' THE,** name of a locomotive built by George Stephenson ; won a prize of £500 in 1829 ; travelled 12m in 53 minutes.

rocket, see FIREWORKS

rocket-plane, see AVIATION

Rockingham, 2ND MARQUIS OF, *rok'ing-am* (1730–82), English Whig politician ; Prime Minister 1765 ; his ministry repealed the Stamp Act ; Prime Minister again for a short time 1782.

rocks, see GEOLOGY

Rocky Mountains, mt. system from north to south of N. America. They run roughly parallel to the west coast. In Canada they are crossed by two passes, Crow's Nest and Kickinghorse. In USA the ranges are known as Kootenay, Wind R., Big Horn Mts, etc. In Wyoming is the volcanic Yellowstone region ; total length *c.*4,000m. The highest peaks in the whole system are Mt McKinley (Alaska) 20,300ft and Mt Logan, 19,539ft.

rodent, *rō'dent* (Latin *rodere,* to gnaw), any animal of the order *Rodentia,* in which the teeth are specially adapted to gnawing, e.g. squirrel, marmot, beaver, rat, mouse, agouti, cavy, hare and rabbit.

Rodin, AUGUSTE, *rō-dan'* (1840–1917), French sculptor, among the greatest of modern times, *b* Paris ; notable for his Impressionist pieces built up in clay and cast in bronze or carved in marble afterwards. Among his masterpieces are *The Burghers of Calais, The Prodigal Son,* and *The Thinker* (Le Penseur).

Rodney, LORD (1719–92), admiral, born near London ; distinguished himself in the battle off Ushant 1747 ; captured Martinique and Santa Lucia, 1762 ; defeated the Spanish fleet off Cape St Vincent 1780. Several British warships have been named after him.

Rogation Days, three fast days of the RC and Anglican churches. They are the Monday, Tuesday and Wednesday following Rogation Sunday, the 5th after Easter ; formerly celebrated by beating the bounds.

Rohmer, SAX, *rō'mĕr* (1886–   ), pen-name of the English writer Arthur Sansfield Ward, author of Oriental mystery stories, e.g. *Dr Fu-Manchu.*

Roland, 8th c. Frankish hero and giant ; fought for Charlemagne ; killed, with many other knights, in the pass of Roncesvalles during an expedition against Saragossa (Spain). His exploits are the subject of many romances, notably the *Chanson de Roland,* a national

French epic of 4,000 lines, written in the 11th century.

Roland, MADAME (1754–93), French revolutionary, *b* Paris. As Marie Jeanne Philipon she married Roland de la Platière, both becoming prominent among the Girondins, the party holding moderate republican views. When the Girondins fell from power, Madame Roland was guillotined, her last words being :

Oh, Liberty, what crimes are committed in thy name !

Rolland, ROMAIN, *rŏ-län* (1866–1944), French author ; wrote several notable books, of which *Jean-Christophe* is possibly the chief, though *Péguy* ranks very high. He was awarded the Nobel Prize for literature 1915.

Rolls, CHARLES STEWART (1877–1910), engineer, *b* London ; did much to make motor-cars popular in Britain. With Sir Frederick Henry Royce (1863–1933) he founded the famous firm of Rolls-Royce Ltd, makers of cars and aero-engines.

Romaic, see GREEK

Roman Britain, see BRITAIN

Roman Catholic Church, part of the Christian Church which acknowledges the pope as supreme head ; has *c.*400,000,000 adherents, largely in America, Poland, Spain, Italy and France, with *c.*2,400,000 in England and Wales, 614,000 (mainly Irish) in Scotland, and over 3,111,000 in Ireland. In England and Wales there are 4 archbishops and 14 bishops ; in Scotland 2 archbishops and 6 bishops ; and in Ireland 4 archbishops and 24 bishops. The pope, who lives in the Vatican, Italy, is assisted by a college of 70 cardinals. Cardinal Pacelli succeeded to the Papacy as Pius XII in 1939.

The RC Church claims to be *the* Church. It is catholic because its members are found the world over. It is apostolic because its popes claim to be in unbroken succession from St Peter. Its members venerate the Virgin Mary, believe in seven sacraments (baptism, confirmation, the Eucharist, penance, extreme unction, holy orders and matrimony), in the sacrificial meaning of Mass, in purgatory, in Transubstantiation, i.e. in the changing of bread and wine into the body and blood of our Lord when taken as a sacrament, and (since 1870) in the infallibility of the pope in matters of faith and morals. See REFORMATION

romance, *rŏ-mans'*, properly an epic in a Romance language (i.e. one derived from Latin, e.g. French, Spanish and Provençal), as, say, early legends of King Arthur. More generally, any popular epic of modern Europe. Still more recently, an imaginative tale, usually with much adventure and a strong love interest.

Romance, see LANGUAGE

Roman emperors, see ROME

Roman Empire, see ROME

Roman numerals :

I =	1	XX	=	20
II =	2	XXX	=	30
III =	3	XL	=	40
IV =	4	L	=	50
V =	5	LX	=	60
VI =	6	LXX	=	70
VII =	7	LXXX	=	80
VIII =	8	XC	=	90
IX =	9	C	=	100
X =	10	CC	=	200
XI =	11	CCC	=	300
XII =	12	CCCC or CD	=	400
XIII =	13	D	=	500
XIV =	14	DC	=	600
XV =	15	DCC	=	700
XVI =	16	DCCC	=	800
XVII =	17	CM	=	900
XVIII =	18	M	= 1,000
XIX =	19	MM	= 2,000

Romans, EPISTLE TO THE, letter written by St Paul from Corinth. It is one of the books of the NT.

Rome, sometimes called the Eternal City, cap. of Italy since 1871 ; *c.*17m from the mouth of the R. Tiber ; pop.1,550,000.

Traditionally founded by Romulus 753BC, the city began as a settlement on the Palatine, one of the Seven Hills of Rome (Palatine, Capitol, Aventine, Caelian, Esquiline, Viminal and Quirinal). The first walls were built after its capture by the Gauls 390BC, and the first aqueduct and military highway (*Via Appia*) begun *c.*312BC. Julius Caesar largely remodelled the city ; Pompey erected the first notable public buildings ; and of Augustus it has been said that he found the city of brick and left it of marble. Vespasian (acceded AD69) raised the Colosseum for chariot races and gladiator fights, and rebuilt the temple of Jupiter. Hadrian (AD117) built the Pantheon in its present form. Trajan and Marcus Aurelius erected monumental columns ; Diocletian and Caracalla built immense public baths. The first Christian churches (basilicas) in the city were the work of Constantine ; and the catacombs (underground churches and tombs of the Christians) still remain.

Great structural improvements have been carried out since 1871, including those ordered by Mussolini. Today Rome is a popular tourist centre, also a place of pilgrimage for Roman Catholics, having Vatican City (the home of the pope), and also St Peter's, generally regarded as the noblest church ever built. Rome is also a centre of art and scholarship, and notable for fine modern buildings. During World War II the city's railway yards were bombed by the Allies (1943) who liberated Rome from German domination June 1944.

The history of Rome may be summarised as having four phases : (i) foundation and regal period ; (ii) progress (510–30BC) as cap. of a growing republic ; (iii) supreme importance as

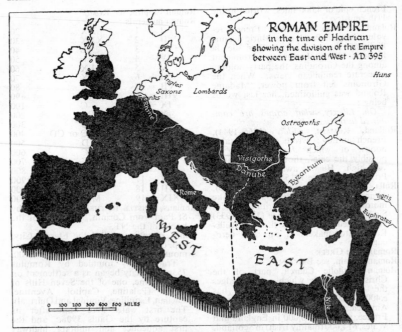

ROMAN EMPIRE
in the time of Hadrian
showing the division of the Empire
between East and West · AD 395

THE ROMAN EMPIRE

The Roman Empire reached its greatest extent (black on the map) under Hadrian, Emperor AD117–138. The dotted line shows how in 395 the Empire was divided into two parts, Eastern and Western. The Goths, Lombards, Franks, Angles, Saxons and Huns are shown approximately in the areas they occupied or had reached just before the barbarian invasions which occurred in the 4th and 5th centuries.

centre of the W. Roman empire, which ended AD476, though the eastern empire continued to 1453 ; and (iv) revival as the Holy Roman Empire, dating from the crowning in St Peter's of Charlemagne, AD800 to 1806, the states within the empire including what are now Germany, Austria, Switzerland, Czechoslovakia and Belgium.

The growth of Rome was at first gradual. In early years two rulers shared in the government, aided by two *praetors* (later known as *consuls*). Having gained control of the Latins, the Romans controlled Campania and the cities of the Etruscans, and by the 3rd c. BC governed the whole peninsula now called Italy. Carthage was ·destroyed 146BC, and Greece, parts of Asia Minor, and Spain were conquered in the 2nd c. BC. The conquest of Gaul (now France) began as early as *c.*133BC.

The republic may be said to have ended with the death of Julius Caesar 44BC, and the imperial age to have begun with the victory of Augustus at Actium 31BC. For 200 years the vast Roman empire (with lands on both sides of the Mediterranean) enjoyed comparative peace and immense wealth. Great

soldier-emperors arose, e.g. Trajan, Hadrian ; but after Marcus Aurelius the legions (as widely separated as the Rhine, Danube, and Euphrates) strove to make their respective commanders emperor, while barbarians (e.g. Goths, Franks, Alamanni, etc.) threatened an empire over fond of luxury.

Decay within was arrested by Diocletian (AD284), whose genius for a time restored the fortunes of the empire. He created mobile armies on the frontiers, instituted an empire council, began a reform of the coinage and revised taxes, but in spite of these wise and far-reaching measures, the government weakened. After his day the central power robbed local authorities of their civic rights, and a kind of caste system grew up, land-workers becoming little more than tax-paying serfs. Intrigue was rife at court and in political circles. Oriental influences crept more and more into Roman life and thought when Constantine removed his capital from Rome to Constantinople, and after his death (AD337), revolt followed revolt. Alaric, the Gothic chief, sacked Rome AD408. Attila invaded Italy AD452. The last of the Roman emperors, Romulus

Augustulus, was pensioned (AD476) by the barbaric leader Odoacer.

Our debt to Rome is immense. The modern world owes the basis of its laws, its conception of order and its ideas of justice to the Romans, whose code was first set down in writing by the *Decemvirs* in the 5th c. BC. The Romance languages (e.g. English, French, Spanish and Italian) spring from Latin. Roman military highways not only meant that Roman authority could be exercised in countries as far away as Britain and Egypt, but that new possibilities of trade and commerce were opened up, i.e. civilising influences were encouraged. Learning and art flourished, and Roman literature has enriched succeeding generations with poetry, drama and prose. Greatest among Roman poets were Lucretius, Catullus, Horace, and above all Virgil. The best prose writers were Cicero, Livy and Tacitus.

ROMAN EMPERORS
First Century

Augustus	27BC–AD14
Tiberius	AD14–37
Caligula	37–41
Claudius	41–54
Nero	54–68
Galba	68–*69
Otho	*69
Vitellius	*69
Vespasian	*69–79
Titus	79–81
Domitian	81–96
Nerva	96–98

* ' year of the Four Emperors '

Second Century

Trajan	98–117
Hadrian	117–138
Antoninus Pius	138–161
Marcus Aurelius	161–180

*Remainder with dates of accession :
the most important in capitals*
180 Commodus, 192 Pertinax, 193 L. Septimius SEVERUS, 211 Caracalla and Geta, 217 Macrinus, 218 Heliogabalus, 222 M. Aurelius Severus, 235 Maximinus, 235 Balbinus and Pupienus, 238 Gordianus, 244 Philippus, 249 Decius, 251 Gallus, 254 Valerian, 260 Gallienus, 268 Claudius, 270 Aurelian, 275 Tacitus, 284 DIOCLETIAN, 305 Constantius and Galerius, 306 ‧CONSTANTINE, 337 Constantine II, Constantius II, Constans, 350 Constantius II, 361 Julian, 363 Jovian.

Division of Empire

West (Rome)		East (Byzantium)
364	Valentinian I	364 Valens
375	Gratian and	
	Valentinian II	379 Theodosius I
383	Valentinian II	392 Theodosius I
395	Honorius	395 Arcadius
		408 Theodosius II
		450 Marcion

West (Rome)		East (Byzantium)
455	Maxinus	
455	Artus	
457	Majorian	457 Leo I
465	Authemius	
472	Olybrius	
473	Glycernio	
474	Julius Nepos	474 Leo II
475	Romulus Augustulus	

Romford, *rŭm'fĕrd,* town, Essex ; pop. 58,000.

Rommel, FIELD-MARSHAL ERWIN (1892–1944), German soldier ; commanded the Afrika Korps so successfully that he became Germany's most popular soldier in World War II. A master of tank warfare, he surprised Lord Wavell's forces near El Agheila 1941 ; defeated the British 8th Army at Bir Hacheim (Libya) 1942 and pushed them back to Alamein, where however they stood. Rommel was driven out of N. Africa by Field-Marshal Montgomery after his victory at Alamein, Oct 1942. Rommel poisoned himself in order to avoid being arrested for alleged participation in the Generals' plot 20 July 1944.

Romney, GEORGE (1734–1802), English painter, born in Lancashire. Though poor and uneducated he became the rival of Sir Joshua Reynolds, and was notable for subject pictures and portraits.

Romulus, *rom'ū-lŭs,* legendary founder of Rome, twin brother of Remus, and declared in old tales to have been the son of Mars, the War-god. Left to die in the open-air, he and his brother were adopted and suckled by a wolf, and later brought up by a shepherd. Romulus is said to have killed Remus for jumping over a wall of the city (Rome) he was founding *c.*753BC.

Roncesvalles, *rŏn-thes-väl'yäs,* valley of the Pyrenees ; scene (according to tradition) where part of Charlemagne's army was destroyed by the Basques, the hero, Roland, being slain, AD778.

Ronsard, PIERRE DE, *rŏn-sär* (1524–85), French Renaissance poet ; popular at court, a friend of Queen Elizabeth of England and Mary Queen of Scots. He did much to revive French poetry, and is especially notable for his sonnets and lyrics.

Röntgen, WILHELM KONRAD, *rŭnt'gen* (1845–1923), German scientist ; discovered Röntgen rays (later called X-rays) 1895 ; awarded the Nobel prize for physics 1901.

rood, old name for a cross or crucifix, especially one above the rood-screen in many English churches, usually put there between the 14th c. and Elizabeth's day. The word survives also in Holyrood (formerly Haly Rude), i.e. Holy Cross.

rook, see CROW

Rooke, SIR GEORGE (1650–1709), English admiral ; famous for his victories at La Hogue 1692, and Vigo 1702.

Roosevelt, FRANKLIN DELANO, *rōz'velt*
(1882–1945), 32nd President of the USA,
son of James Roosevelt, *b* Hyde
Park, New York ; practised as a
lawyer ; did much to combat the
submarine menace in World War I ;
shared President Wilson's enthusiasm
for the League of Nations.

At 39 he became a victim of infantile
paralysis ; only his indomitable spirit
saved him from becoming a helpless
cripple. As a Democrat, and as Governor of New York State, he attacked the
problems of unemployment, graft and
corruption. Elected President of the
USA 1932 during the worst of the
Great Slump, he proved himself a great
leader ; took USA off the gold standard,
and inaugurated the vast experiment
of the New Deal in conjunction with his
National Industrial Recovery Administration (NRA) ; made trade treaties
abroad ; showed himself a man of
immense courage, vision, tact and
energy in his politics of reconstruction.

In World War II Roosevelt gradually
swayed American opinion from isolationism towards friendly assistance for
Britain, and after the disaster of Pearl
Harbour (Dec 1941) he led the USA into
war against Japan and Germany.
Between Franklin Roosevelt and Winston Churchill there was perfect understanding, which did a great deal to
encourage complete co-operation between Britain and America in military,
naval and air attacks ; the planning of
campaigns in N. Africa, Italy, and the
assault (1944) on Occupied France, as
also in economic matters, e.g. Lend-
Lease. Roosevelt proved also to be a
faithful and able ally to Russia. By his
broadcast addresses (fireside talks) he
welded the American people into a
single weapon against the enemy.

He died during his third term of

FRANKLIN D. ROOSEVELT 1882–1945

THE WILD DOG-ROSE

office as President. A series of films
illustrating his life has been made, and
a statue in his memory was erected and
unveiled (by Mrs Roosevelt, his wife)
in London 1948. The statue was designed by Sir William Reid. It is in
Grosvenor Square.

Roosevelt, THEODORE (1858–1919), American Republican statesman, *b* New York ;
26th President of the USA 1901, and
again 1904 ; attacked political corruption ; made possible the building of the
Panama Canal ; built up the American
navy. As a man he was vigorous and
decisive, fond of adventure, travel and
hunting.

root, in mathematics, the converse of a
power, i.e. the *n*th root of a given number
is the number which, multiplied by
itself *n* times, gives that number, e.g.
$2^5 = 32$, therefore 2 is called the 5th
root of 32 ; and in general, if $a^n = b$,
a is the *n*th root of *b*, written $\sqrt[n]{b}$ or $b^{\frac{1}{n}}$.

rope, thick cordage ; made by hand till
the 18th c., Edmund Cartwright inventing a rope-making machine 1792. Rope
is usually manufactured from jute, coir,
hemp, cotton, sisal and, more recently,
nylon ; three strands make a hawser,
two hawsers twisted together make a
cable. Wire ropes are used in such work
as quarrying, and in January 1949 an
invention for cleaning and oiling wire
ropes was tested and found satisfactory.
In seven minutes it cleans and oils as
much wire rope as previously took a
whole day to do by hand.

rope trick, claimed as a performance by
Indian jugglers in which apparently a
rope, thrown in the air, remains erect
while a boy climbs to the top. It is very
doubtful if the trick is anything more
than a legend.

Rorke's Drift, see ZULULAND
rorqual, see WHALE
Rosa, CARL (1842–89), German concert
director ; formed the Carl Rosa Opera
Company 1875.

Rosario, river port, Argentina ; important

railway centre ; exports wool, hides and cereals ; pop.522,000.

rosary, see BEADS

Roscommon, county, Eire, in the province of Connaught ; co.tn Roscommon.

rose, shrub or tree (family *Rosaceae*), its flower being the emblem of England (see EMBLEM). The wild dog-rose or briar has curved prickles, toothed leaflets (in groups of 5) ; sweet-scented pink or white flowers with 5 petals. Bright red, pear-shaped fruit called hips appear in autumn. These are used medicinally in the form of rose-hip syrup. Cultivated varieties are grouped as tea, hybrid, climbing and rambler roses.

Rosebery, ARCHIBALD PHILIP PRIMROSE, 5TH EARL OF (1847–1929), statesman, *b* London ; Foreign Secretary 1886 ; Prime Minister for a short time after W. E. Gladstone's retirement 1894. One of the founders of the Liberal League, he was a great Imperialist

rose-hip syrup, see ROSE

rosemary, evergreen shrub introduced into Britain in the 16th c. ; has purple flowers. The leaves yield a constituent of eau de Cologne.

Roses, WARS OF THE (1455–85), struggle for the kingship in England between members of the house of York (whose emblem was a white rose) and the house of Lancaster (red rose).

In the early years of Henry VI's reign, Richard Duke of York was heir to the throne. When Henry had a son of his own, Richard took up arms with the support of the Earl of Warwick, the 'king-maker,' against Henry and his chief adviser, Edmund Beaufort, Duke of Somerset. Somerset was killed and Henry taken prisoner at St Albans 1455, Richard becoming Protector. The queen (Margaret of Anjou) then supported Henry's cause. Defeated at Blore Heath (1459), she was victorious at Wakefield (1460), where Richard was killed, and at St Albans (second battle), but was defeated by Warwick at Mortimer's Cross, Richard's son, Edward, being proclaimed king as Edward IV.

He and Warwick defeated the Lancastrians at Towton (1461), and then crushed other Yorkist rebellions. Later, Edward quarrelled with Warwick, who fled to France, and joined with the queen. He returned to England and drove Edward from the country, proclaiming Henry VI king once more. Edward IV, however, returned and defeated and killed Warwick at Barnet 1471. After his victory at Tewkesbury, he killed the young prince, Edward V, and probably murdered the insane Henry VI, and ruled as king, being followed by his son Richard III, whose bad government caused the Lancastrian, Henry Tudor, to take up arms. Henry defeated Richard III at Bosworth, 1485, and became Henry VII, the first Tudor king. By marrying Elizabeth, daughter of the Yorkist Edward IV, he joined the houses of Lancaster and York, and took as the emblem of England the Tudor rose, i.e. a red rose within a white one.

Rosetta, town on the delta of the Nile. Here 1799 was found the Rosetta Stone, a large slab of black basalt with inscriptions in Egyptian demotic, Egyptian hieroglyphic and Greek of a decree given at Memphis 196BC. Comparison of the three versions of this text on the Rosetta Stone enabled scholars for the first time to decipher ancient Egyptian writing. The stone was brought to the British Museum 1802.

Ross, SIR JAMES CLARK (1800–62), nephew of Sir John Ross ; made several Arctic expeditions ; discovered the magnetic N. Pole 1831. He commanded an Antarctic expedition 1839, discovering Victoria Land and Mt Erebus.

Ross, SIR JOHN (1777–1856), English explorer ; attempted to find the NW. Passage 1818, and again 1829 ; went in search of Sir John Franklin.

Ross, SIR RONALD (1857–1932), British doctor ; discovered the malaria parasite in mosquitoes *c.*1897 ; awarded the Nobel prize for medicine 1902. See MOSQUITO

Rossall School, English public school 3m from Fleetwood, Lancashire ; founded 1844.

Ross and Cromarty, *krom'ĕr-ti,* county of N. Scotland ; generally mountainous with extensive deer forests ; co.tn Dingwall.

Rossetti, CHRISTINA GEORGINA, *rō-set'i* (1830–94), poet, sister of Dante Gabriel Rossetti, *b* London ; lover of books, animals and flowers ; wrote graceful mystical lyrics, often about death, but in spite of sorrow and suffering she was cheerful and courageous. Her books of poetry include *Goblin Market* ; *The Prince's Progress* ; and *Sing-Song.*

Rossetti, DANTE GABRIEL (1828–82), poet and artist, brother of Christina Rossetti, *b* London of parents who were refugees from Naples. As a poet he is notable for his sonnets, e.g. *The House of Life*, and his translations of Dante and the early Italian poets, his work being full of rich imagery. As an artist, he was the pupil of Ford Madox Brown, and the friend of Holman Hunt, Millais, William Morris and Burne-Jones. He was the chief founder of the Pre-Raphaelite school of painting which revived the devotional spirit in art.

Rossini, GIOACHINO ANTONIO, *rŏs-sē'ni* (1792–1868), Italian composer ; won fame with his operas *The Barber of Seville* ; *William Tell.*

Ross Island, see POLAR REGIONS

Rosslare, see WEXFORD

Ross Sea, part of the Antarctic between S. Victoria and King Edward VII Land.

Rostock, town, Mecklenburg, Germany ; exports grain and flax ; pop.122,000.

Rostov-on-Don, *ros-tŏf',* industrial city and port, USSR, *c.*34m east of Taganrog ; trades in grain; pop.510,000.

Rosyth, *rō-sīth'*, naval base, Firth of Forth.

Rotary International, organisation founded 1905 by Paul Harris of Chicago ; introduced into Britain 1911. Each club comprises members representative of various trades and professions. The total number of clubs is over 3,000. The Rotary motto is *Service, not Self.*

rotation of crops, see AGRICULTURE

Rothamstead Experimental Station, *roth'-am-sted*, agricultural station near Harpenden, Hertfordshire ; founded 1843 ; notable for its scientific investigation of farming and similar problems.

Rotherham, *rothĕr'am*, town, near Sheffield, W. Yorkshire ; on the rivers Rother and Don ; noted for iron, pottery and chemicals ; pop.76,000.

Rothschild, name of a famous Jewish banking family, the first of note being Amschel Moses Rothschild (*d* 1754), a moneychanger of Frankfort (Germany). The founder of the great banking house of Rothschild was Mayer Amschel Rothschild (*d* 1812), who provided vast sums for the wars against Napoleon. His five sons extended the business over Europe. Later Rothschilds were Nathaniel Mayer (1840–1915), President of the British Red Cross Society, and Baron Henri de Rothschild, a famous Paris doctor and dramatist.

Rotifera, *rō-tif'ĕr-ä*, group of animalcules found in ponds and (in a few instances) in sea-water. The largest is just visible with the naked eye. Under the microscope they are of exceptional interest, and the movements of their cilia, which draw food to the mouth, remind the observer of a revolving wheel, hence the name. Most are free-swimming, but some are attached to plants. They possess a rudimentary brain and very simple eyes.

Rotorua, town of N. Island, NZ, noted for volcanoes and hot springs, etc. which are near by.

At the moment NZ is planning a vast undertaking whereby its thermal springs will be used for generating electricity.

Rototherm, see THERMOMETER

rotten boroughs, see REFORM ACTS

Rotterdam, Netherlands port on the R. Maas ; noted for shipbuilding, distilling and many other industries ; suffered much in World War II ; pop.612,000.

Roubaix, *roo-bā*, town, France, *c.*6m from Lille ; manufactures woollen goods ; also grows early tomatoes ; pop.107,000.

Rouen, *roo-än*, cathedral city and port, France, on the R. Seine ; *c.*87m northwest of Paris. A beautiful old town, with fine churches, it is noted for textiles. Here William the Conqueror died, and in the market-place Joan of Arc was burned 1431 ; pop.123,000.

roulette, *roo-let'*, gambling game especially associated with Monte Carlo, the hazard being decided by the position of a white ball after it comes to rest on one of 37 spinning compartments.

round, see SINGING

rounders, outdoor game popular in Britain in the 18th c. ; now usually played on a diamond-shaped field with 10 players a side, each of the batting side striking the ball with a ' bat ' 35in long and 3½in wide. The fielders attempt to catch the ball, or to throw it so as to hit the batsman as he runs round the ' odds ' or ' bases ' ; in either case he is out. A run is scored whenever a member of one batting side completes the circuit. If the last man completes the circuit, his side has another innings.

It was from this game that base-ball was developed in USA.

Roundheads, see CIVIL WAR

Round Pond, see LONDON

Round Table, see ARTHUR

Round Table Conference, see INDIA

Rousseau, JEAN JACQUES, *roo-sō* (1712–78), French political philosopher and writer, *b* Geneva (Switzerland) ; had much charm of manner, but was suspicious, quarrelsome, and grew melancholy in later life. His greatest book, *Le Contrat Social* (The Social Contract), became the ' Bible ' of many leaders of the French Revolution, his basic belief being that the common man counts, and that government should be the expression of the general will, not the will of a few only, hence it is a plea for democracy. His novel *La Nouvelle Héloïse* gave rise to the romantic movement in France.

Rovering, see BOY SCOUTS

Rowallan, LORD (1895–   ), Chief Scout 1945.

rowan, *row'-an*, a small tree with slender, upward branches, its leaflets often in sprays of 13 or 15 ; the flowers are cream-coloured ; in autumn they give way to clusters of bright red berries. Though called in England the mountain-ash, the rowan-tree is not an ash. It is common in Scotland.

Rowley Regis, *row'li rē'jis*, town, Staffordshire ; noted for iron, pottery and chains ; linked with Dudley ; pop. 45,000.

Roxburghshire, *roks'bŭ-rŭ-*, sheep-grazing border county, Scotland. Jedburgh is now the co.tn.

Royal Academy, see PAINTING

Royal Academy of Music, founded 1822 to provide musical education for professional students. The HQ are in Marylebone Road, London, NW1.

Royal Air Force, see RAF

Royal College of Music, (Prince Consort Road, South Kensington, London, SW7), founded 1883.

' **Royal George,'** British man-of-war that capsized at Spithead 1782, Admiral Kempenfelt and 800 men being drowned.

Royalists, see CIVIL WAR

Royal National Lifeboat Institution, see LIFEBOAT

Royal Oak Day, see CALENDAR

Royal Observatory, astronomical observatory, Greenwich, founded 1675 by Charles II. The Observatory is now being removed to Hurstmonceux, Sussex. The reason for the removal of the

Observatory from Greenwich to Sussex
is the glare over London at night.
There are royal observatories also at
Edinburgh and the Cape of Good
Hope. See GREENWICH

Royal Society, THE, chief scientific society
of the UK ; founded 1662 ; encourages
scientific investigation by awarding
medals, e.g. the Copley, Davy and
Darwin awards ; equips scientific expeditions. A Royal Society having similar aims was founded in Edinburgh 1783.
It is known as the Royal Society of
Edinburgh.

Royal Standard, the king's own banner ;
bears the arms of England, Scotland
and Ireland ; flown over buildings
where the king is in residence.

Royce, SIR F. H., see ROLLS, C. S.

Royden, MAUDE (1876–), English
social worker and preacher (City Temple,
London, 1917–20) ; supported the campaign for votes for women.

RSFSR, short for the Russian Socialist
Federal Soviet Republic. See USSR

rubber or **indiarubber,** at one time known
as caoutchouc, elastic product of various
trees from which, when cut, there flows
a milky juice. Such trees grow in
tropical and sub-tropical climates, notably in Central and S. America, where
for long Brazil was the chief source of
rubber, the best being exported largely
from Pará. India, W. Africa, Ceylon
and especially Malaya, e.g. British
Malaya and the Netherlands E. Indies
are sources of immense quantities of the
finest rubber, a large proportion of
which is now exported via Singapore.

Chemically rubber consists of very
long molecules (a 5-carbon group) in
tangled chains, the main constituent
being a polymer of isoprene, from which
synthetic rubber is manufactured.

Once used almost wholly for rubbing
out pencil marks, rubber has grown in
importance since *c.*1840, and is now of
immense value in industry, though the
use of pure rubber has given place, to a
great extent, to that of so-called vulcanised rubber, i.e. rubber mixed with
sulphur, an invention of the American,
Charles Goodyear. This, combined
with heat, produces greater elasticity,
one of its most important uses being the
making of tyres, elastic, waterproofing,
soles and heels for shoes, etc.

A rubber plantation may have from
70–100 trees per acre. The trees are
tapped when they are from 5 to 6 years
old, and upwards, i.e. when they are
25–30in round the trunk. A cut is made
in the bark at about 3ft and an angle
of 45°, and the sap (latex) flows into a
cup. A good yield for a young tree is
3lb of dried rubber per year. In Malaya
(prior to World War II) the annual
production of rubber amounted to
*c.*500,000 tons out of a world-total of
1,150,000 tons, the average yield *per
acre* being *c.*425lb. Many Malayan
estates are now replacing old trees by

budded trees (derived from exceptionally
fine stock), and the expected yield is
1,000lb of rubber per acre. See BRAZIL;
MALAYA

Rubbra, EDMUND (1901–), composer,
b Northampton ; notable for his
symphonies.

Rubens, PETER PAUL (1577–1640), Flemish
artist, lived much in Antwerp ; painted
*c.*1,200 pictures and portraits, all aglow
with rich colour, and instinct with movement. His flesh-tints are masterly, and
some of his huge canvases are among the
world's greatest pictures, e.g. *The Birth
of Venus* and *The Holy Family.*

Rubicon, see CAESAR, JULIUS

rubidium, *roo-bid'i-ŭm,* white metal and
element, Rb ; atomic weight 85·48 ;
atomic number 37 ; resembles sodium ;
discovered 1861.

Rubinstein, ANTON, *roo'bin-stīn* (1829–94),
Russian pianist ; best known for his
piano compositions and songs.

ruby, precious stone ; a red, transparent
variety of corundum, Al_2O_3.

rudd, British fresh-water fish resembling
the roach ; has red fins and eyes.

rue, *roo,* shrub with bluish-green leaves
and small yellowish flowers, emblems of
bitterness and grief. It has a powerful
odour.

ruff, starched linen or lace collar worn in
the 16th c. ; especially characteristic of
Elizabethan dress.

ruff, bird (now a rare summer visitor to
Britain) akin to the sandpiper ; has
plumage mottled grey, brown, and black
with buff underparts. In the breeding
season the male has a broad ruff or
collar of feathers.

Rufus, see WILLIAM II

Rugby, town, Warwickshire, on the R.
Avon ; famous for its public school ;
noted for engineering, motor cars, etc.,
and as an important railway centre ;
pop.43,000.

Rugby football, see FOOTBALL ; RUGBY
SCHOOL

Rugby School, public school founded 1567
by a grocer ; became famous under
Dr Thomas Arnold, headmaster 1827–42;
notable as the scene of the popular book
Tom Brown's Schooldays by Thomas
Hughes, an old boy who became a
barrister.

Rugby football is named after Rugby
School, where it was first played. In
the ' Close ' there is an inscription to
William Webb Ellis, who 1823 ' with a
fine disregard for the rules of football as
played in his time, first took the ball in
his arms and ran with it, thus originating
the distinctive feature of the Rugby game.'

Rügen, *rü'gen,* German island in the
Baltic Sea.

Ruhr, *roor,* tributary of the R. Rhine ;
flows through the world's richest coalfield, its valley having many industries,
especially iron and steel.

Ruislip, *rīs'lip,* growing residential district
between Harrow and Uxbridge, Middle-
sex ; pop. (with Northwood) 66,000.

' Rule Britannia,' see ARNE, T. A.

Rum, island of the Inner Hebrides ; area 42sq.m.

rum, intoxicating liquor distilled from cane-sugar, or artificially made with rum essence Rum distributed in the Royal Navy is still known as grog, after Admiral Vernon (nicknamed Old Grog from his grogram cloak).

Rumania, *roo-mā'niä,* republic of SE. Europe, anciently comprising Dacia and Scythia ; now includes Wallachia and Moldavia ; has been independent since 1878. The area is *c.*92,000sq.m ; pop. 17,000,000. Much of the rich agricultural land is in peasant proprietorship, cereals being grown on a vast scale. The country has exceedingly valuable oil wells near Ploesti. Minerals include petroleum, salt, coal, lignite and mica. The country suffered severely during World War II. It was deprived of its agricultural machinery, and in 1947 the people faced famine. Bucharest, the cap., was liberated from Nazi occupation 1944.

Rumford, COUNT VON, *rŭm'fĕrd* (1753–1814), American soldier and scientist, *b* Massachusetts. In the American War of Independence he fought for the British ; entered the Bavarian service ; and founded the Rumford medal of the Royal Society. He is remembered as a pioneer of the theory that heat is a form of energy.

ruminant, *roo'mi-nant,* group of hoofed animals (with even toes) that chew their cud, i.e. they eat hastily and watchfully, and then retire to bring up their food and masticate it at leisure. Examples are oxen, sheep, goats, deer and camels.

Rump, THE, see LONG PARLIAMENT

Runciman, VISCOUNT (1870–1949), Liberal politician, *b* S. Shields ; President of the Board of Education 1908, later of the Board of Trade, where he had much to do with tariffs. Head of a British mission to Czechoslovakia 1938 during the crisis preceding the Munich Agreement, he was instrumental in persuading Czechoslovakia to give way.

Runcorn, port, Cheshire, on the R. Mersey ; noted for shipbuilding, chemicals, alkali, etc. ; has a fine transporter bridge to Widnes; pop.23,000.

runes, letters of the Runic alphabet of ancient Scandinavia, Britain and Ireland ; much used for inscriptions on stones from about the 3rd c. AD.

Runnymede, name of a meadow along the south bank of the Thames, *c.*20m from London ; scene 1215 of King John's agreement to the principles of *Magna Carta.*

rupee, *roo-pē',* Indian silver coin usually valued at *c.* 1s 5d, or say *c.* 13·5 Rs to £1. A *lakh* of rupees is 100,000 written (Indian notation) Rs1,00,000.

Rupert (1619–82), German prince, son of the Elector Palatine, Frederick V, his mother being a daughter of James I. As nephew of Charles I, he fought for the Royalists at Edgehill, Marston Moor and Naseby. He was the founder of the Hudson's Bay Company.

Rushmore, MOUNT, see SCULPTURE

Ruskin, JOHN (1819–1900), writer and lover of beauty, *b* London ; travelled much in France, Switzerland and Italy ; inherited 1864 his father's fortune of £150,000; in later years lived at Coniston in the English Lake District.

A great Victorian, Ruskin condemned sham and ugliness ; wished to do much to improve the lot of the working man ; fought for honesty of purpose in craftsmanship, and for the creation and preservation of beauty. He wrote many books, e.g. *Modern Painters* ; *The Stones of Venice* ; *The Seven Lamps of Architecture* ; *Unto This Last* ; *Time and Tide* ; *Sesame and Lilies.* He founded in Sheffield the Ruskin Museum. At Oxford is Ruskin College (1899) founded to help working men and women to fit themselves for public life.

Russell, 1ST EARL (1792–1878), best known as Lord John Russell, Whig statesman, *b* London ; introduced the Reform Act 1832 ; supported free trade from 1845 ; succeeded Palmerston as Prime Minister 1865–66. A great reformer, he was later unpopular because of his mismanagement of the Crimean War.

Russell, 3RD EARL (1872–   ), better known as Bertrand Russell ; notable as (*a*) a philosopher who has written several important books on the subject ; (*b*) a mathematician who collaborated with A. N. Whitehead in *Principia Mathematica,* a treatise on higher mathematics ; (*c*) a scientist, his books including studies of atoms and Relativity ; and (*d*) a pioneer in social theories expressed in books on education and industrial civilisation.

One of Bertrand Russell's most brilliant books is his *History of Western Philosophy* (1947).

Russell, GEORGE WILLIAM (1867–1935), Irish poet, better known by his penname AE ; wrote many lyrical poems, usually mystical.

Russell, WILLIAM CLARK (1844–1911), English novelist, *b* New York ; a sailor for seven years ; author of *The Wreck of the ' Grosvenor.'*

Russia, see USSR

Russo-Japanese War (1904–5), begun by Japan when Russia failed to leave Korea and Manchuria ; ended in Japan gaining most of her demands by the *Treaty of Portsmouth.*

Russo-Turkish wars, three 19th c. wars between Russia and Turkey : (*a*) 1827–29, leading to independence for Greece ; (*b*) 1854–56, see CRIMEAN WAR ; and (*c*) 1877–78, resulting in independence for the Balkan states.

rust, generally regarded as a hydrated oxide of iron (chiefly $2Fe_2O_3.3H_2O$) formed when iron is exposed to air, damp and carbonic acid. Iron does not rust in dry air, or in water that is free from dissolved oxygen. The presence of carbon dioxide is also probably necessary. Rusting is usually prevented (*a*) with paint, (*b*) with another metal, e.g. zinc or tin, but Canadian scientists have claimed very recently to have discovered an anti-rust material of great importance.

rust, plant parasite or fungus, especially wheat rust. Red rust on wheat comes from spores that have ripened on the barberry.

Ruth, OT character whose story is told in the beautiful *Book of Ruth*. She married Boaz.

ruthenium, rare metal and element, Ru ; atomic weight 101·7 ; atomic number 44.

Rutherford, LORD (1871–1937), better known as Professor Rutherford, scientist, *b* Nelson, NZ ; followed Professor J. J. Thomson at the Cavendish Laboratory, Cambridge ; notable for remarkable achievements in physics; predicted the discovery of the neutron ; may be regarded as the father of the investigations into the nature of matter and energy which led to atomic fission, and so to the atom-bomb of 1945.

Rutherford, MARK (1831–1913), pen-name of William Hale White, *b* Bedford ; author of novels dealing with moral problems, e.g. *The Autobiography of Mark Rutherford.*

Rutherglen, *ruth'ĕr-glen*, town adjoining Glasgow ; makes chemicals, dyes and paper ; pop.25,000.

Rutland, smallest county in England (area 152sq.m) ; is east of Leicestershire ; co.tn Oakham.

Ruwenzori, *roo-wen-zō'ri*, mt. range, Uganda ; rises 16,000ft ; earlier known as the Mts. of the Moon ; discovered by Stanley 1887–89.

Ryde, holiday town and yachting centre, I. of Wight.

Rye, town near the Sussex coast ; one of the Cinque Ports.

rye, cultivated grass (*Secale cereale*) yielding the grain from which the so-called ' black bread ' of N. Europe is made ; largely grown in Scandinavia, N. Germany and the Netherlands. Although it thrives in comparatively poor soil, it is *c*.90 % as nourishing as wheat. In Britain rye is grown largely as forage and a milling crop, either as summer or winter rye, the latter ripening in August. Rye bread is becoming increasingly popular in Britain.

Rylands, JOHN (1801–88), merchant, *b* St Helens, Lancashire ; founder of an immense cotton factory. His widow built the John Rylands library, Manchester, as a memorial. Opened 1899, it has over 250,000 books, including rare Bibles.

ryot, see INDIA

Ryswick, TREATY OF, signed near The Hague, 1697, after a war in which England, Holland, Germany and Spain fought against France, compelling Louis XIV to surrender all his conquests except Strasbourg, and to promise not to support James II.

S

S, chemical symbol for sulphur.

Saar, *zär*, river of France and Germany ; flows 152m to the Moselle. The SAAR BASIN, governed by the League of Nations after World War I, was returned to Germany, 1935. After World War II the people voted for economic union with France.

Saarbrücken, *zär-brü'ken*, town in the Saar Basin (Germany) ; surrounded by coal mines and an industrial region ; pop.135,000.

Sabatini, RAFAEL (1875–1950), writer and dramatist, son of Italian and English parents ; author of over forty books, most of them thrilling historical tales. e.g. *The Sea Hawk* and *Captain Blood.* Many have been filmed.

Sabines, *sab'īns*, people of ancient Italy. Long at war with Rome, they were conquered *c*.290BC.

sable, *sā'b'l*, Siberian animal rather like the marten ; *c*.18in long ; has very valuable silky, brown fur.

sabotage, *sab'ō-täj*, methods of retarding industry or business by smashing machinery, buildings, or otherwise preventing progress. In World War II people in countries under Nazi rule did all they could to hinder the Germans, and many acts of sabotage were committed, such as derailing troop-trains, blowing up munition factories, etc.

saccharin, *sak'ă-rin* (Greek *saccharon*, sugar), sulpho-benzimide *c*.560 times sweeter than cane sugar ; manufactured from toluene.

Sachs, HANS, *zäks* (1494–1576), German cobbler who won fame as a singer, poet and playwright ; *b* Nuremberg ; he was stirred by the spirit of the Reformation and left over 4,000 popular songs.

Hans was a Meistersinger, i.e. he belonged to a guild of master singers and poets. With his humour, skill and charm he taught the Meistersingers to sing happily and to write poems everyone could understand. He is immortalised in Wagner's opera *Die Meistersinger*.

sackbut, 14th c. wind instrument rather like a trombone. The sackbut mentioned in Daniel 3 was a *stringed* instrument.

Sackville-West, VICTORIA (1892–   ), writer and poet, *b* Knole, Kent ; author of *Heritage, The Edwardians, All Passion Spent,* and other well-known novels.

sacrament, religious ceremony regarded by some Christian churches as an act which is performed merely as an outward sign of inward grace, by others as actually the means whereby grace is communicated to those taking part in it. The RC church recognises seven sacraments : baptism, confirmation, the Mass, penance, ordination, marriage and extreme unction. Most Protestant churches recognise only baptism and holy communion. About communion many views are held, ranging from those who regard it as the sacrament of the Lord's Supper, in which sharing the bread and wine is an act of fellowship reminding us of our fellowship in Christ who gave his blood and body that men might live ; to those who maintain that in the sacrament the bread and wine without visible change are turned into the same substance as Christ's body and blood.

Sacramento, river flowing *c.*400m in California ; also the cap. California, USA ; has flour mills and canning factories ; pop.106,000.

sacrifice, offering to God. The Jews at one time sacrificed burnt offerings. Some savage peoples at one time believed in human sacrifice, e.g. the ancient Druids and the Mexicans of the 15th c., thus hoping to win favour with their gods.

Sadducees, see JEWS

Sa′di, *sä′dē* (*d* 1291), Persian poet, *b* Shiraz ; his best known works are *The Fruit Garden* and *The Rose Garden*.

saffron, small plant with a corm like that of the crocus. The flower, which blooms in autumn, is purple with orange-red stigmas.

saga, *sä′gä,* prose story of ancient Icelandic heroes. Many sagas were written by unknown authors, some by Ari (1067–1148), others by Snorri Sturlason, *d* 1241. Among the most famous are the sagas of Egil, and those of the Volsungs. Early sagas were recited by skalds, i.e. poets.

sage, small shrub with a woolly stem, wrinkled leaves, and purple flowers. It is used by cooks for seasoning.

sago, starchy food from the pith of the sago palm, a tree *c.*30ft high, and abundant in Malaya and Borneo.

Saguenay, *sag-ĕ-nā′,* tributary of the St Lawrence, Quebec; length 120m

Sahara, *sä-hä′rä,* desert of N. Africa ; area *c.*3,500,000sq.m (seventy times that of England) ; much of it is sand, but there are granite rocks, mts. rising over 9,000ft, deep valleys and dry river beds. There are a few oases. The daytime heat is usually fierce, but at midnight there may be several degrees of frost.

Great caravan routes cross the desert, and there are regions suitable for grazing herds of cattle. The ruins of many cities are to be found, proving that at one time the rainfall was considerable in parts.

Plans have been discussed for making much of this vast wilderness into arable land, the construction of a canal 200m long, it is said, serving to flood a wide area and to irrigate a region capable of supporting 100,000,000 people.

Saigon, *sī-gon′,* cap. and port, Cochin-China ; pop.190,000.

sainfoin, pea-like plant with pink flowers. Grown for grazing purposes, it is a valuable fodder plant ; thrives on dry soil.

St Abb's Head, headland on the Berwickshire coast.

St Albans, city, Hertfordshire ; has remains of the Roman Verulamium. Francis Bacon is buried in St Michael's church. Here, in the Wars of the Roses, the Yorkists defeated the Lancastrians 1455, but suffered defeat 1461. The modern city has breweries and printing-works, also a fine cathedral ; pop. 42,000.

St Andrews, royal burgh and watering place, Fife ; has ruins of a 12th c. cathedral and a 13th c. castle. The university (oldest in Scotland) was founded 1411. St Andrews is Britain's foremost golfing centre. See WISHART, GEORGE

St Asaph, *as′af,* cathedral city, Flintshire.

St Austell, town, Cornwall ; long noted for china clay ; pop.22,000.

SAFFRON

St Bartholomew, MASSACRE OF, *bär-thol'ō-mū*, massacre in France 1572, when *c.*25,000 Huguenots were ruthlessly massacred by the Roman Catholics.

St Bartholomew's Hospital, London hospital founded (together with a priory) 1123 ; now notable for its medical school ; usually spoken of as ' Bart's.'

St Bernard, *bŭr'nĕrd*, name of two passes over the Alps : (*a*) the Little St Bernard, rising to 7,176ft ; (*b*) the Great St Bernard, between Valais (Switzerland) and Piedmont (Italy), rising to 8,110ft. Here is the St Bernard monastery (or hospice) with rooms for 175 travellers.

St Catherine's College, college of Cambridge University ; founded 1473 ; popularly known as ' Cat's.'

St David's Head, most westerly point of Wales. It is on the coast of Pembrokeshire.

St Denis, *san dĕ-nē'*, town, France, on the R. Seine ; burial place of many kings of France.

St Dunstan's, see PEARSON, SIR A.

Sainte-Beuve, CHARLES AUGUSTIN, *sant bŭv'* (1804–69), French novelist, essayist, historian, and the most impartial critic France has had. A man of penetrating insight, his prose is admirably lucid.

St Elmo's fire, bluish electrical discharge sometimes seen above a mast, spire or tree in thundery weather. See ELECTRICITY

St Étienne, *san tā-tyen*, town, France, 36m south-west of Lyons ; noted for coal and iron, also for its textiles, including silks and ribbons ; pop. 190,000.

St George's Channel, channel between Ireland and Wales.

St Gothard, *sānt goth'ĕrd* ; *got'-*, pass over the Alps from Switzerland to Italy ; rises to nearly 7,000ft. The St Gothard Tunnel, 9¼m, is only one of 80 tunnels through which a railway runs.

St Helena, *sānt hĕ-lē'nä*, British volcanic island in the S. Atlantic, 1,140m from the African coast ; area 47sq.m ; pop. 4,700. Napoleon died in exile here 1821. Flax (phormium) is manufactured.

St Helens, *-hel'enz*, town, Lancashire ; has collieries, iron-works, and is noted for glass ; pop.107,000.

St Helier, *-hel'yĕr*, port and chief town, Jersey (one of the Channel Is.) ; pop. 28,000.

St James's Palace, see LONDON

Saint Joan, see JOAN OF ARC

St John, river of N. America ; flows 450m to the Bay of Fundy.

St John, important winter port and CPR terminus, New Brunswick (Canada) ; pop.52,000.

St John of Jerusalem, name of an order of knighthood founded at Jerusalem *c.*1070, part of their work being to protect pilgrims. Driven from the Holy Land, they settled in Rhodes, and finally at Malta 1530. The English order, revived 1834, devotes itself to Red Cross work,

ST JOHN'S WORT
The plant and its seed, the leaf and the the stamens

notably the St John Ambulance Association. See NURSING

St John's, port and cap., Newfoundland ; pop.63,000.

St John's College, college of Oxford University, founded 1555. The gardens are perhaps the most beautiful in Oxford.

St John's College, college of Cambridge University, founded 1511.

St John's Wood, district of London, north-west of Regent's Park.

St John's Wort, *-wĕrt*, tall, flowering plant of the hedge-bank ; has a star-like, short-stalked flower with five pale yellow petals. The smooth leaves are in pairs.

St Kilda, island of the Outer Hebrides, uninhabited since 1930.

St Kitts, island of the British W. Indies (Leeward group) ; area 68sq.m ; pop. 30,000 ; noted for cane sugar ; cap. Basseterre.

St Laurent, LOUIS (1882–   ), French-Canadian lawyer, who became Prime Minister in 1949.

St Lawrence, *-lŏ'rens*, river of N. America ; issues from L. Ontario ; flows 1,900m to the Gulf of St Lawrence, an arm of the N. Atlantic. The river, frozen in winter, is partly the boundary between USA and Canada. It drains the Great Lakes.

St Leger, *-lej'ĕr*, horse race at Doncaster (Yorkshire) held in September.

St Louis, *-loo'is* ; *loo'i*, river port, Missouri USA ; on the R. Mississippi ; noted for tobacco, meat-packing, smelting and printing ; pop.813,000.

St Lucia, *-lū'shi-ä*, largest of the Windward Islands (British W. Indies). The USA leased seaplane bases here 1940. The island, famed for its lovely scenery, is mountainous, and exports sugar, limes, lime-oil, coconuts, copra and bay rum ; cap. Castries.

St Malo, *san* *mä-lō,* port and holiday town on the NW. coast of France.

St Margaret's, London church near Westminster Abbey ; is the official church of the House of Commons. There are memorials of Sir Walter Raleigh.

St Martin's-in-the-Fields, 18th c. church in Trafalgar Square, London. Destitute people may sleep in its crypt.

St Mary-le-Bow or **Bow Church,** church built *c.*1671, Cheapside (London). People born within sound of its bells are known as Cockneys. The church suffered severely from bombing in World War II.

St Moritz, *sänt mō'rits,* town, Switzerland ; has medicinal springs ; popular for winter sports.

St Nazaire, *san nä-zār',* port for Nantes, France ; on the R. Loire ; famous for shipbuilding ; used by the Nazis as a U-boat base in World War II, and practically wiped out by continuous bombing ; its river exit was blocked 1942 ; pre-war pop.44,000.

St Patrick, ORDER OF, see CHIVALRY

St Paul, city, Minnesota, USA ; on the Mississippi R. ; great railway and commercial centre ; pop.288,000.

St Paul's Cathedral, see LONDON

St Paul's School, public school founded 1509. The original building, close to St Paul's Cathedral, London, was destroyed in the Great Fire 1666. The school is now at Hammersmith.

St Peter Port, cap. of the island of Guernsey.

St Peter's, see ARCHITECTURE ; ROME

St Petersburg, see LENINGRAD

Saint-Pierre, JACQUES DE, *san pyär* (1737–1814), French writer, *b* Havre ; wrote *Paul et Virginie,* a tale of two lovers on the island of Mauritius.

St Quentin, *san kän-ta*n, town, France ; on the R. Somme ; manufactures textiles ; pop.49,000.

saints, in the NT means simply members of the Christian church ; now applied especially to good men and women who have tried to serve God in some particular way, e.g. the mother of Jesus, his disciples, St Paul, St George, St Patrick, St Augustine and St Joan. Men and women who have died for their faith are regarded as martyrs, and may become saints. For Roman Catholics a saint is one who, after his life has been examined by the pope, has been canonised. ' S ' or ' St ' is short for saint ; *san, santa* and *santo* are the Spanish and Italian equivalents.

Saint-Saëns, CHARLES CAMILLE, *san säns'* (1835–1921), French composer, *b* Paris ; wrote several operas of which *Samson and Delilah* (1877) is the most famous.

St Swithin's Day, see CALENDAR

St Thomas's Hospital, hospital by the Thames, London. The present buildings were opened 1871 ; notable for its medical school. The hospital was severely bombed in World War II.

St Valentine's Day, see CALENDAR

St Vincent, one of the Windward Is., British W. Indies ; exports include cotton, copra, rum, molasses and spices. It is subject to volcanic eruptions. The capital is Kingstown, a busy port.

St Vincent, headland on the south-west coast of Portugal. Naval battles fought nearby include those of (*a*) 1693, when the British were defeated by the French ; (*b*) 1780, when Admiral Rodney defeated the Spanish ; (*c*) 1797, when Earl St Vincent (*d* 1823) shattered a Spanish fleet with the aid of Nelson, who disobeyed orders but turned defeat into victory.

St Vincent, JOHN JERVIS, EARL OF, *jär'vis ;* *jŭr'-* (1735–1823), British admiral ; shared in the capture of Quebec 1759, and in the relief of Gibraltar, but most famous for his brilliant victory off Cape St Vincent, 1797, when he defeated a Spanish fleet.

St Vitus's dance, popular name for *chorea,* a nervous complaint causing twitching and restlessness.

saké, *sä'ki,* Japanese intoxicating drink made chiefly from rice.

saki, *sä'ki,* monkey with a yellow or whitish face ; found only in S. America.

sakiya, see FELLAH

Sakkar'a, Egyptian village on the left bank of the R. Nile. It is noted for twenty pyramids, among them the famous stepped pyramid of Tcheser.

salaam, *sä-läm',* form of greeting in many countries of the East. Indians salaam by bending the head and body, and placing the right hand against the forehead. ' Salaam aleikum ' is Arabic for ' Peace be with you.'

Saladin, *sal'ä-din* (*d* 1193), Moslem soldier of fine character and great skill ; lived much in Damascus (Palestine) in his youth ; became Sultan of Egypt and Syria ; conquered Palestine by capturing Jerusalem 1187 ; opposed at Acre by Richard Coeur de Lion. To finance the third crusade the Saladin tithe was levied 1188 in England. See CRUSADES

Salamanca, town in W. Spain; pop.72,000; scene 1812 of Wellington's victory over the French.

salamander, see AMPHIBIAN

Salamis, *sal'ä-mis,* rugged Greek island ; has a naval base. Hereabouts, 480BC, a battle was fought between the Greeks with 360 ships and the Persians (under Xerxes) with *c.*1,000. The Greeks, led by Themistocles, pretended to sail away, later turning on their enemies, who lost 200 ships in the Straits of Salamis, and were compelled to retire.

Sale, town, Cheshire, adjoining Manchester ; pop.43,000.

Salem, *sä'lem,* ancient city of the Jebusites ; may possibly have been on the site of the later city of Jerusalem.

Salem, town and port, Massachusetts, USA ; manufactures cotton ; once notorious for its persecution of so-called witches ; pop.41,000.

Salerno, port, Italy ; 34m south-east of Naples. Its medical school was famous in the Middle Ages ; noted for cotton-spinning and printing ; pop.68,000.

Salford, *sŏl′fĕrd*, city, Lancashire, on the R. Irwell ; adjoins Manchester, and has the docks of the Manchester Ship Canal ; pop.174,000.

Salic Law, 5th c. code of laws of the Franks, a people who lived by the Rhine. One of their laws prohibited women from ruling.

Salisbury, *sŏlz′ber-i*, city, Wiltshire ; on the R. Avon ; laid out in squares known as chequers ; famous for its 13th c. cathedral with a spire 404ft high. Salisbury is actually New Sarum, Old Sarum being close by ; pop.31,000.

Salisbury, cap., S. Rhodesia ; stands high on the Mashonaland plateau ; airport on the London–Johannesburg route ; pop.52,000.

Salisbury, FRANK O. (1874–   ), English artist, especially noted for portraits of famous people, and for his historical pictures.

Salisbury, LORD (1830–1903), *b* Hatfield, Hertfordshire. He was a Conservative statesman whose two chief aims were peace and power for the British Empire. A scholar and devout churchman, he did not believe in democracy. Foreign Secretary 1878, he was Leader of the Conservatives 1881 ; Prime Minister 1885, also 1886–92 and 1895–1902, and was a rival of Gladstone.

Salisbury Plain, chalk region, Wiltshire, *c*.20m by 15m. Here is Stonehenge.

Sallee, see BARBARY

sallow, see WILLOW

Sallust (86–34BC), Roman historian ; governor of Numidia (a Roman province in N. Africa) in consequence of his friendship with Julius Caesar ; afterwards returned to Rome with immense wealth. Sallust wrote *Bellum Catilinarium* and *Bellum Iugurthinum*. He is best known for his *Historiae*, a history of Rome 78–67BC. He was always careful to make sure of his facts. His style is crisp and vivid.

salmon, a pink-fleshed fish greatly in demand as food. It hatches out of eggs laid between October and January in fresh water, e.g. the rivers Tweed, Tay, Dee, Don, Deveron and Spey in Scotland, the Wye and the Severn in England. In the first year of its life it is known as a *fry*, in its second as a *parr* and in its third as a *smolt*. At this stage it leaves its native river for the sea, returning to fresh water in later life to spawn. A fish returning to fresh water in the fourth year of its life is known as a *grilse* and weighs 2¼–5¼lb ; above this age the fish is regarded as an adult salmon and may then weigh anything from 6 to 45lb or more. Its age and life history may be ascertained by examining its scales under a microscope, since its rate of growth increases greatly in salt water, thereby increasing the space between the rings on its scales, and always remains greater in summer than in winter. On its return to fresh water its growth ceases. A salmon returning to the sea after spawning is known as a *kelt* and may not be killed ; the rate of mortality among kelts is very high, and few fish return to spawn a second time.

Rod-fishing for salmon provides excellent sport ; on most Scottish rivers the fishing season extends from 11 Feb. to 31 Oct. The use of salmon as food has been largely commercialised, and nets operate on the mouths of almost all British rivers ; in British Columbia the netting and canning of salmon is an important industry.

Salmon may be distinguished from sea trout, a fish of generally similar habits, by its relatively large and coarse scales ; these are usually 10 to 12 in a vertical line between the dorsal fin and the lateral line.

Salop, short for Shropshire.

salt, in chemistry, compound formed when all or part of the hydrogen of an acid is replaced by a metal ; thus, ferrous sulphate, $FeSO_4.7H_2O$, is an iron salt of sulphuric acid. In acid salts only part of the replaceable hydrogen has been replaced ; basic salts are those in which only part of the hydroxyl group of a base have been replaced.

salt, sodium chloride, $NaCl$; found in sea-water, brine, rock salt ; mined in Northwich, Cheshire ; Droitwich, Worcestershire ; also in large quantities in Germany, Russia, Spain and USA ; deposits may be layers many thousands of feet thick. Near Cracow, Poland, are salt-mines in which hundreds of people not only work but live.

The Romans believed that upsetting salt was a sign of misfortune, hence Leonardo da Vinci in his picture *The Last Supper* shows an overturned salt-cellar near Judas.

Tablets of pure salt are now being consumed by people who work in intense heat, thus replacing the salt content of the body previously lost by perspiring.

Salt, SIR TITUS (1803–76), *b* Morley, Yorkshire ; invented a way of using alpaca (a kind of wool from the S. American alpaca) ; built Saltaire, 14m from Bradford.

Saltaire, see SALT, SIR T.

Salt Lake City, cap. Utah, USA ; noted for meat-packing, oil-refineries, etc. ; pop.150,000.

saltpetre, *sŏlt-pē′tĕr*, potassium nitrate or nitre, KNO_3 ; white crystalline salt found in Spain and India ; used in the manufacture of gunpowder. Chile saltpetre, sodium nitrate ($NaNO_3$), is used as a fertiliser and in making nitric acid. See SODIUM

Salus, *sal-ūs*, Roman goddess of health and prosperity, the Greek Hygieia, from which comes *hygiene*, the science and practice of preserving health and preventing disease.

Salvador, see CENTRAL AMERICA

salvage, *sal'vij*, anything saved from loss or destruction. The salvaging of a wrecked ship is now often accomplished by divers who seal up holes in the hull so that air may be pumped in to make her rise to the surface.

Salvation Army, see BOOTH, ' GENERAL ' W.

sal volatile, *sal vō-lat'i-lē*, ammonium carbonate. Spirits of salts (possibly containing alcohol also) are used as smelling salts.

Salween, river of Asia ; rises in Tibet ; flows through the Shan States to Lower Burma, entering the Gulf of Martaban near Moulmein after 1,800m. Much teak is floated down the river. The Burma Road crosses the Upper Salween at Tengyueh, scene of bitter fighting in World War II.

Salzburg, *zälts'bur*ch, tourist resort, Austria ; pop.77,000.

samar or **sambur**, large Indian deer, sometimes 4½ft at the shoulder ; has branched antlers.

Samaria, ancient province of Palestine. The inhabitants (Samaritans) were despised by the Jews ; yet Jesus told the story of the Good Samaritan, Luke 10.

samarium, *sä-mā'ri-ŭm*, rare element, Sm ; atomic weight 150·43 ; atomic number 62.

Samarkand, second largest town, Uzbekiston (USSR) ; formerly the capital ; has a mausoleum to Tamerlane ; manufactures textiles and has a large trade in fruits and cereals ; now called Zarafshan ; pop.155,000.

Sambre, *sän'br*, river of France and Belgium ; flows 112m to the Meuse at Namur.

sambur, see SAMAR

Samian ware, *sä'mi-an*, red or black glazed earthenware made in the Roman empire, but named after Samos, a Greek island.

Sammons, ALBERT (1886–), violinist, *b* London ; almost self-taught ; notable as an interpreter of Elgar and Delius.

Samoa, *sä-mō'ä*, group of islands in the W. Pacific, some (e.g. Upolu, where R. L. Stevenson died) governed by NZ, the rest (e.g. Tutuila) belonging to USA. Apia is the chief town of the British islands. Copra, bananas and rubber are exported.

Samos, *sä'mos*, Greek island of the Aegean Sea ; colonised by Ionians *c*.1000BC ; was Roman from 84BC. The island, long famous for Samian ware, i.e. unglazed earthenware, now produces raisins, wine, oil and cotton.

samovar, *sam'ō-vär*, Russian urn in which tea is brewed ; usually of copper ; the fuel is charcoal.

Samoyeds, *sam-ō-yeds'*, primitive people, rather like the Finns, inhabiting Arctic Russia.

sampan, Chinese or Japanese sailing boat *c*.15ft long ; often used as a house-boat.

samphire, *sam'fīr*, fleshy-leaved plant of British and Mediterranean coasts. Its blue-green leaves are made into a kind of pickle.

sampler, embroidery on canvas or silk worked by a girl as an example (or sample) of her skill ; fashionable from the 17th–19th centuries.

Samson, strong man of whom we read in the OT. An Israelite, he was betrayed by Delilah, and captured by the Philistines, who put out his eyes, though he destroyed many by wrecking a theatre, the upper storey of which rested on two pillars which he broke.
Read Judges 13–16 and *Samson Agonistes* by Milton.

Samuel, first prophet of Israel, and last of the judges. As a child he served in the Temple, where God spoke to him ; chose Saul and then David as kings of Israel ; died *c*.970BC. His story is told in the OT books, 1 and 2 Samuel.

San Antonio, city, Texas, USA. It is a noted health resort in a region producing oil ; pop.253,000.

San Carlo Opera Company, operatic company associated with the San Carlo theatre, Naples. The theatre, damaged in an air raid 1943, was later restored, and there, during World War II, Italian singers entertained over 4,000,000 Allied troops.

Sanctions, name for a method of political economic boycott of any nation going to war contrary to the Covenant of the League of Nations. Sanctions were half-heartedly imposed on Italy for invading Abyssinia (1935), and had they been widely and firmly applied they might have crippled the country. Actually, the exporting of goods to Italy continued with only slight reductions ; hence the effect was negligible.

sanctuary, sacred place, especially that part of a church where the altar stands. At one time a criminal might find safety for forty days from his pursuers if he could reach a place of sanctuary, e.g. Durham Cathedral (which still keeps its sanctuary knocker), Beverley Minster (Yorkshire), or Westminster Abbey. The custom was abolished in England in the 17th century.

sand, particles of rock (not exceeding 0·5mm in diameter), especially quartz, felspar and mica. Sandstone comprises layers of sand, the grains being cemented with calcium carbonate, or perhaps silica or iron oxide.

Sand, GEORGE, *sand* ; *sän* (1804–76), pen-name of Amandine Lucile Aurore Dupin, Frenchwoman, *b* Paris ; wrote letters, novels, plays, all showing her wide sympathies, love of art, and varied emotions.

sandalwood, small evergreen tree of the E. Indies. The wood has a sweet perfume and is used as incense.

sanderling, seashore bird, rather like a plover ; has grey and brown plumage above, white below ; visits Britain August–April.

Sandhurst, town, Berkshire, *c*.4m from

Wokingham ; has a Royal Military Academy (founded 1799) training candidates for the cavalry, infantry, and Royal Engineers, etc. The former College was amalgamated with the Royal Military Academy (Woolwich) 1946.

sandpiper, -pī'pĕr, bird rather like the plover. Brown above, it is greyish below, and has a white chin. A summer visitor to Britain, it lays reddish-white eggs with brown spots, and is found near rivers or by the seashore.

Sandringham, village, Norfolk, famous for Sandringham House, a royal residence built c.1870.

sandstorm, high wind that raises sand in vast clouds in desert areas, the sharp granules causing agony to unfortunate travellers. Sahara sandstorms are often caused by the simoom, a hot wind.

Sandwich, town, Kent ; on the R. Stour and 2m from the sea ; one of the Cinque Ports.

Sandy Hook, peninsula of New Jersey, USA.

San Francisco, city and port, California ; on San Francisco Bay, approached from the Pacific through a strait called the Golden Gate, now crossed by a bridge 8¼m long, having a single span of 2,310ft. San Francisco was severely damaged by earthquake and fire 1906, but has since been handsomely rebuilt. It has a vast trade, is an important railway terminus, and its industries include shipbuilding, meat-packing and sugar-refining ; pop.635,000.

San Francisco Conference, meeting of the United Nations, June 1945, at which matters of international peace, security and world co-operation were discussed. See UNO

sanhedrin, see JEWS

Sankey, JOHN (1866–1948), lawyer ; b Moreton, Gloucestershire ; Lord Chancellor 1929 ; a viscount 1932 ; Chairman of the Coal Mines Commission 1919, being in favour of nationalisation.

San Marino, sän mä-rē'nō, small republic (c.38sq.m ; pop.16,000) near Rimini on the Adriatic ; produces wine, cereals and lime ; cap. San Marino.

San Remo, -rä'mō, town, Italy ; on the Riviera ; has a climate suitable for sufferers from lung-trouble ; pop.32,000.

San Salvador, -säl-vä-thŏr', capital of the republic of Salvador, Central America ; pop.110,000.

San Sebastian, -sä-bäs-tyän', port and health resort, Spain ; on the Bay of Biscay ; pop.104,000.

Sanskrit, ancient sacred language in which the literature of the Hindus, e.g. hymns and religious books, are written. Many European languages are derived from the same language as Sanskrit. Famous examples of Sanskrit literature are the epic poems : (a) Mahabharata, crowded with stories of Hindu gods and goddesses ; (b) Ramayana, written perhaps 3,000 years ago, a tale of the wanderings and adventures of a prince.

Santa Cruz, san'tä krooz, port, Teneriffe, Canary Is. ; exports silk, sugar, tomatoes, bananas and potatoes ; pop. 73,000.

Santa Fé, sän'tä fä, city, Argentina ; pop.154,000.

Santa Filomena, see NURSING

Santander, sän-tän-där', port and holiday town, Spain ; on the Bay of Biscay ; has a large export trade ; pop.102,000.

Santayana, GEORGE, sän-tä-yä'nä (1863–), American thinker, b Madrid, but in early life went to USA ; travelled much ; author of the exquisite Sonnets and Other Poems ; notable for his philosophical books, especially The Life of Reason.

Santiago, cap. Chile ; manufactures textiles and leather goods ; pop.953,000.

Santiago, port, Cuba ; manufactures cigars ; pop.107,000.

Santo Domingo, former name (still used sometimes) for the republic of Dominica, W. Indies. The Dominican Republic, in the east portion of Haiti, was for many years the scene of warfare between Spaniards and Negroes, but today the region of c.19,000sq.m is well governed. There are excellent roads, and the republic produces sugar, cocoa, coffee, tobacco and timber. The pop. is c.2,053,000 ; cap. Ciudad Trujillo, a town that was founded by the brother of Christopher Columbus, and is the oldest town of European foundation in the New World.

Santos, -tus, Atlantic port, Brazil ; exports coffee ; pop.170,000.

Saône, sōn, French river flowing to the Rhône, which it joins at Lyons.

São Paulo, sown pow'lu, city, Brazil ; has Santos (45m away) as its port ; trades in coffee ; noted for fine buildings ; pop.1,269,000.

São Salvador, see BAHIA

Sapper, pen-name of Cyril McNeile (1888–1937), writer of thrilling adventure stories, e.g. Bulldog Drummond, 1920. He wrote a series of Bulldog Drummond books, many of which have been used as material for films.

sapper, rank in Royal Engineers corresponding to that of private soldier in infantry. Originally a sapper cut saps, i.e. ditches. In the army the Corps of Royal Engineers is usually referred to as ' the Sappers.'

sapphire, saf'īr, cornflower-blue gem ; actually a variety of the mineral corundum. The best sapphires come from Siam and Ceylon.

Sappho, saf'ō, 6th c. BC Greek poetess ; styled by Byron (The Isles of Greece) ' burning Sappho ' ; her verse, exquisitely graceful, is full of passion.

Saracens, Mohammedans, especially the Arabs who fought against the Crusaders.

Saragossa, city in NE. Spain ; cap. of the province of Saragossa and former cap. of the kingdom of Aragon ; on the R. Ebro ; noted for silk, woollen cloth and leather ; when besieged 1808–9 during the Peninsular War, a Spanish girl who then showed great courage, earned the name of the Maid of Saragossa ; pop. 284,000.

Sarajevo or **Serajevo**, *să'ră-ye-vō*, town, Yugoslavia ; pop.80,000 ; scene of the assassination of the Archduke Francis Ferdinand (28 June 1914) which hastened the outbreak of World War I.

Saratoga, BATTLES OF, *sar-ă-tō'gă*, battles during the War of American Independence : (*a*) 1777, when General Burgoyne (British) fought an indecisive battle with General Gates ; (*b*) also 1777, when Burgoyne attacked the Americans and was thrown back from Saratoga, finally surrendering to General Gates 17 Oct., thus bringing the war to an end. Saratoga Springs is a town in New York State, *c*.40m from Albany.

Sarawak, see BORNEO

Saraz, lake among the Pamirs ; appeared suddenly 1911, and is now over 37m long.

sard, beautiful reddish stone, a variety of cornelian.

sardine, see PILCHARD

Sardinia, island of the Mediterranean, south of Corsica ; area *c*.9,300sq.m ; cap. Cagliari ; noted for wine, minerals, timber and fisheries ; has belonged to Italy since 1859.

Sardis, capital of the ancient kingdom of Lydia ; captured by the Persians 546BC, and by Alexander the Great 334BC ; destroyed (15th c.) by Tamerlane.

sardonyx, white and brown gem, a variety of onyx. See PLATE XII

Sargasso Sea, *săr-gas'ō*, region of the N. Atlantic, roughly lat.25°–30°N ; comprises a vast area of seaweed floating in comparatively calm water. Columbus was the first to sail this way, and since then many strange tales have been told of ships caught in the weed. Actually sailors have little to fear.

Sargent, JOHN SINGER (1856–1925), American artist (*b* Florence, Italy) ; lived most lyin Chelsea ; famous for his portraits of Edwardian society figures.

Sargent, Sir MALCOM (1895–), English conductor ; conducts philharmonic and other orchestras.

Sargon, King of Assyria 722–705BC. A great soldier, he captured Babylon 709BC.

Sark, GREAT AND LITTLE, islands of the Channel Is. ; noted for fine coastal scenery. The islands were under German control during World War II.

sarsaparilla, *săr-să-pă-ril'ă*, cooling drink made from the boiled roots of a S. American vine.

Sartre, JEAN-PAUL, see EXISTENTIALISM

Sarum, *săr'ŭm*, Latin name for Salisbury, Wiltshire ; Old Sarum, actually 2m away, is now deserted. Inhabited in the Stone Age, it was a city on the Middle Ages, and had two Members of Parliament as recently as 1832.

The *Sarum Use* is an 11th c. collection of Church rules made at Salisbury, a

model for the compilers of the *English Book of Common Prayer.*

Saskatchewan, *sas-katch'ē-won*, river of Canada ; flows from the Rockies in two great streams (N. and S.) which unite to reach L. Winnipeg.

Saskatchewan, province of Canada between Manitoba and Alberta ; area 252,000sq.m ; pop.896,000. Saskatchewan is the largest wheat-growing province of Canada ; cap. Regina.

Saskatoon, second largest town, Saskatchewan, Canada ; noted for wheat and wool ; pop.43,000.

Sassoon, *sa-soon'*, Jewish family of merchants and bankers. The founder was David Sassoon (1792–1864), a merchant in Baghdad who built up a huge business in Bombay. SIEGFRIED SASSOON (1886–) became known as a poet during World War I. He wrote *Counter Attack* ; *Memoirs of a Foxhunting Man* ; and *Old Century.*

satellite, *sat'ĕ-līt*, small companions of large objects, e.g. the moon is the earth's satellite. The word is often used in Town and Country Planning in connection with satellite towns.

satin, glossy silk fabric made in China long ago ; first manufactured in England by French Protestant refugees in the 17th c., notably at Spitalfields (London).

satire, *săt'īr*, prose or verse ridiculing what is wrong, stupid or a sham. Usually the satirist ridicules the foolish manners or vices of his day, e.g. Lucilius, Horace and Juvenal, all famous Roman satirists. In English literature satire appears in the works of Pope, Dryden and Swift ; the most telling satire in English today is found in *Punch.* French satirists include Boileau, Molière and Voltaire.

satrap, *să'trap* ; *sat'rap*, provincial governor in ancient Persia.

saturated compound, in chemistry, a compound with no free valency.

Saturn, see ASTRONOMY

Saturnalia, *sat-ĕr-nā'lia*, annual festival in ancient Rome in honour of Saturn, god of agriculture ; held in December. Slaves were then waited on by their masters. The word now means merrymaking without restraint.

satyr, *sat'ĕr*, in old Greek tales, a woodland god with the horns and tail of a goat. A somewhat similar creature was known to the Romans as a faun.

Saudi Arabia, see ARABIA

Saul, first King of Israel ; son of Kish ; led armies against the Philistines, defeating them at Gibeah. Saul was moody, but David could often please him by playing the harp (1 Samuel 16). Finally he became insane, and died *c*.1010BC.

Sault Sainte Marie, *so sănt mä-rē*, town, Ontario, separated from a town of the same name, USA, by St Mary's R. ; hereabouts is a canal to avoid rapids in the river ; pop.28,000.

Saunders, HILARY AIDAN ST GEORGE

(1898–   ), writer, sometimes under the pen-name Francis Beeding or David Pilgrim ; author of several Ministry of Information publications, e.g. *Battle of Britain.*

savanna, see GRASS

Savannah, *sä-van'ä,* city, Georgia, USA ; near the mouth of the Savannah R. ; noted for cotton and lumber ; has naval stores ; pop.96,000.

' Savannah,' see SHIPS

Savings Certificates, see NATIONAL SAVINGS CERTIFICATES

Savonarola, GIROLAMO, *sav-ō-nä-rō'lä* (1452–98), Italian reformer, *b* Ferrara ; became a monk; was a famous preacher ; tried as a heretic, and strangled. Read George Eliot's *Romola.*

Savoy, *sä-voi',* formerly a duchy in SE. France, now the departments of Haute-Savoie and Savoie, a region notable for fine mountain scenery. The house of Savoy recalls wide territories in the 12th c., reduced 1720 to Sardinia, the Duchy of Savoy, Piedmont. Savoy was ceded to France 1860, and the remainder merged into the Italian kingdom under Victor Emmanuel.

A district of the Strand, London, is called the Savoy from a palace built there 1245, prison-home of John of France, captured at Poitiers 1356.

Saxe, MAURICE, *säks* (1696–1750), French soldier ; earned a deservedly high military reputation ; created Marshal of France 1743 ; won the notable victory of Fontenoy 1745.

Saxe-Coburg-Gotha, *saks kō'būrg gō'tä,* former state of the German empire. See VICTORIA

saxifrage, *sak'si-frij,* name of several rock-plants with a circle of leaves near the ground, e.g. London pride, the flower of which has white petals dotted with red.

Saxon architecture, see ARCHITECTURE

Saxons, warlike Teutonic people who, as pirates, sailed the N. Sea and English Channel *c.*AD286. They had conquered part of what is now Germany by 350. In the 5th c. they were settled in Germany and Gaul ; later they and the Jutes (founders of Jutland, a part of Denmark) and Angles invaded Britain. See ANGLO-SAXONS

Saxony, former German state ; area 5,856 sq.m ; pop.5,200,000 ; cap. Dresden. The area is now in the Russian Zone.

saxophone, *sak'sō-fōn,* brass musical instrument invented by Adolphe Sax (1814–94), who also invented the saxhorn. Though a brass instrument, the saxophone has a reed.

Sayers, DOROTHY (1893–   ), English writer whose brilliant mystery stories have great charm, e.g. *Strong Poison* ; *Lord Peter Views the Body.* She caused a stir with her broadcast play *The Man Born to be King,* 1942.

Sb, chemical symbol for antimony (*stibium*).

scabious, *skā'bi-ŭs,* common British field plant, usually with blue flower-heads ; leaves opposite and lobed. There is also the Devil's-bit scabious.

Scafell Pike, see LAKE DISTRICT

scale (Latin *scala,* a ladder), in music, order of notes in a chosen key. The commonest in modern European music is the diatonic (one of 5 tones and 2 half-tones or semitones, the 8th note being the octave, i.e. the beginning of the scale in a higher or lower key). The 12 notes of the octave of a piano make the *chromatic scale,* each being a half-tone above the one before.

scalene triangle, see TRIANGLE

scallop, see MOLLUSCA

scalping, old custom among some N. American Indians of taking off (with its hair) the skin of the head of a vanquished enemy as proof of a brave's success in battle.

Scandinavia, name for part of Europe comprising Norway and Sweden; it sometimes includes Denmark, Finland and Iceland.

scandium, rare element Sc ; atomic weight 45·1 ; atomic number 21.

Scapa Flow, British war station between Pomona and Hoy (Orkneys) ; scene of the scuttling of the German fleet 21 June 1919, and of German U-boat raids in World War II. The *Ark Royal* was sunk here by a U-boat 14 Oct 1939.

scapula, see SKELETON

scarab, ornament (stone, metal or gem) in the shape of a beetle ; worn as a lucky charm in ancient Egypt.

Scarborough, *skär'bŭ-rŭ,* port and holiday town on the N. Yorkshire coast ; pop. 38,000.

Scarlatti, ALESSANDRO (1659–1725), Italian composer ; wrote church music, 500 cantatas and *c.*100 operas.

scarlet fever (*scarlatina*), infectious disease characterised by a bright red rash.

scarlet pimpernel, see PIMPERNEL

scenario, *sē-nä'rio,* outline of a film (also a play), giving plot, characters and scenes so that the producer can work from the script.

scent or **perfume,** often distilled from plants, e.g. lavender, otto (or attar) of roses (prepared in Damascus, Cashmere, etc.). Scents may be artificially prepared from coal-tar by-products. Eau-de-Cologne (water of Cologne) has been manufactured at Cologne (Germany) since 1709.

sceptre, *sep'tĕr* (Greek *skēptron,* staff), a king's emblem of power. Egyptian rulers had sceptres ; the king of Great Britain holds three at his coronation : (*a*) St Edward's staff ; (*b*) a rod with a golden dove ; (*c*) a rod with a globe and cross.

Schelde, *schel'de* ; *skelt,* river rising in France, and flowing 250m through Belgium and Holland to the N. Sea.

scherzo, *sker'tsō* (Italian, a joke), musical term for a light or humorous movement in a symphony, usually the third of four movements, as introduced by Beethoven.

20

Schiller, JOHANN VON (1759–1805), German romantic poet and dramatist, b Marbach, Württemberg. Of his many plays (including one about Joan of Arc) the greatest is *William Tell*. He is regarded by the Germans as their national poet.

Schleswig-Holstein, *shlās'vich hōl'shtīn*, former province of Germany ; is the south part of the Jutland peninsula.

Schneider Trophy, *shnī'dĕr trō'fi*, international aviation trophy for seaplanes ; value £1,000 ; presented 1913 by Jacques Schneider, a French flying enthusiast ; won outright by Britain 1931 with a speed of 340·0mph.

School Certificate, see EXAMINATIONS

schools, see EDUCATION

schooner, *skoon'ĕr*, sailing ship, usually with 2, 3 or 4 masts, rigged fore-and-aft.

Schopenhauer, ARTHUR, *shō'pen-how-ĕr* (1788–1860), German thinker with an unhappy outlook on life ; b Danzig ; friend of Goethe.

Schubert, FRANZ PETER, *shoo'bert* (1797–1828), Austrian composer who in his 31 years wrote 8 symphonies, over 30 orchestral pieces, 13 operas, many cantatas, quartets, piano-solos and over 600 songs ; born near Vienna ; composed a fantasia when only 13. Always poor, he suffered hardship and disappointment, but found consolation in music. He had a genius for writing songs, linking sound and sense better than almost any other composer, e.g. his setting for Shakespeare's *Who is Sylvia?* His *Unfinished Symphony* is of exceptional distinction. He died in poverty.

Read *Schubert*, Otto Erich Deutsch (translated by Eric Blom) ; *Schubert*, Norman Flower.

Schumann, ROBERT, *shoo'män* (1810–56), German composer of outstanding genius; b Saxony. An injury to his right hand caused him to spend the remainder of his life writing, rather than playing, music, e.g. orchestral, chamber, pianoforte and especially songs. He died in an asylum.

Schuman Plan, name for a scheme devised by Robert Schuman, French Foreign Minister. Basically it proposed (May 1950) that coal and steel production in France should be controlled by an international authority subject to the Council of Europe, and that, if willing, other European countries should participate in the plan, all uniting in a common effort. Though largely approving of the scheme, the British Government felt unable to participate in it. In Aug 1950 the Consultative Assembly of the United Nations approved the plan, and since then France has proposed a similar scheme for European agriculture.

Schuschnigg, KURT VON, *schoosh'nig* (1897–), Austrian statesman ; succeeded Dollfuss as Chancellor 1934 ; imprisoned during World War II. See AUSTRIA

Schweitzer, ALBERT, *shvī'tsĕr* (1875–), German doctor, missionary, thinker, author and musician, b Kaiserberg, Alsace (France). As a young man he was ashamed of the white man's treatment of less civilised races, and went as a medical missionary to the Congo (Central Africa). He was known as a brilliant organist and as an authority on Bach. He was the author of *My Childhood and Youth* ; *My Life and Thought* ; *On the Edge of the Primeval Forest* ; and a startling study of Christ.

Read *Albert Schweitzer : The Man and His Mind*, George Seaver.

science (ultimately from Latin *scire*, to know), exact and well-arranged knowledge in agreement with general laws. E. N. da C. Andrade has said : *Pure science is not so much a matter of subject as a matter of treatment—it is a particular method and point of view. Its aim is not to tell us why things are as they are, but how things work.* The

SCHUBERT 1797–1828

scientist endeavours to find truth by weighing and measuring, and by proceeding logically step by step, continually testing by practical experiment every theory.

Though pure science deals with abstract knowledge, theory leads to practical results since all applied science is based on careful and exact inquiry. While scientists are usually thought of as investigating heat, light, sound, electricity, magnetism, mechanics, chemistry, astronomy, geology, biology, psychology, etc., it should be noted that there is a scientific approach to *every* aspect of knowledge ; thus the musician may regard music as one of the arts, the scientist may examine its structure, re-

garding music merely as sound. Note
also that the poet, the devout believer in
religion, and the scientist are not opposed to one another, but are, rather,
complementary, all glimpsing truth from
different approaches.

Consult *A Dictionary of Science*,
E. B. Uvarov ; and read *Essays in
Popular Science*, Julian Huxley ; *The
Mysterious Universe*, Sir James Jeans ;
Why Smash Atoms? A. K. Solomon ;
Limitations of Science, J. W. N. Sullivan ;
Science and the Modern World, A. N.
Whitehead ; *Science and Everyday Life*,
J. B. S. Haldane ; *Science for the
Citizen*, Lancelot Hogben ; *The World
of Science*, Sherwood Taylor ; *The
Cavendish Laboratory*, Alexander Wood ;
also *Discovery*, a monthly magazine.

Scilly Isles, *sil'i*, group of *c*.35 islands
c.25m from Land's End ; noted for
early flowers and vegetables. The only
town is Hugh Town in St Mary's.

Scipio, *sip'i-ō*, name of several Roman
soldiers and statesmen, e.g. Publius
Cornelius Scipio, died 183BC, known
as Scipio Africanus Major ; led an
army to Carthage (N. Africa) and
defeated Hannibal 202. See PUNIC WAR.
Also Scipio Africanus Minor, governor
of N. Africa, ended the 3rd Punic War
by capturing Carthage 146BC ; *d*.
129BC. Gnaeus Scipio, and another
Publius Cornelius Scipio (*d* 211BC),
his brother, fought the Carthaginians.

SCM, see YOUTH ORGANISATIONS

Scone, *skoon*, town, Perthshire ; scene of
the crowning of early Scottish kings.
Its Coronation Stone, removed from
Scone by Edward I, was stolen from
Westminster Abbey on Christmas Day
1950.

scorched earth, name given to military
tactics adopted 1937 by the retreating
Chinese. The burning of cities and the
destruction of factories, farms, shipping,
vehicles and crops made advance by the
Japanese slow and costly. This policy
was brilliantly executed by the Russians
in their retreat before the Germans
June 1941–42, a strategy, incidentally,
employed by them during Napoleon's
invasion of 1812. It was also the policy
followed successfully by Robert the
Bruce and other Scottish leaders in
their Wars of Independence against the
English.

score, term (mathematics) for 20. To
find the cost of a score of articles, reckon
every shilling as £1 ; e.g. 1 article at
5s 8d = 5⅔s, i.e. £5⅔ or £5 13s 4d for 20.

scoria, ashes thrown out by a volcano
while in eruption ; also the crust
formed on cooling lava.

scorpion, creature belonging to a group
including spiders. Somewhat like a
small lobster, it has a jointed tail ending
in nippers and a very poisonous sting.
It is found in dark places and under
stones in S. Europe, E. Indies, S.
America and Africa. It feeds on insects.

Scotland, kingdom of Great Britain,

THE SCORPION

north of the Cheviot Hills ; area 30,410
sq.m ; pop.5,030,000.

The mainland of Scotland is divided
into three parts : (*a*) *Highlands*, divided
by the Great Glen, along which runs the
Caledonian Canal : the central masses
of these heather-clad mountains are the
Grampians, with Ben Nevis (4,406ft),
the highest point in the British Is. ;
(*b*) *Central Lowlands*, mainly the valleys
of the rivers Tay, Forth and Clyde, a
densely-populated region where most of
the coal is found, especially in Clydesdale, also rich in iron ; and (*c*) *S.
Uplands*, region with grassy hills, which
provide rich grazing for sheep. The
many islands of Scotland include the
Orkneys, Shetlands (northern) ; Hebrides,
Mull, Skye, Arran (western) ; the
extremely indented west coast resembles
Norway's fiords. Rivers (mostly short
and swift) include the Forth, Tay, Dee,
Spey, Tweed and (most important)
Clyde. Many Scottish rivers are noted
for salmon. Hydro-electric power is
being developed on a large scale, e.g.
at the Falls of Foyer, Loch Ness ; the
Galloway and the Grampian schemes.
The Tummel-Garry and Gairloch scheme
was undertaken 1945. Lochs (lakes)
are a feature of Scotland, the largest
being Loch Lomond.

For the tourist, Scotland offers many
attractions, e.g. the beauty and romance
of the Border country, a land of ballads
immortalised by Sir Walter Scott ; the
magnificence of the Highlands with
glens (valleys), bens (mts.), lochs, deer
and ancient Highland customs and dress.
Such sport as grouse-shooting, deer-
stalking, fishing and climbing may be
enjoyed and indulged in to the full.
Cities and charming villages rich in
historical interest and steeped in tradition abound, while in the extreme north
and north-west, Gaelic is still spoken in
everyday life, and ancient crafts are still
practised.

The climate is mild and moist in the
west, dry and bracing in the east. Some
75 % of the land is officially described as
' rough mountain pasture, moor and
waste,' but it is possible that increased
hydro-electric power and planned
afforestation may bring new prosperity
to areas at present almost unproductive.
Scotland is famous for sheep (especially
the black-faced mountain breeds), cattle

(e.g. Aberdeen-Angus, Ayrshire and Highland breeds), and also for Clydesdale horses. Crops include oats, barley and potatoes (grown extensively in the east and south-east). The chief industrial area is in the W. Central Lowlands, of which Glasgow is the busy centre. Here, on the Clyde, are great shipbuilding yards (where the *Queen Mary* and *Queen Elizabeth* were built). Glasgow is also noted for cotton ; Paisley for cotton-thread; Dundee for jute; Lanarkshire and Ayrshire for coal. Aluminium is manufactured near Ballachulish ; whisky is distilled in the glens ; tweeds are made in and near the Tweed valley, and in the island of Harris ; granite is mined in the Aberdeen area ; and many east coast towns and villages are noted for fishing.

The chief towns are Edinburgh (cap.), Glasgow (the principal commercial and industrial centre), Dundee, Aberdeen, Paisley, Greenock, Motherwell and Clydebank, also Inverness.

Scotland is represented in Parliament by over 70 members in the Commons, and by 16 peers in the Lords. There has been a Secretary for Scotland since 1885, the office being a Secretaryship of State since 1926. Scots law differs profoundly from English, as also does Scottish education, the country having one of the finest educational systems in Europe.

Among a host of famous Scotsmen may be noted Robert Burns, Sir Walter Scott, David Hume, Thomas Carlyle, R. L. Stevenson, Adam Smith, James Hogg, John Knox, David Livingstone, J. L. McAdam (pioneer of modern roads), Lord Kelvin, Sir James Young Simpson (anaesthetics), William Murdoch, Andrew Carnegie, Ramsay MacDonald, Earl Haig, William MacTaggart (painter), Allan Ramsay (poet) and Allan Ramsay (painter), Sir R. A. Watson-Watt and Lord (formerly Sir John) Boyd-Orr.

The Romans knew the country (which they called Caledonia) as the home of the Picts, and though they conquered what is now England, they never succeeded in quelling the wild tribes north of Hadrian's Wall. The Scots, a Gaelic-speaking Celtic race, came from Ireland in the 6th c. AD, and later united with the Pictish Celts to found the Kingdom of Scotland. Christianity reached S. Scotland as early as AD380, but tribal warfare continued among Picts, Scots, Brythons, etc. till Kenneth Macalpine won a measure of control in the 9th c., and Scotland became one kingdom.

In later centuries England made repeated attempts to conquer the Scots, and bitter enmity continued till the 17th c., hence the Border raids, and the Wars of Independence, in which the Scots were led by William Wallace (1297), and Robert Bruce, who defeated the English at Bannockburn 1314. The flower of Scotland perished at the battle of Flodden 1513, but even so Scotland maintained full independence until 1707. For many years Scotland was allied with France against England, hence the marriage of Mary Queen of Scots to the French Dauphin. At the Reformation Scotland became Presbyterian, England remaining Episcopalian, a difference of profound significance, especially in the development of Scottish character, in which religion and a genius for philosophy seem inherent.

With the crowning of James VI of Scotland as James I of England (1603) a step towards happier relationships was taken ; and though this was followed by Scottish anger at the religious policy of Charles I, and by the stern measures of Cromwell, the parliaments of England and Scotland were united 1707. Even this was followed by the Jacobite rebellions of 1715 and 1745 ; but, in the main, after 1707 Scottish history is merged in that of Great Britain.

Read *Scotland*, ed. H. W. Meikle (Nelson). See CELTI ; COVENANT ; UNITED KINGDOM

Scotland Yard, popular name for New Scotland Yard, HQ since 1890 of the London Metropolitan Police. It is on a site by the Thames, where once stood a palace of the kings of Scotland. It is noted for its detectives, and ' the black museum ' with relics of many crimes.

Scott, SIR GEORGE GILBERT (1811–78), architect, *b* Buckinghamshire ; an exponent of the neo-Gothic revival, he restored many English churches and designed the Albert Memorial, London.

Scott, SIR GILES GILBERT (1880–   ), architect, grandson of Sir George Gilbert Scott ; designed the immense Anglican cathedral, Liverpool, 1903.

Scott, PETER (1909–   ), artist ; son of Captain Scott, the explorer ; specialises in studies of birds and in portraits ; author of *Morning Flight* and *Wild Chorus*. In May 1949 he went to the NW. Territories, Canada, to study wild ducks, etc.

Scott, CAPTAIN ROBERT FALCON (1868–1912), explorer, born near Plymouth, Devon. As a boy he went aboard the training ship *Britannia*. When little over 30 he became a commander, and was chosen by Sir Clements Markham to lead an expedition to the S. Polar regions, sailing from London in the *Discovery* 1901.

Scott discovered the volcanoes Erebus and Terror on Ross I. ; learned what lay beyond the Great Ice Barrier (a vast frozen plain and a desert of snow); made a remarkable sledge journey ; and returned 1904. He sailed again for the Antarctic 1910 in the *Terra Nova* ; heard that Roald Amundsen (the Norwegian) had already set out to reach the S. Pole, but hoped to get there first. After a hard struggle he reached the Pole 17 Jan 1912, only to find that Roald Amundsen had beaten him by a few days. The story of his failure to return is told in POLAR REGIONS. Read Apsley Cherry-Garrard, *The Worst Journey in the World.*

Scott, SIR WALTER (1771–1832), novelist, sometimes called the Wizard of the North, *b* Edinburgh, limped from childhood ; became a lawyer ; appointed Deputy Sheriff of Selkirkshire ; later, Clerk of Session in Edinburgh.

As a youth he had loved visiting villages and towns on the Scottish Border, there hearing folk-ballads which he wrote down in his book *The Minstrelsy of the Scottish Border,* published by his friend, James Ballantyne. Its success prompted him to write romantic epic poems of the old days in Scotland, e.g. *The Lay of the Last Minstrel* (1805) ; *The Lady of the Lake* ; *Marmion* ; and *Rokeby.* Becoming rich, he bought an estate by the R. Tweed, and began building a great house, Abbotsford, where he lived like a Scottish laird of earlier days, and always had many guests. He was happy with his wife and children, delighted in his horses and dogs, was kind to his servants, and was esteemed by all.

The story is told that Scott was one day looking for some fishing tackle when he came on part of a tale he had written years before. He read it, enjoyed it, and finished writing it in three weeks. It was published anonymously in 1814 as *Waverley,* and was a tremendous success, being a happy mixture of romance and adventure. It did not become known generally until much later that Scott was the author of *Waverley.* Other novels came quickly from his pen, e.g. *Guy Mannering* ; *The Antiquary* ; *The Black Dwarf* ; *Old Mortality* ; *Rob Roy* ; and *The Heart of Midlothian,* all in the style of *Waverley* ; yet others include *Ivanhoe* ; *Kenilworth* ; *The Pirate* ; *The Fortunes of Nigel* ; *Quentin Durward* ; and (perhaps best of all) *Redgauntlet.*

Scott was created a baronet 1820, but at 55 misfortune overtook him when James Ballantyne went bankrupt. As Scott was a partner in the firm he, too, shared in the disgrace. A sum of £250,000 was owing, *and Scott set to work to pay every penny.* With courage and energy he kept on at his task. His wife died ; he became ill ; visited Rome ; and returned to Abbotsford where he died. His son-in-law, John Gibson Lockhart (1794–1854) was with him at the end, and wrote the life-story of Scotland's greatest historical novelist. Both are buried at Dryburgh Abbey.

Read *Sir Walter Scott,* John Buchan.

Scouts, see BOY SCOUTS

'scrap of paper,' see BELGIUM ; WORLD WAR I

screw, see MECHANICS

Scriabin, ALEXANDER, *skr-yä-been'* (1872–1915), Russian composer, *b* Moscow ; wrote mystical music, e.g. *The Divine Poem.*

scribe, one who writes. Among the Jews, the Scribes were men who made copies of the law of Moses and lectured about it ; they were bitter enemies of Christ.

scriptorium, room in a monastery where manuscripts were copied.

Scrope, RICHARD (*d* 1405), Archbishop of York ; rebelled against Henry IV 1405 ; beheaded near York.

scrub, land covered with bushes and small trees.

sculling, propelling a light boat with the use of sculls, which are shorter and more curved than oars. The Wingfield Sculls for amateurs takes place on the Thames between Putney and Mortlake ; the Diamond Sculls contest is held at Henley.

sculpture, art of carving or shaping figures, usually in stone, wood or metal. The first sculptors were perhaps men of the Stone Age. The Egyptians carved colossal figures 3500BC, also statuettes of men, women, animals, birds, though all their human figures were shown standing upright, and were without even a hint of action. Assyrian sculptors portrayed battle-scenes, warriors, and winged animals with human heads.

The best ancient Greek sculpture belongs to the 6th c. BC. Myron was a sculptor well known in the 5th c. BC, his most renowned work including the famous *Discobolus,* a young man throwing the discus, i.e. a round stone used in a competitive sport. In the glorious age of Pericles (*c.*500–429BC) the greatest Greek sculptor was Pheidias, the Athenian. He was given the task of gathering sculptures for the adornment of buildings on the Acropolis, where his own statue of the goddess *Athena,* over 40ft high, was among the outstanding masterpieces of Greek art ; and his gigantic statue (in ivory and gold) of *Zeus* was certainly among the wonders of the ancient world. Another Greek sculptor was Praxiteles (*d c.*340BC), famous for his statuary group *Hermes with the Infant Dionysus.* Later Greek carvings include the *Winged Nikē of Samothrace* ; *Apollo Belvedere* ; *The Dying Gaul* (known as *The Gladiator*) ; and *The Laocoon,* discovered in Rome 1506, a group showing a Trojan priest and his two sons being crushed to death by serpents.

Greek sculpture, which has never been surpassed, has a unique beauty ; and even today the perfect human form is taken to be that shown by Greek sculpture, e.g. Polyclitus, or that master craftsman who, in the 2nd c. carved the unrivalled *Venus of Milo,* found 1820 at Melos (now Milo), a Greek island.

Roman sculpture excelled in carving portrait busts, i.e. head and shoulders only.

The Renaissance in Europe (15th c.) produced a number of notable sculptors, e.g. (*a*) Donatello (*d* 1466), an Italian, *b* Florence (possibly the greatest sculptor

SCULPTURE

(left) The Winged Nikē (Victory) of Samothrace   *(right) Epstein's Madonna and Child*

SCULPTURE

Khafra, Pharaoh of Egypt 2900–2750 B.C.   *The goddess Demeter, Greek, c. 350* B.C.

SCULPTURE
3rd c. Roman marble bust of Caracalla, Roman Emperor, A.D. *186–217*

since classical times) whose works include a famous figure of *St George* on the first horse ever cast in bronze, also a bronze figure of *David* ; (*b*) Andrea del Verrocchio (1435–88), also *b* Florence, a pupil of Donatello and master of Leonardo da Vinci : best remembered for his equestrian statue of *Bartolomeo Colleoni*, an Italian soldier ; (*c*) Michelangelo, the painter, who was also a matchless sculptor ; his marble group *La Pietà* (in St Peter's, Rome) is world famous. See MICHELANGELO

Other and later sculptors of note include Antonio Canova (1757–1822), an Italian ; the English sculptors John Flaxman (1755–1826), and Sir Francis Chantrey (1781–1841), *b* Norton, near Sheffield, who was befriended when poor and unknown by John Flaxman, and won fame for his statues of the *Duke of Wellington* ; *James Watt* (in Westminster Abbey), and, most of all, his exquisite carving of *The Sleeping Children* in Lichfield Cathedral.

In more recent years sculpture has been redeemed from the commonplace by François Auguste Rodin (1840–1917), a vigorous French sculptor, *b* Paris ; famous for his rough, dramatic and impressive statues, e.g. *Burghers of Calais* and *The Thinker* ; Constantin Meunier (1831–1905), a Belgian sculptor who made a stir with his statues of workers in mines and factories, and on farms ; Jacob Epstein, son of Russian and Polish parents, *b* New York 1880 ; settled in London 1905. His works, especially his busts, are often beautiful as well as full of strength and character ; but some of his carvings (e.g. *Night*, or *Christ*, carved 1920), seem uncouth, and have caused great differences of opinion among art critics. An especially noted English sculptor of today is Henry Moore (*b* 1898), a Yorkshireman whose works express deep emotion. Few women have successfully taken up sculpture, an exception being Barbara Hepworth (1903–) Wakefield, Yorks.

The largest sculptures in the world are the heads of four American presidents (Washington, Jefferson, Lincoln and Theodore Roosevelt) carved in the living rock, 3,000ft long and 800ft high, Mt Rushmore, S. Dakota.

As a rule a sculptor begins by making a clay model built on an iron skeleton (armature) ; this may be baked to form a terracotta model, or from it a mould may be made in plaster of Paris, and another plaster model fashioned, which the sculptor copies in marble. Modern sculptors often use a pointing machine that cuts into stone to the correct depth. A sculptor who chisels direct into marble must be an exceedingly fine craftsman, otherwise he may easily ruin a costly piece of stone. Bronzes are cast from moulds.

Scunthorpe, growing town, N. Lincolnshire ; has iron and steel works ; pop.46,000.

scurvy, disease due to lack of fresh fruit and vegetables, or (more accurately) to a lack of vitamin C which these supply. At one time ships' crews almost always suffered from scurvy during long voyages, i.e. the gums became spongy, the skin spotted. A pioneer in the abolition o scurvy was Captain Cook, who proved that the disease could be cured or prevented by eating fresh fruit and vegetables. See VITAMINS

scutage, *skū'tij*, or **shield-money** ; payment made in wartime by a feudal knight to his lord for the privilege of staying at home instead of going to fight. The custom began in England in Henry II's day and ended in the 14th century.

Scutari, *skoo'tä-rī*, town facing Istanbul, of which it is a suburb ; manufactures

SCULPTURE
Bronze statue of Colleoni, a 15th c. Italian soldier of fortune. This statue, which is the work of Verrocchio (1435–88), is one of the finest of its kind in the world.

SEALS

(1) *The Sea-lion*   (2) *The Grey Seal and Young*   (3) *The Walrus*

silks, cottons and muslins ; scene of the hospital established by Florence Nightingale during the Crimean War ; pop. 130,000, mostly Turks ; also a town in Albania (the ancient cap., Illyria), pop.30,000.

Scylla and Charybdis, *sil'ä* ; *kä-rib'dis,* in old Greek tales, two dangers of the Straits of Messina between Sicily and Italy : (*a*) Scylla, a sea monster with 12 feet and 6 heads ; (*b*) Charybdis, a whirlpool. To be between Scylla and Charybdis, therefore, is to be between two dangers.

scythe, *sīth,* farm implement for cutting long grass or corn. The wooden handle is a snaith ; the blade is sharpened with a whetstone. A motor scythe will cut 4 acres in 8 hours, using only 1½ gallons of fuel.

Scythia, *sith'i-ä,* region north and northeast of the Black Sea ; anciently the home of a nomadic tribe of Scythians.

Se, chemical symbol for selenium.

sea, part of an ocean, e.g. the N. Sea, Caribbean Sea ; also an inland area of water, e.g. the Dead Sea, Caspian Sea. Sea-water is denser than river water, 3·5% being composed of various salts, including sodium chloride (common salt), sulphates of sodium, magnesium and potassium, also bromides and carbonates.

sea anemone, *ä-nem'ō-nē,* flower-like animal (polyp) attached by a sucker to a rock under water ; has a short, thick tube, leathery skin, and a mouth ringed with tentacles. It is often of beautiful and varied colours.

sea bass, fish *c.*2ft long ; is bluish-grey paling to silver beneath ; found in the Mediterranean and off the south coast of Britain.

sea bream, British food fish, red above, silvery below ; has a black spot over each gill. The young are called chads.

Sea Cadet Corps, British youth organisation, which trains boys for the Royal or Merchant Navy.

sea-cow, see MANATEE

sea horse, curious fish *c.*7in long, shaped like a horse's head and neck ; swims in an upright position, and has only one fin. The tail, curled inwards, is used as an anchor. Found chiefly in the Atlantic and Mediterranean, it is related to the pipe-fishes, which are long and slender, and have bony plates.

seal, sea-mammal found chiefly in the Arctic and Antarctic, though the monk seal belongs to the Mediterranean, and many seals frequent British waters. The tapering body is covered with coarse hair and a layer of blubber. The limbs are largely hidden under the skin. The young are born on land.

Seals found on British shores include the harbour seal ; great grey seal, seen off the Scottish and Irish coasts ; Greenland seal, and hooded seal, which is able to puff out its face to an immense size.

The SEA-LION, a kind of seal, has

close, woolly fur from which sealskin coats are made. It abounds in Alaska, Bering Sea and Labrador. The WALRUS, similar to the sea-lion, is usually bigger and heavier ; when full grown it is recognised by its large tusks curving down from its upper jaw. It may be 12ft long, and weigh over a ton.

seal, mass of wax (or sometimes lead) on which a sign, initial or design, usually with an inscription, has been impressed by a matrix of metal or stone. Many documents, especially those of corporations, and the deeds made by lawyers, are sealed for security.

sealed orders, secret orders given in a sealed envelope to the captain of a ship or commander of a submarine ; opened only when the voyage has begun.

seance, *sā'äns* ; *sā-äns,* meeting at which psychical phenomena are supposed to occur, e.g. those present believe themselves to be mystically in communication (through a medium) with the spirits of the dead.

sea otter, animal (*c.*3ft long) hunted in Alaska and the Aleutian Is. for its valuable fur.

seaplane, see AVIATION

seasickness, temporary illness actually due to the motion of a drop of liquid in the ear, now largely obviated by taking a pill, the composition of which is due to Canadian doctors.

sea-snake, reptile of the Indian and Pacific Oceans ; usually brightly coloured ; may be from 3–8ft long ; has highly poisonous fangs.

seasons, periods of the year known as spring, summer, autumn and winter. These are due to the tilting of the earth's axis ; summer is *not* (as is often supposed) due to the earth approaching the sun, and therefore receiving more heat, but to the tilting of the axis *towards* the sun, with the result that one half of the globe faces the sun more directly, and accordingly receives more heat and has a longer period of daylight.

Astronomically speaking, summer begins in the northern hemisphere when the sun appears overhead at noon along the Tropic of Cancer a line, 23½°N of the Equator. This is on 21 June (summer solstice). By 21 Sept. (autumn equinox) the sun is overhead at noon at the Equator ; by 21 Dec. (winter solstice) it is overhead at noon along the Tropic of Capricorn (23½°S) ; and by 21 March (vernal or spring equinox) the sun appears to be overhead at noon at the Equator again. The summer solstice gives us our longest day in the northern hemisphere *c.*21 June, the winter solstice our shortest day, *c.*21 Dec., when we have only 8 hours daylight.

sea trout or salmon trout, fish found in British waters and the Mediterranean ; silvery in colour ; is often 3ft long.

Seattle, *sē-at'l,* city and port, Washington, USA. It has shipbuilding yards and canning factories ; pop.368,000.

sea urchin, creature of the starfish family. The skin, covered with prickles, is rather like that of the hedgehog.

seaweeds, sea plants belonging to a larger group of aquatic plants called algae, among them dulse and laver. A form of synthetic silk is now being manufactured from seaweed.

Sebastian (AD255–88), Christian saint and martyr, *b* Narbonne, France ; put to death by order of the Emperor Diocletian.

Sebastopol, *sē-bas-tō'pul,* Crimean grain-exporting port, USSR ; scene of a famous siege (1854–55) in the Crimean War ; also of severe fighting in World War II ; pop.112,000.

secant, see CIRCLE ; TRIGONOMETRY

Second Republic, period of French history from 24 Feb 1848, when King Louis Philippe abdicated, to 2 Dec 1852, when Louis Napoleon (Napoleon III) was made emperor.

secretary (Latin, *secretarius,* confidential officer), one who attends to the financial business of a company and represents it in financial and business matters. In order to become a qualified Company Secretary it is necessary to pass the examinations of such public bodies as the Chartered Institute of Secretaries, and/or the Institute of Company Accountants.

A private secretary is one who assists an individual with his or her work. The secretary should be able to take shorthand notes at a reasonably high speed, be a good typist and book-keeper. It is also advisable and useful to become proficient at an additional subject such as a language, journalism, or better still, both.

Anyone applying for a private secretarial post should be able to produce a certificate of proficiency obtained after a course of instruction at a recognised secretarial college.

Secretary of State, director of a government department, e.g. the Secretary of State for Foreign Affairs, and those for War, Air and for Commonwealth Relations. Each is a member of the Cabinet.

secret messages, see CIPHERS AND CODES

secret police, see GESTAPO

Secret Service, department of most governments ; organises a system of espionage, i.e. employs spies to gather information secretly from other countries. See CIPHERS AND CODES

secret societies, groups of people, often rebels, who desire to bring about changes in religion, politics, etc. by unconstitutional methods, e.g. the notorious Ku-Klux-Klan of USA (founded 1865) which sought to prevent coloured people sharing in government affairs.

During World War II many German-occupied countries had ‘ underground movements,’ i.e. groups of saboteurs. See SABOTAGE

sector, see CIRCLE

Security Council, see UNO

Sedan, *sē-dan',* cloth-manufacturing town, France ; on the R. Meuse, and 164m north-east of Paris ; notable for the crushing defeat of the French by the Germans 1870.

Sedan chair, kind of upright box with seat, door and windows ; carried by two men who hold the ends of two poles. Said to have been invented at Sedan, France, it was used in England early in the 17th century. Such chairs were hired until the 19th c. much as taxis are hired today.

Sedbergh, *sed'bĕr,* town, Yorkshire, famous for its public school founded *c.*1525 ; refounded 1552.

Sedgemoor, *sej'moor,* area of marshy land, Somerset ; scene of the defeat of Monmouth by James II, 1685.

see, see CHURCH

seeds, see BOTANY

seeing, see EYE

Seeland, see ZEELAND

Seeley, SIR JOHN (1834–95), historian, *b* London ; wrote *The Expansion of England* ; *The Growth of British Policy* ; also *Ecce Homo* (i.e. *Behold the Man!*) a study of the human side of Jesus.

segment, see CIRCLE

Segrave, SIR HENRY (1896–1930), speed expert born in USA of Irish ancestry ; drove a car at Daytona, USA, at 231mph (1929) ; killed on L. Windermere while travelling 100mph in a motor-boat.

Seine, *sān,* river of France ; rises north-west of Dijon, and flows 480m to the English Channel.

seismograph, *sīz'mō-gräf,* record of an earthquake made by an instrument (seismometer) that produces a straight line (drawn or photographed) on a moving strip until an earth tremor occurs, causing the instrument to record a wavy line.

Selángor, see MALAYA

Selassié, HAILE, *hīl sel-as'i* (1892–   ), Negus (King) of Ethiopia from 1928 ; proclaimed Emperor 1930 ; exiled 1936–40, when the Italians occupied the country ; restored 1941. His eldest son is Crown Prince Asfa Wossen, *b* 1916.

Selborne, village, Hampshire ; home of Gilbert White, the naturalist. See WHITE, GILBERT

Selby, town, W. Yorkshire ; on the R. Ouse ; noted for its fine abbey.

Selene, *sē-lē'nē,* in old Greek tales, goddess of the moon, and a daughter of Hyperion.

selenium, *sē-lē'ni-ŭm,* non-metallic element, Se, discovered 1817 ; atomic weight 78·96 ; atomic number 34 ; found in several forms, chiefly as a brick-red powder, or as a so-called metal which burns with a reddish-blue flame. Selenium is curious for the way in which it is acted on by light, metallic selenium conducting electricity much more effectively when light shines on it, a property that enables scientists to use it in several ways, e.g. in the optophone, an instrument enabling blind people to 'read' ordinary print; in photo-electric cells, television and burglar-alarms.

selenium cell, see PHOTO-ELECTRIC CELL

Selkirk, ALEXANDER, see DEFOE, DANIEL

Selkirkshire, inland county, Scotland; part of the ancient forest of Ettrick; co.tn Selkirk, 40m south-east of Edinburgh; once famous for brogue shoes, now noted for tweeds.

Sellafield, site of a large-scale atomic-pile, Cumberland. Known as Windscale Works, this vast atomic energy production factory incorporates the latest equipment for the production of plutonium etc. Though still incomplete, it has a chimney rising 400 feet above buildings of concrete and glass. See ATOMIC PILE; HARWELL

selling price, see PROFIT

selvas (Spanish, forests), tropical forests, especially in the Amazon region of S. America; also of the Guinea coast and Congo region.

Selwyn, GEORGE AUGUSTUS (1809-78), English churchman; went to NZ as a missionary bishop 1841. Selwyn College, Cambridge University, was founded in his memory 1882.

semaphore, *sem'ä-för,* signalling instrument. Also a system of signalling, especially between ships; now largely replaced by the electric telegraph and radio.

Semitic, see LANGUAGE

semi-water gas, fuel made by passing air and steam through incandescent coke.

semolina, *sem-ō-lē'nä,* coarser part of wheat set aside during grinding.

sen, see YEN

senate (Latin *senatus,* council of elders), a meeting. In early Rome the senate was a kind of city council; later it became the empire parliament with 600–1,000 representatives, i.e. *senators,* directing public affairs, religion, money, preparations for war, affairs of other nations, government and law-making.

Today the upper chamber in the parliaments of Canada, Australia, S. Africa, USA is known as the senate. Some universities are managed by a committee called a senate.

Seneca the Elder, *sen'ē-kä* (*d* c.AD38), Roman orator, famous for his remarkable memory.

Seneca the Younger (*d* AD65), son of Seneca the Elder. Tutor to the Emperor Nero, he gained such control over the young ruler that, at first, Nero governed more or less wisely; later Nero compelled his old tutor and friend to commit suicide.

Seneca, whose fortune is said to have amounted to £3,000,000, was a thinker, statesman and playwright; nine of his tragedies (sadly undramatic) may still be read. His prose is full of noble thoughts finely expressed.

Senegal, river of French W. Africa; reaches the Atlantic at St Louis, capital of the colony, which is noted for ground-nuts.

Senlac, old name for the spot in Sussex where the battle of Hastings was fought 1066.

Sennacherib, *se-nak'ĕr-ib,* King of Assyria 705–680BC; campaigned against many Middle-Eastern countries, including Palestine (2 Chronicles 32); destroyed Babylon; made Nineveh a great city. See ASSYRIA

Sénnar, town on the Blue Nile. Hereabouts is the Sénnar Dam, 200m south-east of Khartoum.

sensitive plant, prickly plant of tropical America. At the slightest touch its leaves fold up and droop.

sentence, in law, the penalty imposed on a criminal by a judge.

Senussi, *se-noo'sē,* Moslem sect founded c.1843 in Libya by the Sheikh es Senussi. In World War I the Senussi fought against Britain, but in World War II they supported Britain against the Italians. After World War II Britain adopted the policy of aiding them to live their own way without foreign interference.

Seoul, *se-ool',* cap. of Korea (Chosen). It was the scene of bitter fighting against Communists in 1950; pop.1,142,000.

sepia, *sē'pia,* brown colour used by artists; made from the ink of cuttle-fish, or from the juice of walnuts.

sepoy, *sē'poi,* Indian foot-soldier in a European army; first enlisted in the 18th c. to guard factories of the E. India Company.

septicemia, *sep-ti-sē'mia,* generalised form of blood-poisoning due to harmful bacteria in the blood-stream.

sequoia, *sē-kwoi'ä,* huge evergreen tree found chiefly in California (USA); may be called (*a*) *big tree,* specimens of which have reached 320ft in height, with a girth of c.110ft; or (*b*) *redwood,* one of the biggest trees in the world, sometimes 340ft high. A redwood in Yosemite National Park (USA) has a motor-road through the trunk. Sequoias and redwoods are probably the oldest living things, several being c.1,500 years old, possibly more.

The trees are named after Sequoia (*d* 1843), a cripple of the Cherokees (American Indians) who invented a Red Indian alphabet of 85 letters, and thus gave the Indians a written language and literature.

Seraing, *sĕ-rän',* town, Belgium; on the R. Meuse; famous for its engineering works; pop.45,000.

Serajevo, see SARAJEVO

Serbia, see YUGOSLAVIA

serf (Latin *servus,* slave), in feudal (or Norman) times, a peasant compelled to cultivate the land of his lord or master. He could not leave the land without his lord's permission, and paid a rent, either in money or produce. Serfdom amounted almost to slavery. The Black Death (c.1350) began its gradual abolition in England, though in Scotland a form of serfdom (e.g. among colliers) lingered till the 18th century. In Russia 23,000,000 serfs were emancipated 1863.

serge, woollen cloth, usually dyed dark blue or black.

series, in, see ELECTRICITY

Seringapatam, town, Mysore (India) ; fortified by Tippoo Sahib, who was killed during the British siege 1799.

Sermon on the Mount, see CHRIST

serpent, see SNAKE

serpentine, hydrated silicate of magnesium. It is green, and is easily carved with a knife.

serum, *sēr'ŭm* (a) yellowish watery fluid which remains when blood clots, (b) fluid prepared for immunisation and vaccination.

serval, African wild cat 4–5ft long ; is brownish with black spots.

servant, one who works for or serves another, e.g. (a) a domestic servant, (b) a member of the Civil Service, who is styled a civil servant.

Note that after the Last Supper, Jesus washed the feet of His disciples to show that to serve is noble ; hence *Ich Dien* (German, I serve) has become the motto of the Prince of Wales.

Service, ROBERT WILLIAM (1874–), Canadian poet, b Preston, Lancashire ; had an adventurous life ; best known for his *Rhymes of a Rolling Stone.*

service tree, tree rather like the rowan, but the greenish-brown fruit, spotted with red, is larger.

Servius Tullius, legendary king of ancient Rome 578–534BC ; said to have enclosed the hills with a ditch and rampart, i.e. the Servian Wall.

sesame, *ses'ă-mē,* plant grown in India for its seeds, from which oil is pressed.

Seth-Smith, DAVID (1875–), English naturalist ; well known as 'the Zoo Man,' and as a popular broadcaster.

Seton, ERNEST THOMPSON, *sē'tŭn* (1860–1946), writer, born in England ; went to Canada as a child ; became a naturalist. His books include *Wild Animals I Have Known* ; *Woodcraft and Indian Lore* ; and *Wild Animals at Home.* His boys' organisation, Woodcraft Indians, founded 1902, was actually the inspiration of Baden-Powell's Boy Scout movement.

Settlement, ACT OF, measure passed 1701 to settle the crowns of England, Scotland and Ireland on the Electress Sophia of Hanover and her Protestant heirs.

Seven Weeks' War, fought between Prussia and the combined armies of Austria and some German states 1866, Prussia emerging as a leading state.

Seven Wonders of the World, in ancient times were : the Hanging Gardens, Babylon ; the Pyramids of Egypt ; the Temple of Diana, Ephesus ; the statue of Jupiter, Athens ; the Colossus of Rhodes ; the Pharos (lighthouse), Alexandria ; and the mausoleum at Halicarnassus.

Seven Years' War, (1756–63) between (a) Great Britain, Prussia and Hanover,

and (b) France, Austria, Poland, Russia, Sweden, Saxony and (later) Spain. It amounted to a fight for existence on the part of Prussia, whose enemies were on every side. Overseas, it was a duel in which France and England fought for power in Canada and India.

The results were that Prussia kept Silesia, which she had at the beginning ; and that in consequence of (a) General Wolfe's victory over the French at Quebec 1759, (b) Admiral Hawke's victory in Quiberon Bay, also 1759, and (c) Robert Clive's victory at Plassey (India) 1757, the British drove the French out of Canada and India, thus securing valuable territories, a triumph largely due to the elder Pitt.

Severn, river rising in Wales, flows 220m to the Bristol Channel ; noted for its tidal bore, sometimes 9ft high. The Severn Tunnel (Bristol–Cardiff line) is 4m 634yd long.

Plans for the Severn Barrage, costing *c*.£50,000,000, were approved 1945, a scheme to harness the falling tide, and develop over 2,200,000,000 kilowatt-hr. of electric power per year, the hydro-electric plant having 32 turbines.

A suspension bridge (Aust–Beachley) is now being built at a cost of over £15,000,000.

Severus, LUCIUS SEPTIMIUS, *sē-vē'rŭs* (AD146–211), Roman emperor from AD193 ; made notable conquests in the east (Babylon, etc.) ; led an expedition to Britain 207, quelling the rebellious Brigantes and rebuilding Hadrian's Wall. Shortly before he died at York (Eboracum), he called for the urn in which his ashes were to repose, and said : *I have been all, and am no better for it ; this urn will soon hold what the whole world could not contain.*

Seville, *sev'il,* city and port of Spain ; on the R. Guadalquivir ; famous for its magnificent 15th–16th c. cathedral, and for the Alcazar, a palace of Moorish and Spanish kings. It was the birthplace of Murillo and Velazquez. Its university dates from 1256. Manufactures include cigars, textiles and machinery ; pop. 370,000.

Sèvres, *sā'vr,* French town on the R. Seine ; famous for beautiful porcelain.

Sewell, ANNA, *sū'el* (1820–78), b Yarmouth ; remembered for her popular book, *Black Beauty,* the story of a horse.

sewing machine, *sō'ing,* machine for facilitating the use of needle and thread ; greatly accelerates all sewing processes. The idea may be said to have begun with Thomas Saint, an Englishman. He was followed by Barthélemy Thimonnier (1793–1857), a French tailor whose wooden machine caused much opposition, and who died in poverty. Great improvements were effected by Walter Hunt (d 1859), a New York Quaker, and also by the American Elias Howe (1819–67), though to Isaac Merritt Singer (1811–75) goes the credit of developing the first successful machine for domestic use.

The modern Singer for school and home has several variations, the class 201K being among the latest. This has a reverse feed enabling the operator to sew either backwards or forwards ; mechanism facilitating linen darning and embroidery ; a hinged presser foot, and a special stitch regulator. There are also easy attachments for binding, hemming, ruffling and quilting. A fascinating innovation is ' Singercraft ' for making rugs and mats.

Valuable instructional booklets are provided by Singer Sewing Machine Company, Ltd, also a variety of 16mm instructional films, e.g. *The Birth of a Sewing Machine* ; *A Sewing Machine Lesson* ; *Binding* ; *Hemming* ; *Ruffling* ; *Darning and Embroidery*.

sex, distinction between male and female in living things, including not only animals, but also plants. Certain primitive forms of life, e.g. bacteria, the sea-anemone, amoeba, etc. are asexual, i.e. they reproduce by splitting in two or growing a ' bud ' that later becomes a perfect creature ; but most other forms (plants, animals, human beings) reproduce their kind by a sexual act in which the male fertilises the female.

Sexagesima, *sek-sä-jes′i-mä*, second Sunday before Lent.

sextant, instrument for measuring angles, especially for the navigator of a ship, who uses it to measure the apparent height of the sun at noon so that he may calculate his latitude at sea.

Seychelles, *sä-shel′*, group of *c.*90 British islands in the Indian Ocean. Mahé is noted for its giant tortoises and a curious double coconut. Exports include cereals, sugar, cotton goods ; cap. Victoria (on Mahé).

Seymour, *sē′mor*, name of an English family, including Edward Seymour (*d* 1552). He became Protector for the young king, Edward VI ; ruled more or less wisely, introducing changes in Church matters which led to the revised *Prayer Book*. He was beheaded. His sister, JANE (*d* 1537), was Henry VIII's third wife, and mother of Edward VI.

Sforza, COUNT CARLO, *sfor′tsä* (1873–   ), Italian statesman, Foreign Minister 1947 ; one of a famous family which held the duchy of Milan in the 15th century and for long encouraged art.

Shackleton, SIR ERNEST (1874–1922), Antarctic explorer, *b* Kilkee, Ireland ; joined Captain Scott's Antarctic Expedition 1901 ; commanded the British Antarctic Expedition 1907–9. Sailing in the *Nimrod*, he and some of his companions made a gallant attempt to reach the S. Pole. He sailed south in the *Endurance* 1914, when he and his crew lived on a drifting ice-floe for 16 months. They finally reached Elephant I., from which (1916), Shackleton and 6 men set out across angry seas in an open boat only 22ft long, and after one of the most terrible adventures in history arrived at S. Georgia, and were later joined by the remainder of the expedition.

Shackleton sailed from London (1921) in the *Quest* bound on another Antarctic expedition, but died in S. Georgia, and was buried there.

Read his book, *The Heart of the Antarctic*.

shadow, dark area, and the simplest proof that light normally travels in straight lines. The darkest part of a shadow is the *umbra* ; lighter parts towards the edges are the *penumbra*.

shaduf, *shä-doof*, primitive means of raising water still employed, notably in Egypt. It consists of a bucket suspended by a cord from the end of a long lever.

Shaftesbury, LORD, *shäfts′bĕri* (1801–85), friend of the poor. Anthony Ashley-Cooper, 7th Earl of Shaftesbury, lived as a child in a great house, Grosvenor Square, London. He was neglected by his mother, but cared for by his father's old housekeeper, Maria Millis, and to his dying day wore the watch she gave him. While a schoolboy at Harrow he happened to witness a pauper funeral, and there determined to fight for better conditions for the working classes.

Succeeding to his father's earldom 1851, he lived at a time when children were used as sweeps and sent up chimneys, or were compelled to work 16 hours a day in factories ; when women toiled in the mines, and when there was abject poverty, pitiful ignorance, and much cruelty. Shaftesbury was bitterly opposed by mill-owners and mine-owners who fought against every reform he tried to introduce. He was often defeated, but kept on. The friend of Queen Victoria, he walked and talked with peers, yet spent most of his life pleading in Parliament for shoeblacks, thieves, chimney-sweeps, lunatics, poor women and children. He became poor himself, but was greatly loved and highly respected. He saw the reforms he had pleaded for gradually maturing, and his name is always linked with the Ragged Schools, which provided free education, and sometimes food and lodgings, for waifs and strays.

Shaftesbury, first President of the Ragged School Union, was largely responsible for the Factory Acts of 1833 and 1842, protecting children in factories, and prohibiting underground labour for women and children ; also the Act of 1847 reducing the working day for women and children to 10 hours. He introduced reforms for the care of young law-breakers ; also the Lodging House Act 1872. He laid the foundation-stone of the Shaftesbury Park Estate, Battersea, with 1,200 houses for 8,000 poor persons. A leader of the Evangelical party in the Church of England, Shaftesbury was called ' good St Anthony of England.'

Read *Lord Shaftesbury*, J. L. and B. Hammond.

shagreen, *shä-green'*, untanned leather, made often from shark skin, but also from that of the horse, the ass or the camel ; usually dyed green ; is rough and pitted.

shah, *shä*, Persian word for king.

Shah Jehan, *shä ja-hän* (*d* 1666), Mogul (Indian) emperor 1628–58 ; a great military leader ; gave India two of her most beautiful buildings : the Taj Mahal and the Pearl Mosque, Agra. He founded the 17th c. city of Delhi, where his peacock throne is said to have been valued at £6,000,000.

Shakespeare, WILLIAM (1564–1616), poet and dramatist, described by Ben Jonson as ' Soul of the age, the applause, delight and wonder of our stage ' ; born, it is thought, St George's Day (23 April) at Stratford-on-Avon, Warwickshire. Little is known of his life.

His father was a dealer in skins, corn and timber, and though at one time well-to-do and either bailiff or mayor of Stratford, he later became poor.

William was educated at Stratford Grammar School, which he left when *c*.14 ; married Anne Hathaway (8 years his senior) before he was 20 ; had 3 children : Susanna, Hamnet and Judith.

The story is told that at this time young Shakespeare was caught poaching in the grounds of Charlecote Park, property of Sir Thomas Lucy, and that to avoid imprisonment he fled to London *c*.1586, but we do not know how much of this is true. He became an actor ; won his way on the stage ; improved the plays in which he acted, adding his own speeches ; and finally wrote his own masterpieces.

The company of players to which he belonged enjoyed royal favour and was known as the King's Servants. With others, Shakespeare shared in building the famous Globe theatre *c*.1598, which quickly attracted large audiences. Becoming rich, he was later able to buy New Place at Stratford, where he died on St George's Day 1616. He is buried in the parish church of Stratford, a town with much to remind us of him, e.g. the house in which he was born, still with the desk he used when he had trudged unwillingly to school ; also the only letter now in existence that certainly was penned by him. His school, with a red roof and timbered walls, was built 1428. A mile or so away is Anne Hathaway's cottage at Shottery ; by the Avon rises the massive block of the Shakespeare Memorial Theatre built with money raised by admirers of Shakespeare the world over ; reopened 23 April 1932, the earlier building having been destroyed by fire. It includes a museum, an art gallery, and a valuable library of books about Shakespeare ; has what is believed to be the only genuine portrait of the dramatist.

WILLIAM SHAKESPEARE 1564–1616

The ' Baconian theory ' may be summed up by saying that some scholars (especially in USA) have tried to prove that Shakespeare never lived, and that what are called Shakespeare's plays were actually written by Francis Bacon, who signed himself Will or William Shakespeare.

Shakespeare's plays are usually grouped as tragedies, histories, comedies, but Shakespearean comedy is not what we call comic. Whether a play by Shakespeare is a tragedy or a comedy is made clear to the audience only in the 4th act ; in the 5th (and last) the hero or heroine dies or is in some way overcome by the villain if the play is a tragedy, whereas in a comedy the last act shows the hero or heroine enjoying good fortune. Shakespeare rarely invented a plot for himself, but chose rather to take some old tale or piece of history, altering it to suit his requirements ; some of his plays about ancient Rome have plots taken from Plutarch's *Lives*.

Shakespeare's plays (in the order in which he is believed to have written them) are as follows :

Titus Andronicus
King Henry the Sixth (part 1)
Love's Labour Lost
The Comedy of Errors
The Two Gentlemen of Verona
A Midsummer Night's Dream
King Henry the Sixth (parts 2 and 3)
King Richard the Third
Romeo and Juliet
King Richard the Second
King John
The Merchant of Venice
King Henry the Fourth
King Henry the Fifth
The Taming of the Shrew
The Merry Wives of Windsor

Much Ado About Nothing
As You Like It
Twelfth Night
Julius Caesar
Hamlet
All's Well that Ends Well
Measure for Measure
Troilus and Cressida
Othello
King Lear
Macbeth
Antony and Cleopatra
Coriolanus
Timon of Athens
Pericles
The Winter's Tale
Cymbeline
The Tempest
Henry the Eighth
The plays were first collected 1623, when a folio edition was issued ; a copy of this, now in the British Museum, was bought for £5,250.

Shakespeare's poems include *Venus and Adonis* (1593) ; *Lucrece* (1594) ; and *The Passionate Pilgrim* (1599). As a poet he is at his best in his *Sonnets*, in which he often refers to a lady who remains a mystery ; we have no certain clue to her identity. No English writer has been quoted so often as Shakespeare, who has given noble expression to innumerable thoughts, e.g.

How far that little candle throws his beams!
So shines a good deed in a naughty world. (*The Merchant of Venice*)
Who steals my purse steals trash ;
'tis something, nothing ;
'Twas mine, 'tis his, and has been slave to thousands ;
But he that filches from me my good name
Robs me of that which not enriches him,
And makes me poor indeed. (*Othello*)
There is a tide in the affairs of men,
Which, taken at the flood, leads on to fortune. (*Julius Caesar*)

Shakespeare ranks among the world's supreme dramatists because his plots are usually superbly unfolded ; because his mastery of characterisation is unsurpassed ; because his language is noble, vivid and full of poetry ; because his themes, based on fundamentals of human life and experience, reveal amazing insight into men and women of all sorts and conditions, and are therefore timeless ; and because his imagination and skill have produced plays which have the overwhelming reality of life itself.

From what others have said about Shakespeare we may note

There, Shakespeare, on whose forehead climb
The crowns o' the world. Oh, eyes sublime
With tears and laughter for all time.
(*E. B. Browning*)
Our myriad-minded Shakespeare.
(*Coleridge*)

What point of morals, of manners, of economy, of philosophy, of religion, of taste, of the conduct of life, has he not settled ? What mystery has he not signified his knowledge of ? What office or function, or district of man's work, has he not remembered ? What king has he not taught state, as Talma taught Napoleon ? What maiden has not found him finer than her delicacy ? What lover has he not out-loved ? What sage has he not outseen ? What gentleman has he not instructed in the rudeness of his behaviour ?
(*R. W. Emerson*)
Read *Life in Shakespeare's England*, J. Dover Wilson ; *Introducing Shakespeare*, G. B. Harrison.

shale, layer, or layers, of clay. Most shales contain fossils ; bituminous shale may be rich in oil.

shallot, see ASCALON

Shalmaneser, *shal-mä-nē′zĕr*, name of five kings of Assyria, the earliest *c.*1300BC ; the last (who besieged Samaria) *d* 722BC.

Sha-mo, see GOBI

shamrock, plant of the pea family. The leaves are usually in three parts. The plant is the national emblem of Ireland.

Shanghai, *shang-hī′*, port and chief commercial city, China ; 12m from the coast and 160m south-east of Nanking ; on Wu-sung R. ; linked by canals with the interior ; exports tea, silk, cotton and rice ; occupied by the Japanese 1938, and by the Chinese Communists 1949 ; pop.3,550,000.

Shanklin, seaside town, I. of Wight.

Shannon, largest river of Ireland ; flows 240m into a wide estuary between Kerry and Clare. A dam near Limerick gives a fall of 100ft ; here is the Shannon hydro-electric power station which supplies most of Eire.

Shannon, world's first free airport. It is 15m from Limerick, and has been customs-free since 1947.

Shan States, see BURMA

Shantung, *shän′dung*, province of China by the Yellow Sea ; cap. Tsi-nan-fuo. The region (*c.*42,000sq.m) has pop. 36,500,000, and is one of the most densely populated areas in the world. The silk material, shantung, was first made here.

shares, see STOCKS AND SHARES

shark, sea-water fish, generally fierce and powerful ; has usually five pairs of gills and several gill-slits on each side of its head ; it has also a mouth, on the underside of its head, with many strong teeth. Species found in British waters include hammer-headed shark ; blue shark ; tope ; porbeagle (often 10ft long), and thrasher, sometimes 15ft long, including its remarkable tail. Of man-eating sharks the great white shark of tropical seas is perhaps the most terrible ; but the whale shark, often 60ft, is the least harmless. The angel-fish is a kind of shark ; so, also, is the dog-fish.

Sharon, PLAIN OF, *shār'on*, region of Palestine noted for its fertility. The rose of
Sharon (Song of Solomon, 2) was probably the narcissus.

Sharp, CECIL JAMES (1859–1924), English
musician and writer ; collected 5,000
folk-songs and folk-dances ; founder
1911 of the English Folk-Dance and
Song Society. See FOLK-SONGS

Sharp, WILLIAM (1855–1905), poet and
novelist, *b* Paisley ; best known for his
Celtic stories written under the pen-name
of Fiona Macleod.

Shasta Dam, immense dam on the Sacramento R., USA ; completed 1944. The
dam is 602ft high ; and the hydro-
electric plant generates 150,000 kilowatts.

Shaw, AIRCRAFTSMAN, see LAWRENCE OF
ARABIA

Shaw, ALFRED (1842–1907), English
cricketer ; played seven times for
England against Australia ; famous as a
slow bowler.

Shaw. BERNARD (1856–1950), dramatist,
b Dublin. He was christened George
Bernard, and has long been known as
G. B. S., though in later life he wished
to be known simply as Bernard Shaw.

Coming to London as a young man,
he identified himself with the Fabian
Society. He won fame as a music, and
then as a drama, critic and was still
more successful as a dramatist, his plays,
startlingly unorthodox in theme, abounding always in that particularly brilliant
and challenging wit which is now known
as Shavian. The introductions to many
of his plays are among the most
notable literary triumphs of this century,
and these, together with the plays (and
a variety of books) reveal Shaw as a
rebel against convention, and as one
delighting to stab others broad awake.
From the first he was a Socialist, a fearless (but always witty) denouncer of
muddled thinking, smug respectability,
and hyprocrisy in politics, religion and
social ideals.

Among a host of his plays may be
mentioned *Man and Superman* and
Back to Methuselah, in both of which
Shaw propounds his belief in a ' life-
force ' capable of raising mankind to a
nobler level. Other plays include *Saint
Joan* (1924), a powerful historical drama ;
Pygmalion ; *The Apple Cart* ; *Candida* ;
John Bull's Other Island ; and *Androcles
and the Lion.*

Among various books may be noted
*Adventures of a Black Girl in Search of
God* ; *The Intelligent Woman's Guide to
Socialism and Capitalism* ; *Everybody's
Political What's What.*

With his caustic wit and unconventional manners, Shaw was something
of a legend 20 years before his 90th
birthday (1946), which was marked by
the publication of many of his plays in
cheap editions, also the publication of
G. B. S. 90, a volume of tributes to the
veteran dramatist by twenty-seven of his

younger contemporaries. Shaw was
a vegetarian from youth. As a tall,
erect old man, with a flowing white
beard he was one of the best-known of
literary figures.
Typical quotations from his works are:
A man of great common sense and
good taste—meaning thereby a man
without originality or moral courage.
How can what an Englishman believes be heresy ? It is a contradiction in terms.
If you strike a child, take care that
you strike it in anger, even at the risk
of maiming it for life. A blow in cold
blood neither can nor should be for-
given.
A lifetime of happiness : No man
alive could bear it : it would be hell
on earth.

Shawcross, SIR HARTLEY (1902–   ),
British lawyer and Labour politician ;
MP for St Helens and Attorney-General
1945.

shawm, *shaum*, old musical instrument now
replaced by the oboe. In the *Prayer
Book* shawm should actually be *shofar*,
an instrument (still used in Palestine)
that is usually made out of a ram's horn.

Sheba, name given to two ancient kingdoms
(*a*) in S. Arabia, (*b*) in Ethiopia. We
do not know from which the Queen
of Sheba travelled to visit Solomon
(1 Kings 10).

Shechem, *shek-im*, ancient name for a town
(now Nablus) north of Jerusalem.

Sheen Palace, see RICHMOND (SURREY)

sheep, animal found wild in parts of Europe
and Asia, but now largely domesticated
in most parts of the world and reared
chiefly for its wool and flesh (mutton).
Among breeds of British sheep are
Leicester, Lincoln, and Wensleydale, all
with long wool ; short wool breeds
include Down, Suffolk and Dorset Horn;
mountain breeds include Cheviot, Blackface, Lonk and Welsh. Wild sheep
(both male and female) have horns, but
most domestic breeds are without.
A male sheep is a *ram*, or, if not
intended for breeding, a *wether* ; a
female is a *ewe*. The Merino has fine
white wool. A cross between a Leicester
and Merino is said to give the finest
fleece. In Britain, shearing occurs May–
July. Australia, NZ, S. Africa and
Argentine have immense flocks.
The substitution of sheep-farming for
an agricultural system of small-holdings
caused untold misery among country-
people in England in the early 16th c.
and in the Scottish Highlands during the
19th c., where the development was
known as the ' Clearances,' i.e. of people
off the land. See PLATES 17 (*bottom*),
19, 20, 21 (*top*)

Sheerness, port, Kent ; at the mouth of
the Medway and on the I. of Sheppey ;
has naval docks and storehouses.

Sheffield, city, W. Yorkshire, where the
rivers Don and Sheaf meet. Its cathedral was damaged by German bombs in

RADIO   *plate 61*

Top : A B.B.C. Transmitter Control Room, from which four transmitters can be remotely operated. The picture shows the control desk, fault indicator panel and programme input equipment. *Bottom :* A programme operator at the panel in a listening cubicle. In the studio behind the panel are four actors reading a script. (Both *B.B.C.*)

plate 62   TELEVISION CAMERA

A B.B.C. Television unit in action with an ' Emitron ' camera. (*B.B.C.*)

TELEVISION AND BROADCASTING

plate 63

Bottom : The ballet *Les Sylphides* being televised in a specially built television studio at Radiolympia, London. *Top left :* One of the largest types of high-power water-cooled transmitter valves ; *right :* ' the programme was recorded . . .' A B.B.C. Type D recording unit. (*B.B.C.*)

plate 64   RADIO

Radio brings men of all nations closer to one another, in some ways, than ever before. The 500 foot mast of the B.B.C.'s London Transmitting Station at Brookmans Park, Herts. (*B.B.C.*)

SHEEP

(1) *The Leicester*   (3) *The Suffolk*
(2) *The Blackface*   (4) *The Merino*

World War II. Noted for its cutlery, the city is also world-famous for steel, machine tools, armour plates, guns, turbines, boilers and railway material ; also for silver-plated goods and glass. The university was founded 1905 ; pop.512,000.

Sheffield plate, copper utensils (e.g. candlesticks and chafing dishes) plated with silver by a process discovered *c.*1742 by a Sheffield workman, Thomas Boulsover (1704–88) ; now replaced by electroplate.

sheikh, *shāk,* Arabic word for old man ; used as a title for an Arab chief, preacher or saint.

shekel, ancient Jewish measure of weight, *c.*10dwt Troy ; also a coin worth *c.*2s. 8d if silver, £2 if gold.

sheldrake, British wild duck. The common sheldrake, *c.*26in long, has a dark green head, is black and white on the wings, and has a bright red beak.

shellac, substance formed on the bark of certain trees by an insect (the stick-lac). When refined it is used for varnishes.

Shelley, PERCY BYSSHE (1792–1822), English poet, *b* Warnham, Sussex. A rebel at Oxford, he was eager to put the world right, but his university career was cut short because of his pamphlet on atheism (disbelief in God) published 1811. In disgrace, he was compelled to live in lodgings in London, where he fell in love with Harriet Westbrook, then only 16, with whom he ran away to Scotland.

They were married, but the marriage proved unhappy.

Meanwhile, Shelley mixed poetry with politics, and eloped (1814) with Mary Wollstonecraft Godwin. He left England for ever 1818, seeking improved health in Italy, chiefly Rome and Florence. He learned Greek, and was led to enjoy the classics by his friend, Thomas Love Peacock. Shelley was drowned while sailing (as he loved to do) from Leghorn to Spezia, his body being cremated in the presence of Lord Byron and Leigh Hunt.

Shelley's poetry, like his life, is full of passion and idealism. Much of it preaches that imagination is the great instrument of goodness. His *Revolt of Islam* ; *Prometheus Unbound* ; *The Cenci* (a tragedy) are all great poetry ; but he is remembered most for his *Adonais* (prompted by the death of John Keats), and his glorious lyrics, e.g. *The Cloud* and *To a Skylark.*

Mary Wollstonecraft Shelley, his second wife (1797–1851), wrote *Frankenstein,* a gruesome tale.

shells, see MOLLUSCA

shepherd's purse, common wayside plant ; the rough-haired leaves are (*a*) those near the ground in a rosette, each long and narrow, (*b*) those farther up the stem and like arrow heads ; the small white flowers give place to heart-shaped fruits.

Sheppey, ISLE OF, island in the estuary of the Thames. It is a part of Kent, from which it is separated by the R. Swale, spanned by a bridge ; the chief town is Sheerness.

Sheraton, THOMAS (1751–1806), cabinet-maker and drawing-master, b Stockton-on-Tees, Durham ; was poor all his life. His fame rests on his designs for furniture. The Sheraton style is notable for simple outlines, square form and straight legs.

Sherborne, town, Dorsetshire. Its noted school was founded 1550.

Shere Ali, *shār ä'lē* (1825–79), Ameer (ruler) of Afghanistan, whose opposition to the British 1878 led to the Afghan Wars.

Sheridan, RICHARD BRINSLEY (1751–1816), dramatist and politician, b Dublin ; entered Parliament 1780 ; made a masterly speech during the trial of Warren Hastings. His greatest fault was a passion for gambling, and he was heavily in debt when he died.

One of the wittiest men of his day, Sheridan is remembered for his plays, *The Rivals* (1775) ; *The School for Scandal* ; and *The Critic*.

sheriff, i.e. shire-reeve, one who looks after a shire.

A reeve, as we read in Chaucer's *Canterbury Tales*, was at first a steward or bailiff of an estate, a kind of fore-man ; shire-reeves became important in Henry II's day, but now in England the office of sheriff is little more than an honour conferred on worthy citizens.

In Scotland, however, the sheriff has a function corresponding to that in England of a county-court judge. In this capacity he has considerable powers.

Sheriffmuir, barren spot, c.5m north-east of Stirling ; scene 1715 of an indecisive battle between Jacobites led by the Earl of Mar, and Hanoverians led by the Duke of Argyll.

'Sherlock Holmes,' see DOYLE, SIR A. C.

Sherman, WILLIAM TECUMSEH (1820–91), American soldier, b Lancaster, Ohio ; notable for his share in the American Civil War ; was of great use to General Grant ; invaded Georgia 1864, beginning his famous march to the sea in November, an episode that prompted Henry Clay Work (1832–84) to write the words and tune of *Marching through Georgia*.

Sherriff, ROBERT CEDRIC (1896–   ), English dramatist and novelist ; was a captain in World War I ; won fame with his play, *Journey's End*, produced in London 1929. Other plays include *Badger's Green* and *Windfall*. His novels include *The Fortnight in September* and *Greengates*.

sherry, Spanish white wine named from Jerez, a town in the province of Cadiz.

Sherwood, forest (of which only a little remains), Nottinghamshire ; associated with Robin Hood.

Shetland Islands, c.100 islands roughly 50m north of the Orkneys (north of Scotland) ; total area c.550sq.m ; cap. Lerwick. Fair Isle and Unst are noted for hand-knitted woollens. The islands give their name to a hardy breed of ponies.

shield, protective armour to ward off arrows or blows from sword or spear. Bronze Age shields had a boss (in the middle) and many studs ; the Greek shield was often round, with a leather apron ; the Roman (*scutum*), oblong and convex, was of wood covered with leather ; Norman shields were kite-shaped.

Shields, name of two towns (a) N. SHIELDS (Northumberland), now part of Tyne-mouth and on the north bank of the Tyne ; exports coal, has shipbuilding yards ; pop.65,000 ; and (b) S. SHIELDS (Durham), south of the Tyne ; has a fine harbour with docks and wharves ; manufactures glass, chemicals, boilers and cables ; pop.103,000.

Shillibeer, GEORGE, see ROADS

Shillong, capital of Assam.

Shintoism, *shin'tō-izm*, ancient national religion of Japan, largely the worship of nature, but long associated with the teachings of Buddha and Confucius, and in some respects similar to Chinese ancestor worship. State Shinto was different, being used from 1868 as a political means of inducing fanatical worship of the emperor. A mixture of traditional religion, myth and politics, its priests were paid out of state funds, and from the 19th c. Japanese youth was imbued with wild dreams of conquest, resulting in the war of 1941–45. State Shinto was abolished by General MacArthur after Japan's defeat 1945.

shinty, game, rather like hockey and hurling, played on a field (e.g. 250yd by 100) with goals (known as hails) 12ft wide, 10ft high, each with a net at the back. The 12 players on each side use a caman (or club) with a triangular head. The ball, c.2in in diameter, is of cork covered with leather. Shinty, played in Ireland and the Scottish Highlands, is known in Gaelic as *Camanachd*.

shipbuilding, see SHIPS

Shipley, town, W. Yorkshire ; on the R. Aire ; manufactures woollens and worsteds ; pop.30,000.

Ship Money, see HAMPDEN, J.

ships, vessels intended for navigation, particularly sea-going vessels ; evolved from the prehistoric log, raft, dug-out canoe ; may be grouped as : (I) sailing ships ; (II) power-driven ships.

(I) SAILING SHIPS are known to have been in regular service on the R. Nile 4000BC. The Greeks who fought at Troy c.1200BC had *galleys* with sails, also two rows (or banks) of oars. These were *biremes*. A *trireme* had three banks of oars, a *quadreme* four, a *quinquireme* five. Triremes, deadliest of all ancient Greek battleships, had a pointed ram. *Roman galleys* (often 150ft long) were driven by gangs of slaves toiling at the oars. The *long ships* or *dragons* of the Vikings had sometimes 60 oars and one large sail ; the prow was carved in the shape of a dragon or serpent.

EGYPT: SEA-GOING SHIP c. 2600 B.C.

MODEL OF A VIKING LONG SHIP c. A.D. 1000

13th c. KING'S SHIP OF WAR

16th c. WARSHIP "HARRY GRACE A DIEU"

18th c. NAVY FRIGATE

19th c. TOPSAIL SCHOONER "MARY" (1835)

19th c. TEA CLIPPER

FULTON'S "CLERMONT"

SHIPS

iling Ships are known to have been in use since 4000BC. Here are some examples showing development
m 2600BC to the 19th century. Their varying shapes and sizes show how, with growing experience
the sea, there evolved the knowledge that compactness and streamlining make for greater safety
and speed. Fulton's ' Clermont ' was one of the first ships to be fitted with steam engines.

British seapower began with King Alfred, who built fine ships to fight the Danes. Crusaders saw the three-masted ships then sailing the Mediterranean between Venice and Genoa, but it was not till the 16th c. that we built vessels of similar size, e.g. the *Great Harry*. English ships of the 13th c. had a kind of upper deck (the castle) either fore or aft, sometimes ridiculously high. By Armada year (1588) the English had learned that smaller and more compact ships were quicker and also easier to handle. In the 17th c. the *E. Indiaman* (trading with India and China) was one of the swiftest and most useful ships at sea, and in the next century three-masted *sloops* and *frigates* were among our most successful battleships. All had carved figure-heads at the prow. Sailing ships reached the height of their glory in the 19th c., and *c.*1850 British and American *clippers* were travelling 300m a day. These were graceful vessels with three masts, great spread of sail, and a hull with slim, clean lines. The tea clippers made astonishing records, e.g. the *Cutty Sark*, built Dumbarton 1869, probably the fastest ship then afloat ; sailed from Sidney to London in 75 days.

The first iron ship was built in England *c.*1770, but even *c.*1850 the navy still comprised fleets of wooden ships. With the invention of the steamship, however, wooden vessels began to fall into disuse, though happily some are with us yet, and we may still see the sun on white sails as trim yachts speed before the wind. See PLATE 31

(II) POWER-DRIVEN SHIPS :

As early as 1802 William Symington, a Scottish engineer, fitted a steam engine to a boat and thus towed two heavy barges on the Forth and Clyde Canal, but the owners of the canal declared that his ship would damage their property, and Symington died in poverty. The first to make steam navigation practicable was Robert Fulton (1765–1815), an American who astonished New York with the *Clermont* 1807, fitting her with steam engines made in Scotland. In spite of jeering crowds, his ship steamed 150m along the Hudson R. in 32 hours. A Scotsman, Henry Bell (1767–1830), built the *Comet* 1812, plying between Glasgow and Greenock 7 years before the *Savannah*, fitted with a small engine, crossed from America to Liverpool partly under steam, mostly under sail.

The most memorable year in the history of British steamships was 1838 when the *Great Western* and the *Sirius* crossed the Atlantic under steam, though it is not generally known that a Dutch steamer had succeeded in doing this 11 years earlier. The *Great Western* (1,340 tons), built by Isambard Kingdom Brunel, sailed 4 days after the *Sirius*, but both arrived at New York about the same time. Prior to 1836 steamers were driven by paddle-wheels, but Captain

John Ericsson (1803–89), a Swedish soldier in America, invented the propeller or screw which changed the whole course of ocean navigation. Brunel's *Great Eastern*, with paddles and screw, crossed the Atlantic 1860.

Meanwhile, Sir Samuel Cunard (1787–1865) had founded (1839) the British and N. American Royal Mail Steam Packet Co., with ships carrying letters and parcels across the Atlantic, this leading to the formation of the Cunard Line 1878, known since 1934 as the Cunard-White Star Line. All ships of the Cunard Line had names ending in *-ia* ; those of the White Star Line (founded 1871) ending in *-ic*. The first Cunarder was the *Britannia* (a paddle-steamer), in which Charles Dickens crossed to America 1842 ; an early White Star liner was the *Britannic* which (1890) made the crossing in slightly over 7 days, thus beating all records. The *Turbina* (45 tons, driven by turbines invented by Sir Charles Parsons) made history 1894 by travelling at 38 knots, her engines being designed so that expanding steam, directed against the blades of a series of cylinders, caused them to revolve at high speed, a principle now employed in almost all fast liners and battleships.

Among notable liners may be mentioned : (*a*) *Titanic*, 46,000 tons, declared unsinkable because she was divided into many water-tight compartments, but sank after collision with an iceberg during her maiden voyage 1912 ; she was 852ft long, with engines of 70,000hp, and a speed of 21 knots ; (*b*) *Mauretania*, 44,000 tons, 790ft long ; held the Blue Riband of the Atlantic for 20 years, i.e. she remained the fastest trans-Atlantic vessel, averaging 26 knots ; (*c*) *Lusitania*, 31,500 tons, sunk 1915 by a German submarine, 1,198 passengers and crew losing their lives ; (*d*) *Queen Mary* (launched on the Clyde 1934) ; 80,000 tons, 1,018ft long and 118ft wide ; has 4 sets of turbines developing 200,000hp : 3 funnels, each 30ft in diameter ; a rudder weighing 140 tons : 30,000 electric lamps ; made her maiden voyage 1936 ; her sister ship (*e*) *Queen Elizabeth*, launched during the war of 1939–45, made a secret crossing to New York in spite of German U-boats. She came into civilian commission 1946. See PLATES 52, 53

Today shipbuilding in Britain is carried on beside the Clyde, Mersey, Humber, Tyne, Wear and Tees. The old method of using red-hot rivets is giving place to welding ; and many types of ships are now being built of concrete on prefabrication lines. This method of greatly increasing the speed of production was developed in USA and Britain during World War II. Marine types of powerful Diesel engines are being used on an increasing scale. Navigation is also in transition, the introduction of radar lessening the need of lighthouses and lightships, and simplifying much of the routine of the chart-room, besides minimising the danger of navigation at night and in fog.

The atomic ship may be expected within the next 5 or 10 years, though atomic energy is likely to be used in naval ships before others. The greatest difficulty to be overcome is the screening of the power-unit from the crew.

When we speak of the *tonnage* of a ship we recall the old custom of measuring her size by the number of ' tuns ' of wine she could carry. Today we have (a) *gross tonnage*, the measure of the inside capacity of a ship in cu.ft divided by 100, so that 1 ton = 100 cu.ft ; (b) *net tonnage* (on which harbour dues are paid) found by subtracting the total volume of space taken up by machinery and crew accommodation from the gross tonnage ; (c) *displacement tonnage* (sometimes called simply displacement), meaning the actual weight in tons of the ship and cargo when at sea ; (d) *deadweight tonnage*, the weight in tons of the load, including cargo, coal or oil, and stores.

NAUTICAL TERMS, especially those belonging to the days of sailing ships, include : *aft* or *astern* = in the rear ; *forrard* = in front ; *forecastle* or *fo'c'sle* = the seamen's quarters at the fore ; *amidships* = near the middle of the vessel ; *galley* = kitchen, usually on the main deck ; *cockpit* = a room in a man-of-war where the doctor attends the wounded ; *companion* = a wooden projection over steps from deck to cabin ; *hold* = part of the ship where the cargo is stowed ; *hatch* = the cover over a hold. To *batten the hatches* was to fasten them securely so as to keep the cargo dry. *Poop* = the raised stern deck, its railing being the *taffrail* ; *steerage* = the part in front of and below the poop ; *portside* (or *larboard*) = left side, looking towards the prow ; *starboard* = right side ; *scuppers* = gutters for carrying water from the decks ; *bulwarks* = wooden or metal walls or rails ; *gunwale* = the top rail of the bulwark ; *crow's nest* = a kind of box on a mast (it is used as a shelter for the look-out) ; *helm* = wheel or machinery for steering ; *lee side* = the side away from the wind, i.e. the sheltered side ; *windward* = the windy side ; *log-book* = a diary of the voyage kept by the captain or master ; *mast* = support for the sail or sails. Note that in a four-masted ship the front mast is the fore-mast, the second the main mast, third the mizzen mast, fourth the jigger mast, and that each mast has (a) lower mast, (b) top-mast, (c) top-gallant mast (d) royal mast, (e) skysail mast. The *yards* = wooden or iron spars slung across the mast ; *shrouds and stays* = wire ropes supporting the masts and forming part of the *rigging*, as also the *halliards*, i.e. the ropes for hoisting and lowering sails ; *boom* = a long pole to which the bottom of the main sail is fastened. To *furl a sail* = to tie it up to the mast or yard ; to *hoist a sail* = to spread it to the wind ; a *jib* = a triangular sail. To *sail close to the wind* = to sail as nearly as possible in the direction the wind is blowing. *Capstan* = a metal drum for hauling up anchors. In modern vessels it is driven by steam or electricity ; in old sailing ships it was turned by sailors using a *capstan-bar* ; a *windlass* is similarly used for lifting weights, cables, etc. *Tacking* = steering first in one direction, then in another while sailing against the wind ; *to veer* = to turn the stern to the windward ; *to heave to* = to slow down the speed of the ship. A vessel is on her *beam-ends* when she leans too far over to the side. *Davits* = arms from which lifeboats are lowered ; *to scuttle* a ship is to open cocks or make holes below water, and thus sink her ; a *stowaway* = one who hides in a ship hoping to secure a free passage. The PLIMSOLL MARK, painted on the hull of any vessel of 80 tons, or more, shows if a ship is laden more deeply than the Board of Trade allows ; it is named after Samuel Plimsoll (1824–98).

Speed at sea is measured in *knots*, a knot being 1·1515m or 6,080ft per hour ; hence we speak of a ship travelling so many knots, but we do *not* say so many knots *per hour*. See NAVY

ship-shore radio, communication between those ashore and those at sea by telephone and radio, first introduced (as radiotelephone) in the British Isles 1930 when it became possible to ' ring up ' the *Majestic*. Later it was much extended, and the service now includes Atlantic liners, the telephone subscriber being linked via Rugby Transmitting Station (shortwave radio) or Baldock, through Faraday Building, London ; coastal and short-voyage ships in British waters may be communicated with via stations at Humber, Portpatrick and Seaforth, the range being c.150m. See TELEGRAPH

Shiraz, *shē'räz*, town, Iran ; trades in wine, cotton, carpets and opium ; pop.130,000.

shire or **county**, in England or Wales or in Scotland the largest local unit of administration. Shire is possibly from OE *scir*, a province ; county from Norman France *comte*, count, i.e. a ruler of a district.

A shire is nominally under the care of a sheriff (shire-reeve). In early times the Saxons held a shire-moot twice a year. Many shires cover much the same area as the old kingdoms of Britain. From Tudor times each shire has had its lord-lieutenant in its co.tn ; also its county court. By the Local Government Act 1888 large towns (now any place with over 50,000 people) became county boroughs or administrative counties. Cornwall is actually a duchy, i.e. Edward III's gift to his son the Black Prince 1336. The duchy of Lancaster was given to his brother, John of Gaunt. By 'ENGLISH HOME COUNTIES' we mean those near London, generally regarded as Middlesex, Essex, Kent, Hertfordshire, Surrey and Buckinghamshire. COUNTIES PALATINE (Latin *palatinus*, belonging to a palace), e.g. Durham, Lancashire and Cheshire were once governed by feudal lords charged with the defence of England against Scottish or Welsh invaders. See LOCAL GOVERNMENT

Shirley, JAMES (1596–1666), dramatist and poet, *b* London. Of his plays *The Lady of Pleasure* (comedy) and *The Traitor* (tragedy) are perhaps the best. His fine lyrics include *The glories of our blood and state.*

shoddy, material made from old woollen goods and tailors' clippings of new cloth ; carried on at Batley, Ossett, Dewsbury (Yorkshire). A variety is known as MUNGO.

shoebill or **whale-head,** kind of N. African heron. A large bird, it is found among reeds by rivers. It has grey plumage, and is notable for its long legs and exceptionally large bill, shaped somewhat like a shoe or boat.

Shoeburyness, town, Essex ; long noted for its school of gunnery.

shofar, see SHAWM

shooting stars are otherwise called *meteors* (if they fail to reach the earth) or *meteorites* (if they strike its surface). Invisible while hurtling through space, they are seen soon after entering our atmosphere because friction with the air causes them to blaze to a white heat. Thought to be fragments of disrupted comets, they travel at 60mps, or faster, and are usually small, though some may weigh several tons. A meteorite weighing probably 130 tons fell near Vanovara, Siberia, 1908, destroying trees for 20m round. The so-called BARRINGER METEOR, buried 600ft deep in Arizona, was probably actually the head of a comet.

shop, place where goods are sold. Since 1893 there have been many Shop Acts for improvements in the conditions under which assistants work. By the Shop Act of 1912 (since amended) no one under 18 could be employed in a shop for more than 74 hours a week, including meals, and must have at least one free half-day ; and later Acts (e.g. that of 1934) have reduced this to 48 hours.

Multiple stores, a feature of recent years, present good chances of promotion to smart and ambitious young men and girls ; but such stores menace the small trader because they are able to buy more cheaply and to sell more cheaply, since even a small profit on a large turnover brings good returns.

Since about 1948 some shops have introduced the ' help yourself ' system, which seems to be growing in popularity.

Shorter, CLEMENT (1857–1926), English journalist, *b* London ; editor of various periodicals. He was an authority on George Borrow, Napoleon and the Brontës.

shorthand or **stenography,** system of speedwriting much used in business and reporting. Using shorthand a trained writer can take down words as quickly as they are uttered, and accurately transcribe what has been said.

A form of shorthand was known to the Romans. Modern shorthand began 1588 with Dr Timothy Bright's system, followed by those devised by Shelton and John Byrom. Great improvements on earlier systems were made by Sir Isaac Pitman (1813–97) who called his system *phonography* (i.e. sound writing) and gave each sound a sign of its own. The ' outlines ' (characters) of Pitman's shorthand are based on the use of straight lines, shallow curves, hooks and circles. Gregg's shorthand was invented 1888 by John Gregg. Yet another system was introduced 1916 by Reginald J. G. Dutton ; this has only 29 characters, 6 rules for abbreviations, and 75 word-signs to learn by heart.

In spite of many new systems those of Pitman and Gregg have withstood the test of time and have retained their leading positions as yet unrivalled. Pitman's in particular has gained universal recognition.

Ability to write shorthand at high speeds is of immense value, particularly to journalists, business men, secretaries, office workers and students. Shorthand theory is taught and speed classes are held at secretarial colleges and schools of commerce throughout Britain, while correspondence classes in shorthand theory may be taken with various colleges.

Both theory and speed certificates (elementary, intermediate and advanced) are granted by the Royal Society of Arts, the London Chamber of Commerce besides various other Public Bodies. In addition Pitman's hold shorthand examinations for the Pitman method, and *Pitman's Office Training* is published weekly.

short story, popular form of fiction brought to a fine art during the 20th century. Brief tales were told by the ancient Egyptians, by Jesus in the form of parables, by Aesop in fables ; but the modern short story was largely moulded in USA, notably by Edgar Allan Poe, and in France, especially by Balzac, Hugo, Dumas and (most of all) by Guy de Maupassant. British masters of the art include (among many) Guy N. Pocock, Sheila Kaye-Smith, Jan Struther, H. G. Wells, John Buchan, Virginia Woolf, G. K. Chesterton, Francis Brett Young and Rudyard

Kipling. Anton Tchekhov in Russia and O. Henry in USA had an immense influence on the development of style and technique.

Shottery, village, Warwickshire. It is near Stratford-on-Avon, and has Ann Hathaway's cottage. See SHAKESPEARE, WILLIAM

Shovell, SIR CLOUDESLEY, *shŭv'el* (1650–1707), admiral, *b* Cockthorpe, Norfolk, took part in the capture of Gibraltar 1704. After the battle of Toulon 1707 his ship was wrecked in the Scilly Is., where Shovell is said to have been killed for the sake of his emerald ring.

shoveller, *shŭv'lĕr,* exceptionally handsome broad-billed duck ; winters in Britain. The drake has a green head, blue shoulders, dark brown back, brown and white wings and chestnut breast.

shrew, *shroo,* small animal similar to a mouse, though the snout is usually longer ; it is found in temperate and in tropical regions. The three British species are : (*a*) COMMON SHREW, *c.*3in long, usually brownish grey, with round ears ; burrows in banks ; lives on insects, worms and snails ; (*b*) PYGMY SHREW, our smallest British animal, 2in long, with bright silky fur ; rare in England ; (*c*) WATER SHREW, 3in long, grey above, whitish below, rare in Scotland, unknown in Ireland.

Shrewsbury, *shrōz'bĕri* ; *shrooz'-*, co.tn, Shropshire ; on the R. Severn ; noted for stained glass, malting, iron-founding ; pop.43,000. Its public school (founded 1552) is at Kingsland, close by.

Shrewsbury, BATTLE OF, fought 1403 between Henry IV of England and the rebels led by Sir Henry Percy (Hotspur) with a number of Scots, and a Welsh army under Owen Glendower. The rebels were defeated, and Hotspur killed.

Shrewsbury, EARL OF, English title given to Roger Montgomery by William I ; revived 1442 for John Talbot, and has been retained by the family of Talbot ever since. ELIZABETH, COUNTESS OF SHREWSBURY (1518–1608), known as Bess of Hardwick, built Hardwick Hall and Chatsworth House.

shrike, name of several birds, e.g. (*a*) BUTCHER-BIRD, which hangs insects on thorns near the nest ; a winter visitor to Britain, it has grey, white, and black plumage ; (*b*) RED-BACKED SHRIKE, visits this country Apr.–Sept. : the nest, usually in a bush, is lined with hair ; the eggs are white, tinted blue or green ; (*c*) WOODCHAT, a rare visitor.

shrimp, sea creature (Crustacean), *c.*2in long ; found in shallow water ; is brown, but turns red when boiled. The PRAWN, similar but *c.*4in long, has a jointed greenish-grey shell.

Shropshire, county of England on the Welsh border ; mainly agricultural, and noted for sheep ; known as Salop for short ; co.tn Shrewsbury.

Shrove Tuesday, see CALENDAR

shuttle, see WEAVING

Shwe Dagon pagoda, see BURMA

Si, chemical symbol for silicon.

Siam, *sī'am,* kingdom known as ' the land of Free Men,' once called *Thailand* ; lies east of Burma ; area 198,247sq.m ; pop.14,500,000 ; largely mountainous in the north, and has teak forests ; the south is mostly flat, the chief crops being rice, sugar, cotton, also rubber, all thriving in the tropical conditions of heat and the heavy rains brought by the monsoons. Minerals include wolfram and tin. Rubies and sapphires are found. Transport is still mainly by means of elephants and buffaloes, though railways are being built, and Bangkok (pop.684,000), the commercial cap. and chief port, is linked by air with India, China and Australia. Often styled ' the Venice of the East,' Bangkok is on the R. Menam.

The people include Siamese, Chinese and Shans. The king, Phumiphon Aduldet, *b* 1928, succeeded 1946.

siamang, long-armed ape or gibbon of Sumatra and the Malay Archipelago ; *c.*3ft high, has black hair. At dawn and dusk siamangs howl in chorus while inflating a large sac on the neck.

Sibelius, JEAN, *si-bā'li-us* (1865–), Finnish musician with a romantic style, though many of his compositions are too complex to be popular. The spirit of his country, with its severe winters and gay summers, inspires all his music, e.g. symphonies, tone-poems, orchestral pieces, operas and songs. His *Valse Triste* and *Finlandia* are favourites.

Siberia, *sī-bēr'iä,* vast region in the north of USSR, comprising all N. Asia between the Urals and the Pacific, roughly 5,000,000sq.m ; is mainly tundra in the far north, the ground being frozen for several inches below the surface except when thawed in summer to form marshes. The region near the Urals, and in the Yakutsk republic, are both rich in minerals, and in recent years the Russians have developed large areas in a remarkable way, e.g. the coalfields of east and west Siberia, and the newly opened-up areas where potatoes, carrots, turnips, radishes, swedes and cattle-fodder are grown within the Arctic Circle, notably the Kola Peninsula, Murmansk, Khibin and near the new town of Igarka on the R. Yenisei. The chief railway is the Trans-Siberian from Chelyabinsk to Vladivostok.

sibyls, *sib'ils,* in old Greek and Roman tales, prophetesses, of whom the most famous was the Cumaean Sibyl (from Cumae in Campania, an old Italian province).

Sicily, *sis'i-li,* Italian island of the Mediterranean. Separated from the ' toe ' of Italy by the narrow Strait of Messina, its area is *c.*9,950sq.m. Mt Etna, an active volcano, rises 10,800ft, and the island exports sulphur, tunny, sponges and sardines. The capital is Palermo.

The island was invaded by the United Nations' army of liberation July 1943.

Sickert, WALTER (1860–1942), British Impressionist artist ; an expert in painting indoor scenes with remarkable lighting effects, also outdoor scenes with hidden sunshine.

Siddons, SARAH (1755–1831), actress, *b* Brecon, S. Wales ; made her first stage appearance at Drury Lane (London) as Portia 1775 ; became the greatest tragic actress of her day.

siderostat, instrument by means of which light from a star is automatically directed continuously down the shaft of a fixed telescope, the plane mirror being moved by clockwork or electricity.

Sidi Barrani, *sid'ē bä-rä'nē,* settlement on the coast of Egypt ; scene of tank warfare in World War II.

Sidlaw Hills, range of hills north of the Tay between Perth and Dundee, Scotland.

Sidney, SIR PHILIP (1554–86), among the most illustrious of courtiers, *b* Penshurst, Kent ; went to school at Shrewsbury ; travelled in Europe ; beloved by the people of Holland, where William the Silent praised his genius ; MP for Kent ; Governor of Flushing ; at Chartley (Staffordshire) met Penelope Devereux, the Stella of his famous sonnets ; ambassador at Prague 1577. A brilliant courtier and fine soldier, it was while fighting the Spanish (then trying to conquer Holland) that he received a fatal wound at the battle of Zutphen, where, a little later, feverish and in great pain, he gave a water-bottle to a common soldier, with the immortal words, *Take it, thy necessity is greater than mine.* He was buried in St Paul's Cathedral, London, and among the rich and noble mourners were 31 poor men, one for each year of his life.

Sir Philip Sidney, soldier and statesman, was also an author and a poet. His sonnets set a fashion in Shakespeare's day ; his *Apologie for Poetrie* was the first book of its kind in England ; his *Arcadia* written for his sister, Countess of Pembroke, was published 1590, and is said to have been read in prison by Charles I.

Sidney Sussex, college of Cambridge University ; founded 1596 ; largely rebuilt *c.*1821 ; attended by Oliver Cromwell.

Sidon, *sī'don,* ancient town of Phoenicia ; now a notable port, Syria and Lebanon ; pop.20,000. TYRE, a smaller port, is *c.*20m away.

Sidonia, MEDINA, see ARMADA

siege, *sēj,* surrounding a fortified place with troops, or ships, so as to cut it off from outside help in the hope that starvation will compel the besieged to surrender, or with the intention of attacking and forcing an entry. If the attacking force is compelled to retire it is said to *raise the siege.* Notable sieges include those of Syracuse, Orleans, Gibraltar and, during World War II, Tobruk.

Siemens, *zē'mens,* name of an Anglo-German family of inventors and engineers. ERNST WERNER VON SIEMENS (1816–92), invented an electro-plating process, laid many telegraph lines, and (most important of all) manufactured improved dynamos. His brother, KARL WILHELM SIEMENS (1823–83), won fame by his invention of a new type of furnace of great value in manufacturing iron and steel. ALEXANDER SIEMENS (1847–1928), specialist in laying electric cables, was an expert in electric lighting.

Sienkiewicz, HENRYK, *shen-kyä'vich* (1846–1916), Polish novelist ; won fame with three books *Fire and Sword* ; *The Deluge* ; and *Pan Michael* (describing Poland in the 17th c.). His *Quo Vadis?* (Latin *whither goest thou?*) published 1895 and translated into 30 languages, has been dramatised.

sierra, *si-er'ä* (Latin *serra,* saw), Spanish name for a rugged mt. chain, e.g. Sierra Nevada.

Sierra Leone, *-lē-ō'nē,* British colony on the west coast of Africa ; area *c.*2,500 sq.m ; pop.122,000 ; with the Protectorate the area is 28,000sq.m ; pop.1,934,000. Commerce is increasing as roads and railways are built ; exports (mostly from the capital, Freetown) include iron ore, palm kernels, diamonds, gold and raw cocoa.

sight, see EYE

Sigismund, *sij'is-mŭnd* (1368–1437), German king from 1411, when he was virtually Holy Roman Emperor, but not crowned till 1436. Though a champion of reform in the Church, he was indirectly responsible for the death of John Huss.

Sikh, *sēk,* member of a large military and religious community of India. The Sikh states include Patiala, Jind and Nabha in the Punjab, now partly in India, partly in Pakistan. Founded by Baba Nanak (1469–1539), the movement was entirely religious till the early 18th c. Led by Ranjit-Singh, the Sikhs became a powerful body which opposed British rule in the Sikh wars 1845 and 1848, when Ranjit's son, Dhuleep-Singh, was exiled in England, and the Punjab became British. Later some of the best recruits in the Indian army were Sikhs.

Si-kiang, *shē-käng',* province of Tibet.

Si-kiang, river of S. China ; flows *c.*1,250m to Canton, and has a wide delta.

Sikkim, Indian state east of Nepal ; area 2,745sq.m.

Sikorski, WLADYSLAW, *shi-kor'ski* (1881–1943), Polish general and statesman ; Prime Minister 1922–33 and 1939.

silage, *si'lāg ; -lij* (Greek *siros,* pit for corn), mass of herbage mixed with molasses and stored in a silo for use as winter fodder on farms. Fermentation is due to bacteria. Silage (or ensilage) was first used in Britain *c.*1880, the idea coming from France.

Silesia, *sī-lē'zhiä* region of Europe shared (since 1919) among : (*a*) Poland, having (prior to 1938) *c.*1,630sq.m ; (*b*) Prussia, having *c*.14,000sq.m, including an important industrial district, the chief town being Breslau ; and (*c*) Czechoslovakia (*c*.1,700sq.m).

silica, see SILICON
silicates, see SILICON
silicon, non-metallic element, Si ; atomic weight 28·06 ; atomic number 14 ; discovered 1823 ; not found as a mineral, but its dioxide (silica) is one of the most abundant of all compounds ; much used for hardening alloys.

Impure silicon (a brown powder) may be prepared by heating sand with magnesium powder ; crystalline silicon results from the action of aluminium on potassium silico-fluoride.

SILICA is the chief constituent of sandstone and felspar ; its purest form is rock crystal, a colourless quartz. Coloured forms include agate, jasper, onyx, opal and flint ; white sand is almost pure silica, SiO_2. See PLATE XII

Silicon carbide or CARBORUNDUM, SiC, specific gravity 3·23 at 15°C, appears as fine blue, green, or brown crystals unchanged by heat up to 2,220°C ; extremely hard, and useful as an abrasive ; accidentally discovered by an American chemist, Edward Acheson (1856–1931) ; salts of silicic acid H_2SiO_3 are known as SILICATES, occurring abundantly in rocks ; ordinary glass is actually a mixture of sodium silicate and calcium silicate. See GLASS
silicones, see PLASTICS
silk, fabric woven from threads spun by the silkworm, i.e. the caterpillar of the silk moth, *Bombyx mori.* The caterpillars are fed on young mulberry leaves till they begin to spin a cocoon with 300–400yd of silk. After treatment, this is spun into thread and woven into a beautiful and durable material.

The manufacture of silk began in China, reaching Europe in the 6th century. Silk is now made in China, Japan, Italy, France (especially in the neighbourhood of Lyons), also in Britain, the chief centres being Bradford, Braintree, Coventry, Macclesfield, Derby, Manchester, Nottingham and London ; also Ayrshire, Scotland. The first silk-throwing machine in England is believed to have been set up in Derby 1714 by Sir Thomas Lombe. See PLATES 27 (*bottom*), 28

Artificial silk or rayon is now manufactured on an immense scale. The inventor may be regarded as Count Hilaire de Chardonnet, who attracted attention at the Paris Exposition 1889. See CELLULOSE
silk, TO TAKE, see KING'S COUNSEL
silkworm, see SILK
Siloam, *sī-lō'am,* pool or reservoir outside the walls of Jerusalem. It was made in the time of Hezekiah (*c*.700BC).
silt, sand and mud at the mouth of a river or near the banks after overflowing, e.g. the vast deposits of fertile mud left behind every year by the Nile floods.
silver, metallic element, Ag (Latin *argentum*) ; atomic weight 107·88 ; atomic number 47 ; specific gravity 10·5 : melting-point *c*.950°C ; found as cubic crystals in large masses or in silver ores. Combined with sulphur, the ore is known as silver glance or argentite (Ag_2S) ; it is also found alloyed with other metals, e.g. lead, mercury, copper. Silver is mined chiefly in USA, Mexico, S. America, Canada (especially Ontario), Peru, Japan, Australia (New S. Wales), and Britain. It is the best of all conductors of electricity. Soft when pure, it is alloyed with copper for coins.

Silver oxide, Ag_2O, a dark brown powder, gives a yellow tinge to glass ; silver nitrate is $AgNO_3$; SILVER BROMIDE, AgBr, is sensitive to light, hence its use in photography. It is a pale yellow salt. Potassium argentocyanide, $KAg(CN)_2$ is used for silver plating by electrolysis.
silver bromide, see BROMINE
' **Silver Jubilee,**' see RAILWAYS
silver weed, plant (*Potentilla anserina*) of damp meadows, The flower (June, July) has five flat yellow petals. The leaves, silvery below and deeply toothed, grow in pairs.
simile, see FIGURES OF SPEECH
Simla, town, Punjab, India ; is built, 7,000ft above sea-level, on a spur of the Himalayas ; long the HQ of the British administration May–October.
Simnel, LAMBERT (*d* 1525), handsome youth who posed as the Earl of Warwick, and was crowned as Edward VI in Ireland. He landed in England, heading a rebellion against Henry VII, was defeated at Stoke, near Newark, 1487, and pardoned.
Simon, SIR JOHN, *sī'mon* (1873–), English politician and lawyer. *b* Bath ; entered Parliament as Liberal MP 1906 ; knighted 1910 ; in the Cabinet 1913 ; Home Secretary 1915–16 ;

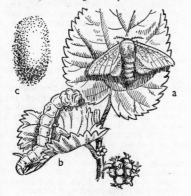

THE SILK WORM
(*Bombyx Mori*)
(a) *the Moth*   (b) *the Caterpillar*
(c) *the Cocoon*

visited India 1928–29, and was responsible for the important survey of Indian affairs popularly known as the *Simon Report.* Secretary of State for Foreign Affairs 1931–35, he was Chancellor of the Exchequer 1937–40 ; Lord Chancellor 1940, when he was created Viscount Stackpole Elidore. He was Chairman of the commission on population 1944.

Simonides, *sī-mon'i-dēz* (556–468BC), Greek elegiac and lyric poet, *b* Ceos ; wrote odes, hymns, epitaphs and epigrams ; popularly said to have been the first Greek poet to write for money. He wrote a famous epitaph on the Lacedaemonians (Spartans) killed at Thermopylae :
  Tell them in Lakedaimon, passer-by,
  We did our duty by them : here we lie.

simoom, see SANDSTORM

simple interest, see INTEREST

Simplon, *san-plön,* Swiss pass (rising to 6,582ft) over the Alps, leading from Brieg to Piedmont, Italy. The Simplon Road (begun by Napoleon 1800) is 42m long. A Simplon tunnel was opened 1906 ; another 1921.

Simpson, SIR JAMES YOUNG, *sim'son ; simp-* (1811–70), Scottish surgeon, *b* W. Lothian ; best remembered as a pioneer in the use of anaesthetics, and may be regarded as the discoverer of chloroform in this connection. He announced his discovery 1847. See ANAESTHETICS

Simpson's Line, see TRIANGLE

Sinai, *sī'nī,* peninsula of Asia, east of the Red Sea. The Mt Sinai of the OT, one of eight mts. hereabouts, was traditionally the place where Moses received the Tables of the Law.

Sinclair, UPTON (1878–   ), American writer, *b* Baltimore, USA ; author of over 100 books or plays ; a fighter against social evils. He won fame with *The Jungle* (1906), an exposure of the Chicago meat-packing industry, a book that led to the passing of the Pure-Food Legislation ; and he is author also of *The Metropolis* ; *King Coal* (based on mining conditions in USA after the strike 1914–15) ; *Jimmie Higgins* (in which the author upholds pacifism) ; *The Goosestep,* an attack on higher education ; *World's End* ; and *Wide is the Gate.*

Sind, once a British province in Bombay Presidency, now a province of Pakistan ; area 48,136sq.m ; pop.4,535,000, chiefly Moslems speaking Sindhi. The most important town and port is Karachi, now the capital of Pakistan. Sind was conquered 1843 by Sir Charles Napier, who is said to have announced his triumph by sending a message of one word, *Peccavi,* Latin for ' I have sinned.'

sine, see TRIGONOMETRY

Singapore, see MALAYA ; RAFFLES, SIR S.

Singer, ISAAC MERRITT (1811–75), American inventor, *b* New York State ; improved earlier forms of sewing machines; patented a single thread and chain-

stitch machine that brought him a fortune.

singing, as a way of expressing emotion, is possibly older than speech. Singing in public requires a good voice, the careful study of voice-production, correct breathing and articulation. The compass of the average voice is 1½ octaves ; a mixed choir may range over 3 octaves.
  A solo is for one voice, a duet for 2 voices, a trio for 3 and a quartet for 4. It is usual to distinguish voices as soprano and contralto (women), tenor and bass (men), treble and alto (boys).
  Since the early days of Jewish worship in the Temple, singing has been a part of almost all religious services. Handel did much in 18th c. Britain to make congregational and choir singing popular ; in more recent times gramophone and radio have encouraged the public to appreciate singing intelligently.
  Singing includes the CONGREGATIONAL SINGING of psalms and hymns ; COMMUNITY SINGING of a great variety of songs and hymns. MADRIGALS are short lyric pieces, often pastoral in theme, the words ranking high as poetry. The best madrigals date from *c.*1550 to *c.*1630. GLEES (most popular from 1750 to 1830), unaccompanied songs chiefly for male voices, are usually harmonic rather than contrapuntal. Somewhat similar is a ROUND, a short song with a simple air easily picked up and often repeated. A good example is *Three Blind Mice,* popular in England since the 16th c. The CATCH is almost identical, except that it introduces a pun, i.e. it is humorous.
  Famous singers include Jenny Lind, Galli-Curci, Madame Patti, Clara Butt, Enrico Caruso, Isobel Baillie, Roy Henderson, Grace Moore, Richard Tauber, Paul Robeson, Chaliapin.
  Those who wish to derive as much pleasure as possible from singing, or to become proficient in the organisation of singing festivals, should read *Youth and Music,* Desmond Macmahon (Nelson). For singing as a career, first consult a professional teacher of singing, later the Royal Academy of Music.

Sing Sing, state prison of USA, 30m from New York ; built 1825 ; named from Sin Sinck Indians.

Sinhalese, natives of Ceylon, descendants of colonists from the valley of the Ganges (India) *c.*540BC. The Sinhalese speak an Indo-Aryan language, have a rich and ancient literature, practise a form of Buddhism.

sinking fund (*a*) in government finance, a fund for paying off the national debt ; usually derived from the excess of revenue over expenditure ; (*b*) in industry, a fund set aside to pay for the repair and replacement of machinery.

Sinn Fein, *shin fān,* Gaelic for *Ourselves Alone,* a motto chosen by the Irish Nationalist Movement early this century as a summary of their ideals. At first

the movement was for a revival of
Gaelic language and literature only ;
later it came to stand for intensely
national feeling in political and economic
affairs, and grew increasingly anti-
British under the presidency of Eamonn
de Valera. By 1918, 73 out of 105
Irish Members of Parliament were also
members of Sinn Fein, these becoming
the governing council (*Dail Eireann*) ;
hence the Irish republic, now the
independent democratic state of Eire.

Sioux, *soo,* N. American Indian tribe found
chiefly in S. Dakota and Nebraska.

Sioux City, city, Iowa, USA ; on the
R. Missouri ; makes bricks and tiles ;
pop.82,000.

siphon, see PUMP

siren, in old Greek tales, a sea nymph
whose enchanting song lured sailors to
leap overboard, e.g. the sirens mentioned by Homer in the *Odyssey.*

siren, mechanical device used in World
War II to warn civilians of approaching
enemy aircraft. Two electrically driven
fans produced (*a*) a wailing note (the
Alert), and (*b*) a steady note giving the
Raiders Past signal, i.e. the All Clear.

Sirius or Dog Star, brightest star in the
sky, its light being 26 times that of the
sun, from which it is *c.*9 light-years
distant. It was worshipped by the
ancient Egyptians ; the Greeks regarded
it as one of Orion's hounds.

' Sirius,' see SHIPS

sirocco, Mediterranean warm south wind,
usually (but not always) very dry ;
harmful to vegetation ; also a warm
south wind in USA.

sisal, *sī'sal,* plant named from Sisal, a
seaport of Yucatan. Botanically it is
the agave, and is often wrongly termed
hemp. It is grown in immense quantities
in British E. Africa, and is used for
making twine, e.g. that used in harvesting machines.

siskin, kind of finch ; plumage brown and
grey with a green bar across the wings ;
visits Britain in winter. The siskin
bought as a cage-bird is usually the
offspring of a siskin and a canary.

Sistine chapel, see VATICAN

Sittingbourne, town and port, Kent ;
pop.20,000.

Sitting Bull (*d* 1890), American Indian
chief, Tatanka Yotanka, *b* N. Dakota ;
rebelled against the government ; killed
while trying to avoid arrest.

Sitwell, literary family, namely a sister and
two brothers : (*a*) EDITH, *b* Scarborough,
Yorkshire, 1887, unconventional poet,
accomplished prose-writer and critic ;
(*b*) SIR OSBERT, *b* 1892 ; served in World
War I ; writer of bitter satire in prose
and verse ; especially notable for his
brilliant series of autobiographical books,
e.g. *Left Hand! Right Hand!, Great
Morning,* etc. ; (*c*) SACHEVERELL, *sä-
shev'ĕr-el,* *b* 1897, poet, short-story
writer and music critic, notable for
books on Mozart and Liszt.

Siva, see BRAHMANISM

Skagerrak, strait between Norway and
Jutland.

skald, see SAGA

skate, British food fish of the ray family ;
greyish above with small black spots ;
from 2 to 4ft long ; is flat, with broad
fins and a tail like a whip.

Skeat, WALTER WILLIAM (1835–1912),
British authority on Anglo-Saxon.

skeleton, the bony framework of vertebrate
animals. The human skeleton comprises
skull and lower jaw ; backbone or spine
(i.e. *c.*33 small bones, or *vertebrae,* giving
protection for the spinal cord) ; chest,
a kind of cage with 12 pairs of ribs,
7 of them attached (at the front) to the
sternum or breast-bone ; shoulder bones
(*a*) collar-bone or *clavicle* (often broken
in sport), and (*b*) shoulder-blade or
scapula. The arm comprises the *humerus*
(upper bone), and the 2 lower bones,
i.e. the *radius* (thumb side) and *ulna* ;
the hand has 27 bones ; the leg bones
are attached to the great haunch-bones
of the pelvis, and comprise (*a*) thigh-
bone (*femur*) separated from (*b*) the
shin-bone (*tibia*) and the brooch-bone
(*fibula*) by the knee-joint. The foot has
26 bones. Altogether the human skeleton
has *c.*200 bones, these being largely
composed of calcium phosphate with
calcium carbonate and magnesium
phosphate.

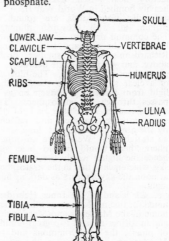

THE HUMAN SKELETON

In addition to being a framework for
flesh, fat and organs, certain bones serve
as levers on which the muscles act.
See SPINAL COLUMN

Skelton, JOHN (*d* 1529), English poet ;
rector of Diss, Norfolk ; wrote a satire
on Cardinal Wolsey. His works include
The Death of Philip Sparrow ; *Colyn
Cloute* ; and a morality *Magnificence.*

ski, *shē* (Norwegian), *skē,* a snow-shoe
of ash or hickory ; usually *c.*90in long,

4–6in wide. The heel is flat, the toe pointed and turned up. The runner uses two poles with metal discs, as aids in climbing and as brakes in descent ; downward jumps of over 140ft may be made. Ski-ing is a winter sport in Norway, Switzerland and Canada.

Skiddaw, see LAKE DISTRICT

skin, covering of the body in two layers : (a) epidermis or cuticle ; (b) dermis, or true skin, a mass of fibrous tissue. Below is the subcutaneous tissue, in which lie blood vessels and hair roots. The dermis has sebaceous glands containing fat (sebum), and sweat-glands, i.e. coiled tubes which reach the surface of the epidermis and are vitally important in regulating the temperature of the body. The skin is also crowded with minute nerve-ends sensitive to touch and temperature.

DERMATITIS, inflammation of the skin, includes : nettle-rash, erysipelas, eczema, impetigo, ringworm and lupus.

Skin diseases are now often successfully treated by X-rays, arc-lamp, mercury vapour lamp, Finsen light (which employs ultra-violet rays), radiant-heat baths, and radium (radium bromide).

Skipton, historic town, W. Yorkshire ; in the Aire valley ; manufactures textiles.

Skoda Works, shkō-dä, great munitions factory, near Pilsen, Czechoslovakia ; heavily bombed in World War II.

skua, gull ; four kinds are found in Britain, all with brownish plumage. The common or great skua, 25in long, known in the Shetland Isles, is rare ; Richardson's skua is smaller, dusky above, and yellowish-white below.

sky, apparent space above. The blueness of a clear sky is due to the fact that light from the sun is broken up as it passes through the atmosphere. The shorter waves (the blue end of the spectrum) are scattered and reflected by the atmosphere above : long waves go straight on. Were there no atmosphere there would be no blue sky, hence the higher we fly the darker the sky, which means that in the stratosphere at noon the sky appears as dark as midnight.

Skye, skī, island of the Inner Hebrides ; noted for fine mt. scenery ; is the ancient home of the Macleods and Macdonalds, and in former days of two great families of pipers, the MacCrimmons and the MacArthurs. To this day the people speak Gaelic and have preserved many ancient songs and traditions of their race. The chief town is Portree, port and business centre of the island.

skylark, see LARK

Skyros, skē'rōs, Greek island of the Aegean Sea ; has goats and vineyards ; notable as the burial-place of Rupert Brooke, the poet.

Slade, FELIX (1790–1868), English collector of fine glass and pottery, old manuscripts and engravings ; bequeathed most of his collection to the British Museum ;

founded the Slade School of Art, London.

slag, top layer of impurities (chiefly silicates) formed during smelting and refining metals.

slaked lime, see CALCIUM

slander and **libel,** purposely defaming someone's character, business or profession. In England, if spoken, it is termed slander ; if written, libel. The author (or artist) and the publisher of a newspaper or magazine may be sued for libel ; the injured person may, if the case be proved, receive damages, i.e. recompense, sometimes amounting to thousands of pounds.

Slaney, river, Eire ; flows 60m to Wexford Harbour.

slang, colloquial form of speech or writing not recognised as the standard language of the time ; usually avoided by people of good taste.

In the 17th c. slang was the jargon of rogues and vagabonds ; and some of our modern slang has come from tinkers, Gypsies (whose Romany words are chiefly of Hindi and Persian origin), public schools, universities, technical expressions, USA, and World Wars I and II, e.g. chump for 'simpleton,' boss for 'chief,' blighty for 'home' ; lead up the garden path for 'deceived' ; OK for 'all right.'

Sometimes slang wins its way into the King's English, but as a rule such words and phrases die a natural death.

slate, form of clay (or shale) that has been heated and compressed ; splits readily ; may be grey, bluish, green, red or mottled. Some of the best comes from N. Wales, but there are slate quarries in Ireland, Scotland, Cornwall, Germany and USA.

Slav, name given to peoples (mostly of E. Europe) who came originally from north of the Carpathians, and speak dialects of the Slavonic class of Indo-European languages, e.g. Poles, Czechs, Slovaks, Yugoslavs and Russians.

slavery, forced labour without payment.

The daily life of the early Greeks and Romans was dependent on slaves, but in Greece slavery was often tolerable ; slaves were allowed to marry, they could appeal against cruel masters, and if they worked hard might save enough money to buy their freedom, or freedom might be granted to them. In the Roman empire slaves were not so fortunate, as we gather from the story of Androcles and the Lion. Roman slave-owners had the power of life and death, though in some circumstances the slave could buy his freedom after six years. It must not be forgotten that both Greek and Roman slaves were often kindly treated, sometimes being regarded as members of the family ; indeed the slave of a kindly owner might well enjoy life.

Nevertheless, the idea of slavery (even at its best) is obviously wrong, since freedom is the right of all.

Whatever may be said of slavery in ancient times, it is undeniable that more recently it was wholly a bad thing, and that the discovery of America led to a new and cruel form. Owners of cotton and other plantations in N. America required labour, and the cheapest was slave labour. Thus began the SLAVE TRADE, i.e. European traders (e.g. Spanish, Dutch and English) raided W. Africa, captured Negroes, crowded them into ships, and sold them in America, a shameful form of trading that brought great profits to Liverpool and Bristol merchants, especially in the 18th century.

A pioneer in the abolition of slavery was Granville Sharp (1735–1813), b Durham. Hearing the story of a slave who had been almost flogged to death, Sharp devoted his life to freeing slaves. The story goes that one day a runaway slave in England was about to be taken back to the W. Indies, when Sharp climbed over the side of the ship, showed the captain a legal document (a writ of *Habeas Corpus*), rescued the slave, went to court on his behalf, and finally 1772 obtained (from Lord Chancellor Mansfield) the important pronouncement that by English law any slave was free the moment he set foot on English soil. Sharp, Thomas Clarkson and William Wilberforce founded the Association for the Abolition of Slavery 1787.

Wilberforce (1759–1833) stirred the country to a new sense of right and wrong. Even as a schoolboy at Pocklington he had called slavery an *odious traffic in human flesh* ; as a man he gained the support of his friend William Pitt, and in 1789 Parliament condemned the slave trade. Then in 1833, only a few days before Wilberforce died, came the Emancipation Act, when Parliament abolished slavery throughout the British Empire, the cost of compensating the slave-owners being £20,000,000.

Much had still to be done. Slavery went on in the USA, where slaves found a champion in William Lloyd Garrison (1805–79), b Newburyport, Massachusetts. With the help of a number of Quakers he began to make a stir, and after imprisonment continued lecturing on slavery. He came to England, met Wilberforce, and founded a paper, *The Liberator.* Meanwhile, gallant but impetuous John Brown died in the cause of freedom, and the song, *John Brown's body lies a-mouldering in the grave, but his soul goes marching on,* roused all America. Another cause of the change of heart which swept over millions in USA was a book written by Harriet Elizabeth Beecher, who married Calvin E. Stowe. As Harriet Beecher Stowe she wrote *Uncle Tom's Cabin* (1852) and almost everyone in America read about Topsy and Uncle Tom. But the Southern States still insisted that slavery should continue, and the American Civil War

(1861–65) was fought partly over the question of freeing the slaves. Finally, the Northern States won, owing in great measure to the leadership of Abraham Lincoln. Slavery in USA was abolished 1865 ; but in one form or another it still exists in a few parts of the world. Many slaves have won fame, e.g. Aesop ; Epictetus ; Cervantes, the Spaniard who wrote *Don Quixote* ; the first bishop of the Anglican Church, W. Africa, Samuel Adjai Crowther (d 1892). Booker Washington (1858–1915), described as the most distinguished Negro of modern times, was at one time a plantation slave. A great scholar, he did much for his own people, and helped to educate the Red Indians.

See LINCOLN, ABRAHAM ; NEGROES ; NEPAL ; ZANZIBAR.

sledge or **sleigh**, vehicle drawn or pushed about on runners instead of wheels. In cold lands, e.g. Arctic Russia, sledges drawn by men, dogs or reindeer are often the only means of transport over the snow ; sledges driven by propellers may be seen on Swiss lakes during winter sports. The Canadian and N. American sledge, called a *toboggan*, has iron runners 4 to 8ft long ; on the Swiss toboggan, c.4ft long, the rider lies face downwards ; speed may reach 70mph.

sleep, period of rest when we are unconscious. During sleep less blood flows to the brain, the pulse is slower, we breathe more deeply, the temperature of the body is slightly reduced, and the brain and other tissues are repaired ; but even in profound sleep *part* of the brain is active. Adults need 7–8 hours sleep a day as a rule.

Sleeplessness (*insomnia*) may be due to ill-health, and especially to anxiety or mental strain.

sleeping sickness, tropical disease, especially of W. Africa, the Congo, W. Indies, caused by a microbe (*trypanosoma*) carried by the tsetse-fly, a brown insect roughly the same size as the common house-fly. Sir David Bruce did fine work in discovering the cause, thus leading the way to the cure of this dread disease.

Since 1948 antrycide has been found useful in immunising cattle from infection, and there is now hope of raising great herds in areas of Africa where the tsetse-fly is found. The immunisation of cattle with antrycide is now being extensively carried on in N. and E. Africa and in Northern Nigeria.

Sleeping sickness must not be confused with SLEEPY SICKNESS, an acute infectious disease chiefly affecting the nervous system.

sleigh, see SLEDGE

Slessor, MARY (1848–1915), missionary, b Aberdeen, worked as a mill-girl in Dundee ; went to Nigeria 1876. She was known as Mary Slessor of Calabar, where she did fine work.

Slieve Bloom, mt. range, Eire, between Offaly and Leix.

Sligo, *slī'gō,* county of Connaught, Eire. Its co.tn is the port of Sligo at the mouth of the R. Garavogue.

Sloane, SIR HANS, see LONDON (MUSEUMS)

sloe, see BLACKTHORN

sloop, sailing ship with one mast, fixed bowsprit, and a jib (or stay) from the masthead to the bowsprit. Warships ranking below frigates were at one time called sloops.

sloth, *slōth,* animal found only in S. and Central America ; has a large body, small head, fore-limbs longer than the hind ones ; feet (with long claws) turned inwards so that it shuffles clumsily on the ground but is active when, *upside down,* it climbs the branches of trees. The shaggy hair is brown or greyish. Both 3-toed and 2-toed sloths feed on leaves and fruit.

sloth bear or **honey bear,** animal of the mountainous parts of India and Ceylon ; has shaggy black hair ; lives on honey, fruit and insects.

Slough, *slow,* town, Buckinghamshire ; 2m from Windsor ; noted for engineering ; pop.60,000.

Slovakia, see CZECHOSLOVAKIA

slow-worm, see LIZARD

slug, see MOLLUSCA

Sluys, BATTLE OF, *slois,* sea fight 1340 in which the English, under Edward III, beat the French off the mouth of the R. Sluys (Flanders).

smack (Dutch), usually a fishing boat with sails ; more correctly a decked trawler.

small holdings, plots of cultivated land, larger than allotments, and held by people who make them their chief source of income. The Small Holdings and Allotments Act 1907 provided facilities for intensive production of vegetables and crops.

smallpox, see VACCINATION

Smeaton, JOHN (1724–92), engineer, *b* Austhorpe, near Leeds ; showed remarkable mechanical ability as a boy. He built the Forth and Clyde Canal. His fame rests on his successful erection of the 3rd Eddystone lighthouse (off Plymouth), completed 1759. He founded 1771 an engineering club that later became the Institute of Civil Engineers.

smell, SENSE OF, see NOSE

smelting, see IRON AND STEEL

Smiles, SAMUEL (1812–1904), writer and social reformer, *b* Haddington ; had much to do with railways ; author of many books, including *Self Help,* showing how men with grit and determination make a success of life.

Smith, ADAM (1723–90), *b* Kirkcaldy, Scotland ; professor of logic and philosophy ; travelled abroad (1764) with the Duke of Buccleuch ; had many distinguished friends. His fame rests on his *Wealth of Nations* (1776), a remarkable and (at that time) exhaustive survey of political economy. Modern economists have travelled far beyond the principles he laid down, but students today need a working knowledge of his book, which had an enormous influence on political economy and practical politics in the 18th and 19th centuries. Adam Smith was one of Hume's best friends, and after Hume's death wrote a famous letter vindicating his character against those who disliked (but could not refute) his views on questions of natural theology.

Smith, DODIE, Lancashire playwright noted for her plays *Autumn Crocus* and *Dear Octopus.*

Smith, CAPTAIN JOHN (1580–1631), romantic figure in the story of British colonisation, *b* Willoughby, Lincolnshire ; ran away from Louth Grammar School ; was a soldier in France, Flanders and the Middle East. In 1607 he went to Virginia, where he proved to be the life and soul of a small company of colonists. His life-story reads rather melo-dramatically, but it seems that he was captured by Red Indians whose chief, Powhattan, condemned him to death. Smith was saved by the pleadings of Powhattan's daughter, Pocahontas, who (being told later that Smith was dead) married John Rolfe, a colonist from Norfolk, with whom she came to England, where (1616) she met her former lover, Smith, in London.

Read *Pocahontas,* David Garnett.

Smith, SYDNEY (1771–1845), churchman, lecturer, author, wit and a noted Whig, *b* Woodford, Essex ; canon of St Paul's, London ; one of the founders and first editor of *The Edinburgh Review.*

Smith, SIR WILLIAM, see BOYS' BRIGADE

Smith-Dorrien, GENERAL SIR HORACE LOCKWOOD (1858–1930), soldier ; served in Zululand, Egypt, Sudan, S. Africa ; was Adjutant-General in India 1901–3. In World War I he had to make a momentous decision at Mons during the retreat August 1914. His decision to give battle at Le Cateau was condemned by Sir John French, though the opinion now is that Smith-Dorrien was right.

Smithfield, London district where, during the Tudor persecution of Protestants, martyrs were burned at the stake. Today the Smithfield meat market covers 10 acres.

Smithsonian Institution, educational and research institution, Washington, USA ; founded 1846 with funds from the bequest of James Smithson (1765–1829), a British scientist.

smoking, see TOBACCO

Smolensk, city, USSR, on the R. Dnieper. It is an important railway centre ; pop.130,000. During World War II Hitler made the city the HQ of the German defences in Russia.

Smollett, TOBIAS (1721–71), Scottish novelist, *b* Dalquhurn, Dumbartonshire ; surgeon in the navy 1739–44, lived much in Italy in later life. His books include *The Adventures of Roderick Random* ;

The Adventures of Peregrine Pickle ; and *The Expedition of Humphry Clinker.* The latter, his masterpiece, is written in letter-form. All Smollett's books are full of rollicking though coarse fun.

smuggling, offence of avoiding the lawful customs duties on goods brought into or taken from a country. When duties were high the smuggler found the risk of evading the coastguards (or preventive men) well worth while e.g. notably in William III's day when the smuggling of tea, tobacco, wines, etc., was carried on in many coastal areas, compelling Parliament 1736 to reduce the duties on wine and tobacco and increase the penalties. Smuggling was almost a 'regular employment' for many seafaring families in Yorkshire, Cornwall (where the Carters ' operated ' in Prussia Cove), Devon, and especially last century, Kent and Sussex.

Read *Mary Anerley*, R. D. Blackmore ; *Guy Mannering*, Sir Walter Scott ; and *Dr Syn*, Russell Thorndike.

smut, disease of corn causing the grain to become a black powder ; brought about by a fungoid parasite.

Smuts, FIELD-MARSHAL JAN CHRISTIAAN (1870–1950), statesman of S. Africa, *b* Bovenplaats, Cape Colony, of Boer parents. As a young and brilliant lawyer in Cape Town he took a great interest in politics and journalism. In the Boer war he fought against the British, but later did all he could to establish lasting peace.

Smuts helped to give self-government to the Transvaal and Orange Free State, and was a great power in S. Africa 1913. During World War I he led the S. African party which eventually crushed a revolution engineered by Germany, thus enabling S. Africa to play a vital part for the Allies. He attended the Imperial War Conference, London 1917 ; was given a seat in the Cabinet ; had much to do with laying the foundations of the League of Nations ; was Prime Minister of S. Africa 1919–24 ; shared the office with General Hertzog 1933 ; and won fame as a statesman with a deep sense of the need for empire unity. In World War II he led S. Africa to make great sacrifices for the fight against Germany, became leader of the Opposition when Dr Malan was elected Prime Minister 1948.

There is no doubt that Smuts was a man of vision, and that the Commonwealth's debt to him is incalculable.

Smyth, DAME ETHEL MARY, *smith* (1858–1944), only British woman composer of note ; *b* London ; studied at Leipzig ; won fame with her *Mass in D*, 1893. Her operas include *Fantasio* ; *Der Wald* ; and *The Wreckers*, possibly her masterpiece. Her work, which has had greater popularity in Germany than in Britain, has a hint of Beethoven, but is original and personal in conception and treatment.

Smythe, FRANCIS SYDNEY (1900–1949), mountaineer, *b* Maidstone, Kent; author of *Kamet Conquered*, etc.

Sn, chemical symbol for tin ; Latin *stannum.*

snail, see MOLLUSCA

snake or **serpent,** reptile without legs. All snakes, except sea-snakes, have small, overlapping plates above, broad plates below ; are without eyelids, and have, therefore, a fixed and glassy stare ; move with a rippling motion of the lower plates ; are flesh-eaters able to swallow their prey whole, even if it is very bulky because the bones of the jaw (and some of the head) are joined by a kind of elastic membrane and because the teeth point backwards. Many snakes inject poison into their victims as they bite. The tongue may be shot out without opening the mouth ; the young are born in eggs with soft shells, though in some species they are hatched in the parent's body. From time to time the old skin cracks, and the snake wriggles out.

The largest snakes belong to tropical regions. There are no snakes in Ireland, and only three kinds in Britain (*a*) GRASS SNAKE (unknown in Scotland), greenish-grey with black bands and two white, or yellowish, spots behind the head ; often 3–4ft long ; harmless ; (*b*) SMOOTH SNAKE, harmless, *c.*2ft long, has a grey back with dark spots ; (*c*) ADDER or viper, our only poisonous snake. See ADDER

Well-known snakes of other lands include the COBRA, found in Asia and Africa ; noted for its ability to distend the skin of the neck into a kind of hood. The black cobra of India, often 6ft long, is greatly feared ; the king cobra, 14ft long, is one of the most deadly.

FIELD-MARSHAL SMUTS 1870–1950

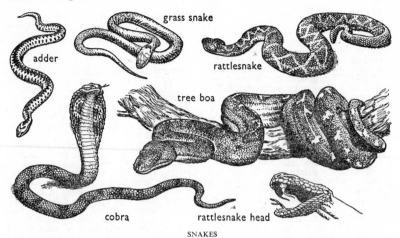

SNAKES

Of British snakes the Adder *is the only poisonous one ;* Grass snakes *are harmless. Warning of the* Rattlesnake's *approach is given by the rattle of the peculiar horny tail rings from which it is named : the head shows the poison fangs. Loose skin round the* Cobra's *neck is distended when this very venomous snake is about to strike. The non-poisonous* Tree Boa *kills its victims by squeezing them.*

The RATTLESNAKE, sometimes 8ft long, is found in N. America   The rattle is caused by the shaking of the horny tail. BOAS are snakes that kill their prey by crushing it to death.   Of these, the PYTHON, found mostly in India, Africa and New Guinea, usually hangs from a tree near a river ; attacks deer, goats, etc. ; may be 30ft long.

snake charming, art long practised in Egypt and India, etc., the charmer claiming that he has some mystical power over his snakes, usually cobras, but this has yet to be proved.   As a rule he uses snakes from which the poison fangs have been drawn ; or, if not, he has inoculated himself with an antidote to snake poison.

snapdragon, British plant (order *Scrophulariaceae*) with lance-shaped leaves, and usually purple or reddish flowers that open like a mouth ; the garden variety is antirrhinum.

snipe, name of a group of British birds much like plovers, e.g. COMMON SNIPE, a winter visitor with a long beak ; plumage, mottled black and brown above, white bars on flanks, white below ; is 10in long.   The JACK SNIPE, smaller, is buff, brown and black, with a purple sheen.

snow, water-vapour freezing in the atmosphere at a temperature below 32°F, when it forms 6-sided crystals.   One foot of snow represents *c.*1in of rainfall. Snow does not usually lie for more than a few weeks in Britain, but in USSR and Canada it remains most of the winter.   In Arctic and Antarctic regions the snow-line (the height at which snow remains all the year round) is at sea-level ; at the equator, *c.*16,000ft.

Snowden, PHILIP (1864–1937), Cabinet minister and author, born near Keighley, Yorkshire ; Labour MP for Blackburn 1906–18 ; for Colne Valley (Yorkshire) 1922 ; first Labour Chancellor of the Exchequer 1924, again 1929 ; wished to keep the country on the Gold Standard ; created Viscount 1932 ; resigned from the government as a protest against the abolition of free trade 1932 ; had great ability in the economic field.   A man of indomitable will, he fought unceasingly against a spinal disease.

Snowdon (Welsh, *eagle top*), highest mt. of Wales (Caernarvonshire) ; 3,560ft.

snowdrop, very early spring flower much praised by poets ; grows from a bulb ; has spear-like leaves, and a white drooping flower.

snow leopard, see OUNCE

snuff, powdered tobacco inhaled through the nose.   Snuff-taking was especially common in the 17th and 18th centuries.

Soane, SIR JOHN, *sōn* (1753–1837), architect, *b* Whitchurch, near Reading ; rebuilt the Bank of England 1800 ; gathered pictures, antiques, MSS, for his house in Lincoln's Inn Fields, London, which he presented (1833) to the nation.

soap, cleansing substance replacing ashes of wood boiled with lime, the only ' soap ' known in ancient times, and also the 18th c. ' soap,' made from the ashes of burned seaweed.   Soap is now manufactured from a variety of animal and vegetable oils, including tallow (chiefly from USA and Australia), other animal fats, coconut oil, especially from Cochin and Ceylon, palm-oil from W. Africa and the E. Indies ; palm-kernel oil, cottonseed oil from USA, Egypt,

India, S. America, S. and W. Africa, soya-bean oil, imported chiefly from China, Manchuria and Japan, olive oil (particularly useful in manufacturing toilet soaps), and resin, largely derived from pine forests in America, France and Spain.

One or more of these fats are boiled (i.e. saponified) with an alkali, either (a) caustic soda for hard soaps, as laundry soaps, or (b) caustic potash for soft soaps. Saponification is done in huge pans holding over 60 tons of soap. These are heated by admitting steam ; the fatty acids combine to form soap, the lye is run off separately. From it glycerine is ultimately obtained. Toilet soaps are coloured and perfumed.

The greatest romance of soap-making is the story of the way in which Lord Leverhulme began with a factory making 20 tons of soap a week, and went on to build Port Sunlight, where 4,000 tons are manufactured weekly.

Soar, river, England ; flows 40m to the Trent.

Sobranyé, *sō-brän'ye,* Bulgarian parliament or National Assembly.

soccer, see FOOTBALL

Socialism, political doctrine of those who maintain that control of all economic activities should be entrusted to the State. In Britain this doctrine is advocated by the Labour Party ; steps taken to realise it include the nationalisation (1945–49) of coal, electricity, railways, gas, etc.; and the establishment (even before 1945) of a vast system of government controls for banking, finance and foreign trade.

In the history of Socialism as a worldwide movement, two trends can be distinguished. *Social Democracy* (or democratic Socialism as practised in Britain) is a form of Socialism in which no effort is made to abolish parliamentary government. The State takes possession of the means of production and distribution : but Parliament continues to be elected as before, and the bodies appointed by government to operate nationalised concerns and undertakings are responsible to Parliament.

Communism is a form of Socialism inspired by the writings of Karl Marx (1818–83) and practised in Russia and Russian-dominated countries—China, and Eastern and Central Europe. Under Communism, the State takes possession of all economic units, and usually there is much propaganda to the effect that now at last government of the people by the people has been really and truly established. In fact, however, government of the people is carried on by the Communist Party, which is a small minority, elected by itself, acting mainly in its own interests, and subject in no way to popular control.

Social Survey, see GALLUP, DR GEORGE

Society Islands, French islands of the Pacific, including Tahiti.

Society of Friends, small Christian community founded in the 17th c., chiefly as a result of the preaching of George Fox, who believed that God had spoken direct to him, as to the Bible prophets. Many who were persuaded that he had ' seen the Light ' became known as Children of the Light, and began preaching that all men may have a direct and personal experience of God. These were popularly known as Quakers, the nickname (it is said) being due to the way in which early Friends trembled or *quaked* when moved by the inward spirit.

GEORGE FOX (1624–91), *b* Fenny Drayton, Leicestershire, began to preach 1648 ; used ' thee ' and ' thou ' ; refused to take oaths ; condemned war ; entreated men to live and dress simply. Fox married Margaret Fell of Swarthmore Hall (Lancashire) 1669.

Friends believe that God is in the soul of every man ; that public worship should be a simple, patient waiting for guidance ; that kindness should be shown to all, hence much of the philanthropy that has made the Friends universally respected, e.g. the freeing of slaves in America, and, in England, Elizabeth Fry's lead in prison reform. Famous Friends include Gurney, William Penn, John Woolman, John Bright, the Cadburys and Rowntrees.

sociology, scientific study of society, sometimes called social science. Sociology began with Plato and Aristotle, but the word itself was first used by Auguste Comte (1798–1857). Noted sociologists include Herbert Spencer, William James, William M'Dougall, Sir James Frazer and Patrick Geddes. Modern students regard the science as embracing anthropology, social psychology, the study of social institutions, citizenship and the bearing on these of economics and heredity.

In recent years the rise of what are known as totalitarian states is a complete reversal of the fundamentals of society laid down by, say, Herbert Spencer in his *Principles of Sociology* : *Living units* (i.e. individuals) *do not and cannot lose individual consciousness. This is an everlasting reason why the welfare of citizens cannot rightly be sacrificed to some supposed benefit of the State, but why, on the other hand, the State is to be maintained solely for the benefit of the citizens.*

In Mussolini's Italy and Hitler's Germany the totalitarian State became one political party, the individual counting for nothing, the State for everything.

sockmen, see VILLEIN

Socrates, *sok'ra-tēz* (*c.*470–399BC), Greek thinker, *b* Athens, son of a sculptor ; became a sculptor himself ; at one time a soldier ; fought at Delium (424BC) ; married Xanthippe, who is said to have been bad-tempered.

21

SOCRATES *c.*470–399 B.C.

Socrates, who seems to have been ugly but of great physical strength, never wrote a book, but had always time to talk with anyone anywhere. He gathered round him in Athens the intellectual youth of his day, putting questions to them in such a way that they were compelled to revise their beliefs. His followers included Plato and Alcibiades. As an old man, he was accused of disbelief in the gods of the Greeks, and of corrupting youth. His judges were Athenian citizens, 280 voting for his death, 230 against. A month later he calmly drank the cup of hemlock. Plato, who was present, tells us in his *Phaedo* :

Now the hour of sunset was near. ' Yet,' said Crito, ' the sun is still upon the hilltops ; do not hurry—there is time enough.'

' Yes Crito,' said he, ' but I do not think I should gain by sparing a life which is already forfeit ; please do not refuse me.'

Crito made a sign to the servant who was standing by, and he went out and returned with the jailor carrying the cup. Then, raising the cup to his lips quite readily and cheerfully, he drank off the poison.

Hitherto most of us had been able to control our sorrow, but now when we saw him drinking, and saw that he had finished the draught, we could no longer forbear, and in spite of myself my tears were falling fast, so that I covered my face and wept. Socrates alone remained calm, walking about till his legs began to fail. Then he lay on his back. He was beginning to grow cold about the groin when he uncovered his face (for he had covered himself up) and said, ' Crito, I owe a

cock to Asclepius, will you remember to pay the debt ? '

' The debt shall be paid,' said Crito. ' Is there anything else ? '

There was no answer to this question.

Even from childhood Socrates had been more than a thinker, for he was acutely aware of spiritual voices, as he called them, and he believed in the immortality of the soul. He also believed that before we can hope to gain knowledge we must realise how ignorant we are ; and he brought to the cold theories of the Greeks the warmth of a great faith. His way of compelling others to discover their own ignorance or confusion of thought by asking simple questions is known as the *Socratic method.*

We should, however, note that a modern critic, Bertrand Russell (*History of Western Philosophy*) has said of Socrates : ' His merits are obvious. He has some very grave defects. He is dishonest and sophistical in argument, and in his private thinking he uses intellect to prove conclusions that are to him agreeable. . . . As a man, we may believe him admitted to the communion of saints ; but as a philosopher he needs a long residence in a scientific purgatory.' See PLATO

soda, see SODIUM

Soddy, FREDERICK (1877–   ), scientist, *b* Eastbourne ; worked with Lord Rutherford ; added much to our knowledge of radioactivity ; was a pioneer in atomic disintegration ; predicted the existence of isotopes, and proposed the name.

sodium, *sō'di-ŭm,* element Na ; atomic weight 22·997 ; atomic number 11 ; melting-point 97·9°C ; soft, white metal first isolated 1807 by Sir Humphry Davy by electrolysis ; tarnishes rapidly on exposure to air ; burns with a bright yellow flame ; displaces hydrogen from water, giving sodium hydroxide and hydrogen ; occurs widely in nature, e.g. in sea-water and rock-salt as sodium chloride (common salt), NaCl, and is obtained industrially by the electrolysis of fused caustic soda or sodium chloride; is essential to life.

Important compounds include sodium hydroxide (CAUSTIC SODA), NaOH, produced as a by-product of the Leblanc process for the production of sodium carbonate, or by the ammonia-soda process, or the electrolysis of sodium chloride solution ; forms a strongly alkaline solution with water. Caustic soda is used in the manufacture of soap. Sodium carbonate (WASHING SODA), $Na_2CO_3.10H_2O$, is the crystalline substance used for household work ; sodium sulphate $Na_2SO_4.10H_2O$, is known as GLAUBER'S SALTS ; sodium thiosulphate is commonly called ' hypo ' by photographers ; sodium silicate, Na_2SiO_3, is the common household

' WATER-GLASS ' ; sodium nitrate, $NaNO_3$, is found in nature as Chile saltpetre, and is an important fertiliser ; it is also much used in making nitric acid. Sodium burned in air forms the yellow powder, sodium peroxide, Na_2O_2. Sodium bicarbonate, $NaHCO_3$, is used in making baking powder ; when mixed with dough and heated it gives off carbon dioxide, this causing the dough to ' rise.'

Sodom and **Gomorrah**, *sod'ŭm* ; *gō-mor'ä*, towns of ancient Palestine ; destroyed by fire (Genesis 19). They may have been near the Dead Sea.

Sofia, *soff'ē-ä*, cap., Bulgaria ; on the R. Isker and the railway to Istanbul ; pop.400,000 ; has been largely modernised and westernised ; noted for textiles, leather and its hot springs.

Soho', district of W. London (near Oxford Street), notable for literary, artistic and musical associations.

soil, formed by the weathering of rocks ; comprises (*a*) small grains of rock, especially sand, clay, carbonate of lime, etc. ; (*b*) humus, i.e. decayed plant and animal matter ; (*c*) bacteria.

soil erosion, see TENNESSEE VALLEY AUTHORITY

Soissons, *swä-sön*, town, France, on the R. Aisne ; noted for textiles.

Sokol, *sō'kōl* (Czech, *falcon*), health and patriotic organisation founded 1862, the movement spreading through Bohemia (and elsewhere) with mass meetings and gymnastic displays. Members wear a loose fawn jacket, red shirt and round fawn cap with a Sokol feather ; after World War I the Sokols helped to secure the establishment of the Czechoslovak Republic.

solan goose, see GANNET

solar plexus, network of nerves in the abdomen and behind the stomach. A blow (as in boxing) in the pit of the stomach temporarily paralyses this sensitive region, the largest area of sympathetic ganglia.

Solar System, see ASTRONOMY

solder, see METALS

sole, valuable British food fish *c*.12in long. It is flat ; dark brown on the right (upper) side, white beneath. Caught in a trawl, it is often called Dover sole to distinguish it from LEMON SOLE, a kind of dab that is brownish yellow with many spots.

Solemn League and Covenant, see COVENANTERS

solen, see MOLLUSCA

solenoid, cylindrical coil of insulated wire forming a magnetic field when an electric current flows through it, most of the lines of force being parallel to the axis. An elaborated form is applied to magnetic brakes, motor-starters and soft-iron instruments, e.g. ammeters and voltmeters.

Solent, west end of the channel between the I. of Wight and Hampshire. It is a great yachting centre.

Solferino, *sol-fair-ē'no*, small Lombardy town ; scene 1859 of a victory of the French over the Austrians, witnessed by a young man in a white coat. He was Jean Henri Dunant, founder of the Red Cross. See RED CROSS

solicitor, *sō-lis'it-ĕr* (Latin *sollicitare*, to plead), member of the legal profession who may act in a lower court as a client's advocate, barristers alone pleading in higher courts. The old name was attorney. Solicitors deal with much legal business, e.g. conveyancing, advocacy, making and proving wills, administering trusts and bankruptcy. Since 1919 women have practised as solicitors.

As a career, one must serve articles to a solicitor for three or five years after passing the Preliminary Examination of the Incorporated Law Society, or its equivalent. The stamp duty on the Articles is £80 ; Intermediate and Final examinations must be passed. Varying premiums are payable to solicitors to whom law students are articled.

In Scotland before 1939 solicitors were known as Writers or Law Agents. Many Edinburgh solicitors belong to the Signet Society, and if so they are known as Writers to the Signet (WS).

Solicitor-General, law official who ranks in England second to the Attorney-General; in Scotland next to the Lord Advocate. He is a Barrister or Advocate, and usually a Member of Parliament ; he has much to do with managing the country's legal business.

solidus, *sol'i-dŭs*, Roman gold coin used in Britain till the 7th c. ; later replaced by a silver coin worth 1/20th libra.

Solingen, *zō'ling-en*, town, British Zone, Germany ; manufactures steel and cutlery ; pop.139,000.

solitaire, *soli-tār'*, extinct flightless bird of roughly the same size as a turkey ; had brownish-grey plumage ; last seen in the island of Rodrigues 1691.

Sollum, *sol-oom*, small town and port in W. Egypt ; scene of bitter fighting 1940–42 during World War II.

Solomon (*d c*.937BC), 3rd King of Israel, son of David and Bathsheba ; ruled forty years ; maintained peace with other countries ; had many wives ; built the Temple at Jerusalem ; also a great palace. Wealthy but extravagant, he was renowned for his wisdom. Solomon may have written part of the Book of Proverbs (see 2 Chronicles 1–9).

Solomon (1902–   ), pianist, *b* London. He made his first public appearance at the Queen's Hall when only eight ; is now notable as a leading interpreter of Beethoven.

Solomon Islands, group of islands *c*.500m east of New Guinea, the islands of the north being under Australian mandate. The British Protectorate in the south includes GUADALCANAL, invaded by Japan 1942. The islands are volcanic, have tropical vegetation, and are inhabited by Melanesians.

Solomon's temple, see TEMPLE

Solon, *sō'lon* (*c*.638–558 BC), Athenian statesman, one of the 'Seven Wise Men' of ancient Greece. As archon (chief magistrate) he divided the Athenians into four groups according to their wealth ; abolished the custom that enabled a creditor to make a slave of his debtor ; devised many excellent new laws, and a new system of democratic government. He was author of the saying ' Call no man happy until he is dead.'

solstice, see SEASONS

solute, see SOLUTION

solution, in chemistry, a homogeneous mixture, e.g. a liquid in which some solid, liquid or gas is dissolved, say salt in water, where the salt is the *solute*, water the *solvent*.
Solubility is expressed as the number of grams of a solute that will dissolve in 100 grams of a particular solvent at the given temperature. The rate usually increases with a rise in temperature, but not always. When a solvent cools, a solid solute generally appears in the form of crystals.

solvent, chemically, a liquid that dissolves a substance. The most powerful is probably selenium oxychloride, a straw-coloured liquid discovered 1937 ; it will dissolve almost any substance except glass, platinum and tungsten. The commonest solvent is water. Others are petrol, carbon tetrachloride, etc.

Solway Firth, inlet of the Irish Sea between Scotland and NW. England.

Somaliland, *sō-mä'li-*, British possession, Africa, south of the Gulf of Aden ; area (without the former Italian region) *c*.68,000sq.m ; pop.700,000, mostly nomadic. Somaliland exports meat and leather ; the mountainous interior is believed to have coal and oil ; famous for its game, e.g. lion and gazelle. The chief town is Berbera, a port.
FRENCH SOMALILAND (9,000sq.m) is west of the British possession ; cap. Jibuti.

Somers, LORD JOHN (1651–1716), statesman, born near Worcester ; helped to draw up the *Declaration of Right* 1688 ; was one of William III's most trusted ministers.

Somers Islands, see BERMUDAS OR SOMERS ISLANDS

Somerset, *sŭm'ĕr-set*, south-west county of England, with a coastline on the Bristol Channel ; co.tn Taunton.

Somerset, EDWARD SEYMOUR, DUKE OF (*d* 1552), statesman who served Henry VIII and Cardinal Wolsey ; proclaimed the young Edward VI king 1547 ; was created Duke of Somerset and made Lord Protector of England. Somerset encouraged Protestantism, and was responsible for the revised *Prayer Book* 1552. He insisted on the use of English instead of Latin in church services. In an unsuccessful attempt to force the Scots to agree to a marriage between Edward

VI and Mary Queen of Scots, he invaded Scotland, and won the battle of Pinkie 1547. Plots against him (fostered by landlords who resented his attempts to prevent the enclosure of common lands) led finally to his being sent to the Tower of London, and his execution.

Somerset House, Victoria Embankment, London ; built 1776–86 ; contains government records, registers of births, marriages, deaths and copies of wills. It is named after a palace built 1549–52 by Edward Seymour, Duke of Somerset.

Somme, *sŏm*, river, France ; flows 150m from the neighbourhood of St Quentin to the English Channel ; scene of bitter fighting in World War I, especially July–Nov 1916.

Sonar, see ECHO

sonata, *sō-nä'tä*, musical composition (for a solo instrument or with piano accompaniment) in three or four parts, called movements, usually (*a*) quick, (*b*) slow, (*c*) minuet, scherzo, or light or graceful piece, (*d*) a lively finale. Of these (*a*) and (*d*) are in the same key, (*b*) and (*c*) in related keys.
Musicians began writing sonatas in the 17th c., when any piece of instrumental music was called a sonata (sonata meaning music played on an instrument, as opposed to cantata, sung music), the *sonata da camera* being chamber music, the *sonata da chiesa* for church services. Later, the sonata became a piece of music with two main themes, the various movements making up a *suite*. Pioneers of the sonata were Andrea Gabrieli and the two Scarlattis ; while Haydn, Mozart and Beethoven vastly developed it, and its present form may be said to have come into being in this period.

sonnet, see POETRY

Soong, T. V. (1891–   ), Chinese statesman ; Prime Minister 1944–47.

Sophia, ELECTRESS OF HANOVER, *sō-fī'ä* (1630–1714), daughter of the Elector Palatine, who married Elizabeth, daughter of James I of England. Sophia's son was George I, King of Great Britain and Ireland.

sophists, *sof'ists* (Greek *sophistes*, wise man), Greek teachers (first notable in the 5th c. BC) who specialised in practical arts, e.g. public speaking, politics, as Protagoras, Gorgias, Hippias. The sophists challenged accepted views, and encountered much hostility : sophistry has thus come to mean thinking which, though clever, is superficial. Nevertheless, it is probably true that the modern world owes a great deal to the Sophists. Socrates himself was something of a sophist, though represented by Plato as one of their chief opponents.

Sophocles, *sof'ō-klēz* (495–406BC), ancient Greek dramatist, the peer of Aeschylus and Euripides.
He was *b* Colonus, near Athens, son of a rich metal-worker. Handsome and graceful as a youth, he was at

15 chosen to lead the chorus in a song of triumph in honour of the Greek victory at Salamis. He defeated Aeschylus in a competition 468BC for tragic drama, and took his full share of civic duties in his long life. Kindly in disposition, he was a favourite with the people. It is said that as an old man he was declared by his son Iophon to be insane, and that the only defence Sophocles made was to recite a chorus from his latest play with such brilliance that the judges dismissed the case.

Of over 120 dramas by Sophocles only 7 survive, all teaching self-control and the acceptance of God's will. Finely proportioned, notable for restraint and harmony, his plays are of interest for their plots, which are masterpieces of construction ; their dialogue in superb iambic verse ; their intensity, and the dramatist's employment of a third actor, painted scenery, and skilful use of the chorus, which is more a part of the general theme than in most Greek plays of the period. His extant plays are *Antigone, Electra, Trachiniae, Oedipus Tyrannus, Ajax, Philoctetes, Oedipus Coloneus.* Though *Oedipus Tyrannus* failed to win the prize when presented at the Dionysia, it is now usually regarded as the outstanding masterpiece of Greek tragedy ; it is based on the legend of Oedipus, son of Laïus, King of Thebes. Sophocles made great use of exquisite choric odes in all his plays.

Sophocles is more human than, say, Aeschylus, but even his characters are the playthings of the gods, hence :

Ye citizens of Thebes, behold : 'tis Oedipus that passeth here,
Who read the riddle-word of Death, and mightiest stood of mortal men.
And Fortune loved him, and the folk that saw him turned and looked again.
Lo, he is fallen, and around great storms and the outreaching sea !
Therefore, O Man, beware, and look toward the end of things that be,
The last of sights, the last of days ; and no man's life account as gain
Ere the full tale be finished and the darkness find him without pain.

The translation above (from *Oedipus the King*) is by Gilbert Murray. Note also

Χάρις χάριν γάρ ἐστιν ἡ τίκτουσ' ἀεί

For kindness is ever the begetter of kindness.

soprano, *sō-prä'nō,* highest female voice.
Sorbonne, *saur-bon',* French centre of education ; founded by Robert de Sorbonne *c.*1250 ; rebuilt (1629) by Cardinal Richelieu ; again rebuilt in impressive style 1885 ; has housed the university of Paris since 1896.
Sordello, 13th c. Italian troubadour ; hero of one of Robert Browning's poems.
sorghum, grass, one type of which is Indian millet. It is an excellent food crop for animals, and is being grown in Queensland (Australia) on an increasing scale.

sorrel, name of a group of weeds, e.g. COMMON SORREL, often 2ft high ; has arrow-shaped leaves ; spikes of reddish-green flowers June–July ; SHEEP'S SORREL, much smaller ; DOCK, with tall stem and greenish flowers. The WOOD SORREL, a different genus, has a creeping root-stock from which the white flowers rise on slender stalks.

S O S, Morse signal code ($\cdots$ $-$ $-$ $-$ $\cdots$) issued since 1912 by ships or aircraft in distress. It is *not* (as some imagine) an abbreviation for *save our souls.*

soul, that part of us which may be aware of God, and of things spiritual. It seems to be more than mind and is believed to be immortal. St Paul (1 Corinthians 3) says : *Know ye not that ye are the temple of God, and that the spirit of God dwelleth in you?*

Soult, MARSHAL, *soolt* (1769–1851), one of Napoleon's most brilliant generals ; was at Austerlitz ; commanded troops in Spain and Portugal during the Peninsular War, his armies facing those of the Duke of Wellington.

sound, form of non-electromagnetic vibration which causes the sensation of hearing (see EAR ; WAVE-MOTION). The source of sound is always a body in rapid vibration, e.g. a vibrating string (say, that of a violin), a vibrating column of air, as in an organ pipe or whistle or the human larynx, or a vibrating diaphragm, e.g. a telephone or a radio loud-speaker. Any of these sources of sound may be set in motion by mechanical means (e.g. a rotating toothed wheel impinging on a card, a gramophone needle) : or by electrical means, including the action of light on selenium ; but in every case the source, by its movement, sends pulsations (or waves) through the medium surrounding it.

That medium may be a solid, or a liquid, or a gas (including air). Unlike electromagnetic waves, sound waves cannot travel through a vacuum, a fact indicated (to some extent) by placing a clock under a bell-jar, and pumping out some of the air, whereupon the ticking of the clock becomes fainter.

The velocity of sound-waves depends on the density and elasticity of the medium through which they travel, and the velocity (V) in any medium is found by the formula $V = \sqrt{\dfrac{E}{D}}$, where E is the bulk modulus of elasticity of the medium, D its density. For a gas $V = \sqrt{\dfrac{\gamma P}{D}}$, where P is the pressure of the gas, and γ the constant depending on the number of atoms in the molecule. For air this is 1·41 ; thus, incidentally, we may find the number of atoms in the molecule of a gas by determining the speed of sound in it.

In air the velocity of sound is independent of pressure, since both P and D are changed proportionally when the temperature is changed, but proportional to the root of the absolute temperature ; hence velocity is less in the cold upper atmosphere than nearer the ground. Roughly, the velocity of sound in air at 0°C is 700mph, or 1,030ft per sec. For small rises of temperature the velocity increases c.2ft per sec. per degree C. The velocity of sound in glass is c.18,000ft per sec. ; in water (at 8°C) 4,708ft per sec.

A sound is heard when sound-waves actuate a suitable receiver, i.e. the ear, causing the drum to vibrate with the same frequency as the source. The ear transmits these vibrations to the brain, and then only is the sound 'heard,' i.e. interpreted. Below c.30 vibrations a sec. the ear begins to be aware of the separate pulses, while above c.30,000 per sec. the human ear will not respond, and the sound becomes inaudible, though it is believed that bats are sensitive to these high frequencies, and recent research has suggested that they owe their uncanny ability to avoid obstructions in the dark by sending out supersonic waves which, being received again after reflection by obstructions, enable them to judge their speed of approach. It would thus appear that bats have long been using a practical application of the Doppler effect, and have long applied the principles of radar.

Noise is the result of *irregular* sound-waves reaching the ear ; musical sounds are the result of *regular* waves. The latter differ (*a*) *in pitch*, which is dependent on the number of vibrations per sec. ; the greater the number, the higher the pitch, e.g. the highest note of a piccolo is 4,752 vibrations per sec., the lowest note of an organ 32·7. If two notes vibrate together, the frequency of one being in simple proportion to that of the other, the ear regards them as being *in harmony*. If they are not in some simple proportion (say, 1:2 or 3:4), the two sounds together produce a *discord*. Middle C on the piano tuned to normal diapason pitch vibrates 256 times per sec. (*b*) *Musical sounds differ in loudness or intensity*. This, due to the energy in the waves, is measured in phons (see PHON). The intensity of a sound at any given point varies inversely as the square of the distance from the sounding body, and directly as the square of the amplitude of the vibrations. (*c*) *Musical sounds differ in quality or timbre* ; thus, middle C on the piano sounds different from a note of the same pitch on a violin or trumpet. All three instruments give the same note, but each sound has differing *overtones* which combine to produce a different quality in the note.

The frequency of a note emitted by a wire or string kept under constant tension varies inversely as the length, *l* ;

i.e. the fundamental frequency (*n*) is $n \propto \dfrac{1}{l}$. To double the frequency of a wire of constant length, the tension must be increased 4 times, i.e. $n \propto \sqrt{T}$, where T = tension. If M = mass of 1cm in grams, T the tension in dynes (in grms wt $\times$ 981) and *l* the length in cms, then $n = \dfrac{1}{2\,l}\sqrt{\dfrac{T}{M}}$, when the wire is vibrating with its fundamental frequency.

In a vibrating wire the point of greatest movement is the *antinode* ; the point of rest the *node*.

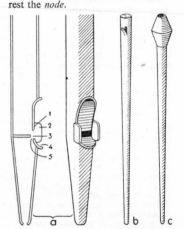

SOUND : ORGAN PIPES

(a) *the large metal flue-pipe as used for diapason stops :* (*1*) *upper lip* (*2*) *ear* (*3*) *languid* (*4*) *lower lip* (*5*) *windway or airway*
(b) *Orchestral Oboe fully 'capped', i.e. closed at the top*
(c) *Cor Anglais—open at the top*

Organ pipes may be (*a*) *open*, i.e. the top is open, or (*b*) *stopped*, i.e. the top is closed.

In a sounding organ pipe the column of air is in vibration rather like a helical spring, i.e. to and fro along the pipe. In a flue pipe the air is kept vibrating by blowing across a lip or 'knife edge' at the open end of the pipe. This is also the principle of the flute and piccolo. On large organ pipes and some wind instruments (e.g. clarionet, oboe, saxophone), the air column is set in vibration by a reed which is caused to vibrate by forcing air past it. The timbre of the note is greatly influenced by the type of reed and the material and shape of the pipe. The pitch of the note depends on the length of the air column, and in wind instruments this is varied by stopping or uncovering holes in the pipe, or, with horns, by varying the length of pipe used by means of valves.

The frequency formula for the fundamental of a closed pipe is as follows :

$$n = \frac{v}{4\,l}$$

where v is the velocity of sound in air, and l is the length of the effective part of the pipe.
Read *The World of Sound*, Sir James Jeans. See DOPPLER, C. J. ; MICROPHONE

sound films, see FILMS

sounding at sea, see ECHO

South Africa, see UNION OF SOUTH AFRICA

South African War, see BOERS

Southall, *sowth'öl*, town, Middlesex ; manufactures chemicals and cars ; pop.50,000.

Southampton, *sowth-amp'tŭn*, town and port, Hampshire. At the head of Southampton Water, it has a great trade and passenger services with America and the Far East. Its docks accommodate trans-Atlantic liners, e.g. the *Queen Mary*. Southampton was repeatedly bombed during World War II.
The city has recently built a new passenger terminal, a marine air terminal for BOAC, and a huge cold-storage depot ; pop.170,000.

Southampton, HENRY WRIOTHESLEY, 3RD EARL OF (1573–1624), courtier who befriended Shakespeare ; imprisoned for sharing in Essex's rebellion.

South Australia, state of Australia between W. Australia and New S. Wales ; area 380,000sq.m ; pop.637,000. The north is partly desert ; the only notable river is the Murray, but there is a water pipeline 235m long from Morgan to Whyalla. The exports include agricultural products and some minerals. The cap. is Adelaide.

South Carolina, *-kar-ō-līn'ä*, Atlantic state of USA ; noted for cotton ; cap. Columbia.

South Dakota, *-dä-kō'tä*, north-west state of USA ; noted for wheat ; cap. Pierre.

Southend-on-Sea, holiday and seaside town, Essex ; pop.144,000.

Southern Rhodesia, see RHODESIA

Southey, ROBERT, *sowth'i* (1774–1843), poet and author, *b* Bristol. In early life he was a rebel in religion and politics, and was much influenced by the French Revolution. He travelled in Spain and Portugal ; was friendly with Wordsworth and (for a time) with Coleridge. He was made Poet Laureate 1813. He wrote much prose and verse but is remembered chiefly for his *Life of Nelson*. He died insane.

Southgate, town, Middlesex ; pop.74,000.

South Georgia, British island of the S. Atlantic ; 800m south-east of the Falklands ; has a whaling station. See SHACKLETON, SIR E.

South Island, largest of the three chief land masses of NZ ; mainly agricultural ; towns include Christchurch and Dunedin.

South Kensington Science Museum, see LONDON

South Orkneys, islands of the S. Atlantic. Dependencies of the Falkland Is., they have an important meteorological station owned by Argentina.

South Pole, see POLAR REGIONS

Southport, holiday and seaside town, Lancashire ; on the R. Ribble estuary ; noted for its great annual flower show ; pop.84,000.

South Sea Bubble, nickname for a trading venture founded as the S. Sea Company 1711 by English Tories, for trade with S. America, the profits to liquidate the national debt. The price of stock rose rapidly till £1,000 had to be paid for a £100 share. Mismanagement and fraud brought about the collapse of the company 1720, with consequent suffering for thousands of investors. Sir Robert Walpole showed great skill in making what restitution was possible.
The *Mississippi Scheme*, a similar speculative undertaking by John Law, also collapsed 1720.

South Shetland, group of British islands in the Antarctic, 580m from Cape Horn ; important as a base for sealing and whaling.

South Shields, see SHIELDS

South Uist, *yoo'ist* ; *oo'-eesht*, island of the Outer Hebrides ; pop.4,200, chiefly crofters and fishermen.

Southwark, *sŭth'ĕrk*, often called ' the Borough,' borough of London, south of the Thames.

Southwell, cathedral city, Nottinghamshire.

South-West Africa, see UNION OF SOUTH AFRICA

sovereign, see MONEY

Soviet, see USSR

sow thistle, British wild plant (2–3ft high) with hollow, juicy stems, alternate toothed leaves, yellow flowers, and a fruit with silky hairs.

THE SOW THISTLE

soya bean, see BEAN

Spa, *spä*, town, Belgium ; a noted inland watering-place.

Spaak, PAUL-HENRI, *späk* (1899–), Belgian prime minister 1938–39 and from 1947 ; president of UNO 1946–47.

space, see RELATIVITY

space ship, craft designed for interplanetary travel. Many hypothetical

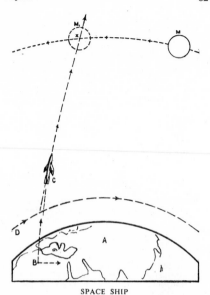

SPACE SHIP

(A) *Earth* (B) *Base from which Space Ship is launched* (C) *the Space Ship* (D) *the atmosphere surrounding the Earth* (M) *the Moon* (M$_1$) *the Moon's position at the time of the Space Ship's arrival* (X) *the point at which the paths of the Moon and the Space Ship cross each other*

craft of this kind have been designed, but that of Mr W. Kennedy shown at the *Britain Can Make It* exhibition (1946), is the first based on the use of atomic energy. A sphere, its motors would raise the machine at *c*.60mph at first, the speed increasing to 25,000mph to enable the 'ship' to overcome the earth's gravitational pull. In theory, such a machine might reach the moon in *c*.2 days, landing being accomplished by projecting a cushion of air. This atomic rocket, jet-propelled, is not the fantastic idea of a writer of boys' stories, but the planned product of a scientific brain.

Spain, national state in the Iberian peninsula of SW. Europe, i.e. south of the Pyrenees, which separate it from France, and with a coastline washed by the Atlantic and the Mediterranean ; area 196,700sq.m ; pop.27,000,000. The country is largely a lofty plain with parallel mt. ranges (*sierras*) mostly west to east, and including Sierra Morena, Sierra Nevada (rising to 11,420ft), and the rivers Ebro, Guadalquivir, Guadiana, Tagus, Douro and Minho, few of them of any great use to shipping.

It has been said that Europe ends at the Pyrenees, and in a sense this is true, for Spain is in some ways much more like Africa than Europe. Its climate is one of great extremes, especially in the interior where winters are intensely cold, summers very hot, hence the old rhyme :
> The air of Madrid is as keen as a knife,
> It won't snuff a candle, but blows out your life.

The central table-land is mostly a dreary plain, often swept by sandstorms, but Andalusia, one of the southern provinces, is typical of the delightful and colourful sunny Spain with a fertile soil yielding a rich variety of crops. S. Spain is noted for mulberries, Valencia being famous for silks ; and the region is still better known for its many wines, including sherry, named from Jerez. Olives, lemons, oranges, almonds, dates, cereals, cane sugar and grapes are produced in Spain, also cork, wine, hemp, sardines, tunny, silk and wool. The mineral wealth is considerable, and iron, copper, lead, wolfram, mercury, silver and salt are mined. Glass, tobacco, leather goods and sugar are manufactured. Onions are exported. The *peseta* is valued at approximately 8d.

The capital is Madrid, almost in the centre of the country. It is linked by rail (and in some cases by air) with the chief cities and industrial centres, e.g. Barcelona, Valencia, Seville, Granada. In the extreme south is the rocky fortress of Gibraltar, a valuable British possession.

Spain is of great historical importance. The Phoenicians visited it for its supplies of iron and tin. It was colonised by the Carthaginians, who were displaced by the Romans *c*.201BC. The Vandals and Visigoths followed the Romans, and after them came the Moors, a vigorous race which not only conquered Spain in the 8th c., but vastly improved it, advancing farming, introducing metalwork and enriching the country with superb examples of Moorish architecture (e.g. the Alhambra at Granada) which provides much of the charm of many Spanish cities and towns today. The Moorish dominance of Spain ended in the 13th c., and in the 15th and 16th Spain was supremely rich and powerful because of her immense sources of wealth in the New World, discovered 1492 by Columbus. Moreover, the country became a united kingdom with kings ruling (as did Charles V) Naples and Sicily, Milan, the Netherlands. Spain came to stand for the RC religion, and for the persecution of Protestants, hence the bitter enmity between Elizabethan seamen and the Spaniards. Decay set in after the defeat of Philip II, whose Armada came to grief 1588. Since then Spain has been a third-rate power. The last king, Alfonso XIII, left the country 1931 when Spain became a republic, but (1947) General Franco announced that Spain should again become a kingdom, though not in his lifetime. From 1936 there was bitter civil war, resulting in General Franco becoming head of a Fascist government 1939.

Spanish overseas possessions today include the Balearic and Canary Is. Her colonies include Ceuta, Spanish Guinea, Spanish Morocco, also 100,000 sq.m of the Sahara ; but gone is the might and splendour of the 16th c. when Spain was powerful in S. and Central America, her galleons proudly sailing the Spanish Main with cargoes of gold, silver and precious stones.

Famous Spaniards include Ignatius Loyola, Francis Xavier ; the artists Murillo and Velazquez ; Pizarro (conqueror of Peru), Cortes, conqueror of Mexico ; Cervantes, author of *Don Quixote.*

Spalding, *spaul'ding,* town among the Fens, Lincolnshire ; noted for bulbs.

Spanish-American War, struggle 1898 in which USA aided the people of Cuba to throw off the Spanish government, a Spanish fleet being defeated in Manila Bay and again after escaping from Santiago. Spain thus lost both Cuba and the Philippines.

Spanish Armada, see ARMADA

Spanish Guinea, *gin'i,* islands on the west coast of equatorial Africa ; area *c.* 10,000sq.m ; export cocoa ; cap. Santa Isabel on the island of Fernando Póo.

Spanish Main, former name for the Caribbean Sea ; more correctly the Spanish possessions in S. America from the R. Orinoco to Darien (Panama).

Spanish Succession, WAR OF THE, fought 1702–14 by France, Spain and Bavaria against the Grand Alliance formed 1701 by William III of England, and comprising Britain, Austria, Prussia, Holland, Denmark, Portugal and (later) Savoy, a part of Italy.

Charles II of Spain died in 1700, whereupon Louis XIV of France decided that his own grandson, Philip of Anjou, should become King of Spain (with the title of Philip V). This decision met with Spanish approval, and caused little comment elsewhere ; but when Louis declared that by being King of Spain, Philip did not thereby forfeit his claim to the throne of France, feeling was aroused in England and in other countries against the idea that two such powerful countries should be united.

To prevent this union England sent the Duke of Marlborough with an army to the Continent where, in collaboration with the Dutch, he defeated the French in the Spanish Netherlands ; marched to the Danube ; joined forces with Prince Eugène of Savoy, defeated the French at Blenheim, 1704 ; and returned to Flanders, where (1706) he won the battle of Ramillies (12m from Namur) with Dutch help. Meanwhile, Prince Eugène had beaten the French in Italy, and Britain had captured Gibraltar (1704). The French had some successes, but Marlborough crushed their forces at Oudenarde (Flanders), 1708, afterwards capturing Lille, and thus forcing Louis XIV to sue for peace.

The terms proposed by the Allies were too severe, and the war dragged on After the capture of Tournai, Marlborough won (1709) the fierce battle of Malplaquet. The Tory government then dismissed Marlborough (1710) and made an armistice with France (1712), leaving Holland, Savoy and Prussia to continue the fight until the TREATY OF UTRECHT (1713) by which Britain gained Nova Scotia, Hudson Bay, New Foundland, Gibraltar and Minorca, also valuable trading rights ; Philip of Anjou became King of Spain on condition that one person should never rule France and Spain together ; Charles of Austria received Naples, Milan and Sardinia ; and the Duke of Savoy became King of Sicily.

sparking-plug, see ELECTRIC SPARK

sparrow, group of finches including the HOUSE SPARROW (a small brown bird streaked with black), whose untidy nest is lined with feathers. The eggs, white tinged with blue or green, may be spotted or streaked with brown or purple ; three or four broods are raised each year.

THE HOUSE SPARROW

The TREE SPARROW, another member of the family, is brown with a white collar and two white bars on the tail. The nest is often in a hollow tree ; the eggs are dull white with brown spots.

sparrow-hawk, see HAWK

Sparta (Lacedaemon), renowned city of ancient Greece, cap. of Laconica. The Spartans were famous 700BC for their efficiency as soldiers. They scorned comfort and spoke little.

When Xerxes invaded Greece they helped the Athenians to fight the common enemy, 300 winning immortality in the famous pass of Thermopylae 480BC, where they were killed to the last man. The Persians marched on, but the courage and sacrifice of the immortal Three

Hundred became a glorious tradition among the Spartans.

At Plataea 479BC the Spartans enabled the Greeks to compel the Persians to retreat. Led by Lysander 405BC the Spartans overthrew Athens, and for twenty-five years were supreme in Greece ; but eventually they were overcome by the city of Thebes 371BC, and finally crushed by Philip of Macedonia 338BC.

The frugal life and the invincible courage of the ancient Spartans became proverbial, hence even today we speak of a man who bears pain unflinchingly as being ' a Spartan.' Sparta is also the classical example in antiquity of a city in which the rights of individuals were completely subordinated to the interests of the State.

speaking clock, see CLOCK

special constables, officers appointed to help the regular police in emergencies, e.g. the General Strike 1926 and in time of war. Their duties were first stated in the Special Constables Act 1831.

specific gravity, ratio between weights of equal volumes of any substance and a chosen standard substance, e.g. hydrogen or air for gases, water at 4°C for liquids and solids. The sp.gr. of a gas may be found by filling a glass sphere first with hydrogen, then with a gas of unknown sp.gr. at the same pressure, and weighing both, when

$$\text{sp.gr. of gas} = \frac{\text{Wt of gas}}{\text{Wt of equal vol. of hydrogen at same pressure}}$$

The sp.gr. of solids may be found by the method devised by Archimedes, i.e. weighing a solid in air and then in water, when :

$$\text{sp.gr. of solid} = \frac{\text{Wt of solid in air}}{\text{Wt of equal vol. of water}}$$

i.e.

$$\frac{\text{Wt of solid in air}}{\text{Wt of solid in air} - \text{Wt in water}}$$

The sp.gr. of liquids may be found (a) with a specific gravity bottle (usually c.50cc) having a small hole in the stopper. The bottle is weighed empty, then full of water, finally, when full of liquid of unknown sp.gr. Then :

$$\text{sp.gr. of liquid} = \frac{\text{Wt of liquid}}{\text{Wt of equal vol. of water}}$$

or (b) by using a hydrometer, i.e. an instrument with a bulb (to make it buoyant) and a graduated rod. If, when the hydrometer floats in the liquid, it reads, say, 60 on the graduated rod (water giving 100), then the sp.gr. of the liquid is 100/60, i.e. 1·67. Some hydrometers give direct sp.gr. readings.

Useful sp.gr. values (water=1·000) include

alcohol (ethyl)	0·789
aluminium	2·705
copper	8·95
glass (approx.)	2·89

gold	19·4
ice	0·916
lead	11·3
mercury	13·6
silver	10·5

The term relative density is often used for specific gravity.

specific heat, amount of heat, measured in calories, required to raise the temperature of 1 gram of a substance through 1°C (at any given temperature). The specific heat of a solid is found by heating a mass of the solid to a known temperature, and immersing in water in a vessel called a calorimeter ; the temperature is noted before and after.

The specific heats of some common substances are :

air	0·238
carbon	0·225
copper	0·095
glass	0·19
hydrogen	3·4
ice	0·5
lead	0·031
mercury	0·033
methylated spirit	0·615
nitrogen	0·44
oxygen	0·24
steam	0·49
sulphur	0·20
turpentine	0·426
water	1·000
wrought iron	0·114

See HEAT

spectacles, see EYE

Spectre of the Brocken, see BROCKEN

spectroscope, see SPECTRUM

spectrum, if visual, a coloured band formed when, say, sunlight is dispersed by rain to produce a rainbow, or when light passes through a prism. See PLATE IV

Sir Isaac Newton, the first to examine the phenomenon, placed a prism in a beam of sunlight, and noted that the white light was (a) deflected from its normal path, and (b) spread out in a band of colours, namely, red, orange, yellow, green, blue, indigo and violet.

The explanation of the phenomenon is that white light actually comprises an infinite variety of wave-lengths, these together giving what appears white. Separated, they produce the hues of various groups with approximately the same wave-lengths, i.e. the wave-lengths giving shades of, say, orange, are in a group removed from those giving, say, indigo.

The study of the spectrum (spectrum analysis or spectroscopy) requires a spectroscope, i.e. an optical instrument for viewing dispersed light. This, when fitted with a camera, becomes a spectrograph, and a spectrometer if combined with measuring apparatus.

In a simple spectroscope light passes through a narrow slit and then along a collimator, which gathers up the rays into a parallel beam ; then to one or more prisms arranged to disperse the light as much as possible, and, finally, to a telescope so that the band may be observed, photographed, or measured. In some spectroscopes prisms are replaced by a *diffraction grating*, i.e. a glass slide on which are over 20,000 diamond-cut lines per inch. The diffraction grating can spread the colours more than a prism, enabling the observer to concentrate on the analysis of a minute portion of the spectrum.

Though Newton discovered the spectrum of sunlight (1672), investigation of spectra advanced little till 1815, when Joseph Fraunhofer (1787–1826), a German scientist, discovered what are known as *Fraunhofer's lines*, and spectrum analysis became a science only when Gustav Robert Kirchoff discovered (1859) the meaning of these lines.

If, say, sodium, is burned, and its spectrum examined, a brilliant double vertical line is observed in the yellow portion ; similarly, other elements have a characteristic form. When we examine the spectrum of sunlight we see two dark vertical lines precisely where the bright lines appear in the sodium spectrum, and we conclude that sodium is in the sun ; hence we have a method of discovering the composition of the sun and stars by observing their light. We know also that whereas white-hot solids give a continuous spectrum, glowing gases give isolated bright vertical lines. Much information has been gleaned from examination of the sun by its calcium wave-length (the K line) ; and Sir William Huggins (1824–1910) showed that displacement towards the red in the spectrum of a star may indicate that it is travelling *away* from us. Spectrum analysis has more recently revealed binaries, i.e. double stars revolving about each other ; also that the sun is travelling *c*.13mps towards the constellation Hercules.

Beyond the visible spectrum is the invisible, i.e. the infra-red (heat rays) with a length greater than 7,600AU (see ANGSTRÖM UNIT) ; and the ultra-violet, with wave-lengths of 3,900–2,000AU.

Spectroscopy has led to a new knowledge of atoms. The spectrum of hydrogen (the simplest of all spectra) has a single series of lines in the visible region proceeding from the visible red to the ultra-violet, and *regularly diminishing* in wave-length. To explain this simple sequence has required a revolution in scientific thought as startling as Relativity, with which it is closely associated. See LIGHT

'Speedbirds,' see BRITISH OVERSEAS AIRWAYS CORPORATION ; and PLATE 59 (*bottom*)

speedwell, common wayside plant with oval opposite leaves, strongly toothed, and with bright blue tubular flowers.

Speke, JOHN HANNING (1827–64), explorer, *b* Somerset ; accompanied Sir Richard

Burton to Somaliland 1854 and with him (1857) reached L. Tanganyika. Speke pushed on alone to Victoria Nyanza, and later proved that the Nile flows out of this lake.

Spenborough, woollen-manufacturing town, W. Yorkshire ; pop.36,000.

Spencer, HERBERT (1820–1903), thinker and scholar, *b* Derby ; devoted himself to literature, his chief books being *First Principles* ; *Principles of Psychology* ; *Principles of Sociology* ; *Principles of Ethics* ; *Education* ; also his *Essays*. In these he outlined the science and thought of his day.

Spencer, STANLEY (1892–), English painter ; combines a modern style with that of the early mystical painters.

Spender, STEPHEN (1909–), British poet ; an authority on Spain ; has published *Poems* ; *The Destructive Element* ; and *The Burning Cactus*.

Spennymoor, town, Durham ; has coal mines and iron and steel works.

Spenser, EDMUND (1552–99), poet, *b* London ; friend of the Earl of Leicester, Sir Philip Sidney and Sir Walter Raleigh. He went to Ireland 1680 as secretary to the Lord Deputy (Lord Grey de Wilton), and was given a large estate and castle (Kilcolman) where he lived for several years before the Irish rebellion 1597, when the castle was set on fire. It is believed that one of Spenser's children was burned to death. The poet died in London, and at his funeral noted writers of his day dropped their pens into his open grave in Westminster Abbey.

Of Spenser's poems the two most famous are *The Shepherd's Calendar*, not unlike some of Virgil's poems ; and *The Faerie Queene*, a kind of pageant gathered round Queen Elizabeth. The latter introduces the virtues Holiness, Justice and Courtesy as characters, and tells us the adventures of Una and the Red Cross Knight. The poem is written in nine-lined (Spenserian) stanzas.

The following lines are from *Epithalamion* :
Wake now, my love, awake ! for it is time ;
The Rosy Morn long since left Tithones bed,
All ready to her silver coche to clyme ;
And Phoebus gins to shew his glorious hed.
Hark ! how the cheerefull birds do chaunt theyr laies
And carroll of Loves praise.
The merry Larke hir mattins sings aloft ;
The Thrush replyes ; the Mavis descant playes :
The Ouzell shrills ; the Ruddock warbles soft ;
So goodly all agree, with sweet consent,
To this dayes merriment.
Ah ! my deere love, why doe ye sleepe thus long.

Spey, *spā*, swift Scottish river flowing 110m to Moray Firth ; noted for salmon.

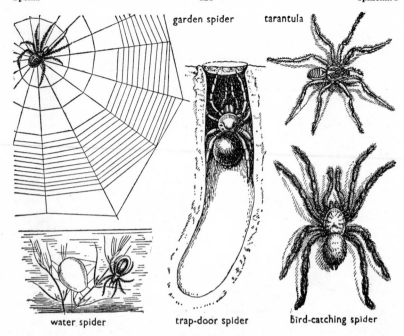

garden spider   tarantula

water spider   trap-door spider   bird-catching spider

SPIDERS

Shown here is part of the round web woven by the Garden Spider *; ready to open the hinged door of its burrow, the* Trap-door Spider *lies in wait for its prey ;* Tarantula Spiders *weave no webs but capture their prey by running : according to superstition, their bites cause epilepsy ; the* Water Spider *weaves a silken under-water nest : the spider here is carrying down an air bubble ; members of the* Bird-Catching Spider *family come from various parts of the world and are among the largest spiders known : the largest is 2 inches long.*

Spezia, *spet'syä,* city, port and naval base, Italy ; noted for shipbuilding, machinery and olive oil ; pop.121,000.

sphagnum, see MOSSES

sphere, see AREA ; VOLUME

Sphinx, *sfinx,* a monster carved in stone, especially the Great Sphinx of Gizeh near Khafra's Pyramid, Egypt. This is in the form of a man-headed lion, and is 187ft long, the top of the head being 66ft above the base, the face 14ft wide. Its age is uncertain, but Thothmes had it dug out of drifted sand as far back as 1400BC, so that it is probably 5,000 years old or more.

Spice Islands, old name for the Moluccas, Netherlands E. Indies.

spices, products of plants that are aromatic and pungent, e.g. allspice, pimento, cinnamon, clove, ginger, mace and nutmeg.

spiders, group of creatures (Arthropoda) with jointed feet. They are not true insects, and are closely related to scorpions. The head and chest (*cephalothorax*) are in one piece separated from the abdomen by a narrow waist. Some spiders are poisonous. Spiders have 8 legs, each with 7 joints ; the males are often smaller than the females. Unlike insects, the young hatch as small spiders, not as grubs.

The GARDEN SPIDER weaves a web in the dark, the silk coming from 4 small spinnerets at the rear of the body, the liquid silk hardening instantly.

The BIRD-CATCHING SPIDER of some tropical lands (especially in S. America) is large and hairy. It weaves a strong web in which not only insects but even humming-birds are caught. The TRAP-DOOR SPIDERS make burrows with a hinged door of silk and soil ; kill insects, and even small animals. The TARANTULA, a kind of wolf-spider found in S. Italy, is named after Taranto, the Italian port. The S. American tarantula is fierce, and its bite is extremely poisonous.

WATER SPIDERS, found in ponds and streams, are remarkable for their stiff hair which holds a bubble of air when they dive, thus enabling them to breathe under water. They build a silken diving-bell at the bottom of a pond, lay eggs there, and carry bubbles of air to it.

spiel, see CURLING

spikenard, Indian plant from which, in

Bible times, a costly ointment, curative and fragrant, was made. The ointment is mentioned in John 12.

spinach, *spin'ij* ; *-ich*, plant grown as a vegetable in Britain since *c.*1568.

spinal column, *spī'nal*, backbone of vertebrate animals. In man it supports the trunk (upper part of the body) ; comprises 24 separate bones (*vertebrae*), with 5 more at the lower end that eventually unite to form the *sacrum*, and another 4 very small vertebrae uniting to form the *coccyx*. The vertebrae are separated by cartilage, and each has a backward curve forming a bony canal in which the spinal cord lies.

spinet, see HARPSICHORD

spinning, action of drawing, twisting and combining animal or vegetable fibre (e.g. wool or cotton) into continuous threads. At first this was done by hand with the aid of a spinning wheel, the wheel in improved types being revolved by a treadle (e.g. later Saxon spinning-wheels). The material to be spun was wound on a distaff held under the arm. One thread only could be spun at a time on such machines, but James Hargreaves (1766) invented a spinning-jenny with which one person could spin as many as 16 threads at a time ; this was improved by Sir Richard Arkwright. Samuel Crompton invented the spinning mule.

Spinoza, BARUCH (1632–77), philosopher, *b* Amsterdam, Holland, son of a Portuguese Jew. As a result of reading the works of Descartes he abandoned the Jewish faith. His great work on ethics was published after his death. Spinoza believed in tolerance, contemplation, endurance in misfortune, and in right living ; his philosophy in some points resembles that of Plato.

Spion Kop, *spē-on' kop*, battle of the Boer War in which the British suffered defeat, 1900.

spiritualism, belief held by many people that the living are unconsciously influenced by the spirits of the dead, and that we may converse with them through a medium, i.e. some person who, when in a trance, passes on messages from the spirit world. The belief is satirically dealt with in Noel Coward's play *Blithe Spirit.*

Spiritual Peers, see PARLIAMENT

' Spitfire,' see AVIATION ; RAF

Spithead, sheltered waters between the I. of Wight and Hampshire ; much used by ships of the Royal Navy.

Spitsbergen, group of islands in the Arctic governed by Norway, known also as Svalbard. The islands, rich in coal, were the scene of a daring raid by Allied forces 1941.

spleen, organ of the body, and largest of the ductless glands. In man it is as big as a fist, weighs 6–8oz, and acts as a reservoir for red blood corpuscles.

splint, see STADER SPLINT

Split, formerly Spalato, port, Dalmatia, Yugoslavia ; important in the days of ancient Rome ; trades in wine, grain and oil ; pop.45,000.

sponge, *spŭnj*, animal (order *Porifera*) found in water ; may be a single simple creature taking in minute particles of food through the pores of its skin, and having no internal organs except specialised cells ; but is usually found in a colony. It builds up a horny or flinty skeleton which forms the common sponge used for washing. Sponges come chiefly from the coasts of the Mediterranean and Florida, USA.

SPONGES

spontaneous combustion, see COMBUSTION

spoonbill, bird related to the ibis ; *c.*32in long ; has white plumage, and a long black bill, somewhat spoon-shaped. It is found in Asia and Europe, and very occasionally in Britain.

Sporades, *spor'ă-dēz*, two groups of islands in the Aegean Sea. Those in the south belonged to Italy prior to 1946 ; all are now Greek.

sports equipment, see YOUTH ORGANISATIONS

spot transaction ; in commerce, one requiring immediate cash payment.

Spree, *sphrā*, river of Germany ; flows 230m via Berlin to join the R. Havel.

spring, see SEASONS

Spring, HOWARD (1889–), novelist, *b* Cardiff ; author of *My Son, My Son* ; *Fame is the Spur*, etc.

springbok, African gazelle ; *c.*30in high ; has yellowish hair with white hairs along the back, and a black line on the flank. Its lyre-shaped horns are *c.*15in high.

THE SPRINGBOK

Springfield, name of several towns in USA, e.g. the cap., Illinois, noted for flour, cotton, paper and coal ; pop.75,000 ; also a city of Massachusetts, manufactures textiles ; pop.150,000 ; and a machinery-manufacturing town, Missouri, pop.61,000. Also an important railway centre, Ohio ; pop.71,000.

Spring-Rice, SIR CECIL (1859–1918), British ambassador to USA during World War I.

spruce, see FIR

Spurgeon, C. H., see BAPTISTS

Spurn Head, sandy point north of the mouth of the Humber. Its lifeboat crews have rendered conspicuous service.

square, in mathematics, a number raised to the second power, e.g. $5^2 = 5 \times 5$, i.e. 25.

SQUARES 1 TO 30

$1^2 =\ 1$	$11^2 = 121$	$21^2 = 441$
$2^2 =\ 4$	$12^2 = 144$	$22^2 = 484$
$3^2 =\ 9$	$13^2 = 169$	$23^2 = 529$
$4^2 = 16$	$14^2 = 196$	$24^2 = 576$
$5^2 = 25$	$15^2 = 225$	$25^2 = 625$
$6^2 = 36$	$16^2 = 256$	$26^2 = 676$
$7^2 = 49$	$17^2 = 289$	$27^2 = 729$
$8^2 = 64$	$18^2 = 324$	$28^2 = 784$
$9^2 = 81$	$19^2 = 361$	$29^2 = 841$
$10^2 = 100$	$20^2 = 400$	$30^2 = 900$

Note.—The above table can be used in reverse as a rough guide for any square root between 1 and 900. For example, it tells us that the square root of any number between 841 and 900 lies between 29 and 30.

square root, in mathematics, that number whose square is equal to the given number, e.g. $6^2 = 36$, hence the square root (written $\sqrt{36}$) of 36 is 6. Note the following :

$$\sqrt{2} = 1 \cdot 4142136$$
$$\sqrt{3} = 1 \cdot 7320508$$
$$\sqrt{4} = 2 \cdot 0000000$$
$$\sqrt{5} = 2 \cdot 2360680$$
$$\sqrt{6} = 2 \cdot 4494897$$
$$\sqrt{7} = 2 \cdot 6457513$$
$$\sqrt{8} = 2 \cdot 8284271$$
$$\sqrt{9} = 3 \cdot 0000000$$
$$\sqrt{10} = 3 \cdot 1622777$$

Note also that $10\tfrac{1}{2} = \sqrt{10}$, i.e. $3 \cdot 1622777$

squaring the circle, see CIRCLE

squash rackets, see RACKETS

squire, shortened form of *esquire*, originally one who bore a shield for a knight. Legally, in England, esquires are the sons of peers, eldest sons of baronets and knights, justices of the peace ; but in England the term was long used for the chief person in a village, as delightfully portrayed in the character of Sir Roger de Coverley in the *Spectator*.

Squire, SIR JOHN COLLINGS (1884–), English poet.

squirrel, British animal of the rodent group. The common squirrel (*Sciurus vulgaris*) is *c.*8in long, with a bushy tail *c.*7in ; the coat is brownish red in summer, the tail partly buff ; in winter the sides are grey. The animal, common in

THE SQUIRREL

wooded districts of England and Wales, is somewhat rare in Scotland. The nest is in a fork or hole in a tree, and the squirrel may sleep for some weeks in winter. It lays up a store of nuts for winter use, hiding these in several places.

The grey squirrel, introduced from N. America, is rapidly reducing the number of red squirrels, especially in the London area.

Srinagar, *srē-nŭg'är*, carpet-manufacturing city, and cap., Kashmir, India ; pop. 208,000.

SS, short for Schutzstaffel, *shuts'shtä-fel*, a part of the German army during the Nazi régime. The SS were a bodyguard for ' der Führer,' and were known also as Blackshirts.

Stacpoole, HENRY DE VERE, *stak'pool* (1865–1951), British author of many popular stories, including a romance of the S. Seas, *The Blue Lagoon* and *The Story of My Village*.

Stader splint, metal splint invented by the American, Dr Otto Stader *c.*1931 ; much used for war casualties 1942–45 ; now coming into increasing favour ; enables a patient to work or play while a broken limb is healing.

stadtholder, *stat'hŏl-dĕr* (Dutch, *deputy*), chief magistrate of the Netherlands : a title discontinued 1802, but revived (as Statthalter) by Hitler.

Staël, MADAME DE, *stä'el* (1766–1817), French writer ; fled from Paris during the Revolution ; inherited an estate at Coppet ; remembered for her novel *Corinne* (1807) and other works ; regarded as one of the most influential of all French women.

Staffa, basaltic island on the west coast of Scotland ; notable for Fingal's Cave. See BASALT

Staffordshire, midland county, England ; mainly watered by the R. Trent ; its two coalfields include the Potteries (N) and the Black Country (S) ; co.tn, STAFFORD, noted for machinery, cars and especially boots and shoes ; pop. 34,000.

stag beetle, insect, common in S. England ; *c.*2in long. The mandibles are somewhat similar to the antlers of a stag. The larvae live in decaying oaks.

stage-coach, see ROADS

Staines, growing residential town, Middlesex, on the R. Thames ; pop.38,000.

stainless steel, see IRON AND STEEL

stalactite, *stä-lak′tīt,* limestone formation, usually like an icicle, found most commonly in limestone caves, e.g. in the Peak and Cheddar districts, England. Water dripping from the roof leaves behind a minute coating of calcium carbonate, $CaCO_3$; such accumulations over long periods build up a pendant, i.e. a stalactite. If water drips from this, a STALAGMITE may be slowly built up, the two possibly uniting to form a pillar.

stalagmite, see STALACTITE

Stalin, JOSEF, *stä′lēn* (1879–   ), formerly Joseph Vissarionovitch Djugashvili, Russian statesman, *b* Gori (Georgia); son of a peasant. Prior to 1917 he was continually in and out of prison (and once exiled to Siberia) for agitating in favour of Socialism ; became a friend of Lenin ; was a member of the Bolshevist party, and editor of *Pravda.* Gradually he won increasing power, and in 1927, after Lenin's death and Trotsky's banishment, became virtual dictator of Russia.

His gigantic and daring experiment was, not to improve the existing social system, but to replace it with an entirely new system. To do this he began (1929) his famous (*First*) *Five Year Plan,* during which, with the aid of experts from other countries, he reorganised

STALIN 1879–

labour and industry on a vast scale. In the early days he was ruthless in eliminating opponents, justifying his name, for Stalin means ' man of steel.' He employed the Ogpu (secret police) to guard against revolts. Over 30,000,000 copies of his history of the Communist Party have been sold. In World War II he contributed to the defeat of Hitler ; conferred with Churchill and Roosevelt, and chose excellent generals. He became Marshal of the Soviet Union 1943. It seems probable that he lost prestige after the war, but in any case his policy seemed to be one of opposition to UNO, hence innumerable difficulties and delays in the restoration of Europe from 1945 onwards.

Read *Stalin : A Political Biography,* Otto Deutscher. See USSR ; WORLD WAR II

Stalingrad, *-grad′,* city on the R. Volga, USSR ; manufactures machinery, especially tractors. The city (pop. 450,000) was superbly defended during World War II, Aug–Nov 1942, the ' steel-hearted ' citizens being presented 1943 by Britain with a sword of honour, a tribute to their courage.

stallion, see HORSE

Stalybridge, *stä′li-,* town, Cheshire ; manufactures cotton goods, and has ironfoundries ; pop.23,000.

Stambul, see ISTANBUL

Stamford Bridge, village of E. Yorkshire ; scene 1066 of the defeat of Harold Hardrada by Harold of England. Tostig (Harold's brother) was killed, and Hardrada ' received 7ft of English earth,' because he was unusually tall.

Stamp, SIR JOSIAH (1880–1941), British economist ; held various university lectureships and government positions ; was Chairman of the LMS Railway, and Director of the Bank of England. An expert on financial matters, he had a great influence on industrial development after World War I.

Stamp Act, act 1765 requiring all legal documents to bear a stamp obtainable only on payment of a fee (stamp-duty) to the Crown. The Act was applied to the American colonies, but the colonists opposed it on the ground that they were not represented in Parliament, and the Act was repealed 1766.

stamp collecting, world-popular hobby also known as *philately* ; dates from the introduction of the penny post in this country (1840), when the first adhesive postage stamp was issued. Brazil and Switzerland followed with similar stamps 1843, USA, Trinidad and Mauritius 1847, France, Belgium and Bavaria 1849.

Stamps are printed in sheets. In early days the sheets were not perforated, but scissors were used to cut them up. A method of dividing the sheets known as rouletting (now almost obsolete) was done with a wheel, later replaced by the method of perforating now in common use.

Stamp collectors often choose to concentrate on the stamps of one country only. Others collect only air stamps, or such stamps as have an error of printing or perforating. Specialists pay great attention to the watermark in the paper, a device to prevent forgery. If a watermark is difficult to see when the stamp is held to the light, it may be detected by placing the stamp face downwards on a black surface, and pouring a drop of benzine on it.

Famous stamps include the 'Penny Blacks' and the triangular Cape of Good Hope stamp.

One of the most useful books for stamp collectors is *Stamp Collecting*, Stanley Phillips. Stamp catalogues include those published by Stanley Gibbons Ltd, London, publishers also of a monthly magazine.

Standard, BATTLE OF THE, fought 1138 near Northallerton, Yorkshire, when the Scots were defeated by the English, who gathered round a consecrated standard of the four saints of N. England.

standardisation, uniformity in type and quality, especially as applied in industry and engineering. Towards the end of the 19th c. USA and Germany (in competition for the world's markets) began to standardise many mechanical parts, with the result that more could be produced, the speed of production was increased, and therefore cheapened, and interchange was possible. The motor-car industry is now a notable example of standardisation of parts ; the electrical trade is another.

Standish, MILES, see PILGRIM FATHERS

Stane Street, Roman road from Chichester to London. Traces still remain.

Stanhope, LADY HESTER (1776–1839), traveller ; born in Kent. Tall and adventurous, she inherited 1806 a large fortune from her uncle, William Pitt, and settled in Syria 1813, where she lived in Oriental style.

Read *Eothen*, A. W. Kinglake ; *Lady Hester Stanhope*, Joan Haslip.

Stanley, SIR HENRY MORTON (1841–1904), British explorer, *b* Denbigh, Wales ; lived in extreme poverty as a child ; became a journalist in USA, and was sent to find David Livingstone in Africa. He met Livingstone at Ujiji 1871, greeting him with the famous words, 'Dr Livingstone, I presume?' Later he undertook the exploration of the Congo, and after founding British activity in the Sudan, led a further exploration which resulted in the colonisation of a wide area of the Congo by Belgium. In spite of great dangers and difficulties he succeeded 1887 in relieving Emin Pasha who had been cut off by a Mahdist rising. His books include *Through Darkest Africa*.

See LIVINGSTONE, DAVID

stanza, see METRE ; POETRY

starch, carbohydrate stored in plants, especially rice, cereals and potatoes ; when digested the molecules reform to make malt-sugar and then glucose, the change being effected by enzymes. Dextrin is the result of the hydrolysis of starch.

Star Chamber, COURT OF, court founded by Edward III. Remodelled by Henry VII, it did good service in maintaining law and order, especially in checking the power of the great nobles. Its use by the Stuarts, notably Charles I, led to injustices, and it was abolished by the Long Parliament 1641. Star Chamber was named from a room in the Palace of Westminster which had a ceiling decorated with stars.

starfish, popular name for a sea animal, shaped like a star, several species being found along British coasts. The 'rays' have small suckers enabling the creature to move slowly. It feeds on shellfish.

starling, British bird (*Sturnus vulgaris*), *c*.8in long ; has black plumage with green and purple reflections, upper feathers tipped with buff, under tail coverts edged with white. When singing or whistling it often imitates the notes of other birds. The nest of grass, twigs and moss, may be in a tree or under the eaves of a house ; 4–7 pale blue (or bluish-green) eggs are laid.

stars, see ASTRONOMY

Stars and Stripes, see FLAG

Star Spangled Banner, see ANTHEM

Staten Island, *stat'en*, island, 14m long, partly in the city of New York, USA.

State-ownership, see CAPITAL

States-General, political body representing the clergy, nobility and commons of the French kingdom ; first called by Philip IV 1302 ; became the National Assembly 1789.

The government of the Netherlands is still known as the States-General.

State Shinto, see SHINTOISM

static electricity, see ELECTRICITY

Stationery Office, British government department (founded 1786) ; publishes and distributes government publications.

Statue of Liberty, metal figure of a woman holding a torch aloft. The world's biggest statue, it stands on Bedloe's I., at the entrance to New York harbour, and was presented to America by the French. It was the work of Auguste Bartholdi (1834–1904), and was completed 1884. From heel to head the figure is 111ft ; the hand is 16ft long ; index finger 8ft ; right arm 42ft ; each eye 30in across ; thumb 12ft round. The statue stands on a pedestal, and from the base of the pedestal to the top of the torch is 305ft.

Stavang'er, port on the south-west coast of Norway ; noted for its fisheries and two fine harbours ; pop.47,000.

steam, water, H_2O, in a gaseous state, i.e. water above its normal boiling-point of 100°C (212°F). By increasing the pressure, the temperature of steam may be raised, and above 374°C steam cannot be condensed to liquid water

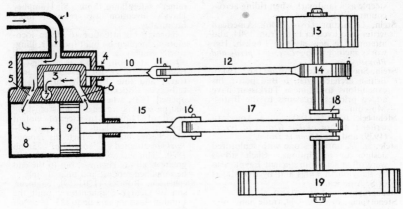

STEAM ENGINE

(1) *Steam Pipe* (2) *Steam Chest* (3) *Slide Valve* (4) *Gland* (5, 6) *Ports* (7) *Exhaust Pipe joins here* (8) *Cylinder* (9) *Piston* (10) *Valve Rod* (11) *Crosshead* (12) *Eccentric Rod* (13) *Driving Wheel for Belting* (14) *Eccentric* (15) *Piston Rod* (16) *Crosshead* (17) *Connecting Rod* (18) *Crank* (19) *Fly Wheel*. *The arrows indicate the movement of the steam.*

by pressure, hence this is termed the *critical temperature.* The pressure of steam at 100°C is normally 14·7lb per sq.in ; but at 215°C the pressure rises to 300lb per sq.in. What is called *superheated steam* is steam heated above the temperature of saturated steam, i.e. above the temperature at which steam is formed from water.

Steam is invisible. Strictly speaking, the white cloud coming from a boiling kettle or from a locomotive is not steam, but a collection of minute drops of water condensed from steam.

steam engine, machine for changing heat energy into mechanical energy. Apart from early experiments like those of Hero of Alexandria (*c.*130BC) and Giovanni della Porta, the chief pioneers were Thomas Savery, who patented an engine *c.*1698, Thomas Newcomen, Denis Papin (a French engineer), and James Watt (1736–1819), father of the modern steam engine. Richard Trevithick (1804) first applied steam to transport ; George Stephenson improved the locomotive.

The basic principle of the steam engine is that the expansive energy of steam is made to move a piston while seeking an exit from a cylinder. If the exhaust steam is led to a second (and larger) cylinder, the engine is of the compound expansion type ; if into a third cylinder, of the triple expansion type. Such engines are called reciprocating, and change about 20% of the heat energy employed into mechanical energy ; but the STEAM TURBINE, invented by Sir Charles Parsons, gives 30% efficiency, and is almost ideal as a marine engine and for driving dynamos.

In principle the turbine is a machine in two parts, the immovable *stator*, and the *rotor*, i.e. a series of cylinders lined with blades or flanges more or less at right angles. When steam at high temperature and great pressure enters the first and smallest cylinder, it impinges on the blades, gives the rotor a circular motion, and continues to exercise driving force in the other and larger cylinders, thus causing the rotor to revolve at high speed. A system of gearing down is used in marine engines. See WATT, JAMES

steam hammer, power-driven hammer invented *c.*1842 by James Nasmyth. The hammer (weighing 100 tons or more) may fall by gravity or with the addition of steam pressure. Steam is now sometimes replaced by compressed air.

steamships, see SHIPS

stearic acid, *stēr'ik*, one of the fatty acids, $C_{17}H_{35}COOH$.

steel, see IRON AND STEEL

Steele, SIR RICHARD, see ADDISON AND STEELE

steelyard, form of weighing machine, especially suitable for heavy goods. The article to be weighed is hung from a hook (or in a pan) near the fulcrum, and a movable weight is pushed along a graduated arm to a point where it balances the load.

steeplechasing, may be either (*a*) horse-racing across country, i.e. over natural hedges and streams, or along a course with artificial obstacles, as in the Grand National at Aintree (Liverpool), or (*b*) cross-country running for athletes. The name comes from the custom in early days of taking some prominent steeple as a landmark when riding across country on horseback.

Stein, GERTRUDE (1874–1946), American writer who lived in Paris from 1904, and attempted a new style in English. Her works include *Three Lives* ; *Operas and Plays.*

Stein, SIR MARK AUREL, *stīn* (1862–1943), British archaeologist, *b* Budapest ; his expeditions to Chinese Turkistan have added priceless treasures to the British Museum.

Steinbeck, JOHN E. (1902–   ), American writer ; author of *The Grapes of Wrath* (1939) and *The Moon is Down.*

stele, *stē'lē,* upright stone with sculptured designs or inscriptions. Such stones were often set up in ancient Egypt, also by Babylonian kings and by the Mayas of S. America.

stenography, see SHORTHAND

Stenotyping, *sten'ō-tīp-ing,* trade name of a method of speech-recording that is in no way related to shorthand. The Stenotypist uses a small machine (a Palantype) with keys by means of which sounds are transcribed direct into the letters of the alphabet in such a manner that anyone trained in Stenotyping can immediately read the typescript. Steno-typing applies equally to all languages, and a skilled Stenotypist can record speeches at 200 words a minute. For particulars apply to the London School of Stenotyping.

Stentor, in old Greek tales, herald of the Greeks in the Trojan war. He had a very loud voice, hence our word *stentorian.*

Stephen, *stē'ven,* first Christian martyr ; joined the Christian society in Jerusalem after the death of Jesus ; chosen (Acts 6) to care for the poor ; stoned to death (Acts 7).

Stephen (*d* 1154), King of England from 1135, son of William the Conqueror's daughter ; seized the crown on the death of his uncle, Henry I, who had intended that his daughter, Matilda, should succeed him. Matilda raised forces to support her claim, and having taken Stephen prisoner (1141), was proclaimed ' Lady of England ' ; but civil war broke out, Matilda leaving England 1147. By the *Treaty of Wallingford* 1153 Matilda's son (later Henry II) agreed to leave Stephen in authority on condition that he became king at Stephen's death.

Stephen was utterly unsuited to rule (though a gallant and chivalrous knight), and his reign of ' 19 long winters,' characterised by the worst features of feudalism, was a period of lawlessness.

Stephens, JAMES (1882–1950), poet, *b* Dublin ; wrote *The Crock of Gold* and several volumes of poetry.

Stephenson, GEORGE (1781–1848), engineer, *b* Newcastle-on-Tyne ; learned to read and write at a night school ; earned his living as a youth by working colliery engines ; won fame by inventing a miner's safety lamp, though Sir Humphry Davy's invention was received more favourably.

Turning his attention to steam loco-motion, Stephenson built for the Killingworth colliery a locomotive that drew 30 tons at 4mph. He was the first to realise the need for a suitable iron track, and thus built the first of all railways (Stockton to Darlington), opened 1825, when his train (carrying 600 passengers) reached the astonishing speed of 15mph. In face of violent opposition, he laid the Liverpool–Manchester line, on which his famous *Rocket* attained a speed of 35mph 1830. This success made him the world's greatest railway engineer, but to the end he remained modest and unassuming.

Stephenson, ROBERT (1803–59), engineer, son of George Stephenson ; built the London–Birmingham line 1833–38 ; won fame also as a builder of bridges, e.g. the Menai Straits bridge.

steppe, see GRASS

stereotype, see PRINTING

sterling, see MONEY

Stern, GLADYS BRONWYN (1890–   ), author, *b* London ; her novels include *Tents of Israel.*

Sterne, LAURENCE, *stŭrn* (1713–68), humor-ous writer, *b* Clonmel, Ireland ; became a clergyman ; travelled abroad for his health ; *d* London. His fame rests on two books : (*a*) *Tristram Shandy* (written at Shandy Hall, a quaint old house still to be seen at Coxwold, Yorkshire), a tale full of wit and wisdom, with such characters as Uncle Toby, Corporal Trim, the Widow Wadman ; (*b*) *The Sentimental Journey,* an account of Sterne's wanderings in France and Italy.

Stern Gang, terrorist organisation in Palestine founded by Abraham Stern, and responsible for riots against the Allied forces during World War II. Later the band attempted to secure Jewish freedom. It was responsible for the murder of Count Bernadotte, 1948.

stethoscope, *steth'ō-skōp,* medical instru-ment, invented by René Laennec (1781–1826), a French doctor. It amplifies a person's heart-beats and breathing, thus enabling the physician to hear both quite clearly.

Stettin, *shte-tēn',* river port, on the R. Oder, formerly in Germany, now in Poland ; *c.*60m from Berlin ; has ship-building yards ; manufactures chemicals and bricks ; now called Szezecin ; pop.73,000.

Stevenage, *stē'ven-ij,* small town, Hertford-shire, now being developed in the Greater London plan. The pop. will be increased to *c.*60,000.

Stevenson, ROBERT LOUIS (1850–94), author, *b* Edinburgh ; went to Edinburgh University and later became an advocate at 25 ; although he never enjoyed good health he loved to travel. After visiting Belgium, he returned to write *An Inland Voyage* and *Travels with a Donkey.*

Stevenson sailed for N. America 1879, and was ill while in California, where (1880) he married Mrs Osbourne, mother of Samuel Lloyd Osbourne. All three lived for a time near Calistoga, described in *The Silverado Squatters*. Later he returned to Scotland with his wife and stepson. He added immensely to his reputation by *Treasure Island* (1882) ; but his health was poor, so he was ordered south. He wrote *A Child's Garden of Verses* ; several plays (in collaboration with his friend W. E. Henley) ; *The Strange Case of Dr Jekyll and Mr Hyde*, and (1886) his popular adventure story, *Kidnapped*, also many other stories, and his famous essays *Virginibus Puerisque*.

Illness compelled Stevenson to search for health in more genial latitudes, and after again visiting America (1887), where he wrote *The Wrong Box* and began *The Master of Ballantrae*, he sailed for the Pacific, stayed six months at Honolulu, and reached Samoa 1889. There he bought an estate (naming it Vailima) at Apia. He lived happily among the natives, wrote more books (e.g. *The Ebb Tide*), and died suddenly.

Stevenson's masterpiece is *Weir of Hermiston*. It is unfinished, and he was working on it when he died. Like *Kidnapped*, it is a novel set in Scotland. Competent critics are of opinion that in R.L.S. (as he is sometimes called) a Scottish theme and Scottish language liberated deeper and more potent powers of expression than anything in his 'English' novels. His influence was great on English writers, but as a great imaginative writer he belongs more truly to Scottish than to English literature.

Stevenson's famous epitaph (written by himself and wrongly quoted on his grave) is :

Under the wide and starry sky
Dig the grave and let me lie.
Glad did I live, and gladly die,
And I laid me down with a will.

This be the verse you grave for me :
Here he lies where he longed to be ;
Home is the sailor, home from sea,
And the hunter home from the hill.

Read *R. L. Stevenson*, by David Daiches.

stibnite, widely distributed ore of antimony.

stick insect, straight-winged insect closely resembling a twig or leaf, and not easily detected among foliage. Of about 600 species, the majority live in the tropics where some have been found to measure 13in in length.

stickleback, fish that may be (*a*) 3-spined stickleback, *c*.2–3in long, found in British streams and ponds ; (*b*) 10-spined stickleback, also found in fresh water ; or (*c*) 15-spined stickleback, found only in sea-water. All make nests and lay yellow eggs.

Stigand (*d* 1072), English churchman ; made Archbishop of Canterbury by Edward the Confessor.

sting ray, fish occasionally found in British waters, but most common in the tropics ; the whip-like tail has a sharp spine.

stipendiary, *stī-pen'di-ĕr-i*, magistrate who, in London and various other English towns, receives a stipend, i.e. a salary. His duties are the same as those of a Justice of the Peace, the latter sitting in the smaller courts.

Stirlingshire, county, Scotland. Between Perthshire and part of Lanarkshire (it divides the Highlands from the Lowlands), it has coal and iron mines. The co.tn, STIRLING (' Gateway to the Highlands '), is noted for its castle standing on a high rock and for its industries which include the manufacture of carpets, tweeds and tartans ; pop.23,000.

stiver, *stī'ver*, old-time Dutch silver coin ; 1/20th of a gulden ; worth about a penny.

stoat, fierce animal of the weasel tribe ; *c*.10in long, with a tail 4½in long ; has reddish-brown fur in summer, ears with white edges and tail tipped with black. The coat changes little in winter in England, but in Scotland, and in far northern countries, it becomes snow-white, except for the black tip of the tail, and is then known as ERMINE, the best coming from Alaska. Ermine is much used for civic robes.

stock, garden plant (family *Cruciferae*), more correctly called stock-gillyflower ; may have single or double flowers ; includes a great variety of colours. All are fragrant, especially the night-scented stock. Virginia stock (introduced from the Mediterranean) is a favourite.

Stock Exchange, market for invested

THE STOAT

(*above*) *in Summer*   (*below*) *in Winter*

capital. The most famous stock exchanges are the London Stock Exchange (Throgmorton Street), the Bourse (Paris) and the New York Stock Exchange (Wall Street).

Membership of the London Stock Exchange, where stocks and shares are sold, is strictly regulated, members being either brokers or jobbers. Stockbrokers are agents who act between the jobbers and the public, taking a commission for doing so. As agents they are liable for their clients. Orders from the public are given to brokers and not direct to the jobbers. The latter, who speculate on stocks and shares, make their profits by the 'jobbers' turn,' i.e. the difference between the buying and selling prices they quote to the broker for stocks.

'Bulls' are speculators who buy stocks in the hope of selling them to another person at a higher price before the next settlement, which comes, as a rule, every fortnight ; ' bears ' are those who sell in the hope of buying back the stock later at a lower price.

Stock'holm, port and exceptionally beautiful cap., Sweden. It is on the mainland and also 9 islands of the Baltic. Though frozen for *c.*3 months in winter, the port is an extremely busy one, and the manufactures include textiles, sugar and iron. Among many handsome buildings is the City Hall, one of the noblest modern erections in Europe ; pop. 614,000.

Stockport, town, Cheshire ; manufactures include cotton, iron and brass ; pop. 125,000.

stocks, wooden or metal structure for keeping a man prisoner by the feet ; used as a punishment for minor offences from Saxon times to the 19th c. Many English villages still have their stocks, sometimes with a whipping-post attached.

stocks and **shares,** terms used in commerce to denote the parts into which capital or property is divided.

In order to begin or extend a company money is needed for buildings, machinery, advertising, trading expenses, etc. ; this is called *capital.* It may be divided into *shares* which the public are invited to buy in the hope that the company will make a profit and thus pay *dividends* to the *shareholders.* Some companies issue several kinds of shares, e.g. Preference, Ordinary or Deferred. The holders of Ordinary and Deferred shares do not receive any dividend until the Preference shareholders have received a certain percentage, so that, in the event of a years' trading profits being small there may only be a small sum left to share among the Ordinary shareholders. If the profits are large, the Ordinary shareholders may receive more than the holders of Preference shares.

Once a company is established its shares may rise or fall in price according to the amount they are earning and to the degree of confidence the public has in the directors, and other factors.

Some companies do not issue shares, but divide their capital into *stock.* Shares are numbered, and may be issued in denominations of, say, £10, 10s or even 1s, but stock is *not* numbered. £100 stock is thus equivalent to 100 £1 shares or 1,000 2s shares. In either case the company issues a certificate to the holder stating that he has so much stock or so many shares, and his name is registered in the company's books.

Some companies and governments issue ' bearer bonds ' which have no name registered in the company's books, but each is a certificate, the owner (bearer) being able to claim any dividend which may be due to him.

Registered stock- and share-holders receive their dividends by cheque payable to themselves or their banks ; bearer bond holders cut a ' coupon ' from their bond (a supply of coupons being printed for some years in advance), and this is then cashed by the company or government issuing the bond. When all the coupons on a bond are used, a special kind of coupon called a ' talon ' is cut off which entitles the holder to a new sheet of coupons for future use.

When a government or city wishes to borrow money (e.g. to build houses) it issues stock to the public in much the same way as a company, and pays interest or dividends out of taxation or rates.

' Debentures ' are not actually stocks or shares but acknowledgments of *loans* made to the company. The holders are known as ' secured creditors,' i.e. even if the company goes bankrupt some of the assets (buildings and machinery) may be realised by the debenture holders.

Some stocks are ' redeemable,' i.e. the capital they represent will be paid back at a certain date ; but most commercial stocks and shares have no such proviso. If, therefore, the holder wants his money back at any time, he must sell his stocks and shares on the Stock Exchange, when he will receive the ' market price,' which has nothing to do with the price he paid for them, since once a share is issued its value depends on what others will pay, and *that* in turn depends on the prosperity of the company. See Stock Exchange

Read *Stock Exchange,* W. T. C. King.

Stockton-on-Tees, town and port, County Durham ; noted for iron and steel, shipbuilding, etc. The first passenger railway in the world was the Stockton to Darlington line, opened 1823 ; pop. 68,000.

stoic, *stō'ik,* one who, in ancient times, accepted the Greek philosophy that happiness depends, not on conditions outside a man, but on inward virtue ; hence the mistaken modern idea that a stoic is one who is indifferent to pain or misfortune. See Zeno of Citium

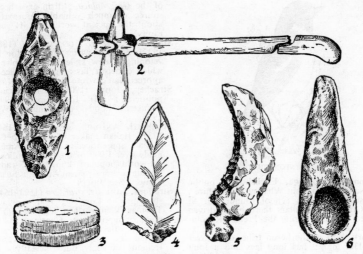

STONE AGE IMPLEMENTS

(1) A perforated flint pick from Paris   (2) A stone celt in its original shaft, from the Solway Moss   (3) A perforated axe-hammer from Kieff, Russia   (4) A graver and end scraper from Suffolk   (5) A chipped stone knife from Japan   (6) A clay spoon from Hassocks, Sussex

Stoke, BATTLE OF, fought in Nottinghamshire 1487 between the followers of the rebel, Lambert Simnel, and Henry VII's forces, which were victorious.

Stoke Poges, *stōk pō'jis,* Buckinghamshire village ; burial place of the poet Thomas Gray, who is believed to have had its churchyard in mind when he composed his famous *Elegy written in a Country Churchyard.*

Stoke-upon-Trent, city, Staffordshire, includes the ' Five towns ' of Burslem, Hanley, Longton, Tunstall, Fenton ; centre of the ' Potteries ' ; immortalised in Arnold Bennett's novels ; pop. 277,000.

stomach, see DIGESTION

stomata, see BOTANY

Stone Age, THE, prehistoric period when, as far as is known, man had no knowledge of metals. The period is usually divided into : (*a*) the *Eolithic*, thought to have ended *c.*600,000BC ; (*b*) the *Paleolithic* (Old Stone Age), which may have ended *c.*100,000BC, weapons being chipped at first, but improved in (*c*) a later period (the *Mesolithic*), which lasted till *c.*10,000BC ; (*d*) the *Neolithic* period (New Stone Age), with weapons showing finer finish. This period may be said to have lasted at least 5,000 years.

Eolithic man had at first no fire, no domestic animals ; he knew nothing of farming, and was a hunter only. Later Stone Age men used bows and arrows and sharp flint daggers. Their women sewed skins with bone needles. Some of their cave dwellings were adorned with remarkably fine pictures of men and animals, e.g. bears, wolves,

reindeer and mammoths. Possibly *c.* 15,000 years ago the weather was less severe in Europe, and Stone Age men, some of whom by now used flint knives with ground edges, lived not only in caves, but (in some areas) in LAKE-DWELLINGS, i.e. groups of wooden huts on platforms resting on piles driven into the bed of a lake. Remains of lake-dwellings have been found in Switzerland, and also in Britain, e.g. in E. Yorkshire. Men now used wooden pitchers and spoons, earthenware and pottery ; they domesticated certain wild animals, e.g. the dog, cow and sheep ; buried their dead in mounds (barrows), and are thought to have worshipped in open-air temples, e.g. the stone circles of which remains abound in Britain, including Stonehenge and Avebury, Wiltshire.

stonechat, bird (*c.*5in long) of the thrush family. It is mainly black and white ; found on commons ; feeds on insects and worms. The egg, pale pink to blue, is very slightly speckled.

Stonehenge, prehistoric circle of standing stones, Wiltshire, 7m from Salisbury ; a national monument since 1918 ; comprises an outer circle, 100ft in diameter, once with 30 upright stones 16ft high, each pair originally with a massive stone at the top ; also an inner circle with stones 6ft high, and remains of a horseshoe of stones, including a pair of uprights 21ft high. The Circle, believed to be at least 4,000 years old, may have been used for worship by early Bronze Age men, also for checking the calendar.

THE STONECHAT

Stonyhurst College, English RC public school *c.*4m from Whalley, Lancashire ; successor to a school founded at St Omer, the scholars there being driven to England during the French Revolution.

stork, bird of the heron tribe, often over 43in long ; has long legs and a long beak. The white stork has a few black feathers on the wings ; red legs and beak ; it migrates from N. Africa, and is common in Holland and Germany, where it nests on roofs and towers. The black stork, less common, is very occasionally found in Britain.

Stormont, district near Belfast. Here since 1932 the Parliament of Northern Ireland has met.

storm trooper, member of the Brownshirts or Sturmabteilung formed by Adolf Hitler *c.*1923 ; disbanded 1934 ; sometimes written S.A. or SA.

Stornoway, fishing town and cap., Isle of Lewis, Scotland.

Storrs, SIR RONALD (1881–   ), British administrator in Egypt, Jerusalem, Cyprus ; noted as a broadcaster, lecturer and writer.

Stour, *stowr* ; *stoor*, Kentish river flowing 40m near Canterbury to the N. Sea ; also one flowing 47m via Harwich ; also a tributary of the R. Avon.

Stourbridge, town, Worcestershire. It is on the R. Stour, and manufactures iron, glass and fireclay ; pop.33,000.

stout, variety of black beer, an alcoholic drink made from hops, malt and also roasted malt ; manufactured chiefly in London and Dublin.

Stow, JOHN, *stō* (*d* 1605), English antiquarian, *b* London ; best known for his *Survey of London,* giving us a valuable picture of the city in the 16th century.

Stowe, HARRIET BEECHER, *stō* (1811–96), American writer, *b* Litchfield, Connecticut ; married the Rev. Calvin Stowe. She is remembered as the author of *Uncle Tom's Cabin* (1851), a novel that did much to induce Americans to abolish slavery. See SLAVERY

Strabo, *strā'bo* (*d* AD19), Greek traveller and writer ; author of historical memoirs almost all of which are now lost ; and

of the *Geographica,* still in existence, a source of much valuable information about the ancient world and its geography.

Strachey, GILES LYTTON, *strā'chi* (1880–1932), English writer notable for developing a new style in biography in which criticism has as great a place as appreciation ; wrote *Eminent Victorians.*

Strachey, JOHN (1901–   ), Socialist politician ; MP for Dundee 1945 ; Minister of Food 1946 ; Minister of War 1950.

Stradivari, ANTONIO, *strad-i-vär'i* (1644–1737), Italian maker of violins, *b* Cremona ; apprenticed to Nicholas Amati ; made over 1,000 of the finest violins in the world (popularly known as ' Strads'), signing each instrument Antonius Stradivarius. See VIOLIN

Strafford, EARL OF, *straf 'ĕrd* (1593–1641), statesman, *b* London ; first known as Thomas Wentworth ; led the parliamentary opposition to Charles I and his minister, Buckingham, but later supported the king. Strafford governed Ireland ruthlessly but efficiently. He was created Earl 1639, and was the king's chief adviser. In 1640 he was impeached by the Long Parliament. His trial (on a charge of treason) began 1641, and to his lasting disgrace, King Charles signed the death-warrant of his trusted servant.

A man of outstanding ability, Strafford's motto was ' Thorough ' ; but his loyalty brought his downfall, and the bitter words : *Put not your trust in princes.*

Stralsund, *shträl'zunt,* manufacturing town and port, Germany (Russian Zone) ; pop.53,000.

Stranraer, *stran-rär',* historic royal burgh and port, Wigtownshire ; has a steamer service to Northern Ireland.

Strasburg, historic town, France ; noted for leather goods, machinery, cutlery and beer. From 1870 it was the capital of German Alsace-Lorraine ; restored to France 1919 ; famous for its Gothic cathedral ; pop.174,000. The first meeting of the Council of Europe was held here in August 1949.

Stratford-on-Avon, *strat'fĕrd on ā'vŭn,* town, Warwickshire ; pop.12,000. See SHAKESPEARE, WILLIAM

Strathclyde, *strath'klīd,* from the 8th c. a British kingdom also called Cumbria. It included the Clyde district, Ayrshire, and at various periods Cumberland and Westmorland.

Strathmore, fertile valley running southwest through Angus and SE. Perthshire, Scotland, into Strathearn and Strathallan, the whole forming a system of straths or valleys *c.*100m long from Dumbartonshire to the N. Sea. Its northern slopes form the foothills of the Highlands.

stratosphere, layer of the upper atmosphere, approximately 7–50m above the earth ; has a temperature much below zero. See ATMOSPHERE

Strauss, JOHANN, *shtrows* (1804–49), Austrian composer of *c.*250 dance pieces. His son Johann (1825–99) was still more notable, his 400 dance tunes including the famous *Blue Danube* waltz. Eduard (1835–1916) and Joseph (1827–1870) were also celebrated musicians.

Strauss, RICHARD (1864–1949), German composer ; pioneer of new orchestral forms ; noted for his tone-poems and his operas, e.g. *Salome* and *Elektra*.

Stravinski, IGOR FEDOROVITCH, *strä-vin'skē* (1882–), Russian composer ; introduced a new technique ; created a sensation with his remarkable orchestration, his ballets (e.g. *The Fire Bird* and *Petroushka*), and his symphonies.

strawberry, delicately flavoured soft, red fruit of a plant with a trefoil leaf, rough, toothed and hairy on the underside. The five-petalled flowers are white. Garden varieties are derived from the wild strawberry. New plants arise from buds on special creeping stems called runners.

THE WILD STRAWBERRY

streamlined, constructed so as to offer the minimum resistance to air or water, especially planes, ships and cars.

Street, ARTHUR GEORGE (1892–), English farmer who won fame as a journalist, and also as an author of books about country life, e.g. *Farmer's Glory* ; *Strawberry Roan* ; and *Ditchampton Farm.*

streptomycin, *strep-tō-mī'sin* recently discovered drug somewhat akin to penicillin. Derived from a soil organism midway between a fungus and a bacterium, it is as yet in the experimental stage. It is known to be useful against typhoid, meningitis, whooping cough, etc. ; and there is reason to hope that it may be successfully used against tuberculosis.

Stresemann, GUSTAV, *shrtā'ze-män* (1878–1929), German statesman ; leader of the National Liberal party in Germany ; founded the People's Party 1918 ; had much to do with the Locarno Pact.

strike, refusal to work, a method much used by workers in capitalist countries to secure better conditions, especially higher wages. In an official strike employees leave the task of negotiating with their employers or the government to those who represent their union. British strikes of recent years include the railway strikes of 1911, 1919 ; transport and dockers' strikes of 1912, 1945, 1949. The coal miners' strike of 1926 developed into a general strike, other unions coming out in sympathy. This resulted in legislation which made sympathetic strikes illegal. The steelworkers' strike of 1946 was one of the biggest in USA.

Stromboli, *strom'bō-lē,* island north-west of Sicily ; its volcano is almost always in eruption.

Strong, LEONARD ALFRED GEORGE (1896–), author of many books ; popular broadcaster ; his novels include *The Garden* ; *The Brothers* ; *Sea Wall* ; other books are *Common Sense about Poetry* ; *English for Pleasure* ; *King Richard's Land* ; *The Fifth of November* ; and *Mr Sheridan's Umbrella.*

strontium, *stron'shi-ŭm,* metal and element, Sr ; atomic weight 87·63 ; atomic number 38 ; discovered 1808 ; resembles calcium. A hard white substance, its compounds are used in fireworks to give a crimson glow.

Stroud, *strowd,* Cotswold town, Gloucestershire ; noted for woollen cloth.

Struther, JAN, pen-name of Mrs Maxtone Graham (1901–), journalist, poet and author ; won fame with her novel *Mrs Miniver,* 1939.

strychnine, *strik'nin* ; *strich'-,* alkaloid poison derived from the seeds of the plant *nux vomica.*

Stuart, surname of a line of Kings of Scots (and from 1603 of Great Britain) who were descended from Walter the Steward (1293–1326) who fought at Bannockburn. Stuarts who ruled Scotland were as follows :

Robert II 1371–90 ; Robert III 1390–1406 ; James I 1406–37 ; James II 1437–60 ; James III 1460–88 ; James IV 1488–1513 ; James V 1513–42 ; Mary 1542–87 ; James VI 1587–1625.

Many of these Stuarts had great personal charm, but they were wayward and very unfortunate : James I and James III were murdered ; James IV fell at Flodden Field ; Mary was beheaded. In 1603 James VI succeeded to the throne of England, and the two Kingdoms were thereby united. Stuart rulers of the United Kingdom were as follows :

James VI and I 1603–25 ; Charles I 1625–49 ; Charles II 1660–85 ; James VII and II 1685–88 ; Mary 1688–94 (with William of Orange, *d* 1702) ; Anne 1702–14.

In 1714 the succession passed from the Stuarts to the House of Hanover, but James Stuart (known as the Old Pretender) son of James VII and II, laid claim to the throne. Three Jacobite rebellions (1715, 1719 and 1745) were instigated by him during his lifetime (1688–1766) ; all failed. After the death of the Old Pretender his son Charles Edward Stuart (the Young Pretender, 1720–88) continued to claim the throne, but with no prospect of succeeding after the failure of the ' Forty-Five.'

Student Christian Movement, see YOUTH ORGANISATIONS

students, see YOUTH ORGANISATIONS

sturgeon, *stŭr'jŭn*, fish of the N. Atlantic ; may be *c.*9ft long ; ascends rivers in the spawning season. In England sturgeon have been regarded as fish royal since Edward II's day, but any taken above London Bridge belong to the Lord Mayor of London. CAVIARE is made from the salted roe.

Sturmabteilung, see NAZISM

Sturt, CHARLES (1795–1869), British explorer, *b* India ; discovered the rivers Darling and Murray, Australia.

Stuttgart, *shtut'gärt*, cap., Württemberg, Germany ; notable for its sale of books, the manufacture of chemicals, textiles, beer, pianos and jewellery, also for the fine scenery round about ; pop.460,000.

Stylites, ST SIMEON, see HERMIT

styrene, see PLASTICS

Styria, *stir'i-ä*, province of Austria.

Styx, *stiks*, in old Greek tales, river with poisonous waters, across which the dead are ferried by Charon.

subconscious, see BRAIN ; PSYCHOLOGY

sublimation, in chemistry, the vaporisation of a solid without the intermediate formation of a liquid.

submarine, vessel capable of travelling below as well as on the surface of the water. Pioneers of the submarine were Robert Fulton and J. P. Holland. The first British submarine was launched 1901. In World Wars I and II German submarines were known as U-boats, and certain British vessels (camouflaged) hunting them were known (in the earlier war) as Q-boats. Typical U-boats of World War II were of, say, the U-27 type, a submarine of 500 tons displacement ; length 206⅜ft ; hp2,000/750 ; speed 16 knots.

British submarines today may have a displacement of 1,354 tons. The *Black Swan* class have a displacement of 1,300 tons. With a length of 229½ft, they have geared turbines developing 3,600hp, and a speed of 19·25 knots. Their guns include 6 4-in AA guns. Improvements have been made recently, e.g. the ' T ' class (*Tribune, Trident*, etc.) with a displacement of 1,000 to 1,575

tons, and hp up to 2,500. These are 265ft long, have 10 21-in torpedo tubes, carry 210 tons of fuel, and a complement of 53. Still more recent are the ' A ' class (e.g. *Affray*, laid down 1944, *Alaric* of 1946, etc.).

Small submarines were of great use in World War II ; and the Japanese had ' one-man ' types.

Future submarine warfare is certain to be more complex and deadly than ever before, especially now that improvements include the Schnorkel breathing device ; the use of a chemical oxidant enabling submarines to remain almost permanently under water and to travel at, say, 25 knots ; and also the use of more deadly torpedoes. Incidentally, it seems that a submerged submarine is the safest retreat from atomic missiles. In 1947 the British submarine *Alliance* remained submerged for several weeks. At the moment the United States Tang type of submarine has probably the highest under-water speed.

subpoena, *sub-pē'nä*, in England a writ (or order) commanding a person to appear in a law court as a witness.

subsidy, payment for goods out of national taxation, the reason being to maintain low price-levels, and thus to prevent inflation, hence British food-subsidies during and after World War II.

substantive, see NOUN

Success, LAKE, see UNO

Suckling, SIR JOHN (1609–42), English poet and witty courtier ; chiefly remembered for his lyrics, e.g. *Why so pale and wan, fond lover ?*

Sudan, *soo-dan'*, two regions of NE. Africa. The ANGLO-EGYPTIAN SUDAN, a part of the British Empire, lies between the southern boundary of Egypt and French Equatorial Africa ; area *c.*967,500sq.m ; pop.7,600,000, mainly Arabs, Negroes and Nubians. The chief waterway is the R. Nile. Products include dura (millet), cotton, gum-arabic, senna, ground-nuts, timber, wheat, maize, hides and honey, also gold and salt. The cap. is Khartoum. The country is administered by a governor-general for Britain and Egypt.

For some years two parties in the Sudan pressed for independence, one (National Front) demanding self-government in union with Egypt ; the other (Independent Front, including the Umma, i.e. *people*) aiming at complete independence.

The FRENCH SUDAN, a French colony between Algeria and Nigeria, includes much of the Sahara ; area *c.*582,000sq.m ; pop.3,600,000 ; produces maize, rice, cotton, ground-nuts, also cattle, camels and asses ; cap. Bamako.

Sudetenland, *soo-dā'ten-*, frontier area of Czechoslovakia ; occupied by Germany 1938 after the Munich Agreement, returned to Czechoslovakia 1945.

Suez, *soo'ez*, gulf of the Red Sea between the Sinai peninsula and Egypt.

Suez, town, Egypt, at the south end of the Suez Canal ; linked by rail with Cairo and Port Said. It is an ancient trading centre, but is badly built ; pop.50,000.

Suez Canal, see CANALS ; DISRAELI, B.

Suffolk, *sŭf'ŭk,* county of E. England, with a coastline of 62m washed by the N. Sea ; grows much wheat and sugar-beet ; co.tn Ipswich (E. Suffolk), Bury St Edmunds (W. Suffolk).

suffragan bishop, see BISHOP

Suffragettes, see ELECTION

sugar, general name for a sweetening substance once derived wholly from the sugar-cane, grown chiefly in British India, Cuba, E. Indies, W. Indies and Brazil, with a total of about 17,000,000 tons a year, but now derived in increasing quantities from sugar beet (see BEET), especially in USSR, Germany, USA, Britain, etc. to the extent of about 10,000,000 tons a year.

The sugar-cane, a cultivated grass often 20ft high, is crushed and the juice boiled. Beet is soaked and allowed either to diffuse slowly, or to pass through a cylinder in a stream of hot water, being later separated with lime and then filtered. Both cane and beet sugar are refined to produce 4-sided prisms that melt at 160°C. *Treacle* is made from a sweet syrup (molasses) derived in the refining process. See PLATE 12 *(top)*

In chemistry sugars are sweet-tasting crystalline substances of the mono-, di-, and tri-saccharide groups, e.g. glucose, etc.

sugar-beet, see BEET

Suleiman I, *soo-lā-män'* (*d* 1566), Sultan of Turkey, known as the Magnificent ; succeeded 1520 ; raised the Ottoman empire to its greatest glory ; crushed rebellions in Egypt and Syria, drove the Knights of St John from Rhodes, and advanced far into Europe.

Sulgrave, village, Northamptonshire ; has Sulgrave Manor, home 1539–1610 of the Washingtons, ancestors of George Washington, first President of the USA.

Sulla, LUCIUS CORNELIUS (138–78BC), Roman statesman ; became dictator 82BC. A master of war and statecraft, he was a brilliant organiser and scholar, but without morality.

Sullivan, SIR ARTHUR (1842–1900), composer, *b* London ; notable for hymn-tunes, settings for Shakespeare's plays, overtures ; and many songs (including *The Lost Chord*). His fame is shared by Sir W. S. Gilbert, who was his collaborator in producing a brilliant series of comic operas (see GILBERT, SIR WILLIAM SCHWENCK), all of which are still immensely popular.

sulphate of ammonia, see MANURES AND FERTILISERS

sulphonamides, *sŭl-fon-am'īds,* various powerful anti-bacterial drugs found in recent years to be of immense value in treating certain diseases, their action being to interfere with or slow down growth or multiplication of infectious

bacteria, thus giving the white cells of the blood assistance in self-defence. The sulphonamides include : (*a*) *sulphaguanidine,* used in dysentery and cholera ; (*b*) *Prontosil,* and its variations *Prontosil-soluble* and *Prontosil album* (or *sulphanilamide*), of great value in treating flesh wounds, as proved during World War II ; (*c*) *sulphapyridine,* better known as M and B 693, now very widely used in treating pneumonia and meningitis. *Sulphanilamide* is used especially in treating septicemia and sore throats.

sulphur, *sŭl'fĕr,* chemical, non-metallic element, S ; atomic weight 32·06 ; atomic number 16 ; found in many regions of volcanic activity, but comes mostly from Mediterranean countries and Texas, USA ; often brought to the surface by pipes filled with hot water. One form (flowers of sulphur) is a yellow powder ; another is in sticks or rolls known as brimstone. Sulphur melts at 113°C ; is insoluble in water ; is used in vulcanising rubber ; burns with a blue flame, producing sulphur dioxide, SO_2, which, dissolved in water, forms sulphurous acid, H_2SO_3.

Sulphur trioxide, SO_3, and water form SULPHURIC ACID (oil of vitriol), H_2SO_4. Concentrated sulphuric acid has specific gravity 1·84 ; boils at 338°C ; generates heat when mixed with water. Sulphates, e.g. Epsom salts and ammonium sulphate, are salts of the acid.

Sulphide ores include galena or lead sulphide, PbS ; iron pyrites, or iron bisulphide, FeS_2 ; cinnabar or mercury sulphide, HgS. SULPHURETTED HYDROGEN, or hydrogen sulphide, H_2S, is found in the waters of some spas, e.g. Harrogate.

sulphuric acid, see SULPHUR

sultan, Mohammedan title meaning ruler, especially used by foreigners for the ruler of the Turkish empire, though the title is now abolished. The feminine is *sultana.*

sumac or **sumac,** *shoo'mak,* small tree, one variety of which yields a material used in tanning leather.

Sumatra, see NETHERLANDS

Sumer, *sū'mĕr,* ancient name for the region later known as Babylonia. Sumerian civilisation was at its height c.3500–2500BC, as excavations at Ur of the Chaldees by Sir Leonard Woolley have shown.

Sumerians, see BABYLONIA ; SUMER

summer, see SEASONS

Summer Time, see CALENDAR

summoner, see CHAUCER, GEOFFREY

sun, see ASTRONOMY

Sunda Islands, *sŭn'dä,* Dutch islands of Sumatra, Java, Borneo, Bali and Lombok from the Malay Peninsula to the Moluccas.

Sundar Singh, *sŭn'dä sing* (*d* c.1933), Indian mystic who became a Christian ; wandered as a preacher in India ; went to Tibet as a missionary ; visited England

and America 1920 ; set out on a second missionary tour in Tibet 1929, and was not heard of again.

· **Sunday School,** Church institution where children are given religious instruction. The movement began with Robert Raikes, who opened a Sunday school in Gloucester 1780, and was encouraged by the Sunday School Society, founded by William Fox 1785, and by the Sunday School Union formed in London, 1803. New methods, such as the grading of scholars into (*a*) beginners, (*b*) primary, (*c*) junior, (*d*) intermediate, and (*e*) senior departments, were popularised in Britain *c.*1902. From the first the movement was vigorous and progressive in USA. Today there is a serious decline in membership. The term ' Junior Church ' is now preferred by many.

Sunderbunds, jungle region of the lower part of the Ganges delta, home of snakes and tigers.

Sunderland, port at the mouth of the R. Wear, County Durham ; noted for shipbuilding, machinery and chemicals ; has extensive docks and a remarkable aluminium bascule bridge opened 1948 ; exports coal ; pop.178,000.

sundew, insect-eating plant with small white flowers on stalks 4–6in long, springing from a rosette of leaves that have crimson threads tipped with gummy fluid. The leaf tentacles close on an insect, and a liquid is poured on the victim, which is thus digested.

sundial, device for telling the time by the position of the shadow of an upright or projecting piece of metal, called a *stile* or *gnomon.*

sun fish, fish that is almost spherical except for the fins and tail ; may be 7ft long ; one species is sometimes found in British waters.

sunflower, garden plant (family *Compositae*) introduced into Britain from N. America *c.*1596 ; may be 6ft high ; has rough oval leaves, and a huge yellow flower-head producing grey seeds valuable as poultry food, and for oil.

sunlight, see SPECTRUM

sunspot, apparently dark area on the sun, actually the mouth of a ' funnel ' up which gases are rushing ; moves with the rotation of the sun, but has its own motion also. There may be several sunspots at once, and about every eleven years a period of exceptional activity produces more than usual, with consequent increase of magnetic storms on the earth. A sunspot (1921) had an area of 1,800,000,000sq.m. (The earth could have been dropped into it like a pill into a bassoon.)

Sun Yat Sen, *soon'-yät-sen* (1866–1925), Chinese doctor who became a political agitator after visiting Japan, England and USA ; raised a revolutionary party which deposed the Manchu line of kings 1911 ; became first President of the Chinese republic ; later organised new revolts, and (1923) established the

supremacy of the Chinese Nationalist party.

' **Super Fortress,**' see AVIATION

Superior, L., world's largest freshwater lake. Between Canada and USA, its area is 31,820sq.m ; length 383m ; has many islands ; abounds in fish.

supersonic, in physics, vibrations in all respects similar to sound waves, but having frequencies greater than those that can be heard by the human ear, say a frequency greater than 20,000 per sec. Planes travelling at over 40,000 ft reach supersonic speed at *c.*675mph, e.g. a De Havilland in 1948.

Super-Tramp, see DAVIES, WILLIAM HENRY

Suraj-ud-Dowlah, *su-rä'jä ud dow'lä* (1757), Nawab of Bengal from 1756. A tyrant, he attacked Calcutta 1756, and was responsible for the incident known as the Black Hole. Defeated by Clive at Plassey, he took flight, and was executed by his rival, Mir Jafar.

Surat, port, Bombay Presidency ; site of the first English settlement in India (1613) ; manufactures textiles, and exports grain and cotton ; pop.171,000. See EAST INDIA COMPANY

surd, in mathematics, an irrational and incommensurable root, e.g. $\sqrt{2}$, or any root that cannot be worked out exactly.

Surgeons, ROYAL COLLEGE OF, corporation founded London 1800 with HQ at Lincoln's Inn Fields, WC2. That of Edinburgh is at 18 Nicolson Street. The Royal College of Surgeons in Ireland has HQ at 123 St Stephen's Green, Dublin.

F.R.C.S. stands for Fellow of the Royal College of Surgeons ; when ' E ' is added to these letters it means that the degree has been obtained in Edinburgh.

surgery, treatment of disease or injury by manipulation, if possible, i.e. without cutting (e.g. massage, radium treatment, etc.) ; or by cutting if necessary. Surgery appears to have been known even in the Stone Age, when trephining operations (making a hole in the skull to relieve pressure on the brain, or, possibly, to allow an imaginary demon to escape) were apparently successfully performed. It was brought to a fine art by the ancient Greeks, but lost to a great extent in Europe in the 7th century. Revived by Ambroise Paré (1510–90), a French surgeon, it was very considerably advanced by John Hunter in the 18th century.

In more recent times surgery has been immensely improved, due partly to a fuller knowledge of anatomy, and to the use of anaesthetics, care in avoiding infection (the result of the pioneer work of Pasteur and Lord Lister), the discovery of X-rays, which now enables the surgeon to see the part of the body on which he is operating, even though deeply hidden, also blood-tests, methods of cutting without loss of blood, and of sewing up wounds. Scrupulous cleanliness in the operating theatre, the prevention of shock, improved instruments (all of which are sterilised before use), the employment of drugs (e.g. penicillin), all aid the surgeon in his work. Microscopical examination of blood, and chemical tests, are of great value in diagnosis. Plastic surgery has made rapid strides recently.

Surinam, see NETHERLANDS

surplice, *sŭr'plis,* vestment of white linen with full sleeves. In the Roman church it is usually ornamented with lace, but is shorter than the knee-length surplice worn by clergy, choristers and readers in the Anglican Church.

Surrealism, see ART

Surrey, English county between Kent and Hampshire. Much of it is beautifully wooded. The county hall is at Kingston-on-Thames, but Guildford is the co.tn.

Surrey, HENRY HOWARD, EARL OF (*d* 1547), English courtier. A quarrelsome man, he was falsely accused of treason, and was executed. With Sir Thomas Wyatt he made the sonnet popular, thus giving English poetry a new grace.

surtax, direct tax on high incomes, the highest paying as much as 10s 6d in the £1.

surveying, measurement of an area of the earth's surface, and a necessary preparation for building or map-making. The surveyor makes great use of the chain (100 links or 22yd), and the theodolite, a type of telescope with a graduated scale for reading off the angle through which it has been moved. For large areas the method of triangulation from a given base-line is now being superseded by aerial photography.

The survey of Britain is done by the Ordnance Survey. For particulars of surveying as a career, write to the Secretary, Chartered Surveyors' Institution.

Susquehanna, *sŭs-kwē-han'ă,* river of USA, flowing 422m into Chesapeake Bay.

Sussex, SE. coastal English county ; has sheep on the Downs ; administered from Lewes and Chichester.

Sutcliffe, HERBERT, *sŭt'klif* (1894–), cricketer, born near Leeds (Yorkshire) ; appeared in 27 Test matches against Australia 1924–34 ; frequently partnered with J. B. Hobbs.

Sutherland, county of N. Scotland ; has wild scenery, deer forests and grouse moors ; co.tn Dornoch. Scene 1814 and 1919 of the Sutherland Clearances, when hundreds of crofters were evicted from their holdings with much brutality to make room for sheep-walks.

Sutlej, river flowing from the Himalayas to meet the R. Indus after *c.*900m.

Sutro, ALFRED, *soo'trō* (1863–1933), dramatist, *b* London of Jewish descent ; notable for his comedies, e.g. *The Walls of Jericho* and *Living Together.*

suttee, see BENTINCK, LORD WILLIAM CAVENDISH

Sutton, town, Surrey ; pop. with Cheam 70,000.

Sutton Coldfield, town, Warwickshire, a suburb of Birmingham ; has a television transmitter ; pop.42,000.

Sutton Hoo, see ANGLO-SAXONS

Sutton-in-Ashfield, town, Nottinghamshire; manufactures silks, woollen goods and hosiery ; pop.38,000.

Suva, see FIJI

Svalbard, see SPITSBERGEN

Swabia, *swā'bi-ă,* formerly a duchy of south-west Germany.

Swaffer, HANNEN (1879–), journalist, *b* Lindfield, Sussex ; won fame as a critic in the *Daily Express,* being outspoken and severe when writing of plays and actors.

Swale, river of Yorkshire ; flows 60m to join the R. Ouse.

swallow, *swol'ō,* migratory bird (*Hirundo rustica*) ; visits Britain Apr.–Sept. Black above, with a patch of russet on the head, it has a red chin, under parts cream with a deep black collar ; the tail forked. The swallow, living wholly on insects taken on the wing, builds a saucer-shaped nest of mud ; lays 4–6 white eggs spotted with reddish-brown.

THE SWALLOW

Somewhat similar is the HOUSE MARTIN, smaller than the swallow, and pure white below. The nest of mud and hair is built against a wall. The SAND MARTIN, mouse-coloured above, white below, nests in burrows.

swallow-tail butterfly, large black and yellow butterfly found only in Norfolk and Cambridgeshire. The hind wings have a rust-red spot and 7 blue spots. The green caterpillar is belted with black and blue.

swan, bird related to the duck and goose ; has a long neck, short legs with webbed feet, no feathers on the front of the face. In winter three species of swans visit Britain, but the mute swan (*Cygnus olor*) is the only one to nest here. It has a black nob at the base of its orange bill, holds its wings slightly raised, and has the neck arched. It lays 5–10 greenish-white eggs.

A male swan is called a *cob* ; a female a *pen* ; young swans are termed *cygnets.*

Swan, J. W., see LIGHTING

Swansea, *swon'zē*, port, S. Wales (Glamorganshire) ; has a fine harbour, spacious docks ; exports steel, tin, coal and iron ; is possibly Britain's busiest oil port ; pop.152,000.

swastika, *swos'ti-kä*, cross-like design formed of equal arms with right-angled continuations ; used as a symbol as early as the Stone Age, chiefly by the Aryan race, but found in regions as far apart as France, Troy, Buddhist India, China and Japan. The swastika, notorious as the Nazi symbol, appeared on the German flag after Hitler rose to power *c*.1933.

Swatow, *swä-tow'*, port, China, at the mouth of the Han R. ; pop.200,000.

Swaziland, *swä'zē-*, protectorate of the British Empire in S. Africa ; area *c*.7,000sq.m ; pop.160,000, chiefly Bantu. Though mountainous in the west, the soil is fertile and the climate healthy. Swaziland is noted for sheep, cattle, maize, beans, pumpkins and sweet potatoes ; the minerals include tin ; administrative HQ Mbabane.

Sweden, *swē'den*, kingdom of N. Europe. It is in the Scandinavian Peninsula, and is east of Norway, from which it is separated by mts. Rivers and lakes are numerous, and forests cover 50 % of the area of 173,345sq.m, these providing timber, wood-pulp, cellulose, pitch, tar and the raw materials for the manufacture of paper and matches. Sweden is exceptionally rich in iron of the finest quality, also zinc, sulphur and lead. Of the pop. of *c*.6,770,000, *c*.35 % are engaged in agriculture, e.g. growing sugarbeet, potatoes and grain in the south.

Sweden, one of the most progressive countries in Europe, has a large mercantile fleet, growing industries, and a contented people, chiefly Lutherans in religion, almost all able to read and write, many having been exceptionally well educated. The country's architecture is remarkably fine, many of its schools, theatres and factories being excellent examples of successful modern design. Infant mortality (1943) was the lowest ever recorded in Europe.

The government consists of a Diet (*Riksdag*) with two chambers. The king is a descendant of Bernadotte, a French soldier who succeeded Charles XIII by invitation 1818, and an uncle of the late Count Bernadotte, Palestine mediator who was murdered in Jerusalem, Sept. 1948. Exports include timber, woodpulp, paper, machinery, matches, iron ore and agricultural produce. The cap. is Stockholm.

Swedenborg, EMANUEL, *svē'den-böri* (1688–1772), Swedish scientist who wrote notable scientific works, but later became a religious mystic. After he died (London) the New Church, founded on his religious system, was organised.

sweepstake, see GAMBLING

sweet-pea, see PEA

sweet potato, plant of S. America and other warm regions ; has trailing stems, triangular leaves, and funnel-shaped flower; produces tubers (*batatas*) called sweet potatoes.

sweet william, garden plant with stiff, jointed stems, lance-shaped leaves in pairs, and a cluster of flowers at the top. They are generally white, pink, crimson, or two-coloured. The scent of the flowers is sweet and heavy.

Sweyn, *swän* (*d* 1014), King of Denmark from 986 ; was the father of Canute. Sweyn raided England, especially after Ethelred the Unready's massacre of the Danes 1002.

swift, swallow-like bird noted for its rapid and acrobatic flight ; glossy black except for a grey patch under the chin ; the wings are long and narrow. Visiting Britain Apr.–Aug., it builds a nest of straw, grasses and feathers, gummed together with saliva, usually built under the eaves of a house or in a church tower ; lays two white eggs ; feeds wholly on insects ; screams joyously in flight.

Swift, JONATHAN (1667–1745), author, *b* Dublin ; became secretary to Sir William Temple ; at whose home (Moor Park, Surrey) he met Esther Johnson, with whom he later fell in love, and about whom he wrote in his *Journal* (where he refers to her as Stella), and also in his *Sonnets*. His friends included Addison and Pope. He took part in English politics, going over from the Whigs to the Tories ; became Dean of St. Patrick's Cathedral, Dublin, in 1713. Always liable to fits of depression, he was mad in later life.

Swift's writings, almost all of them satires, include *The Battle of the Books*, *A Tale of a Tub*, *Drapier's Letters*, and his clever and humorous prophecies supposed to have been written by Isaac Bickerstaff ; his *Journal to Stella* was not intended for publication. He is best remembered for *Gulliver's Travels* (1726). Part I is supposed to be the adventures of Lemuel Gulliver, a ship's doctor, wrecked on the island of Lilliput, where the people are no more than 6in high ; Part II is the story of Gulliver's adventures among the giants of Brobdingnag ; in Part III Gulliver finds himself on the flying island of Laputa ; Part IV describes the land of the Houyhnhnms (*hoo-in'ums*), i.e. horses with reasoning powers, and the Yahoos, men in the shape of beasts.

swimming, method of propelling oneself through water, employing, say, the breast stroke, requiring simultaneous movement of arms and legs ; or a speed stroke, e.g. the over-arm, trudgeon, or the Australian crawl, in which the face is submerged except when the swimmer turns it sideways to breathe deeply.

The first to swim the English Channel (*c*.40m, allowing for drift) was Captain Webb (1875). In 1949 an English schoolboy, F. Mickman, swam the

Channel ; the present world record is held by the Egyptian, Hassan Abd-el Rehim, who crossed, 1950, in 10hr 50min.

Swinburne, ALGERNON CHARLES, *swin'bĕrn* (1837–1909), poet, *b* London ; a little man with very small hands and feet but a large, weak-chinned head, greenish eyes and a mass of flaming hair. He lived wildly but wrote amazingly imaginative verse, being especially famous for his lyrics.

Swindon, town, Wiltshire ; has railway workshops ; pop.62,000.

Swing, RAYMOND GRAM (1887–), American journalist, author and broadcaster, who was highly popular in Britain as commentator for the BBC on American affairs from 1935.

swing music, see JAZZ

Swinnerton, FRANK (1884–), English writer ; notable as a literary critic, and for his many novels, e.g. *The Merry Heart* ; *Elizabeth* ; and *Thankless Child.*

Swinton, town, Lancashire ; manufactures cotton ; pop. (with Pendleton) 41,000.

Swinton, VISCOUNT (1884–), formerly Sir Philip Cunliffe-Lister, politician ; President of the Board of Trade ; Colonial Secretary ; Minister for Civil Aviation 1944.

Swiss Family Robinson, THE, island story by J. R. Wyss (1781–1830), a Swiss pastor.

Switzerland, inland country of Europe. Of its area of *c.*16,000sq.m no less than 73 % is mountainous (chiefly the Alps, but also, in the north-west, the Jura). The valleys, however, are highly productive, being exceedingly well farmed, and agriculture includes cereals, fruits, including grapes. The large number of dairy farms supply great quantities of milk which is exported in the form of condensed milk. Forests cover *c.*1/5th of the country.

Switzerland is the home of a skilled and hard-working people (pop.4,266,000) who produce for export many varieties of textiles (especially silks and rayon), machinery, paper, chemicals, chocolate, clocks and watches. German, French, Italian and Romaunsch are spoken. Education has long been exceptionally successful. The republic, divided into twenty-five cantons, is governed by a president and a Parliament comprising two Chambers, known together as the Federal Assembly. The cap. is Berne. Greatly favoured by tourists, Switzerland is renowned for its Alpine peaks, e.g. Mont Blanc, Jungfrau and Matterhorn ; beautiful lakes (e.g. Zurich, Lucerne, Constance, Geneva), and has been called the ' playground of Europe ' from the number of visitors attracted by its scenery and its facilities for sport, e.g. mt.-climbing and ski-ing. The pure mountain air is ideal for people threatened with consumption.

In spite of wars in Europe, Switzerland has for long remained neutral.

sword, *sörd*, weapon of personal offence and defence ; that used by ancient Greeks and Romans was short and pointed, meant to cut rather than stab. Norman swords (with long, wide blades) were for slashing ; 15th c. English swords had long, tapering blades ; those of the 16th c. had guards over the hilt. Rapiers (much used in duelling in the 16th–17th c.) were light and finely tempered. Other swords include broadsword, falchion, sabre and the Oriental scimetar.

sword-fish, Atlantic fish from 4–15ft long, with the upper jaw prolonged to form a sword-like weapon sometimes 3ft long.

sycamore or **great maple,** *sik'ä-mör*, quick-growing tree reaching *c.*80ft in 50 years ; has a mass of foliage. The leaves, growing in bunches, have 5 points ; the flowers are yellowish tassels ; the winged fruits are U-shaped.

THE SYCAMORE

The leaves, the flowers and the winged seed

Sydney, *sid'ni*, port and cap., New S. Wales, Australia ; on what is probably the finest harbour in the world, and in a superb setting ; has five graving docks, one opened 1945. The north and south shores are linked by the Sydney Harbour Bridge, a superb example of engineering (see BRIDGES) ; has vast shipping trade ; refuels with oil or coal, and loads grain with modern plant ; is a great railway centre. The manufactures include clothing, cars and pottery. The National Park here has an area of 34,392 acres ; and in Koala Park we may see native bears. Taronga Park, with its plants, animals and fish is a fascinating spot ; pop.1,400,000

Sydney, port, Cape Breton, Nova Scotia ; has a fine harbour. Coal is mined near by, and there are large iron and steel works ; pop.28,000.

Sydney Harbour Bridge, see BRIDGES and PLATE 56

SYHA, see YOUTH ORGANISATIONS

syllogism, *sil'ō-jizm*, in logic, form of deductive reasoning in which from two statements or premises a conclusion is drawn, the conclusion being necessarily true if the premises are true. A typical syllogism is :

1 All men are mortal
2 Socrates is a man
3 Socrates is mortal

1 and 2 are the premises : 3 is the conclusion, which cannot but be true if the premises are true. See LOGIC

symbiosis, see PARASITE

symbols (chemical), see ELEMENT

Symington, WILLIAM, *sīm'-* (1763–1831), Scottish engineer, *b* Leadhills ; notable as the first engineer in Britain to build a steamer, the *Charlotte Dundas*, launched 1802.

symphony, *sim'fö-ni*, musical composition, essentially a sonata for orchestra ; usually has four movements, the first being the chief, the second usually slower and lyrical, the third often with dance rhythms ; the fourth akin to the first, but generally lighter, often in rondo form. Haydn has been styled the father of the symphony. Of Mozart's 41 symphonies those in G minor, E flat, and C are the most famous. Beethoven's 9 symphonies are classics. Other composers of the symphony include Schubert, Schumann, Mendelssohn, Brahms, Tchaikovsky, Dvórak, Elgar, Sibelius, Vaughan Williams, Bliss, Goossens and Shostakovich.
Read *The Symphony*, Ralph Hill.

synagogue, see JEWS

synchrotron, machine for producing 30,000,000 volt X-rays by accelerating electrons. The experimental machine completed 1948 and now at the University of Glasgow is a pioneer, and later models are expected to develop ten times as much energy. They will be used for treating tumours.

syncopation, *singkō-pā'shon*, displacement of either the beat or the normal accent of a piece of music, i.e. prolonging a sound from a weak place in the bar to a stronger one. Syncopation has long been used by composers, and is found in folksong. Taking a hint from the rhythms of African music as preserved by Negroes in USA, American composers *c*.1915 made great use of syncopation in dance music, hence jazz and swing.

syndicalism, *sin'dik-al-izm*, system advocated by some revolutionaries who hold that trade unions should own and manage industry, and that shareholding should be abolished.

Synge, JOHN MILLINGTON, *sing* (1871–1909), Irish dramatist ; lived for a time in the Gaelic-speaking community of the Aran Is. His plays are in English, but their inspiration is mainly Gaelic. They are deeply tragic in feeling, but full of rich humour, especially *The Playboy of the Western World*, which caused an uproar when first performed at the Abbey Theatre (Dublin) in 1907.

synthesis, *sin'thē-sis*, Greek *syn-* (*with* or *together*) and *thesis* (*putting*) ; in chemistry, the building up of a compound from its elements. Thus synthetic rubber is an artificial substitute for natural rubber (it is made from isoprene).
Synthetic chemistry has revolutionised industry in recent years. Once he knows the chemical formula of a natural substance, the chemist is often able to build it up in the laboratory. When it was realised that eventually the supply of Chile saltpetre would become exhausted, with a consequent loss of the natural source of nitrates, Birkeland and Eyde found a means of producing synthetic nitrates from the nitrogen in the atmosphere ; similarly many dyes, once largely obtained from plants, are now made from coal-tar products. Drugs and antiseptics are frequently synthetic productions ; sugars and perfumes are built up artificially ; essences from esters, also plastics and rayon.

Syracuse, *sī'rä-kūs*, ancient city on the coast of Sicily and the island of Ortygia ; was at the summit of its greatness *c*.390 BC ; conquered by the Romans 212BC ; destroyed by the Saracens AD878. Today there is a modern city on Ortygia ; pop.54,000.

Syracuse, city, New York state, USA ; noted for steel ; pop.206,000.

Syria and the Lebanon, *sir'i-ä* ; *leb'ä-non*, formerly under French mandate, but independent since 1946, each with a president. The combined area is *c*.60,000sq.m ; combined pop.3,050,000. Much is desert ; the people are chiefly Moslem. The cap. of Syria is Damascus, pop.230,000 ; other towns include Aleppo, Jebel Druze (government HQ). The cap. of the Lebanon, Beirut (pop. 160,000), is an important port.
Syria and the Lebanon are rich in archaeological remains, e.g. Damascus, at least 4,000 years old ; also the towns of Baalbek and Palmyra.
Read *Syria*, Robin Fedden.

Szegedin, *se'ged-in*, second largest city, Hungary ; noted for its river-trade (on the Rs. Maros and Tisza) ; pop.140,000.

T

Taal, see AFRIKAANS

Tabernacle, portable wooden temple, hung with curtains at one end, which was set up within an enclosure at some distance from the camp of the Israelites as they journeyed from Egypt towards Palestine. First set up by Moses in Mt Sinai, the Tabernacle had a Holy Place containing a golden altar for incense, shrewbread and a golden candlestick ; and a smaller portion, the Holy of Holies, separated by a veil, and entered by the high priest only.

The setting up of this temporary structure was the work of the family of Aaron, i.e. the Levites. See Exodus 25.

Table Mountain, flat-topped mt. rising steeply 3,582ft above Cape Town, S. Africa, and overlooking Table Bay.

tables, see BACKGAMMON

tables, see MULTIPLICATION ; WEIGHTS AND MEASURES

tabor, see PIPE AND TABOR

Tabriz, *tă-brēz'*, city, Iran ; manufactures carpets and cotton goods ; has much trade ; pop.214,000.

Tacitus, CORNELIUS, *tas'i-tŭs*, Roman historian, died early in the 2nd c. AD. His writings include the *Dialogue on Orators* ; the *Histories* (only 4 of the original 12 remaining) ; the *Annals* ; the *Germany* ; and the *Life of Agricola*. In the main he was an accurate as well as a vivid writer, and though his *Germany* is often geographically incorrect, his *Life of Agricola* is interesting for its account of Roman Britain. The *Annals* deal with the period AD14-68. His work abounds in epigrams.

Not only has Tacitus left us a fascinating sidelight on Britain as it was in the days of his father-in-law, Agricola, but he was the writer of the first biography of classical times. Bitter and critical, his style is unlike that of any of his contemporaries. We may note : *Atque omne ignotum pro magnifico est ; sed nunc terminus Britanniae patet,* i.e. ' For wonder grows where knowledge fails. But now the very bounds of Britain are laid bare ' (*Agricola*). Also the bitter remark attributed by Tacitus to Galgacus who led the Caledonians against the Romans in Scotland ; *Ubi solitudinem faciunt, pacem appellant,* i.e. ' Where they make a wilderness they call it peace.'

Tacoma, port on Puget Sound, Washington, USA ; exports agricultural and mining products of the district ; pop. 109,000.

Tadcaster, town, W. Yorkshire ; brews beer.

tadpole, see AMPHIBIAN

Taff Vale Judgment, see TRADE UNIONS

Taft, WILLIAM HOWARD (1857–1930), American statesman, *b* Cincinnati, Ohio ; made a great reputation as a judge ; elected President of the USA 1908, but his tariff acts (1910) were unpopular.

Taganrog, *ta-gan-rŏk'*, USSR port on the Sea of Azov ; trades in agricultural products ; pop.160,000.

Tagore, SIR RABINDRANATH, *tä-gör'* (1861–1941), Indian writer, *b* Calcutta; founded a famous school 1901 ; notable as a poet (e.g. *Gitanjali* and *The Crescent Moon*), and as a writer of plays and novels. He was a man of wide sympathies and deep spiritual qualities.

Tagus, *tä'gŭs*, river of Spain and Portugal, flows 565m via Lisbon to the Atlantic.

Tahiti, *tä-hē'tē*, island of the Society Is. ; a French possession since 1880 ; produces cotton, sugar, copra, mother-of-pearl and phosphates.

tailor bird, bird *c.*6in long, with greenish plumage ; found in India and China : named from its habit of sewing two long leaves together with cocoon silk or fibre, and building a nest of grass and hair in the pocket thus formed.

Taine, HIPPOLYTE ADOLPHE (1828–93), French historian ; author of a *History of English Literature*, the finest of its kind by a foreigner, and famous for his masterly survey of the history of France, *Les origines de la France contemporaine.*

Taiwan, see FORMOSA

Takoradi, port, Gold Coast ; opened 1928.

Talavera, *tä-lä-vä'rä*, town, Spain ; on the R. Tagus ; scene of a costly victory gained by Wellington over the French 1809.

Talbot House, *tol'bŭt*, soldiers' rest-house in World War I ; popularly known as Toc H. See CLAYTON, P. T. B.

talc, French chalk, i.e. hydrated magnesium silicate.

talent, unit of weight and money among the ancient Greeks ; worth 60 minae, roughly £240. The Attic talent weighed *c.*57¾lb. The talent mentioned in the Bible was a mass of gold (108lb) worth *c.*£6,000, or 96lb silver worth *c.*£410.

talisman, Arabic word for a charm, often a jewel engraved with mystic words or signs.

Talleyrand-Périgord, CHARLES MAURICE DE, *tä-le-rän pä-rē-gör* (1754–1838), French statesman ; belonged to the old nobility, *b* Paris ; lamed in boyhood ; became a bishop, but resigned and was given important but unofficial duties as a diplomat abroad, including England. He returned to France after the Reign of Terror, and became Foreign Minister 1797.

Though a friend of Napoleon, Talleyrand disapproved of military schemes, and desired peace with England. After Napoleon's defeat in 1815 he did much to raise France to a position of importance among the European nations. A man of outstanding charm of manner, his policies were always designed to further what he considered to be the best interest of his country.

Tallinn, formerly Reval, cap. of Estonia. A busy Baltic port (trading in cereals, timber and cement), it is linked by rail with Leningrad ; pop.147,000.

Talmud, THE, see JEWS

tamandua, see ANT-EATER

tamarind, tropical tree ; may be 50–60ft high ; has leaves comprising 20–24 leaflets in two rows ; fragrant red and yellow flowers ; bean-like pods containing hard seeds.

tambourine, musical instrument comprising a wooden ring over which skin is stretched. This is beaten with the hands. The metal discs in the rim are called jingles.

Tambov, *täm-böf'*, town, USSR, 300m south-east of Moscow ; has grain and cattle markets ; pop.102,000.

Tamerlane (1336–1405), Tartar conqueror, born near Samarkand ; became ruler of Turkestan 1369 ; led victorious armies into Persia ; reached the Caspian Sea ; invaded India ; sacked Delhi ; defeated the Turks and Egyptians, and was planning an invasion of China when he died. His name is immortalised in Marlowe's tragedy, *Tamburlaine the Great.*

Tamil, language of *c.*21,000,000 people in S. India and Ceylon ; has added such words as *cheroot, curry* and *pariah* to English.

Tamm'any Hall, HQ in New York of the Tammany Society, a political organisation founded *c.*1789 in favour of the Democrats.

tam o' shanter, loose woollen cap with a knob or tassel, so named from the humorous and weird poem *Tam o' Shanter* by Robert Burns.

Tampa, port, also a holiday town, Florida, USA ; noted for cigars ; exports oil ; pop.108,000.

Tampico, port, Mexico ; exports asphalt ; pop.124,000.

Tanganyika, *tan-gan-yē'-kä*, lake, Central Africa ; area 12,700sq.m. Discovered by John Hanning Speke and Richard Burton, and explored by David Livingstone.

Tanganyika Territory, known as German E. Africa till 1918 ; has 500m of coast on the Indian Ocean, and an area of *c.*360,000sq.m. The pop. of *c.*6,000,000 includes *c.*17,000 Europeans. Largely mountainous, there are vast forest reserves (including cedar and ebony) ; cotton, coffee, ground-nuts and sisal are grown, also kapok and pyrethrum. Gold and diamonds are exported, also tin and wolfram. There are *c.*6,000,000 cattle. The cap. is Dar-es-Salaam. See PLATE 10 (*top*)

tangent, see CIRCLE ; TRIGONOMETRY

tangent galvanometer, see ELECTRICITY

tangerine, see ORANGE

Tangier, *tan-jēr*, port, Morocco ; cap. of the International Zone established 1925 ; pop.100,000. There is a considerable shipping trade. Tangier was a British possession 1662–83.

tank, an armoured fighting vehicle with caterpillar tracks instead of wheels ; first used (by the British Army) in World War I, it went into action for the first time during the battle of the Somme, 1916.

Early tanks (both British and German) were normally *c.*26ft long, weighed *c.*27tons, with motors of *c.*150hp.

In World War II tanks played a decisive part, especially in N. Africa, where desert warfare depended largely on them. The German Panzer divisions there won success with the Mark III, and later with the Mark IV, which carried a 75mm cannon ; our Valentines weighed 16 tons, travelled at 15mph, and were of some value in Libya despite the fact that they only carried 2-pounders ; the Crusader of 18 tons had a maximum speed of 30mph ; and the Matildas (26 tons) were 19ft long and carried 2½in armour plates. All British and American tanks kept in touch with higher HQs by radio.

In 1942 the General Grant tank with the aid of the General Sherman class knocked out the German Mark IV class. A speed of 40mph is not uncommon for the most modern tanks, which have a range of 150m or more. Flame-throwing tanks and amphibious types (especially useful for crossing rivers) are important variations.

That tanks have changed modern military tactics is undoubtedly true. Their importance in World War II may be judged from the epic story of Montgomery's victories in N. Africa.

Read *Tanks*, Professor A. M. Low.

Tannenberg, *tän'en-ber*ch, village of E. Prussia, scene 1914 of a German victory over the Russians.

Tannhäuser, *tän'hoi-zēr*, hero of a German legend of the Middle Ages. The tale has been immortalised by Wagner in his opera *Tannhäuser.*

tanning, see LEATHER

tansy, British plant (family *Compositae*) of waste ground ; may be 3ft high ; has large leaves deeply cut feather-wise ; dull yellow flowers in clusters blooming in August.

tantalum, rare metal and element, Ta ; atomic weight 180·88 ; atomic number 73 ; has a high melting-point (2,850°C) ; used in alloys and lamp filaments.

Tantalus, *tan'tä-lŭs*, in old Greek tales, son of Zeus ; condemned to stand in water with fruits above his head, but prevented from either drinking or eating ; hence our word to *tantalise.*

Taoism, *dow'izm*, mixture of philosophy, religion and magic that has long found favour with millions of Chinese ; derived from Lao-tze ; now mixed with Confucianism and Buddhism.

Tapajos, *täpä-jōs'*, tributary of the R. Amazon, Brazil ; flows over 1,000m.

tape machine, instrument (known in USA as the ticker) that translates telegraphic messages relayed from a central exchange into printed messages on a moving strip of paper ; used in newspaper offices, clubs and hotels.

tapestry, hand-made fabric in which designs are woven ; the art of making tapestries was known in ancient Egypt and Greece. London and Paris were famous for their tapestries in the 14th c. ; Arras still more so. Brussels tapestries were in vogue to the end of the 18th c. ; and Gobelins (i.e. tapestries in the style of those made by the famous French dyers in the 15th c.) are regarded as the finest of all. See PLATES VI, VII

tapioca, S. American plant with deeply lobed leaves and yellowish flowers ; the starchy tapioca food comes from the root.

tapir, *tā'pĕr*, large and clumsy animal of S. and Central America, Java, Borneo ; has a very short trunk and brownish hair ; feeds on vegetation.

tar, black, oily liquid, largely a mixture of hydrocarbons derived from the destructive distillation at high temperature of wood (notably pine), shale and coal ; hence it is a by-product of gas-works. Coal-tar is the source of benzene, toluene, xylene, phenol, naphthalene, creosol and also pitch, and indirectly of dyes, disinfectants, poison gas, insecticides, perfumes and many drugs.

Tara, hill, County Meath, Eire ; legendary home of the kings of Ireland in Celtic times.

Taranaki, region of NZ, in the south-west of N. Island ; noted for forests and iron-sand.

Taranto, *tär'än-tō*, port and chief naval base, S. Italy ; near the Gulf of Taranto. Anciently it was the chief city of *Magna Graecia*. Much damage was done to Italian vessels by a British attack from the air 1940 ; pop.180,000.

THE TANSY

tarantula, see SPIDERS

Tarbes, *tärb*, historic town, France, on the R. Adour ; manufactures paper and flax ; pop.32,000.

Tardieu, ANDRÉ, *tär-dyŭ'* (1876–1945), French politician, *b* Paris ; Prime Minister 1929, 1930 and 1932.

tare, among British plants, a flowering vetch of the pea family ; in the East, DARNEL, a species of grass closely resembling wheat ; hence the NT parable of the wheat and the tares. The seeds of darnel are poisonous.

tariff-reform, see FREE TRADE

tariffs, see FREE TRADE

tarpon, food fish with a long, slim body, large scales, and of a silvery hue. Though belonging to the herring family it may weigh over 100lb, and affords excellent sport to anglers in S. Atlantic waters.

Tar'quin, or more fully Tarquinius Superbus, 7th and last of the legendary kings of Rome ; said to have ruled 534–510BC. Banished, he attempted to return but was defeated at the battle of L. Regillus *c*.496BC.

Tarragona, *tä-rä-gō'nä*, Mediterranean port, Spain ; manufactures silk, wine and jute ; has Roman remains ; pop.31,000.

Tarshish, town, probably a Phoenician city of SW. Spain. It is often mentioned in the OT.

Tarsus, birthplace of St Paul ; is in Asia Minor ; trades in cotton, grain and hides ; was of great importance in Roman times.

tartan, woollen cloth with a coloured check pattern, especially as used for the kilt and plaid of the national dress of the Highlanders of Scotland, various patterns indicating different clans, e.g. Campbell of Argyll, MacGregor, Buchanan, Graham of Montrose, MacPherson, etc. Red, blue, yellow, green, black and white are the chief colours. A black and white checkered plaid is called a shepherd's tartan.

Tartar, *tär'tĕr*, name in the Middle Ages for the mounted nomads (wandering tribes) of central Asia, Tartary being, vaguely, the region between the Pacific and the R. Dnieper. Jenghiz Khan established a Tartar empire which dominated E. Europe 1238–1462. Today one of the republics of USSR is known as Tartar. Its capital is Kaxan.

Tartu, city, Estonia ; pop.60,000.

Tashkent, cap., Uzbekistan (USSR) ; pop.585,000 ; manufactures silk and leather.

Tasman, ABEL JANSZOON (*d* 1659), Dutch explorer ; commanded (1642) an expedition during which he sailed round Australia, discovered Van Dieman's Land (renamed Tasmania 1853), and went on to discover NZ, the Friendly and the Fiji Islands.

Tasmania, *taz-mā'niä*, island, separated from S. Australia by Bass Strait (140m wide). Named after Abel Tasman (*d* 1659), the Dutch explorer, Tasmania

22

has an area of 26,215sq.m, and a pop. of *c*.245,000. Much of the island is mountainous. There are valuable forests. Cheap electric power generated by water-power has encouraged industry, e.g. logging, wood-pulping and woollen manufacture. Many fruits are grown, especially apples. The climate is excellent, though the west has a heavy rainfall. Tasmania has been a state of Australia since 1901. The cap., Hobart, was founded 1842.

A feature of Tasmania is its English appearance, due in part to its lanes and hedges, also its houses in the English style of last century.

Tasmanian devil, fierce, flesh-eating animal of the kangaroo species ; is *c*.28in long, with a tail 12in ; lives in a burrow ; feeds at night, especially on poultry ; common in Tasmania.

Tasso, TORQUATO (1544–95), Italian poet, *b* Sorrento ; first entered the service of Alfonso II, Duke of Ferrara and later was kept in an asylum for seven years, his *Gerusalemme Liberata* (an epic finished 1574) and his sonnets being published without his knowledge. An unhappy genius, Tasso is little read today, though remembered for his narrative poem *Rinaldo*, his pastoral drama *Aminta*, and for his epic, *Gerusalemme Liberata* (Jerusalem delivered), the story of the First Crusade.

taste, see TONGUE

Tate Gallery, gallery of British Art, Millbank, London, opened 1897, the gift of Sir Henry Tate (1819–99). There are over 3,000 works of art by British artists and sculptors, 500 by foreign artists.

tattooing, custom of adorning the skin with coloured designs, usually by puncturing and rubbing in powdered charcoal and other pigments ; still practised (especially from superstitious motives) by primitive peoples, e.g. in SE. Asia, Borneo, New Guinea, Polynesia ; also favoured by sailors. Tattooing is now usually done with an electric needle.

Tauber, RICHARD, *tow'bĕr* (1893–1948), Austrian tenor singer, *b* Linz, Austria ; first appeared in England 1931.

Taunton, co.tn, Somerset ; manufactures gloves, hosiery, silks and cider ; has much agricultural trade ; pop.32,000.

Taurus, mt. range of Asia Minor from the R. Euphrates to the Aegean Sea. The pass called the Cilician Gates leads to the valley of Adana.

taxes, payments on property, articles, or income as a means of supplying the government with money to meet its expenses, e.g. education, Parliament, defence (army, navy, air force, etc.), building and repair of roads and administration.

In Norman times the king demanded money from his people as he needed it, but gradually taxation came under the control of Parliament, and the levying of taxes has been solely in the hands of the House of Commons since Stuart times. A tax may be direct, as income tax or property tax, or indirect when in the form of excise and customs duties or entertainment tax.

Local taxation is in the form of RATES, the money thus collected being used for the immediate urban or rural area, and not for national affairs. Much of the government's income is derived from indirect taxes, such as those on beer, wines, spirits and tobacco, from stamps affixed to legal documents and from death duties. Thus, when a man buys an ounce of tobacco, part of the sum he pays goes to the shopman and to the wholesaler or manufacturer, and the other part to the government. Prior to 1947 cars in Britain were taxed according to hp. Now there is a uniform tax of £10 per year on all cars bought after the new system came into operation.

INCOME TAX has been continuously imposed since 1842. It was as low as 2d in the £1 in 1874, rising in 1941 to 10s in the £1. Two kinds of income are recognised, *earned* (by people who receive wages or salaries), and *unearned* (by people who receive dividends from money invested), the tax on unearned income being higher than on earned for higher incomes.

Not *all* an earned income is taxed, however. People whose incomes do not exceed *c*.£110 a year pay no income tax. At present, people earning more than this sum are allowed £80 if single, and £140 if married, tax-free ; that is to say, a man with an income of £400 pays income tax on £400−£80, i.e. £320 if single, and on £400−£140, i.e. £260 if married. There is a further allowance of £50 for each child.

Since 1945 wage-earners of less than *c*.£600 come under the scheme known as ' PAY AS YOU EARN ' (PAYE), a plan worked out by Sir Kingsley Wood. The person who earns, say, £300 a year receives, weekly or monthly, not his actual wage, but his wage *minus* the appropriate amount of income tax. The benefit of this is that he is then free to spend *all* the money he receives, and has not to be prepared to pay back some of it as tax.

Tay, river, Perthshire ; flows 118m to the N. Sea, entering by a wide estuary. The river, noted for salmon, is crossed at Dundee by a railway bridge, built 1882–87 to replace the first Tay Bridge, blown down in a storm 1879, while a train was crossing it.

Taylor, SAMUEL COLERIDGE- (1875–1912), composer, *b* Croydon, son of an English mother and a W. African Negro father ; noted for his cantata *Hiawatha's Wedding Feast*, and much chamber music.

Taylor, JEREMY, *tā'ler* (1613–67), English churchman, *b* Cambridge. An eloquent preacher, he was the author of two devotional books, *Holy Living* and *Holy Dying.*

TB, see Tuberculosis

Tchaikovsky, Piotr Ilyich, see Tschaikovsky, P. I.

Tchekhov, Anton Pavlovich, *che-*chōf (1860–1904), Russian writer, *b* Taganrog (S. Russia) ; won fame as an author of humorous short stories, but later dealt psychologically with sad themes, especially in his plays, though his one-act plays *The Bear* and *The Proposal* are masterpieces of broad humour. His play, *The Cherry Orchard,* is a powerful mixture of tragedy and comedy, but *The Seagull* is one of deep gloom. Of his short stories *A Dreary Story* ; *My Life* ; *Peasants* ; *The New Villa* ; and *The Bishop,* are typical examples. His stories and plays have had a great influence on English literature.

tea, evergreen plant ; has a white, fragrant flower and spherical seeds. The leaf has saw-like edges, and from this comes the tea (Chinese, *cha*) which forms a stimulating beverage. The young leaves of the tea-plant are exposed to the air after being gathered, and are then roasted, rolled and dried. Green tea is made from leaves exposed to the air for a short time only. Most teas are blended in warehouses by wholesalers. Introduced into Britain *c.*1650, tea was at first very expensive, the retail price being between £6 and £10 per lb. The tea-drinking habit grew slowly, but *c.*10 times as much tea is drunk today as was consumed 100 years ago, the amount in Britain being *c.*9·02lb per person per year. Formerly imported almost wholly from China, tea is now imported mainly from India and Ceylon, though the demand for China tea is increasing again. See Plate 11 (*bottom*)

teaching, as a career offers fair rates of pay followed by superannuation. Training is given in (*a*) a two-year training college (in certain cases the student can remain to take a specialised third-year course, or proceed to another college for this purpose), or (*b*) a University course, followed by a year's training at a University Training Department, or (*c*) a specialist college for women, e.g. domestic science or physical training, the course being three years. See Education ; Technical Education

teak, large and valuable timber tree cultivated in India, Burma and Java ; may be 100–150ft high ; has opposite oval leaves, white flowers, and bladder-like fruit. The close-grained timber is exceedingly valuable, especially in building and shipbuilding.

teal, small duck common at the mouths of British rivers. The male is buff dappled with brown ; it has also a jagged black and white line along the wing, and a reddish head with green and buff at the sides. The eggs are cream.

teasel or **teazel,** tall British plant with a stiff stem, prickly ribs, leaves in pairs, and small purplish flowers.

Technical Colleges, see Technical Education

technical education, term which includes a wide range of instruction, given either in technical, art, or commercial colleges, or in evening institutes. Most of this type of education is part-time, undertaken in evening classes or during the day when employers release their employees for the purpose. Some of the larger firms have their own schools. Junior Technical Schools came into being *c.*1905, and give a two or three year course from the age of *c.*13. Under the Education Act of 1944, as Secondary Technical Schools, they will admit pupils at 11, giving a general education, with a bias in the direction of industry (including agriculture) or commerce.

Technical Colleges offer a wide range of courses, leading in some cases to university degrees and to certificates awarded by certain national institutions, e.g. the City and Guilds of London Institute, or the Institute of Bankers. A student can, therefore, find in Technical Colleges courses for such subjects as bricklaying, photography, automobile engineering, public health work, or breadmaking.

Details of courses may be obtained from the local Secretary or Director of Education.

Students may well seek advice from the Advisory Director of the British Institute of Engineering Technology or the British Tutorial Institutes.

See Education ; Examinations

Technical School, see Education ; Technical Education

technical training, see Apprentice

Technicolour, in cinema photography, trade name for three-colour cinematography based on three-colour analysis, i.e. the combination of three separate films.

Teck, formerly a castle of Württemberg, Germany ; gave its name in the 12th c. to a duchy. Mary, Queen of George V of England, was a daughter of Francis, Duke of Teck.

Tedder, Air Chief Marshal, Lord (1890–), served in World Wars I and II ; held important posts in the RAF ; in the latter war he was brilliantly successful in the Middle East.

Teddington, parish, Middlesex. It is on the Thames, which is tidal as far as Teddington Lock ; pop.23,000.

Te Deum Laudamus (Latin *We praise Thee, O God*), name (from the opening words) of a hymn or canticle in the *English Book of Common Prayer.*

Tees, river forming the boundary between County Durham and Yorkshire ; flows 80m to the N. Sea.

teeth, hard bony structures in the jaws of vertebrate animals. They are adapted to the manner and type of food eaten, e.g. the front teeth of gnawing animals, the hinged teeth of cod and hake.

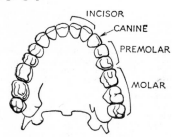

PERMANENT HUMAN TEETH (UPPER JAW)

In man, a tooth comprises a crown and root, the crown being coated with enamel, largely calcium and magnesium. Below is the *dentine*, a form of ivory. In all, a child has 20 milk teeth which give place (about the 7th year) to 32 permanent teeth, 16 in each jaw, the 4 central teeth being *incisors* (chisel-shaped), with a *canine* at each side (called an eye-tooth in the upper jaw) ; then 2 *premolars*, and 3 *molars*. Brushing the teeth to remove decaying matter is supremely important.

Tegucigalpa, *tā-goo-sē-gäl'pä,* inland town and cap., Honduras ; pop.56,000.

Tehran, *tē-rän,* walled but modernised cap., Iran ; noted for carpets and silks ; scene 1943 of a war conference attended by President Roosevelt, Marshal Stalin and Mr Churchill ; pop.699,000.

Teign, *tān,* river, Devon ; flows 30m to the English Channel.

Teignmouth, *-mŭth,* holiday town and port, Devon ; on the estuary of the R. Teign ; noted for china clay.

Tel-Aviv, *tel-ä-vēv',* all-Jewish city on the coast of Palestine, north of Jaffa ; founded *c.*1908 ; planned on modern lines with imposing public buildings, wide streets ; has over 70 industries, great export trade (e.g. hosiery, tailoring, knitted fabrics, silk and cotton goods) ; pop.185,000. It is now the capital of the State of Israel.

telefilm, see BAIRD, SIR J. L.

telegraph and **telephone,** methods of communication between points linked by wires carrying electric current.

The *telegraph* comprises a transmitting end at which electrical impulses are sent by means of a key. By depressing the key (by hand or mechanically) an electric circuit is closed, causing a current to flow through the conducting wire (or cable) to the receiver. By varying the length of the depression the operator sends a series of Morse ' dots ' and ' dashes.' The electric impulses may be very feeble when they arrive at the receiving apparatus, due to the resistance of miles of wire, but they are strong enough to operate a relay, thus closing a local and much more powerful circuit. This controls an electromagnet which, in response to the ' stepped-up ' impulses, controls an inking apparatus with a steadily unrolling strip of paper. The modern multiple method of transmitting messages by Morse is a development of the system invented 1844 by Samuel Breese Morse.

Long-distance telegraph lines are strengthened with frequent relays ; submarine cables, however, may have to carry an el=ctric impulse 4,000m without reinforcement.

The modern telegraph includes the TELEPRINTER, an instrument which transposes electric impulses into typewritten words at the rate of 65 words a minute. The tape-machine is another variation of a telegraphic receiving apparatus.

The *telephone,* invented by Alexander Graham Bell, requires a current along a wire connecting two instruments operated by sound-waves. Lifting the receiver of a telephone closes a circuit, and speaking into the mouthpiece causes the delicate aluminium diaphragm of the microphone to vibrate in response to the sound-waves of speech. The diaphragm moves a piston that presses against small grains of carbon. When the grains are tightly packed they convey an electric current more effectively than when loose, hence the current in the wire is controlled by their compression. After passing along the wire, the electric impulses reach the receiver's telephone, where they are changed to sound waves by a telephone earpiece, actually a small permanent magnet in a coil of wire, this causing a thin iron plate to vibrate.

The AUTOMATIC TELEPHONE is a device for enabling a subscriber to ring, via the exchange, any other subscriber on that exchange. See Diagram on page 653.

In 1951 there were over 5,000,000 telephones in Great Britain.

It is now possible to telephone to ships at sea, the telephone subscriber being linked to exchange, then (possibly) to some other exchange directly linked with a radio station, where the electric impulses caused by his voice are changed into radio impulses which, being picked up at sea, are again converted into sound-waves aboard ship.

It is possible that the present form of telephone will soon be a museum piece, having given place to the VISUAL TELEPHONE, an instrument in which, when you lift the receiver, you will both see and hear the speaker.

See PLATE 60

Tel-el-Kebir, BATTLE OF, *-ke-bēr',* victory by a British force, led by Sir Garnet Wolseley, over Egyptian rebels (led by Arabi Pasha) 1882.

Telemachus, *tē-lem'ä-kŭs,* in old Greek tales, the loving and dutiful son of Odysseus and Penelope.

telephone, see TELEGRAPH AND TELEPHONE

teleprinter, *tel'ē-,* instrument used in modern telegraphic communication (see TELEGRAPH), comprising electric machines, like typewriters, at each end. Each can receive and send messages.

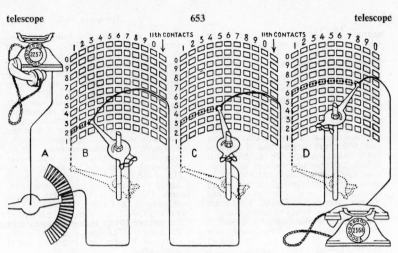

THE AUTOMATIC TELEPHONE

A *line-switch* (*one to each Subscriber*)   B *the first selector*   C *the second selector*
D *the final selector*

Suppose the Subscriber wishes to call 2368.   On lifting the receiver the Subscriber is automatically switched through by his line-switch to a disengaged first selector (B in the diagram) and receives the ' dialling tone.'   On dialling digit 2, two impulses are sent which raise the first selector wipers to level 2.   The wipers then automatically find a disengaged link to a second selector (C) on that level.   The Subscriber then dials digit 3 and three impulses are sent which raise the second selector wipers to level 3.   The wipers again automatically find a disengaged link to a final selector (D) on that level.   The Subscriber then dials digit 6 and the final selector wipers are raised to level 6.   The Subscriber then dials digit 8, which turns the wipers round to number 8 contact of level 6, which is connected to the required Subscriber's telephone.   If the line is free a ringing current is sent to the required Subscriber, and a ' ringing tone ' signal is received by the calling Subscriber.   If the required Subscriber's line is engaged, the ' engaged tone ' signal is sent to the calling Subscriber.   The ' engaged tone ' signal will also be sent if all the ten outgoing links from any level are engaged.   The wipers will then step on the eleventh contacts and send the signal.

By depressing the keys the operator causes the messages not only to be printed on her own machine but to appear on the machine at the receiver end exactly as she sends it.   The ' receiver ' can become ' transmitter ' whenever the operator at the other end stops using the machine, and an answer to her message may be sent immediately. The machine is capable of recording up to 65 words a minute.

telescope, optical instrument for viewing distant objects more distinctly.   There is reason to believe that Roger Bacon (*d* 1294) knew something of the principle of the telescope, but the invention is usually attributed to a Dutchman, though Galileo was probably the first to make practical use of the astronomical telescope.   Kepler, Newton and Herschel were all pioneers in improving the instrument.

The fundamental principle of the working of a telescope is as follows : more or less parallel rays from a distant object are focussed by the objective lens, forming an inverted image.   A second lens, the eyepiece, gives a magnified image, so that the distant object is seen

enlarged.   This is the *refracting telescope* in its simplest form.   To eliminate a blurred image and chromatic aberration (coloured bands), the modern telescope of this type has an eye-piece consisting of two lenses.   Such telescopes are useful in viewing stars and planets, and the fact that the object viewed is seen upside down does not matter.   If adapted for viewing objects only a few miles away, a further lens is employed to re-invert the image.

In the *reflecting telescope* the object lens is replaced by a concave mirror, thus eliminating chromatic aberration at this stage.   The larger the mirror, the more light is gathered from a distant object, hence stars too small or too distant to affect the retina of the human eye become visible in such telescopes.

The largest astronomical telescopes use reflecting mirrors, light being focussed along the instrument from a travelling *coelostat*, which moves by clockwork or electricity in such a way that a chosen star is kept in view in spite of the movement of the earth.   At the Mt Wilson Observatory (California, USA) is a reflecting telescope with a mirror of 100·4in diameter. The telescope weighs 100 tons, and is swung on a split polar axis. Other gigantic telescopes are employed at the Lick and Yerkes Observatories, USA ; but the largest of all is in the Hale Observatory, on Mt Palomar, California. It is a 200in reflecting telescope, 55ft long, and weighing 110 tons. This is housed in a circular and domed building, and has a Pyrex reflector weighing 20 tons. The telescope makes a distant star appear c.640,000 times larger than it appears to the naked eye, and Dr Hubble of Mt Wilson Observatory declares that with it we could see a candle 20,000m out in space, and that through it the moon seems to be only 25m away. Star clusters over 1,500,000,000 light-years distant are now being photographed.

By replacing the human eye with a camera, permanent photographs are obtained ; a telescope may be used in connection with a spectroscope.

television, see BAIRD, SIR J. L.

Telford, THOMAS (1757–1834), Scottish engineer ; constructed the Caledonian Canal ; was responsible for the improvement of c.1,000m of roads in Britain ; humorously nicknamed ' the Colossus of Roads.'

Tell, WILLIAM, hero of 14th c. Swiss folklore, according to which Tell refused to salute the hat of Gessler, bailiff of the Duke of Austria. Condemned to death, he was offered a pardon on condition that he should (with bow and arrow) attempt to shoot an apple placed on his son's head. He succeeded in this. Later he killed Gessler, and raised a rebellion resulting in Swiss independence. The story is the subject of an opera by Rossini.

Tell-el-Amarna, group of ruins near the Nile, 196m from Cairo. Here stood a city built c.3,300 years ago. Excavations have been made by Sir Flinders Petrie and Sir Leonard Woolley.

tellurium, element, Te ; atomic weight 127·61 ; atomic number 52 ; discovered 1798.

temperature, see HEAT ; ZERO

temperature of the body, in human beings is normally c.98·4°F. This is maintained by oxidation of food, and is regulated by a sensitive nerve centre in the brain controlling the capillary blood-vessels and sweat glands.

tempering, process of hardening metal, especially steel, by raising it to a known temperature (sometimes roughly estimated according to the colour the steel assumes) and plunging it into water, or oil. The surface colours are oxides. Quenching when blue gives a very hard but brittle temper for fine cutting edges and springs. Quenching when straw-coloured gives a slightly less hard but less brittle temper suitable for screwdrivers.

temple, building dedicated to the worship of a god or goddess, e.g. ancient Egyptian temples, as at Karnak ; Indian temples, sometimes hewn out of rock, and often fantastically adorned with carvings ; Buddhist temples, as the pagoda at Madura ; Greek temples, as the Parthenon at Athens ; and Roman temples. See PLATES 66, 67

The Jewish temple, built on Mt Moriah, Jerusalem, was a magnificent structure with outer courtyards, and a central holy place where the Ark of the Covenant was kept. Solomon's temple, destroyed by Nebuchadnezzer 586BC, was rebuilt c.520BC. It was again destroyed, being later partly rebuilt by Herod the Great c.20BC, his work being finally swept away by the Romans AD70.

Temple, DR WILLIAM (1881–1944), English churchman, b Exeter. Archbishop of York 1929–42, he was Archbishop of Canterbury 1942. He sympathised with the claims of Labour, and worked for Christian witness and improved social conditions.

Temple, SIR WILLIAM (1628–99), English diplomat ; b London ; sat in the Irish Parliament ; was England's representative at the Hague ; lived at Moor Park, Surrey, where Jonathan Swift was his secretary.

Temple, INNER AND MIDDLE, district of London in the neighbourhood of Fleet Street and the Thames ; was the property 1184–1313 of the Knights Templars. Its church (one of four round churches in England) was built by the Knights Templars in the 12th century. It was severely damaged in World War II.

tempo, see TIME (MUSIC)

tenant, see HOUSE

tench, British fresh-water fish c.18in long ; may weigh 3–4lb. Olive green above, paling to grey below, it has reddish fins.

Tenchebrai, BATTLE OF, tŏnsh-e-brā, fought 1106 in Normandy between Henry I of England and his brother Robert, Henry securing Normandy.

Teneriffe, ten-ĕr-ēf', largest of the Canary Is. ; noted for the Peak of Teneriffe, rising 12,100ft. The cap. is Santa Cruz. The island is noted for tomatoes, bananas, lace and wine.

Teniers, DAVID, ten'yĕrz (1582–1649), Flemish painter. He excelled as a painter of landscapes. His son, David (1619–90), was also a noted artist.

Tennessee, ten-e-sē', central state of USA ; cap. Nashville ; see TENNESSEE VALLEY AUTHORITY.

At Oak Ridge is an atomic energy plant near the hydro-electric power stations of the Tennessee Valley Authority. The plant cost £200,000,000. The town of Oak Ridge has pop.78,000.

Tennessee Valley Authority (usually known as TVA), agency of the USA government with authority since 1933 to develop the Tennessee valley by preventing destructive flooding of the river, controlling navigation, building hydro-electric stations and distributing electricity, taking steps to prevent soil erosion and marketing the produce of the rapidly growing community. The whole plan, one of the most amazing and successful ventures of its kind, has resulted in vastly improved conditions for agriculture and industry, and in increasing the happiness of the people in the area.

Tenniel, SIR JOHN, *ten'yel* (1820–1914), artist *b* London ; noted for his political cartoons in *Punch* and for his illustrations of *Alice's Adventures in Wonderland.*

tennis, game differing from lawn tennis in having complicated rules and a special form of scoring. The amateur needs expert tuition by a coach. Tennis is not to be confused with LAWN TENNIS.

Tennyson, ALFRED (1809–92), poet, born at the rectory, Somersby, Lincolnshire ; educated at Louth Grammar School.

At Cambridge he became the friend and admirer of Arthur Henry Hallam (1811–33), who early showed promise of genius, knew several languages and wrote plays and poems. Hallam died suddenly at Vienna, a tragedy that profoundly shocked Tennyson. Eventually (1850, the year in which he was made Poet Laureate) Tennyson published his long poem *In Memoriam,* a tribute to his friend.

Tennyson was raised to the peerage when 75.

Notable poems are *The Princess* (1847); *Maud,* a poem of love and war ; and the group of stories known as *The Idylls of the King,* i.e. tales of King Arthur and the Knights of the Round Table. Written in blank verse, the *Idylls* are full of noble thoughts exquisitely expressed. His shorter poems include *The Lady of Shalott ; The Lotos Eaters ; Break, Break, Break ; The Brook ; Ode on the Death of the Duke of Wellington ; The Charge of the Light Brigade ; Flower in the Crannied Wall ; The Revenge.* His last poem, *Crossing the Bar,* was sung at his funeral in Westminster Abbey.

As examples of Tennyson's poetry we may note the following :

Now fades the last long streak of snow,
Now burgeons every maze of quick
About the flowering squares, and thick
By ashen roots the violets blow.

In Memoriam

The splendour falls on castle walls
And snowy summits old in story :
The long light shakes across the lakes,
And the wild cataract leaps in glory.
Blow, bugle, blow, set the wild echoes flying ;
Blow, bugle ; answer echoes, dying, dying, dying.

The Princess

And slowly answer'd Arthur from the barge :
The old order changeth, yielding place to new,

*And God fulfils himself in many ways,
Lest one good custom should corrupt the world.*

The Passing of Arthur

tenor, in singing, male voice between bass and alto.

tent, portable shelter, generally of canvas ; may be a bell-tent, i.e. supported by a central pole, the lower edge pegged down in a circle ; square, i.e. having a ridge-pole resting on two uprights ; marquee, a large tent suitable for flower-shows, etc.

terbium, element Tb ; one of the rare earths ; atomic weight 159·2 ; atomic number 65.

Terceira, *ter-sā'rä,* Portuguese island of the Azores ; produces fruits (oranges especially) and grain ; cap. Angra, a flourishing port.

teredo, see MOLLUSCA

Terence (*d c.*159BC), Roman dramatist ; said to have been born at Carthage, and for a time to have been a slave in Rome ; won fame as a writer of comedies with clever plots and excellent characterisation. His plays include *Andria ; Hecyra ; Heauton Timorumenos ; Eunuchus, Phormio* and *Adelphi.*

Note. *Fortis fortuna adiuvat,* i.e. Fortune aids the brave. (*Phormio*)

termites, insects with net-veined wings ; better known as white ants, though they are distinct from true ants. They live underground in tropical lands, lining their tunnels with a hard substance ; and they sometimes build tall cone-like hills popularly called ant-hills. Their communities contain large queens and smaller males, workers and soldiers, the latter having very large heads and jaws. Termites are extremely destructive ; they eat their way through the walls of wooden houses, etc.

tern, see GULL

Terni, *ter-nē,* town, Italy, *c.*50m north-east of Rome ; manufactures munitions and steel ; pop.70,000.

terracotta, unglazed red or yellow earthenware of fine clay.

terrestrial magnetism, see MAGNETISM

Territorials, see ARMY

Terror, MT, extinct volcano (*c.*11,000ft) in Ross I., Antarctica.

Terry, DAME ELLEN (1848–1928), actress, *b* Coventry ; superb in Shakespearean plays.

Terry, FRED (1863–1933), actor, *b* London, brother of Ellen Terry ; excelled as Blakeney in *The Scarlet Pimpernel ;* married the actress Julia Neilson, and was the father of Dennis and Phyllis Neilson-Terry, both successful on the stage.

Terylene, *tĕr-i-lēn',* trade name of a recently invented fibre. Largely made from terethalic acid (derived from coal and oil) and from ethylene glycol, Terylene can be made up into clothes.

Test Act, act 1673 ordering every holder of an office under the English crown to take the sacrament according to the rules of the Church of England, the aim being to eliminate Roman Catholics and dissenters from such offices. See JAMES II

testator, see WILL

Test Match, cricket match played between England and either an Australian, Indian or a S. African team.

tetrarch, *tet-rärk,* originally one of four rulers of a region ; later any minor ruler, especially in Syria, during the Roman occupation, e.g. Herod Antipas.

Tetuan, *te-twän',* cap. of the Spanish Zone, Morocco ; pop.50,000.

Teutoberger-Wald, *toi'tō-bair-gĕr vält,* forested mt. range, NW. Germany ; scene of a victory by the Germans over the Romans AD9.

Teutonic race, race probably of Scandinavian descent, characterised by tall stature, oval face, blue eyes, blond hair and skin, and a narrow nose. The race spread from the region which is now Germany and Scandinavia, and advanced at the breaking up of the Roman Empire into Central, S. and W. Europe. It included Goths, Franks, Angles, Saxons, Jutes, Danes, Norwegians and Normans.

The Teutons lived mostly in village communities ; had kings, loved poetry, and held folk-moots. They were nature-worshippers, their gods including Odin, Thor and Frigg.

TEUTONIC is a sub-family of the Indo-European speech, including Scandinavian, High and Low German, and Gothic, now lost.

Teviot, *tē'vi-ŭt,* salmon and trout river flowing *c.*37m in Roxburghshire to meet the Tweed.

Tewkesbury, *tūks'beri,* agricultural town, Gloucestershire ; noted for its Norman abbey.

Texas, largest state in USA ; has *c.*400m of coastline on the Gulf of Mexico ; much stock is raised ; cap. Austin.

Texel, Netherlands island in the Zuyder Zee.

Thackeray, WILLIAM MAKEPEACE (1811–63) English novelist, *b* Calcutta ; inherited £500 a year as a young man ; became a journalist and editor ; won fame after 1837 with his stories, verses, caricatures and reviews, mixing humour with satire in such writings as *The Yellowplush Papers* ; *The Paris Sketch Book* ; and *The Snobs of England.* He lectured in USA on *The English Humorists* (1852) and again on *The Four Georges.* His wife became insane 1840, four years after their marriage, and for the rest of his life Thackeray lived mostly at the Garrick Club.

It is as the author of *Vanity Fair* ; *Pendennis* ; *The Newcomes* ; *The Virginians* ; and *Henry Esmond* that Thackeray is chiefly remembered. These masterpieces reveal him as second only to Dickens in his portrayal of character and the social life and manners of his day. While Dickens was most successful in drawing characters taken from the lower classes, Thackeray excelled when

laying bare the weaknesses of the upper classes. Though he attacked snobbery ceaselessly, he was, without knowing it, a snob himself, yet warm-hearted and kindly.

Thailand, see SIAM

Thales, *thā'lēz* (640–546BC), Greek thinker, *b* Miletus, Asia Minor, regarded as chief of the Seven Wise Men of Greece. He was the first to break away from superstition, and to attempt a scientific explanation of the universe. He was also a pioneer in abstract and practical geometry, algebra and astronomy, foretelling an eclipse of the sun 585BC. One of the sayings attributed to him is : *Seize time by the forelock.*

thallium, rare metal and element, Tl ; atomic weight 204·39 ; atomic number 81 ; discovered *c.*1862 ; resembles lead.

Thames, *temz,* longest river in England ; rises in the Cotswolds, and flows (via Oxford, Reading, Windsor and London), *c.*250m to the N. Sea. It is tidal as far as Teddington, 80m from the sea.

thane or **thegn,** in Anglo-Saxon England, a person below an earl and above a ceorl, usually a military leader and a holder of land. If a king's thane, he had special privileges. The title disappeared in England soon after the Norman Conquest (1066) but remained (for royal tenants) for some centuries in Scotland.

Thanet, *than'it,* area, Kent, separated from the mainland by the R. Stour.

theatre, *thē'ätĕr* (Greek *theatron,* seeing), building where plays are presented on a stage. The earliest Greek theatres were built about the 6th c. BC ; that of Dionysus (4th c.) was of stone ; all (open to the sky) were more or less semicircular, some seating 20,000 spectators. Roman theatres were somewhat similar.

For over 1,000 years after the fall of Rome no theatres were built in Europe. In England, miracle plays were acted in churches or churchyards. The guilds had movable platforms called *pageants* ; and the secular plays of the 16th c. were sometimes presented in inn-yards. Burbage's Globe Theatre (with which Shakespeare was closely associated) was built *c.*1599 in Southwark, London. Today a theatre may seat several thousand people (the audience), and have an elaborate stage with built-up scenery, drop-curtains and varied lighting effects.

Many countries now have a *national theatre,* usually with State aid for the promotion of the cultural life of the community, e.g. the Théâtre Français, Paris.

By *repertory theatre* (locally often spoken of as ' The Rep '), is meant a theatre with a company of actors and actresses regularly attached to it, a different play being performed at intervals, possibly weekly. Interest in repertory theatres has greatly increased in recent years. The repertory is the opposite of theatres (such as those in the West End of London) where a single play performed by a special company may have a run of a year or more, according to its popularity.

Possibly the finest theatre in Europe is the one opened 1946 at Malmö, Sweden. Its architecture is superb, and it has an auditorium that can be adjusted to seat 400, 800 or 1,200 people.

England's first children's theatre was opened 1947 in London (St Marylebone), the plays being for children between 6 and 12. See PLATE 78

Thebes, *thēbz,* formerly a great city, Egypt, *c.*300m south-east of Cairo ; known to have flourished over 4,400 years ago, and was probably at the summit of its greatness *c.*1600–1100BC, when many of its remarkable temples, tombs and statues, now in ruins, were among the wonders of the ancient world. Today the villages of Luxor and Karnak are on the site.

Thebes, formerly the capital of ancient Boeotia, Greece. It stood *c.*44m from Athens, and was destroyed by Alexander the Great 336BC.

thegn, see THANE

The Hague, *hāg,* seat of the Netherlands government, though the cap. is Amsterdam. The Hague, 2m from the N. Sea, is notable for handsome buildings, bridges, streets shaded with lindens. The industries include copper and lead smelting ; pop.476,000. International conferences are frequently held at the Hague, where is the Palace of Peace. The Hague Tribunal (1899 and 1907) considered reductions in armaments, and here the International Court of Justice meets.

The Helder, fortified port of N. Holland ; pop.34,000.

Theiss, river of Central Europe ; flows *c.*740m to meet the Danube.

Themistocles, *thē-mis'tō-klēz* (*d* 449BC), far-sighted Athenian statesman. By astute political moves he opposed Aristides, and succeeded in carrying out a vast shipping programme in Athens, with the result that when the Persians attacked, they were defeated at the naval battle of Salamis 480BC. It was due to his diplomatic skill that the Spartans united with Thebes to help Athens against the Persians in their triumph at Plataea 479BC.

Themistocles went on to make the harbour of Piraeus, and to build fortifications round Athens, but his wealth and incivility made him many enemies, and finally he found refuge with his former enemies, the Persians. Nevertheless, he laid the foundations . of Athenian sea-power and commerce.

On one occasion Themistocles is said to have declared : ' I never learned how to tune a harp or play upon a lute, but I know how to raise a small and inconsiderable city to glory and greatness.'

On another occasion a man from Seriphus (a tiny island) said to Themistocles : ' If you did not belong to a great city like Athens you would not be famous.' To which Themistocles replied : ' No, it is quite true ; if I had belonged to Seriphus I would never have been famous ; but if you were an Athenian, you would have been no more famous than you are ! '

The Naze, headland on the coast of Essex.

The Needles, group of chalk rocks off the west coast of the I. of Wight.

The Nore, sandbank at the mouth of the R. Thames. The Mutiny of the Nore (disaffection in the British fleet stationed there) occurred 1797.

Theocritus, *thē-ok'ri-tŭs,* 3rd c. Greek poet, probably *b* Syracuse ; author of pastoral poems, hymns, lyrics and epigrams, abounding in exquisite passages. The 30 poems that have come down to us are the *Idylls,* models for Virgil, Spenser and Milton.

Note the following :

'Ες Τροίαν πειρώμενοι ἦλθον 'Αχαιοί.

By trying, the Greeks got into Troy.

theodolite, *thē-od'ō-līt,* instrument largely used by a surveyor, enabling him to measure horizontal and vertical angles with great accuracy. It consists of a small telescope that may be turned horizontally and vertically on graduated circles, and is generally provided with levels and a compass. Angular displacements are read on a micrometer scale.

Theodoric the Great, *thē-od'ō-rik* (*d* 526), King of the Ostrogoths or E. Goths ; became King of Italy after 4 years of war, and ruled wisely for 33 years. He is the hero of many German legends.

Theodosius I, *thē-ō-dō'shi-ŭs* (AD346–395), Roman emperor of the East from 379. Christianity flourished during his reign.

theorem or **proposition,** general statement of a geometrical fact or truth, e.g. *the sum of the angles of a triangle is equal to 2 right angles.* The formal proof of a theorem requires (*a*) a statement of the facts given, (*b*) a statement of the facts to be proved, and (*c*) a logical proof of (*b*) based on the truths given in (*a*). Note that (*a*) is the *hypothesis,* (*b*) the *conclusion.*

therm, practical unit of quantity of heat = 100,000 British Thermal Units (B.Th.U.), or 25,200,000 calories (small); used for measuring consumption of coalgas for domestic purposes, where (*a*) number of therms in 1,000cu.ft of gas of 500 B.Th.U. per cu.ft is

$$\frac{1,000\text{cu.ft} \times 500 \text{ B.Th.U.}}{1,000} = 5 \text{ therms}$$

(*b*) number of cu.ft of gas that will produce 1 therm is

$$\frac{100,000}{500} = 200\text{cu.ft.}$$

See HEAT

thermionics, science concerning the emission of electrons as a result of heat.

thermionic valve, fundamentally important

22 *a*

valve in radio ; consists of a vacuum tube containing practically no air, and having a heated filament as cathode, emitting electrons collected by a metal plate (anode), the flow being controlled by intervening wire mesh electrodes called grids. The earliest valve of this type was the invention of Sir John Ambrose Fleming. A small electrical potential applied to the grid controls releases a relatively large electric current between filament and anode, the energy of which is derived from a high tension supply to the receiver. The valve is thus primarily an amplifier.

thermit or **thermite,** aluminium powder and the oxide of a metal. If ignited with magnesium, great heat and a brilliant white light are produced ; used for welding iron rails.

thermochemistry, *thŭr-mo-,* science concerned with the heat changes that take place in chemical reactions, e.g. the combustion of fuels, or the formation of water-gas when steam passes over white-hot coke.

thermodynamics, *-dī-nam'iks,* science, established by James Prescott Joule, dealing with energy, work and heat. It has much to do with the laws of gases, and has had considerable influence on the development of steam, and other heat-engines.

The two best-known laws of thermodynamics are : (*a*) *There is an exact equivalence between heat and work. If a certain amount of work is used entirely to produce heat, the same amount of heat is always produced, and conversely, when heat is entirely transformed into work the same amount of heat performs the same amount of work* ; (*b*) *Heat cannot be made to flow from a low temperature to a high temperature without expenditure of energy.*

If this Second Law of Thermodynamics were the only operating factor throughout the universe it would mean that the temperature would steadily fall till all the heat reached a uniform low temperature. No heat could then be converted into work and the universe would have ' run down ' like a clock that had not been wound up. Whether there is any active principle that is rewinding it is a matter for speculation.

The mechanical equivalent of heat expressing law (*a*) experimentally and mechanically says that one calorie is equivalent to $4 \cdot 2 \times 10^7$ ergs.

thermo-electric couple, two metals joined together and heated or cooled at one junction, thereby causing an electric current to flow through a suitably arranged circuit. The current thus produced is called thermo-electric current. The principle involved is practically applied in, say, the THERMOPILE, an instrument for detecting and measuring heat radiations. This usually comprises rods of antimony and bismuth. The current generated as a result of heat

(even the small amount radiated by a distant star) is measured by a delicate galvanometer.

thermometer, instrument for measuring temperature ; a glass tube with a very fine bore ending in a bulb filled with alcohol, or more often with mercury. Heat causes the liquid or mercury to expand along the tube, and the amount of this expansion is read off a graduated scale marked in degrees.

Scales of calibration include : (*a*) *Fahrenheit,* an adaptation by G. D. Fahrenheit, a German scientist, of one invented by Sir Isaac Newton ; it shows freezing-point of water as 32°, its boiling-point as 212° ; (*b*) *Centigrade,* showing freezing-point as 0° (zero), boiling-point 100° ; temperatures below zero are minus, e.g. $-12°C$ is 12°C of frost ; (*c*) *Réaumur* (after René de Réaumur, *d* 1757, French scientist) ; freezing-point 0°, boiling-point 80° ; conversion of F to C or C to F is effected by

$$\frac{°F - 32}{9} = \frac{°C}{5}$$

The clinical thermometer, used by doctors, reads 95–110°F, and is so made that the mercury does not run back after the thermometer is taken from the patient. Gardeners use a maximum and minimum thermometer. Exceedingly low temperatures are read off with a hydrogen thermometer ; exceedingly high temperatures with, say, a ROTO-THERM bimetallic thermometer, based on the expansion of iron and aluminium. A common high temperature thermometer is the thermocouple. The platinum resistance type is also used. See HEAT ; PYROMETER

thermopile, see THERMO-ELECTRIC COUPLE

Thermopylae, *thĕr-mop'i-lē,* pass, North Greece, leading to Thessaly ; scene 480BC of the heroic defence made by the Spartans against the Persians. See SIMONIDES OF COS

Thermos flask, see VACUUM FLASK

thermostat, instrument for regulating temperature ; applied especially to gas-cookers, hot water cylinders, boilers and radiators. The principle is that by expanding or contracting, a metal bar or coil regulates the supply of gas or electricity.

Theseus, *thē'sūs,* hero of many old Greek tales ; son of Aegeus, King of Athens ; slew the Minotaur, finding his way out of its lair (the labyrinth) with the aid of a thread given him by Ariadne.

thesis, generally a written work, the result of research by a student or specialist ; especially a study submitted by a candidate for scholastic honours.

Thespis, 6th c. BC Greek poet and dramatist ; founder of Greek drama, and inventor of the prologue ; probably the first to introduce an actor into the choric festivals.

Thessalonians, see THESSALONICA

Thessalonica, *thes-ā-lon-ī'kä,* old name for

Salonica, busy Greek port ; pop. 240,000. St Paul's two letters to the Thessalonians were written to the Christians there *c*.AD52. Modern Salonika, on the Aegean, was a base in World War I for an unfortunate Allied invasion of Bulgaria 1915.

Thessaly, region of ancient Greece between Epirus and the Aegean Sea. Modern Thessaly consists of Larissa and Trikkala.

The Wash, east coast estuary, England, between Lincolnshire and Norfolk ; receives the waters of the Ouse, Nen, Welland and Witham. Since 1947 *c*.12m of new coastline have been added and over 3,000 acres of rich agricultural land reclaimed.

Thiers, LOUIS ADOLPHE, *tyār* (1797–1877), French statesman ; compelled to accept 1871, on behalf of France, the terms of a disastrous peace after the Franco-Prussian War. He was first President of the Third Republic.

thigh bone, see FEMUR

thinking, see BRAIN ; LOGIC ; PHILOSOPHY ; PSYCHOLOGY

third degree, method used by the police in various countries (including USA) when examining accused persons, e.g. questioning for many hours, while depriving them of sleep.

Third Programme, name for a programme broadcast by the BBC since 1946. On the whole it provides somewhat more educational or classical features, e.g. broadcast versions of Greek plays and music not usually heard on the more popular programmes ; it is, therefore, designed for the more discriminating listener.

Third Reich, *rīch*, German for Third Empire, name given to the German totalitarian state under the dictatorship of Adolf Hitler 1933–45, and having only one political party. The ' first German ' Empire was that of Charlemagne. That founded by Bismarck was the second.

Third Republic, name of the period of republican government in France 1871–1941.

Thirlmere, lake of the English L. District. It is in Cumberland, and supplies water to Manchester, 105m distant.

Thirty Years' War, series of religious wars 1618–48, causing intense and widespread suffering in Germany. They began (Bohemia) between Protestants and Catholics. Denmark intervened 1624. Gustavus Adolphus of Sweden joined the Protestants 1630 (killed at Lützen 1632), and (1635) Richelieu supported the Protestants against the Catholic Hapsburgs. The *Treaty of Westphalia* (1648) prevented the unification of Germany for 300 years but guaranteed religious toleration. It also recognised the independence of Holland and Switzerland.

Thisbe, see PYRAMUS

thistle, national emblem of Scotland. The plant (family *Compositae*) has many species including : spear thistle with prickly stem and leaves, a flowerhead with purple florets above a hard ball covered with prickly bracts. Associated with the thistle is Scotland's national motto *Nemo me impune lacessit* (' Nobody who provokes me goes unpunished ' ; or as it has been translated in Scots : ' Wha daur meddle wi me ? ').

Thistle, ORDER OF THE, see CHIVALRY

Thomas, *tom'ăs*, saint and apostle, called Didymus (twin) in Greek ; often referred to as ' doubting Thomas ' because he would not believe in the Resurrection till he had seen Christ (John 20).

Thompson, DOROTHY, *tom'sŭn* (1894–   ), American journalist and radio commentator ; noted for her social work and as a traveller.

Thompson, FRANCIS (1859–1907), poet, *b* Preston ; educated for the RC priesthood, later as a doctor, but suffered extreme poverty and starvation in London. His poems, devotional and full of rich religious imagery, include *The Hound of Heaven.*

Thomson, SIR GEORGE PAGET (1892–   ), professor of physics, son of Sir J. J. Thomson ; associated with the production of the 1945 atom-bomb ; awarded the Nobel prize 1937.

Thomson, JAMES, see ARNE, T. A.

Thomson, SIR JOSEPH JOHN (1856–1940), scientist, *b* Manchester ; was Cavendish professor of experimental physics, Cambridge, 1884–1918. To his remarkable researches we owe the discovery of the electron, the development of the ionic theory of electricity ; awarded the Nobel prize (physics) 1906.

Thoreau, HENRY DAVID, *tho'rō* (1817–62), American naturalist and thinker, *b* Concord, Massachusetts. A great friend of Ralph Waldo Emerson, he wrote several delightful books, including *Walden, or Life in the Woods.*

thorium, see RADIUM

Thornaby-on-Tees, iron-founding and shipbuilding town, N. Yorkshire ; pop. 21,000.

Thorndike, DAME SYBIL (1882–   ), actress, *b* Gainsborough ; famous for her performances in classical plays, e.g. Shakespeare's *Macbeth*, and Shaw's *St Joan.*

Thorne, *thörn*, town, W. Yorkshire ; builds barges and manufactures ropes.

thoroughbred, see HORSE

Thoth, Egyptian god who weighed the souls of the dead.

Thothmes, name of four Egyptian kings of the XVIIIth dynasty (*c*.1540–1411BC). Thothmes III, the Napoleon of his day, defeated the Syrians at Megiddo, and compelled the Assyrians and Hittites to pay him tribute. He built the vast temple of Thebes. His mummified body may still be seen in the museum at Cairo.

Thrace, name given by the Greeks and Romans to a region north of Macedonia. Somewhat mountainous, it is now shared by Greece, Turkey and Bulgaria.

three-ply, see PLYWOOD

Throgmorton, FRANCIS (1554–84), English conspirator ; headed a RC plot to replace Queen Elizabeth by Mary Queen of Scots.

Thrums, see BARRIE, J. M. ; KIRRIEMUIR

thrush, popular name for several perching birds common in Britain, e.g. (*a*) MISTLE THRUSH (*Turdus viscivorus*), resident ; may be 11in long, plumage reddish-brown above, yellowish-white with black triangles on throat and neck ; lays 4–7 eggs (greyish, clouded with brown marks) in April ; usually nests in a tree ; the powerful and sweet song is heard as early as Feb. ; feeds on insects and berries, especially the mistletoe, hence the name ; and (*b*) SONG THRUSH or MAVIS (*Turdus musicus*), resident bird *c*.9in long ; brownish, with white throat mottled brown ; sings nearly all the year ; the nest (usually of grass and moss plastered with mud) is in a thick bush ; lays 4–6 eggs (greenish-blue with a few dark spots).

THE SONG THRUSH

thrust, in mechanics, total force acting on the whole surface of a liquid, i.e. average pressure × area.

Thucydides, *thū-sid'i-dēz* (*d c*.400BC), historian of the Peloponnesian war, a 27 years' fight between Athens and Sparta for supremacy in the Greek world. Little is known of his life. He was probably born in Athens ; had associations with Thrace, where he possessed gold mines ; knew intimately all the famous people of his day.

His failure to save Amphipolis from the Spartans 424BC led to his banishment from Athens. While in exile he wrote his famous history, prefacing it with a survey of ancient Greece. He took pains to be accurate and impartial. He gives dramatic reality to his record by quoting speeches, e.g. the funeral oration of Pericles. He omits all unimportant details, and by masterly analysis reveals the inner meaning of events. His style is always superb.

Thugs, see BENTINCK, LORD WILLIAM CAVENDISH

thulium, element, Tm ; atomic weight 169·4 ; atomic number 69.

thumbscrew, instrument of torture for pressing or breaking the thumb ; much used by the Spanish Inquisition ; revived by the Nazis.

thunder and **lightning**, phenomena still only partially explained. Negative charges of electricity on the upper parts of clouds can be accounted for, but we do not know how positive electricity occurs on raindrops during a moderate shower.

It seems that a thunder cloud receives negative charges in one part, positive in another, and that the accumulation continues until the insulation of the air is broken down by a flash of lightning, often developing 1,000,000 kilowatts, i.e. several times the capacity of the Battersea Power Station. According to George Kimble and Raymond Bush (*The Weather*) there is (*a*) a downward flash (or quick succession of flashes) developing millions of volts ; (*b*) a surge of high-voltage electricity from the earth up the newly-blazed trail ; and (*c*) a current that melts or ignites an object struck. Thunder is the noise of exploding air temporarily heated and therefore expanding. Since sound travels in air about 1 mile in 5 secs., while the light arrives almost instantaneously, we have a simple method of judging the distance of the storm by the interval between sight and sound.

Ferro-concrete buildings are safe during thunderstorms, as the electric discharge is earthed by the iron or steel. Out of doors, avoid high ground, and do not shelter under lofty and isolated trees, especially oaks.

Dr Schonland of S. Africa calculates that lightning is responsible for the natural fixation of nitrogen in the air, say 100,000,000 tons a year, which reaches the earth, thereby enriching plant-life, by solution in rain.

Lightning conductors were invented by Benjamin Franklin 1772. The conductor, consisting of sharp metal points suitably earthed, is fixed to the highest part of a building. A passing thunder cloud produces a discharge of electricity of opposite charge from the conductor, the strength of the electric field near the points becoming great enough to make the air a conductor, hence a stream of opposite charge to that of the cloud, and thus a gradual neutralisation.

Thursday Island, island, belonging to Queensland (Australia), in Torres Straits ; area only 900 acres ; has pearl fisheries.

Thurstan (*d* 1140), Archbishop of York from 1114 ; refused to admit that York was under the authority of Canterbury, thus causing a quarrel involving Henry I and the pope.

thyme, see WILD THYME

thymol, *thī'mol*, mild antiseptic derived from oil of thyme.

thyroid gland, see GLANDS

Tiber, *tī'bĕr*, river, Italy, flows *c*.245m from the Apennines to the Mediterranean, which it enters *c*.15m below Rome. It is navigable for 100m, and brings down much yellowish mud.

Tiberias, *tī-bĕ'ri-as*, town, Palestine. On the shores of the Lake of Galilee, it was named after the Roman Emperor Tiberius ; pop.12,000. It is now included in Israel.

Tiberius, *tī-bēr'i-ŭs* (42BC–AD37), Roman emperor ; succeeded Augustus AD14 ; suspicious and gloomy.

Tibet, see CHINA

tibia, *tib'iă,* front or shin bone of the leg, to the outer side of which is the *fibula.*

ticker, see TAPE MACHINE

ticket-of-leave, see PRISON

tides, periodic rising and falling of the waters of the oceans, due in some measure to the attraction of the sun and in greater measure to that of the moon (actually about twice that of the sun). High spring tides are the result of the combined attraction of the sun and moon (when in a straight line with the earth) ; low neap tides the result of the sun and moon being relatively at right angles.

Actually the time-lag of the moving mass of water is so great that there is low water when the moon is above a given area, high water at places 90° away. The land masses of the earth, ocean depths, also wind pressure cause infinite variations in the tides, a complete theory of which has not yet been given. Rising tides are said to flow, falling tides to ebb.

Tientsin, *tin-tsin',* river port, China, *c.*70m from Peiping ; in Japanese hands for some years after 1937 ; pop. 1,400,000.

Tierra del Fuego, *ti-er-rä del fwā'gō,* group of islands south of S. America, from which they are separated by the Strait of Magellan. Mostly barren, the islands are inhabited by wandering Indians who rear flocks of sheep.

Tiers État, *tyär zā-tä',* French for Third Estate, i.e. the burghers, as represented before 1789 in the Estate of the Realm. In medieval kingdoms the Three Estates comprised the Lords Spiritual (bishops, etc.), the Lords Temporal (the nobility) and the burghers. The common people were not represented.

Tiflis, *tē-fli-ēs',* university town and cap., Georgia, USSR ; pop.520,000 ; noted as a trading centre and for its silversmiths. Now sometimes known as Tbilisi.

It is worth noting that the public baths in Tiflis are heated by the sun's rays directed on water pipes covered with blackened aluminum.

tiger, flesh-eating animal of the cat family ; its body may be 6ft long, with a tail 3ft long ; has reddish-fawn fur paling to white below, with black stripes, its coat being an excellent camouflage in the jungle. It is found in most parts of Central and S. Asia, and though common in India is unknown in Ceylon. It preys at night on cattle and deer, and does not usually attack men. The cubs remain with the parents for three years.

Tigris, *tī'gris,* river, Iraq, rising in the mts. of Kurdistan, and flowing 1,100m to join the R. Euphrates. On its banks are Baghdad, Mosul and the ruins of Nineveh.

Tilbury, town, Essex ; north of the Thames ; has spacious docks and much overseas trade.

tilde, see ACCENT

Tillett, BENJAMIN (1860–1943), Labour leader, *b* Bristol ; organised the Dockers' Union 1887 ; MP 1917–24 and 1929–31 ; chairman of the TUC 1928–29.

Tilsit, *til'zit,* town now in USSR, on the R. Niemen ; manufactures chemicals and machinery ; pop.57,000.

Tilsit, PEACE OF, concluded 1807 between France and the allied Russians and Prussians after the defeat of the Russians at Friedland, Prussia losing certain possessions (including part of Poland), while Napoleon gave Russia a free hand in Sweden and Turkey.

Tiltman, HUGH HESSELL (1897–   ), author and war correspondent, has travelled widely in E. Asia and the Pacific ; joint-author with T. C. Bridges of *Heroes of Modern Adventure.*

TIM, see CLOCK

timbre, see SOUND

timbrel, ancient musical instrument much like the tambourine.

Timbuktu, chief town, French Sudan. On the borders of the Sahara, it is a great trading centre, and the place from which caravans set out for many areas of N. Africa.

time, fundamental in nature which, like space, we all feel we understand but cannot define. Obviously time is measurable only when there is movement, e.g. the sun or the hands of a clock, and movement requires space, so that time and space are closely related. Measuring time is one thing, saying precisely what it *is,* another. A complete agreement about the nature of time may be long delayed.

It is fairly certain that man's first conception of the passage of time was governed by the change of night and day, and by the passing of the seasons. The day and the year are still our units of time. The solar day is the time taken from one noon (when the sun is apparently highest) to the next noon. The solar day varies slightly during the year, and the average (or mean solar) day is the standard we divide into 24 hours, each hour into 60 minutes, each minute into 60 seconds.

The day is, therefore, the time taken by the earth to go round once on its axis. Actually, if the datum point from which the rotation of the earth is checked is the sun there is a small error due to the movement of the earth round the sun during the year, hence our planet does not quite complete a full revolution on its axis in a solar day. The time of complete rotation can only be judged when the stars are used to measure, hence the sidereal day, of great importance in astronomy.

The sun appears to be overhead at the same time only for places on a line of longitude (meridian), i.e. for places north and south of each other. If ' noon ' is occurring in E. England, people in W. England must wait till the earth in its rotation has brought them directly ' under ' the sun before it is true noon for them. If every meridian had its exact proper time there would be confusion ; so, in England, we all set our watches by the meridian that runs through Greenwich Observatory, and such time is called Greenwich Mean Time (GMT). If New York adopted GMT, however, the sun would not be overhead till 5pm, so New York adopts a noon 5 hours later than GMT.

By the INTERNATIONAL DATE LINE we mean chiefly long.180°, though this is actually regarded as curving in the neighbourhood of the Aleutian Is. (N. Pacific) and Fiji (S. Pacific) to enable people living close together on these, and neighbouring islands, to have the same day. Ships crossing the Date Line adjust their clocks, since one side may be, say, Monday, the other Tuesday. At 12 noon GMT the time is :

   21.14 at Adelaide (Australia)
    6.54 at Baltimore
   12.54 at Berlin
   16.51 at Bombay
    8.08 at Buenos Aires
   14.05 at Cairo
   20.00 at Canton
   13.14 at Cape Town
   11.35 at Dublin
   11.47 at Edinburgh
   11.45 at Madrid
   14.40 at Moscow
    7.04 at New York
   21.00 at Osaka
   12.10 at Paris
   19.46 at Peiping
    7.00 at Philadelphia
   12.49 at Rome
    3.49 at San Francisco .
   20.00 at Shanghai
   22.05 at Sydney
   21.00 at Tokyo

The BBC TIME SIGNAL has been 6 pips since 5 Feb 1924, the *last* pip (or dot) giving the exact time. Until recently the pips were the result of closing an electric circuit by the movement of an escape wheel in a pendulum-controlled clock at Greenwich Observatory, and the pip was correct to 1/20th sec. Now a clock governed by a rapidly vibrating quartz crystal is used. The removal of the Observatory to Hurstmonceux does not alter GMT.

time, in music, used : (*a*) for the pace or *tempo* at which the music is to be played, e.g. *allegro moderato*, i.e. moderately quick ; *adagio*, slow ; (*b*) for the TIME-SIGNATURE, expressed as a fraction, and indicating the number of beats in a bar,

e.g. $\frac{2}{2}$, i.e. 𝅝 𝅝 or $\frac{2}{4}$ i.e. 𝅘𝅥 𝅘𝅥

both simple duple ; or simple triple,

e.g. $\frac{3}{2}$ i.e. 𝅗𝅥 𝅗𝅥 𝅗𝅥. The time value of notes in music is based on the semibreve (written 𝅝) = 2 minims (𝅗𝅥) = 4 crotchets (𝅘𝅥) = 8 quavers (𝅘𝅥𝅮 or 𝅘𝅥𝅮𝅘𝅥𝅮 etc.) = 16 semiquavers (𝅘𝅥𝅯 or 𝅘𝅥𝅯, etc.) = 32 demisemiquavers (𝅘𝅥𝅰 or 𝅘𝅥𝅰 or 𝅘𝅥𝅰, etc.). A dot after a note increases its value by half, e.g. 𝅘𝅥. = 𝅘𝅥 𝅘𝅥𝅮 (though there are exceptions) ; a double dot increases its value by a half + a quarter, e.g. 𝅗𝅥.. = 𝅗𝅥 𝅘𝅥 𝅘𝅥𝅮. The breve is rarely used.

time (table of), see WEIGHTS AND MEASURES

' Times, The,' British newspaper founded 1 Jan 1785 by John Walter ; has been the leading newspaper in Britain since 1847. From 1812 it had an exceptionally fine system of gathering foreign news, and printed details of the battle of Waterloo before the government received any particulars of it. It was the first paper to be printed by steam-driven presses. Its most famous editor was John T. Delane (1817–79).

Published at Printing House Square, London, E.C.4, *The Times* (together with its many supplements) remains the world's premier newspaper, its leading articles having great influence on the public and the government.

Time Signal, see CLOCK ; TIME

Timisoaora, *tē-mish-wä'rä*, city, Rumania ; manufactures leather ; pop.90,000.

Timor, *tē-mor* ; *tī'mor*, island of the Malay Archipelago ; area 12,581sq.m, divided into : (*a*) *Portuguese Timor* in the north ; cap. Dilly ; and (*b*) *Netherlands Timor* ; both export coffee, sandalwood and wax.

Timor Sea, shark-infested area of the Indian Ocean, north-west of Australia.

Timoshenko, MARSHAL, *tim-ō-shen'kō* (1895–), Russian general ; People's Commissar of Defence of USSR 1940– 1941 ; had a great part in defeating the Germans in World War II.

Timothy, Christian missionary ; accompanied St Paul in Europe (e.g. Athens, Corinth, Rome), and became bishop of Ephesus. See PAUL

tin, metallic element, Sn ; atomic weight 118·7 ; atomic number 50 ; melting-point *c.*230°C. It is soft and easily hammered into shape. One of the first metals used by man, it was obtained from Britain by the Phoenicians in pre-Roman times ; now it is chiefly derived from the ore known as cassiterite, mined in Malaya, Australia, Bolivia and Britain (especially Cornwall) ; from this it is extracted by roasting, then by smelting in a reverberatory furnace.

A silvery-white metal, tin gradually changes at low temperatures to a powdery form called grey tin. It is much used in alloys, e.g. pewter, solder, etc. ; used as 'silver paper' for wrapping chocolates and cigarettes ; iron coated with tin becomes tin-plate. Much so-called tin is actually tin-plate.

tinder, see FIRE

Tintagel, *tin-taj'el,* coastal village, Cornwall. It has a ruined castle traditionally the birthplace of King Arthur.

Tintern Abbey, ruined Cistercian abbey by the R. Wye, 5m from Chepstow, Monmouthshire ; founded 1131, dissolved 1537.
Read Wordsworth's poem, *Lines Composed a Few Miles Above Tintern Abbey.*

Tintoretto, *tēn-tō-ret'ō* (1518–94), Italian artist, b Venice ; painted huge canvases in the style of Titian and Michelangelo.

Tipperary, *tip-ĕr-ār'i,* midland county, Eire, in the province of Munster ; noted for dairy farming ; cap. Clonmel.

Tippoo Sahib (1749–99), sultan of Mysore, son of Hyder Ali ; fought the British.

Tipton, town near Dudley, Staffordshire ; manufactures iron goods, chemicals, cement and bricks ; pop.36,000.

Tirana, *tē-rä'nä,* cap., Albania ; pop. 31,000.

Tirconaill, see DONEGAL

Tirol, district in Austria and Italy famous for its Alpine scenery. Largely an Austrian province, it is a great tourist centre, and produces wine, silk and wool. The chief town is Innsbruck.

Tirzah, first capital of ancient Israel, and home of the Israelite kings after the division of Solomon's kingdom. The site, certainly 6,000 years old, was unearthed 1946 by Father Roland du Vaux. It is a few miles from Mt Ebal, and west of the R. Jordan.

tit or **titmouse,** British bird with a small body and rather long tail ; varieties include : (*a*) BLUE TIT or TOMTIT, 4½in long ; has blue crown, white cheeks, greenish back, blue wings and tail, white breast with a blue line ; often visits gardens ; nests in trees ; lays

THE BLUE TIT

faintly greenish speckled eggs ; (*b*) LONG-TAILED TIT, one of our smallest birds ; plumage mainly black and white ; found in small flocks in woods ; builds a dome-shaped nest lined with as many as 1,000 feathers ; (*c*) GREAT TIT, has black head with white cheeks, greenish back ; (*d*) MARSH TIT ; (*e*) CRESTED TIT, has black and white crest ; very rare, but found in pine forests in N. Scotland ; (*f*) BEARDED TIT, also rare near the Norfolk Broads ; climbs like a parrot ; (*g*) COAL TIT, brown and white with black head ; feeds on caterpillars and insects.

Titan, *ti'tan,* in old Greek tales, one of a family of giants.

' Titanic,' see SHIPS

titanium, *tī-tā'ni-ŭm,* metal and element, Ti ; atomic weight 47·90 ; atomic number 22. This useful metal is being increasingly used in industry.

Titian, *tish'an* (d 1576), Italian artist ; spent the greater part of his life in Venice. His pictures express the joy of living characteristic of the Renaissance, and are rich in colour, e.g. bright blues and reds predominating in his early works, more sombre colours later.

Titicac'a, S. America's largest lake. Over 130m long, it is between Bolivia and Peru, in a mt. hollow 12,640ft above sea-level. Here steamers may be seen above the clouds.

Tito, MARSHAL (1892–), Croat peasant with a chequered career ; joined the Red Army 1917 ; imprisoned for Communist activity in Yugoslavia ; led underground movement against Germany in World War II ; elected Marshal of Yugoslavia and President of National Liberation Committee 1943 ; Prime Minister 1945 ; allied himself with Stalin but in 1948 stubbornly and successfully resisted Russian attempts to absorb Yugoslavia into the Soviet Union, or at any rate to reduce her national independence to a mockery. By the autumn of 1949 the rift between the two countries was openly acknowledged.

Tito's decision to make a stand against Russia made it inevitable that he should look to the West for military and economic aid : but it was no part of his intention that Yugoslavia should be given a democratic government on Western lines. In private life before the war, Tito's name was Josip Broz.

Titus, *ti'tŭs,* Christian missionary ; accompanied St Paul to Jerusalem. One of the NT books is a letter of Paul to Titus.

Titus, FLAVIUS SABINUS VESPASIANUS (AD40–81), Roman emperor, styled the Magnificent ; captured the Temple and sacked Jerusalem AD70 ; succeeded his father, Vespasian, AD79 ; was one of the most popular of all Roman emperors, except among the Jews.

Tiverton, lace-making town, Devon ; has Blundell's School, founded 1604.

Tivoli, *tēv'ō-lē,* residential town amid fine scenery 18m from Rome. A summer resort of wealthy Romans in ancient times, it was praised by Horace in his poetry.

TNT, short form of trinitrotoluene, a high explosive manufactured by mixing concentrated nitric and sulphuric acids and toluene. The formula is $C_6H_2(CH_3)(NO_2)_3$ or

$$NO_2-C \underset{C}{\overset{C}{\underset{\underset{NO_2}{|}}{\overset{\overset{CH_3}{|}}{|}}} C-NO_2$$

toad, see AMPHIBIAN

toadstool, see FUNGUS

tobacco, plant cultivated in temperate and warmer climates. It grows to a height of about 6ft, and has yellow or reddish flowers, the leaves forming a valuable industrial crop. When the leaves are ripe they are cured, graded, packed tightly into bales and stored in warehouses, where they are left for several years to mature. The tobacco is then ready to be made into cigars, cigarettes or pipe tobacco.

It is popularly believed that Sir Walter Raleigh introduced tobacco into England. In the 17th and 18th centuries, Virginia supplied our limited needs, but in the 19th and 20th centuries we had to import tobacco from Turkey, Rhodesia, etc.

After its introduction, tobacco quickly became popular, and today a vast number of people find it practically indispensable. The cigarette is said to date from *c.*1799. Nicotine, an alkaloid present in tobacco, is poisonous.

Tobago, see TRINIDAD

toboggan, see SLEDGE

Tobruk, town and port on the Mediterranean coast of Libya. At the beginning of World War II it was Italy's chief Libyan naval base, and was the scene of repeated attacks during the N. African campaign. It was besieged Apr–Dec 1941.

Tocantins, *tō-kän-tēns,* river, Brazil ; flows 1,700m to the mouth of the Amazon.

Toc H, see CLAYTON, REV. P. T. B.

toddy, intoxicating drink made from the fermented sap of various palms, especially the toddy palm of India and Ceylon. In Scotland toddy is a mixture of whisky, sugar and hot water.

Todmorden, *tod'mor-den,* town, W. Yorkshire ; on the R. Calder ; has coal mines ; manufactures cotton goods ; pop.18,000.

toga, *tō'gä,* outer garment worn by men in ancient Rome, usually a woollen cloak, 4–5yd long, draped over the tunic, and wrapped round the body so as to fall in folds to the ankles. The toga was forbidden to slaves and foreigners. In the later republic it became a ceremonial garment, emperors wearing a purple embroidered toga.

When a Roman boy was about 16 he discarded his scarlet-bordered gown and put on the black *toga virilis,* indicating that he had reached the age of responsibility.

Togliatti, PALMIRO, *tol-yä'tē,* Italian Communist ; was vice-premier 1944, Minister of Justice 1945–46,

Togoland, see GOLD COAST

Tokyo, cap., Japan ; on Honshu I. ; pop. (1940) 6,779,000. Formerly called Yedo, it has many canals, and is partly on the delta of the R. Sumida. It was almost destroyed by an earthquake 1923, but has since been rebuilt. There are few manufactures, but an important university. It is the residence of the Emperor. During World War II a large part of the city was destroyed by bombs.

tolbooth, *tōl-,* especially in Scotland, temporary shed or tent at a fair where tolls or dues were paid and offenders against the fair regulations detained ; hence tolbooth came to mean the town prison, the best known being that in Edinburgh, which stood near St Giles's church from the 15th c. to 1817, the site now being marked by a heart let into the causeway.

Read *Heart of Midlothian,* Sir Walter Scott.

Toledo, *tō-lē'dō ; tō-lä'thō,* town, Spain ; on the R. Tagus ; has many beautiful and historic buildings, notably the cathedral, and has been famous for swords since Roman times ; pop.25,000.

tolls, see ROADS

Tolpuddle, village, Dorset ; home of six farm workers who, for banding themselves together in order to plead for an increase in wages, were sentenced 1834 to seven years' transportation to Australia, and became known as the Tolpuddle Martyrs. Their example inspired later generations of Trade Unionists.

Tolstoy', COUNT LEO (1828–1910), Russian author and reformer, born on his father's estate at Yasnaya Polyana in the province of Tula, 130m south of Moscow. Coming of a noble family, he received a good education, served in the Crimean War ; disliked Western ideals ; settled on his estate 1861, and was at first

COUNT LEO TOLSTOY 1828–1910

Plate XIII

COLOUR IN PAINTING

As a first step towards fuller appreciation, colour in painting may be considered from several points of view.

(*a*) In so far as the colours in a picture merely depict things seen, just as they might appear to us ' in real life,' we may say they are used *descriptively*. (*b*) At the same time, these colours themselves may give rise to certain emotions and feelings, whether *directly* (as in the case of the proverbial bull made ' angry ' by the sight of a red rag), or *indirectly* (as when, by the association of ideas, a ' warm ' yellow evokes ideas of ' sunshine ' and ' enlightenment ' and ' happiness '). In so far as the colours in question give rise to emotions and feelings (i) directly or (ii) indirectly, we might say that they are used (i) *emotively* or (ii) *evocatively*. In point of fact, the evocative is usually experienced as an overtone of the emotive, or (so to speak) as an additional charge on it ; and in most actual cases it is not possible to draw a clear distinction between the two. In this discussion the word ' emotive ' is to be understood as including the evocative.

Further (*c*), on looking at a particular painting, we may be impelled to say that it contains ' too much red ' or ' too little of that particular yellow ' or that ' this blue doesn't go with that particular green.' Alternatively, we may judge that the total effect of the colours used in this particular picture is ' just too lovely for words.' Though crudely expressed, such judgments show that we are also able to consider the colours in a picture as elements in a formal whole or pattern. The fact that there *is* this wholeness is in itself a source—and to those who value painting and the arts generally chiefly because they enable us to perceive the ' one ' in the ' many,' the chief source—of value. Essentially, this value is *positive* ; and in so far as the colours, by their harmony, their contrast, their balance, their rhythm, help to create it, we may say that the painter has used them *formally*. [*Continued on Plate XVI*

Plate XIV

Plate XV

Plate XVI

COLOUR IN PAINTING—*continued*

Finally, it must be stressed that these ways of considering colour in painting are not exclusive of one another, and that in order to achieve full appreciation it is necessary to combine them.

Plate XIII : ' Hay Harvest ' (*in the Prince Lobkowitz Collection, Raudnitz ; reproduced by permission of the Pallas Gallery*), by Pieter Bruegel (1530–69). Here there is a certain emphasis on description ; but colour is also used emotively (e.g. the glowing foreground, the cool blue distance) and formally (e.g. the bold and essentially simple arrangement in pleasantly contrasting bands of orange, yellow-green, green-grey, blue and blue-violet).

Plate XIV, top : ' Flatford Mill ' (*National Gallery, London*), by Constable (1776–1837). Here, as in Bruegel's picture, the scene itself is highly evocative, and the colours are used largely in order to describe it, but with marked formal emphasis. *Plate XIV, bottom :* ' Chestnut Trees at Jas de Bouffan ' (*in the Minneapolis Institute of Arts ; reproduced by permission of the Soho Gallery, Ltd*), by Cézanne (1839–1906). Here there is a subtle progression of colours (yellow, yellow-green, green-grey and grey-violet) and the emphasis is on colour used formally.

Plate XV, top : ' Les Alpilles ' (*in the Kröller-Müller Museum, Otterlo, Holland ; reproduced by permission of the Pallas Gallery*), by Van Gogh (1853–90). Within a complex formal pattern, the colours themselves have violent emotive force. *Plate XV, bottom :* ' Cornfield and Cypresses ' (*Tate Gallery, London*), also by Van Gogh. Here the colours are still strongly emotive, but they are used more descriptively, and also more formally, than in ' Les Alpilles.'

Plate XVI : ' Fuji above the Lightning ' (*British Museum*), by Hokusai (1760–1849), the Japanese master. He does not depict, he *evokes*, a scene of forbidding grandeur. The colours he uses are deeply emotive, his use of them severely formal.

intensely happy with his wife (Sophie Behrs), although later they quarrelled and were very unhappy.

His life falls mainly into two divisions (*a*) the period in which he was content to enjoy the best himself, and share it with his family ; and (*b*) the later period in which, ashamed of living to apparently little purpose, he strove to find a new way of life based on universal love, on the belief that the kingdom of God is within us, and that greed and force must be abolished. The benevolent landlord and contented husband thus became an idealistic reformer.

Tolstoy's many books deal with social matters, non-resistance, religious principles and his own individual interpretation of Christianity, themes which appear in his plays and short stories ; but he is most famous for two of his novels : (*a*) *War and Peace* (1866), a story of the Napoleonic wars, having hundreds of characters, all intensely alive, a masterly revelation of his belief that true success and failure depend on loyalty to an inner truth ; (*b*) *Anna Karenina* (*an'ä kären'yi-nä*) (1877), depicting the soul-struggle between passion and duty, its characterisation perhaps even superior to *War and Peace*.

Tolstoy, great-hearted and with a giant intellect, was the victim of his own emotions. He stirred the world, but he remained unpractical. He lived simply, toiling in his fields, renounced wealth and wore peasant dress.

toluene, *tol'ŭ-ēn*, hydrocarbon, $C_6H_5.CH_3$, found in coal-tar ; used in manufacturing drugs, dyes and TNT.

tomahawk, hatchet-like weapon of some N. American Indians ; had a horn, stone or iron head with a wooden handle.

tomato, trailing or climbing plant (family *Solanaceae*) with a soft stem, winged leaves, and a red fruit of considerable size when cultivated ; comes from S. America ; introduced into Britain 1596.

Tomlinson, HENRY MAJOR (1873–), English writer with a fine prose style ; author of exquisite essays and many sea-stories. His books include *All Our Yesterdays* ; *Out of Soundings* ; *The Wind is Rising* ; and *The Turn of the Tide*.

Tomsk, town, Siberia (USSR) ; on the trade-route to China ; pop.150,000.

ton, *tŭn*, measure of weight = 20cwt ; 2,240lb (long ton) ; 20 centals, each of 100lb in the short ton, i.e. 2,000lb. The long ton = 1·015 metric tons or 1,016·6 Kilograms ; the short ton = 0·9072 metric tons or 907·2 Kilograms. A shipping ton is 40cu.ft of goods ; a ship's displacement ton is 35cu.ft.

Note, a ton of water is 35·943 cu.ft, i.e. 224 gallons.

Tonbridge, *tŭn'brij*, town, Kent ; on the Medway ; noted for its public school founded in the 16th century.

Tonga Islands, see FRIENDLY ISLANDS

tongue, *tŭng*, muscular organ connected at its base with the *hyoid bone, epiglottis,* the soft palate, and the *pharynx* ; enables man and the higher animals to masticate food and swallow it, and has delicate *papillae* in its mucous membrane which are organs of taste, those near the front detecting sweet tastes, those at the back bitter ones. In man the tongue is important in forming sounds.

Tonic Sol-fa, scientific method of writing music with letters, especially useful for teaching children to sing at sight. First used, in a simple form, by Elizabeth Glover of Norwich, it was perfected and successfully popularised by a Yorkshireman, John Curwen (1816–80).

tonnage and **poundage,** *tŭn'ij,* duties levied 1347 and 1373 at English ports, the revenue being for defence ; claimed and levied 1628 by Charles I without the consent of Parliament ; granted to Charles II by Parliament 1660 ; abolished 1787 in favour of customs and excise.

tonnage (of ships), see SHIPS

tonsils, small almond-shaped masses in the membrane between the mouth and the *pharynx*. Their function is to serve as germ-filters. Should the tonsils become inflamed or septic, they serve, not as germ filters, but to encourage germs and are therefore better removed. Inflammation of the tonsils is tonsillitis. *Adenoids,* often associated with tonsils, are an overgrowth of gland-like tissue behind the nose and throat, which causes somewhat muffled speech, breathing through the mouth and snoring during sleep— they too are better removed if at all troublesome.

tonsure, ceremonial shaving of the top of the head, practised by some orders of RC priests and monks. The idea is to distinguish clergy from laymen.

topaz, *tō'paz,* yellow, green, blue or red gem-stone found in gneiss and granite, some of the finest specimens coming from USSR and Brazil ; actually crystalline alumina.

Topeka, *tō-pē'kä,* cap., Kansas, USA ; manufactures textiles and machinery ; pop.68,000.

tor, pillow-shaped rock or peak sometimes found in weathered granite regions, notably on Dartmoor.

tormentil, dainty heath and woodland plant, family *Potentilla* ; each small 4-petalled yellow flower has its own stalk ; the compound leaves have 3 leaflets and 2 stipules.

tornado, *tor-nā'dō,* destructive whirlwind, usually accompanied by a dark, funnel-shaped thunder cloud, the ascending vortex of wind travelling at 20–40mph. Tornados are especially frequent in the Mississippi and Ohio regions of USA. A tornado at sea causes a waterspout.

Toronto, city and cap., Ontario, Canada ; on the coast of L. Ontario. The chief industries include printing and publishing and, most important, meat-packing. A handsomely built city, Toronto is a

great banking and railway centre, and
has much shipping ; pop.697,000.

torpedo, weapon of war fired from a ship,
submarine or aircraft, and aimed at an
enemy vessel. It is in the form of a long
metal tube with high explosives in its
' war-head,' behind which is powerful
machinery governed by controls so that
speed, depth and direction may be
accurately adjusted beforehand. The
Whitehead torpedo (invented *c.*1866 by
Robert Whitehead, born in Lancashire
1823, *d* 1905) is the standard pattern,
though modern torpedoes are now much
more formidable, e.g. the Mark II,
which is 21in in diameter. With a range
of 15m, this is driven by compressed
air, develops 250hp ; has a balance
chamber, and is gyroscopically self-
controlled.

Torpedo bombers of the Fleet Air
Arm use 18-in torpedoes.

The so-called homing torpedo (designed to correct its own course) is now
beyond the experimental stage. It is
known also as the acoustic torpedo.

Torquay, *tör-kē´,* popular holiday resort on
the S. Devon coast ; overlooks Tor
Bay ; has a mild climate ; pop.46,000.

torque, see TORSION

Torquemada, THOMAS DE, *tör-kä-mä´thä*
(1420–98), Spanish inquisitor, *b* Valladolid ; revived the Inquisition for the
torture and execution of heretics. He
is believed to have condemned 2,000
victims to the stake, and was responsible
for persecuting Jews, 160,000 of whom,
it is said, fled from the country, causing
its financial ruin.

Torrens, shallow salt lake, S. Australia.
It is *c.*130m long, but is often almost dry.

Torres Strait, *tör´ez,* channel, *c.*90m wide,
between Queensland (Australia) and
New Guinea.

Torres Vedras, *tör´rezh vä´thräsh,* town,
Portugal, *c.*25m north of Lisbon ;
scene of Wellington's defence 1810 of
fortifications dug across a narrow
isthmus.

Torricelli, EVANGELISTA, *tör-rē-chel´lē*
(1608–47), Italian scientist ; assistant to
Galileo ; famous for his discovery 1643
of the principle of the barometer.

torsion, *tör´shon,* in mechanics, strain
produced by twisting a thin wire or bar.
If, say, a wire is twisted by a force
(' couple '), the torque (or twist) is proportional to the moment of the force ;
and the angle through which the wire
twists varies directly with the length of
the wire multiplied by the force, and
inversely as the 4th power of the radius
multiplied by a constant depending on
the material of which the wire is made.
Quartz, glass and steel will suffer considerable torsion and return to normal,
though glass does not completely recover at once. Lead does not recover
after twisting.

Torsion bar springing is being used
now on motor-car suspension systems.

tortoise, *tör´tŭs,* land reptile with part of

THE TORTOISE
A popular garden pet

the skeleton forming an outside cover
(*carapace*) into which the limbs and
head may be retracted ; has gums of
horn in place of teeth ; feeds mostly
on vegetable matter. Varieties in S.
Europe are from 6–10in long, and have
yellow and black carapaces. The giant
tortoises of the Galapagos Is., and other
islands of the Pacific, may live for over
125 years.

Most so-called tortoise-shell actually
comes from TURTLES, the sea variety of
the tortoise. These have feet modified
to act as paddles. They live entirely in
water except when laying eggs in sand.
The green turtle (used for turtle soup)
belongs to the tropics.

torture, pain deliberately caused as punishment for a prisoner, or to make him
confess ; much used by the Spanish
Inquisition when dealing with heretics ;
frequently employed in England in the
15th c., though never sanctioned by
English law, and declared illegal 1628.
Torture was revived in Germany and in
German occupied countries by the Nazis.
Forms of torture included thumbscrew,
rack, boot and mutilations.

Tory, old-fashioned name for the Conservative or Unionist party in England
and Wales or Scotland.

Toscanini, ARTURO, *tōs-kä-nē´nē* (1867–
), Italian, *b* Parma ; conductor of
the orchestra at La Scala Opera House,
Milan 1898–1908, later of the New York
Philharmonic Society. He returned to
Milan 1946.

Tostig (*d* 1066), Anglo-Saxon earl, son of
Earl Godwin and brother of Harold II.
Outlawed for his harsh government of
N. England, he joined Harold Hardrada
in an invasion of Yorkshire 1066, and
was slain at Stamford Bridge.

totalisator, nicknamed the 'tote,' automatic
system of registering bets on horse and
dog races, and of calculating the odds
on winners ; introduced into Britain
1929. See GAMBLING

totalitarian state, nation governed by a
single party or group under a dictator,
and having no means of voicing the
political views of other parties or
groups ; e.g. Nazi Germany, Fascist
Italy. See FASCISM ; NAZISM ; POLITICS

' **tote,**' see TOTALISATOR

totem, usually an animal or plant venerated,
and sometimes worshipped, by primitive
tribes in Africa, America and Australia.
In the totem the life or spirit of the tribe

is thought to be indwelling. Some tribes regard themselves as descended from their totem, hence a totem kinship, and a refusal to kill or eat the totem. Many set up totem poles with grotesque carvings. Totemism is often associated with magic.

toucan, fruit-eating bird of Brazil, related to the woodpeckers ; notable for its light but very large curved bill which is usually gaily coloured.

touch or **tactile sensation,** one of the senses. In man it is most highly developed at the tip of the tongue.

Toulon, *too-lön'*, Mediterranean naval base, France ; manufactures lace and wine ; pop.150,000 ; scene of the scuttling of the French fleet November 1942 during World War II.

Toulouse, *too-looz'*, university city, France ; on the R. Garonne. It is served by railways and canals, and is notable for its cathedral ; pop.213,000.

Tourcoing, *toor-kwan'*, town, on the Belgian frontier of France ; manu-

factures textiles ; population 79,000.

tournament, in the Middle Ages, a mock battle between mounted men ; grew in popularity in France and England from the 11th c., and was at its height in England in Henry II's reign. In single combat one knight tried to unhorse another with his lance, and sometimes two bodies of knights attacked each other. By the 16th c. tournaments had degenerated into pageants. For a vivid description of a tournament in Richard I's day, read Sir Walter Scott's *Ivanhoe.*

Tours, *toor*, city, France ; on the R. Loire ; manufactures silk and woollen goods ; notable for its Gothic cathedral; pop.84,000.

Tower Hill, see LONDON

Tower of London, THE, see LONDON

Tower, PRINCES IN, see EDWARD V

town planning, i.e. *planning* rather than (as so often in the past) allowing a town to grow in a haphazard manner ; involves carefully considered lay-out, wide streets, parks, a centralised shopping district, control of architecture so that ugliness and bad building are avoided, provision of a green belt or of easy access to the country, and of ample light and air. Care is taken that workers' homes are within reasonable distance of their work, and that factories (as far as possible) are grouped together and made healthy and attractive.

    A pioneer in town planning was Sir Ebenezer Howard (1850–1928), an Englishman inspired by the American, Edward Bellamy, whose book, *Looking Backward,* is the story of Boston in the year AD2000. Bellamy's vision of a fairer and happier city gave Howard his life's mission, prompting him to write *Garden Cities of Tomorrow,* from which came the garden cities of (*a*) LETCH-

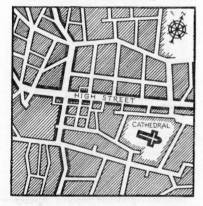

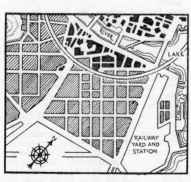

TOWN PLANNING

(Above, left) sketch-plan of the old town of Winchester, built on the remains of a Roman Camp. (Below, right) sketch-plan of a section of a modern garden suburb of Antwerp. (Below, left) sketch-plan of Lucerne, which shows two distinct types of planning—ancient and modern. The old town is within the circle.

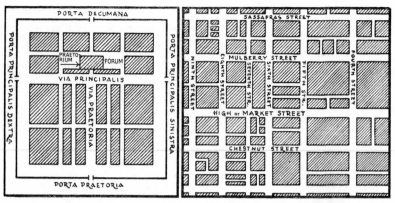

TOWN PLANNING
(left) *Plan of a typical Roman Camp*
(right) *Sketch plan of modern Philadelphia, U.S.A.*

WORTH, begun 1904 ; set amid lovely Hertfordshire scenery 34m from London; and (*b*) WELWYN (1919), also in Hertfordshire and 25m from London ; now noted for its film studios.

Howard did more : He roused men and women to demand better housing conditions, resulting in the Town Planning Acts 1909 and 1932. Since then most cities have begun turning themselves inside out, i.e. people have left the old houses and narrow streets and gone to live on the outskirts, where many new building estates have been successfully planned by architects and others imbued with a desire to ensure the health and happiness of the community. Devastation caused by bombing during World War II gave those responsible for town planning a unique opportunity to carry out bold rebuilding schemes, e.g. those of London, Hull and Coventry.

Something of what can be done by town planning on a small scale may be seen at Bournville, a Worcestershire village planned 1895 by George Cadbury ; New Earswick, near York, built by Joseph Rowntree ; and Port Sunlight, Cheshire, laid out 1888 by Lord Leverhulme.

The tendency today is to build towns with a pop. not exceeding 60,000 ; and the Reith Committee (1946) recommends new towns amid green fields, e.g. at Stevenage, Hemel Hempstead and E. Kilbride (Scotland). The Ministry of Town and Country Planning was created 1943, and the Act of 1947 made counties and county boroughs the local planning authorities.

Read *Town Planning*, Thomas Sharp ; *Living in Cities*, Ralph Tubbs ; *The Anatomy of the Village*, Thomas Sharp ; *Town and Country Tomorrow*, G. Boumphrey (Nelson).

Townsville, *townz'vil*, port on the north-east coast of Queensland, Australia ; pop.37,000.

Towton, village in Yorkshire, scene 1461 of the defeat of the Lancastrians by the Yorkists.

Toynbee, ARNOLD (1852–83), English reformer ; lectured on industrial and social problems ; associated with Toynbee Hall (1885), the first educational and social settlement in E. London.

Trabzon, -*zōn'*, port, Turkey ; formerly Trebizond ; pop.33,000.

trachea, see LARYNX ; LUNGS

tractor, power unit for haulage, especially motor tractors used on farms and by contractors ; may have metal, rubber-tyred wheels, or caterpillar track.

Trade, BOARD OF, British government department concerned with trade and commerce ; deals with industries, manufactures, export and import ; development.

Trade Union Congress, see TRADE UNIONS

trade unions, associations of workers formed for the purpose of securing good working conditions and adequate rates of pay. Such associations grew out of loose combinations of workers in the 18th c. In spite of stern Combination Acts (e.g. that of 1800) these organisations expanded in the 19th c., such inhuman prosecutions (in the name of the law) as those meted out to the Tolpuddle Martyrs (1834) serving rather to strengthen than to weaken the cause of unions. Terrible working conditions during the 19th c. Industrial Revolution fostered the growth of trade unions, hence the Amalgamated Society of Engineers (known as the ' new model '). This accumulated large funds, some of which were devoted to ' friendly benefits,' e.g. sick pay and pensions for members.

From 1871 (when the Trade Union Act apparently gave full legal status to trade unions) to 1913 a battle for full freedom was fought, e.g. the Taff Vale judgment (1901), which made trade unions liable for damage caused by strikes, a disability removed by the Trade Disputes Act (1906) and the Osborne Judgment of 1909. The Trade Union Congress (TUC), founded 1868 (most other unions being now affiliated), called the General Strike 1926, which brought the economic life of the country to a temporary standstill. A Trade Unions Act was passed (1927) declaring a general strike illegal and making it difficult for Trade Unions to collect funds to be used for political purposes. In 1946 this act was repealed, and it has still to be decided whether a general strike is legal or not.

The pressure exerted by the British Trade Union movement has been responsible for great improvements in the living conditions of British workers and their families, and it has been partly responsible for the redistribution of the national income in favour of lower-income groups which makes it probable that in future government action to check unemployment may be more effective than it has been in the past. The Trade Unions in Britain have grown up in circumstances somewhat different from those by which they are now surrounded. It remains to be seen whether a movement which came into existence in order to extract concessions from independent employers will successfully adapt itself to the structure of a nationalised economy. See CLOSED SHOP

trade winds, see ATMOSPHERE

Trafalgar, BATTLE OF, *trä-fal'gĕr* ; *traf-al-gär'*, naval battle fought as a consequence of Napoleon's determination to invade England. This meant ferrying troops across the English Channel, which was constantly patrolled by the British fleet. Napoleon's plan was to draw off our ships by sending a squadron, commanded by Admiral Villeneuve, towards the W. Indies, with orders (*a*) to entice our fleet to pursue, (*b*) to hurry back to protect the little ships in which the invading French soldiers were to cross the Channel. (*a*) was successful ; Villeneuve with 33 French and Spanish ships, and 2,640 guns, lured our warships west, but on the way back he was challenged off Cape Trafalgar (south-west coast of Spain) by Nelson, with 27 ships and 2,138 guns. Nelson's plan was to split the enemy into three formations, his flag-ship *Victory* leading one attack, Admiral Collingwood, in the *Royal Sovereign* leading the other.

The signal for battle was given soon after 6am 21 Oct 1805, but the first shot was not fired till noon. The famous signal, *England expects that every man will do his duty*, was given with 31 flags. The battle, brief but furious, ended in utter defeat for the French, but Nelson was fatally wounded.

The victory put an end to Napoleon's hopes of invading England, made the French powerless at sea for the rest of the war, and left the British navy without a rival in the world.

Trafalgar Square, see LONDON

traffic lights, see ROADS

tragedy, see DRAMA

Traitor's Gate, see LONDON

Trajan (AD53–117), Roman emperor. A Spaniard born near Seville, he won distinction as a soldier ; succeeded Nerva AD98, and proved one of the ablest of all Roman rulers. Though he tried to suppress Christianity, he did not persecute Christians ; he administered the empire wisely, and extended it beyond the Danube into Dacia (now Rumania), also into Armenia and Assyria.

trans-Atlantic flight, see AVIATION

Transfiguration, incident in the life of Christ when (according to Matthew 17, Mark 9 and Luke 9) Christ appeared in glory in company with Moses and Elijah in the presence of Peter, James and John.

transformer, electrical device, similar to the induction coil, for stepping up or down in voltage an alternating current without changing the frequency.

The transformer consists of a primary coil wound together with a secondary coil and a laminated soft iron core. The input is connected across the primary coil, and the output is taken from the secondary coil. If the secondary winding has *more* turns than the primary, the voltage will be stepped up ; if the secondary winding has *less* turns than the primary, the voltage will be stepped down.

Transformers are much used since it is more economical to carry current long distances at high voltage than at low, transformers enabling, say, a current of one ampere at 130,000 volts to be stepped down for domestic and other use to one of 650 amperes at 200 volts.

transit of Venus, see ASTRONOMY

Transjordan, see PALESTINE

transport, see ROADS

transportation, system of sending convicted criminals abroad to live and work for a number of years or for life. British convicts were sent to work on the plantations in N. America in Charles II's day. After the War of American Independence English convicts were transported to Botany Bay, Australia. England abolished transportation 1853, but the system continues in France, where certain types of convicts are sent to Devil's Island and other penal settlements overseas.

transubstantiation, see ROMAN CATHOLIC CHURCH

Transvaal, see UNION OF SOUTH AFRICA

Trapani, *trä'pä-nē*, handsome and busy port, Sicily ; exports cereals and olives ; pop.64,000.

trapezium, see QUADRILATERAL FIGURE

Travancore, *trav-an-kör'*, state in SW. India ; associated with the Madras Presidency ; pop. (chiefly Hindus) *c.*6,070,000.

trawler, vessel, now usually a small steamer, used in trawling, i.e. fishing with a large net, especially for cod, plaice, turbot, whiting, sole, haddock, ling and skate. In war trawlers have given fine service, as mine-sweepers, in clearing minefields. See PLATES 13, 14.

treadmill, wheel turned by treading with the feet ; said to have been invented by the Chinese, and used by them for drawing water for irrigation ; later employed as punishment in some British prisons, but discontinued *c.*1900.

treason, generally regarded as an act of betrayal, high treason being disloyalty to the reigning sovereign, an act of rebellion.

Under English law, treason was punishable by hanging and disembowelling. In 1715 this barbarous practice was introduced also into Scotland. Since 1870 the punishment has been death by hanging.

Treasury, British government department responsible for managing national financial affairs, and also for preparing the annual statement of revenue and expenditure known as the Budget. The Treasury has to estimate future expenditure, find ways and means of raising the money required, the official chiefly concerned being the Chancellor of the Exchequer, though the nominal head of the department is the First Lord of the Treasury, who is usually the Prime Minister.

Methods of raising money include taxation ; treasury bills, i.e. documents issued in return for money borrowed on short-term loans at low rates of interest ; treasury bonds, i.e. securities for money borrowed by the Treasury, usually for five years, and generally (but not always) repayable at par. The Treasury is also responsible for the issue of treasury notes, i.e. currency notes for £1 and 10s, first issued 1914 in place of sovereigns and half-sovereigns, but replaced 1928 by notes for the same amounts issued by the Bank of England, over which the Treasury has control, and the nationalisation of which was accomplished by the Labour government of 1945. The expenditure of other government departments are all supervised by the Treasury.

treaty, formal agreement between two or more governments ; may conclude a war ; give mutual promises to stand by each other if one of the signatories is attacked ; establish mutually beneficial trade and commercial arrangements.

Treaty of London, see WORLD WAR I

treaty-port, name given to ports in China opened to British trade after the Opium War 1840–42, e.g. Hong Kong, Canton, Amoy, Foochow and Shanghai.

Trebizond, see TRABZON

Tree, SIR HERBERT BEERBOHM (1853–1917), actor and theatre-manager, *b* London ; immensely popular in Shakespearean plays, and also in modern productions.

tree creeper, British climbing bird, the common variety, *c.*5in long, being chiefly brown and white in colour ; has a long, curved beak with which it picks insects from the bark of trees.

THE TREE CREEPER

tree pipit, see PIPIT

trees, with shrubs, are regarded by the botanist as plants. Some live over 1,000 years, e.g. oaks, giant redwoods of California, etc. They yield timber, cellulose, medicines, dyes and food, so that it is not surprising that on a tree in a Spanish park are these words :

Ye who pass by and would raise your hand against me, hearken ere you harm me. I am the heat of your hearth on cold winter nights ; the friendly shade screening you from the summer sun ; and my fruits are refreshing draughts quenching your thirst as you journey on.

I am the beam that holds your house, the board of your table, the bed on which you lie, and the timber that builds your boat. I am the handle of your hoe, the door of your homestead, the wood of your cradle, and the shell of your coffin.

Harm me not.

Trees may be (*a*) deciduous (shedding their leaves in the autumn), e.g. oak and beech ; (*b*) evergreen (never without leaves), e.g. holly. Coniferous trees (cone-bearing) are almost all evergreens, e.g. pines, firs and yews ; all yield resin, turpentine and pitch.

The planting of trees is more necessary now than ever. Forests have a noticeably beneficial effect on climate ; tree products (especially cellulose from the soft-woods) are in increasing demand. The care of trees is the concern of *Men of the Trees,* a society founded in Kenya (E. Africa) 1922, and in Britain 1924, by Richard St Barbe Baker.

Read *Trees, Shrubs, and How to Grow Them,* W. H. Rowe, and see PLATES 29, 30

Trelawny, SIR JONATHAN (1650–1721), churchman, *b* Cornwall ; Bishop of

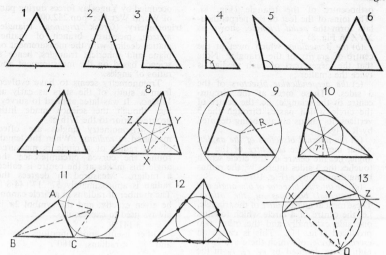

Diagram of the triangles explained in the text

Bristol 1685. His opposition to the sale of indulgences led to his imprisonment by James II, and (it is said) to the writing of the song *And Shall Trelawny Die?*

Trent, river flowing *c.*120m from Staffordshire to the Humber.

Trent or **Trento,** town once in Austria, now in Italy ; on the R. Adige ; scene of the RC Council 1545–63.

Trenton, cap., New Jersey, USA ; noted for pottery ; pop.125,000.

trephine, *trē-fīn'*, surgical instrument for cutting a hole in the skull to perform an operation on the brain ; also the operation itself.

Trevelyan, GEORGE MACAULAY, *trē-vel'yan* (1876–   ), historian, author of several books on Garibaldi ; *Life of John Bright* ; *British History in the Nineteenth Century* ; and (most important of all) his *History of England* (1926), a masterly study, and *English Social History* (1946).

Trevithick, RICHARD, *trev'i-thik* (1771–1833), inventor, born in Cornwall ; greatly improved steam-engines, being the first to ally steam to locomotion successfully.

trial, in law, examination of a prisoner before a judge and jury. In England the case is called, the jury empanelled (i.e. enrolled), and the counsel for the prosecution opens with a speech explaining the whole matter, after which he calls various witnesses, and examines them by asking questions. The plaintiff's counsel then cross-examines the witnesses in an attempt to get facts in favour of his client. The counsel for the prosecution may then re-examine the witnesses, as also may the plaintiff's counsel. Then the defending counsel opens his case, calling on witnesses in a similar manner. Finally, the judge sums up the case, and directs the jury to the salient points, after which the jury (which may or may not retire) gives its verdict and the judge pronounces sentence.

In Scotland there are usually no opening speeches.

triangle, in geometry, etc., a plane figure bounded by 3 straight lines, all the angles totalling 180° or 2 right angles. If the triangle is denoted by A B C, then *a, b, c* are the sides opposite the angles A, B, C.

Names given to triangles on account of their *sides* are :

(*a*) *equilateral,* with 3 sides equal (Fig. 1)

(*b*) *isosceles,* with 2 sides equal (Fig. 2)

(*c*) *scalene,* with 3 unequal sides (Fig. 3)

Names given to triangles on account of their *angles* are :

(*d*) *right-angled,* with one right angle (Fig. 4)

(*e*) *obtuse-angled,* with one angle obtuse (Fig. 5)

(*f*) *acute-angled,* with all angles acute (Fig. 6)

The side opposite to (or *subtending*) the right angle in Fig. 4 is called the *hypotenuse* (see PYTHAGORAS) ; the *perimeter* is the sum of the sides ; an *altitude* is a line drawn from a vertex (or apex) perpendicular to the opposite side ; a *median* is a line joining a vertex to the middle point of the opposite side (Fig. 7).

Concurrent lines of a triangle are lines which pass through a common point, and we may note especially :

(*a*) *the 3 altitudes,* which meet at the

orthocentre of the triangle (Fig. 8). (The joins of the feet of the perpendiculars form the *pedal triangle*, shown as XYZ in Fig. 8) ;

(*b*) *the 3 medians*, which meet at the centre of gravity of the triangle. Note that the larger part of each median is twice the smaller ;

(*c*) *the perpendicular bisectors* of the 3 sides. These meet at the circumcentre of the triangle, i.e. the centre of the circle which passes through the 3 vertices, its radius always being denoted by R (Fig. 9) ;

(*d*) *the internal bisectors of the angles*, which meet at the *in-centre* of the triangle, i.e. the centre of the circle which touches the 3 sides internally, the radius being denoted by *r* (Fig. 10) ;

(*e*) *the internal bisector of one angle and the external bisectors of the others*. These meet at an *ex-centre* of the triangle, i.e. the centre of a circle which touches one side externally and the other two produced (Fig. 11). This is called an *escribed circle*, of which there are 3, the radii being denoted by r_1, r_2, r_3 in the angles BAC, ABC, BCA respectively.

Note also the *nine-points' circle* (Fig. 12), i.e. the circle which passes through (i) the mid-points of the 3 sides of a triangle, (ii) the feet of the altitudes, and (iii) the mid-points between the 3 vertices and the orthocentre. The centre of the nine-points' circle is midway between the cicumcentre and the orthocentre of the triangle, and its radius is half the radius of the circumscribed circle, and therefore $= \dfrac{R}{2}$.

Note also *Simpson's Line* : If perpendiculars X, Y, Z be drawn from any point O on the circum-circle of a triangle to the 3 sides, the feet of the perpendiculars are in a straight line (Fig. 13). This is a notable theorem on *collinearity*.

Trichinopoly, town, Madras Presidency, India ; noted for its Hindu temples ; pop.143,000.

tricolor, see FRENCH REVOLUTION

trident, *trī′dent*, in old Greek tales, the three-pronged spear of Poseidon, god of the sea (the Roman Neptune), a symbol now carried by Britannia, the idea being that Britain rules the waves.

Triennial Act, act of Parliament (1641) declaring that Parliament must meet at least every three years ; also an act (1694) limiting the length of any one Parliament to three years. The Septennial Act (1716) extended this to seven years ; and this was revised (1911) to a period of five years, except in an emergency, e.g. during war.

Trier, *trē′er*, city, Germany ; on the R. Moselle ; has Roman remains and an 11th c. cathedral ; industries include textiles ; pop.68,000. (French name Trèves.)

Trieste, *trē-est′*, Adriatic port, Italian till 1947, when it became a free territory ; industries include shipbuilding. There is a spacious harbour. Trieste was occupied by Yugoslav forces during part of World War II ; pop.252,000.

trigonometry (Greek *trigōnon*, triangle, *metron*, measure), branch of mathematics dealing with the measurement of plane and spherical triangles, hence a science based on the measurement and ratios of angles.

Trigonometry seems to have evolved from a study of the stars as early as 1700BC. It was later applied to surveying, though the science made little progress prior to the 17th c.

In trigonometry angles are often measured in *radians*. When the length of the radius of a circle is measured round the curved circumference the angle this makes at the centre is called a radian. Measured in degrees the radian is approximately 57° 17′ 44·8″. The number of radians in a circle cannot be given exactly, and the symbol 2π is always used to express it.

$$\pi = 3{\cdot}14159 \ldots$$

Other useful approximations are $\frac{22}{7}$ and $\frac{355}{113}$. π radians $= 180°$.

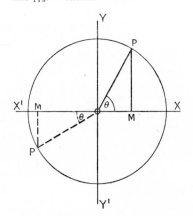

FUNDAMENTAL RATIOS

Note also the following *fundamenta ratios*, illustrated by the diagram, in which XOX′ and YOY′ are lines at right angles ; P is any point on the circumference of a circle having O as centre. PM is perpendicular to X′OX. Then, if the angle XOP be called θ, the *sine* (sin) of θ is $\dfrac{\text{PM}}{\text{OP}}$; the *cosine* (cos) $\dfrac{\text{OM}}{\text{OP}}$; and the *tangent* (tan) $\dfrac{\text{PM}}{\text{OM}}$. The reciprocals of these ratios give *cosecant* (cosec) $\dfrac{\text{OP}}{\text{PM}}$; *secant* (sec) $\dfrac{\text{OP}}{\text{OM}}$; and *cotangent* (cot) $\dfrac{\text{OM}}{\text{PM}}$.

The following useful equations given on the next page can easily be proved :

$\cos A \times \sec A = 1$ $\tan A = \dfrac{\sin A}{\cos A}$

$\sin^2 A + \cos^2 A = 1$

$\sin A \times \operatorname{cosec} A = 1$ $\cot A = \dfrac{\cos A}{\sin A}$

$\tan^2 A + 1 = \sec^2 A$

$\tan A \times \cot A = 1$

$\cot^2 A + 1 = \operatorname{cosec}^2 A$

Trigonometrical values of certain angles are :

degrees	0°	30°	45°	60°	90°
radians	0	$\dfrac{\pi}{6}$	$\dfrac{\pi}{4}$	$\dfrac{\pi}{3}$	$\dfrac{\pi}{2}$
sine	0	$\dfrac{1}{2}$	$\dfrac{1}{\sqrt{2}}$	$\dfrac{\sqrt{3}}{2}$	1
cosine	1	$\dfrac{\sqrt{3}}{2}$	$\dfrac{1}{\sqrt{2}}$	$\dfrac{1}{2}$	0
tangent	0	$\dfrac{1}{\sqrt{3}}$	1	$\sqrt{3}$	0
cotangent	∞	$\sqrt{3}$	1	$\dfrac{1}{\sqrt{3}}$	0
secant	1	$\dfrac{2}{\sqrt{3}}$	$\sqrt{2}$	2	∞
cosecant	∞	2	$\sqrt{2}$	$\dfrac{2}{\sqrt{3}}$	1

Complementary angles :
$\sin(90°-\theta) = \cos\theta$, $\cos(90°-\theta) = \sin\theta$, $\tan(90°-\theta) = \cot\theta$, $\operatorname{cosec}(90°-\theta) = \sec\theta$, $\sec(90°-\theta) = \operatorname{cosec}\theta$, $\cot(90°-\theta) = \tan\theta$.

Supplementary angles :
$\sin(180°-\theta) = \sin\theta$, $\cos(180°-\theta) = -\cos\theta$, $\tan(180°-\theta) = -\tan\theta$, $\operatorname{cosec}(180°-\theta) = \operatorname{cosec}\theta$, $\sec(180°-\theta) = -\sec\theta$, $\cot(180°-\theta) = -\cot\theta$.

Note also :

$\sin 15° = \dfrac{\sqrt{6}-\sqrt{2}}{4}$

$\cos 15° = \dfrac{\sqrt{6}+\sqrt{2}}{4}$

$\tan 15° = 2 - \sqrt{3}$

$\cot 15° = 2 + \sqrt{3}$

$\sin 18° = \dfrac{\sqrt{5}-1}{4}$

$\cos 18° = \dfrac{\sqrt{10+2\sqrt{5}}}{4}$

$\tan 18° = \tfrac{1}{5}\sqrt{25-10\sqrt{5}}$

$\cot 18° = \sqrt{5+2\sqrt{5}}$

(a) Fundamental formulae :

(i) $\sin(A+B) = \sin A \cos B + \cos A \sin B$

(ii) $\cos(A+B) = \cos A \cos B - \sin A \sin B$

(iii) $\sin(A-B) = \sin A \cos B - \cos A \sin B$

(iv) $\cos(A-B) = \cos A \cos B + \sin A \sin B$

(v) $\sin(A+B)\ \sin(A-B) = \sin^2 A - \sin^2 B = \cos^2 B - \cos^2 A$

(vi) $\cos(A+B)\ \cos(A-B) = \cos^2 A - \sin^2 B = \cos^2 B - \sin^2 A$

(vii) $\sin C + \sin D = 2\sin\dfrac{C+D}{2}\cos\dfrac{C-D}{2}$

(viii) $\sin C - \sin D = 2\cos\dfrac{C-D}{2}\sin\dfrac{C-D}{2}$

(ix) $\cos C + \cos D = 2\cos\dfrac{C+D}{2}\cos\dfrac{C-D}{2}$

(x) $\cos D - \cos C = 2\sin\dfrac{C+D}{2}\sin\dfrac{C-D}{2}$

(xi) $2\sin A\cos B = \sin(A+B) + \sin(A-B)$

(xii) $2\cos A\sin B = \sin(A+B) - \sin(A-B)$

(xiii) $2\cos A\cos B = \cos(A+B) + \cos(A-B)$

(xiv) $2\sin A\sin B = \cos(A-B) - \cos(A-B)$

(xv) $\tan(A+B) = \dfrac{\tan A + \tan B}{1 - \tan A\tan B}$

(xvi) $\tan(A-B) = \dfrac{\tan A - \tan B}{1 + \tan A\tan B}$

(xvii) $\sin 2A = 2\sin A\cos A$

(xviii) $\cos 2A = \cos^2 A - \sin^2 A = 1 - 2\sin^2 A = 2\cos^2 A - 1$

(xix) $\sin 2A = \dfrac{2\tan A}{1 + \tan^2 A}$;

     $\cos 2A = \dfrac{1 - \tan^2 A}{1 + \tan^2 A}$

(xx) $\tan 2A = \dfrac{2\tan A}{1 - \tan^2 A}$

(xxi) $\sin 3A = 3\sin A - 4\sin^3 A$

(xxii) $\cos 3A = 4\cos^3 A - 3\cos A$

(xxiii) $\tan 3A = \dfrac{3\tan A - \tan^3 A}{1 - 3\tan^2 A}$

(b) Formulae for triangles :

A, B, C are the angles ; a, b, c the sides ; s is half the sum of the sides ; R the radius of the circumscribed circle, and r the radius of the inscribed circle ; Δ is the area.

(i) $\dfrac{\sin A}{a} = \dfrac{\sin B}{b} = \dfrac{\sin C}{c}$

(ii) $\cos A = \dfrac{b^2 + c^2 - a^2}{2bc}$

     $\cos B = \dfrac{c^2 + a^2 - b^2}{2ca}$

     $\cos C = \dfrac{a^2 + b^2 - c^2}{2ab}$

(iii) $\sin\dfrac{A}{2} = \pm\dfrac{\sqrt{(s-b)(s-c)}}{bc}$

     $\cos\dfrac{A}{2} = \pm\dfrac{\sqrt{s(s-a)}}{bc}$

$$\tan \frac{A}{2} = \pm \frac{\sqrt{(s-b)\,(s-c)}}{s(s-a)}$$

(iv) $\sin A = \dfrac{2}{bc} \sqrt{s(s-a)\,(s-b)\,(s-c)}$

$\qquad \sin B = \dfrac{2}{ca} \sqrt{s(s-a)\,(s-b)\,(s-c)}$

$\qquad \sin C = \dfrac{2}{ab} \sqrt{s(s-a)\,(s-b)\,(s-c)}$

(v) $a = b \cos C + c \cos B$
$\quad b = c \cos A + a \cos C$
$\quad c = a \cos B + b \cos A$

(vi) $\Delta = \sqrt{s(s-a)\,(s-b)\,(s-c)}$

$\qquad = \tfrac{1}{2}bc \sin A = \tfrac{1}{2}ca \sin B = \tfrac{1}{2}ab \sin C$

$\qquad = \dfrac{abc}{4R}$

(vii) $R = \dfrac{a}{2 \sin A} = \dfrac{b}{2 \sin B} = \dfrac{c}{2 \sin C} = \dfrac{abc}{4\Delta}$

(viii) $r = \dfrac{\Delta}{s} = (s-a) \tan \dfrac{A}{2}$

$\qquad = (s-b) \tan \dfrac{B}{2} = (s-c) \tan \dfrac{C}{2}$

(c) *Area of quadrilateral inscribed in a circle*
$$= \sqrt{(s-a)\,(s-b)\,(s-c)\,(s-d)}$$

(d)   (i) $\sin \alpha + \sin (\alpha + \beta) + \sin (\alpha + 2\beta)$
$\qquad\qquad + \ldots$ to n terms

$$= \frac{\sin \left\{ \alpha + \dfrac{n-1}{2}\beta \right\} \sin \dfrac{n\beta}{2}}{\sin \dfrac{\beta}{2}}$$

(ii) $\cos \alpha + \cos (\alpha + \beta) + \cos (\alpha + 2\beta) + \ldots$ to n terms

$$= \frac{\cos \left\{ \alpha + \dfrac{n-1}{2}\beta \right\} \sin \dfrac{n\beta}{2}}{\sin \dfrac{\beta}{2}}$$

trillion, in Britain, a million million million, i.e. 10^{18} ; in USA, a million million, i.e. 10^{12}.

Trinidad, island of the W. Indies ; discovered by Columbus 1498 ; ceded to the British 1802 ; notable for its sugar, cocoa, rum, copra, limes and grape-fruit; especially for its remarkable asphalt lake of 114 acres, from which over 30,000 tons are exported yearly, the supply being continually maintained. The chief town and port is Port of Spain, a handsome modern city with a pop. of over 105,000. Tobago, an island 21m north-east, has a pop. of 33,000.

Trinity, mystery of one God in three persons, i.e. God the Father, Son and Holy Ghost.

Trinity College, college of Cambridge University, founded by Henry VIII 1546. Its mastership is in the gift of the Crown.

Trinity College, college of Oxford University ; founded 1555.

Trinity Hall, college of Cambridge University ; founded 1350.

Trinity House, corporation given a charter 1514 by Henry VIII. It is responsible for the upkeeping of over 60 lighthouses and over 40 lightships in England and Wales, and has legal powers concerning those of Scotland and Ireland and Gibraltar ; controls also the pilots of the UK ; and contributes towards the aid of aged and distressed mariners. The governing officers are known as Elder Brethren.

Trinity Sunday, Sunday after Whit Sunday.

Tripartite Pact, agreement to stand by each other signed 27 Sept 1940 by Germany, Italy and Japan ; later by Hungary and Rumania.

Triple Alliance, any alliance among three countries, but especially that of England, Holland and Sweden, against Louis XIV (1668) ; of Austria, Britain and Russia 1795 ; and of Germany, Austria and Italy 1882.

Triple Entente, *än-tänt'*, agreement between Britain, France and Russia, 1907–17 ; a development of the *Dual Alliance* between France and Russia 1890–93, and the *Entente Cordiale* 1904 between France and Britain.

Tripoli, see WORLD WAR II

tripos, *trī'pos*, once the three-legged stool on which Cambridge candidates for degrees sat when being examined ; now means Honours examinations for the degree of BA at Cambridge University.

triptane, hydrocarbon, an aviation petrol with a high octane superiority, one of many discoveries of Professor Vladimir Ipatieff, a Russian who became a naturalised American. His pioneer work on butadiene led to the modern method of making synthetic rubber.

trireme, see SHIPS

Tristan da Cunha, *tris-tän dä koon'yä*, lonely British island (area 44sq.m) in the S. Atlantic, 2,000m west of the Cape of Good Hope ; pop.220 ; cap. Edinburgh ; now has a meteorological and radio station.

Trojan horse, *trō'jan*, wooden horse which, according to Virgil's *Aeneid*, the Greeks besieging Troy left near the gate when they pretended to sail away. The Trojans hauled it into the city, and men hidden inside the horse opened the gates at night, thus enabling the Greeks to capture Troy.

Trojan War, although it is better known to us as the subject of ancient Homeric legends, was probably an actual struggle between prehistoric Greeks and peoples of Asia Minor for control of the Dardanelles. In the Homeric legend it is said to have lasted ten years, and to have been caused by Paris, who ran off with Helen of Troy. It forms the story of Homer's *Iliad*. See HOMER ; TROY

Trollope, ANTHONY, *trol'ŭp* (1815–82), novelist, *b* London ; for many years in the Post Office ; led a busy life, but found time to hunt, to play whist and to write over 50 novels, of which those in the Barchester series are the most famous, i.e. *The Warden* ; *Barchester Towers* ; *The Small House at Allington* ; *Dr Thorne* ; *Framley Parsonage* ; and *Last Chronicle of Barset*. They are neither deep nor exalted, but give a faithful and detailed account of life among the clergy in mid-Victorian England. Interest in Trollope's novels was revived by broadcasts 1945–46.

Tromp, MARTIN (1597–1653), Dutch sailor, sometimes confused with his son Cornelius van Tromp. One of the finest of all Dutch admirals, Martin Tromp won over 30 naval battles, defeated the English admiral Blake off Dungeness 1652, and is said to have sailed the English Channel with a broom at his masthead, a sign that he had swept his enemies from the seas.

Tromso, fishing port of Norway ; port for Spitsbergen.

Trondhjem, *tron'yem,* port, Norway ; trades in fish, timber and copper ore ; was formerly the cap. ; pop.55,000.

Tropic of Cancer, see SEASONS

Tropic of Capricorn, see SEASONS

troposphere, layer of the atmosphere below the stratosphere, i.e. the region where temperature decreases with height ; extends roughly 7–10m. See ATMOSPHERE

Trossachs, THE, name for a region of Perthshire regarded as one of the finest in Scotland ; notable for mt. scenery, forests, lakes and crags, much of it described by Sir Walter Scott in *The Lady of the Lake* and *Rob Roy*. The lakes include Loch Katrine, source of Glasgow's water supply.

Trotsky, LEON, *tröt'skē* (1877–1940), assumed name of a Russian revolutionary, collaborator with Lenin in the new socialist order of the USSR ; part organiser of the successful revolution of Nov 1917. He may be regarded as the founder of the modern Soviet army.

When Stalin came to power after the death of Lenin, he gave up the policy of trying to create a world-wide revolution and concentrated instead on consolidating the revolution in Russia itself. Trotsky maintained that this policy was at variance with the dogmas of Marx and Lenin, but he was denounced as a 'deviationist ' (the Communist term for a ' heretic ') and in 1927 had to flee the country. He died in Mexico.

troubadours, *troo'bä-dörs,* singers of the Middle Ages, especially (1090–1290) in Languedoc and Provence, though they flourished also in Italy and Spain. Troubadours composed elaborate poems and sang them to the accompaniment of a viol-like 5-stringed instrument, often in praise of a woman or a lord, or telling of romance and chivalry.

trout, fresh-water food fish of British streams ; greenish-brown above paling to a dull white, dotted in parts with X-shaped black spots ; average weight 2lb, but may weigh as much as 12lb or

more. The sea trout is a distinct species, similar to the salmon in its general characteristics but differing from it in appearance by the greater number of scales on its body. The average number of scales between the dorsal fin and the lateral line is between 14 and 18, and the average weight of the adult fish is about 3lb.

Trowbridge, *trō'brij,* cloth-manufacturing town, Wiltshire.

Troy, *troi,* city, New York state, USA ; on the Hudson R. ; manufactures include hosiery ; pop.70,000.

Troy or **Ilium,** *īl'i-ŭm,* ancient city 3½m from the mouth of the Dardanelles ; immortalised by Homer in the *Iliad* as Priam's city. Apparently nine inhabited places have stood on the site at different times, the first a Stone Age encampment; the sixth being Priam's fortified city. Later cities included those built by Alexander the Great and Julius Caesar. The capture of Troy by the Greeks opened up the Black Sea (Euxine) to trade. See HOMER ; TROJAN HORSE

Troyes, *trwä,* city of France, on the R. Seine, *c.*100m from Paris. For the first *Treaty of Troyes* see HUNDRED YEARS' WAR ; the second treaty was signed 1564, England and France agreeing to trade freely with each other. Troy weight is named from this town ; pop. 60,000.

Troy Town, see FOWEY

Truman, HARRY S. (1884–   ), born in Missouri ; became Vice-President of USA 1944, and President at the sudden death of Franklin D. Roosevelt 1945. Favouring world co-operation, he is a man with deep religious convictions.

What has now become known as the *Truman Doctrine* is, in effect, a reversal of the Monroe Doctrine, namely, that USA prosperity since World War II can only be secured by aiding free peoples to maintain their free institutions and their national integrity against aggressive movements that seek to shape them as totalitarian states.

In 1948, Truman was elected President for a further four-year period. His success surprised the commentators and greatly enhanced his prestige. In Nov 1950 two Puerto Rican Nationalists made an attempt on his life ; in Dec. Mr Attlee visited him for talks on Far East problems. Mr Truman dealt vigorously (1951) with the Korean war, and continued to support ' Aid for Europe.'

Truro, *troo'rō,* cathedral city and port, Cornwall ; exports local tin and copper.

trust, term now commonly used for a combine or cartel, i.e. an amalgamation of industrial firms for the purpose of eliminating competition, and thus controlling prices ; an outstanding example being the Standard American Oil Trust. Commercial trusts are a feature of USA.

Shareholders in a trust deposit their shares in the hands of trustees, and receive a certificate, the trustees actually managing the business and distributing dividends to the shareholders.

trustee, one appointed in a will to administer property left *in trust* until certain events occur ; hence a trustee may have to invest money, which he can only do in trustee securities, i.e. investments listed under the Trustee Act (1925) as investments open to trust funds, e.g. government stock, stock in the Bank of England and certain other stocks.

trypsin, *trip′sin,* enzyme of the pancreas ; changes proteins into amino-acids.

Tschaikovsky, PIOTR ILYICH, *chī-kŏf′skē* (1840–93), Russian composer and conductor ; famous for his songs and his piano and chamber music, especially his *Sixth Symphony* (*Pathétique*), his Piano Concerto in B flat minor, and '*1812*' *Overture.*

tsetse-fly, see SLEEPING SICKNESS

Tse-Tung, MAO (1893–   ), Chairman of the Central People's (Communist) Government Council of China since 1949. Tse-Tung's victory ended Chiang Kai-shek's Kuomintang ; the new government was recognised 1950 by Britain

TT, see MILK

Tubby Clayton, see CLAYTON, REV. P. T. B.

Tube, see LONDON

tuberculosis, *tū-bĕr-kū-lō′sis,* disease caused by a bacillus, *B. tuberculosis* (first isolated by Koch), infecting any one of many parts of the body, e.g. the spine, the hip-joint, the intestines, and especially the lungs. Knowledge of bacteriology has done much in recent years to combat the disease (often called TB, and responsible for one in ten of all deaths in Britain), but the best means of fighting it are preventive, e.g. ensuring an adequate amount of fat in the diet, improved housing conditions, disinfection and inspection of milk supplies. Doctors are hopeful that DIASONE, a drug of the sulfa family, will prove highly effective in combating this dread disease. In the experimental stage in 1942, diasone had apparently great possibilities. Regular radiographs of workers is one method advocated for discovering TB in its earliest stages. STREPTOMYCIN, isolated in USA, is said to be successful in treating the disease.

BCG (Bacillus Calmette Guerin), a mild strain of tubercle bacilli, is claimed to strengthen resistance to infection, and has reduced TB in Sweden.

Tübingen, town, Württemberg, Germany ; has a 15th c. university ; notable for printing and dyeing ; pop.24,000.

TUC, see TRADE UNIONS

Tudor, name of a famous Welsh family, one member being Owen Tudor, beheaded by the Yorkists at Mortimer's Cross 1461. His son Edmund (*d* 1456), became Earl of Richmond, and married Margaret Beaufort. Their son, Henry, became Henry VII (1485), first Tudor king of England. His Tudor successors were Henry VIII, Edward VI, Mary and Elizabeth (*d* 1603).

Tugela, *too-gē′lä,* river, Natal ; flows 300m from the Drakensbergs to the Indian Ocean.

Tuileries, *twē′lĕr-ē,* palace in Paris, built 1564 on the site of some tile-yards (*tuileries*) ; home of many French kings ; burned 1871. Only the gardens remain.

tulip, plant (family *Liliaceae*), brought to Britain from Holland in the 16th c. ; grown from bulbs largely in Holland and Lincolnshire. There are many varieties of tulips of all colours ; they bloom in spring, each stalk bearing one cup-shaped flower.

Tulle, *tūl,* town, France, 45m from Limoges ; once manufactured a fine silk fabric (tulle) used for veils and trimmings.

Tulsa, city, Oklahoma, USA ; manufactures bricks and glassware ; pop. 142,000.

tumbril, cart in which, during the French Revolution, prisoners were taken to the guillotine ; also a covered vehicle used to transport army stores.

tumulus, see BARROW

Tunbridge Wells, fashionable inland health resort, Kent ; has mineral springs ; pop.35,000.

tundra, wide barren lowlands bordering the Arctic in N. America, Europe and Asia. The winters are long and severe, the rainfall slight (say 10in a year), hence the tundra is actually a cold desert, having only stunted bushes, mosses and lichens. It is inhabited by a few Eskimos (N. America), by Finns and Lapps (Europe), and by Samoyedes in Siberia. Reindeer and caribou are found.

tungsten, metal and element, W (wolfram) ; atomic weight 183·92 ; atomic number 74 ; found as wolfram in China, Burma, USA, Bolivia, Portugal, Malay States, Argentina, etc. and to some extent in Cornwall and Devon. Its high melting-point (*c.*3,370°C) makes it useful for filaments in electric lamps ; it is also much used in steel alloys, especially high speed steels. Tungsten carbide is used for cutting tools.

Tunis, see TUNISIA

Tunisia, *tū-nis′iä,* French protectorate between Algeria and Tripoli, N. Africa ; area *c.*45,000sq.m, some of which is desert, though there are regions producing cereals, olives and vines, and supporting cattle and sheep. Minerals include coal, copper, lead and phosphates. The capital is Tunis, on a site near that of Carthage.

Tunisia was the scene of the spectacular German retreat before British and Allied troops 1942–43.

tunny, large marine fish of the mackerel family ; found in British waters ; may be 10ft long and weigh over 1,000lb. Tunny fishing is an exciting sport.

turban, Mohammedan headdress, consisting of a long scarf of silk, cotton or muslin wound round the head, the manner of folding depending on rank.

turbine, see SHIPS

turbine (gas), see GAS ENGINE

turbot, British food fish of great delicacy. A flat fish, it is greyish-brown, and may be 3ft long.

Turenne, VICOMTE DE, *tū-ren'* (1611–75), Marshal of France, *b* Sedan. A great soldier and a master of military manoeuvres, his strategies were copied by Napoleon. He won fame in the Thirty Years' War.

Turgenev, IVAN SERGEIEVITCH, *tur-gen'yef* (1818–83), Russian novelist ; often melancholy, but wrote with fidelity of the people he knew. His book *A Sportsman's Sketches* depicted Russian peasant life, and contributed towards the emancipation of the serfs. He won European fame with *A House of Nobles* ; but his greatest work of fiction is *Virgin Soil.* Another of his novels is *Fathers and Sons.*

Turin, city, N. Italy ; manufactures textiles, motor cars and rayon ; famous for its 15th c. cathedral enriched with frescoes ; pop.659,000.

Turkestan, ill-defined region shared between USSR and Afghanistan ; home of Mongols and Aryans, most of whom were nomads till recent years. The area is now being opened up industrially, and Western customs are being adopted.

Turkey, republic comprising (*a*) Turkey in Europe (area *c.*9,250sq.m ; pop. 1,266,000), a region bordering on Bulgaria and Greece ; and (*b*) Turkey in Asia (Anatolia), area *c.*285,000sq.m, pop.15,000,000. Though agriculture is still somewhat primitive, there are great herds of goats and cattle, also large numbers of sheep. Cereals, raisins, figs, olives and cotton are grown, and especially tobacco. The forests yield much timber ; mulberry trees are grown. The mineral wealth (now being increasingly exploited) includes chrome ore, zinc and manganese. The capital is Ankara.

The Turks once owned much more land than they do now, and for centuries the people remained little affected by the march of civilisation, but in recent years amazing changes have taken place, due in large measure to Kemal Ataturk (*d* 1938). The caliphate has been abolished, traditional costume discarded, the alphabet reformed and education made compulsory. Railways have been built, lines extended and built, e.g. the line to Iran. Though the former Ottoman Empire (once styled ' the sick man of Europe ') decayed for three centuries, the future of Turkey now seems full of promise.

turkey, bird of the pheasant family brought from N. America to Britain ; has a long featherless blue-red neck. The plumage, generally bronze with black, has also some white feathers. The turkey weighs up to 50lb and lays brown-spotted whitish eggs.

Turkish bath, see BATHS

Turkomans, wandering race of Mohammedans in N. Iran and neighbouring regions. Many have become settled farmers in recent years.

Turku, formerly the cap., Finland ; once called Abo ; pop.74,000.

Turner, SIR BEN (1863–1942), Labour leader, *b* Yorkshire ; entered Parliament as Labour MP 1922. One of the founders of the Labour Party, his chief work was associated with the National Union of Textile Workers.

Turner, JOSEPH MALLORD WILLIAM (1775–1851), artist, regarded by some as the world's greatest landscape painter, *b* London.

Turner, who was a barber's son, made drawings even as a boy ; exhibited in the Academy when only fifteen ; tramped round England sketching scenery, and studying the details of landscape and the effects of changing skies ; elected RA 1802. He made many foreign tours, e.g. Germany, and especially Italy, where the old masters and the brilliant colour of the sunny land inspired him to paint more vividly. He greatly advanced the art of engraving.

Though he amassed a huge fortune, Turner remained a lonely genius. He never married, and his scanty education made him painfully reserved. He is said to have summed up his art in the words, ' Well, painting's a rum thing.' He died at Chelsea, and left his pictures to the nation.

Turner excelled in watercolour and oils. His hundreds of pictures of English and foreign scenes are all masterly. He is notable for his painting of seascapes. During the height of his career he delighted to paint in oils brilliant sunsets, seascapes and dramatic pictures of classic subjects, e.g. *Ulysses Deriding Polyphemus.* His amazing mastery of atmosphere and colour is seen in *Sun Rising in a Mist* (1807) ; his superb sea and sky effects are revealed in *Calais Pier* ; and his sense of the dramatic is shown in his famous *Fighting Téméraire Towed to Her Last Berth.*

It is, however, as the first painter who found subjects among the surroundings and scenery of industrialised England, that Turner is most remarkable.

The story is told that a lady once remarked critically, ' I have never seen a sunset like that, Mr Turner.'

' No, madam,' was the reply. ' But don't you wish you had ? '

turnip, fleshy-rooted plant long cultivated as a root crop. The two chief varieties are (*a*) *white-fleshed,* generally of low-feeding value, and liable to be injured by frosts ; (*b*) *yellow-fleshed,* of slower growth, but more robust, and superior in feeding value, also less susceptible to frosts, and capable of being stored for longer periods.

turnpike, formerly a gate across a road, opened only when a toll was paid ; hence turnpike roads, i.e. those repaired with money collected at turnpikes.

turpentine, crude or distilled liquid derived from the resin of pine trees and other conifers ; much used for making varnishes and paints.

Turpin, DICK (1706–39), highwayman, born in Essex ; became a cattle thief ; later chief of a gang of robbers. After accidentally shooting his friend, Tom King, at Whitechapel (London), he escaped to York, but was later arrested and hanged.

Many thrilling tales have been invented about Dick Turpin, and he has been pictured as a fine character who, like Robin Hood, robbed the rich to help the poor ; but apparently all such stories are legends, and it is not true that he made the famous ride to York on Black Bess.

turquoise, *tŭr′koiz,* blue or green gem ; found in Iran and Mexico.

turtle, see TORTOISE

turtle dove, very shy species of pigeon, a summer visitor in England but not in Scotland ; has a reddish tinge on head and neck, a black and white collar, and black spots on the rust-coloured wings.

Tuscany, department of north-west Italy, formerly a grand duchy ; corresponds more or less to the ancient Etruria.

Tussaud's, MADAME, see LONDON

Tutankhamen, *tŭt-änk-ä′men* (*d* c.1353BC), Egyptian king of the XVIII dynasty ; he was buried in the Valley of the Kings at Thebes, and from the excavation of his tomb in 1923 by Howard Carter a fabulous hoard of treasure was recovered. His was almost the only one of the tombs of the kings that had not been broken into in ancient times by robbers.

TVA, see TENNESSEE VALLEY AUTHORITY

Twain, MARK (1835–1910), pen-name of Samuel Langhorne Clemens, American humorous writer, *b* Missouri ; worked as a printer ; became the pilot of a steamer on the R. Mississippi, then a reporter, miner, journalist and traveller. His book *Innocents Abroad* (1869) won him fame. He is noted for *The Adventures of Tom Sawyer* and *The Adventures of Huckleberry Finn,* both published in cheap editions by Thomas Nelson ; he wrote also *A Tramp Abroad* ; *The Prince and the Pauper* ; and *A Connecticut Yankee at the Court of King Arthur.* While Mark Twain was still alive, a newspaper published mistakenly the report that he was dead. Mark Twain's comment was, ' The report of my death is greatly exaggerated.'

Tweed, river flowing c.97m through beautiful scenery in S. Scotland to Berwick. The woollen cloth now called tweed was formerly known as tweel. The modern name arose from the error of a clerk who knew that the cloth in question came from Tweedside, and thought that it ought to be called tweed.
See PLATES 21 (*bottom*), 22

Tweedsmuir, LORD (1875–1940), better known as John Buchan (*buch″n*), *b* Peeblesshire ; became a lawyer ; joined the firm of Thomas Nelson ; Unionist MP for the Scottish Universities 1927 ; Governor-General of Canada 1935 ; author of stirring novels, e.g. *The Thirty-Nine Steps* ; *Greenmantle* ; *Mr Standfast* ; also *Midwinter* ; *Witch Wood* ; and the popular adventure story, *Prester John,* published 1910, one of many stories that have centred round the original Prester John, a 12th c. priest-king long associated with Ethiopia.

Twelfth Day, see CALENDAR

Twelve Apostles, see APOSTLE ; CHRIST

' Twentieth Century Ltd,' see RAILWAYS

Twickenham, town, Middlesex ; on the R. Thames ; HQ of Rugby football ; pop.106,000.

Tyler, WAT, *tī′lĕr* (*d* 1381), English rebel ; led a rising of Kentishmen to demand the abolition of the poll tax ; met by young King Richard II at Smithfield, and was there killed by Sir William Walworth, Lord Mayor of London.

Wat Tyler's rebellion was similar to many ' *jacqueries* ' or peasants' risings that occurred on the Continent.

Tyndale, WILLIAM (*d* 1536), English scholar severely persecuted for daring to translate the Bible ; lived for a time at Antwerp, where he was put to death. See BIBLE

Tyne, *tīn,* river forming the boundary between Northumberland and County Durham ; flows c.63m to the N. Sea. A tunnel between Howden and Jarrow is under construction.

Tynemouth, port, Northumberland, at the mouth of the R. Tyne ; exports coal, and has shipbuilding yards ; pop.65,000.

Tynwald, *tin′wold,* name for the Parliament of the I. of Man.

type metal, alloy of 60% lead, 30% antimony, 10% tin ; used in making printers' type.

typewriter, machine invented c.1843, and later much improved, especially by E. Remington, whose first machine came on the market 1874. Today machines with many refinements, adjustments and special gadgets are available. There are standard and portable typewriters ; also silent models.

A good typist should be able to type 50–60 words a minute, but a speed of 150 words a minute has been attained.

typhoid fever, *tī-foid,* infectious disease resulting from the bacterium *Bacillus typhosus.* Very similar are the diseases paratyphoid A and B. Typhoid is most common in tropical regions, though immunity is almost assured after injection with a suitable vaccine. A more serious disease, typhus fever (communicated by body lice) has caused many epidemics in Europe. It has recently been shown that by killing certain body insects and organisms, DDT is a valuable preventative of typhus fever.

typhoon, see HURRICANE

typhus, see TYPHOID

Tyre, *tīr,* port of the Lebanon ; pop.6,000 ;

formerly a city of Phoenicia, rich in the days of David and Solomon ; captured 332BC by Alexander the Great ; came under Roman rule ; once traded in glass-ware and purple dyes. See SIDON

tyre, metal, solid rubber, or air-filled rubber rim of a wheel, e.g. the metal rim of a wooden cartwheel, made slightly smaller than the circumference of the wheel, heated and shrunk on the wood, thus tightening all the joints. A similar process is used in shrinking tyres on railway wheels, or the wheel is cooled excessively. Solid rubber tyres were once common on cycles. The pneumatic (i.e. air-filled) tyre for cycles, cars, lorries and planes was invented by J. B. Dunlop (*d* 1921), the outer cover protecting an inner tube. A non-puncture tyre is now being made.

Tyrone, *tī-rōn'*, county of Ulster, Northern Ireland ; co.tn Omagh.

Tyrrhenian Sea, *ti-rē'ni-an*, part of the Mediterranean west of Italy.

U

U-boat, German *Unterseeboot*, a German submarine. U-boats were active in World Wars I and II.

Udaipur, *ood'i-pore*, native state of Rajputana, India.

Udall, NICHOLAS, *ū'dal* (1506–56), playwright, probably *b* Hampshire ; best known as the writer of our earliest English comedy, *Ralph Roister Doister*.

Uganda, *ū-gan'dă*, British protectorate between Kenya and the Sudan, Africa ; area *c*.94,000sq.m ; pop.4,000,000. Both the government and agriculture are largely in native hands. Products include raw cotton, cotton-seed, sugar, gold, tin ore, timber and hides. The HQ of the British administration are at the cap. Entebbe.

Uitlander, *oit'ländĕr*, name in the S. African Republic for white people other than Boers. By refusing civil rights to Uitlanders (chiefly British) the Boers did much to bring about the S. African war, 1899–1902.

UK, see BRITISH ISLES ; UNITED KINGDOM

Ukraine, *ū-krān*, republic of USSR, area 225,000sq.m ; pop.41,000,000. The Ukraine, north of the Black Sea, has fertile soil, hence its great wheat harvests. Sugar-beet is also extensively grown ; coal, iron, manganese and quicksilver are mined. The cap. is Kiev, captured by the Nazis, but liberated 1943.

ukulele, *ū-kă-lā'lĭ*, 4-stringed musical instrument ; might be called the Hawaiian guitar ; first played in Portugal, and became popular in USA *c*.1925.

Ullswater, beautiful lake, Cumberland, in the English L. District. It is over 7m long.

Ulm, German port on the R. Danube ; noted for its cathedral with a spire 528ft high ; pop.62,000.

ulna, see SKELETON

Ulster, region of Ireland comprising (*a*) Northern Ireland, (*b*) a province of Eire, including the counties of Cavan, Donegal and Monaghan.

Ultima Thule, *ŭl'ti-mä thū'lē*, name given by ancient writers to a remote island in the far north, possibly one of the Orkney or Shetland Is. ; first mentioned by Pytheas, a 4th c. Greek traveller ; hence the ' end of the world.'

ultra violet rays, electromagnetic waves in the region of the solar spectrum beyond the violet ; are responsible for vitamin D in the human body and in fruit.

Ulysses, *ū-lis'ēz*, Latin form of the Greek Odysseus, chieftain of Ithaca, and one of the heroes of the Trojan war. The story of his return from Troy forms the theme of Homer's *Odyssey*. See HOMER

Umberto II, *oom-ber'tō*, King of Italy for 29 days, 1946 ; went into exile after a referendum.

umbra, see SHADOW

umbrellas, said to have been introduced into England by Jonas Hanway (1712–1786), traveller and philanthropist. They are an adaptation of the parasol known in ancient Babylon.

Umbria, department of Italy, comprising Perugia and Terni. In ancient Italy Umbria was the territory of the powerful Umbri, subdued by the Romans *c*.307BC.

Umma, see SUDAN

Uncle Remus, *rē'mŭs*, pen name of Joel Chandler Harris (1848–1908), American writer ; author of *Uncle Remus*, delightful Negro tales of Brer Rabbit and Brer Fox. Walt Disney's film *Song of the South* is a fascinating if fanciful interpretation of these stories, the part of Uncle Remus being played by James Basket.

Uncle Sam, nickname for the USA.

Underground, see LONDON

underground movement, see SECRET SOCIETIES

Underhill, EVELYN (1875–1941), English woman writer on mysticism.

under the counter, phrase much used towards the end of World War II, and after. Scarcity of goods led to the practice of keeping goods under the counter (or out of sight), and producing them for favoured customers only.

underwriter, person, almost always a member of Lloyds, prepared to take a risk in insurance. He writes his name under the policy to guarantee payment of the money. Formerly underwriters insured only ships and their cargoes, but now their business is more general, and includes buying all the shares of a company or municipality not subscribed for by the public. He does so in return for an agreed commission.

Undset, SIGRID, un'set (1882–   ), Norwegian novelist ; best known for her study of Scandinavian life in the Middle Ages, *Kristin Lavransdatter.*

UNESCO, short for United Nations Educational, Scientific and Cultural Organisation, an attempt since *c.*1945 to banish ignorance, and to encourage education on broad and international principles. During World War II (and for some years before) propaganda did much to spread wrong conceptions among hundreds of millions of people, and among the tasks of UNESCO are those of flooding many countries of the world with books (especially textbooks), films and broadcasts calculated to combat ignorance and prejudice, and to foster culture of every kind. UNESCO's 4th session met in Paris 1949, its 5th in Florence 1950. Its activities now include Germany and Japan.

unicorn, *ū-ni-korn,* imaginary animal with a horn in the middle of the head ; probably derived from old tales of the rhinoceros.

Unified Field Theory, see EINSTEIN ; RELATIVITY

Uniformity, ACT OF, name of three acts (*a*) 1549, enforcing the use of the English *Prayer Book,* (*b*) 1559, the same as (*a*), but fining people who did not attend church ; and (*c*) Act of 1662 regulating the form of church service in England, and thus causing many clergymen to become Nonconformists.

Union, ACTS OF, in British history, see UNITED KINGDOM

Union Day, general holiday in S. Africa, the anniversary of the establishment of the Union of S. Africa, 31 May 1910.

Unionists, party in British politics arising from a desire among Liberals (led by Joseph Chamberlain) to preserve the union of Great Britain and Ireland, and therefore opposed to Home Rule 1885 for Ireland. Later these Liberals formed with the Conservatives a coalition government under Lord Salisbury (1895), and by 1912 the two parties were united. In Scotland the name Unionist is still used for the Conservative Party. See PARLIAMENT

Union Jack, see FLAG

Union of South Africa, self-governing territory of the British Commonwealth ; extends from the most southern point of Africa to the Limpopo R. ; area *c.*790,000sq.m.

Largely a tableland, S. Africa has step-like ranges in the south-west separated by plateaux (Great Karroo and Little Karroo), rising to the Drakensberg Mts, sometimes 11,000ft. The ' high veld ' of the Transvaal, Orange Free State and Cape Province (north) is almost treeless grassland, giving place (towards the Limpopo) to bush veld. A feature of the scenery is the flat-topped (and often cloud-hidden) *kopje,* Dutch for a little head, e.g. Table Mt. The Kalahari Desert has pasture part of the year. On the whole, the climate is excellent. The pop. comprises *c.*2,200,000 Europeans ; 8,770,000 non-Europeans, chiefly Africans (Bantu, Zulu and Hottentot) and Indians (who are traders and merchants). In 1949 there were outbreaks of violence at Durban, in which many people were killed when Zulus and Indians, inflamed by racial hatred, fought in the streets.

Under Dr Malan vigorous steps were taken against Communist agitation ; but the ' colour bar ' question became increasingly formidable. The passing (July 1950) of the S. African Group Areas Bill, preceded by widespread unrest, seems unlikely to provide a solution to the difficult problem how the different races are to live together.

The government cap. is Pretoria ; the legislative cap. Cape Town. Small towns are called *dorps.*

The Union has five Provinces : The CAPE OF GOOD HOPE (area 277,000sq.m ; European pop.800,000 ; cap. Cape Town) has hot summers, and is largely covered with scrub. There are sheep and ostrich farms. The products include diamonds (Kimberley), mohair, goats' hair, wool and hides. See PLATE 6 (*top*)

NATAL (area 36,000sq.m ; pop. 220,000 Europeans ; cap. Pietermaritzburg) has 360m of coast bordering the Indian Ocean ; it is noted for fruits, tea, sugar and wattle (for tanning) ; also for sheep, cattle, cereals, coal, iron and copper ; chief shipping port Durban ; also *Zululand,* annexed 1897, with the grandson of Cetewayo as Paramount Chief.

TRANSVAAL (area 110,000sq.m, pop. 950,000 Europeans) is the home of many Dutch farmers raising stock ; it is famous for Kruger National Park, a vast reserve for game. The Transvaal's chief wealth is gold, notably in the Rand, or Witwatersrand, ridge, 40m long, its reefs containing probably the largest amount of gold ore in the world, and now producing over 10,000,000oz per annum. The chief town of the goldfield is Johannesburg. The capital however is Pretoria, a centre of the steel industry. See PLATES 6 (*bottom*), 33, 34

The ORANGE FREE STATE (area 50,000 sq.m; pop.200,000 Europeans) is noted for diamond mines, sheep-raising, cattle, horses and ostriches ; cap. Bloemfontein.

EGYPTIAN ARCHITECTURE   *plate 65*

hypostyle or pillared hall of the Great Temple at Karnak (1350–1330 B.C.) is an example
ost-and-lintel construction.   The pillars, decorated with flat-relief carvings of figures
inscriptions, are closely spaced because the roof slabs are not strong enough to span
a wider gap.   (*Courtauld Institute*)

plate 66   EGYPTIAN AND GREEK ARCHITECTURE

Top : The Temple at Edfu, Egypt, built between 237 and 42 B.C. The picture shows the end of the pillared hall, which faces a cloistered forecourt. *Bottom :* One of the Greek temples at Paestum, Italy (6th century B.C.), a notable example of the Doric Order.

(Courtauld Institute)

THE ACROPOLIS AT ATHENS
plate 67

Top : The Parthenon, dedicated to Pallas Athene, was built 447–432 B.C. after the devastation of the Acropolis by the Persians. The style is Doric. *Bottom :* The Erechtheum, 420–393 B.C., is Ionic, with slender columns having the characteristic volute or scroll capital. On the left side of the temple can be seen the famous portico of six ' Caryatids ' supporting the marble roof. (Both *Professor T. E. Jessop*)

plate 68   EARLY CHRISTIAN CHURCHES—ROMAN AND BYZANTINE

Top : The church of Santa Sabina in Rome (A.D. 425) shows how the shape of the Roman basilica (law court) was adapted to the needs of Christian worship. (*Rev. J. P. Sumner*).
Bottom : The church of San Vitale at Ravenna, Italy, built A.D. 527–574 at a time of strong influence from Byzantium (Constantinople). The whole structure is designed to support a central dome, richly decorated with mosaics.   (*Courtauld Institute*)

—AND THEIR RAMIFICATIONS

plate 69

Top : Traces of Roman and Byzantine influence can be seen even in this very oriental-looking church at Yaroslavl, Russia. (*Eric Byron, Esq.*). *Bottom :* Southwell Minster (12th–13th century) shows how the basilica has been carried forward into the cruciform or cross-shaped church in medieval Europe. Note how the round gives way to the pointed arch in windows cut in the 15th century.

(*National Buildings Record*)

plate 70   ROMANESQUE OR NORMAN ARCHITECTURE—DOMESTIC

The Castle at Hedingham in Essex was built in the early 12th century by Aubrey de Vere, whose father had come to England with William the Conqueror. This picture shows part of the great semi-circular archway which spans the Banqueting Hall of the 'Keep'. Note the arched fireplace and window recesses with typical Norman chevron or zig-zag mouldings.
(Royal Commission on Ancient Monuments.   H.M.S.O.)

NORMAN ARCHITECTURE—ECCLESIASTICAL   *plate 71*

This view of heavy pillars and deeply recessed arches was taken in Durham Cathedral, which was built during the 11th and 12th centuries. The ribbed cross-vault of the ceiling became an important feature of most churches and halls in the subsequent Gothic period.

(Rev. J. P. Sumner)

plate 72

GOTHIC ARCHITECTURE

Top : Lincoln Cathedral (12–13th centuries) was built during the 'Early English' period of Gothic architecture. The layout is cruciform with two towers flanking the west front and a central tower—the highest of all English cathedrals. (*Raphael Tuck and Sons*).
Bottom : The Queen of Sheba, Samuel and other figures form part of the piers flanking the deeply recessed portals of Reims Cathedral (A.D. 1212–1241). (*Cliché Doucet*)

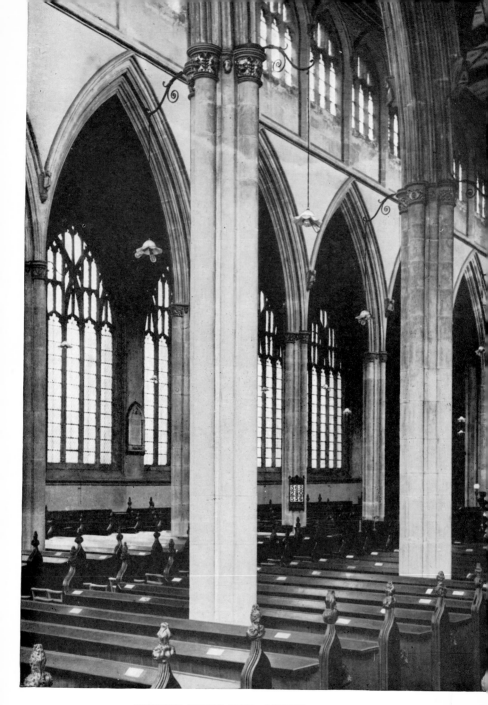

ENGLISH DECORATED GOTHIC   *plate 73*

Church of the Holy Trinity, Hull (14th century). Compare this with the view of Durham
Cathedral on Plate 71. The columns are more slender and formed of a bundle of shafts,
the arches are wider and pointed, and the solid walls have given way to large tracery windows.
The whole effect is light, spacious and graceful. (*F. H. Crossley, Esq.*)

plate 74   THE RENAISSANCE

Top : Hampton Court Palace, built early in the 16th century by Cardinal Wolsey and
Henry VIII, a splendid example of the harmonious combination of brick and stone
in a strictly ordered whole. (*Royal Commission on Ancient Monuments. H.M.S.O.*)
Bottom : Mapledurham, a relatively modest country mansion of the kind built in Elizabethan
and Jacobean times. Large square-headed windows divided by stone mullions are
characteristic of ' Early Renaissance ' architecture   (*National Buildings Record*)

CLASSICAL INFLUENCE

plate 75

Top : The Quirinal Palace in Rome dates from the 15th and 16th centuries. The straight façade, overshadowed by a large cornice, depends for its effect on the repetition of window units which are varied for each floor. On the left is one of the obelisks taken from Egypt under the Roman Empire. *Bottom :* Moor Park in Hertfordshire, built in the 18th century, shows classicism in England at its height. Yet, designed to fit into the English landscape, the English garden and mansion of the 'Late Renaissance' or Georgian period developed a character of their own and became famous throughout Europe. (*Batsford Ltd.*)

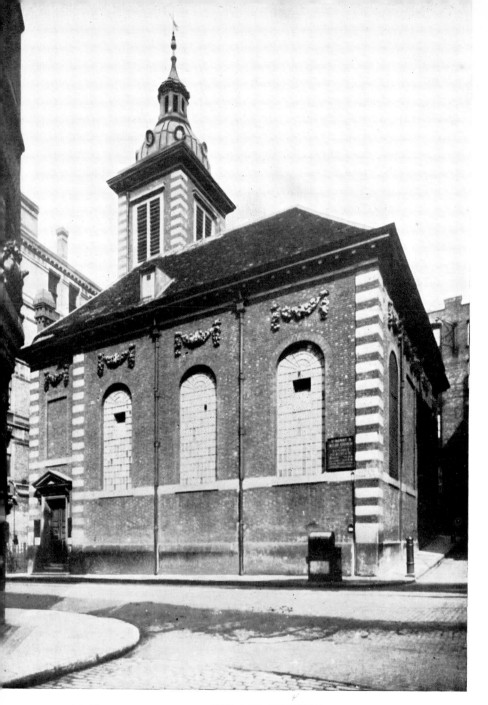

plate 76   THE AGE OF WREN

After the Great Fire of London (1666) Wren was called upon to rebuild many of the City's churches. St. Benet's Welsh Church at Paul's Wharf (rebuilt 1683–84), shown here, is one of the smallest of these churches. The design, almost austere, relies for effect on the warm colour of handmade bricks contrasted with grey stone dressings at the corners. Relief is introduced by the festoons of carved flowers above the windows, an entablature above the door and the heavy cornice at the eaves. (*Batsford Ltd.*)

THE AGE OF THE ADAM BROTHERS

plate 77

In the century after Wren the Adam Brothers were among the most distinguished architects, known for their designs of civic buildings and country mansions as much as for their fine work of interior decoration. The Radcliffe Observatory at Oxford, built in 1772, is reputed an example of Robert Adam's work. It shows his careful placing of windows in panels which are defined by horizontal string courses and ionic pilasters, cornice and balustrade. Typical Adam features are the panels or plaques of carved stone above the windows.

(A. F. Kersting, Esq.)

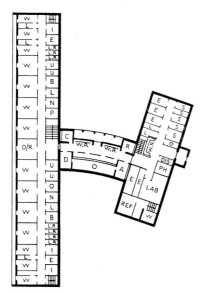

KEY (*Left and Above*)

(*A*) Administrator. (*B*) Bathroom. (*C*) Conference room. (*D*) Director. (*DIS*) Dispensary. (*D/R*)Day-room. (*E*)Examination. (*I*)Isolation. (*L*) Lavatory. (*LAB*) Laboratory. (*L.R*) Linenroom. (*N*) Nurse's room. (*O*) Office. (*P*) Pantry. (*PH*) Pharmacy. (*R*) Records. (*REF*) Refectory. (*S*) Surgery. (*U*) Utility (*W*) Ward. (*W.R*) Waiting-room.

KEY (*Opposite*)

Front : (1) Exhibition Gallery. (2) Foyer. (3) Auditorium. (4) Lavatory. (5, 6, 7) Alternative Prosceniums. (8) False proscenium. (9)Stage Boxes. (10) Wings. (11) Dressing-room (*spare*). (12) Lavatory. (13) Green-room. (14) Sewing-room. (15) Wardrobe.

Back (*Greek Theatre*) :   (16) Upper Stage. (17) Lower Stage (Orchestra). (18) Auditorium.

plate 78

Above : Model and sketch plan (ground floor) for a Naval Hospital at Athens, designed by A. Kriesis. The form of the building is chiefly determined by two factors—(*a*) adaptation to function, which underlies the arrangement in three blocks, (*b*) the shape of the site, which accounts for the slight curving of the central administrative block—and simplicity is the keynote of the design.

F. Gibberd, Esq.

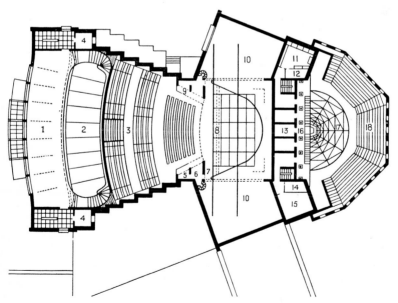

plate 79

Above : Project for a Drama Theatre at Oxford University, by Frederick Gibberd. Here the design is more elaborate, but once again the form of the building is determined mainly by functional considerations. Particularly notable are the incorporation of an open-air theatre for Greek plays, and (inside) the provision of three proscenium arches, so that the producer has a choice between Elizabethan, Restoration and modern stages for the performance of English drama.

plate 80   **EDINBURGH**

Moray Place, Edinburgh, is one of a group of squares built by James Gillespie Graham in the early 19th century when the city expanded rapidly. On account of the adjoining street layout, Moray Place is five-sided with symmetrical façades looking on to a central enclosed garden. At intervals groups of massive columns rise above the heavy masonry of the ground floor with its round headed windows : yet, with great restraint in the use of ornamentation, the effect is harmonious and dignified. (*R. Adam, Esq.*)

SW. AFRICA, a territory mandated to the Union, has an area of 318,000sq.m. Much of the land is barren. For Basutoland and Swaziland, protectorates outside the Union, see BASUTOLAND ; SWAZILAND.

The Cape of Good Hope was discovered 1488 by Bartholomew Diaz, a Portuguese navigator. Table Bay was taken by the Dutch 1652. The Cape Province became British 1814. Natal, discovered Christmas Day (Christ's *natal* day) by Vasco da Gama 1497, was first settled by the English 1824. Dutch Boers (*Voortrekkers*) trekked into the Transvaal from English colonies, fought the natives, and settled beyond the Vaal R. The Boer Wars (1880–81 and 1899–1902) resulted in the S. African Republic becoming part of the British Commonwealth 1910. Since 1933 Dr Malan (Prime Minister from 1948) has advocated a South African republic.

The makers of modern South Africa include Louis Botha, Cecil Rhodes, Sir Harry Smith, Paul Kruger and Field-Marshal Smuts.

See ALL-AFRICA HIGHWAY

Read *Union of South Africa*, Julian Mockford (Nelson) ; *The Story of an African Farm*, Olive Schreiner ; *Jock of the Bushveld*, Percy Fitzpatrick ; *The City of Gold*, Francis Brett Young ; *Prester John*, John Buchan ; *King Solomon's Mines*, Rider Haggard.

unitary method, see RATIO

United Kingdom (UK), consists of England and Wales, Scotland and Northern Ireland. England absorbed Wales by conquest in the 13th c. Scotland's Parliament survived the Union of the Crowns 1603, when James VI of Scots became James I of England ; it was abolished by the Act of Union 1707, and Scotland was incorporated with England in the kingdom of Great Britain. By a similar Act, Ireland was united with Great Britain 1801, thus forming the United Kingdom (of Great Britain and Ireland). The Irish Act of 1801 was dissolved 1922 after the Irish Rebellion and Civil War. Northern Ireland (the six counties of Ulster, cap. Belfast) was then given its own Parliament but remained part of the United Kingdom ; the rest of Ireland became the Irish Free State, now Eire, which likewise has its own Parliament, but does not belong to the United Kingdom.

In Scotland after World War II there was increasing support for the view that the settlement of 1707 should be modified, and that Scotland should once more have a Parliament of its own.

United Nations, see UNO ; WORLD WAR II

United Nations, CHARTER OF THE, see DUMBARTON OAKS

United Nations Organisation, see UNO

United Provinces, province of India (since 1902) comprising Agra and Oudh ; is south of the Himalayas ; towns include Lucknow, Cawnpore, Agra, Allahabad and Benares.

United Services Museum, see LONDON

United States of America, written USA for short, republic between Canada and Mexico (1,600m north to south), and between the Atlantic and Pacific (2,700m east to west) ; area 3,026,789sq.m, without Alaska (586,400sq.m) and other possessions.

A country of vast distances, the USA has *c*.13,000m of coastline ; the Rockies, a mt. range more or less parallel to the Pacific coast ; an immense central plain separated from the Atlantic mainly by the Appalachian Mts ; the Great Lakes (Superior, Michigan, Huron, Erie and Ontario) with a total area of over 98,000sq.m ; the spectacular Grand Canyon (Arizona) ; immense rivers, e.g. Mississippi and Missouri, together flowing 4,502m to the Gulf of Mexico, and many great cities, e.g. New York, Chicago, Philadelphia, Detroit, these four alone having a combined pop. of over 18,000,000.

The forests of the east include beech, oak, pine and spruce ; farther south are magnolias and tulip-trees. Though wide areas are naturally desert, or have been denuded of vegetation in recent years, some of these are now being made productive by the building of huge dams, e.g. Boulder Dam, Grand Coulee and Shasta, the reclamation of the Tennessee Valley (see TVA) being an outstanding example of what can be done when irrigation and hydro-electric power are provided by public enterprise. See PLATE 42 (*bottom*)

Transport and travel are facilitated by 3,000,000m of roads, including the Alaska Highway, part of the 17,000m Inter-American Highway from Alaska to the Argentine. There are 248,040m of railway ; and interstate and overseas airways are being rapidly developed and extended. Of a total of *c*.46,000,000 motor vehicles in the world, over 32,000,000 are in the USA.

The cap., Washington, in the federal district of Columbia (DC) has the government buildings where Congress meets. New York, America's greatest port and most important city, is famous for its waterfront backed by towering skyscrapers ; Detroit, manufacturing millions of motor vehicles, is the scene of Henry Ford's pioneer experiments in mass-production ; Chicago has huge grain elevators, and a maze of stockyards where cattle, sheep and pigs are herded before being made into canned meat, an industry for which (with fruits and fish) America is especially noted.

A country extending from sub-arctic to sub-tropical zones, USA has every variety of region, e.g. New England (near the Atlantic seaboard), in many respects intensely English in appearance and tradition ; the Middle W., hot in summer, dry and cold in winter ; the

23

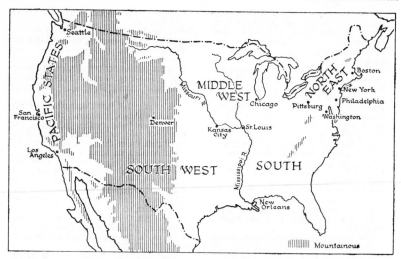

THE UNITED STATES OF AMERICA
Showing the main regions and some of the principal cities

Pacific coast, notably California, where the dry climate and brilliant sunshine have made possible the film industry of Hollywood ; the Rockies with their rugged pinnacles and great forests with saw-mills and lumber camps ; the oil-lands, e.g. Texas, producing not only petroleum but also helium ; the south-west, where (in, say, Arizona, Colorado and Utah) the cactus thrives, and cow-boys round up thousands of cattle on the spacious ranches ; the south-east, e.g. Louisiana, Mississippi and Alabama, famous for cotton, the crop being largely gathered by Negroes ; and what has been called the playground of America, i.e. Florida, where flowers and fruits abound.

As an agricultural country, the USA has over 6,000,000 farms, many of 10,000 acres and more. Maize is grown in vast quantities, and a good harvest of wheat may total 1,140 million bushels, the wheat-belt stretching across N. and S. Dakota, Kansas, Montana and Nebraska. Other products include cane and beet sugar, fruits, e.g. apples, oranges and grapefruit. Reckless exploitation of the soil during the last 70 years has ruined vast tracts of the best land in the USA, a fact which will adversely affect the world's food supply if some remedy cannot soon be found for it. See PLATE 2 (*bottom*)

The vast mineral wealth includes almost all the important metals, e.g. copper, nickel, molybdenum, manganese, gold, silver, lead, zinc, tin and especially iron, hence the great iron and steel industries of Pittsburgh and Cleveland. Coal is abundant, and includes anthracite. Half the world's

total of petroleum (*c.*63,000,000 gallons) is produced in USA. See PLATE 35

Among the exports may be mentioned motor vehicles, aircraft, chemicals, coal, copper, cotton, fruits, tinned goods, iron and steel, machinery (especially precision-made instruments), petroleum, tobacco, wheat, flour and maize.

The government of the USA is based on the constitution drawn up (1787) by George Washington, Thomas Jefferson, Alexander Hamilton and others. Congress comprises two houses : (*a*) a *Senate*, to which each state elects two members (senators) for six years, and (*b*) a *House of Representatives* elected every second year by popular vote. The President, elected every four years, resides, while in office, in the White House, Washington. The chief political parties are Democrats and Republicans.

The unit of currency is the dollar ($) of 100 cents, the sterling value varying according to the rate of exchange, but since 1949 established in the neighbourhood of $2·87 = £1.

Education is compulsory, and a large proportion of young people attend one or other of the many universities, e.g. Harvard, Yale or Columbia.

The USA has a pop. of *c.*140,000,000, including *c.*13,000,000 Negroes, and 376,000 Red Indians, the latter chiefly in reserves in Oklahoma, Arizona and New Mexico. The pop., exceedingly mixed, includes people of Austrian, French, German (over 1,230,000 in 1940), Italian, Irish, Scottish, English, Dutch, Scandinavian stock, and many others.

Apart from the District of Columbia (DC), the USA has 48 states :

Alabama (Ala.) ; Arizona (Ariz.) ; Arkansas (Ark.) ; California (Cal.) ; Colorado (Colo.) ; Connecticut (Conn.); Delaware (Del.) ; Florida (Fla.) ; Georgia (Ga.) ; Idaho ; Illinois (Ill.) ; Indiana (Ind.) ; Iowa ; Kansas (Kan.) ; Kentucky (Ky.) ; Louisiana (La.) ; Maine (Me.) ; Maryland (Md.) ; Massachusetts (Mass.) ; Michigan (Mich.) ; Minnesota (Minn.) ; Mississippi (Miss.); Missouri (Mo.) ; Montana (Mont.) ; Nebraska (Nebr.) ; Nevada (Nev.) ; New Hampshire (N.H.) ; New Jersey (N.J.) ; New Mexico (N. Mex.) ; New York (N.Y.) ; North Carolina (N.C.) ; North Dakota (N. Dak.) ; Ohio ; Oklahoma (Okla.) ; Oregon (Oreg.) ; Pennsylvania (Pa.) ; Rhode Island (R.I.) ; South Carolina (S.C.) ; South Dakota (S. Dak.) ; Tennessee (Tenn.) ; Texas (Tex.) ; Utah ; Vermont (Vt.) ; Virginia (Va.) ; Washington (Wash.) ; West Virginia (W.Va.) ; Wisconsin (Wis.) ; Wyoming (Wyo.).

These comprise continental USA, but in addition there are outlying territories and possessions, e.g. Alaska, Hawaii, Puerto Rico, Guam, the Panama Zone and Samoa. Prior to 1946 the Philippines belonged to the USA, but these islands are now independent.

Columbus led the way to S. America ; John Cabot discovered N. America, reaching Cape Breton I., 1497. English colonisation of what is now the USA began with Raleigh's Virginia, followed (1620) by the settlement of the Pilgrim Fathers. Massachusetts was colonised 1629, and by 1643 the colonists formed the confederacy of New England, i.e. a region on or near the Atlantic seaboard. Later settlements included those of Pennsylvania (by the Quaker, William Penn), S. Carolina and Georgia, all the New England colonies having democratic government and institutions. The Dutch settled in New Amsterdam (now New York) *c.*1664. Colonists from Scotland and France followed ; and later generations (born and bred in America) pushed steadily west.

In the 18th c. the Americans resented George III's attempt to tax them without representation, hence the war of American Independence 1775–83, the *Declaration of Independence* (1776), and the drawing up of a new constitution. George Washington, who had guided the young nation to independence, became the first President of the USA, 1789, thirteen states comprising the original nation.

From this period Americans became intensely patriotic, and it is not surprising that (1823) President Monroe propounded the doctrine that no European power should acquire territory in the American continent.

The gold rush to California (1848) hastened exploration in the west, but political discontents, and the question of slavery, led to the unhappy and costly American Civil War 1861–65, in which the southern states were prevented from leaving the union by the skill of Abraham Lincoln, who also succeeded in abolishing slavery.

Since then the USA has had a meteoric rise to greatness. A world power to be reckoned with long before the close of last century, she contributed towards the defeat of Germany in World War I, though she did not support her own President Wilson in his outline for the League of Nations.

From 1919 to 1933 the USA tried the experiment of Prohibition (i.e. making the sale of intoxicants illegal), and *c.*1929 began the period of industrial and trade depression which caused widespread unemployment till President Franklin D. Roosevelt (1933) instituted his National Recovery scheme which, to some extent, gradually restored prosperity.

The outbreak of World War II (1939) found America firmly isolationist, i.e. determined not to be involved in European disputes, but under President Roosevelt's masterly guidance the country gradually agreed to render increasing assistance to Great Britain, e.g. Lend-Lease. With Japan's attack (7 Dec 1941) on Pearl Harbour, an American naval base in the Pacific, the USA came wholeheartedly into the war against the Axis powers. She enlisted nearly 7,000,000 men in the army, over 3,790,000 of all ranks in the navy, 2,400,000 in the air arm, while civilians supplied huge quantities of food and munitions to the Allies. From 1950 the USA prosecuted the war against N. Korea with the utmost vigour (see KOREA) ; and in 1951 the nation was preparing to defend democracy in the Far East and in W. Europe should need arise.

USA has long been the home of skilled inventors, engineers, scientists and doctors. Many of the inventions of the last 150 years have been American, as also a host of scientific discoveries, improved medical and surgical methods, together with much pioneer work in astronomy, agriculture and town-planning.

In literature we think of quaint old Benjamin Franklin (who was also a statesman and inventor), of Harriet Beecher Stowe, author of *Uncle Tom's Cabin* ; of Washington Irving, Mark Twain, Herman Melville, Oliver Wendell Holmes ; of the short story writers, e.g. Edgar Alan Poe, Nathaniel Hawthorne, Bret Harte and O. Henry ; of the poets Henry Wadsworth Longfellow and Walt Whitman ; and of such novelists as (to name a few only) Henry James, Theodore Dreiser, Joseph Hergesheimer, Sinclair Lewis, Upton Sinclair, Ernest Hemingway, Thornton Wilder (e.g. *The Bridge of San Luis Rey*), Pearl Buck (*The Good Earth*), Robert

Sherwood, Eugene O'Neill, John Steinbeck (*The Grapes of Wrath*), Margaret Mitchell (*Gone With the Wind*). Read *USA*, D. W. Brogan ; *Inside USA*, John Gunther.

units (electrical), see ELECTRICITY

universe, see ASTRONOMY

universities, educational establishments, the two chief functions of which are (*a*) research, i.e. the pursuit of knowledge for its own sake ; (*b*) teaching, i.e. passing on knowledge to students ; thus, each university becomes a corporation or society of scholars, and includes professors, lecturers, research students and undergraduates. Degrees are conferred on students who have qualified by passing certain examinations. What are known as Pass degrees (e.g. BA, B.Comm, B.Sc) are usually obtained after studying for three years ; an Honours degree may take longer, and is awarded to a student who has specialised in one or two subjects. A degree in medicine usually takes a minimum of five years. Post-graduate degrees, denoting success in advanced study, may be taken after two or more further years of study. See EXAMINATIONS

Some universities, especially Oxford and Cambridge, are almost entirely residential, i.e. the students live together in colleges during term time. Others have some college or hostel accommodation, but are largely non-resident, students living at home or in private lodgings. All universities in the UK, except London, demand that the student shall live near enough to the university to attend lectures and take part in university life. In addition to academic studies there are opportunities for students to enjoy games and athletics of all kinds, and to join in debating and other societies, and in many forms of social activity. The social and athletic side of university life is usually controlled by a Students' Union, and the Unions of the different universities are co-ordinated by, and represented on, the National Union of Students, a body which discusses any topics of general interest to students, and is regarded as the official organ of student opinion.

Uniquely among British Universities, London University confers degrees on external as well as internal students, and courses for these degrees may be taken either at various colleges and university colleges throughout the country, or by private study and correspondence courses.

There are universities in Aberdeen, Belfast (Queen's University), Birmingham, Bristol, Cambridge, Dublin (Trinity College), Durham, Edinburgh, Glasgow, Leeds, Liverpool, London, Manchester, Oxford, Reading, St Andrews, Sheffield, Wales (colleges at Aberystwyth, Bangor and Cardiff) ; and there are university colleges (i.e. colleges which have not yet received a Royal

Charter and, therefore, cannot yet confer their own degrees, but whose students take London degrees) at Exeter, Hull, Leicester and Southampton. The four Scottish universities were all founded before 1600. All the English universities, except Oxford and Cambridge, were founded after 1800.

Most universities, in addition to the courses for their own students, organise extra-mural lectures and University Extension classes. Particulars of these courses may be obtained from the Director or Secretary of the university concerned. (See a useful list in *Whitaker's Almanack*.)

Famous English-speaking universities overseas include the University of S. Africa ; the universities of Calcutta, Bombay, Allahabad and Madras (India); McGill, Toronto and Dalhousie in Canada ; Melbourne, Adelaide, Sydney and Perth (Australia).

Famous foreign universities include Salerno, Padua, Bologna, Siena, Naples, Rome, Perugia, Florence, Turin, in Italy ; Paris, Orleans (France) ; Prague ; Vienna, Heidelberg, Cologne, Tübingen, Königsberg, Jena, Göttingen, Bonn (Germany and Austria) ; Louvain (Belgium) and Leyden (Holland) ; in USA, Princeton, Yale and Harvard.

A most useful guide for the new student at a university is *First Year at the University*, Bruce Truscot. See EDUCATION ; EXAMINATIONS

University College, college of Oxford University ; believed to have been founded prior to 1249.

University Extension classes, see UNIVERSITIES

Unknown Warrior, soldier of World War I who fell in France. Though his name and his rank are unknown, his remains were solemnly reburied in Westminster Abbey, 11 Nov 1920, as a tribute to the fallen.

UNO, short for United Nations Organisation, an international committee that first met in London 1946 to deal with world problems after World War II. The foundations of the organisation were laid at Moscow 1943, and the principles then agreed upon were developed at Dumbarton Oaks (Washington, DC) 1944, and at the San Francisco Conference 1945. UNO (representing 51 states) came into existence 24 Oct 1945, and its flag (The Four Freedoms) has 4 vertical red stripes on a white background. UNO replaced the League of Nations, which held its final assembly 1946.

At the first meeting of the General Assembly (London) M. Paul H. Spaak (Belgium) was elected President.

The permanent HQ of the General Assembly is in Manhattan (New York), the building having been in use since 1951. Meanwhile, delegates (now from 55 countries) meet either at Flushing Meadows, Long I., *c.*15m from Central New York, or at Lake Success, *c.*15m from Flushing Meadows. Delegates wear so-called ' walkie-talkie ' sets, i.e. radio receiving sets with headphones, these enabling them to hear simultaneous interpretations of speeches in one of the four official languages used. UNO publishes a weekly magazine about its many activities.

Important tasks are performed in UNO by the Security Council (chiefly responsible for world peace, and advised by military experts and by an Atomic Energy Commission) ; the Economic and Social Council, dealing with international economic, social, cultural and other matters ; the International Court of Justice ; the Secretariat. Controlled by UNO are such bodies as UNESCO (see UNESCO) ; FAO, i.e. Food and Agriculture Organisation of the United Nations, which has an annual conference, and is organising a very necessary World Food Board ; ECO, i.e. European Coal Organisation, designed to increase Europe's total coal output and direct the coal to countries in greatest need ; ECITO, i.e. European Central Inland Transport Organisation, thus far dealing chiefly with railways ; PICAO, i.e. Provincial International Civil Aviation Organisation ; and UNRRA, i.e. United Nations Relief and Rehabilitation Administration which, by June 1947, when its activites ceased, had repatriated over 7,000,000 displaced persons, and shipped to needy countries supplies valued at over £900,000,000.

Several nations have joined the United Nations since it came into being 24 Oct 1945, but the 51 original members were : Argentina, Australia, Belgium, Bolivia, Brazil, Byelorussian Soviet Socialist Republic, Canada, Chile, China, Colombia, Costa Rica, Cuba, Czechoslovakia, Denmark, Dominican Republic, Ecuador, Egypt, El Salvador, Ethiopia, France, Greece, Guatemala, Haiti, Honduras, India, Iran, Iraq, Lebanon, Liberia, Luxemburg, Mexico, Netherlands, New Zealand, Nicaragua, Norway, Panama, Paraguay, Peru, Philippine Commonwealth, Poland, Saudi Arabia, Turkey, Ukrainian Soviet Socialist Republic, Union of S. Africa, USSR, United Kingdom, USA, Uruguay, Venezuela, Yugoslavia.

Read *The United Nations,* Louis Dolivet.

UNRRA, see UNO
untouchable, see PARIAH
Upanishads, see HINDU
upas tree, *ū'pas,* tree found in Java ; sometimes 60ft high ; noted for the exceedingly poisonous milky juice which flows when the bark is cut. Metaphorically, ' upas tree ' means any sinister or harmful influence.
Upolu, *oo-pō'loo,* most fertile island of W. Samoa (part of the dominion of NZ) ; produces copra, bananas and rubber ; Robert Louis Stevenson's

burial place ; has the harbour of Apia.
Uppingham, town, Rutlandshire ; has a boys' public school founded 1584.
Uppsala, *ūp-sä'lä,* town, Sweden, 45m from Stockholm ; famous for its cathedral and university ; pop.40,000.
Ur, ancient Sumerian city on the R. Euphrates in what is now Iraq ; once the home of Abraham ; noted for ruined temples and other traces of an ancient civilisation of 7–5000BC. Some of its buildings were discovered 1944.
Read *Ur of the Chaldees,* Sir Leonard Woolley.
Ural, *ū'ral,* river flowing 1,500m from the Urals to the Caspian Sea.
Urals, mt. range of USSR, rich in metals, coal and precious stones, extending from the Arctic to the Caspian Sea. Huge oil deposits have been found recently.
uranium, see GREAT BEAR LAKE ; LEAD ; RADIOACTIVITY ; RADIUM
Uranus, see ASTRONOMY
Urban, *ūr'ban,* name of eight popes, among them URBAN II (*d* 1099) who preached the first crusade ; URBAN VI (1318–89), who by his tactless behaviour brought about the great schism 1378, i.e. the scandal of two popes, one in Rome, the other at Avignon ; URBAN VIII (1568–1644) who supported Richelieu of France in the Thirty Years' War.
Ure, *ūr,* river, Yorkshire ; flows 50m from the Pennines and through Wensleydale to meet the R. Swale.
Ur of the Chaldees, see SUMER ; UR
Ursa Major and **Minor,** see GREAT BEAR
Uruguay, *ū-ru-gwā'* ; *ū-ru-gwī',* smallest but most advanced republic of S. America ; is north of the Rio de la Plata ; area *c.*72,000sq.m ; pop. 2,185,000, of whom 770,000 live in Montevideo, the cap. The wide pampas supports vast herds of cattle and flocks of sheep. The exports are frozen and packed meat and hides. Uruguay has been a republic since 1830. A bridge carrying road and rail traffic over the R. Uruguay now links the country with Brazil.
USA, see UNITED STATES OF AMERICA
USA, PRESIDENT OF, see PRESIDENT
Ushant, *ūsh'ant,* rugged island off the west coast of France.
Usk, river flowing 70m through beautiful scenery, chiefly in Monmouthshire, to the Bristol Channel.
USSR, i.e. Union of Soviet Socialist Republics, formerly Russia, an imperial kingdom ruled by tsars ; now comprises RSFSR (i.e. Russian Socialist Federal Soviet Republic), area 6,372,860sq.m ; pop.109,280,000, and 15 other republics, e.g. the Ukraine, Byelorussia, Armenia, Georgia, Lithuania, Latvia and Estonia, the total area of all 16 republics being 8,336,510sq.m, with an estimated pop. of 193,000,000.

Almost three-quarters of Russia is an immense plain with steppes in the south, tundra towards the Arctic north. The mts. include such ranges as the Caucasus,

Urals (separating European from Asiatic Russia), the Pamir, Tien and Shan ranges. The rivers include the Volga, Don, Dnieper (Europe), Ob, Yenisei and Lena (Asia). The climate is continental and extreme, Moscow having a winter temperature of 12°F, rising in summer to 68°F ; while Verkhoyansk (NE. Siberia), the coldest place in the world, has 81° of frost in Jan., and a temperature of 70°F in July, a difference of c.120°. In spite of weather conditions in the far north, the Soviet has built towns there, developed agriculture and mining to an extraordinary extent, and annexed (1937) large uninhabited areas round the N. Pole. The far northern towns of Kirovsk (pop.40,000), Amderma, Igarka and Duninka are all new. All are busy centres, and in them are hardy people working in Arctic conditions. Tomatoes are grown in lat.70°N in electrically warmed soil.

Agriculture, the chief occupation of the people, has been vastly improved in recent years, farming being on the collective system. Immense wheat harvests are gathered from the ' black earth ' regions, also rye, oats, barley, millet, maize, sugar-beet, potatoes, cotton, flax and hemp. The great forests include coniferous trees in the north, where fur-trapping is important. The fisheries include herring and cod, and sturgeon (especially for caviare) from the Volga. The Soviet's mineral resources are enormous, e.g. the Ural region, where gold, platinum, iron (chiefly in the Ukraine), copper, mercury, asbestos, magnesite and coal are mined. Coal is also mined in the Donetz region, and the Soviet's supplies comprise one-fifth of the world total. Oil is found in the Caucasus, at Baku, and notably in the region between the Volga and the Urals, e.g. Syzran. Plans are now in progress for increasing production of all mineral resources, these being aided by the construction of new railway lines, canals and roads and airways. Railways include the Trans-Caucasian line, the Trans-Caspian, the Trans-Siberian ; while gigantic waterways, completed or in process of construction, link Moscow with the Baltic, White, Black and Caspian Seas, and provide a valuable network. Hydro-electric power is generated on a huge scale.

The largest republic (RSFSR) is in the east of European Russia and the north of Asiatic Russia, and has 17,000m of Arctic coastline. Its mineral wealth is enormous, including oil. Here is the capital (Moscow).

Among other republics of the Soviet may be noted : (*a*) UKRAINE, a great cereal-growing district in the southwest, cap. Kiev ; (*b*) WHITE RUSSIA (Byelorussia), cap. Minsk ; (*c*) AZERBAIJAN, by the Caspian Sea, important for its mineral wealth, especially oil at Baku, the capital ; (*d*) GEORGIA, south

of the Caucasian Mts, which has the richest supplies of manganese ore in the world, also coal and petroleum deposits, and produces great quantities of boxwood ; cap. Tiflis ; (*e*) LITHUANIA, a Baltic republic, annexed to the USSR 1940, area c.20,000sq.m ; pop.2,450,000; produces rye, wheat, barley, and exports bacon, dairy produce, cellulose and timber ; cap. Vilnius ; (*f*) LATVIA, east of the Gulf of Riga ; area c.25,000 sq.m ; pop.2,000,000 ; annexed to the USSR 1940 ; mostly a flat and marshy region exporting flax, timber, dairy produce and paper ; cap. Riga ; (*g*) ESTONIA, annexed to the USSR 1940 : an agricultural republic producing rye, oats, flax, butter and bacon, and manufacturing cotton and woollen goods, paper and matches : cap. Tallinn ; (*h*) other republics, e.g. ARMENIA, UZBEKISTAN.

Large cities of the Soviet include Leningrad, previously known as St Petersburg, then (1914–24) as Petrograd; Gorki (formerly Nijni-Novgorod) ; Rostov on Don ; Stalingrad ; Kuibyshev ; Kazan ; Sverdlovsk ; Novosibirsk ; Saratov ; Voronezh ; Omsk ; Archangel ; Astrakan ; Moscow the cap. of the RSFSR, has pop.4,137,000 and was founded c.1147. Though St Petersburg was the capital from 1703, Moscow again became the capital 1918, and now the vast Palace of the Soviets rising in its midst is destined to be the tallest building in the world, 1,365ft, with a stainless steel statue of Lenin 325ft high.

For long centuries only partly civilised, ruled by tsars who crushed the peasantry with taxes, and banished all political agitators to the dreary wastes of Siberia, Russia remained a backward nation till the Socialist revolution of 1917, when Tsar Nicholas II abdicated, and a republic was declared. Lenin steered the new republic through difficult years till his death 1924, when Joseph Stalin became leader. By a series of harsh but effective ' Five Year Plans,' Stalin enabled the Soviet to weather the storms of party strife and Trotsky revolutions, and to build up an immense co-operative system of production, providing farms with machinery, improving transport, establishing mills and factories, advancing teaching by leaps and bounds, opening up new mineral deposits, developing hydro-electric power, statecontrolling the cinema, press, trade, and thus marshalling the nation's energies and resources so that, when invaded by Nazi Germany 1941 (though at first overrun, huge areas being devastated by the scorched-earth policy, and the enemy penetrating as far as Stalingrad, Moscow and the Urals) the USSR was finally able to roll back the Germans, and liberate occupied areas.

The USSR is nominally a democracy, but in fact a totalitarian state. Only one party, the Communist Party, exists. The Union is governed by the Communist Party through the Supreme Council of the USSR, comprising (*a*) the Council of the Union, i.e. 569 members representing the various republics, and (*b*) the Council of Nationalities, i.e. 574 members. The Third Communist International or Comintern, founded 1919, was dissolved 1943. Villages, districts, regions and republics all elect by direct vote their councils, i.e. *soviets*, and each has its own council of commissars. It is very difficult for anybody who is not a member of the Communist Party to be elected. Though once abolished, religion is not now forbidden.

After World War II ideological differences between Russia and the democratic peoples of the West became more apparent. Hopes of avoiding war diminished—hence the huge armament plans of W. Europe and the USA.

Russia has produced many notable men, e.g. in music such names as Borodin, Rimsky-Korsakov, Rubinstein, Tschaikovsky, Rachmaninoff and Stravinski ; among authors and poets Pushkin, Gogol, Turgenev, Dostoievski, Tolstoy, Tchekhov, Gorki and Andreyev. The people delight in films, plays, chess, dancing, and especially ballet ; in recent years immense strides have been made in science and engineering, though the country as a whole lacks technicians. In war (e.g. that of 1939–45) the Red Army proved invincible and heroic, its generals (under Marshal Stalin) developing pioneer methods of attack, and employing military tactics, new types of tanks and planes, with the utmost skill.

Read *Life in the USSR*, Beatrice King (Nelson) ; *Land of the Soviets*, James Gregory ; *An Atlas of USSR*, James Gregory and J. F. Horrabin.

See STALIN, J. ; WORLD WAR II

Utah, *ū'tä*, state, USA. It is north of Arizona, has great mineral wealth, and is famous for cereals, vegetables, cattle and sheep ; cap. Salt Lake City.

Utica, *ū'ti-kä*, city, New York State, USA ; noted for textiles, including knitwear ; pop.101,000.

Utopia, *ū-tō'piä* (Greek *ou*, not, *topos*, a place), title of a book by Sir Thomas More (published in Latin at Louvain 1516 ; first English translation 1551), the story of a perfect state on an imaginary island. It may be compared with Plato's *Republic* ; Augustine's *The City of God* ; Bacon's *New Atlantis* ; Samuel Butler's *Erewhon* (anagram of 'Nowhere') and *The World Set Free*, H. G. Wells.

See MORE, SIR THOMAS

Utrecht, *ū'trekt*, city, Netherlands, *c.*21m north-east of Rotterdam ; manufactures machinery, chemicals and glass ; pop. 164,000.

Utrecht, TREATY OF, see SPANISH SUCCESSION, WAR OF

Uxbridge, town, Middlesex ; pop.51,000.

Uzbekistan, *ŭz-bek-i-stän'*, region of USSR, comprising the former states of Bokhara and Khiva ; total area 66,400sq.m ; pop.6,300,000. North of Afghanistan, it exports silk, cotton (the Khiva region having notable cotton lands), wheat and rice ; cap. Tashkent. One of the most striking features is the Great Ferghana Canal (188m), of much aid to irrigation.

Uzziah, *ŭz-ī'ä*, King of Judah ; said to have reigned 52 years ; became a leper (2 Kings 14–15 ; 2 Chronicles 26).

V

' V,' in World War II, symbol of victory ; indicated faith in ultimate triumph for the Allied Nations. The sign given with two fingers by Winston Churchill, was adopted by underground movements working against the Nazis. The Morse equivalent (· · · —), the opening bars of Beethoven's *Fifth Symphony*, and such verses as

> Do not give way,
> Never despair ;
> We'll get them yet,
> Hitler beware,

were all variations on a victory theme which helped to unite and encourage people in occupied countries. The ' V ' campaign was organised by Colonel Britton.

V2, see AVIATION

Vaal, *väl*, tributary of the Orange R. ; separates the Transvaal from the Orange Free State, S. Africa ; length *c.*560m.

vaccination, *vak-si-nā'shon*, precautionary treatment against smallpox, a disease which, in the 18th c., was responsible for many deaths a year in Britain, and for the disfigurement of many people. Edward Jenner (1749–1823) discovered *c.*1796 that calves suffer from cow-pox, which is identical with smallpox, and that by inoculating a child with lymph taken from such diseased calves it is possible to produce in the child anti-toxins that form a lasting defence against smallpox, giving immunity for 5–6 years, and ensuring that the disease will never be severe enough to leave disfiguring scars. Vaccination was compulsory in England from 1853 to 1948.

Similarly, other inoculations are now used, e.g. for diphtheria (known as immunisation), and for preventing tetanus, cholera, typhoid and whooping cough. See JENNER, EDWARD

vaccine, vak'sēn, either lymph, containing a virus, taken from an animal suffering from cow-pox, see VACCINATION, or any preparation of a virus or fluid containing dead bacteria injected into the body to produce a degree of immunity from certain diseases.

vacuum, vak'ū-ŭm (Latin vacuus, empty), empty space. We may consider a perfect vacuum in theory, but in practice we may construct only a partial vacuum, e.g. by means of an exhaust pump and mercy air-pumps. Vacuum-tubes always contain at least some molecules of air. A good vacuum in a cyclotron contains 1/100,000,000th of an atmosphere.

vacuum flask, storage vessel invented by Sir James Dewar, the principle being adapted (as in the Thermos flask) for storing hot liquids. The flask has double walls, the facing surfaces silvered to diminish loss of heat by radiation, the space between being a partial vacuum to reduce convection and conduction, and the points where the vessel touches the container being as small as possible to reduce loss by conduction. Evaporation is prevented by closing the top with a cork.

Note : The vacuum flask will also keep cold things cold, and was, in fact, invented for this purpose. See DEWAR, SIR J.

VAD, see NURSING

Valdai Hills, väl-dī', low hills in the neighbourhood of Leningrad, USSR.

Valencia, väl-en'shiä, city c.3m from the mouth of the R. Guadalaviar, Spain ; manufactures silk, cigars and leather goods ; produces oranges ; once the cap. of the Moorish kingdom of Valencia ; pop.400,000.

Valenciennes, vä-län-syen', town, France, on the R. Schelde and 20m from Douai ; once famous for lace ; now manufactures chemicals ; pop.42,000.

valency, vä'len-si, combining power of a chemical element, expressed in relation to the number of atoms of hydrogen, or other monatomic elements or groups, with which one atom of the element will combine or will replace. An element may be monovalent or a monad (e.g. chlorine in HCl), or bivalent, i.e. it combines with two atoms of hydrogen (e.g. oxygen in H_2O), or trivalent, e.g. nitrogen in NH_3. If an element does not combine with another (e.g. argon) it is non-valent.

The electronic theory of valency in its simplest form supposes three main types of union.

(a) In *Electrovalency*, electrons are given by one atom to another, so producing electrified particles called ions.

(b) In *Covalency*, electrons are shared usually in pairs, one electron in each pair being provided by one atom.

(c) In *Semipolar Valency*, electrons are shared likewise in pairs, but both electrons are provided by one atom. In all these cases the atoms reach the stable condition of eight electrons in their orbits.

The tendency at present is to X-ray solids and find how the atoms are actually arranged, thus securing a clue to the essential nature of valency. See ELEMENT

Valens, FLAVIUS, vä'lenz (d AD378), Roman emperor ; ruled from 365 ; killed at the battle of Adrianople.

Valerian, val-ee'ri-an (d. AD266), Roman emperor ; an able administrator ; fought against the Goths, and was taken prisoner by the Persian conqueror Sapor.

valerian, name of various plants (family *Valerianaceae*), including the common valerian, with deeply lobed leaves that are not quite opposite, and masses of clustered pink or white tubular flowers at the top of the stem.

VALERIAN
The flowering plant and the seed

Valhalla, see BRUNHILD

valkyre, see BRUNHILD

Valla, LORENZO, see CONSTANTINE, DONATION OF

Valladolid, välyä-thō-lēth', university and cathedral city, Spain ; pop.116,000. Columbus died here.

Valletta, cap. and port, Malta ; a British naval base and military station ; has the palace of the Knights of St John ; pop.23,000.

Vallombro'sa, beauty-spot 21m from Florence, Italy. It is among the pine forests of the Apennines.

Valmy, BATTLE OF, val-mē, 1792, named from a village in NE. France, where the French defeated a German invading army.

Valois, väl-wä, name of a famous French

family, members of which were kings 1328–1589, Philip VI (1293–1350) being the first, Henry III the last.

Valparaiso, *văl-pă-rā'zō*, city and chief port, Chile. Though repeatedly shaken by earthquakes, it is a handsome and prosperous port ; linked by rail with Buenos Aires ; pop.216,000.

vampire, once regarded by many peoples of Europe as a demon, especially one occupying the body of a dead person. See BAT

vanadium, white metal and element, V ; atomic weight 50·95 ; atomic number 23. The hardest metal known, it is much used in steel alloys.

Vanbrugh, SIR JOHN, *van'brŭ* (1664–1726), architect, *b* London ; built Castle Howard and Blenheim Palace ; also noted for his witty plays.

Vancouver, chief port of British Columbia and W. Canada. Has a magnificent harbour and a vast trade, being the western terminus of the CPR ; deals in grain ; noted for brewing, shipbuilding, sugar refining and flour milling ; pop. 275,000.

Separated from the mainland by Queen Charlotte Sound is VANCOUVER I., 278m long ; rich in timber and minerals (e.g. coal, iron and copper). Its largest town, Victoria, is the cap. of British Columbia. See PLATE 30 (*bottom*)

Vandals, barbaric Teutonic people associated in their migrations with the Goths ; migrated in the 3rd c. from the shores of the Baltic Sea to the Danube ; then, in the 5th c., into Gaul (France) ; thence to Spain and N. Africa. In these countries they helped to overthrow what was left of the Roman Empire.

Vanderbilt, name of a family of American business-men. The founder, CORNELIUS VANDERBILT (1794–1877), *b* Staten I., New York, started a ferry at sixteen. Later he owned fleets of ships and controlled many railways ; died leaving £20,000,000 ; endowed Vanderbilt University. His son, WILLIAM HENRY (1821–85), left £40,000,000. William's son, CORNELIUS (1843–99), was director of thirty-five railways.

Van Dyck, SIR ANTHONIS, *van dīk* (1599–1641), Flemish artist, *b* Antwerp ; spent much time in England, painting many portraits of Charles I and his court ; noted for his skill in painting hands.

Vane, SIR HENRY (1589–1654), English politician ; at first one of Charles I's counsellors, though he later supported Parliament. His son, SIR HENRY VANE (1613–62), a Puritan, was Governor of Massachusetts. He served the Parliamentarians, but disapproved of the execution of Charles I ; reorganised the navy and enjoyed Cromwell's favour. Being accused of plotting rebellion after the Restoration, he was unfairly tried for treason, and executed.

Van Gogh, VINCENT, *văn chŏch* (1853–90),

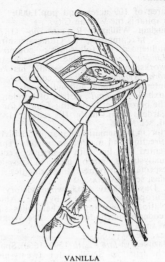

VANILLA
A pod, the buds, the flower and a leaf

Dutch artist ; often insane, but a superbly sincere and passionate revealer of nature in vivid colour. See PLATE XV

vanilla, climbing plant of Central America. Its pods are used for flavouring various foods.

Van Loon, HENDRICK (1882–1944), Dutch-American historian ; won fame 1922 with his book *The Story of Mankind*, followed by *Ancient Man* and *The Home of Mankind*.

vaporisation, see LATENT HEAT

vapour, *vā'pĕr*, gas below the critical temperature ; may be liquefied by increasing the pressure without altering the temperature.

Varna, thriving Black Sea port, Bulgaria ; pop.78,000.

Vasco da Gama, *gä'mä* (*d* 1524), Portugese sailor who, 1497, went in search of a sea-route to India, rounded the Cape of Good Hope, and reached Calicut. He made a second voyage 1502.

Vatican, official home of the pope and seat of papal government in Rome, a group of palaces, courts, chapels, offices and gardens, covering 13½ acres, all on a low hill (the ancient *Mons Vaticanus*) immediately north of St Peter's. Most of the buildings were begun by Pope Nicholas V, 1450. Some of the 7,000 rooms have rich decorations by Perugino, Raphael and Fra Angelico. Of the many chapels, the *Sistine*, built in the time of Pope Sixtus IV (say, 1480), is notable for its glorious frescoes by Michelangelo. Art treasures are to be seen in the north wing (the Belvedere) over 400yd long, among them the *Apollo Belvedere* and *Laocoon*. The Vatican Library has *c.*35,000 MSS and 250,000 books.

The VATICAN, or PAPAL STATE, has an

area of 109 acres, and pop.1,000. Its capital is the Vatican City.

Vaughan Williams, RALPH, *vŏn-* (1872–), composer, *b* Gloucestershire ; influenced by folk-songs ; composed *Linden Lea* ; notable for orchestral works, symphonies (especially his *Pastoral Symphony*), piano concertos, all intensely national and individual.

Vauxhall, *voks-haul'*, district of London in the borough of Lambeth ; famous for its gardens from Charles II's reign to 1859.

veal, see MEAT

vector, in mathematics, a quantity involving direction and magnitude, usually represented by a line with an arrow. Vector analysis is much used in physics, especially for representing velocities.

Vedas, see BRAHMANISM

VE Day, 8 May 1945, when victory in Europe was secured by the Allied Nations, Germany and her allies surrendering unconditionally. See WORLD WAR II

Vega, see ASTRONOMY

Velazquez, *vā-läth'kwäth* (1599–1660), Spanish artist, *b* Seville ; for twenty-nine years court painter to Philip IV ; friend of Rubens ; excelled as a portrait painter, though his *Surrender of Breda* is regarded as one of the finest of all historical pictures.

veld, see GRASS

velocity, in physics may be of (*a*) *sound*, (*b*) of *light*. The velocity of sound in any medium is expressed in the formula

$$V = \sqrt{\frac{E}{D}},$$ where V = velocity, E =

modulus of elasticity of the medium,

D = its density. For a gas $V = \sqrt{\frac{\gamma P}{D}}$

where P is the pressure of the gas, γ a constant depending on the number of atoms in its molecule (for air $\gamma=1\cdot4$). The approx. velocity of sound in air at (60°F) = 1,120ft per sec., or $c.12\frac{1}{2}$ miles per min ; this increases approx. $1\cdot1$ft for each degree rise in temperature. The velocity of sound in water (at 15°C) = $c.4,780$ft per sec.

The velocity of *light* (in a vacuum) = 186,282mp.sec. For acceleration, see ACCELERATION

velour, fabric of linen, cotton and mohair. It resembles felt, but has a pile like velvet.

velvet, silken fabric with a short, thick pile. It was introduced into Europe from the Far East in the 13th c., Spain and Italy later being famous for velvets. The revocation of the *Edict of Nantes*, 1685, drove many French Protestant refugees to England, where they began manufacturing velvet, especially in Spitalfields, London.

Vendôme, DUC DE, *vän-dōm'* (1654–1712), French soldier, *b* Paris. A brilliant leader, he captured Barcelona 1697, but was defeated by Marlborough at Oudenarde 1708.

Venezuela, *ven-ē-zwē'lä*, republic of S.

America, It is north of Brazil, and largely comprises the basin of the R. Orinoco, the source of which was discovered 1944. The climate is tropical, the hot wet season being Apr.–Oct., and though there are dense forests the llanos (open prairie) cover large areas. Products include rice, coffee, wheat, maize, sugar, tobacco, cotton, rubber and gums. Petroleum is important. The area is $c.364,000$sq.m ; the pop.4,100,000. The cap., Carácas, is the burial place of Bolivar, to whom the republic owes its independence from Spain.

Venice, city and Adriatic port, Italy. It is built on $c.80$ islands and on piles, and many of its ' streets ' are canals or waterways along which move gondolas and motor launches. A naval base, it has shipbuilding yards. Much favoured by tourists, it is famous for its beautiful buildings, e.g. the cathedral of St Mark, the church of St Maria della Salute, the Palace of the Doges (magistrates), old houses, the Bridge of Sighs ; also the Rialto. Prior to the discovery of a route to India via S. Africa, Venice was, from the 5th c., a great market for goods from the east. The pop. is 267,000.

venison, see MEAT

' veni, vidi, vici,' see CAESAR, JULIUS

Venizelos, ELEUTHERIOS, *ven-ē-zē'lōs* (1864–1936), Greek politician, *b* Crete, the independence of which he secured 1897. Prime Minister of Greece 1910, 1917, he formed the Balkan League against Turkey ; and in spite of opposition in World War I, forced King Constantine to abdicate, and Greece to co-operate with the Allies. Prime Minister again 1928, he made treaties with Italy, Yugoslavia and Turkey.

ventilation, method of circulating pure air in buildings.

When people are in a room or hall the air tends to become vitiated because oxygen is being used up and also because carbon dioxide (CO_2) is being breathed out (the presence of as little as $0\cdot5\%$ CO_2 is harmful). Moreover, the temperature tends to rise. Ventilation must ensure a sufficient supply of oxygen, the carrying off of CO_2, a comfortable temperature without draughts, and the correct humidity. This may be achieved by keeping windows open at the top ; or, as in air-conditioned buildings, by a system of circulating cleaned and warmed air by means of electric fans. Scientific ventilation is now an important item not only in buildings, e.g. factories, schools, theatres, cinemas, hotels, administrative offices, but in travelling vehicles and aircraft.

Ventnor, *vent'nēr*, health resort, I. of Wight.

ventricle, see BLOOD

Venus (goddess), see APHRODITE ; (planet), see ASTRONOMY

Venus de Milo, see APHRODITE ; SCULPTURE

Vera Cruz, *vā'rä kroos*, thriving port, Mexico ; on the Gulf of Mexico ; pop.71,000.

Verdi, GIUSEPPE, *vār'dē* (1813–1901), Italian composer ; most famous for his operas, e.g. *Rigoletto* (written when he was 38) ; *Il Trovatore* ; *La Traviata* ; *Aida*, all notable for their exquisite arias.

Verdun, see WORLD WAR I

Verity, CAPTAIN HEDLEY (1905–43), Yorkshire left-arm bowler ; died when a prisoner of war.

Vermeer, JAN, *fer-mār'* (1632–75), Dutch artist, *b* Delft, where he died. Greatest of the so-called ' little masters' of Dutch art, a lovely radiance suffuses all his pictures, whether sunlit scenes out of doors, or exquisitely simple and beautifully lighted interiors. After World War II, a remarkable series of paintings, supposedly the work of Vermeer, proved to be forgeries by the Dutch painter Van Meegeren (*d* 1947). This caused a sensation among art-lovers the world over, because Van Meegeren's forgeries were virtually indistinguishable in appearance from genuine paintings by Vermeer.

Vermont, New England state, USA ; noted for butter, cheese and maple sugar; cap. Montpelier.

Verne, JULES (1828–1905), French writer, *b* Nantes ; had a rare gift for storytelling, and wrote tales in which he combined adventure and great scientific knowledge, e.g. *Five Weeks in a Balloon* ; *Twenty Thousand Leagues under the Sea* ; and *A Journey to the Centre of the Earth*.

vernier, device for giving accurate fractional readings of measurement ; much used in micrometers ; named from Pierre Vernier (*d* 1637). The vernier comprises (in one type, the sliding vernier) a scale giving tenths of inches, and a sliding jaw with 10 divisions equal to 0·9in each, therefore, giving 0·9 of 0·1in. In the diagram, though the jaw has passed the inch mark it has not reached 0·1in beyond, but the 7 line corresponds with 0·7 on the main scale, hence the vernier reads 1·07in.

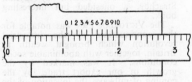

THE VERNIER

Vernon, MOUNT, see WASHINGTON, GEORGE

Verona, *ve-rō'nă*, town, Italy ; on the R. Adige ; noted for Roman remains, fine churches ; suffered severely in World War II ; pop.163,000.

Veronese, PAOLO, *vā-rō-nā'sā* (1528–88), Italian artist, named from his birthplace, Verona ; did magnificent historical and mythical wall-paintings, notably in Venice ; also many easel-pictures renowned for their flesh tints and draperies.

Verrocchio, ANDREA DEL, *ver-rōk'kiō* (*d* 1488), Italian artist and sculptor, *b* Florence ; famous for his equestrian statue of Colleoni, regarded by some critics as the finest of its kind in the world. See SCULPTURE

Versailles, *věr-sä'y*, town, France, 10m south-west of Paris ; chiefly famous for its 17th c. palace, scene 1919 (in the Hall of Mirrors) of the signing of the international treaty between the Allies and Germany. See AMERICAN CIVIL WAR ; WORLD WAR I and II.

verse, see POETRY

vers libre, poetry without a regular metrical structure.

vertebrae, see SKELETON

Verulam, LORD, see BACON, FRANCIS

Verulamium, Roman city near the site of which St Albans (Hertfordshire) now stands.

Vespasian, *ves-pā'zhian* (AD9–79), Roman emperor. A great military commander, he was proclaimed emperor by his troops AD69 (the ' Year of Four Emperors ') ; gave the empire a period of peace and order ; lived simply ; improved finance and administration ; remodelled the senate, and governed as one of Rome's most enlightened emperors.

Vespucci, AMERIGO, *ves-poot'chē* (1451–1512), Italian navigator, *b* Florence ; set up in business in Seville (Spain), and became a naturalised Spaniard ; probably made four voyages to the New World, and claimed to have set foot on the mainland 1497 before Cabot. The claim is now discredited, but the new continent may possibly have been named after him.

Vesta, in old Roman tales, goddess of the hearth. Her temple had a sacred fire tended by vestal virgins.

vestry meeting, see LOCAL GOVERNMENT

Vesuvius, Italian volcano 7m from Naples. It is *c*.3,000ft high and has two active cones. Serious eruptions occurred 1634 and 1906, but the worst was AD79, when two cities were destroyed. On this occasion, *Herculaneum* (*hur-kū-lā-nē-ŭm*) was buried in lava and ashes to a depth of 40–100 ft. Its houses, streets, frescoes and art-treasures have been brought to light by patient excavation since 1706. *Pompeii* (*pom-pā-yē*), a seaport and holiday resort on the Bay of Naples, had been previously shaken by an earthquake AD63. Partly rebuilt, it was likewise overwhelmed by the eruption of Vesuvius in AD79. Many of its houses and temples have been excavated since 1748. See PLINY THE YOUNGER

vetch, name of many plants of the pea family, including TUFTED VETCH, a climbing plant with leaflets in groups of ten pairs, ending in a spiral tendril ; the flowers (July, Aug.) are blue or purple.

veterinary surgeon, *vet'ěr-in-eri*, one who treats diseases in domestic animals. The course must be taken at a college affiliated with the Royal College of Veterinary Surgeons. namely that at Camden Town, London, and those of Liverpool, Edinburgh, Glasgow and Dublin ; or the degree of B.Sc or D.Sc. in Veterinary Science may be taken at the universities of London, Edinburgh or Liverpool.

veto (Latin, I forbid) ; right to prevent an enactment, e.g. the right of the House of Lords in the British Parliament to suspend all legislation by the House of Commons except that dealing with finance. The veto is used in the Security Council of UNO.

Via Sacra, *vē'a sä'kra* (Latin for Sacred Way) ; one of the chief streets of ancient Rome. Once enriched with sacred monuments, it led from the Capitoline Hill to the Colosseum.

Viborg, see VIIPURI

vibrations, see WAVE-MOTION

vicar, see CHURCH

viceroy (Latin *vice*, in place of, *roi*, king), one who governs on behalf of a king, e.g. (before 1948) the Viceroy of India.

Vichy, *vē'shē*, health resort, France, 75m from Lyons. Water from its thermal springs is bottled and sold. The town was the seat of the Vichy Government (pro-German) in World War II.

Victor Emmanuel II (1820–78), first King of Italy ; ruled through a difficult period of change, but remained popular, and was declared king of a *united* Italy 1861.

Victor Emmanuel III (1869–1947), King of Italy ; succeeded King Umberto 1900 ; assumed command of the Italian armies during World War I (supporting the Allies), but supported Mussolini's Fascist regime from 1922. He was proclaimed Emperor of Ethiopia 1936 ; abdicated 1946.

Victoria (1819–1901), Queen of Great Britain and Ireland, Empress of India, b Kensington Palace (London), daughter of the Duke of Kent (4th son of George III) and Princess Victoria of Saxe-Coburg-Gotha, sister of Leopold, King of the Belgians.

Victoria, brought up largely under German influences, became queen 20 June 1837. She married Prince Albert of Saxe-Coburg-Gotha 1840, her husband being known as the Prince Consort. Though her love for him was genuine, she could never forget that she herself took pride of place in affairs.

After the death of Prince Albert (1861) Victoria long refused to appear in public, and was more intimate with her Scottish ghillie, John Brown, than with anyone else. Her most trusted ministers were Lord Palmerston and her beloved Disraeli (' Dizzy ') to whom (1877) she owed the title of Empress of India. She consistently opposed Gladstone in his reforms.

Long hidden from her people, she was for a time unpopular but came to be regarded as the symbol of an amaz-

QUEEN VICTORIA 1819–1901

ingly progressive age—the Victorian era —and was wildly cheered at her jubilee 1887, and at her diamond jubilee 1897.

Under 5ft in height, Victoria was, at the end of her long reign (63 years), a lonely but dignified old lady, certainly much more than a figurehead, and exercising her powers as a constitutional monarch to the full. When she disapproved of a policy she put every obstacle she could in its way.

Among Victoria's nine children were (a) *Princess Victoria* (Princess Royal) (1840–1901), mother of William II, who was German emperor 1888–1918 ; (b) *King Edward VII* (1841–1910), father of George V ; and *Princess Alice* (1843–1878).

Read *Queen Victoria,* by Lytton Strachey, a onesided but interesting book.

The VICTORIAN ERA was notable for the continuation of the industrial revolution which brought wealth to Britain, together with abominable social conditions. It was marked by the growth of our export trade, by the coming of railways, the invention of the electric telegraph and telephone, pioneer work in radioactivity and X-rays ; the launching of the first screw-driven ship, and the introduction of the Bessemer process of making steel. The first Atlantic cable was laid, the Suez Canal opened, the Forth Bridge built. In Victoria's reign empire expansion in Australia, China, India and Africa took place. New gold supplies were found in Australia, British Columbia and S. Africa. Her reign saw the Penny Post established, free trade adopted

(1846) ; the repeal of the Corn Laws ; the Great Exhibition (Hyde Park) 1851 ; the Indian Mutiny ; the cotton famine in Lancashire ; compulsory education for England (1870) ; the Crimean, Afghan, Zulu and Boer wars.

Famous men of the age were Gladstone, Lord Melbourne, Lord Palmerston, Disraeli, Curzon of Kedleston ; Darwin, Huxley, Wallace ; Sir John Franklin, Livingstone, Speke ; Lord Roberts, General Gordon, H. M. Stanley ; Dickens, Thackeray, George Meredith, Lewis Carroll, Swinburne, Hardy, R. L. Stevenson, John Stuart Mill, Thomas Carlyle, J. R. Greene, Charles Reade, Matthew Arnold, James Anthony Froude, John Ruskin ; the Earl of Shaftesbury was a great reformer; famous women included Charlotte Brontë and Florence Nightingale.

Victoria, smallest mainland state of Australia ; south of New S. Wales ; area 87,884sq.m ; pop.2,000,000. Almost half the cultivated area is devoted to wheat and oats. Wine is produced. The minerals include gold (but the output is decreasing), coal, tin, gypsum and bauxite ; cap. Melbourne.

Victoria, cap, British Columbia, Canada ; on Vancouver I. ; manufactures clothing, leather goods, machinery, biscuits and soap ; cans fish ; pop.44,000.

Victoria, cap., Hong Kong ; has a naval dockyard ; manufactures sugar, cotton goods, etc. ; pop.429,000.

Victoria and Albert Museum, see LONDON

Victoria Cross, highest decoration for valour awarded to officers and men of the British Navy, Army and Air Force. The medal, instituted by Queen Victoria 1856, is given only for acts of conspicuous bravery. It is popularly known as the VC.

Victoria Falls, spectacular falls (236–354ft high) on the Zambesi R., S. Rhodesia. The river is over a mile wide at this point, and the falls were discovered by David Livingstone 1855.

Victoria Nyanz'a, lake, 200m long ; area 26,200sq.m (nearly half the size of England and Wales). On the equator, it is in east Central Africa. Discovered by John Hanning Speke 1858, the lake is now regarded as the chief source of the R. Nile.

Victoria regia, see WATER LILY

Victory, wooden battleship launched at Chatham 1765 ; became Nelson's flagship 1803. Nelson died aboard her at Trafalgar 1805. She is now in dry dock at Portsmouth.

Vienna, vē-en'ä, cap., Austria ; near the R. Danube ; has many manufactures, e.g. textiles, chemicals, jewellery, scientific instruments, linen, carpets and cinema films. The old part of the city is noted for its Renaissance buildings and art treasures. The Prater is a magnificent park.

The Congress of Vienna met 1814–15 after Napoleon's defeat. Vienna was the scene of bitter fighting April 1945 (World War II) when it was occupied by the Nazis. The pop. of 1,860,000 includes 178,000 Jews.

Viet-Namh, republic of Indo-China established after World War II by Nationalists desiring to be politically independent of the French ; pop.20,000,000. See ANNAM

vigil, see KNIGHT

Vigo, vē'gō, port and holiday town, northwest Spain ; pop.66,000.

Viipuri, vē-pu-rē (formerly Viborg), port, Finland ; pop.82,100. Viipuri was ceded to Russia 1940.

Vikings, vī-, Scandinavian adventurers who raided the coasts of Britain from the 8th to the 10th century.

villa, see HOUSE

Village College, centre for educational and recreational activities, usually carried on in the evening, and sometimes in connection with the extra-mural studies of a university ; students are 15 years and over ; subjects differ widely from WEA courses to cookery, country dancing, Young Farmer's Clubs and dramatics. A fine example is at Impington, Cambridge.

villein, vil'in (11th–15th c.) one who could not leave the land to which he was ' bound,' but had a right to share in the common land of the manor. He was sometimes sold by his lord ; his children were born villeins, and (like the father) were obliged to work on the land at certain times. Gradually the old feudal customs were relaxed, and the manorial system began to break down. Villeins became freemen if they lived a year and a day in a chartered town ; and the whole system of villeinage was eventually ended by the Black Death (1348), and the Peasants' Revolt (1381), after which labourers became free to choose their masters and to work for money wages.

From the 11th c. England had been divided into estates called *manors*, the idea having probably been borrowed from the village communities of the early Teutons. Each manor had its lord, each lord his villeins ; and each manor had its *demesne* (i.e. land belonging exclusively to the lord), though there was also arable land and meadow (one for ploughing, the other for grazing sheep and cattle) belonging, in part, to the lord, in part to the villeins, who also shared in the woods and commons. Each villein or tenant had the same number of strips of land, but some strips were in one part of the manor, others in another, hence no villein had *all* the good land, and no one had all the poor land. *Sockmen* were freemen who held land on condition that they rendered military service when required.

During the period of villeinage, local disputes were settled in the manorial court, where wrong-doers were tried, the lord's steward usually presiding in the presence of the bailiff (the lord's representative) and the reeve (chosen by the villeins). Even today manorial courts are to be found here and there.

Villeneuve, PIERRE, *vēl-nŭv* (1763–1806), French admiral who reluctantly carried out Napoleon's plan to draw off Nelson to the W. Indies. He was defeated 1805 at the battle of Trafalgar.

Villon, FRANÇOIS, *vē-yön* (*b* 1431), French poet and vagabond ; *b* Paris ; often imprisoned ; banished 1465, after which nothing more is known of him ; wrote many exquisite *ballades.*

Vilna, *vēl'nă,* town, Lithuania, though Polish for some time prior to 1944 ; pop.200,000.

vinculum, see BRACKETS

vine, climbing shrub (family *Vitaceae*) with slender stems supported by tendrils ; has large, lobed leaves with toothed edges ; green flowers ripening to berries (grapes) with two or four seeds, and valued as (*a*) *grapes* ; (*b*) when dried, as *currants, raisins* or *sultanas* ; (*c*) *for making wine.* The chief vine-growing regions include Rhineland, France, Italy, Portugal, Spain and (more recently) S. Africa (see PLATE 6, *top*), Australia and California. In Britain, grapes are grown in hot-houses. The famous vine at Hampton Court was planted 1768.

vinegar, sour liquid obtained from the fermentation of malt, wine, sugar, etc. ; contains 3–6% acetic acid.

vinyl plastics, plastics derived from vinyl acetate producing a clear, glass-like substance ; also vinylidene chloride plastics, much employed in America for strong ' silk ' fabrics and for moulded articles ; also polyvinyl acetals, a type of plastic which, as butaldehyde, is used for laminated safety glass.

violet, modest plant (family *Violaceae*) ; includes SWEET VIOLET with heart-shaped leaves ; 5-petalled purple flowers (sometimes white) blooming in March, April ; DOG VIOLET (unscented) ; flowers light purple ; PANSY or HEARTS-EASE, oval leaves with wavy edges ; 5-petalled flowers (summer) of varied hues.

violin, stringed musical instrument with a sounding-box, finger-board, neck (ending in a scroll) and four strings (usually of catgut) passing tightly over the bridge. The player uses a horse-hair bow.

Andrea Amati, an Italian who lived at Cremona in the 16th c., made excellent instruments ; also his sons Antonio and Geronimo, both excelled by Andrea's grandson, Nicolo, who died 1684.

Most famous of all violin makers was Nicolo's pupil, Antonio Stradivari (1644–1737), *b* Cremona. His instruments are known as ' Strads,' and the best are worth several thousand pounds.

The relation of the violin to similar instruments is best understood by reference to their names in Italian. *Violino* (violin) is the diminutive of *viola* (viola) : it means therefore a dimunitive viola. In Italian the suffix *-one* denotes some-

thing *bigger* than the object to whose name it is affixed. Thus *violone* (double-bass) signifies a *big* viola, and from this (by using another diminutive suffix, *-cello*) we get *violoncello* ('cello), which therefore denotes a diminutive double-bass. This instrument is obviously bigger than a viola, because its name still contains a vestige of the suffix *-one.*

viper or **adder,** only poisonous snake in Britain ; is 20–25in long ; has a flat head marked with a dark V, and a zigzag line down the back.

virgate, see DOMESDAY BOOK

Virgil, *ver'jil* (Publius Virgilius Maro ; 70–19BC), greatest of Latin poets. Born near Mantua, N. Italy, possibly of Celtic stock, he received a good education, and soon became one of the leading poets in Rome. Most of his life was spent in Rome and Naples, and he was one of the brilliant circle of writers gathered by Maecenas (the patron of Horace) to celebrate the glories of the newly founded Roman Empire.

Virgil's works comprise the *Eclogues,* the *Georgics* and the *Aeneid.* The *Eclogues* are a collection of short pastoral poems or idylls somewhat in the manner of the Greek poet Theocritus. They are notable for a gracefulness and elegance not previously attained in Latin poetry. The *Georgics* is a longer poem in four books. A poetical treatise on husbandry, it deals with such topics as the cultivation of grain crops, olives, timber, vines ; stock-raising (horses and cattle) ; and beekeeping. These themes enable Virgil to sing the praises of Italy as a country not only fertile but beautiful ; but he does more than that. Italy had been racked for two generations by unrest and civil war, and the empire newly founded by Augustus seemed to promise an age of tranquillity and plenty. In the *Georgics* Virgil expressed a universal feeling of hope and thankful-ness, and in the *Aeneid,* by far his greatest poem, this also is one of his deepest motives.

The *Aeneid* is an epic poem in twelve books. In it Virgil tells how Aeneas (legendary founder of Rome) fled from Troy after its destruction to Sicily and Carthage ; how he fell in love with Dido the Carthaginian queen ; how in order to fulfil his destiny he left her ; how he visited the nether world and there heard prophecies of the future greatness of Rome ; and how at last he managed to establish the Trojan refugees on the mainland of Italy. In all this it is Virgil's object, which he accomplishes with supreme skill, to display the foundation of the Empire as a fulfilment of the destiny fore-shadowed in the wanderings of Aeneas.

By Christians in the Dark Ages (AD400–1000) Virgil's *Aeneid* (and some of his other works, notably the Fourth Eclogue) were regarded as in some ways a divinely-inspired prophecy of the

coming fusion of Christianity with the imperial tradition of Rome. More than any other single writer of antiquity, Virgil helped to create the idea of civilisation ordered, all-embracing, dedicated to a higher purpose. This idea is perhaps the greatest legacy of Rome ; and that is why Dante in his *La Divina Commedia* makes Virgil the Guide and Master who conducts him through Hell and Purgatory to Paradise. Dante honours him as the greatest of all poets :
di cui la fama ancor nel mondo dura
e durerà quanto il mondo lontana
(i.e. *whose fame endures yet in the world, and will endure as long as the world remains*). Considering that Virgil was not a Christian, and that Dante's poem is one of the greatest expressions of Christianity in the Middle Ages, this is possibly the highest praise ever lavished by one great poet on another.

virginal, *vŭr'ji-nal,* 16th c. name for the spinet and harpsichord.

Virginia, *vĕr-jin-iă* (so named by Sir Walter Raleigh in honour of Queen Elizabeth, the ' Virgin Queen '), state, USA, on the Atlantic seaboard ; noted for tobacco ; cap. Richmond. Virginia, founded by Raleigh, was the first English colony in N. America.

virginia creeper, climbing plant often seen clinging to walls ; has large, hand-like leaves that turn red or flame-coloured in autumn.

Virgin Islands, group of small islands in the W. Indies, some, e.g. Tortola, owned by Britain ; others, e.g. St Thomas, St John, etc., by the USA. The climate is delightful, especially in winter.

virus, see BACTERIA

viscount, *vī'kownt,* in the British peerage, a title of nobility between an earl and a baron. Children of a viscount use the prefix Hon., i.e. Honourable.

Vishnu, see BRAHMANISM

Vist'ula, river of Central Europe ; flows *c.*630m to Danzig on the Baltic.

vitamin D, see RICKETS

vitamins, *vīt'a-mins,* accessory food factors. These may be contrasted with enzymes (see DIGESTION). Minute quantities of both are required, but enzymes are produced *in* the body, vitamins (as a rule) are supplied only by the food eaten. If they are absent from diet serious results follow. Most vitamins, it seems, are unaltered by cooking. Only one part of Vitamin D is found in 4,000 million parts of fresh milk.
VITAMIN A, found in animal fats, e.g. milk, egg-yolk, butter, cod-liver oil, halibut oil protects the lungs and eyes. VITAMIN B is not yet completely understood. B_1 occurs in most foods, notably the husk and germ of seeds (rice and wheat), and continued eating of polished rice or *white* bread (both lacking the husk) leads to various diseases, e.g. (in tropical countries) beri-beri. Vitamin B_2 promotes growth in young people. VITAMIN C prevents scurvy. It is found in fresh fruits and vegetables. VITAMIN D may be made by the body itself if it receives the ultra-violet light that comes naturally from clear skies ; children in smoke-darkened cities suffer from rickets because bone-formation is retarded by lack of this vitamin. Other vitamins include VITAMIN K, responsible for clotting when blood flows from a wound. Precisely how vitamins work in the body remains a mystery. See SCURVY

Vitor'ia, Basque city, Spain, 30m south of Bilbao ; scene 1813 of Wellington's victory over the French ; pop.50,000.

vitriol, concentrated sulphuric acid, H_2SO_4; sometimes called oil of vitriol.

vivisection (Latin *vivus,* alive, *secare,* to cut), operation on a living animal for the purpose of gaining physiological knowledge. Legally it must be done

VITAMIN TABLE

Vitamin	Where present	Importance of
A	Butter, milk, cheese, eggs, cod-liver oil, liver, carrots, green vegetables	1 Assists growth 2 Protects against certain eye diseases 3 Resists colds
B	Oats, wholemeal bread, yeast, pulses, cabbage, lettuce, watercress, milk, liver	1 Prevents beri-beri 2 Assists growth
C	Cabbage, lettuce, oranges, lemons, grapes, potatoes, currants	1 Keeps blood vessels and gums healthy 2 Prevents scurvy
D	Cod-liver oil, herring, halibut oil, salmon, milk, cream, butter, egg yolk, animal fats	1 Is necessary for building good bones and teeth 2 Gives protection against rickets

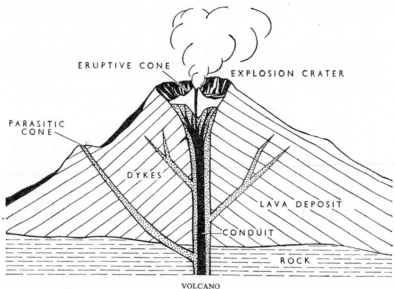

VOLCANO
The internal structure

while the animal is under an anaesthetic. The practice is opposed by various anti-vivisection societies.

vizier, Oriental title, especially in Turkey, where the sultan's chief minister was formerly called the grand vizier.

VJ Day, 15 Aug 1945, when fighting in World War II was brought to an end by the unconditional surrender of Japan. See WORLD WAR II

Vladivostok, port, Siberia, USSR. It is the Pacific terminus of the Trans-Siberian Railway. The fine harbour is blocked with ice in winter, though ice-breakers usually keep an open channel ; pop. 206,000.

vocal cords, see LARYNX

vodka, Russian drink containing 40–60% alcohol ; distilled from potatoes, rye, barley and oats.

Vogler, GEORG JOSEPH, *fō'glĕr* (1749–1814), German musician ; became a priest, and was known as Abt (i.e. Abbot) Vogler ; composed many psalms, hymns and masses. He is the subject of a well-known poem by Robert Browning.

volcano, *vol-kā'nō*, outlet on the earth's surface (on land or under water) through which, during an eruption, quantities of hot gas, steam, molten rock and fragments of solid matter are ejected. Strictly speaking, any vent in the surface from which molten rock pours is a volcano, though popularly it is thought of as a mountain, i.e. a solidified cone of cooled-off ash and lava, with a depression (crater) near the top. A volcano may be active, i.e. giving evidence of internal activity by earthquake shocks in the neighbourhood, by steam rising from its crater or craters, and by overflowing lava ; or it may be presumed to be extinct, though some volcanoes, once imagined to be extinct because inactive for long periods, have suddenly burst into vigorous action.

The products of an eruption are steam, various gases (e.g. sulphur dioxide, sulphuretted hydrogen), ashes, cinders, scoriae, all forms of lava, i.e. molten rock, usually granite or basalt. This may flow for miles as a glowing river of death, and in earlier geological ages vast areas of lava shaped portions of what is now the N. American continent. When Mt Laki (Iceland) erupted 1783 an area as big as London was covered to a depth of 50ft.

The cause of volcanic eruptions is not altogether explained. The interior of the earth at a depth of possibly 20m has a temperature of *c.*1,000°C, the molten granite or basalt being infused with various gases at immense pressures. Hence, a local increase of pressure, or a fault in the upper strata, may result in the gases forcing a way out, often by an earlier volcano-shaft after blowing off the topmost mass of cooled lava.

Among active volcanoes may be mentioned STROMBOLI, one of the Lipari islands, off Italy ; 3,000ft, and always rumbling ominously ; VESUVIUS (Italy), *c.*3,700ft ; HECLA (Iceland), 5,100ft, frequently active since the 11th c. ; and LLULLAILACO (Chile), ASAMA (Japan) and MT WRANGEL (USA).

Other volcanoes (some active now or active fairly recently) are ETNA (Sicily), 10,800ft, with *c*.200 cones. It caused enormous loss of life 1693. MAUNA LOA (Hawaii) is 13,675ft ; KRAKATOA, between Sumatra and Java, caused an explosion 1883 which was among the biggest ever recorded. It blew an island, 18sq.m and 1,400ft high, out of existence, the dust and ashes making the sky at midday as dark as midnight even 150m away. MT PELÉE (Martinique) erupted 1902, a vast quantity of fiercely hot gas and steam escaped through a fissure, the scorching blast instantly killing all the inhabitants of St Pierre (*c*.26,000 people) with the exception of a man who, being condemned to death, was awaiting sentence in a cell below ground-level. Later in the year the pressure below the volcano temporarily thrust up a vertical column of rock (800ft high and 350ft across) weighing *c*.8,000,000 tons.

In Hawaii is KILAUEA with a crater of 4sq.m, a seething and glowing mass of basalt. COTOPAXI, 19,612ft, one of the most remarkable volcanoes in the world, rises among the Andes in an almost perfect snow-covered cone. On the high slopes one may thrust a stick through the snow to the molten lava beneath—proof that lava is a poor conductor of heat.

Among volcanoes presumed to be extinct may be mentioned Fujiyama (Japan) ; Chimborazo ; Aconcagua ; Popacatapetl ; Elbruz ; and Britain has volcanic rocks in S. Scotland and NE. Ireland, e.g. the basalt columns of the Giant's Causeway. Charnwood Forest, the Lickey Hills, the Breidden Hills (Wales) are the results of pre-historic volcanic eruptions.

vole, small gnawing animal distinguished from rats and mice by its short tail and blunt head. Varieties include : (*a*) FIELD-VOLE or FIELD MOUSE, brown above, whitish below ; (*b*) BANK VOLE, yellowish-red, with white feet ; and (*c*) WATER VOLE, commonly called water rat, *c*.8in long ; has soft yellow-brown fur.

Volga, river of USSR. The longest in Europe, it flows over 2,000m from the Valdai Hills to the Caspian Sea, and is navigable almost all the way. Linked by canals with the R. Neva, it is a great highway for transport, and abounds in salmon and sturgeon.

volt, *vōlt*, in electricity, unit of electro-motive force and potential difference (PD), defined as the electromotive force which, when steadily applied to a conductor having resistance of 1 ohm, will cause a current of 1 ampere to flow ; approx. 10^8 CGS electromagnetic units. When 1 coulomb falls 1 volt in electrical level, 1 joule of work is done, hence volts are joules per coulomb. See ELECTRICITY

Volta, COUNT ALESSANDRO, *vōl'tä* (1745–1827), Italian scientist ; experimented with electricity ; invented a type of electroscope and also the voltaic battery. The volt is named after him.

voltaic pile, *vol-tā'ik*, in its simple form as devised by Volta, is a number of cells joined in series, each comprising plates of zinc and copper separated by cloth moistened in sulphuric acid. Zamboni's is a dry series.

The first electric battery ever con-structed, Volta's original pile, still rings a bell in an Oxford laboratory.

Voltaire, *vōl-tār*, assumed name of François Marie Arouet (1694–1778), French writer, *b* Paris ; several times exiled because of his witty attacks on the institutions of his day. Visiting England 1726–29, he met Horace Walpole, Pope and Swift, and was favourably im-pressed by the British constitution. He amassed a fortune by lucky speculation, and for a time lived at the court of Frederick the Great of Prussia ; but he spent his last years at Ferney, near the Swiss border, there setting up successful industries, e.g. the manufacture of watches, silk stockings and lace.

His popularity grew tremendously. He was the richest, most celebrated, and busiest writer in the world of his day ; but the cheers of admirers were too much for him when a crown of laurel was placed on his head after the pro-duction of his last play (*Irène*) at the Comédie Français, Paris (1778), and he died shortly afterwards.

Voltaire's motto was *Écrasez l'infâme*, i.e. crush or overwhelm the infamous, and his life was spent in ridiculing with perfect irony and deadly wit the vices, follies and injustices of 18th c. France. A little man with a hook nose and brilliant eyes, he was unlovable and dishonest, but he remains one of the outstanding French writers.

Of his fifty plays, his comedy *Nanine* is perhaps the best ; of his many poems the *Henriade* and *La Pucelle* are brilliant criticisms of the age, though scarcely poetry ; of his prose tales *Candide* is the most brilliant and satirical ; of his historical works the *Siècle de Louis XIV* and the *Siècle de Louis XV* are the most valuable. He has lost his fame as a philosopher, but his immense corres-pondence remains of great interest even now. Read (in translation) *Candide*, edited by John Butt.

Note Voltaire's irony in : *Ce corps qui s'appelait et qui s'appelle encore le saint empire romain n'était en aucune manière ni saint, ni romain, ni empire*, i.e. This agglomeration which was called and which still calls itself the Holy Roman Empire, is neither holy, nor Roman, nor an empire. Also (of John Byng, English admiral) : *Dans ce pays-ci il est bon de tuer de temps en temps un amiral pour encourager les autres*, i.e. in this country it is thought well to kill an admiral from time to time so as to en-courage the others.

voltameter, see VOLTMETER

voltmeter, instrument for measuring difference of voltage or electrical potential. Somewhat similar to the ammeter, it is calibrated in volts, offers a high resistance to current flowing in parallel, and is not to be confused with the VOLTAMETER, an instrument that measures current by the amount of metal deposited or gas liberated in an electrolytic cell. See ELECTRICITY

volume, measure of bulk or space occupied by a body, e.g. solid, liquid or gas.

If b = breadth, h = perpendicular height, l = length, r = radius, π = 3·1416, then the volume of various solid figures is found thus :

$cone$: $\frac{1}{3}\pi r^2 h$
$cube$: l^3
$cylinder$: $\pi r^2 h$
$rectangular\ solid$: lbh
$sphere$: $\dfrac{4\pi r^3}{3}$

volvox, minute organism partly plant (having chlorophyll) and partly animal ; found in ponds ; may comprise a colony of 10,000 one-celled organisms, e.g. *Volvox globator.*

Vortigern, *vör'ti-gĕrn,* local king in England, *c.*AD450. In the age after the withdrawal of the Roman legions it was he, it is said, who invited Hengist and Horsa to settle in Kent, thus opening the way for the Saxon invasions that overwhelmed what was left of Roman culture.

Vosges, *vōzh,* mts., France, between the rivers Moselle and Rhine ; rich in minerals, e.g. lead, silver, copper and rock salt.

voting, see ELECTION

vowels, in English, the letters a, e, i, o and u, and sometimes w (as in *aw, ou,* etc.) and y. The other letters are consonants.

Vulcan, *vŭl'kan,* in old Roman tales, god of fire.

vulcanised rubber, see RUBBER

vulcanite, see EBONITE

Vulgate, see BIBLE

vulture, bird of prey ; has a neck more or less bare of feathers (except in one species). All varieties have long hooked beaks and powerful, sharp claws ; all feed on decaying flesh. The black vulture is found in S. Europe ; American species include the condor.

Vyshinsky, ANDREI JANUARIEVICH (1883–), Soviet statesman ; Deputy Commissar for Foreign Affairs 1946 ; succeeded Molotov as Soviet Foreign Minister in 1949. For an account of Vyshinsky as prosecutor in the Moscow purge trials 1937–38, read *Eastern Approaches,* Fitzroy Maclean.

W

W, chemical symbol for tungsten (Latin *wolframium*).

WAAC, short for Women's Auxiliary Army Corps, founded 1917. See WOMEN'S ROYAL ARMY CORPS

Wade, GEORGE (1673–1748), British field-marshal ; suppressed the Jacobite Rebellion 1715 ; notable for the military roads which he built in the Highlands after that ; unsuccessful as commander of government troops in the Highlands 1745 ; replaced by the Duke of Cumberland.

Wade's roads did more in the long run than Cumberland's severity to pacify the Highlands. By our standards they were mere cart-tracks, but of them it was said :

If you had seen this road before it was made,
You would lift up your hands and bless General Wade.

Read Neil Munro, *The New Road.*

Wadham College, college of Oxford University, founded 1612.

wadi or **wady,** Arabic word for a river bed that is dry except immediately after rain ; used chiefly in N. and E. Africa.

Wagner, W. RICHARD, *väg'nĕr* (1813–83), German musical composer, *b* Leipzig ; was poor for the greater part of his first 50 years ; suffered defeat after defeat in his attempts to win fame. A revolutionist in opera, he wedded music, poetry and drama, and at first shocked the musical world. His operas include *Rienzi, Lohengrin, Tristan and Isolde, Tannhäuser, The Flying Dutchman,* and *The Mastersingers of Nuremberg,* all of which failed to attract much attention before his immense *Ring of the Nibelungen* was produced 1876 in a theatre specially built for the purpose at Bayreuth. The success of *Parsifal* was instantaneous.

His son, Siegfried (1869–1930), was notable as a conductor of his father's operas at Bayreuth.

Wagram, *vä'gräm,* village, 11m from Vienna ; scene (1809) of Napoleon's victory over the Austrians.

wagtail, name of several British birds, all insect-eating. They do not hop, but run, their tails dipping and wagging up and down, hence the name ' wagtail ' ; found chiefly in meadows and by streams.

WAGNER 1813–83

The pied wagtail, almost wholly black above, is greyish below ; lays 4–6 blue and speckled eggs in a nest on the ground.

Waikato, *wä'ē-kä-tō*, river, N. Island, NZ; flows 170m to the Tasman Sea.

Wakefield, town, W. Yorkshire ; on the R. Calder ; has a 15th c. cathedral with a lofty spire ; manufactures chemicals, worsted and soap ; scene of the battle of Wakefield (Wars of the Roses) in which the Lancastrians were victorious 1460 ; pop.60,000.

Wakefield, BATTLE OF, fought between the Yorkists and the victorious Lancastrians 1460.

Wakefield, 1ST VISCOUNT (1859–1941), a noted philanthropist ; organised C. C. Wakefield & Co., manufacturers of Castrol oil ; promoted speed-records, e.g. Mollison's Cape Town flight, Seagrave's car races ; endowed Talbot House (Toc H).

Wake Island, USA island, area *c*.1sq.m.

THE GREY WAGTAIL

It is *c*.2,000m from Hawaii, and on the route to Hong Kong. It was occupied by the Japanese 1941, and recaptured by USA forces 1945.

Walcheren, *väl'che-ren*, island, Netherlands, in the estuary of the Schelde ; scene of the useless Walcheren expedition 1809, a British attempt to aid Austria.

Its dykes were weakened by bombing in World War II and the sea flooded the island. The dykes were later repaired. Middleburg, cap. of Zeeland, is on Walcheren.

Waldensians, stout-hearted Protestant sect founded *c*.1170 by Peter Waldo, a rich merchant of Lyons who, like St Francis, sold his goods and gave the proceeds to the poor. Waldo had the NT translated into Provençal, the language of the people, and taught that the Word of God as recorded in Scripture was as good as the tradition of the Church. For this he was excommunicated 1184.

For maintaining that it is wrong to inflict capital punishment and that the Church of Rome was not the Church of Christ, the Waldensians were persecuted by the Inquisition. Driven out of the towns, they settled in Alpine valleys on the borders of France and Italy. In 1487 the pope ordered their extermination, but an army which he set against them was defeated. In 1532 the Waldensians finally parted with the Church of Rome and joined the Protestant Reformation of Switzerland.

In 1655 the Duke of Savoy sent an army of French and Irish into the mountains against the Waldensians, and a terrible massacre ensued. (This is the massacre referred to in Milton's sonnet *Avenge O Lord thy slaughtered saints*.) Persecuted again in 1685 by the French, a remnant of the Waldensians found refuge in Geneva, but led by Pastor Arnaud 800 of them marched back into the valleys of the Vaudois (Fr. for Waldensians) and reconquered them. From 1655 until well on in the 19th c., the Waldensians received frequent help from Protestants in Britain. There is still a Waldensian Church in Italy, but it is a dwindling minority.

Wales, strictly the Principality of Wales and Monmouthshire, western division of Great Britain ; area 8,006sq.m ; borders the English counties of Cheshire, Shropshire and Herefordshire ; has 12 counties, excluding Monmouthshire but including the county of Anglesey, an island linked to the mainland by the Menai suspension bridge. The total pop. (with Monmouthshire) is *c*.2,523,000.

Largely mountainous (Snowdon, the highest mt., being 3,560ft), Wales is noted for its fine scenery, especially in the north, which is a favourite tourist centre ; it has a rugged coast, old castles, historic towns and lovely valleys, e.g. the Vale of Clwyd. There is a fine breed of mt. sheep. S. Wales, with its coalfield (including anthracite), is rich in iron, copper, and has the important ports of Swansea and Cardiff. Wales has many rivers, e.g. Severn, Wye, Usk, Dee, Taff, Towy ; its largest lake is Bala.

The Welsh, a distinct nation, are Celtic, and in the days of Llewelyn the Great (d 1240) the country seemed politically secure ; but intrigues by Llewelyn ap Gruffydd led to Wales being compelled to submit to English authority, Edward I's son (later Edward II) being declared Prince of Wales at Caernarvon 1301. Most of the present-day Welsh are Nonconformist, and the people, justly proud of their great traditions and romantic history, delight in song and story, nearly a million of them still speaking Welsh, though English is also spoken throughout the country. In Wales there is a growing movement in favour of a larger degree of self-government than the country is allowed at present.

Wales, PRINCE OF, title borne by the eldest son of the British sovereign ; created 1301 by Edward I for his son, afterwards Edward II. Legend says the king presented the infant to the Welsh. The motto is *Ich Dien*, i.e. I serve.

Wales, UNIVERSITY OF, founded 1903 ; comprises colleges at Aberystwyth, Bangor, Cardiff, Swansea.

wallaby, see KANGAROO

Wallace, ALFRED RUSSELL, *wol'is* (1823–1913), naturalist, *b* Usk, Monmouthshire ; accompanied H. W. Bates on an expedition to the Amazon, and later collected insects in Malay, also studying plant and animal life ; discovered the principles of evolution at the same time as Charles Darwin. Among his books are *Darwinism* ; *Travels on the Amazon*.

Wallace, EDGAR (1875–1932), journalist, author and dramatist ; found when nine days old by a Billingsgate fish-porter; was an errand boy ; sold newspapers ; became a newspaper corrrespondent, and won success with his 150 books, most of them detective tales. His best work is seen in his earlier stories of Africa, e.g. *Sanders of the River*.

Wallace, SIR WILLIAM (?1270–1305), heroic leader of Scottish national resistance against King Edward I. Born in SW. Scotland of Celtic stock, Wallace was educated near Stirling. Here he learned one thing that he never forgot, the Latin verse *Dico tibi verum, Libertas optima rerum* (*I am telling you the truth, liberty is best of all things*). At 18 Wallace killed one of the English garrison of Dundee in a personal quarrel, and went into hiding. Eight years later (1297) he emerged at the head of a band of 30 men, burnt Lanark and killed the English sheriff Hezelrig. Followers flocked to join him, and he began to build up a large-scale movement of national resistance.

An English army was sent to Scotland to capture Wallace. He defeated it at the Battle of the Bridge of Stirling, and invaded the North of England. In 1298 Edward himself marched into Scotland, and defeated Wallace at Falkirk. The Norman nobles of Scotland changed sides frequently during the struggle, and Wallace's defeat at Falkirk was due in part to the defection of Sir John Comyn just before the battle.

Wallace had been acting in the name of John Balliol as Guardian of Scotland. He now resigned and went into hiding. For seven years he was hunted high and low, and in the end he was caught (probably through the treachery of Sir John Monteith, whose name was ever afterwards reviled in Scotland). Wallace was brought to London and tried in Westminster Hall. To the accusation that he had committed treason against the King of England, he replied with truth that he had never been a subject of King Edward's. This plea was brushed aside. Wallace was sentenced to death and executed with the utmost savagery the same day.

By his heroic though unsuccessful resistance, Wallace inspired the Scots to go on fighting until they had secured their independence. His exploits are recorded in a long poem by Blind Harry the Minstrel, and the memory of them remains in Scotland to this day.

Wallachia, *wo-lā'kiä*, region which later became part of Rumania.

Wallasey, *wol'ä-si*, residential town, Cheshire, in the Wirral Peninsula ; pop.99,000.

Waller, EDMUND (1606–87), poet, *b* Buckinghamshire. He attempted in the Civil War to secure London for Charles I, for which he was fined and banished, but at the Restoration he sat in Parliament. As a poet he is famous for his musical lyrics, e.g. *Go, lovely rose*.

wallflower, plant (family *Cruciferae*) ; flowers in spring ; has four petals to each scented flower ; the colour varies ; the leaves are dark and strap-like.

Wallingford, *wol'ing-fėrd*, town, Berkshire. The *Treaty of Wallingford* 1153 made peace between King Stephen and Matilda.

Walloons, French-speaking pop. of Belgium. Many Walloon Protestants settled in Canterbury as refugees in Elizabeth's day. They were silk-weavers and cloth-makers.

Wallsend, mining town, Northumberland ; on the R. Tyne ; noted for shipbuilding and metal work. It is at the east end of Hadrian's Wall, hence the name ; pop.45,000.

Wall Street, street in New York. Here is the Stock Exchange, and the name Wall Street now stands for the American stock market.

Walmsley, LEO, *wölms'li* (1892–   ), English author of many novels, e.g. *Three Fevers* (filmed) and *Sally Lunn*.

WALNUT

*The flowers and the leaves : (top left) a
female flower and half seed : (bottom left) a
whole fruit and the ' nut '*

walnut, *wŏl′nut,* nut of the large and
handsome tree found in Britain and
especially Italy and France. The nut,
inside a rough, hard shell, has a fine
flavour. The timber of the walnut tree
is used in making furniture.

Walpole, SIR HUGH, *wŏl′pōl* (1884–1941),
English novelist. His books include a
series dealing with London life, e.g.
The Prelude to Adventure ; *Fortitude* ;
The Young Enchanted ; his best work is
the saga of the Herries family told in
Rogue Herries ; *Judith Paris* ; *The
Fortress* ; and *Vanessa.* Other books are
the delightful tales of his youth, e.g.
Jeremy ; *Jeremy and Hamlet.*

Walpole, SIR ROBERT (1676–1745), statesman, *b* Houghton, Norfolk ; entered
Parliament 1701 as a Whig ; rose rapidly
to power in George I's reign ; Chancellor of the Exchequer 1715 ; gave
warnings of the impending disaster of
the S. Sea Company, and when the
' Bubble ' burst was given the task,
1721, of repairing the country's finances.

From 1721–30 he shared the government of the country with Viscount
Townsend ; and from 1730–41 ruled
alone. He refused a peerage 1723
because he wished to remain in the
House of Commons, though he was
created Earl of Orford 1742.

Walpole had no high ideals, but in an
age when corruption was rife, he was
above party politics. He put the
country's interests before his own,
secured sound finance, stood for a
degree of religious tolerance, and avoided
war as long as he could. He introduced
free trade principles ; but he is most
memorable as *Britain's first Prime
Minister,* being the first Englishman of
modern times to be sole leader of a
ministry. He also helped to make the
Commons the most powerful political
body in the land.

Walpole used the phrase ' The balance
of power,' during a speech in the
Commons 13 Feb 1741 ; and on being
created an earl, and therefore promoted
to the House of Lords, he remarked to
the Earl of Bath, ' My Lord Bath, you
and I are now two as insignificant men
as any in England.'

walrus, see SEAL

Walsall, *wŏl′sŏl,* town near Birmingham ;
noted for making leather goods, harness
and hardware ; pop.110,000.

Walsingham, SIR FRANCIS, *wŏl′sing-am*
(*d* 1590), English statesman, *b* Chisle-
hurst, Kent. He was sent abroad on
important diplomatic errands, but was
most successful as organiser of secret
police, and in discovering plots against
the life of Queen Elizabeth.

Waltham, *wŏl′tham,* watch-making town,
Massachusetts, USA ; on the Charles
R. ; pop.40,000.

Walthamstow, *-stō,* town, SW. Essex ;
actually a residential suburb of London ;
pop.124,000.

Walton, IZAAK, *wŏl′tŭn* (1593 – 1683),
writer and angler, *b* Stafford ; made a
fortune as an ironmonger in London,
retiring *c.*1644.

Walton spent his leisure in writing
delightful biographies of some of his
friends, but is especially remembered as
an expert angler, and for his charming
book *The Compleat Angler* (1653), our
first nature book. In it three characters
talk about the country, *Piscator* (the
angler), *Venator* (huntsman) and *Auceps*
(falconer). His style is simple, his
humour kindly. One of his most
famous sayings is : *We may say of
angling as Dr Boteler said of strawberries:
' Doubtless God could have made a better
berry, but doubtless God never did ' ; and
so God never did make a more calm,
quiet, innocent recreation than angling.*

Walton-on-Thames, residential town, Surrey ; pop. (with Weybridge) 37,000.

Walton, WILLIAM TURNER (1902–),
English composer, *b* Oldham ; composed his Symphony and violin concerto,
1947 ; recognised as an outstanding
modern composer, and a writer of
incidental film music.

waltz, *wŏlts,* dance in 3–4 time ; popular
since the 19th century.

Walvis Bay, *wŏl′vis,* small but important
whaling and fishing port, SW. Africa.

wampum, see AMERICAN INDIANS

Wandering Jew, character in several
legends, one German tale declaring that
he was a cobbler in Jerusalem, and that
because he refused to allow Christ to
rest by his shop, he was condemned to
wander for centuries. The theme was
dramatised 1920 by E. Temple Thurston.

Wandsworth, *wŏnz′wĕrth,* largely residential
borough of SW. London.

Wanganui, *wŏn'gä-noo-ē,* port, N. Island, New Zealand ; population 26,000.

Wanstead and **Woodford,** *won'sted,* residential district, Essex ; pop.60,000.

Wantage, -*tij,* town, Berkshire ; birthplace of King Alfred.

wapiti, *wop'i-ti,* large Californian deer ; chiefly reddish in colour ; notable for its handsome branching antlers.

THE WAPITI

war, state of affairs in which two nations or group of nations resort to armed conflict in an attempt to resolve their differences, instead of continuing to seek a settlement by reaching some agreement.

Civil war is fighting between opposing factions in one country. Formerly wars were fought with armies on land, navies at sea ; now war is largely a series of combined operations—army, navy and air forces. Atomic warfare and bacterial warfare loom ahead, and in both the civilian population is likely to suffer, hence the dire need of international understanding and co-operation.

The following is a list of important wars, their chief battles being given in brackets :

BC

499–478 GRECO-PERSIAN ; Persian invasion of Greece repelled (Marathon, 490BC ; Thermopylae and Salamis, 480BC ; Plataea, 479BC)

431–404 PELOPONNESIAN ; Athens defeated by Sparta

334–323 MACEDONIAN, leading to Alexander's conquest of Persia (Granicus, 334BC ; Issus, 333BC ; Arbela, 331BC)

264–146 PUNIC : (*a*) *First,* 264–241BC, Carthage defeated by Rome ; (*b*) *Second,* 218–201BC, Carthage defeated by Rome ;

(*c*) *Third,* 149–146BC, Carthage destroyed

58–51 GALLIC, establishing Roman influence over W. Europe

50–30 ROMAN CIVIL WARS, Octavius creating the Roman Empire after the battle of Actium, 31BC

AD

1066 NORMAN INVASION OF ENGLAND

1096–1270 CRUSADES

1337–1453 HUNDRED YEARS' (Crécy, 1346 ; Poitiers, 1356 ; Agincourt 1415 ; siege of Orleans 1429)

1455–1485 WARS OF THE ROSES

1588 SPANISH ARMADA, the power of Spain being crippled

1618–1648 THIRTY YEARS'

1642–1649 ENGLISH CIVIL, establishing the Commonwealth (Marston Moor, 1644 ; Naseby, 1645)

1701–1714 WAR OF THE SPANISH SUCCESSION (Blenheim, 1704 ; Ramillies, 1706 ; Oudenarde, 1708 ; Malplaquet, 1709)

1740–1748 WAR OF THE AUSTRIAN SUCCESSION (Fontenoy, 1745)

1756–1763 SEVEN YEARS' (Plassey, 1757; Quebec, 1759)

1775–1783 AMERICAN INDEPENDENCE, resulting in the creation of the USA (Lexington, 1775 ; Saratoga, 1777 ; Yorktown, 1781)

1789–1799 FRENCH REVOLUTION, leading to the Reign of Terror and to France becoming a republic

1796–1815 NAPOLEONIC (Nile, 1798 ; Marengo, 1800 ; Trafalgar, 1805 ; Austerlitz, 1805 ; Jena, 1806 ; Wagram, 1809; Waterloo, 1815)

1808–1814 PENINSULAR

1854–1856 CRIMEAN (Sebastopol and Balaclava, 1854)

1859–1861 ITALIAN, resulting in the foundation of a new kingdom of Italy (Solferino, 1859)

1870–1871 FRANCO-PRUSSIAN (Sedan, 1870)

1899–1902 BOER (sieges of Ladysmith and Mafeking, 1899)

1904–1905 RUSSO-JAPANESE

1914–1918 FIRST WORLD WAR (see WORLD WAR I)

1935–1936 ITALIAN INVASION OF ETHIOPIA

1936–1939 SPANISH CIVIL WAR

1937–1945 SINO-JAPANESE, i.e. Japanese attacks upon and invasion of China

1939–1945 SECOND WORLD WAR (see WORLD WAR II)

1950– KOREAN

Warbeck, PERKIN (*d* 1499), pretender. He was declared by the Irish Yorkists 1492 to be the younger son of Edward IV (believed to have been murdered in the Tower of London). After landing at

Whitesand Bay, Cornwall, 1497, he led an army, and proclaimed himself as Richard IV of England. He was defeated, and hanged.

warbler, general name for 11 species of birds nesting in Britain, and for 9 visiting birds. They resemble thrushes, and include the whitethroat, blackcap, garden warbler, sedge-warbler, reed-warbler and grasshopper-warbler. Most are song birds, and the plumage is usually greenish brown.

THE WILLOW WARBLER

war criminals, see NUREMBERG

Ware, town, Hertfordshire ; once noted for the Great Bed of Ware, removed from the Saracen's Head hotel to the Victoria and Albert Museum (London). Made of oak in 1463, the bed holds twelve people. It is said to have belonged to Warwick ' the King-Maker.'

War Office, administrative HQ of the British army. It is directed by the Army Council, formed 1904, and comprising the Secretary of State for War, and various under-secretaries and field-marshals.

Warrington, town, Lancashire ; on the R. Mersey ; manufactures soap, glass and ironware ; pop.79,000.

Warsaw, cap., Poland ; on the R. Vistula ; linked by rail with Berlin, Leningrad and Moscow. The scene of much fighting, it has been in Russian, French and German hands. Its cathedral and university are famous, and it has a great variety of industries ; pop.479,000, including many Jews.

Wartburg, *värt'bur*ch, castle near Eisenach, Germany. Here while in hiding Luther translated the Bible into German.

wart-hog, see PIG

Warwick, RICHARD NEVILLE, EARL OF, *wor'ik* (1428–71), English soldier and statesman, known as 'the King-Maker,' and a great figure in the Wars of the Roses. A Yorkist, and nephew of Richard Duke of York, Warwick did much to bring about the Yorkist victory at St Albans 1455, and was made Governor of Calais and High Admiral. With Edward Earl of March he defeated the Lancastrians at Northampton 1459, taking Henry VI prisoner. He proclaimed his cousin Edward king in London (as Edward IV) ; crushed the Lancastrians at Towton 1461, and for the next four years was virtual ruler of England. Quarrelling with Edward, he withdrew to France, later invading England, and defeating the king. Edward, however, raised an army, and compelled Warwick again to fly to France, where he allied himself with the Lancastrians, landed in Devonshire, compelled Edward to fly, and restored Henry VI to his throne. Finally, Edward returned. Landing in Yorkshire (Ravenspurn) 1471 he defeated and killed Warwick at Barnet. See ROSES, WARS OF

Warwickshire, midland county, England ; much of it is beautiful pastoral land, but there are densely peopled industrial areas, e.g. Birmingham and Coventry. The co.tn, WARWICK, on the R. Avon, has ruins of a 14th c. castle, once the home of the Earls of Warwick.

washing soda, see SODIUM

Washington, *wosh'ing-tŭn,* mining town, County Durham ; on the R. Wear.

Washington, cap., USA, in the Federal District of Columbia (DC) ; on the R. Potomac ; founded 1791, and has been the home of the Government since 1800. Here is the huge domed Capitol where Congress meets ; also the Supreme Court. The White House, residence of the President, is about a mile away ; pop.663,000.

Washington, north-west state of USA, with a coastline on the Pacific ; noted for lumbering, mining and fishing ; cap. Olympia.

Washington, BOOKER (1858–1915), Negro, *b* Virginia, USA ; was a plantation slave ; became principal of the Tuskegee Institute for Negroes (Alabama), and strove to secure a better understanding between Negroes and white people. See SLAVERY

Washington, GEORGE (1732–99), first President of the USA, called the ' father of his country,' soldier and statesman, *b* Virginia.

Descended from English ancestors, Washington had little education ; showed skill as a soldier as early as 1754 when he defeated an army of French and Indians. Having served with distinction as an officer, he retired to his home at Mount Vernon, married a rich widow (Martha Custis), and became one of the wealthiest men in America. A man of unimpeachable integrity, he was a good business-man, a kindly slave-owner, a local politician, a hospitable host. Over 6ft in height, he was dignified, calm, haughty and therefore more respected than loved. He had the gifts of patience and perseverance, and was admirably suited for the position of Commander-in-Chief of the American armies in the bitter War of American Independence 1775–83.

In that struggle Washington had not only to fight the armies of George III, but to organise home affairs, to control opposing factions and by stern rule to unite a disunited people. For the story of the battles of the period, see AMERICAN INDEPENDENCE, WAR OF

Washington rendered great service to

GEORGE WASHINGTON 1732–99

the young nation in the peace that followed. Having resigned his commission, he returned to Mount Vernon 1783, but was called on (1787) to draw up the American constitution. Though Hamilton and Jefferson had much to do with framing the government of the country, Washington had also a large share. He was elected first President of USA 1789, and for a second term of office (four years) 1793. He refused to stand for a third term and died two years after his retirement. George Washington was undoubtedly the creator of America's independence and of her constitution. Someone said of him that he was ' first in war, first in peace, and first in the heart of his countrymen ' ; and Gladstone declared ' Washington is to my mind the purest figure in history.'

Washington Conference, conference 1921 when the limitation of armaments and Pacific problems were discussed by USA, Britain, Italy, France and Japan, the powers signing a treaty by which they undertook to limit their navies.

wasp, name given to the social wasp (of which there are seven British species), but applied also to solitary wasps, wood wasps and sand wasps.

The social wasp (*Vespa vulgaris*), in many respects akin to the bee, has four transparent wings folded lengthwise, and a thick hind-body connected with the thorax by an exceedingly narrow waist. The female has a sting, and is larger than the male, the male being larger than the worker.

A colony of wasps begins when a queen lays eggs in spring, having constructed a few six-sided cells of a kind of paper, actually a mixture of wood-shavings and saliva. The eggs hatch in about a fortnight, and in another fourteen days, or so, the workers appear, these carrying on the business of building more cells and nursing the grubs. Social wasps feed mainly on other insects and caterpillars, and the nests are often in trees or holes in the ground.

Among hundreds of species of solitary wasps are the carpenter and mason wasps, which show remarkable skill in building tunnels and cells for their young. But perhaps the most astonishing is a digging wasp that uses a fragment of stone to hammer down the soil over her nest.

One of the wonders of the solitary wasp is that it provides its grub with food, e.g. a caterpillar or spider or fly, sealing it in the cell after stinging it in precisely the right place (a region of the nervous system) so that the victim is

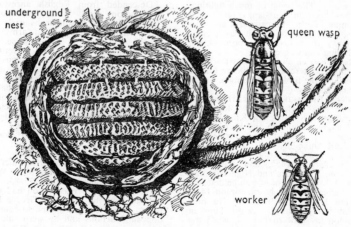

WASPS
Underground nests are made from chewed wood by the wasps ; the insects have distinctive black and yellow stripes

helpless but not dead, and will not, therefore, decay before the grub feeds on it. See Hornet

watches at sea, see Bell

water, liquid ; when pure is the chemical compound H_2O, i.e. by volume two parts of hydrogen to one of oxygen, or eight parts of oxygen to one of hydrogen by weight ; increases in density as the temperature decreases from boiling-point (100°C or 212°F) to 4°C (39·2°F) when it reaches its maximum density. If cooled further, water *expands*, hence ice floats. As the coldest water is at the top, only the surface of rivers and lakes freezes. Were these to freeze solid, life in them would perish. Taking the form of ice or snow at low temperatures, water becomes vapour or steam at 100°C when at a pressure of 29·9in of mercury.

Water or ice covers *c.*0·75 of the earth's surface, and forms *c.*0·875 of all animal-life, and 0·9 of all plant-life. It is almost incompressible and almost colourless and tasteless ; has a specific gravity of 1 at 4°C (39·2°F) ; is the standard to which all liquids and solids are referred ; is a bad conductor of heat and electricity.

In nature water is never found pure, even rain water containing carbonic acid gas. Spring water contains dissolved salts, e.g. chlorides, sulphates, etc. ; and sea-water contains a great variety of salts in solution, e.g. common salt (sodium chloride, NaCl) magnesium, potassium, calcium, the total weight of salts being 3·5% of any given quantity, hence sea-water is denser than rain water. It is estimated that in a cubic mile of sea-water there is gold valued at £5,000,000. See Heavy Water

water, Hardness of, see Calcium

water-beetle, see Dysticus

Waterbury, city, Connecticut, USA ; manufactures watches, brassware and metal goods ; pop.99,000.

watercress, plant growing in or near water ; has a creeping stem, somewhat heart-shaped leaflets, and small white flowers. It is often cultivated for use in salads.

water crowfoot, plant (family *Ranunculaceae*). It is actually a white buttercup. The leaves under water are like hairs, those above are glossy, roundish and in three parts.

water equivalent, see Heat

waterfall, perpendicular fall of a river or stream. Famous falls include Victoria Falls, N. Rhodesia, 1,500yd wide and 354ft deep ; Niagara, between Canada and USA, one part being 1,300yd wide, with a drop of 175ft. Hereabouts is the largest hydro-electric power plant in the world. Other falls are the Ribbon Falls, Yosemite, USA, 1,612ft high ; Upper Yosemite, 1,430ft ; Uitshi, British Guiana, 1,200ft ; Takakaw, Canada.

Waterford, county, Munster, Eire ; noted for dairy farming and fisheries ; co.tn Waterford.

water gas, gas produced by the action of

THE WATERHEN

steam on incandescent coke. It is a mixture of carbon monoxide and hydrogen, and is used as a fuel.

water-glass, see Sodium

waterhen or **moorhen,** British bird ; dark olive brown above, dark grey on the head, neck and underparts ; has a red frontal plate above the beak. It builds a nest among reeds, and is an expert diver and swimmer.

water lily, family of *c.*60 species of water plants, the flowers usually being white, pink, red or yellow. The commonest in Britain is *Nymphaea alba*, found in many garden ponds ; the most remarkable is the *Victoria regia*. A native of shallow S. American lakes, it has floating leaves 4–12ft across, the edges turned up several inches. The white or red flowers are 15–18in wide. Fine examples may be seen at Kew Gardens.

Waterloo, Battle of, fought 18 June 1815 ; named after a Belgian village *c.*11m south of Brussels. Opposing the Allies (Prussians commanded by Blücher ; British, Dutch, etc. commanded by Wellington) were the French, led by Napoleon. The British and their allies were commanded by the Duke of Wellington at Brussels. Marshal von Blücher commanded a Prussian army at Namur. On 16 June, Blücher was attacked by the French at Ligny, and compelled to retreat towards Wavre. Meanwhile a British detachment had a sharp encounter with the advance guard of Napoleon's main body at Quatre Bras. Under cover of this the concentration of Wellington's army was successfully achieved at Waterloo, a few miles to the north of Quatre Bras. Wellington had 67,000 men facing 74,000 of the French, whose cavalry and artillery were superior. The Allies were strongly posted just behind the crest of a long ridge.

Fighting began *c.*11.30am on 18 June. Much of the fiercest of it raged round a British advanced post down in the valley, at Haye Sainte, where the British made a magnificent stand. Later the French charged repeatedly up the hill, and actually pierced the centre of the allied line, which had taken a hard pounding from the French artillery. In the afternoon the Prussians by a brilliant manoeuvre and by hard marching attacked on Napoleon's right flank, and turned the scales against him. Towards evening Napoleon made his final bid for victory, ordering his famous Imperial Guard to advance. They did so, but Wellington ordered a charge, the British guards surging forward and forcing back the French at the moment when Blücher's delayed army arrived in time, as it happened, to share in the scattering of the retreating French. British and allied losses amounted to 37,000 men ; the French had about as many.

This battle proved to be Napoleon's final defeat. He was exiled to St Helena, and for long there was much-needed peace in Europe.

Waterloo Bridge, see LONDON

water polo, game played in a swimming bath between 2 teams of 7 players. It lasts 14 minutes. The idea is to knock (with one hand only) a football into your opponents' goal.

water spider, see SPIDERS

waterspout, see TORNADO

Waterton, CHARLES (1782–1865), naturalist, born in Yorkshire ; spent *c*.12 years in British Guiana and Brazil collecting birds and animals ; made his home (Walton Hall, near Wakefield) a sanctuary for birds ; author of *Wanderings in South America.*

Watford, town, Hertfordshire ; manufactures paper and silk goods, etc. ; pop.73,000.

Watling Street, see BRITAIN

Watson, SIR WILLIAM, *wot'sun* (1858–1935), poet, *b* Yorkshire ; notable for his lofty thoughts exquisitely expressed, e.g. his poems on *Wordsworth's Grave* ; *Lachrymae Musarum,* etc.

Note, as an example of his style :

We are children of splendour and flame,
Of shuddering, also, and tears ;
Magnificent out of the dust we came,
And abject from the spheres.

watt, *wot,* unit of electric power, i.e. rate of work done expressed in joules per sec. ; or the energy expended per sec. by an unvarying electric current of 1 ampere flowing across a potential difference of 1 volt ; equivalent to 10^7 ergs, or 1 joule per sec. Note that 1hp = 746 watts. A *watt-hour* = the work done by 1 watt acting for 1 hr, is thus equal to 3,600 joules, or $3 \cdot 6 \times 10^7$ ergs ; hence the *Kilowatt* (i.e. 1,000 watts), and the *Kilowatt-hour* (KWH), which is the Board of Trade practical unit of work done when a rate of work of 1,000 watts is maintained for 1 hr ; it is equal to 3,600,000 joules. See ELECTRICITY

Watt, JAMES (1736–1819), Scottish engineer, *b* Greenock ; apprenticed to a maker of scientific instruments, London ; made

instruments for Glasgow University, where, 1764, he repaired Newcomen's steam engine, which led him to seek ways of obviating the very considerable waste of steam.

In Newcomen's engine steam was allowed to enter the cylinder, the inlet was then closed, and the cylinder cooled to condense the steam and produce a partial vacuum that caused the piston movement. At every stroke, therefore, steam was wasted in reheating the cylinder. Watt's great contribution was the use of a separate condenser communicating with the cylinder. This enabled the cylinder and piston to be kept hot, and thus avoided waste of steam.

In this way Watt laid the foundations of the practical application of steam to industry. For many years he worked in partnership with Matthew Boulton of Birmingham. He made a host of other improvements, e.g. parallel motion, centifrugal governors, steam indicators and the double-acting cylinder. It is interesting to note that, shrewd though he was, Watt refused to believe that steam locomotion was possible, and he had no interest in high-pressure steam. See STEAM ENGINE

Watteau, JEAN ANTOINE, *vä-tō'* (1684–1721), imaginative French artist and engraver ; *b* Valenciennes ; gave his name to a period and style of French painting in which grace and movement lend charm.

watt-hour, see WATT

wattle, see ACACIA

Wattle Day, see AUSTRALIA DAY

Watts, GEORGE FREDERIC, *wots* (1817–1904), artist, *b* London ; famous for his portraits, and later, his allegorical pictures, e.g. *Hope.* He was also notable as a sculptor, e.g. *Physical Energy.*

Watts, ISAAC (1674–1748), Nonconformist minister, *b* Southampton. Of his many hymns *O God our help in ages past* is perhaps the most famous.

Waugh, EVELYN, *wau* (1903–   ), author, *b* Hampstead. His irony is displayed in such books as *Black Mischief* ; *A Handful of Dust.* His brother, ALEC WAUGH (1898–   ), author of many novels, wrote an unusual story of school life *The Loom of Youth.*

Wavell, FIELD-MARSHAL VISCOUNT, *wāv'el* (1883–1950), soldier, statesman, author, *b* Colchester ; served in the S. African War, and in World Wars I and II, being Commander-in-Chief Middle East in the latter, later Commander-in-Chief in India ; became Viceroy of India 1943. He wrote *The Palestine Campaign,* and compiled *Other Men's Flowers,* an anthology of poetry, 1944.

wave-motion, series of pulsations. The basic idea comes from waves of the sea, which *appear* to roll towards the shore, though actually no individual drop of water has, on the whole, any forward movement. Surface waves on a liquid

WAVE—MOTION

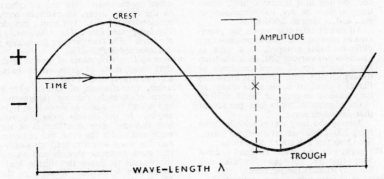

are due to each particle performing a circular or elliptical movement, hence a floating cork swings back and forth as it rises and falls. *but does not advance.* Similarly, by jerking a rope we may cause waves to travel along its length, but any one point in the rope has merely an up and down movement. Hence wave-motion (apart from electromagnetic waves) is a regular disturbance through a medium, the particles vibrating (or oscillating) and thus transmitting energy from place to place without disturbance of the medium.

This transmission of energy through a vibrating but otherwise stationary medium is the fundamental miracle of wave-motion. For visual waves (e.g. waves of the sea, ripples on a pond, waves in a rope) *wave-length* is the distance from one crest to another ; *frequency* is the number of crests passing a point in a given time, e.g. 240 crests pass a given point in one second, then the frequency is 240 per second ; *amplitude* is half the height from crest to trough.

Sound waves are caused by vibrations, as when a violin string compresses molecules of air. These do not return to normal immediately, but ' swing ' a little too far, thus causing compression waves or impulses. The molecules of air remain more or less stationary, but the wave passes through the vibrating molecules at *c.*331 metres per sec., or 700mph. In solids, sound waves travel faster than in air (14 times faster in steel). Since a compression wave depends on the vibration of particles in a medium, it cannot travel through a vacuum. See SOUND

Electromagnetic waves (actually not waves at all, though they act as such) travel best through ' empty ' space, the various forms of matter tending to hinder their passage by absorbing them. Precisely how they travel in a vacuum remains a mystery. At one time scientists assumed the existence of a substance called the ether as an explanation of their transmission, but the existence of the ether has never been proved, and it is possible that the waves are actually particles (e.g. cathode rays) which act in the way we should expect waves or vibrations to act. We think of them, therefore, as electric and magnetic fields travelling 186,282mp.sec. Unlike visible waves they have no crests or troughs, but we represent them as if they had, since every electromagnetic wave reaches a climax (crest) and dwindles to a minimum (trough), and its amplitude is the difference of energy between maximum and minimum.

For all waves we find that if λ = wave-length, v their velocity, n their frequency then $v = n\lambda$; and if T is the time of one complete vibration, then $T = \frac{1}{n}$.

Electromagnetic waves may be several thousand miles long or shorter than 1/30th the diameter of an atom. Among them are (*a*) *X-rays*, often only 1/2,000,000,000cm in length with a frequency of as much as 6×10^{18} (that is 6,000,000,000,000,000,000 vibrations per sec.), capable of penetrating all kinds of matter ; (*b*) *ultra-violet light*, with a wave-length up to 1/4,000cm, and a frequency from 10^{17} vibrations per sec. ; (*c*) *light* (i.e. visible light) with a wave-length between 1/25,000 and 1/12,500cm, and vibrations from 8×10^{15} to 4×10^{15} per second ; these rays are produced by hot bodies, e.g. the sun, electric lamps and ionised gas ; (*d*) *infra-red rays*, wave-length up to 1/25cm, and a frequency as low as 7×10^{11} per second ; these are produced by hot bodies but are invisible to the eye ; (*e*) *Hertzian waves* from 1/10mm to 20 miles, and with frequencies as low as 10,000 per second. They are produced by electric sparks and oscillating electrical circuits. They may cause electrons to move. There are also smaller and larger wave-lengths, e.g. the γ rays, i.e. electromagnetic radiation waves, shorter than X-rays, caused by radioactive substances or by bombardment with electrons ; and, among larger wave-lengths, are those produced by a coil rotating in a magnetic field, sometimes as slow as, say, 100 vibrations per sec., and as long as 2,000 miles.

All electromagnetic waves are generated by moving electric charges, but they differ by being grouped, as it were, in ' packets ' of varying size, each quantum being made up of some hundreds or thousands of waves. What is known as Planck's constant is the total energy of the quantum in ergs, i.e. $(6 \cdot 55 \times 10^{-27})$ $\times$ the number of vibrations per sec. of that particular wave.

Among the long waves (chiefly those from 200–2,000 metres) are radio waves. See QUANTUM ; RADIO ; SPECTRUM

Waveney, *wāv'en-i*, river, England ; flows 50m (mostly between Norfolk and Suffolk) to meet the R. Yare.

wax, solid fatty substance ; melts at a low temperature (usually below 100°C) ; may be either *animal wax* (e.g. that derived from sperm oil, wool-fat or lanolin, beeswax, etc.) or *vegetable wax* (e.g. that derived from certain Brazilian trees and myrtle-wax) ; or, finally, *paraffin wax.*

Wayland the Smith, see ASHDOWN

Weald, *wēld*, district, Kent, Surrey and Sussex ; once covered by a forest, most of which was cut down for smelting iron with charcoal.

wealth, see ECONOMICS

Wear, *wēr*, river, County Durham ; flows 65m from the Pennines to the N. Sea at Sunderland.

weasel, flesh-eating animal *c.*9in long ; has bright reddish fur above, white beneath. In cold regions the fur turns white in winter, e.g. the north of Scotland. The weasel lives in holes in the ground, making a nest of grass and leaves ; kills rats, mice and rabbits.

weather and weather forecasts, see CLIMATE

Weatherhead, LESLIE D. (1893–   ), Minister of the City Temple, London,

THE WEASEL

since 1936 ; popular broadcaster ; noted psychologist. He was an officer in the Indian army, chaplain in Iraq, missionary in India. His books include *Psychology and Life* ; *The Afterworld of the Poets* ; *The Transforming Friendship* ; *It Happened in Palestine.*

weaver bird, *wēv'ĕr*, name of several birds that build nests of grass-woven bags, e.g. the weaver bird of India.

weaving, manufacture of fabric with a warp of threads running lengthways, and a weft (or woof) of threads at right angles. In the earliest loom the weft was threaded over one thread of the warp and under the next, but centuries ago the warp was arranged on *heddles* that raise alternate threads and enable the weaver to throw the shuttle backwards and forwards. Weavers of the Middle Ages used a ball of thread ; later the web was wound round a spool in the hollow of a shuttle (a boat-shaped piece of wood with metal ends) and as this flew from side to side it left a trail of thread.

John Kay (*d* 1764) invented a fly shuttle *c.*1733 ; this was highly successful, but Kay died in poverty. His idea was improved by Robert Kay, who (1760) invented the drop-box, enabling several shuttles to be used, thus making possible a quicker means of pattern weaving. The power-loom, invented *c.*1785 by Edmund Cartwright, was a machine in which the heddles were raised and lowered and the shuttle thrown mechanically. Cartwright set up his first power-loom at Doncaster, Yorkshire ; workpeople wrecked the looms there, and elsewhere, fearing that the new invention would rob them of their livelihood.

Early in the 19th c., Joseph Marie Jacquard (1752–1834), *b* Lyons, invented an improved loom, forerunner of the machines in use today. Automatic looms are now used in Britain and USA, these ingenious machines refilling their own shuttles, and weaving intricate patterns, first planned on squared paper, and then transferred to the loom, which is guided on much the same principle as that of a pianola.

C. H. Baddeley of Bradford has recently perfected a shuttleless loom likely to revolutionise textile weaving.

Webb, MARY (1881–1927), *b* Leighton, Shropshire ; wrote several novels before she won instant fame with *Precious Bane* 1924. Her other stories include *The Golden Arrow* ; *The Spring of Joy* ; *Gone to Earth* ; *The House in Dormer Forest.* All are full of passion and tinged with tragedy, and all reveal an amazing capacity for vivid characterisation, and a feeling for the beauty (and often the mystery) of nature. Her descriptive powers are superb. Her work is akin in treatment to that of Thomas Hardy, and the setting for her plots is that of her native countryside.

Webb, CAPTAIN MATTHEW (1848–83), swimmer, *b* Dawley, Shropshire. He swam the English Channel 1875 in 21¾ hours, and was drowned while attempting to swim the rapids below Niagara.

Webb, SIDNEY JAMES, see PASSFIELD, LORD

weber, *vā'bĕr* ; *wē'bĕr*, magnetic unit of pole strength. A pole of *m* webers will repel a unit pole 1cm distant (in air) with a force of *m* dynes. See MAGNETISM

Weber, CARL VON (1786–1826), German composer, wrote masses, cantatas, symphonies, songs, but was most famous for his operas, e.g. *Der Freischütz* ; *Euryanthe* ; *Oberon* ; regarded as the founder of the German romantic opera. His most popular composition is *Invitation to the Waltz.*

Weber, WILHELM EDUARD (1804–91), German scientist ; devised the fundamental units used in measuring electrical quantities. See MAGNETISM ; WEBER

Webster, DANIEL (1782–1852), American statesman, *b* Salisbury, New Hampshire, USA ; had great gifts as an administrator ; best remembered for his many eloquent speeches.

Webster, JOHN (*d* 1625), English dramatist, probably *b* London ; friend of Dekker, Middleton ; noted for his mastery of gruesome and macabre effects. His best known play is *The Duchess of Malfi.*

Weddell Sea, *wed''l,* bay, Antarctica ; named after James Weddell, a British explorer.

Wedgwood, JOSIAH (1730–95), potter, *b* Burslem, Staffordshire ; brought pottery-making to an art, much of his ware being enriched with raised ornament in classic style ; opened the Etruria works ; famous for the so-called jasper ware in various colours. See PLATE VIII

Wednesbury, *wednz'bĕr-i,* town, Staffordshire ; long noted for iron and steel, hardware and boiler-plates ; pop.32,000.

weevil, name for many British beetles with a long snout. All are vegetable eaters, and their grubs do much damage in gardens and to crops.

weight, see MATTER

weights and **measures,** standards of size, weight and value. These differ in various parts of the world, but we may consider here two systems of weights and measures (*a*) the British ; (*b*) the Metric.

(*a*) The British System is based on two units of measurement, the *yard* and the *pound.* The yard is the unit of length ; the pound is the unit of weight ; and from the latter is derived the *gallon,* the British unit of capacity.

Originally the length of the king's arm, the yard is defined as the distance between two hairlines on two gold plugs in a bar of iridio-platinum kept by the Board of Trade, though recently the National Physical Laboratory has sought to make this standard more precise by defining the yard as a length based upon the wave-length of light emitted by a cadmium filament. From the standard

yard are derived such lengths as the inch and mile, and thus also all our measures of area and volume.

The British standard avoirdupois pound (from the French *avoir de pois,* i.e. goods of weight) is related to the standard yard by the fact that one cubic foot of distilled water at standard temperature and pressure *weighs* 62·321lb. The Board of Trade standard pound is a platinum cylinder weighing 7,000 grains, the Troy pound being 12 ounces.

The gallon is the volume occupied by 10lb of distilled water at 62°F and 30in barometric pressure, and is equal to 277·274 cubic inches.

(*b*) The Metric System (used generally in France and elsewhere and by scientists, engineers, etc. in *all* countries) is a decimal system, i.e. all units are related to one another by being multiples or sub-multiples of 10, thus greatly simplifying calculations. The system was devised in France during the Revolution, and was adopted there in 1801.

The basic unit of measurement in the Metric system is the *metre,* a length originally defined as 1/10,000,000th of the distance from the N. Pole to the Equator (the line being presumed to pass through Paris) ; but it was later found that the calculation of this distance was slightly inaccurate, and for all practical purposes the standard metre is now determined by a measured length (at 4°C) on a registered bar of platinum kept in Paris. This standard metre is equivalent to 1·0936143yd.

The basic Metric unit of mass (i.e. weight) is the *gramme,* defined as the weight of 1 cubic centimetre of pure water at 4°C. (The gramme is equivalent to 0·00220462231lb.)

The basic Metric unit of capacity is the *litre,* defined as the volume of 1,000 grammes of pure water at 4°C and 760mm pressure, often regarded as 1,000cc, but actually 1,000·027cc.

The relation of smaller and larger units to the basic unit in any table in the Metric System is shown by the following prefixes : (*a*) the Latin prefixes *milli-* (1/1000th) ; *centi-* (1/100th) ; *deci-* (1/10th) ; (*b*) the Greek prefixes *Deka-* (10 times), *Hekto-* (100 times) ; *Kilo-* (1,000 times), and *Myria-* (10,000 times).

Note : the *long* ton has 2,240lb, but the *short* ton has 2,000lb, i.e. 20 centals of 100lb or 0·907 metric tonne ; the long ton equals 1·016 metric tonnes ; 1 gramme is 0·03215oz Troy ; the Troy oz is the same as the Apothecaries' oz, i.e. 480 grains or 31·1035 grammes ; the quintal is 220·46lb or 1·968cwt ; a bar of gold weighs 400oz Troy, but a bar of silver weighs *c.*1,000oz Troy ; the bushel varies locally ; a minim is more or less a single drop of liquid ; the nautical mile is 6,080ft ; the metre is 39·3701inches. See pages 710, 711.

TABLES OF WEIGHTS AND MEASURES

1. British (or Imperial) with Metric Equivalents

Avoirdupois Weight

16 drams (dr)	=1 ounce (oz)	=	28·350 grammes
16 oz	=1 pound (lb)	=	0·4536 Kg
14 lb	=1 stone (st)	=	6·350 Kg
2 st (28 lb)	=1 quarter (qr)		
4 qr (112lb)	=1 hundredweight (cwt)	=	50·80 Kg
20 cwt (2,240lb)	=1 ton		=1016·00 Kg

Measure of Capacity

4 gills	=1 pint	=0·56792 litre
2 pints	=1 quart	=1·136 litre
4 quarts	=1 gallon	=4·5456 litre
2 gallons	=1 peck	=9·092 litre
4 pecks	=1 bushel	=3·637 Dl
8 bushels	=1 quarter	=2·900 Hl

Note—These are the tables of measurement most widely used in trade and commerce. They are based on the pound and gallon, by which they are linked with the tables of measurement used by chemists and apothecaries.

Apothecaries' Measure of Weight			*Apothecaries' Measure of Capacity*	
20 grains	=1 scruple (Ə) =	1·296 grm	60 minims	=1 fluid drachm
3 scruples	=1 drachm (ℨ) =	3·888 grm	8 fluid drachms	=1 fluid ounce
8 drachms	=1 ounce	= 31·1035 grm	20 fluid ounces	=1 pint
12 ounces	=1 pound	=373·2420 grm	8 pints	=1 gallon

Measure of Length

12 inches (in)	=1 foot (ft)	=	0·30480 metre
3 ft	=1 yard (yd)	=	0·914383 metre
5½yd	=1 pole	=	5·0292 metre
22 yd	=1 chain or 100 links	=	20·1168 metre
10 chains	=1 furlong		=201·168 metre
8 furlongs or 1,760yd	=1 mile (m)	=	1·6093 Km

Square Measure

144 sq.in	=1 sq.ft	=	9·2903 sq.dm
9 sq.ft	=1 sq.yd	=	0·8361 sq.m
30¼sq.yd	=1 sq. pole	=	25·293 sq.m
40 sq. poles	=1 rood	=	10·117 ares
4 roods	=1 acre	=	0·40468 Hectare
640 acres	=1 sq.m		=259·00 Hectares

Note—An acre is the area of a square surface of which one side is 69·57yd ; it contains 4,840sq.yd.

Cubic Measure	*Nautical Measure*

1,728 cu.in	=1 cu.ft	=0·028317 cu.m
27 cu.ft	=1 cu.yd	=0·764553 cu.m

6 ft	=1 fathom
100 fathoms	=1 cable's length
10 cables	=1 nautical mile (approx.)

Note—1 cu.ft of pure water weighs 62·32 lb.

Angular Measure

60 seconds ('')	=1 minute (')	
60 minutes	=1 degree (°)	
90 degrees	=1 right angle or quadrant	
4 quadrants	=1 circumference	

Time

60 seconds	=1 minute (min)	
60 min	=1 hour (h or hr)	
24 hr	=1 day (d or dy)	
365 days	=1 year (yr)	
366 days	=1 leap year	
100 years	=1 century (c)	

2. Metric with British (or Imperial) Equivalents

Measure of Length

10 millimetres (mm)	=1 centimetre (cm)	=	0·3937 in
10 cm	=1 decimetre (dm)	=	3·937 in
10 dm	=1 metre (m)	=	1·0936 yd
10 m	=1 Dekametre (Dm)	=	10·936 yd
10 Dm	=1 Hectometre (Hm)	=	109·36 yd
10 Hm	=1 Kilometre (Km)	=	0·6214 mile

Square Measure

100 sq.mm	=1 sq.cm	=	0·1549 sq.in
100 sq.cm	=1 sq.dm	=	15·5 sq.in
100 sq.dm	=1 sq.m	=	10·764 sq.ft
100 sq.m	=1 are	=	119·6 sq.yd
100 ares	=1 Hectare (Ha)	=	2·471 acres
100 Ha	=1 sq. Km	=	0·386 sq. mile

Measure of Capacity

10 centilitres (cl)	=1 decilitre (dl)	=0·176 pint
10 dl	=1 litre (l)	=1·759 pints
10 l	=1 Dekalitre (Dl)	=2·2 gallons
10 Dl	=1 Hectolitre (Hl)	=2·75 bushels

Cubic Measure

1,000 cu.cm	=1 cu.dm	=61·024 cu.in
1,000 cu.cm	=1 cu.m	=35·315 cu.ft

Weight

10 milligrams (mmg)	=1 centigram (cg)	=0·1543 grain (Troy)
10 cg	=1 decigram (dg)	=1·5432 grains (Troy)
10 dg	=1 gramme (grm)	=0·0353 ounce (Avoir)
10 grm	=1 Dekagram (Dg)	=0·3527 ounce
10 Dg	=1 Hectogram (Hg)	=3·527 ounce
10 Hg	=1 Kilogram (Kg)	=2·205 pounds
100 Kg	=1 quintal	=1·968 cwt
1,000 Kg	=1 tonne	=0·9842 ton

Useful Approximations

To convert
POUNDS (Avoirdupois) to KILOGRAMS, multiply by 11 and divide by 5.
KILOGRAMS to POUNDS (Avoirdupois), multiply by 5 and divide by 11.
INCHES to CENTIMETRES, multiply by 5 and divide by 2.
CENTIMETRES to INCHES, multiply by 2 and divide by 5.
LITRES to GALLONS, multiply by 50 and divide by 11.
GALLONS to LITRES, multiply by 11 and divide by 50.

Weimar, *vī'mär*, city, Germany ; on the R. Ilm ; noted as a railway junction and as a centre of book publishing. Here is Goethe's house, now a museum ; pop.40,000.

The WEIMAR CONSTITUTION is the name given to the democratic republican constitution established in Germany after World War I, and destroyed by Hitler 1933.

welding, joining two pieces of metal when in a semi-molten state ; may be done by a blacksmith after heating the metal in a forge ; by means of a blow-pipe and oxy-acetylene flame ; by electric welding, in which, as a rule, one of two methods is employed : (i) a current passes through the two pieces of metal to be joined, the resistance they offer generating sufficient heat to melt them ; or (ii) arc welding (especially suitable for repairs) the work itself being the nega-tive electrode, the positive usually a thin iron bar. The welder wears blue glass over his eyes to protect them from ultra-violet rays ; he keeps his + electrode about ⅛in from the work, causing intense heat in the arc, and so fusing the metal. This method has now been adapted to replace riveting, a most important advance in shipbuilding.

well, hole in the ground from which water or oil is drawn. We read of (water) wells in the Bible and Aesop's fables ; but ARTESIAN WELLS are comparatively modern, taking their name from Artois, France, where they were first sunk, the principle being that a bore is made, a narrow pipe being sunk till it taps a supply of water flowing underground *from a higher level than the well,* with the result that water rushes up the pipe, and, if not controlled, spouts into the air. Such wells are common in Australia. One in Queensland is 7,009ft deep.

Welland, river, flows 70m, mainly through Lincolnshire to the Wash.

Welland Canal, see CANALS

Wellesley, MARQUIS OF, *welz'li* (1760–1842), elder brother of the Duke of Wellington ; born in County Meath, Eire. An able statesman and administrator, he was Governor of India 1797–1805, and may be regarded as the organiser of the Indian empire. He destroyed the power of the French, and that of Tippoo Sahib.

Wellingborough, town, Northamptonshire, noted for boots and shoes ; pop.29,000.

Wellington, port and cap. (since 1865), NZ; is in N. Island ; has the Government offices ; manufactures soap and woollen goods ; pop.186,000.

Wellington, DUKE OF (1769–1852), soldier and statesman, often called the Iron Duke ; *b* Dublin ; began life as Arthur Wellesley ; won fame as a soldier in India, where his campaigns were bril-liantly successful, e.g. the storming of Seringapatam, his battles against the Mahrattas (when in 1803 he made a remarkable journey of 600m) and his victory at Assaye, all largely due to his

care of the troops, his able organisation and his strategy. As Napoleon's op-ponent in Spain 1808–14, he fought the Peninsular War with stubbornness though at great sacrifice of manpower, his victories including those of Talavera (1809) and Salamanca (1812). His holding of the lines of Torres Vedras ranks as a major military triumph.

Created Duke of Wellington 1814, he shared with Blücher the decisive victory of Waterloo, 1815, thus putting an end to Napoleon's conquests in Europe. His approach-march and con-centration were jeopardised by careless-ness, but his choice of ground and the disposition of his troops on the battle-field were masterly.

From 1815 Wellington was a states-man rather than a soldier. A Tory, and one of the greatest figures in the Europe of his day, he had immense influence. He enabled France to recover from her long series of wars by withdrawing foreign troops three years before the stipulated time ; he went on diplomatic missions to foreign powers ; became Prime Minister 1828 ; repealed the Test and Corporation Acts, passed the measure for Catholic Emancipation, and stoutly opposed the Reform Bill. He did much to secure the repeal of the Corn Laws 1846. In later life he lived chiefly at his home, Strathfieldsaye, Hampshire, but died at Walmer Castle, and was buried in St Paul's, London.

Wellington appeared to the world as a hard, cold man who gave orders briefly and expected unquestioning obedience. From his soldiers he required discipline above all things ; in national affairs he stood for order. He disliked change, but was willing to make changes slowly. In private life he was much less the 'iron' duke than was popularly imagined. He loved children, and was beloved by them. He was scarcely a genius, but he was great because of his sincerity, truthful-ness and personal unambition. Perhaps his greatest quality was commonsense.

Wellington College, English public school founded as a memorial to the Duke of Wellington. It is near Wokingham, Berkshire.

Wells, HERBERT GEORGE (1866–1946), author, historian, pioneer and dreamer, *b* Bromley, Kent ; worked in a chemist's shop, then in a drapery store ; won a scholarship to London University ; became a lecturer in biology ; and was later a journalist. He won fame with his scientific novels ; e.g. *The Time Machine* ; *The Invisible Man* (filmed 1934) ; *The First Men in the Moon* ; *The Food of the Gods* ; *The War in the Air* ; and revealed his gift of humour in his masterly short stories. His story *Kipps* (1905) also *Bealby* (1915), show that he might have been great as a novelist purely and simply ; but he became increasingly eager to set before men the shining ideals of a well-planned and reasonable world, hence his books of a Utopian nature, e.g. *The World Set Free* ; *The New Machiavelli* ; *Men Like Gods* ; *The Shape of Things to Come*.

It was a daring thing for him to attempt his group of books *The Outline of History* (1920), *The Science of Life*, written with the help of Julian Huxley, and *The Work, Wealth and Happiness of Mankind*. Even these did not complete his vision of what the world might be, and he went on to write *The World of William Clissold* ; *The Open Conspiracy*.

A master craftsman, H. G. Wells preached largely through his stories. He richly entertained his own generation, and (more than that) he made them think.

Welwyn Garden City, see TOWN PLANNING

Wembley, town, Middlesex, actually a residential suburb of London ; scene 1924 of a great Empire exhibition. At its stadium (accommodating 100,000 spectators) are played the Association Football Cup finals ; pop.134,000.

Wenceslas, *wen'ses-läs* (*d* 929), Duke of Prague and Bohemian saint ; murdered for attempting to convert his people to Christianity ; is the ' Good King Wenceslas ' of the Christmas carol.

Wener, largest lake, Sweden ; linked by canal with the Baltic.

Wensleydale, upper valley of the R. Ure, N. Yorkshire.

Wentworth, THOMAS, see STRAFFORD, EARL OF

Weser, *vā'zĕr*, river, Germany ; flows *c*.300m to the N. Sea.

Wesley, CHARLES, *wes'li* (1707–88), churchman and poet, younger brother of John Wesley, *b* Epworth, Lincolnshire. While at Oxford he gathered round him a number of undergraduates who studied and also planned their days *methodically*, hence the name Methodists. He accompanied his brother to Georgia, N. America ; began an evangelical revival in England, and is best remembered for his hymns (possibly *c*.6,000), including *Jesu, Lover of my Soul*.

Wesley, JOHN (1703–91), evangelist and founder of Methodism, *b* Epworth, Lincolnshire ; educated at Lincoln College, Oxford, where he joined a group of young men known as the Holy Club, but nicknamed Methodists because they were *methodical* in all they did. Becoming a clergyman, Wesley went as a missionary to Georgia. He passed through a great spiritual crisis at a meeting in Aldersgate Street, London, 1738, during which he ' felt his heart strangely warmed,' and became convinced that salvation from sin was possible through faith in Christ alone. Hence began the amazing preaching campaign which was his life's work.

Though frail in body, he travelled 250,000m (mostly on horseback) ; crossed the Irish Sea 42 times ; preached over 40,000 sermons ; rose at 5 o'clock every morning ; kept a journal ; translated books, and instituted social reforms. As a result of being prohibited from preaching in churches, he preached in the open air, in private houses and later in the chapels which were built by the Methodists themselves. Wesley's religious revival spread like wildfire across England, then to Scotland and N. America. His doctrine was simply that Christ forgives sins, and that in His strength men and women may live better and more joyous lives. He preached his last sermon at Leatherhead.

After his death the work he had begun continued to flourish, and today there are over 2,260,000 members of the Methodist Church in Britain, and over 21,000 churches ; world Methodism has nearly 12,000,000 members and 94,000 churches.

Wessel, HORST (1907–30), German writer of a Nazi rallying song ; *b* Bielefeld. A limestone cairn erected to his memory by the Nazis was destroyed by British sappers 1946.

Wessex, kingdom of the W. Saxons ; established in what is now Hampshire in the 6th c. AD ; later it was extended till under Alfred (9th c.) it occupied more or less all England.

As used by Thomas Hardy, the name is applied chiefly to Dorset, scene of his novels.

West, REBECCA (1892–   ), writer, born in County Kerry, Ireland ; noted for her forceful and constructive magazine articles, especially those on political questions ; author of many books, e.g. *The Thinking Reed*.

West Bridgford, suburb of Nottingham. Here is the Nottinghamshire County Cricket ground (Trent Bridge) ; pop. 21,000.

West Bromwich, *-brŭm'ich*, busy ' Black Country ' town, Staffordshire ; manufactures bricks, machinery and iron goods ; pop.81,000.

Western Australia, large but sparsely inhabited state, Australia ; area 975,920 sq.m ; pop.503,000. Mostly a tableland, W. Australia has a temperate climate and is chiefly pastoral. It has 11,000,000 sheep, and nearly 900,000 cattle, and is notable for hardwood forests and eucalyptus trees. Exports include wheat, wool, hides, timber and gold, also meat, butter and honey. The state is rich in flowers, some of which are rare and, frozen in ice, are frequently sent overseas for exhibition purposes, e.g. pitcher-plants and orchids. The cap. of W. Australia is Perth.

Western Desert, name given to the desert area west of the R. Nile. It is in Egypt and Libya, and extends to the Mediterranean coast ; scene of fighting in World War II, when the coastal towns (e.g. Mersa Matruh, Sollum, Sidi Barrani, etc.) were of great importance to British and Allied armies. Several times the British forces advanced into Libya, even as far as Benghazi and El

Agheila, but every time they were thrown back. In July 1942 they made a final stand at Alamein, from which they advanced in November 1942 in a successful campaign that drove the Germans out of North Africa.

The stand at Alamein was made about the time of the Russian stand at Stalingrad. Together they marked the turning of the tide against Germany in World War II.

Western Union, see EUROPE ; NORTH ATLANTIC PACT

West Ham, river port, Essex ; on the Thames ; has many industries and large docks ; pop.174,000.

West Indies, group of islands in the Atlantic Ocean between N. and S. America, so named (1492) by Columbus, who imagined he was approaching India. Most are British, but some belong to the USA and the Netherlands ; others are independent. See BAHAMAS ; CUBA ; JAMAICA ; LEEWARD ISLANDS ; and PLATE 12 (*top*)

Westinghouse, GEORGE (1846–1914), American engineer who made many improvements in railway signalling, and invented the Westinghouse air brake 1868.

West Lothian, *lō'thi-an,* county of Scotland south of the Firth of Forth ; coal, iron and oil are worked ; co.tn Linlithgow.

Westmeath, inland county in the province of Leinster, Eire ; co.tn Mullingar.

Westminster, city and borough of the county of London ; includes Whitehall, the Houses of Parliament ; Government offices, Buckingham Palace. See LONDON

Westminster Abbey, see LONDON

Westminster Cathedral, cathedral of the RC Archbishop of Westminster, London. A brick building in a revival of the Byzantine style, with a domed tower 283ft high, it was consecrated 1910.

Westminster Hall, see LONDON

Westminster School, English public school developed from a school attached to Westminster Abbey. Boys gaining scholarships on the Elizabethan foundation are known as King's scholars. One of the features of the school is tossing the pancake on Shrove Tuesday.

Westminster, STATUTE OF, see BRITISH COMMONWEALTH OF NATIONS

Westmorland, county of NW. England. It is mountainous, and includes part of the L. District ; co.tn Kendal.

Weston-super-Mare, *-sū'pĕr mār,* holiday town, Somerset ; overlooks the Bristol Channel ; pop.40,000.

Westphalia, *west-fā'li-ä,* formerly a duchy, now with N. Rhine a German state.

Westphalia, TREATY OF, 1648, ended the Thirty Years' War, giving a measure of religious liberty to Catholics and Protestants, and perpetuated the separation of Germany into a number of petty kingdoms. See THIRTY YEARS' WAR

West Point, US military academy, New York state.

West Virginia, state of USA ; it is north-west of Virginia ; produces coal and petroleum ; cap. Charleston.

Westward Ho!, beautiful seaside town, Devonshire, on Bideford Bay ; named after Charles Kingsley's novel. It is immortalised by Rudyard Kipling in *Stalky & Co.*

wether, see SHEEP

Wetter, *vet'ĕr,* lake, Sweden ; fed by hidden springs and has clear blue water ; area 733sq.m.

Wetterhorn, *vet'ĕr-,* peak of the Bernese Oberland, Switzerland ; rises 12,166ft.

' wet water,' see FIRE

Wexford, county of Leinster, Eire ; has 90m of coastline ; co.tn WEXFORD, on the R. Slaney, linked by rail with its harbour at Rosslare.

Wey, *wā,* tributary of the Thames, flowing 35m in Surrey and Hampshire.

Weygand, MAXIME, *vā'gän* (1867–   ), French soldier, *b* Brussels ; did brilliant work in World War I ; Commander-in-Chief of the defeated French army 1940.

Weymouth, *wā'muth,* holiday town, Dorset coast ; pop.37,000.

whale, sea mammal (*not* a fish) ; comes to the surface to breathe ; gives birth to fully formed calves, feeding them with its own milk ; has a thick coating of fat (blubber) ; is warm-blooded.

Largest of the *toothed whales* is the SPERM WHALE or CACHALOT, often 60ft long ; usually found in schools (groups) of *c.*100 ; hunted for sperm oil (from the blubber), for ivory taken from its 20–24 teeth, and for spermaceti, a kind of wax in the skull. The DOLPHIN, *c.*8ft long, is common round British coasts. The most notable was known as PELORUS JACK. He piloted ships through Cook Strait, NZ, for many years and was last seen 1914. Another dolphin took his place some years later, and continued to pilot ships through the Strait. The PORPOISE is like the dolphin, but smaller. The NARWHAL, from 12–15ft, is a small whale of the Arctic, notable for its tusk, often 7ft long. Besides these there are the *toothless whales.* These have plates of whale-bone, and include the *true whale* or RORQUAL, with over 300 whalebone plates (which are known as baleens). This whale may be over 70ft long.

Whales have long been hunted, and whaling has been carried on by Norwegians, Dutch, Americans and especially the British, notably from Hull. Whalers now sail in whaling factories, i.e. ships of over 20,000 tons, e.g. the *Southern Venturer.* Harpooning by hand has given place to firing the harpoon from a gun, the whale being killed by an explosive charge in the barb. Some whaling vessels now have asdic (directional soundings through the sea) with which to locate whales.

Whales are now much hunted in the S. Atlantic and Pacific.

Read *Moby Dick,* Herman Melville ; *Peter the Whaler,* W. G. Kingston ;

THE WHALES

(1) *Porpoise*   (2) *Dolphin*   (3) *Narwhal*   (4) *Bottlenose*   (5) *Cachalot or Sperm Whale*
(6) *Beluga*   (7) *Right whale showing Baleen plates*   (8) *Rorqual or Blue Whale*

The Cruise of the Cachalot, F. T. Bullen ;
The Whale Hunters, J. J. Bell.

whaling, see WHALE

Wharfe, *wörf*, river, W. Yorkshire ; flows 60m to join the Ouse.

Wharton, EDITH, *hwör'tŭn* (1862–1937), American novelist ; author of *The Age of Innocence.*

whaup, see CURLEW

wheat, *hwēt*, cereal forming the principal food of mankind, more wheat being milled than all other cereals combined. A cultivated grass (family *Gramineae*), wheat has been harvested since the Stone Age, and was being cultivated in China as early as 3000BC, and also in ancient Egypt.

The stalks of wheat support spikes on which flowers are formed, the kernels (or grains) being enclosed in scale-like coverings (*glumes*) that in threshing form chaff. Approx. 71·2% of the grain is carbohydrates, 11% proteins, the remainder water, fat and mineral. The coatings, when ground, form bran.

Wheat grows to a height of from 3 to 5ft according to climate, and thrives best in stiff soil. It may be sown in winter or spring, and is harvested (in Britain) in July and Aug. British wheats are, on the whole, deficient in gluten, and are styled ' soft ' or ' weak ' ; but Canadian and N. American imported wheats are ' hard ' or ' strong ' ; thus a British wheat gives flour that makes a 2lb loaf with a volume of 2,000cc, but a Canadian wheat will make a 2lb loaf with a volume of 3,000cc. British wheats yield an average of 17½cwt per acre, while Canadian wheats average 9½cwt, and Australian and Argentine wheats only 6¾cwt.

Great advances in wheat production have been made in the last fifty years, due largely to the discoveries of Mendel, and to the experiments of Professor Biffen of Cambridge ; hence such varieties as Yeoman, Squarehead, Victor, Holdfast and Little Joss. Yellow rust, smut and bunt are wheat diseases liable to do much damage to crops, but dry disinfectants are now being used against these. See PLATES 2, 3, 4

wheatear, insect-eating bird visiting Britain from early March. It is *c.*6in long, grey above, with black on the wings, and black and white on the tail, though in autumn it is chiefly reddish.

Wheatstone, SIR CHARLES (1802–75), scientist, *b* Gloucester ; notable for many electrical devices, e.g. those connected with the electric telegraph, rheostat, and Wheatstone's bridge for measuring electrical resistance ; recognised the importance of Ohm's law, and did much to develop the dynamo.

Wheatstone's bridge, see ELECTRICITY

wheel, *hwēl*, mechanical device of supreme importance. In relation to the axle, a wheel is an adaptation of the lever, with the advantage of continuous circular motion. See MECHANICS

THE WHINCHAT

Wheeling, town and great railway centre, W. Virginia, USA ; pop.61,000.

whelk, see MOLLUSCA

whey, see MILK

Whig Party, see PARLIAMENT

whinchat, small British migratory bird with yellowish plumage above, white throat, reddish breast ; found in hedges and furze bushes ; builds in a hollow under a tuft of grass ; lays 4–6 blue eggs.

whip, in British politics, an officer whose business it is to see that there is a good attendance of his own party when an important debate is to take place in the House of Commons. He is usually a junior minister, and acts as a teller when there is a division, i.e. when members have to vote.

whippet, dog that is a cross between one of a greyhound breed and a terrier ; weighs *c.*20lb ; is exceedingly swift, hence its use in racing and for rabbit coursing.

whip-poor-will, N. American night bird *c.*9in long ; has a peculiar call rather like *whip-poor-will*, hence the name.

Whipsnade, extension of the London Zoological Gardens, opened 1931 in a delightful spot 3m from Dunstable (Bedfordshire). Here wild animals are not confined in cages, but are allowed a measure of freedom ; they may be seen in surroundings very similar to their natural haunts.

whisky, drink containing 40–50% alcohol. Whisky is chiefly distilled from malted barley in Scotland and Ireland, and from Indian corn or rye in N. America.

THE WHEATEAR

It is colourless and raw at first, but after maturing for three years or more in barrels it gains an amber hue and becomes mellowed.

Whispering Gallery, see LONDON

Whistler, JAMES MCNEILL (1834–1903), American artist ; lived much in England, and died Chelsea. Greatly criticised, especially by John Ruskin, Whistler painted pictures revealing his fine sense of colour, and giving a feeling of space and airiness, often with a hint of Japanese art, e.g. *Old Battersea Bridge* ; *The Pool* (London) ; *The Music Room* ; *Portrait of the Painter's Mother.*

Whistler had a ready wit, e.g. when a lady said that a scene reminded her of his pictures, he replied, ' Yes, madam, Nature is creeping up.'

Whistler, LAURENCE (1912–   ), writer ; also engraves on glass ; author of several books, e.g. *Four Walls*, a book of poetry.

Whitby, romantic old seaside town and port, N. Yorkshire ; once notable for jet ; has a ruined abbey ; associated with Caedmon, who was a monk here ; also with Captain Cook.

White, GILBERT, *hwīt* (1720–93), naturalist ; *b* Selborne, Hampshire, where he was curate, and where he died.

A patient observer of birds, flowers, trees and animals, he wrote *The Natural History and Antiquities of Selborne*, probably the most popular book of its kind ever written.

Those interested in birds, flowers, trees, animals of our countryside will find it worthwhile to compare their own nature calendars with the one compiled by this careful observer.

whitebeam, tree common in Britain (especially in chalky pastures) and in France ; named from the white and woolly buds and young oval leaves. The fruit turns red.

Whitefield, GEORGE, *hwit'fēld* (1714–70), preacher, *b* Gloucester. At Oxford he joined the Wesleys as a ' Methodist,' and went with John and Charles Wesley to Georgia, where he founded an orphanage. Prevented from preaching in the churches at home, he made evangelical tours in which he preached out of doors, and did much to kindle new religious fervour in England, Scotland and S. Wales. He founded the Moorfields Tabernacle, London. Whitefield had a powerful voice and was a born orator. His followers form the Calvinistic Methodist Church.

Whitehall, see LONDON

Whitehaven, port, Cumberland ; has coal and haematite mines, blast furnaces, etc.; pop.21,000.

Whitehead, ALFRED NORTH (1861–1947), thinker and mathematician ; collaborated with Bertrand Russell in writing *Principia Mathematica.*

Whitehead, ROBERT (1823–1905), inventor, *b* Lancashire. He improved silk-weaving machinery, but is most famous as a pioneer in torpedo construction.

white horse, large design formed on a chalk hillside by removing the turf, e.g. the white horses of Uffington (Berkshire) ; Bratton (Wiltshire) ; Kilburn (Yorkshire). The Uffington horse is 355ft long.

White House, THE, official home in Washington of the president of the USA. The foundation stone was laid by George Washington, and the house was first occupied by John Adams, 1800. The exterior stone walls are painted white. See UNITED STATES OF AMERICA

White Russia, republic of USSR, otherwise called Byelorussia ; area *c.*81,000 sq.m ; pop.10,558,000 ; cap. Minsk. See USSR

White Sea, inlet of the Arctic Ocean, USSR ; frozen nine months in the year ; chief port, Archangel.

White Star, see SHIPS

whitethroat, song bird visiting Britain in summer ; may be 5in long ; has reddish plumage above, pinkish white below. Often found in thickets and gardens, it lays greyish speckled eggs.

THE GREATER WHITETHROAT

whiting, food fish of the cod family, found in British waters ; weighs *c.*2lb.

Whitley Bay, *hwit'li*, seaside town, Northumberland ; pop.30,000 with Monkseaton.

Whitman, WALT (1819–92), American poet, *b* Long I., New York ; was teacher, journalist, editor, tramp, carpenter and army nurse. He died poor but famous, and is remembered for his book of poems, *Leaves of Grass.* His verse, lacking rhyme or metre, is full of rich cadence. Only towards the end of his life was his greatness recognised, but he is now famous for his idealism and sympathy, his discovery of God in nature, the city street, and human experience. Today he is regarded as America's democratic poet. As a typical example of his verse note :

I think I could turn and live with animals, they are so placid and self-contain'd ;
I stand and look at them long and long.
They do not sweat and whine about their condition,
They do not lie awake in the dark and weep for their sins,
They do not make me sick discussing their duty to God ;
Not one is dissatisfied, not one is demented with the mania of owning things,
Not one kneels to another, nor to his kind that lived thousands of years ago;

Not one is respectable or unhappy over the whole earth.

Whitstable, *hwit'stä'bl,* seaside town, Kent; noted for oysters.

Whit Sunday, see CALENDAR

Whittier, JOHN GREENLEAF (1807–92), American Quaker poet, *b* Massachusetts. He did much to bring about the abolition of slavery ; wrote many fine nature poems, also *Maud Muller, Barbara Frietchie,* and *Snow-Bound,* a vivid picture of New England life.

Ichabod is generally regarded as his greatest poem.

Whittington, RICHARD (*d* 1423), prosperous business-man who was Lord Mayor of London 1397, also 1398, 1406 and 1419. He lent large sums of money to Richard II, Henry IV and Henry V. The story of Whittington and his cat seems to have been first told in 1605.

Whittle, AIR COMMODORE SIR FRANK (1907–   ), pilot who entered the RAF at Cranwell ; was a Group Captain 1943 ; long devoted his attention to the problem of jet-propulsion, the first flights of his Gloster jet-propelled plane being made 1941, though he had lodged his patent as early as 1930. His invention revolutionised aircraft construction, and led the way to greater speeds and longer flights ; he was knighted 1948. See AVIATION

Whitworth, SIR JOSEPH (1803–87), engineer, *b* Stockport ; invented improved machine tools ; standardised the measurements of screw threads ; manufactured cannon of cast steel. His engineering firm was amalgamated with that of Sir William Armstrong 1897.

whooping cough, disease characterised by catarrh of the respiratory organs and a peculiar and prolonged cough. A considerable degree of immunity is assured by injecting a suitable vaccine.

whortleberry, see BILBERRY

Whymper, EDWARD (1840–1911), English mountaineer and explorer ; remembered as leader 1865 of the first successful attempt to climb the Matterhorn. From the top Whymper looked over and saw another party still some way below the summit. Two days later the second party found a way to the top, but meanwhile disaster had overtaken their rivals. On the way down, one of Whymper's party of 7 slipped, dislodging 3 others. Whymper and the 2 remaining members of the party clung to the rock-face, but the rope broke, and the 4 who fell were killed on the glacier 4,000ft below. Later it was discovered that the rope was an old one that ought not to have been used, but allegations that it had been cut are unfounded. The story is told in Whymper's *Scrambles,* one of the most thrilling adventure stories ever written.

Whymper did no more climbing in the Alps, but later he took an expedition to Ecuador and led the first recorded ascent of Chimborazo.

He was not only an able mountaineer but also a writer of vigorous and exciting books.

Read especially *Scrambles Amongst the Alps.*

Wick, co.tn, Caithness ; noted for its herring fisheries.

Wicklow, *wik'lō,* county in the province of Leinster, Eire ; favoured by tourists for its mt. scenery ; co.tn Wicklow.

widgeon, *wij'ŭn,* British wild duck *c*.18in long ; has a white forehead, chestnut cheeks and neck, greyish back. It is brown on the wings and tail. Found in winter, usually near the coast ; it breeds in Scotland and Ireland.

Widnes, town, Lancashire ; noted for chemicals and copper ; pop.42,000. See RUNCORN

Wiesbaden, *vĕs'bä-den,* town, Germany, *c*.6m from Mainz, and amid beautiful scenery ; has *c*.30 hot springs, and is a highly popular health resort ; pop. 172,000.

wig, false hair ; worn in ancient Egypt and by Greeks and Romans ; became popular in France in Louis XIII's day, and among gentlemen in England *c*.1660, the full wig being later replaced by the smaller peruke or tie-wig. From *c*.1750 powdering the hair took the place of wigs, though the Speaker of the House of Commons, judges and barristers and town clerks still wear wigs when officially engaged.

Wigan, town, Lancashire ; has coal mines; manufactures cotton ; pop.85,000.

Wightman Cup, see LAWN TENNIS

Wigtownshire, county of SW. Scotland ; co.tn Wigtown.

Wilberforce, WILLIAM (1759–1833), reformer, *b* Hull (Yorkshire), for which town he became MP 1780. His life's

WILBERFORCE 1759–1833

work was the abolition of slavery. He had condemned Negro slavery as an 'odious traffic in human flesh' even as a schoolboy, and with the help of his friends Pitt, Clarkson, Fox and Burke, he succeeded in persuading Parliament to pass an act 1807 ending the exportation of slaves. The emancipation (freeing) of slaves in the British Empire was assured by the act of 1833, passed three days before Wilberforce died. See SLAVERY

Wilde, OSCAR (1856–1900), Irish writer, *b* Dublin ; in London became leader 1870–95 of the 'aestheticist' literary movement of the time (i.e. literature written in accordance with the motto 'Art for Art's Sake'). Wilde was overtaken by disasters largely of his own making and died soon after serving a sentence in prison. His plays (*The Importance of Being Earnest* ; *Lady Windermere's Fan,* etc.) are witty but superficial : his novel *Dorian Gray* is interesting but unconvincing. He wrote also some poetry of little contemporary importance.

wildebeest or **gnu,** *wil'de-bēst,* African antelope ; is 4ft at the shoulder ; remarkable for its heavy head and neck. The horns curve down and then up and backwards. It has an erect mane.

Wilder, THORNTON, *wīl'dĕr* (1897–), American author, *b* Madison, Wisconsin ; travelled in Italy and China. A fine literary craftsman, his novels include *The Cabala* ; *Heaven's My Destination,* his masterpiece being *The Bridge of San Luis Rey.*

wild mustard, plant with dusty green leaves, and clusters of four-petalled bright yellow flowers ; the fruit is a thin green pod.

wild thyme, *tīm,* small, trailing plant. The edges of the leaves are rolled back ; the small purple flowers (June–Aug.) are in a funnel-shaped calyx. It is common in mountainous districts and chalky pastures.

Wilhelmina, *vil-hel-mē'nä* (1880–), Queen of the Netherlands ; *b* The Hague ; succeeded 1890 ; married Henry, Duke of Mecklenburg-Schwerin (1876–1934). Her daughter Juliana was born 1909. During World War II Wilhelmina found refuge in England ; abdicated after celebrating her Diamond Jubilee (1948) in favour of her daughter Princess Juliana.

Wilkes, JOHN, *wilks* (1727–97), politician, *b* London ; founded *The North Briton* 1762 in which, as a Whig and freethinker, he mercilessly attacked the Tories, and even criticised the king's speech 1763, for which he was imprisoned. Elected MP, he clamoured for the abolition of rotten boroughs, and for votes for the lower classes. He did much to establish the principle of the freedom of the Press, and the right of a member to sit in Parliament if duly elected.

Wilkins, SIR GEORGE HUBERT (1888–),

Australian explorer ; made a flight (1919) from England to Australia ; took part in several Antarctic and Arctic expeditions 1920–31, his exploits making him world famous ; author of *Flying the Arctic* and *Under the North Pole.*

Wilkinson, ELLEN (*d* 1947), English politician associated with votes for women, trade unions, the Socialist movement. Labour MP 1924, she was notable for her interest in social work, and as a brilliant speaker. She was Minister of Education in the Labour government returned 1945.

will, in law, a document declaring how a person wishes his *estate* (i.e. his money, property, investments and perhaps personal belongings) to be disposed of after his death.

In English law, it must be signed by him (the *testator* or, in the case of a woman, the *testatrix*) in the presence of two *witnesses,* all of whom must see each other sign. An adult who fails to make a will is said to die *intestate.* The testator may leave sums of money to a number of *legatees,* and the remainder of his estate (the *residue*) to some person or persons. If, after the will has been signed and witnessed, an addition is made, the new paragraph is called a *codicil.* When money is left in trust, it is necessary to appoint two people as *executors and trustees* to see that the testator's wishes are faithfully carried out, or the Public Trustee may be appointed for this purpose.

The duties of a trustee include, very often, the administration of the estate for the benefit of children till they are old enough to administer it themselves, i.e. when they reach the age of 21.

A copy of any English will made since 1858 may be seen at Somerset House, Strand, London, or the District Registry, for a fee of one shilling, and the original will for 2s. Obtaining *probate* means filing a will in the Probate Division of the High Court of Justice and obtaining a certified copy for the trustees.

In Scotland a widow is entitled to one-third (*jus relictae*) of the deceased husband's 'moveable' estate, and the children collectively to another third of it (*legitim* or 'bairns' pairt'). If there are no children, the widow is entitled to one-half of the moveable estate, and so are the children if there is no widow. A husband who survives his wife has the same rights in connection with his dead wife's moveable estate. *Thus there is only one third of the moveable estate* ('*deid's pairt*') *that can be left as the testator pleases.* A husband may leave his 'heritable' (i.e. real) property as he pleases, except that the widow may claim a life-rent on one third of it. The general effect of the Scots testamentary law is to secure the interests of the surviving spouse and his or her children : in Scotland a man cannot 'cut off his son with a shilling.'

Scots law is more flexible than English law as to the *form* of the will, which if *holograph*, i.e. in the testator's own handwriting, even *without witnesses*, may be perfectly valid. Scottish wills are registered in the Register House, Edinburgh.

Willenhall, town, Staffordshire ; manufactures brassware and iron goods, notably locks and bolts ; pop.30,000.

Willett, WILLIAM, see CALENDAR

William (1143–1214), King of Scots, known as William the Lion ; grandson of David I ; succeeded his brother Malcolm IV, 1165 ; allied Scotland with France.

William I (1027–87), King of England, known as William the Conqueror, son of a Norman duke ; *b* Falaise ; became Duke of Normandy 1035 ; married Matilda, daughter of the Count of Flanders (and a descendant of Alfred the Great) ; showed himself an able soldier in his battles against various rebels.

When Harold, the brother-in-law of Edward the Confessor of England, was wrecked on the coast of Normandy 1063, William compelled him to promise (by swearing on the bones of many saints) that at Edward's death he would aid William to become king of England ; but when Edward died, Harold himself became king. William at once prepared to invade. Landing at Pevensey, he met Harold at Senlac (near Hastings) 1066, and by his victory put an end to Anglo-Saxon history and began the Norman period. He was crowned, in Westminster Abbey, Christmas Day 1066.

For some time William's authority extended only over S. England, where he built many castles, and took power from the Anglo-Saxons, giving it to his Norman followers ; otherwise he interfered comparatively little with the normal life of the people. He crushed rebellions in the north 1069, laying waste wide regions 1070–71, and finally stamped out the last embers of revolt by defeating Hereward the Wake. He developed the feudal system, and took care that no baron had too much land in one place or too much power. He had the *Domesday Book* compiled 1085 ; made few alterations in church affairs, but with the aid of Lanfranc, Archbishop of Canterbury, prevented the pope from gaining too great a hold on the Church.

William II (*d* 1100), King of England, called William Rufus, having a ruddy complexion ; second son of William I, whose eldest son, Robert, was Duke of Normandy. Cruel and tyrannical, William II overruled the feudal laws, revived severe punishments for minor offences, and quickly lost the loyalty of the barons, who, led by Odo of Bayeux, revolted in favour of Robert. William crushed the rebellion, invaded Scotland, and later compelled Robert to do homage. While riding in the New

WILLIAM OF ORANGE 1650–1702

Forest he was killed by an arrow, whether by accident or design it is impossible to say.

William III (1650–1702), King of Great Britain, born at The Hague, son of William, Prince of Orange, and Mary, daughter of Charles I of England ; elected Stadtholder 1672.

Though William lost almost every battle he fought, he was superb in defence, coming out of every reverse stronger than before. Ruler of the Dutch, he spent his whole life in checking the power of France, outwitting Richelieu, Mazarin and Louis XIV ; and proving a masterly diplomat.

Discontent in England and Scotland led to his being invited to become king. William landed at Brixham with an army 1688. James II fled, and William and his wife, Mary (daughter of James II) became king and queen. William, stern and silent, was never popular in England. He did not understand our politics, but he acted promptly when Ireland declared for James II, and won his only victory at the battle of the Boyne 1690. He must be held responsible for the massacre of Glencoe 1692. He ruled prudently during a difficult period of change ; and perhaps, after all, he regarded England and her affairs as of secondary importance to his life's task of checking French power.

William IV (1765–1837), King of Great Britain and Ireland ; third son of George III ; known as the ' sailor prince ' ; entered the House of Lords as Duke of Clarence ; married Adelaide, princess of Saxe-Meiningen 1818 ; ruled from 1830, taking little active part in politics apart from his desire to prevent the passing of the Reform Bill 1832.

William I (1797–1888), German emperor, *b* Berlin, son of Frederick William III of

Prussia ; proclaimed German emperor 1871 by Bismarck.

William II (1859–1941), German emperor, better known as the Kaiser ; *b* Berlin. He ascended the throne 1888 at 29 ; believed in the Divine Right of kings ; had romantic visions of a great German empire ; quarrelled with Bismarck, who resigned 1890 ; was opposed to democratic principles. He built up a powerful fleet and army, and in his foreign policy gradually alienated all British sympathy. His dream of German expansion led to World War I. He abdicated 1918, and afterwards lived in retirement at Doorn, Holland. Conceited, impatient and without any real genius for administration or military affairs, he failed as a ruler.

His son, FREDERICK WILLIAM (1882–), the Crown Prince, a popular commander in World War I, but without notable ability, became an enthusiastic supporter of the Nazi policy.

William the Silent (William I of Orange) (1533–84), Prince of Orange ; named the Silent because, as a diplomat, he spoke rarely ; eventually became Stadtholder of the Netherlands. He led his countrymen against the Spaniards, but was assassinated before he completed his task.

Williams, EMLYN (1905–), Welsh dramatist, *b* Mostyn, Flintshire ; appeared as an actor on the London stage 1927 ; later acted for the films ; won fame with his plays *Spring* ; *The Late Christopher Bean* ; and *The Corn is Green*.

Williams, JOHN (1796–1839), missionary, *b* London ; sent by the London Missionary Society to the Society Is. 1816 ; murdered by cannibals.

Williamson, HENRY (1897–), writer, *b* Bedfordshire ; author of *Tarka the Otter*, and of many novels, e.g. *The Linhay on the Downs* ; *The Story of a Norfolk Farm*, etc. In his book *The Beautiful Years* he reveals his admiration for Richard Jefferies, the naturalist.

Read *Salar the Salmon* ; *The Lone Swallows* ; *The Old Stag*.

will-o'-the-wisp (or *ignis fatuus*), pale flickering flame sometimes seen hovering over ponds ; is due to the presence of marsh-gas or methane. In medieval times it was thought to lure benighted travellers in the fen-country to their destruction.

Willoughby, SIR HUGH, *wil'ō-bi* (*d* 1554), English explorer ; attempted to find the north-east passage to India and China (Cathay), sailed 1553 ; perished in Lapland, but opened the way to trade with Russia.

willow, name of a number of trees including : (*a*) WHITE WILLOW (*Salix alba*), the young leaves covered with white hairs ; usually found near streams, often pollarded (or lopped) to increase the growth of its pliant branches used in basket-making ; (*b*) WEEPING WILLOW ;

(*c*) BAY-LEAVED WILLOW with fragrant leaves ; (*d*) GOAT WILLOW or SALLOW, which gives us ' palm ' for Easter ; (*e*) a hybrid of the white willow that supplies timber for cricket bats, hence the nickname ' King Willow ' for the game of cricket. See OSIER

willow herb, tall, thin plant. Species include the GREAT WILLOW HERB, 4–6ft high, with large rose-coloured flowers (July). The leaves clasping the stem are narrow and saw-edged ; both leaves and stems are downy.

Wills, WILLIAM JOHN, see BURKE, ROBERT O'HARA

Wilmington, city and port, Delaware, USA ; noted for shipbuilding and paper ; pop.113,000.

Wilson, THOMAS WOODROW (1856–1924), American statesman, born in Virginia, USA ; Democratic President of USA 1913 ; he was re-elected 1917. A lover of peace, he attempted to keep America out of World War I, but the sinking of the *Lusitania* (1915) and the increasing menace of German submarine activities, compelled him to support the Allies 1917. He appointed General Pershing as supreme commander of the USA army, and united Democrats and Republicans in the war effort.

After the war he drew up an outline of his proposed League of Nations (his famous *Fourteen Points*), but though fundamentally right as an idealist, he failed in practical details, not only being swayed by determined statesmen like Clemenceau of France, but unable to rouse enthusiasm in USA, hence America's refusal to enter the League.

WOODROW WILSON 1856–1924

24*a*

It was said of him that he always did the right thing in the wrong way ; but his conception of the League was an inspiration to the world, and a valuable experiment in securing international peace.

Wilton, town, Wiltshire ; *c*.3m from Salisbury. Wilton carpets are now made elsewhere.

Wiltshire, county of S. England. Here is Salisbury Plain, also a part of the New Forest. The county is chiefly pastoral. The administrative offices are at Trowbridge.

Wimbledon, residential town, Surrey ; noted for its common of over 1,000 acres, and also as the HQ of the All-England Lawn Tennis Club ; pop. 60,000.

wimshurst, see ELECTRICITY

Winant, JOHN GILBERT, *wī'nant* (1889–1947), USA ambassador in London 1941.

Winchester, city, Hampshire, of which it is the co.tn ; noted for its cathedral and public school (Winchester College, founded 1385) ; pop. 26,000. Winchester was the capital of England before the Norman Conquest.

Winchester College, one of the oldest English public schools, founded by William of Wykeham 1385 ; has always been closely associated with New College, Oxford. Many of the buildings are 14th century. Those who have been educated at Winchester are known as Wykehamists.

wind, see ATMOSPHERE

Windermere, largest lake in England ; is on the borders of Lancashire and Westmorland ; length 10½m.

windflower, see ANEMONE

Windhoek, *vint'huk*, cap., SW. Africa ; is 5,500ft above sea-level.

windmill, mill, usually for grinding corn, driven by wind acting on sails. An old type was the post-mill, revolving on a central post to face the wind, later largely replaced by tower mills with a revolving top and generally four sails. Windmills for pumping water are usually of the American or annular type, having a wheel with light metal vanes. Plans to generate electricity on a national scale by making use of wind-power have recently been put forward. Britain has a research station in the Orkneys.

windpipe, see LARYNX

Windsor, family name of the ruling royal house of Great Britain and Northern Ireland ; formerly known as the house of Saxe-Coburg-Gotha, but in 1917 King George V assumed the surname of Windsor.

Windsor, town, Berkshire, 22m west of London, and on the R. Thames ; famous for its castle and royal palace, founded by William I on the site of an older fortress ; largely rebuilt by Edward III. Its beautiful St George's Chapel, added by Edward IV and completed by Henry VIII, is famous for its magnificent vaulted roof. The living quarters

of the castle are handsomely furnished and contain rare art treasures. In the Home Park is Frogmore House. The Great Park (1,800 acres) has many fallow deer. Pop.22,000.

Windsor, town, Ontario, Canada ; manufactures motor vehicles ; pop.117,000 ; linked by tunnel with Detroit, USA.

Windsor, DUKE OF (1894–   ), eldest son of King George V. As Prince of Wales he was for years one of the most popular world-figures. He visited many parts of the Empire ; succeeded as King Edward VIII 20 Jan 1936 ; abdicated 11 Dec 1936 (in order to be free to marry Mrs Wallis Warfield) ; became Duke of Windsor, and was appointed Governor of the Bahamas 1940.

Windward Islands, group of British islands in the W. Indies, e.g. St Vincent, St Lucia, Dominica, Grenada, total area 813sq.m ; pop.252,000.

GRENADA, discovered by Columbus, was at first called Conception ; it produces cane sugar, coffee and cotton ; cap. and chief port, St George's.

DOMINICA, *c*.29m long, has a fine climate ; produces limes, lime-juice, fruits and vanilla ; the chief town is the port of Roseau.

wine, drink made from fermented grape-juice, It was known to the ancient Egyptians, Jews, Assyrians, Greeks and Romans. Wine may form its own alcohol or have spirit added ; and it may be bottled 40–50 years. The chief wines include Spanish and Portuguese (e.g. port, sherry and madeira) ; German (e.g. hock, moselle) ; French (e.g. champagne, burgundy). Australian wines are now winning favour. See VINE

Wingate, MAJOR-GENERAL ORDE CHARLES (*d* 1944), one of the most remarkable soldiers of modern times ; suppressed revolts in Palestine 1936 ; brilliantly successful in guerilla tactics against the Italians in Abyssinia ; best remembered as the astonishing British leader of the Chindit Expedition in the Burma Campaign (World War II), his so called ' Circus ' comprising soldiers (nicknamed Chindits) selected for ability and courage. The campaign, unique in history, was a penetrating operation depending on radio and airborne supplies.

Read *Wingate's Phantom Army*, W. G. Burchett.

Wingfield Sculls, English Amateur (Sculling) Championship rowed on the Thames, Putney to Mortlake, in July.

Winnipeg, cap., Manitoba, Canada. It is at the junction of the R. Assiniboine and the Red R., and on the CPR ; industries include sawing timber, leather goods and clothes, but it is chiefly notable for its trade in grain gathered from the prairie provinces. From 1763 there was a trading station here called Fort Garry ; modern Winnipeg is finely planned, and has wide straight streets and many handsome buildings, including the city hall ; the population is *c*. 230,000.

Winstanley, HENRY (1644–1703), engineer ; built (1700) the first Eddystone lighthouse (of wood), in which he perished.

winter, see SEASONS

winter aconite, *ăk'on-īt*, common plant of the buttercup family ; has a bright yellow cup-like flower above a green ring or frill of leaves ; flowers Jan.–Mar.

wireless, see RADIO

wireworm, larval form of several British beetles ; usually brown, slender and the same width from end to end. The wireworm lives in the soil, doing much damage to plants on which it feeds.

Wirral, see CHESHIRE

Wisbech, *wiz'bēch*, town with agricultural trade, Cambridgeshire ; noted for bulb-growing and fruit-canning.

Wisconsin, north central state, USA ; richly agricultural, but has lumber-yielding forests and supplies of lead and copper ; cap. Madison.

Wishart, GEORGE (*d* 1546), Scottish Protestant martyr. Charged with heresy for teaching the Greek Testament, he took refuge in England, and there being similarly charged, fled to Germany and Switzerland. After his return to Scotland he was burned at St Andrews.

Wishaw, part of Motherwell, Lanarkshire ; has iron works ; repairs railway rolling stock.

wistaria, *wis-tār'iä*, Chinese flowering shrub (family *Leguminoseae*) commonly grown against walls in Britain ; has long leaves comprising *c*.6 pairs of oval leaflets, and sprays of blue, purple or white flowers.

witan or **witenagemot**, see PARLIAMENT

witchcraft, rites, supposedly magical, practised by believers in a primitive fertility religion widespread in Western Europe even at the beginning of the 17th c. Margaret Murray has suggested that the witch-cult was a survival of the pre-Christian religion of Western Europe. The gods worshipped by members of the witch-cult were identified by Christians with the Devil. The witch-cult was particularly active in the late Middle Ages, and even became a threat to the existence of the Christian Church. For this reason hundreds of witches were brought before the Inquisition and other tribunals and burnt at the stake. The witch-cult was finally suppressed in the 18th c. and today it survives only in a few meaningless superstitions. Read *The Witch-Cult in Western Europe*, by Margaret Murray.

Witney, small town, Oxfordshire ; noted for blankets.

Witt, JAN DE, *vit* (1625–72), Dutch statesman ; became virtual ruler of Holland from 1653, restoring peace and prosperity, fostering Dutch commerce and (after war with England) concluding an alliance with England and Sweden. He and his brother, Cornelius, lost popularity during the war with France, and were torn to pieces by a mob.

Wittenberg, *vit'en-berch*, historic town, Saxony (Germany) ; on the Elbe ; burial place of Martin Luther, who nailed his ' Ninety-five Theses ' against indulgencies on the door of the castle church, hence the town has been called ' the cradle of the Reformation.'

Witwatersrand, see RAND

woad, *wōd*, British plant (family *Cruciferae*) with small yellow flowers, and oval ground-leaves from which the Ancient Britons made the blue dye mentioned by Julius Caesar. The plant was grown in England till 1932.

Wodehouse, PELHAM GRENVILLE (1881–), English writer ; author of *The Inimitable Jeeves* and the Psmith series ; was in German hands during World War II, about which he has since written.

Woking, *wō'king*, growing residential town, Surrey ; pop.47,000.

wold, *wōld*, in England, open, hilly country, e.g. the Lincolnshire and Yorkshire Wolds, the latter of chalk hills rising to 800ft.

wolf, fierce member of the dog family ; found in N. Europe and N. America ; common in England prior to *c*.1509 ; vanished from Scotland and Ireland in the 18th century. The wolf (*Canis lupus*), usually brownish-grey, lives mainly in forests. In winter wolves hunt in packs. The Alaskan wolf may be over 30in at the shoulder and 6ft long, including the tail.

Wolfe, HUMBERT, *wulf* (1885–1940), British writer ; won a reputation as a poet with *London Sonnets* and *Kensington Gardens*. His later poems include *Requiem* ; *The Uncelestial City*.

Wolfe, JAMES (1727–59), *b* Westerham, Kent ; fought in Flanders, Prussia (being present at Dettingen), and at Falkirk and Culloden ; had command of a brigade in N. America 1758.

As Major-General, 1759, he took a force up the R. St Lawrence, and directed operations against the French in Canada. The enemy, believing that in defending Quebec they need take no steps to guard against attack from the cliffs—the Heights of Abraham—thereby gave Wolfe his chance. Scaling the cliffs, Wolfe's men reached the plain, took the French by surprise, and defeated them. Both Montcalm, the French commander, and Wolfe were killed. By this victory Wolfe secured Canada for the British Empire.

The story is told that while being rowed to the attack on Quebec, Wolfe repeated almost the whole of Gray's *Elegy*, adding that he would rather have been its author than beat the French.

Wolseley, VISCOUNT GARNET, *wulz'li* (1833–1913), soldier of English ancestry born in County Dublin ; served in the Burmese war 1852–53, the Crimea, the Indian Mutiny ; completely subdued the country in the Ashanti campaign ; quelled the rebellion of Arabi Pasha at Tel-el-Kebir, Egypt, 1882 ; and went to the relief of Gordon.

Wolsey, CARDINAL THOMAS, *wul'zi* (*c.*1475–1530), attended Magdalen College, Oxford ; became Chaplain to Henry VII ; distinguished himself in several diplomatic missions ; made a Privy Councillor by the young King Henry VIII, who readily used his industry and organising ability. For securing favourable peace terms after the war with France, 1514, he was made Archbishop of York. He became a Cardinal, and was made Lord Chancellor 1515. Papal Legate, 1518, his foreign policy was that of keeping the balance of power. He chose to support the Hapsburg Charles V of Spain (Holy Roman Emperor) against France in the hope that by thus currying favour he might become pope. The victory of Charles at Pavia 1525 led to increased power for the Hapsburgs and decreased power for England, a serious blunder on Wolsey's part.

Meanwhile, his popularity at home was steadily waning. It was he who taught Henry VIII to rule without a Parliament ; to make use of the court of Star Chamber. Wolsey's disregard of church matters was a byword. His love of pomp and show (as shown by his staging of the Field of the Cloth of Gold, 1520, his building of Hampton Court Palace, and the regal style in which he lived) made him enemies everywhere. Rather than protest against Henry VIII's dissolution of the greater monasteries, he lined his own pockets with some of their confiscated wealth. He had no friend but the king, and when, over the question of Henry's divorce from Catherine of Aragon, Wolsey was unable to obtain the pope's consent, his doom was sealed.

Charged with treason, Wolsey was arrested in Yorkshire, missing execution by dying at Leicester when on his way to attend his trial in London. Shakespeare makes him say

Had I but serv'd my God with half the zeal
I serv'd my king, he would not in mine age
Have left me naked to mine enemies.

Wolverhampton, chief manufacturing town of the Black Country, Staffordshire ; amid coal and iron mines ; noted for locks and keys, also hardware ; pop. 156,000.

wolverine or **glutton,** *wool'vĕr-ēn,* animal of the weasel group found in the forests of Europe, Asia and N. America. Heavily built and *c.*3ft long, it has dark brown fur and a bushy tail ; feeds at night on small animals, notably rabbits ; is now extinct in Britain.

wombat, bear-like burrowing animal of Australia and Tasmania ; *c.*2ft long ; has short ears ; the fur is thick and coarse. The young are carried in a pouch. Wombats feed on grass and roots.

Women's Land Army, body of farmworkers organised during World Wars I and II to aid agriculture. Members, commonly known as Land Girls, wore a distinctive green and buff uniform ; they numbered (1939–45) *c.*80,000.

Women's Royal Air Force (WRAF), formerly Women's Auxiliary Air Force (WAAF), women's branch of the RAF, refounded 1939.

Women's Royal Army Corps, organisation known until 1945 as the Auxiliary Territorial Service (ATS) ; established 1938.

Women's Royal Naval Service, women's service which co-operated with the Royal Navy during World War II.

Women's Voluntary Service, organisation founded 1938 and popularly known as WVS ; helped to care for evacuees in World War II, attended air-raid victims, etc.

Wood, SIR HENRY (1869–1944), conductor, *b* London ; composed songs and orchestrations ; helped to found the promenade concerts (the ' Proms ') in Queen's Hall, London, 1895, and continued to conduct them for fifty years ; introduced many foreign composers to the British public. Sir Henry always wore a carnation in his buttonhole.

Wood, SIR KINGSLEY (1881–1943), English politician ; introduced the Early Closing Bill 1920 ; became Postmaster General 1931 ; did much to improve the Post Office ; Chancellor of the Exchequer 1940, and responsible for ' pay as you earn ' (PAYE) in income tax.

woodchat, see SHRIKE

woodchuck, see MARMOT

woodcock, British bird (*c.*14in long), closely related to the snipe ; plumage mainly reddish-brown striped with black ; has long, straight beak ; nests in a hollow in the ground.

THE WOODCOCK

Wooderson, SYDNEY C., English runner ; works in a solicitor's office, training in the evenings and at week-ends ; has a stride of 6ft 6in. His world record (1937) of a mile in 4 minutes 6·4 seconds has since been broken, though he holds the world record (1938) for 880 yds in 1 minute 49·2 seconds.

THE GREAT SPOTTED WOODPECKER

Woodford, growing residential suburb of NE. London ; pop.24,000.

Woodhouse Grove, public school (since 1942) ; founded 1812 ; reorganised 1883 ; is at Apperley Bridge, near Bradford, Yorkshire.

woodlark, see LARK

woodpecker, family of wild birds with feet adapted to climbing. The British woodpeckers include : (*a*) GREEN WOODPECKER (*Picus viridis*), olive green above, head crimson and black ; yellow on the rump ; nests in a hole in a tree ; taps on the bark and picks off insects with its long tongue ; (*b*) GREAT SPOTTED WOODPECKER, plumage black with white and crimson ; (*c*) LESSER SPOTTED WOODPECKER, *c*.5in long ; black above with white bars ; red crown.

wool, curled hair of various animals, especially the sheep, one of the finest wools for woollen goods coming from the Merino. British sheep supply wool (in part) for hosiery, flannel, dressgoods, worsted serges and high-class tweeds.

After being cleaned to remove dust and grease, wool is spun into yarn, and then woven into cloth (see WEAVING) and dyed. The introduction into Australia of the Spanish Merino sheep has given that country immense flocks, and today we import large quantities of Australian wool (see PLATE 21, *top*), also wool from NZ and S. Africa. Woollen goods are manufactured in the W. Riding of Yorkshire (e.g. Huddersfield, Halifax, Dewsbury, Batley and Keighley), Bradford being the world's largest wool market ; also in S. Scotland and the west of England.

The woollen industry in England has long been important, hence the WOOL-SACK in the House of Lords. It is a large square cushion filled with wool. Reserved for the Lord Chancellor, this seat is said to have been first used in Elizabeth's day when wool was England's chief industry.

WORSTED takes its name from the Norfolk village of Worsted, noted for woollen goods in the 14th century.

Within recent years research at Leeds University has resulted in the production of *unshrinkable wool*, the fibres having synthetic resins inside. The tickle was taken out of wool *c*.1944 by the use of sodium bisulphite and the enzyme papain, this giving a silkiness to the fibre. In 1949 Air Vice-Marshal Geoffrey H. Ambler of Yorkshire announced a device to revolutionise wool spinning by eliminating three or four processes.

Woolf, VIRGINIA (1882–1941), author, *b* London ; wrote many novels, including *The Voyage Out* ; *Night and Day*. Her later books deal more with psychology.

Woolley, FRANK EDWARD (1887–), left-handed cricketer, *b* Tonbridge, Kent ; played in 32 matches against Australia.

Woolley, SIR LEONARD (1880–), British archaeologist ; excavated the Hittite ruins of Carchemish, the Egyptian city of Tell-el-Amarna, and revealed the ancient glories of Ur ; author of such fascinating books as *Ur of the Chaldees* ; *Digging up the Past.*

woolsack, see WOOL

Woolton, LORD (1883–), English business-man ; rendered great services to the nation as Minister of Food during World War II, instituting a system of rationing by which everyone had a fair share of available foodstuffs.

After the triumph of the Labour Party (1945) he did much to rouse the Conservatives to new endeavour, and was instrumental in launching a campaign (at the Brighton Conference, 1947) for a £1,000,000 fighting fund. His efforts to raise the Conservative votes were not so successful in by-elections as had been hoped.

Woolwich, *wul'ij*, borough of SE. London; has a military arsenal ; manufactures guns and ammunition. The Royal Military Academy, founded 1741, was moved to Sandhurst 1946 ; pop.147,000.

Woolworth, FRANK WINFIELD (1852–1919), American business-man ; opened a store in Utica with a capital of £60, the maximum price for any one article being 10 cents. By 1934 the company owned 1,954 stores in USA and Canada, and 600 in the UK. He built the Woolworth Building, New York, and died leaving a fortune of £9,000,000.

Worcester, *woos'tĕr*, city, Massachusetts, USA ; manufactures textiles and tools ; pop.194,000.

Worcester College, college of Oxford University, founded 1714. The head of the college is known as the provost.

Worcestershire, English county in the valley of the R. Severn. Industrial in the north (The Black Country), it is famous in the south for its hop-gardens and orchards. The co.tn, Worcester, is noted for its cathedral and for gloves. It has long been famous for porcelain ; pop.51,000.

Wordsworth, D., see WORDSWORTH, W.

Wordsworth, WILLIAM (1770–1850), poet, *b* Cockermouth, Cumberland ; an orphan at 14 ; delighted to wander alone in the L. District ; became a deep lover of nature. He joined with Samuel Taylor Coleridge in publishing *Lyrical Ballads* 1798, in which the aim was to free poetry from the stilted language and the learned manner then in vogue, and to write of common things and ordinary events in a way that simple folk could understand. His 13 months in France ended at the beginning of the French Revolution, which stirred him to demand freedom for mankind.

Wordsworth lived for a time at Grasmere (Westmorland) ; married Mary Hutchinson 1802, and settled at Rydal Mount 1813. He was fortunate in the love and devotion of his wife (described by him as 'a phantom of delight When first she gleamed upon my sight '), and that of his gifted sister, DOROTHY (1771–1855), famous for her journals. He became Poet Laureate 1843.

Wordsworth did good service to English literature by reviving a love of nature, and bringing simplicity and naturalness to poetry. He excels in his nature poems, e.g. *To Daffodils* ; and he taught us that flowers and trees may bring ' thoughts that do often lie too deep for tears.' But sometimes Wordsworth was too simple, and still more often he was too wordy, saying in poetry what would have been better said in prose. He rises to great heights in his sonnets, e.g. *On Westminster Bridge.* His poems include *The Prelude* ; *The Excursion* ; *Sonnets on the River Duddon* ; and *Ode on the Intimations of Immortality.*

As examples of Wordsworth at his best we may take these lines composed a few miles above Tintern Abbey :
> I have learned
> To look on nature, not as in the hour
> Of thoughtless youth ; but hearing oftentimes
> The still sad music of humanity,
> Nor harsh nor grating, though of ample power
> To chasten and subdue. And I have felt
> A presence that disturbs me with the joy
> Of elevated thoughts : a sense sublime
> Of something far more deeply inter-fused,
> Whose dwelling is the light of setting suns,

> And the round ocean and the living air,
> And the blue sky, and in the mind of man ;
> A motion and a spirit, that impels
> All thinking things, all objects of all thought,
> And rolls through all things.

Also his sonnet inspired by an early-morning view of London as seen from Westminster Bridge :
> Earth has not anything to show more fair :
> Dull would he be of soul who could pass by
> A sight so touching in its majesty :
> This city now doth like a garment wear
> The beauty of the morning ; silent, bare,
> Ships, towers, domes, theatres and temples lie
> Open unto the fields and to the sky,
> All bright and glittering in the smoke-less air.
> Never did sun more beautifully steep
> In his first splendour valley, rock, or hill ;
> Ne'er saw I, never felt, a calm so deep !
> The river glideth at his own sweet will :
> Dear God ! the very houses seem asleep,
> And all that mighty heart is lying still !

work, see MECHANICS

Workington, port, Cumberland ; has ship-building yards, engineering works, also coal and iron mines ; pop.28,000.

Works, MINISTRY OF, British government department in charge of royal palaces, public offices and ancient monuments, with offices in London and Edinburgh.

Worksop, town, Nottinghamshire ; manu-factures chemicals ; pop.28,000.

World, see EARTH

World Bank, THE, bank known officially as the International Bank, established 1944 by UNO. Its capital was 9,100,000,000 dollars. It exists to facilitate international loans during the recovery period after World War II.

World Council of Churches, organisation largely inspired by Archbishop William Temple, and formally inaugurated at its first assembly at Amsterdam 1948. The HQ are at Geneva, and the Council represents Christian thought and activity.

World Fair, see EXHIBITIONS

World War I (1914–18), struggle resulting from Germany's desire to conquer Europe.

The immediate cause of the war was apparently the assassination (28 June 1914) at Sarajevo, Serbia (now part of Yugoslavia), of the Archduke Francis Ferdinand, heir to the Austrian throne. As Germany and Austria were allies, the two countries made war against Serbia, ostensibly to avenge the murder of the Archduke, actually as a pretext for attacking Russia, which aided Serbia, and France, Russia's ally.

The easiest route to France was through Belgium, but Germany (then ruled by Kaiser William II) had promised by the *Treaty of London* 1831 never to invade that country. Nevertheless, she tore up what she was pleased to call ' a scrap of paper,' and sent her troops into Belgium. Britain, having promised to support Belgium, kept her promise, declaring war on Germany 4 Aug 1914.

Germany and Austria, aided by Turkey and Bulgaria, formed the Central Powers. The Allies were Britain and the British Empire, with France, Russia for a time, Serbia and Belgium. Japan and Italy joined the Allies 1915, Rumania 1916, the USA 1917. Britain and France fought chiefly on what was called the western front ; Russia on the eastern front ; and fighting went on on the Italian frontiers, in the Balkans, Egypt and Palestine.

Belgium's gallant resistance against German forces barely gave the British 3 weeks to rush 60,000 men towards Mons. These, and others, were compelled to retreat to the Marne, the Germans entrenching along the Aisne while attempting to win the Channel ports of Dunkirk and Calais, also Zeebrugge, which became a German submarine base. Von Hindenburg's brilliant victory over the Russians at Tannenberg (E. Prussia) made him the idol of the German people.

Trench warfare was the main feature of 1915, the trenches on the western front extending from the Belgian coast to Switzerland. The Germans began using poison gas at Neuve Chapelle in April ; and about the same time began our disastrous attempt to separate Germany and Turkey by the Gallipoli campaign, in which the British, Australians and New Zealanders won glory in the Dardanelles Peninsula, but were compelled to evacuate the Peninsula at the end of the year.

By May 1916 voluntary recruitment in Britain was found to be inadequate, and conscription replaced recruiting.

In France the first battle of Verdun opened 1916, followed by the historic battle of the Somme, in which (14 Sept.) tanks were employed for the first time. The tanks achieved local successes, but there were not nearly enough of them to force a break-through. A year of disappointment for the Allies, 1916 saw Russian resistance broken, the German submarine attacks increasing, our forces in Mesopotamia weakening ; also the death of Earl Kitchener, drowned when on his way to Russia. In addition, German aircraft were raiding British towns.

There was bitter fighting along the western front 1917, e.g. the second battle of the Aisne, third battle of Ypres, Cambrai, etc. The Italians lost 200,000 men at Caporetto. For all that, General Allenby was winning in Palestine, and

the torpedoing of the *Lusitania* (1,198 people being drowned) brought the USA into the war.

Overwhelmed at St Quentin in the spring of 1918, the Allies fighting on the western front seemed about to suffer final defeat. The French were compelled to retreat to Paris ; fierce fighting raged in the regions of the Somme, Aisne, Marne, Arras and Ypres, the Germans, led by General Ludendorff, advancing steadily. So desperate was the Allied position that (11 April) Sir Douglas (later Earl) Haig issued his famous order of the day :

Every position must be held to the last man. With our backs to the wall, and believing in the justice of our cause, each one of us must fight on to the end.

But it was not till August that Sir Douglas Haig and the French general, Marshal Foch, compelled the Germans to retreat, rolling them back till they sued for an armistice, granted 11 Nov 1918.

The war at sea included the German submarine campaign against Allied shipping, also the battles of Heligoland, Coronel and the Falkland Isls., all 1914 ; Dogger Bank, 1915 ; and the somewhat inglorious battle of Jutland 1916, in which Admiral Beatty and Admiral Sir John Jellicoe lost touch with the enemy, though, as a result of the engagement, the German fleet never again put to sea. One of the most brilliant naval successes was the blocking of Zeebrugge harbour 23 April 1918.

A feature of World War I was the use of aircraft. The first German airraid on Britain was on Christmas Eve 1914. Zeppelin raids accounted for 556 deaths in all ; raids by planes for 857.

The end of the war brought many problems. The peace terms were discussed at Versailles, a town *c*.10m from Paris. Representatives from the Allied countries met in Conference Jan 1919, the chiefs being Lloyd George, M. Clemenceau (Premier of France), and President Wilson (USA). The map of Europe was reshaped ; Germany was garrisoned by an army of occupation, ordered to pay £1,000,000,000 in gold or goods before May 1921, and forbidden to raise an army or manufacture munitions. The German battle fleet was to surrender at Scapa Flow (in the Orkney Is.), and this was duly carried out, though the Germans scuttled most of their ships.

The Versailles Conference had good intentions, but not all its decisions were wise. Given little opportunity for trade, Germany had less for paying her debts ; and no doubt the *Treaty of Versailles* (signed 10 Jan 1920) was in some measure responsible for World War II.

The men who attempted to punish Germany attempted also to build a safer world. They hoped this could be done by mean of the LEAGUE OF NATIONS, which came into being 1920, and had HQ at Geneva. A kind of world-brotherhood, the League was the inspiration of President Wilson, though the USA refused to become a member of it. Its basic ideal was the preservation of world peace by bringing international disputes before arbitrators. Based on President Wilson's famous Fourteen Points, the League was, in theory, an excellent plan, and for many years (till replaced 1946 by UNO) it rendered good service, especially in minor disputes, in the realms of law, commerce and medicine, but it failed to prevent the outbreak of World War II.

For some account of the political consequences of World War I, see WORLD WAR II, POLITICAL BACKGROUND

World War II, conflict 1939–45 in which the Axis powers (Nazi Germany and Fascist Italy, later joined by Japan, Hungary, Rumania, Slovakia, Bulgaria, etc.) were defeated by the United Nations (Britain and the British Commonwealth, Russia and the United States, together with forces gathered from countries occupied by Axis powers. Early in the war France was compelled to make a separate peace with Germany, but (along with many other occupied countries) she was liberated 1944–45.

Among Allied war leaders were Winston Churchill (Prime Minister from 1940), General Wavell (later Viscount Wavell), and Field-Marshal (later Viscount) Montgomery, in close co-operation with President Roosevelt and General Eisenhower, both directing USA affairs. Marshal Stalin was responsible for Russian strategy ; General de Gaulle led the Free French, and General Chiang Kai-Shek was responsible for China's resistance to the Japanese. Axis leaders included Adolf Hitler in Germany, Mussolini, dictator of Italy, etc.

It should be noted that Germany's early successes in the war were largely due to (a) her mass-produced mechanised forces, e.g. tanks, aircraft, guns, army vehicles, etc., and (b) the inevitable time-lag before Britain and the Common-wealth and her later Allies could manu-facture similar or improved war material on mass-production lines. World War II was pre-eminently a war of machines, and the individual courage and skill of soldiers, sailors and airmen availed little if equipment was inadequate or in-sufficient. Before the end of the war amazing advances in mechanical devices and their rapid production were achieved by the United Nations. Their aircraft outrivalled that of the Axis both in number and in fighting qualities, and there can be no doubt that scientific development and speed in manufacture of such war material as bombs, tanks, radiolocation, etc. were in large measure responsible for ultimate victory.

The war was also a war of ideologies, that is a struggle between totalitarian and democratic rule. Germany and Italy (and later Japan) aimed at world domination, whereas Great Britain and USA desired no territorial gains, their aims being those set forth in the *Atlantic Charter*, namely to preserve for mankind freedom of thought and speech, freedom for religious conviction, and freedom from fear. In a sense, therefore, the United Nations were crusading against the gangster methods of dictatorship.

The main causes of World War II were (1) Germany's determination to reverse her defeat in World War I by establishing German superiority over all other nations, and (2) the failure of the victorious Allies of World War I to control the international situation brought into existence by cause (1) and by other results of the Versailles settle-ment of 1918.

Led by Hitler, the Nazi party came to power in Germany 1933, and the main object of Nazi foreign policy was to secure a revision of the Versailles, and other treaties, which had deprived Germany of her colonies and forbidden her to have a large army. Italy had emerged from World War I nominally victorious, but exhausted and im-poverished, and had not benefited under the Versailles settlement. Under Musso-lini, Italy, like Germany, aimed at re-vision of the treaties.

The Western Allies—France, Britain and the USA—refused to consider any major revision of existing treaties, but they failed to display the strength and unity of purpose that would have been necessary in order to maintain the Versailles settlement once it was seriously challenged. In 1936 Hitler's troops re-occupied the Rhineland, which had been demilitarised in 1918. Britain and France failed to intervene at this crucial moment. Germany accordingly began open re-armament.

In the Spanish Civil War (1936–39) Germany and Italy gave much aid to the Fascist revolutionary forces of General Franco. Again Britain and France followed an ineffective policy of non-intervention. This gave much encouragement to Hitler and Mussolini, and caused misgivings in Russia, where the Communist regime was naturally opposed to Fascist and Nazi aggres-sion.

In March 1938 Germany annexed Austria, a flagrant breach of the peace. Britain and France again failed to do anything ; they did, however, intervene when Hitler began his diplomatic on-slaught on Czechoslovakia (August 1938), but German rearmament had by then outstripped their strength, and they were forced to accept the humiliat-ing Munich Agreement, whereby Czecho-slovakia was made defenceless. In March 1939, Germany completed the conquest of Czechoslovakia, and began to threaten Poland.

Soviet Russia was the only anti-Fascist power that could have rendered effective military aid to Czechoslovakia or Poland. In Britain and France, many of the political leaders hated and feared Communism so greatly that they would not have been sorry to see Germany attacking Russia. Britain and France gave guarantees for the territorial integrity of Poland, but they failed to reach any agreement with Russia for military co-operation in the event of further aggression by Germany. In August 1939 Russia (with gross cynicism) made a non-aggression pact with Germany, and Germany invaded Poland, whereupon Britain and France declared war on Germany (3 Sept 1939).

Poland was quickly overrun. By agreement with Germany, Russian forces occupied the eastern half of her territory. Russia thus gained depth for her defence against a possible German invasion of her own territory. During the winter, Russia attempted to invade Finland, so as to block that avenue of approach. Russian troops were remarkably unsuccessful in these operations, but after a few months Finland made peace and Russia gained what she wanted. Meanwhile French and British troops manned the French frontier. It was obvious that Germany would sooner or later invade Belgium, but Belgium refused to give her any pretext for doing so, and therefore declined to make any military agreement with the Allies.

In April 1940 Germany attacked Denmark and Norway. The British failed in their attempt to aid the Norwegians, and King Haakon of Norway and his Government found refuge in Britain, whither also, before long, came the Governments of Holland, Belgium, Free France, Poland, Czechoslovakia, Greece and Yugoslavia.

Britain's defeat in Norway led to a change of Government, Winston Churchill replacing Neville Chamberlain as Prime Minister of a 3-party Coalition Government 10 May 1940, the day on which Hitler launched his attack in the West. Bombing Belgium and Holland in a lightning attack, he poured mechanised forces (preceded by paratroops) across these countries, compelling the Belgian army to surrender, and pinning down British and other forces on the beaches of Dunkirk, whence 224,524 British and 112,546 other troops (mainly French) were rescued by 1,000 ships early in June. General Weygand's attempt to reorganise French resistance failed, and with the Germans in Paris and also with the Italians attacking in the south (Italy having declared war on France 10 June), the Pétain-Weygand Government of France capitulated to the Germans. Britain and the Common-wealth then stood alone against the combined might of the Axis.

Since all the ports from Norway to the south of France were in Axis hands, it seemed that Germany and Italy could easily destroy Britain, where mass-production of war material was still not forthcoming. Hitler therefore decided to invade. As a preliminary he began a large-scale bombing attack on the south of England, hence the Battle of Britain in which British pilots succeeded in defeating the *Luftwaffe* (German air force), thus compelling Hitler to postpone the actual invasion, though night-bombing was maintained for nine months, over 1,500,000 houses in London alone being damaged. Other important centres were attacked, and by 1941 some 43,000 civilians had been killed and more than 50,000 seriously injured.

Meanwhile Italy's entry into the war had threatened the British sea-route of the Mediterranean, and in Nov 1940 General Wavell's small force attacked Italian troops in Libya and drove them back in a brilliant campaign to Benghazi and El Agheila. Meanwhile (28 Oct.) Italy had invaded NW. Greece, but the Greeks held them near the frontier. Early in 1941, German armies passed through Hungary, Rumania and Bulgaria to invade Yugoslavia and Greece, and in N. Africa German armoured forces surprised the British and drove them back to Egypt, failing however to seize Tobruk, in which a British garrison remained. Accepting the situation on this front, the British Middle East Command sent troops that could ill be spared to Greece, but Greek resistance was quickly overwhelmed and in May German airborne forces completed the conquest of the Balkans by their successful invasion of Crete. During this period only the British naval victory over the Italians at Cape Matapan, the garrison of Malta, and the forces in the Western Desert, checked enemy operations in the Mediterranean.

Thus far Britain and the Common-wealth were still alone in the fight against the Axis. By invading Russia (22 June 1941), however, Germany at once increased her liabilities and Britain received a powerful ally. Russia's early tactics were those of the 'scorched earth policy,' i.e. retreat after destroying or removing everything likely to be of value to the advancing enemy, and these tactics were maintained until the Germans approached both Leningrad and Moscow. There is no doubt that Russia's superb efforts and the brilliance of her generalship contributed very largely to the defeat of Germany.

On 7 December 1941 Japan attacked without warning the chief USA naval base in the Pacific, namely Pearl Harbour, an action which at once caused America to enter the war as Britain's ally. Not even the additional menace of the Japanese (powerfully equipped with ships and aircraft) shook the confidence of the Allied Nations in ultimate victory, and, in January 1942, 26 countries at war with the Axis powers pledged themselves in the *Declaration of the United Nations* to stand together in war, to unite in order to help each other when peace was declared, and to carry out the spirit of the *Atlantic Charter* (see ATLANTIC CHARTER).

In the Far East and the Pacific Britain and America were ill-prepared. By mid-1942 Japanese forces had overrun Burma, the Andamans, Malaya, Sumatra, Java, Timor, Borneo, the Philippines, Hong Kong, Formosa. Before the end of the year they had occupied the Solomon Islands, thus directly threatening US communications with Australia, and had gained a footing in New Guinea: but in May they had been defeated in a great naval battle in the Coral Sea, and their lengthy sea-communications were exposed and overstrained. The British navy had been strained to the utmost in the Atlantic, where the German U-boat offensive was at its height, but in the Pacific, American sea-power soon began to tell.

During the winter the British Eighth Army had advanced in Libya, freeing Tobruk, and had established a line running near Gazala across the Libyan peninsula. In early summer 1942 German armoured forces under Rommel attacked this forward position, and drove back the British in headlong retreat towards Alexandria. In July began the British stand at Alamein, little more than 50 miles west of Alexandria.

In Russia the German advance continued, and the Germans were within sight of a break-through at Stalingrad, which would have taken them across the R. Volga, thus cutting the supply-route to Moscow from Iraq and Persia. But at Stalingrad (Sept–Nov 1942) the Russians stood. The Russian and British stand at Stalingrad and Alamein may be regarded as the turning point of the war in the west.

It was in November 1942 that General Montgomery, supplied with new equipment (including American Sherman tanks), began a sensational series of victories from El Alamein. Driving the Germans (under Rommel) and Italians beyond El Agheila, Benghazi and into Tripoli (i.e. 1,350m in 82 days) he planned to meet British and American troops landed, under the command of General Eisenhower, in French North Africa. Though General von Arnim attempted to stem the advance, all Axis forces were finally driven out of North Africa in May 1943.

Fighting against the Japanese in the tropical jungles of Burma and in the Pacific proved unsuccessful at first, but gradually the Japanese were robbed of their gains, the US navy taking heavy toll of the Japanese navy and air force, and securing (Feb 1943) Guadalcanal in the Solomons, a valuable springboard for later island-hopping tactics across the Pacific.

The invasion of Axis-controlled Europe began with Allied attacks on Sicily, conquered in 38 days. In Sept 1943 Italy surrendered, later declaring war against Germany.

Meanwhile the Russians had been equally successful. Counter-attacking at Stalingrad Nov 1942, and again after the German summer offensive 1943, they brilliantly defeated the Germans not once but many times, and came within striking distance of the Carpathians March 1944, and in Sept 1944 they broke through into the plains of Hungary, liberating Belgrade, and laying siege to Budapest, which fell in Feb 1945. Before the end of 1944 Russian troops in Poland had reached Warsaw and were preparing for a dash towards Berlin.

But the might of Germany could not be broken without reaching German soil. To do this a way must be blazed through France, and hence on 6 June 1944 (the so-called D-Day) immense forces began to land in Normandy in a combined operation (navy, army, air force) which succeeded in gaining a foothold. Some 4,000 vessels were employed. A prefabricated harbour (Mulberry Harbour) was towed across the English Channel in sections and quickly built on the French coast, and men and equipment were landed in spite of enemy opposition. General Eisenhower was in supreme command of the armies which henceforth battled their way to the Rhine ; French resistance movements organised insurrections to hinder the Germans, and at a later stage millions of gallons of petrol were delivered to Frankfurt by means of pipelines under the Channel. With men, aircraft, tanks and munitions in abundance, the Allied armies swept irresistibly forward, crossing the Rhine in March 1945, and advancing steadily to meet the Russians from the east. Subsequent events have shown that had D-Day been postponed, Germany's new rocket warfare might have hampered, if not destroyed, the Allied invasion effort. The Germans, indeed, had hopes of perfecting atomic warfare, but these hopes were destroyed by the speed of the advances upon the last Nazi strongholds. Hitler's death was announced on 1 May 1945, and within a few hours Berlin surrendered to Russian forces. Four days later all German forces in north-east Germany, also those in Holland and Denmark, surrendered unconditionally to Field-Marshal Montgomery, and by 7 May the war in the west was over.

The Japanese war continued, however. Having driven the Japanese out of

Burma, and thus opened the Burma Road again from Lashio (Burma) to Kunming (China), the Allied forces had steadily strangled Japanese sea communication with the East Indies, so recapturing the Philippines by Feb 1945. US troops seized key islands commanding the approaches to Japan itself, capturing Iwojima (an island 800m southeast of Tokyo) in March 1945, and taking Okinawa (only 350m from the mainland) in June. These gains enabled American bombers to raid the Japanese homeland. On 6 Aug 1945, a single atomic bomb was dropped on Hiroshima, an industrial city of 340,000 inhabitants ; the city was almost entirely destroyed, and 160,000 people were killed. On 9 Aug. a second atom bomb was dropped on Nagasaki with equally devastating effects. On 14 Aug. the Japanese Emperor announced Japan's unconditional surrender. Meanwhile (8 Aug.) Russia had declared war on Japan, and Russian troops were soon occupying the whole of Manchuria.

Thus, after nearly six years of struggle on a scale and with a ferocity never known before, World War II came to an end, leaving a host of problems for the statesmen of disrupted nations to deal with in the hope of establishing order and securing a permanent peace. Europe was starved, blasted and in chaos ; countries were clamouring for their rights ; multitudes of people were homeless, without transport or food or money ; some millions of ' displaced persons' required the aid of UNRRA and IRO, and social, economic, political and other questions were of major importance and demanded speedy attention. (See UNO)

Meanwhile Germany was divided into (a) the Western zones, under separate American, British and French administrations, and (b) an Eastern zone under Russian occupation. In Berlin a Four-Power administration was set up, but the city itself was within the Russian zone, and in 1948 the Russians virtually laid siege to it in the hope of forcing the Western Powers to withdraw. The original Four - Power administration broke down, and Berlin was split in two, the Western Powers supplying their sectors by air (see BERLIN). The impossibility of co-operation between the Western Powers and Russia led also to Western Union in Europe, and to the setting up in Bonn (1949) of a German Federal Government as far as Western Germany was concerned. Within a few days after taking office, the new government of Western Germany had declared that its intention was ultimately to recover the territories east of the Oder-Neisse line. Thus it seemed probable that the post-war partition of Germany had sown the seeds of a further conflict. (See NORTH ATLANTIC PACT)

Immediately after the war Russian forces occupied the northern part of Korea, and American forces occupied Japan. Civil war continued in China, where Chinese Communists were encouraged and supported by Russia, while the USA supported the anti-Communist ' Nationalists' under General Chiang Kai-Shek. But in Feb 1949 the ' Nationalists ' collapsed, and the USA withdrew her support. In the Far East, therefore, as in Europe the post-war years brought friction between Communists and anti-Communists, a situation which can be understood only if we examine the political background to World War II.

POLITICAL BACKGROUND

States and empires were severely strained by the upheaval of World War I. In the defeated countries they collapsed altogether. This weakening of the established order facilitated the growth of revolutionary movements arising out of economic distress and misery. The revolutionary driving-force was international Communism, which in turn provoked the anti-Communist revolutionary movements known as Fascism and Nazism.

In Russia (defeated by Germany 1917) Communist revolutionaries seized power and held it. In Germany, Austria and Hungary the victorious Allies set up parliamentary governments ; but in these countries parliamentary democracy never really took root, partly because it had been imposed from outside, and partly because it became involved in the disastrous American economic crisis, 1929–36, and was therefore discredited. Underlying the outward appearance of democratic politics in Germany (1920-1933), and also in Austria (1927-34), there was therefore a ruthless struggle for power between Communist and anti-Communist revolutionary movements. Both sides aimed at the destruction of parliamentary democracy and subsequently of each other.

In Italy a similar struggle had led, 1922, to the establishment of a Fascist state with Mussolini as dictator. Fascism was established in Austria by Dollfuss 1934, only to give way, 1938, to Nazism, which had meanwhile been established in Germany by Hitler 1934. (Fascism was the form taken by the anti-Communist revolutionary movement in countries where the Roman Catholic Church was especially powerful, as it was in Italy, and also in Austria until 1936, when German rearmament outstripped Italy's military power.)

In Britain and America the existing regimes were parliamentary. They survived the strains and stresses of 1929–36, but some headway was made by both Communist and anti-Communist revolutionary movements. In France parliamentary government survived the inter-war period, but gains were made by revolutionary movements of both kinds.

In World War II, Germany everywhere supported anti-Communist revolutionary movements. (The ' quisling ' governments set up by Germany in Norway, France, Hungary, etc. were all of this type.) That the wartime co-operation of Russia and the Western Allies represented an unstable combination of revolutionary and anti-revolutionary forces became clear after World War II. In all the countries (e.g. Hungary, Poland) in which her influence was dominant, Russia imposed revolutionary regimes ; whereas Britain and America, in the countries they controlled, did all in their power to establish and support anti-Communist governments that were in some cases far from ' democratic ' (e.g. Greece, China).

Nobody foresaw this situation more clearly than Hitler, who prophesied shortly before his death that after World War II there would be a further conflict between Russia and the West, and that if Germany's conquerors set out to destroy one another, not they, but Germany, would be victorious in the end. World War II caused immense destruction, and there can be little doubt that a third world war will be much more terrible. But humanity is faced with problems even graver than atom bombs and possible world wars.

Shortage of food is one of the root-causes of political unrest all over the modern world. Millions were killed in World War II, but world-population did not decrease, it *increased*. Meanwhile the world's food-productive capacity is actually declining (see AGRICULTURE). Possibly the most disastrous consequence of World War II is that the numerous problems created by it tend to distract attention from the problem, even more serious, of world food-supply.

Read *A Miniature History of the War*, R. C. K. Ensor, and the various volumes of Winston Churchill's memoirs of the World War ; also *The Report of the Supreme Commander to the Combined Chiefs of Staff on the Operations in Europe of the Allied Expeditionary Force*.

worsted, see WOOL

Worthing, seaside town, Sussex ; pop. 46,000.

WRAC, formerly ATS, see WOMEN'S ROYAL ARMY CORPS

WRAF (formerly WAAF), see RAF ; WOMEN'S ROYAL AIR FORCE

wrangler, *rang'glĕr*, at Cambridge University, one who disputed ; later an undergraduate taking a first class in the public examination for honours in the mathematical tripos. Prior to 1909 successful candidates were listed in order of merit, the first on the list being known as senior wrangler ; now the list is in alphabetical order.

Wrekin, *rē'kin*, isolated hill, Shropshire, height 1,335ft.

THE BROWN WREN

wren, *ren*, name of several perching birds, all exceedingly small, with slender beaks, short rounded wings and mottled plumage. They hold the tail erect. The common wren, *c*.4in long, has reddish-brown plumage ; builds a small domed nest ; lays bluish-white speckled eggs. The GOLDEN-CRESTED WREN, actually of the warbler family, and the smallest British bird, is 3½in ; yellowish-green plumage above, reddish-white below ; frequents trees ; the nest (sometimes domed) hangs from a branch and has 6–10 eggs.

Wren, SIR CHRISTOPHER (1632–1723), *b* E. Knoyle, Wiltshire. Though best known to us as an architect, he was eminent in his day as an MP ; also as a scientist, a brilliant mathematician and an inventor far ahead of his contemporaries, e.g. his plans for blood transfusion, for fumigation, for deriving fresh water from sea-water, for an agricultural implement to plough, harrow and sow in one operation, and for an improved winch.

As an architect he was greatly influenced by Greek and Roman styles, though later he appreciated Gothic designs. He had designed Pembroke College, Cambridge, and the Sheldonian Theatre, Oxford, before the Great Fire of London, 1666, gave him his chance to rebuild fifty city churches and thirty-six halls, besides a host of other buildings (see PLATE 76). His plans for a spacious new London were unfortunately rejected, and his original design for the new St Paul's had to be remade. Nevertheless, it remains his greatest triumph. He is buried in his own masterpiece, and his epitaph reads : *Si monumentum requiris, circumspice*, i.e. If you seek a memorial, look around you.

wrestling, athletic sport requiring strength and agility. The aim is to compel your opponent to touch the ground with any part of his body other than the feet. This is the Cumberland style. In the West Country style, two shoulders and one hip, or two hips and one shoulder, must touch the ground. There is also a Lancashire style, and the ' all-in ' style,

a

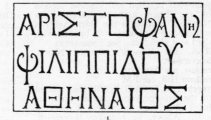

b

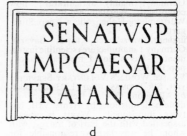

c

d

WRITING

(a) *Egyptian Hieroglyphics* (b) *Alphabetic Greek*
(c) *Chinese Ideographs* (d) *Roman Alphabet*

favoured in the USA. Wrestling is closely related to ju-jitsu.

Wrexham, *rek'sam,* mining town, Denbighshire ; pop.26,000.

Wright, WILBUR (1867–1912) and ORVILLE (1871–1948), American inventors. They repaired cycles at Dayton, Ohio, but from 1900 devoted themselves to building the first power-driven heavier-than-air machine. This made its first flight of 852ft, in 1903. In 1905 Wilbur made a flight of 24m in 38 minutes. See AVIATION

writ, *rit,* legal term in England for an order issued by a court. It is the first step in almost all legal cases, e.g. a writ of summons is served on a defendant who must appear in court ; or the writ fi. fa. (*fieri facias*) authorising the seizure and disposal of a debtor's goods.

Writer to the Signet, see SOLICITOR

writing, any generally accepted system of signs drawn on paper, stone, clay, bark or other durable smooth surface to record and represent words thought or spoken. The chief kinds of writing are (1) *hieroglyphic* (used by the ancient Egyptians), in which each syllable is represented by a single sign ; (2) *ideographic* (used in China and Japan), in which each sign stands for a particular idea ; (3) *alphabetic* (used by ourselves and in ancient times by Greeks and Romans). In alphabetic writing each sign stands in its context for a single sound ; which means in practice that an efficient alphabet can be constructed

out of less than thirty signs or characters, whereas hundreds of hieroglyphics or ideographs may be necessary in order to represent all the possible syllables or ideas in any particular language.

Before the invention of writing man applied his intelligence to a body of traditions handed down orally from father to son, and by this the growth of knowledge was both limited in its extent and retarded in its rate of progress. The invention of writing relieved man's memory of heavy burdens, and made it possible for him to use his mind more freely. The earliest systems of writing were those (hieroglyphic) invented *c.*3000BC by the Egyptians and in Mesopotamia by the Sumerians. By 1500BC these systems had been adopted, or new ones invented, all over Asia Minor. These early systems were all very complicated. After 1500BC the Phoenicians (Semitic sea-traders in Syria and Palestine) invented a simpler system (alphabetic). The Semitic alphabet was taken over by the Greeks and modified to suit their own language. From the Greek alphabet the Latin alphabet (and therefore our own) developed.

Other important systems of writing at the present time are *Arabic* (derived like Greek from early Semitic writing) ; *Russian,* derived from Greek, on which it was based by St Cyril (9th c. AD), therefore being also known as *Cyrillic* ; and *Chinese and Japanese.* Gothic (a somewhat crabbed and illegible version of the Latin alphabet invented in Northern Europe in the Dark Ages) is still used in Germany side by side with the Latin alphabet. See ENDPAPERS

WRNS, see WOMEN'S ROYAL NAVAL SERVICE

Wroclaw, see BRESLAU

Wrotham Hill, see FM

wryneck, *rī'nek*, small British bird related to the woodpeckers ; named from its habit of twisting its neck as it picks up ants. Above, its plumage is greyish, spotted and barred with brown ; below it is whitish.

Württemberg, *vür'tem-bārch*, former state, Germany, mainly agricultural ; now comprises Württemberg-Baden and Württemberg-Hohenzollern ; cap. Stuttgart.

Würzburg, *vūrts'burch*, town, Bavaria, Germany ; manufactures scientific instruments ; has a noted medical school ; pop.108,000.

WVS, see WOMEN'S VOLUNTARY SERVICE

Wyatt, SIR THOMAS, *wī'at* (1503–42), poet, *b* Allington Castle, Kent ; sent on diplomatic missions by Henry VIII, but twice imprisoned. Wyatt is always associated with the Earl of Surrey, with whom he was largely responsible for introducing the sonnet into English literature.

Wyatt, SIR THOMAS (*d* 1554), English conspirator ; son of the poet ; attempted to prevent Mary Tudor marrying Philip of Spain, and to crown Elizabeth as queen. He was defeated and later beheaded.

wych elm, see ELM

wych hazel, see HAZEL

Wycliffe, JOHN, *wik'lif* (*d* 1384), styled the ' Morning Star of the Reformation,'
b N. Yorkshire ; fellow and Master of Balliol College, Oxford ; became a parish priest ; finally held the living of Lutterworth, Leicestershire, from 1374. Courageous, scholarly, a genius in controversy, he was early persuaded that much of the religion of his day was fundamentally wrong ; hence he became the brains of the Parliamentary party opposed to the pope. By his brilliant writings he brought a new spirit to the religious beliefs then held by the Church; and by sending out preachers (known as Lollards) he revealed to common folk the need for new spiritual values, though perhaps he did not realise that his teaching would be confused in the popular mind with the Peasants' Revolt 1381, and that his preachers would be regarded as political agitators.

His greatest and most daring task was to translate the Bible into English, a work begun, with the help of assistants, *c*.1378. By so doing, he made it ultimately possible for ordinary people to read the Bible for themselves, instead of receiving its truths at second hand from priests. In this way Wycliffe foreshadowed the Reformation proper, which began, not in England, but on the Continent, where John Huss and Martin Luther used Wycliffe's torch to set Europe ablaze. Wycliffe's translation is important also as an early example of superb and melodious English prose. See BIBLE

Wye, *wī*, river of England and Wales ; flows 130m, mostly through beautiful scenery, to the R. Severn.

Wyoming, north-west state, USA ; has wild mt. scenery and several geysers. The state includes the famous Yellowstone National Park. Petroleum is produced ; cap. Cheyenne.

X

Xavier, FRANCIS, *zav'i-ĕr* (1506–52), Spanish saint, *b* Xavier, Navarre ; friend of Ignatius Loyola ; travelled as a Jesuit missionary in India, Ceylon and China.

xenon, *zen'on*, inert gas and element, Xe ; atomic weight 131·3 ; atomic number 54 ; found in very small quantities in the atmosphere.

Xenophon, *zen'ō-fon* (430–354BC), Greek soldier and writer. As a pupil of Socrates, he fought for Cyrus of Persia (*see below*) ; was in the service of Agesilaus, King of Sparta, and seems to have spent his last years writing books, e.g. *Hellenica*, a history of Greece, and *Memorabilia*, in which he tells us about Socrates. His *Symposium* is a lively account of the conversations
of Socrates. But his greatest work was his *Anabasis*. If *Anabasis* seems tedious to the student of Greek, he should read about in in T. R. Glover's book *The Ancient World*. The author says :

> For many it is a dismal memory, with its *parasangs* and its repeated phrase ' Thence he marches.' But for anyone who likes a good story that carries one along, a first-hand tale of real adventure, there are few to match it.

T. R. Glover then goes on to give a vivid and exciting summary of this great epic written by Xenophon, the general who succeeded in bringing home the

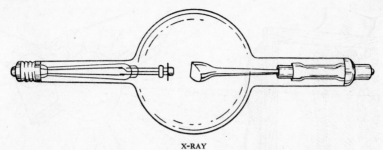

X-RAY

A Coolidge Tube

famous 10,000 Greeks who, 401BC, enlisted in an army raised by the Persian, Cyrus the Younger, against his brother Artaxerxes. Setting out from Sardis, Asia Minor, the expedition won a victory at Cunaxa, 50m from Babylon, where, however, Cyrus was killed. To Xenophon fell the stupendous task of guiding the 10,000 home, a journey of 1,000m through enemy country. Every difficulty imaginable was in his way. His men lost heart and were ready to stone him ; they had to negotiate mountainous country ; they were repeatedly ambushed ; they ran short of food and water ; they quarrelled among themselves, but by patience and skill Xenophon somehow led them to the Bosphorus, a military feat that still stirs us to wonder. Once we realise how great an adventure this march of the 10,000 actually was, the *Anabasis* becomes nothing less than the thrilling story of a magnificent achievement.

For *Catabasis*, see a brief note under ANABASIS. Sayings from Xenophon include :

Δοκεῖ δέ μοι χαλεπώτερον εἶναι εὑρεῖν ἄνδρα τἀγαθὰ καλῶς φέροντα, ἤ τὰ κακά. It seems to me harder to find a man who bears good fortune well, than one who bears evil well.

Ἥδιστον ἄκουσμα ἔπαινος. The sweetest sound is praise.

Οὕτως χρὴ ποιεῖν, ὅπως ἕκαστός τις ἑαυτῷ ξυνείσεται τῆς νίκης αἰτιώτατος ὤν. We must so strive that each man may regard himself as the chief cause of the victory.

Xerxes, *zŭrk'sēz* (d 465BC), Persian king, son of Darius I, whom he succeeded 485BC ; devoted all his energies to carrying out the invasion of Greece planned by his father. He put down a revolt in Egypt, destroyed the kingdom of Babylon, gathered 500,000 men, built a vast fleet, cut a channel near Mt Athos, bridged the Hellespont, signed a treaty with Carthage, and then, having all his immense preparations ready, began the attack.

So formidable was his war machine that it appeared invincible. Crossing the Hellespont in the spring of 480BC, he secured the pass of Thermopylae in spite of Leonidas and the 300 courageous Spartans who defended it until betrayed. He then conquered Elatea, Thebes and Athens. In the moment of victory he received a message from Themistocles, the Athenian soldier and statesman, who appeared to be currying favour with the Persians by advising them, as a traitor, to attack the Greeks at Salamis. Xerxes took this advice, but his fleet, crowded into a narrow space, was defeated, and thus, at the eleventh hour, all his plans came to nothing. With his fleet destroyed, and supplies cut off, Xerxes was compelled to retreat. Next year (479BC) his army of occupation was routed at Plataea, the final blow to his dreams of conquest. Xerxes never again attempted to invade Greece ; indeed Persia was too poor as a result of defeat to stage further military expeditions during his reign.

X-rays, electromagnetic waves discovered 1895 by Wilhelm Konrad Röntgen, and named X-rays because they were not then understood. Of a similar nature to light rays, but of smaller wave-length ($0\cdot5$–$1,000$AU, frequency from 6×10^{18} to 3×10^{15} per sec.), they penetrate many substances opaque to light, e.g. flesh ; bone they do not penetrate so easily, hence their wide use in aiding the surgeon to see deep into the body. Barium sulphide is impervious to these rays, and by swallowing this, the stomach and intestines may easily be seen on a fluorescent screen or in X-ray photographs. The rays penetrate steel and reveal flaws, and there are now innumerable adaptations of X-rays in industry.

The modern X-ray tube is shielded by lead to give operators protection from the rays which, though they will in some circumstances alleviate cancer, may also, if prolonged, cause a fatal disease.

The X-ray spectrometer consists o an X-ray tube, the rays from which strike a crystal and then pass through an ionisation chamber to the crystal under examination. By this means

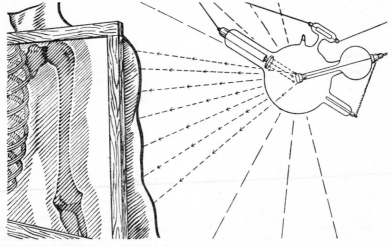

X-RAYS

much has been learned of the nature of atoms. See RÖNTGEN, W. K. ; SYNCHROTRON ; WAVE-MOTION

Xylene, *zī'lēn,* liquid hydrocarbon obtained from coal-tar.

Xylonite, *zī'lon-īt,* British-made plastic of the cellulose type, a mixture of pyroxylin and camphor.

xylophone, *zīl'ō-fōn,* musical instrument with from 27 to 50 bars above resonators. Struck with two light hammers, they give a tinkling, clattering sound.

Y

yacht, *yot,* light vessel built for speed. As a sailing ship, she carries an immense spread of canvas ; but there are also steam and oil-burning yachts. Yachting for pleasure began with the formation of the Cork Club 1720. The Royal Yacht Club, founded 1817 at Cowes, later became the Royal Yacht Squadron. There are about 60 other yacht clubs in Britain. Yacht racing is a feature of summer-time regattas at many ports and holiday resorts. See AMERICA CUP

yak, ox-like animal found only in Tibet and parts of China. It is a massive animal with brown shaggy hair and short legs. The bull has upward-curving horns. The Tibetans use the domesticated yak as a beast of burden.

yakalo, *yak'ä-lō,* hybrid offspring of a yak and a bison or buffalo ; such hybrids are bred in W. Canada.

Yale University, American university in Connecticut, named after Elihu Yale (1648–1721). Founded 1701, it was not declared a university till 1887.

Y-alloy, see ALUMINIUM

Yalta, port and holiday resort, Crimea, USSR ; scene (Feb 1945) of a meeting during World War II of Mr Churchill, President Roosevelt and Marshal Stalin, plans being made for compelling Germany to surrender unconditionally.

yam, tropical climbing food plant of the E. Indies and Philippines. Largely cultivated in the W. Indies, it has twining stems, heart-shaped leaves and tubers similar to those of the potato.

Yangtse-Kiang, *yäng-tsē' kī-äng',* China's greatest river ; flows 3,400m from Tibet to the Yellow Sea near Shanghai. Though unnavigable in parts, it is a great waterway, and its valley is densely peopled, especially in the delta region. American engineers have already begun part of a vast scheme for controlling the river, and thus preventing it flooding the valley where 350,000,000 people live, most of them peasants. A dam is being built near Ichang.

Yarmouth, port and seaside town, Norfolk; on the R. Yare ; best known for its great herring fleet, and for its dried

herrings (bloaters). The old town has very narrow streets called rows, some damaged by German raids in World War II ; pop.49,000.
Read *David Copperfield*, Charles Dickens.

Yarrow, tributary of the R. Ettrick ; flows 25m, chiefly in Selkirkshire ; praised by Wordsworth.

Yates, DORNFORD (1885–   ), pen-name of Cecil William Mercer, British writer notable for his novels, e.g. *As Other Men Are* ; his adventure tales, e.g. *Blind Corner* ; *Fire Below* ; and particularly his ' Berry ' series.

yawl, small sailing boat ·with a tall main mast, and a mizzen-mast with a sail well out beyond the stern.

year, see CALENDAR

yeast, *yĕst*, minute fungi which, with sugar, form the enzyme zymase, causing fermentation, the sugar decomposing into alcohol and carbon dioxide. Yeast is much used in brewing and baking. Since *c.*1940 a British chemist, A. C. Thaysen, has developed the production of flavoured yeasts exceedingly rich in vitamin B. Concentrated doses supplement poor diet. Later, Carl Lindegren, an American chemist, began the production on an immense scale of a new synthetic food, basically yeast, though flavoured to taste like meat, cheese, etc.

Yeats, WILLIAM BUTLER, *yates* (1865–1939), Anglo-Irish poet, *b* Dublin. His early poetry was somewhat wistfully tinged· with Irish literary romanticism. Of this manner *Innisfree* is a well-known example. Between 1900 and 1914, however, Yeats began to be affected by contemporary realities, especially by those of Ireland's struggle for independence. The execution of the leaders of the Easter Rebellion (1916) and the imprisonment of some of his friends had an even deeper effect on him, and the poetry that he wrote after that was his best. He was deeply conscious of living in a world that was falling to pieces, and all his life he was seeking for new symbols to express this unparalleled experience. His later poetry has none of the delicate refinement of his first period. It is robust and rough, but at the same time powerfully eloquent. The following is an example of his later style :

I fasted for some forty days on bread
    and buttermilk,
For passing round the bottle with girls
    in rags or silk,
In country shawl or Paris cloak, had
    put my wits astray,
And what's the good of women, for all
    that they can say
Is fol de rol de rolly O.

Yeats-Brown, FRANCIS (1886–1944), British writer, *b* Genoa ; noted for his book *Bengal Lancer.*

Yedo, see TOKYO

yellow fever, see MOSQUITO

yellow-hammer, see BUNTING

Yellowhead Pass, pass in the Rockies by which the CPR enters British Columbia from Alberta.

Yellow River or Hwang-ho, river in China. Rising in Tibet, it winds 2,600m to the Gulf of Pe-chi-li, in the Yellow Sea ; often causes floods, hence it is sometimes called ' China's sorrow.' Its valley may have been the cradle of Chinese civilisation. The name is due to the yellow mud brought down in vast quantities.
Japanese invaders broke its banks, 1936, causing immense floods, but under the direction of UNRRA engineers have turned the river to its old course.

Yellow Sea, part of the Pacific bounded by Manchuria, China and Korea, so named from the great quantities of yellow mud brought down by the Yellow R. (Hwang-ho).

Yellowstone National Park, tourist region of *c.*3,350sq.m in Wyoming, USA ; renowned for its forests and animal life, including bison, its magnificent and often rugged scenery, its hot springs and geysers. The Yellowstone R. flows through the reserve.

Yemen, kingdom of SW. Arabia, the name meaning ' the land on the right hand ' (of Syria) ; area *c.*74,000sq.m ; pop. 3,500,000 ; cap. San'a ; products include cereals and coffee.

yen, Japanese gold coin minted at 5, 10 or 20 yen. The yen is divided into 100 sen.

Yenisei, *ye-nē-se´ē*, river of Soviet Asia ; flows over 3,000m from N. Mongolia to the Arctic Ocean.

yeoman, *yō´man*, word meaning originally a countryman. A retainer in Chaucer's day, he was later a small freeholder, i.e. between the gentry and the labourers.

Yeoman of the Guard, see BEEFEATER

Yeovil, *yō-vil*, town, Somerset ; noted for gloves ; pop.20,000.

yerba maté, see ILEX

Yerkes, CHARLES TYSON, *yŭr´kēz* (1837–1905), American business-man who endowed the Yerkes observatory.

yew, *yū*, bushy evergreen tree common in churchyards ; usually has several trunks growing from one root ; may live 500 years or more. The dark green foliage is poisonous, and the deep red timber was once prized for making bows.

YHA, see YOUTH ORGANISATIONS

Yiddish, dialect, or group of dialects, spoken by Jews ; a mixture of approx. 70% German, 20% Hebrew and 10% other words ; commonly spoken among Jews in Europe, USA and especially the East End of London.

YMCA, short for Young Men's Christian Association, founded 1844 by Sir George Williams (1821–1905), *b* Dulverton, Somerset. A world-wide organisation, the YMCA began with a group of twelve young men in London. The badge is a red triangle. The YWCA (Young Women's Christian Association) was founded 1855. Its sign is a blue triangle.

Yoga, *yō´gä*, Indian cult or belief in which a knowledge of spiritual truth and power

YEW
A thicket of evergreen Yew Trees

is sought by practising control of the mind and body, e.g. concentrating the thoughts, regulating the breathing, fasting, etc. One who practises this cult is called a Yogin or Yogi.

Yokohama, *yō'kō-hämä,* city, Japan. An important port on Tokyo Bay (Honshu), it trades in silk, tea, cotton and tobacco. Though almost destroyed by an earthquake 1923, it was rebuilt, but suffered severely from US bombing in World War II ; pop.968,000.

Yonkers, city, New York state, USA ; has various industries ; pop.143,000.

York, walled city and cap., Yorkshire ; on the R. Ouse ; notable for narrow streets and old houses, also for Clifford's Tower (Norman), many churches, and especially its minster, founded AD627. One of the largest and finest churches in England, the minster has much old glass in its windows. Industries include sweets and chocolate, and the city is a great railway centre. The Archbishop of York lives at Bishopthorpe, close by. The Roman name was Eboracum ; pop.105,000.

York, DUKE OF, title often borne by the second son of the king of England. Henry VIII, Charles I, James II, George V and George VI were each known as Duke of York before becoming king.

York, RICHARD, DUKE OF (1411–60), English soldier and statesman ; opposed Edmund Beaufort, Duke of Somerset, in Henry VI's reign ; defeated Somerset at the battle of St Albans, the first in the Wars of the Roses ; claimed the throne, but was killed at the battle of Wakefield.

Yorkshire, largest county in England (area 6,081sq.m), divided into three ' ridings ' (N., E. and W.) ; the word *riding* means ' thirding ' or third. The cap. is York. Though mainly agricultural, Yorkshire has the Cleveland mining district (north) and a great coalfield in the industrial west, famous for its woollen and worsted industries. Its most important port is Hull.

Yorktown, see AMERICAN INDEPENDENCE, WAR OF

Yosemite Valley, *yō-sem'i-tē,* spectacular gorge, California, USA, included in Yosemite National Park, of 1,126sq.m. The valley is remarkable for its brilliantly coloured rocks, foaming R. Merced, and waterfalls.

Young, ANDREW (1885–), poet, *b* Elgin, but brought up in Edinburgh. He wrote *Nicodemus* (a religious play), and such books of verse as *Winter Harvest* and *Collected Poems.*

Young, ARTHUR (1741–1820), writer, *b* London ; gave a forward movement to English agriculture by his many books on scientific farming.

Young, EDWARD (1683–1765), poet, *b* Upham, Hampshire ; wrote *Night Thoughts on Life, Death and Immortality,* a poem full of sententious reflections.

Young, FRANCIS BRETT (1884–), author, born in Worcestershire ; famous for his many novels with a fine literary style, e.g. *My Brother Jonathan* ; *The House Under the Water* ; *Far Forest* ; has also published volumes of exquisite verse.

Young Farmers, see YOUTH ORGANISATIONS

Younghusband, SIR FRANCIS EDWARD (1863–1942), British explorer, *b* India ; entered the army ; led expeditions into central Asia ; author of *India and Tibet* and *The Heart of a Continent.*

Young Pretender, see JAMES EDWARD

Youth Camping Association, see CAMPING ORGANISATIONS

Youth Hostels Association, see YOUTH ORGANISATIONS

youth organisations, societies for training youth in various ways, and providing planned social activities in leisure time.

Apart from voluntary work, e.g. through churches and such organisations as Boy Scouts, Girl Guides, YMCA clubs, little was done in the UK before 1939, though national youth movements were fostered in Italy and Japan, and especially in Nazi Germany, from *c.*1933. The Ministry (then the Board) of Education encouraged local authorities to form Juvenile Organisation Committees (1916) to cater for the social welfare of young people, and some help was thus given to voluntary work. A National Fitness Council was organised 1936, though the work had to be abandoned 1939, when the Board issued various circulars urging local authorities to form Youth Committees to provide young people (14–20) with recreation and training, particularly on club lines, and (1941) the Board further stimulated organisations such as the ATC, JTC, Sea Cadets, WJAC and GTC.

Though youth organisations are numerous and varied, catering for many interests both indoors and out, membership is not compulsory. It seems that when County Colleges are established for the further education of young people, these will become the focal-points of almost all youth activities.

Youth associations are too numerous to give in full, but representative types include :

Air Training Corps
Association for Jewish Youth
Boys' Brigade
Boy Scouts Association
Christian Endeavour Union
Church of Scotland Youth Department
English-Speaking Union
Girls' Friendly Society
Girl Guides Association
International Student Service
Junior Bird Recorders' Club
National Federation of Young Farmers' Clubs
National Union of Students (of the Universities and Colleges of England and Wales)
St John Ambulance Brigade (Cadets)
Student Christian Movement
Sunday School League
Young Men's Christian Association, see YMCA
Young Women's Christian Association, see YMCA
Youth Department of the British Council of Churches
Youth Leaders' Association

Excellent guides to, and summaries of, the work of youth movements will be found in (a) Youth Organisations of Great Britain (Jordan and Sons, Ltd) ; and (b) Youth Service Handbook (W. Walker and Sons, Ltd).

Books likely to be of use to club leaders include :
How to Lead Discussion Groups, E. M. Hubback (English Universities Press)
Young Citizen, A. E. Morgan (Penguin Special)
Commonsense About Drama, L. A. G. Strong (Nelson)
Acting for All, Robert Newton (Nelson)
Let's Do A Play, Rodney Bennett (Nelson)
New Fellowship Song Book, Sir Walford Davies (Novello)

Daily Express Song Book
National Youth Song Book, D. MacMahon
Let's Get Up a Concert, R. Bennett and H. S. Gordon (Nelson)
English Country Dance Tunes (Novello)
Let's Go Camping, D. Raven (Nelson)
The Service of Youth Book, D. Edwards-Rees
Club Leadership, B. L. Q. Henriques
In the Service of Youth, J. Macalister Brew (Faber and Faber)
Games Worth Playing, D. MacCuaig and G. S. Clark (Longmans)
Youth and the Village Club, Edith M. Clark (Nelson)

Note also various Ministry of Education circulars, e.g. Service of Youth (No. 1486) ; Youth Service Corps (1543); Pre-Service Training Organisations (1603) etc. ; also Club News, a monthly magazine published by the National Association of Girls' Clubs and Mixed Clubs ; and, somewhat similar, The Boy, a magazine published by the National Association of Boys' Clubs.

Provision is made on a liberal scale for youth on holiday, e.g. hiking and cycling, etc. Membership of the following associations is inexpensive, and the facilities are many :
Holiday Fellowship (known as HF)
Co-Operative Holiday Association (CHA)
Youth Hostels Association (YHA)
The Scottish Association (SYHA)
Cyclists may well join the CTC (Cyclists' Touring Club). A useful Cycling Manual is published by the English Universities Press.

For youth keen on camping, membership of the Youth Camping Association of Great Britain and Ireland is useful, and enables the camper to get the utmost out of his holiday under canvas. The association's Handbook of Camping is admirable.

For plays, see DRAMA

For music and art, apply for guidance to the Council for the Encouragement of Music and Arts.

For magazines, see NEWSPAPERS. See also EDUCATION

Ypres, ē′pr, town, Belgium, c.36m from Bruges ; noted for textiles ; suffered severely in World War I and gave its name to several battles.

Ypres, EARL OF (1852–1925), better known as Sir John French, British soldier, b Ripple, Kent ; fought in the S. African War, gallantly relieving Kimberley. He was Commander-in-Chief of the British Expeditionary Force in the early and difficult first year of World War I, though he did not work well with the French generals. He was created Earl of Ypres (in memory of the battle of Ypres) 1921.

ytterbium, i-tŭr′bi-ŭm, rare earth and element, Yb ; atomic weight 173·04 ; atomic number 70.

yttrium, it′ri-ŭm, rare earth and metal,

Y or Yt ; atomic weight 88·92 ; atomic number 39.

Yucatan, peninsula of Central America separating the Gulf of Mexico from the Caribbean Sea. It is c.400m long, and notable for its mahogany forests. Maize and indigo are produced.

Yugoslavia, yū-gō-slä′via, one of the Balkan states, known since 1945 as the Federal People's Republic of Yugoslavia, King Peter (who assumed power 1941) being deprived of his rights. The country comprises Serbia, Montenegro, Croatia, Slavonia, Bosnia, Herzegovina, part of Dalmatia, Slovenia, etc. ; area c.96,000sq.m ; pop.16,000,000. It has a seaboard on the Adriatic ; its great river is the Danube. The country produces maize, wheat, timber, and is largely agricultural, but coal, lignite, copper-ore, lead, zinc and bauxite are mined. Belgrade, the cap., was freed from Nazi rule 1944. Though in the Russian zone of influence since World War II, Yugoslavia has been governed by Marshal Tito, its Prime Minister, in a singularly independent way.

Religion plays an important part in the life of the people, the Serbians being chiefly Orthodox Church. Bosnia has many Mohammedans ; Croatia and Slovenia are largely RC, and as a result there is much unrest and division among the people.

Yukon, inhospitable territory, NW. Canada; area 207,000sq.m. The region attracted many adventurers during the Klondike gold rush 1898 onwards, and once had a pop. of 27,000, now reduced to under 5,000 ; produces gold and silver ; cap. Dawson.

Yukon, river, Alaska, flows 2,300m to Bering Sea ; abounds in salmon.

Yunnan, yun-nän′, south-west province, China.

YWCA, see YMCA

Z

Zagreb, zä′greb, formerly Agram ; town, Yugoslavia ; a great market for wheat, maize, sugar beet and tobacco ; pop. 186,000.

Zama, site in what is now Algeria (French NW. Africa) of a battle fought 202BC between the Carthaginians (led by Hannibal) and the victorious Romans under Scipio.

Zambesi, zam-bē′zi, river, Africa, flows 1,600m from the region of the Belgian Congo to the Indian Ocean. In its course are the famous Victoria Falls.

Zamora, thä-mō′rä, town, Spain ; on the R. Douro ; manufactures textiles ; now much less important than when peopled by the Moors.

Zanté, zän′tä, Ionian island ; noted for currants.

Zanzibar, British protectorate in E. Africa; includes the island of Zanzibar, the island of Pemba, and a strip of the mainland coast, total area 1,020sq.m, pop.235,000, mostly Arabs. Zanzibar is governed by a sultan. With a tropical climate, the protectorate produces coconuts, copra, rubber, and is the world's greatest source of cloves. The city and port of Zanzibar has a pop. of 45,000. Slavery was abolished 1890.

zebra, horse-like animal found only in Africa. The common or mt. zebra (Equs zebra) has black stripes on a tawny pelt. The QUAGGA or WILD ASS, now possibly extinct, was similar, but had stripes on the head and neck only.

zebu, zē′bū, humped and horned domesticated ox, chiefly of India ; is usually white or grey ; capable of withstanding intense heat, and is immune from tropical diseases. It is also found in E. Africa and China.

Zechariah, zek-ä-rī′ä, 6th c. BC Hebrew prophet, author of part of the OT book that bears his name. A contemporary of Haggai, he encouraged the Jews to rebuild the Temple in Jerusalem.

Zedekiah, zed-ē-kī′ä, last king of Judah ; lived in the 6th c. BC ; taken prisoner by Nebuchadnezzar.

Zeebrugge, zä′brug-e, town, Belgium ; the port for Bruges ; linked with Harwich by ferry ; famous for an incident in World War I when (1918) the Vindictive stormed the mole, and two cruisers were sunk as blockships at the mouth of the canal, thus preventing German submarines using the base.

Zeeland, province of the Netherlands. Middelburg, on Walcheren Island, is the capital.

Zeiss, CARL, zīs (1816–88), German optician, b Weimar ; founded 1846 a famous optical instrument factory at Jena.

zenana, ze-nä′nä (from the Persian), term for a Hindu harem, i.e. the part of a house where the women live ; also used collectively for the women themselves.

Zend-Avesta, zend ä-ves′tä, sacred books of the Parsees, more correctly Avesta and Zend, i.e. law and commentary ; written originally in Zend, a language similar to Sanskrit, possibly in part by Zoroaster.

Zenobia, zē-nō′bi-ä, 3rd c. queen of Palmyra (a city 150m north-east of Damas-

ZEBRA
(1) *Quagga*   (2) *Mountain Zebra*

cus). Though conquered by the Roman emperor (Aurelian) her beauty, courage and strength of character caused him to allow her to live in comfort in Italy.

Zeno of Citium, *zē'nō* (*d* 264BC), Greek thinker; taught in the *stoa poïkile* (painted porch), Athens, hence his philosophy is called *stoicism*; believed that there is a reason (*logos*) for everything; that the wise man is neither pleased nor grieved by what happens; and that all things work together for good if we do good.

Zeno of Elea, 5th c. BC Greek thinker; famous for his eight paradoxes, among them (*a*) that however quickly Achilles may run he can never overtake a tortoise, (*b*) that if an arrow in flight cannot be said to be in any *one* place at any given moment, it does not exist. These, and other theories, were long debated and long ridiculed; but it would seem that they have in them the germ of the ultimate realities of time, space and matter as revealed, at any rate in part, by the most modern scientific theories, e.g. Relativity and the ultimate structure of atoms. The resolution of paradox (*b*) above is that *at* any given instant the arrow *does not exist*. It *takes time* for it to exist, the time taken being governed by the periodicities of the particles of which it consists. Thus the arrow exists *in* a moment of time, but not *at* an instant.

zeolite, hydrated silicate of sodium (or potassium) and aluminium; also a substance used to soften 'hard' water.

Zephaniah, *zef-ä-nī'ä*, 7th c. BC Hebrew prophet, i.e. in the days of King Josiah. He was author of the OT book that bears his name.

Zephyrus, *zef'i-rŭs*, in old Greek tales, the west wind, son of Eos (Dawn); hence *zephyr*, a gentle wind.

zeppelin, see AVIATION

Zeppelin, COUNT VON, *zep'e-lin* (1838–1917), German inventor; from 1900 designed rigid dirigibles (airships or zeppelins), a class of aircraft which ultimately gave place to heavier-than-air machines. See AVIATION

Zermatt, *tser-mät'*, village and noted tourist centre, Switzerland.

zero, in physics, absolute zero is regarded as the temperature at which the molecules of a perfect gas would be without kinetic (i.e. heat) energy. In theory this temperature is taken to be $-273 \cdot 13°$C, and is therefore the lowest temperature possible. Solid helium melts at the low temperature of $-272°$C. It seems unlikely that we shall ever succeed in reaching absolute zero, but low temperatures have been reached by making use of the curious fact that some substances are warmer when magnetised and become cooler again when not magnetised. By cooling these in 'boiling' helium, and shutting off a magnetic field, a temperature within $0 \cdot 0044°$ of absolute zero has been attained.

Zeus, *zūs*, in old Greek tales, the supreme god; known to the Romans as Jupiter. He was god of the weather, especially of thunder and rain, and was associated with Mt Olympus. The oak was sacred to him. Zeus was regarded as the father of the human race.

Zimbabwe, *zim-bä'bwä*, ruins, S. Rhodesia, probably built by 14th c. gold-seekers. The name means *houses of stone*.

zinc, metal and element, Zn; atomic weight $65 \cdot 38$; atomic number 30; found naturally as calamine, $ZnCO_3$, and as zinc sulphide (or zinc blende), ZnS, which is smelted by roasting in air and then heating with coke to form commercial zinc, known as spelter.

A hard, bluish metal with a melting-point of 420°C, zinc has a specific gravity of 7. It is much used for making galvanised iron, i.e. iron dipped in molten zinc ; another method is by means of the metallisation pistol, zinc wire being melted by an oxygen-gas flame, and sprayed at pressure on metal, e.g. the plates of a ship's hull.

Zinc is of great importance in making various alloys, especially brass, and in the die-casting industry, where use is made of super-pure zinc (nicknamed ' four nines,' i.e. over 99·99 % zinc), giving highly reliable results.

Zinzendorf, COUNT VON, *fon tsin'tsen-dörf* (1700–60), German religious reformer ; friend of John Wesley ; founded a Moravian settlement in N. America ; wrote many hymns.

Zion, see JEWS

zip fastener, invention, also called the Lightning Fastener, due to an Alsatian named Aronsen, whose fastener, produced c.1893, was improved 1915 by his son-in-law, Gideon Sundback, a Swedish engineer, but did not become popular till 1925. Zip fasteners are now made in an immense variety of sizes by intricate machinery. The basic principle is that opposite metal numbers interlock only when brought together at the correct angle, this being accomplished by means of the slider.

zirconium, rare metal and element, Zr ; atomic weight 91·22 ; atomic number 40 ; has a high melting-point ; used for photo-flash bulbs, in the rayon industry, and for various steels.

zither, stringed musical instrument popular in Bavaria and the Tirol. A shallow box, it has 30 to 45 wires.

Zn, chemical symbol for zinc.

Zodiac, *zō'di-ak*, that part of the sky (c.18° wide) through which the sun moon and planets appear to pass. The ancient Babylonian astronomers divided this into twelve parts (houses), each with a name and sign taken from one of the constellations in it. These are :

Aries ♈	the Ram
Taurus ♉	the Bull
Gemini ♊	the Twins
Cancer ♋	the Crab
Leo ♌	the Lion
Virgo ♍	the Virgin
Libra ♎	the Balance
Scorpio ♏	the Scorpion
Sagittarius ♐	the Archer
Capricornus ♑	the Sea Goat
Aquarius ♒	the Water Bearer
Pisces ♓	the Fishes

Zola, ÉMILE, *zō'lä* (1840–1902), French writer of Italian and Greek ancestry, *b* Paris ; lived for a time in dire poverty, an experience that enabled him to understand the hardship and suffering of life ; eventually earned sufficient money as a journalist and author to devote the rest of his life to three tasks : (*a*) the greatest, the writing of twenty novels telling the story of the Rougon-Macquart family, a kind of immense *Forsyte Saga*. In this series *La Fortune des Rougon* ; *L'Assommoir* ; *La Débâcle* ; *Germinal* ; *La Terre* ; and *Le Docteur Pascal* are among the most noteworthy ; (*b*) a series of three books : *The Three Cities* (Lourdes, Rome, Paris), the story of a priest ; and (*c*) *The Four Gospels*, the last volume of which he did not live to finish.

In all these books Zola revealed with amazing skill and through a vast number of characters, the follies, weaknesses, injustices and sufferings of his day. He spared nothing of which he did not approve, and in a sense publicly whipped humanity for its sins. His books sold in immense numbers, and he was one of the most talked-of men of his day, intensely admired and intensely hated.

In the famous Dreyfus case in which (as it was ultimately proved) Albert Dreyfus was unjustly condemned to imprisonment on Devil's I., Zola caused a sensation by his open letter headed *J'accuse* (I accuse), in which he accused those who gave evidence against the prisoner.

Zomba, see NYASALAND

Zoo, THE, see LONDON

zoology, *zō-ol'ō-ji* (Greek *zōon*, animal, *logos*, discourse), science of all living things except plants ; hence it includes the study of such life-forms as man, elephant, whale, dog, rabbit, snake, frog, fish, snail, oyster, spider, crab, insect, worm, starfish, sea-anemone, coral, sponge, and various microscopic creatures.

Note that the word *animal* is popularly used for a four-footed creature, e.g. horse and cat, but to the zoologist *all* creatures mentioned above are animals.

It is important to note also that animals and plants are alike in many ways : Both change food into tissue ; plants do this by taking carbon dioxide from the air and absorbing mineral salts from the soil in order to build up their food, whereas animals use inorganic substances only after they have been changed into organic compounds by plants, i.e. plants *produce* food, animals *consume* it.

For the history of animal development from simple one-celled creatures to the various complex forms of today, see EVOLUTION.

It is interesting to note that man, as an animal, is inferior in some respects to some animals. Thus, his sense of smell is not as acute as that of a dog, nor is his sight as keen as that of a vulture. Whereas, however, an elephant can draw only 0·72lb for every lb of its own weight, a man can draw 1·16lb.

More important still : human intelligence far exceeds that of the most intelligent of the lower animals. In assessing animal intelligence we have to differentiate between intelligence, i.e. quickness of apprehension, and *instinct*, a sort of race memory which enables animals to perform apparently skilled actions without conscious thought, e.g. the sparrow's ' cleverness' in building its nest is actually an instinctive operation. Instinct, inborn and requiring no practice, enables a spider to spin a perfect web at the first attempt.

Man, too, has many instincts, e.g. that of self-preservation. On the whole, preservation of the race depends on successful adaptation to environment which brings about variations in structure and behaviour.

Aristotle (*d* 322BC) proposed a rough classification of animals. After that zoology advanced little until the 18th c. when Linnaeus established a new classification. Further advances were made by Lamarck and Darwin ; and the principles of heredity were discovered by Mendel *c*.1866. See BIOLOGY ; EVOLUION ; HEREDITY

' Zoo Man, The,' see SETH-SMITH, DAVID

Zoroaster (Zarathustra), founder of Zoroastrianism (Mazdaism), the religion of ancient Persia. He probably lived *c*.1000BC. The religion founded by Zoroaster was based on a more primitive religion, that professed by the Aryan forefathers both of the Persians and the Indians. Zoroastrianism has many features in common with Indian religion, except that the good spirits and deities of Indian religion are the evil spirits in Zoroastrian mythology. This is because Zoroaster regarded the primitive Aryan polytheism (belief in many gods) as idolatrous, and based his own teaching about God on opposition to it.

The most important aspect of Zoroastrian religious teaching is its *dualism*, i.e. the doctrine that there are *two* supreme spirits : one God (Ahura Mazda, the Wise Lord) who is good, the other Ahriman, who is evil. According to Zoroaster God is powerful, but not all-powerful, inasmuch as his purposes are continually thwarted by Ahriman. Christians believe that God is sole creator of the world and that in totality it is good. Zoroaster taught that God is *moved* to create the world as a means of overcoming Ahriman, and that he will prevail only in the end. Christians believe too that God forgives the sins of those who truly repent, but in older Zoroastrianism God has no power to forgive sins. When a man dies, his good deeds are counted against his bad ones, that is all, and if the good outweigh the bad, he goes to heaven ; if not, to hell.

A Zoroastrian Church grew up in Persia after the death of Zoroaster. Later it was overthrown by Mohammedanism (AD636), and survives only in the religion of the Parsees. *Mithraism*, a form of sun-worship, derived from Zoroastrianism, became a popular religion in the Roman Empire, especially among the troops, and before the conversion of Constantine (early 4th c. AD) was almost as important as Christianity.

Zululand, once a country ruled by Zulu chiefs, but since 1897 a province of S. Africa (included in Natal) and in the region of the Tugela R. and the Indian Ocean. The area is *c*.10,000sq.m. The Zulus (of the Bantu-Negro race) are a fine people with great physical and intellectual powers. King Cetywayo (*d* 1884) was a man of outstanding ability, and was responsible for wars with the British, hence the battle of RORKE'S DRIFT, fought by the Tugela R. 1879, where no more than 80 British soldiers (half of them hospital cases) threw back the repeated attacks of 4,000 Zulus. The grandson of Cetywayo (Mshiyeni Zulu) was proclaimed Paramount Chief of the Zulus 1939.

Zurich, *tsū'rich*, name of (*a*) a lake, Switzerland, 25m long, (*b*) a city overlooking the lake ; manufactures textiles ; has a cathedral and university ; pop.336,000.

Zutphen, *zŭt'fen*, town, Netherlands ; important railway centre ; scene 1586 of a battle in which Sir Philip Sidney (in command of English forces against the Spaniards) was fatally wounded.

Zuyder Zee, *zī'der*, Netherlands inland sea, an inlet of the N. Sea, including the islands of Texel and Ameland. The area would have been wholly reclaimed by 1941 but for the German invasion of the Netherlands in World War II. See NETHERLANDS

Zwingli, HULDREICH, *tsvin'gli* (1484–1531), Swiss reformer, son of a peasant ; became a parish priest 1506 ; denounced the authority of the pope in political matters and in matters of faith ; exposed the superstitious practices of the Church ; declared that churchmen might marry, and that fasting was absurd ; went further even than Martin Luther in his demands for a complete change in Church government. Zwingli invented the Lutheran doctrine of consubstantiation, the view that in the Lord's Supper, the ' substance' of bread and wine exists side by side with that of the body and blood of Christ.

zymase, *zī'mās*, enzyme that causes the alcoholic fermentation of carbohydrates ; is found in yeast. See DIGESTION ; YEAST

PRINTED IN GREAT BRITAIN AT
THE PRESS OF THE PUBLISHERS